Chronicles
of the
SCOTCH
SETTLEMENT
in
VIRGINIA

Extracted from the Original Court Records of
Augusta County, 1745 - 1800

By
Lyman Chalkley

Complete in Three Volumes

VOLUME III

CLEARFIELD

Originally published: 1912

Reprinted by Genealogical Publishing Co., Inc.
Baltimore, Maryland
1965, 1966, 1974, 1980, 1989, 1999

Reprinted for Clearfield Company by
Genealogical Publishing Company
Baltimore, Maryland
2010

Library of Congress Catalogue Card Number: 65-15351
ISBN, Volume III: 978-0-8063-0895-1
ISBN Set: 978-0-8063-0069-6

Made in the United States of America

HONOR ROLL

Subscriptions received since September, 1912.

MISS LELIA S. HATHAWAY, Owensboro, Kentucky.
W. S. MOORE, Manila, Iowa.
PANAMA JEWELRY COMPANY, Panama, Florida.
HORACE E. HAYDEN, Secretary and Historian Wyoming Historical and Geological Society, Wilkesbarre, Pennsylvania.
FREE PUBLIC LIBRARY, Portsmouth, Ohio.
M. M. SPITLER, Nevada, Missouri.
W. H. BEEBE, Ravenna, Ohio.
MRS. ANNA M. B. MILLER, Atlanta, Georgia.
H. D. SPEARS, New York City.
LEXINGTON PUBLIC LIBRARY, Lexington, Kentucky.
BURROWS BROTHERS, Cleveland, Ohio.
MRS WILLIAM T. LOGGINS, Greenwood, Mississippi.
MRS. CHARLES W. RICHARDSON, Washington, D. C.
MISS SUSIE E. HALL, Fairmont, West Virginia.
DANVILLE LIBRARY ASSOCIATION, Danville, Kentucky.
MRS. J. R. RICH, Bandy, Virginia.
MRS. BYRON BLACKBURN, Chanute, Kansas.
SARAH MCCALLA CHAPTER, D. A. R., Cameron, Texas.
BOUTWELL DUNLAP, San Francisco, California.
MRS. WILLOUGHBY WALLING, Chicago, Illinois.
REV. B. L. ANCELL, Yangchow, China.

ADDITIONAL MEMBERS OF THE EXECUTIVE COMMITTEE.

MRS. DANIEL MANNING, Ex-President General N. S. D. A. R., Albany, N. Y.
MRS. JULIUS C. BURROWS, Kalamazoo, Michigan.
MRS. CHARLES W. RICHARDSON, Washington, D. C.
MRS. NOBLE N. POTTS, Washington, D. C.
MRS. GEORGE C. CLEMENT, Cameron, Texas.
MISS LIZZIE A. LYLE, Lexington, Kentucky.
MRS. WILLIAM LINDSEY, Frankfort, Kentucky.

Cincinnati Chapter, Cincinnati, Ohio, desires its name erased from the Honor Roll in the first volume, having rescinded its vote for subscription.

ABSTRACTS OF WILLS OF AUGUSTA COUNTY, VIRGINIA.

AUGUSTA COUNTY COURT.

WILL BOOK No. 1.

Page 1.—James Knox, Jno. Brown, Andrew Pickens, bond, 11th February, 1745 (1746). James Knox qualifies guardian of Ann Jenny Usher.
Page 1.—Robert Willson, in Shanadore in Virginia, will dated 3d November, 1745. Wife, Jane; estate except such as is nominated of the *hole head* to son John. Son, John; daughter, Jannet Holmes, 20 shillings; daughter, Catrin Bell, 20 shillings; nephew (?), Robert Holmes; daughters, Elizabeth, Jane, Frances. Executors, Wm. Long and James Alexander. Teste: Jno. Patterson, Gabriel Holmes, James Bell. Proved, 11th February, 1745, by John Patterson. Proved, 16th April, 1745, by Gabriel Holmes.
Page 3.—John Wilson qualifies administrator, c. t. a., of above, with sureties, viz: Robert Cunningham and Wm. Henderson, 11th February, 1745.
Page 4.—Andrew Pickens qualifies administrator of Joseph Martin with sureties, viz: John Brown and Hugh Thompson. Bond, 12th February, 1745.
Page 4.—Peter Roughenough qualifies administrator of Abraham Strickler, with sureties, viz: Mathais Selzer, John Lionberger. 14th April, 1746.
Page 7.—7th March, 1745-6. Inventory of Joseph Martin appraised by Wm. McFeeters, John Trimble and Jno. Risk. Cross-cut saw and 2 pocket knives, 1 glass bottle. Recorded, 16th April, 1746.
Page 8.—3d November, 1743. John A. Dobikin's will, of Orange County, farmer. Wife, son John, executors. Teste: Wm. Jeames, Wm. Galenbe, Samuel Brown. Proved, 12th May, 1746, by Wm. Jeames.
Page 9.—12th May, 1746. John Dobikin and Mary Dobikin qualify executors, with sureties Benj. Allen, Tunis Hood.
Page 10.—12th May, 1746. Robert Kirkum qualifies administrator of Michael Kirkum, with sureties Henry Kirkum, Richard Woods.
Page 12.—19th April, 1746. Abraham Strickler's inventory appraised by Jeremiah Sutton, Paul Long, Rudolph Maag. Recorded, 18th June, 1746.
Page 15.—William Hutchison qualifies guardian of Aaron Jackson, orphan of Christopher Jackson, with surety Jno. Lewis, 19th June, 1746. Aaron chose his own guardian.
Page 16.—26th June, 1746. Robert Sayers, late from Pennsylvania. Will—Sons, William, Alexander; wife, Cathren; daughters, Margaret, Ann, Elizabeth. Executors, John Buchanan and Joseph Culton, Gent. (desiring

Col. Patton to assist if he will grant me the favor). Teste: Jno. Buchanan, Wm. Adair, Francis McCown, Thos. Beard. Proved, 20th August, 1746, by all except Beard. Wm. and Alex. Sayers qualify executors 20th August, 1746, with sureties John Buchanan and John Hays.

Page 19.—19th February, 1746-7.—Thomas Grubbs qualifies guardian of Abraham Drake, orphan of Abraham Drake, with sureties Abraham Jobe, James McCoy.

Page 21.—19th February, 1746-7. Thomas Grubbs qualifies administrator of Abraham Drake, with sureties as above.

Page 22.—19th February, 1746-7. Reuben Allen qualifies administrator of Benj. Allen, with sureties Wm. White, Thomas Moore.

Page 24.—16th November, 1746. Robert Crockett's will—Wife, Margaret; sons, John, Asbal (Arsble), land on cow pasture joining James Measl; daughter, Jean; sons, Samuel, Robert (infant), James (infant), Alexander. Executors, wife and Robert Davis. Teste: Thos. Gillham, James McCorkle, Robert Bratton. Proved by all witnesses, 19th February, 1746, and both executors qualified, with sureties James McCorkle and Robert Bratton.

Page 27.—19th February, 1746-7. Robert Graham qualifies administrator of Christopher Graham, with sureties Wm. Smith, Robert Bratton.

Page 28.—20th February, 1746. James Patton qualifies administrator of John Jannet, with sureties Peter Scholl, Robert Cunningham.

Page 29.—13th March, 1747. Appraisement of Abraham Drake's estate by Jno. Davis, Alex. Mathes, Daniel Strofer. Recorded, 18th March, 1746.

Page 31.—12th June, 1746. John Dobikin's appraisement by Wm. White, Wm. Carrill, Wm. James. Recorded, 18th March, 1746.

Page 32.—18th March, 1746. James Burk qualifies administrator of Isaac Bean, with sureties Humberston Lyon, Wm. Armstrong. Acknowledged, 18th March, 1746.

Page 33.—18th February, 1746. Elizabeth Skileren qualifies administratrix of her husband, Wm. Skileren, with sureties Robert Black, Jno. Miller. Recorded, 18th March, 1746.

Page 34.—William Skileren made a will dated 6th January, 1744-45, wherein he appointed executors, viz: James Patton, Peter Jefferson, Thos. Meriwether, Thomas Skilson. James Patton proved the will, but did not qualify, and now Elizabeth qualifies as above. Teste: Jno. Christian, Ro. Campbell, Geo. Robinson, Jno. Buchanan, Jno. Willson, Jno. Buchanan.

Page 35.—22d May, 1747. Abraham Drake, Sr., qualifies administrator of Abraham Drake, with sureties Peter Scholl and Gabriel Jones.

Page 36.—21st May, 1747. Elizabeth Watson qualifies administratrix of husband, Joseph Watson, with surety Ralph Laverty.

Page 37.—21st May, 1747. Sarah Hays qualifies administratrix of George Hayes, with surety Patrick Hayes.

Page 39.—21st May, 1747. Peter Dyer qualifies administrator of John Taylor, with surety James Samuel Scott.

Page 40.—1st May, 1747. Isaac Bean's appraisement by Ephraim Vause, James Neelley, Erwin Patterson. Laboring wages from Robert Ellison.

Page 41.—21st May, 1747. Wm. Thompson qualifies guardian of Martha Camell, orphan of John Camell.

Page 41.—26th October, 1746. Receipt by Sarah Bogert (Bugard), widow of Johannes Bugard, of the South Branch, for articles willed by her husband from the executors Able Westfall and Anthony Bogard, and her bond to preserve the estate to the children. Teste: Abraham Vanderpool, Laya Westfall.

Page 42.—21st May, 1747. Abel Westfall qualifies executor of John Bougard, with sureties Thomas West and John States. Teste: Samuel Porteus.

Page 43.—4th September, 1746. Johannes Bougard's will, of the South Branch—Wife, Sarah, big with child, who must be brought up in her father's house; brother, Anthony Bougard, shoemaker's teather; daughter, Anna Bougard. Executors, Abell Westfall and Anthony Bougard. Teste: Abraham Vanderpool, John Westfall, Jacob Westfall. Proved by Jacob Westfall, 21st May, 1747. Proved by other witnesses, 28th June, 1747.

Page 45.—18th June, 1747. Anthony Bougard qualifies executor as above.

Page 46.—17th June, 1747. James Young (I) qualifies administrator of John Young, with sureties Partt Martin, Robert Young.

Page 47.—3d August, 1747. Jean Bohannan. Will—Son, John; granddaughter, Mary Bohanan (daughter of John); eldest daughter, Elizabeth Bohanan; granddaughter, Jean Bohannan; second daughter, Margaret Campbell, the tablecloth I brought from Ireland; granddaughter, the bay colt that was lately put to Elizabeth Bochanan; granddaughter, Mary Bochanan. Executors, Joseph Culton and Robert Edmiston. Teste: Joseph Culton, Robert Edmiston, Francis McCown, John Betty. Proved, 19th August, 1747, by Francis McCown.

Page 48.—21st August, 1747. Settlement of accounts by Robert Cravens, guardian of Thos. and John Levistone, orphans of Robert Levistone. To money received by Nelson. Paid Hugh Douglass. Paid Samuel Hull. Lending to Opackon for ye plot.

Page 48.—19th August, 1747. Ro Edmiston ( ) qualifies executor of Jean Bochanan above.

Page 49.—19th August, 1747. Robert Crockett's Inventory: By Henry Gay, Wm. Elliott, Jno. Gay.

Page 51.—3d August, 1747. Account of debts payed by Margaret Crockett that were owing by the estate of Robert Crockett.

Page 51.—18th August, 1747. George Hays' appraisement: By Jno. Stevenston, John Paul, Nathl. Evans.

Page 52.—19th August, 1747. Abraham Drake's appraisement: By John Davis, Jacob Burner.

Page 53.—20th August, 1747. John Taylor's appraisement: By Robert Hooks, John Stevenson, Robert Scott.

Page 54.—21st August, 1747. Mary Cunningham qualifies administratrix of Samuel Cunningham, with sureties Geo. Robinson, Robert McClenahan.

Page 55.—11th August, 1747. Joseph Watson's appraisement: By Hugh Coffey, Wm. Dougherty, Andrew Moldrow.

Page 56.—17th September, 1747. Samuel Cunningham's appraisement.

Page 59.—17th September, 1747. Benj. Borden on behalf of his wife, Magdalene, qualifies administrator of John McDowell, with sureties Richard Woods, Peter Wallace. Teste: Benj. Johnston.

Page 60.—17th September, 1747. Eleanor Taylor qualifies administratrix of John Taylor, with surety Robert Caldwell.

Page 61.—17th September, 1747. Robert McClenachan qualifies guardian of Margaret Cunningham, orphan of Samuel Cunningham.

Page 62.—17th September, 1747. Andrew Mitchell in behalf of his wife, administratrix of Samuel Cunningham, qualifies; sureties Jno. Pickens, **Jno. Moffett.**

Page 63.—18th September, 1747. Andrew Mitchell qualifies guardian of Margaret, orphan of Samuel Cunningham.

Page 64.—14th September, 1747. David Steele's will—Farmer, son Robert, plantation; wife; son, Nathaniel; daughters, Martha Teas, Isabella McCluer, 5 shillings; daughters, Rebecka, Jannet. Executors, Samuel Doak and Robert Ramsey; refused to execute. Teste: Wm. Steel, Geo. Brakenridge, Robert Alexander. Proved, 18th November, 1747, by Brakenridge and Alexander.

Page 66.—18th November, 1747. Jannet Steel qualifies administratrix on above with sureties Wm. Henderson, David Camell.

Page 67.—19th November, 1747. Robert Brakenridge qualifies guardian of Lettice Brakenridge, orphan of Alex. Brakenridge, with surety James Bell. Lettice chose her guardian.

Page 68.—26th November, 1747. David Steel's appraisement by James Fulton, Charles Campbell and John Mitchell. Books. Cash due by Isaac Roads. Cash due Jno. Teas. Cash due executors of Thos. Steel, deceased. Cash due to Thos. Johnston. Recorded, 17th February, 1747-8.

Page 70.—11th October, 1747. Jannet and Frances Hutchinson's will. Sisters of George Hutchinson. Nuncupative will spoken in Scotch not easily understood **in English.**

Page 71.—18th February, 1747. George Hutchinson qualifies administrator of above, with sureties Wm. and Samuel Henderson.

Page 72.—19th February, 1747. Elizabeth Preston qualifies administratrix of Jno. Preston.

Page 74.—8th March, 1747. Benj. Allen's appraisement by John Ruddle, Sr., Daniel Holman, Wm. James, John Ruddle, Jr.

Page 75.—**Vestell's bond due.**

Page 76.—17th March, 1747. John Young's appraisement.

Page 76.—5th August, 1747. Appraisement of Jean Buchanan, of Borden's tract, by Alexander Walker, Isaac Anderson, Isaac Taylor.

Page 77.—29th April, 1748. Johannes Bogard's appraisement by Michael Harnis, Michael Stump, James Simpson. Money due by Jacob Bogard.

Page 78.—18th May, 1748. Isaiah Harrison qualifies administrator of Jos. Harrison, with sureties Jeremiah Harrison and Wm. White.

Page 79.—18th May, 1747. Nathl. Steel qualifies guardian of Rebecca Steel, orphan of David Steel, with sureties David Dryden and Moses Steel. **Rebecca chose her guardian.**

Page 80.—18th May, 1748. Settlement of George Hays' estate by Sarah Hays, administratrix. To Thos. Paxton, Joseph Lynn, Jno. Mahey, Hugh **Bolle.**

Page 80.—18th May, 1748. Peter Thorn qualifies administrator of John Woolffallier, with sureties William Walling.

Page 81.—22d March, 1747-8. **Jennet and Frances Hutchinson's appraisement.** Due from Samuel McCrown by Jno. Pickins, Wm. Baskins, James Lastly, appraisers.

Page 82.—26th February, 1746-7. Isaac Bean's estate; settlement. Sworn to 16th May, 1748. May 16th, 1748. Received of James Burk full satisfaction for the within account I say received by me.—Moses McClure.

Page 83.—18th May, 1748. Margaret Adams' bond as administratrix of Samuel Adams, with sureties Richard Dicton, Samuel Wilkins.

Page 84.—27th July, 1748. Joseph Harrison's appraisement by Samuel Wilkins, Wm. MaGill, David Logan.

Page 85.—24th October, 1747. John Taylor's Inventory by Thomas Looker, Wm. Carrel, Thomas Milsap. To an improvement of land sold by his widow, now administratrix.

Page 86.—18th August, 1748. John Campbell's estate; settlement by Wm. Thomson.

Page 87.—18th August, 1748. Jacob Glaspy's bond as guardian of James Humphreys, orphan of Wm. Humphreys, with surety John Davies. James chose his guardian.

Page 87.—10th August, 1748. Daniel Monahan's appraisement by James Davies and Mark Evans.

Page 89.—Sale bill of above estate, 13th December, 1744, purchasers, viz: James Price, Wm. Akers, Pat Shirkey, Chas. Ewing, John Thomas, Mary Akers, Nicholas Harford, Mary Kinder, Wm. Armstrong, Wm. Carson, Archibald Grimes, Wm. Mills, James Burk, Bryan Cuff, Wm. Armstrong, Henry Brown, Daniel Creeley, Pat Shirkey, Mark Cole, George Barberer, Simon Akers, Peter Kinder, Joseph Love, Methusalem Griffith, Tobias Bright, Jno. McFall, Wm. March, Mark Cole, Jasper Terry, Henry Brown, Jr., Wm. Terry, Stephen Rentfro. 1740—The estate of Daniel Monahan, Dr. Cash paid Joseph Tate. Cash paid Edmond Cartledge. 1743—Cash paid Andrew Gaughagin.

Page 91.—Cash for John Jennet. Cash for thrashing grain. Cash paid Jno. Boyd. Cash for Jno. Finley. Edmond Smith's account. Cash paid Robert Looney, Robert Rowland, Jno. Bramham. Cash paid Andrew Clemons. 18th June, 1747—Daniel Monahan to Simon Akers, 1 year's keeping his child, £4. 7, 6. Paid John Bird. (Here James Porteus begins to be scribe, *vid.*, page 282.)

Page 93.—16th January, 1748-9. Rudal Brock's will—Son, Frederick; son, George; daughter, Christiana Funkhouser; daughter, Julian Brock; daughter, Eve. Executors, John Dobikin and Wm. James. Teste: John Henry Neff, Peter Gartner, Hans Ber. Proved, 15th February, 1748, by Peter Gartner and John Bare.

Page 94.—15th February, 1748. Executors qualify as above, with sureties Samuel Newman, Jacob Woodley.

Page 95.—26th January, 1749. Johannes Hockman, will (in German)—Wife, Barbara, all estate. Teste: Henry Pfifer, Henry Gochenour, Christian Harnish (ess), Ulrick Hockman. Proved, 15th February, 1748.

Page 97.—15th February, 1748. Jane Skaine's bond as administratrix of Mathew Skaine.

Page 98.—15th February, 1748. Swain Rambo's bond as administrator of Barbara Rambo.

Page 99.—15th February, 1748. Jonathan Cobourn's bond as administrator of James Cobourn, with sureties John Dobikin and Michael Stump.

Page 100.—15th February, 1748. Samuel Newman's bond as administrator of Jonathan Newman.

Page 101.—15th February, 1748. John Stevenson's bond, £500, as administrator of John Hindman, with sureties Henry Downs, Thos. Stevenson, Samuel Givins.

Page 102.—15th February, 1748. Ann Mary Freedley's bond as administratrix of Lewis Freedley, with surety Peter Gartner.

Page 104.—2nd February, 1748. David Moore's will—Sister, Mary Edmiston and her daughter Eleanor, all proper. Executors, Thos. Beard, Ro. Ramsey. Proved, 15th February, 1748.

Page 105.—15th February, 1748. Executors qualify as above.

Page 106.—15th February, 1748. Daniel Stover qualifies guardian of John, Mary and James Campbell, orphans of John Campbell, with sureties Abraham Strickler, George Leath.

Page 106.—26th August, 1748. Samuel Adams' appraisement by George Forbush, John States, Wm. Walling.

Page 107.—15th February, 1748. Daniel Holdman and Peter Gartner's bond as guardian of Julia, George and Elsye Brock, orphans of Rudal Brock.

Page 108.—15th February, 1748. Christopher Graham's appraisement by Wm. Elliott, John Gay, Thos. Femster.

Page 109.—15th February, 1748. Jane Cook's bond as administratrix of Patrick Cook, with sureties Hugh Young, Robt. Young, John Spear.

Page 110.—16th February, 1748. Mary Dyer's bond as administratrix of Peter Dyer, with sureties Samuel Wilkins and Samuel Scott.

Page 111.—16th February, 1748. Mary Smiley's bond as administratrix of Alex. Smiley.

Page 113.—11th December, 1748. John Willey (Wiley)'s will—Daughters, Jean and Margaret; son, George. Executors, Alexander Mathews and George Leath. Jean is aged 7 years 13th of next June. Margaret is aged 5 years 23d of next April. George is aged 2 years 23d of next April. Teste: Thos. Brown, William Beames.

Page 114.—16th February, 1748. Executors qualify on above, with sureties Daniel Stover, Peter Rufenough (signed Peter Ufner).

Page 115.—16th February, 1748. Jane Grimes' bond as administratrix of William Grymes, with sureties John Graham, James Mays.

Page 116.—16th February, 1748. Danl. Evans, administrator of Mark Evans, with sureties Archd. Grymes, John Robinson.

Page 117.—16th February, 1748. James Robinson's bond as administrator of James Robinson, with sureties Jno. Robinson, David Trimble.

Page 118.—14th September, 1748. Nathan Lusk's will—Wife, Elizabeth; son, John; daughter, Agness, wife to Mathew Young; son, James Lusk. Executor, son James. Teste: Pat. Martin, Patrick Cook, Martha Martin. Proved, 16th February, 1748, by Patrick and Martha Martin.

Page 119.—16th February, 1748. James Loosk qualifies as above, with sureties James Phillips.

Page 119.—17th January, 1748-9. William Cowden's will—Sons, James and William, plantation when they are sixteen; wife, Jane. Executors, James Eakin, Jno. Moore. Teste: Walter Eakin, Alex. Moore, Saml. Moore. Proved, 16th February, 1748, by Saml. and Alex. Moore.

Page 121.—16th February, 1748. Executors qualify as above, with sureties John Moore, Joseph Kennady.

Page 122.—10th March, 1746-7. Robert Wilson's appraisement by Jno. Black, James Alexander, Wm. Long. Debts due to John Holmes, Wm. Darlington, Wm. Branston.

Page 123.—12th December, 1748. Patrick Cook's will—Wife, Jane; daughter, Mary (infant); son, John (infant). If children die in infancy, care to be taken to find the nearest blood relations, and, in their default, then the estate to be given in care to the Presbytery of New Castle to be laid out in pious uses and to support the gospel here. Executors, James Lockhart and Patrick Martin. Teste: John Risk, Pat Martin. Proved, 17th February, 1748, by both witnesses.

Page 124.—17th February, 1748. Pat Martin qualifies as above.

Page 125.—No date. Martin Kaufman's will in German and translated— 1. She, herself, shall administer; my brother shall be her bondsman; the appraisers shall be out of the brotherhood. 2. She to have the estate until the eldest son comes of age. 3. Sons and all the children. Teste: David Kaufman, Michael Kaufman, Hans Root. Proved, 17th May, 1749, by Michael Kaufman and John Root. Widow Barbara granted administration.

Page 126.—17th May, 1749. Barbara's bond as administratrix above, with surety David Kaufman.

Page 127.—17th May, 1749. Eleanor Draper's bond as administratrix of George Draper, with sureties James Davis, Robert Looney, Jr.

Page 128.—23d December, 1748. John Johnston's will—Wife, Hannah. Executors, wife and John Dobins. Teste: Adam Reder, Mathias Reeder, Wm. James. Proved, 17th May, 1749, by all witnesses. Both executors granted administration.

Page 129.—17th May, 1749. Administration bond as above, with sureties James Robinson, Valentine Sevier.

Page 130.—10th May, 1749. Ludwick Freedley's appraisement by Alexander Herring, John Bryant, Cornelius Bryant.

Page 131.—17th May, 1749. Lydia Elswick's bond as administratrix of John Elswick, with sureties Richard Ratliff, Ebenezer Westcoat.

Page 132.—27th January, 1748. William Hill's will—Weaver; children, Sarah, James, Mary, John, Joseph, Hannah, Rachel, Elizabeth; wife, Mary. Executors, wife Mary and Thomas Moore. Teste: Wm. Carroll, Isaac Johnson, Jno. Dobikin. Proved, 17th May, 1749, by Jno. Dobikin and Isaac Johnson. Both executors granted administration.

Page 133.—17th May, 1749. Executor's bond as above, with surety Wm. White.

Page 134.—25th January, 1748-9. John Cumberland's will—Brother James Cumberland, 1 shilling; wife, Catherine, executrix. Teste: Wm. White, Saml. Brown, Wm. James. Proved, 17th May, 1749, by all witnesses, and Catherine granted administration.

Page 135.—17th May, 1749. Catherine Cumberland's bond as above.

Page 136.—19th April, 1749. Patrick Cook's inventory and appraisement by Wm. McPheeters, Wm. McCutchen, Wm. Ledgerwood, Jno. Trimble.

Page 140.—16th March, 1748. Samuel Scott's will—Wife, Ann; son, John, 400 acres on Cub Run, slave negroes; daughters, Mary and Jean (infants), slaves, negroes; mother, Jean Scott; brother's son, Samuel Scott. Executors, Robert Scott and Robert Hook. Teste: Robert McFerson, George Scott, George Scott. Presented 17th May, 1749, in Court by executors and proved by all witnesses. Ann refuses to abide by the will.

Page 141.—17th May, 1749. Executor's bond as above, with sureties Wm. Lamb, Mathew Thompson.

Page 142.—17th May, 1749. Mary Moffett's bond as administratrix of John Moffett, with sureties Robert and Wm. Christian.

Page 143.—9th February, 1747-8. Isaac Anderson's will—To be buried where his son John is buried; wife, Martha, and her daughter Elizabeth; son, Isaac; son, James; son, Jacob; daughter, Elizabeth; daughter, Mary. Executors, wife Martha and Hugh Martin. Teste: Hugh Martin, James Anderson. Presented 17th May, 1749, by widow Martha and proved by Hugh Martin and Jacob Anderson. Hugh Martin refuses to execute.

Page 144.—17th May, 1749. Martha Anderson's bond as above, with sureties Francis McCown, Andrew Hays.

Page 145.—17th May, 1749. Elizabeth Taylor 's bond as administratrix of Thomas Taylor, with sureties Thomas Paxton and Thomas Paxton, Jr.

Page 146.—14th December, 1748. Robert Kirkham's will—Wife, Sarah; son, Henry; daughter, Nancy; daughter, Elizabeth; daughter, Margaret; daughter, Sarah. Debt to be paid to Elizabeth Sommers. Executrix, wife Sarah. Teste: Jno. and Ro. Moore, Saml. McCluer, James Trimble. Presented 17th May, 1749, by Sarah, and proved by all witnesses.

Page 147.—17th May, 1749. Sarah Kirkham's bond as executrix, as above.

Page 148.—13th December, 1748. Archibald Clendenning's (of Cowpasture) will—Wife, Esther; son, John; son, Archibald, Jr. To James Burnsides, the plantation in the new found land. To James Burnsides' sister, Rachel Burnsides, under 18. To wife's children, Margaret and John ("youngest daughter named here Margaret Clendenning"). Executors, Thos. and Wm. Galespy. Teste: Wm. Dogherty, Andrew Muldrow, Michael Reamey. Proved, 17th May, 1749, by all witnesses, and executors to be summoned.

Page 150.—17th May, 1749. Ann Hungate's bond as administratrix of Charles Hungate, with sureties John Robinson, Peter Kinder (Günder).

Page 151.—9th March, 1748. Simon Aker's will—Wife, Mary Akers; sons, William and Thomas, and their younger brother and sister, Uriah Acres and Ruth Acres. Executors, wife Mary and son William. Teste: Wm. Armstrong, Susanna Armstrong, Nicholas Haile. Presented, 17th May, 1749, by Mary and William Acres. Proved by Wm. and Susanna Armstrong, and lie for further proof.

Page 152.—17th May, 1749. Mary and William Aker's bond as above, with surety John Mills.

Page 153.—13th May, 1749. Nathan Lusk's inventory and appraisement by John Shields, Saml. McCutchen, Robt. Robinson.

Page 155.—17th May, 1749. James Robinson's inventory and appraisement by Ephraim Vause, John Meason, Richard Hall.

Page 156.—12th April, 1749. Alex. Smiley's inventory and appraisement.

Page 157.—17th March, 1748-9. David Moore's inventory by James Fulton, John Mountgomery and Patrick Hays. Ro Coulton, due for 2 gallons whiskey at 3 shillings; Jno. Shields, due; Jno. Carr, due; Jas. Aikin, due; Benj. Watson, due; Jonathan Brown, due; James Walker, due; John Lowry, due; Jno. Edmiston, due; Wm. McCreerey, due; James Shields, due; Wm. Worthclaw, due.

Page 158.—19th April, 1748. John Patterson's will—To be buried in the graveyard that is hard by Francis McCown's; wife, Agness; son, John (infant); son, George; daughter, Agness; legatee, John Green. Executors, Francis McCown and wife. Teste: Francis McCown, Robt. Gamell, John Betty, 18th May, 1749. Will not proved because witnesses not present, but administration, c. t. a., granted Agness.

Page 159.—18th May, 1749. Agness Patterson's bond as administratrix as above, with sureties Joseph Cannady, Charles Berry.

Page 160.—18th May, 1749. Jacob Thomas' bond as administrator of Jacob Thomas, with sureties Jacob Coger (Kogar), Ludwick Franciscus.

Page 161.—22d December, 1748. Will of Andrew Moore—500 acres to Alex. and Saml. Moore and their mother; James Moore, a cow; William Moore, 5 shillings; John Moore, 5 shillings; Quanten Moore, 5 shillings; David Moore, 5 shillings. Teste: Robert Breckinridge, George Henderson. 19th May, 1749, having been proved last February. Court proved by George Henderson, is now proved by Robert Breckinridge.

Page 162.—19th May, 1749. Alex. and Saml. Moore qualify administrators above, with sureties Nathanl. Evins, Jno. Makey.

Page 163.—19th May, 1749. James Lockhart's bond as executor of Patrick Cook, with sureties Henry Downs and Jno. Smith.

Page 164.—18th August, 1749. Thomas Taylor's inventory and appraisement by Nathaniel Evans, Wm. Caruthers, Mathew Lisle.

Page 165.—19th April, 1749. James Coburn's appraisement. Settled with Andrew Knoling, Peter Tustee, Henry Sheplar, Geo. Sea, Fredk. Sea, Thos. Dove. Due from James Kuykendall, Saml. Coburn. Due from Christian Ewigh, Joel Hornback. Due from Jacob Coburn, Wm. Leane, Isaac Coburn. Due from Henry Femster, John Ryon, Aaron Price. Due from Jno. Collins, Jno. Warwell, Richd. Field. Due from Henry Cartwright, Garrett Decker. Due from Danl. Richardson, John Kuykendall. 21 lbs. nails. By Abraham Vanderpoole, James Simpson, Michael Horn.

Page 169.—9th August, 1749. William Hill's appraisement by Wm. White, John Daubekins, Reuben Allen.

Page 170.—16th August, 1749. John Johnston's appraisement by John Miller, Adam Rider, Thomas Moore.

Page 170.—13th July, 1749. William James' (of Smith's Creek) will—Yeoman; wife, Sarah, estate until eldest son Thomas James comes of age; three sons, Thomas, Joshua and Joseph. Executors, wife and Thomas Moore. Teste: John Dobikin, Daniel Holdman, Jno. Ruddell, Sr. Presented, 22d August, 1749, by Thomas Moore and proved by all witnesses.

Page 172.—22d August, 1749. Thos. Moore's bond as executor, with surety Wm. Karroll.

Page 173.—17th August, 1749. Jno. Cumberland's appraisement—1 servant man, 4 years to serve. Debt due from Wm. Magee.

Page 174.—15th May, 1749. Peter Dyer's appraisement by Robert Cravens, Thomas and Jeremiah Harrison.

Page 175.—22d August, 1749. Leah Tyler's bond as administratrix of Wm. Tyler, with sureties Robert McKay.

Page 176.—26th July, 1749. John Ruddle, Jr.'s (of Smith's Creek), will—Yeoman; father, John Ruddle, Sr.; mother, Mary Ruddle; brothers, Archibald and Stephen Ruddle, and brothers and sisters. Robert Wilson to share with brothers and sisters. Executor, father John. Teste: Andrew Bird, Andrew Bird, Jr., Edward Ryan. 22d August, 1749, proved by Andrew Bird, Sr., and Edward Ryan.

Page 177.—22d August, 1749. John Ruddle's bond as executor as above, with sureties Daniel Davisson, Samuel Lockhart.
Page 177.—22d August, 1749. Wm. Cowden's appraisement by John Huston, Robert Dunlapp, Joseph Kennedy.
Page 178.—22d August, 1749. Andrew Moore's appraisement.
Page 179.—16th August, 1749. John Wiley's appraisement by Saml. Odell, Josiah Parent, John Davis. Work done for Barney Regan.
Page 180.—22d August, 1749. Thomas Beard's bond as administrator of James McNutt, with sureties Thos. Beard, James Buchanan, David Stuart.
Page 181.—21st August, 1749. Robert Kirkum's appraisement.
Page 182.—20th March, 1749. John Campbell's sale bill—To George Shuneman, Stephen Phillips, Barbara Job. To John Barrenhinsell, James McNeal, Anthony Strother, Thos. Dolson (Dottson), Fredk. Freeling, George Neel, Thos. Harmon.
Page 182.—5th April, 1749. Mathew Skeen's appraisement by William Carroll, Wm. James, Robert Colwell.
Page 184.—8th April, 1749. Barbara Rambo's appraisement by Saml. Newman, Peter Scholl, John Ruddell, Sr., 1 sorrel horse lost by Robert Milsaps.
Page 185.—19th August, 1749. John Patterson's inventory.
Page 186.—23d August, 1749. Isaac Anderson's appraisement by Hugh Martin, Francis McCown, Andrew Hays.
Page 187.—14th March, 1749. Robert King's will—Miller; 30 shillings to the Meeting House; son, John; wife, Catherine, plantation on Falling Spring; daughters, Sarah, Elizabeth and Catherine. Executors, Robert Poage and John Anderson. Teste: John Poage, John Young and John Anderson. 23d August, 1749, proved by John Poage and John Anderson.
Page 188.—23d August, 1749. Executors qualify as above, with sureties John Smith and Wm. King.
Page 189.—24th August, 1749. Esther Clendenning's bond as administratrix, c. t. a., of Archd. Clendenning, with sureties Wm. Aylett (signed Wm. Elliott), John Gay.
Page 191.—10th March, 1748. Mark Evans' appraisement by Ephraim Vause, James Nelley, Joseph Robinson.
Page 192.—25th August, 1749. Margery Sharpe's bond as administratrix of John Sharpe, with sureties Jno. Smith, Jno. Warnock.
Page 194.—29th November, 1749. Widow King's (Robert King's) appraisement.
Page 195.—16th June, 1749. Martin Kaufman's appraisement, by Daniel Stover, Jacob Borner, Jno. Holdman.
Page 198.—29th November, 1749. Rev. Jno. Hindman's inventory, by Ro. Hook, Ro. Cravens, Wm. Williams.
Page 200.—9th November, 1749. Wm. Graham's appraisement, by Saml. Hodge, John Miller, Wm. Elliot.
Page 201.—29th November, 1749. Elizabeth E. Berry's bond as administratrix of James Berry, with sureties Thomas and Charles Berry.
Page 202.—10th October, 1749. William Magill's will—Wife, Margaret, and her son, David Gass; sons, James and William, adjoining Charles Campbell; son, John; grandchild, James' son; daughter, Elizabeth. Executors, Robert Cravens, Hugh Campbell. Signed William Magill, Margaret

Magill. Teste: Andrew Erwin, Charles Campbell. Proved, 29th November, 1749, when Margaret renounced the will.

Page 203.—29th November, 1749. Executor's bond as above, with sureties Andrew Erwin, Charles Campbell.

Page 205.—30th November, 1749. Alex. Wright's bond as administrator of Jacob Kinder, with sureties John Harvie, Robert Breckinridge.

Page 206.—10th November, 1749. William Taylor's appraisement, by Samuel Odel, Thos. Grubbs, Abraham Job. To Samuel Denton, Philip Crum.

Page 208.—1st September, 1748. Vendue held at house of Samuel Stewart of goods of Joseph Harrison sold by Jeremiah Harrison. To Timothy Convey, Samuel Harrison, Samuel Monsey, Arthur Johnson, Abraham Smith, Tunis Wood, Samuel Hull, Edward McGinnis, Archibald Buchanan, Aaron Oliver, Ephraim Love, Solomon Turpin, Samuel Wilkey.

Page 209.—30th November, 1749. Patrick Martin's bond as administrator of Andrew Martin.

Page 210.—1st December, 1749. Jacob Miller's bond as administrator of Christian Miller, with surety Theobald Carlock.

Page 211.—22d December, 1743. Daniel Denniston's will of Beverley Manor in Augusta County—Wife, Sarah; son, Daniel (unmarried); daughter, Ann Gilaspy and her children; son-in-law, Patrick Gilaspy; granddaughter, Sarah Gilaspy; granddaughter, Jean Gilaspy. Executors, John Lewis and Ro. Poage. Teste: John Henderson, James Trimble.

Page 213.—24th February, 1749. Codicil to above. Daughter, Ann Gilaspy's 4 sons; 10 shillings to the Meeting House he now belongs to. Teste: John Anderson, Elizabeth Poage. Proved, 1st December, 1749, by all witnesses.

Page 213.—1st December, 1749. Executor's bond as above; surety, Samuel Doake.

Page 214.—2d December, 1749. John Christian's bond as administrator of John Davison, with sureties James Bell, Robert McClenachan.

Page 215.—6th November, 1749. John Woolf's appraisement, by Michael Harnis, Michael Stump, James Simpson. Note of Peter Hart. Note of Nicholas Snider. Sale to Ellis Seller.

Page 217.—27th February, 1749. Francis McBride's bond as administrator of Benj. McBride, with sureties Jno. Dunbarr, Daniel Morley.

Page 218.—27th February, 1749. Hugh Martin's bond as administrator of Martha McCord, with sureties Charles and Andrew Hays.

Page 219.—28th February, 1749. Jane Shield's bond as administratrix of James Shields, with sureties Robt. Campbell, John Shields.

Page 220.—3d April, 1749. Jonathan Newman's appraisement, by Capt. Peter Scholl, John Ruddle, Sr., Wm. James.

Page 221.—28th February, 1749. John Moffett's appraisement, by John, William and George Anderson.

Page 222.—28th December, 1749. William Magill's appraisement, by John Seawright, John Erwin, Charles Campbell. Cash by Hugh Dever and Hugh Ross.

Page 225.—21st December, 1749. Charles Hungate's appraisement, by John Mason, Tasker Tosh, Wm. Armstrong.

Page 226.—28th October, 1749. James McNutt's appraisement, by James Trimble, Joseph Coulton, John Roseman. Notes of Philip Chittam, Jas. Davis and Arthur Miliken.

Page 227.—24th February, 1749-50. Christian Miller's appraisement, by Joseph Langdon, John Cook, Joseph Cokenour.

Page 228.—1st March, 1749. Andrew Martin's appraisement, by Andrew Pickens, James Walker, James Coulter.

Page 229.—2d March, 1749. Peter Kinder's appraisement.

Page 231.—2d March, 1749. Mathew Edmiston, Danl. Harrison, Gabriel Pickens, farmers. Mathew's bond as guardian of Robina, daughter of James Patterson. Robina did not chose guardian.

Page 232.—11th December, 1749. Saml. Crockett's will, of Reed Creek, farmer—Wife, Esther; executors, Wife and James Montgomery; son, John; five sons; some of children are infants; daughters, Agness, Jane, Catherine; guardian of children, Joseph Crockett. Teste: Joseph Crockett, John Noble, John Downing. Proved, 22d May, 1750, by Joseph Crockett and Jno. Noble; and both executors qualify, with surety Joseph Long.

Page 234.—6th December, 1749. Samuel Brown's will, farmer—Brother. Henry Brown, colt that runs at Round Oak; two youngest brothers, Daniel and David; wife, Mary, mare bought of Robert Gay; two children, Adam (eldest) and Henry Brown, infants. To eldest born, Adam, house and land at Round Oake. Executors, Adam Dickinson and brother Henry Brown. Teste: Benj. Hardin, John Dickinson, Isaac Scholley. Proved, 22d May, 1750, by Hardin and Dickinson.

Page 236.—22d May, 1750. Executors qualify on above, with sureties Jno. Pickins and Wm. Acres.

Page 237.—6th January, 1749-50. John Woodley's will—Son, Jacob, 5 shillings; son-in-law, Nicholas Seahaven. Executor, Nicholas Seahaven. Teste: Daniel Holdman, John Rudle, Hans Heinrich Neff. Proved, 22d May, 1750, by all witnesses, and executor qualifies.

Page 239.—11th September, 1749. Mathusalem Griffie's will, of Round Oak, farmer—Wife, Lucretia; youngest son, John; three sons; eldest son, Morrice Griffie, 300 acres on Meason's Creek by the Lick; executors, son Morrice and wife; son, Benjamin; daughter, Elizabeth Griffie, under 21; daughter, Hannah, infant; daughter, Lucretia, under 25. Teste: Thomas Tosh, Tasker Tosh, Thos. Acres. Proved, 22d May, 1750, by Thos. Acres, and others to be summoned.

Page 240.—22d May, 1750. Elizabeth Barber's bond as administratrix of George Barber, with sureties Jno. Smith, Robert Looney.

Page 241.—6th April, 1749. Robert Edmiston's will—Wife (Jean?); legatee, Jean Edmiston; daughter, Dorothy Edmiston; son, James; son, William. Executors, Thos. McSpaden, Wm. Edmiston. Teste: Jno. Edmiston, Samuel Buchanan. Proved, 22d May, 1750, by Buchanan, and Edmiston summoned.

Page 242.—22d May, 1750. Elizabeth Lucas' bond as administratrix of Richard Lucas, with sureties Maurice O'Freel, Joseph Crockett.

Page 244.—26th February, 1749. Andrew Boyd's will, farmer—Wife, Rebecca; two sons, Thomas and John; cousin, Jno. White, 1 cow, if he come to live here. He is to live 3 or 4 years at a Spring between (betwixt) Andrew's dwelling house and the Half Way Creek. Executors, wife and James Fulton. Teste: Wm. Hay, Jennat Boggs, Robert Alexander. Proved, 22d May, 1750, by Hay and Boggs, and both executors give bond, with sureties Patrick Hays. Rebecca's mark——

Page 246.—22d May, 1750. Archibald Clendenning's appraisement, by Hugh Coffey, Alex. McCray, John Cartmel. Books.
Page 247.—4th August, 1749. George Draper's appraisement, by Richard Hall, Wm. Ingless, Thomas Ingless.
Page 248.—23d May, 1750. William Henry's bond as guardian of James McCord, orphan of Wm. McCord, with surety Francis McCown.
Page 249.—25th May, 1750. John and Eleanor Fletcher's bond as administrators of John Hindman, clerk, whereof John Stevenson was administrator, with sureties John Lewis, Wm. Hamilton, Jno. Graham.
Page 250.—7th March, 1750. James Berry's appraisement by Thomas Beard, James Trimble, David Hays.
Page 252.—2d July, 1750. Richard Ticktom's will—Wife, Rose, the mare that was Frederick's; son, Joseph; son, Richard; daughter, Mary; daughter, Nanny (the horse at John Miller's, and cow at Ben Hass). Teste: Wm. Miller, Thos. West, John States. Presented by Rose Ticktom, 28th August, 1750, and witnesses summoned. Proved, 20th February, 1750, by States, and Rose qualified administratrix, with sureties Daniel Love, James Hamilton. (No bond here.)
Page 253.—Shannandore, 4th June, 1750. Caleb Job's will—Wife, Barbary; four children, Samuel, Jacob, Nathan, Elizabeth. Executors, wife and Ephraim Leith. Teste: Abraham Job, Moses McKay. Proved, 28th May, 1750, by Job and McKay, and both executors gave bond (no bond recorded).
Page 254.—10th August, 1750. Andrew Boyd's appraisement, by James Fulton, Wm. Moore and Robert Alexander. Jennet Steel's note; Alex. McCorkle's note; David Moore's note.
Page 255.—28th August, 1750. Daniel Holdman's account against estate of Rudy Brock for services done to the children—3d November, 1750, cash paid for George Brock's land; Efey Brock's share of grain.
Page 255.—28th August, 1750. Ephraim Leath and Barbary Job's bond as executors of Caleb Job.
Page 257.—20th August, 1750. Appraisement of James Shields, cordwinder, by John Wilson, Wm. McCutchen, David Karr.
Page 259.—4th July, 1749. Samuel Scott's appraisement, by Wm. Lamb, James Beard, Mathew Thompson.
Page 262.—29th August, 1750. Hugh Parker's bond as administrator of James Rutledge, Gent., deceased, with sureties Jno. Stephenson, Hans Baumgartner.
Page 263.—29th August, 1750. Wm. Edmondson's bond as executor of Robert Edmondson, deceased, with surety John Edmondson.
Page 265.—30th August, 1750. William James' appraisement, by Wm. White, John Rudle, Reuben Allen.
Page 266.—27th December, 1749. Simon Acres' appraisement, by Erwin Patterson, Joseph Robinson, John Meson.
Page 267.—27th November, 1750. Paul Lung's bond as administrator of Rudy Mauck, with sureties Frederick Fraelich (Frailey), Peter Scholl.
Page 268.—18th July, 1750. George Barber's appraisement, by Henry Houlston, Robert Williams, William Terry, Joseph Robinson.
Page 269.—25th July, 1750. Abraham Job's will—Wife, Elizabeth; son, Elisha, trustee for the widow, and after her widowhood, equal executor with her; children Rebecca, Isaac (infant), Phoeby, David (infant), Hannah;

daughter, Mary McCoy, and her son, Isaac McKay; son Isaac to be bound to James Brown, a hatter; son David to be bound to a saddler in that County which is called West Nottingham. Proved, 27th November, 1750, by Henry Netherton. Elizabeth, the widow, qualified executrix, c. t. a., nuncupative will.

Page 270.—27th November, 1750. Elizabeth Job's bond as above, with Henry Netherton, Robert McCoy.

Page 271.—3d November, 1750. Mathew Shaup's will—Eldest sons-in-law, Michael Carn, George Carn, the full estate their own father left them; one-third to be divided between 8 children; one-third to be divided between his own 6 children; two eldest sons, John and Adam Shaup. Executors, George Carpenter, Jacob Pence. Teste: Henry Dickey (Dickins), Jacob Nicholas, George Bernhart Mann. Proved, 28th November, 1750; proved by Nicholas, and others summoned.

Page 272.—4th November, 1750. John Lawrence's will (in German and signed Hans. Lawrentz)—Jacob Nicholas to have his choice of the two places, and of testator's place 100 acres to be added to Felty's place, and the remainder to be divided among the childen in Pennsylvania. His estate in Germany, Jacob Nicholas and the other heirs of those that are alive of brother's and sister's children, either in America or Germany, shall have equal shares. Teste: Valentine Bentz, Michael Carn, Henry Burgie. Proved, 28th November, 1750, by Burgie and Bence, and others to be summoned. Proved, 27th February, 1750, by Michael Carn, and Jacob Nicholas qualifies administrator, c. t. a. (no bond appears here).

Page 273.—23d November, 1750. John Woodley's (of Smith's Creek) appraisement by Hans Heinrich Neff, Daniel Holdman, John Ruddell.

Page 274.—14th November, 1750. Charles Gallagher's will (Gallaghar)—Beloved friend, Rev. Mr. William Wappaler, £10; beloved friend, Rev. Mr. Taylor, £10; beloved friend, William Hopkins; beloved friend, Samuel Cerrel; beloved friend, Ephraim Love, executor. Teste: William Hopkins, Isaiah Shipman, Jennet Love. Proved, 28th August, 1750, by Wm. Hopkins, and others summoned. Proved, 26th February, 1750, by other witnesses, and Ephraim Love qualified executor.

Page 275.—15th September, 1750. John Greer's nuncupative will—Debts to be paid to William Long, William Nul, John Kennedy, Nathaniel Patterson; son Alexander to be bound to a trade; one child to be bound to John Mitchell; one child to be bound to S D; oldest girl to go to some descent woman to learn housewifery. Executors, John Mitchell and Samuel Doak. Teste: James Cowin, Jno. Mitchell, Saml. Doak, Francis Beatey. Proved, 28th November, 1750, by Cowin and Beatey.

Page 275.—28th November, 1750. Sale bill of Ann Hungate's vendue—To William Alexander, Joseph Milikin, Malcom Campbell, Wm. Carson, Wm. Armstrong, James Neeley, John Lawler, Jacob Patton, Uriah Acres, Archibald Grimes.

Page 276.—4th July, 1749. John Elswick's appraisement, by Thomas Ingliss, James Scaggs, Ebenezer Westcoat.

Page 278.—28th November, 1750. Francis McCown's bond as guardian of James McCord, orphan of William McCord, with surety Jno. Weiley. James chose his guardian.

Page 279.—29th November, 1750. William Baskins' bond as administrator of Robert Baskins.

Page 280.—30th November, 1750. John Lynn (Linn), Jr.'s, bond as guardian of Sarah Bennett, orphan of Richard Bennett, with surety John Lynn, Sr., Jas. McCorkle. Sarah chose her guardian.

Page 281.—No date. New Kent—Thos. Wadle, Dr., to James Renalds; Mathew Young, Dr., to James Renalds; Charles Hays, Dr., to James Renalds, 1 doubloon, 2 maydores, 1 pistole, 2 pieces of silver; Robert Armstrong, Dr., one bufelow, £3, £12. James Rannald's will (Renalds)—Wife and children; two eldest sons. Teste: Charles McAnally, Rebeckah Buchanan. Executors, John Hays and James Thompson. Proved, 30th November, 1750, by Rebeckah Buchanan, and Charles to be summoned.

Page 282.—26th February, 1750. Charles Gallagher's appraisement, by Jeremiah Harrison, Daniel Harrison, Robert Cravens. (Here James Porteus ceases to be scribe, *vid.* page 93, *supra*.)

Page 283.—27th February, 1750-51. Magdalene and Andrew Bird's bond as administrators of Andrew Bird, with sureties John Dobikin, Samuel Newman.

Page 284.—22d February, 1750. Benj. Kerkendall's bond as administrator of John Mills, with sureties Anthony Bogart, Jno. Dunbar.

Page 286.—2d July, 1750. Richard Tictom's will, *vid.* page 252, *supra*.

Page 287.—27th February, 1750. Rosamond Tacton's bond as executrix of Richard Tacton, with sureties Samuel Love, James Hamilton.

Page 288.—27th February, 1750-51. Phoebe Davison's bond as administratrix of Daniel Davison, with sureties John Harrison, Samuel Newman.

Page 289.—26th February, 1750. Asabel Hodge's bond as administrator of John Hodge.

Page 291.—25th December, 1750. John Hays' will, plantationer—Wife, Rebecca; three sons; son, Andrew; son, Charles; son, John (land on Roanoke joining William Miller's plantation); nephew, John Hays, Jr. (Rebecca Hays, daughter to son John); daughter, Jenett Mills; nephew, (?) Rebeckey Guines; nephew, Robert Lusk; nephew, James Hays, son to son James; legatee, Robert Lusk; legatee, Abigail Hayes, alias Kinseys. Executors, wife Rebecky and sons Charles and Andrew. Teste: James Buchanan, Saml. Hayes, James Moore. Proved, 26th February, 1750, by all witnesses, and Charles and Andrew refuse to administer, and Rebecca qualifies with sureties (no bond appears).

Page 294.—29th August, 1750. Gilbert Campbell's will, of Forks of James River, plantationer—Wife, Prudence Campbell, alias Osran; son, George (infant); son, Charles (infant); daughter, Elizabeth Woods, alias Campbell; son, James; daughter, Prudence Hays; daughter, Sarah Campbell; daughter, Lattice Campbell. Executors, James Trimble, Thomas Stuart and Andrew Hays. Teste: James Thompson, Robert Allison, Alex. McMullen. Proved, 26th February, 1750, by Thompson and Allison, and probate granted to Andrew Hays.

Page 297.—26th February, 1750. John Mason and James McKachey's (Keachey) bond as administrators of Wm. Alexander, with Erwin Patterson and Joseph Love.

Page 298.—29th January, 1750-51. William Alexander's appraisement, by Thomas Tosh, Wm. Akers, James Neeley.

Page 300.—26th February, 1750. Elizabeth Crawford, George Anderson, Robert Patterson's bond as administrators of James Crawford, with surety Patrick Crawford, Mathew Robinson.

Page 301.—8th February, 1750-51. Mathias Shaup's appraisement, by John Stevenson, Wm. Williams, Henry Downs.

Page 304.—8th February, 1750. John Lawrence's appraisement.

Page 305.—27th February, 1750-51. Valentine Pence's bond as administrator (executor) of Jacob Pence.

Page 306.—26th February, 1750. Mathias Selzer's bond as executor of Michael Rynard.

Page 307.—27th February, 1750-51. Rebecca Hays' bond as executor of John Hays, with sureties James Walker and James Buchanan.

Page 308.—27th February, 1750-51. Andrew Hays' bond as executor of Gilbert Campbell, with sureties Charles Hayes, James Walker.

Page 309.—26th February, 1750. Ephriam Love's bond as executor of Charles Gallagher, with sureties Isaiah Shipman, Andrew Lewis. By John Anderson, Robert Pog, John Peterson.

Page 312.—26th February, 1750. Jacob Nicholas and Valentine Pence's bond as administrators of Mathew Shaup, with sureties Wm. Williams and James Downing.

Page 313.—27th February, 1750. Jacob Nicholas' bond as executor of John Lawrence, with surety Jacob Miller.

Page 314.—27th February, 1750-51. Sarah Thorn's bond as administratrix of Henry Thorn, with sureties Peter Thorn, John Dunbarr.

Page 315.—13th November, 1750. Henry Thorn's will—Wife, Sarah, with child; father, Peter Thorn. Teste: James Scott, Henry Sheabler, Hunkrist Carlock. Proved, 27th February, 1750, by Carlock, and others to be summoned.

Page 317.—27th February, 1750-51. James Thompson's bond as executor of James Rennald, with sureties John Lyle and David Moore.

Page 318.—8th February, 1750-51. James Randall's appraisement, by Wm. Hall, Robert Allison, Nathaniel McClure.

Page 319.—28th February, 1750-51. James Berry's bond as guardian of John, James and William Berry, orphans of James Berry, with surety Wm. Martin, George Berry; guardian appointed.

Page 319.—28th February, 1750. Jonathan Newman's estate; settlement by Samuel Newman. To Joshua Potts, Eleanor Taylor, John Hodge, John Ruddle, Jr., Wm. Carryl, John Henry Neff.

Page 320.—28th February, 1750. Robert Edmiston's appraisement by John Moore, John Edmiston, Joseph Kennedy.

Page 321.—10th August, 1750. Appraisement of Saml. Brown, on Round Oak, by Ephraim Vause, Wm. Buis, Thomas Buis. 7th November, 1750. Appraisement of above on Cowpasture, by Hugh Coffey, Elicksander Mealray, Jno. Donaley.

Page 322.—1st March, 1750-51. John Wilkins' ( ) bond as administrator of Thos. Wilkins, with sureties Daniel Harrison, Robert Young.

Page 324.—27th February, 1748-9. James Bell's will—Wife, Rachel; son, William (infant); son, James, under 23, 400 acres on Jenning's Branch, and one plantation on a branch of Cathey's River near testator's home place, where he lives; cousin, Andrew Foster. testator has sold him a tract on a spring branch of Cathey's River, called McClure's Run; daughters, Margaret, Elizabeth, Mary Ann and Jean Bell; nephews, William and James Bell, tract on which they dwell known by name of Smith's Spring. Executors, wife Rachel and nephew James. Teste: Alexander Crawford,

Robert Renick, Saml. Bell. Proved, 28th May, 1751, by all witnesses, and executors qualified, with sureties John Archer and Thos. Armstrong.

Page 327.—9th April, 1751. James Robinson's will, yeoman—Wife, Mary, and her daughters; two youngest sons, Isaac and Jonathan (Isaac is the older); son, James; son, David, 200 acres on Shanando River where he now lives. Executors, wife Mary and son David. Teste: James Williams, John Miller, John McDonald. Proved, 28th May, 1751, by McDonald and Miller, and Mary qualifies executrix, with sureties John Bryan and John Dobikin.

Page 330.—30th March, 1751. Cornelius O'Bryan's will, yeoman ( )—Wife, Rebecca; son, John; son, Cornelius; son Thomas' eldest son Benjamin; remainder of children. Executors, wife Rebecca and son John. Teste: James Williams, Joseph Bryan, Jacob Gum. 28th May, 1751, proved by Joseph Bryan, and lie for further proof. 27th August, 1751, proved by Jacob Gum.

Page 331.—23d August, 1750. Jacob Goldman's will—Wife; son, John; son, Jacob; youngest child shall have her share as well as the oldest; executors, Frederick Stern, Humphrey Baker; daughter, Mary. Teste: Humphrey Baker. Presented, 28th May, 1751, but witnesses fail to appear, and lies for proof.

Page 332.—22d March, 1751. John Bumgarner's will—Son, John; son, Christian; daughters, Mary, Elizabeth and Madley; grandson, Jacob Burner; sons to be put to school until they can read and write, and then to trades. Executors, Mathais Selzer and Jacob Burner. Teste: Benj. Barger, Charles Burk, Geo. Shuneman. (No certificate of probate of any kind.)

Page 333.—28th May, 1751. Isabella and James Edmondson's bond as administrators of David Edmondson, with sureties Wm. McFeaters and Wm. Henderson.

Page 335.—28th May, 1751. Ingbor Allen's bond as administratrix of Reuben Allen, with surety Cornelius Ruddle.

Page 338.—28th May, 1751. Edward Williams' bond as administrator of Isaac Jones, with sureties Peter Thorn, Abel Westfall.

Page 337.—28th May, 1751. Alice Cherry's bond as administratrix of Edward Cherry, with sureties Robt. Rennick, Abraham Vanderpoole.

Page 339.—25th May, 1751. John Hays' appraisement, by Joseph Coulton, Alex. Walker, James Moore.

Page 341.—28th May, 1751. Jane Jackson's bond as administratrix of Wm Jackson, with sureties John Dickinson, George Wilson.

Page 342.—13th March, 1751. Michael Rinhart's inventory, by John Dobkin, Nicholas Seehorn, David Magit, George Shuneman.

Page 346.—7th March, 1750. Rude Mack's inventory, by Mathias Selzer, Daniel Stover, Jacob Burnet.

Page 348.—28th May, 1751. Abraham Job's appraisement, by Henry Netherton, James McCoy, Frederick Frailey.

Page 349.—18th May, 1751. James Crawford's appraisement, by Robt. Poage, Thomas Gordon, Saml. Henderson, John Anderson.

Page 351.—29th May, 1751. Susannah Carson's bond as administratrix of Henry Carson, with sureties Jacob Woodley, Clement Dixon.

Page 352.—30th August, 1750. Samuel Crockett's appraisement, by James Callhoon, John Noble, Wm. Sayers. Paid Robert Miller, Robert

Alcoran, James Ryne. To William Mountgomery. Due by Peter Harman, Jno. Thompson, Jr., Joseph Crockett, Andrew Gaughagen.

Page 356.—29th May, 1751. Jackson and Joseph Allen's bond as administrators of Mary Allen.

Page 358.—29th May, 1751. Lucretia Griffith's bond as executrix of Mathusalem Griffith, with sureties Erwin Patterson and Tasker Tosh.

Page 359.—22d May, 1751. Improvements valued on Samuel Porter's plantation, by John Poack and James Davis, on Buffelow Creek.

Page 360.—29th May, 1751. Robert Rose's bond as guardian of Wm. Rieley, orphan of John Rieley, deceased, appointed guardian.

Page 361.—23d May, 1751. Improvements valued of William Henderson's plantation on North Branch of James River, by John Mathews and John McClure. (Sworn by John Mathews, Sr.)

Page 361.—20th April, 1751. Andrew Bird's appraisement, by Wm. White, Wm. Carrol, John Ruddle.

Page 362.—29th May, 1751. Appraisement of Jacob Pence, by Robert Hooks, Wm. Williams.

Page 366.—15th August, 1751. Reuben Allen's appraisement, by John Ruddle, Daniel Holdman, Michael Waren.

Page 367.—27th August, 1751. James Bell's appraisement, by John Archer, Wm. McPheeters, Samuel Wallace.

Page 368.—6th August, 1751. James Robinson's appraisement by Thos. Moore, John Bryant, John McDonal. Due by Daniel Murley and John Patton.

Page 370.—27th August, 1751. John Hodge's appraisement, by Wm. Draper, Robert Caldwell, Wm. McGee. Due from John Lee, Robert Caldwell, Nicholas Seahorn.

Page 372.—27th August, 1751. David Edmondson's appraisement, by Wm. Finley, Wm. Jonston, Samuel McCune.

Page 372.—23d May, 1751. Gilbert Campbell's appraisement, by Alex. McMullan, Robert Allison, James Thompson, Andrew Hays.

Page 373.—23d May, 1751. Appraisement of goods left by Gilbert Campbell to his wife, Prudence Campbell, alias Puran.

Page 374.—27th August, 1751. Thomas Housen's (signed Joho Housen) bond as administrator of James Porteus, with sureties David Kingkade, W. Russell.

Page 375.—27th August, 1751. Frederick Sea's bond as administrator of George Sea, with surety Andrew Lewis.

Page 377.—24th August, 1751. Inventory of Richard Ticktum from the gap of the North Mountain upon Shannadore, by Charles Dayly, John Steats, Uriah Humble, all of the place aforesaid.

Page 379.— —— Daniel Gibson's will—Wife, Elizabeth Gibson, executrix. Teste: Alex. Blair, John Nickel, Robert Gambell. 28th August, 1751, no probate order.

Page 379.—28th August, 1751. John Scot's bond as administrator of Alex. Scot.

Page 381.—28th August, 1751. Thomas Lewis' bond as surveyor, with sureties Andrew Lewis, Jno. Madison.

Page 381.—28th August, 1751. Andrew Lewis' bond as deputy surveyor.

Page 382.—28th August, 1751. James Trimble's bond as deputy surveyor, with sureties Silas Hart, Robert Breckinridge.

Page 383.—28th August, 1751. Peter Moser's bond as administrator of Daniel Mouse, with sureties Frederick Sea, John Scott.

Page 384.—28th August, 1751. Andrew Hay's bond as guardian to Robert Lusk, orphan of John Lusk; appointed.

Page 385.—28th August, 1751. John Moore's bond as guardian of Margaret Bell, orphan of James Bell; appointed.

Page 386.—28th August, 1751. Archibald Graham's bill of sale of a negro boy, 11 years old, to Robert Bratton. Teste: W. Wilson, Ralph Laverty.

Page 386.—29th August, 1751. John Graham's bond as guardian to James and David Graham, orphans of Wm. Graham; appointed.

Page 387.—10th January, 1751. Robert Davison's will, yeoman—Son, John Davison, 13½ pence; daughter, Mary Huston, 13½ pence; wife, Ann. Executrix, Ann. Teste: John Mackey, William Lusk. 29th August, 1751, proved by all witnesses. Ann refuses to execute, and administration granted to John Davison.

Page 388.—4th September, 1751. Vendue by George Anderson and Robert Patterson upon estate of James Crawford. To Wm. Bell, Mathew Armstrong, Thomas Story, Edward Ritledge, Robt. Craig, Saml. Mullene, John Patterson, Saml. Keer, Pat Crawford, James Henderson, Timothy Coll.

Page 390.—17th October, 1751. John Rutledge's will—Aged father; nephew, George Rutledge, was partner with James Bell in a tract of land; 400 acres on Long Glade conveyed to them by Thos. Gilespy; brother, Wm. Rutledge; brother, Thomas Rutledge; sister, Catherine Marshal; sister, Jean Rutledge. Executors, Thomas Rutledge and James Bell. Teste: William Armstrong, John Flood, Hugh Means. Proved, 26th November, 1751, by all witnesses, and Thomas Rutledge qualifies executor, with sureties Wm. Thompson, Wm. Preston.

Page 392.—6th June, 1751. Appraisement of Isaac Jones by Abram Vanderpool, Henry Shipler, John McDade.

Page 393.—26th November, 1751. Jacob Thomas' bond as administrator of John Windlekite, with sureties Henry Long, Jacob Miller.

Page 394.—26th November, 1751. John O'Briant's bond as executor of Cornelius O'Briant.

Page 395.—27th November, 1751. Robert Davison's appraisement by Mathew and Daniel Lyle and James Edmondson.

Page 396.—23d April, 1751. John Gray's will, yeoman—Wife, Agness; son, Jacob; son, William; son, David; son, Joseph; son, Benj.; daughter, Ann Gray; son, Saml.; son, John; daughter, Elizabeth. Executors, son Samuel and John Lyle. Teste: Archd. Alexander, James McClung, Daniel Lyle. 27th November, 1751, proved by all witnesses, and both executors qualify, with sureties Archd. Alexander and James McClung.

Page 399.—23d April, 1751. Appraisement of Daniel Davis by Wm. White, John Ruddle, Michael Waren.

Page 400.—10th August, 1751. Edward Cherry's appraisement by Abel Westfall, Peter Thorn. Due by Loury Myers. Due by Abra. Hite.

Page 401.—27th November, 1751. John Archer and John Pickins' bond as guardians of Elizabeth and Catherine King, orphans of Robert King with surety John King, Robert McClenachan, appointed.

Page 403.—28th November, 1751. Robert Bratton and James McCorkle's bond as guardians of Archd. Crockett, orphan of Robt. Crockett, with sureties James Lockhart, Jno. Henderson, appointed.

Page 402.—28th November, 1751. George Breckinridge's bond as administrator of James Connelley, with sureties Robt. McClenachan, Ro. Breckinridge.

Page 405.—29th November, 1751. Joseph Carpenter's bond as guardian (appointed) to James, Benjamin and John Scot, orphans of John Scot, with surety John Lewis.

Page 405.—27th November, 1751. John McGill's bond as guardian (appointed) to James Patterson, orphan of James Patterson, with surety Mathew Armstrong.

Page 406.—19th November, 1751. Mathew Armstrong's bond as guardian (appointed) to Saml. Patterson, orphan of James Patterson, with surety Mathew Edmondson.

Page 407.—29th November, 1751. Judith Scot's bond as administratrix of John Scot.

Page 409.—22d June, 1751. John Miles' appraisement by James Simpson, Michael Harnis, Jacob Westfall.

Page 409.—22d August, 1751. Henry Carson's appraisement by John Dobikin, Adam Reader, Alex. Painter.

Page 410.—30th November, 1751. David Stewart's bond to collect the County proportion, with sureties Wm. Henderson, Thos. Stewart, Jno. Trimble.

Page 411.—20th November, 1752. Anne Wright's bond as administratrix of Thomas Wright, with surety John Jackson, James Jackson.

Page 412.—17th December, 1751. Alexander McCleary's will, yeoman—Wife, Margaret; daughter, Rachel, infant. Executors, Archd. Alexander and Robt. Huston. Teste: Samuel Gray, Moses Whitesides, Thos. McSpeaden. Proved, 20th May, 1752, by all witnesses, and executors qualify.

Page 414.—20th May, 1752. Improvements on John Hogshead's plantation. £40, by Simpson and John Archer. 21st May, 1752, John Gray's appraisement by Danl. Lyle, William Caruthers, Archd. Alexander.

Page 417.—25th January, 1752. Cornelius O'Bryan's appraisement, by Peter Scholl, John Miller, Michael Warren.

Page 417.—31st January, 1752. Valuation of David Cloid's 2 tracts—400 acres, stock and improvements, £62; 260 acres, stock and improvements, £75. Both tracts on Pessimon Run. By Joseph Robinson, Tobias Smith.

Page 417.—21st May, 1752. James Connelly's (Conly's) appraisement, by Thomas Ingles, Tobias Bright, Richard Hall.

Page 418.—9th April, 1752. Nathan Patterson's will, freeholder—Wife, Isabell; sons, John, Mathew, Robert (John is oldest), Mathew 2d; daughter, Isabell; daughter, Sarah; daughter, Martha. Executors, wife, John Wilson, Robert Campbell. Teste: Robert Campbell, Mathew Wilson, Wm. Wilson. Proved, 21st May, 1752, by Robt. Campbell and Wm. Wilson, and to lie for further proof, and executors qualify, with surety Alexander Richey.

Page 421.—21st May, 1752. Eleanor Boyd's bond as administratrix of Robert Boyd, with sureties Robert Poage, Mathew Armstrong.

Page 422.—8th February, 1752. Valuation of Robert Rennix' improvements on plantation, formerly called John Harrison's place, by John Maxwell, Samuel Walker, John Smith.

Page 423.—3d September, 1751. Mary Allen's inventory, by Wm. White, Danl. Holdman, John Ruddell.

Page 424.—15th June, 1752. Valuation of John Lowry's 250 acres on North Branch James River, by Thomas Paxton, John Berrisford.

Page 424.—2d February, 1752. Elizabeth Hodge's will—(Executors live at great distance, Gabriel Jones). Lands now in law with Asahel Hodge to be recovered; two youngest sons, Jonathan and Jacob; children, David (eldest); Elizabeth, Ruemia, Rachel, Hannah; eldest son, David, to be apprenticed to Thos. Rees, blacksmith; second son, Jonathan, to be apprenticed to Andrew Bird to learn trade of weaver; youngest son, Jacob, to be bound to Samuel Newman to do laboring work; daughter, Rachel, to be bound to Momas Looker; daughter, Hannah, to be bound to Wm. Draper. Teste: Wm. Draper, Edward Davis, Andrew Bird, Samuel Newman. Proved, 17th June, 1752, by witnesses, except Davis. Gabriel Jones refuses to execute, and administration granted Peter Scholl and Samuel Newman, with surety Thomas Looker.

Page 427.—17th June, 1752. Martha Mahan's bond as administratrix of Patrick McClure, with sureties Patrick Martin, Wm. McFeeters.

Page 428.—17th June, 1758. Elizabeth Thommer's bond as administratrix of Jacob Thommer, with surety John Crum.

Page 429.—18th June, 1752. Jacob Lorton and Jacob Harman's bond as administrators of Israel Lorton, with sureties Tobias Bright and Wm. English.

Page 431.—18th June, 1752. John Graham's bond as guardian (appointed) to Thomas Mann, orphan of John Mann, with surety Adam Dickinson.

Page 432.—18th June, 1752. Alexander Gibson's bond as administrator of Daniel Gibson, with sureties John Patterson, Sampson Archer.

Page 433.—18th June, 1752. James Bell's further appraisement. Due by James Kirk, Andrew Foster, James Callison, Thomas Armstrong, Daniel McNaire, Andrew Kinkade, Charles Clendennin.

Page 433.—16th August, 1751. Methesalem Griffith's appraisement, by Henry Brown, Jr., Neal McNeal, Wm. Carvin. Due by Malcom Campbell, Benj. Halter, Henry Brown, Sr., Isaac Taylor, Alex. Ingrem, Geo. Robinson, Edward McDonald.

Page 435.—7th October, 1746. Robert McKay, Sr.'s, Will—Daughter, Margaret; wife of Joshua Job, tract called Joshua's Bottom; sons, Robert, James, Zachary, Moses. (Tract given to Margaret is part of Order Council for 100,000 to testator and Jost Hite, first, and afterwards renewed by testator, Hite, Green, and Duff). Daughter, Hannah, wife of George Hollingsworth; daughter, Leah, wife of Wm. Taylor. Daughter, Mary, wife of George Robinson, of Penna. Daughter, Elizabeth. Son, Zachary—plantation known as Nathan Calbreath's Bottom. Executors, Robert, James, and Moses. Teste: Gabriel Jones, David Vance, Abraham Hite, 7th October 1746.—Codicil, wife. Proved 19th August, 1752, by Jones and Vance. Zacharay McCoy refuses to execute, and other executors qualify (Jones makes oath, but Moses and Robert are Quakers) with sureties, Moses McCoy, David Vance, Chas. Burk.

Page 439.—19th August, 1752. Daniel Gibson's appraisement, by Alex. Crawford, Andrew Foster, James Sayers.

Page 440.—20th August, 1752. Elizabeth Thomas' bond as administatrix of John Windlekite, her former husband, with witnesses John Crum, Jacob Miller.

Page 441.—16th August, 1752. Ann Wright's appraisement by John McCreery, Wallace Estill, Alexander Black.

Page 442.—20th August, 1752. John Goldman's bond as administrator of Jacob Goldman, with surety Adam Harman.

Page 444.—22d August, 1752. Alexander McCleary's appraisement, by Mathew and Daniel Lyle, Wm. Caruthers.
Cash due from Nancy.

Page 446.—21st September, 1750. John Greer's vendue. Sold to John Lockhart, John Roseman, Sarah Lynn, John Teat, John Mitchell, Christopher Kelly, George Breckinridge, Thos. Scott, James Lynn, Thos. Teat, Francis Beaty, John Mitchell.

Page 447.—24th August, 1752. John Mitchell and Samuel Doage's bond as guardians (appointed) of Rebecca, Alexander, Martha, Mary Greer, orphans of John Greer, deceased, with sureties Francis Beatey.

Page 448.—15th November, 1752. Andrew Bird and Mary Rease's bond as executors of Thomas Rease, with sureties Samuel Newman and Wm. Draper.

Page 449.—15th November, 1752. Daniel Richardson's bond as admnistrator of Robt. Fryer, with sureties Andrew Lewis, Peter Scholl.

Page 451.—15th November, 1752. Mary Noble's bond as administatrix c. t. a. of John Noble, with sureties Will Callhoun, Patrick Callhoun.

Page 452.—14th November, 1752. Nathan Patterson's appraisement by Andrew Steel, Saml. McCutchon, Thos. Kirkpatrick, James Clark. Due by Robert Plesent, Jane Jackson, Geo. Wilson, and James Mease.

Page 455.—1st September, 1752. Thomas Reese's will. Blacksmith. Wife, Mary, executrix with Andrew Bird. Deed for land bought from Valentine Severe, to be made to wife, Mary, and Andrew Bird. Son, Joseph Reese, infant. Teste: Saml. Newman, Wm. Draper, Ralph Rund. Proved, 15th November, 1752, by all witnesses, and both executors qualify.

Page 456.—29th September, 1752. Jacob Goldman's appraisement (he died 12th December, 1750). To books by James Miller, Robert Norris, John Bigman.

Page 457.—15th November, 1752. George Zee's appraisement by John Cunningham, Daniel Richardson, Henry Kearr.

Page 459.—26th November, 1751. David Stewart's bond as sheriff, with sureties Andrew Lewis, James Lockhart, Wm. Lewis, Daniel McAnare.

Page 460.—15th November, 1752. Jacob Gogure, Jacob Miller, Solomon Bryan appraise John Windlekite's estate at his house, and also at Michael Gommers and John Grumbs the part that is in their hands, and produced by Eve Elizabeth, widow of said Windlekite and Jacob Thomas, deceased.

Page 461.—15th November, 1752. Jacob Thomas' appraisement.

Page 461.—31st October, 1752. Israel Lorton's appraisement by Richard Hall, Benj. Ogle, Thos. Ingles.

Page 463.—16th November, 1752. Pat McCue's appraisement, by Samuel Wallace, Moses Ofrel, John Trimble.

Page 463.—10th June, 1752. John Noble's will. Wife, Mary. Son, Alexander. Land at Cripple Creek, at Big Spring. Son, James; son, Patrick; son, Ezekiel (infant). Daughter, Jean. Executors, wife, Mary, and testator's brother, James Callhoun. Teste: Wm., Patrick, Agnes Callhoun. Proved, 16th November, 1752, by Wm. and Patrick Callhoun, and executors qualified with sureties Wm. and Pat. Callhoun.

Page 465.—No date. George Rutledge's bond to make title to Darby Hanly to 2 tracts in Forks of James. George is about to move to Carolina and appoints Wm. Preston and Ro. Cunningham his attorneys. Witnesses, James Miller, James Moffett. Acknowledged and recorded 16th November, 1752.

Page 466.—16th November, 1752. Robert Christian's bond as guardian (appointed) to Mary and Robert Moffett, orphans of John Moffett, with sureties John and William Christian.

Page 466.—16th November, 1752. John Christian's bond as guardian (appointed) of Catherine, Wm., and Hannah Moffett, orphans of John Moffett, with sureties Francis F. McCown, Robert Brown.

Page 467.—16th November, 1752. William Christian's bond as guardian (appointed) to George and John Moffett, orphans of John Moffett, with surety James Lockhart.

Page 468.—17th November, 1752. David Stewart's bond for collection of County proportion, with sureties James Robinson, Robert Bratton.

Page 469.—17th November, 1752. James Patton's bond as administrator of Daniel Murphy.

Page 470.—20th November, 1752. William Preston's bond as assistant surveyor, with sureties John Patton, Wm. Baskins.

Page 471.—27th November, 1752. Valuation of improvements on Alexander Brownlee's 400 acres on North Branch Shanado by John Finley, John Hogshead.

Page 471.—21st March, 1753. Anthony Strother's bond as administrator of James Rutledge, with surety Thomas Lewis.

Page 472.—20th December, 1752. William Jamison's will. Wife, Sarah, executrix. Eldest son, John; 237 acres on Jackson River. Sons, George and Andrew. Son, William. Teste: Saml. Hodge, Thos. Gillham. 21st March, 1753, proved by both witnesses, and Sarah qualified, with sureties David Dryden, Robert Armstrong.

Page 474.—21st March, 1753. Elizabeth Carlile and James Carlile's bond as administrators of James Carlile, with sureties William Smith, Robert Bratton.

Page 476.—25th December, 1752. Peter Cotner's will. Yeoman. Eldest son, George; 2d son, Peter. Daughter, Mary, infant, under 18. Wife, Mary. Four children. (George is to pay his youngest brother £—— of coming of age). Teste: Michael Waren, Samuel Holdman, Thos. Moore. Executors, wife, Mary, and Adam Rider. Proved, 21st March, 1753, by all witnesses; Danl. Holdman and executors qualify, with surety Jacob Bare.

Page 478.—21st March, 1753. Elizabeth Moore and David Moore's bond as administrators of Saml. Moore, with sureties Joseph Kennerley, John Moore.

Page 480.—9th February, 1753. Richard Luke's appraisement by Joseph Crockett, James Callhoun, John Montgomery.

Page 485.—27th October, 1751. James Scot's will.. Of South Branch of Potomac. Sister, Sarah Scot. Two mares bought of Even Hughes. Sister, Phebe Scot; sister, Rachel Scot. Three cousins (nephews?), James, Joseph, and Jacob Scot (sons of Bro. John?). Two brothers, Adonijah Scot and David Scot. Brother, Benjamin Scot. Two brothers are infants. Teste: Joel Hornback, John Frazier. Codicil, horses left to Bro. John Scot's children to be taken by Benj. Scot until they are of age. Proved, 22d March, 1753, by John Frazier and Ridle Hyer, and Benj. Scot qualifies administrator with sureties Henry Lancisco, Peter Mauzie.

Page 487.—21st July, 1752. Elizabeth Hodge's appraisement by Danl. Holdman, John Ruddell.

Page 488.—1st December, 1752. Thomas Reese's appraisement by Thos. Moore, Samuel Newman, Nicholas Roberts.

Page 489.—15th March, 1753. Robert Fryer's (Tryer?) appraisement by James Simpson, Peter Thorn, Francis McBride, and vendue by Israel Ward. To Daniel Richardson, John McDoyle, Israel Ward.

Page 490.—22d March, 1753. Michael Harns' bond as administrator of Euric Westfall, with sureties Henry Curdsake, Benj. Scot.

Page 491.—22d March, 1753. Benjamin Scot's bond as administrator c. t. a. of James Scot, with sureties Michael Harness, Henry Curtract.

Page 492.—23d March, 1753. John Black's bond as administrator of Michael Railey.

Page 493.—11th June, 1751. William Jackson's appraisement by Ralph Laverty, George Wilson, Archibald Elliott. Note of James Ewin, Charles Whitacre, Lofftus Poland. Cash recovered by James Lockridge; cash recovered by Adam Dickinson; by John Ward; by Robert Armstrong; by Thomas Thompson.

Page 480.—16th January, 1753. John Noble's appraisement, by Robt. Norris, Saml. Montgomery, John Montgomery. Note of John McFarland, Joseph Crockett, Robert Allcorn, John Hatthorn, James and John Miller, James Callhoun, Nathaniel Welshar, Wm. Montgomery, Wm. Callhoun. To butter money, cash. Philip Snider's bond. Due John McFarland for 106 acres land at £5 per 100. Due to the remainder of land. William Callhoun, Widow Lukes.

Page 483.—27th December, 1752. Valuation of improvements on Benj. Borden's 400 acres on Borden's Run, a branch of James River; 312 acres on Borden's Run, a branch of James River; by David Cloyd, John McClenachan.

Page 484.—22d March, 1753. James Connerley's appraisement by Joseph Kennedy, John Maxwell, James Campbell. Vendue by George Breckinridge, administrator.

Page 496.—23d March, 1753 (by Court Order of 28th May, 1751.) Valuation of improvements of William Carravin on 254 acres and 172 acres, both on waters of Roanoke, by Wm. Graham, Richard Kerr: 2 negros, 1 house—17½ x 14 ft.—114 fruit trees.

Page 497.—19th December, 1751. John Jacob Rothgab's will. Settled and living at South Shanado. Written in High Dutch and translated by How Dickins. Son, John George (infant). Son, Peter. Daughters, Elizabeth, Anna, Barbery, Catherine. Wife, Anna. Executors, wife. Anna, and Paul Lung. Teste: John Spiller, John Taylor, Martin Forelight. Proved, 16th May, 1753, by John Taylor, who declared the other witnesses dead, and widow, Anna, qualified. (Signed Ann Holloback) with surety Peter Rufner.

Page 498.—16th May, 1753. James Lockhart and Robert Christian's bond as administrators of John Flood, with sureties John Anderson, Samuel Henderson.

Page 499.—12th March, 1753. Mathew Thompson's will. Son, Mathew, executor. Wife, Martha Thompson. Grandson, Mathew, son to son, Mathew. Son, William. Son, John. Legatee, John Davison. Daughter, Margaret Thompson's 5 children. Teste: Patrick Frazier, Mary Thompson, George Vance. Proved, 16th May, 1753, by all witnesses, and Mathew Thompson qualified, with sureties Pat. Frazier, James Beard.

Page 501.—16th May, 1753. Elizabeth Thomas and John Jones' bond as administrators of Morgan Thomas, with sureties Wm. White, Wm. Moore.

Page 502.—16th May, 1753. Paul Long's bond as guardian (appointed) to Conrad and Jacob Cood, orphans of Caspar Fought, deceased, with surety John Taylor.

Page 502.—22d March, 1753. Sarah McCord's nuncupative will. Sister, Mary. Brother, Adam. Teste: John, Robert, and Wm. Christian. Debts due by Sarah to Israel Christian, Wm. Henderson, Thos. Rutledge. Debts due to Sarah by Daniel Cidney, Jean Rutledge. Proved, 19th May, 1753, and John Christian qualified administrator.

Page 503.—15th August, 1753. Michael Rady's appraisement by James Bell, William Long, Thomas Stewart, and vendue, to William Bishop, Ezekiel Eurman, Wm. Carr, Jacob Gray, Wm. and James Robinson, John Cunningham, James Gilespy, due by John Black. Received from Edward Hall.

Page 505.—10th August, 1753. Jacob Rodgab's appraisement by Mathias Selzer, Jacob Halterman, Christian Magret.

Page 506—15th August, 1753. Peter Cottner's appraisement.

Page 508.—15th August, 1753. Morgan Thomas' appraisement.

Page 509.—15th August, 1753. Mathew Thompson's appraisement by Evan Evans, John Davison, Robert Shankland; Dr. Housing; Christopher Finey.

Page 511.—18th July, 1752. James Fulton's will, farmer—Son, Hugh, 250 acres joining Samuel Steel's line. One horse died in New England, and 1 horse died here. Son, James, to take care of the widow for her life. Son, William. James to take care of the 2 young boys, David and Thomas, and 3 daughters, Elizabeth, Elliner, and Jane. Son, John. To daughter, Elizabeth, a mare brought from New England. Son, David. Wife, Sarah, and son, Hugh, executors. Teste: Robert Ramsey, Thomas Beard, Robert Alexander. Proved, 15th August, 1753, by all witnesses, and executors qualify with sureties John Brownlee, Thos. Beard.

Page 513.—15th September, 1748. Andrew Baxter's will. Wife, Margaret. 100 acres during her life, then to Andrew Stevenson, adjoining Wm McClung. Legatee, Nathaniel Evans; legatee, Andrew Evans; legatee, John Pal; legatee, Jacob Anderson. Teste: Wm. McClung, George Stinson, David Moore. Proved, 15th August, 1753, by all witnesses; administrator granted Andrew Stevenson, who qualifies, with sureties Geo. Stevenson, David Moore.

Page 515.—23d May, 1751. James McNutt's orphans. Settlement by

Thos. **Beard**, administrator. Paid Mr. Burden for 185 acres bought by my wife (Thos. Beard's?) now, but before marriage. 17— to Mr. Burden quit rents on 85 acres for 10 years. 1747 to Mr. Downs for quit rents. 1744 to Mr. Burden for quit rents, 300 acres. December 20th, 1748, paid David Hays rents debt due before marriage. Paid Wm. Nutt debt. 8th May, 1749, paid Wm. Hunter for work. 4th February, 1747, paid John Huston, debt. 9th December, 1748, paid John Roseman, debt. 10th May, 1748, paid Saml. Wilson, for bringing some linen from Penna. Paid to Widow Sheals, a debt. Paid to Robt. Alexander, for schooling James and Robert McNutt. Paid to James Dobbins, for schooling Alex. McNutt. Paid one new Bible, for Alex. McNutt. Paid one new Testament, for James McNutt. Paid one new spelling book, for the children.

Page 516.—15th August, 1753. John Brownlee's bond as guardian (appointed) to Alexander McNutt, orphan of James McNutt, with sureties Samuel Doake and Arthur Hamilton.

Page 516.—15th August, 1753. Esther Robinson's bond as administratrix of James Robinson, with surety Wm. Robinson.

Page 518.—27th November, 1753. Robert Breckinridge's bond for collection of the County proportion, with sureties Robt. McClenachan, Andrew Lewis.

Page 518.—20th June, 1751. John Patterson's vendue by Agnes Patterson. To George Henderson, John McCroskry, Robt. Stewart, Wm. Henry, James Anderson, Wm. Laughridge, John Moore, Jacob Anderson.

Page 519.—16th August, 1753. John Smith's bond as guardian (appointed) to Catherine King, orphan of Robt. King, with surety Samuel Stalnaher.

Page 520.—17th August, 1753. Thomas Fulton's bond as guardian (appointed) to William Kinkade, orphan of Thos. Kinkade, with sureties Robert Bratton, Wm. Hamilton.

Page 520.—15th August, 1753. Executors' account against the Estate of David Moore. Paid to James Buchanan for note due to John Kirkpatrick.

Page 521.—18th August, 1752. James Campbell's bond as administrator of Patrick Lynch, with sureties John Smith, Wm. Anderson.

Page 522.—21st November, 1753. Michael Realy's estate and appraisement. Robert Campbell, North Mountain, owes. 15th September, 1753, vendue at house of John Black. Patrick and David Campbell owe.

Page 522.—7th August, 1753. Daniel Richardson's will—farmer. Wife, Elizabeth. Executor, Thos. Parsons. Children. Teste: John Knowls, Hunkrist Carlock, John Scull. Proved, 21st November, 1753, by Knowls and Scull, and executor qualifies with surety Benj. Scot and John Patton.

Page 524.—21st November, 1753. Blandena Westfall's estate appraised by John Cunningham, Henry Lancisco, Peter Thorn, John Scull.

Page 525.—21st November, 1753. Alexander Thompson's bond as guardian (appointed) to Benj. Bennet, orphan of Richard Bennet, with surety Wm. Thompson.

Page 526.—21st November, 1753. Patrick Lynch's appraisement by Henry Brown, James Neeley, Wm. Bryan.

Page 527.—10th November, 1753. James Scott's appraisement and division of estate by John Willson (Welton), John Cunningham, Conrad

Harness. To Benjamin, ¼ part of a wagon, to be divided between Benjamin, Adonijah, and David Scot.

Page 528.—10th November, 1753. Alexander Scott's appraisement. 21st November, 1753. Abraham Brown's bond as administrator of Drury Bailey, with sureties Wm. Davis, George Wilson.

Page 530.—22d November, 1753. Elizabeth and Edward Edward's bond as administrators of Hugh Edwards, with sureties Hugh Gay, William Elliott.

ABSTRACTS OF WILLS OF AUGUSTA COUNTY, VIRGINIA.

AUGUSTA COUNTY COURT.

Will Book No. 2.

Page 1.—30th March, 1753. Benjamin Borden's will, Gent. Stepsons, Sam'l. McDowell and James McDowell. Stepdaughter, Sarah McDowell. Wife, Magdalen. Negro wench named Moll. Daughter, Martha; daughter, Hannah. Executors, John Lyle, Archibald Alexander, and wife, Magdalen. Father, Benj. Borden. Brothers. Brother, Joseph. Teste: Roger Keys, John Keys, Jacob Gray. Proved, 21st November, 1753, by all witnesses. John Lyle refuses to execute, others qualify, with sureties John Lyle. Andrew Hays, Thos. Paxton.

Page 4.—22d November, 1753. John Patterson's account of estate by Joseph Kennedy. Charles Berry. To Joseph Kennedy for 18½ gallons liquor. To Dr. Flood. To John Moore for making coffin.

Page 4.—22d November, 1753. George Trout's bond as administrator of Nicholas Trout, with sureties Christian Clemmons, Valentine Pence.

Page 5.—22d November, 1753. Thomas Reedy's bond as administrator of John Richman, with sureties John Collier, William Hall.

Page 6.—27th November, 1753. Andrew Lewis enters 400 acres on head of Peters Creek, which forks from Adam Dickinson's meadows joining waters of Greenbrier, called 2d Creek, on James River Waters. David Stewart.

Page 7.—27th November, 1753. Robert Breckinridge's bond as sheriff with sureties Robt. McClenachan, Thos. Gorden.

Page 7.—19th January, 1754. Andrew Lewis enters 400 acres on Peters Creek, a branch of James River, between the upper survey of Adam Dickinson's and the Indian Patch, also 200 acres on the Warm Springs mountain joining tract formerly Harden's, etc.; three 400 surveys on head branches of James River near a survey made for Wm. Warwick and on some of the head branches of the Back Creek, and Thomas Lewis's 200 acres on the Cow Pasture where John Shaw lives and 200 acres where Harklas Wilson lives, and 200 acres in the Bull Pasture at the foot of the mountain. Robert McClenachan.

Page 8.—28th February, 1754. Thos. and Andrew Lewis, 200 acres of land joining Harcklas Wilson on the cow pasture and two 200 surveys near John Shaw's land, two 200 acres joining Lewis' line near head of Bull Pasture, and two 200 surveys near foot of mountain, north side of Bull pasture not far from Bodkin's land, and 200 acres joining George Wilson, and a survey of the Reed Hole and towards Hicklin's land, and 200 acres at a small meadow between the Warm Springs and Jackson's land, and 200 acres about 5 miles from the Warm Springs near the path from said Spring to Harden's land on the mountain, and one survey on Cedar Run near a survey made on said Run, and 200 acres in the Calf Pasture joining the west and north lines of Samuel Gay, and 200 acres on a ridge near Dunlap's old place where Meek made some improvements. Robert McClenachan.

Page 8.—6th March, 1754. Andrew Lewis enters two 200 surveys on Bratton's Run in the Calf Pasture which runs through that place of Dunlap's where he last lived and 100 acres on the Little River between McCutchen's land and Clendenning's old place, and 200 acres joining south side of McCutchen's land below Wm. Smith's, and 200 acres at a meadow on a branch of the Great River of the Calf Pasture near a mile northwest from Saml. Tencher's, and 200 acres joining the southwest end of James Gay's land in the Cow Pasture, and 200 acres on the Glady land at the sulfer mine on south side Warm Spring Mountain Gap on both sides the path, and 100 at the foot of the Warm Spring Mountain, north side, about two miles from said Spring, northeast course, and 200 acres joining the survey at the Warm Spring and down the branch, and 200 acres about two miles, more or less, from the Warm Springs, southwest course, and 200 acres in the Cow Pasture side of the Warm Springs Mountain at the foot of said mountain about three miles near a west course from James Gay's.

Page 9.—2d September, 1753. William Clark, Sr.'s, will, farmer—Wife, Elizabeth Clark; son, John; son, William. Executors, wife Elizabeth and son William. Teste: John White, William White, John Ruddle. Proved, 20th March, 1754, by John and Wm. White. Son William qualifies, with sureties Moses and Abraham Bird.

Page 11.—14th March, 1754. Valuation of improvements on 280 acres on Bull Pasture of William Wilson's by James McCleary, John Clark.

Page 11.—20th March, 1754. John Ruckman's appraisement, by Joseph Long, John Hanna, James Bets, Henry Kirkum.

Page 12.—19th January, 1754. Nicholas Trout's appraisement. To Nicholas Milberry, to widow Trout.

Page 13.—5th June, 1753. Philip Chittam's will—Sons, John and William. To son John, a horse bought of Sampson Mathews for to schooling. To daughter Eleanor. Wife. Teste: John Smith, George Wilson, Samuel Walker. Proved, 20th March, 1754, by all witnesses, and widow Mary qualifies administratrix, with sureties Jno. Smith, Robert Rennix.

Page 15.—20th March, 1754. Anne Copland's bond as administratrix of Benj. Copland, with sureties Michael Warren, Abraham Smith.

Page 16.—20th March, 1754. John Erwin's bond as administrator of Geo. McSwine, with sureties Andrew Erwin, Robert McClenachan.

Page 17.—20th March, 1754. John Erwin's bond as administrator of Robert Foil, with surety Robert Brown.

Page 19.—15th March, 1754. James Trimble, Assistant Surveyor, enters 200 acres of vacant land on a branch of Buffalo Creek above Saml. Gabeson's 3 or 4 miles; also 150 acres between South Mountain and South River above the Narrow Passage, and 100 acres joining his own land on a branch of Buffalo Creek, and 100 acres between his own land and Michael Finney's extending along his own line.—James Patton.

Page 19.—14th March, 1754. James Trimble, Assistant Surveyor, enters 200 acres on head of South Branch of Potomac, 200 more above the Indian Plains on the South Branch, 200 at a place called the Indian Camp, opposite a gap in the mountain on the head of the South Branch water. All these entries are above the Crab Apple Bottom. Also 400 acres on head of South Fork of Potomack joining survey of Col. Wood's grant upon Clover Creek Road.—James Patton.

Page 19.—13th March, 1754. Valuation of improvements on four tracts of Joshua Hadley and his expenses in coming to Virginia and moving his family there: 115-acre tract, called the Halfmoon; 186-acre tract, called Long Bottom; 400-acre tract at mouth of Craig's Creek; 50-acre tract, called Pound Bottom; 6 weeks' journey in coming to and going from Virginia at 5 shillings per day. To coming with his wagon stock and family six weeks at 26 shillings per day. By Joseph Robinson, David Robinson, Edmund McDonald.

Page 20.—21st March, 1754. Susannah Patton's bond as administratrix of Jacob Patton, with sureties John Smith, Geo. Wilson.

Page 21.—1753. James Carlile's appraisement, by Robert Gay, James Campbell, Jacob Clements.

Page 22.—6th February, 1754. Benj. Borden's appraisement, by Jno. Paxton, Daniel Lyle, John McAkee, James Trimble. Due by Jacob Gray, Roger Keys.

Page 26.—14th December, 1750. William McBride's will, laborer—Wife, Sarah; son, Francis. Executors, son Francis and Joseph How. Grandchildren, Margaret and Sarah McBride, 1 plantation between Francis McBride and the Bigg Cow Run on Capecappen in Augusta County. Teste: William Warden, Mary McBride, Ann Dunbarr. Proved, 21st March, 1754, by Mary and Ann. Joseph How refuses to execute and Francis McBride qualifies, with sureties Jacob Gum and James Thomas. Francis' mark.

Page 28.—21st March, 1754. Thomas Wright's bond as administrator of Isaac Scooly, with sureties Jas. Carlile. Wm. Smith.

Page 30.—15th March, 1754. Valuation of improvements on John Mathews' place in Forks of James River, by Jno. Poage, Jno. Maxwell, Jno. Hargar.

Page 30.—20th March, 1754. Drury Bealy's (Bailey) appraisement, by John Lapsley, Saml. McClure, John Paxton.

Page 31.—21st March, 1754. John Miller's bond as administrator of Jas. Jones, with sureties David Stewart, Walter Davis.

Page 32.—25th March, 1749. John Young's estate, Dr. to James C. Young, administrator: To funeral charges, £4. To cash, by Henry Downs, Capt. Danl. McAnare, Capt. John Brown, Hugh Young, Robt. Scott, Robt. Boyd, John Davis.

Page 32.—5th November, 1753. James Campbell's will—Aged about 71 years: To son Daniel, 200 acres, part of tract testator lives on; to Margaret, a horse running at John McClure's; to grandchild, Elizabeth White, a child, to be cared for by Margret; to grandson, James Steel, a horse until testator's son, Daniel, comes of age; to son, John; to son-in-law, Isaac White; to son-in-law, Saml. Steel and Isaac White, executors. Teste: Robt. Cunningham, Benj. Stewart. Proved, 22d March, 1754, by the witnesses. Executors qualify, with surety Jno. Ramsey.

Page 35.—23d March, 1754. John Madison's bond as guardian (chosen) to Agnes Welsh, orphan of James Welsh, with surety Alex. Wright.

Page 36.—March, 1754. James Robertson's inventory by Jas. Campbell, Ephraim Voss, John Robeson.

Page 36.—23d March, 1753. Halberd McClure's will, gentleman—Wife, Agnes; brother, John's son Halberd; sons; son Alexander, son Nathaniel, executors. Teste: Baptist McNabb, Jno. Davison, Saml. Lyle. Proved, 15th May, 1754, by Davison and Lyle, and executors qualify.

Page 39.—24th April, 1748-9. John Huston's will—Wife (to act with advice of John Moore); sons, Samuel and Mathew (infant); rest of children; Mary Blair to have a share with the rest (of the children). Executors, wife and John Moore. Teste: James Eakin, Joseph Kennedy, Walter Eakin. Proved, 15th May, 1755, by the witnesses; wife Margaret and John Moore qualify, with sureties Mathew Lyle and Wm. Lockridge.

Page 41.—22d April, 1754. James Campbell's appraisement, by John Finley, Archd. Stewart, Thos. Stewart, Wm. Finley.

Page 42.—15th May, 1754. Saml. McClure's bond as guardian (appointed) to Halbert McClure, orphan of Jno. McClure, with sureties Richd. Woods, David Dryden.

Page 43.—16th May, 1754. David Miller's bond as administrator of Wm. Miller, with sureties Geo. Henderson, Jno. Allison.

Page 43.—5th January, 1754. William Burk's will—Sons, John and William, tract purchased of John and Lewis Neal; son, Thomas, tract purchased of George Hayl, and entry adjoining called Long Meadow, 400 acres; daughter, Catherine Burk, alias McCommus; daughter, Judea Burk (infant), tract at mouth of Naked Creek. Judea is to be under care of Mrs Matteson. Thomas is to be under care of Mr. John Matteson. Testator's (?) Thomas' (?) interest in estate of David McCommus. Son William to learn trade of blacksmith. Sister Bridget Burk, living out of this Colony. Executors, John Matterson and Gabriel Jones. Teste: Nicholas Null, Thos. Smith, Daniel Remy. Proved, 16th May, 1754, by all witnesses.

Page 45.—16th May, 1754. Margaret Reburn's bond as administratrix of Edward Reburn, with sureties Robert McMahon, Henry Reburn.

Page 46.—14th April, 1754. William Preston enters 400 acres on head of Pott's Creek, and 400 acres on the first large bottom on Pott's Creek above Potts' improvement, 400 acres formerly entered for Tobias Bright on Craig's Creek, two 400-acre tracts at the forks of Tom's Creek, 400 acres on the next large bottom above Col. Patton's uppermost survey on Craig's Creek.—James Patton.

Page 46.—17th May, 1754. Jane Fraim's bond as administratrix of James Fraim, with surety Robert Rennick.

Page 48.—11th April, 1754. Robert Foil's appraisement and sale bill, by Chas. and Robt. Campbell, Wm. Magill. 19th April, 1754. Vendue of above. By Jno. Erwin. Robert Foil's estate in account with Jno. Erwin.

Page 50.—11th April, 1754. George McSwine's appraisement, by same as above. 17th April, 1754, sale bill of above.

Page 51.—17th March, 1754. Hugh Edward's appraisement, by Joseph Mays, George Lewis, Ralph Laverty.

Page 51.—20th May, 1754. John Madison's bond as guardian (appointed) to Judith Burke, orphan of Wm. Burke.

Page 52.—21st May, 1754. James Brown's sale bill of household goods to John Cochran. Teste: Robert Hastings, Wm. McClintock.

Page 52.—22d May, 1754. Richard Wood's bond as guardian (chosen) to Saml. McDowell, orphan of Jno. McDowell, with sureties Wm. Preston, Robert McClenachan.

Page 53.—22d May, 1754. Robert Breckinridge's bond as administrator, c. t. a., of Wm. Burke, with surety David Stewart.

Page 54.—May, 1754 (?). Halbert McClure's appraisement.

Page 55.—14th May, 1754. James Trimble, Assistant Surveyor, enters 200 acres on a branch that runs into the main river at or in Given's place formerly entered and gave up by Joseph Long. And a tract of 200 acres joining his own land upon a branch of Buffalo Creek that runs through Hugh Lusk's land.

Page 55.—15th May, 1754. Hugh Young's bond as guardian (appointed) to Mary and John Cook, orphans of Patrick Cook, with sureties Robert Patterson, William Hamilton.

Page 56.—16th May, 1754. Robert McMahon's bond as administrator of Saml. McMahon, with sureties Archibald Hamilton, Thomas Story.

Page 57.—16th May, 1754. Persilla Rees' bond as administratrix of Thos Rees, with sureties David Cloyd, Stephen Renfro.

Page 58.—16th May, 1754. David Miller's bond as administrator of Wm. Miller, with sureties Geo. Henderson, Jno. Allison.

Page 59.—6th June, 1754. Halbert McClure's appraisement, by John Paxton, John Moore, Joseph Walker.

Page 60.—10th August, 1754. John Huston's appraisement, by Jas. Eakin, Wm. McCaules.

Page 61.—21st August, 1754. Francis McCown's bond as guardian (chosen) to Edward Faris, orphan of Wm. Faris, with sureties William Young, Samuel Crawford.

Page 62.—4th May, 1754. John Wilson's will, farmer—To son James Wilson (infant), 400 acres adjoining Duncan's line, and field commonly called Patterson's; to William (infant); to wife Anne; daughter Mary to live with her step-mother until of age; daughter Agness. Executors, Roger Keys and wife Anne. Teste: Alex. McMullen, Esther McMullen, Sarah Keys. Proved, 21st August, 1754, by Esther and Sarah. Roger Keys refuses to execute, and Anne qualifies, with sureties Roger Keys, Thomas Storey.

Page 64.—15th June, 1754. Wm. Clark's appraisement, by John Ruddle, William White.

Page 64.—29th May, 1754. Benjamin Copeland's appraisement, by Robert Patterson, Joseph Bryan, John Brown.

Page 65.—22d August, 1754. Walter Davis' bond as guardian (appointed) to Caleb Harman, orphan of John Harman, with surety James Lockhart.

Page 66.—5th August, 1754. James Frame's appraisement, by James Arbuckle, Robert Gallon, John Scot.

Page 67.—22d August, 1754. John Bowyer's indemnifying bond to Archibald Alexander, with sureties James Lockhart, Andrew Hays, Wm. Woods. Alexander had given Bowyer power of attorney to act for him in signing deeds to the Borden lands. Teste: Francis Bealey (Beaty), Jas. Thomson, Daniel Harrison.

Page 68.—1751. John Scot's appraisement, by John and Mathew Patton, Daniel Richeson.

Page 69.—8th May, 1754. Philip Chittam's inventory, by John Maxwell, Saml. Walker, Michael Dougherty. Note—(Spinning wheel in nearly all inventories).

Page 70.—14th August, 1754. John Black's accounts drs. to Michael Bealey's estate: To Wm. Bishop, to Ezekiah Inman, Edward Hall, Joseph Love, George Caldwell. Estate of Michael Realey to John Black, administrator; 1 day's work to my son. John's mare at hay and grain in my stable. To entertaining 20 men and horses at sundry times. To attendance on his death bed 17 days. To light, wake and burying. To making a bier for carrying his body. To fine muslin stock. To washing and dressing his clothes. To paling his grave and 1 walnut coffin. To my son Anthony, 20 days hunting a colt. To owing at George Caldwell's. To viewing of work at David Cunningham's.

Page 71.—19th September, 1754. William Scot's (yeoman) bill of sale to John Maxwell (yeoman). Teste: Richard Borton, John Smith, Mathew Campbell.

Page 72.—11th September, 1754. James Robertson's will—To wife (with child); sons, George and Alexander; to each of daughters (?) 'till the heirs come of age. Executors, Mathew Robertson, John Poage. Teste: Wm. Robertson, Alex. Matheson, Jno. Craig. 20th November, 1754. Proved by Rev. Jno. Craig and Robertson. Executors refused to execute, and widow Elizabeth qualified executrix, with sureties John Poage and Saml. Henderson. Elizabeth's mark.

Page 74.—9th September, 1754. John Wilson's appraisement, by Saml. Buchanan, Andrew Duncan, John Logan (Loggan).

Page 75.—10th November, 1754. Robert Armstrong's will—Daughter, Hannah Kircum, ⅓ of tract he now lives on bought of Col. Patton; daughter, Catherine Finney, 1 English shilling; sons, John and Robt., tract on Mill Creek bought of John Allison; sons (and daughters), infants, viz: James and Benjamin; daughters (under 18); to son, James, entry on head of McClure's Run; wife, Martha, executrix; daughters, Martha, Alice and Agnes, infants. Teste: John Mathews, Sr., William Woods, John Mitchell. Proved, 21st November, 1754, by Mathews and Mitchell, and Martha qualifies executrix, with sureties John and Joshua Mathews.

Page 78.—21st November, 1754. Hannah Kirkam's bond as administratrix of Robert Kirkam, with sureties John and Joshua Mathews.

Page 79.—18th September, 1754. Edward Labourn's appraisement, by Hugh Thompson, James Craig, Saml. Henderson, Henry Downs, Jr.

Page 80.—3d May, 1753. Samuel Moore's appraisement, by Patrick Hays, William McCanless, Samuel Lanlap (Dunlap?).

Page 80.—21st November, 1754. Daniel Love's bond as guardian (appointed) to Joseph Dictom, orphan of Richd. Dictom, with sureties Uriah Humble, Robt. Ralston.

Page 81.—22d November, 1754. Burr Harrison's bond as Assistant Surveyor, with sureties Gabriel Jones, Francis Tyler, W. Russell.

Page 82.—21st November, 1754. Archibald Boreland's accounts as administrator, vs. estate of Wm. Jackson—Paid Andrew Dunlap, John Harden, Robt. Duffels, Archd. Elliot, Wm. Davis, Alex. Wright, Alex. McAllroy, Michl. Harper, Jno. Carolile, Samuel McAlvery, Jno. Graham, Joseph Mays, Samuel Ferguson, Wm. Elliott, Stephen Wilson, Alex. Gillespy, Naphtalin Gregory, Jno. Warwick, John Crockett, Charles Dunlap, Geo. Lewis, Thos. Bryan, Nathan Patterson, James Boreland, Wm. Hamilton, James Brown, James Lockridge, John Williamson, David Stanley; cash paid James Armstrong; 7 gallons whiskey for 2d vendue; to Jinney Boreland's account proved.

Page 84.—18th November, 1754. William Preston, Assistant Surveyor, enters 400 acres below the survey made on the Forks of John's Creek; 200 acres above the uppermost survey on South Fork of John's Creek; 200 acres above the survey made on the North Fork of said creek; two 400-acre tracts between Bradshaw's survey and Adam Looney's land; 200 acres called the sugar land; 200 acres called the Mill place joining Jacob Patton's old place; 200 acres at a spring below Henry Holston's joining Frederick Hartsough's land; two 400-acre surveys between the Spreading Spring Draft and George Burdwell's; 400 acres at the Poplar Spring joining Dayley's land; 200 acres on the west end of Dayley's; 200 acres between John McGowin's and Nathaniel Evans' land; two 400-acre tracts below the Laurel Gap on Pott's Creek; 400 acres on the next large bottom above said Gap; 400 acres on Purgatory Creek on north side of James River; 200 acres on east side of the Long Bottom; 400 acres between William Hutchinson's and James Moore's on the Path; 400 acres between Priscilla Reese's and James McAfee's land; 200 acres at head spring of little Catabo.—James Patton.

Page 84.—19th March, 1755. Daniel Love's bond as guardian (chosen) to Margaret Donelson, orphan of Andrew Donelson, with sureties Ephraim Love, David Ralstone.

Page 85.—19th March, 1755. Daniel Love's bond as administrator of James Hamilton.

Page 86.—15th March, 1755. Benjamin Copeland's additional appraisement, by Robert Patterson (mark), Jos. Bryan (mark), John Brown—Daniel Henderson's note; John Macau's note; Gabriel Pickin's note; John Shaw's note (run away); James Gamble's note; Alex. Craig's note; Repentance Townsend's note; Henry Cryswell's note; Joseph Write's bonds.

Page 87.—19th March, 1755. Ann Ralstone's accounts as administratrix of Benj. Copeland—Paid Susan Shannon, Jacob Gum, John McDonnel for one testament; paid John Davis for molasis; paid Mr. Hall for schooling the children; paid Thomas Underwood, Hugh Douglass.

Page 88.—21st February, 1755. John Sprout's will (is this Sproul?)—Executors, wife and daughter Mary; sons, John and Jace, infants. Mary and Martha and Sarah to have what is their own. Additional executor, Robert Renick. Teste: Jas. Morson (Morrison), Saml. Walker, Mathew Vance. Proved, 19th March, 1755, by Walker. Jane and Mary Sprout qualify with sureties Saml. and Joseph Walker.

Page 89.—18th March, 1755. James Fulton's appraisement taken by Hugh and Sarah Fulton, executors, appraised by Alex. Brownlee, Patrick Hays, Robert Alexander.

Page 91.—19th March, 1755. James Buchanan's bond as administrator of David Ray, with sureties John Buchanan, Alex. Richey.

Page 92.—25th December, 1754. John Peter Salling's will, farmer—To daughter, Catherine Fooler, 1 shilling; to daughter, Mary Elizabeth Burton, 1 shilling; to John Salling, son of daughter Catherine that she had soon after she married Henry Fooler, 100 acres known as the Meadow entry; to sons, George Adam and John Salling; to son, John, tract testator lives on, and also tract Peter Crotingal lives on, and horse bought from Joseph Burton, and a horse running at Hart's Bottom. John is infant. Executors, George Adam Salling. Teste: Jos. Bryan (Ryan), James Randal, Richard Borland (is this Borland? Burton? Boston?). Proved, 19th March, 1755, by Ryan and Randal.

Page 93.—19th March, 1755. Robert Kirkham's appraisement, by Joseph Lapsley, James Simpson, John Paxton.

Page 94.—19th March, 1753. Robert Armstrongs' appraisement, by same as above.

Page 95.—5th March, 1755. Daniel Richardson's appraisement, by John Willson, John Cunningham, Conrad Harness. John Ryan's note, Solomon Hedges, John Scoot, John Reager, George Youckam.

Page 96.—19th March, 1755. James Robertson's appraisement, by Robert Patterson, Wm. Baskins, Danl. Denison.

Page 97.—20th March, 1755. Daniel Harrison's bond as guardian (chosen) to John Scot, orphan of Saml. Scot, with sureties David Stewart, Robert McClenachan.

Page 98.—20th March, 1755. Patrick Lynch's additional appraisement, by James Nealey, Henry Brown, Wm. Bryan, Jr.

Page 98.—18th September, 1754. Valuation of improvements (with regard to expense) on 3 tracts called the Naked Farm on Roanoke formerly belonging to Daniel Evans, now Peter Evans—100 fruit trees; 1 log house 15 ft. by 10; 1 house 22½ x 12; 1 corn crib 15 ft. long and 4 ft. wide; 1 spring house 18 ft. x 12 ft.; 1 wagon. Certificate by George Robinson, 15th March, 1755, that William Carraven, Neal McNeal, James Bean qualified as such appraisers before him.

Page 99.—20th March, 1755. John Gay's bond as guardian (appointed) to Samuel, James, Alexander and Andrew Crockett, orphans of Robt. Crockett, deceased, with sureties John Ramsey, James Boreland.

Page 100.—1st October, 1754. Appraisement of Jacob Patton's estate, by James Mountgomery, Henry Houlston, Wm. Plummer.

Page 100.—21st March, 1755. William Burk's appraisement.

Page 102.—24th March, 1755. James Bell's estate, settlement by James Bell, Rachel Bell. To Wm. McAghan. To money ordered to be paid to James Bell, son of decedent, in lieu of the land willed to him by his father. Cash in hands of Andrew Kinkade.

Page 103.—25th March, 1755. Robert Breckinridge's bond for collection of County levy, with sureties John Brown, Robert McClenachan.

Page 104.—25th March, 1755. Same's bond as sheriff, with sureties John Anderson, Robert Christian.

Page 104.—26th January, 1755. John Glass' will—Wife, Sarah; children, Samuel, John, William, Elizabeth, Sarah and Mary. The 100 acres lying between Joseph Glass and John Bukket; gives testator's part to John Bukket. The 150 acres lying between David Glass' line and Mr. Wood's, also to John Bukket. Executors are Wm. Wright, wife Sarah, Richard Pillson. Teste: James Caldwell, Andrew Alexander, John States. Proved, 21st May, 1755, by all witnesses, and all executors qualify.

Page 107.—19th April, 1755. David Rhey's (Ray's) appraisement, by James McCown, Saml. Keys (Hays?), Robert Bell.

Page 108.—21st May, 1755. John Ramsey's bond as guardian (appointed) to Samuel, James, Alexander and Andrew Crockett, orphans of Robert Crockett, with sureties Thomas Fulton, John Gay.

Page 109.—19th May, 1755. Samuel McMahon's appraisement, by Thos. Stevenson, John Campbell, David Stevenson, and accounts—Paid Saml. McMahon, George Bowman, Jno. Reybourn. To Robert McMahon, Cr., 21st May, 1755, by appraisement.

Page 110.—15th April, 1755. William Miller's appraisement, by Wm. Carraven, Hugh Mills, Richard Carr—3 bonds on Richard Reed, Edward McDonald; 3 bonds on William Beard, Wm. Miller, Jr.

Page 111.—5th April, 1755. John Sprout (Sproul?) appraisement, by John McAxwell, Michael Dougherty.

Page 111.—22d May, 1755. George Adam Salling's bond as executor of John Peter Salling, with sureties James McDowell, Robert Renick, Joshua Mathews. (Note—2 pages, each numbered 112 and 113.)

Page 113.—28th November, 1754. Robert McClenachan enters: 1. On Jackson's River about 2 miles above John Davis' mill at a rich (?) bottom; 2. On both sides of Fitzpatrick's path at a branch about 1½ miles from Davis' mill; 3. On both sides of said path at the forks of two drafts about half way between Davis' mill and Fitzpatrick's mill.

Page 113.—9th May, 1755. William Gay's will of the Calf Pasture—Wife, Margaret; eldest son, John, the plantation George Campbell lives on, formerly held by James Stevenson; to son, Robert, plantation testator lives on; to daughter, Mary; to daughter, Agness. Executors, wife and brother John Gay. Teste: Wm. Elliot, Jno. Fulton, James Stevenson. Proved, 20th August, 1755, by all witnesses. Executors qualify, with sureties Wm. Eliot, Ro. Campbell, Robert Gay.

Page 113.—18th August, 1755. Benj. Copland's additional appraisement, and accounts of estate.

Page 114.—20th August, 1755. John Buchanan's bond as administrator of Saml. Stalnaker, with sureties Israel Christian, Pat. Martin.

Page 115.—22d August, 1755. Sarah Haw's bond as administratrix of Henry Haws, with sureties Mathew Patton, Jas. Callison.

Page 116.—22d August, 1755. Alexander Wright's bond as administrator of Wm. Wright, with sureties John Harvie, Gabriel Jones. Teste: John Semple.

Page 118.—19th November, 1755. James Hambleton's appraisement, by James Beggs, Nicholas Cain.

Page 118.—20th June, 1755. Vendue of James Hambleton, by Daniel Love—In the Gap of the North Mountain upon Shanandoah. To Henry Abrams, James and Isaac Johnston, Wm. Claypole, John Dunbar.

Page 119.—19th November, 1755. William Gay's (of Calf Pasture) appraisement, by James Lockridge, Saml. Hodge, Joseph Vachub.

Page 120.—Joseph Paxton's will—Brothers, Samuel and William; mother; sister's two children, 1 pistole each to be sent the first opportunity. Executors, brother John and cousin Thomas Paxton. Teste: James Eakin,

Jos. Paxton. Proved, 19th November, 1755, by both witnesses. John and Thomas Paxton qualified executors, with sureties Joseph and Thos. Paxton

Page 122.—19th November, 1755. Margaret Fulton's bond as administratrix of Thomas Fulton, with sureties John Kinkade, Samuel Tincher.

Page 123.—19th November, 1755. Edward Hall's bond as guardian to Daniel Plummer, orphan of Robert Plummer, with sureties John Ramsey, Wm. Beard.

Page 123.—19th November, 1755. Adam Miller's bond as guardian to Michael Cogar, orphan of Nicholas Cogar, with sureties William Oller (Owler, Wilhelm Ohlner), Henry Miller.

Page 124.—26th July, 1755. John Peter Salling's appraisement by

Page 125.—20th November, 1755. William Davis' bond as administrator of John Thomas, with surety James Lockhart.

Page 126.—19th September, 1755. Thomas Wright's will—Executors. brothers Peter and James Wright. To Thomas Wright, son to Peter. To James Wright, son to Peter. To sisters Reatchel and Deborah Wright. Teste: James Dunlap, John Dickinson, Edward Mullin. Proved, 20th November, 1755, by Dickinson and Dunlap.

Page 126.—20th November, 1755. Mary Sorn's bond as administratrix of Jacob Sorn, with sureties Jacob Syver, John Duncan.

Page 127.—21st October, 1754. Robert Mean's will—To John McClung. Money in hands of Edward Thomson and Thomas Thomson. To the said Thomas McClung, the note of James Nilly, which is in hands of Thos. Black; wife a keeping, to said John. Teste: James Gay, Jenot Warrick. Proved, 21st November, 1755, by the witnesses; administration granted Thomas Thompson, nephew and heir-at-law of Robert Means, who qualified with sureties Hugh Hicklin and George Wilson.

Page 129.—19th November, 1755. James Lockhart's bond as collector of quit rents during his sheriffalty, with sureties John Brown, James Callison, David Moore, Hugh Young, James Neeley, John Lewis, Robert Christian.

Page 129.—19th November, 1755. James Lockhart's bond as sheriff with same sureties.

Page 130.—5th December, 1754. Appraisement of Richard Tictom, in the Gap of the North Mountain upon Sorondo, sold by Daniel Love, 5th December, 1754 To James Bagge, Jacob Richards, Nicholas Mase, Uriah Humble, Ephraim Love (part of a tramble), Daniel Love, Wm. Pickins, John Davis, Howel Jones, Jacob Bear, Robert Denton, John O'Neal, John Miller, Edward Megary, Mathew Waters, James Bryant, Jacob Sword, Robert Williams, William Carrill, Thomas Wast, Zephli Joseph, Mathew Waters, Joseph Zrepbli, Andrew Seduskay, Charles Witman, Abraham Bird, Nicholas Custert, Arnold Custard, Jacob Richards, James Claypole.

Page 131.—1st September, 1750. James Patton's will—Daughter, Mary, wife to William Thompson, 1 negro woman; tract called Spring Hill; 3,000 acres on which Saml. Stalnaker and others is living, known by name of Indian Fields, on waters of Houlston's river, a branch of the Missisipio. Grandson, James Thompson, infant, remainder in above in fee tail. Daughter, Margaret, now wife of Col. John Buchanan. To son-in-law, William Thompson, the tract called Springfield, joining where widow Gouldman now lives and on which Henry Patton lives. William is to keep the estate intact for his son, James, until 1772. To Margaret, tract called Cherry tree bottom, near Robert Looney's tract at mouth of Purgatory, tract on which there is a small stone house. Margaret's daughter, Mary; sister, Preston, and her son, William Preston, £10 to be paid to Rev. John Craig, pastor at Tinkling Spring, to pay his stipends from 1740 to 1750, to be paid by the congregation out of the money advanced by him to help build the meeting house. £10 of same to be laid out for a pulpit and pulpit cloth. John Preston's bond to be given up to his son, Wm. Preston. All debts due by George Wilson, who is married to testator's wife's niece, Rebecca Vicers (Viers?), to be given up. Granddaughter, Mary Buchanan. Executors, John Buchanan, Wm. Thompson, nephew, Wm. Preston, Silas Harte. All disputes between executors to be left to arbitration of the minister and elders of Tinkling Spring church. Testator was agent for John Smith, Zachery Lewis, Wm. Waller, Wm. Green, Wm. Parks for the Roanoke and James River grants. As to the Great Grant on the waters of Misicipia, James Gordon, James Johnston, John Grimes, John ———, Richard Barns, Robert Gilchrist, James Bowre, Robert Jackson, have assigned their parts to testator. Richard Winston's part is assigned to little John Buchanan. To Mary Preston, horses. Teste: Thomas Stewart, Edward Hall, John Williams. Proved, 26th November, 1755, by Stewart and Hall. Wm. Preston refuses to execute, also Silas Harte. Buchanan and Thompson qualify, with sureties David Stewart, Joseph Culton, Wm. Preston, Edward Hall, Thomas Stewart. 16th August, 1769, Wm. Preston qualifies executor.

Page 135.—17th March, 1756. Margaret Looney's bond as administratrix of Robert Looney, Jr., with sureties Rob. Rowland, John Looney.

Page 136.—3d December, 1754. William Smith's will—farmer. Child yet unborn; wife's young son, Thos. Steel; step-daughter, Jannet Steel; stepson, Robert Steel; stepson, Thomas Steel. Executors, Samuel Steel and wife Janet. Teste: Patt. Campbell, Wm. Steel, Robert Alexander. Proved, 17th March, 1756, by Campbell and Alexander. Executors qualify, with surety John Ward.

Page 137.—17th March, 1756. Wm. Edmondson's bond as guardian (chosen) to James Hays, orphan of Geo. Hays; Andrew Steel, John Loggan, sureties.

Page 138.—17th March, 1756. Samuel Newman's bond as administrator of Caspar Utt, with sureties Michael Warren, Jacob Woodley.

Page 139.—17th March, 1756. Jacob Woodley's bond as administrator of George Handy, with surety John Harrison.

Page 140.—17th March, 1756. Joseph Paxton's appraisement by John Smiley, Moses McCluer, John McClure. 18th March, 1756. John Bowyer's bond as guardian (chosen) to James McDowell, orphan of John McDowell, with sureties Joseph Lapesly, Richard Woods.

Page 141.—4th August, 1755. John Glass' appraisement by James Caldwell, Andrew Alexander, John Shields. John Glass' estate due to Patrick Kenan, Thomas Shields, Robert Moody, Wm. Long, Jas. Moody, Jno. Bigam, Samuel Downy, Thos. Brown, Jas. McLong, Arthur Hamilton, Wm. Karr.

Page 142.—20th March, 1756. Peter Wright's bond as executor of Peter Wright, with sureties George Wilson, Thomas Hughart.

Page 143.—4th December, 1753. Joseph Tees' will. To sons, William and Charles, plantation and negroes. Wife. Charles is 16 years old. To daughter Mary, the place bought from John Wilson; to daughter Eleanor and her children, the place bought from James Hamilton. Executors, wife, overseer, Wm. Henderson. Teste: John Campbell, Andrew Campbell, Walter Sorals. Proved, 17th March, 1756, by John and Andrew Campbell, and Jane Tees qualifies executrix, with sureties Wm. Henderson, John Campbell.

Page 144.—18th March, 1756. John Graham's bond as administrator of Wm. Johnston, with sureties John Graham, John Gay.

Page 145.—15th May, 1756. Robert Looney, Jr's., appraisement by William Harbison, John Bowen, Robert Rowland, Hugh Caruthers.

Page 146.—17th May, 1756. William Smith's appraisement, by John Mitchell, Robert Wilson, Robert Alexander—Widow Howston, Thomas Tate, Jno. Brownlee, widow Fulton, owe by accounts.

Page 147.—30th July, 1755. Daniel (Dan) Evans' will—Wife, Rhoda; brother, Nathaniel Evans; brother, Peter; Susannah Griffith to remain with Rhoda during Rhoda's widowhood, or until she arrives at 21. Executors, brother Peter Evans and Mark Cole, inhabitant in Bedford County, and wife Rhoda Evans. Teste: Caleb Powell, Erwin Patterson, Lawrence Stephen. Proved, 19th May, 1756, by Erwin Patterson. Peter Evans refuses to execute. Rhoda qualifies, with surety David Bryan.

Page 148.—19th May, 1756. Joseph Tays appraisement, by John Finley, Wm. Thompson, Saml. Steel, Wm. Finley.

Page 149.—19th May, 1756. John Bingaman's bond (with Jacob Nicholas, Henry Seller) as administrator of Jno. Bingaman.

Page 150.—19th May, 1756. Mary Cook's bond (with John Bingaman and Hance Magot) as administratrix of Henry Cook.

Page 151.—19th May, 1756. Janet Craig's bond (with Robt. Gibson and Robt. Thompson) as administratrix of John Craig.

Page 152.—21st May, 1756. Mary Johnson's bond (with Robt. and John Graham) as administratrix of John Johnson, deceased.

Page 153.—22d May, 1756. George Handy's appraisement, by Reuben Harrison, Thomas Lookey, Zabulon Harrison.

Page 153.—18th August, 1756. John Ramsey's bond (with Israel Christian) as guardian (chosen) to Alex. McDonall, orphan of Randall McDonall.

Page 154.—18th August, 1756. John Meason's (Mason) bond (with William and John Robertson) as administrator of Joseph Cummings.

Page 155.—4th December, 1755. John Thomas' appraisement, by Jeremiah Seeley, James Dunlap, Peter Wright.

Page 155.—18th August, 1756. John Craig's appraisement, by (?).

Page 155.—22d January, 1756. John Smith's will—To John Smith, son of brother Daniel Smith, the plantation on North River, Shanedoe, which testator bought of Silas Hart; to brother Daniel; to brother Abraham Smith; to brother Henry Smith. Executor, brother Daniel Smith. Teste: Thomas Sewell, Benj. Kinley (Kinsey), Daniel Smith. Proved, 18th August, 1756, by Benj. Kinsey, and to lie for further proof. Daniel Smith qualifies with Silas Harte and Robert Harrison.

Page 156.—19th August, 1756. Frederick See's bond (with Adam and John Dickinson) as administrator of John See.

Page 157.—19th August, 1756. John Man's bond (with Adam and Jno. Dickinson) as administrator of Moses Man.

Page 158.—12th August, 1756. John Johnston's appraisement, by Andrew Russell, Wm. Johnson, John Hutchison, Jr.

Page 159.—19th August, 1756. Jacob Zorn's appraisement, by Jacob Sivart, John Dunkell, Charles Wolson. Also additional appraisement, by Bouston Hover, Mark Swatley, Christian Eavach.

Page 161.—April, 1750 (doubt about the date). Thomas Fulton's appraisement, by Andrew Hamilton, John Graham, Daniel O'Hara. (Subscribers acknowledge this to be a true copy of our judgment according to our best knowledge of the worth and value and estate of Thos. Fulton. Witness 18th August, 1756.)

Page 162.—2d January, 1756. John Hogshead's will—Son, James; son, John, the bark house and tan yard and 2 acres of meadow joining Robert Gilkeson's line; son, David; son, Michael; daughter, Rebecca Hogshead; to grandson, Wm. Allen. Executors, David and Michael Hogshead. Teste: James Bell, John Archer, James Allen. Proved, November, 1756, by Allen and Bell. Both executors qualify with James Allen and Wm. Hind.

Page 164.—27th May, 1756. Casper Utt's appraisement, by Uriah Humble, John Thomas, Arnold Kurter.

Page 164.—17th November, 1756. Mary Robinson's bond (with John Robinson, John Miller) as administratrix of Jno. Robinson.

Page 165.—26th June, 1754. Accounts against estate of James Hamilton—To a cryer, 12 pence in the pound; to the corroner, £1, 2, 8. Going to Balhaven for Dunbar's deed. List of proven accounts vs. James Hamilton's estate—Wm. McGee; Jno. Miller, Danl. Cummings, John Dunbar.

Page 166.—17th November, 1756. John Dean's bond (with John Dickinson, Wm. Dean) as administrator of George Kinkade.

Page 167.—17th November, 1756. William Johnston's appraisement, by Robt. Graham, Archd. Armstrong, William Elliott.

Page 167.—17th November, 1756. James Boreland's bond (with John Graham and Jas. Arbuckle) as administrator of John Bird.

Page 168.—17th November, 1756. David Sayer's bond (with David Hays, Jno. Hunter) as administrator of Robert Sayers.

Page 169.—17th November, 1756. William May's bond (with Andrew Muldrough, Joseph Wahob) as administrator of James Mays, deceased.

Page 170.—11th August, 1756. Samuel Paxton's will—Plantation called Broad Spring to be sold. Wife, Mary; brother, Thomas Paxton, second son Samuel; son, Samuel, plantation testator lives on, 212 acres. Executors, brother Thomas Paxton and James Trimble. Teste: James Moore, Archd. Alexander, John Moore. Proved, 17th November, 1756, by Archd. Alexander and James Moore. Executors qualify with John Paxton and James Moore.

Page 171.—17th November, 1756. David Stuart's bond (with John Madison and James Lockhart) as administrator of John O'Neal.

Page 172.—17th November, 1756. John Maxwell's bond (with John Ramsey) as guardian ( ) to John Campbell, orphan of Jno. Campbell.

Page 173.—17th November, 1756. Felix Gilbert's bond (with Hugh Hicklin, Robert Armstrong) as administrator of Nicholas Nutt.

Page 174.—4th September, 1756. Alexander Matheson's will, doctor—To William Robertson, his rifle gun and flowered plush jacket; to John Robertson, great coat, saddle and bridle, course stockings and course shirts; to James, son of Mathew Robertson, cutlass; to Mathew Robertson, £6; to

Silas Hart, £6; to brother Gilbert Matheson, 5 shillings; to brother **Mathew Matheson**; to father, John Matheson, 5 shillings and remainder of the estate. Executors, Mathew Robertson and Silas Hart. Teste: James Henderson, James Robertson, Wm. Bell. Proved, 18th November, 1756, by Henderson. Mathew refuses to execute. Silas Hart qualifies with James Allen and Daniel Smith.

Page 176.—19th November, 1756. Ann Mountgomery's bond (with John Dickinson and James Simpson) as administratrix of James Simpson.

Page 177.—21st August, 1756. John Bingaman's appraisement, by Jacob Miller, Hance Magot, Francis Kirtley.

Page 177.—21st August, 1756. Henry Cook's appraisement, by Jacob Nicholas.

Page 178.—3d September, 1756. Robert Sayers' nuncupative will—To second son Robert (infant), all real estate bought from his brother David Sayers; father was testator's security in above purchase; to son Robert, a saddle which Wm. Scott is making; son, David (infant), which is a fool. Proved, 20th November, 1756, by Jno. Christian, John Hunter, Chas. Campbell. Was objected to by David Sayers, to whom administration was granted, because the will was not signed, but as Campbell and Hunter testified that the testator acknowledged it as his will, it is recorded and administration is rescinded; then administration is granted David as next of kin (Hannah, the widow, refusing to qualify), who qualifies with Jno. Ramsey and **John Hunter.**

Page 179.—30th October, 1756. Daniel Evans' appraisement, by Wm. Graham, James Bean, Wm. Carvin.

Page 180.—24th November, 1756. James Lockhart's bond (with John Trimble, Wm. Long, Danl. Harrison) for collection of County levy.

Page 180.—15th December, 1756. Adam Dickinson's bond (with Wallace Estill, Danl. Harrison) as administrator of Humphrey Madison.

Page 181.—23d February, 1757. John Hogshead's appraisement, by John Archer, Sampson Archer, Thomas Armstrong.

Page 182.—16th March, 1757. Peter Vaneman's (Venman) bond (with Jacob Sybert, Michael Ahart) as administrator of Mark Miller.

Page 183.—16th March, 1757. James Mountgomery's appraisement, by Francis McKowan, John McKowan, Jacob Anderson, Jno. Buntin.

Page 183.—2d January, 1756. John Gatton (signed Patton and order says Patton). John Patton's will—To wife, Agness; five children, viz, William, James, Margaret, Isabell, Agness (infants); elder children are already portioned off. Executors, wife Agness, Alex. Miller, John Wardlaw. Teste: Wm. McClung, Jno. Stevenson, Mathew Lyle. Proved, 16th March, 1757, by the witnesses. Alex. Miller refuses to execute. **Agness** qualifies with Mathew Lyle and Alex. Miller.

Page 185.—16th March, 1757. John Hinton's bond (with Daniel Harrison, Sampson Archer) as guardian (chosen) to Thomas O'Neal (**aged** 16), orphan of **John O'Neal.**

Page 186.—16th March, 1757. Joseph Cummings' appraisement, by Neal McNeal, Thomas Tosh, William Hugens (Hogens).

Page 187.—17th March, 1757. Christopher (Stophel) White's bond **(with** Thos. Hugart, Jno. Davis) as administrator of George White.

Page 188.—26th January, 1757. Robert Sawyer's appraisement, by Robert Christian, William Long, James Alexander.

Page 188.—12th March, 1757. John Robinson's appraisement, by Neal McNeal, Tasker Tosh, Thomas Tosh.

Page 189.—30th November, 1756. Alexander Matheson's appraisement, by John Anderson, George Anderson, James Henderson.

Page 190.—16th June, 1757. Adam Dickinson's bond (with John Harvie) as administrator of Henry Lawless.

Page 191.—22d January, 1757. James Maze's appraisement, by Elijah McClenachan, Ralph Laverty, Adam Dickinson.

Page 192.—16th June, 1757. John Patton's appraisement, by John Lyle, John Stevenson, Wm. McClung.

Page 193.—21st March, 1757. Marks Miller's appraisement, by Sampson Archer, Jno. Huston, Jno. Cravens.

Page 193.—January, 1757. Saml. Paxton's appraisement, by James Walker, Andrew Hays, Alex. Walker.

Page 194.—16th June, 1757. John Smith's appraisement, by John Malkem, Hugh Douglass, John McClure.

Page 194.—17th June, 1757. James Hamilton's estate—Accounts by Daniel Love, administrator.

Page 194.—17th June, 1757. Thomas Thompson's bond (with Wm. Elliott, Ralph Laverty) as administrator of John Moore.

Page 195.—25th July, 1757. William Bell's will—To be buried at Stone Meeting House by side of wife lately ceased; to son Joseph, plantation if he die before he come home from Carolina; daughter Mary, gold ring he did usually wear; to son Edward Baird; sons, William, David, Saml. Bell and Edward Baird; leaves to every one of my other children 1 shilling. Teste: Robert McHan, John Theobald Maighan. Proved, 17th August, 1757, by the witnesses. David Bell is not in this Colony. Edward Beard qualifies with Henry Rayburn, James Craig.

Page 197.—21st May, 1757. Bryan McDonald's will—To son Bryan McDonald, ½ of testator's land where he (Bryan, Jr.) used to live; to son-in-law John Armstrong, other half of plantation above where testator now lives; to daughter Prisla, bed she now lieth upon; to wife Catherine; to son Richard, 5 shillings; to sons James, Edward, Joseph and Bryan McDonald, remainder of estate; to daughters Rebecca Bean, Catherine Armstrong, Mary Smith. Executors, wife Catherine and son-in-law John Armstrong. Teste: Joseph McDonald, George Robinson, Edward McDonald. Proved, 18th August, 1757, by Edward and Joseph McDonald. Both executors qualify with Edward McDonald and Joseph McDonald.

Page 198.—18th August, 1757. John O'Neal's appraisement by Ephraim Love, Thomas Gordon, Daniel Love.

Page 200.—2d July, 1754. William Burk's estate—Accounts. By Robert Breckinridge. October, 1754. Suit vs. Shildrick Brown, Hanover. To James Brown's account; to Henry Dick; to Peter Scholl, coroner for inquest. January, 1756. To John Burk, expense of trip over the mountain. August, 1754. To Wm. Burk, Jr., for expense. June, 1756. To Adam Ollar by judgment of Court.

Page 201.—Estate of William Burk—Debts recovered 1754 and articles sold; to James Neal, John Harman, Nicholas Brook, Margaret Douglass, Christian Grubb, Thomas Smith, Sarah Stern, Daniel Sink, Stephen Johnston, Saml. Thornhill, Jeremiah Earley, Andrew Scott, David Logan, John Early.

Page 201.—21st June, 1757. John O'Neal's additional appraisement, by same as before.

Page 202.—26th August, 1751. William Paul's will—To daughter Margaret, all estate; to son John, 5 shillings; son James, 5 shillings. Executors, Charles Hays, James Moore. Teste: James Lee, Samuel Linsey. Proved, 16th November, 1757, by the witnesses. Chas. Hays qualifies with James Trimble, Saml. Linsey.

Page 203.—16th November, 1757. Jannet McDonald's bond (with John Wright, Danl. Smith) as administrator of Randall McDonald.

Page 204.—17th November, 1757. Esther (Easter) Brown's bond (with Robert Moody, James Moody) as administratrix of Henry Brown.

Page 205.—20th April, 1757. John Mathews' will, of Forks of James River, Gent.—To son John, tract where on son John lives; to son Joshua, tract whereon son Joshua lives for life with remainder to Joshua's 2 children, Anna and Elizabeth, both infants; if they die in infancy, then to their uncle George, and Archer, and William; son Richard, 1 shilling; to son Sampson, tract called Kelley's entry on Borden's Branch, 350 acres; to son George, 1 shilling; daughters, Jane, Anne, Rachel, 1 shilling each; daughter Elizabeth, infant; sons William and Archer, infants; wife, Anne; to poor of Augusta Parish provided it is not divided before testator's death. Executors, sons Sampson and George, who are to convey to Wm. Bradshaw a tract sold to Bradshaw. Teste: Mathew Campbell, Anna Kelley, Jno. Poage. Proved, 16th November, 1757, by Campbell and Poage. Executors qualify with John Poage, John Mathews.

Page 207.—16th November, 1757. Elizabeth Couts' (late widow of Jno. Harmantrout) bond as administratrix of John Harmantrout, with sureties Henry Perkey, Nicholas Null.

Page 208.—26th August, 1757. Gilbert Mills' will, planter—To son William, note on James Staret living in Refoe township, Pennsylvania; son Alexander, clothes; granddaughter Agnes Mills, residuary legatee. Executors, Isaac White, Edward Hall. Teste: Henry Davis, Eleanor Tear Proved, 16th November, 1757, by the witnesses. Executors qualify, with Alex. Richey, Robert McClehenny.

Page 210.—11th September, 1757. Joseph Long's will—To son Samuel, tract at the Welch cabins; to son Henry, tract near place called Billar Spring; to son Joseph, infant, tract where testator lives; to son John, tract at the Big Spring known as Island Ford. (All these tracts now are in one, and these are appointed to divide, viz: Richard Woods, John Hannah, James Beats, James Alexander); to wife Anna; to daughter Agness Cohoun, 5 shillings; to daughter Gennet Long; to daughters Gennet, Elizabeth, Ann, Ruth. Executors, wife Anne and son Henry. Teste: John Long, Wm. Long, Thos. Stewart, James Alexander. Proved, 16th November, 1757, by Wm. and Jno. Long, and James Alexander. Henry Long refuses to execute. Ann qualifies with Richard Woods, Robert Young, Alex. Ritchey.

Page 212.—16th November, 1757. Joshua Mathews' bond (with William McElhenony, Alex. McKorkle) as administrator of Robert Renix.

Page 213.—11th July, 1757. Robert Bell's will, plantationer—To son John (infant), ½ plantation testator now lives on; to five infant daughters; to son Robert (infant), other half of above plantation; to wife Elizabeth, ⅓ of plantation testator lives on. Executors, wife Elizabeth, James Mc-

Coven, Alex. Buchanan. Teste: James, John and William Buchanan. Proved, 16th November, 1757, by James and Jno. Buchanan. Elizabeth qualifies, with James Buchanan, Andrew Hays.

Page 214.—The other executors refusing to qualify.

Page 215.—2d October, 1757. William Bell's appraisement, by Andrew Leeper, James Leeper, Hugh Donohy.

Page 215.—17th November, 1757. Ann Stewart's bond (with John Dickinson, Geo. Wilson) as administratrix of James Stewart.

Page 216.—5th September, 1757. John Wilson's will, shoemaker—To wife Agness; to daughter Sarah; to brother Robert Wilson and brother James Wilson's son John; to brother James' son William; to James McKnut, ½ of shoemaker's tools. Teste: John Christian, John Brownlee, Alex. Brownlee. Proved, 18th November, 1757, by John Christian and Jno. Brownlee. Agness renounces the provisions, and Agness qualifies, with Robt. McClenachan, Richard Woods.

Page 218.— —— November, 1756. John Bird's estate, settlement by James Boreland, administrator—12th January, 1757, paid J. D. Wilper, John Dean, John Sempell, Andrew Hamilton.

Page 219.—18th November, 1757. Michael Reiley's estate, vendue—To William Bishop, Ezekiah Inman, Wm. Kerr, Jacob Gray, Thos. Sheils, Robert Campbell, of No. Mountain. Amounts sworn off said Rieley's estate according to law by these persons. Charles Dalhouse and many others. Paid Joseph Love for venduing the estate. Paid Secretary Nelson for recording Rieley's certificate. Paid James Lockhart by order of John Flood. Paid Robert Gibson for making the grave.

Page 220.—18th November, 1757. Israel Christian's bond (with Chas. Campbell, Abraham Smith) as administrator of John Smith, now a Captain in the French Dominions.

Page 221.—16th November, 1757. Richard Wood's bond as sheriff (with John Bowyer, Joseph Lapsley, Mathew Lyle, Saml. McDowell, John Gilmore, Henry Kirkam.

Page 222.—16th November, 1757. Richard Wood's bond (with sureties above) to collect officers' fees, &c.

Page 223.—21st December, 1757. Richard Wood's bond (with Robert McClenachan, John Bowyer) for collection of County proportion.

Page 223.—15th March, 1758. John Armentrout's appraisement for John Kouts, executor, by Henry Downs, Jacob Nicholas, Augustine Price. Sold by Adam Kittrick before appraisement.

Page 224.—15th March, 1758. Michael Thorn and Anthony Reeger's bond (with Philip Mason, Isaac Johnson, Philip Moore) as administrators of Christian Tosher.

Page 225.—15th March, 1758. Jacob Siver's bond (with Sampson Archer, Ephraim Love) as administrators of Henry Lawrence.

Page 226.—15th March, 1758. Wm. McGill's (Magill) bond (with Daniel Smith) as guardian (chosen) to John Berry, orphan of James Berry.

Page 227.—15th March, 1758. Gilbert Mill's appraisement, by Saml. Steel, Wm. Finley, John Finley, James Gilespy.

Page 227.—21st March, 1757. Marks Miller's appraisement, by Sampson Archer, John Cravins, John Hinton.

Page 228.—6th March, 1758. Joseph Long's appraisement, by Peter Wallace, James Beats, Henry Kirkcum, Joseph Lapsely.

Page 229.—15th March, 1758. Robert Sayer's estate appraisement.

Page 230.—15th February, 1758. John Black's will, yeoman—Wife, Isabell; sons, David and John, executors; son, Samuel; son, William Brown Teste: Adam Thompson, Moses Thompson, Andrew Cowan. Produced 16th March, 1758, and not being signed, Samuel Black, the heir-at-law, gave his consent. It was then proved by Adam Thompson and Cowan. David Black qualified.

Page 231.—31st October, 1757. Bryan McDanniel, Sr.'s, appraisement, by David Cloyd, Saml. McRoberts, William Snodgrass.

Page 232.—1st December, 1757. William Paul's appraisement, by Andrew Hays, Joseph Culton, Alexander Walker.

Page 233.—16th March, 1758. Martha Claypole's bond (with Daniel Harrison) as administratrix of William Claypole.

Page 234.—19th January, 1758. Robert Bell's appraisement, by Jno. Wallace, Saml. Hays, James McCown, Alex. Buchanan.

Page 255.—1st March, 1758. John Mathews' appraisement, by Alex. Beggs, Jno. Maxwell, James Simpson.

Page 236.—16th March, 1758. John Davis Wilper's bond (with Alex. Galespy, Robt. Allen) as administrator of Henry Baughman.

Page 237.—14th March, 1758. James Stewart's appraisement, by Ralph Laverty, James McCoy, Henry Cartmell.

Page 237.—16th March, 1758. Alexander Gilespy's bond (with Jas. Lockhart, Geo. Moffett) as administrator of Mathias Teter.

Page 238.—17th March, 1758. By order of Court November, 1757, Robt. Cravens, Hugh Campbell, Arthur Johnson, chosen by the old Court to appraise the estate of Randall McDonald.

Page 238.—17th November, 1758. John Trimble's bond (with John Anderson, John McCreary) as guardian (appointed) to Hannah Moffett, orphan of John Moffett.

Page 239.—19th March, 1750. Henry Lawless' estate to Adam Dickinson, administrator—Paid McAlvane, Jacob Parsinger, David Meriwether, Peter Wright.

Page 240.—17th May, 1758. John Moore's bond (with Joseph Kennedy, Andrew Steel) as guardian (chosen) to James Bell, orphan of James Bell.

Page 240.—12th May, 1758. Henry Brown's appraisement, by John Ramsey, Wm. Johnston, Wm. Logan.

Page 241.—17th May, 1758. Rachel Bell's bond (with Jas. Sayers, Jno. Henderson) as guardian (chosen) to Mary Anne Bell, orphan of James Bell.

Page 241.—17th May, 1758. Thomas Thompson's bond (with Patrick Martin, Edward Thompson) as guardian (chosen) to James Crockett, orphan of Robt. Crockett.

Page 242.—17th May, 1758. Saml. Craig's bond (with Jno. Young, Alex. Blair) as guardian (appointed) to Jane Bell, orphan of James Bell.

Page 243.—17th May, 1758. George Campbell's bond (with Robert McElheny, Robt. Moore) as guardian (chosen) to Lettice Campbell, orphan of Gilbert Campbell.

Page 244.—18th May, 1758. Wm. McFeeters' bond (with Jno. McFeeters, Jno. Elliot) as guardian (appointed) to Andrew Crockett, orphan of Robert Crockett.

Page 244.—18th May, 1758. Michael Mallow's bond (with Daniel Smith, Philip Harper) as administrator of Peter Moser.

Page 245.—17th May, 1758. Daniel Smith's bond (with Michael Mallow, Peter Venneman) as administrator of Jacob Sivers.

Page 246.—18th May, 1758. Michael Mallow's bond (with Daniel Smith, Peter Venneman) as administrator of George Mouse. (Is the name Mouse the same as Moser?)

Page 247.—18th May, 1758. Philip Harper's bond (with Michael Mallow, Peter Vennamen) as administrator of George Moser.

Page 248.—18th May, 1758. Felix Gilbert's bond (with Jno. Risk, Adam Dickinson) as administrator of Jno. Hutcheson.

Page 249.—12th December, 1756. Nicholas Nutt's appraisement, by Edward Mullin, Edward Thompson, Joseph Carpenter.

Page 250.—18th May, 1758. John McFeeters' bond (with James Philips, Robt. Campbell) as guardian (appointed) to Alex. Crockett, orphan of Robt. Crockett.

Page 250.—19th May, 1758. John Wilson's account, by Ann Wilson, administratrix—Paid Edward McColgan, Edward Tar, Samuel Buchanan, John Jones, Wm. Adair.

Page 251.—19th May, 1758. Mathew Patton's bond (with Abraham Smith, Sampson Archer) as administrator of Jno. Reager.

Page 252.—20th May, 1758. Jacob Patton's estate to Susan Patton, administratrix—To Edward McDonald, Joseph Love, Wm. Plummer, George Tar, Henry Campbell, Jno. Potts, Robt. Williams, Philip Watkins, Reece Watkins, John Walker, Christopher Cunningham, John Patton, Robt. Mountgomery, Robt. Looney, Wm. Lusk, Wm. Graham.

Page 253.—20th May, 1758. Mathew Patton's bond (with Jas. Lockhart, Sampson Archer) as guardian (appointed) to Hanna Hause, orphan of Henry Hause.

Page 253.—16th August, 1758. Agness Patton's bond (with John Mathews, Jno. Wardlaw) as administratrix of Jno. Snodgrass.

Page 254.—14th February, 1758. John Lyle's will, yeoman—Wife, Jean; sons, John and William, 524 acres; four daughters, Martha, Elizabeth, Sarah, Esther. Executors, wife Jean, Danl. Lyle, Archd. Alexander. Teste: Mathew Lyle, Samuel Lyle, Robert Lusk. Proved, 16th August, 1758, by the witnesses. Executors qualified, with Samuel and Mathew Lyle.

Page 257.—16th August, 1758. Thomas Meek's bond (with Jno. Ward, Jacob Martin) as administrator of Moses Moore.

Page 258.—16th August, 1758. Thomas Gregg's bond (with Saml. Semple) as administrator of Wm. Woods.

Page 259.—2d March, 1753. Alexander Campbell's will—To son (youngest) Alexander, plantation testator lives on; to wife, maintenance; to daughter Florence; to daughter Mary; to daughter Jane. Executors, son William, and William Ledgerwood. Teste: Pat. Cunningham, Robt. Campbell, Walter Davis. Proved, 16th August, 1758, by Cunningham and Davis. Executors qualified with Hugh Young, Pat. Campbell.

Page 260.—16th August, 1758. John Dean's bond (with John Stuart, Thomas Hugart) as guardian (?) to Sarah Bird, orphan of John Bird.

Page 261.—16th August, 1758. Catherine Goodman's bond (with Jacob Goodman, John Colley) as administratrix of Michael Frise.

Page 262.—16th August, 1758. John Ward's bond (with Israel Christian, Jno. Dickinson) as administrator of Samuel Moore.

Page 263.—16th August, 1758. Robert Bratton's bond (with Robert McClenachan, Jno. Gay, Ralph Laverty) as administrator of James Dunlap.

Page 264.—17th August, 1758. Margaret Dyer's bond (with Daniel Harrison, Mathew Patton) as administratrix of Wm. Dyer.

Page 265.—29th May, 1758. Samuel Mountony's (Mounthany) will— To John Carlile, of Calf Pasture, all estate; executor. Teste: William Preston, Charles Lewis, David Long, Thomas Lloyd, George Skilron, Philip Phegan. Proved, 17th August, 1758, by Preston and Lloyd. Executor qualified, with Thos. Hugart and Samuel Wilson.

Page 267.—17th August, 1758. Peter Kender's (Kinder? Ginder?) estate, account with Alex. Wright, administrator—To sundries from 22d August, 1748, to 22d August, 1749. Paid Erwin Patterson, Patrick Vance, for wages. Paid Alex. Ingram (4 days writing). Paid Ephraim Vause for crying the vendue. Paid Francis Cyphers, Henry Brown, Geo. Griffith. These did not pay for goods bought at vendue, viz: Joseph Kimmins, James McAfee, Jean Patterson, John Gold, Joseph McDonald, David Robinson.

Page 269.—27th January, 1757. James Mays' estate in account with William Mays, administrator.

Page 270.—18th August, 1758. Felix Gilbert's account of estate of Nicholas Nutt.

Page 270.—18th August, 1758. Wm. McBride's appraisement, by John Dunbar, Robert Denton, James Thomas.

Page 271.—19th August, 1758. James Boreland's settlement of estate of John Bird—Paid John Hart.

Page 271.—19th August, 1758. John Bowyer's bond (with Israel Christian) as guardian (?) to Caleb Harman, orphan of John Harman.

Page 272.—8th November, 1758. George Mouse's appraisement, by Ephraim Love, Daniel Love, Arthur Jonson.

Page 272.—8th November, 1758. Capt. Jacob Siver's appraisement, by same as above.

Page 272.—8th November, 1758. Peter Moser's appraisement, by same as above.

Page 273.—15th November, 1758. William Dyer's appraisement, by Alex. Harron (Herring), Daniel Love, Arthur Johnson.

Page 273.—15th November, 1758. John Black's appraisement.

Page 274.—15th November, 1758. John Lyle's appraisement, by John Lapsley, Robt. Lusk, Jno. Mahey, Robt. Huston.

Page 274.—15th September, 1758. Henry Baughman's appraisement, by Valentine Pence, Daniel Price, Peter Selers (Silers?).

Page 275.—11th November, 1758. Alex. Campbell's appraisement, by David Cunningham, Jas. McCutchen, Saml. McCutchen.

Page 275.—11th November, 1758. Michael Freez's (Frise) appraisement, by Peter Hole (mark), Paul Shever, Loudwick Waggner—Paid Geo. Homs, Valentine Goyle, Jacob Harper.

Page 276.—6th May, 1758. John McCroskry's (signed Coskry) will, planter—To wife Elizabeth, Thomas Hill's bond; to daughter Elizabeth; to son James, 10 shillings; to son William, 10 shillings; to son John, 10 shillings; to son-in-law, William Caruthers; to son-in-law Saml. Huston; to son Alex. McCroskry, 10 shillings; to son Samuel, 10 shillings; to son

David, 10 shillings; to son-in-law James Hope, 10 shillings; to granddaughter Margaret Hope and her two brothers; Saml. and David to pay the bonds assigned to James and William in case they lose not their lands by the enemy; Robert and Alexander Tedford's bonds to pay Margaret Hope; James and Isaac Anderson's bond to be divided between sons and daughters. Executors, son Samuel, Andrew Hays, Alex. Miller. Teste: James Moore, Jno. Maskamell, Alex. McCroskry. Proved, 15th November, 1758, by Moore and McCroskry. McCroskry and Miller qualified (the other not appearing), with Samuel Huston, John Cunningham.

Page 278.—15th November, 1758. James Wilson's bond (with Alex. Hamilton, Archd. Armstrong, Andrew Muldrough) as administrator of Josiah Wilson.

Page 279.—12th November, 1758. John Gay's receipt to Alex. Hamilton for what was in his and his wife's hands belonging to the children of William Gay.

Page 279.—15th November, 1758. Settlement of John Craig's estate, by Jennet Craig, his widow and sole executrix. Due Margaret Thompson, widow. Due Saml. Davison, Rev. Jno. Craig, Saml. Frasure, Ro. Moody, Isbell Frasure (widow), John Baskins.

Page 280.—15th November, 1758. Accounts against estate of William Magill paid by Hugh Campbell and Robt. Cravens. Legacies paid, viz: To James, John, William, Margaret McGill, Hugh Campbell, John Jones, Robert Dickson, John Berry, Ro. Fouller (to each of these £9, 1, 6).

Page 280.—15th November, 1758. Abraham Smith's bond (with Robert Cravens, Ephraim Love) as administrator of Ludwick Fulk.

Page 281.—15th November, 1758. John Hamilton's bond (with Samuel Young, Alex. Galespy) as administrator of John Gay.

Page 282.—15th November, 1758. Jacob Peterson's bond (with Abraham Smith, Ephraim Love) as administrator of Nicholas Frank.

Page 282.—15th November, 1758. Michael Mallow's bond (with same as above)as administrator of John Blair.

Page 283.—15th November, 1758. Barbara Wingord's bond (with Chas. Rush, Jacob Parsinger) as administratrix of John Wingord.

Page 284.—16th November, 1758. Israel Christian's bond (with John Trimble, Pat. Martin) as administrator of Joseph Bell.

Page 285.—16th November, 1758. Woolrick Conrod's bond (with Daniel Smith, Jno. Dunkle) as administrator of Hance Conrod.

Page 286.—16th November, 1758. Daniel Smith's bond (Woolrick Conrod, Jno. Dunkle) as administrator of Henry Lawrence.

Page 287.—3d July, 1758. Henry Brown's further appraisement, by Saml. McCune, Wm. Logan, Wm. Johnson.

Page 287.—17th November, 1758. Benj. Copland's estate settlement, by Ann Ralston (late Anne Copland). 19th March, 1755, former account. John Shaw's note (he ran away). Paid Thos. Pointer for one-half year schooling of Jacob and Mary Copland £1. Credits since 23d September, 1757—To Hannah Copland, Sarah Copland, Anne Ralston, David Ralston, Samuel Semple, Thomas Gregg, Samuel Hull, Robert Patterson, Edward McGeery, David Berry, Daniel Henderson, Peter Trader.

Page 288.—20th November, 1758. John Bowyer's bond (with Robt. Breckinridge, Robt. McClenachan) for collection of County proportion.

Page 289.—20th November, 1758. Same (with same and Jno. Dickinson) for collection of taxes on tithables and land.
Page 289.—7th March, 1759. John Gay's appraisement, by Alex. Galespy, Hugh Young, Samuel Young.
Page 289.—21st March, 1759. James Hunter's bond (with Wm. Hunter and Alex. Hamilton) as administrator of Thos. Caddon.
Page 290.—1st January, 1759. John McCroskry's appraisement, by Andrew Steel, James Pollock, Charles Hays.
Page 291.—21st March, 1759. Bridget Custard's bond (with Thos. Bryan, Michael Warren) as administratrix of Arnold Custard.
Page 292.—21st March, 1759. Charles Hays' bond (with James Buchanan, David Hays) as administrator of James Lee.
Page 293.—7th February, 1759. John Wingord's appraisement, by Archd. Huston, Jacob Nioles (Nicholas?), Valentine Pence (Bentz).
Page 294.—27th April, 1753. Henry Thorn's appraisement, by Jas. Simpson, Michael Harnes, Coonrod Harnes. Cash due by the widow.
Page 294.—16th November, 1758. Hance Reager's appraisement, by Abraham Smith, William Stephenson, Robt. Harrison.
Page 295.—29th March, 1759. Humphrey Madison's appraisement, by James McCoy, Ralph Laverty, Alex. McElroy. Sold to Mary Madison.
Page 295.—24th March, 1759. Samuel Hays' bond (with Jas. Buchanan) as administrator of Jno. Culliland.
Page 296.—1st February, 1759. James McCutchen's will, freeholder—To wife Grisal and youngest son James, the tract testator lives on; to oldest son John and second son Patrick, 343 acres in Calf Pasture; to son William, if he lives to age, land; to elder daughter Sarah, second daughter Elizabeth. Executors, wife Grisal, Patrick Campbell, Samuel McCutchen. Teste: Robt. Campbell, W. Christian, Chas. Campbell, James Campbell. Proved, 16th May, 1759, by Wm. Christian and Ro. Campbell. Executors qualified.
Page 298.—21st December, 1758. Rees Thomas' will, farmer—To wife Jean, tract of patent land on Brock's Creek, 350 acres, until son Evan Thomas shall be of age; to son Rees Thomas; to son John Thomas; to son James Thomas; to his daughters and his wife's daughters. Executors, wife Jean and son John. Teste: John Alderson, Elizabeth Kimsey, William Bodeker. Proved, 16th May, 1759, by Alderson and Bodeker. Executors qualified, with Ephraim Love and Abraham Bird.
Page 299.—24th September, 1757. William Stephenson's will—Wife, Sarah; ratifies former gifts to children; sons, David and Mathew; daughter, Sarah. (John Davis to advise about division of land.) (Tract of land on the Gum Run Meadow.) To sons, Adam and John, what Arthur Trader owes testator. All children, viz: Adam, John, James, William, David, Elizabeth, Mathew, Sarah, probably all infants (girls under 18). John Davis to have the care, guardianship and tuition of children. Executors, wife Sarah and son Adam. Teste: Silas Hart, Henry Smith, Jno. McCoy. Proved, 16th May, 1759, by Hart and McCoy. Executors qualify, with Abraham Smith, Mathew Patton.
Page 301.—16th May, 1759. Thomas Hicklin's bond (with James Hall, Robert Hall) as administrator of John Smith.
Page 301.—24th February, 1757. Roger Dyer's will—To wife Hanna, one-third of estate in this Colony, or any other; to son James, infant;

executrix, wife Hanna; to son William; to three daughters; to daughter Hanna Gester, 427 acres in Hampshire; to grandson Roger Dyer, son of William Dyer; to daughters Hester Patton, Sarah Hays. Teste: Wm. Miller, Adam Hider, William Gibson. Further proved, 16th May, 1759, by Adam Hider, and recorded. Executrix qualifies. Proved, 21st March, 1759, by William Gibson.

Page 303.—29th December, 1757. Andrew Muldrough's will—Executors, James Simpson and Wm. McMory; wife, Jane; two sons, Hugh and John, infants. Teste: Hugh Martian, John Dickinson, Wm. Davis. Proved, 21st March, 1759, by William Davis. Proved, 16th May, 1759, by Hugh Martin. Executors, Simpson and McMurry, qualified, with Geo. Wilson and Jno. Handly.

Page 305.—1st February, 1758. Martha Mitchell's will, widow—Son, James Mitchell. As her son David Mitchell, through the necessity of the times, hath been forced to leave his own habitation, he is to live with James until it pleases God to restore peace to the land. Executors, David and James Mitchell, her sons. Teste: Jno. Fulton, Hugh Fulton, Robert Alexander. Proved, 16th May, 1759, by the Fultons. The executors qualify, with John Hugh Fulton, John Fulton.

Page 306.—10th December, 1757. Christian Doscher's (Dosher, Dorcher) appraisement, by Michael Stump, Leonard Neave, Peter Horse. Due by Charles Wilson, Christian Crose. Due Wm. Darline, John Welton, Anthony Reager.

Page 307.—3d December, 1757. Vendue held at Michael Stump's, on South Fork in Hampshire County, by Anthony Reager, Peter Thorn, administrators of Christian Dousher—To Peter Heath, Thos. Crawford, Tobias Thorn, Michael Oxer, Lazarus Thorn, Philip Moore, Jr., Jno. Welton, Henry Couchman, Simon Hornback, Philpole Yeokham, Abraham Wise, Jno. Cock, Adam Rutherback, Harmus Hook, Conrad Moore, Thomas Singleton, Martin Job, James Hornback, Adam Harpole, Jonathan Coburn, Leonard Knave, Thos. Parsons, Sr., Nicholas Smith, Gaisper Reed, Michael Earsest, Sr., James Taff, Henry Miars, Ruda Bozard, Wm. Jennings, Jno. Varrill, James Parsons, Solom Hedges, Windle Miller, Peter Hive, Henry Shipler, Peter Andrew, Stophel Hoofman, Thos. Crawford, Benj. Scott, Andrew Byarly, Mary Smith, Henry Mook, Philip Hupp, John Mason.

Page 309.—30th March, 1758. William Claypole's appraisement, by Francis McBride, Andrew Sadowski, Jno. McDonald.

Page 310.—12th May, 1759. Arnold Kester's appraisement, by Andrew Sadowski, Abraham Bird, John Thomas.

Page 311.—17th May, 1759. Alexander McDonald's bond (with John Ramsey, Jno. Poage) as administrator of Joseph McClelhill.

Page 311.—17th May, 1759. Samuel Scott's estate settlement, by Robert Scott and Robert Hooks, executors. Paid Thos. Stevenson, Christopher Zimmerman, Robt. McFarson, David Nelson, Henry Downs, Saml. Wilkins, Wm. Craig, Wm. Snodon, Margaret Fowler, William Jordan, Jno. Vought, Patrick Cain, Doctor Harrison, Hugh Thompson, Jonathan Gibson, Jas. Beard; 1 coffin for Samuel Scott; 1 coffin for George Scott; keeping 3 negroes one year, nine months, by R. Scott. Vendue to, viz: David Crighton, Jno. Paul Fought, David Logan, Jas. Underwood, James Berkley, widow McDonald, Patrick Quin, Joseph Kinkade, John Love, Bernard Man, Jacob Pence, John Wilkins, Ann Scott.

Page 313.—18th May, 1759. William Wilson's bond (with Sampson Archer, Jno. Mathews) as administrator of Joseph Bell.
Page 314.—18th May, 1759. John Smith's bond (with Abraham Smith, Danl. Smith) as administrator Jno. Witchell (Mitchell?).
Page 315.—18th May, 1759. Same (with same) of John Bell.
Page 316.—18th May, 1759. Same (with same) of John Tracey.
Page 317.—18th May, 1759. Thomas Fulton's estate settlement—Debts paid to Charles Goodall, Saml. Hodge, Robt. Gween, Thos. Weems, Hugh Young.
Page 318.—17th May, 1759. Andrew Cowan's bond (with Jno. Bigam, Samuel Black) as administrator of John Mentire.
Page 319.—18th May, 1759. George Wilson's bond (James Huston, David Stewart) as administrator of John Cain.
Page 320.—19th May, 1759. James Bane's bond (with Jno. Smith, Wm. Lusk) as administrator of Christopher Hicks.
Page 321.—30th May, 1759. James McCutchen's appraisement, by James McCleerey, James Lockhart, Wm. Ledgerwood.
Page 322.—15th August, 1759. Catherine Miller's bond (with Jacob Miller, Jno. Miller) as administratrix of Henry Miller.
Page 323.—14th August, 1759. Martha Mitchell's appraisement, by John Mitchell, Jas. Cowan, Wm. Ledgerwood.
Page 324.—28th June, 1759. Rees Thomas' appraisement, by Francis Green, Thos. Bryan, Jno. Miller—One quarto folio Bible, £1, 4, 0; 1 quotation Bible, £0, 2, 6; 1 Young Man's Companion; 1 Psalm Book; 2 small books; a few old volumes of books; a parcel of Welsh books; 1 spoke sheaver.
Page 325.—15th August, 1759. William Buchanan's bond (with Jas. and Jno. Buchanan) as administrator of James Buchanan.
Page 325.—20th January, 1759. Arthur Jonson's will—To sons John and Andrew Jonson, tract testator now lives on, with adjoining survey called Hunter's Gulley; to son Arthur, tract adjoining Ellick Herrin's line; to wife (pregnant), executrix (estate, if she do not marry); to remaining children, viz: Jane, Sarah, Mary Jonson. Teste: Danl. Harrison, Saml. Hemphill, Edward McGarry. Proved, 15th August, 1759, by Harrison and Hemphill. Widow, Margaret qualified, with Daniel Love and Robert Cravens.
Page 327.—15th August, 1759. Margaret Clarke's bond (with Jno. Smith, Jas. Davis) as administratrix of Robert Clarke.
Page 328.—5th July, 1759. Andrew Muldrough's appraisement, by William Galespy, James Scott, James Simpson.
Page 328.—20th September, 1758. Vendue of John Snodgrass' estate, by Agnes Patton—To David Edmund, Wm. Parris, Robt. McRandolph, John Wardlaw, Wm. Adair, Peter Angel. Paid to John Mountgomery, Edmond Tarr, James Henry, Jno. Rosamond, Patrick Hays, James McCown, Andrew Steel.
Page 329.—16th August, 1759. John Poage and Samuel Henderson's bond (with James Bell, Wm. Roberson) as administrators of Elizabeth Robertson.
Page 330.—14th August, 1759. Roger Dyer's appraisement, by Daniel Harrison, Mathew Patton—To gold coin, £24, 13, 10; cash, £42, 0, 0; Christian Graft's bond; Michael Graft's bond; Herman Shout's and Nich-

olas Smith's bond; David Nelson's bond; Peter Horse's note; Pat. **Frasure's** bond, Frederick Keyster's note; William Semples' bond; Johnston Hill's bond; Michael Dicken and Wm. Correy's bond; John Salsberry's bond; Joseph Kyles' note.

Page 330.—16th August, 1759. John Bowyer's bond (with Richard Wood, Israel Christian, Felix Gilbert) as guardian (?) to Martha Borden, orphan of Benj. Borden.

Page 331.—16th August, 1759. Mathew Lyle's bond (with Richd. Woods, Jas. Gilmer) as guardian (?) to Saml. McMurty, orphan of Alexander McMurty.

Page 331.—20th August, 1759. Erwin Patterson's bond (with Thos. Tosh, Wm. Carson) as administrator of James McGee.

Page 332.—29th August, 1759. Vendue of Bryan McDonald's estate— To Bryan McDonald, Edward McDonald, William Graham (a large sermon book), James Bean (Drilincourt on Death), Geo. Robinson (a large Prayer Book) James Litherdale (a conc shell), Catherine McDonald.

Page 333.—22d September, 1759. James Buchanan's appraisement, by James McCown, Jno. Wallace, Wm. Reach—In Capt. John Buchanan's hands of his pay.

Page 333.—21st November, 1759. William Stephenson's appraisement, by John Malkem, Thos. Gordon, Ephraim Love.

Page 334.—21st November, 1759. Saml. Gray's bond (with Patt. Hays, Jno. Allison) as guardian (?) to Joseph Gray, orphan of John Gray.

Page 335.—21st November, 1759. William Preston's bond (with William Thompson, Robert Breckinridge) as sheriff.

Page 335.—Ditto to collect the quit rents.

Page 336.—29th July, 1759. Martha Fruit's will (widow)—To Jean Logan, all concerns except one bed and a horse; to Wm. Care, one bed and a horse. Teste: Jno. Shanklin, Benj. Logan, Jannet McDonnald. Proved, 21st November, 1759, by the witnesses. Jane Logan qualified executrix, with Danl. Love, Charles Campbell.

Page 337.—1st September, 1759. Jacob Clements' will—Wife; youngest children, Ruth, Isabella Clements; three daughters, Ann Burnet, Mary McKnight, Rachel Barnet; daughter, Sarah Clements; five daughters, Margaret, Elizabeth, Rebecca, Ruth, Isabel Clements. Executors, Thos. Gillham, James Campbell. Teste: Andrew Hamilton, Robert Lockridge, Thomas Lloyd. Proved, 21st November, 1759, by Lockridge and Hamilton. Executors qualify, with Andrew Hamilton and Robert Lockridge.

Page 338.—21st November, 1759. Robert Hall's bond (with Jno. Bigham, Saml. Tencher) as administrator of Ro. Ramsey.

Page 339.—21st November, 1759. William Gray's bond (with Patrick Hays, Saml. Paxton) as guardian (?) to Benj. Gray, orphan of John Gray.

Page 340.—21st November, 1759. George Kinkade's appraisement, by James Ward, Andrew Gillespie, Robt. Allen.

Page 341.—7th October, 1759. James Armstrong's nuncupative will— Wife, Sarah (pregnant); daughters, Liddy and Jean. Executors, wife Sarah and Bro. Robt. Armstrong. Teste: Thomas Lloyd, Samuel Archer. Proved, 21st November, 1759, by witnesses, and executors qualified, with Sampson Archer, James Bell.

Page 342.—22d November, 1759. Thomas Gilmore's bond (with William Elliott, Jno. Gay) as administrator of John Gilmore.

Page 343.—5th October, 1754. William Campbell's will—To sons James and John; to daughters Mary Clements, Margaret Gillham, Elizabeth Price, Mary Ann Ashton, Rachel Carlile; son-in-law Thos. Gillham; daughter Margaret Gillham's children, 100 acres, part of testator's home plantation; son, Samuel. Executrix, Sarah. Teste: Jacob Clements, Chas. Gillham. (No certificate of Probate.)

Page 344.—22d November, 1759. Saml. Campbell's bond (with James Carlile, Geo. Wilson) as administrator of Wm. Campbell.

Page 344.—22d November, 1759. Daniel Smith's bond (with Jno. Christian, Jno. Scott) as guardian (?) to Jane Scott, orphan of Samuel Scott.

Page 345.—22d November, 1759. John Conrad's appraisement, by Abram Smith, Mathew Patton, Michael Mallow.

Page 345.— —— October, 1759. Henry Lawrence's appraisement, by same as above.

Page 345.—23d November, 1759. George Handy's estate settlement—Paid Thos. Ellwick, paid Margaret Caldwell, paid John Pennywait; Turner's tools, chair frames, chairs—no purchaser.

Page 346.—6th December, 1758. John Wilson's appraisement, by Wm. Wilson, Saml. Steel, Jno. Fulton.

Page 346.—30th August, 1759. Elizabeth Robertson's appraisement, by Archibald Hamilton, Wm. Baskins, Geo. Anderson.

Page 347.—23d November, 1759. Jno. Smith's bond (with William Preston, Jno. Stevenson) as administrator of Benj. Davis.

Page 348.—15th September, 1759. Henry Miller's appraisement, by Jacob Nicholas, August Price, John Dunkell. Jacob Miller's note.

Page 348.—21st February, 1756. William (his "a" mark) Craig's will, yeoman—Wife, Janet; eldest son, Robert Craig; 3 sons, Robert, James and John. Executors, Robert and James Craig. Teste: Geo. Crawford, James Leard. Proved, 26th November, 1759. James Craig refused to execute. Robert qualifies, with Jas. Craig, Geo. Crawford.

Page 349.—26th November, 1759. William Preston's bond (with Felix Gilbert) for collection of County Proportion.

Page 350.—18th March, 1760. James Armstrong's appraisement, by John Finley, Sampson Archer, James Hogshead, Andrew Foster.

Page 351.—18th March, 1760. Robert Ramsey's appraisement, by Andw. Hamilton, Jas. Carlile, Jas. Campbell.

Page 351.—11th March, 1760. Jacob Clements' appraisement, by Andw. Lockridge, Robt. Gay, Robt. Bratton.

Page 352.—18th March, 1760. Hugh Cunningham's bond (with John Gilmore, Jno. Collier, Jas. Gilmore) as administrator of Jacob Cunningham.

Page 353.—18th March, 1760. William Campbell's appraisement, by Andw. Hamilton, Jas. Carlile, Daniel O'Hara.

Page 353.—14th March, 1760. William Craig's appraisement, by Saml. Henderson, Jas. Beard, Andw. Leeper. John Craig, debtor; James Craig, debtor.

Page 354.—19th March, 1760. Arthur Johnston's appraisement, by Danl. Harrison, Saml. Hemphill, Jno. Cravens.

Page 354.—18th March, 1760. David Cloyd's bond (with Andw. Hays, Peter Hog) as administrator of John Cloyd.

Page 355.—7th March, 1760. Samuel Wilson's will—Two cuzens, Thomas and Saml. Wilson, plantation in Borden's grant. Brother Robert

Wilson, executor. Teste: Wm. Wilson, Ann Wilson, Thos. Wilson. Proved, 19th March, 1760, by witnesses. Executor qualified, with Thomas and William Wilson.

Page 357.—12th February, ——. Martha Fruit's (widow) appraisement, by Robt. Cravens, Edwd. Shanklin, Wm. Logan.

Page 358.—14th May, 1760. James Buchanan's further appraisement, by Jno. Wallace, Steth (Streth, Heth?) Wilson, William Reah.

Page 358.—8th February, 1759. Vendue of John Wingord's (Vinegard) estate—To Henry Colar, Christopher Kishlinger, Christopher Wingord, Ludwick Francisco, Augustine Price, Tetrach Couch, Conrad Bloze, Frederick Ermantrout, Jacob Nicholas, Margt. Wilmouth, Brice Russell, Alvenus Byar, Jacob Parsinger, Charles Man, Nicholas Millberry, Jno. Craig, Danl. Price, Jno. Fuge, Jacob Man, Henry Perkey, Nicholas Null, Jas. Laird, Charles Ty (Fy?), Paslin Hover, Valentine Cough, Valentine Cook, Valentine Pence, Robt. Scott, Jacob Man, Stephen Conrad, Christian Tetrach, Valentine Butcher, Peter Herman, Wm. Beard, John Couch.

Page 360.—20th May, 1760. Above estate in account with Alvenus Byar (Boyer), administrator.

Page 361.—6th December, 1759. Jno. Gay's will—To son Henry Gay (infant), part of 347 acres promised to John by his (testator's) father, Henry Gay; to wife, Mary Gay; to father, Henry Gay, all wearing apparel; to be educated in reading and writing (this must refer to son Henry). Executor, father Henry. Teste: Arthur Hamilton, Fras. McDonald, Nathanl. Davis. Proved, 20th May, 1760, by the witnesses. Executor qualified (his "H" mark), with Francis McDonald, James Lockhart.

Page 363.—20th May, 1760. Thomas Cadden's estate in account with James Hunter.

Page 363.—20th May, 1760. Jean Cunningham's bond (with John Mathews, Jno. Bowen) as administratrix of Isaac Cunningham.

Page 364.—18th February, 1759. Andrew Moldrow's appraisement, by James Simpson, William Galespy, James Scott.

Page 365.—20th May, 1760. Mary Thompson's bond (with John Hutcheson, Jno. Gray) as administratrix of Thos. Thompson.

Page 366.—22d March, 1760. Robert Gibson's will, yeoman—Wife, Isabella Gibson, executrix; son, Robert Gibson, executor; son, George Gibson, 190 acres between here and Spring Hill; son, James Gibson; son, John Gibson (if he be alive or comes to demand it). Teste: A. Thompson, Wm. Johnston, Zechariah Smith. Proved, 20th May, 1760, by the witnesses. Executors qualified (Isabella's mark "E"), with John Gray, Zechariah Smith, Wm. Palmer.

Page 368.—30th October, 1759. Thomas Millsap's will—To wife, Mary; to sons, Robert and Thomas; to daughters, Elinor and Mary; to daughter, Jean Macgee; to daughter, Elizabeth Dillen; to sons, Joseph and William, Joseph to have "Robbin's Cabin" joining William Carrol. Teste: Andrew Bird, John Phillips. Proved, 20th May, 1760, by the witnesses. Executors qualified, with Mounce Bird, Wm. Magee.

Page 371.—20th May, 1760. William Shannon's bond (with John Brown, Hugh Young) as administrator of James Young.

Page 372.—15th May, 1759. James Lee's appraisement, by Alexander Walker, Jacob Anderson, Isaac Anderson.

Page 374.—20th May, 1760. John Buchanan's bond (with **Wm. Preston**) as administrator of Abraham Duncleberry.

Page 375.—26th January, 1760. George Rankin's will—Wife, **Martha**; sons, Thomas, William, John, James, Robert; daughters, **Jean** and **Mary**. All children infants? James and Robert are younger sons. Executors, Saml. Henderson, Thos. Patterson. Teste: James Craig, Robt. Craig, Theobald Maighan. Proved, 20th May, 1760, by the witnesses. Executors qualified, with James Craig, Wm. Preston.

Page 378.—16th April, 1760. William Long's will, of Staunton—Wife, Margaret; son, William, lands and lots in and about Staunton and Jackson's River; brothers, Thomas Lewis and Charles Lewis, to be executors. Teste: William Lewis, William Stewart. Proved, 20th May, 1760. Executors qualify, with Andrew and William Lewis.

Page 380.—11th December, 1759. Robert Clark's appraisement, by Peter Luney, Thos. Ramsey, John Potts. To bills against the country. Cash. Two Bibles and other old books.

Page 380.—18th October, 1759. John Smith's appraisement, by Loftus Pullen, Jno. Carlile, Richard Bodkin—Shoemaker's tools; cash received of Capt. Preston.

Page 381.—21st May, 1760. Samuel Scott's estate settlement, by Robert Scott and Robert Hooks—To keeping 2 negroe children, Venus and Peter, from May, 1759, to May, 1760. By judgment vs. Ann Scott, the widow.

Page 381.—21st May, 1760. Martha Stevenson and John Stevenson's bond as administrators of James Stevenson, with John Gay, James Gay, Wm. Elliott.

Page 383.—21st May, 1760. Catherine Dickinson's bond (with Wm. McFeeters, Thos. Weems, Archd. Armstrong, Ralph Laverty) as administratrix of Adam Stevenson.

Page 384.—9th December, 1759. John Colley's will—Daughters, Susan, Catharn, Mary; son, Christian, to mall 5,000 rails; wife, land he bought of Mr. Courts (Curts?); son, Peter; wife and her children, and Mary, Barbery, Margt., Elizabeth, Clorah, Peter. Executors, Ludwick Franciscus, Christopher Ermantrout. Teste: Thos. Poynter, Valentine Mitsker, Wm. Beard. Proved, 20th May, 1760, by the witnesses. Christopher Armentrout (the other refusing) qualified, with Augustine Price, Frederick Armentrout, Jno. Couts.

Page 387.—21st May, 1760. Wm. Thompson's bond (with Wm. Ledgerwood, Jas. Mitchell) as administrator of Wm. Read.

Page 388.—21st May, 1760. James Dunlap's appraisement, by Jno. Brown, Wm. McFeeters, Saml. Wilson—One negro man.

Page 388.—21st May, 1760. Daniel Richardson's estate settlement, by Thomas Parsons, administrator—Paid Philip Halbert; Jno. Vanvill (for a negro), sheriff for 2 levies for 1753; Conrad Huffman, Adam West, Benj. Scott, Peter Reed, Joel Hornback, Henry Shippley, Geo. Bush, Jonathan Coburn, the widow, Leonard Reed, Joseph Skidmore, Austin Scoolcraft, Mr. Churchill, fee in Leonard Reed's suit; Dennis Sullivan's bond (insolvent); Mathias Yeoman (Yeokum?).

Page 389.—26th ———, 1760. Lodwick Foalke's appraisement, by Danl. Smith, Gabrial Pickins, Michael Mallow—Cash.

Page 390.—23d May, 1758. Thomas Gardner's will—To my beloved wife, Ann Gardner, and to my beloved wife, Mary Gardner, all estate

(Mary is the daughter). Brother's son, Thos. Gardner, Jr., and wife, Ann, executors. Teste: Philip Eastin, Cathrine Garman. Proved, 19th August, 1760, by the witnesses. Executors qualify, with Jas. Bell, Alex. Crawford.

Page 391.—28th May, 1760. Samuel Wilson's will, of Staunton—Wife, Martha, to educate the children; oldest daughter, Elizabeth Wilson; daughter, Martha. Executors, John and Thos. Wilson, and wife Martha, or any two. Teste: James Hughes, Robt. Reed, Wm. Preston. Proved, 19th August, 1760, by the witnesses. Thomas and Martha qualify, with Jno. and Robt. Wilson. Teste: H. Churchill.

Page 393.—30th May, 1760. John Spear's will—Wife, Jean; sons, Hugh. Executors, wife Jean and Alex. McFeeters. Teste: Jno. Brown, James Gilmer, James Phillips. Proved, 19th August, 1760, by Gilmer and Phillips. Both executors qualified. Jane Spear, Alex. McFeeters, Jas. Gilmer.

Page 396.—20th September, 1759. Vendue of James Buchanan's estate, purchasers, viz: John, Archibald, William, Buchanan. In hands of Capt. John Buchanan, his pay. Paid Thomas Dredan.

Page 396.—28th May, 1760. Thomas Thompson's appraisement, by Wm. Johnston, John Graham, John Cochran.

Page 397.—19th August, 1760. Susanna Powers' bond (with Christopher Ermantrout, Jno. Couts) as administratrix of Christian Gally.

Page 398.—20th August, 1760. Frederick Mouse's bond (with Lewis Stephens, Wm. Preston) as administrator of George Mouse.

Page 400.—19th June, 1760. John Colly's appraisement, by Archd. Huston, Wm. Beard, Jacob Parsinger.

Page 402.—20th August, 1760. Mary McDonald's bond (with Geo. Robinson, Francis Livers, Malcom Campbell) as administratrix or Edward McDonald. Teste: H. Churchill.

Page 403.—20th August, 1760. Widow Swoob's appraisement, by Jos. Carpenter, Peter Wright, Jno. Mann.

Page 404.—20th August, 1760. Jacob Parsinger's bond (with Christopher Wingord, Lawrence Huntsman) as administrator of Philip Parsinger.

Page 405.—20th August, 1760. Christopher Wingord's bond (with Jacob Parsinger, Lawrence Huntsman) as administrator of Mark Tallard.

Page 406.—20th August, 1760. Adam Dickinson's bond (with Andrew Sitlington, James Gilespy, John Young).

Page 407.—20th August, 1760. Thomas Stuart's bond (with Thomas Fulton, Jno. Sprowl) as administrator of Wm. Hart.

Page 409.—20th August, 1760. Margaret Barrier's bond (with Christopher Wingord, Lawrence Huntsman) as administratrix of Casper Barrier.

Page 410.—21st August, 1760. Ann (Ane) Roger's bond (with Wm. McCanless, Walter Smiley) as administratrix of James Rogers.

Page 412.—21st August, 1760. Robert Gibson's appraisement, by Jno. Finley, Geo. Caldwell, Wm. Caldwell.

Page 413.—8th July, 1760. Robert Ramsey's additional appraisement and sale bill, by Andw. Hamilton, James Calile, James Campbell—To Robt. Hall, James Given, James Hall, James Shaw, Daniel Harrah (O'Hara); to liquor at the vendue; balance due the orphans.

Page 414.—26th March, 1760. Joseph Bell's (the malloto) appraisement, by Jno. Sale?, Robt. Wilson, Saml. Steel.

Page 415.—27th April, 1754. Charles Dalhouse's will (the paper is first a power of attorney to Archd. and Thos. Stewart and Edward Hall to make all demands for him and answer all against him in any of His Majesty's Dominions, and second, a will)—Three sons, George, James and John, to be educated. Executors, attorneys above. Teste: Hugh McClure, Benj. Stewart. Proved, 18th November, 1760, by the witnesses. Archd. Stewart refuses to execute; the others qualify, with Alex. Kelly, Benj. Stewart.

Page 418.—18th November, 1760. Jacob Cunningham's appraisement, by Jno. McCown, Jno. Willey, Andrew Hays—The following notes against Daniel and Samuel Lyle, Edward Fearis, Wm. Davis, Jno. Delap, James Brains, Francis McCown, Robert Moore, Francis Randall, Neaiell McClister, Robert McKeney, David Tallford, James and John Gilmer, Jno. Dunlap, French McKown, Wm. Olley, Richd. Brush, Samuel Horad, Alex. Dell, Edward Bovill, 1 neager fellow.

Page 419.—18th November, 1760. Mark Tallard's inventory, by Wm. Henderson, Wm. Palmer, Patrick McCollom.

Page 420.—19th November, 1760. John Gay's appraisement, by Robert Bratton, Jacob Martin, Joseph Wacob—Fures (furs?).

Page 421.—18th November, 1760. Margt. Luney's bond (with James Litherdale, Jno. Miller) as administratrix of Peter Luney (Looney).

Page 422.—19th November, 1760. David Luney's bond (with Wm. Preston, Jno. Poage) as administrator of Daniel Luney.

Page 424.—19th November, 1760. David Luney's bond (with James Litherdale, Wm. Preston) as administrator of Thos. Luney.

Page 425.—19th November, 1760. Jacob Anderson's bond (with Saml. Henderson, Robt. Talford) as administrator of Stophel White.

Page 426.—19th November, 1760. Margaret Ramsey's bond (with Abram Smith, Jno. Davis) as administratrix of James Ramsey.

Page 428.—7th June, 1760. Thomas Milsap's appraisement, by Michl. Waren, Abraham Bird.

Page 429.—19th November, 1760. Thomas Gardner's appraisement (Thos. and Ann Gardner, executors) by Sampson Archer, Andrew Foster, John Finley.

Page 430.—25th July, 1760. James Young's appraisement, by John Trimble, James Pol (Paul?), Morris O'Freal.

Page 431.—19th November, 1760. George Rankin's appraisement, by Wm. Lamb, Geo. Crawford, Robt. Craig.

Page 432.—19th November, 1760. William Long's appraisement, by David Stewart, Robt. Breckinridge, Felix Gilbert.

Page 434.—20th November, 1760. Barbara Harmon's bond (with Francis Tyler, Christopher Bingman, Henry Price) as administratrix of John Harman.

Page 435.—21st November, 1760. William Hart's appraisement, by James Alexander, Jno. Black, Saml. Black.

Page 435.—16th May, 1760. Thomas Cadden's appraisement, by Robt. Campbell, Jno. Risk, Jno. Cark (Clark?).

Page 436.—24th November, 1760. Casper Barger's appraisement, by George Trout, Wm. Kerr, George Patterson.

Page 437.—12th January, 1760. Deed of apprenticeship—William Hays, son of Patrick Hays, binds himself to William Wilson, taylor, to be taught the said trade, service and occupation of a taylor for 18 years. Signed,

Patrick Hays, William Wilson. Teste: James Stevenson, James Hughes, Wm. Lusk.

Page 438.—20th May, 1760. John Poage's bond (with David Stewart, James Hughes) as Assistant Surveyor.

ABSTRACTS OF WILLS OF AUGUSTA COUNTY, VIRGINIA.

AUGUSTA COUNTY COURT.

WILL BOOK NO. 3.

Page 1.—28th September, 1760. James Rogers' appraisement, by James Eakin, William Moore, David Moore.
(Note.—These dates should be 1761?)
Page 1.—17th February, 1760. John Speer's appraisement.
Page 4.—17th February, 1760. Eve Aphinger's bond (with Jno. Smith, Jacob Parsinger) as administratrix of Peter Apinger.
Page 5.—17th February, 1761. Robert Breckinridge's bond (with Jno. Poage) as administrator of Pharaoh Ryley.
Page 6.—18th February, 1761. James Ramsey's appraisement, by Jno. Malkem, William Cunningham, Jno. Cunningham—One Joynter; cash from Daniel McKnight.
Page 7.—14th February, 1761. Adam Dickinson's additional appraisement, by Andw. Sitlington, John Young.
Page 7.—18th February, 1761. Robert Graham's bond (with James Carlile, Thos. Thompson) as administrator of Florence Graham.
Page 8.—18th February, 1761. William Guy's bond (with Ralph Laverty, Joseph Wachob (Waughope) as administrator of John Meaks.
Page 9.—17th February, 1761. Phillip Persinger's appraisement, by Wm. Preston, Ro. Reed, James Hughes—Current money.
Page 10.—19th February, 1761. Samuel Willson's appraisement, by same as above—Many items and (2d October, 1760, 60 gallons whiskey).
Page 10.—18th February, 1761. William Preston, Assistant Surveyor, enters 3 tracts, 400 acres each, between lands of David Cloyd, James Johnston, Wm. Ralston; a survey for John Mills, David Miller, Wm. Armstrong and said Preston's land whereon Rentfro formerly dwelt. Also 400 acres on a small branch of Craig's (Creek?), above Jacob Patton's old place, known by the name of the Mill Place.
(Note at top of page 109.—Zachariah Johnston's wife was Ann Robinson, sister of Alex. and James Robinson; Jane Robinson, Ann's sister, married John Blair. Both James and Alex. went to Kentucky, Jessamine County? from Geo. Armentrout.)
Page 11.—18th February, 1761. Nicholas Salles' (Solley) bond (with George Skilleron) as administrator of Jno. Wall.
Page 12.— —— October, 1760. John Guy's estate settlement (the name is Gay in the order), by Henry Gay, administrator—Sold to Francis Donnally, Martha Guy, Henry Guy, Arthur Greer, widow Sayers, Wm. Bunt-

ing, Agnes Guy, Jean Moffet, Mary Guy, James Borling, Thos. Brown, Timothy Sullivan. Sundries to Elizabeth Gay, Ann Gay. Paid to John Vance, Nathaniel Lyon, John Neall, John Jamison, James McCoy, Arthur Hamilton, Maj. Brown, Commadore Brown.

Page 14.—24th November, 1760. Stophel White's appraisement, by David Telford, James McCampbell, Andrew McCampbell.

Page 15.—13th December, 1760. John Herman (Harmon's) appraisement, by John Coutz, Adam Hettrick, Valentine Pence.

Page 16.—4th April, 1761. Patrick Young's will—Wife, Esibala (Isabella) and Joseph Walker, executors; son, James; 3 daughters, Sarah, Jannet and Allas. Teste: Wm. Hall, Jas. Campbell, Saml. McMurty. Proved, 19th May, 1761, by the witnesses. Executors qualify, with John Bowyer, Jno. Collier, James McKee. Isabella's mark ( ).

Page 18.—5th February, 1761. Nathaniel McClure's will—Wife, Mary; eldest son, Holbert, £10 to cure his sore leg, above his share; sons, James and Nathan? (their young brother and sisters). Rest of children, viz: Halbert, Mary, Alexander, Hanah, Thomas, Margaret, Dorothy, Moses Young sons to be put to trades. Executors, Alexander and Moses McClure and Archd. Alexander. Teste: David Dryden, Wm. Carleton, Hannah Allison. Proved, 19th May, 1761, by Dryden and Carleton. Executors refuse. Administration granted widow Mary, who qualifies, with John Allison, Saml. McClure, Baptist McNabb. Mary's mark ( ), Allison's mark ( ), McNabb's mark ( ).

Page 20.—11th September, 1760. Robert Huston's will, farmer—Wife, Mary; son, John (infant), 95 acres on Collier's Creek; son, James (infant), 200 acres adjoining place testator lives on; son, Samuel (infant), plantation testator lives on, 307 acres; daughter, Elizabeth, 5 shillings, already provided for; daughters, Ann, Esther, Margaret, Mary. Wife, Mary; son, John; brother, Samuel Huston, executors. Teste: Daniel Lyle, Moses Trimble, Saml. McCoskey. Proved, 19th May, 1761, by Lyle and Trimble and executors qualified (Mary's mark), with Daniel Lyle, John Huston, Jno. Lowry (Lowny).

Page 23.—19th May, 1761. Archibald Buchanan's (Bohannon) bond (with Jno. and Wm. Buchanan) for Archibald and Agnes Buchanan (late Agnes McFerrin) administration of estate of James McFerrin.

Page 24.—13th March, 1760. John Bowen's will—Wife, Lillis (Lillie), sole executor and guardian; daughter, Mary, 1 malato slave; son, Charles. Teste: Jno. Smith, Margaret Smith, Peter Luney, Walter Crockett, Jonathan Smith, Jno. Buchanan. Proved, May 19th, 1761, by Jno. and Jonathan Smith and Jno. Buchanan. Lillie qualifies (her mark), with Jonathan Whitley, Wm. Buchanan.

Page 26.—18th May, 1761. John Culliland's appointment, by Alex. Buchanan, Jno. Wallace, Wm. Buchanan—Cash in Capt. Christian's custody; cash in Capt. Hog's hands.

Page 26.—19th May, 1761. Mary Brown's bond (with Jno. Collier, James Campbell) as administratrix of William Brown.

Page 28.—28th June, 1758. Peter Moser's estate settlement, by Michael Mallow, allowed 19th May, 1761—To Cathron Moser, Jno. Hopkins, Danl. Love, James McDole, Jno. Wright, Fardrick Kestor, Jacob Harper, Andrew Arewen, Powl Shaver, Eaform Love, Nickles Hofman, Edward McGary. (2nd vendue held 8th November, 1758?) To Alex. Miller, James McGill,

Jno. McCoy. (3d vendue held 3d October, 1760.) Credit by Patterkole money received on Peter Moser's account. From Jno. Madison, from George Caplinger, from Henry Carr, from Captain Cartley (Keartley), Capt. Abraham Smith (patterole money), from Captain Smith, for provender; from Captain Smith, on account of Wm. Wood; from Jno. Hogleer; from Capt. Ephraim Love, for provender and paterrole (patrol) money; from Capt. Smith, patterole money. Paid Jacob Rolman, paid Daniel Smith for clorking, paid Fredk. Opp for schooling, paid Fredk. Easter for salt and store goods, paid Johnson Hill for weaving, paid John Hughes, paid Stephen Conrad, the blacksmith.

Page 30.—28th June, 1758. George Mouse's estate settlement, by Michael Mallow. Allowed 19th May, 1761. Sold to Cateren Moser, Jacob Cutman, Chas. Deavier, Seasor (Caesar) Brown, Henry Banener. Second vendue, 8th November, 1758, to Felty Mack, Jno. Arewen, Thos. Peterson, Robt. Mines, Andrew Arewen. Third vendue, 1st October, 1760, to Geo. Caplinger, Michael Props. Received from Geo. Madison for Providen (provender). Received from Capt. Smith, patterole money. Received from Capt. Smith for provender. Received from Abraham Smith, patterole money. Received from Frank Cartley. Received from Henry Fletcher. Paid Gabriel Gile for horse hunting. Paid John McCoy. Paid Andrew Smith for spinning. Three days driving cows from Trout Rock to Cartley's Fort.

Page 32.—21st January, 1761. Alexander McFeeters' will—Executors, wife and John Buchanan; son, Alexander; daughters, Janet, Ann, Martha, Rebecka; grandson, Alex. McFeeters; daughter, Elizabeth Speers. Teste: Wm. McFeeters, Elijah McClenachan, Alex. McFeeters. Proved, 19th May, 1761, by Wm. McFeeters and Elijah McClenachan. Executors qualify, with Wm. Ledgerwood, Wm. Ray (Reah). (Martha's mark .)

Page 34.—15th April, 1761. John Meek's appraisement, by John Gay, Alex. Hamilton, John Stevenson.

Page 35.—13th November, 1759. John Cloyd's appraisement, by Edward, Joseph and Bryan McDonald.

Page 37.—19th May, 1761. John Smith's estate to Thos. Hicklin, administrator—Paid Bowd Estill for 66 lbs. flour to make cakes at the burial. Paid James Burnsides; various articles given to the brother of deceased.

Page 37.—20th May, 1761. Lilley Bowen's bond (with John and Wm. Mathews) as administratrix of Moses Bowen.

Page 39.—20th May, 1761. Benj. Harrison's bond (with Daniel Smith) as administrator of Gideon Harrison.

Page 40.—22d May, 1761. Naomi Hill's bond (with Felix Gilbert and Jno. Fowler) as administratrix of Johnston Hill.

Page 41.—8th July, 1761. John Cally's appraisement by Archd. Huston, Wm. Beard, Jacob Parsinger.

Page 42.—11th December, 1760. Christian Gally's appraisement, by same as above.

Page 43.—24th September, 1760. Edward McDonald's appraisement, by David Cloid, James Cloid, Samuel McRoberts—One wagon, currier's tools, 8 vols. of Spectator, The Body of the Virginia Laws, 2 prayer books, 1 Bible, 2 primers, 1 dictionary, The Complete Tradesman, other small books, 2 moon knives, 19 hides tanned leather, 16 sides soal leather, 11 sides bridle leather, 1 calf skin.

Page 45.—18th August, 1761. Isaac Cunningham's appraisement, by Jno. Maxwell, Joseph Lapsely, Jno. Moore, Jno. Paxton.

Page 46.—18th August, 1761. John Bowen's appraisement, by Jno. Dailey, Jno. McClure, (Neaiell) Neal McCluster.

Page 47.—11th June, 1761. Moses Bowen's appraisement, by same as above.

Page 47.—23d September, 1756. James McClure's will, taylor, of South Carolina—Son, James, Bible and big pot; son, Samuel, next biggest pot; wife, Agness, to have use of both pots; sons, John and Andrew; daughters, Eleanor, Jean, Esther. Executors, Wm. Givens, Wm. McClure. Teste: Wm. Hanna, Wm. Beard, Wm. McClure. Proved, 18th August, 1761, by Wm. Hanna, other witnesses are dead. James, eldest son and heir, appears and waives objection to proving the will. Executor Wm. McClure is dead. William Givens lives in South Carolina. Administration granted to son, James McClure, who qualifies, with Andrew and Hugh McClure.

Page 50.—9th October, 1759. Johan Paul Faught's (John Bellfaught) will—Wife, sole executrix; wife, Mary Katrine; 3 children, Katrine Cleman, Andrew and Casper Faught. Teste: Archd. Huston, Peter Funk, Catrine Funk. Proved, 18th August, 1761, by Huston and Peter Funk. Mary Catrine qualifies, with Christian Cleman, Geo. Trout (signed, Cath. Fought).

Page 52.—12th October, 1760. John Mason's will, farmer—To son, John, 270 acres on Mason's Creek; to son, James, 150 acres on Back Creek; to son, William, 250 acres on Grassy Hill Branch; to youngest son, Joseph, 135 acres where testator lives; to mother, Leah; to daughter, Jannet; to daughter, Mary; to daughter, Margaret. Executors, William Boyd, of North Fork of Otter River in Bedford County, and brother-in-law James Keachey. Teste: Margt. Boyd, Wm. Ritchie. Proved, 18th August, 1761, by the witnesses. James McKatchey qualifies (Boyd lives in Bedford), with Geo. Robinson, John Miller, James Bane.

Page 54.—18th August, 1761. Daniel Looney's (Luney) appraisement, by George Adams, Thos. Ramsey, John Miller—Two nurseries of apple trees. Due by John McFall.

Page 55.—18th August, 1761. Peter Luney's appraisement, by Geo. Adams, Thos. Ramsey, Robt. Montgomery—Cash, etc. Due by Jno. Miller, Thos. Ramsey, Joseph McMortry, Wm. Boyd, Wm. Bird, James Ledderdale, David Luney.

Page 56.—18th August, 1761. Peter Absheir's (Appinger) appraisement, by Robt. Mountgomery, Robt. Rowland, David Luney.

Page 57.—19th July, 1761. Francis Donnally's will—Wife, Sarah (and the child she now bears); six sons, Samuel, Henry, Francis, William, John, James; daughter, Mary. Executors, wife, Wm. Ledgerwood, James Callison. Teste: John Berryhill, David Scott, Alex. McFeeters, Archibald Armstrong. Proved, 18th August, 1761, by McFeeters and Armstrong. Executors qualify, with Thomas Meek and Hugh Martin. Sarah's mark ( ). Callison's mark ( ). Meek's mark ( ). Ledgerwood's mark ( ).

Page 60.—4th May, 1761. Robert Harrison's will—Father, Daniel, best hat; brother, Jesse, £10 for Jesse's daughter Ann when she arrives to 18; brother, Daniel; brother-in-law, Daniel Smith, watch and £20 for schooling Smith's son, Robert Smith; brother, Benjamin; sisters, Mary and Abigail. Executors, Daniel Smith and Jesse Harrison. Teste: Silas Hart, Hugh

Hamilton, Wm. Minter, Wm. Gragg. Proved, 18th August, 1761, by Hamilton and Minter. Executors qualified, with Wm. Preston and Michael Warren.

Page 62.—15th August, 1761. James McFerrin's appraisement, by Andw. Hays, Charles Hays, John McCoven—Thomas Dolly's bond, John Eccles' bond.

Page 63.—18th August, 1761. John McFerrin's bond (with Thos. McFerrin, Wm. Preston) as administrator of Jno. McFerrin, Jr.

Page 64.—18th August, 1761. Mark Miller's estate to Peter Vaneman, administrator—Due to Elizabeth Vaneman, Henry Barringer, Michl. Arehart, Mathias Dice, Henry Puckett, George Mouse, Borket Rider, Geo. Harris, George Caplinger, Looney Higher, Jacob Jobe, Philip Huffman.

Page 64.—9th June, 1761. Patrick Young's appraisement, by Richd. Woods, Wm. Hall, John Paxton, John Wiley.

Page 66.—18th August, 1761. George Moser's sale bill recorded—To Nicholas Hufman, Philip Harper. Cash by Smith and Love for Peter Roling. Paid Ephraim Love, Arthur Johnson, Thos. Wilmouth, to nursing deceased 5 weeks when he was under the doctor, and taking care of his creatures.

Page 67.—25th May, 1761. Valentine Pence's will—Wife, Cathrine; brother's son, Jacob Pence; first born son, Adam Pence. To Jacob Nicholas, deed to be made for land sold, viz: One-half of a tract of 168 acres devised to him by Stophel Francisco. Lawfully begotten children, viz: Adam, Jacob, Henry, John, Catherine, Sarah, Barbara and Mary, and one in the womb. Executors, Jacob Nicholas, Peter Miller, they to sell tract on Nelson's Run joining David Logan's land. Teste: Jno. Craig, Jacob Nicholas. Proved, 18th August, 1761, by the witnesses. Nicholas refuses to execute. Miller qualifies, with Christopher Harmentrout, Jacob Parsinger, Fredk. Harmentrout.

Page 69.—18th August, 1761. Nathaniel McClure's appraisement, recorded.

Page 72.—18th August, 1761. Jacob Siver's appraisement, recorded.

Page 73.—19th August, 1761. John Miller, David Miller, George Adams' bond for Mary Miller's administration of John Ingles' estate.

Page 74.—19th August, 1761. Elizabeth Black's bond (with James Black, Saml. Craig) as administratrix of Anthony Black.

Page 75.—19th August, 1761. Daniel Smith's settlement of estate of Jacob Sivers approved—Paid Woolrick Conrod, Gabriel Kyle; paid 1 clerk's note for swearing into your commission; paid Jno. Wright for crying the vendue; paid Henry Pircy for liquor; paid David Rule; paid Christian Lower (Sower?); paid Paul Shaver; paid Horrical Hufman; paid Henry Baninger; paid Sarah Harrison for liquor for vendue; paid Margaret Johnson for appraising the estate. Sale bill, viz: To John McCoy, Valentine Butcher, Henry Smith, Wm. Snodon, Saml. Briggs, Robt. Gragg, Jno. Dunkle, Ludwick Waggoner, Jno. Skidmore, Jonas Friend, Nicholas Havener. Received of Benj. Hagler, Robt. Minnis, Henry Penigar.

Page 75.—19th August, 1761. Daniel Smith's settlement of estate of Henry Lawrence approved and recorded—Paid Gabriel Pickins, Hugh Hamilton, Windle Siver, Peter Finiman (Vaneman?) Sale bill, viz: To David Nelson, Thos. Feemster, Martin Shoob, Jacob Peters, Jacob Goodman.

Page 78.—15th August, 1761. Johnston Hill's estate appraised by Abraham Smith, Daniel Harrison, Adam Stevenson—James Lawrence's note; Wm. Ingles' ditto; cash in Daniel Ponder's hands; cash in hands of Jonathan Douglass.

Page 79.—19th August, 1761. Mary Jackson's (late Mary Claypole) settlement of estate of William Claypole recorded—To Jno. Wright, Francis McBride, Jno. Dunbar, Jno. and Jos. Claypole, Mr. Johns, Evan Thomas. Sale bill, viz: To Robert Williams, Jersmons Peir, Arthur Trader, Moses Samples, John Douglass, Jno. Arshers, James Cohoon, Dennis Henry, Wm. Cimsey, Andw. Sedusky, Rees Thomas, Henry Harvey.

Page 81.—20th August, 1761. John Wall's appraisement, by James Hamilton, Jno. Hamilton, Geo. Martin. Recorded.

Page 81.—4th July, 1745. John Malckom's will, (mark)—To son, George; to son, John; to daughter, Eleanor McNelie; to daughter, Margaret Wright; to grandson, Wm. Wright; to wife, Margaret. Teste: Andrew Scott, Thos. Scott, Silas Hart. Proved, 20th August, 1761, by Silas Hart and recorded. Wife Margaret refuses to execute, and administration granted Jno. Malkem, who qualifies with Daniel Smith.

Page 83.—17th September, 1761. Valentine Pence's estate appraised, by Archd. Huston, Jacob Nicholas, Geo. Carpenter.

Page 87.—5th September, 1759. Archibald Stewart's will—Wife, Janet; son, Thomas, his Great Bible; daughter, Eleanor, 5 shillings; son, Alexander, tract adjoining Andw. McClure's land; grandson, Archibald Stewart, £10 when aged 10 years; son, Benj. Stewart. Executors, Thos. Stewart, Edward Hall. Teste: Jno. and Andw. Campbell, Jno. Finley. Proved, 17th November, 1761, by Jno. and Andrew Campbell. Executors qualified, with Jno. Campbell, Andrew Campbell.

Page 89.—17th November, 1761. Alexander McFeeters' appraisement, by Thos. Teat, Jno. Bigham, Wm. Currey recorded.

Page 90.—10th August, 1761. Robert Patrick's will—Sons, Charles and John Patrick; son John's son, Robert; daughter, Martha Black, and her 2 sons, Robt. and John; daughter, Isabell McCulloch, and her daughter, Rachel; wife, Rachel. Executors, sons Charles and John. Guardian, wife Rachel. Teste: James Wharey, John McCulloch. Proved, 17th November, 1761, by the witnesses. Charles Patrick refuses to execute. Jno. Patrick qualifies, with Jno. McFeeters, Wm. McFeeters.

Page 92.—17th November, 1761. Robert Harrison's appraisement by Hugh Hamilton, John Hopkins, Robt. Cravens. Recorded.

Page 93.—17th November, 1761. Gideon Harrison's appraisement by Daniel Love, Saml. Hemphill, Wm. Gragg. Recorded.

Page 94.—9th October, 1761. Francis McCown's will, farmer—wife, Margaret; sons, George and Francis; son, Malcom, the plantation formerly belonging to Mathew Young; son, James, the plantation in the Forks; daughters, Margaret, Nancy, Katrine; son, James, the plantation Saml. Norwood formerly lived on, and to pay Malcom £5 when come to age of "menuarty"; daughter, Isbell. Seven children. Executors, wife Margaret and son George. Teste: John Cunningham, Wm. McKemey, John McNabb. Proved, 18th November, 1761, by the witnesses. Margaret refuses to execute. George qualifies, with John McCown, Robt. Christian, George Moffett.

Page 96.— —— September, 1761. Robert Huston's appraisement made by John Macky, Daniel Lyle, Mathew McClure.

Page 98.—18th November, 1761. John Buchanan's bond (with Wm. Preston, Israel Christian) as sheriff.

Page 100.—10th September, 1761. John Faught's (Bellfaught) estate appraised by Archd. Huston, Gasper Kinder, Peter Funk.

Page 101.—18th November, 1761. John Bowen's additional appraisement by John Dayley, John McClure, Neal McNeal. Recorded.

Page 101.—18th November, 1761. John McFerrin, Jr.'s appraisement, Robt. Mountgomery, Saml. McRoberts, John Mountgomery.

Page 102.—14th November, 1761. Thomas Thompson's estate settlement by Mary Thompson, administratrix—Paid Margaret Thompson, Archd. Bryce, Robert Moody, Ephraim Wilson, Saml. McCune, John Cloyd.

Page 102.—10th November, 1761. Wm. Reed's estate, appraised by James Cowin, Thos. Brown, Andrew Alexander.

Page 103.—18th November, 1761. John McIntire's appraisement, by John Buchanan, John Colter, James Moody. Recorded—In hands of Andrew Cowan.

Page 103.—30th October, 1761. Patrick Inglish's will—Debts to Major John Brown and Samuel Moore to be paid first for reasons best known to testator; wife, Else, and his poor babes. Executors, John Brown and Saml. Moore. Teste: Geo. Wilson, Henry Maurray. Proved, 20th November, 1761, by Geo. Wilson, and recorded. Saml. Young qualified with Saml. Moore, William Wallace.

Page 105.—21st November, 1761. John Buchanan's bond (with Wm. Preston) for collection of County Levy.

Page 106.—17th February, 1762. Adam Dean's bond (with John Dean, Robt. Allen) as administrator of James Bourland.

Page 107.—13th October, 1761. Henry Perkey's (German) will, farmer—Wife, Margaret; eldest son, Jacob, tract purchased of Mary Pond, 360 acres on the tract purchased of John Wilson if other is lost; daughters, Mary, Margaret, Elizabeth; daughter, Elizabeth, 135 acres on Lick Run joining Nicholas Null; daughter, Ann, a tract on Shanando joining Elizabeth; sons, John and Henry. Executor, wife Margaret. Dated at end 2d November, 1761. Teste: Robt. Hook, James Bruester, Patrick Wilson. Proved, 17th February, 1761 (should be 1762), by the witnesses. Margaret qualified, with James Waite, James McClure. Margaret's mark ( ).

Page 109.—29th June, 1761. William Brown's estate, appraised by John Summers, Wm. Hall, Jas. Davis.

Page 110.—17th February, 1762. Margaret Gay and Andw. Lockridge's bond (with Wm. and Robt. Lockridge), as administrators of Robert Gay.

Page 111.—17th February, 1762. David Stewart, Walter Cowdon and Saml. Cowdon's bond (with Chas. Lewis, Wm. Crow, Robt. Reed), as administrators of James Leister.

Page 113.—17th February, 1762. Christopher Hicks' appraisement by Stephen Rentfro, David Luney, John Luney, recorded—His pay for ranging. Cash he left when he was "tuck prisoner."

Page 113.—17th February, 1762. Robert Patrick's appraisement, by John Finley, John Hamilton, John Thompson, recorded.

Page 114.—17th February, 1762. Sebastian Hover's bond (with Francis Kirtley), as administrator of Michael Ryan.

Page 116.—9th December, 1761. Francis McCown's estate appraised, by Jacob Anderson, Archd. Buchanan, Hugh Cunningham.

Page 117.—21st February, 1762. James Lockhart's accounts of estate of Dr. John Flood, recorded—Paid Elizth. Preston.

Page 118.—19th February, 1762. John Bowyer's bond (with James McDowell, Saml. McDowell, James McGavock) to indemnify Israel Christian as John's surety on bond as guardian for Martha Borden.

Page 119.—18th May, 1762. Henry Perkey's appraisement, by Robt. Hook, John Stevenson, James Bruester, recorded—3 negroes, Joseph Jenkins' note, 1 wagon.

Page 120.—2d January, 1761. William Johnston's will, yeoman, aged about forty years—Daughter, Mary Johnston, 2 years old last June. Executor, Walter Davis. Teste: Wm. Scott, Michl. O'Donnell, John Cunningham, Robt. Cunningham, John Sorel. Proved, 18th May, 1762, by Scott, John Cunningham, and Sorel. Executor qualified, with Thomas Rutledge and Wm. Scott.

Page 122.—2d October, 1761. Robert Cravens' will—Mark. Executors, wife, and son, John Cravens; wife, Mary, a negro wench called Knelly. To son William, tract called the Great Meadow, 141 acres. To daughter Mary, 124 acres she now lives on. To grandchildren, Zebulon and Robt. Harrison, 200 acres on east side Linville's Creek. To daughter Margaret Harrison. To daughter Agnes, tract she lives on. To Magee (Maggie?). To son Robert. To daughter Elizabeth Cravens. To grandson Robert Cravens, 160 acres, called Wait's Cabin, on the Creek below Joseph Cravens. To grandson John Cravens, brother of Robert above. To granddaughter Mary Black, 470 acres where Saml. Monsey lives to be sold. Nine (9) children, viz: (?) Teste: Archd. Huston, Mathew Thompson, Daniel Love. Proved, 18th May, 1762, by Archd. Huston and Danl. Love. Executors qualify, with Edward Shanklin, Andrew Erwin, Mary ( ) her mark.

Page 125.—28th March, 1762. John Peery's will—To Thos. Kirkpatrick, £10; to brother, James Peery; to Mary Peery and her children. Remaining time James Gilmer has to serve to be disposed of. Executors, John Kirkpatrick, John Peery. Teste: Saml. Downey, Saml. Kinkead, John Campbell. Proved, 18th May, 1762, by the witnesses. Executors qualify, with Thos. Kirkpatrick, John Jamison.

Page 127.—4th September, 1761. Anthony Black's estate appraised by John Finley, James Sayers, Daniel ———.

Page 129.—18th May, 1762. Roger Dyer's sale bill and settlement of estate by Hannah Dyer, administratrix, approved and recorded—To Wm. Samples, Wm. Gregg, Margaret McGlaughlan, David Nelson, Pat Frazier, John Cunningham, Robt. Ralston, Johnston Hill, John Cravens, Jesse Harrison, Bryce Russell, Robt. McGarry, John Dunkle, John Montgomery. Paid John Wright, Ro. Minnis (for whiskey). Sarah Stevenson (for whiskey for vendue); paid Wm. Gibson, Adam Harper, James Dyer.

Page 131.—1st October, 1761. William Wardlaw's will—In Borden's tracke, planter. Executors, Jeannet Wardlaw and John Wardlaw. To wife, Jeannet; to son, John; to ? James Wardlaw; to son, Hugh Wardlaw; to ? Joseph and Wm. Wardlaw, the plantation testator lives on; to daughter, Margaret Wardlaw; to son, Robert Wardlaw, the plantation of woodland lying beside Samuel Buchanan. Teste: Robt. Weer, Jas. Wardlaw, John Wardlaw, Hugh Wardlaw. Proved, 18th May, 1762, by Robt. Weer, Jas. and John Wardlaw. Executors qualified, with James and Hugh Wardlaw. Janet ( ) her mark.

Page 133.—The last will and testament of John Davison, being taken suddenly ill of a colick and departed this life the 11th of April, 1762, expressed these words (to wit): that all his just debts should be paid and Elizabeth, his wife, should have her share as the law directed, and all the rest to be equally divided amongst his four children—Thos. Paxton, David Gray. Proved, 18th May, 1762. Elizabeth Davison ( ) and Danl. Lyle qualify, with Thos. Paxton and David Gray.

Page 135.—11th April, 1762. Andrew Duncan's will—To wife, Jennet, negro slaves; to 5 daughters, Elizth., Mary, Jennet, Jean, Florence; to brother's son, James Duncan; to son, Andrew, infant, testator's home plantation. Executors, John Moore, Joseph Culton. Teste: John McNutt, Hugh Wardlaw, David Sayers. 18th May, 1762, proved, by Davis Sayers, John McNutt. Executors refuse to execute. Administration granted Jennet Duncan, the widow, who qualifies (her mark), with Andw. Russell, John Moore.

Page 137.—26th November, 1761. John Lowry's will—Executors, wife, Elizabeth, and John Moore; to wife, Elizabeth; to son, William, 160 acres joining Robt. Lowry; to daughter, Rebeckah Lowry; to sons, John and Robert Lowry, £6 sent with William Parris to Ireland with the benefit of the return and £16 Lake (?) money, to be taught trades; to daughters, Jennet and Elizabeth Lowry, to be paid when of age by their young brothers, David and James Lowry; to sons, David and James, infants, plantation testator lives on. Teste: John Wardlaw, Jas. Kennedy, Hugh Wardlaw, James Wardlaw. Proved, 18th May, 1762, by John, James and Hugh Wardlaw. John Moore refuses to execute. Elizabeth qualifies, with John Moore, Robt. Lowry.

Page 139.—18th May, 1762. William Carvin's bond (with Jas. Davis, Geo. Parris) as administrator of William Carvin.

Page 140.—19th May, 1762. George Wilson's bond (with James Lockhart, John Dickinson) as administrator of James Simpson.

Page 141.—18th May, 1762. Robert Gay's appraisement, by Robert Bratton, Jno. Graham, Andw. Fulton returned and recorded.

Page 143.—15th November, 1761. Francis McDonald's estate, appraised by Saml. Downey, Thos. Teat, Thos. Brown.

Page 144.—20th February, 1750-51. Sale of personalty of Mathias Shaw, by James Nicholas, executor—Recorded 18th May, 1762, viz: Sold to Jno. Craig, Wm. Frazier, Jas. Downey, Jno. Love, David Nelson, Henry Dooley, William Craig, Bernard Man, Joseph Wait, Saml. Muncy, Joseph Muncy, Casper Faught, Owen Reed, Joseph Wait, Jacob Harmon, Jno. Stevenson, Jacob Nicholas, Peter Herman, James Beard, Cathrine Pence, Michael Carn, William Williams. 5th May, 1755—2d sale, to viz: Jacob Nicholas, Henry Dooley, David Nelson, Peter Miller, Conrad Kimsley, Catrine Shawp (3 books), Michael Carn, Francis Kirtley, Jno. Davison, Margaret Shawp, Jno. Davis, Charles Man, Joseph Cravens, Jno. Couch, Robt. Craig, Jacob Courtsious, Simon Powell, Geo. Carn, Henry Long, Evan Evans, Conrad Backfish, Patrick Wilson, Jno. Hetrick, Nicholas Brock, George, Robert, and widow Scott. By sundries received of the estate of the deceased Jacob Pence.

Page 147.—5th April, 1751. Sale held of the estate of Jacob Pence, and settlement of estate by Peter Miller, executor of Val. Pence, who was executor of Jacob Pence, recorded 18th May, 1762. Sold to Henry Dooley, James

Bartley, Wm. Craig, Jno. Fudge, James Downey, Joseph Wait, Repentance Townsend, Jacob Harman, Saml. Muncy, Robt. Hook, Danl. Love, David Logan, Wm. Beard, Johnston Hill, David Crighton; to cash. Paid Jno. Wright, Henry Perkey, Jno. Maggart, Andw. Faught, Jacob Pence, Nicholas Trout, Thos. Crawford, Archd. Huston.

Page 150.—18th May, 1762. Florence Graham's appraisement, by Wm. Elliott, Archd. Armstrong, Jno. Graham, Jr., recorded. Acct. vs. Joseph Vachub, John and Robert Graham.

Page 150.—24th February, 1762. James Leister's estate, appraised by Jno. Hughes, Sampson Mathews, Mathew Reed.

Page 154.—19th May, 1762. Alex. McFeeters' additional appraisement, by Jno. Bigham, recorded.

Page 154.—20th May, 1762. Settlement of Stophel White's estate by Jacob Anderson, recorded—Funeral charges, viz: 1 shirt, £1, 0, 0; muslin for a cale, £5, 0; 1 sheet, 5 yds., £17, 6; 7¾ gallons liquor, £1, 3, 3; 6 lbs. cheese, £3.9; bords and cofen and nails; £13, 6; 1½ bu. flour (75 lbs.), £7, 3; 6 lbs. for shortening for said bisket, £0, 3, 5; vendue liquor, 2 gals., 1 pt., £6, 4½. Paid James Arbuckle, David Galloway. Stophel White's vendue, sold to viz: David Drein, Jacob Anderson, Alex. Miller, Isaac Anderson, Marion Crawford, Alex. Telford, David Dryden, Baptist McNabb, David Telford.

Page 156.—6th February, 1762.—James Litster's estate sold to, viz: James Ward, Geo. Wilson, Mathew Reed, Wm. Cabeen, Chas. Donnally, Ro. Armstrong, Edward Long, Pat. Cunningham, Andw. Greer, Thos. Fulton, Margt. Cameron, Jno. Stewart, Ro. Reed, Geo. Francisco, David Bell, Wm. Poage, Wm. Crow, Luke Bowyer, Abraham Thornton, Wm. Henderson, Jno. Buchanan, Thos. O'Neal, Alex. Gibson, Alex. Wright, Jno. Francis, James Simpson, Geo. Weaver, Philip Helveston, Jno. King, Geo. Anderson, Rev. Mr. Craige, Andw. Russell, Saml. Caldwell, Joseph Roberts, Jno. Gregory, Jno. Lucas, Mathew Clark, Jno. Anderson, Jr., James Robinson, Jacob Parsinger, Saml. Moore, Christopher Vinyard, Thos. Patterson, the Widow Bell, Ralph Gorrell, Jos. Russell, James Gilmore, Simon Robertson, James Hughes.

Page 157.—24th May, 1762. Adam Dickinson's additional appraisement, by Catherine Dickinson, administratrix, recorded.

Page 158.—17th August, 1762. Andrew Duncan's appraisement, by Wm. Edmondson, Jno. Edmondson, Saml. Buchanan, recorded.

Page 159.—24th May. John Davis' estate, appraised by Samuel Lyle, Alex. McFeeters, and recorded 17th August, 1762.

Page 162.—5th July, 1762. Robert Craven's estate, appraised by Mathew Thompson, Archd. Huston, Jno. Stewart. Bonds due by Ro. McGarry, John Crow, Wm. Cravens.

Page 165.—5th August, 1761. John Mason's estate, appraised by Thos. Tosh, James Bein, Neal McNeal.

Page 167.—17th August, 1762. Agnes Tosh's bond with Jno. Armstrong and James McKeachy, as administratrix of Tasker Tosh.

Page 168.—24th November, 1760. John McCinney's will—Plantationer. To wife, Mary; to son, Alexander; to daughter, Margaret Stuart; to son John; to daughters, Ann, Sarah, Mary. Executors, wife, Mary and son, John. Neighbor, James Phillips to make division of estate. Teste: Jno.

Phillips, Jas. Phillips, Chas. Phillips. Proved, —— August, 1762, by James and John Phillips. Executors qualified with Jno. Trimble. Mary's mark, John McCinney's (McKinney) mark.

Page 170.—15th September, 1758. William Dryer's estate sold to viz: Jno. Mooberry, Ephraim Love, Wm. Cunningham, Wm. Craig, Richard Shanklin, David Nelson, Edward McGary, Charles Differ, Jno. Hughbanks, John Cravens, Thos. Fulton, Wm. Ingles (English), Jas. Thomas, Andrew Erwin, Margt. Dyer, Mathew Black, John Herman, Wm. Brown. Sold and appraised, 5th December, 1759, viz: John Farris, Hugh McGary, Robt. Minnis. Cash due by John Cally. Settlement by Margaret Cravens, late Margaret Dyer, administratrix.

Page 172.—25th January, 1762. William Buchanan's will—Planter. To wife, Rebecka; to son, James; to daughters, Merian, Ruth, Rebeckah, Hannah. Executors, son, James and Andrew Hays. Teste: Alex. Miller, James McCampbell, Jno. McCoskey. Proved, 18th August, 1762, by McCampbell and McCoskey. James Buchanan refuses to execute. Andrew Hays qualifies, with Nathaniel Evans, John Hunter.

Page 174.—13th May, 1762. Andrew Smith's will: to wife, Mary, 1 sermon book; to children, books. Teste: Henry Banniger, Woolrick Conrod, Valentine Gile (Coil). Proved, 18th August, 1762, by Conrod. Henry Penniger qualifies administrator c. t. a., with Woolrick Conrod, Sebastian Hover. Proved, 18th November, 1762, by Valentine Coil.

Page 176.—12th August, 1762. William Wardlaw's estate appraised by Andrew Steel, Jno. Logan, Jno. Moore.

Page 176.—17th June, 1762. John Lowney's estate appraised by Wm. Moore, Wm. McCanless, Walter Eakin: 1 Bible and other sermon books, 6 chairs, 1 table linings.

Page 178.—19th April, 1755. Mathew Erwin's will: to wife, Elizabeth; to daughter, Gennet Erwin, alias Johnson; to daughter, Jean Erwin, alias Jamison; to daughter, Agnes; to daughter, Mary Erwin, alias Francis; to daughter, Ellinor Erwin, alias Patterson; to daughter, Elizabeth Erwin; to daughter, Ann Erwin, alias Anderson. Executrix, wife Elizabeth. John Francis to be overseer. Teste: James Bell, Alex. Blair, Edward Warner. Proved, 18th August, 1762, by Bell and Warner. Elizabeth refuses to execute. Administration granted John Francis, who qualifies, with James Bell, William Frame.

Page 180.—13th August, 1762. Arthur Johnston's estate, appraised by Samuel Hemphill, Daniel Harrison, John Cravens.

Page 180.—18th August, 1762. Mary Gregory's bond (with James Gray, Andrew Sitlington), as administratrix of Naphtalum Gregory.

Page 181.—26th April, 1757. Hugh Thompson's will—To wife, a note due him by his son, Bryce Russell, the Great Bible and books; to son, James, the Great Bible and Confession of Faith, and the Whole Duty of Man; to daughter, Eliner, her Bible, Allen's Call to the Unconverted, and Thompson's Catechesm; to grandson, Hugh Russell, a small Bible; granddaughter, Isabella Helena Russell; to daughter, Mary, now in Ireland; grandchildren, Hugh and Elizabeth Leeper; granddaughter, Rachel Russell, a note on Anthony Thorn; grandson, George Russell; grandson, James Leeper; grandson (daughter?), Jean Leeper; to Mary Scott. Teste: Jacob Sink (Link?), Jas. Craig, Jno. Craig. Executors, Wm. Thompson, Samuel Henderson. Proved, 19th February, 1762, by John Craig, and on 18th

August, 1762, by James Craig. Executors qualify, with Wm. **Baskins,** James Bell.

Page 184.—14th August, 1762. Arthur Johnston's estate sold, settlement by Margaret Gragg, late Johnston, executrix. Recorded, 19th August, 1762. Sold, viz: To David Williams, Israel Young, Robt. and Wm. Gregg, John Magill, Michael Warren. Paid Samuel Samples, Charles Campbell, Adam Stevenson, Robt. Moore, John Cathern, James Allen.

Page 185.—28th May, 1762. Entered for James Trimble, Assistant Surveyor, 200 acres of vacant land on the west line of his own land between him and Saml. McClure, and 100 acres upon the head of Borden's Creek joining his own land, and also 100 acres on Hugh Luok's (Snok's?) Run adjoining to his own land, and likewise 150 acres joining McDowell's line and Saml. Moore's line towards his own land. The above entries made with me this 28th day of May, 1762.—Archd. Alexander. Recorded, 19th August, 1762.

Page 186.—18th August, 1762. Joseph McClolon's appraisement, by Thomas Thompson, Jno. Gray, Andw. Russell, presented and recorded.

Page 186.—19th August, 1762. Robert Christian's settlement of estate of Dr. John Flood recorded 1752, to cash lent.

Page 186.—17th August, 1762. John Poage enters 200 acres on south side of South Branch, opposite Shelton's tract on Earhart's Branch.—John Archer.

Page 187.—17th August, 1762. Same enters 1,000 acres on head branches of Wolf Creek and Sinking Creek, branches of Greenbrier and New River.—John Archer.

Page 187.—20th August, 1762. James Simpson's appraisement, by Jas. Wood, Wm. Crow, Saml. Cowden. Recorded.

Page 187.—5th October, 1762. John McCinney's estate appraised, by Jas. Sayers, Thos. Gardner, Wm. Magill.

Page 188.—25th May, 1760. Thomas Paxton's will—To wife, Sarah; to son, Thomas, executor; to son, Samuel; to son-in-law, Mathew Robinson; to granddaughter, Elizabeth Eakin; to grandson, John Robinson, Teste: Mathew Lyle, Alex. Smiley, Andw. Smiley. Proved, 16th November, 1762, by Lyle and Alex. Smiley. Thos. Paxton qualifies, with Andw. Hays, Mathew Lyle.

Page 190.—16th November, 1762. William Wilson's bond (with Robt. Cravens) as administrator of John Brooks.

Page 191.—16th November, 1762. Saml. Young presented his accounts as administrator of Pat. Ingles. Recorded. Sale bill, viz: To Jno. Jamison, Saml. Cloyd, Alice English, Geo. Francisco, Ro. Reed, Wm. Earls, Andw. Greer, Saml. Moore. Paid Henry Murray, Edward Thompson, Robt. Scott.

Page 192.—16th February, 1762. Robert Mountgomery's bond (with Saml. McRoberts, Thos. Ramsey) as administrator of Jas. Gatlive.

Page 193.—16th November, 1762. John Poage entered 3 full entrys of land on a branch of Back Creek called the Valley, opposite to Jno. Miller's on Jackson River.—James **Lockhart.**

Page 193.—16th November, 1762. Naphtalum Gregory's appraisement, by Alex. Galespy, Jno. Warwick, Jas. Hamilton. Recorded. Some histories and other books.

Page 193.—27th September, 1762. John Wright's will—To wife, Lidy; to eldest son, Abraham, 300 acres called Ball Hill; to second son, James, 175 acres patented in name of testator's father, James Wright, and 30 acres adjoining the Bald Hill part of the Bear Wallow; to child wife is big with, remainder of Bear Wallow tract; to daughters, Elizabeth, Mary, Sarah, Janet, Easter and Lydia Wright, tract called Perish Lines; to third son, Joshua, 170 acres; to farther son, John, infant. Executors, wife Lydia and Daniel Smith. Teste: Michael Warren, Jno. Hughes, Egniar Virden. Proved, 18th November, 1762, by Michael Warren and Egniar Virden. Executors qualified, with Jno. Bowyer.

Page 195.—18th November, 1762. Pharaoh Ryley's appraisement, by Geo. Robinson, Joseph McDonald, Bryan McDonald, Joshua McCormick. Recorded.

Page 196.—18th November, 1762. Joseph Walker and Isabella Young's settlement of estate of Patrick Young. Recorded. Paid John Law, Jno. Taylor, Thos. Stuart, Jno. Hall and Saml. McMurty, James Todd, Gilbert Crawford, Stephen Orson, Jno. Hickman, David Dryden, Hugh Cunningham, Ro. McElhenny, Wm. Hall. Sale bill to Jno. Collier, Jas. Davis, Andrew Hall, Jas. O'Bryan, Saml. McMurty, Geo. Gibson, Isabella Young.

Page 197.—19th November, 1762. John Smith's bond (with Henry Smith) as administrator of James Lawson.

Page 198.—19th November, 1762. John Peery's appraisement, by James McCleery, Jno. Jamison, Mathew Wilson. Recorded.

Page 198.—15th February, 1761. John Erwin's will: to son Edward, part of plantation adjoining William Correy. Sons and daughters and wife. Executors, Andrew Erwin, Jean Erwin and son Edward. Overseers, brother Edward and Francis. Teste: James Oliver, William Curry, David Williams. Proved 19th November, 1762, by the witnesses. Edward Erwin qualifies executor (the others refusing) with Henry Smith, William Curry.

Page 200.—19th November, 1762. Robert Kinkhead's bond (with William Wilson) as administrator of Joseph Henderson.

Page 201.—20th November, 1762. John Buchanan's bond (with Charles Lewis, William Preston), as sheriff to collect tithables.

Page 202.—17th February, 1758. Colonel James Patton's estate; appraised by Thomas Stewart, John Ramsey, Edward Hall. List of bonds, bills, &c., due the estate: James Wiley's, 3rd May, 1754; Wm. Leppard's, 15th February, 1753; John Die and Wm. Leppard's, 2nd February, 1754; William Byers, 15th February, 1754; Ernest Sharp, John Sharp and Martin Loy, 15th February, 1753; Thomas Ose, 8th February, 1754; Alexander Sayers, 22nd April, 1751; Daniel McNaire, 29th November, 1753; Frederick Stern, 12th February, 1754; Elizabeth Sumpter, 12th November, 1754; Patrick Callhoun, 20th April, 1751; Jacob Larton, — June, —; John Cook, 6th February, 1754; James McCaul, 9th April, 1751; John Wilson, 13th August, 1753; Conrad and Michael Kinder, 6th February, 1754; John Goldman, 17th December, 1750; George Stevenson, 8th December, 1752; Daniel Brown, 5th February, 1754; John Adams, 1st February, 1754; James Scaggs, 12th February, 1753; Luke McCherry, 22nd February, 1755; John Miller and Charles Springer, 1st April, 1751; Andrew Evans, 29th January, 1753; James Miller, of Reed Creek, ...; William, Henry and James Bates, 13th August, 1752; William Henry's note; Mathew Patton,

17th December, 1753; Paul Garrison, 16th February, 1754; John Brinegar, 20th April, 1753; John Stedham, Jacob Patton, and Peter Tar, 18th December, 1753; Thomas Lutterington and John Brinegar, 3rd January, 1754; Robert Williams, 17th December, 1753; Thomas English and John Medley, 9th February, 1754; John McCurry and Samuel Jackson, 27th September, 1752; William Lees, 17th December, 1753; Errick Bright, 18th February, 1753; Francis Cypher, 18th February, 1753; Henry and William Ledford, 3rd January, 1754; Henry Holston, 17th December, 1753; Conrad Harchy, 18th December, 1753; Nathan Nicholas, 14th January, 1755; Thomas Hill, 18th February, 1753; John Medley, 11th April, 1748; Samuel Jackson, 25th September, 1753; Plackard Siller (Scilar), 18th December, 1753; Peter Upsher, 20th December, 1753; Benjamin Ogle, 18th February, 1753; Elisha Isaac, ——, 1753; Patrick Downey and Adam Looney, 4th October, 1753; Tobias Bright, 13th December, 1752; Thomas English, 13th December. 1752; Peter Looney, 6th March, 1754; Hance Maurice, 20th December, 1753; George Peter Tar and Henry Holston, Sr., 17th December, 1753; William Graham, 13th August, 1753; William McCurry, 2nd January, 1754; John Brinegar, 3rd January, 1754; Michael Finney, 12th December, 1752; Peter Looney, 6th March, 1754; John McCurry, 25th ——, 1753; Thomas Wilson, 28th January, 1754; John Kighter, 21st April, 1753; John Brinegar, 25th April, 1753; Richard Kerr, 13th September, 1748, 20th September, 1753; John Thompson, 20th November, 1753; William Scott, 4th April, 1748; James Hollis, 4th April, 1753; Hugh McDonald, 19th February, 1749; David Miller, 20th February, 1755; Hugh Mills, 13th April, 1748; William Graham, John Mills and Erwin Patterson, 3rd August, 1753; George Reed, 13th December, 1752; John Welsh, 20th September, 1753; John Donaly, 4th February, 1754; Adam Wall, 26th March, 1751; William Plummer, 18th December, 1753; Thomas Camp, 16th December, 1754; John Moore, 7th February, 1755; Palser Melser, 17th January, ——; Ephraim Vause, 10th October, 1754; Walter Welsh, 20th December, 1753, 24th January, 1754; Charles Milligan, 3rd October, 1753; Henry Holston, 4th October, 1753; Charles Milligan, 13th April, 1748, 20th December, 1753; Stephen Arnold, 6th February, 1749-50; John Robinson, 16th February, 1753; Henry Holston, 4th October, 1753; Henry Zinn, 10th January, 1754; Ben. Watson and Ro. Rennix, 15th November, 1754; William Pepper, 13th February, 1753, 18th February, 1753; John Thompson, 20th November, 1753; Samuel Arnold, 15th March, 1751; Robert Box, 8th February, 1754; Frederick Hartsough, 18th December, 1753; William Ritchie, 2nd December, 1751; Patrick Downey and Adam Looney, 4th October, 1753; George Reed, 13th December, 1752; James and William Gorrell, 18th February, 1753; James Neely, 16th July, 1752; Edward Moore and James Neely, 18th October, 1754; George Stevenson, 8th December, 1752; William Ledford, 21st December, 1752; Thomas English, 15th December, 1752; Francis Cyphers, 18th February, 1753; Thomas Hill, 18th February, 1753; Errick Bright, 18th February, 1753; Elijah Isaac, 18th February, 1753; Benjamin Ogle, 18th February, 1753; Tobias Bright, 18th February, 1753; John Mills, 18th February, 1753; Robert Kirkham, 18th February, 1753; Gilbert Crawford, 1st March, 1753; William Armstrong, 3rd May, 1753; John McCully, 20th April, 1753; Stephen Rentfro, 5th May, 1753; Edward McDonald, 20th December, 1753; Henry Holston, 13th December, 1753; Robert Williams, 17th December, 1753; Mathew and Jacob Patton, 17th December, 1753; Reece Watkins, 17th December, 1753; George Peter Tarr, 17th December, 1753; William Plummer, 10th December, 1753; Plackard Scilar, 18th December, 1753.

Page 205.—Frederick Hartsough and Plackard Scilar, 18th December, 1753; Conrad Harchy, 18th December, 1753; John Stedham, Jacob Patton, George Peter Tarr, 19th December, 1753; Peter Upsher, 20th December, 1753; Hance Maurice, 20th December, 1753; Charles Mitts, 20th December, 1753; William Ralston and James Moore, 2nd September, 1761; Michal Dougherday, 12th September, 1750; John Maxwell, 26th August, 1752; John Robinson, 16th February, 1753; James Armstrong, 13th August, 1753; William Foster, 1st February, 1755; Jacob Brown, 18th February, 1753; James Armstrong, 2nd December, 1751; David Kinkade, 23rd January, 1751; James Price and Arthur Walls, 4th October, 1754; Major John Smith, 4th October, 1754; William Ritchie and James Brice, 4th October, 1754; John Bowen, 15th April, 1748; Nathaniel Wilcher, 24th January, 1755; Colonel John Buchanan, 17th January, 1755; Hugh Caruthers, 6th May, 1754; Jacob Harman, Jr., and Adam Harman, 12th February, 1753; William Carvin, 12th February, 1753; Neal McNeal, 3rd May, 1753; Robert McFarland, 30th January, 1753; Wm. Snodgrass, 4th October, 1753; John Poage and Alexander Miller, 3rd February, 1752; John Mills, 28th December, 1753; Thomas Ramsey, 13th December, 1753; John Berrisford, 4th December, 1753; Archibald Graham, 18th December, 1753; Ben Watson and Robert Rennix, 15th March, 1754; James Bane, — October, 1753; James Kerr, — October, 1753; Bryan McDonald, — ——, 1754; Joseph Potts, 1st January, 1753; Peter Upsher, 18th December, 1753; Thomas Brinegar, 25th April, 1753; Henry Holston, 4th October, 1753; John Mills, 20th February, 1753; John Poage and Alexander Walker, 3d February, 1752; John Downey, 7th August, 1754; Thomas Ramsey, 14th April, 1748; William Ingles, 11th February, 1754; Henry Switsard, 24th February, 1755; Josiah Ramsey, 24th February, 1755; Samuel McRoberts, — ——, 1754; Isaac Taylor, — ——, 1755; John Collier, — ——, ——; Loftus Pullen, — ——, ——; John Smiley, — ——, ——; Robert Galloway, — ——, ——; John Anderson, 13th August, 1753; Walter Smiley, — ——, ——; Nathaniel Evans, 17th July, 1753; Francis McCown, 13th August, 1753; Augustine Price, 11th November, 1754; Francis McCown, 22nd November, 1753; Michael Price and Philip Harles (Hales), 11th November, 1754; Jacob Lingell, 1st November, 1753; John and Christian Bingaman, 17th June, 1753; Augustine and Daniel Price, 1st March, 1753; William Buchanan, — ——, ——; William, Hall, — ——, ——; John Craig, — —— ——; Edward Hall, — ——, ——; John McClure, 13th August, ——; Jacob Patton, — ——, ——; James Moore, — ——, ——; Patrick Sharkey, — ——, ——; James Armstrong, 13th August, 1753; William Patterson, 13th August, 1753; Daniel Droudy, 13th August, 1753; James Lockhart, 13th August, 1753; John Rorty, 13th August, 1753; Walter Davis, 13th August, 1753; Charles Patrick, 13th August, 1753; Robert Christian, 13th August, 1753; John Sprout, 13th August, 1753; Andrew Haislip, 13th August, 1753.

Page 208.—5th January, 1763. John Wright's estate; appraised by John Cravens, Thomas Harrison, John Shalpman: Daniel Young's note; David Smith's ditto; Soloman Turpin's ditto; Peter Watkins' note; John Stewart's ditto; Thomas Bryant's ditto; Skidmore Muncy's note; William Shull's ditto; Charles Differ's ditto; Robert. Williams' ditto.

Page 209.—7th January, 1763. John Brooks' estate, appraised by John Cravens, Mathew Black, James Hemphill; due by Henry Caully.

Page 210.—15th February, 1763. Mary and John Greenlee's bond (with Archibald Alexander, James Lockhart) as administrator of James Greenlee.

Page 210.—13th December, 1762. John Erwin's estate, appraised by Edward Shanklin, Robert Fowler, Charles Campbell.

Page 214.—15th February, 1763. Martha M. Gatlive's bond (with Jno. Smith, Geo. Wilson) as administratrix of Jas. Gatlive.

Page 215.—15th February, 1763. Samuel Huston's bond (with James Pollock, Patrick Lowney), as administrator of Alex. Anderson.

Page 216.—25th November, 1762. Joseph McCord's will, farmer: To wife, Mary; to children, as well unborn, as born; to brother John, executor's wife, Mary and brother Jno. McCord, who are to make Mathew Molar title for the land testator sold him near Moorman's River, in Albemarle; guardian of children, Hugh Cunningham. Teste: Robt. Hamilton, Jno. McKee, James Logan. Proved, 15th February, 1763, by McKee and Logan. Executors qualified with Jno. McKee and Jno. Ramsey. (Mary's mark).

Page 217.—20th March, 1763. Thomas Peerie's will: (Mark): To wife Mary; to son John; to daughter Elizabeth; to children, Margaret, Agness, Thomas, George, William, Robert and Mary. Teste: Moses Williams, Henry Cartmill. Proved, 15th February, 1753, by the witnesses. Mary qualifies (her mark), with James Young, James Peerie.

Page 219.—16th February, 1763. John Lowraine's bond (with John Bowyer), as administrator of David Lowraine.

Page 219.—18th November, 1762. Anto. (Antoine) Bogest (Bogard's) will: To wife Anna; to brother Warner Bogard, 1 pistol. Teste: Jeremiah Osburn, Charles Wolson, John Francklin. Proved, 16th February, 1763, by Osburn and Wolson. Ann qualifies (her mark), with Chas. Wolson and Jeremiah Osburn.

Page 221.—28th February, 1761. John Lewis' will: Wife, Margaret; son, William, tract with the mills, called Mill Place, which John holds under lease from Beverley; grandson, John, son of Andrew; daughter, Margaret Crow; to each of children and grandchildren of same name as self and wife, mourning rings; to son Charles £10 to purchase a watch on which testator's name shall be engraved in testimony of esteem; to Patrick Barnet, all wearing apparel; to Betty Taylor, to be rewarded over and above her wages. Executor's sons, Thomas, Andrew, and William. Teste: Chas. Lewis, Thos. Rafferty, Betty Taylor. Proved, 18th November, 1762, by Betty Taylor, and on 16th February, 1763, by Thos. Rafferty. Executors qualified with John Madison.

Page 223.—16th February, 1763. John Bingaman presented his settlement of John Bingaman's estate: Paid Patton's executors my father's bond with interest to 10th December, 1762; paid Mathias Carsh (Kersh); paid Wm. Leppard, Nicholas Keys, Conrad Bloss, Henry and Christian Bingaman.

Page 224.—17th February, 1763. Daniel Smith (on behalf of Margaret Van Pelt's) bond, (with Francis McBride) as administrator of Peter Bowman.

Page 225.—10th June, 1763. Joseph Herndon's estate: In hands of Robt. Kinkead, administrator; appraised by Samuel Wilson, Samuel Moore, George Wilson.

Page 226.—21st February, 1763. John Bowyer's bond (with John Madison) as administrator of Caleb Harman.

Page 227.—16th August, 1759. John Bowyer's bond (with Richard Woods, Israel Christian, Felix Gilbert), as guardian of Martha Borden, orphan of Benjamin Borden.

Page 228.—21st November, 1759. William Gray's bond (with Patrick Hays, Samuel Paxton), as guardian (chosen) to Benjamin, orphan of Jno. Gray.

Page 229.—21st November, 1759. Samuel Gray's bond (with Patrick Hays, Jno. Allison), as guardian (chosen) to Joseph Gray, orphan of Jno. Gray.

Page 229.—22nd November, 1759. Daniel Smith's bond (with John Christian and Jno. Scott), as guardian (chosen) to Jane Scott, orphan of Samuel Scott.

Page 230.—18th March, 1760. David Cloid's bond (with John Bowyer, James McGavock), as guardian (appointed) to Mary Cloyd, orphan of John Cloyd.

Page 231.—18th March, 1760. David Cloid's bond (with Thos. Paxton), as guardian (chosen) to Jno. Cloyd, orphan of John Cloyd.

Page 231.—18th March, 1760. George Moffett's bond (with Wm. Anderson), as guardian (chosen) to William Moffett, orphan of John Moffett.

Page 232.—18th November, 1760. Samuel Steel's bond (with Thomas Paxton, Pat. Campbell), as guardian (chosen) to David Steel, orphan to Thomas Steel.

Page 233.—20th November, 1760. Abraham Bird's bond (with Mount Bird, Wm. Poage), as guardian (chosen) to Conrad Custard, orphan of Arnold Custard.

Page 233.—17th February, 1761. Uriah Humble's bond (with Thomas West), as guardian (chosen) to Catherine Morly, orphan of Daniel Morley.

Page 234.—18th February, 1761. William Man's bond (with William Elliott, Joseph Vachub), as guardian (chosen) to David Grimes, orphan of William Grimes.

Page 235.—19th May, 1761. Thomas Gardner's bond (with Jas. Bell, Alex. Crafford), as guardian (appointed) to Mary Gardner, orphan of Thomas Gardner.

Page 235.—19th May, 1761. John Harrison, Jr.'s bond (with Thos. Moore), as guardian (chosen) to Josiah Davison, orphan of Daniel Davison.

Page 236.—21st May, 1761. Samuel McDowell and Richard Woods' bond (with David Stewart), as guardian (appointed) to Samuel, Arthur, Esther, Elizabeth, and Charles Woods, orphans of Charles Woods.

Page 237.—22nd May, 1761. John Bowyer's bond (with Gabriel Jones), as guardian to Luke Bowyer, orphan of Michael Bowyer (chosen).

Page 237.—18th August, 1761. Thomas Meeks' bond (with Jno. Davis, Jas. Risk), as guardian to Jno. Meek, orphan of Wm. Meek.

Page 238.—18th August, 1761. Frederick Easter's bond (with Philip Harper, Geo. Harmer (Hammer), as guardian (appointed) to Daniel and Catherine Mouse, orphans of Daniel Mouse.

Page 239.—18th August, 1761. Archibald Buchanan's bond (with Jno. Maxwell, Chas. Hays), as guardian (appointed) to Jno. McFerrin, orphan of James McFerrin.

Page 239.—19th August, 1761. John Skeen's bond (with Michael Warren), as guardian (appointed) to Eleanor Milsap, orphan of Thos. Milsap.

Page 240.—19th August, 1761. Daniel Smith's bond (with Ephraim Love), as guardian (chosen) to Robert Hill, orphan of Johnston Hill.

Page 241.—19th August, 1761. Daniel Harrison's bond (with John Trimble), as guardian (appointed) to Jane Claypole, orphan of Wm. Claypole.

Page 241.—17th February, 1762. Robert Armstrong's bond (with John Archer, Samuel Wilson), as guardian (appointed) to Jane and James Armstrong, orphans of James Armstrong.

Page 242.—17th February, 1762. Roger Keys' bond (with Samuel and James McDowell) as guardian (chosen) to William Wilson, orphan of John Wilson.

Page 243.—17th February, 1762. Henry Murray's bond (with Thos. Armstrong) as guardian (chosen) to Jno. Stewart, orphan of James Stewart.

Page 243.—17th February, 1762. John Hamilton's bond (with Robt Stewart) as guardian (chosen) to Jas. Stewart, orphan of James Stewart.

Page 244.—17th February, 1762. Robert Stewart's bond (with John Hamilton) as guardian (chosen) to Ralph Stewart, orphan of James Stewart.

Page 245.—18th May, 1762. William Pickins' ( ) bond (with John Miller, Andrew Bird) as guardian (appointed) to Samuel Scot, orphan of Samuel Scot.

Page 245.—18th May, 1762. John Moore's bond (with John Handley) as guardian (appointed) to John Duncan, orphan of Andrew Duncan.

Page 246.—18th May, 1762. David Sayers' (Sayer) bond (with Jno. Moore) as guardian (appointed) to Joseph Duncan, orphan of Andrew Duncan.

Page 247.—18th May, 1762. Jannet Duncan's bond (with John Handly) as guardian (appointed) to James Duncan, orphan of Andrew Duncan.

Page 247.—21st May, 1762. James Young's bond (with Samuel Young, Joseph Hannet) as guardian (chosen) to Robt. Young, orphan of Robert Young.

Page 248.—19th August, 1762. David Scott's bond (with Mathew Patton, Jno. Davis) as guardian (chosen) to James and Joseph Scott, orphans of Benj. Scott.

Page 249.—18th November, 1762. John Carlile and Mary Carlile's bond (with Wallace Estill, Thos. Hugart) as guardians (appointed) to Ruth and Isabella Clements, orphans of Jacob Clements.

Page 249.—18th November, 1762. John Summers' bond (with Jas. McDowell, Jas. Trimble) as guardian (appointed) to Sarah, James, Jannet and Alex. Young, orphans of Patrick Young.

Page 250.—17th February, 1763. Daniel Smith's bond (with Jno. Madison) as guardian (chosen) to John Johnson, orphan of Arthur Johnson.

Page 251.—22d February, 1763. Alexander Anderson's estate appraised, by Jas. Eakin, Wm. McCanless, Jno. Montgomery, Mathew Huston.

Page 251.—19th April, 1762. Settlement of Alexander Anderson's estate by Saml. Huston approved and recorded—To attending the said Anderson, nursing and boarding him three weeks in his sickness, £1, 1, 0; to 6 gallons peach brandy for him during his sickness, and at the funeral; paid note to John Jeremiah.

Page 252.—19th April, 1763. John Dunlap's bond (with Jno. Clark, Robt. Clark) as guardian (chosen) to Alex. Dunlap, orphan of Alex. Dunlap.

Page 252.—27th March, 1753. Robert Armstrong's will, yeoman—Eldest son, James, possessed of 350 acres for which the Government is paid, therefore testator gives him no more; son, Robert, all lands and moveables; executor, wife Lydia. Teste: Jno. Jones, Jhorn (?) Armstrong, Sampson Archer. Proved, 20th April, 1763, by Jones and Armstrong. Executor qualified (with Jho. Armstrong, James Gamwell).

Page 254.— —— April, 1760. Anthony Bowyer's estate appraised, by Gabriel Pickens, Jno. Davis, Jas. Dyer.

Page 255.—20th April, 1763. John Mason's appraisement, approved and recorded, by Thos. Tosh, Neal McNeal, Jas. Bean.

Page 256.—20th April, 1763. Henry Gay's settlement of estate of John Gay recorded—To Eleanor Weems; to recording the will of Willms Burgh; paid Jacob Martin; paid Wm. Coven.

Page 256.—10th March, 1763. Additional appraisement of Robt. Cravens' estate, by Jno. Stewart, Mathew Thompson, Archd. Huston.

Page 256.—15th November, 1762. Hugh Thompson's estate appraised, by Brice Russell, Geo. Crawford, Jas. Craig.

Page 257.—25th April, 1763. John Greenlee's bond (with James McDowell) as guardian (appointed) to Mary Greenlee, orphan of Jas. Greenlee.

Page 258.—1st July, 1762. Thomas Fulton's bond to William Howard, of Albemarle, to convey a lot on Water Street in Staunton, being the upper end of the lot whereon Fulton formerly lived, and is the only lot having a poplar tree standing on it in the town. Also 12 acres woodland adjoining Wm. Lewis and commonly called Murray's place. Teste: Robt. McClenachan, Sampson Mathews, Mary Mathews. Proved, 26th April, 1763, by McClenachan and Sampson Mathews.

Page 259.—21st June, 1763. Charles Dalhouse's appraisement (by Jno. Black, Isaac White, Jno. McClure), approved and recorded.

Page 260.—21st June, 1763. Archibald Stewart's appraisement (by James Galespy, Saml. Steel, Wm. Finley, John Finley), approved and recorded.

Page 260.—2d June, 1762. James Armstrong's will—To James Armstrong, son to son William; to son William; to Geo. Rutledge, son to Thos. Rutledge; to Elizabeth Rutledge; to Thos. Rutledge and Wm. Armstrong, what remains in Carlany; wife. Executors, Walter Davis and Jas. Bell. Teste: Jno. Coulter, Geo. Marshall, Thos. Rutledge. Proved, June 21, 1763, by Jno. Coulter and Geo. Marshall. Executors refused to execute. Administration granted eldest son William, who qualifies with Abraham Smith, Saml. Cloyd, Ninian Cloyd.

Page 262.—21st June, 1763. Margaret Leeper's bond (with Saml. Henderson, Jno. Seawright) as administratrix of Jas. Leeper.

Page 263.—21st June, 1763. William Beard's bond (with Archd. Huston) as administrator of John Sheldon.

Page 264.—18th June, 1763. Joseph McCord's estate appraised, by Robert Erwin, Nathanl. Davis, Jno. Gilmer—John McCord's, Jr., note; Benj. McCord's note; Jno. McCord's, Sr., note; Adam McCord and James McCord's note; William Little's note; Robt. Miller's note; Thos. Grubbs' note; Wm. McCord's note. Cash, Mary Brown, debtor; Elizabeth Woods, Dr. Jno. Scott, dr.

Page 266.—22d June, 1763. William Buchanan's appraisement (by Jas. McCampbell, Isaac and Jacob Anderson) approved and recorded—One mill, £28; sundry books; Robt. Allison's bond; judgment vs. Wm. Burk and Richd. Burtain.

Page 266.—14th June, 1763. James Gatlive's estate appraised (by Jno. McFerrin, Thos. McFerrin, Pat Shonkey).

Page 266.—23d February, 1761. Malcom Campbell's will—Wife, Isabella; son, Archibald, tract adjoining the Long Lick and tract on Mill Creek; son, William; four daughters, Elizabeth, Mary, Jean and Rebeckah. Executors, son Archd. and Saml. Lyle. Teste: Archd. Alexander, Danl. Lyle, Nathan Peoples. Proved, 22d June, 1763, by Alexander and Lyle Executors refuse to execute. Isabella also refuses. Administration granted Elizabeth Campbell, who qualifies with Pat. Sharkey, Jno. Neeley, Adam Dean.

Page 268.—10th December, 1762. James Dunlap's estate appraised, by Jno. Dickinson, Ralph Laverty.

Page 269.—28th December, 1762. Col. Jno. Lewis' estate appraised, by Felix Gilbert and Robt. Reed.

Page 270.—23d June, 1763. Robt. Bratton's settlement of estate of James Dunlap, approved and recorded—Paid Hugh Wardlaw, Ro. Lusk, Lettice Breckinridge, Joseph Wahob (Wauchut), Jas. Simpson, Thos. Gillespy, Jos. Mays, Henry Cartmill, James Means, David Dryden, Jas. Burnsides, Thos. Vance, Archd. Clendenning, Lawrence Huntsman, Thos. Thompson, John Low. Received from Capt. Christian, being arrears due Capt. Dunlap. Received from Capt. Hog, due for pay. Received from George Jameson. Received from Capt. Hog, account of James Ramsey.

Page 272.—19th March, 1763. George Robinson's will—Wife, Martha; eldest sons, James and Samuel, to clothe and school all the younger children; younger sons, George and William, infants, to be bound to trades; eldest daughter, Sarah; daughters, Catherine, Priscilla, Martha, under 18. Executors, wife and sons James and Samuel. Teste: William Preston, Wm. Graham, Jos. Robinson, Jno. Robinson, Francis Graham. Proved, 25th June, 1763, by Wm. Preston, Wm. Graham, Joseph Robinson. Executors qualify, with Joseph Robinson, Wm. Graham.

Page 274.—25th June, 1763. James Reyburn's bond (with John Nickel) as guardian (chosen) to Henry Reyburn, orphan of Edward Reyburn.

Page 275.—16th August, 1763. Ann Clendenning's bond (with Felix Gilbert, Wm. Mays) as administratrix of Archd. Clendenning.

Page 276.—20th September, 1763. Ann Kinkead's bond (with Thomas Stevenson, Joseph Kinkead) as administratrix of Burrows Kinkead.

Page 277.—20th September, 1763. Rebecca Dougherty's bond (with Edward Rutledge, Henry Campbell) as administratrix of Charles Dougherty.

Page 278.—20th September, 1763. Lilley (Lily) Bowen's settlement of estate of Moses Bowen, approved and recorded—Paid Wm. Casil, Rees Bowen, Jane Cunningham, Doctor Loyd. Cash lent Jno. Bowen, deceased.

Page 278.—20th September, 1763. James Wardlaw's bond (with James Steel, Andw. McCampbell) as administrator of Thos. Jones.

Page 279.—20th September, 1763. James and John Gilmore's bond (with James McGavock, Jno. Bowyer) as administrators of John Gilmore.

Page 280.—20th September, 1763. William Gilmore's bond (with Jas. Gilmore, Alex. Dale) as administrator of Wm. Culberts.

Page 281.—21st September, 1763. Samuel McDowell's bond (with Jos. Lapsely) as administrator of John Woods.

Page 282.—21st September, 1763. Felix Gilbert's bond (with Benj. Estill) as administrator of John Murphy.

Page 283.—21st September, 1763. Same, as administrator of John Williams.

Page 284.—21st September, 1763. Same, as administrator of Lawrence Huntsman.

Page 285.—21st September, 1763. Patrick Frazier's bond (with Jno. Davison) as administrator of James Underwood.

Page 286.—26th February, 1763. Robert Graham's will—Wife, Jean; son, Thomas, infant; daughters, Elizabeth and Margaret, Rebecca and Jean; son, Christopher Graham; brother, Jno. Graham. Executrix, wife. Teste: Jno. Carlile, Robt. Carlile, Thos. Hicklin. Proved, 21st September, 1763, by the witnesses. Jane qualifies, with Jno. Graham, Hugh Hicklin.

Page 288.—21st September, 1763. John Cravens' settlement of Robt. Cravens' estate, approved and recorded—Paid Saml. Hemphill, Ro. Cravens, Pat. and Jno. Frazier, Margaret Perkey, Pat. Given, John Stewart, Mathew Black, Wm. Minter, Jno. Brown, Wm. Cravens. Cash paid widow Mary. Cash paid John Cravens. Legacy of negro delivered to Zebulon Harrison for his 2 sons. Legacy to Elizabeth Cravens. Legacy to Robt. Black in part of his wife's legacy.

Page 289.—16th April, 1763. James Greenlee's estate appraised, by Saml. McDowell, Jno. McClung, Jas. McDowell—Negro slaves; Robt. Brownfield's note, Robt. Telford's note, Geo. Seaton's note, David Griffey's note, Lewis Morgan's note, Jno. Logan's note, Jno. Skilton's note, Robt. Bradshaw's note; debt vs. Thos. Cottrel. Insolvent notes of Lawrence Moiren, Joseph and Robt. Tarr, Ezekiel Clements, Jno. Ross, Thos. Taylor, Lawrence Moiren, Patrick Downing, Wm. Centern.

Page 291.—22d September, 1763. Sale and inventory of Robert Rennix's estate (by David Stuart, Wm. Lewis, Jno. Poage) presented and recorded.

Page 292.—26th September, 1763. Naphtalim Gregory's appraisement and settlement of estate recorded—Debts due the estate, by James Rusk, Jno. Rusk, Jno. Martin's estate. Account of sales on 13th September, 1763—To Jas. Williams, Michael Weaver, Wm. Fitzjarrell, Thos. Kirkpatrick, Richd. Morrison, Jno. Jordan, Joshua Ewing. Articles kept in hands of widow Mary—Some books. Paid Jno. Humphries.

Page 294.—17th October, 1763. William Adair's will—Daughter, Sarah Keys; to Roger Keys; to John Keys; to Saml. Keys; to Benj. Keys; to Sarah Keys; to Margaret Keys; to Wm. Wilson, Ann Poage, Nancy Wilson, the note of James Park, the money due by David Dredan; to Alex. McMolan; to Wm. McMolan; to William Wolson; to Ann Poage and Easter

McMolan, Easter McMolan Poage, Ann Poage Baxter; to John Rays, whom I appoint executor. "Wolison on ye Sacrament." Executors, Roger Keys. Teste: John Paul, Sarah Keys, Margt. Keys. Proved, 15th November, 1763, by the witnesses. Executor qualified, with John Paul.

Page 296.—23d August, 1758. John Harrison, Jr.'s will, yeoman—Brother Zebulon, eldest son of Jno. Harrison, tract on Smith's Creek, 400 acres; to Phel Harrison, eldest daughter of Zebulon; to sister Phebe Moore, and her daughter; Ann Davison, and to her daughters; Phebe Davison; to brother, Reuben. Executors, brothers Zebulon and Reuben. Teste: Jonathan Douglass, Jno. Hopkins, James Breame (?). Proved, 15th November, 1763, by Jno. Hopkins, and 16th November, 1763, by Jonathan Douglass. Executors qualified (Zebulon's mark), with Danl. Love, Robt. Cravens.

Page 298.—16th November, 1763. Thomas Gilmore's appraisement (by Archd. Alexander, Saml. Lyle, Saml. McDowell). Recorded.

Page 299.—16th November, 1763. Will Calbert's (Alvard) appraisement, by same as above. Recorded.

Page 300.—16th November, 1763. John Woods' appraisement, by Joseph Lapsely, Jno. Gilmore, Archd. Alexander. Recorded.

Page 300.—16th November, 1763. John Bowyer's bond (with Wm. Preston, Jas. McDowell, Saml. McDowell, Wm. Crow) to collect officers' fees.

Page 301.—16th November, 1763. Same to collect quit rents.

Page 302.—16th November, 1763. Same to collect tithables.

Page 302.—16th November, 1763. Same to collect taxes.

Page 303.—16th November, 1763. Blakeley Brush's bond (with Samuel Norwood, Wm. McCanless) as administrator of Richd. Brush.

Page 304.—16th November, 1763. Michael Dougherty's appraisement (by Jos. Culton, Jno. McKee, Jno. Gilmore, William Edmondston). Recorded—Cash due by Wm. Christy.

Page 306.—17th November, 1763. James Finley's bond (with Jno. Stewart, Jno. Allison, Nathan Gilliland, Wm. Kerr) as administrator of Robt. Finley.

Page 307.—8th November, 1763. George Robinson's estate appraised, by Robt. Breckinridge, Jno. Neelley, Bryan McDonald—Danl. McCormick's bond; Jno. Bare's (?) note; Robt. Galloway's note; Wm. Roseby's 3 notes; Arthur Wats' note assigned by James Price; Charles Mills' (?) note assigned by Jno. Lowry.

Page 308.—18th November, 1763. Margt. Risk's bond (with John and Robt. Risk) as administratrix of James Risk.

Page 309.—20th December, 1763. George Mathews' bond (with James Lockhart, Jno. Archer, Jno. Poage) as administrator of Joshua Mathews.

Page 309.—29th November, 1763. William Adair's (Gentleman) estate appraised—Watt's Philosophical Essays; 1 Medical Dictionary; 1 Ambrous Looking to Jesus; 1 Practical Physician; 1 Baley's Dictionary; 1 Complete English Dispensitory; 1 Landon Dispensitory; 1 Art of Surgery; 1 Confession of Faith; 1 The Divine Attributes; 1 The ———— of the Sacraments; 1 Arithmetic; 1 The Dying Man's Testament; 1 Collection of Sermons; 1 The Sovereignty and Wisdom of God; 1 Death and Heaven; 1 Medicinal Experiments; 1 The Intrist of England; 1 Being Born Again; 1 Hyme Book; 1 Music Book; 1 Christian's Interest; Explanatory Chatechasm; 1 The Return of Prayer; The Demision of Sin and Grace; 1 Psalm Book;

Direction to Communicants; 1 Durbam on Death; 1 Divine Breathings; 1 The Wars of England; 1 Sacramental Directory; 1 To Walk with God; 1 Eleven Sermons; 1 Free Happiness; 1 The Free Nonconformist; 1 The Sacrifices of Moses; 2 bookcases.

Page 310.—20th March, 1763. John Davis' bond (with James Stevenson, Jno. Buchanan) as guardian (chosen) to Jacob Scott, orphan of Jno. Scott.

Page 311.—4th May, 1761. Margaret Anderson's will—Granddaughter, Margaret Anderson, alias Clendennin, and her daughter Hannah Anderson and her son John Clendennin. Executors, Jno. Francis and Jno. Poage. Teste: Jas. Bell, Isaac Carson, Mary Francis. Proved, 20th March, 1764, by Bell and Carson. Executors qualified, with James Bell, Michael Dickey.

Page 312.—12th September, 1763. James Leeper's estate appraised, by Michael Dickey, Jno. King, Andrew McComb.

Page 314.—2d November, 1763. Joseph McCord's vendue—Sold to Patrick Finley, Joseph Walker, James Logan, James Moore, Mary Brown, Jno. McCord, James McCallister, Alex. Telford, Jno. Somers, Mary Ann Clendennin, David Telford, Wm. McKee, Charles Boyles, W. Wolsy, James Gordon, Thos. Grubbs, Elizabeth Woods.

Page 315.—20th March, 1764. Burrow Kinkead's appraisement (by Saml. Steel, Jno. Finley, Wm. Christian). Recorded.

Page 317.—10th March, 1764. John Harrison's appraisement, recorded (by Danl. Smith, Michael Warren, Michael Shirley). Due by Jonathan Langdon.

Page 318.—21st March, 1764. Thos. James' appraisement (by Jno. Logan, Wm. Kennedy, Saml. Steel). Recorded.

Page 318.—21st March, 1764. Charles Lynch's bond (with Wm. Thompson, Alex. Thompson) as administrator of Valentine Yoacum.

Page 319.—21st March, 1764. Same, bond as administrator of Frederick Sea.

Page 320.—21st March, 1763 (1764?). John Griffith's bond (with Jno. Smith, David Looney) as administrator of Morris Griffith.

Page 321.—21st March, 1764. Jno. Griffith's bond (with John Smith and David Looney) as administrator of Benjamin Griffith.

Page 322.—21st March, 1764. James Trimble's bond (with Wm. McKee) as guardian (appointed) to Ann and Lydia Berrisford, orphans of John Berrisford.

Page 323.—4th March, 1762. Michael Rhine's (Ryan) estate appraised.

Page 324.—22d March, 1764. Michael Rhine's vendue recorded—To Nicholas Havener, Henry Flesher, Jacob Rolman, Frederick Opp, Thos. Miller, John Davis, Adam Stroud, Henry Stone, Castle Hover, Wm. Robinson, Jacob Bour, Paslin Hover, Elizabeth Rhine, Leonard Props, Jno. Dunkle, Peter Smith, Geo. Bush, Nicholas Summers, Mark Swatley, Henry Pickle, Francis Evick, Leonard Simmons.

Page 325.—27th February, 1764. Jane Young's (wife of Saml. Young) confession of scandalous words. She said that Major John Brown's waggon drove by his son or sons did bring from the Meeting House, commonly called Brown's Meeting House, a waggon load of lime belonging to the Congregation. Teste: Robt. Wilson, Henry Cresswell, Thos. Brown, Jas. Brown.

Page 325.—22d March, 1764. Sebastian (Bosten) Hover's settlement of estate of Michael Rhine (Ryan) recorded—Paid Elizabeth Hope.

Page 326.—24th March, 1764. Henry Stone's settlement of estate of Jacob Zorn (Sorn) recorded.

Page 327.—22d March, 1764. James Stewart's appraisement (by James McCoy, Henry Cartmill, Ralph Laverty). Recorded.

Page 328.—27th November, 1761. John Mathews' will, farmer—Wife, Ann, 2 gold rings made by Mr. John Hanna; son, Edward, infant, tract called Poplar Spring, and a negro man named Fryday; daughters, Lettis, Jane, Ann, when 18; son, John, tract called Little Bottom; son, George, tract bought of John Maxwell. Executors, wife Ann and brothers Sampson and George. Teste: Wm. Patton, Joseph Gamwell, Richard Wilson. Proved, 22d March, 1764, by the witnesses. Ann is dead; other executors qualify, with Jno. Madison, Thos. Stewart.

Page 330.—30th September, 1763. James Underwood's estate appraised, by Bryan Russell, Jno. Davidson, Jas. Belshe.

Page 330.—24th March, 1764. Henry Horse's vendue bill recorded— To Charles Kilpatrick, Jno. Water, Jno. Malkem, Jas. Reyburn, Danl. Love, Chas. Dever, Edward McGarry, Wm. Dyer, Sarah Nare, Ezrah Shipman, Roger Dyer, Jno. Dunkell, Michael Props, Benj. Scott, Peter Nare, Elizabeth Wilfong, Henry Wagener, Christian Goose, Michael Rhine (Ryan), Adam Roudenboush, Michl. Mallow, James Knox, George Scott, Peter Smith.

Page 331.—Settlement of Henry Horse's estate, by Sarah Horse, recorded—Cash paid Leonard Seamon, Thos. Singleton's note of hand; cash paid Hans Michael Seamon; cash paid Christopher Hoofman; cash paid Adam Brudeback; cash paid Charles Wilson; cash paid Henry Shipler; cash paid Hannah Dyer; cash paid John Duncan. Credit by Leonard Seamon for 3 years' rent of the plantation, the valuation of the improvement on the plantation made by the deceased, Henry Horse, which is now conveyed to Robert Davis, who is married to the widow of said Henry.

Page 332.—21st November, 1763. John Murphy's estate appraised, by Thos. Stewart, Peter Wright. 3d April, 1763—Settlement of said estate, by Felix Gilbert, administrator, to Peter Wright for bringing in the goods from Fort Young.

Page 333.—24th March, 1764. Lawrence Huntsman's appraisement.

Page 333.—30th August, 1759. James Robertson's estate sold at vendue— Zachariah Smith, David McNeeley, Mathew Harper, Charles Mehafey, Saml. McCown, Timothy Cole, Thos. Baskins, Jno. Cloyd, Thos. Fulton, Robert Brown, Robt. Adair, Ben Herbert, George Woldridge, Nate Dunlap, Dan. Kidd, Thos. Galbreath.

Page 334.—25th June, 1757. James Moffett's will, farmer—Sons, John and James Moffett, the plantation to be divided between them by a line beginning at middle of Wm. Ledgerwood's pasture, cross the Hasle Bottom, thence to James Carr's land; to daughter, Elizabeth; daughter, Mary; son-in-law, John Berryhill, and his wife, Rachel Berryhill; son James is infant; daughters, Martha and Elizabeth; daughter, Jane; to son-in-law Wm. Campbell and his wife Margrett; to Ann Miller, 1 dollar. Executors, Wm. Ledgerwood and James Mitchell. To son-in-law James Berryhill. Teste: Wm. Edmiston, Arthur Hamilton, Robt. Alexander. Proved, 26th March, 1764, by Edmiston and Hamilton. Executors refuse to execute and

James Moffett is granted administration, who qualifies with Arthur Hamilton and Walter Smiley.

Page 337.—15th May, 1764. Alexander Painter's bond (with Henry Long) as administrator Catherine Painter.

Page 337.—18th September, 1761. Jacob Harman, Sr.'s will—To wife Catrina, tract adjoining where son Peter lives; to son Jacob, 134 acres, with a mill adjoining Peter Miller; to son Teawalt, 50 acres joining Shawp's line, against the Peaked Mountain; to son John's son, Peter Harmon; to son Peter; to 4 daughters; to daughter Elizabeth; to 5 grandchildren, Philip, William and Madlina Price; to the church near the Meeting House now built, 2 acres. Executors, wife Catrina and son Peter.—Jacob Harman. Teste: Archd. Huston, Jacob Parsinger, Peter Miller (German). Proved, 15th May, 1764, by the witnesses. Executors qualify, with George Man. Peter ( ) his mark. Cath. ( ) her mark.

Page 340.—19th June, 1764. Rebecca (mark) Gardner's bond (with (mark) Thos. Bradshaw, Francis Gardner) as administratrix of Thos. Gardner.

Page 341.—19th June, 1764. Richard Brush's appraisement (by Moses, John and Malcom McCown) recorded.

Page 341.—24th May, 1764. Jacob Harman's estate appraised, by Archd. Huston, Jacob Persinger, Peter Miller.

Page 343.—19th June, 1764. John Ramsey's bond (with Jno. Gay, Jas. McCoy) as guardian to Mary, John, Francis, Hugh, Rebecca, William, Elizabeth and Samuel McDonell, orphans of John McDonell.

Page 344.—19th June, 1764. John McCaslin's bond (with Henry Gay, Jas. McCoy) as administrator of Wm. Fitzjarrell.

Page 345.—23d November, 1763. Adam Wall's will—To sister, Apell (Apol ?), Wall, ½ of his estate which is 150 acres on New River, her part joining on Strupel's Creek; to brother's son, John Wall; to eldest brother's son, Andrew Wall; to Jacob Nomel (?); to sister, Apell Wall, £20 in Adam Harman, Sr.'s hands, and also what is due from Wm. Ingles for beef. Teste: James Calloway, Thos. Ingles, Ezel Morris. Proved, 19th June, 1764, by James Calloway. Apple Wall qualifies administratrix, with Pat. McCollom, Andrew Evans. (Apple's mark).

Page 346.—19th June, 1764. Susannah Hall's bond (with John Handley, Jno. Campbell), as administratrix of James Hall.

Page 347.—19th June, 1764. Augustine Price and Fredk. Ermantrout's bond (with Jacob Nicholas), as administratrix of Jno. Collier.

Page 348.—18th February, 1764. James Rusk's estate appraised by Robt. Campbell, Mathew Wilson, James McClearey.

Page 350.—30th September, 1763. Settlement of James Underwoods' estate, by Patk. Frazier. John Barrett.

Page 351.—22d June, 1764. Jane Thompson and Edward Thompson's bond (with Jno. Cartmill, Jno. Handley), as administrators of Thomas Thompson.

Page 352.—22d June, 1764. Felix Gilbert's bond (with Gabriel Jones), as administrator of John Loumer.

Page 353.—5th April, 1764. Archd. Clendenning's appraisement (Ann Clendenning, administratrix), by Jno. Fulton, Samuel Steel, Nathaniel Steel, Robert Alexander, 1 tomhawk, pipe, and pistole. Walker & Cabell's receipt for provisions; 1 cow wounded with an arrow. Carrington & Walker's receipt for provisions.

Page 353.—21st August, 1764. John Young's bond (with Jas. Young, Saml. Vance), as guardian (chosen), to Elizabeth Fulton, orphan of Jno. Fulton.

Page 354.—21st August, 1764. Elizabeth Wallace's bond (with Wm. and Jas. Bell), as administratrix of Samuel Wallace.

Page 355.—23d March, 1764. Andrew Steel's will—To son, Robert; to "my sun Saml. and Alexand (er) Moore, John Foulton and James Wardlaw, &c."; to daughters, Sarah and Elizabeth. Executors, Alex. Moore and Jas. Wardlaw. Teste: Hugh Wardlaw, Andrew Kennedy, Joseph Wardlaw, Wm. Wardlaw. Proved, 21st August, 1764, by Hugh and William Wardlaw and Kennedy.

Page 356.—21st August, 1764. Alex. Moore and Jas. Wardlaw's bond (with Wm. and Hugh Wardlaw, Andw. Kennedy), as executor of Andrew Steel above.

Page 356.—21st August, 1764. John Bowen's bond (with Jas. Edmiston, Edmond Crump), as administrators of Isaac Stover.

Page 367.—21st August, 1764. James Young's bond (Jno. Young, Jno. Young, Robt. Young, Jno. Kirkpatrick), as guardian (chosen) to Wm. and Hugh Young, orphans of Robt. Young, and (appointed) to Joseph Young, orphan of Robt. Young.

Page 358.—21st ———, 1764. Cathrine Painter's estate appraised by Adam Rider, Mathias Beder.

Page 358.—18th August, 1764. We, Amy Frazier, David Frazier, do make over the administration of Wm. Frazier, estate deceased unto James Frazier. Teste: Michael Coker, Robt. Frazier, Michl. Coager.

Page 358.—22d August, 1764. James Frazier's bond (with Michael Coager, Stephen Conrad), as administrator of Wm. Frazier.

Page 359.—22d August, 1764. Thomas Gardner's appraisement (by Jno. Finley, Jno. Buchanan, Jas. Hugart), recorded.

Page 360.—23d August, 1764. Settlement of George Mouse's estate, by Michael Mallow, recorded—1761, May 26th, paid by order by Fredk. Mouse, present administrator.

Page 360.—24th August, 1764. George Mathews' bond (with John Paxton), as guardian (appointed) to Thomas Rennix, orphan of Robt. Rennix.

Page 361.—31st August, 1764. Samuel Wallace's estate appraised by Robt. McClenachan, Jno. Henderson, Jos. Ewing.

Page 361.—20th November, 1764. William Black's bond (with Jas. Knox, Jno. Miller), as administrator of Alexander Black.

Page 362.—20th November, 1764. John McCollom's bond (with John Moore, Pat. McCollom), as administrator of Saml. Hunter.

Page 363.—20th November, 1764. John McFeeters' bond (with A. Thompson, Saml. McFeeters), as administrator of Alex. Crawford.

Page 364.—20th November, 1764. James and Mary Trimble's bond (with James Gilmore, Ben. Estill, Geo. Moffett, David Trimble), as administrators of John Trimble.

Page 365.—20th November, 1764. John Sheldon's appraisement (by Jos. English, Geo. Carpenter, Jas. Leard), and settlement of estate, recorded. Wm. Beard, administrator. To attendance given while sick, myself and family, 3 weeks. Cash paid Robert Elliott.

Page 365.—10th August, 1764. Adam Wall's estate, appraised by Wm. Poage, George Salling, Nathaniel ———.

Page 366.—11th October, 1764. William Fitzjarrell's estate appraised, by James McCoy, Thos. Gillespey, Chas. Donnally. Vendue bill recorded 21st November, 1764; to Jno. McCaslin, Thos. Spencer, Geo. Lewis, Francis Jackson; to Timothy Sullivan.

Page 367.—29th November, 1760 (?). Malcom Campbell's estate appraised by Wm. Bryan, Neal McNeal, James Neelley.

Page 368.—18th September, 1764. Additional appraisement of above. 9th October, 1764—Additional appraisement of above.

Page 369.—21st November, 1764. Joseph Lapsley's bond (with James McGavock) as guardian (chosen) to Mary McBride, orphan of Thomas McBride.

Page 369.—21st November, 1764. Settlement of John Scott's estate, by Jno. Davis and Judith, his wife, administrators, recorded—Paid Joseph Carpenter, guardian to Joseph, James and Jacob Scott. Cash paid Ellis Hogles, Michael Hider, Aaron Ryley, Jonathan Arnold, Thomas Parsons.

Page 370.—21st November, 1764. Silas Hart's (sheriff) bond (with Danl. Harrison, Andw. Erwin, Jno. Hopkins, Archd. Hopkins, Geo. Anderson, Wm. Anderson) to collect officers' fees.

Page 370.—21st November, 1764. Silas Hart's (sheriff) bond (with Danl. Harrison, Andw. Erwin, Jno. Hopkins, Archd. Hopkins, Geo. Anderson, Wm. Anderson) to collect taxes.

Page 371.—21st November, 1764. Silas Hart's (sheriff) bond (with Danl. Harrison, Andw. Erwin, Jno. Hopkins, Archd. Hopkins, Geo. Anderson, Wm. Anderson) to collect quit rents.

Page 371.—1st November, 1764. Andrew Steel's estate appraised, by Wm. McCutchen, Saml. Steel, John Fulton.

Page 372.—27th September, 1764. William Frazier's estate appraised, by Jacob Miller, Jacob Persinger, Archd. Huston—Henry Layburn's note.

Page 374.—9th April, 1764. Received of John Bowyer the sum of £588, 9, 9. in full of my wife's estate which he was guardian for, pay received by me.—Benjamin Hawkins.

Page 374.—24th November, 1764. Robert McClenachan's bond (with Thos. Bowyer, Robt. Breckinridge) as administrator of James Simpson.

Page 375.—24th November, 1764. John Cloyd's estate settlement and vendue bill recorded—1759, 24th November, 2 gallons brandy for ye vendue; 1760, 27th December, 5 shillings paid Francis Lewis (Lever?); 1761, paid for making a coat for James; 1761, 14th April, cash paid widow Gatlive; 1761, 6th April, cash to Joseph Robinson; 1763, 11th August, paid Robert Pepper, Jno. Armstrong for making 3 pair Suse; amount of necessary bought for children; 1759, 29th November, sold to Jas. Cloyd, Jr.—John Cloyd. Settled by David Cloyd, administrator.

Page 375.—25th November, 1763. Silas Hart's bond (with Wm. Thompson, Pat. Campbell) for collection of County proportion.

Page 376.—8th January, 1765. Samuel Hunter's estate appraised, by James Davis, Peter Wallace, Pat. McCollom—Debts due to estate, viz: Paul Whitey, Joseph Robinson, Margaret Clark, Geo. Clark, Thomas Foster, Jno. Smiley, Jno. McCollom, Andrew Smithers, Mathew Galbreath. Debts due by estate—To Mary Clark, Saml. Newberry, Richd. Woods.

Page 377.—19th March, 1765. James Hall's appraisement, recorded, by Thomas Feemster, John Lewis.

Page 377.—19th March, 1765. Alexander Black's appraisement (by Jno. McCreery, Jno. Carlile, Geo. Lewis): Money, silver money, gould money.

Page 379.—9th June, 1761. James Buchanan's will—To son Alexander Buchanan; to son Archibald Buchanan; to son John Buchanan; to sons Wm. and Robt. Buchanan; to wife Mary Buchanan; to sons Geo. and David Buchanan; to daughter Rebecky Buchanan. Executors, wife Mary and son Alexander. Teste: Daniel Nerrity, Jas. McCown, Wm. Scott. Proved, 19th March, 1765, by Daniel Harrison and Wm. Scott. Executors qualified, with Jno. Wallace, Jno. Buchanan. (Mary's mark).

Page 381.—7th January, 1765. James Eakin's will—To wife Agness; to daughter Mary; to son John, 30 acres that John's uncle Walter formerly lived on; to daughter Margaret; to son James; to young sons Andrew and Samuel; testator's brother, Walter Eakin, and Jno. Wardlaw. Teste: Jno. Wardlaw, Jno. Montgomery, Jno. Eakin. Executors, Agnes Eakin, Mathew Huston.

Page 382.—19th March, 1765. Executors above qualify, and will proved by the witnesses. Sureties, Wm. Lockridge, James Henry.

Page 382.—16th January, 1760 (33d year of Reign). James Cunningham's will, of Colony and Dominion of Virginia—To wife Margaret; to son Moses, infant; to Hugh Cunningham, 1 shilling; to daughter Elizabeth, 1 shilling; to James Cunningham, son to son Jacob; to John Cunningham, son to son Isaac; to daughter Mary; to daughters, each and every of them, 1 shilling. Executors, wife and son Moses. Teste: Malcom Allen, Robt. Bowen, Lilly Bowen. Proved, 19th March, 1765, by Malcom Allen and Lilly Bowen. Margaret is dead. Moses qualifies, with Hugh Cunningham, Geo. Dougherty.

Page 384.—23d February, 1764. Philip Charles Vangemunday's will (signed I. C. P. Van Gemunday), minister of the Gospel in the County of Augusta—To wife Mary Philip Charles Van Gemunday, the tract he bought from Jno. Frazier and joining Jas. Johnston, under North Mountain, 1 Testament and 1 Song Book, also 2d Bessell or Bible; to eldest son Henry, 2d Boy's Bible; to every son a small Bible; to wife and children, his high Dutch books. Latin and low Dutch books to be sold by auction. Bequeaths his son, George Frederick Peter, to Col. Peter Scholl. Bequeaths son, Charles Mathias, to Mathias Lear. Teste: Peter Scholl. Proved, 19th March, 1765, by Peter Scholl and Mathias Lear (Lair). Administration granted widow Mary, who qualifies with Peter Scholl, Jacob Persinger.

Page 385.—19th March, 1765. Archibald Huston's bond (with Pat. Frazier) as guardian (chosen) to Esther Boyd, orphan of Robert Boyd.

Page 386.—19th March, 1765. Francis and Alexander Gardner's bond for Francis Gardner's guardianship (appointed) to Robt. Boyd, orphan of Robt. Boyd.

Page 386.—1st February, 1765. John McNeill's will, late Major in Virginia Regiment—All estate to be sold and proceeds put in hands of friend, Mr. Andrew Sproul, of Gosport, merchant, to and for the sole use and benefit of my father if he should be living at the time of my death; if dead, then to be given to brother Hector McNeill, on condition that he get his discharge from the Army within 12 months; if Hector refuse, then to be given to Aunt Henrietta McNeill. To Miss Jenny McClenachan, her choice of the horses he bought from her brother when they came from Carolina; also an antient family white stone ring, set in gold, which I hope she will wear as a memorial of the great esteem and affection I have long had for her. To good friends, Colonel Andrew Lewis and George Weedon—to former, best set of pistols; to latter, his sword. Hopes the following will accept and wear, for the sake of him who has long esteemed them, a plain mourning golden ring, viz: Thos. Lewis, Jno. Madison, Gabriel Jones, my cousin, Annabella McNeill, and Mr. Andrew Sproul. Executor, Col. Andrew Lewis. Teste: Gabriel Jones, Felix Gilbert, Jno. Madison. Proved, 19th March, 1765, by Jones and Madison. Executor qualifies, with Jno. Madison.

Page 388.—9th March, 1765. Alexander Crawford's estate appraised, by Jno. Trimble, Geo. Berry, Jas. McClearey.

Page 389.—19th March, 1765. John Trimble's appraisement (by Jno. Finley, Jno. Trimble, Jas. Sayers), recorded—Two negroes, 2 bound servants; cash due by Henry Cresswell, Chas. Clendenning; to Jno. Price's service under the command of Capt. Wm. Christian, 184 days.

Page 390.—19th March, 1765. Saml. Henderson, executor's account of estate of Hugh Thompson, recorded—Paid James Allen for the coffin; to the widow, for the gold left her; to Eleanor Thompson, the daughter, her legacy; to James Thompson, his legacy; to Hugh Russell, his legacy; to Geo. Russell, his legacy; to Isabella Russell, her legacy; to Rachel Russell, her legacy; to James Leeper, his legacy; to Hugh Leeper, his legacy; to Elizabeth Leeper, her legacy; to Mary Scott, her legacy.

Page 391.—20th March, 1765. Settlement of Randall McDonall's estate, recorded—Due by estate to, viz: John Pleasant, merchant; Wm. Bean.

Page 392.—20th March, 1765. John Craven's bond (with Abraham Smith) as guardian (appointed) to Roger and John Dyer, orphans of Wm. Dyer.

Page 392.—26th March, 1765. Robt. Finley's estate appraisement (appraised 1764 by Michl. Bowyer, Wm. Crow, Thos. Bowyer), recorded.

Page 392.—21st May, 1765. James Eakin's appraisement, recorded, by Thos. Beard, Jno. Lusk, Wm. McCanless.

Page 393.—21st May, 1765. Jno. Dunkle's bond (with Michl. Mallow, Geo. Hammer) as guardian (chosen) to Elizabeth, orphan of George Mouse.

Page 394.—27th August, 1764. Abraham Bess's (Biss) will—To son James, infant, 131 acres adjoining James Johnson; to eldest daughter Margaret, infant; to eldest of surviving children at Margaret's death; tract in Forks of James to be sold. Wife Isabell Biss, executrix. Teste: Joseph Cloyd, Wm. Beard, Jno. Bradley. Proved, 21st May, 1765, by Cloyd and Beard. Isabella qualifies (her mark), with Jno. Smith, David Mitchell.

Page 395.—21st May, 1765. John Archer's bond (with Geo. Skileron) as administrator of Thomas Davis.

Page 396.—20th May, 1765. The within account is given upon oath by us of ye improvements and effects found on John Lewis' land.—Thomas Turk, James Turk.

Page 396.—22d May, 1765. Joseph Cloyd's bond (with James McGavock, Jas. Cloyd) as administrator of Saml. Flowers.

Page 397.—14th May, 1765. Received of Samuel McCutchen the full balance of a bond £8 bearing date February, 1763, which he sayeth is lost.—William Martin. Teste: Pat. Martin, Wm. McCutchen.

Page 397.—23d May, 1765. Eliza Moser's bond (with Danl. Smith, Philip Harper) as administratrix of Eliza Moser (?).

Page 397.—15th May, 1765. James Cunningham's estate appraised, by Jno. McKee, Jno. Gilmore, Robt. Erwin.

Page 398.—24th May, 1765. Andrew Smith's appraisement, by Jos. Skidmore, Carl. Gammen, Michael Mallow—24 apple trees.

Page 399.—24th May, 1765. Jacob Martin's bond (with James Burnsides) as administrator of Jacob Martin.

Page 400.—27th March, 1765. Col. John McNeill's estate appraised, by Alex. McClenachan, Wm. Cunningham, John McClenachan, William Crow. 25th May, 1765, 1 negro woman appraised.

Page 403.—18th June, 1765. James Lockhart's bond (with Sampson Mathews, Jno. Anderson) as collector of that part of the Public Levy to be raised in Augusta.

Page 403.—27th October, 1760. John Colyer's will—To wife Sisley; to son Alexander, 400 acres adjoining James Davis; to son John, place testator now lives on (infant); to son Moses, tract called Boyd's Entry; to son Aaron; to son (daughter?) Margaret. Executors, wife Sisley and James Gilmore. Teste: Jno. Summers, Jno. Wiley. Proved, 20th August, 1765, by the witnesses. Cicely (her mark) qualifies, with Jas. Trimble, John Summers.

Page 404.—15th June, 1765. Thomas Jones' estate appraised, by Jno. Logan, Wm. Kennedy, Saml. Steel.

Page 405.—Whereas a certain difference happened to arise between my wife and Thomas Foster's wife, and unfortunately to me I did espouse my wife's cause, for which I am sorry, and in order to satisfy him, the said Thomas and his wife Elizabeth, we do hereby acknowledge that we have injouresly wronged her, the said Elizabeth Foster, in imputing stealing to her, and by these presents do declare that we are sorry for what we have done and said in regard to that. Given under our hands this 9th day of August A. D., 1765.—Saml. Newberry, Rosanna Newberry. Teste: Jas. Trimble, Jno. Paxton, Joseph Walker, James Gilmore.

Page 405.—6th March, 1765. Henry Kirkham's will—Wife, Mary; son, Robert, the land at the Great Spring; son, Samuel, a mare bought from Edward Gill; son, Michael, 50 acres between John Collier (Colyer) and John Wiley; son, John, 100 acres near John Collier's (Colyer) on the Dry Creek side; sons, Henry and Joseph, infants, land testator lives on to be divided by Richard Woods and Jno. Summers; to daughter Jane; to infant in wife's womb; daughters, Margaret and Elizabeth. If any of the heirs by former wife die infants. Executors, wife, Peter Wallace and Jno. Summers. Peter Wallace has authority to bind son John to his brother Samuel. Teste: Robt. Kirkham, Alex. Collier, Michl. Kirkham. Proved, 20th August, 1765, by Robert and Michael Kirkham. Peter Wallace refuses to execute. Others qualify, with Alex. Dale, Wm. Scott, Robt. Young.

Page 407.—20th August, 1765. James Buchanan's appraisement (by David Hays, Jno. Wallace, Archibald Reaugh), recorded.

Page 408.—20th August, 1765. John Peary's bond (with John and Wm. Jamison) as guardian (chosen) to Thomas Peary, orphan of Thomas Peary.

Page 408.—19th August, 1765. Thomas and Andrew Lewis enter 400 acres on the northwest side of the Warm Springs Survey, and 400 acres on southwest side of same, and 400 acres on south side Warm Springs Mountain.—Wm. Preston.

Page 408.—21st August, 1765. James McDowell's bond (with William Bowyer, Alex. McClenachan) as guardian (chosen) to Jno. Kirkham, orphan of Henry Kirkham.

Page 409.—20th August, 1765. Margaret Robinson's bond (with Wm. Bowyer, James Robertson, Wm. Christian) as administrator of Wm. Robinson.

Page 410.—20th August, 1765. Susanna Shaddon's (Shawdon) bond (with Wm. Preston, Jas. Snodgrass) as administratrix of Mathias Shaddon.

Page 411.—20th August, 1765. Mary Magdalene Kimberland's bond (with Jos. Robinson) as administratrix of Jacob Kimberland.

Page 412.—20th August, 1765. William Preston's bond (with Chas. Lewis) as administrator of John Donaley.

Page 413.—20th August, 1765. John Finley's bond (with David Trimble) as guardian (chosen) to Mary Gardner, orphan of Thomas Gardner.

Page 413.—21st August, 1765. David Nelson's bond (with John Madison) as administrator of John Nelson.

Page 414.—21st August, 1765. Felix Gilbert's settlement of estate of John Williams recorded.

Page 415.—21st August, 1765. Susanna Cochran's bond (with John Stewart) as administrator of John Cochran.

Page 416.—16th August, 1765. Estate of Elizabeth Moser, deceast, daughter of Geo. Moser, deceast, appraised by Peter Vaneman.

Page 416.—This day Lanty Armstrong maed oath that sum time in the fall of the year 1764 the deponent and John Neeley, Jr., was conversing about Mrs. Margaret Cloyd, the deponent asked said Neeley if he was not going to be married—Mrs. Cloyd. Neeley replyed not; that she was not the gurl he took her to be; that he had seen her drunk sundry times and one in particular at his father's, and this deponent further sayeth not. Sworn before me this 4th day of May, 1765.—Lanty Armstrong. Robert Breckinridge.

Page 416.—The deponent being in company with John Neeley, Jr., on the 1st January, 1763, and, after some discourse, asked said Neeley if Miss Margaret Cloyd and him was not going to be married; Neeley replyed not, for she was losing her character. The deponent asked how. Neeley replyed she was too much given to liquor and that she was seen several times when it was plenty so taken she was obliged to leave the company, and further sayeth not, June 8th, 1765.—James McAfee. Samuel McDowell.

Page 416.—Augusta S. S. This day John Neeley, Jr., made oath before us he never said or reported that Margaret Cloyd, daughter of David Cloyd, was guilty of getting drunk; nor that Lanty Armstrong ever had any criminal conversation with her; nor that he had of his own knowledge the least foundation for reporting such things of her in case he had reported them. As witness my hand, John Neeley, Jr. Sworn before us April 17th, 1765. Robert Breckinridge, William Preston.

Page 417.—23d August, 1765. Sale bill of John **Reager's** estate, recorded—To Edward McGary, Jno. Hardman, David Barry, Samuel Patterson, James Magill, Geo. Scott, Hugh Maglaken, Daniel Henderson, David Nelson, Peter Steenberger. Settlement of said estate by Mathew Patton. Paid Jno. Wright for vendue cryer. Paid Jacob Everman, Jno. Dunkle, Hans Colley. Retained in my hands as guardian of ——— Haws.

Page 418.—30th May, 1765. Andrew **Erwin's** will, farmer—To wife Ann, to son Francis (unmarried), executors, entire estate. Teste: Andw. Scott, Saml. Corry, Benj. Erwin. Brother Edward and brother Francis to be overseers. Proved, 15th October, 1765, by Scott and Erwin. Executors qualify (Ann's mark), with John King, Samuel Patterson.

Page 420.—15th October, 1765. Jane **McCown's** bond (with Robt. Young, Jno. Young, Peter Wiley) as administratrix of Moses McCown.

Page 421.—27th September, 1765. John **Cochran's** estate appraised, by Jno. Anderson, Thos. Stevenson, Jas. Allen, Sr., James Allen, Jr.

Page 422.—12th October, 1765. Thomas **Thompson's** estate appraised, by James, Robert and Henry Gay—One nursery of young apple trees, etc.

Page 423.—19th September, 1765. Henry **Kirkham's** estate appraised, by Jno. Wiley, Peter Wallace, Wm. McKee.

Page 423.—24th September, 1765. Appraisement (by Peter Wallace, Jas. Bets, Wm. McKee) of John **Collier's** estate, recorded.

Page 424.—15th October, 1765. Thomas **Lorrimer's** bond (with Felix Gilbert, Jno. Botkin) as administrator of John Lorrimer.

Page 425.—6th October, 1765. Samuel **Wallace's** will—Daughter, Jennet; to wife and son Joseph (if wife has a child); to son Samuel's 2 children; son Robert to have James Ralston and teach him to be a shoemaker. Executors, wife and James Sayers, Jr. Teste: Morris (Maurice) O'Freel, Wm. Magill. Proved, 15th October, 1765, by the witnesses. Sayers refuses to execute. Widow Elizabeth qualifies (her mark), with Sampson Mathews.

Page 426.—27th April, 1765. William **Robertson's** will—To wife and children. Executors, wife Isabella and son John. Teste: Alex. Walker, James Robson, James Moore. Proved, 16th October, 1765, by the witnesses. Executors (Isabella her mark) qualify, with Alex. Walker, Jno. Buchanan.

Page 428.—16th October, 1765. George **Skileron's** bond (with John Madison) as guardian (appointed) to John Wall, orphan of John Wall.

Page 428.—16th October, 1765. Robert **Graham's** estate appraised, by Thos. Feemster, Jno. Hicklin, Jno. Carlile.

Page 428.—7th October, 1765. John **Nelson's** estate appraised, by Jno. Cravens, Jno. Ralston, ——— Metzger (German).

Page 429.—16th October, 1765. Capt. Daniel **Smith's** settlement of estate of Robert Harrison allowed and recorded—Paid George Skilerton (Skileron?); paid Edmond Pendleton, Joseph Langdon, Jno. Stewart, Felix Ohlpman, Capt. Francis Thornton, Solomon Turpin, George Lindwad, Christian Groob, Christian Wilson, Henry Flesher, Doctor Caulval, Peter Watkins, John Crow, Jeremiah Ragen, William Grad, Wm. Minter, Jno. Phears, Isaac Johnston. Sale bill of above estate to, viz: Dennis Henry, Wm. Marks, Wm. McMullen, Toms Thomas, Capt. Waran, Arthur Trader, Neil Linch, Jno. Gum, Ezeriah Worden, Zebulon (Binenran) Harrison. To attendance and necessaries found for the deceased during the time he remained sick at my house, where he did from the 10th February to 25th May, 1761, being 3 months and 15 days.

Page 433.—18th October, 1765. David Looney's bond (with James McDowell) as guardian (appointed) to Margaret Looney, orphan of Daniel Looney.

Page 435.—21st October, 1765. Sale bill recorded of William Culberts, by Wm. Gilmore, administrator, to, viz: Mary Brown, Margaret McCown, Patrick Denny, Andw. Fitzpatrick, Mary Boyls, Mary Ann Crawford, Jas. Logan, Wm. McCanless, David Guin, Jane Scot, Wm. Ooley, Jno. Selone, Jas. McCampbell, Richard McGee, Jean Muldrach, Alex. Dale, Chas. Boyles. Paid William Naper, Jannet Gilmore, Samuel Norwood, Blakeley Brush, Isabell Summers, Elizabeth Woods, Mary McCown, Sarah Davis, John Hays, Cryer of Vendue; James McNabb.

Page 436.—22d October, 1765. Estate of James Leister in account with David Stewart and Saml. Cowdon, administrators, recorded.

Page 437.—23d December, 1763. Joshua Mathews' estate appraised, by ———.

Page 438.—12th August, 1762. James Boreland's estate appraised, by Jno. Shields, Saml. Steel, Wm. Teas.

Page 439.—22d October, 1765. Joshua Mathew's estate settlement, by George Mathews, recorded—25th December, 1764, paid Edward Sharp; 16th March, 1765, paid Darby Shay; 7th June, 1765, paid Benj. Bennett; 23d August, paid Jas. Hartgrove; November, 1764, paid Wm. Saxton, Alex. Baggs, Danl. Goodwin, Stephen Arnold, Sarah Sproul, John Sawyers; paid George Darr, per Col. Preston. Contra—19th October, 1764, by Capt. Audley Paul's bill; Jacob Click's; Jeremiah Dennis' bill; Edmond Crump's; Benj. Watson's.

Page 441.—22d October, 1765. Silas Hart's bond (with Wm. Preston, Jno. Thomas) as sheriff, to collect County proportion.

Page 442.—22d October, 1765. Settlement recorded of estate of John Mathews, by Sampson and George Mathews—19th July, 1764, to 1 bad double loon (doubloon) passed by Jas. Huston, and returned; 17th November, paid Stephen Arnold a debt due his son James; 4th December, paid James Trimble for holding 2 inquests and constables' fees; paid Alex. Walls. Contra—18th April, 1764, by gold sold; 1st September, 1764, by burned silver, by Randall Lafone (?), by Christian Miliron (uncertain whether can be got).

Page 443.—22d October, 1765. Margaret Leeper's settlement, recorded of estate of James Leeper—Paid to the heirs, viz: To Isiah Curry, Andrew Leeper, Wm. McMullen, Geo. Leeper, Jno. Seawright, Nicholas Leeper, Jno. Leeper, Margaret Leeper, Jr., Saml. Henderson, Jas. Leeper, Jr., in his life time.

Page 444.—20th May, 1766. Margaret Clark's bond (with Wm. McCutchen, Jno. Clark) as administratrix of Wm. Clark.

Page 445.—30th October, 1765. Moses McCown's estate appraised, by Richd. Woods, Peter Wallace, Wm. Davis—A certificate for 161 days patrolling at 1/10 per day. 4th March, 1766. 2d appraisement by same—Wm. Bunting owes, Thos. Bates owes, Charles Lockhart owes, Mathew Arbuckle owes, Walter Cowdon (supposed insolvent).

Page 446.—7th November, 1765. The widdow Wallace's (Saml. Wallace) estate appraised, by Jno. Trimble, Maurice O'Freel, Jas. Sawyers.

Page 447.—6th December, 1753. Sale bill of Nicholas Trout's estate to, viz: Jno. Love, Jno. Hales, Patrick Wilson, Jno. Walles, Valentine Pence, Wm. Logan, Gasper Faught, Jacob Sink, Andw. Faught, Evan Evans, Pat. Kinney, widow Trout, Nicholas Millberry, Thos. Crawford, Geo. Trout, Jno. Craig. Setttlement of above estate by Geo. Trout, administrator, recorded 21st May, 1766—Cash paid for liquor at the vendue, 5 gallons at 3/; cash paid for liquor at a grubbing frolick, 6 quarts at 9 per quart, £0.5.6.; cash paid for 6 quarts liquor at the funeral, £0.4.6.; paid Teter Couts, Bernard Man. Contra—Received from John Capebritton.

Page 448.—10th September, 1761. John Bellfaught's estate sold at vendue—To Catrina Faught; to Henry Lynor; to Andrew Faught; to Peter Funk; to Caspar Faught; to Henry Colar; to Elizabeth Bruester; to James Waite; to Alex. Kile; to Geo. Trout; to Robt. Reyburn; to Jno. Hines, Geo. Martin, Peter Miller, Robt. Stevens, Edward Rutledge, James Cover, David Menerley. Cash paid Christian Clements for 1 year's board of the widow. Balance due the legatees to be equally divided between Andrew Faught, Casper Faught, and the wife.—Christian Clements. Recorded, 21st May, 1766.

Page 450.—21st May, 1766. William Martin's bond (with David Trimble, Jas. Burnsides) as administrator of Hugh Martin.

Page 451.—21st May, 1766. Felix Gilbert's bond (with Gabriel Jones) as administrator of Geo. Bowman.

Page 452.—19th August, 1766. Mary Owler's bond (with Nichs. Null, Calem Price) as administrator of Wm. Owler.

Page 452.—11th October, 1765. Felty Goil's will—(Goil vid Kyle—Coil—Gile)—To wife, Margaret; eldest son, Gabriel; son, Jacob; son, George; son, Martin, 130 acres; to daughters Barbary and Elizabeth (unmarried). Executors, Geo. Hammer and son George. Teste: Geo. Teter, Paul Teter, George Woldridge. Proved, 19th August, 1766, by Geo. and Paul Teter. Executors qualify (George his mark), with Henry Stone and Sebastian Hover.

Page 454.—19th August, 1766. Hugh Martin's appraisement (by Wallace Estill, Dawson Wade, Saml. Wilson), recorded.

Page 454.—19th August, 1766. William Sampson's bond (with Stephen Trigg, Is. Christian) as administrator of Henry Fields.

Page 455.—25th March, 1760. Thomas Thompson's will—Brother, James Thompson, 200 yekers which belonged to my father, Jno. Thompson. Executors, Wm. Johnson and Jno. Gray. Teste: Andw. McClure, Isabell Hutchinson, Wm. Logan. Proved, 19th August, 1766, by the witnesses. Executors qualified, with Alex. McDonall, Wm. Martin.

Page 457.—19th August, 1766. Vendue bill recorded of Wm. Woods' estate—James Thomas, David Berry, Samuel Samples, Jeremy Harrison. Settlement of above estate, by Thos. Gregg, administrator. Paid Joseph Skidmore, Moses Semples. Credit by balance of pay received of Capt. Abraham Smith.

Page 457.—9th July, 1766. David Viers' (Viars—Viurs—Via—Wivs) will—Wife, executrix, 1 bond due for John Lancaster, and 1 note of Henry Harris.—Frances Viers. Teste: Chas. Knight, Edward Warner, Adam Reaburn. Proved, 19th August, 1766, by Warner and Reaburn. Frances Via qualifies executrix (her mark), with James Beard, David Lard (Laird).

Page 459.—9th November, 1765. Wm. Robertson's estate appraised, by Jno. Moore, Jas. Walker, Alex. Walker.

Page 460.—19th August, 1766. Andrew Miller's bond (with Israel Christian, Benj. Hawkins) as administrator of Jno. Miller.

Page 461.—4th April, 1766. John Henderson's will, farmer—Wife, Rose; son, William; daughters, if either die, the other to enjoy her share. Teste: John Davidson, Robt. Finley. Executors, brother James and wife's brother, John. Proved, 20th August, 1766, by the witnesses. James Henderson and John Finley qualified executors, with Adam Dean and Wm. Finley.

Page 462.—21st August, 1766. Andrew Boyd's bond (with Andw. Lewis, Wm. Preston, Robt. Breckinridge, Wm. Ingles, Benj. Hawkins, David Robinson) as administrator of Alexander Boyd.

Page 463.—The full account of the estate of Mary Gardner paid to me by her former guardian's widow.—John Finley. Recorded, 21st August, 1766.

Page 463.—21st August, 1766. Wm. McBride's bond (with Jno. Bowyer) as guardian (chosen) to Joseph McBride, orphan of Thomas McBride.

Page 463.—21st August, 1766. Mathew Shaddon's appraisement, recorded.

Page 464.—22d August, 1766. Thomas Davis' appraisement (by Jas. Reyburn, Jos. Reaburn, Wm. Mathews), recorded.

Page 464.—23d August, 1766. Daniel Davidson's estate settlement, by administrator, recorded—Paid Saml. Lusk for Smith's work; paid John Ridle for linen; paid David Jones for assisting to take care of creatures; to trouble and expenses in going to the Jerseys.

Page 465.—18th November, 1766. Andw. Lewis' bond (with Jno. Buchanan, Jno. Bowyer) as sheriff to collect officers' fees, &c.

Page 467.—Same as above, to collect quit rents. Same as above, to collect taxes.

Page 467.—18th November, 1766. Robert Brown's bond (with Jno. Finley, Saml. Love) as guardian (appointed) to Francis and Saml. Gardner, orphans of Thomas Gardner.

Page 467.—25th September, 1766. Alexander Boyd's estate appraised, by Francis Smith, Wm. Bryan, James Roberts.

Page 474.—28th September, 1765. William Frazier's estate sold at vendue—To, viz: Hance Magot, Wm. Hook, Wm. Patterson, John Ferrell, Jacob Herrberrger, Michael Coker. Settlement of above estate, by James Frazier—4 gallons liquor at the funeral, 6½ gallons for vendue.

Page 477.—19th November, 1766. Thomas Joans' (Jones) estate settlement, by Jas. Wardlaw, recorded.

Page 477.—19th November, 1766. William Herbert's bond (with Israel Christian, Andw. Boyd) as administrator of Robt. Andrews.

Page 478.—19th November, 1766. William Clark's appraisement (by Thos. Berry, Robt. Gay, Saml. McCutchen), recorded—One smoothing iron; 2 boxes of silver and other bullion and cash. James Ward, Dr.; Jno. Cowarden, Dr.; David Williams, debtor.

Page 479.—19th November, 1766. Daniel Pierie's (Pierce?) bond (with Peter Hog) as administrator of Jacob Goodpasture.

Page 480.—19th November, 1766. William McCutchen's bond (with Andw. Hays) as guardian (appointed) to Jno. Duncan, orphan of James Duncan.

Page 481.—19th November, 1766. Thomas Thompson's further appraisement (by Robt., James and Henry Gay), recorded.

Page 481.—19th November, 1766. Henry Gay's bond (with Jas. Frazier) as guardian (chosen) to David Moore, orphan of David Moore.

Page 481.—24th September, 1766. John Henderson's estate appraised, by Jno. Poage, Jno. Ramsey, Jno. Graham.

Page 482.—17th October, 1766. William Oaler's estate appraised, by Michl. Coger, Jacob Shull, Jno. Fults.

Page 483.—25th September. David Via's estate appraised, by Samuel Henderson, Wm. Lamme, Andw. Leeper.

Page 484.—20th November, 1766. George Robinson's appraisement, recorded (by Jas. and Saml. Robinson, and Martha McCormick, late Robinson, executors)—Paid Francis Livers, Francis Delaney, Robt. McGitre, James Hollis. Credit by Danl. McCormick, Adam Beard, Robert Galloway.

Page 485.—21st November, 1766. Settlement recorded of Robert Finley's estate, by James Finley—Paid Saml. Rippy, expenses travelling from Carlile, expenses traveling from Staunton to New London, from New London to Halifax; paid Jas. Bratton; paid Mr. Ravelet, Mr. Finney, Nathanl. Gilliland; paid Jno. Ramsey, Calfpasture; James Branan. Contra—1764, by Cash received of Wm. Carroll, Middle River; by cash received of Wm. McFeeters, Sr.

Page 486.—21st November, 1766. Danl. Smith, executor of John Smith, Jr., settles his accounts and recorded—Cash paid Abraham Smith, his legacy; cash paid Henry Smith, John King; cash paid Hanna Dyer; to going 3 times to Wms. Burg to attend ye Assembly getting my brother's pay allowed; to cash received of Col. Smith, being the pay of my brother while in the Service.

Page 486.—24th November, 1766. Andrew Lewis' bond (with Geo. Moffett) for collection of County proportion.

Page 487.—20th January, 1767. John Colley (Cawley), aged 20 years, deposes, that being in the presence and company of James Hughs, deceased, during the time of his last sickness in the dwelling house of the said James, he heard him say that should will and bequeath by his last testament all his substance that he was possessed of to his wife Euphemia during her natural life, except a house and lot to his daughter Euphemia, as also the wearing apparel of his first wife, mother of Margt. Kennedy, which he should give and bequeath to the said Margaret, together with her mother's riding saddle, and that this conversation was had with the said decedant James about two days before his ———, which happened on Thursday morning, the 18th inst., and further sayeth not. Randolph Lockhart, aged 30 years, deposes to same effect. Proved, 20th January, 1767. Administration granted widow Euphemia and Sampson Mathews.

Page 488.—20th January, 1767. Above bond with Peter Hog and George Mathews.

Page 488.—17th March, 1767. Jane Davis and Saml. Davis' bond (with Jno. McKee, Robt. Young) as administrators of Jas. Davis.

Page 489.—17th March, 1767. Tasker Tosh's appraisement (by David Bryan, Wm. Bryan, Wm. Culton), recorded.

Page 491.—12th November, 1765. Malcom Campbell's estate appraised, by ———. Word "filly" appears at this time.

Page 491.—17th March, 1767. James Davis' bond (with Wm. McBride, Jno. Thompson) as administrator of John Cryton (Carington).

Page 492.—24th August, 1761 (Record says 1760) and in the first year of the Reign, &c., George III. Charles Campbell's will, of Manor Beverley—To son, William, tract called Asp Bottom on middle branch of Indian River, commonly called Holstein's River; to 3 eldest daughters, Elizabeth, Jean and Margaret, infants, tract called Campbell's Choice on north branch of Holstein's River; to daughter, Ann Campbell, tract called Papa Bottom on North Branch Holstein. Executrix, Margaret. Teste: David Robinson, Jno. Buchanan, Elizabeth Buchanan. Proved, 17th March, 1767, by Jno. Buchanan and David Robinson. Margaret (her mark) qualifies, with Wm. Christian, Robt. Campbell, Jno. Ramsey, Daniel McNaire.

Page 495.—17th March, 1767. Saml. Pepper's bond (with James (his mark) Ledderdale, Jno. Craig) as administrator of James Carty.

Page 496.—17th March, 1767. Vendue recorded of Francis McCown's estate to, viz: Wm. Naper, David Dredan (vid Dryden), James Bets, Richd. Bush, Pat. McCampbell, Wm. Taylor, David Gum, Wm. Napen (Naper?), David Quin, William Wooley, Wm. Culbert. Settlement of above estate—Paid Jno. McNabb, Francis Randalls, Robt. McKeney, Saml. Gest, James Telford.

Page 498.—17th March, 1767. Robert Cravens' estate settlement, by the executors, recorded—Paid Saml. Monsey (?), Rev. Alex. Miller, Wm. Logan, Robt. Belshe.

Page 500.—19th February, 1767. James Trimble, Assistant Surveyor, enters 400 acres on Bratton's Run from Dickinson's Path down the Branch, and 400 below the above, and 300 joining, and 200 adjoining another of Trimble's tract on Camp Mountain Run above Lawrence's Mill Place.

Page 500.—9th March, 1767. Same enters 200 acres on lines of David Trimble's land, 400 acres joining the Chalk Banks, including the Ponds, 16th March, 1767.

Page 500.—18th March, 1767. Robert Breckinridge's bond (with Malcom Allen, Richd. Woods) as guardian (chosen) to Robert Sayers, orphan of Alex. Sayers.

Page 501.—18th March, 1767, recorded. Valentine Pence's estate to Peter Miller, executor—Paid Henry Long, who married one of Valentine's daughters, her legacy; paid Jacob and Adam Pence, their legacies; paid Jacob Nicholas as exla of Mathew Sharpe. Received from Conrad Peterfish, Jno. Counts, Christian Teter, Jacob Moyer, Christopher Reisling, Nicholas Null.

Page 503.—18th December, 1766. David Bryan's will, of Roanoke—Executors, wife, brother William and John McClung; to daughter, Mary, infant; to son, William; to son, David; has sold tract to William Cox, deed to be made to him. Teste: Thos. Barnes, Thos. Lloyd, Wm. Bryan. Proved, 18th March, 1767, by Barnes and Bryan. Elizabeth (her mark), the others refusing, qualifies, with Wm. Christian, Walter Crockett, Robt. Breckinridge.

Page 506.—20th November, 1766. Credit due to Capt. Robt. Bratton on account of Capt. James Dunlap's estate since his last settlement with the Court.

Page 506.—12th January, ——. Joseph Crockett's will, farmer—Executors, sons Walter and Joseph; wife, Jean, one-third of land he lives on on South Fork of Roanoke joining Mr. Matteson's line; son, Hugh; son, Walter; son, Joseph; son, Samuel, survey on Cedar Run above Willey's plantation; son, Robert, tract on head of Peak Creek, and a tract on head of Camp Run above Saml. Mountgomery's; to Walter and Joseph and Robert, tract on head of South Fork of Holston River; to daughter, Martha; daughter, Elizabeth; daughter, Agness; daughter, Mary. Teste: Phil Love, James Bryan, Joseph Colven. Proved, 17th March, 1767, by Love and Bryan. Walter Crockett qualifies (Joseph refuses), with Wm. Christian, David Looney, Thos. Barnes.

Page 509.—23d August, 1767. David Stewart's will—To wife Margaret, and to her oldest daughter, Mary Pall, 1 tract lying over James River, 100 acres; to son, John; to daughter, Sebing (?), 219½ acres purchased from Andw. Johnston; to daughter, Elizabeth, tract on Round Oak and part of a lot in Staunton (no buildings on it) between Saml. Cowdon and me, and the lot that Jno. Stuart now lives on to be sold; to son, John, plantation testator lives on with 2 negros, goot from Greor formerly Patrick Martins. Executors, George Mathis and Wm. Lewis. Teste: Joseph Ray. Proved, 19th March, 1767, wholly in testator's handwriting. Executors refuse. Administration granted George Mathews and Andw. Lewis, who qualify with Sampson Mathews, Robert Breckinridge.

Page 511.—20th March, 1767. Settlement of Johnston Hill's estate, recorded—Paid James Haith; credit by Aney Hill, John Pheus, Daniel Ponder, Chas. Davis, Hugh McGary, Wm. McMullen, Robt. Hill, Chas. Smith, Peter Watkins, Solomon Turpin, James Lawrence.

Page 513.—7th January, 1767. Jacob Goodpasture's estate appraised, by Thomas Poage, Daniel Dennison, Wm. Wallace.

Page 513.—24th January, 1767. James Hughes' estate appraised, by Robt. McClenachan, Wm. Crow, Robt. Reed, Walter Cunningham.

ABSTRACTS OF WILLS OF AUGUSTA COUNTY VIRGINIA.

AUGUSTA COUNTY COURT.

Will Book No. 4.

Page 1.—15th May, 1767. James Davis' estate appraised, by Jno. McCollom *et als.* Neal Casedy's bond; Martha Goldbreath; Robt. Shannan's bond; bonds of, viz: Jno. Neeley, Jno. Wiley, Andw. Smithers, Moses Coiler (Collier?).

Page 4.—19th May, 1767. John McClenachan's bond (with Jno. McCreerey) as guardian to Elizabeth Edwards, orphan of John Edwards.

Page 5.—9th September, 1766. John Miller's estate appraised, by James Rowland, Saml. McRoberts *et als.*

Page 7.—4th May, 1767. Dower assigned to Margaret Leeper in land of James Leeper, allowing Hugh Donotho the benefit of the timber on the Bigg Spring.

Page 7.—19th May, 1767. James Buchanan's estate settlement, by David Ree, recorded.

Page 8.—19th May, 1767. Jacob Lockhart's bond (with Mathew Arbuckle, Isaac Ward) as administrator of Chas. Lockhart.

Page 9.—19th September, 1766. Henry Field's estate appraised, by James Neeley, Wm. and Edward Carvin—Paid accounts to, viz: Wm. Simpson, Stephen Trigg, Henry Paullen.

Page 11.—13th May, 1767. John Creighton's estate appraised by Wm. McKee, Robt. Young, Jno. McKee.

Page 12.—20th May, 1767. Mathew Harper's bond (with Andrew Russell, Wm. Jameson) as administrator of Michael Harper.

Page 13.—20th May, 1767. John Miller's estate settled by Israel Christian and Andrew Miller, executors—To Dr. Thos. Loyd.

Page 14.—9th September, 1766. Valentine Giles' estate appraised, by Jonas Friend, Geo. Dise, Michl. Mallow: Due by Geo. Teter, Francis Jackson, Henry Peskels, Moses Elsworth, Youst Hinkele.

Page 15.—25th May, 1767. Andrew Lewis' bond (with Abraham Smith) to collect the public levy.

Page 16.—7th April, 1767. Col. David Stewart's estate appraised by &c ———.

Page 18.—18th August, 1767. Nathaniel Evans' bond (with Stephen (mark) Arnold) as guardian to Mary Reynolds, orphan of James Reynolds.

Page 19.—19th May, 1767. Charles Kilpatrick's will: To son Roger Kilpatrick, 5 sh.; to son-in-law, Jno. Hogshead, 5 sh.; to son-in-law, Robt. Cunningham, 5 sh.; to son Alexander, plantation; to wife, Elizabeth; to daughter, Elizabeth. Executors, wife Elizabeth and son Alexander, —— Gardens, Jno. McKenny and Roger Kilpatrick. Teste: Jno. and Wm. McKenny. Proved, 18th August, 1767, by the witnesses. Elizabeth refuses to execute. Alexander qualifies, with Jas. Hogshead, Pat. Cunningham.

Page 22.—18th August, 1767. John Wahub's bond (with Joseph Vachub, Henry Gay) as administrator of Wm. Gay.

Page 23.—16th December, 1766. William Ralston's will: Wife Eleanor, executrix. Son Robert, 10 sh.; son David, 10 sh., to be overseer. Teste: Samuel McFeeters, Wm. and Samuel Ralston. Proved, 18th August, 1767, by the witnesses. Executrix qualifies (her mark), with Saml. and Wm. Ralston.

Page 26.—18th August, 1767. James Cloyd's bond (with Mathew Arbuckle, Joseph Richison) as administrator of Jno. Cloyd.

Page 27.—18th August, 1767. Skidmore Monsey's bond (with Wm. Dunlap, Geo. Spears) as guardian to Saml. Scott, orphan of Samuel Scott.

Page 29.—18th August, 1767. James Burnsides' bond (with Robert Patterson, Jno. Vachub, Saml. Clark) as administrator of Martha Patterson.

Page 30.—11th February, 1767. James Huggart's will—Wife, Agness, negros; son, James, sole executor, 400 acres in Cowpasture; rest of the children; to sons, William and Thomas, and daughters, Jenny and Nancy, each 10 shillings. Teste: Chas. Knight, James McClearey. Proved, 19th Henry Gay.

Page 33.—13th August, 1767. Charles Lockhart's estate appraisement, by James Ewing et als—To James Ward, Sr.

Page 34.—19th August, 1767. Samuel Todd's bond (with Robert Young, Jno. Lowry) as guardian to Sarah, James, Jannet and Elizabeth Young, orphans of Patrick Young.

Page 35.—19th August, 1767. Settlement of Valentine Coil's estate, by Geo. Hammer and Geo. Coile—Cash paid Gabriel Coile, George Caplinger; cash paid Francis Evick, Geo. Tice, Woolrick Conrod; cash paid Colien Havenor, Nicholas Havenor, Jno. Murray, Henry Stone, Mark Swatley, Christian Grod, Barned Lince, Martin Coile.

Page 37.—19th August, 1767. Archd. Clendenning's estate settlement, by Ann Clendenning, recorded—Paid Ash Claftrock, John Clendenning, Wm. Galespie, Zopher Carpenter, James Furguson, David Galloway, James Millican, Robt. Galespie, Geo. Roberts, Benj. Kimsey, John Baller, John Jeremiah; paid by Jeremiah Seeley.

Page 38.—4th August, 1767. Wm. Preston, Assistant Surveyor, enters 2 tracts, 400 acres each, on north and west sides of James McMillin's lands on waters of Craig's Creek, Catawbo and Roanoke; also 200 acres on both sides of Craig's Creek, above land of Wm. Plummer; 300 acres on both sides of Barbours Creek between lands of Wm. Lee and Wm. Rowland; 2 tracts, each 200 acres, adjoining Henry Switchard on a branch of Catawbo; also 3 tracts of 200 acres each between the Crab Tree Orchard and the Paint Banks on Potts Creek; also 4 tracts of 200 acres each between Paint Banks and Potts improvements; also 400 acres above and on south side of Israel Christian's land on Craig's Creek where Simon Dehart lives; also 400 acres above Thos. Toshe's land on Neely Creek.

Page 39.—17th August, 1767. Michael Harper's estate appraised, by Will and James Henderson, Thos. Rutledge.

Page 39.— —— ——, ——. Estate of Col. James Patton, deceased, to Jno. Buchanan, Dr.—To six slaves purchased by Buchanan in compliance with Patton's will and applied to use of Buchanan's eldest daughter Mary and annexed to her lands on James River. 22nd January, 1767.

Page 40.—24th August, 1767. Account of administration of estate of Col. John McNeill, recorded—Cash paid Wm. Duncan for board of servants under cure; to gold watch sold George Weedon. 1765, April 1st—Cash paid Joseph Gamble for riding express for Col. McNeile to Dr. Jameson. July 4th—Cash paid in part of Farghagh Cambel's account. November 5th—Cash paid James Hughes the balance of Farghagh Camil account. Cash paid Hector McNeil. 1766, January 1st—Cash paid Mr. James Melvin. 1766, January 9th—To cash paid Wm. Lewis for 750 pounds flower for ye use of ye detachment Col. McNeil marched to Fort Pitt. July 2d—Cash paid John Coke. Credits—1765, February, by 5 ounces, 3 pennyweights of gold, £25.16.0.; by 35 dollars and 2 half johannos, £14.13.9.; by 1 moidon, 6 Inglish shillings; by cash from Col. Bouquet, £90.0.0.; by cash from Capt. Walter Cunningham, £12.16.9.; by cash from John Mann. August 20th, by cash from Edward Long for blankets. 1766, May 22d, by cash from Wm. Hyde.

Page 44.—24th August, 1767. George Mathews' bond (with Wm. McClenachan) as guardian to Elizabeth Mathews, orphan of Joshua Mathews.

Page 45.—23d September, 1767. Mary McClure's settlement of estate of N. McClure—Cash paid for funeral expenses for my child; cash paid for schooling the children; cash paid Halbert McClure, one of the heirs; cash paid Joseph Reed, one of the heirs; cash paid James McClure, his part; cash paid Nathl. McClure, his part; cash paid Jno. Smiley, his part; cash paid Thos. McClure, his part; cash paid Margt. McClure, her part; cash paid Moses McClure, his part. Recorded on motion of Baptist McNabb.

Page 46.—25th October, 1767. Catherine Conrad, widow of Stephen Conrad, on account of ill health and age refuses to administer on Stephen's estate and asks to have her eldest son George Conrad appointed. Teste: Jacob Purkey, Henry Lung.

Page 47.—17th November, 1767. George qualifies as above.

Page 48.—17th November, 1767. Halbert McClure's bond (with Samuel McClure) as guardian to Thomas McClure, orphan of Nathaniel McClure.

Page 49.—17th November, 1767. Halbert McClure's bond (with Samuel McClure, John McClure) as administrator, c. t. a., of Nathl. McClure.

Page 51.—17th November, 1767. Samuel Davis' bond as guardian to James Casety, orphan of Neil Casety.

Page 51.—17th November, 1767. Samuel Davis' bond (with Richd. Woods) as administrator of Neil Casaty.

Page 53.—17th November, 1767. John Montgomery's bond (with Mallcom Allen, Saml. McRoberts) as administrator of Alexander Bruce.

Page 55.—13th November, 1767. Martha Patterson's estate appraised (by James Ewing, John McPheeters, James McCleerey, John McCleerey).

Page 55.—17th November, 1767. Appraisement of Wm. Rallstone's estate (by Moses Hall, Adam Stephenson, Samuel McPheeters), recorded.

Page 57.—10th September, 1767. Mary McClure's (mark) will—To son, Thomas, for his schooling; to son, Moses, for his schooling; to daughter, Margaret, for her schooling; to son, James, 5 shillings. Executors, Joseph Walker and Saml. Lyle. Teste: James McDowell, Saml. McDowell, Alex. McCluer. Proved, 17th November, 1767, by James and Saml. McDowell. Executors refuse. Administration granted Halbert McClure, who qualifies with Saml. (mark) and John (mark) McClure.

Page 59.—18th November, 1767. John Harrison's estate settlement, recorded—Cash paid Iowel (Joel) Roboson, Thomas Wales. Sold, viz: to John Nedomtoone, John McDonnald, Alex. McDonald, Robert Dickey, Joseph English, John Needham, Jacob Decoson, Jacob Grub, Joseph Langdon, Danl. Prentice, Danl. Ponder, Jonathan Langdon, Jacob Peters.

Page 61.—Mr. Smith, Sir: Whereas I am incapable at present of administering on my ded husband estate and my son also and I am informed you are the bigest creditor we desire that you would administer for your own and our good the sooner the better for we cannot at present so therefore we leave it to the mercy of you and the Court so no more at present from your friends. November 16th, to Daniel Smith. George Null, Margaret Null.

Page 61.—18th November, 1767. Daniel Smith's bond (with John Malcom, Benj. Logan) as administrator of Nicholas Null.

Page 63.—20th November, 1767. Charles Campbell's appraisement (by Wm. Wright, Jno. Brownlee, William Kerr), recorded.

Page 65.—16th November, 1767. John Archer's improvements examined and valued.

Page 66.—21st November, 1767. Mary O'Donnal's bond (with Jno. Buchanan, Thos. Stewart) as administratrix of Michl. O'Donnal.

Page 67.—21st November, 1767. William Ingliss' bond (with Israel Christian) to keep the public ferry established on his land across New River.

Page 68.—23d November, 1767. Saml. Wallace's estate settled—Paid to, viz: Elizabeth Wallace, Robert Phillips, Francis Gardner, Saml. Bell,

Robt. Wallace. Trustees of Ye Meeting House, Mary Ann Bell, John Vance (for a coffin), Jane Hamilton, Charles Phillips.

Page 69.—29th January, 1767. Robert Andrews' estate appraised, by Humberston Lyon, George Horbush (Forbush?).

Page 70.—Settlement of above estate, by Wm. Herbert—1766, paid Jesse Townsend for corn; paid Rees Bowen, John Jankins, Fredk. Homs, Geo. Yeates. To my commission (?) to Humberston Lyon, Jr. Paid David Duttose.

Page 71.—Contra—By Thomas Hobbes, John Drake, by Thos. Jones, Charles Duerson, James Adames, Wm. Dean, James Nelley, James Waady.

Page 71.—24th November, 1767. James Hughes' estate settlement, recorded—Paid for making cakes for funeral. 1767, February 11th, by received from Saml. Hughes; by received from Andrew Russell, Sr. March 30th, by received from Wm. Dunlap, Jr. March 30th, by received from John Verner. July 25th, by received from Andrew Russell, Jr. July 27th, by balance for nursing a child. July 29th, by Wm. Howard's account; by James Colton's account. September 28th, by Jeremiah Edward's account. Oct. 7th, by remainder Saml. Hughens' bill. Bills due the estate that are doubtful: John Craney's, James Hill's, John Lindsey's, Jno. McNulty's, Hector McNeil's, Robt. Adair's, Benj. Woods, Richd. Dunn, Saml. Cloyd, Jno. Lucases, James Shaw's.

Page 75.—24th November, 1767. Andrew Lewis' bond (with Jno. Madison) for collection of County proportion.

Page 76.—8th March, 1768. Valuation of stock on John Archer's 75 acres and 245 acres by George Francis, James Reaburn, Adam Reaburn.

Page 77.—15th March, 1768. Isaac Robinson's bond (with Adam Miller) as administrator of George Gost.

Page 78.—18th March, 1768. Saml. McClure's bond (with Arthur McClure, Thomas Vance) as guardian to Moses McClure, orphan of Nathl. McClure.

Page 79.—16th March, 1768. John Mann's bond (with Wm. Mann) as administrator of Caleb Moy.

Page 80.—16th March, 1768. Estate of Peter Looney, Dr., in account with James McCain and Margaret, his wife—Cash paid David Smith; cash paid Robert, Abraham and David Looney; cash received from James Holles; cash received from Benj. Estill for Abraham Haines.

Page 82.—16th March, 1768. Saml. Paxton's estate in account with Thos. Paxton and James Trimble, executors. John Paxton's proven account. Prudence Campbell's proven account. Received from Hugh Kelsey.

Page 84.—20th October, 1767. William (mark) Talor's will, farmer—To son, Isaac, infant, tract adjoining Mill Creek, corner in the Warm Run, corner before Andrew Taylor's door, William Lusk's line; to son, William, infant, tract testator lives on, joining Daniel Lyle; to son, James, infant; to 3 daughters, Martha, Isbell and Jemmina, infants; to youngest son; to wife, Elizabeth, executrix. Teste: Wm. Lusk, Daniel Lyle, James Lyle. Proved, 16th March, 1768, by Wm. Lusk and Danl. Lyle. Executrix qualified (mark), with Saml. and Danl. Lyle.

Page 87.—16th March, 1768. Thomas Dryden's bond (with Joseph Reed, Patrick (mark) McCollom) as guardian to Margaret McClure, orphan of Nathl. McClure.

Page 88.—18th March, 1768. George Moffett's bond (with John Christian) as guardian to James Trimble, orphan of John Trimble.

Page 89.—15th March, 1768. Halbert McClure's bond (with Thomas Vance, Robert Young) as guardian to Margaret and Moses McClure, orphans of Nathaniel McClure.

Page 91.—4th March, 1768. Mary McClure's estate appraised, by William Ramsey, James Thomson, Alex. McClure.

Page 92.—18th March, 1768. John Lyle's bond (with James Lyle, Saml. McDowell) as guardian to Mathew Eaken, orphan of Walter Eaken.

Page 93.—16th March, 1768. James McKain and Jonathan Smith's bond to James Ledderdale to secure Ledderdale, who with John Miller (now deceased) was surety of Margaret Looney as administratrix of her late husband, Peter Looney.

Page 94.—17th March, 1768. Jonathan Smith's bond (with Joseph Luney) as guardian to Peter Looney, orphan of Peter Looney.

Page 95.—17th March, 1768. John Jackson's (mark) bond (with Isaac Robinson) as guardian to Jane Claypole, orphan of Wm. Claypole.

Page 96.—24th November, 1767. Stephen Conrod's estate appraised, by Jacob Bare, Mathias Kersh, Archd. Huston.

Page 99.—3d December, 1767. Nicholas Null's estate appraised, by Jacob Nicholas, John Couts, Archd. Huston.

Page 101.—9th June, 1767. David Bryan's estate appraised, by James Neeley, Thos. Barnes, John Bowman—Accounts due to David Bryan's estate from, viz: James Carty, Christian Lockmier, Wm. Thornton, Lenard Huff. The congregation: Danl. McNeil, Richd. Doggett, Joshua Johns, Wm. Simpson, Wm. Cocks, Wm. Halley, Edward Springer.

Page 104.—29th March, 1768. William Crawford's bond (with Robt. Clark, John Thompson) as guardian to Mary, orphan to Alex. Crawford.

Page 105.—30th October, 1765. John Donilly's estate appraised, by Bryan McDonald, John Armstrong.

Page 106.—17th May, 1768. James Hugart's estate appraisement, by James McCoy, Charles Donnerley, John Cartmill, recorded.

Page 107.—21st November, 1772. David Henderson, son of Danl. Henderson, puts himself apprentice to William Young, blacksmith, to learn his art, trade or mystery for 4½ years. Teste: Wm. Robertson, Wm. Anderson.

Page 108.—17th May, 1768. Sale bill and settlement of estate of Andrew Smith, recorded, Henry Penninger, administrator, c. t. a.—Sold to, viz: Mark Swedley, Joseph Skidmore, Jr., Mathias Dice, Ludwick Wagener, Jones Friend, John Dunkle, Jacob Peters, Philip Props, Powel Shanour, Christian Grace (Grad?), Geo. Dunkle, William Waiett, Christian Rolsman, Valentine Gile, Charles Power, Martin Shob, Leners Seaman.

Page 111.—26th November, 1767. Neal Cassedy's estate appraised—One souz press.

Page 112.—27th November, 1767. William Gay's estate appraised.

Page 113.—17th April, 1766. William Kelly's will—To wife, Margaret; to son, Samuel; to son, Anthony; to son, John; to daughter, Margaret; to daughter, Elizabeth McElwrath; to daughter, Rebecca. Executors, wife Margaret, son Anthony and Andw. Hays. Teste: John Hays, John Moore, David Scott. Proved, 17th May, 1768, by Hays and Moore. Margaret and Anthony Kelly qualified, with Alex. Walker and James Coulter.

Page 116.—18th May, 1768. Robert Graham's appraisement (by Thos. Feamster, John Carllile), recorded.

Page 116.—18th September, 1767. John Cloyd's estate sold at vendue—To George Poage, Thos. Arbuckle, John Man, Andw. Wilson, Josiah Crawford, Robert Kirkham.

Page 117.—18th May, 1768. Robert and Mathew Reed's bond (with John Ramsey) as administrator of George Rodgers.

Page 118.—18th May, 1768. Alexander Walker's bond (with Thomas Hudson, John Wallace) as administrator, c. t. a., of James Rutherford.

Page 119.—18th May, 1768. James Rutherford's will was presented by Wm. Buchanan, one of the executors, who refused to execute. It is proved that Margaret, the widow, likewise refuses. Will is proved, by William Buchanan (another witness, James Buchanan, being dead). The other witness, Archibald Buchanan, is ordered summoned. Administration granted Alex. Walker.

Page 119.—7th May, 1768. Robert Fillson's will—To sister, Florans Fillson, all estate. Executors, John Givens, Saml. Henderson. Teste: Saml. Bell, John Henderson, John Givens. Proved, 18th May, 1768, by Givens and Bell. Executors refused to execute. William Robertson qualifies, with Saml. Henderson, George Crawford.

Page 121.—19th May, 1768. Mathias Lair's bond (with John Gratton, Danl. Smith) as administrator of Ferdinando Lair.

Page 123.—19th May, 1768. Bond as above as guardian to George, Ferdinando, Margaret, Cathorine and Mathias Lair, orphans of Ferdinando Lair.

Page 124.—22d March, 1768. John Cockran's estate settled—Paid John Gentry, James Maurry, Mathew McCullough, Alexander Baine.

Page 125.—15th July, 1767. James Carty's estate appraised, by John Blackmore, Frederick Stern, Edmond O'Neal. Saml. Pepper, administrator.

Page 126.—14th May, 1768. William Taylor's estate appraised, by David Gray, Henry McClung, William Lusk.

Page 127.—21st May, 1768. Thomas Bowyer's bond (with John Madison) as administrator of James Jackson.

Page 128.—17th May, 1768. William Crawford's bond (with Charles Campbell, Saml. McCutchen) as guardian to Rebecca, orphan of Alex. Crawford.

Page 129.—16th August, 1768. Catherine Miller's bond (with George Martin) as executrix of Jacob Miller.

Page 130.—16th August, 1768. Francis Smith's bond (with Benjamin Hawkins, George Skillern, Patrick Shirkey) as administrator of David Miller.

Page 132.—6th July, 1768. William Kelly's estate appraised, by James Walker, Alex. Walker, Sr., Alex. Walker, John Moore.

Page 134.—24th December, 1760. James Rutherford's will, weaver—Wife, Margaret; son, Samuel, deaf and dumb. My son, John Wallace, and my ———, Thos. Hudson. Executors, wife Margaret and Wm. Buchanan. Teste: William Thompson, Archibald Buchanan, James Buchanan, Wm. Buchanan. Proved, 17th August, 1768, by Archibald Buchanan.

Page 135.—7th July, 1768. James Rutherford's estate appraised, by Joseph Culton, John Berry, John Walker; John McCampbel's bond; Thos. Hutson's; Mat. Moorehead's.

Page 136.—27th July, 1768. John Bowen's will—Three sons, John, Moses and William Bowen; 3 daughters, Ann, Rebecca and Elizabeth; wife, Rachel. Executors, wife Rachel, Wm. Mathews, Wm. Bowen. My trusty and well-beloved brothers. Teste: John Smith, Joseph Luney, Richd. Mathews, Malcom Allen. Proved, 17th August, 1768, by Mathews and Allen. William Mathews and Wm. Bowen qualified executors.

Page 139.— —— ——, 1768. George Rodgers' estate appraised, by James Buchanan, Hugh Johnston, Thos. Bowyer.

Page 143.—1st September, 1767. Sale bill of Michael Harper's estate—James Shoemaker, Saml. Furguson, Robt. McKim, Wm. Jameson. Settlement of above estate, by Mathew Harper. For going to the South Branch, to where he died, 5 days.

Page 144.—22d August, 1768. Jacob Goodpasture's estate settled, by Daniel Pierce—Paid Isaac Blackfild; paid John Bealey.

Page 145.—19th August, 1768. Margaret (her mark) and Hugh Campbell's bond (with Charles Campbell) as administrators of Robert Campbell.

Page 147.—19th August, 1768. Mary Wilson's bond (with John Christian, James McCleerey) as administratrix of James Wilson.

Page 148.—10th May, 1767. Isaac Bracpeil's (Barefield, Brackfield?) (his mark) will, farmer—Wife, Catherine; youngest son; oldest daughter, Elizabeth, now married and living in Pennsylvania, and her oldest daughter, Catherine; 3 sons, Stophel, Jacob and Isaac; 2 youngest daughters, Catherine and Barbary; to son, Stophel, ⅔ of home place; to son, Jacob, tract on Slate Lick Branch. Executors, Jacob Miller and Catherine Brackpiel. Teste: Abm. Bird, Jacob Trumbo. Proved, 15th November, 1768, by Andrew Bird and Trumbo. Executors qualify (Cathorine Brackfield).

Page 152.—7th April, 1768. James Robinson's will, weaver—To son, James Robinson, Jr.; to sons, John and David, 200 acres on North River; to son, Samuel, 60 acres on North River; to daughters, Rachel, Hanna and Jane. "I give to my dearly beloved wife Hanna, Isabella, Margaret, each ⅓ of the remainder of my estate after the above is paid off." Executors, wife Hanna and James Edmiston Miller. Teste: Saml. Moore, Jas. Welsh, Wm. Napier. Proved, 15th November, 1768, by Moore and Welsh. Edmiston qualifies, with James Trimble and Robt. Thompson.

Page 154.—15th November, 1768. Robert Campbell's appraisement (by Wm. McPheeters, Morris O'Freil, John Mophet), recorded.

Page 155.—15th November, 1768. James McDowell's bond (with Pat. Martin) as administrator of Wm. Wilson.

Page 157.—2d February, 1767. Thomas Lorimor's will, in the Black Thorn in Augusta County—To Hugh Botkin, 100 acres now in possession of Hugh on the Black Thorn on South Branch. Teste: John Botkin, Robert Harper. Proved, 15th November, 1768, by the witnesses. Administration granted Hugh Botkin, who qualifies with John Botkin, James Byrnsides.

Page 159.—29th October, 1768. Henry Bowen, heir-at-law of John Bowen, to Lilly Bowen, widow of John—Since John's death the slave left to Lilly had had a child, and, in order to settle the question of the title to that child, Henry conveys the slave's increase to Lilly, who has conveyed to him 400 acres. Teste: Malcom Allen, Robt. Bowen.

Page 161.—9th September, 1768. Robert Wilson's will, farmer—To son, David, 260 acres I live on; wife; son, William (unmarried, infant) (?); daughter, Lettice, unmarried; daughter, Ann, unmarried; son, Robert, infant (?); sons, Thomas, Samuel, James, have already had their shares. **Executrix**, wife Mary. Teste: Robert Mitchell, John Tate, Sr., John Tate, Jr. Proved, November 16th, 1768, by John Tate, John Tate, Jr. Mary Wilson qualified, with James Ewing, William Crow, Arthur Graham.

Page 163.—16th November, 1768. John Crington's estate, in account with James Davis—A sheet for a funeral, £0.12.0.; 1 gallon of liquor, £0.3.0.; 3 weeks' attendance, £0.9.0., to a coffin, £0.15.0.

Page 164.—12th November, 1768. James Wilson's estate appraised, by John Brownlee, Wm. Brown, Robert Christian, James Gillmore.

Page 165.—16th November, 1768. John Davis' bond (with Halbert McCluer, Hugh Cunningham) as guardian to John, Daniel and Michael Higins, orphans of Daniel Higins.

Page 166.—2d September, 1768. Malcom Campbell's estate settled, by William Simpson and Elizabeth, his wife, administrators—Paid Francis Deleney, Saml. Flours, Adam Baird, Saml. Drake, Archibald Lamb, George Dare for Col. Preston, William Haley, Anthony Bledsoe for 8 gallons rum for vendue; James McNeil, for catching horses; Austin Brumbly, for catching horses; Peter Dyerly, Abraham Moon. Sale at vendue November 29th, 1763.

Page 168.—11th November, 1768. Jacob Miller's estate appraised, by Benj. Logan, Francis Stuart, Joseph Cravens.

Page 168.—9th November, 1768. George Ghost's estate appraised, by Cornelius Ruddell. John Thomas—Funarrall of William Munsey for the use of Geo. Ghost, deceased; to 1 winding sheet, £0.16.6.; to 1 shirt, £0 14 0.; to making a coughing, £0.5.0.; to 5 quarts whiskey, £0.5.0.; to trouble of sickness and attendance.

Page 170.—12th January, 1768. William Stewart's will, freeholder—To sister Jane, lands and chattels left to me by my father in the town land of Raffrey, was married to Wm. Marshall; to Ann Stewart, married to Thomas Osborn; to Mary Stewart, married to Andw. Shaw; to Elizabeth Stewart, married to John Patton; to Francis Stewart; to William Stewart, infant, when at age my land on Middle River, formerly owned by James Henderson; to brother John Stewart, executor. Teste: Thomas Stewart, Thomas Thompson, John Petter, Robert Hamilton. Proved, 18th November, 1768, by Thos. Stewart, John Peters. John Stewart qualifies executor, with Thos. Stuart and John Bowyer.

Page 172.—19th November, 1768. James Cartie's estate—Sale bill, Saml. Pepper, administrator, recorded—To Levy Smith, Saml. Cloyd, Anthony Blather, Ellis Bean, Thos. Grisom, Fred Starn, Jacob Lorton, Anthony Blather, Edmond O'Neal, James Jonston, Isaac Job, Casper Wever, Henry Francis, John Taylor, James Hogg, Henry Skeggs, Saml. Ewing, Jacob Harmon, Roger Tap, Saml. Scott.

Page 173.—18th January, 1768. Alex. Bruce's estate appraised, by James McDowell, Anthony Bledsoe, Josiah Ramsey.

Page 174.—— ——— ———, 1768. Jacob Pence's estate settled, by Valentine Pence—Paid Jacob Pence remainder of his portion of his father's estate; paid George Pence, John Pence, Wm. Pence. Errors excepted by Peter Miller, executor of Valentine Pence.

Page 175.—16th November, 1768. John Bowyer's bond (with Saml. McDowell, James McDowell, William Bowyer, Michael Bowyer) as sheriff.

Page 178.—21st March, 1769. Jane Grymes' bond (with Joseph Warhop, Robert Dunlap) as administratrix of David Grymes.

Page 179.—23d May, 1768. John McCreerey's will, carpenter—To wife Agness; children; to son Robert; to son John; to son Robert's son, John. Executors, sons John and Robert. Teste: Chas. Lewis, John Kinkead. Proved, 21st November, 1769, by the witnesses. John and Robert qualified.

Page 181.—21st March, 1769. William McClenachan's bond (with Thos. Madison, Jno. Neeley, Baptist Armstrong) as guardian to Susannah Evans, orphan of Daniel Evans.

Page 182.—29th August, 1768. John Bowyer's estate appraised, by Jonathan Smith, Walter Stewart, William Rowland.

Page 184.— —— August, 1764. Valentine Yoacon's estate appraised, by John Candler, Robt. Brooks, Zachariah Moorman, Chas. Lynch, administrator.

Page 185.— —— August, 1764. Frederick See's estate appraised, by above.

Page 185.—21st March, 1769. William McPheeters' bond (with Jno. Patrick, Archd. Reaughe) as guardian (appointed) to Alexander and Robert Crawford, orphans of Alex. Crawford.

Page 186.—21st March, 1769. William Wilson's appraisement (by Wm. Edmiston, Saml. Buchanan, Charles Campbell, Robt. Steel), recorded.

Page 187.—22d March, 1769. John Gilmore's bond (with John McCown) as administrator of Margaret Lynn.

Page 188.—2d October, 1768. John Shanklin's will—To sister, £5; to sister Margaret, £4; to cousin Elebth Evans; to cousin Richard Shanklin; to Margaret Shanklin; to sister Ann; to cousin Joseph; to cousins Evan and Jonathan; to brother Edward, executor. Teste: John Fairbairn, Wm. Snodon. Proved, 22d March, 1769, by the witnesses. Edward Shanklind qualified, with Wm. Snodon, Andw. Johnston.

Page 191.—20th March, 1766. Robert Shanklin's will—To brother Edward's five daughters; to Elizabeth Evans; to brother Thon; to Edward and his son Robert and his youngest sons; to brother Jhon; to Richd. Shanklin; to Jonathan Evans; to Elizabeth Evans; to sister Margaret; to Robert and John Shanklin; to brother John; to Ro. and John Edwards' two sons and his son John. Teste: John Fairbairn, Darkis Snodon. Proved, 22d March, 1769, by the witnesses. Edward Shanklin qualified executor, with Wm. Snodon, Andrew Johnston.

Page 193.—31st January, 1769. James Leister's (Liser) will—Three children, John, Jean and Martha Lister. Executors, John Paxton, Saml. McDowell. Teste: Henry Campbell, William Hill, James Wallace, Saml. McDowell. Proved, 22d March, 1769, by Campbell and McDowell. Saml. McDowell refuses to execute. Paxton qualifies, with Samuel McDowell.

Page 195.—22d March, 1769. Settlement recorded of John Trimble's estate, by Mary and James Trimble, administrators—By John Prise' (Price?) weges and bounty, £12.0.0. Cash of John Bigham on Geo. Bighams. By Henry Criswell's bond. Paid Andw. Baskin, Alex. McKinsey, John Boswell, Saml. Davison, Thos. Gardon on Bigham's account.

Page 197.—22d March, 1769. Settlement recorded of Jacob Harmon's estate, by Peter Harman—Paid Margaret Perkey, Phillip Williams; paid to Henry Bingaman, part of his legacy; paid to Phillip Williams in cash in part of his legacy; paid to Catherine Harman in cash and goods sold at sale; paid to George Man; paid to Henry Null, part of his legacy.

Page 198.—July, 1756—September, 1757. Christian Dosher, Dr., to Michael Thorn, account proved in Hampshire County before Jonathan Heath. 1st February, 1769.

Page 199.—22d March, 1769. Settlement recorded of Christian Tosher's (Dosher, Dasher?) estate—1757, to 1 bond; 1759, February, paid Henry Shepter; paid Mary Smith, Mary Fitzpatrick, Henry Make.

Page 199.—14th November, 1768. Received of Peter Miller, executor of Valentine Pence, who was executor of Jacob Pence, £2.18.6½, being the ballance due me on settlement of my father's estate.—Yacob bru— (Pence). Ditto, similar receipt from George Pence.

Page 200.—Ditto, similar receipt from Johann. Ditto, similar receipt from William. Ditto, similar receipt from Christian Parsinger for his wife Barbara's portion of her father's estate.

Page 200.—15th March, 1769. James Robinson's estate appraised, by Wm. Foster, Jno. McNutt, Saml. McCluer.

Page 203.—2d February, 1769. Robert Wilson's estate appraised (Mary Wilson, executrix), by John Tate, Robert Alexander, John Fulton, David Doack.

Page 204.—11th January, 1769. Adam Thompson's will—Wife, Naomie; Son, Andrew; daughters, Margaret and Rebecca. Teste: Samuel Downey, Andrew Scott, Thos. Scott. Executors, Saml. Downey, Andw. Thompson. Proved, 22d March, 1769, by Scott. Executors qualified, with John Thompson, John Handly.

Page 206.—23d March, 1769. David Miller's appraisement, by John, David and William Robinson, recorded.

Page 207.—14th February, 1769. James Trimble, Assistant Surveyor, enters 400 acres in a valley of the Camp Mountain on a branch of the James River on a branch that runs into Clenup Branch, a branch of James River.

Page 207.—27th March, 1769. Francis Smith's bond, with George Skillern as administrator of Francis Kidd.

Page 209.—10th April, 1769. Isaac Brackfield's estate appraised, by Adam Reider, John Thomas, Rudie Mauk.

Page 211.—11th December, 1768. Joseph King's will (his mark)— Eldest son Joseph left in care of wife; children Nicholas and Nelly left to Thomas Hugart; youngest son John left to John Carlile. All to be brought up to the rules of the Church of England. Teste: Saml. Vance, Mary Gregory. Proved, 20th June, 1769, by the witnesses. Administration granted Thos. Hugart, who qualifies with Wm. Hugart, Wm. Kinkead.

Page 213.—5th April, 1769. Nicholas Havenor's will—To wife Elizabeth, ⅓ of all estate whether in this Colony or any other, and his iron stove, executrix; to son Jacob, executor, land on South Fork, wagon and geers, ½ of cuper tools; to son Frederick, part of tract on South Forke on which testator lives, and a tract purchased of Robert Davis; to daughter Catren; to daughter (?). Teste: Mathew Patton, Robert Davis, James Stephenson. Proved, 20th June, 1769, by Patton and Davis. Executors qualify, with Robert Davis, Henry Stone.

Page 216.—22d June, 1769. Settlement recorded of William Robinson, deceased—Paid James Calloway, James Orrey, Richard Doged; cash received of Capt. Israel Christian; cash received of Col. Preston.

Page 217.—26th September, 1765. William Robinson's (above) estate appraised, by Walter Crockett, William Bryan, James Neely.

Page 219.—28th May, 1769. John McMahan and Samuel Erwin appraise the improvements of John King on a tract bought by him of William Watterson, 30 cattle valued at sixty pounds.

Page 219.—17th June, 1769. Margaret Rutherford's receipt to Alexander Walker, executor of James Rutherford, for her portion of her husband's estate. Teste: William Buchanan, Thos. Hutson, John Wallace.

Page 220.—9th May, 1769. Robert Shanklin's estate appraised, by Daniel Smith, John and Joseph Cravens—Cash of Grany McDonald.

Page 221.—9th May, 1769. John Shanklin's estate appraised, by same—William Loagen's note; Benj. Loagen's note.

Page 222.—23d June, 1769. John Lewis' bond (with Andw. Lewis, Jas. McDowell) as Assistant Surveyor.

Page 222.—24th July, 1769. Robert (mark) Allison's will—To son James, has received his part; to daughter Mary Davison, has received her part; to son John, 10 shillings; to daughter Agness; to son Robert, infant, testator's home plantation; to son Francis, infant, 250 acres on Mill Creek; to son Halbert, received his part already; to wife Hannah; to daughter Janet. Teste: Alexander (mark) McClure, Arthur McClure, Joseph Walker, Joseph Walker, Jr. Proved, 15th August, 1769, by all except Joseph Walker, Jr. Hannah Allison qualifies, with Alex. and John McCluer.

Page 225.—15th August, 1769. James Sawyer's bond (with John Archer, Wm. Mathews) as administrator of George Brown.

Page 226.—5th August, 1769. Dr. the estate of Henry Kirkham in account with John Summers and Mary Evans, late Mary Kirkham, administrator c. t. a.—Cash paid Ann Long, Saml. Todd, Alex. Collier, John Wiley, James Bambridge, Abram Brown, John Hickman, Saml. Kirkham's legacy; Paul Whitley, for malt for the vendue; James Beats, for stilling liquor for the vendue; Robert Shannon, for crying for vendue. By Saml. Sharp's bond; Saml. Mann's account. By Jeremiah Seeley's note, insolvent. By Israel Burnley's note, insolvent.

Page 228.—16th August, 1769. Settlement recorded of Robert Shanklin's estate (Edward Shanklin, executor)—Paid Jane Logan for 12 gallons whiskey; paid Joseph Peace for making a coffin and plank.

Page 229.—16th August, 1769. John Shanklin's estate settled, by Edward Shanklin, executor.

Page 230.—16th August, 1769. William Preston's renunciation of executorship of George Darr's estate provided the Court will grant administration to Capt. Francis Smith, but if they will not, then Wm. will qualify. Teste: Arthur Campbell.

Page 230.—8th September, 1766. George Darr's will—Debts and funeral charges to be paid, and if anything remains, his will is that Col. Wm. Preston have it who has for many years past during my misfortune treated me with great friendship and humanity. Wm. Preston to be executor. Teste: Francis Smith, Henry Carter. Proved, 16th August, 1769, by Henry Carter. Francis Smith qualifies, with John Mills.

Page 233.—16th August, 1769. William Preston and William Campbell's bond as administrators of John Buchanan (with William Thompson, Robert Breckinridge, William Christian, Patrick Campbell, John Mills, David Robinson, John Taylor).

Page 234.—26th August, 1769. William Preston's bond (with Robert Breckinridge, John Mills, David Robinson, Wm. Campbell, George Skillern, John Taylor, Patrick Campbell) as executor of James Patton.

Page 235.—17th August, 1769. The estate of Col. James Patton, Dr.— To William Thompson, an executor, 1757, cash paid Col. Wm. Walker, cash paid Col. Green, cash paid Richard Vernon, James Coyle. 1762, February 10th, by to Banyans appraised. Cash of Doctor Walker on account of Jacob Harmon in full of the Horseshoe bottom. Cash of John Roerty, Andrew Haislip, Jacob Larton, Jacob Shull, James Hollis, Daniel Brown. By cash of Thos. Henry, rent of land in Louisa; Jno. Sprout, John and Christian Bigaman, Wm. Ledford, Jno. Ledford, Michl. Dougherday, Hugh Mares, Wm. Lepperd and Jacob Dye. James Hutton, Jno. Wiley for Jno. Ruckman, John Douglas for a tract of land in Louisa since Col. Patton's death.

Page 237.—By cash from, viz (apparently in payment of piece of land belonging to Col. Patton's estate): Robt. Armstrong, Wm. Foster, Michl. Dougherty, Danl. Droudy, James Wiley (by James Davies), James Campbell. Wm. Preston (in part for Dayley's and Wat. Welshe's bond whose lands he purchased), David Robinson (part of William and James Gorrel's debt), Wm. Ingles (on Jno. Medley's bond), Alex. Dall, John Thompson, John Robinson, Hugh Mills, John Stephenson, Wm. Patterson, Wm. Buchanan, Augustine Price, Jacob Shull, Philip Harless, Michl. Price, James Kerr, Jno. Craig, Edd. Hall, James Coyle, Wm. Sawyers, James Davies (on Wm. Hall's bond), Pat. Sharkey, James Moore, James Armstrong, James Neeley (on Moore's bond), James Hollis, Danl. Brown, Adam Wall, Wm. Sawyers (account of Saml. Crockett's heirs), Thos. Henry (rent of land in Louisa), Pat McCollom, Casper Barrier, Henry Brown, John Sprout, Michl. Finney, Wm. Ingles, Robt. Galloway, Isaac Taylor, Neil McNeil, Wm. Carven, Wm. Ralston, Dr. Walker (for Tobias Bright), Jno. Collier, Jno. Smiley, Jno. McClure, Wm. Fleming, David Kinkead, Wm. Graham, James Scraggs, Jno. Armstrong (for Geo. Reed's bond), Jacob Brown, John Draper (for land sold since death of Col. Patton). Robert Armstrong for a tract called McCord Mill sold since Col. Patton's death.

Page 239.—15th August, 1769. Thos. Hugart certifies that as administrator of Joseph King he can find no estate.

Page 239.—17th August, 1769. Settlement recorded of estate of Stephen Conrad (Geo. Conrod, executor)—Paid, viz: Jacob Bear, John Fudge, Jno. Michl. Stophelmire, Mathias Kersh, Michl. Summy, Jno. Seller, Valentine Mitcher, Paul Lingal, Mauks Swadley, Jacob Archinbright, Peter Smith, Saml. Maggot, Michl. Shirley, Jacob Shell, Christian Pikle, Jacob Peters, Conrad Peterfish, George Fullingar, Geo. Mallo.

Page 241.—26th November, 1767. Stephen Conrad's estate sold to, viz: John Coutch, Lewis Fisher, Stephen Hensbengar, Zachariah Rexrode, Henry Tamewood, Peachey Gilmore.

Page 245.—17th August, 1769. Additional appraisement, recorded, of Mathew Shaddon, by Bryan McDonald, John and Lanty Armstrong.

Page 245.—14th June, 1769. Francis Kidd's estate appraised, by Robert Breckinridge, Bryan McDonald, John Nelly—Consists only of one silver watch.

Page 246.—30th December, 1767. Wm. Preston, Assistant Surveyor, enters 250 acres between Gilbert Marshall and James Alexander on Back Creek, 400 acres joining Jasper Tarry, James Neely and Andrew Wilson, 400 acres on Potts Creek joining and above the Paint Bank.

Page 246.— —— October, 1767. Dr. James Henderson and John Finley—To estate of John Henderson, deceased. 1769, 26th March, paid Saml. Love of the estate of John Montague; paid Edwd. Waldon.

Page 248. 17th October, 1769. Saml. Erwin's bond (with Hugh Donaghe, Joseph Reburn) as administrator of James Frew.

Page 250.—17th October, 1769. John Young's bond (with John Handley, William and James Bell) as guardian (appointed) to James Young, orphan of James Young.

Page 251.—17th October, 1769. Samuel McRoberts' bond (with John Mountgomery, John Bowyer) as administrator of Chas. McGee.

Page 252.—10th July, 1769. Nicholas Havener's estate appraised—Mathias and George Dyce's accounts.

Page 254.—26th September, 1769. John Dilling's will—To sons William and Thomas; to wife Elizabeth, executrix. Teste: John Sevier, Michael Rork, Margaret Heath. Proved, 18th October, 1769, by Rork and Heath. Elizabeth qualifies, with William McDowell, Robt. Rutherford.

Page 257.—18th October, 1769. John Neilley's bond (with Wm. McClenachan, John Bowyer) as guardian (appointed) to Catharine Evans, orphan of Daniel Evans.

Page 257.—15th May, 1769. Thomas Beard's will—To wife, all cleared land where house stands to clear land for turnips where they last grew; to daughter Fane; to daughter Jane; to wife, his elbow chair, negroe boy; to son Hugh, cleared land; to grandson Thomas, son of Hugh, 170 acres lying next John Montgomery's Thomas Hill; to grandchildren, viz: Thomas Alexander, Thomas (page 259) Beard (William's son), Thomas Mitchell, Thomas Dunlap, £10 each; to Robert Ramsey's children (testator's grandchildren), £12.10.0.; to son William; to daughters Ester Alexander, Elizabeth Mitchell, Mary Dunlap; to grandchildren Ann Alexander, Martha Mitchell. (Frequent provision for such issue in case daughter Jane have issue.) Executors, James Mitchell, Thos. Hill. Teste: John, James, Andrew Eakin. Proved, 18th October, 1769, by John and James Eakin. Executors qualify, with William Alexander, Wm. Kennedy, Hugh Beard.

Page 261.—19th October, 1769. George Mathews, William Mathews, John Maurray's bond (with Sampson Mathews, John Bowyer) as guardians (appointed) to John, Moses, William, Ann, Rebecca, Elizabeth Bowen, orphans of John Bowen, Jr.

Page 263.—5th September, 1768. James Gilaspey's will, farmer—To wife Jennet; to son John, plantation John now lives on; to son James, plantation James now lives on; to son William, plantation William now lives on, but if William should die before his present wife, then to William's children; to brother John's children, if they should come for it (they are in Ireland); to 5 children, viz: John, James, William, Agness and Elizabeth. Executors, sons John, James, William Gilaspy and Edward Hall. Teste: Elenor Hall, Sarah Hall, Ben. Stewart. Proved, 20th October,

1769, by Elenor Hall and Benj. Stewart. Edward Hall and Wm. Gillespey qualify, with Ben. Stewart and John Hamilton.

Page 265.— —— ——, 1767. Dr. the estate of Col. David Stewart, in account with Andw. Lewis and Geo. Mathews, administrators—Paid Silas Hart on account of Wm. McClenachan's going to Wmsburg to sign the writ of election; to paid the men that brought in the Corps; to expenses to Maryland in 1767 and 1768; to expenses to Carolina. 1767, by cash from Thos. Bowyer for a sword; by rent of a Dutchman (Andw. Clinc); by cash from Thos. Sumter.

Page 268.—21st November, 1769. Appraisement recorded of James Gillespie's estate, by John Ramsey, John Black, John Davidson, Jr.

Page 269.—21st November, 1769. Settlement recorded of estate of Robert Filson in account with William Robertson, administrator—Cash paid Saml. Bell for attendance on intestate while sick; cash paid Dr. Watkins for medicines while sick. By Saml. Burnes' note for £50 South Carolina currency when recovered.

Page 270.—3d November, 1769. David Black's will—To wife Elizabeth; to children. Executors, Saml. Black and John Bigham. Teste: John Henderson, Jno. Black, Wm. Cowan. Produced 19th December, 1769, by Samuel Black. John Bigham refuses to execute. Widow Elizabeth objected on the ground the testator was not in his right senses, but the will is declared good, and Saml. Black qualifies, with John Black and Michael Bowyer.

Page 273.—9th October, 1769. George Ghost's estate settled, by Isaac Robinson.

Page 274.—19th December, 1769. William Bowyer's bond (with Robert McClenachan, Alex. McClenachan, Michl. Bowyer, John Bowyer) as sheriff.

Page 275.—19th December, 1769. William Bowyer's bond (with Robert McClenachan, Alex. McClenachan, Michl. Bowyer, John Bowyer), bond to collect quit rents.

Page 276.—20th March, 1770. William Stewart's appraisement (by Wm. Robertson, Jno. Givens, Hugh Allen), recorded.

Page 276.—28th November, 1769. Thomas Beard's estate appraised (by John Montgomery, Wm. Moore, Thomas Wilson). James Mitchell and Thomas Hill, executors.

Page 277.—24th May, 1769. Jonathan Cunningham's will, of Carr's Creek—To wife Mary; to dutiful father, Hugh Cunningham. Executors, father Hugh and William McKee, testator's brother-in-law. Teste: Hugh Weir, Nathan Peoples, Cornelius Docherty, Robert Hamilton. Proved, 20th March, 1770, by Weir and Peoples. William McKee refuses to execute. Hugh Cunningham qualifies, with Wm. McKee, John McKee.

Page 280.—20th March, 1770. George Brown's inventory (by Danl. McNare, Robert Armstrong, James Kirk), recorded.

Page 281.—20th March, 1770. John Stephenson's bond (with Alex. Hamilton, Robert Clark) as guardian to James Rusk, orphan of James Rusk.

Page 282.—20th March, 1770. John Colley's estate settled, by Christopher Ermentrout—Paid Valentine Butcher, Paul Shover, Jacob Goodman, Ludwick Fridley, Peter Hole, Jacob Grub, Jacob Fred. Couters, Michl. Hornbeck, Anthony Hornbeck, Mary Colly, Elizabeth Colly, Wm. Glassgo, Susannah Powers; paid Elizabeth Glassgow the specific legacies due by the will of her deceased husband.

Page 283.—20th March, 1770. Christian Colly's estate settled, by Christopher Ermantrout—Paid Pat Wilson, Matt. McDowell, Danl. Stringar, Jacob Ruh.

Page 285.—20th March, 1770. Elizabeth Rutherford's bond (with Jacob Woodle, John Phillips) as administratrix of Thomas Rutherford.

Page 286.—20th March, 1770. James Frew's (True?) appraisement (by John Stewart, John Burnside, Hugh Allen), recorded.

Page 287.—20th March, 1770. John Kerr's bond (Archibald Hamilton, Wm. Robertson) as administrator of James Kerr.

Page 288.—21st March, 1770. John Dilling's appraisement (by Andrew Huling (Heeling?), Lewis Circle, Jacob Rambo), recorded.

Page 289.—24th November, 1769. Charles McGee's estate appraised, by Robert, Saml. and James Montgomery.

Page 289.—13th March, 1770. Alexander Bruce's estate settled, by John Montgomery, administrator—Paid Joseph Montgomery, Walter Stewart, Anthony Bledsoe, John and Andrew Crockett, Wm. Sawyers, Thos. Ramsey, Andrew Lyday. Received from James Allison for improvements and right of entry of land sold Allison. Due the estate from Benj. Rutherford, John Rutherford and Wm. Herbert.

Page 291.—25th August, 1769. Col. Abraham Smith's plantation at South Branch, near Paul Shever's, containing 140 acres; there are 28 fruit trees planted, 4 acres cleared land and 5 acres fenced, a very good house worth £5, about 30 fruit trees planted. By John Poage, James and John Skidmore.

Page 292.—21st March, 1770. Alexander McClenachan's bond (with Robert McClenachan) as guardian to John, Andrew, James, Elizabeth and David Black, orphans of David Black.

Page 293.—16th March, 1770. Nicholas Null's estate sold at vendue—To Abram Wright, Augustine Price, Henry Null, Honekil Hoofman, Paushton Ostler, Gill Price, Ponshton Hostler, John Ferrel (Terril), Hauverstine Price, Patrick Dickson, George Null, William McBush, Peter Brinninger, Windle Weaver, Francis Kirtley, Wm. Munger, Alvenious Bowyer, Samuel Muncey, Peter Bunginger, Thos. Birk, Philip Williams, Henry Bingaman. Cash from Charles Fry, John Couch. By Windle Sivers' bond, from Archibald Hughston. By Charles Rush's note, Nicholas Shirley.

Page 296.—23d March, 1770. James Kerr's estate appraised, by George Elliott, Benj. Yardley, John Givens.

Page 297.—7th January, 1770. Jacob Warren's will, yeoman—To son Thomas; to daughter Elizabeth; to daughter Hannah; to son John; to wife Anna, and granddaughter Ann Warren, 275 acres. Executors, wife Ann and Abraham Lincoln. Teste: Abraham Lincoln, Michael Warren, Edmon Warren. Proved, 26th March, 1770, by the witnesses. Lincoln refuses to execute. Ann qualifies, with Michael Warren, Danl. Smith.

Page 299.—28th April, 1769. Adam Thompson's estate appraised, by John Buchanan, James Callison, John Handly.

Page 301.—3d September, 1744. Margaret Adams' will, of Orange County—To son Robert Patterson and his children; to Mary Patterson, daughter of son Robert Patterson; to daughter Jane Love; to granddaughter Margaret Dollinson; to granddaughter Ester Harrison; to daughter Elizabeth; to son-in-law Daniel Love; to son Samuel Adams. Executors, Robert Patterson and Samuel Adams. Teste: Saml. Hull, Jacob Green (Gum?),

Thomas Lunday. We, the children of Margaret Adams, have reseved of the exter the full of all legsy I say revd. accordin to her desiare and will.—Danl. Love, Jane (mark) Love, Ester Harrison. 15th September, 1744. These are to certify to all persons whom, &c., that I, Robert Patterson of North Carolina, Tryon County, son of William Patterson, deceased, do disclaim any right or title that is or may be alledged belonging to me of a certain tract of land lying and being in Augusta County upon a small branch on the south side of Linvell's Creek, which said land was taken up by Margaret Adams, the widow of John Adams, deceased.—Robert R. Patterson. 1st February, 1770. Teste: Francis Adams, J. P., North Carolina, Tryon County. Certifies that Francis Adams is a magistrate. Ezekiel Polk, C. C. Proved, 15th March, 1770, by Samuel Hull and Jacob Gum. Samuel Adams qualifies executor, with Joseph Dictum, John Madison, Jr.

Page 304.—15th May, 1770. John Madison's bond (with Thomas Madison) as guardian to Catherine Madison, orphan of Humphrey Madison.

Page 305.—17th March, 1770. John Patterson's will—To wife Jane; to grandson John Patterson, son of son Robert; to son John; to son William; to son James; to son Robert; to daughters Agness, Rebecca, Elizabeth. Teste: George Taylor, John Wiley. Proved, 28th March, 1770, by the witnesses. 19th June, 1770, Jane Patterson is granted administration and qualifies (mark), with Thos. Patterson, John Allison.

Page 308.—26th May, 1770. John Lowry's will—To wife Jean; to son Melvin; to son Patrick; to son-in-law Saml. Todd; to son John, executor. Teste: Archd. Alexander, Moses Trimble, Saml. Lyle. Proved, 19th June, 1770, by Trimble and Lyle. Executor qualifies, with Nathl. Evans, Samuel Lyle.

Page 310.—9th May, 1770. Thomas Redford's estate appraised, by George Carpenter, James Bruster, Archd. Huston.

Page 311.— —— ———— ——. John Brown's will—To wife Margaret; to son Thomas; to son James; to daughter Elizabeth Skillern; to son Hugh (infant), land adjoining the Meeting House; to son John. Land in Greenbrier to be divided between the 4 sons. Executors, wife Margaret and son James. Teste: John Poage, Jacob Lockhart. Proved, 19th June, 1770, by the witnesses. James Brown refuses to execute. Margaret (her mark) qualifies, with Thomas Brown, James Brown.

Page 315.—19th June, 1770. Dorothy Caplinger's bond (with John Poage, Peter Vaneman) as administratrix of Saml. Caplinger.

Page 316.—20th June, 1770. Mary Stevenson's bond, Andw. Hays' bond (with Saml. McDowell, Jacob Anderson) as administrators of John Stevenson.

Page 318.—28th October, 1769. Saml. Caplinger's estate appraised. by Francis Arvig (Awigand?) and George Hammer and Jacob Peterson.

Page 318.—21st August, 1770. Martha and Alexander Walker's bond (with Thos. Connly, John and Robert Campbell) as administrators of Alexander Walker, Jr.

Page 320.—21st August, 1770. Jane Martin's renunciation of right to administer in favor of George and Andrew Martin. Test: Joh Pettrson, Michael Harra, David Hays, Thomas Berry.

Page 320.—19th September, 1769. Patrick Martin's will: To wife, Jane; to sons, George and Andrew; to sons, Joseph and James; to daughter, Mary Patterson. Executors, wife, Jane, and George Martin. Teste:

George Jameson, James McNutt, Alex. Montgomery. Proved, 21st August, 1770, by Jameson. George Martin qualifies executor, with Joseph Berry, James Buchanan, Alex. McNutt.

Page 323.—22d August, 1770. Felix Gilbert's bond (with John Madison) as administrator of William Sallix.

Page 325.—18th August, 1770. James Hogshead, Jr.'s, improvements valued—89 acres joining James' other land and Thomas Bradshaw, by Roger Kilpatrick, William McKemey, Wm. Anderson.

Page 325.—4th November, 1769. George Darr's estate, appraised by Robert Breckinridge, John Nelly, Joseph Cloyd.

Page 326.—22d August, 1770. William Sharp's bond (with John Poage) as guardian to Jane Meek, orphan of John Meek.

Page 326.—22d August, 1770. Michael Mallow's bond (with Jno. Poage, Danl. Smith) as administrator of Noah Roundtree.

Page 328.—22d August, 1770. Jacob Warren's appraisement (by Jno. Henton, David Ralstone, Reuben Harrison) recorded.

Page 329.—7th July, 1770. Jacob Warren's estate sold by Anne Warren—To Alexander West, Michael Warren, John Werren, Timothy Warren, Edmond Warren, John Broion, Robert Mathes, Abriham Lincoln, Mary Warren, Methias McGlamry.

Page 331.—3d August, 1770. John Brown's estate, appraised by James Ewing, William McPheeters, John Buchanan.

Page 334.—11th April A. D., 1769 (vid p. 150, *supra.*). The moveable effects of Isaac Brackfield, deceased, sold at public auction as follows, viz: Drs. William Barefield, John Bear, Anthony Rader, Michael Lamb, Jacob Holman, Mathias Rader, Jacob Miller, Conrad Humble, Michael Kintner, Thomas Pickens, James Johnson, Christopher Brackfield, George Kintner, Saml. Nicholas, Rese Thomas, Martin Craider, Adam Rader, Sr., George Trumbo, James Cain, James Beggs, Michael Hannegam, Jacob Brackfield.

Page 328.—Isaac Brackfield's estate settled by Jacob Miller—Paid a minister's stipend.

Page 339 (vid pp. 409-10).—25th August, 1770. Benj. Harrison's bond (with Andw. Bird and David Bell) as administrator of Danl. Harrison.

Page 340 (vid pp. 409-10).—25th August, 1770. Sarah Harrison's bond (with Abrm. Smith) as executrix of Daniel Harrison.

Page 341.—27th August, 1770. Mathew Shaup's estate in account with Jacob Nicholas.

Page 342.—20th April, 1770. Division line between Augusta and Botetourt, beginning on South Mountain by a spring of Pedlar Creek on Amherst line where South River or Mary Creek empties into North Branch of James River, up the river to Kerr's Creek, up the creek to its upper fork at Gilmore's Gape, crosses Cowpasture River in Donnelly's place, crosses road between Hot and Warm Springs, crosses Jackson's River in John Dean's place, crosses Back Creek to Anthony's Creek Mountain.

Page 343.—31st October, 1768. Michael O'Donley's estate, appraised by John McClure, Saml. Black, Wm. Black.

Page 344.—20th November, 1770. George Mathews' bond (with Sampson Mathews, John Archer, Pet. Hog) as sheriff.

Page 347.—20th November, 1770. Thomas Hicklen's bond (with Hugh and John Hicklin) as guardian to Christopher Graham, orphan of Robert Graham.

Page 347.—20th November, 1770. Charles Rush's bond (with Daniel Sink, Peter Miller) as administrator of Nicholas Hoffman.

Page 349.—20th November, 1770. Elizabeth Coffman's bond (with Sebasten Hover, Adam Rodeback) as administratrix of Henry Coffman.

Page 350.—2d September, 1770. William Henderson's will, aged about 71 years—To wife; two sons, William and David Henderson; to son, James; to three sons-in-law, David and Joseph Bell and John Leeper; to Shusanna Henderson, daughter of son John Henderson; to Shusanna Finley, daughter to daughter Martha; to granddaughter, Jeen Teas. Executors, wife, and brother, Samuel Henderson, and testator's son, James Henderson. Teste: Walter Davis, John Carlile. Proved, 20th November, 1770, by the witnesses. James Henderson qualifies executor, with Samuel Henderson, John Carlile.

Page 353.—21st November, 1770. Thomas and Charles Lewis' bond (with John Bowyer, John Madison) as guardian to William Long, orphan of William Long.

Page 354.—14th August A. D., 1770. John Stephenson's estate, appraised by Thomas Wilson, John McClung, James McCampbell, James Buchanan—William Chambers' account, insolvent; John Michel Siver's bond, not all solvent; Eracker Smith, James Doearn.

Page 357.—21st November, 1770. Alexander Robertson's appraisement (by John McMahon, Robt. Stevenson, James Allen, Arthur Conoley).

Page 358.—30th August, 1770. John Smith's estate, appraised by Robert McClenachan, Pat. Buchanan, Jno. Buchanan.

Page 360.—26th November, 1770. Alex. McClenachan's bond (with John McClenachan) as guardian to Elizabeth and Martha Wilson, orphans of Saml. Wilson.

Page 361.—27th November, 1770. George Brown's estate in account with James Sawyers.

Page 361.— — November, 1770. George Rodgers' estate, settlement recorded—1769, 23d March, cash paid Thomas Smith for Coffin; cash paid Thomas Poage for flour and butter at the funeral; 1768, 30th June, cash paid Robert Philips for hunting horses; 1768, 10th October, cash paid Hugh Johnston for the corps, cash paid Robert Hartgrove for warning to the funeral; 1769, October, cash paid Owen Sullivan for drawing this account; cash paid for washing, fire, candles, and attendance the corps two days and a night; cash paid Caleb Foulke's bond; cash paid Saml. Hudson's bond; cash paid Andrew Tybout's bond; cash paid Dr. John Watkins; 1768, 16th November, cash received of Benj. Early, James Lessley's wife, ditto Philip Harly.

Page 364.—29th November, 1770. George Mathews' bond (with Samp. Mathews, Thos. Madison, John Madison, Jr.) for collection of County proportion.

Page 365.—15th January, 1771. John Frogg's bond (with John Madison, Jr., Sampson Mathews) as administrator of Arthur Frogg.

Page 367.—19th March, 1771. William Bowyer's bond (with Michael Bowyer, Thomas Madison) as administrator of William Christian.

Page 368.—26th May, 1770. John Smith's will—To wife, Barbara; to son, Jacob, 80 acres of the plantation already bought; to sons, John and Peter Villortin; to daughter, Margaret Penner; to daughter, Madline Howe

(Hone). Executors, wife Barbara and son Jacob. Teste: Jon. Henderson, James Buchanan, Thomas Scott. Proved, 19th March, 1771, by James Buchanan and Scott. Both executors qualify (Barbara, her mark), with John Poage.

Page 370.—13th December, 1770. Henry Coffman's estate appraised, by Abraham Bird, Jacob Miller, &c.

Page 372.—30th November, 1770. John Nicholas Coffman's estate appraised by Jacob Nicholas, Daniel Price, &c.

Page 374.—20th March, 1771. Margaret Linsey's estate settled by John Gilmore—Paid Alexander Deal, John Beaty, Robt. McLehenny, Timothy Ryan, Wm. Porter, Alex. and Robt. Tedford.

Page 375.—28th August, 1770. Patrick Martin's estate appraised by Thomas Berry, Saml. McCutchen, Geo. Jameson.

Page 377.—20th March, 1771. John Patterson's appraisement (by George Eliot, James Gambel, John Hall) recorded.

Page 378.—23d September, 1769. Robert Allison's estate appraised by William Hall, Joseph Walker.

Page 379.—22d March, 1770. John Donnelly, Sr.'s, estate settlement recorded—William Preston, administrator, 1765. 1765, cash paid Saml. Piper for making a coffin. 1765, 29th October, cash paid Joseph Cloyd for rum for vendue. Cash paid Drewry Puckett, James McAffee, David Fleming, Joseph McDonald, Conrad Wall, James Cloyd, administratrix of Abraham Biss. Has paid the widow her thirds, and three of the children. Estate sold at vendue to, viz: Danl. McCormick, Walter Stewart, Drury Puckett, Archd. Fisher, Michael Reesener, James Laughlin, Elizabeth Hance, George Darr, Wm. Thornton.

Page 381.—27th November, 1770. William Henderson's estate appraised by Walter Davis, Thomas Rutledge, Alex. Long—Bonds of Lazarus Inman, Sith Rodgers, Andrew Russell, Sr. and Jr.

Page 383.—21st March, 1771. James Patton's settlement of estate recorded—John Buchanan, executor; 1758, 22d April, paid Francis Riely; 1765, 5th June, to putting Ratclif's place into the office where it was tossed, for the estate; 1761, 14th August, cash paid Dr. Thomas Walker for his claim to Burke's Garden; 1761, 26th June, cash paid Zachariah Lewis for his 6th share of the Roanoke and James River Grant, which share is annexed to the estate of Col. Patton; 1761, 27th June, to my third of 182 acres on ye North Fork of Roanoke sold to James Bryans for £150; 1766, September, to cash paid John Moffett for 170 acres, part of which had been surveyed for and sold to Michael Dougherday by Col. Patton by mistake; 1756—8th September, by cash of Wm. Armstrong (Roanoke); 20th September, Wm. Ralston; 1757—7th February, Wm. Snodgrass; 19th February, John Marshall; 23d April, James Hutton; 13th January, John Stevens; 1758—20th February, Ester Sawyers; 22d April, John Potts; 1759—17th May, Hugh Carruthers; 1760—25th February, Wm. Carravin; 25th August, Peter Ipsher; 1761—11th July, James Bane; 14th November, Jacob Harmon, Sr., for the Horse Shoe Bottom; 1763—16th June, Joseph Crockett on account of John McCurry; 1764—16th November, Nicholas Welsh on account of Placeard Scilor; 1767—Frederick Stern by John Taylor, who has purchased his land; 5th March, widow Bowen, Sr.; 1768—12th September, by cash of Danl. Goodwin for Mathias Vance's old place sold him;

1768—27th January, John Peary for land sold him, formerly sold to Kemp; 22d February, Thos. Goodson for Wm. McCurry and Thos. Wilson.

Page 389.—12th September, 1767. John Donelly's estate appraised by James McCown, Lanty Armstrong, John Armstrong, Bryan McDonald.

Page 389.—14th October, 1769. Col. John Buchanan's estate appraised by John Blackimore, Jos. How, Saml. Pepper.

Page 391.— — 1769. William Salix's estate in account with Felix Gilbert.

Page 392.— — 1770. David Black's estate in account with Saml. Black, administrator.

Page 394.—24th March, 1771. Saml. Floyd's bond (with Robert Armstrong, Charles Floyd) as administrator of William Floyd.

Page 396.—22d March, 1771. Elliott (Ellet) Rutherford's bond (with Daniel Smith, John Gratton) as guardian to Robert, Joseph, Reuben, Mary Rutherford, orphans of Thomas Rutherford.

Page 397.—26th March, 1771. Henry King's bond (with Saml. .McKee) as guardian to John Cockran, orphan of Jno. Cockran.

Page 398.—30th July, 1769. John Harrison's will, cordwinder—To wife, Phoebe; to son, Zebulun; to son, Reuben, the Long Meadow plantation; to daughter, Pheby Moore; to daughter, Ann Langdon. Executors, sons Zebulon and Reuben. A Baptist minister to preach his funeral sarment. Teste: Felix Sheltman, John Ray, John Harrison, Jr. Proved, 21st May, 1771, by Ray and Harrison. Executors qualify with Archibald Huston, James Beard.

Page 401.—16th May, 1771. Bill of sale by Andrew Boyd to William Preston, executor of James Patton, of 5 negro slaves and sold by Preston to Andrew Boyd and Mary Boyd, his wife, eldest daughter of Col. John Buchanan, deceased, and Margaret, his wife, in compliance with the will of James Patton.

Page 402.—21st May, 1771. Robert Risk's bond (with Moses Moore, Danl. Meek) as guardian to James Risk, orphan of James Risk.

Page 403.— — May, 1771. Archibald and John Hopkins' (commissioners) assignment of dower to Sarah Harrison (widow) recorded.

Page 404.—10th October, 1770. John Berry's will—To daughter, Mary; to John Nesbit; to John Berry, son of James Berry, deceased; to John Berry, son of William Berry; to John Berry, son of William Berry; to John Berry, son of Francis Berry; to Francis Berry, wheelwright; to Mary Berry, daughter of Wm. Berry, and her sister Elizabeth; to Elizabeth Berry, daughter of Charles Berry; to daughter, Rebecca Berry. Executors, Alexander Walker, wheelwright, and Wm. Edmastonn. Teste: John Walker, Jr., James Walker, Francis Berry. Proved, 22d March, 1771, by John, John (Jr.), and James Walker. Executors qualify (Edmiston's mark —) with John Walker, Jas. Crawford.

Page 407.—23d May, 1771. Estate of John Cloyd, Dr., to James Cloyd—To paid Martin Allen, cryer of vendue.

Page 408.—8th June, 1767. Daniel Harrison's will—To wife; to Sarah Stevenson, his wife's daughter; to son, Benjamin Harrison, youngest son; to children. Teste: Andrew Johnson, John Johnson, Robt. Brown, Andrew Johnson's deposition taken in Culpeper County, 13th May, 1771, before James Barbour, Jr., and Robert Throckmorton. Proved, 25th August,

1770, by John Johnson. Executors qualified as above, vid., pages 339, 340.

Page 411.—13th August, 1771. John Berry's estate appraised by Joseph Culton, John Walker, John Stewart—Bonds of Hugh and Francis McClung; Wm. McGaughey, not solvent; Robert Farice, not solvent; Peter Cutwright, solvent; Robt. Buchanan, solvent.

Page 412.—3d June, 1769. David Graham's estate appraised by John Davis, Archibald Smithers, Wm. Hutcheson. Accounts against, viz., Job Fletcher, Thomas Mann, Robert Vachob, Jas. Fitzpatrick.

Page 414.— — 1776. Later appraisement of Wm. Fitzgeral's estate—To a cow killed for use of soldiers at Fort McNeil.

Page 414.—20th August, 1771. Mary M. Gregory's bond (with John McClenachan, Saml. Vance, Henry Gay) as administratrix of James Gregory.

Page 415.—20th May, 1771. Mary Dice's bond (with George Hammer, Mathias Dice) as administratrix of George Dice.

Page 417.—7th July, 1771. William Elliott's will—To wife; to son, James; to son, John; to son, William; to rest of the children; to son, Archibald, schooling and smith's trade; to son, Lanty, schooling and choose a trade. Executors, wife Jane and son John. Teste: Robert Clark, John Stephenson, James Clark. Proved, 21st August, 1771, by the witnesses. Executors qualify (Jane's mark —) with Archibald Armstrong, Jno. Dickinson.

Page 420.—21st August, 1771. Michael (Micael) Mallow petitions that one Noah Rountree was murdered on his plantation by the barbarity of one Jes (Ies) Townsend, who was tried in this court and sent to Williamsburg. Micael has buried the corpse and had the estate appraised and sold and holds, subject to the court's order, viz: Sold to George Cauger, Saml. Skidmore, by expense of burying.

Page 421.—21st August, 1771. A general account of debts paid due from the estate of Wm. Fitzjeral, deceased, by John McCaslin, administrator. 1776, August, to Edward Simpson for his son. Credit by the sale bill, viz: To Thomas Spencer, Francis Jackson, Timothy Sulivan, Edward Thompson.

Page 423.—2d May, 1771. William Lusk's will—To sons, John and William Lusk, in Carolina, 5 shillings each; to daughter, Mary Philips; to son, Joseph; to wife, Elizabeth; to daughters, Elizabeth, Sarah, and Margaret. Executors, wife Elizabeth, with Andrew Hays, Sr., and Saml. Lyle. Teste: Archd. Alexander, Daniel Lyle, James Lyle, Jr. Proved, 20th August, 1771, by Daniel and James Lyle, and on 21st August, 1771, and Saml. Lyle and Andrew Hays qualify with Andrew Mc(Mis)Campbell, Thomas Vance.

Page 425.—27th June, 1766. William Johnson's will (about to remove out of Virginia to Pennsylvania)—To brother, Michael Johnston, now living in Upper Freehold in East Jersey; to only daughter, Mary Johnston, when she comes to age of 18, which will be in 1776. Executors, Alexander Thompson. Teste: John Thompson, Sarah Thompson, James Thorp. Proved, 21st August, 1771, by John and Sarah Thompson. Executor qualifies with Robert and John Thompson.

Page 428.—4th April, 1771. John Stuawart's (Stewart) will, of the Middle River of Shanadoe—To wife, Mary; to Saml. Henderson and Geo.

Crawford, all his lands in trust until testator's son John reaches 20 years; to children under age, two white servants, Wm. Kelly and Danl. Huggen; to daughter, Jane; to son, William, when he attains 20 years; to eldest son, William, the plantation devised to him by his Uncle William Stewart, deceased; to second son, John, plantation testator lives on; to third son, James; to above trustees, the tract on Middle River bought of Wm. Robertson; to daughter, Jane Stewart, unmarried, under 25; to daughters, Mary and Elizabeth, under 18. Executors, the trustees above. Teste: Hugh Allen, William Kerr, Thomas Frame. Proved, 21st August, 1771, by Allen and Frame. Executors qualify with Hugh Allen and Thomas Frame.

Page 434.—6th August, 1771. John Robertson's will—To wife; to son, Alexander, infant; to children; to six daughters. Executors, wife Mary and nephew Alex. Robertson, son of brother Mathew Robertson. Teste: Silas Hart, Mathew Robertson, Matthew Matthewson. Proved, 21st August, 1771, by the witnesses.

Page 436.—Mary qualifies (her mark —) with Wm. Hutcheson, John Lessley, Jos. Gamwell.

Page 438.—21st August, 1771. Daniel Harrison's appraisement (by Solomon Tirpin, Robert Craven, John Gratton) recorded.

Page 441.—21st August, 1771. Jane Graham settles David Graham's estate—By Wm. Follin's note; Uriah Humphrey's; paid Jacob Salmons, David Floyd, Christopher Vachob, Mathew Morehead, Nansey Hamilton, Jacob Keyls.

Page 443.—21st August, 1771. Samuel Craig's bond (with William and James Bell) as guardian to John Black, orphan of Anthony Black.

Page 444.—14th February, 1771. John Mitchell's will, farmer—To wife, Elizabeth, plantation hired (?) from his mother by verbal will; to third son, John; to fourth son, James, executor; to youngest daughter, Elizabeth; to eldest son, Thomas; to eldest daughter, Elenor Wilson; to second son, Robert; to second daughter, Mary Right. Teste: John Tate, Andrew Moore, Thos. Wilson. Proved, 20th August, 1771, by Moore and Wilson.

Page 446.—9th August, 1771. Estimate of funeral and other charges due Wm. Berry and Alex. Walker, executors from the estate of John Berry, by James Walker, James McCampbell, Alex. Walker, Andrew Hays

Page 447.—19th November, 1771. Charles Rush's bond (with Jacob Nicholas) as administrator of Lodwick Fridley.

Page 448.—20th November, 1771. William Elliot's appraisement by James Graham, Christopher Vachub, John Graham, recorded—Jane and John Elliot, executors.

Page 452.—29th July A. D., 1771. John Graham's will—To oldest son, Lanty; to wife, Elizabeth; to James Graham's son, John; to Lanty's brother John's son, John; to daughter Anne; to Jane Lockridge; to Rebecca and her son, John; to Robert Graham; to daughters, Florence and Betty; to sons, Robert and John; to Lanty's daughter, Rebecca; to daughters, Flory, Jane, Betty, and Anne. Executors, wife and son Lanty. Teste: Joseph Robinson, John Kinkead, John Armstrong. Proved, 19th November, 1771, by Kinkead and Armstrong. Executors qualify with James Gay, Wm. Young.

Page 454.—7th September, 1771. Thomas (mark) Hicklin, Sr.'s will, of the Bull Pasture—To son, Hugh; to son, John, Thomas; to daughters,

Rosannah Johnston, Jane Laverty; to daughters, Dinah Botkin, Sarah Black. Executor, eldest son Hugh. Teste: James Bradshaw, Agness Bradshaw, Wm. Steward. Proved, 20th November, 1771, by the witnesses. Executor qualifies with Charles Lewis, John Wilson.

Page 457.—20th November, 1771. John Robertson's appraisement by Jno. Malcom, John Davis, John McCay, Adam Stephenson, recorded.

Page 459.—16th March, 1771. Settlement of Henry Coffman's estate— By bonds of, viz: James Sears and Michael Thorn, David Cradock, Christopher Yeasill and Philip Crites, Mary Tasher and Michael Thorn, Henry Coffman and Michael Stump, Elizabeth Tasher and Michael Thorn, Peter Shook and James Sears, Joseph Wilson, George Yeokim and Michael Thorn, John Rorebough and Martin Jobb, John Higgens and Ignetius Coombs, Danl. McNeil and John Westfall, Michael Moore and Geo. Yeokim, John Spelman and John Roreback, Job Wellton and Thos. Parsons, Thos. Parsons and Robert Cunningham, Jacob Bogard and Michael Harness, Martin Jobb and Adam Rydebogh, Elizabeth Tosher and Michael Thorn. By cash received at vendue as follows, viz: Richard Byrn, Jacob Break, John Our, Philip Crites, Lanie Hire, Leonard Knave, Charles Smith, Lewis Shriver, Jacob Rabuck, Richard Byrn, Michael Drum (Dunn?), James Willkie, Conrad Moore, Christale Tasher, Abigail Coffman, John Gradner. Debts due by Jacob Reiger. Debts due to, viz: Peter Haws, Cathrine Stump, Malldlin Break, Chas. Lynch. Cash paid as follows, viz: To Richard Brynns, James Willy, Madlin Coofman.

Page 464.—20th November, 1771. John Willson's estate, Dr., to John Dean, settlement.

Page 465.—22d November, 1771. Elizabeth and Samuel McDowell's bonds as administrators of James McDowell.

Page 466.—21st November, 1771. Appraisement recorded of John Harrison's estate by Michael Warren, John Hinton, Wm. Henton.

Page 468.—21st November, 1771. Recorded. Charles McGee's estate, Dr. to Saml. McRoberts, administrator—Paid to, viz: Robert Montgomery, John McRoberts, Joseph Montgomery, James Montgomery, Wm. Caruthers. Received, viz: John Coonby's note, James Jervis' note, Josiah Ramsey's note.

Page 469.—5th September, 1771. Recorded. Settlement of estate of Alex. Crawford, by John McPheeters—1st November, 1764, vendue, sold to, viz: John Windor, Alex. Kelly, Alex. Leget, Nancy Berry, Hugh Kellsey, Adam Morrow. Paid John Elliott for Isabella.

Page 473.—28th November, 1771. George Mathews' bond (with Sampson Mathews, John Madison, Jr., Thomas Madison) for collection of County Levy.

Page 473.—17th March, 1772. Paul Custard's (signed Kuster) bond (with Jacob Miller) as administrator of nuncupative will of Conrad Custard.

Page 475.—17th March, 1772. Recorded. Michael O'Donnel's additional appraisement—Cash from Robert McClinken, Pady Curren, Maley Burbeg, executor of Gerd Coldu.

Page 475.—17th March, 1772. Henry McDonald's bond (with Thos. Kinkead, Saml. Kelly) as administrator of Saml. McDonald.

Page 477.—11th January, 1772. Be it known to all persons to whom it may Concern, that whereas Simon Casedy hath taken a Liberty to spread some Slanderous Reports upon John Hall's Daughter concerning her Chastity and on Robert Wiley Concerning Stealing or taking of Bells Clendestantly, and, on being Convicted thereof, he doth hereby freely Acknowledge his fault that what he said was Positively false, malicious and without foundation, and that he is Heartily sorry for the same to which he hath subscribed this 11th of January, 1772.—Simon Casidy. Teste: John Poage, Moses Wall, Chas. Harris, and several others.

Page 478.—23d January, 1772. Michael Coiner's recantation of slanderous words as above. Teste: Henry Cresswell.

Page 478.—12th September, 1771. William Lusk's estate appraised by Henry McClung, Daniel Lyle, Wm. Ramsey. Statement of the part of above estate willed to wife, Elizabeth Lusk.

Page 480.—13th January, 1772. Edward Erwin's will, of Long Glade—To sons, Edward and Francis Erwin; to Francess Brown, bed and furniture, if she behaves well and marry by consent; to son-in-law, Robert Law. Executors, sons Edward and Francis. Teste: Edward Erwin, Robt. Curry, John Erwin. Proved, 18th March, 1772, by Edward and John Erwin. Executors qualify with Wm. and Saml. Corry.

Page 483.—28th December, 1771. Halbert McClure's will—to wife, Mary, executrix; to 3 daughters, Mary, Isabella, Phebe. Teste: Archd. Alexander, Robert Feris, Wm. Alexander. Proved, 18th March, 1772, by Fearis and Alexander (Wm.). Mary (her mark) qualifies with Thos. Vance, John Young.

Page 485.—31st January, 1772. Jos. Hicklin's, Sr., estate appraised by Robert Carlile, John Carlile, James Bradshaw.

Page 486.—18th March, 1772. John Graham's appraisement by Thomas Hugart, John Kinkead, Andrew Hamilton.

Page 488.—19th March, 1772. John Carlyle's bond (with John McCreery, John Graham) as administrator of William Gwynn.

Page 490.—26th September, 1771. Col. John Buchanan's estate on Reed Creek appraised.

Page 491.—21st March, 1772. Recorded. George Dice's appraisement by Ulrunk (Alrunk?) Conrat, Jacob Freind.

Page 492.—Culpeper, 21 Nov., 1771. Kind Sir: I received yours a few days ago wherein you let me know you were a little uneasy at my long stay. I am sorry I could not be over before now. If Capt. Peter Hog will bind my son Samuel to you, shall take it a favor of him. I expect to be up between this and the 25th of next month and, if possible, will bring you some Cash, if you desire. My son should be bound before I come up. This is to Empower Captain Peter Hog to do it according to your Request. I am with Sincerity, Your ever Well Wisher, Wiat Coleman. P. S.—My compliments to Mrs. Mathews and all other Friends. To Mr. Sampson Mathews. Favor Capt. James Kenerley.

Page 493.—Whereas Robert Cowdon has for some time Past reported and said that William Ledgerwood was a convict, he does now Acknowledge it to be False Report and that he had no Grounds for saying so of him. As witness my hand this 30th day of March, 1772.—Robert Cowdon. Teste: Hugh Young, John Young.

Page 493.—21st March, 1772. Phillip Harles' will—Executors, Mathias Kersh and Augustine Price; to wife, Margaret; to son, Martin Harless, tract on Sinking Creek called Clover Bottom, in Botetourt County; to son, Immanuel, infant, 600 acres where testator lives; to son, Philip, 113 acres in Botetourt; to son, David, 300 acres in Botetourt on Tom's Creek; to son, Henry, cash; to daughter, Margaret; to daughter, Mary. Teste: Archd. Huston, Samuel Bell, Margaret Bell. Proved, 19th May, 1772, by Huston and Bell (Saml.). Augustine Price qualifies with Charles Rush, Henry Price, Danl. Price.

Page 497.—5th November, 1771. Saml Doak's will, farmer—To wife, Jane; to daughter, Elinor, unmarried; to wife, to have disposal of all household furniture at her Pleasure to her 3 daughters, Elinor, Mary, Isbel; to son, John; to oldest son, David, plantation David now lives on as Robert Doak laid it off; to son, Samuel, plantation at head waters of Rockfish in Amherst; to son, John, plantation testator lives on; to son, Robert, tract testator formerly lived on in Rockfish, joining Capt. Crawford; daughters, Jane and Elizabeth. Executors, wife Jane, son David, son-in-law Wm. Brown. Brother-in-law John Finley and John Tate to advise executors. Teste: John and James Mitchel, William Tate, John Tate, Jr. Proved, 19th May, 1772, by James Mitchel and the Tates. David Doack qualifies with John Tate, Nathaniel Steel.

Page 500.—31st March, Ano Domino, 1772. Jane Patterson's will, formerly wife of John Patterson—To son, William Patterson; to son, James Patterson's son John; to daughter, Elizabeth; to daughter, Mary; to son, Robert's daughter Jean; to son, James' daughter Jean; to daughter, Janet. Son-in-law Thomas Dixon and son James to make division. Executors, son James and son-in-law Thomas Dixon. Teste: James Gambel, Robert Gambel. Proved, 19th May, 1772, by the witnesses. Thos. Dixon refuses to execute. James qualifies (his mark) with Thomas Patterson, Alex. Thompson.

Page 503.—18th May, 1772. William Johnston's estate appraised by George Caldwell, Wm. Palmer, John Caldwell.

Page 503.—10th April, 1772. We, the subscribers being first sworne to appraise the estate of Conrad Coustar, deceased, Feb. 1st, 1772, as followeth, appraised by us April 10th, 1772—Uriah Humble, Jas. Marsall, Abraham Bird.

Page 505.—19th May, 1772. Appraisement recorded of John Stewart's estate by Wm. Robertson, James Kerr, John Givens—In James Gildart's hand in Liverpool Sterling.

Page 506.—19th May, 1772. John Trimble's bond (with James Trimble, Saml. McDowell, Elijah McClenachan) as Assistant Surveyor.

Page 507.—2d April, 1772. Thomas Hutcheson's will—To wife, Sarah, plantation and the boy, Thomas Rhoads (if she gives up Thomas Rhoades, then John Hamilton is to have him); to daughters, Agness and Sarah. Executors, Andrew McClure and John Hamilton. Teste: Zach. Johnston, Francis Alexander, John Williams. Proved, 20th May, 1772, by the witnesses. Both executors refuse to execute. Administration granted Sarah Hutcheson, who qualifies (her mark) with William Scott, William Scott.

Page 510.—11th April, 1769. James Knox's will—Executors, John Dickinson, John Cartmill, Sr.; to wife, Jane; to son, James; to son, John, £5, if he comes for it; to son, Robert; to daughter, Jean; to daughter, Abigail; to daughters, Elizabeth, Mary. Teste: John Dickinson, Daniel

Workman, Martha Dickinson. Proved, 20th May, 1772, by John Dickinson.

Page 512.—20th May, 1772. William Gwynn's appraisement (by Robert Carlile, John Carlile, Loftiss Pulland) recorded—1 nursery of peach trees.

Page 512.—21st May, 1772. Robert Graham's estate settled; Ralph Laferty, administrator. 1766, August—Paid Mathew Wilson, Richard Ellet.

Page 514.—10th December, 1771. Loudawick Fridley's estate appraised by Archibald Huston, Augustine Price, George Mallow.

Page 515.—23d May, 1772. Adam Thompson's estate settled—Paid John Kitchey, Wm. Macwill. Joshua Russell, Dr.

Page 519.—23d May, 1772. George Mathews' bond (with Samp. Mathews, John Madison, Jr., Thos. Madison) for collection of Public Levy.

Page 520.—10th June, 1772. Saml. Doack's estate appraised by John Ward, James Mitchell, James Meteer.

Page 521.—2d June, 1772. David Dryden's will—To wife, Dorothy, large Bible to be left by her to Nathaniel, and also both Boston's Works; to son, Thomas, 1 dollar; to son, James, 1 dollar; to son, David, 1 dollar; to daughter, Elinor; to daughter, Jane; to daughter, Elizabeth; to sons, Nathaniel and William. Executors, Saml. Lyle and son James. Teste: John and William Thompson, John Moor. Proved, 18th August, 1772, by J. and W. Thompson. Executors qualify.

Page 524.—18th August, 1772. Iseble Stewart's bond (with Henry Cresswell, John Elliott) as administratrix of James Stewart.

Page 526.—6th May, 1772. John Taylor's will—To wife, Esther, executrix; to eleven children; to son, John, £5 more than the others. Teste: Archibald Huston, James Waite, John Stephenson. Proved, 18th August, 1772, by Waite and Huston. Esther qualifies (her mark) with James Waite, Archd. Huston.

Page 528.—12th August, 1772. Robert Stephenson's will—To wife, Martha; to son, Thomas, all lands; to each of living daughters, $1; to "my Mary Rankin, my daughter-in-law"; to grandchildren and Mary Rankin. Executors, John Polock and James Allen, Jr. Teste: James Anderson, Joseph (his — mark) Reaburn, James Allen, Sr. Proved, 18th August, 1772. James Poage ("executor therein named") and James Allen qualify with Jno. Anderson, James Allen.

Page 531.—18th August, 1772. Elizabeth Shaver's bond (with Jacob Harper, Peter Vaneman) as administratrix of Paul Shaver.

Page 533.—18th August, 1772. Settlement of estate of Saml. Caplinger by Dorraty Likens, administrator.

Page 533.—18th August, 1772. Ditto of John Nicholas Hophman by Charles Rush. Paid Michael Shally, Catrine Lumenberger.

Page 534.—17th August, 1772. John Lewis, Deputy Surveyor, enters 400 acres on North Side Middle River Shenandoah between the land James Carr purchased of Nicholas Sallas, and Beverley Manor up the River from Sallos; also 400 acres on South Side Middle River opposite the above.

Page 535.—4th June, 1772. John Trimble, Assistant Surveyor, enters 100 acres on the Walnut Hollow on a ridge between some of the southermost branches of Irish Creek; also 200 acres on another ridge about a northeast course from the above and about 2 miles distant.

Page 535.—18th August, 1772. John Shull's bond (with Michael Abecost, Leonard Seeman) as administrator of Sebastian Neigley.
Page 536.—18th August, 1772. Sebastian Hover's and Mathew Patton's bond (with Jacob Nicholas, James Dyer) as administrators of Mark Swadley.
Page 538.—19th August, 1774 (1772?). Jacob Gillespy's bond (with John Malcom, John McCay) as administrator of Jacob Galespy.
Page 539.—19th August, 1772. Halbert McClure's appraisement by William and Joseph Alexander, Joseph Reed, and settlement of estate recorded—Accounts, viz: James Bunting, Jesse Maupin, Francis Taplett, Thornton Fanow.

ABSTRACTS OF WILLS OF AUGUSTA COUNTY, VIRGINIA.

Will Book No. V.

Page 1.—9th January, 1772. Samuel Nicolas' will, farmer—To wife, Mary; to son, Phillip; to daughter, Elizabeth Nicolas; to son, Margaret Nicolas; to youngest son, John. Executors, son Philip Nicholas and John Thomas. Teste: John Dunbarr, James Thomas, John Bailey. Proved, 19th August, 1772, by the witnesses. Executors qualified with John Miller, John Miller, Jr.
Page 4.—20th June. Bulpasture. Wm. Given, his vendue. Recorded, 19th August, 1772.
Page 4.—19th August, 1772. John Henderson's bond (with John Malcom, John McCoy) as administrator of Daniel Henderson.
Page 6.—19th August, 1772. John Gillmore and John Thompson's bond (with Robert Thompson and Alex. Thompson) as guardians to John Gilmore, orphan of Thomas Gilmore.
Page 7.—19th August, 1772. John Gratton's bond (with John Dunbarr) as guardian to Jane Claypole, orphan of Wm. Claypole.
Page 8.—20th August, 1772. Recorded. Thos. Hutcheson's appraisement by Walter Davis, Andrew McClure, John Hamilton.
Page 9.—20th August, 1772. Thomas Stewart's bond (with George Mathews, David Henderson) as guardian to Charles O'Donald, orphan of Michael O'Donald.
Page 10.—28th ———, 1772. Philip Harles' estate appraised by Archd. Huston, Frederick Ermantrout, Peter Miller.
Page 13.—22d August, 1772. Sampson Mathews' bond with Geo. Mathews as guardian to Martha Mathews, orphan of Joshua Mathews.
Page 13.—28th August, 1772. John Thomas Breden (Bratton? Thomas Bratton? Thomas Braton?) will, yeoman—To wife, Catherine; to wife and children, proceeds of sale of entry for a tract on Stuart's Creek at the Fork of the road leading to Dickinson's and Capt. Lewis. Wife to bind out children to trades in Frederick County or elsewhere. Teste: James

Steel, Robert Scott, James Hill. Proved, 20th August, 1772, by the witnesses, and wife Catherine qualifies (her mark) with Peter Hog and Sampson Mathews.

Page 16.—17th November, 1772. Jane Hook and Thomas McClulock's bond (with John Davidson, John Finley) as administrators of Robert Hook, Jr.

Page 17.—24th September, 1772. Robert Turk's will—To son, Thomas, all estate, executor; to son, James, 1 English shilling. Teste: Charles Teeas, Thomas Turk, Elizabeth Gleave. Proved, 17th November, 1772, by Teas and Turk. Thomas Turk qualifies with John Madison, Jr., John Hind.

Page 20.—17th November, 1772. Andrew Sutlington's bond (with James Gay, Archibald A. Smithers) as administrator of William Sutlington.

Page 21.—17th November, 1772. Christian Roleman and Henry Stone's bond (with John Skidmore, George Kile (Coile)) as administrator of Jacob Roleman.

Page 23.—17th November, 1772. Recorded. James McDowell's appraisement by Archibald Alexander, John McClung, Alex. Stewart, John Lyle—7 negroes, 1 weaver called Christopher Lightfootder, 1 servant boy called Jack McGuire.

Page 27.—17th November, 1772. Recorded. Thomas Bradon's appraisement by James Steel, John Coulter, Hugh McClure.

Page 29.—9th October, 1772. John Taylor's estate appraised by John Stephenson, James Bruster, John Young.

Page 30.—29th October, 1772. Daniel Henderson's estate appraised by Abrum Smith, John Coraford, John Davis.

Page 32.—18th November, 1772. Recorded. Jacob Gillasppey's appraisement by Jarod Erwine, Henry Black, John Craford.

Page 33.—18th November, 1772. Francis Gardner's bond (with Thomas Bradshaw) as guardian to Francis and Samuel Gardner, orphans of Thomas Gardner.

Page 34.—18th November, 1772. Daniel Smith's bond (with Felix Gilbert, Sampson Mathews, Abram Smith, Robt. McClenachan, Wm. McDowell) as sheriff.

Page 35.—Bond as above to collect quit rents, &c.

Page 36.—19th November, 1772. Joseph Kinkead's bond (with Sampson Mathews) as contractor for a jail, price, £268.0.0. Plan annexed—stone stairs run up in the jail; 2 stoves, 1 upstairs and 1 downstairs, to be finished before 1st November, 1773. Undertaker has advantage of the old jail, which is built of stone and has a great quantity of iron and iron doors.

Page 39.—19th November, 1772. William Teas' bond (with Joseph Love) as contractor to repair the road over the Mountain at Rockfish Gap for sum of £30, for the first year and £6.17.6 annually for seven years.

Page 40.—19th November, 1772. Recorded. Prais Bill of Nagle's Estate diseased, by Henry Penaner, George Nickls, Barnit Louts—A membram of old debts. Joseph Ham, Joseph Benit, Jr. and Sr.; Wm. Smith, Old Lanbert, Leg in fot (Seg in fot?), Adam Pour, Sun Volt.

Page 41.—19th November, 1772. Hugh Bodkin's recantation of slanderous words about John McMahon. Teste: Felix Gilbert, David Laird, Joseph Reaburn, David Bell.

Page 42.—20th November, 1772. Thomas Hicklin's estate to Hugh Hicklin: 1771—Paid Thomas Neil for a coffin, paid Dr. Arch. Decon, paid Mrs Jane Laverty, paid my daughter's attendance on said Hicklin in the time of his sickness, 3 months at 12/0.

Page 43.—21st November, 1772. David Henderson, son of Daniel Henderson, apprentices himself to William Young, blacksmith, for 4 years.

Page 44.—21st November, 1772. Recorded. James Gregory's appraisement by William Hutcheson, Archibald Smithers, John Vance.

Page 45.—21st November, 1772. Memorandum of agreement between Sampson and George Mathews with their servants, Denis Callahan, Mary Jackson, and John Welsh, viz: Said Callahan is to teach Mary in his art and mystery of britches-making, also John Welsh; the Mathews are to allow Denis the benefit of Mary's work for six months; Mary is to serve the Mathews 8 months after present time of service has expired.

Page 46.—26th August, 1772. John Poage enters 200 acres joining his own, John Anderson, and Beverley Manor.

Page 46.—21st November, 1772. Daniel Smith's bond (with Felix Gilbert, Abraham Smith) for collection of County proportion.

Page 47.—16th March, 1773. Nicholas Butcher's bond (with John Poage, Nicholas Harpole) as administrator of Valentine Mischorls Butcher.

Page 49.—10th February, 1772. George Fults's (Foltz) will—To wife, Catharine Barbara, all estate until youngest child Susanna comes to age of twelve years; to oldest son, George; to youngest son, John Phillips, infant; to daughters, Hanna, Eave, Susanna. Teste: Adam Loff, Adam Harpole, Nicholas Oswedy. Proved, 16th March, 1773 (written in the "Garman Tong" and translated by Anthony Ayler) by Adam Lock and Adam Harpole. Widow Catherine Barbara qualified with Nicholas Harpole, Adam Lock.

Page 52.—8th February, 1773. Elizabeth Stalsnaker relinquishes her right to administer on her husband's estate and nominates Charles Rush.

Page 52.—16th March, 1773. Charles Rush's bond (with Daniel Price Danl. Sink) as administrator of Henry Stalsnaker.

Page 53.—16th March, 1773. Robert Davis' bond (with Mathew Patton, Frederick Keester) as administrator of William Davis.

Page 55.—16th March, 1773. Adam Mallow and Fred. Keester's bond (with Henry Stone, John Skidmore) as administrators of Michael Mallow.

Page 56.—9th January, 1773. Thomas Lorrimer's estate appraised by James Hogg, Stoufall Eaye, Joseph Gamwell.

Page 57.—16th March, 1773. Mathew Shawdon's estate to Susanah Shadon, executrix—Cash paid Robert Shipley, Archibald Fisher, James and Joseph Snodgrass, William Bumpass. Whiskey for the funeral, 20/0

Page 58.—30th January, 1773. Robert Turk's estate appraised by James Kerr, William Robertson, John Ramsey.

Page 59.—14th August, 1772. Saml. McDonald's estate appraised by Robert Bratton, Saml. Hodge, Andrew Lockridge.

Page 60.—16th March, 1773. Mathew Wilson's bond (with Alexander Sinclair) as administrator of John Wilson.

Page 61.—21st January, 1773. William McPheeter's, Sr., will (signed also by Mary McPheeters), farmer—To wife, Mary; to "dearly beloved John McPheeters"; to dearly beloved daughters, Martha and Jannet, 1 book "Willison on Affliction," 1 book "Rise and Progress of Religion"; to heir of daughter Mary's estate; to sons, William and Samuel, executors. Teste: William Brownlee, Robert Peerie, John Moffett. Proved, 16th March, 1773, by Brownlee and Moffett. William McPheeters, Jr., qualified with George Berry, John Findly (Friedly).

Page 64.—1st December, 1772. Jacob Roleman's estate appraised by Mathew Patton, Robert Davis, etc.

Page 67.—14th September, 1772. Mark Swatley's estate appraised by Robert Davis, Christian Ruleman, &c. Henry Pickel's bond, George Evab's bond, Godlove Gabert's bond, Frederick Props' bond, William Jordan's accompt, Zeacriah Rexrode's bond.

Page 73.—10th September, 1772. Paul Shaver's estate appraised by Francis Wire (McGuire) Joseph Crouch, Conrad Good.

Page 74.—17th March, 1773. Recorded—Samuel Craig's account of his guardianship of the estate of John Black, orphan of Anthony Black, deceased. To rent of plantation on Middle River for 176- and 1764—Samuel Craig; 1765—Hugh Martin; 1766—Robt. Clendennin; 1768, 9, 70, 71—Robert Clendennin; 1772—James Lock; by cash paid Hanah McKanear for stockings; by cash paid Margaret Craig; James Black's payments for the use of the orphans; 1767—paid to Thankful Finley; by cash for rent in 1776.

Page 75.—17th March, 1773. Saml. McPheeters' bond (with William McPheeters, James Seawright) as guardian to Samuel Crawford, orphan of Alex. Crawford.

Page 76.—6th February, 1773. Rebecca Brown, late Rebecca Garner's account against the estate of Thomas Garner, deceased—To my account proven 12th August, 1765.

Page 78.—22d March, 1773. Walter Cunningham's bond (with Robert Armstrong) as administrator of John Cunningham.

Page 79.—23d January, 1773. William Stalp's (Stolp?) will—Executors, wife Elizabeth, son John; blacksmith tools to be sold; to son, John; to daughter. Margaret; daughter, Mary; to son, Hennery, both old and new plantations. "And I further order for my loving wife one-half of the plantation to Adam Orban joining to the County line." "Margaret and Mary to have as much as the two oldest daughters had when they married." To residuary legatees, wife and children John Stalp, Catherine, Elizabeth, Margaret, Mary, Henry. Teste: Adam Reader (and two German names) Proved, 18th May, 1773, by Mathias Lair and Catherine Lair (Leher?). Executors qualify (Catharine her mark) with John Gratton, Mathias Lear.

Page 82.—A copy and translation of the will of Adam Reader, deceased, April 18th, 1773—To wife and true helpmate; to son, Mathias Reader; to son, George Reader; to son, Anthony Reader; to son, Adam Reader; to 3 daughters. Deed to be made for land sold to Nicholas Carn. Abram Bird and testator's son Adam shall pay £20 that they received from Jacob Hite in the name of my daughter Elizabeth, which is to be shared between her 3 children. Teste: Jacob Cepliner, Anthony Reader, Jacob Mire (Moyer). 18th May, 1773—Translation proved by Jacob Moyer and will proved by Jacob Moyer and Jacob Kiplenger. Adam Reader qualified with Jacob Trumbo, Jacob Bear, Abraham Bird.

Page 85.— — May, 1768. Ferdinand Lair's estate appraised and settlement of estate recorded 18th May, 1773—To cash in hands of Andrew Hudlough (Herdlough?); to cash in hands of Conrad Wall; paid Barbara Lair; paid an old account from Germany by Fred Hanger; paid Joseph Cowley, Conrad Weeble, Mathias Rodes, William Stalp, Peater Tirkel's bond.

Page 86.—5th April, 1773. Thomas Wilson's will, farmer—To sons, Mathew and Samuel; to son, Nathaniel, 5/0; to each of five daughters, 5/0, viz: Rebekah, Martha, Elizabeth, Rhoda, and Sarrah; to son, Samuel; to wife. Executors, brother Robert Willson and son-in-law James Wilson. Teste: William Moore, Saml. McDowell, Andrew Moore. Proved, 18th May, 1773, by William and Andrew Moore. Executors qualified with Thomas Tate and Andrew Moore.

Page 89.—18th May, 1773. Peter Vaneman's bond (with Henry Stone) as guardian to Mary Butcher, orphan of Valentine Butcher.

Page 89.—18th May, 1773. Thomas Lewis and Daniel Smith's bond (with Gabriel Jones) as administrator of Thomas Jackson, Clerk.

Page 91.—16th January, 177—. George (his mark) Capliner's will—To son, George Caplener, and his brother, John Caplener, who are to pay each of their brothers and sisters; to wife; to 2 young sons and youngest dafter. Teste: John Skidmore, Frane (his mark —) Evo. Executors, George Hammo, George Dice, 3rd, for administrators after my desass on my estate. I desor that my two sons will lorn the two youngest boys to read through the Salter Poruct and the 2 boys is to live with their elder brothers till they are sixteen years of age. Teste: George Caplener, Jr., John Caplener. Proved, 18th May, 1773, by the witnesses. George Hammer qualifies with John Skidmore, Francis Eve.

Page 93.—18th May, 1773. Archibald Huston's bond (with Charles Rush, Mathias Lair) as guardian to Henry Stalp, orphan of Wm. Stalp.

Page 94.—"The last will and testament of Francis McCown, deceased, was not recorded by reason of its not being proved, but it still remains among the papers of May Court, 1773. Alphabet this."

Page 95.—20th March, 1773. Henry Stulznaker's estate appraised by Jacob Nicholas (2 German names).

Page 97.—26th March, 1773. James Thompson's (in Burden's tract) will—To son, John, 140 acres on which John lives joining Robert Allison; to son, William; to son, James, 238 acres; to son, Joseph; to wife, Mary; to daughter, Mary; to daughter, Catrin; to daughter, Margaret Hall; to daughter, Elizabeth Ward; to grandson, James Hall; to grandson, James Ward. Executors, sons John and James. Teste: Saml. Lyle, Thos. Cunningham, James McCluer. Proved, 19th May, 1773, by Lyle and McCluer John Thompson qualified with Samuel Lyle, Danl. Lyle.

Page 100.—19th May, 1773. Charles Rush in account with the estate of Loudawick Fredley—Paid John Barselinsmayer.

Page 101.—19th May, 1773. Elijah McClenachan's bond (with Joseph Henderson and John Mitchell) as guardian to Sarah Campbell, orphan of Robert Campbell.

Page 102.—10th June, 1772. Jane Patterson's estate appraised by John Blair, James Gambel, Robert Young, William Frame.

Page 104.—19th April, 1773. Thomas Greeg's will—To wife, Elizabeth, the land purchased from Saml. Samples; to the children; executors to make a deed to George Davis for 140 acres; to my three children, Ann, Mary, and Elizabeth. Executors, Daniel Smith and Andrew Erwin. Teste: John Warren, Samuel Samples, George Davis. Proved, 17th August, 1773, by oath of George Davis and affirmation of Jno. Warren. Executors qualify with John Henton.

Page 107.—17th September, 1771. William Dean's will—To wife; to daughter, Mary; youngest daughter, Elizabeth; son, John; to son, Adam, executor. Teste: Saml. McClung, Andrew Bourland, Sarah Bourland. Proved, 17th August, 1773, by McClung and Sarah Bourland. Adam Dean refuses to qualify. Administration granted Sarah, the widow, who qualifies (— her mark) with Adam Dean, Saml. McClung.

Page 109.—17th August, 1773. Walter Davis' bond (with David Henderson, William Scott) as guardian to Mary and Margaret O'Donnell, orphans of Michael O'Donnell.

Page 110.—2d January, 1773. Samuel Downey's will—To wife; to daughter, Margaret; to four youngest children, viz: Elizabeth, Rachel, Samuel, William; to daughters, Mary Ann, Rebecca, and Janet. Executors, wife, William McPheeters, and Charles Campbell. Teste: Charles Campbell, Saml. McPheeters. Proved, 17th August, 1773, by the witnesses. Martha Downey and William McPheeters qualify with Robt. Thompson, and Saml. McPheeters.

Page 114.—27th May, 1772. John Chrisman's will, of Linvel's Creek; to wife, Mary, plantation, and 3 tons of hay yearly until four sons arrive at 21; to four sons, Jacob, Joseph, Abraham, and Isaac. Executors, John Henton, of Linvel's Creek, and Mary Chrisman, wife. Teste: George Chrisman, Tunas Hood, John Smith. Proved, 17th August, 1773, by Chrisman and Smith. John Hinton qualified with George Chrisman and Daniel Smith.

Page 117.—1st December, 1770. Joseph Culton's will—To daughter, Jane Culton, alias Petterson, land on Moffet's Creek; to daughter. Margaret Walker, alias Culton; to son, James Culton. Executors, John Stuart, Jr., and Andrew Hays. Teste: Robert Culton, John Love, John Hays. Proved, 17th August, 1773, by Culton and Hays. John Stuart qualifies with William McPheeters, Samuel Steel.

Page 119.—18th April, 1773. Adam Reader's estate appraised by John Thomas (2 Germans).

Page 121.—17th August, 1773. Augustine Price, administrator, in account with the estate of Philip Horless—To paid Jacob Siler the legacy left to his daughter, £50; paid Henry Horless, his legacy; paid Geo. William the legacy left to his daughter; paid Immanuel Horless; paid Margaret Horless, her legacy.

Page 122.—7th December, 1772. Robert Hook, Jr.'s, estate appraised by Patrick Frazer, John Davidson, Archd. Huston.

Page 125.—8th April, 1773. Michael Mallow's estate appraised by Robert Davis and 2 Germans.

Page 130.—17th August, 1773. William Davis' appraisement recorded.

Page 133.—18th August, 1773. Settlement recorded of Thomas Thompson's estate, Edward Thompson, administrator—To paid John Montgomery,

William Dougherty, Michael Riney, 15 gallons liquor for the vendue; Mary Moore.

Page 135.—18th August, 1773. Recorded. Thomas Wilson's appraisement by James McCrary, Alexander Moore, William Moore.

Page 138.—1st July, 1773. John Brett's will—Executor, David Laird; debts to be paid and remainder to go to his family. Teste: James Hooke, Hannah Harndon. Proved, 18th August, 1773, by the witnesses. David Laird qualifies with John Blair, James Hooke.

Page 139.—2d June, 1773. John Trimble, Assistant Surveyor, enters 400 acres on waters of Irish Creek between Mine Hole Survey and the Deviding Ridge; also 400 acres adjoining to above, including Edmonson's Camping Ground; also 200 acres on the top and both sides of the mountain at Kinkead's Gap.

Page 140.—14th August, 1773. Recorded, viz: A list of the first vendue made by Mary O'Donal the first day of November, 1768; also the second vendue; sold to John O'Dair, Robert Richardson; also the third vendue made by Thos. Stewart 1st July, 1772; a list of whabis (?) to prove of Michael O'Donal's estate; Derby Leary's account; list of debts paid by Mary O'Donal; to Smith Williamson, Dorbe Lary, Rose Keening; whiskey for the funeral, £2.2.6; commissioners distribute the balance of the estate among the children, four in number.

Page 143.—19th August, 1773. Recorded, viz: 1761—The estate of the late William Long, of Staunton, Dr.; paid Barnibas Hughes, Doctor Lyn, clothing Wm. Long nine years. 1760—Contra.

Page 144.—19th August, 1773. Recorded, viz: 1770—Thomas Rutherford's estate, to Evan Price and Elizabeth, his wife. 9th May—To Reuben Rutherford, William West, Dochther Knave, James Bruster. 9th May—By vendue to, viz: Rebecca Paretree, John Dobbins, Evan Philips, Francis Dove, Martin Grider.

Page 146.—19th August, 1773. Recorded. Settlement of Alexander Walker's estate: Vendue 6th September, 1770—To David Laird Cooper. Cormack McCaferty, Henry Demat, Hugh Green, Martha Walker, Wm. Deal, Bryan Kenny. 1773, August—A list of debts paid: To John Adare, James McCall.

Page 149.—A memorandum of an agreement between David Laird, merchant of Augusta, and Henry Mace, blacksmith, formerly servant to said Laird, witnesseth: David has discharged Henry from remainder of his term on condition that Henry shall work under Laird's direction for country customers so as to work out £100 above his board. Henry is to find himself in coals off Laird's land. Teste: John Poage, William Lame.

Page 150.—23d August, 1773. Joseph Bell's bond (with Thos. and John Patterson) as committee of Jannet Patterson, an idiot.

Page 151.—23d August, 1773. John Patterson's bond as committee to Mary Patterson, who is born deaf and dumb.

Page 152.—16th November, 1773. Recorded. Wm. Dean's appraisement by Wm. Christian, Robert Christian. Mat. Thompson, Robt. Wilson.

Page 153.—1st September, 1773. The will of John Bender literally translated—To dear father and mother; to wife, Catharine; to sister, Margaret; to three sisters. Teste: John Bear, Adam Rader, Conrad Holle. Proved, 16th November, 1773. This will of John Bender, alias Painter, proved by Jacob Mayer to be a true translation, and by Bear and Holle. Administration granted Catharine Painter, who qualifies (mark) with John Bear, Nicholas Keern, Christian Painter.

Page 156.—16th November, 1773. Joseph Bell's estate settlement recorded: 1758, June—By 11 days conducting War Hatchet and the Party of Indians. 1758, July—By cash for your Indian account kept by me. 1758, October 24—By provisions allowed you by the Assembly. Settled by Capt. Christian.

Page 158.—Joseph Bell's appraisement, 23d November, 1758. Appraised by James Huges, Saml. Wilson, and Wm. Long.

Page 159.—16th November, 1773. William McPheeters' appraisement recorded, by John Moffett, James McCleerey, John Young—Abraham Jenkin's account, Duval Bosanques account.

Page 162—2d September, 1773. William Stalb's estate appraised by Jacob Mayer, Anthony Reader, Adam Reader.

Page 164.—2d August, 1773. Rev. Thomas Jackson's estate appraised by James Bruster, David Laird, Archibald Huston.

Page 170.—16th November, 1773. Samuel McCutchen's bond (with William McPheeters, Wm. Crawford) as guardian to Martha Crawford, orphan of Alexander Crawford.

Page 171.—16th November, 1773. Charles Campbell's bond (with Wm. McPheeters, Saml. McCutcheon) as guardian to Elizabeth and Rachel Downey, orphans of Saml. Downey.

Page 172.—16th November, 1773. Recorded. Joseph Culton's appraisement by John Huston, Saml. Steel, Joseph Moore.

Page 173.—16th November, 1773. Elizabeth Painter's bond (with Henry Lung, Henry Selzer) as administratrix of Adam Painter.

Page 174.—11th September, 1773. John Chrisman's estate appraised by Francis Green, David Ralstone, Andrew Erwin.

Page 176.—23d January, 1772. John Shield's will, freeholder—To wife Margaret; to son, John; to son, William; to son, Thomas; to son, Robert; to daughter, Mary: "I ordain Thomas Shields and my son William Shields and Wm. Hays my sole executors." Teste: John Shields, William Shields, Wm. Shields, Wm. Hays. 24th January, 1772—Codicil: To son, William, ½ of the tract whereon son John lives. Proved, 16th November, 1773, by John and William Shields. William Shields refuses to qualify. 17th November, 1773—Administration granted Margaret and Thomas Shields, who qualify with Mathew Thompson, William Shields.

Page 180.—4th August, 1768. Aron Oliver's will—To wife; to daughter, Jemima Oliver, executrix; to daughter, Anne Pickens. Teste: Abram Pickens, Henry Black, Margaret Black. Proved, 18th November, 1773, by Smith and Henry Black. Jemima (mark) qualifies with Daniel Smith.

Page 182.—4th December, 1772. William Sitlington's estate appraised by Charles Donelly, Ralph Laverty, William Reach—1 servant man appraised to Dorby Dedy, £18.00.0; 1 servant man, named Joseph, appraised to Blackhouse, £15.10.0; 1 servant man, named Augustine Picket, £14.00.0; 1 servant man, named Richard, appraised to Edwards, £14.00.0; 1 servant woman appraised to £12.00.0.

Page 183.—20th September, 1773. Thomas Gragg's estate appraised by David Ralston, Henry Ewin, John Ewin.

Page 184.—20th November, 1773. Daniel Smith's bond (with Robert McClenachan) for collection of County proportion.

Page 185.—11th October, 1773. James Hardgraves' will—To wife Elizabeth, to son Robert Hardgrave, to son Francis Hardgrave, executors. Teste: John Cawley, Daniel Kidd, Elizabeth Griffin. Proved, 20th November, 1773, by the witnesses. Elizabeth qualifies with John Frogg, James Hill.

Page 187.—November Court, 1773. John Cartmill's will partly proved and lie for further proof.

Page 187.—20th December, 1773. Christofull Kislin's will, of Lick Run—To son, John; to son, Teterick; to wife, Christiana; to son, Mathew, infant; to daughters, Catherine, Elizabeth, and Christiana; to son, Henry, infant. Teste: John Siller, Peter Kinder, and (German). Proved, 15th March, 1774, by the witnesses. Administration granted widow Catherine, who qualifies (mark) with Philip Lingle, John Lingle.

Page 190.—2d August, 1773. Estate of Jacob Caplenger, of South Branch, appraised by Jacob Conrad, Jacob Friend, Wolrie Conrad.

Page 193.—15th March, 1774. Recorded. David Dryden's appraisement by Alex. McClure, James Thompson, Wm. Ramsey—1 note on Patrick Porter, of North Carolina, payable November, 1772. Legacies appraised, viz: To wife, Dorothy, son Nathaniel, son William, son Thomas.

Page 196.—1st November, 1773. Archibald Reach, Jr.'s, will—To wife, Margaret; to children. Executors, wife and Uncle Archibald Reah. Teste: Michael Coulter, William Reah, James Clark. Proved, 15th March, 1774, by Coulter and Reah. Executors qualify (Margaret — her mark) with Thomas Hill, William Reagh.

Page 198.—March Court, 1774. William Dunlap's will proved by one witness and lie for further proof.

Page 199.—15th March, 1774. Recorded. Appraisement of John Shield's estate by Robert Christian, Robt. Wilson, Mathew Thompson, Thos. Shields.

Page 200.—22d November, 1773. John Macky's will—To wife, Mary; to son, Henry, a plantation in Forks of James River in Botetourt County, 170 acres; to son, William, 360 acres the testator lives on; to daughter, Jane; to daughter, Mary; to daughter, Esther; to daughter, Betsy. "Until my children come to full age." Executors, wife Mary, brother-in-law Wm. Porter, Henry McClung. Teste: Archibald Alexander, Joseph Reed, John Peoples. Proved, 15th March, 1774, by the witnesses. Executors qualify (Mary — her mark) with Saml. McDowell, John Porter.

Page 203.—6th July, 1773. Ladowak Shadow's will—Executor, Jacob Doran, sole heir, "loving friend Jacob Doran." Teste: Wm. Mathews, James Reburn, John Nickle. Proved, 15th March, 1774, by Mathews and Nickle. Jacob Doran qualifies with William Mathews.

Page 204.—15th March, 1774. Conrad Kustard's settlement of estate. Contra—Paid to, viz: Thomas Baggs, James Marshal, Morris Custard, John Frank's bond, Henry Runyan, John Steel, Michael Humble. Paul Custard, administrator.

Page 208.—2d July, 1771. James (his — mark) Gregory's will—To mother, executrix; to brother, William. Teste: Saml. Vance, William Fulton (Fullen?). N. B.—My brother Naphtaly is to have £5 and Samuel and John £10 each. Proved, 15th March, 1774, by William Fuller and recorded (formerly proved by Vance).

Page 208.—3d May, 1773. George Fults, of the Walnut Bottom, estate appraised by Robert Davis, Peter Vaneman.

Page 211.—1st April, 1773. Valentine Butcher's (on South Branch) estate appraised by Peter Vaneman, Robert Davis, Adam Louck.

Page 216.—20th 8ber, 1773. Robert Poack's will—To sons, John and Thomas, "My real estate, 260 acres, lying upon a branch of Linvel's Creek; to daughter, Martha Woods, 1 pistole; to sons, Robert, George, and William, 1 pistole; to daughters, Elizabeth Crawford, Margaret Robertson, 1 pistole. Executors, William Lewis and son John Poage. Teste: John Craig, Isabella Helena Craig, Charles Baskin. Proved, 16th March, 1774, by John Craig, Clerk, and Baskins. (No administration order.)

Page 217.—19th August, 1773. Robert Graham's will—To wife; to 3 daughters, Sarah, Rebecca, Jane, infants. Teste: Lanty Graham, James Goy (Gay?), Jean Lockridge. Proved, 16th March, 1774, by Graham and Lockridge. Administration granted Elizabeth Graham, who qualifies (her — mark) with Andrew Lockridge, Andrew Kinkead.

Page 219.—16th March, 1774. John Bigham's bond (with Joseph Henderson, Robert Buchanan) as administrator of John Bigham.

Page 220.—16th March, 1774. George Moffett's bond (with John McMahon) as guardian to Robert Reaburn, orphan of Robert Reaburn.

Page 221.—16th March, 1774. Recorded. Aaron Oliver's estate appraised by Jarad Erwine, Isaiah Shipman.

Page 221.—16th September, 1773. Samuel Downey's estate appraised by John Handly, Alex. McPheeters, Peter Hanger, James Callison—James Porterfield's account.

Page 225.—17th March, 1774. Recorded, viz: The estate of Pollis Negter (Paulus Neghly), Dr., to John Shell Shell. 1773, 19th May—Paid Henry Benninger.

Page 226.—18th March, 1774. Recorded. John Cunningham's appraisement by Daniel Kidd, Alex. Gibson, William Lewis.

Page 227.—26th February, 1774. James Hartgrove's estate appraised by John Griffen, Thos. Smith, John Abney.

Page 229.—18th March, 1774. Samuel McDowell's bond (with John Bowyer) as guardian to James McDowell, orphan of Saml. McDowell.

Page 230.—19th April, 1774. William Crawford's bond (with Pet. Hog, Thos. Hughes) as assistant surveyor.

Page 231.—22d ———, 1774. Christopher Kislinger's estate appraised by Jacob Nicholas, John Seller, Jacob Miller.

Page 233.—16th May, 1774. Isabella Helena Craige relinquishes her right to administer on her late husband's (Rev. John Craige) estate, and nominates James Allen, Jr., and George Moffett, Gent. Teste: Charles Baskin, Geo. Craig.

Page 233.—17th May, 1774. James Allen, Jr., and George Moffett's bond (with George Mathews and James Gambel) as administrators of Rev. John Craig.

Page 234.—15th June, 1773. Mathew Lyle's will—To son, James, executor; to daughter, Elizabeth, now in Ireland—if she do not come in within 3 years, then the land to go to James; to daughter, Martha; to son, John

Teste: Danl. Lyle, Archibald Alexander, John Lyle, Jr. Proved, 17th May, 1774, by Daniel and John Lyle, Jr. James Lyle qualifies with Samuel and Daniel Lyle.

Page 237.—10th February, 1774. John Hunter's will—To son, Robert, 5/0; to daughter, Jane Wallace, 5/0; to daughter, Martha Moore, 5/0; to son, Samuel, 5/0, executor; to son, Hugh, 5/0; to son, Henry, the still and vessels; to son, John, all land testator now lives on; to daughter, Frances Lawrence, 5/0; to wife, Frances, executrix. Teste: Joseph Ray, Saml. Blackwood, Thomas Keor. Proved, 17th May, 1774, by the witnesses. Frances qualifies (her mark) with William Black, John Hunter.

Page 240.—17th May, 1772 (1774?). Jane Risk's bond (with John Alexander, Saml. McCutchen) as administratrix of James Risk.

Page 241.—30th April, 1774. Robert Graham's estate appraised by Robert Bratton, William Lockridge, James Bratton—To money due by Wm. Anderson, overseer for Thos. Adams.

Page 242.—11th February, 1769. Margaret Rutherford's will—Widow, being old and failed in body; to son, Samuel Rutherford, deaf and dumb; to sons, John Wallace and Thomas Hutson; to Rebecca Campbell, after Samuel's death; to James Wallace, £7; to Robert Wallace, £5; to Margaret Hutson, £5; to Isbela Hutson, £5. Executors, Alex. Walker, William Buchanan. Teste: Robert Tedford, George Buchanan, Alex. Tedford, John Tedford. Proved, 18th May, 1774, by all the Tedfords. Executors qualified with David Tedford, John Wallace.

Page 245.—8th November, 1773. Thomas West's will—To wife, Catens; to daughter, Judy Tiswaters (Fiswaters?); to daughter, Christian Narlr; to daughter, Elizabeth. If wife should be with child. Executrix, wife. Teste: Daniel Smith, Paul Kustan (Kester?), Richard Kester. Proved, 20th May, 1774, by witnesses. Cathorine qualifies (signed Caian West) with Paul Keester (Kaster), John Caplinger.

Page 247.—20th May, 1774. Recorded. Archibald Reach's appraisement by Joseph Moore, Hugh Kelso, Alex. McPheeters.

Page 248.—16th August, 1774. Conrad Humble's bond (with John Dunbar, Conrad Custard) as administrator of Martin Humble.

Page 250.—13th August, 1774. Margaret Rutherford's estate appraised by John Walker, Michael Couter, George Jameson—Bonds on Thomas Hutson.

Page 251.—14th May, 1774. Mathias Rodes' will—To son, Mathias; to wife, Barbara; to children. (Copy from the original—a very bad translation of German.) Teste: Jacob Mayer, Nicholas Kern. Valentine Cloninger testifies to correctness of translation. 16th August, 1774, proved by witnesses.

Page 252.—7th March, 1774. James Lusk's will, yeoman—To brother, William, land in Forks of James; to brother, Robert. Teste: James Snodgrass, James Montgomery, George Weir. Proved, 16th August, 1774, by the witnesses.

Page 254.—16th August, 1774. Charles Rush, administrator, settles the estate of Henry Stalsnaker—Paid to the widow, Catharine Pence; paid David Bosang, Michael Milterbarger.

Page 256.—16th August, 1774. Daniel Kid's bond (with John Graham) as administrator of Neil McCan.

Page 257.—17th February, 1774. Henry Dick's will—To wife, Catharine, executrix; to children, viz: John, Runamus, Henry, Jacob, Michael, Charles, Christian, Catharine Dick, when youngest is of age. Teste: Conrad Peterfish, John Kirtley, Charles Foy. Proved, 16th August, 1774, by Peterfish and Foy.

Page 258.—16th August, 1774. Catherine Jack's bond (with Charles Rush, Charles Foy) as administratrix of above estate—Dick, Deck, Tack, Teck, Tick?

Page 259.—28th March, 1774. Archibald Huston's will—To wife, Mary; to son, John, 200 acres, part of Pond Spring tract; to son, Stephen; to James, 250 acres of tract whereon David Gravin now lives; to son, Archibald, infant; to son, George, 360 acres whereon testator lives; to son, Nathan, 100 acres, part of Pond Spring tract; to six daughters, residuary legatees. Executors, sons James and George, and Cap David Leard. Teste: James Bruster, John (his — mark) Stephenson, Jennet (mark) Frazer, Isbell (mark) Campbell. Proved, 16th August, 1774, by Bruster and Stephenson. Mary appears and refuses to execute and renounces the will. David Laird and Geo. Huston qualify with James Bruster and John (mark) Stephenson.

Page 262.—16th August, 1774. Robert Stephenson's estate settled—Paid Thomas Stephens, Sr., Anderson Scoot.

Page 264.—7th June, 1774. Improvements valued on William McKenny's tract joining Robt. Kilpatrick's tract by John Gardner, James Hogshead, James McKemey.

Page 265.—24th March, 1755. John (his — mark) Nichel's will—To wife, Barbara; to eldest son, John; to sons, Joseph and Isaac; to son, Thomas; to daughter, Elizabeth. Executors, wife Barbara and her brother, Andrew McCombe. Teste: Alexander Blair, James Reburn. Proved, 17th August, 1774, by the witnesses. Executors qualify (Barbara's — mark) with John Poage, Joseph Reburn.

Page 267.—17th August, 1774. Recorded. Lodwick Shaddow's appraisement by ——— —Four Duch Books, 15/0; apple trees, 7/0.

Page 268.—27th October, 1773. Robert Scott's will—To Martha McClintock, £5; to executors. all remainder of estate to pay them for their trouble. Executors, Wm. McClintock, John Young. Teste: William McClintock, Jr., Preepare McClintock. Proved, 20th September, 1774, by the witnesses. William McClintock qualifies (his mark) with Mathew Reed, John Clark.

Page 271.—7th October, 1774. Henry Deck's estate appraised by John Seller, Daniel Price, Jacob Bare.

Page 274.—24th August, 1774. John Nickle's estate appraised—Receipts as follows, viz: 27th August, 1774—John Nickle, for his part of his legacy; Thomas, for his part of his legacy. 27th August, 1774—Order by Ben. Lewis to pay to Andrew Ralstone £1.10, part of Ben's part of John Nickoll's estate. 27th August, 1774—Order by Andrew Nickle to pay his part ditto. 27th August, 1774—Order by Elizabeth Nickle to pay her part ditto. 27th August, 1774—Please let Andrew Ralstone have £3.0.0 out of my part of my father's estate.—William Craigg.

Page 278.—8th May, 1773. Conrad Bloze's will—To wife, Mary Catrine; to son, John Adam; to son, George Jacob; to wife, Valentine; to daughter,

Eve Elizabeth. Executors, Jacob Mayer. Teste: Adam (mark) **Hetrick,** Archibald Huston, Rebeka Huston. Proved, 15th November, 1774, by Hetrick. Archibald and Rebecca are dead. Jacob Mayer refuses to execute. *Administration granted Mary Catherine, who qualifies with Anthony Ealer, Alvanious Bowyer, Jacob (mark) Bowyer.

Page 281.—15th November, 1774. Thomas Smith's bond (with Robert Russell) as administrator of Thos. Dunbarr.

Page 282.—4th August, 1774. Francis Kirtley's will—To wife, Elizabeth Kirtley, the tract his youngest son is to have; to son, Francis, tract at foot of the mountains where testator formerly lived, 1,100 acres, and the place Thos. Berry now lives on, and 5 negroes; to son, John Kirtley, 3 tracts in Orange County called, viz: Bryan's Trackt, Golding's Trackt, and Maddey's 600 acres, and also tract called the Grass Thicket in Augusta and the land on Nacked Creek; also testator's part of the land where Ruben Roach lives, and 5 negroes; to daughter, Elizabeth Kirtley, land bought of Eastise's estate called Pinkey's Old Mill Place; to son, Honorius Powell Kirtley, infant, land on Buns Run, being part of land testator lives on; to son, Sinkle Kirtley, other part of the land on Buns Run. (Fifteen negroes bequeathed besides those above.) Brother William Kirtley, if living, to make division. Executors, wife Elizabeth, son Francis Kirtley, son John Kirtley. Teste: William Kirtley, John Caurfey, Jane Crawford. Proved, 15th November, 1774, by the witnesses. Elizabeth refused to execute and renounced the provisions of the will. Francis Kirtley qualified with Thomas Lewis, Daniel Smith.

Page 286.—16th November, 1774. Recorded. John Makey's appraisement by Archibald Alexander, Wm. Alexander, John Lyle, Jr., William McClung.

Page 288.— ———— —, 177—. Robert McClenachan's bond (with John Madison, Jr.) as administrator of Wm. McClenachan.

Page 289.—22d August, 1774. Samuel Wilson's will—Executors, wife Mary and Thomas Hugart; to eldest son, Ralph, 5 shillings; to next eldest son, Elibable, plantation testator lives on; to youngest son, Sampson, £100, infant; to daughter, Ruth, infant; to wife, Mary. Teste: John Jordan, John McCoy, Joseph Gamwell. Proved, 16th November, 1774, by McCoy and Gamwell. Hugart refuses to execute. Mary qualifies with Thos. Hugart, Robert Armstrong.

Page 292.—16th November, 1774. Mary and Michael Aberman's bond (with George Coyle, Robert Minnes, Joseph Croutch, Wm. Gragg).

Page 293.—15th November, 1774. Agatha Frogg relinquishes her right to administer on estate of husband, John Frogg, and nominates John Madison, Jr. Teste: Thomas Jones, Joseph Smith.

Page 293.—16th November, 1774. John Madison, Jr.'s, bond (with Daniel Kidd, Thomas Patterson) as administrator of John Frogg.

Page 295.—1st October, 1774. Robert Patterson's will—To son-in-law, Alexander Stuart, Bible; to son, Thomas; to son, John; to son John's

---

*NOTE.—That with this bond, the Clerk begins to give the date, not only in the month and year, but adds: "And in the 15th year of the Reign of our Sovereign Lord, George III," and so in the bonds following.

children; to granddaughter, Mary Stuart; to grandson, Robert Stuart; to grandson, Robert Patterson. Executor, son Thomas. Teste: John Archer, Daniel Kidd, Edward Hall. Proved, 16th November, 1774, by Kidd, and recorded. Thomas qualified with John Madison, Jr.

Page 297.—17th November, 1774. James Dunwoody's (Dinwody) bond (with Robert Dinwoody) as administrator of John Dunwody.

Page 299.—17th January, 1775. John Christian's bond as sheriff (with William Bowyer, George Moffett, William Christian, Robert Christian).

Page 299.—Ditto for collection of County proportion.

Page 300.—Ditto for collection of quit rents, officers' fees, &c.

Page 301.—15th April, 1774. Thomas Shankland's (his mark) will, farmer—To wife, Eleanor, tract adjoining Thomas Gordon; to grandchildren, viz: Of son Robert's children, viz: Thomas, William, Robert, son John, son ————; son Thomas' son Thomas; to oldest son, Robert. Executors, sons Robert and John. Teste: William and Archibald Hopkins, George Baxter. Proved, 17th January, 1775, by Archd. Hopkins and Baxter. Executors qualify with Archd. Hopkins, Geo. Baxter.

Page 304.—25th June, 1774. John McClenachan's will—To wife, Margaret, tract near Staunton, where Thomas Scott lived, given me by my father in his lifetime; to son, Thomas, above tract after wife's death, 3 negroes; brothers and sisters, to inherit in default of heirs of Thomas; John Frogg, to be fully satisfied for testator's board while at his house. Executors to abide by a memorandum left with John Lewis. Executors, John Hervie, Charles Lewis, Alex. Sinclair. Teste: Margaret Lewis, Wm. Haddon, John Lewis. 16th November, 1774—Widow Margaret Ann appears and renounces the will and its provisions for her. 17th January, 1775—Will and memorandum (follows) proved by John Lewis and Wm. Haddon. Sinclair qualifies with Robert McClenachan, John Dean, Alex. Gibson, Alex. McClenachan. Memorandum mentioned in the will, p. 306, viz:

Page 306.—Captain John Dickinson, Dr., to 2 tickets paid, if not drawn to be repaid; William Bailey's bond for £5 belonging to John Davis; Archer Mathews, Dr., for a piece of land in Greenbrier, £25, 10 years' credit.

Page 310.—10th August, 1774. Charles Lewis' will—To wife, Sarah; to son, John, tract testator lives on, also tract on Greenbryer called the Great Glade, 1,000 acres; to son, Andrew, plantation gotten from John Lewis, George's son, line where his brother's survey begins; also 1 plantation on Greenbrier where Wm. Crane lives; to daughter, Elizabeth Lewis, plantation on Greenbrier where George Lewis lives; to daughter, Margaret, plantation on Greenbrier where Wm. Bleake lives. Wife is now pregnant, to such child, plantation where Mr. Cowordin lives, also Cuthbert's Lick Place on Greenbryer; to sons, the lands coming to testator as an officer. Executors, brothers Thomas and William. Teste: John Dickinson, Hugh Hicklin, Charles Cameron. Proved, 17th January, 1775, by Dickinson and Cameron. Executors qualified, with Robert (mark) Bratton, Andrew Hamilton, Wm. Christian, George Mathews.

Page 313.—17th January, 1775. John Wilson's bond (with Jacob Worwick, Tully Davitt) as administrator of John Williams.

Page 314.—17th January, 1775. Alex. Sinclair and Alex. McClenachan's bond (with John Dean, Robt. McClenachan, Alex. Gibson, John Dickinson) as guardian to John McClenachan, orphan of John McClenachan.

Page 316.—18th January, 1775. William Campbell's bond (with Daniel Smith, John Davis) as executor of Hugh Campbell.

Page 317.—20th March, 1775. Jane and James Allen's bond (with Wm. Lewis, John Hind, Thos. Patterson) as administrators of Hugh Allen.

Page 318.—2d March, 1775. Col. Charles Lewis' estate appraised by John Cowordin, John and Robert McCreery: one white servant man, John Sharpley.

Page 321.—14th April, 1773. Isaac Robinson's will—Being in the Township of Whitpan in County Philadelphia, Province Pennsylvania—To wife, Hannah; to youngest son, Luke, infant, to son, James, under 24, plantation on north side Shanandore, 365 acres; to eldest daughter, Elinner Robinson; to youngest daughter, Hanna; to second daughter, Catherine. Executors, wife Hannah, friend Stephen Riddle, of Hampshire County. Teste: Jonas Supplee, Thomas Fitzwaters. 26th September, 1774—Commission to George Bryan, Geo. Clymer, Justices of Peace; Peter Miller and Lewis Weise, gentlemen of Philadelphia County, Penna., to examine above witnesses. 5th November, 1774—Commission executed and return certified by Bryan and Clymer. 11th May, 1774—Affidavit of above witnesses at Philadelphia before Benj. Chew, Reg. Gen. Both witnesses are Quakers. 16th August, 1774—This will presented by Stephen Riddle and dedimus ordered to issue as above. 21st March, 1774—Proved and recorded. Stephen Ruddle qualifies with Cornelius Ruddle, John Gratton.

Page 326.—20th November, 1774. Alexander Walker's will—To wife, Elizabeth; to son, Robert, negro boy; to daughter, Mary, negro girl; to son, Andrew, 90 acres bought of Joseph Lindel; to daughter, Martha; to daughter, Elizabeth; to daughter, Barbara; to son, John, testator's home plantation; to daughter, Isabell. (Many negro slaves bequeathed.) To daughter, Margaret; to son. Alexander's two children, Jane and Elizabeth Walker. Executors, wife Elizabeth and son Robert. John Campbell to be guardian to children. Teste: Joseph Hannah, Robert Haslet, Thos. Connly. Proved, 21st March, 1775, by the witnesses. Executors qualify with John Hind, Arthur Connaly, John Campbell.

Page 330.—4th May, 1773. Samuel Hodge's will, of the Calf Pasture—To wife, Elizabeth; to daughter, Eleanor, unmarried; to son, John, plantation whereon John lives between Wm. Kinkead and James Gay; to son, James, testator's home plantation; to grandson, Saml. Hodge, "one certain ivory-headed cain"; to daughter, Sarah McDonal; to daughter, Agness Martin; to daughter, Margaret McElvain; to daughter, Cathereen Kelly; to daughter, Elizabeth McCutchen. Executors, wife Elizabeth and John Hodge. Teste: Francis McConnel, Henry McDonnal, Francis McDonnal. Proved, 21st March, 1775, by the McDonalds.

Page 331.—21st March, 1775. Recorded. Capt. Samuel Wilson's appraisement by John McCoy, Joseph Gamwell, Joseph Malcom.

Page 333.—21st March, 1775. Jacob's (Eberman) bond (with Robert Minnes, Joseph (mark) Bennet) as administrator of David White.

Page 334.—21st March, 1775. Morris O'Freil's bond (with John Jameson) as administrator of James King.

Page 335.—21st March, 1775. Recorded. Francis Kirtley's appraisement by Wm. Nalle, Martin Nalle, Jr., John Seller.

Page 337.—21st March, 1775. Peter Hog's bond as administrator of Thos. Hog.

Page 339.—21st March, 1775. John Lewis' bond (with John Warwick (mark) and John Sutlington (mark)) as administrator of Michael Bush.

Page 340.—21st March, 1775. Cathorine Magert's bond (with Jacob Peter, Charles Walker) as administratrix of David Magert.

Page 342.—19th March, 1771. Hugh Campbell's will—To wife, Esther; to 3 sons and 2 daughters, William, Hugh, Charles, Esther, Marthew; to son, Robert. Executors, John Magill, Wm. Campbell. Teste: Andrew Scott, Robert Fowler, John Davis. 18th January, 1775—Dedimus to Danl. and Abraham Smith to examine Robert Fowler. Executed 6th February, 1775. Proved, 17th January, 1775, by John Davis. Dedimus for Robert Fowler who is very sick. Administration granted to William Campbell. no bond. 22d March, 1775—Proved by Fowler's deposition and recorded. John Magill qualifies with Abraham Smith, Saml. Gibson.

Page 345.—16th March, 1775. Hugh Campbell's estate appraised by John Gratton, James Magill, Edward Erwin, Edward Shanklin.

Page 348.— ———— ——, 1772. James Stewart's estate appraised—Notes of, viz: Richard Elliott, Jas. Scoolcraft, Daniel McLean (by the road), Patt. Hamilton by road, Charles Firnelson by road, Darby Connly by road, Geo. Westfall by the road, by a private balance of Ginsang by Ralph Stewart.

Page 350.—21st March, 1775. Recorded. Robert Scott's estate appraisement by James Brown, John Moffett, John Thomas.

Page 351.—5th June, 1774. Elizabeth Armentrout's will, widow—To son, Philip; to children living, being six in number; to grandsons, Henry Armentrout and John Armentrout, sons of her son John, deceased. Executors, son Phillip and friend, Charles Rush. Son Henry Armentrout and Frederick Harris are indebted to her. Teste: Gabriel Jones, John Rush, and (a German). Proved, 20th June, 1775, by Jones and Rush. Charles Rush refuses to execute. Philip qualifies (bond signed Elizabeth Armentrout) with Valentine Cloninger, Frederick Armentrout.

Page 353.—10th February, 1775. John Cawley's will, of Staunton—To wife, Margaret; estate to be divided between children of elder brother, Michael and younger brother, Thomas, and sister Margaret; to brother, Michael; devises to be sold: 3 hides in possession of Harman Lovingood, tanner, also the venire money due from the Colony on account of Bridget Doyle, criminal, also claims against the County for the past expedition; to Valentine Cloninger. Executors, John Poage and Capt. Alex. McClenachan Teste: Saml. Bell, James Culbertson, Daniel Kidd. Proved, 20th June, 1775, by the witnesses. Widow Margaret renounces the provisions of the will. Alex. McClenachan qualifies with William Bowyer, Daniel Kidd. John Poage also qualifies.

Page 357.—20th June, 1775. William Longsdale's bond (with James Eliot) as administrator of John Collins.

Page 359.—20th June, 1775. Samuel Lyle's bond (with Gabriel Jones) as administrator of John Gillespy.

Page 360.— ———— ——, 1774. Dr. the estate of Robert Graham. In account with Elizabeth Graham, executrix. April 30—To wool made use of for children's cloaths; to paid Wm. Kinkead for liquor (son to Andrew); to funeral expenses for a child; to paid for cheese at funeral of Robert Graham; to leather sold John Plunkett.

Page 361.—20th June, 1775. Andrew Lockridge's bond (with George Mathews) as guardian to Sarah and Jane, orphans of Robt. Graham.

Page 362.—5th January, 1775. Adam Hadrick's will, farmer—To grandson, John Ermontrot; to daughter, Elizabeth Coutts; to great grandson, George Ermontrout; to aforesaid John Ermontrout's brother, Henry Ermontrout. Executor, above-named John Ermontrout. Teste: Jacob Nicholas, Felix Gilbert, 3 Germans. Proved, 20th June, 1775, by Nicholas and Gilbert. John Armentrout qualifies with Jacob Nicholas.

Page 365.—24th 7ber, 1772. Robert Gilkeson's will, well stricken in years—To wife, Rebecca; to son, Archibald, and his son, Robert, infant; to daughter, Margrit Hogshead; to daughter, Isabel Brown; to grandson, Robert Gilkison; to child Isabel Brown is now pregnant with. Executors, wife Rebecca and son-in-law David Hogshead. Teste: James Bell, John Hogshead, Michael Hogshead. Proved, 15th August, 1775, by the witnesses. Executors qualify (both with mark) with James Bell, Michael Hogshead.

Page 367.—15th August, 1775. Francis Gorton's (Garthon) bond (with Abraham Smith, Francis Erwin) as administratrix of Elizabeth Garthon.

Page 369.—15th August, 1775. Mary Watson's bond (with Hugh Donaghee, Thomas Hewit) as administratrix of John Watson.

Page 371.—4th June, 1775. David White's (of Tyger's Valley) estate appraised by Elias Baker, John Warrack.

Page 371.—5th November, 1774. Gunrod Blows' estate appraised by (5 Germans).

Page 374.—15th August, 1775. Robert McKittrick's bond (with Alex. Kirk) as administrator of John Potter.

Page 376.—15th August, 1775. George Dice's estate settled by Margaret Dice, administratrix—Cash paid Christian Lower, Leonard Neif, Mich. Misker, Christian Countryman, Paulser Michker, Peter Spears.

Page 377.—3d and 4th August, 1773. George Caplinger's (of South Branch) estate sold at vendue—To Leonard Probst, Jacob Caplinger, Danl. Probst, Henry Caplinger, Cathorine Caplinger, Elizabeth Caplinger, John Caplinger, Geo. Caplinger, Adam Caplinger, Michael Alkeir, Ulrick Conrad, Christian Pickle, Stovel Low, Valentine Post, John Skidmore; to Doctor Neal, Chas. Bowers, Peter Caphart, Aron Skyhaw, Zachoriah Rexrode, Geo. Caplinger (2 crout tubs), Joseph Skidmore, Elizabeth Harbold, Jacob Rude, Jobb Velton, George Ganker, Thomas Willmott, Aron Vansye, Martin Coyle, Danl. Richardson, Danl. Hornbeck.

Page 381.—15th August, 1775. George Caplinger's estate settled by Geo. Hammer, executor; paid John Griffen, Christopher Ove.

Page 382.—15th August, 1775. John Bigham's appraisement (recorded) by John Buchanan, Thos. Scott, James Gilmer.

Page 384.—1st February, 1775. Thomas Shanklin's estate appraised by Ephraim Love, John Hopkins, Jesse Harrison.

Page 386.—17th March, 1775. George Fults' estate appraised and settlement recorded 15th August, 1775—Sold to Henry Judy, Martin Judy, Michael Mannin, Nicholas Judy, Jacob Critchs, Thomas Northon, Richard

Burns, Mathias Dice, Jacob Simond, Jacob Hinkle, Thomas Hall, Joseph Ham, Jacob Ragen.

Page 390.—5th October, 1775. James Lessley's, Jr., will—To wife, Mary, upbringing of the children; to youngest daughter, Agness, under 18. Executors, Mary Lessley, James Kerr, Robert Kinney. Teste: Robert Rodgers, Saml. Lessley. Proved, 21st November, 1775, by the witnesses. James Kerr and Robt. Kinney qualified.

Page 392.—22d November, 1775. David Magget's appraisement (recorded) by Jacob Bare, Henry Millar, Francis Kertley.

Page 393.—13th December, 1774. Thomas Dunbarr's estate appraised by James Hill, Valentine Cloninger, John Abney.

Page 393.—17th March, 1773. Samuel Nicholas' estate appraised by John Dunbarr, William Samples, Michael Warren.

Page 395.—13th September, 1775. Col. Charles Lewis' estate appraised by same as before.

Page 395.—2d September, 1775. Robert Gilkison's estate appraised by Wm. Anderson, James Hogshead, George Moffett.

Page 396.—2d September, 1775. Valued. John Hogshead's improvements on, viz: 1 tract, 300 acres; 2 achors, cleared and under fence.

Page 397.—22d November, 1775. Thomas Hutcheson's estate in account with Sarah Hutcheson, administratrix—Cash paid Alex. St. Clair for liquor at the funeral, £0.15.6.

Page 398.—22d November, 1775. Recorded. Elizabeth Armentrout's appraisement by David Harned, George Carpenter, Jacob Grub.

Page 400.—22d November, 1775. Recorded. John Potter's appraisement by John Kirk, Alex. Kirk, John Beard—"For Sogering mony under Capt. Moffett, £6.7.6."

Page 400.—22d November, 1775. Recorded. John Dunwody's appraisement by Mathew Patton, John Peebles, Loftus Pullen—Samuel Lawrence's note.

Page 401.—22d November, 1775. Recorded. Eliza Garton's appraisement by Alex. Herring, John Magill, John Huston.

Page 402.—11th October, 1775. Adam Hatrick's estate appraised by (3 German names).

Page 403.—23d November, 1775. John Christian's bond (with Daniel Smith, Danl. Kidd) as collector of County proportion.

Page 404.—26th December, 1774. Stephen Hansbarger's will—To wife, Uashel (Rachel?); to sons, Adam, Henry, Stephen, Conrad, Robert. Executor, son Adam. Teste: John Zimmerman, George Zimmerman, Adam Carpenter, Jacob Miller, Leonard Zimmerman. Proved, 19th March, 1776, by Jacob Miller and Geo. Carpenter. Executor qualified.* (No bond recorded.)

*NOTE.—No bonds recorded from this on.

Page 406.—29th February, 1776. John Jameson's will—To wife, Jane; to grandson, John Perry; to granddaughter, Sarah McNabb; to nine children. Executors, Robert Armstrong, Daniel O'Friel. Teste: John Trimble, John Young, Robt. Wallace. Proved, 19th March, 1776, by Trimble and Wallace. Executors qualify.

Page 407.—28th November, 1775. Peter (mark) Hohl's will—To wife, Susannah Margaret, the Pennsylvania mare; to eldest son, Peter; to three eldest daughters; to youngest daughters, infants. Executor, eldest son

Peter, land on Jackson River to be sold. Teste: Bernhard Lentz, Leonard Simon, Peter Fleisher. (True translation by John William Leo.) Proved 19th March, 1776, by the witnesses. Executor qualifies.

Page 409.— ——— —, ——. Jacob Conrad's will—To son, Jacob, testator's dwelling place; to daughter, Barbara, the place she lives on (wife of Charles Hedrick); to daughter, Elizabeth, the place she lives on, bought of Christopher Thompson and James Skidmore, wife of George Fisher; to daughter Mary Conrad's two children, Margaret Barlet, John Clifton, land bought from Saml. Caplinger; to Jonas Friend, a debt to be paid; son to sign his three sisters their deeds by his Earship. Teste: Wolerey Conrad, John Skidmore, George Kile. Proved, 19th March, 1776 (translation by George Carpenter) by the witnesses. Jacob Conrad qualifies administrator.

Page 410.—14th July, 1775. James Davison's will—To wife, Jane; to eldest son, John, infant; to two youngest children; to daughter, Mary; to division "among my children." Executors, Archibald and John Hopkins. Teste: John Hagarty, Wm. Chesnutt, James Dunn. Proved, 19th March, 1776, by Chesnutt and Dunn. Executors summoned. At a Court for Augusta County by authority of the Commonwealth of Virginia, August 20, 1776, Archibald and John Hopkins refuse to qualify executors.

Page 413.—6th July, 1775. John Galaspey's estate appraised by John Montgomery, John Alexander, Saml. Houston.

Page 414.—18th November, 1775. John Watson's estate appraised by David Laird, William Blair, Jeremiah Smith.

Page 415.—19th March, 1776. Samuel Downey's estate settled—Paid John Ager.

Page 420.—18th February, 1775 (heading says 1765, date at end says 1775). John Davis' will, planter. Executrix, wife Elizabeth, all property. Teste: Josiah Davison, John Bannett, Jeremiah Osburn. Proved, 20th August, 1776, by Bannet and Osborn. Elizabeth qualifies.

Page 421.—13th June, 1776. Samuel Sample's will—To wife, Ann; to son, Samuel; to son, Moses; to sons, a division; to son William's son, William, an equal legatee; to son, Robert; to grandson, Thomas Randall. Executors, sons Robert and Moses. Teste: Andrew Erwin, John Brown, Mary Black. Proved, 20th August, 1776, by Erwin and Brown. Executors qualify.

Page 422.—29th April, 1776. Thomas Armstrong's will—To wife, Ann; to son, William; to daughter, Sarah Rutledge; to son, Abel Armstrong, testator's home plantation and the new survey on north side Genning's Branch; to well-beloved son and daughter, Robert and Jane McKitrick; to well-beloved son and daughter, Edward and Jane Rutledge; to well-beloved son and daughter. Henry and Rosanna Murray. Executors, wife Ann and son William. Teste: James Trimble, Robert Armstrong, John Beard. Proved, 20th August, 1776, by Trimble and Beard. Executors qualify.

Page 424.—20th August, 1776. Will of James Robinson was proved by one witness and lie for further proof.

Page 424.—Ditto. Ditto of William Wright. Ditto.

Page 425.—Ditto. Ditto of Mathew Kinkead. Ditto.

Page 425.—7th May, 1776. Francis Miller's estate appraised by Elijah McClenachan, John Paris, Joseph Henderson.

Page 426.—17th August, 1776. Doctor William McClenachan's estate appraised by Thomas Smith, John Abney, Alex. Gibson. Above valued by Doctor John Jackson 20th February, 1776.

Page 427.—15th March, 1776. Thomas Anderson's estate appraised by James Gambel, William Young, Isaac Carson—1 servant man named Peter Charles; James Anderson's (schoolmaster) note; reseved from Capt. Moffett cash, £5.1.4.

Page 429.—20th August, 1776. Recorded. John Watson's appraisement continued—Debts due the estate, from, viz: William Lammar, John McMaster, Patrick Murphy, Nicholas Roap, John Church, George Chuson (Chusour), Nathen Lamm, Benonee Cashaw, David James, Henry Gore, Nicholas Schom, George Jaffrey.

Page 430.—21st May, 1776. Valentine Pence's estate settled by Peter Miller—Paid Henry Pence, legatee, since former settlement; paid John Pence, legatee, since former settlement; paid Henry Swatzer, who married Mary Pence; paid George Probo, who married Barbara Pence; paid Sarah Pence. Received from Henry Metsker.

Page 431.—19th August, 1776. Stephen Conrad's further settlement—To paid John Sworback, the minister, part of the testator's subscription; by a tract of land sold my brother. George Conrad, executor.

Page 432.—27th February, 1775. David Hays' will—To wife, servant girl named Agness McGraw; to daughter, Johanna Buchanan; to daughter, Eloner Paxton; to daughter, Hannah Sawyers; to daughter, Mary Lapsley; to sons, David, William, Joseph, Robert, John, division. Executors, wife Isabella Hays, William Paxton, James Sawyers. Teste: Andrew Kinnear, George Berry, Agness Kinnear. Proved, 21st August, 1776, by solemn affirmation of the Kinnears. Isabella and Sawyers qualify. Paxton to be summoned. 19th August 1777, Paxton qualifies.

Page 434.—23d September, 1776. James Gay's will—To wife, Jean; to son, John, 5 shillings; to son, James, land adjoining John in the Cowpasture; to son, Robert, land testator lives on; to son, Samuel, tract on Mill Creek in Cowpasture; to daughter, Agness; to daughter, Jean; to daughter, Mary; to daughter, Marthew. Executors, wife Jean Gay and Robert Dunlap. Teste: James Elliot, John Dunlap. 19th November, 1776, proved by the witnesses. Executors qualify.

Page 436.—19th November, 1776. Recorded. John Robinson's sale bill to, viz: Jane Robinson, Thos. Tate, Wm. Cook, Wm. Blackwood, Alex. Mitchell, Chas. Herrington, Sarah McMullen, John Carruthers, Samuel Hunter, Peter Kile, David Kile.

Page 438.—18th ———, 1775. Peter Burns' will, of the Cowpasture—Executors, John Cowardin and Chas. Cameron, of the Cowpasture. To John Cowardin, all estate. Teste: James Shaw, Margaret Cowardin, Catron Sevents. Proved, 19th November, 1776, by Cowardin. Executor Cowardin qualifies.

Page 440.—19th November, 1776. Recorded. A list of the sundry articles appraised at Inn Peter Holes in the Crab Apple Bottom by Adam Loch, Leonard Simmons, Henry Bennigar.

Page 444.—11th September, 1776. John Davis' estate appraised by James Dyer, George Duncell, John Garner.

Page 445.—2d June, 1775. Mathew Kinkead's will, farmer—To wife, Elizabeth; to daughters; to children, infants; to eldest son, David, the upper plantation; to son, John, the lower plantation, infant; to child wife now bears; to daughters, Elizabeth and Sarah, Mary Anne. Executors, wife and William McTeer. Teste: William Kinkead, John Hodge, Saml. Lockridge. Proved, 19th November, 1776, by Wm. Kinkead. 19th November, 1776 (?), further proved by John Hodge and Lockridge. Elizabeth qualifies.

Page 448.—29th August, ——. (Recorded, 19th November, 1776.) Thomas Armstrong's estate appraised by James Kirk, William and James Bell.

Page 450.—Vendue bill of above—Sold to, viz: Smith Thomas (Thompson?), Jame Mackitrick, John Joans, James Martin, Martin Dixon, Robt. Ross, Saml. Shannon, Wm. Dabige, Wm. Depreist, Wm. Wildridge, Charles Cousalvan (Consalvan?), Geo. Francey, Elizabeth Stweet (Stivert?), Thos. Rhods, Saml. Moses, Jane Kirk, Richard Spinler.

Page 453.—29th October, 1776. David Hays' estate appraised by George Jameson, Andrew Kinnear, David Buchanan.

Page 455.—5th September, 1776. Samuel Samples' estate appraised by Leonard Herring, Henry and Andrew Ewin—Remainder of the time of Edward Walker.

Page 457.—9th February, 1773. John McCleery's will—To wife, Margaret; to son, James; executors, son James and John Thompson; to each daughter, 1 shilling; to son, John; to son, Samuel. Teste: Robert Clark, Mathew and Robert Patterson.

Page 459.—19th November, 1776. Archibald Alexander's bond as sheriff, with John McClung, Wm. Alexander, Robert Carruthers, James Lyle.

Page 461.—17th December, 1777 (1776?). Recorded. George Robinson's estate appraised by Robert Christian, Alex. Long, James Bell.

Page 462.—11th August, 1775. Sale at vendue of Elizabeth Harmantrout's estate at the house of Philip Harmantrout—sold to, viz: Peater Armantrout, Henry Kiser, Edward Mold, David Harned, Charles Dever, Henry Coler, Jacob Grub, David Jarvin (Garvin?), John Rush, Robt. Sanpils, little Geo. Armantrout, Martin Grider, John Padon (Patton), Geo. Hinton, Chas. Shuls, Peter Nicolas, Thomas Alderson.

Page 466.—17th December, 1777 (1776?). Settlement of above estate—To David Arnet as appraiser.

Page 467.—7th October, 1776. Margaret Cawley's will, of Staunton—To grandchildren, William and Margaret Fulton, children of Thomas Fulton, of Town of Camden, South Carolina, house and half lot in Staunton; to grandson, William Gamel, son of Joseph Gamel; late husband, John Cawley. Executors, Sampson Mathews and her brother, Wm. Patton. Teste: Peter Hog, James Buchanan, Samuel Bell. Proved, 21st January, 1777. Executors qualified.

Page 469.—21st January, 1777. Archibald Alexander's bond for collection of the County proportion.

Page 469.—18th March, 1777. Recorded. David Hays' further appraisement.

Page 470.—11th March, 1777. James Gay's estate appraised by Alexander Hamilton, John Dunlap, James Crockett.

Page 472.—29th November, 1776. Arnest Amone's estate appraised by John Seller, John Huntman, and (German).

Page 474.—29th November, 1776. Above sold at public vendue to, viz: Peter Hershman, John Cotess, John Frye (Feye?), John Byire, Olerick Harshman, Martin Nall, Frederick Hane, John Crotes, Ludwick Rinerd, Mithes Charch, Augustine Priss, Ludwick Shafner, George Blowes, John Fiey, Conrad Shlander, John Burre, John Feny, Adam Blower, Peter Runkel, Charles Fiea.

Page 476.—7th June, 1775. William Wright's will, aged about 68—To wife, mare bought from James Armstrong and the legacy felt her by her father; to son, Samuel; to son, John; to son, William; to each of my four daughters; to sons, James and Alexander, the home place. Executors, wife and son Sammuill. Teste: Walter Davis, John Black. Proved, 20th August, 1776, by John Black, and on 18th March, 1777, by Walter Davis. Samuel refuses to execute.

Page 478.— — ———, 1776. Jacob Conrad's estate appraised—Due by Adam Longh, Thos. Skidmore.

Page 479.—18th March, 1777. Recorded. Steen Hansbaig's appraisement by Geo. Carpenter, John Zöller (Seller?).

Page 481.—4th June, 1775. Robert Campbell's will, farmer—To wife, Sarah, executrix, 390 acres home plantation; Hugh Fulton, son-in-law, executor; to daughter, Mary Richey, daughter Martha Kennedy; to daughter, Sarah Fulton; to Rebecca Crawford, daughter of James Crawford and Isabella Crawford, daughter of testator; to Isabella Crawford, daughter to George and Isabella above; to James Crawford's second wife, 5 shillings to be paid each by Isabella and Rebecca when they come of age; to daughter, Mary Richey, Wm. Kennady, and Hugh Fulton. (Date at end is 4th July, 1775.) Teste: Pat. Buchanan, James Ewing, James Burnsides, Mathew Wilson. Proved, 18th March, 1777, by Buchanan and Wilson. Executors qualified.

Page 483.—11th December, 1770. James Robinson's will, yeoman—To sons, George and David, plantation (bounded by widow Black's field); to wife, Jane; to oldest son, William; to son, James, to son, Joseph; to son, John; to daughter, Sarah McMullan. Executors, James Cowan, Samuel Hunter. Teste: John Black, John Wilson, Wm. Campbell. Proved, 20th August, 1776, by John Black, and on 18th March, 1777, by Wilson.

Page 485.—22d October, 1776. David Williamson's will—To wife, Pernellipy; to daughter, Lurini; to daughter, Lyddy; to daughter, Jennet, unmarried; to son, John, 100 acres joining David Steel on Half Way Creek; to son, David, 150 acres as above; to son, Jonathan, landing including the Old Field and cabin next to Thos. Wilson's land; to son, James, when free of his apprenticeship. Executors, Thomas Wilson, John Boyd. Teste: Andrew Moore, Robert Steel. Proved, 18th March, 1777, by the witnesses. Boyd refuses to execute. Administration granted Penerepy, the widow.

Page 487.—25th August, 1775. John Risk's will—To wife, Margaret, the clock; to son, Robert; to daughter, Mary Risk, alias Hays; to daughter, Hannah Risk, alias Moore; to daughter, Mathew Risk, alias Ellot; to daughter, Margaret Risk, alias Wahub; to nephew, James Risk; to son, William; to son, David; to son, Samuel, home plantation; the plantation in the Calfpasture to be sold; to son, John; plantation joining the one Benj. Kindley did live on, be sold and money divided between nephews, John Risk, son to Robert Risk; John Risk, son to Wm. Risk; to daughter, Elizabeth Risk. Executor, Robert Risk, son. Teste: John Hays, John Richey, Alexander Lowrey. Proved, 19th November, 1776, by John Hays, and on 18th November, 1777, by the other witnesses. Executor qualifies.

Page 489.—18th March, 1777. John Harmon's estate settled—Paid Henry Boraf, Henry Preush, Christian Korp, Phillip Hass. Settled by Barbara Harmantrout, late Barbara Hermon, administratrix of John Hermon.

Page 490.—18th March, 1777. Recorded. Memorandum of widow Cimberland's effects (Jacob Cimberland's appraisement) and settled by Mary Cimmerlan, administrator—Paid Michael Price, Paulser Swelser, Fredk. Artsugh, William Purveance.

Page 492.—18th August, 1775. John Gay's will, of the Calfpasture—To wife, Jean; to daughter, Agness; to son, John; to daughter, Mary; to daughter, Jean; to daughter, Elizabeth. Executors, Robert Dunlap, Samuel Ramsey, James Crockett. Teste: The executors. Proved, 18th March, 1777, by Dunlap and Crockett. Samuel Ramsey to be summoned whether he will execute, and on 20th May, 1777, Ramsey refuses. Administration granted John and Jane Gay, who qualify.

Page 494.—1st March, 1777. Mark Bannister's estate appraised by John Smith, Wm. Herring, Patrick Queen.

Page 495.—19th March, 1777. John Nicholas' estate settled.

Page 495.—19th March, 1777. William Davis' estate in account with Robert Davis, administrator—Paid Robert Snodgrass for funeral charges, £10.17.10, Pennsylvania Exchange; paid Elizabeth Davis, executrix of John Davis; paid Samuel Beale, Charles Smith, Aron Van Sky, Samuel Moore; paid traveling expenses to Pennsylvania; paid Gasper Mickken, John Blizard; cash received at the house in Pennsylvania where intestate died.

Page 498.—19th April, 1777. Joseph Blair's estate appraised by Geo. Berry, Thos. Mitchell, Mathew Thompson.

Page 499.— — ——, ——. John Needham's will—To wife; to daughter, Snier; to daughter, Eliner. Teste: Timothy Waren, John Harrison, William Henton, Peter Henton. Proved, 20th May, 1777, by Warren and Harrison. Administration granted George Henton.

Page 500.—19th March, 1777. Ann Needham's will, wife of the late John Needham—To son, John Car; to daughter, Caterian Warren; to daughter, Sniah Needham; to Sarbrough Sheltman, legacy; to granddaughter, Ann Sheltman; "between my two daughters and son, John Scarbrough, and Catherian"; George Henton to make division. Teste: John Alderson, Jr., Timothy Warren, Jno. Lincoln. Proved, 20th May, 1777, by Warren and Lincoln. George Henton qualified executor.

Page 500.—20th May, 1777. Elijah Garton's estate settled—Paid Sairah Baird; 13th October, 1775, above estate sold at vendue; to Munie Morrison, books 7/0.

Page 502.—20th May, 1777. John Davis' estate settled.

Page 503.—26th May, 1777. Thomas Brown's estate appraised by Thomas Tate, Robert Wilson, Wm. Thompson.

Page 505.—23d June, 1777. Thomas Wilson's estate appraised by Thomas Hill, William and Andrew Moore, Mathew Wilson.

Page 506.—16th August, 1777. David Williams' estate appraised by Robert Wear, Thomas Hill, James Henry.

Page 509.—15th June, 1774. Thomas West's estate appraisement by John Dunbarr, Conrad Humble, Thomas Beggs.

Page 510.—19th August, 1777. Recorded. John Douglass' appraisement by Samuel and Mathew Huston, James Henry, Robert Steel.

Page 511.—15th August, 1777. Robert Campbell's estate appraised by James and John McCleery, Mathew Wilson, Robt. Patterson.

Page 513.—13th May, 1775. Martin Humble's estate appraised by Abraham Miller, James Wright, Joshua Wright—Sworn to before John Canon.

Page 514.—15th May, 1777. David Hays' estate appraised by George Jameson, Andrew Kinneer.

Page 514.—17th April, 1777. Peter Buzzard's estate appraised by Henry Stone, Charles Powers, Robert Davis.

Page 516.—19th August, 1777. Recorded. John Gay's appraisement by Robert Dunlap, James Stevenson, James Elliott.

Page 518.—23d May, 1777. John Needham's estate appraised by Michael Warren, Wm. Hinton, John Harrison.

Page 520.—19th August, 1777. John Needham's, Sr., appraisement (recorded) by same as above.

Page 521.—29th June, 1777. Philip Lingle's will—To wife, Barbary; to sons, Jacob and John, infants, and the child the wife bears; Jacob to learn trade of wheelwright; John, to learn trade of blacksmith. Executors, Jacob Blair, Geo. Koogler, wife Barbary. Teste: Augustine Price, Henry Armantrout, Jno. Armantrout. Proved, 19th August, 1777, by the witnesses. Executors qualified.

Page 523.—19th August, 1777. Recorded. Mathew Kinkead's appraisement by Andrew Hamilton, Lanty Graham, John Wright.

Page 524.—11th January, 1777. Jacob Mark's will—To wife, Margaret; to the three children, if any die before coming to age; to son, Jacob Mark; to daughter, Mary; to youngest son, David; if father should come to this country; to oldest brother. Executrix, wife Margaret. Teste: Charles Mair, Jacob Gum, Samuel King. Proved, 19th August, 1777, by Mair and King. Executrix qualifies.

Page 526.—19th August, 1777. John Galaspy's estate settled by Samuel Lyle—1776, January 24th, received from Capt. Samuel McDowell, his soldier's pay for serving on the Shawney's Expedition; February 8th, by Joseph Wear; 1777, January 25th, by Ebenezer Alexander's note.

Page 527.—19th August, 1777. David Dryden's estate settled by Samuel Lyle—1773, March 2, paid John McCollom, Jr.; legacies paid August 27th, to James Dryden, Elliner Dryden, Thomas Dryden, Nathan Dryden, Wm. Dryden, Dorothy Dryden. David Dryden; 1772, September 10th, received from Thomas Leekey; October 31st, Mathew Elder; 1776, August 27th, Dominick Moran.

Page 530.—28th July, 1774. Thomas Story's will, well stricken in years—To wife, Mary; to son, Thomas; to son, James, 175 acres joining John Stuart and Samuel Hinds; to son, John, 150 acres joining John Givens and Pat. Crawford; to daughters, Rebecca, Martha, Sarah, Elinor, Elizabeth, Mary. Executors, wife Mary and son James. Teste: Edward Rutledge, William Kerr, Samuel Bell. Proved, 20th August, 1777, by Bell and Rutledge. James Story qualifies.

Page 531.—March, 1777. Thomas Andrew's will—To friend and nephew, Peter Hall, son of Henry Hall, carpenter, of Augusta County. "Nephew John Hall, son of said Henry Hall, all pay money, smart money, one smooth bore gun and every thing else that may become due to me while in the cause of my Country in case I should die in the service." To Henry Hall, son of said Henry, 100 acres lying between Warm Springs Valley and a Certain Bullitt. Teste: John Watkins, Valentine Cloninger. Proved, August 20, 1777, by the witnesses. Administration granted Henry Hall.

Page 533.—3d October, 1771. John Harrison's estate sold at vendue—1st sale. 17th October, 1775, John Harrison's estate sold at vendue—2d sale. 1st sale—To Amoziah Davison, Even Henton, Edmund Warren. 2d sale—To Elisha Knox, John Conner, Joseph Scothorn.

Page 534.—19th January, 1771. Above estate settled—Paid Thomas Porter for making one coffin; paid Geo. Speer.

Page 535.—4th September, 1777. Philip Lingle's estate appraised by (3 Germans).

Page 538.—4th September, 1777. Philip Lingle's estate sold at vendue, to, viz—John Peters, Peter Coker, James Madey, Thomas Doolin, Jacob Hamer, Wm. Ludspicke, Peter Bronomer (Brunemer?), Henry Trusler, Augustine Price, Jr., Barbara Lingle, Bartholomew Aulter (Antler), Ab. Rew, Christian Teder, John Fudge.

Page 543.—5th February, 1775. David Bosang's will, of Staunton—To wife, Barbara; to son-in-law, Philip Gruber, Jr.; to my three ———, namely, Margaret Gruber, Henry Lees, John Bosang. Executors, Peter Hanger, Casper Scheyder. Teste: Daniel Kidd, John David Greiner, Valentine Cloninger. Proved, 18th November, 1777, by Kidd and Greiner. Casper Scheyder refuses to execute, and it is proved that Peter Hanger will not serve. Administration granted the widow.

Page 544.—17th February, 1778. Recorded. David Hestin's appraisement by Daniel Kidd, James Hill, Jacob Peck—Above goods were sold on the expedition against the Cherokees, to, viz: To Capt. John Gilmore, Robert McClure, Valentine Jones, Capt. Wm. Christian for Thos. Berry, Gawin Hamilton, Samuel McGill, Samuel Henderson, Wm. Ritchie, James McGlaughlin, James Cuddy, Jos. Guinn.

Page 546.—6th December, 1774. Thomas Watterson's will, farmer—To wife, Mary; to nevey William Watterson. Executors, wife Mary and James Bell. Teste: James Young, Elizabeth (mark) McCamas, George Glenn. Proved, 17th February, 1778, by Young and Glenn. Widow Mary qualifies.

Page 547.—3d February, 1778. Andrew Walker's will—To wife, Margaret, if she has a child to him; to mother-in-law; to brother and sisters. Executors, Thomas Connely and John Burnsides. Teste: John Campbell,

Robt. McCormick, Mary Sevenson. Proved, 17th February, 1778, by Campbell, and recorded. Executors qualify.

WILL BOOK No. VI.

Page 1.—19th November, 1774. David Cunningham's will—To wife, Ann, executrix; to son, David, executor; to son, Patrick, 1 shilling; to son, William, 1 shilling; to daughter, Ann, 1 shilling; to daughter, Mary, 1 shilling; to John, David, James, Alexander, Jane, Sarah, all estate. Teste: James Ewing, Capt. James Ewing. Proved, 17th March, 1778, by the witnesses. Executor qualified.

Page 2.—17th March, 1778. Recorded. Isaac Robinson's appraisement by Waller Moffett, Conrad Humble. Cash received of Michael Henican.

Page 3.—17th February, 1778 (March?). Recorded. John Hays' appraisement by Robert Wilson, Wm. Thompson, Thomas Shields, James Cowan.

Page 4.—20th August, 1774. James Clark's will—To daughter, Jean Clark (Clok), 2 shillings; to daughter, Elizabeth Regh, 2 shillings; to daughter, Sarah Clok, 2 shillings; to son, John, 2 shillings; to son, James, 2 shillings; to son, William's heir, 2 shillings; to daughter, Ane Dunlap, 2 shillings; to son, Alexander, 2 shillings; to son, Samuel, 2 shillings; to son, Robert, 2 shillings; to daughter, Marget, 2 shillings; to wife, Elizabeth. Executors, wife, and son Wm. Regh. Teste: James and John McCleerey, James Ewing. Proved, 17th March, 1778, by James McCreerey and Ewing.

Page 5.—10th August, 1776. William Teas' will—To wife Mary, to Robert Love, £10, to daughter Jane, executors. Teste: Hugh McClure, Robert Love, Hannah Reid. Proved, 17th March, 1778, by McClure. Executors qualify.

Page 6.—17th March, 1778. John Poage's bond as sheriff (with James Allen, Hugh Donaghee, Daniel McNare).

Page 8.—18th March, 1778. John Poage's bond as surveyor.

Page 8.—18th March, 1778. Mark Swadley's estate in account with Mathew Patton and Sebastian Hover—Paid Leonard Simon, Richard Beven, John Jordan, Nicholas Seamans, Christopher Crommett, Margaret Dyche, Peter Smith, Cutlip Gabbart; received William Jordan's account; Lewis Bakers' do.

Page 10.—15th September, 1772. Sale bill of above to, viz: Anthony Regar, Thos. Feemster (Cowpasture), Aron Skihawk, David Whitton, William Darling, David Taylor, Martin Shole, George Bushberry, James Wilke, Jacob Brack, William and James Dyer, Adam Look, Jno. Dunwoodey.

Page 14.—21st April, 1778. Recorded. James O'Neal's appraisement by William Meteer, William Kinkead, John Graham. (Appraised 28th March, 1778.)

Page 15.—27th March, 1778. Above estate sold at vendue, to, viz—Leven Benston.

Page 16.—21st April, 1778. Recorded. David Cunningham's appraisement by James Ewing, Samuel McCutchan, Wm. Hughes.

Page 18.—29th March, 1778. Morris O'Friel's will, farmer—To wife, Catherine, executrix; to son, Daniel; to daughter, Mary; to son, Jeremiah;

to daughter, Eleanor; to grandson, Joseph, 160 acres between William and James Bell; to grandsons, Morris and John Martin, infants, 400 acres, tract in Forks of James; to John O'Friel, survey on McClure's Run. Teste: Walter Trimble, Robert Wallace, Robt. Rennick. Proved, 21st April, 1778, by Trimble, and 19th May, 1778, by the witnesses. Executrix qualifies.

Page 20.—1st May, 1778. William Teas' estate appraised by James Steel, Benj. Stewart, William Gillespy—One convict servant named Wm. Parker.

Page 22.—19th May, 1778. Andrew Walker's appraisement recorded—Thomas Frame, Arthur Connly, John Campbell.

Page 23.—28th July, 1777. James Alexander's will—To nephew, James Alexander, executor, plantation he (decease) lives on, 400 acres in Beverley Manor on Long Meadow. Teste: Samuel Bell, Gabriel Alexander, Richard Madison. Proved, 19th May, 1778, by Alexander and Madison. Executor qualifies.

Page 24.—15th March, 1775. Joseph Skidmore, Sr.'s, will, farmer—To son, Andrew, executor. Teste: Robert Mimes, Jacob Eberman, Elias Barker. Proved, 17th March, 1778, by Minnes, and on 19th May, 1778, by Jacob Eberman. Andrew qualifies.

Page 25.—6th May, 1778. Peter Burns' estate appraised by Leonard Bell, John McRoberts, Jno. McCasslin.

Page 26.—14th May, 1778. Edward (mark) Warner's bill—To wife and daughter, Marthew, all estate. Executors, John Poage and John Burnside. Teste: John Harper, Marthia Burnside, Jacob Campbell. Proved, 19th May, 1778, by John Harper and Campbell, and 21st May, 1778. Executors qualify.

Page 27.—19th May, 1778. Nathan (mark) Reagland's will—To son, John, "the fore neagros left me—my grandfather"; to daughter, Rebecca; to wife, Sackey. Executors, John Poage, James Allen, Jr. Proved, 19th May, 1778, by John Harper and Matthew Burnsides. Teste: Above witnesses and Wm. Hook.

Page 28.—16th September, 1777. James Archer, Jr.'s, will—Father to make distribution of estate among testator's brothers, executor; estate to be divided between father and mother, brothers and sisters; to brother, William, sister Isabella Archer, sister Elizabeth Archer, brother John Archer, brother Edmond Archer. Teste: George Huston, Reuben Crigler, Nathan Huston. Proved, 19th May, 1778, by George and Nathan Huston. Executor qualified.

Page 30.—14th January, 1777. Moses Thomson's will, of Tyger's Valley—To wife, Elizabeth; to children, to be schooled and taught trades; to oldest daughter, Catharine Thomson, her part of estate to be committed to care of testator's sister, Anne Teenan, wife of Robert Teenan, in North Carolina. Executor, Mathew Patton. Teste: David Mathews, Benj. Chaner (Cleaver), Thos. Skidmore. Proved, 19th May, 1778, by Mathews and Chaner. Executor qualified.

Page 31.—19th May, 1778. Christopher Kisling's estate settled—Paid Mr. Gilbert as coroner, Wm. Barrier. Above men paid by the widow, what follows was paid by John Herdman, her present husband—To John Kisling, his part of his father's estate.

Page 32.—19th May, 1778. John Poag's bond as collector of public tax.

Page 34.—19th May, 1778. David White's (of Tygar's Valley) estate appraised, sold, and settled—Vendue, to viz: Cathorine White, Aron Richeson, Samuel Eberman, George Burdon, Michael Austner, 1 gun bought by Catherine White and taken away by force and violence by Wm. White; cash paid Wm. Clover; cash received of the public for pay of the intestate as a spy.

Page 35.—2d May, 1778. John Coutts' estate in Rockingham County appraised by Jacob Nicholas, Chas. Rush, John Rush.

Page 36.—21st May, 1778. John Poage's bond for collection of County proportion.

Page 37.—19th May, 1778. Martin Humble's estate in account with Conrad Humble, administrator—Paid Henry Runnion, Jno. Trumbo, James Devoir; paid Ab. Kuykendall, Richard McMachen's account; paid Jacob Fegley.

Page 39.—16th June, 1778. Robert Poage's bond as assistant surveyor.

Page 39.—1st December, 1777. Edward Hynds' will (of the Bull Pasture)—To wife, Anne, with child; to oldest daughter, Elizabeth, home plantation and all entered land this side of Crab Run; to daughter, Jenny, upper plantation and land on other side of Crab Run. Executors, wife and John Peebles; to servant, Wm. Smith, £10. Teste: Wm. Stewart, John Hicklin, Wm. (mark) McCandless. Proved, 16th June, 1778, by Stuart and Hicklin.

Page 41.—28th March, 1778. John Stewart's estate appraised by Benj. Wilson, John Warrick—Vendue bill of above estate (Wm. Hamilton, administrator); 30th March, 1778, to sold to, viz: Benj. Abot, Alex. Maxwell.

Page 42.—18th August, 1778. Recorded. Edward Warner's appraisement by John McMahon, William Black, John Harper.

Page 43.—3d January, 1778. John Loggan's will—To son, John; to son, Samuel; to son, William; to son, Robert; to son, Joseph; to daughter, Sarah; to wife; to daughter, Mary; to son, Alexander; to son, Jame. Executors, wife and Mathew Huston. Teste: Robert Kenkead, Samuel Huston, Geo. Weir. Proved, 19th May, 1778, by Weir, and 18th August, by Huston. Mary qualifies.

Page 45.—19th August, 1778. John Poage's bond for collection of public tax.

Page 46.—21st April, 1778. Dower laid off for widow of Thomas Story. Report of commissioners, cor. Thomas and John Story and James Story.

Page 46.—17th October, 1778. John Logan's estate appraised by John McKemy, Robt. McNutt, James Montgomery, David Rusel.

Page 48.—17th November, 1778. Recorded. Edward Hinds' appraisement by Thomas Hicklin, Thos. Feemster, James Peebles.

Page 49.—19th June, 1775. Charles (mark) Campbell's will—To wife, Mary; to son, William; to son, Robert, three children—Hugh, Robert, and Sarah; to other children, division to be made by son John, and Charles, executors. Teste: John Wilson, William Campbell. Proved, 17th November, by the witnesses, and Charles Campbell qualifies.

Page 51.—20th May, 1778. John Dunwoody's estate, Dr., to paid by his brother James, administrators of said estate—To Mary Gregory, Francis

Ford's account, Joseph Newton's account, Wm. Almond's account; received James Morrow's account, Henry Morice account; received from the County for service in the Shaney Expedition to the Point; received from the County for one gun and pistol lost in the battle at the Point.

Page 52.—3d August, 1778. Ephraim Richason's will (of Tygart's Valley)—To wife, Rachel; to sons, Aron and Abraham, infants; if children be not well used, they are to be taken by Daniel Richason. Executors, brothers Aaron and Daniel Richardson. Teste: William Blair, Aron (mark) Richardson. Proved, 19th January, 1779, by the witnesses, and 20th January, 1779, administration c. t. a. granted Aron Richason.

Page 53.—22d March, 1776. Thomas (X) Bradshaw's will—To wife; to son, James; to daughter Jane's son, Thomas; to daughter, Jane; to son, Thomas. Executors, sons James and Thomas. Teste: Joseph Wright, Rd. Mathewz, William Mathews, Mary Mathews. Proved, 16th February, 1779, by Richard and William Mathews and Mary Mathews. Executors qualify.

Page 54.—25th August, 1778. Gabriel Alexander's will (of South River of Shanandore)—To wife, Dorcus; to son, James, 5 shillings; to son, Francis, 5 shillings; to daughter, Dorcus Lackey, 5 shillings; to daughter, Margaret; to son, John, 60 acres on South River, part of home plantation joining John's other land and William Long; to son, Gabriel, tract owned by testator and James Bell. Executors, sons Gabriel and James. Teste: **Samuel and David Long, John Bell.** Proved, 16th March, 1779, by John Bell and Samuel Long. Executors qualify.

Page 56.—16th August, 1778. William (mark) Blackwood's will—To wife, Eloner, and her seven children, until youngest is of age; to son, Samuel; to 3 sons—Samuel, William, Joseph. Executors, wife Eloner and Joseph Kerr. Teste: Alexander Long, Samuel Blackwood, Mary Kerr. Proved, 19th March, 1779, by Samuel Blackwood and Mary Kerr. Widow qualifies.

Page 57.—17th March, 1779. Joseph Skidmore's estate settled by Andrew Skidmore—Received from Jno. Hagle, Jno. Alkier, Jno. Yocume.

Page 58.—2d July, 1778. Moses Thompson's estate appraised by William and Benj. Cleaver, Joseph Danaho—1 entry of land at the Cherry Tree Fork; 1 entry of land at Thompson's Meadows; 1 entry of land at Big Lick; 1 plantation whereon dwelling house is.

Page 59.—16th March, 1779. Recorded. Archibald and Lanty Elliot's appraisement by John Vachub, John Meek, Robt. Wallace.

Page 60.—14th August, 1775. Thomas Hogshead's estate appraised by Joseph Bell, John Patterson, Thomas Poage.

Page 61.— — ———, ———. Andrew Lewell's will—To wife, Rebecca; to son, Abraham, infant; if Abraham dies without issue, then to be divided between his brothers and sisters; to 3 younger sons, Andrew, Simon and Peter, infants, to be educated and taught trades; to Abraham's sister; to daughter, Hanah, infant. Executors, wife Rebecca and Charles Yarhoss. Teste: John Poage, Jas. Allen, James Anderson. Proved, 18th May, 1779, by Poage and Allen. Executors qualify.

Page 63.—March, 1779. William Wallace's estate appraised by Joseph and David Bell, Jas. Crawford.

Page 66.—18th May, 1779. Recorded. John Cawley's estate settlement—Paid Bryan Henry (Kenney), Elizabeth Hartgrove, John Yancey.

Page 67.—25th February, 1776. Hugh Allen's estate appraised by Samuel Henderson, William Robertson, James Kerr.

Page 68.—18th May, 1779. Recorded. Andrew Walker's estate settlement.

Page 68.—18th May, 1779. Recorded. Thomas Bradshaw's estate settlement.

Page 69.—18th May, 1779. Recorded. Charles Campbell's appraisement—Appraised by Michael and James Dickey, James and Archibald Henderson.

Page 71.—18th May, 1779. Recorded. John Douglas' estate settlement—Paid George Wear, Mary McMurphey.

Page 72.—22d May, 1779. John Poage's bond (with Thos. Smith, Jacob Grass, David Greiner, Daniel Kidd) for collection of public taxes.

Page 72.—19th January, 1776. James Anderson's will—To wife, Jean; to son, John, 5 shillings; to son, George, 5 shillings; to son, James, 5 shillings; to daughter, Agnis, 5 shillings; to daughter, Jane, 5 shillings; to son, Samuel, whole estate; to son Samuel's son, James, 200 acres, infant. Executors, George Moffett and John Young. Teste: John Blair, Isaac Carson, Peter Challe. Proved, 15th June, 1779, by Blair and Carson. Executors refused, administration granted Samuel.

Page 74.—17th August, 1779. Recorded. William Blackwood's appraisement by Robert Christian, Mathew Thompson, Wm. Kerr.

Page 75.—25th September, 1776. William Christian's will—Executors, "my brothers, Robert and John Christian and Capt. George Moffett"; to son, Patrick, 269 acres whereon Patrick now lives, part of 1614 acres "whereof 538 acres were laid off for my share"; to William Christian (son to Patrick), land, 40 acres of 180 (80) acres; to son, Gilbert; to wife, Mary; the 3,000 acres to which testator is entitled by Proclamation 1763 to be divided between 3 daughters, Margaret, Elizabeth, and Mary. Teste: William Anderson, Patt. Christian, Wm. Scott. Proved, 17th August, 1779, by Anderson and Scott. Moffett refuses to execute; John Christian qualifies.

Page 77.—17th August, 1779. Recorded. David Bosang's estate appraisement by David Greiner, Jas. Hill, Casper Snider, Jacob Grass.

Page 80.—20th July, 1779. Michael Bowyer's bond as escheator.

Page 81.—15th May, 1777. Mary Thompson's estate appraised by Samuel Lyle, Andrew Hall, Alex. McClure—Debt due by John Thompson being a legasie due to Mary Thompson at her deceas.

Page 82.—22d May, 1779. Andrew Lewell's estate appraised by James Allen, John Patterson, Mathew and Robert Kenny.

Page 84.—1st December, 1778. Joel Westfall's estate appraised by Jese Hamilton, Jonas Friend, Aron Richardson (mark).

Page 85.—3d August, 1773. James Stewart's estate appraised—Accounts against, viz: Jas. Schoolcraft, Daniel McCan, Ralph Stewart.

Page 87.—Vendue bill of above James Stewart, deceased, 1772, to, viz: Richard Eliot, Wm. Haddon.

Page 88.—Isabel Barker to the estate of James Stewart, deceased, Dr.

Page 89.—17th August, 1779. Recorded. James Lessley, Jr.'s, appraisement by Wm. Robertson, Thos. Patterson, Mathew Kinney—Cash in hands of James Lessley, Sr.

Page 92.—13th August, 1779. Darby Connly's estate appraised by Wm. Hamilton, John Warwick, John Hamilton—Received from John Hamilton one certificate for nine cattle of said estate that was impressed for the use of the Malitia in actual service and appraised to. Ditto, 9 hogs impressed.

Page 94.—19th June, 1778. Joseph Skidmore, Sr.'s, estate appraised by Benj. Willson, Jonas Friend, Wm. White, Wm. Cbaven.

Page 95.—8th December, 1778. Ephraim Richardson's estate appraised by Daniel Westfall, Francis Wire, Wm. Blair.

Page 96.—Above estate settlement—Due from Watson Clark.

Page 97.—8th December, 1778. Ephraim Richardson's estate sold at vendue, to, viz: Aron Richardson, Anthony Smith, Rachel Richardson, James Lackey, Joseph Pancake, Eliah Fornelson, John Crouch, John Fornelson.

Page 98.—21st March, 1779. Francis Wire's (Were) will—To wife, Hannah; to sons, Daniel and Benjamin, committed to their mother's charge until they are six years old and then to be bound; to four children—Solomon, John, Daniel, Benjamin, infants. Leaves Solomon to Daniel Westfall, to be taught a trade, also a branch of shoemaker's trade. Leaves John to Benj. Wilson, to be taught a branch of weaver's trade suitable to the work of the country, and a branch of the shoemaker's trade. Executors, Benj. Wilson and Daniel Westfall. Teste: Henry Delong, George Shaver, Daniel Westfall, Benj. Wilson. Proved, 18th August, 1779, by George Shaver and Henry Delay. Executors qualify.

Page 100.—4th June, 1778. This is to certify that Casper Eakert, of Augusta County, taner, who is know Going out on Command under Thomas Right in Service against the headin and I do propose to Give unto my Broder fillips Eaker, all my land and crops that is now in the ground, likewise to horses, 8 head of cattle wit the increds (?), &c.—Casper Eakert. Teste: Randell Slack, Sarah (mark) Slack. Proved, 17th August, 1779, by the witnesses. Administration granted Phillip Ekert.

Page 100.—31st August, 1779. John Flasher's will (yeoman, of Augusta County and Province of Virginia)—To wife, Mary Susanna; children to be bound to trades if not well treated by their mother; to son, Henry. Estate to be divided between the 2 children. Teste: Henry Fleisher, Nicholas Seybert. Executors, wife and witnesses. Proved. 16th November, 1779. Nicholas Seybert refuses to execute, other executors qualify.

Page 101.—8th September, 1779. David Allen's will—To wife, Elizabeth; to children; to wife's mother, Mary Allen; to son, Robert, infant, £5 in lieu of a horse left him by his grandfather, Robert Allen; to son, John Crooks Allen, infant; to sons, James and David, infants; to daughter, Mary, infant; to son, James Joseph Allen, infant. Executors, brothers John Allen, in Frederick County, and Thomas Allen, in Shanando. Teste: John Montgomery, James Henry, Patrick Hall, James Givens. Proved, 16th November, 1779, by James Henry and Edward Hall. Executors qualify.

Page 103.—16th November, 1779. Recorded. William Blackwood's vendue—Sold 24th August, 1779, by Eleanor Blackwood; sold to, viz: George Huston, Robert Stewart, John Askins, Robt. Bailey.

Page 104.—16th November, 1779. George Moffett's bond as sheriff.

Page 105.—22d October, 1779. Rebecca (mark) Caruthers' will—To daughter, Esther, all estate, together with £1,200 willed to Rebecca by her husband; mother; care of said child given to executors, for failure then, to John Caruthers; to sisters; to brothers; to brother, William; to brothers, James and John. Executors, father John Moffett. Teste: James Cunningham, James Young, Wm. Moffett. Proved, 16th November, 1779, by Young and Moffett.

Page 107.—16th November, 1779. Recorded. Michael Mallow's sale bill—Sold to, viz: Michael Allgyre, Jacob Bragg, Peter Wineman, Jacob Carpenter, Joseph Bennett, Adam Mallow, Jacob Break, Richard Byrns, Martin Judy, Philip Harper, Jno. Rice; to Nicholas Boucher, Jno. Westfall, Peter Vineman, Jno. Higgins, Jacob Goodman, Jacob Heffenor, Christopher Hoofner, Gasper Bogart, Henry Rule, Abel Griffith, Peter Hald, Peter Segerfoot, widow Moser, Aaron Vanscoy, Thos. Bland, Zachary Retsworth, Sarah Harmon, Ludowick Waggoner, Thos. Wilmot, Adam Lock, Michael Peterson, Geo. Walker, Samuel Morrall, Zachary Retsroth, Henry Judy, Jacob Springstone, Jacob Caplinger, John Server, Eve Moser, Lawrence Causan (Cansen?), Robt. Craigard, Gabriel Cyle (Kile).

Page 112.—Above estate settled—Paid Thos. Branan, John Wiss, Thos. Sumfield, Michael Wilfong, Cathrine Moser, Jacob Stookie.

Page 113.—16th November, 1779. John Graham's estate settled.

Page 114.—16th November, 1779. John Cawley's estate settled—Gerald Phelan's note.

Page 114.—18th November, 1779. David Allen's estate appraised. Appraised by James Tate, Jas. McChesney, Pat. Hall.

Page 116.—29th December, 1779. Lanty Graham's (Grams) will—To wife, Elizabeth; to daughter, Rebecca; to brother John Graham's two sons, John and James Graham; to brother John Graham's son, Lanty; to brother Robert Graham's daughter, Sarah Graham, infant; to mother. Executors, wife, and brother John Graham. Teste: Andrew Lockridge, John Graham, Thos. Hughart. Proved, 15th February, 1780, by Hughart and Lockridge. John Graham appears and refuses to execute. Elizabeth Graham qualifies.

Page 118.—16th March, 1780. Lanty Graham's estate appraised by Andrew Hamilton, Wm. Lockridge, Wm. Meteer.

Page 119.—20th March, 1779. David Bell's will—To wife, Florence; to sons, William, John, James, David; to sons, William and David, the home plantation adjoining Jno. Patterson; to sons, John and James, lands in Kean Tucky, the head of Cow Pasture, Jackson's River, and South Branch; to daughter, Susannah; to daughter, Elizabeth. Executors, wife, and brother Joseph Bell. Teste: James Anderson, Wm. Christian, Wm. Anderson, Samuel Anderson. Proved, 21st March, 1780, by James Anderson and Christian. Executors qualify.

Page 121.—21st March, 1780. Edward Hynds' estate settlement recorded—8th July, 1778, sale at vendue to, viz: John Peebles, Anthony Johnson, Francis Foard, Mathew Pen, Eli Bab Wilson, John Kingin, Thos.

Deverix, Lewis Baker, Wm. McKeamey, Thos. Dugless, Joseph Newton; 1777, John Jordan; paid Elizabeth Peilentine, William Smith's legacy.

Page 124.—21st March, 1780. Jacob Ruleman's estate settled.

Page 125.—28th November, 1779. Thomas Beard's estate appraised by Jno. Montgomery, Wm. Moore, Thos. Wilson.

Page 126.—Above estate settled—Paid Wm. Berkley, Jno. Eakin, Wm. Perrins, Thomas Alexander's and Thos. Beard's legacies; Esther Alexander's legacy; Thomas Mitchell and his mother; Thos. Dunlap and his mother; Robt. Ramsey and children; Martha Mitchell's legacy.

Page 127.—15th March, 1780. John McClintock's estate appraised by Jno. Young, Jno. McPheeters, Ro. Clark.

Page 127.—25th March, 1780. George Moffett's bond for collection of County levy.

Page 128.—29th September, 1779. Catrine Freel's estate appraised by Samuel Craig, James and Wm. Bell.

Page 129.—List of debts paid by Mary Teas to creditors of William Teas to, viz: 1777—Lazarus Inman, George Allist, Bridget Lee, Joel Crawford, Hannah Woods, Francis Hoggs, Mary Page, Alex. Purdice, Doct. Ham, Abner Wood, Gidian Pullen, Benj. Calley, James Lansley.

Page 132.—1st November, 1779. Casper Ekert's estate sold at vendue—Now belonging to his brother, Philip Ekert, by Christian Ruleman, Henry Stone, Michael Willpink.

Page 132.—Vendue bill of Samuel Samples—Jacob Caplin, John Chasm, Elihu Messexs, James Floyd, Wm. Greagg, John McVey, Wm. Pettijohn, Wm. Perrigin, Margaret and James McVey, Felix Sheltman.

Page 136.—Settlement of Samuel Samples' estate—Paid heirs of Thomas Gregg, deceased.

Page 139.—5th December, 1778. Jacob Springstone's estate appraised by Benj. Willson, Jesse Hamilton, Daniel Westfall.

Page 140.—19th July, 1779. George Crawford's will (of Middle River)—To wife, Elizabeth, ½ home plantation; to son, James, ½ home plantation and entry adjoining; to son, George, plantation bought from Joshua Hickman on Littler's Creek; to son, Robert, plantation bought of Brice Russell with addition taken off of Hickman's place on Lettler's Creek; to son, William Crawford, plantation bought of Wm. Baskins; to son, John, ½ home plantation before devised to wife above; to daughter, Margaret Anderson; to daughter, Mary Renkin; to daughter, Elizabeth Crawford; to daughter, Martha; to daughter, Sarah; to daughter, Jane. Executors, sons James and George. Teste: John Givens, John Givens, Jr., Thomas Graham. Proved, 16th May, 1780, by the Givenses. Executors qualify.

Page 142.—16th May, 1780. John Willson's bond as Deputy Surveyor.

Page 143.—12th May, 1780. Joseph Gambell's estate appraised by John McCoy, John Hiner, James Hoge.

Page 145.—20th May, 1780. George Moffett's bond for collection of taxes imposed by Act of Assembly passed at Williamsburg 4th October, 1779

Page 146.—5th Mar., Anno que Domini, 1767. James Lessley's will—To wife, Sarah, to manage plantation and support the children; to son, James, $1, having already provided for him; to son, John; to son, Robert and

Samuel, home plantation; to daughters, Mary Robertson and Mary Roger; to daughters "now with me," Isabella, Dolly, Sarah, Agness, Elizabeth. Executors, wife Sarah, son James, and William Johnston. Teste: John and William Stuart. Proved, 19th August, 1780 (the witnesses being both dead), by witnesses to handwriting. Sarah, the widow, qualifies.

Page 147.—16th August, 1780. Recorded. Peter Hole's estate vendue bill—Sold to, viz: Peter Hole, Paul Summers, Neckless Harper, Wm. Dunwiddy, George Hole, Henry Fletcher, Joseph Ham, John Feris, Wm. McAlly, Barnard Lance, Enees Hole, Elias Painter, George Cowger, Capt. Parsons, Leonard Summons, Peter Segerfeet, Mike Mannen, widow Gregory, Roger Patton, Leasy Hole, James and Thomas Parsons, Conrad Lance, Miss Hole.

Page 151.—Above estate settled by Peter Hole, executor—Paid Peter Smith, George Puffenberry, John Argon, Henry Penegor, Samuel Grutrix. Settled 16th August, 1780.

Page 152.—11th May, 1780. Francis Wire's estate appraised by Jacob Westfall, Aron Richard, John Casety.

Page 154.—19th September, 1780. Recorded, viz: 15th December, 1778, Dr., the estate of Joel Westfall—To Jacob Westfall, Jr., administrator, and Wm. Westfall, administrator.

Page 154.—23d September, 1780. Jacob Seccafoose's estate appraised by Mathew Willson, James Ewing, Samuel McCutchen.

Page 156.—8th May, 1780. John Flesher's estate appraised.

Page 157.—John Flesher's vendue bill, by Henry Flesher, executor—To, viz: Christian Snedecore, Wm. Bennett, John Byrne, Josiah Cochran, Abram Burner, Paulser Flesher, Thomas Hicks, Samuel Crider, Susan Flesher, William Jeines, George Dawson, John Wormsley, Samuel Creedrick, Wm. Jienes, Joseph Lance, Thos. Hix.

Page 158.—29th March, 1779. James Wallace's (mark) will—To grandson, James Wallace, 100 acres which I looked upon in my lifetime to be my part of the tract which we lived upon; to daughter-in-law, Jean Wallace, to live on other part of the plantation; to grandsons, William and Samuel Wallace, infants, 100 acres other part of plantation; to granddaughter, Frances; to granddaughter, Mary. Executors, grandson James Wallace and John Patterson. Teste: David Bell, James Crawford, Joseph Bell. Proved, 19th November, 1780, by the witnesses. John Patterson refuses to execute. James Wallace qualifies.

Page 160.—22d November, 1780. Geo. Moffett's bond for collection of County taxes.

Page 161.—22d November, 1780. Geo. Moffett's bond as Sheriff.

Page 164.—4th December, 1780. Hugh Daniel recants having said Francis Marra was a convict.

Page 164.—20th May, 1780. John Archer's will—To wife, Rebecca; to brother, Sampson Archer; to sister, Elizabeth Stuart; to William Blair's daughter, Rebecca; to John Blayr, son of my friend William Blair; to Mary Ross, wife of Robert Ross; to the poor, whether friends or strangers, remainder of estate. Executors, John Poage, Robert Armstrong. Teste: William Clunie, William Blear, James Anderson, John Richey.

Page 166.—14th July, 1776. James Gamble's will—To wife, Agness, tract cor. Alex. Blair; cor. the land that was Alex. Craig, Sr.'s; the spring house that belonged to Alex. Craig, Jr.; cor. John Young; cor. James Anderson; to son, Robert, tract cor. Alex. Blair, cor. Alex Craig, Sr.; to son, John, land on both sides Middle River; to daughters, Sarah, Agness, Elizabeth, Esther. Executors, John Poage and beloved brother Thomas Bell and son Robert Gamble. Teste: James Bell, William Frame, William Young. Proved, 15th May, 1781, by the witnesses, and Robert Gamble qualifies.

Page 169.— — February, 1781. Archibald Henderson's will—To wife, Elizabeth; to daughter, Eleanor, infant; to brother, William. Executors, Joseph Patterson, John Dickey. Teste: James, Isabella, Eleanor Patterson. Proved, 15th May, 1781, by the witnesses. Executors qualified.

Page 171.—15th May, 1781. Edward Warner's estate settled—3d June, 1778, vendue; paid Edward Barton.

Page 171.—13th February, 1775. John Everman's estate appraised by Ephraim Richardson, Wm. Westfall, George Westfall.

Page 173.—16th May, 1781. Recorded. John Berry's estate settlement— Paid Margret Kirkpatrick, Samuel Neizbitt, Elizabeth Henry. Debts and legacies paid by the executor—To David McCrea for funeral liquor, £1.7.0, Anthony Kelly for a coffin, Margret Rutherford, Capt. John Gilmore, Wm. Berry, James Berry, Rebecca Buchanan, Robt. Fearis, Alex. McIlroy, George and Charles Berry, Robt. Kilpatrick, Rebecca Kelly, Mary Johnson, Elizabeth Bell, Andrew McCampbell for Jno. Berry, Jr., Francis and Elizabeth Berry, Mary Neizbitt, John Berry Shoemaker, Rebecca Gillaspy.

Page 175.—16th May, 1781. Margret Cawley's estate settled—Paid John William Lao, Robt. Histrop; received cash by Wm. Jsaton (Isaton), rum sold.

Page 176.—27th February, 1781. Thomas Nelson's estate appraised by Samuel McCutchen, John Burk.

Page 177.—3d October, 1780. James Tate's will—To wife and children, estate to be kept together for their support and education. Executors, wife Sarah, Benj. Stuart, John Tate, Jr., William Tate. Teste: Thomas Tate, John Tate, Jr., Jenny Tate. Proved, 21st August, 1781, by Thomas and Jane Tate. Executors qualify.

Page 178.—Dr. the estate of Moses Thompson to Mathew Patton, executor—1779, December 6, to Charles Lynch (Synch); 1779, June 8, to David Harmon; 1778, December 13, to Daniel Westfall; 1778, July 10, vendue bill, to Ebenezer Petty, Jacob Root, Thomas and Joseph Summerfield, Andrew Skidmore, Thos. Harrad, Aron Vanskoy.

Page 180.—Estate of William Teas to Robt. Love, executor, Dr.—1778, July 11, paid Francis Hodges for seven days' reaping, £4.4.0; July 17, paid Hugh McGee for six days' reaping; July 20, paid George Sutherland for 7 days' reaping; July 22, paid Wm. Rice for 1 day's reaping; 1779, August 30, cash paid David Henderson on receipt of Miss Teas; 1778, September 8, cash received from Cornelius McFall; September 8, cash received of Andrew Lecky; September 8, cash received from John and Jordon Gibsons, sundries at vendue; September 8, cash received of Charles Kennin, sundries at vendue; 1779, September 8, cash received of Thomas Griff, sundries at vendue.

Page 183.—27th August, 1781. James Gamble's estate appraised agreeable to the rate of 1774, by William Young, James Trimble, Jno. Gardner.

Page 187.—29th January, 1781. William Long's will (of South River, Shanadore)—To wife; to son, Alexander Long, the money that son William had in possession at his decease; to son, William's son, infant; to son, Francis, 100 acres adjoining Jacob Gabhart; to sons, David and Joseph, 400 acres that David lives on; to son, John, if ever he returns home again; to son, James, part of testator's home tract adjoining James Bell; to son, Samuel, other part of tract lying between Francis and James; to daughters, Elizabeth Henderson and Dorcas Barnet, 150 acres on Long Meadow; to grandson, William Long, son of son William, 250 acres on Long Meadow adjoining Andrew McClure and James Alexander. Executors, sons Alexander, Samuel, James. Teste: John Bell, Gabriel Alexander, Joseph Bell. Proved, 18th September, 1781, by John Bell and Alexander.

Page 190.—John McClenachan's estate in account with Alexander St. Clair, executor—1774, July 14, to sundry articles found by myself for use of John McClenachan's heirs, Thomas and John; November 13, for sundries for Thomas when sick; 1774, November 13, to paid sundries for the funeral, viz: 7¾ lbs. cheese; 79 qts. spirrits; 3 gals. wine; 7¾ yds. ribbon; ½ gal. wine; 27 pds. flour; 5 lbs. butter; 3 lbs. sugar; 2 lbs. sugar; 29 yds. holland; 10 yds. scarfing; 1775, October 5, to Thomas Smith for a coffin for Thomas; 1778, November 25, to Smith Tandy for getting a negro child inoculated; 1781, July 20, to Valentine White, 56 days' schooling of John. Contra: 1776, December 30, received Isaac Benlever's account, Alex. Ocheltree's account; 1777, September 10, received Lazarus Barkley's account, Lazarus Murphy's account; by bonds of Christopher Symes, Richard Godall, Charles Symes, Seriah Stratton.

Page 202.—3d October, 1780. James Buchanan's will—To wife, Sarah; to son, Alexander; to daughter, Jean; to mother and sister, Sarah. Executors, Charles Campbell, William and David Buchanan. Teste: David Buchanan, John Yager, Elizabeth Hannah. Proved, 21st August, 1781, by David Buchanan and Hannah. 16th October, 1781, Wm. Buchanan qualifies.

Page 203.—30th October, 1781. Francis Gardner, Sr.'s, will—To wife, Esther; to grandson, Francis Gardner; to grandson, Samuel Gardner. Executors, William and James Bell. Teste: Sampson Sawyers, Wm. Sterrett, Wm. Burgess. Proved, 19th December, 1781, by Sterrett. Executors qualify.

Page 205.—19th December, 1781. Alex. McClenachan's bond as Sheriff.

Page 207.—20th November, 1781. Recorded. Capt. James Tate's appraisement by John Fulton, David Humphrey, David Willson.

Page 208.—8th October, 1781. Elizabeth (mark) Clark's will—To daughter, Jean Elliot's heirs; to well beloved Elizabeth Breath (Reath, Reoth?); to daughter, Sarah Elliot; to daughter, Anne Dounlap; to daughter, Margret Clenkaid; to son, John Gridle; to son, James; to son, Alexander and to Alexander's wife; to four daughters; to son, Samuel; to son, William's heirs; to son, Robert. Executors, son Robert Clark and William Reaoh. Teste: Charles Donally, James McCleerey, Robt. Patterson, Geo. Berry. Proved, 20th November, 1781, by McCleerey and Berry. Robert Clark qualifies.

Page 209.—4th July, 1774. William Thompson's will (of Tinkling)—To youngest son, Robert; to wife; to six children, viz: Alexander, John, Robert, Agnes Edmundson, Rebecca McNeelly, Sarah Hendry. Executors, sons Alexander and Robert. Teste: William and John Caldwell, John Finley. Proved, 20th November, 1781, by Jno. Caldwell and Finley.

Page 211.—20th November, 1781. Recorded. James Buchanan's appraisement.

Page 213.—22d May, 1781. John Archer's estate appraised by Jas. Trimble, William Young, Jno. Gardner, James Kenny.

Page 214.— — September, 1781. John Hogshead's estate appraised at old rates by John Nickle, John Barns, Wm. McKemy.

Page 220.—19th February, 1782. Recorded. Thomas Shield's appraisement by Robt. Christian, Robert Willson, Matthew Thompson.

Page 221.—20th July, 1781. Margret (mark) Spouel's will (of Tinkling Spring)—To be buried at discretion of Alexander Thompson, Sr.; to granddaughters, Agnes, Martha, Margret, Sarah Thompson; to son-in-law, Alexander Thompson, executor. Teste: James Spence, Mary Palmer, Robert Thompson. Proved, 19th February, 1782, by Spence and Thompson.

Page 222.—5th August, 1774. John Estill's will (of Botetourt, yeoman)—To wife, Rebeckah, a survey on New River opposite the Influx of Blue Stone, towards James McGuire's (McGuire) Survey; to daughter, Priscilla Gold, home tract on hands creek joining lands with Bond Estill and James Ellison. Executors, Benj. Estill and Wm. Hutchison. Teste: William Hutchison, Felty Koch (Valentine Cook). Proved, 18th September, 1781, by Hutchison and Cook. Hutchison refuses to execute. 20th March, 1782, administration granted Rebecca Estil; both the executors refused.

Page 224.—15th March, 1782. Jacob Fulwider's estate appraised by John Fulton, Patrick Hall, Gorg. Bright.

Page 224.—2d March, 1782. James Ritchey's estate appraised by Hugh Donaghe, John Lowry, Joseph Campbell.

Page 225.—25th June, 1779. James Hogshead's will (senior)—To wife, Elizabeth, two bound children, viz: Robert and Mary Finney, until they come of age; to son, Robert; to son, James; to son, John; to son, William; to daughter, Mary; to son, David, entry of land adjoining Alexander Gardner. Executors, wife Elizabeth and son James. Teste: David, Michael, John Hogshead.

Page 227.—9th January, 1782. James Fulton's estate appraised by James Brownlee, Robt. Doak, Thomas Boyd.

Page 228.—20th March, 1782. Ann Burk's refusal to administer on husband's estate, William Burk, and nominates eldest son, William Burk. Teste: Edward Burk.

Page 228.—18th March, 1782. Jean (mark) Hind, ditto of her husband, John Hind, and nominates son, Wm. Hind. Teste: James Dickey, John Alexander.

Page 229.—10th April, 1782. Alex. Cunningham's estate appraised by Samuel McCutchan, Wat. Cunningham, David Trotter.

Page 229.—26th June, 1781. Robert Campbell Cutler's will—To wife, Mary; to eldest son, George, the Round Hill plantation, 140 acres joining Geo. Bright and home plantation. Also 200 acres, likewise 50 acres more adjoining Robert Shaw and David Williamson; to 2d son, Robert, home plantation 200 acres; also the Maple Swamp plantation 150 acres; also 200 acres of an entry adjoining Geo. Bright and the Mill place bought of David Williamson; to daughter, Jannett, tract between home plantation and Beverley Manor; to wife. Executors, wife Mary and sons George and Robert and daughter Jannet. Teste: William and Mary Forgason. Proved, 16th April, 1782, by the witnesses. Widow Mary qualifies.

Page 231.—10th August, 1775. Isaac White's will—To wife, Jane, mare bought of Lewis Baker; to sons, viz: David, Isaac, James and Gordon White, if any of them die in infancy; to daughters, Jane, Isabella, Margret, if any die infants; son, Gordon, and daughters, Isabella and Margret, be schooled; to daughters already married, viz: Mary Young, Elizabeth, and Sarah Rodgers. Executors, James Steele, John Young. Teste: Andrew Russell, David White. Proved, 17th April, 1782, by the witnesses. Executors refused to execute. Jane, the widow, relinquished her right. Administration granted David and Isaac White.

Page 234.—25th May, 1781. Archibald Laghlin's estate appraised by Samuel McCutchen, James Ewing, David Trotter.

Page 235.—27th April, 1782. Thomas Tate's bond as Commissioner of Specific Tax.

Page 235.—Ditto, Andrew Anderson's, ditto.

Page 236.—Ditto, Alex. McClenachan's bond for collection of specific tax.

Page 237.—21st May, 1782. Recorded. Archibald Huston's appraisement by John Young, James Laird, Robert Hill—Due from James James, Geo. Keesil, John Logan.

Page 241.—20th May, 1782. John Estill's estate appraised by Walter Davis, Samuel Hunter, James Mitchell, Samuel Gibson.

Page 243.—3d October, 1780. John P. Vance's will (yeoman)—To wife, Martha; to daughter, Margaret; to son, Benjamin; to eldest son, Samuel, plantation on Back Creek; to sons, James and William, tract near Staunton. Executors, John Moffett, Jacob Warrick, John Baller, of Boutetourt County. Teste: Samuel Vance, Wm. Hutchison, Michael Dougherty. Proved, 21st May, 1782, by Hutchison, and on 18th June, 1782, by Dougherty. Executors have refused to execute. Administration granted widow Martha.

Page 245.—5th November, 1780. Archibald Gilkeson's will (farmer)—To wife, Sarah, the land formerly belonging to her on Calfpasture; to sons, Robert, James, and Hugh; to daughter, Rebecca, infant; to mother, Rebecca Gilkison, property left her by his father's former will; daughter Rebecca to be under care of mother and after her death, of Margret Hogshead, daughter to David Hogshead. Executors, William Young, Hugh Brown. Teste: John Gardner, Michael (X) McCluer. Proved, 16th July, 1782, by the witnesses. Executors qualify.

Page 247.—11th July, 1782. John Wamsley's, Sr., will—To daughter, Elizabeth Robinson; to Thomas Wamsley, David Wamsley, Elizabeth Robinson; to Wm. Wamsley. John, James, Joseph, Mathew, Mary, Samuel, Dorcas Wamsley, each child to receive their part by succession. Executors, sons David Wamsley and McKenny Robinson; son Mathew to have one year's schooling, then bound to learn trade of Tayler; son Samuel to have two years, ditto, trade, saddler; daughters Mary and Dorcas to be left in care of McKinney Robinson, one year's schooling for Mary and three for Dorcas. Teste: John Bennet, Thomas Bland. Codicil, 25th July, 1782; to son, John, Ibetroth; to son, James. Teste: Thos. Bland, Margret (mark) Bland. Proved, 20th August, 1782, by Bland and Bennitt. Executors qualified.

Page 248.—19th June, 1782. Joseph Wright's estate appraised by Alex. Hamilton, John Davis, Ephraim Bates.

Page 250.—Joseph Wright's vendue bill—Sold to, viz: Ezekiah Stout, Indian James Tanner, Thomas Galford, John Wades, Jacob Beens.

Page 251.—13th June, 1782. Thomas Cunningham's will—To wife, Elizabeth, daughter Mary to her care and trust as her own; to youngest daughter, Mary; to eldest daughter, Ruth; to second daughter, Sarah; division between wife and three children; to brother, Archibald; to James Harris, care of daughter Ruth; to Mary Berry, Jr., care of daughter Sarah. Executors, wife and brother Archibald. Teste: James Berry, Jacob Pattn, Jas. Harris, Chas. Berry. Proved, 22d August, 1782, by James Berry and Patton.

Page 253.—16th August, 1782. William Burk's estate appraised by John Abney, Peter Hanger, Thos. Scott.

Page 254.—2d September, 1782. Robert Burns' will (of Staunton)—To wife, Isabella; to daughter, Margaret Cunningham Burns, 4,000 acres in Kentucky; to daughter, Mary Burns; to step-daughter, Sarah Lockhart; to son, Thomas Burns, 5 shillings; to son, Henry Burns, 5 shillings. Executrix, wife Isabella. Teste: R. Madison, Will Steel. Proved, 15th October, 1782, by the witnesses. Isabella qualifies.

Page 256.—13th March, 1782. William Wood's will—To wife, Ann; to sons, Searight and Alexander; children to be of age before division of estate. Executors, wife Ann, Alex. Seeright, Wm. Loggan. Teste: Robt. McCormick, James Rowan, Simon Carson. Proved, 15th October, 1782, by witnesses. Logan refuses to execute. Ann qualifies.

Page 258.—20th May, 1782. Samuel Henderson's will—To wife, Jane; to sons, Andrew and Alexander; to daughter, Florence; to son, James, 190 acres purchased from James Thompson; to sons, William and David, plantation purchased of Samuel Givans; to children. Teste: John Craig, Florence Bell, Anne Craig (mark). Proved, 15th October, 1782, by John Craig and Bell. Administration granted James Henderson.

Page 259.—15th July, 1782. John Vance's estate appraised by John Davis, Alex. Hamilton, Richard Eliot.

Page 260.—1st October, 1782. Joseph Gamble's further appraisement by John McCoy, James Hogg, John Hines.

Page 261.—9th September, 1782. John Wamsley's estate appraised by McKenney Robinson and David Wamsley.

Page 264.—25th November, 1782. Alex. McClenachan's bond for collection of County levy.

Page 264.—28th October, 1782. Robert Burns' estate appraised by Robt. McClenachan, Daniel Kidd, Petter Hanger.

Page 267.—29th December, 1782. Inquisition at David Frame's before John McCreerey, one of the Coroners, on view of body of Gerrel Pheland—Witnesses John McRoberts, James Young, that on said day they found said Wheland lying in the Cowpasture River without any wounds. Verdict: He was drowned in attempting to cross the river. Pat. Miller, Andrew Suttlington, Robt. McCreerey, Wm. Black, Alex. Black, Abram Hempenstall, David Frame, Jeremiah Frame, Mathias Benston, Sampson Willson, Chas. Cameron, James Henry.

Page 268.—3d March, 1783. Inquisition at same place before John McCreerey, Coroner. on view of body of John Mitchell—Witnesses Leonard Bell, Van Swearingen et als., believed to have died a natural death at Frame's Still House on 2d March. Leonard Bell, Van Sweoringen, Joseph Mays, Geo. Francisco, John McRoberts, Wm. Young, James Kenny, Robt. McCreery, Jno. Montgomery, Geo. Benston, Jas. Montgomery, Jeremiah Frame.

Page 269.—19th March, 1783. Recorded. John McClenachan's estate, Dr., to Alex. St. Clair—1781, September 7, ¼ year's schooling for Johnny, paid Mr. Mustoe; 1782, December 30; 1774, October —, David Porter's bond uncollected (Carolina).

Page 275.—13th February, 1780. Christian Clemons' (signed in German) will—To wife, Catharine; to son, John, home plantation; to eldest son, Gasper, plantation joining David McNeelly; to my in law, George Trout and his wife, 5 shillings; to Henry Lyner and his wife; to Philip Berger and his wife; to daughter, Catharine, and her son, David Trout; to daughter, Elizabeth. Executors, wife and son-in-law, Henry Lyner. Teste: John Davidson, Robert Stephen, Jno. Surfas. 15th March, 1783, Kathorine refuses to qualify. Teste: Robert Stephen, Jacob (mark) Barrier. Proved, 18th March, 1783, by Robert Stephens and John Surfas. Henry Lyner qualifies.

Page 277.—23d September, 1780. John Mitchell's will—To Ann Russell, £150; to Mary Russell, £150; to Andrew Russell's children; to Esther Turk; to Andrew Russell, but he is to give Ann, Mary, and Mathew their quantity of the legacy and the rest of the childrens, that is to say, William, Betty, Andrew, John, Jean, and James their mentioned parts of the legacy when they are of age; Thomas Turk, father of Esther, is to control her legacy until she is of age; to Mathew Russell; to William Russell; to Ann Russell; to Mary Russell; to Jean Russell. Teste: John Reaugh, Margaret Kirk, Mary Turk. Proved, 15th April, 1783, by the witnesses.

Page 279.—30th January, 1771. Jacob Lockhart's will—To son, James, £10 to be paid by son Jacob Lockhart, and to be allowed a living on testator's plantation if he should be drove away from his home by Indians; to 2d son, Jacob, land on Back Creek; to youngest son, Levy, infant; to daughters, Jane and Elce. Eexcutors, John Moffett and son-in-law Mathew Arbuckle. Teste: Wm. Mitchell, Jno. Kirkpatrick, Robt. Clark. Proved, 15th April, 1783, by Kirkpatrick and Clark. John Moffett appeared and refused to execute.

Page 280.—2—th September, 1782. Will of Samuel Black, aged about 55—To son, John, 300 acres on Niw River where John now lives; to son, William, 300 acres, rest of above tract; to sons, Samuel and James, infants, home place known by name of Pine Knot; to daughters, Margaret, Mary, Martha, Nancy, Jean; to wife. Executors, wife, brother Wm. Black, Wm. Porter. Teste: Walter Davis, Thos. Stuart, Mathew Alexander. Proved, 15th April, 1783, by Stuart and Davis. Executors qualify.

Page 282.—17th February, 1783. Samuel Hamilton's estate appraised by John Rankin, George Crawford, Jno. Craig.

Page 284.—15th February, 1783. John Ramsey's will—To son, Andrew, tract between John Patrick and Jno. Black, also money lent to Andrew to pay Robt. Estham; to son, George, land in Cantuckey; to son, John, 1 French Crown, Patriotism (?); to son, Alexander, 1 French Crown, Patriotism (?); to son, William, 1 French Crown, Patriotism (?); to grandson, John Ramsey, 1 French Crown; to grandson, Alex. Ramsey (?), 1 French Crown; to granddaughter, Mary Ramsey; to grandson, John Steele; to wife, Marey; to son, Daniel, residuary legatee and devisee. Executors, wife Mary, Andrew Ramsey, and Andrew Steele. Teste: John Patrick, John, and Samuel Black. Proved, 15th April, 1783, by Patrick and Samuel Black. Executors qualify.

Page 286.—9th April, 1783. Christian Clemon's estate appraised by James Kerr, Jas. Robertson, Jacob Barger, Alex. Robertson.

Page 287.—12th November, 1780. John Young's will (Junior), on Middle River—Going an Expedition in Service of my Country which may terminate in Death; to wife, Margret; to brother, William; to Margaret Henderson, £20, provided she behave well till free; to brother James Young's son, Andrew Young; to Robert King and his brother George; to John Stiffey; to Sarah Henderson (on good behavior till married); to brothers, James, Robert, William; to sister Rebeckah's son, Andrew McComb. Executors, wife and brother, William Young. Teste: Ro. Gamble, Isaac Carson, John Blair. Proved, 20th May, 1783, by Gamble and Blair. Executors qualify.

Page 289.—24th March, 1780. John Young's will—To son, John Young, part of plantation John, Jr., now lives on; to son, William; two above to pay to each of other children, £1, viz: James, Robert, Isabel, Margret, Rebeccah, Sarah. Executors, sons John and William. Teste: John Poage, Jr., James and Francis Bell. Proved, 20th May, 1783, by Francis Bell and Jno. Poage, Jr.

Page 291.—7th May, 1793. Robert (mark) Caldwell's will—Executors, Samuel Henry and Robt. Thompson; to wife, Agness; to son, David, home place; to other two sons, William and Robert; to daughter, Mary, if she stay with the family. Teste: James Frazer, Sarah Henry. Proved, 20th May, 1783, by the witnesses. Executors qualify.

Page 292.—9th May, 1783. James Kirk's will—To son, Alexander, 10 shillings; to son, John, 10 shillings; to daughter, Martha, 10 shillings; to son, Robert, £5; to wife, Jean, and sons, James and George, all estate. Executors, wife Jan and son John. Teste: Benj. Talmann, Ambros (mark) Jones, James McCan. Proved, 20th May, 1783, by the witnesses. Executors qualify.

Page 294.—7th January, 1754. John Christian's will—To wife, Margret, bearing a child; to eldest son, Robert; to son, William. Executors, brothers Robert and William. Teste: Jacob Van Lear, Israel Christian, Robt. Moffett. Dedimus, 4th May, 1783, to take deposition of Van Lear and Christian, executed 17th May, 1783, as to Van Lear, Sr., aged 78; he remembers nothing of the will, and is blind; can give no testimony. May 20, 1783, one witness being dead and another not appearing, the Court refuses to probate the will as it was made 25 years ago and testator has had five children since. Administration granted son, Gilbert Christian. Widow has refused to execute.

Page 296.—16th May, 1782. John Hind's estate appraised by James Young, Edward Erwin, Hugh Brown.

Page 300.—29th April, 1783. Jonathan Dunbarr's estate appraised by Thos. Smith, John Abney, Wm. Blear.

Page 300.—1st April, 1783. John McDonough's will (sadler)—Executors to sell house and lotts in Staunton and plantation purchased of Capt. Thos. Smith; to Edward Hart McDonough, infant under 14, half of plantation in Albemarle whereon testator formerly lived (dwelt); to Dianah McDonough, under 18; to Edward Simpson, of Fredericksburg; Edward Hart McDonough at 14 to be bound to a sadler, tanner or hatter. Executors, Thos. Smith, John Abney, Richard Madison. Teste: Francis Mara, Robt. Cochran, Wm. Gilham. Proved, 20th May, 1783, by Cochran and Mora. Executors qualify.

Page 302.—9th September, 1774. Archibald Huston's estate appraised and sold, and 21st May, 1783, settled and recorded—Sold to, viz: Stephen Huston, John Peder (Pedan), James Laird, Junior, Henry Coaler, James Waide, Michael Lease, John Hooper, Jno. Craney, Barney McMurry, George Weton.

Page 308.—16th June, 1783. Mary (mark) Donnelly relinquishes her right to administration on her husband's, Charles Donnelly's, estate and nominates Andrew Donnelly, of Greenbrier, and her son, Andrew Donnelly. Teste: James Bleake, William (mark) Gillespey.

Page 308.—15th February, 1779. Charles Donnelly's will (of Cow Pasture)—To wife, Mary; to daughters, Jean Bleake, Mary Brown; to other four children, viz: Andrew, Charles, Ann, Catherine; to sons, Andrew and Charles Donnally, Jr. Executrix, Mary and Col. Andrew Donnally and son Andrew. Teste: James Bleke, John Gay, Wm. (mark) Gillespy. Proved, 17th June, 1783, by Blake and Gillespy. Gay is since dead. The two Andrews qualify.

Page 310.—17th June, 1783. Archibald McLaughland's estate settled.

Page 311.—8th May, 1783. Samuel Black's estate appraised by Cornelius Ruddle, Thos. Rutledge, Alex. Thompson. Continental Loan Office Certificates of June, 1780, for $6,000. James Best's account.

Page 316.—2d June, 1783. Robert Caldwell's estate appraised by James Frazer, Ben. Stuart, Will Caldwell, June (Samuel) McCune (McCune).

Page 317.—31st May, 1780. Leonard Shound's (Shown) will—To wife, Mary; to sons, Andrew and John, home plantation and land purchased of John Black; to son, Isaac, infant, to be supported for his lifetime; son, Henry, to be bound to a trade; to daughter, Catharine; to two married daughters. Teste: Elijah McClenachan, Wm. (mark) Greever, Philip Engleman. Proved, 15th July, 1783, by McClenachan and Engleman. Executors qualify, viz: Sons Andrew and John.

Page 319.—2d September, 1779. Catherine Park certifies the following list to contain all personal estate of Roger North, except debts due on bonds, bills, notes, &c: Sold 18th November, 1777, to, viz: Capt. Smith, Daniel Miller, David Keal, Mary Hayard, John Barkly, Robert Aistrop, Miss Hanley, Mary Coffee, Mary Rackham, John Jasper, Mrs. Parks, Mrs. North.

Page 334.—29th August, 1777. List of those indebted to the estate of Roger North—Molly Mathews, Michael Diveyer, John Paris, Taylor, Edward Brayton, Mary Dillon, Wm. Collen, Carolina; Rev. Adam Smith, Margaret Mountfield, Hannah Sires, Robt. Jameson, Prince Edward; Andrew Cowen, Holstein; John Adkins, going to Carolina; William Loveley, Sally McGraw, servant to Dr. Watkins; James Bowyer (Taylor), John Anderson, Long Glead, Holstein; Joseph Love, Montgomery; Geo. Berry (son to Francis), James Anderson, son of John, M. River; John Henderson, son to David, So. River, dead; John Brown, son to Widow, N. Mtn.; David Steel (tailor), Wm. Jordan, So. River; Wm. Scott (taylor), John Welsh (tailor), Amos Perkins (blacksmith), Michael McEntosh, James Cooper, Forks of James; Mary Blackwood, married to McCrosky; ———— Crawford, brother to Patrick; Wm. Russell, Buchanan's Mill; Charles Philips, Adam Cribb, Eleanor Craig, M. River; Eleanor Dunn at Elijah McClenachans, Robert Patterson, No. Mountain; Nelly Keenan, James Berry, son to Francis, Holst.; John Woods, M. River; Andrew Anderson, son to John; Andrew Jenkins; Major Scott (dead), Mark Hatton, Andrew Campbell, son to John, So. River; Andrew Wilson, reedmaker; James Anderson, M. River; James Kelly (mason), John Cypher, James Brown (dead), John Votaw, Wm. McNab, No. Mountain; Joseph Right, M. River; James Armstrong, Holstein; Wm. Long, Warm Springs; Jean Rush, Evan Griffith, son of Abel, M. River; James Bott, Alex. Reed, Rockfish; Miss Betsey Hughes, Greenbrier; Henry Black, Dutchman; Hugh Divier, No. River; John Smith, son of Daniel, dead; Gasper Carner, Black's Gap; Daniel Meek, Calfpasture; Mary Cawfield, Jacob Kile, No. Mountain; Wm. Rogers, B. M.; John Campbell, No. River; James Edmonson, taylor; Chas. Syms, attorney at law; Nath. Bell Magruder, James Long, Mid. River; Richard Aldeman, Jno. Ehrhard, laberer; James McManis, Amherst; Jno. Todd, attorney at law; Thos. Bird, labourer; Abraham Savage, Thos. Jones, at the Office; Jacob Meckghew, Pr. Edward; Jno. Heany, Miss Jenny Lewis, Thomas' daughter, Jno. Hughson, Mason.

Page 342.—29th August, 1777. Persons to whom Roger North's estate is indebted—Joseph Kinkead, Holstein; John Young, N. M., son to Hugh; Wm. Hutchison, son to George, Greenbrier.

Page 344.—Above estate settled by Catherine North, administratrix—1776, November 7, paid James Clarke for freedom dues; 1777, May 29, paid Alex. Brownlee, 11 months' storekeeping; August 28, paid Mr. Curry for teaching (schooling) Phill.; September 30, paid Michael Bowyer for do; 1777, by cash from Capt. Hays for soldiers; September 2, by cash from Wm. Rush, son to John; by cash from Jno. Jonett.

Page 350.—19th August, 1783. Recorded. Charles Donnally's appraisement by Alex. Crawford, Andrew Sutlington, Ralph Laverty.

Page 352.—22d March 1778. Mathew (mark) Lettimore's will—To James Tate, all estate and executor. Teste: John and Wm. Tate. James Crow. Proved, 19th August, 1783, by J. and W. Tate. Executor is dead. Administration granted Sarah and John Tate.

Page 353.—19th August, 1783. Commissioners report that they are unable to settle James Ralston's estate for lack of vouchers.

Page 353.—23d August, 1783. John Cawley's estate further appraised.

Page 354.—22d March, 1776. Isaac Carson's will—To wife, Rebecca, and children; to son, Abraham; to 3 daughters, Agnes, Jane, Mary; to child of which wife is now pregnant. Executors, Capt. George Moffett, Wm. Young. Teste: John Bleir, James Scott, Samuel Anderson. 19th August, 1783, Col. Geo. Moffett deposes that 3, 4, days before Carson's death Carson showed him above will and stated he wished it altered because it cut out two children, that he wished them to be made equal with the others. John Poage deposes ditto.

Page 357.—16th September, 1783. Recorded. John Michael's appraisement by Wm. Robertson, James and Alex. Robertson.

Page 357.—31st March, 1779. Ambrose (mark) Powell's will—His rifle gun left with John Offill to be given to Jacob Gilasby, son of Jacob Gilasby. To all brothers and sisters, residuaries, except Sarah Haines and her two children, Stephen and Dicey Haines, who are to have an equal part with his brothers and sisters. Executor, Richard Bohannon. Teste: Robert Gaines, John Offill, James Bohannon. Proved, 16th August, 1783, by Gains and Buchanan. Executors qualified.

Page 358.—6th May, 1783. John Christian's estate appraised by Walter Davis, Mathew Thompson, Wm. Shields.

Page 361.—21st February, 1782. James Bell's will, of Long Glade—To wife and children; to children, viz: John, James, Francis, David. Samuel, Thomas, Agnis, Sarah, Rebecca. Executrix. wife. Teste: Michael Hogshead, Isaac Carsen, William and John Hogshead. Proved, 21st October, 1783, by William and John Hogshead.

Page 363.—27th August, 1777. Thomas Story's estate sold at vendue, and settlement—1779, January, paid Gerald Phelan for schooling the orphans; 1781, January, paid John Campbell, collector of additional tax, for raising 80 soldiers in Augusta.

Page 369.—4th March, 1782. John Cochran's (Cohorn) estate appraised by Jno. Poage, Alex. Robertson, Robt. Kenney, Archibald Dickson—Articles to be divided between Cochran's 3 daughters, viz: Martha, Elizabeth, Margaret; certain articles to go to Henry King; Mr. King is to receive, &c., and returned in his step-daughter's name, viz: Martha Cohorn.

Page 370.—Dower assigned to widow of John Cochran above. She is now wife of Henry King.

Page 371.—20th February, 1781. Robt. Alexander's will—To wife, Esther; to daughters, Sarah and Eleanor, unmarried; to sons, Peter, Hugh, James, Peter's tract at Lessley's cabin; James's adjoins John Fulton and James Henry (all sons unmarried); to daughters, Ann and Esther, 5 shillings each; to son, William; to son, Thomas; to son, Robert; to grandchild, Martha. Executors and guardians, wife and son Robert. Teste: Hugh

Fulton, Thos. Stevenson, Thos. Baird. Proved, 18th November, 1783, by Baird and Stevenson. Executors qualify.

Page 373.—18th January, 1782. James Sawyers' will, "in middle of my age"—To dearly and well-beloved Hannah Sawyers, wife; to children, until youngest is 18; to son Thomas, son David, son Geo. Washington; to daughter Ann, daughter Rebeckah (a negro slave, said slave is to attend Mrs. Archer during her life; to daughter Martha, daughter Rachel; to father, negro Nelson to wait on him his lifetime; to sister, Rebecca. Executors, Col. Geo. Mathes, Wm. Crawford, wife, Jno. Sawyers, David McNare. Teste: Sampson Sawyers, Ann Renick, Wm. Crawford, Daniel McNare. Codicil, 9th September, 1782. Teste: Daniel and David McNare. Proved, 18th November, 1783, by Sawyers, Renick, McNare. Widow Hannah, Wm. Crawford, Daniel McNare qualify.

Page 378.—18th November, 1783. John Ramsey's estate appraised by John Black, Wm. Gillespy, Wm. Finley, Thos. Tourk.

Page 380.—29th July, 1783. Jacob Van Lear's will—To wife, Margaret; to son, Jacob, all lands; to son, John, £15; to daughter, Gartry Robinson, 50 shillings; to daughter, Isabel Abney, 50 shillings. Executors, Jacob Van Lear and John Christian. Teste: Patrick and John Christian. Proved, 18th November, 1783, by the witnesses. Jacob qualifies.

Page 382.—28th August, 1783. Robert Gibson's estate appraised by John Blair, Jno. Gamble, Wm. Young.

Page 384.—19th November, 1783. Thomas Hughart's settlement recorded of his guardianship of Ruth Wilson.

Page 384.—19th November, 1783. Thomas Nelson, Jr.'s, estate settled.

Page 385.—19th November, 1783. Jacob Segenfoos' estate settled.

Page 386.—18th November, 1783. Robert Alexander's estate appraised— Due by Hansel Olphid.

Page 388.—18th November, 1783. Allotment of above estate among the legatees—To Ann Balew, wife of Abraham Balew, 5 shillings; to Esther Austin, wife of Wm. Austin, 5 shillings. Signed by all except Austin.

Page 391.—17th December, 1783. Charles Cameron's bond as inspector of hemp, deer skins, &c., at Staunton.

Page 392.—16th December, 1783. Wm. Bowyer's bond as sheriff.

Page 397.—22d October, 1783. William Hook relinquishes to George Hook his right to administer on estate of James Hook. Teste: George Fraizer, Samuel Hill.

Page 397.—16th March, 1784. Recorded. William Woods' appraisement by John Fulton, James Henry, Robert Cooper.

Page 398.—9th June, 1783. John McDonough's estate appraised by David Greiner, John Bosang, Francis Mara.

Page 402.—30th May and 10th June, 1783. John McDonough's estate sold at vendue—Sold to, viz: Robt. Cockbeam (burn? brain? rain?), Robt. Aistrop, Wm. Coursey, Geo. Fergason, Peter Heyn, Owen Owens, Peter Hains, Henry Cook, Thos. Stocton, Alex. Fretwell, Nathaniel Harlow, Jno. Devenport, Daniel White, Mat. Glaves, Goodman Baksdal, Marshal Derret, Solomon Below, Jas. Consolive, Jno. Marks, Meshick Hickcock, Jane E. Kyle, Wm. Gouge (Gonge), Wm. Brisco, Fras. Branum, Math. Montgomery, Thos. Pheemster, James Cole (Cale).

Page 410.—7th February, 1784. James Henderson's will—To wife, Martha; to sons, William and David; to daughter, Sarah Stuart; to other 2 sons, James and Joseph; to James Dickey and John Dickey; to young James Dickey; to son, Archibald's (deceased) daughter, Eleanor, infant; to son, Archibald's (deceased) widow, Elizabeth. Executors, wife and William Dunlop. Teste: James Young, Wm. Alexander, Michael Dickey. Proved, 19th May, 1784, by the witnesses. Martha qualifies.

Page 412.—18th September, 1783. Valentine Cloninger's will—To Nicholas Spring, tract purchased of Robt. Beverley; to Catherine Spring, daughter of Nicholas, tract adjoining above tract John Fudge's and Samuel Leeven's in Beverley Manor; to wife, Catherine, remainder of estate; to nephew, Philip Cloninger. Executors, wife, Thos. Bell, Peter Hanger. Teste: R. Madison, John Bosang, Jos. Buchanan. Proved, 19th May, 1784, by Madison and Bosang. Bell and Hanger refused to qualify. Catherine qualifies.

Page 413.— — ———, ———. Valentine Cloninger's appraisement bill recorded.

Page 415.—1784. Robert Stevenson's estate settlement.

Page 416.—1784. William Sutlington's estate settled—Paid Robt. Dilap (Delapp); to sundry expenses attending his affairs in Maryland—Robert O'Hara's account; Dougan's receipt doctor's fees; received from Susannah Day, Thos. Cartmill, Pet. Upp, George Erskin, John Erskin, Wm. Wildings.

Page 419.—17th February, 1784. Recorded. William Woods' appraisement.

Page 420.—1st September, 1783. Daniel Ramsey's will—To mother, amount in appraisement bill of father; to brother, John Ramsey, Andrew Steel, Alex. Ramsey, Andrew Ramsey, Wm. Ramsey, George Ramsey, Jno. Ramsey (son of James, deceased), equal proportion of remainder; to brother, Andrew, all real estate; of land willed to testator at mother's death to brother Andrew, to be appraised by James Steel, Wm. Finley, Jr., Wm. Gilespey, Jno. Finley; to John Ramsey, son of James, infant; to Alex. Ramsey, son of James. Executors, Andrew Steel, John and Andrew Ramsey. Teste: John Black, Martha Black, Samuel Black. Proved, 15th June, 1784, by John and Samuel Black. John Ramsey and Andrew Steel qualified. Andrew Ramsey refused *in persona*.

Page 422.—21st November, 1783. James Sawyers' estate appraised by William Bell, Benj. Brown, Wm. Starit.

Page 424.—23d January, 1784. John McMahon's will—To wife, Deborah; to daughter, Nancy; to son, William, home plantation, 330 acres, infant; to son, John; to son, Robert; to daughter, Mary; daughter, Elizabeth; to 3 youngest daughters. Executors, wife and son Robert. Teste: William Wilson, John Campbell. Proved, 19th October, 1784 (formerly proved by Rev. M. Wilson), by John Campbell.

Page 425.—19th October, 1784. Recorded. Charles Floyd, inventory and appraisement by John Nickel, John McGlamery, Jno. McKitrick.

Page 427.—19th October, 1784. Recorded. Mathew Kennedy's ditto, by Thos. Rankin, James Craig, Jno. Campbell. Appraisement 1st October, 1784.

Page 429.—6th September, 1784. Thomas Waddle (Waddell), Sr.'s, will—To 3 oldest children, has already given their part; to sons, Thomas and John, 288 acres and a survey adjoining James Curry; to son, Joseph, the land he now cuts; to son, John; to son, Thomas; to wife; to daughter, Elizabeth; to daughters, Martha and Jane; to four daughters. Executors, Joseph, Thomas, and John. Teste: James Waddell, Sarah Persey. Proved, 19th October, 1784, by the witnesses. Joseph and Thomas qualify.

Page 431.—19th October, 1784. Recorded. Archibald Gilkison's appraisement by John Gardner, James McKemy, Samuel Anderson.

Page 433.—16th November, 1784. Recorded. Account of George Searight's estate.

Page 433.—16th November, 1784. Recorded. Robert Campbell's (cutler) appraisement by Samuel Steel, Hugh Fulton, Wm. Forgas, ———, John Boyd.

Page 435.—16th November, 1784. Recorded. John McMahon's appraisement by William Johnston, Arthur Connly, Jno. Campbell, Hugh Donaghe.

Page 437.—15th April, 1784. Jemima Bradley's will—To Samuel Merritt, Military Warrant 1666 for 400 acres; also 1 interest certificate of 86 pounds, all property. Teste: John Griffin, James Stricklar, Jenet Frazer. Proved, 25th December, 1784, by Griffin and Strickland.

Page 438.—9th October, 1784. Adam Broabacks' will—To wife, Elizabeth, farm until children come of age; to son, Philip, homeplace, 85 acres; to daughter, Sarah; to John Osburn, deed to be made by executors for land sold to him in Bedford; deed to be made to the purchaser for the place whereon father lived. Executors, wife and Conrad Slusher. Teste: Samuel McCutchan, Jno. McCutchan, Lawes Geldmaker. Proved, 21st December, 1784, by Jno. McCutchen and Hilmaker. Executors qualify.

Page 439.—24th January, 1785. Adam Brubak's estate appraised by David Steele, David Cunningham, James Crow.

Page 440.—16th September, 1779. John Harrison's estate sold at vendue—To John Reeves, Thomas Alderson. Account of debts paid 1777. Sworn to 18th May, 1784, by Col. Reuben Harrison.

Page 442.— — May, 1784. Recorded. James Gamble's settlement—Paid legacy to Agnes Gamble, daughter to James; paid Sarah Gamble (deceased), her heir.

Page 443.—7th October, 1784. George Hooke's estate sold at vendue to, viz: Martha Kennedy, Wm. Hooke, Wm. Hooke, Jr., Thos. Blackley, Wm. Bean, Daniel Joseph, Daniel Fitzgeral, Robt. Heslip, John Jasper, George Hook Roe (?).

Page 447.—14th April, 1784. Edward Lade's estate appraised by Robert McKitrick, Wm. Armstrong, Samuel Runkel—Note of Anthony Bleomate.

Page 448.—15th March, 1785. Alex. McClenachan's, this day appointed Clerk, bond as Clerk of the County, with Alex. St. Clair, Samuel Lewis, Jno. Dean.

Page 448.—15th March, 1785. William Bowyer's, sheriff, bond to collect taxes.

Page 449.—11th January, 1783. Robert Burns' estate sold at vendue.

Page 451.—Dr. the estate of Major Robert Burns—Paid Major John Belfield. Contra: 1781, September, received Thos. Clark's account (artificer), Richard Hedd's tavern account, Capt. Gaurley's account; 1782, August, received from Capt. Richard Singleton; by one lot known by name of Bessy Bell and Mary Gray containing 560 acres; 1776, by James Burns of Cumberland, County Juniatta; 1771, May, by John Walter Gibbs, Chas. Tours, price bond lost at the battle of Long Island for £250 hard dollars at 8/0; 1780, by General Thompson's account; 1783, April, paid John Brunt's wages; 1783, October, by cash received of William Gilham.

Page 458.—29th September, 1783. Isaac Carson's estate appraised by Robert Gamble, John Gamble, John Blair.

Page 460.—9th May, 1778. Nathan Reagland's will—To son, John, ½ of the 4 negroes left him by his grandfather; to daughter, Rachel; to wife, Susania. Executors, John Poage and James Allen, Jr. Teste: John Harper, Wm. Hook, Mathew Burnside. Proved, 19th April, 1785, by Mathew Burnside, and 17th May, 1785, by John Harper.

Page 461.—28th August, 1782. Thomas Cunningham's estate appraised by Jno. McKeemy, Robt. M. D. Nall, James McClung.

Page 463.—9th April, 1783. Christian Clemons' estate appraised.

Page 464.—17th May, 1785. Recorded. Appraisement and sale bill of Alex. Walker's estate—Charles Fredericksbore's bill due 2d March, 1774.

Page 467.—Sale bill—Sold 17th May, 1780, to, viz: James Craig, son of James.

Page 468.—19th May, 1785. Philip Lingle's estate settled.

Page 470.—24th February, 1785. Andrew Anderson and Mary Patterson depose that on Monday, 21st February, 1785, they were at the house of Richard Madison, then in bed of his last illness. Richard asked to have his will drawn; said he wished his wife, Priscilla Madison, should have all his estate. Richard died on the Wednesday afternoon following. Proved, 21st May, 1785. At Priscilla's request administration granted to Wm. Bowyer.

Page 471.—7th May, 1785. George Searight's additional appraisement.

Page 471.—10th May, 1785. Elizabeth Guy's will—To sister, Rebecca Thompson; to sister Rebecca's daughter, Margaret; to sister Rebecca's 2 youngest daughters; to sister, Martha Gillespy; to sister Martha's oldest daughter, Mary; to sister Martha's daughter, Ann; to nephew, Henry Guy; to niece, Martha Galespy, daughter of Hugh Gillespy; to nephew, Samuel Foger; to nephews, John and Henry Thompson, infants; to brother-in-law, John Gillespy; to Robert Guy; to Archibald Guy. Executors, John Gillespy, James Bleake, James Windon. Apprentice John Windon to be set free. Proved, 21st June, 1785, by James Windon and Samuel Gillespy. Executors qualify.

Page 475.—16th April, 1785. Sarah Hutchinson's estate appraised by James Caruthers, Wm. Black, John Brooks.

Page 476.—28th February, 1776. John Henderson's will, of County and Parish of Botetourt, joiner—To wife, Jean, and 10 children; to son, John, the tract said John, Jr., lives on; to son, Jones Henderson, to son-in-law, Robert Ritchey, executors. Teste: John and Robert Henderson. Codicil, 1st April, 1783. Appoints wife Jean as one of the executors. Proved, 16th August, 1785, by Robert and John McCutchen. Jones Henderson qualifies.

Page 478.—1st March, 1785. Thomas Stevenson's will—To son-in-law, George Poage, 1 shilling; to grandson, George Poage, 1 shilling; to grandson, John Poage; to Agness Reed; to Joseph Hannah; to Deborah Reed; to Isabel Reed; to Alex. Reed; what money Henry King owes to be given to the poor if got from him; 20 shillings to pale in the church yard; to Robert Reed, Jr. Executors, Alex. Reed and David Gibson. Teste: John Campbell, Thomas Willson, Jno. Dixon. Proved, 16th August, 1785, by Wilson and Dixon. Executors qualify.

Page 480.—16th August, 1785. Commissioners report they cannot settle David Hays' estate for lack of vouchers. They report that the administrator of Geo. Waildon was paid in 1779-1780 fifteen pounds more than the estate amounted to.

Page 481.—16th August, 1781. Archibald Scott's bond to celebrate in matrimony.

Page 482.—20th June, 1785. Jacob Grass' estate appraised by John and Wm. Handly, Pat. Buchanan.

Page 483.—September Ct., 1784 (?). Recorded. George Searight's appraisement by Jno. Campbell, Andrew McCampbell, David Gibson, Jas. Dickey.

Page 485.—September Ct., 1784 (?). Recorded. James Bell's appraisement by James Dickey, John Blair, Wm. Young.

Page 488.—2d September, 1783. William McClintock's will—To wife, Martha, and after her death to son, Samuel, sole executrix; to son, William; to son, Samuel; to 3 married daughters, Francis Clark, Margaret Dogherty, Martha Philson; to 2 daughters, Prepare and Elizabeth, 400 acres on Cove Creek in Greenbrier County; to John McClintock, son to William McClintock; to grandson, John McClintock Dogherty. Teste: John Young, Samuel and Wm. Clark. Proved, 17th May, 1785, by Young, and 20th September, 1785, by Samuel Clark. Martha McClintock qualifies.

Page 490.—12th May, 1785. Robert Mill's will—To wife, Susannah; to nephew, John Mills, the plantation on which I and he now live; to nephew, John Mills' oldest son, Robert, infant; to Isabell Hannah, my niece's daughter; to brother John's children, viz: Alexander, Robert, William; to brother William's sons. Executors, nephew Jno. Mills and friend George Moffett. Teste: Isaac Hamm, Jno. Rankin, Rebekah Carson. Proved, 20th September, 1785, by Isaac Hanna and Rebecca Carson. John Mills qualifies.

Page 492.—10th May, 1783, Robert (mark) Bratton's will—To wife, Anne Bratton; to son, James, the land James lives on; to son, George, tract on Jackson River, 240 acres; to son, John, tract on branches of the Little River, 700 acres; to son-in-law, Wm. Givens, and Agnes, his wife; to son, John, in trust, £200 for support of unfortunate daughter Mary; to 4 children, Adam, George, John, and Agnes (Givens); to son, Adam, home plantation, executor. Thomas Adams to be overseer. Teste: Joseph Fauntleroy, Will. R. Fleming, Jno. Dunlap, William Given, Jno. Poage, Wm. Given. Proved, 18th October, 1785, by Poage and Dunlap. Executor qualifies.

Page 495.—18th October, 1785. Recorded. Elizabeth Guy's appraisement by Leonard Beall, Andrew McCaslin, James Gilespy; Henry Guy's legacy; Mary Gillespey's legacy; Martha Gillepsy, Sr.'s, legacy; Ann Gillespy's legacy; Martha Gillespy, Jr.'s, legacy; Archibald Guy's legacy; Samuel Frazer's legacy; Rebecca Thompson's legacy; John Gillespy's legacy.

Page 496.—13th November, 1779. James Gilmore's (Gillmer) will—To wife, Ann; to son, John; to son, James; to son, Alexander; to four daughters, Elizabeth Campbell, Martha Curry, Rebekah Brawford, Janet Peery. Executors, wife Ann and sons John and James. Teste: Elijah McClenachan, Arthur Hamilton, Wm. Blair. Proved, 20th September, 1785, by Hamilton and Blair. John qualifies.

Page 498.—15th November, 1785. Recorded. James Gilmore's appraisement by Wm. Wilson, Samuel Gibson, James Moffett.

Page 499.—14th November, 1782. William Kerr's will—To wife, Mary, executrix; division among all my children. Teste: Joseph Ray, Wm. Mulhallan. Proved, 15th November, 1785, by the witnesses. Executrix qualifies.

Page 501.—15th November, 1785. William Wilson's bond to celebrate matrimony.

Page 502.—15th November, 1785. George Searight's estate settled—Paid Jno. King and Jas. Searight, guardians to orphans.

Page 504.—20th March, 1785. William Burk's bond to keep in repair the bridge on the Creek near Daniel Kidd's in Staunton.

Page 505.—24th June, 1774. Rev. John Craige's estate appraised by Jas. Bell, Jno. Patterson, David Bell, Thos. Poage—Settlement filed 15th November, 1785; paid John King (Holston), Jared Whaling; paid Annalina Atwaters, Joannah Hamilton.

Page 506.—23d November, 1785. William McClintock's estate appraised by John Young, ——— Pallmore, Jno. Handly.

Page 507.—20th December, 1785. Samuel Shannon's bond to celebrate matrimony.

Page 508.—11th October, 1785. Adam Murrey's will—To William Patrick; to Rebeccah Patrick; to Mary Patrick; to John Patrick, executor. Teste: Robt. Craig, Jr., Archibald Rhea, Hugh McAleary. Proved, 17th January, 1786, by Rhea and McAleary. Executor qualified.

Page 510.—14th January, 1786. Thomas Peerey's estate appraised by Francis Erwin, Henry Miller, Francis Erwin.

Page 511.—23d June, 1782. William Johnson's will—To sons, John and Joseph, 20 shillings; to daughter, Jean, 40 shillings; to wife, Eleanor; to daughters, Sarah, Rebeckah, and Margaret; Sarah to have £10 more than the others; daughter Sarah has an injured foot. Executors, James Allen, Jr., and Geo. Moffett. Teste: Andrew Anderson, Alex. Robertson, Robt. Kenney. Codicil, 5th May, 1785, transfers £10 from Sarah to Joseph. Teste: Same as before. Proved, 21st February, 1786, by the witnesses. Executors qualify.

Page 515.—25th January, 1786. Adam Murray's estate appraised by Thos. McCollock, &c.

Page 516.—21st February, 1786. Recorded. George Crawford's estate settlement—1783, paid Thomas Menken who married one of legatees; paid Andrew Anderson, who married one of legatees; paid to legatees, viz: The widow, Ro. Crawford, Wm. Crawford, Jno. Crawford, Elizabeth Crawford; 1780, 12th October, paid for enlisting one 18 months' man, James Crawford, C. P.

Page 518.—22d March, 1786. Thomas Hughart's bond as Sheriff.

Page 520.—18th March, 1777. Thomas Carson's will—Now enlisted in Capt. John Syms' Company of Ragulars as a soldier; Col. Alex. Thompson to take care of his pay while in service, and in case of testator's death, or being killed, then Col. T. is to give his estate to Colonel's daughter, Agness, whom testator appoints his heir. Teste: Alex. Crawford, Samuel Henry. Proved, 21st March, 1786, by the witnesses.

Page 521.—20th March, 1786. William Elliot's estate settled—To legatees, viz: James, William, Jean, Elizabeth, Archibald (dead), Ann, Lanty (deceased in minority), Margaret, Sarah; the estate of Jane Elliot, Dr. To Robert Givens, £33.5; Contra: by one negro, £66.10; to Sarah Elliot, £33.5. We have examined the above account as stated, of John Elliot. guardian to Margaret and Sarah Elliot, and find vouchers for the equal division of the above £66.10 which appears to have been left them by their mother, Jean Elliot, deceased. Given under our hands 20th March, 1786.

Page 522.— — March, 1786. Recorded. Andrew Donnelly's appraisement by John Dickinson, Andrew Sutlington, Alex. Crawford.

Page 523.— — March, 1786. John Estill's estate settled.

Page 524.—25th ———, 1786. Samuel Carrick's bond to celebrate matrimony.

Page 524.—31st January, 1782. John Francis' will—To wife, Mary; to 4 daughters, Ann, Margaret, Martha, and Jean Francis; to 3 daughters, Elizabeth, Agnis, Mary. Executors, John Gardner, James McCamey. Teste: James Patterson, Abel Griffith, Joseph Moss. Proved, 20th June, 1786, by Patterson and Moss. Gardner qualifies.

Page 525.—16th December, 1785. William Burk's will—To brother, Edward Burk, home place; to mother, Ann Burk; to brother, Joseph Burk; to sister, Elizabeth Bosang; to half sister, Mary Grass. Executors, "Brothers Edward and John Bosang." Teste: Elijah McClenchan, Stophel Olinger. Proved, 18th July, 1786, by witnesses. Edward Burk and Jno. Bosang qualify.

Page 526.—18th April, 1786. John Davidson's estate appraised—1773, 13th March, paid John McKeemey, who married Ann, daughter of deceased; paid Samuel Davidson, son of deceased; paid John Davidson, son of deceased; paid John Douglas, schooling of the orphans; 1762, 9th June, to amount of goods this day sold at vendue—To cash received of John Higgins. Errors executed James Lyle, executor of Daniel Lyle, deceased.

Page 527.—5th March, 1786. Barnard Lance's will—To wife, Mary; to son, George, infant; to son, Joseph, tract adjoining Cunningham; to son, Cunrade; to daughter, Elizabeth, 98 acres she now lives on; to daughter, Mary, 98 acres adjoining above; to Martain Life, the place he lives on, 150 acres; to Conrad Buck, 150 acres; to daughters, Margaret, Amy, Chreestiaria. Executors, wife and son Joseph. Teste: Henry Slusher, Sebastian Stone, John Crewger. Proved, 20th June, 1786, by Stone and Flesher. Executors qualify.

Page 528.—28th June, 1786. Robt. Hogshead's estate appraised.

Page 530.—18th March, 1786. Robert Rusk's will—To wife, Elizabeth Rusk; to sons, John (oldest son) and James, infants; to son, John, plantation on Brown's Creek, 358 acres; to daughter, Rachel, under 13 years; 420 acres on Naps Creek to be sold; to oldest daughter, ———, under 18; to nephew, James Rusk, Sr.; to nephew, Robert Rusk; to nephew, Robert O'Dear; to brother, David Rusk; to mother, Margaret Rusk, and brother, Samuel Rusk, land left by father's will; to John Whitman, a debt to be paid; to daughters, Margaret, Jean, Hannah Rusk. Deed to be made to John Wilson, of Rockbridge, for land sold him. Executors, wife Elizabeth, brother John Rusk, and brother-in-law James Moore. Teste: John McKemy, Jno. O'Dair, Elizabeth Adaer, Margaret Rusk. Proved, 18th July, 1786, by Jno. McKemy and the Adairs. Executors qualify. (The name is several times spelled Risk.)

Page 531.—15th June, 1780. Sale of Joseph Gamble's estate—Sold to, viz: Samuel Redman, Capt. Jno. McCoy, Jonathan Shipman, Capt. Jos. Bell, George Dosian. Continued, 1st October, 1782; to Isabell Gamble, Edward Steward, Robert Duffield, Jno. Hiner, Mathew Pen, Moses Knapp, Lewis Mertin, Wm. Blagg, Joseph Breath.

Page 533.—18th July, 1786. John McDonough's estate settled—1784, paid Alex. Fretwell; 1785, received from Chas. Consolvant.

Page 535.—24th June, 1786. Alex. Walker's estate settled—1774, paid to legatees, Robert and Mary Walker; to Thos. Connelly, husband to Margaret; to Isabella Walker; paid John Ervin for teaching the children, 1780; paid James Anderson, ditto, 1782; paid John Young, ditto, 1785. Legatees Andrew and Martha are dead. Legatee Elizabeth is dead.

Page 535.—20th September, 1786. Thomas Scott's estate settled.

Page 537.—20th September, 1786. Roger North's estate settled—1783, cash paid Burns for repairing 2 swords broke by Philip North in Staunton; 1783, cash paid for 1 book (Cicero); 1783, cash paid Dr. Tindall for cleaning his teeth and powder; 1784, cash paid for 2 books—Horace and Cicero; 1786, cash paid for a lawn apron to Miss Timberlake; 1786, cash paid Blair and Timberlake for board and tuition; 1785, cash paid for an Algebra; 1785, cash paid Stephen May for teaching Philip to dance; 1785, cash paid Mr. Wilson for tuition; 1786, cash paid A. M. Onesney for teaching P. N., French. Above is guardian's settlement of accounts of Philip North.

Page 538.—1st August, 1786. Thomas Scott's estate appraised.

Page 539.—1st September, 1786. Robert Bratton's estate appraised.

Page 541.—Dr. the estate of Roger North in account with Sampson Mathews, husband of the administratrix of the deceased—1782, paid Mr. McClure for schooling; 1782, by cash received of Nelly Fleming.

Page 544.—18th February, 1786. Mathew Robertson's will—To son, Alexander; to son, William; to wife, Martha; to son-in-law, John Blair; to son-in-law, Patrick Christian; to son, James. Teste: Robert Kenny, Archibald Dickson, Wm. Trotter. Proved, 20th September, 1786, by the witnesses. Executors William and Alexander qualify.

Page 545.—30th December, 1785. Mary Ramsey's will, of Parish of St. Anne's, Albemarle County—To Alexander Ramsey, son to James Ramsey, infant; to six sons, viz: John, Alexander, Andrew, William, George Ramsey, and Andrew Steele; to Mary Ramsey, daughter to James Ramsey, infant. Executors, son John Ramsey and Andrew Steele. Teste: Samuel

Black, Alex. Cummin, James Perthulls. Proved, 17th October, 1786, by Black and Perthulls. Executors qualify.

Page 546.—27th July, 1786. Thomas Brown's estate appraised by Jno. Young, Jas. Cunningham, Jas. Bell.

Page 547.—18th December, 1786. Mathew Robertson's estate appraised.

Page 548.—1st July, 1786. John Francis' estate appraised—Abel Griffith, Wm. Young, Samuel Anderson.

Page 549.—30th October, 1786. William Woolwine's estate appraised by John Bosang, Peter Hanger, Harman Lovingood.

Page 550.—24th May, 1786. Alex. Kilpatrick's inventory upon taking oath of insolvent debtor.

Page 550.—4th March, 1779. John Anderson's will—To wife, Jane, the mare called the Carolina mare; to son, Robert; to son, William, in case he return from his journey; to son, James; to son, Andrew, tract adjoining John Patterson; to son William's son, John, infant; to son-in-law, James Allen; to son-in-law, Wm. Craig. Executors, sons James and Andrew. Teste: James Anderson, James Blair, George Anderson. Codicil, 17th May, 1786, transfers slave from son James to son Andrew. Teste: James and George Anderson. Proved, 20th February, 1787, by James and George Anderson. Andrew qualifies.

Page 551.—31st January, 1787. Edward Rutledge's will—To wife, Sarah; to daughter, Rebecka Rutledge; to son, James; to daughter, Rosanna; to son, George; to son-in-law, John Allison, for his sons John and James Allison; to 5 children, viz: Lucy Allison (wife of Jno. Allison, Jr.), Rebecca, James, Rosanna, and George Rutledge; to children, viz: Mary Erwin (wife of Wm. Erwin), Sarah McNeeley (wife of George McNeeley). Executors, William Allison, John Allison, Jr., David Stephenson. Teste: D. Stephenson, Gilbert Carr, Samuel Steel. Proved, 20th February, 1787, by Carr and Steele. D. Stephenson qualifies.

WILL BOOK No. VII.

Page 1.—31st January, 1787. Edward Rutledge's will—As above.

Page 3.—11th December, 1786. Robert Moodey's verbal, solemn, and dieing words: Living on ye head of Long Meadow; to nephew, John Frazer, Mansion House and 200 acres, joining Samuel Gilor's, Samuel Frazer's lines; to niece, Ann Frazer, 100 acres joining Samuel Henry, with ye Wallowing Hole Improvements. Teste: Samuel, James, (X) Ann Frazer. Proved, 18th April, 1787, by the witnesses. Administration granted John Frazer.

Page 4.—28th September, 1786. Philip (X) Olinger's will, farmer—To son, Jacob, 186 acres, home place; to wife, Juliana; to son, Stophel; to daughter, Barbara, and her son, John Palmer, infant; to daughter, Katharine; to grandson, Jacob Casner, infant, to be taught both Dutch and English, and to cypher, and a trade; to son, Philip, deed to be made for 148 acres he now lives on. Executors, Jacob Gabord and Augustine Argenbright. Teste: Jacob Maxwell, Wat. Cunningham, Frederick Hanger. Proved, April, 1787, by Cunningham and Hanger. Argenbright qualifies.

Page 7.—12th April, 1787. Philip Olinger's estate appraised by James Peery, Jacob Cale, Frederick Hanger.

Page 10.—24th February, 1787. Edward Rutledge's estate appraised by Gilbert Carr, John Stuart, Robert Heslet.

Page 15.—17th July, 1787. Recorded. Mathew Mathewson's appraisement.

Page 16.—18th April, 1787. James Cartey's estate settled by Samuel Pepper—Sale held 16th June, 1768.

Page 18.—7th April, 1787. Thos. Hutchison's estate settled by Robt. Scott, administrator of Sarah, who was administratrix of Thomas—Paid Wm. Scott for finding Sarah Hutchison in a house to live in and fire wood for near two years. Burial expenses of the said Sarah Hutchison.

Page 19.—April Court, 1787. Recorded. Neal McCann's estate settled by Daniel Kidd—1774, paid burial expenses.

Page 20.—24th March, 1787. Anthony Mustoe's bond as "Land Searcher."

Page 20.—19th March, 1787. Adulf Spindle, claimant's bond to celebrate matrimony.

Page 21.—19th June, 1787. Joseph Bell, Jas. Ramsey, Chas. Cameron took oath as Commissioners of the Tax.

Page 21.—18th September, 1787. James Chambers' bond for celebrating matrimony.

Page 22.—14th July, 1787. John Galloway's estate appraised.

Page 23.—18th September, 1787. Jacob Grass' estate settled by Elizabeth Fogas and Elizabeth Grass.

Page 25.—1st September, 1787. Philip Woolvine's estate sold at vendue—Articles bought by Elizabeth Woolvine, administratrix.

Page 26.—17th July, 1787. William Fleming's estate settled by Margaret, relict and administratrix—1782, 28th March, paid Henry Dache; 18th July, Chas. Hunt; 1787, September 18th, settled by Margaret McGonagal, administratrix.

Page 27.—25th April, 1787. John Ritchey's estate appraised—To account vs. John Ritchey, son of above John.

Page 28.—24th July, 1787. Certificate that Maj. Jno. Wilson, Alex. Crawford, William Monteer are chosen overseers of poor for 2d Battalion; 3d July, 1787, ditto, William Young, Thos. Frame, Wm. Finley at election, 2d July, 1787, at Stone Meeting House, for 2d District; 2d July, 1787, ditto, John Tate, Peter Heiskell, Jno. Christian, for the Southern District.

Page 29.—6th October, 1786. Inventory of Samuel Moses when he took oath of insolvent debtor.

Page 29.—13th October, 1787. Settlement of Thomas Shanklin's estate by John Shanklin, accounts in 1774, and by Robert Shanklin, accounts in 1786. 1774, paid John Fairbern; 1786, paid Elizabeth Shanklin, executrix of John Shanklin, deceased. Commissioners report there is a balance in hands of George Baxter, Thos. Shanklin, and Elizabeth Shanklin (widow), and of Robert Shanklin; all these persons are reported as executors by Andrew Shanklin, who acts for his father, Robert Shanklin.

Page 31.—4th December, 1786. Patrick Crawford's will—To son, George; to son, John; to sons, James and William, twins, tract purchased of Madam Wood; to daughter, Martha; to daughter, Mary; to grandson, George McChesney; other children have received their parts; to four sons. Executors, sons George and John. Teste: Jno. Poage, James Crawford, Alex. Robertson. Proved, 18th December, 1787, by Poage and Robinson and executors qualify.

Page 33.—Above estate appraised by John Givens, Jr., Robert Kenny, James Rankin, George Crawford.

Page 36.—15th November, 1787. Andrew Yeager's estate appraised by Jno. McCoy, Geo. Sheets.

Page 38.—26th June, 1786. Thomas Meck's will (Meek?)—To wife, Agnes, home plantation; to son, Daniel, plantation on which he now lives; to son, Samuel; to four sons and daughters, viz: John and Samuel Meek, Elizabeth Reah, Mary Vachub, Martha Reah, Daniel Meek; James Reah's wife. Executors, John Meek, James Reah. Teste: Thomas Hughart, Samuel Craig, Alex. Stuart. Proved, January Court, 1788, by Hughart and Stewart. Executors qualify.

Page 40.—15th January, 1788. William McPheeters' bond as Sheriff.

Page 43.—4th September, 1785. Jno. Faris' will—To wife, Agnes Feris; to son-in-law, Wm. Feris; to son-in-law, Job Rennolds. Executors, wife Agnes and son-in-law Wm. Faris. Teste: Joseph Waddell, Edward Wealden. Proved, 16th October, 1787, by Joseph Waddell, and 19th February, 1788, by Wealdon, and 17th June, 1788, executors qualify.

Page 45.—David Allen's estate in account with Thomas and John Allen, executors—1779, paid legatees, viz: Robert, Elizabeth, and Mary Allen; receipt to John and Thos. Allen, executors, from Robert Allen, legatee and guardian to James, Mary, and David Allen.

Page 47.—13th March, 1788. Commissioners report the Clerk's office well kept since the present Clerk was appointed.

Page 47.—25th March, 1788. Thomas Meek's estate appraised by Joans Henderson, Jno. Vachub, James Berry.

Page 49.—4th February, 1788. Robert Reed's estate appraised by Harman Lovingood, David Trimble, Alex. Gibson.

Page 150 (vid. page 63 infra.).—19th February, 1788. Zechariah Smith's will—To son, Mathew; to granddaughter, Serah, if she stay with Mathew until she is 18; to daughter, Elizabeth Gibson; to each son-in-law, $1. Executors, son Mathew Smith and Zechariah Johnston. Teste: Margaret Caldbreath, Ann Johnston. Proved, 16th April, 1788, by the witnesses.

Page 51.—Thomas Shanklin's estate to John Shanklin, executor, Dr.—1775, to James McVay for making coffin.

Page 53.—23d September, 1782. Samuel Bell's will, intending to journey shortly to the Kentucky settlement—To brothers, John, Thomas, Joseph; to sister, Sarah. Executors, brothers John and Thomas. Teste: Wm. Steel, Valentine Cloninger. Proved, 15th April, 1788, by Cloninger and hologroph, and 16th April, 1788, executor qualifies.

Page 54.—Jno. McDonough's estate in account with Jno. Abney, continued from 18th July, 1786—Paid Braxton Eastham; 1787, received from Geo. Huddle for rent; Geo. Woland, ditto.

Page 56.—15th March, 1788. Andrew McCombe's will—To wife, Jane; to son, William; to daughter, Barbara Curry; to daughter, Agness Reburn, Mary Young, Jean Curry, deceased (to her 3 daughters), Sarah Gardner,

Martha Dickey; to son-in-law, formerly Robt. Curry, the land Robert lives on that he purchased from testator's son, William, 130 acres; to Robert Curry's children that he had by daughter Elizabeth, viz: Andrew, Margaret, Jean, William, Mary, Robert, Elizabeth, Agnes; to all daughters, viz: —. Executors, wife and sons James Young, Robt. Curry. Teste: Samuel McKee, George Glenn, David Gibson. Proved, 17th June, 1788, by the witnesses. Executors qualify, widow refuses to execute by writing 14th April, 1788.

Page 59.—17th January, 1788. Thomas Caldbreath's appraisement by Christopher Graham, James Frazer, Jno. Hamilton.

Page 61.—25th March, 1788. Thomas Meek's estate appraised by John Vachub, Joans Henderson, James Berry.

Page 63.—Zechoriah Smith's will (see p. 50, *supra*.)

Page 64.—4th February, 1788. Robt. Reed's estate appraised.

Page 65.—8th March, 1788. John Coulter's will, aged about 68 years—To wife; to son, David; to son, John; to 3 daughters, Bety Ray, Bett Best, Nancy Beaton; to daughter, Mary Best; to sons, James and Joseph; to daughters, Nancy Beaton, Bety Reay, Bell Best, Mary Best; to grandson, John Coulter, Joseph's son. Executors, son David and Walter Davis. Teste: Edward Hall, Mathew Allexander. Proved, 17th June, 1788, by the witnesses, and 15th July, 1788, David Coulter qualifies and leave reserved for Davis to qualify later.

Page 67.—7th December, 1787. Agness Corson's (Carson) will—Estate falling to her by her father's will; to brother, Isaac, infant (?); to sister, Rebeckah, infant, under 18; to mother; to friends, Isaac Hannah, executor; to remaining brother and sisters. Teste: Geo. Moffett, Ro. Curry, Jno. Blair. Proved, 17th June, 1788, by Curry and Blair. Executor qualifies.

Page 69.—28th May, 1788. Whereas a report hath prevailed that the child I am big of was got by David Cail. This is to certify that the report is as false as groundless, for the father of said child is Archibald Keasy. Given under my hand, &c.—Margaret Hunter. Teste: A. Mustoe, Wm. Chambers.

Page 69.—17th April, 1788. James Culbertson's will—(Sets out transactions with Maj. Robt. Burns and Isabella Burns in 1782 and since showing indebtedness to him); also that out of his 4,000 acres to which he is entitled as Captain in the Virginia Line, he has sold 1,000 acres to Hugh Donaho, lying near Mouth of Miami; also Thomas Johnston, of Louisa, is to have 800 acres; Richard Bruce, of Albemarle, owes him £4 balance for a watch, &c., after deducting £3.0.0 allowed him to pay his brother, George Bruce. His accounts for services as Commissary and Quarter Master and Forage Master to Polaski's Legion (vouchers in hands of Capt. Geo. Rice (Brice) have not been paid. Also for services as issuing Commissary for the Prisoners stationed at Staunton of Burgoyne's Army (also in hands of Capt. Geo. Brice) also unsettled. Capt. Wm. Long owes £60 for money lent and other transactions in 1776. Robert Draffors (ons), of Charlottesville; Geo. Divers, of Albemarle; Wm. Holliday, of Winchester; Col. Thomas Bell and Mrs. Brice's claim for washing which she has charged to Robert Gamble to be paid. Then all debts to be paid (after deducting his reasonable wages as storekeeper for Gamble; John North). John Parris to be allowed 500 acres military lands for making clothes. Estate to be divided between brothers and sisters, viz: Robert Culbertson, Molly, Anne, and Margaret. Executors, brother Robert Culbertson, of Sherman's Valley, Penna.; Thomas Bell, Anthony Mustoe, Robert Gamble. Teste: Alex. St. Clair, Hugh McDowell, John Boys. Proved, 17th June, 1788. Anthony Mustoe qualifies.

Page 74.—9th March, 1787. David McCoskry's will—To wife, Grisel, until son John arrives to 21 years, executrix; to son, John, testator's plantation; to daughters, Elizabeth, Jean, Martha, Ann, Esher, Agness; to oldest daughter, Elizabeth, daughter, Esther; to wife and children, land on Licking Creek in Kentucky. Executors wife Jonathan Poage, James Tedford. Teste: Jno. McKemey, Wm. Morrows, Robert Cooper, Henry Venus. Proved, 17th June, 1788, by Morrow and Cooper. McKoskry and Poage qualify. Tedford appears and declines to qualify.

Page 77.—16th April, 1788. Joseph Gamble's estate settled by Isabella Gamble, executrix—28th March, paid Lewis Baker, doctor; 1782, received cash from, viz: Wm. Blag, Edward Stuart, Lewis Mertin, Wm. McCanless, Joseph Baith.

Page 79.—27th June, 1788. Andrew McComb's estate appraised by Wm. Young, Jno. Gamble, Jno. Bell.

Page 81.—29th October, 1787. John Townsend's will—To wife; to mother; to brother, Ezekiel; to daughter, Mary. Teste: Wm. Bourk, Sr. and Jr.; Wm. Roberson. Proved, 15th July, 1788, by the Burks. Keziah Townsend qualified.

Page 82.—28th November, 1786. Stephen Beck's (Bek—German) will—To wife, Catherine, £70 out of money due by Peter Frenger; to son, Peter Beck; to daughter, Mary Leedekey; to daughter, Catharine Frenger; to granddaughter, Anna Cleary Beck, daughter of son Peter Beck. Executors, John Hawpe, Jacob Teaford. Teste: James Mitchell, Wat Cunningham, Samuel Hay. Proved, 15th July, 1788, by Cunningham and Hay. Executors qualify.

Page 85.—9th July, 1788. David McKoskry's estate appraised by Robert Cooper, Andrew Kennedy, Robt. Herris (?).

Page 86.—14th June, 1788. John Abney's will—To wife, Isabella; to son, William; to the rest of the children; to son, John; son William to carry on the Hatting Trade. Executrix, Isabella. Teste: Wm. Chambers, Alex. Humphreys. Proved, 16th September, 1788, by the witnesses. Isabella qualifies.

Page 88.—12th May, 1788. Samuel Armstrong's will—To mother, Elizabeth, 30 acres testator lives on; to sister, Mary Armstrong; to sister, Jean Shields. Executors, William Armstrong, Alex. Long. Teste: G. Christian, James Brand, Jr. Proved, 16th July, 1788, by the witnesses. Executor William qualifies. Alexander appears and declines to qualify.

Page 90.—5th October, 1787. Robert Craig's will, farmer—On Middle River; to son, John, 192 acres whereon testator lives and 200 acres adjoining; to daughters, Anne and Rebecca, unmarried; to son, Robert; to each of other two sons; to each of other four daughters. Executors, sons John and Robert. Teste: James Henderson, Andrew and Alex. Henderson. Proved, 16th September, 1788, by James and Andrew. Executors qualify.

Page 96.—16th September, 1788. Recorded. John Coulter's appraisement by Alex. Hall, Hugh McLary, Andrew Fulton, David Colter, executor. These are debtors, viz: Jonathan Boldin, Jno. Bruffy, James West, Robert Sterips.

Page 97.—20th February, 1788. John Miller's estate appraised by Thos. Femster, Jno. Kinkead, William Dickey.

Page 99.—14th October, 1785. Thomas Adams' will, of the Calfpasture, being about to take a perilous journey to the Ohio River; to wife, Elizabeth, lands in Augusta and Amherst; to only brother, Richard Adams; to nephew, William Adams Fry, all lands on Western Waters; to William Smith, son of my highly esteemed and much lamented nephew, William Smith, lately of County of Essex, deceased; to nephew, William Adams; to friend, John Blair, Chancellor, lands he purchased of testator in Albemarle County known by name of Mountain Plains; to Ralph Wanlass, lands whereon Ralph lives and to support Ralph's mother while she lives; to niece, Tabitha Epps; to slave, Joe, freedom—"As there is no man to whom I consider myself under Greater obligations than to my slave Joe." Executors, Maj. Thos. Massie, of Frederick, nephews Wm. Adams and Wm. Adams Fry. Written with own hand. Proved, 22d October, 1788. Executors Massie and Fry qualify; other executor is dead. Handwriting is proved by Thomas Hughart and Archibald Stuart.

Page 101.—The estate of Thomas Shanklin to John Shanklin, Extr. Dr., formerly recorded.

Page 103.—19th October, 1788. Frederick County. William Cocke instructs the Court to add his name as security for Massie and Fry as executors of Adams.

Page 104.—1st September, 1785. Samuel (mark) McCorkle's will, planter—To wife, Sarah (executrix with Patrick Buchanan); to son, John; to daughter, Mary; to daughter, Martha Callesone; to son, Samuel; to son, Robert; to daughter, Sarah Chapman, and her first son; to daughter, Elizabeth McCorkle; to grandsons, Samuel and Wm. McCorkle. Teste: John Wallace, Mary Buchanan, Jno. Heizer. 16th December, 1788, proved by Wallace and Hizer. Executors qualify.

Page 106.—14th May, 1788. Robert Willson's will—To wife, Rachel; to daughters, Rebecca Sharril, Mary Thompson, Sarah Swink; to daughters, Rachel and Martha Willson; to eldest son, William; to youngest sons, James and John. Executors, wife and sons William and James. Teste: Wm. Wilson, Samuel and Jno. Gibson. Proved, 16th December, 1788, by Wm. Wilson and Samuel Gibson. William and James qualify.

Page 107.—10th December, 1788. Robert Craig's estate appraised by James Renkin, James Crawford, Jno. Crawford.

Page 108.—14th June, 1786. Hugh Green's will, of Augusta County and congregation—To wife, Agnus; to housekeeper, Mary Warner; to Nancy Wilson, daughter to Rev. Wm. Wilson; to Robert Ried, son to Robert Ried; to Cormick McCafferty, 13d, and Jinny his wife; to grandson, Hugh McCafferty; to daughter, Mary Gentry, and to each of her sons; to Alex.

Reid; to Jinny Green, daughter of Wm. Green, testator's grandson; to children and wife. Executors, Rev. Wm. Wilson and Robt. Reid, Jr. Teste: William and Elizabeth Wilson. Codicil, 1st February, 1787, revokes legacy to Mary Warner. Teste: Francis Allen and Robt. Campbell Proved, 20th January, 1789, by William and Elizabeth Willson. Both executors qualify.

Page 110.—28th June, 1788. Andrew Alexander's will—To wife, Catherine; to oldest son, James; to grandson, Andrew Hunter; to grandson, John Alexander, infant, son of son Andrew, tract at foot of South Mountain at place called the Wallowing Hole; to granddaughters, daughters of son Andrew above; to Samuel Hunter. Teste: Wm. Thompson, Samuel Wilson, Peter Frenger. Executor, son-in-law Samuel Hunter. Proved, 20th January, 1789, by all witnesses. Executor qualifies.

Page 112.—20th January, 1789. William McPheeters' bond as Sheriff.

Page 113.—14th October, 1788. Thomas Stuart's will—To wife, Elizabeth; to son, James; to grandson, Thomas Stuart; to son, Robert, houses and lots in Staunton; to son, Thomas; to daughter, Elizabeth Paxton; to daughters, Jenny (houses and lots in Staunton), Julia and Mary; to grandson, Stuart Paxton. Executors, son Robert, and Thomas Stuart. Teste: Benj. Stuart, William and Samuel Black, Robert Stuart. Proved, 17th February, 1789, by William and Samuel Black. Robert qualifies, and 22d April, 1789, Thomas Stuart qualifies.

Page 116.—17th October, 1776. Robert Allen, Jr.'s, will, farmer—To wife, Jean, she is to dispose of his lands to his heirs as she directs. Executrix, wife Jean. Teste: Benj. Stuart, James Steel. Proved, 17th February by the witnesses. Jane qualifies.

Page 118.—Isaac Carson's (Corson) estate in account with Wm. Young, executor—1787, paid; 1787, received from Mary, Jane, and Agnes Carson, Samuel Anderson (the less), Samuel Anderson (the big), John Vanskiver, Marcus Cupps, Jno. Gaurner, Geo. Hood, Rebeccah Hannah, relict to ye deceased. This balance in my hands ready to be divided amongst the legatees when it can be legally done, as the two youngest children, owing to the will not being renewed after them two were born, they are not mentioned, and this executor wishes equity to them to take place also.

Page 120.—14th November, 1788. John Abney's estate appraised—50 blacks, &c.

Page 123.—16th February, 1789. Samuel McCorkle's estate appraised by Wm. Wilson, John Wallace, Samuel Heizer.

Page 124.—30th January, 1789. Hugh Green's estate appraised by Thos. Frame and Jas. Allen.

Page 125.—17th February, 1789. Hugh Green's sale bill recorded—John Patterson, dumb.

Page 128.—16th September, 1788. Andrew McCombe's estate appraised.

Page 129.—21st April, 1789. Recorded. Susanna Henderson's estate in hands of William Henderson, Sr., by Walter Davis, Jno. Brooks, Daniel Rea.

Page 129.—21st April, 1789. Recorded. Robert Willson's appraisement by William Gilkeson, Robert Donaldson, Henry Swink.

Page 132.—17th December, 1787. Samuel Braford's will—To wife, Ann; to daughter, Mary Braford, unmarried; to son, John, 209 acres adjoining

Thos. Mitchel; to son, James, 201 acres; to daughter, Ann; to son, Hugh; to son, Samuel; to daughter, Rachel; to daughter, Elizabeth; to grandson, Samuel Hays, son of daughter Elizabeth, infant. If Samuel Hays die infant, then his legacy to go to his sister, Elizabeth Christian. Executors, two sons-in-laws, Patrick Christian, of Augusta County, and Samuel Miller, of Rockingham County. Teste: Wm. Shields, Samuel Hunter, Peter Frenger. Proved, 21st April, 1789, by the witnesses. Executors refuse to qualify. Administration granted John and James Brawford.

Page 137.—21st April, 1789. Recorded. Thomas Rankin appraisement by James and Wm. Craig, Jno. Givens.

Page 139.—22d April, 1789. John Poage's bond as surveyor.

Page 140.—16th February, 1789. John Poage's will—To daughter, Mary Poage; to eldest son, Robert; to son, George, 325 acres on Naps Creek joining lines with Moses Moore; to son, James, tract at Brown's Lick; to sons, John and Thomas, executors; to wife, Mary; to other children, William, Elizabeth, and Ann. Teste: John Gardner, Daniel McNare, Agnis Poage, Wm. Wilson. Proved, 22d April, 1789, by Daniel McNare and Agnis Poage. Executors qualify.

Page 143.—22d April, 1789. Recorded. Samuel Armstrong's appraisement by John Christian, Jacob Van Lear, Mark Hatton.

Page 144.—12th June, 1784. George Anderson's will, Sr.—To wife; to grandson, George, infant, son to testator's deceased son and heir-at-law, William, 100 acres where William lived, adjoining Paterson's Island; to sons, George and James, executors; to grandson, George Anderson, son to testator's deceased son, John, infant; to son William's daughters, sisters of grandson George, *supra;* to son-in-law, Gilbert Christian; to son-in-law, Adam Guthery; to son-in-law, James Andiddle; to son-in-law, Wm. Anderson; to daughter, Jane. Teste: Robert Kenney, James Magonel, Andrew Anderson. Codicil, 9th June, 1788. The 100 acres devised to grandson George is now devided between him and his mother Margaret, and at her marriage or death, then her 50 acres to testator's grandchildren, Elizabeth, Mary, Margaret, Robert, Jane, and Nancy Anderson. Teste: James Anderson, Wm. Anderson, Wm. Brooks. Proved, 21st April, 1789, by Kenny and Anderson, and on 22d April, 1789, executors qualify.

Page 147.—Hugh Allen's estate in account with the administrator—To paid William Craig, who married the widow, her one-third; to paid Capt John Campbell for soldier's bounty; to paid Robt. Rhodes for schooling orphans; to paid Archibald Dixon for soldier's bounty.

Page 153.—30th May, 1789. Robert Allen, Jr.'s, estate appraised.

Page 154.—2d May, 1789. Alex. Humphreys certifies that Elizabeth Bourke is well qualified to practice as midwife in all natural cases.

Page 155.—The praisement of William Chestnut's estate, his deceased. Mary Saphiah, his wife, administered and had it praised. Dr. this 18th December, 1788, by James Stephenson, John Bird, Robert Robinsin.

Page 157.—23d October, 1788. Isaac Waugh's will—To sister, Jean, 60 acres in Cumberland County, Penna., cor. David Bell's fence and James Ellet's line; also one-third of the orchard left him in father's will; "the above land I leave to James' own disposal"; to brother, Samuel; to brother, John. Executrix, sister Jean. Teste: John Campbell, Henry Spering, James

Oliver. Proved, 16th June, 1789, by Campbell and Sherring. Executrix Jane Richardson qualified.

Page 158.—14th November, 1787. James Callison's will (Sr.)—To wife, Isabella; to son, Robert; to daughter, Dorothy; to son, James; to granddaughter, Isabella Callison, daughter to son John, unmarried; to son, John; to son, William; to daughter, Jean; to daughter, Agness; to daughter, Mary; to daughter, Eloner; to daughter, Isabella; to daughter, Margaret. Teste: Wat Cunningham, James Peerey, Joseph Blair. Proved, 16th June, 1789, by Blair and Peery. Executors qualify.

Page 162.—3d July, 1789. John Poage's estate appraised by Andrew Anderson, James Allen, Alex. Robertson.

Page 166.—20th February, 1789. Andrew McClure's will—To son, Joshia (Josiah), 265 acres home place; to son, John; to wife, Elener; to daughter, Elizabeth; to daughter Elizabeth's son, John Trimble. Executors, sons John and Josiah. Teste: Zechariah Johnston, David and John McClure. Proved, 21st July, 1789, by David McClure, and 15th September, 1789, by John McClure.

Page 168.—8th April, 1789. Charles Berry's will (Sr.), farmer—To wife, Mary, and son Robert's support; to son, Robert; to son, John; to son, Charles, tract in Washington County on Houlstone; to daughter, Challe Berry, unmarried; to daughter, Elizabeth Henry; to daughter, Jean Brawford; to son, James; to daughters, Mary, Jean, and Elizabeth, 5 shilling in room of their birthright. Executors, wife Mary and sons James and John Teste: Jo. McKemy, Jacob Patton, Mary Patton, Wm. (mark) Trotter, Henry (X) Minger. Proved, 15th September, 1789, by McKemy and Minger. James and John qualify.

Page 171.—7th May, 1789. James Blear's will—To wife, Jean; to 3 daughters, Elizabeth, Mary, Jean, after marriage or death, of wife Jean; to daughter, Margaret; to son, John; to son, James. Executors, wife and son John. Teste: John Campbell, Samuel King, Thos. Bleakely. Proved, 15th September, 1789, by Campbell and Blakely. Executors qualify.

Page 173.—27th July, 1767. John George Weaver's will (signed in German Waber)—To wife, Christina, after her death division among the children; to son, Andrew, 1 shilling in lieu of birthright; to rest of children, viz: Ann Margaret, Peter, John, George, Mary, Elizabeth. Executors, Thomas Mitchel. Teste: Peter Hanger, Samuel Bell (a German). Proved, 15th September, 1789, by Peter Hanger and Harman Lovingood. 19th January, 1790, Mitchell appeared and refused to execute. Administration granted widow Christiana and son John.

Page 176.—21st December, 1787. William Finley's will—To son, William, land he now lives on; to son, Robert, home place, whereon testator and Robert now live, adjoining John Ramsey, deceased, and son Robert's children; son John has already received land. Executors, 3 sons—John, William, Robert. Teste: William Wallace, Andrew Ramsey, Sarah Finley. Proved, 15th September, 1789, by Ramsey and Wallace.

Page 178.—6th April, 1785. Jacob Grass's will—To daughter, Mary, to live in small house on plantation built by Anthony Mustoe; to son, Peter, daughter, and John Bosang, property in Staunton; to son, Frederick, has sold his share to his brother Peter; to daughter, Barbara; to daughter, Mary.

Executor, son Peter. Teste: John Griffin, Hugh McDowell, Anthony Mustoe. Proved, 21st July, 1789, by McDowell, and 15th September, 1789, by Mustoe.

Page 180.—23d April, 1789. Jennate McCutchen's will—To James Brownlee, Sr., two-thirds of her share of Wm. McCutchan's estate; to the rest of her legatees, tract on Pine Run patented in name of Wm. McCutchan. Teste: John, William, Alexander Brownlee. Proved, 15th September, 1789, by William and Alexander Brownlee. Executor qualifies.

Page 181.—20th April, 1785. Jacob Seyler's (Siler) (German) will (Sr.)—To wife, Dority, after her death to children; to eldest son, Philip, 5 shillings in lieu of birthright; to daughter, Magdalene at death of her husband, and her children; to son, Jacob; to second daughter, Mary Catherine, now married to Martin Yeakly; to daughter, Anna Catherine, now married to John David Griner; to daughter, Anna Mary, now married to Geighford (Geo. Eiford? Ayford?); to daughter, Elizabeth, now married to Monanel Herlis; to daughter, Dorothy, now married to Anthony Mustoe; to daughter, Anna Margaret; to daughter, Eve Margaret, now married to ———— Olinger. Executor, Hermon Levingood. Teste: Elijah McClenachan, Wm. Burk, Edward Burk. Proved, 20th October, 1789, by McClenachan and Burk. Executor refuses; Dorothy also refuses, and administration granted A. Mustoe and George Wiford.

Page 185.—15th April, 1788. John Blair's will—To father; to 3 sisters, Elizabeth, Mary, and Jean; to sister, Margaret; to brother, James; to mother. Executors, father and James Seawright. Teste: John Campbell, Jacob and John Sheetz. Proved, 15th December, 1789, by Campbell and Jacob Sheets. Executor Seawright qualifies.

Page 187.—10th February, 1786. Rebeckah Archer's will—To Anne, Rebecca, Martha, Rachel Sawyers, daughters of James Sawyers, deceased; to Thomas, David, George, and above girls, Sawyers; to brother-in-law, William Blair. Executors, William Crawford, Hannah Sawyers. Teste: David McNare, James McCaa, Alex. Crawford, Rebecca Sawyers. Proved, 15th December, 1790, by Crawford and Sawyers. Executors refused. Administration granted David Sawyers.

Page 189.—20th August, 1789. John McKemey's will (Sr.), farmer—To wife, Agness; to son, James; to daughters, Jean, Agness, Margaret, Elizabeth; to children, viz: William, Jean, John, Agness, James, Margaret, Elizabeth; to son Robert's son, John; "Each grandson named after testator, viz: William McKemey's son, John; John McKemy's son, John; John James McKemy's son, John, and John Cooper, John Bradshaw, John Montgomery, John Woodle." If daughter Jean's part be not demanded before her death, then to her children. Executors, sons William and John McKemy. Teste: Thomas Waddell, John Cooper, Richard Roche, Chas. Hogshead. Proved, 15th December, 1789, by Roche and Hogshead. Executors qualify.

Page 191.—19th January, 1790. Recorded. James Blear's appraisement by Henry King, Thomas Frame, John Harper, Jacob Sheets—28th April, 1789. Samuel Brawford's estate appraised by John Sterling, James Shields, Samuel Hays.

Page 195.—19th January, 1790. James Steele's bond as sheriff.

Page 200.—4th January, 1790. John Renkin's will—To brothers, James and Robert, executors; to brother, Thomas' heirs, Thomas' estate to be cleared of debt to testator's father's estate; to brothers and sisters, viz: William Renken, sister Jane Bell, sister Mary Young, or her heirs. Teste: John Craig, James Henderson, Andrew and Alex. Henderson. Proved, 16th February, 1790, by Craig and James and Alex. Henderson. Executors qualify.

Page 201.—24th July, 1785. Cutlip Black's (Gotelieb Schwartz) will— To wife, Margaret; to son, John, home place, under 24; to daughter, Shusy. Executors, John Tate and Nathaniel Steel, Sr. Teste: Hugh Fulton, John Bright. Produced in Court 16th February, 1790, by Jacob Clyne and proved by Jno. Bright and Philip Battrorff.

Page 202.—16th August, 1789. Samuel Steel's well—Executors, James and Andrew Steel; to son, Samuel; to four daughters, Margaret, Sarah, Martha, and Mary; to sons, James, Andrew, and Samuel. Teste: Samuel Finley, Andrew Ramsey, Jane Fienley. Proved, 16th February, 1790, by Samuel and Jane Finley. Executors qualify.

Page 203.—8th September, 1790. William Tease's estate sold at vendue by Robert Love and Mary Tease, executors—Sold to, viz: James McManners, Wm. Rice, Neal McFaul, Samuel Love, Jourdon Gibson, Cornelius Maupine, Benj. Yearly. Sold, 3d April, 1779, to, viz: Robt. Love.

Page 208.—William Tease's estate settled—1778, 11th July, paid Frank Hodge, Geo. Sutherland ———, ———, paid Solomon Isril, George Holland, Jean Teas (daughter); ——— ———, Mrs. Jean Tease to Mary Tease.

Page 213.—15th January, 1790. John Stuart's will—To wife, Frances; when youngest child arrives at 18; to children, Mary, Margaret, Samuel, and child wife may now be with. Executors, wife, David Stephenson, Robt. Kenny. Teste: George and James Crawford, Mary Stuart. Proved, 16th February, 1790, by Geo. Crawford and Mary Stuart. Frances qualifies.

Page 215.—18th April, 1789. Christian Clemmon's estate appraised by Jas. Kerr, Jacob Barger, Alex. Robertson.

Page 215.—26th March, 1790. John Rankin's estate appraised by James and Robert Rankin—By John Craig, Jno. Crawford, James Craig.

Page 217.—22d October, 1776. John Buchanan's will—To wife, Margaret, executrix; to daughter, Martha, wife of John Buchanan; to son, William Buchanan; to son, Patrick, £3, executor; to son, Robert; to son, John; to son, James, executor; to sons, Alexander and David; to daughters, Mary and Catherine. Robert Gnear (now in my care) to be taught the art and mystery of a Taylor. Teste: Elijah McClenachan, Moses Williams. Proved, 20th April, 1790, by the witnesses. Patrick qualifies. 20th April, 1790. Margaret refuses to execute. Teste: John Gregory and Jno. Wallace.

Page 220.—14th January, 1790. John Givens' will (Sr.)—To wife, Margaret; to son, Thomas, 150 acres, part of home plantation; to son, James; to daughter, Mary; to daughter, Sarah Lofftis; daughter, Ann Henderson; son, John; son, George; son, Samuel; son, William; daughter, Elizabeth Lamme; daughter, Margaret Agnew. Executors, wife Margaret, son James. Teste: D. Stephenson, George and James Crawford. Proved, April 20, 1790, by D. Stephenson and Geo. Crawford. James qualifies. Margaret Givens refuses to execute and nominates son James as sole executor.

Page 222.—25th January, 1788. David Greiner's estate appraised by Robert Douthat, Peter Hanger, Peter Heiskell.

Page 223.—4th February, 1788. David Greiner's estate sold at vendue.

Page 226.—3d May, 1790. Inquest upon body of a man found in a field of Maj. Andrew Anderson. Verdict: Is the body of John Peck, son of Andrew Peck, aged between sixteen and seventeen; died by hand of God— Robert Kenney, Andrew Anderson, James Allen, Jr., Alex. Reed, John Crawford, Thomas Poage, Jr., Jas. Kerr, Jas. Cochran, Thos. Frame, Wm. Crawford, John Campbell, John Gamble. Held in consequence of an order from me in absence of Coroner.—David Stephenson.

Page 227.—Edward Rutledge's estate in account with David Stephenson, acting executor—Paid legatees, viz: Rebecca Rutledge, John Allison. Settled 20th April, 1790.

Page 229.—Specific legacies of above estate—To Sarah Rutledge; to James Rutledge; to Rosaana Rutledge; to books bequeathed to Lucy Allison, Rebecca, James, Rosanna, Geo Rutledge.

Page 230.—1st June, 1785. Thomas Gillespy's will—To wife, Eleanor; to eldest son, John; to son, Thomas; to son, Jacob; to son, Samuel; to daughter, Mary Donally; daughter, Hannah Jones; daughter, Jene ———; to youngest daughters, Eleanor and Ann; to youngest sons, James and William, tract on Stuart's Creek, of Cowpasture River. Executors, sons James and William and wife Eleanor. Teste: William Connell, Zachariah Beall, Leavin Nealls, Andrew McCasling. Codicil, 13th November, 1786— £15 to be taken from Eleanor and given to her son, Thomas, a boy 3-4 year old, for his schooling, and if James shall die without issue, then his part of land to go to William. Teste as before (Leavin Nicalls). Proved, 15th June, 1790, by Connell and McCaslin. William and Eleanor Gillaspey, the surviving executors, qualify.

Page 232.—19th January, 1790. James Sawyers' will—To son, Sampson Sawyers, 5 shillings; to son, James, 5 shillings; to son, John, 5 shillings; to daughter, Rachel Crawford, 5 shillings; to daughter, Rebecca Sawyers, excutrix, all property. Teste: Wm. Sterrett, Wm. Armstrong, Wm. Edmondson, Thos. Sawyers. Proved, 15th June, 1790, by Sterrett, Armstrong, Edmondson. Executrix qualifies.

Page 234.—20th July, 1790. Recorded. John George Weaver's appraisement by Thomas Mitchel, Samuel Hunter, Wm. Shields, James Mitchel, Jr.

Page 235.—1788. The estate of John Coulter, deceased, to David Coulter, executor; 1789, paid Joseph, John, James, Isabella Coulter, David Rhea, James Best, Francis Best, Jno. Bratton.

Page 236.—12th June, 1790. Jennate McCutchen's estate appraised.

Page 237.—12th June, 1789. Thomas Stuart's estate appraised by Walter Davis, Samuel Long, Joseph Colter.

Page 239.—List of debts by bonds, bills, notes, and acceptances due to above estate—By Francis Allison and son, Andrew; George Burton; Francis Bogs, assigned by John Hardy; Thomas Bates (Holston); Wm. Butt; Isaac Burns; John Boal; Jno. Creely; Wm. Currance; David Clerkston; Wm. Dandridge; Jno. Emmitt; Jno. Earskins; Edward Harkins; Jno. Jack; James Walker (Samuel's son).

Page 244.—List of book debts due Thomas Stuart—By John Allison (Middle River); James Bates, Jr.; Manis Burgey; James Buchanan (near John Tate's); ditto (Burden's Land); John Bell, son to the widow; Wm. Burbridge; Wm. Barnett (Rockfish); John Caldwell (son Samuel); John Cock (Mason); Jno. Campbell (son to Henry); Robt. Campbell (son to widow); Robt. Cowan (son to James); William Campbell (Sander's son); Robt. Campbell (Smith); Alex. Elliot (son to George); William Fulton (Bigham's son-in-law); James Frazer (Scotchman); ditto (Long Meadow); William Fulton (schoolmaster); James Henry (son to Samuel); Robt. Hamilton (Doctor); John Henderson (shoemaker); Samuel Hays (blacksmith); Wm. Jamison (son to Robert); ditto (Christian's Creek); Wm. Johnston (Brushy (Brusley?) Neck); John Kilpatrick (son to Thomas); James Kilpatrick (Thomas' son); John Lyle (widow's son); Joseph Long (Forks); Edward Long (taylor); John Montgomery (wagonmaker); Jno. Moore (Abney's place); Robert Mitchell (John's son); James McCroscery (John's son); William Moore (D. brother); Alex. Moore (D. brother); James McClung (John's son); James McCown (Frank's son); Alex. Montgomery (son to John); James Moore (son to widow); Wm. McClenachan (Doctor); James McClure (owned A. Reed's place); Mr. ——— Oglebay (son to James Brady); Wm. Poage (Holston); Robert Patterson (carpenter); Wm. Reed (taylor); John Robertson (Providence); James Stuart (Providence); Samuel Steel (Providence); Charles Stuart (millwright); widow Stuart (Burden's Land); John Stuart (taylor); John Sinters (Suinters) (Patrick Martin's son); Robert Stuart (Pastures); John Shields (son to John); William Stuart (schoolmaster); John Thompson (wheelwright); John Thompson (son to James); Thomas Wilson (Caylor's town); John Walker (Forks); Samuel Wilson (James' brother); Thomas Welson (Chesnut Ridge); John Weir (Smith's cousin); Alex. Walker (farmer); John Wilson (Robert's son); James Weir (Jeremiah Teford's father-in-law); Edward Walton; John Weir (Hugh's brother); Hugh Weir (Smith); John Weir (Robert's son); George Taylor (Botetourt); David Steel (Robert's son); James Walker (son to John); David Robertson (Providence); Jno. Starling (Botetourt); Christopher Migrons; Wm. Napper; Jno. Long (Holston).

Page 260.—15th February, 1788. Andrew Hamilton's will, of the Calfpasture—To wife, Martha; to son, William; to son, Andrew; to each grandson named Andrew, 250 acres in Kentucky; to all my daughters; to sons William and Andrew, all books. Executors, son William and son-in-law Wm. Rennocks, wife Martha. Teste: Wm. Lockridge, Samuel Lockridge, Thos. Adams. Proved, 21st September, 1790, by the Lockridges. Hamilton and Wm. Renocks qualify.

Page 262.— — ———, ———. John Lewis' will—To wife, Margaret, Warm Spring tract, and after her death to son Thomas. Executrix, wife. Teste: Margaret McFarlane, Agatha Frogg, Wm. Long. Proved, 21st September, 1790, by Agatha Stuart (late Agatha Frogg) and Wm. Long. Margaret qualifies.

Page —.—30th June, 1789. John Fulton's will, freeholder—To wife, Mary; to oldest son, James, 200 acres adjoining home plantation; to son, Samuel, 109 acres; to son, William, infant; to son, Andrew, 5 shillings;

to son, Hugh, 5 shillings; to 3 daughters, Sarah, Margaret, Elizabeth, unmarried. Executors, wife Mary and son Andrew. Teste: Thomas Fulton, Samuel McCutchen, Jas. Steel, David Fulton. Proved, 21st September, 1790, by McCutchen, Steel, and David Fulton. Executors qualify.

Page 264.—James Culbertson's appraisement by R. Douthat, P. Heiskell, Jas. Lyle, Jr.—To Thomas Scott; to Christopher Keloffer.

Page 267.—26th ———, 1789. Jacob Syler's estate appraised by ———, Edward Burk.

Page 270.—Greenbrier, June 23, 1790: This is to assart to all parsons to home these presence may consarn that I am informed that sur John Hicklin has been accused of being guilty of Ravishing of my Child which I downt not believe he ever did and that she never Received any Damage by said hicklin to my knowledge. Sartifide by me.—Elizabeth Dey. Teste: James McGooney, Joseph Newton.

Page 270.—15th July, 1790. David Mathews' will—All estate to poor of the Parish in Rev. Archibald Scott's congregation. Executors, John Young, James Brown, Sr. Teste: John Scott, James Williamson, Jean Scott. Proved, 21st September, 1790, by John Scott and Williamson Brown qualified.

Page 272.—19th October, 1786. Thomas Brown's estate sold at vendue, to, viz: Elizabeth Brown, Margaret Brown, Jr.; John Brown, Jr.; Valentine Thorn, Wm. Welch, Nicholas Look, Wm. Forbuss, Henry Fogess.

Page 274.—Thomas Brown's estate settlement by Mrs. Elizabeth Brown—Paid Doctor John Griffith.

Page 277.—26th February, 1790. George Crawford's will—To wife, Florence; to son, Samuel, home plantation after mother's death; to son, James Crawford, tract bought of Jas. Story; to son, William. Before children come to age. Executors, brother James Crawford and brother-in-law James Henderson. Teste: James and Robert Rankin, Alex. Henderson. Proved, 21st September, 1790, by James Rankin and Henderson. James Crawford qualified.

Page 278.—21st September, 1790. Benjamin Hinkle's bond to solemnize matrimony.

Page 279.—Alex. McClenachan, late Sheriff, in account with Augusta County—1782, 26th April, by amount of County levy for 1781 delivered to collect being laid on 2,000 tithables at 1¼ each; to 283 tithables contained in the list of tithables returned for 1782 above the number on which the levy was laid at 1¼ each; 1782, November 22, by amount of claims allowed in the levy for 1781 supposed to be paid to the County creditors; by payment to Alexander Wilson for a waggon and team purchased for the public; 1782, November 23, by amount of County levy for 1782 at 1/0 on 2,283 tithables.

Page 280.—Thomas Hughart's settlement as Sheriff—1785, to amount of County levy for 1785 on 2,090 tithables at 2/9 each; 1786, to amount of County levy for 1786 on 1,860 tithables at 3/0 each.

Page 282.—19th October, 1790. Recorded. John Fulton's appraisement.

Page 284.—19th February, 1790. John Stuart's estate appraised by John Campbell, George Crawford, John Mills.

Page 288.—29th October, 1789. John Trimble, Sr.'s, will—To wife, Ann, son John to support her; to daughter, Margaret McClenachan; to daughter, Mary Philson; to son, Walter; to son, John, home plantation, adjoining plantation testator's son Robert lives on; to grandson, John Trimble, son to son Joseph, deceased, infant, if said grandson demand the same; to son, Robert, plantation Robert now lives on; to Robert's eldest son, James Trimble; to son Robert's widow and children, in case of Robert's death; to daughter, Elizabeth Ellot, and her husband, James Ellot. Executors, son John Trimble and William McPheeters. Teste: Elizabeth McClenachan, Jno. Young, Jno. Moffett, Michael Coalter. Proved, 19th October, 1790, by Young and Moffett.

Page 290.—21st December, 1790. Recorded. John Lewis' appraisement by Samuel Vance, Jacob Warick, Jno. White.

Page 292.—16th November, 1790. James Young's will—To Agnes Miller, wife to Wut Miller, daughter to George Glenn; to James Glenn, son to George Glenn; to William Glenn, son to George Glenn; to Sarah Glenn, daughter to George Glenn; to Martha Glenn, daughter to George Glenn to Hugh Glenn, son to George Glenn; to Mary Glenn, daughter to George Glenn, infant; to Margaret, Esther, Elizabeth, Martha, John, James, William Bing, children to John Bing; to son-in-law George Glenn, to son-in-law John Bing, executors. Teste: Robert Young, Jr.; Robert Young, Sr.; Sarah Young. Proved, 21st December, 1790, by all witnesses. George Glenn and Wm. Young qualified.

Page 295.—17th August, 1790. Robert Astrop's will, of Staunton—To wife, lot opposite the Court House bought of Mustoe and Chambers, lot No. 6 (stable) bought of Wm. McDowell; house, stable and ¼-acre lot above Mr. Mustoe's dwelling house opposite the church; to children, boys or girls, part of lot 2 where testator now lives; to children, alive now, viz: Henry, Jesse, Elizabeth, Polly. Wife, executrix, and Alex. St. Clair and Anthony Mustoe, executors. To James Holmes in July, 1789, I (owe) £30 for one year as storekeeper; son Henry to be brought up as a silversmith, or some light trade; son Jesse to be brought up as a cabinetmaker or shop joiner. Teste: Michael Bowyer, Alex. Gibson, Jr., James Seawright. Proved, 21st December, 1790, by Bowyer and Seawright. Executrix Jane qualified.

Page 298.—12th October, 1786. James Gillespy's will, about to take a journey to Kentucky—To brother William, to brother Samuel (tract left testator by will of father), executors; to mother and sister Anne. Teste: Wm. Connell, Chas. Donally, James Coleman. Proved, 21st December, 1790, by Connell and Donally. William qualifies.

Page 300.—6th November, 1790 Inquisition at Hugh Talbert's before John Tate, upon body of Thomas Stephenson. Verdict: That on the 3d inst. he accidentally fell from his feet against the rute of a saplin and into the water at the same time and so was suffocated and died by the visitation of God.

Page 301.—25th December, 1790. Appraised Andrew Yeager's estate—John McCoy, Joseph Malcom, George Shetes.

Page 301.—Articles sold at vendue by Alex. Craig, administration of

Samuel Craig—To, viz: Margaret and James Craig, Robt. Flitchers, Alex. Dods, John Plunket, Timothy McKnight.

Page 303.—William Blackwood's estate to Elenor Blackwood, executrix—1778, paid funeral expenses; 1777, 6th September, paid Dr. Long for inoculating seven of Wm. Blackwood's family at one pound per patient.

Page 304.—9th December, 1790. Jacob Haldiman's will—To wife, Elizabeth, and hers and my children. Teste: Robt. Porterfield, Nicholas Earhart, Daniel Krouse. Proved, 18th January, 1791, by Earhart and Krouse. Widow qualifies.

Page 305.—7th September, 1790. James Steel's commission as Sheriff.

Page 306.—18th January, 1791. James Steel's bond as Sheriff.

Page 310.—10th July, 1790. Timothy Caul's will—To three sons, Thomas, Hugh, William (William is infant); to wife, Elizabeth, executrix; to daughter, Agnes Caul, unmarried; to daughter, Margaret Caul, unmarried; to daughter, Mary Caul, unmarried; executors, Thomas and Hugh; to son, James, 5 shillings. Teste: Andrew Allison, D. Stephenson, John McClure. Proved, 18th January, 1791, by Stephenson and McClure. Thomas and Hugh qualify.

Page 312.—31st October, 1788. Thomas Adams' estate appraised—19 negro slaves, &c. Above is appraisement of estate in Augusta.

Page 316.—Appraisement, ditto, in Amherst County—12 negro slaves.

Page 317.—Ditto, ditto, in Buckingham County—6 slaves.

Page 318.—12th February, 1791. William Buchanan's estate appraised by James Megongal, John Shannon, Smith Thompson.

Page 318.—6th June, 1781. John Frazer's will, of Rockingham County—To wife, Jennet, all estate whatsoever; to James Walker; to Mary Aderson; to brother, Joseph Fraizer; to brother, George Fraizer; to sister, Molly Galloway; to brother, William; to Andrew Shanklin, son of testator's sister, Molly. Executors, wife Jennett and her brother, James Hooke. Teste: Geo. Huston, Robt. Hook, Wm. Hooke, Isabella Campbell, Elenor Campbell. Proved, 15th February, 1791, by Huston, Robert and Wm. Hooke. Jennett qualifies.

Page 322.—15th February, 1791. Recorded. David Mathew's appraisement by (3 Germans).

Page 322.—23d June, 1783. James Kirk's appraisement bill.

Page 326.—13th March, 1787. William Parrus' will—To my beloved (wife?) Janet (and daughter Elizabeth while in her age); to son, John, £10, to be paid by John's brother, Andrew; to daughter, Elizabeth; to son, Andrew, eldest son, executor. Executrix, wife Janet. Teste: James Henry, Samuel Carson, Mathew Taylor. Proved, 15th February, 1791 (executors qualify), by Henry and Carson.

Page 328.—17th September, 1785. Robert Allen's will, farmer—To wife, Martha, and family; to son, James, 1 shilling; to son, Robert, 1 shilling; to son, John, 1 shilling; to son, William, 1 shilling; to daughter, Mary Malarie, 1 shilling; to daughter, Ann Frazier, 1 shilling; to son, Mountecue Allen; to son, Benjamin Allen; to son, Thomas Allen; to daughter, Elizabeth Meek. Executors, wife Martha and Patrick Buchanan. Teste: James Bell, James Colter, Robert Allen, John Scott. Proved, 15th February, 1791, by Bell and Colter.

Page 331.—1st February, 1791. Eleanor Johnston's estate appraised by Mathew and Robert Kinney, Wm. Robertson.

Page 333.—John McDonough's estate in account with estate of John Abney, executor, deceased.

Page 334.—Inventory of estate of George Kirk, son of James Kirk, deceased, put into my hands as guardian by John and Jean Kirk, executors. 14th February, 1791.—Wm. Moffett.

Page 335.—Ditto of James Kirk, son to James Kirk, ditto.—John Kirk.

Page 335.—2d February, 1791. James Craig's will (Sr.)—To sons, James and William, lands on Middle River; also tract adjoining James Crawford, John Craig, and Henderson's land; to son, George Craig, home tract and that purchased of Jno. Davison, and all lands on east side of South River; to daughter, Sarah Ely, or Sarah Throp; to son, Samuel; frees slaves; to son, James' daughter, Mary; to each grandson named for testator, viz: James Craig's son, James; William Craig's son, James; Samuel Craig's son, James (if he have one); James Ely's son, James; James Anderson's son, James; to heirs of daughter, Mary Craig, deceased; to daughter, Agnes Anderson, and her husband, James Anderson. Executors, James, George, William. Teste: John and Anne Craig, James Patterson. Proved, 15th February, 1791, by John Craig and Patterson. James and George Craig qualify, leave reserved for other executor to qualify.

Page 339.—24th January, 1791. James Lesslie's estate settled by Sarah Lesslie—Isabella Gamble's dower paid at marriage before the appraisement. Dolly Woods, ditto, ditto; paid Mary Robinson, being a legacy formerly left her in the hands of the deceased.

Page 340.—Joseph Lesslie, Dr., in account with Sarah Leslie, executrix of James Leslie; Samuel Lesslie, Dr., in account with Sarah Leslie, executrix of James Lesslie; John Lesslie, Dr., in account with Sarah Lesslie, executrix of James Lesslie.

Page 341.—Executrix to the estate of James Lesslie, Cr.—By his one-eighth part of the net estate as a legatee; by his wife's specific legacy per the will.

Page 342.—Sarah Lesslie, Jr., in account as above; Robt. Lesslie, Jr., in account as above; James Woods, in account as above; Isabella Gamble, in account as above; Dolly Waddle, in account as above; balance due to the heirs of Dolly Waddle.

Page 344.—14th April, 1791. William Purris' estate appraised by Samuel Carson, James Rowan, Robert Henry.

Page 346.—Estate of John Lewis, deceased, in account with Margaret Lewis, executrix.

Page 350.—15th October, 1790. Jacob Leamer's (Lemon) estate appraised by John Dickey, John Lam.

Page 352.—13th July, 1784. Alexander Blair's will, taylor—To son, John, whole estate, he to pay, viz: to son, James, 6 shillings; to sons, William and Samuel (their heirs, as they are deceased), 6 shillings each. Executor, son John. Teste: William Young, Jno. Gamble, Ro. Gamble. Proved, 19th April, 1791, by Young and Jno. Gamble.

Page 353.— —— March, 1791. Maj. Robert Porterfield, Robert Kenney, Jno. Gamble elected overseers of poor at Stone Meeting House.

Page 353.—7th January, 1791. Andrew Lockridge's will—To son, John, 1 crown; to daughter, Elizabeth Gwin, 1 crown; to daughter, Elenor Dinwiddy, 1 crown; to daughter, Margaret Henderson, 1 crown; to son, Andrew, 1 crown; to son, James, 1 crown; to son, William, tract purchased of Thos. Hicklin; to sons, Robert and Lanty, lands in Bullpasture, infants; to wife, Jean; to daughter, Sarah, 1 crown; to daughter, Rebecca; to my seven children, viz: William, Rebecka, Robert, Lanty, Elizabeth Lockridge, Jean, Ann. Executors, sons Andrew and William. Teste: John Montgomery, John Bradshaw. Proved, 19th April, 1791, by Montgomery and Bradshaw. Executors qualify.

Page 355.—Archibald Gilkison's estate to Wm. Young and Hugh Brown, executors, Dr.; November, 1783, paid Enos Jones' account; November, 1783, paid Wm. Jourden account; 8th March, 1791, settled.

Page 357.—21st April, 1791. William Fleming's additional appraisement.

Page 358.—29th March, 1791. Wm. Moffett, Alex. Gibson, Robt. Doak elected overseers of poor.

Page 358.—19th April, 1791. James Sawyers, Sr.'s, estate appraised by Benj. Brown, Wm. Armstrong, Wm. Sterrett.

Page 361.—Dr. estate of Andrew Lewell in account with Chas. Yeorons, executor—Paid Barbara Smith by Gasper Ballinger for land in October, 1779; paid Dr. Erwin for attendance at death bed February, 1779; paid John Erwin for schooling in April, 1781; paid Gilbert Christian for schooling in March, 1781; paid Joseph Oneal for schooling; paid Joseph Erwin the widow's part.

Page 363.—9th April, 1791. Timothy Caul's estate appraised by William Allison, Robert Heslet, John Allison.

Page 365.—12th May, 1791. Andrew Lockridge's estate appraised by John Bradshaw, William Dickey. Robert Carlile.

Page 368.—21st June, 1791. Recorded. Jacob Haldiman's appraisement by Jno. Finley, John and Andrew Ramsey.

Page 371.—28th December, 1790. Elizabeth Crawford's will—To daughter, Mary Rankin, in hands of son, John Crawford, £80; to son, John Crawford; to daughter, Elizabeth Bolling; to daughter, Martha Crawford; to daughter, Sarah Crawford; to daughter, Jane Crawford; to son, James Crawford; to rest of my children. Executors, sons James and John. Teste: James Renkin, Robert Crawford. Proved, 21st June, 1791, by the witnesses. James Crawford qualifies.

Page 372.—1st March, 1791. James Craig, Sr.'s, estate appraised by Jas. Rankin, John Craig, Jas. Crawford.

Page 375.—12th September, 1787. Jno. Bourland's estate appraised by Samuel Vance, John Byrd, Wm. Bourland—Certified to by Betsey Bourland, executrix, 7th June, 1791.

Page 376.—4th May, 1791. Patrick Ryndle's (Reynolds) will, yeoman—To Jean McCreary (McCray), horse and crop of grain on Thos. Beard's place. Executors, Jean McCray and Archibald Rhea. Teste: John Workman, Andrew McElvain, Sina Workman. Proved, 21st June, 1791, by John Workman and McElvain. Executrix qualifies.

Page 378.—10th October, 1785. Thomas Rutledge's will, planter—To wife, Jean, executrix, and sons James and Edward, executors; to wife, Jean, apprentice boy, John Fogle; negro wench, Chloe, to choose which son she will live with, viz: James, John, Thomas, Edward; to sons, Thomas and Edward, home plantation; to sons, James and John, lands in Botetourt County, on Roanoke, on North Fork; to sons, Thomas and Edward, 100 acres in South Carolina on a branch of Fishing Creek; to all four sons; to daughter, Katarine Rutledge; to son, George Rutledge, 1 shilling; to daughter, Elizabeth Armstrong, 1 shilling; to daughter, Ann Henderson, 1 shilling; to daughter, Mary Young, 1 shilling; to daughter, Jean Brooks, 1 shilling. Teste: Patrick Buchanan, Henry Marshall. Proved, 21st June, 1791, by the witnesses. Jane Rutledge appears and refuses to execute. Other executors qualify.

Page 381.—26th October, 1787. John Neal's estate appraised by Thos. Neal, James and Robert Curry.

Page 381.—22d February, 1791. Daniel Miller's will, yeoman—To wife, Mary, until son William is of age; to sons, James and William Miller; to daughter, Margaret Miller, under 18; to sons, Michael, Jacob, Daniel, Samuel, 5 shillings each; to daughter, Catherine Miller, 5 shillings. Executors, wife and Andrew Moore, Sr.; William Buchanan. Teste: J. McKemey, Robt. McChesney, Jan McChesney, Robert Young. Proved, 21st June, 1791, by McKemy and Young. Executrix qualifies.

Page 384.—Dr. the estate of William Fleming in account with James Megongal, and Margaret, his wife, late Margaret Fleming, administratrix.

Page 385.—Dr. County of Augusta in account with James Steel, Sheriff, 1790, 2397 tithables at 2/9.

Page 386.—19th July, 1791. Elizabeth Crawford's appraisement recorded by Jas. Rankin, George Crawford, James Givens.

Page 388.—19th July, 1791. Recorded. John Bourland's appraisement by same as above.

Page 388.—Dr. estate of John Hind in account with William Hind, administrator—1788, paid Archibald Hopkins as per son Ephraim; 1788, paid Daniel Kidd, bond given in 1772 as per Dutchman's receipt.

Page 402.—Appraisement of Barnet Lance's estate by Peter Hull, Jno. Gum, Sr.; Michael Armengash. Recorded, 20th September, 1791.

Page 403.—Account of sales of above to, viz: George and Peter Hull, Thomas Galford, Thomas Mullenax, John Mullinax, John Gum, Sr.; Martin Life.

Page 404.—17th April, 1791. John Finley's will, farmer—To wife, Thankful, living out of land devised to son David; to sons, George, Robert, and daughter, Margaret Shields, each 5 shillings; to son, Thomas; to son, John; to daughter, Jean and her son, John Trimble; to son, David, sole executor; to daughter, Thankful McKarter. Teste: David McNair, Jno. Thomas, Jno. Wilson. Proved, 20th September, 1791, by all witnesses. David qualifies.

Page 407.—Adam Stephenson's appraisement by Wm. Hogshead, John Erwin, John Bing. Recorded. 20th September, 1791.

Page 411.—Sale bill of estate above—Sold, 12th May, 1790, to, viz: Rebecca Stephenson, Wm. Freeholder, Edward Collins.

Page 413.—Appraisement of Daniel McNair's estate recorded 20th September, 1791—Note on John Knowles, account vs. George Leburn, Owen Colley, Michael Dwier, Niclas Suesanger, Tolly Divat.

Page 414.—18th March, 1791. Agreement between James Brownlee, John McCutchan, and John McCutchan, Jr. (teste: James Wardlaw, Samuel McCutchan, Asher Waterman). Commissioners appointed on motion of James Brownlee, administrator of Andrew Duncan, to examine the accounts of the estate, report that they find the accounts in confusion on account of the marriage of Andrew Duncan's widow with William McCutchan, and also confused the accounts of above McCutchan, Jr. and Sr., administrators of William McCutchan, who is dead; they agree to leave all questions (including estate of the deceased wife of both Duncan and McCutchan) to these, viz: Zachariah Johnston, Jno. Tate, Joseph Bell, Jr.; Michael Coulter, John Cunningham. The(y) report there is the sum of £21.12.9 coming to each legatee of Duncan. Elizabeth Buchanan has received £34.6.1. Mary Craig has received £26.11, Janet Edminston £26.6/0, Jane McKiney £22, Florence Brownlee £23.10/0. Jane McKinney shall receive £4 more than others due from David Craig and that his receipt be delivered to Mr. John McKinney for that purpose.

Page 419.—5th August, 1791. Francis Erwin's will—To wife, Jean; to daughter, Susannah; to 3 sons, John, William, Francis; to daughter, Frances, and her elder sister, Jean; to daughter, Susannah; two daughters in Cellibacy, Frances and Susanna; to daughter, Elizabeth Nickel, now married; to daughter, Mary Ervin, married; to daughter, Jean Ervin, married. Executors, sons John and William Ervin. Teste: James Young, Robert Curry, Alexander Curry. Proved, 18th October, 1791, by Young and Robt. Curry.

Page 422.—28th April, 1788. James Allen's will (Sr.), farmer—To children of daughter, Rachel Thomson, 5 shillings each; to daughter, Margaret Bell, 5 shillings; to daughter, Agnes Shields, 5 shillings to son, William Bell, 5 shillings; to daughter, Rebecca McClure, 5 shillings; to daughter, Elizabeth McNair, 5 shillings; to daughter, Mary Allen, 5 shillings; to son, Francis Allen, £50; to son, James, home plantation. Executors, wife Mary, son-in-law David McNaire, son James. Teste: Wm. Wilson, James Allen, John Hartsook, Wm. Baker. Codicil, 24th March, 1789. Teste: Wm. Wilson, John Hartsook, Wm. Baker. Proved, 18th October, 1791, by Hartsook and Baker.

Page 424.—15th April, 1791. Moses Williams' will, planter—Executors, sons David and Alexander; to 3 sons, David, Alexander, John, home plantation, 300 acres; David's part where Gabriel Pendle now lives; Alexander's part where he now lives; John's part where he now lives; to daughter, Ana Williams; to daughter, Flow Lindsey, 5 shillings; to daughter, Margaret Pendle, 5 shillings; to 3 sons, David, Alexander, John. Teste: Patrick, Mary, David Buchanan. Proved, 18th October, 1791, by Patrick and David Buchanan.

Page 427.—James Young's estate appraised 8th January, 1791.

Page 428.—19th October, 1791. Nuncupative will of Dennis Burns who has for a considerable time had his residence and boord with John Bell—To John Bell, all estate; he died 24th October, 1791. Teste: Edward Erwin, Rebeckah Stephenson, James Stephenson. Proved, 20th December, 1791, by the Stephensons.

Page 428.—23d April, 1791. Jno. Crawford's will—To wife, Rachel, executrix; to child, if he have one living; to Mary Rankin's six children. Teste: Andrew Anderson, James Crawford, Wm. Crawford. Proved, 20th December, 1791, by all witnesses. Executrix qualifies.

Page 431.—John Finley's appraisement by David McNair, James Willson, Jno. Thomas—Recorded, 20th December, 1791.

Page 432.—12th August, 1791. John Oliver's will—To son, Robert Willson's son, John Willson; to granddaughters, Elizabeth, Margaret, and Martha Willson, daughters to Robert Willson, infants. Executors, son-in-law, Robert Wilson. Teste: Wm. Young, Hugh and Francis Brown. Proved, 20th December, 1791, by all witnesses. Executor qualifies.

Page 434.—7th June, 1791. Robert McClenachan's will—To wife, Sarah; to daughters, Agnes Dean, Jene Sinclair, Lettis Kizer; to son, Alexander, plantation in Rockbridge whereon Robert Shaw lives; to grandsons, John and Robert McClenachan, sons of son Robert McClenachan, deceased, all Kentucky lands. Executors, Alex. McClenachan and Alex. St. Clair. Teste: Michael Bowyer, Alex. Humphreys, James St. Clair. Proved, December Court, 1791, by two of the witnesses.

Page 436.—7th October, 1791. Jno. Christian's will—To wife, Rachel, executrix, bonds on Phillemon Richards, Jr., and John Gum; to sister, Isabella, bonds on Wm. Forbes. Teste: Jos. Ray, Jas. Burke, Thos. Ray. Proved, December Court, 1791.

Page 438.—Thomas Rutledge's appraisement by Walter Davis, George Marshall, David Harbison, Hugh Gilkeson. Recorded, December, 1791.

Page 440.—8th September, 1791. Joseph Bell's commission as Sheriff.

Page 441.—17th January, 1792. Joseph Bell's bond as Sheriff.

Page 446.—2d January, 1792. Frances Erwin's appraisement by John Bell, Jno. Hogset, David Bell.

Page 452.—22d February, 1792. Alexander Gibson, Jr.'s, qualification as Commissioner of Tax.

Page 453.—Thomas Rankin's appraisement by Wm. Craig, James Craig, Jno. Givens.

Page 456.—14th November, 1792. James Allen's estate appraised.

Page 458.—11th February, 1792. John Oliver's estate appraised by Jacob Sheets and Anthony Ailer.

Page 461.—18th August, 1786. Robert Armstrong, executor of John Archer, executes the power in the will by giving one-half of the residuum of the estate to John Archer, nephew of John Archer, deceased, and the other half to be divided between Sampson Archer, Sr., and Sampson Archer, Jr., children—induced to do this because they are relatives and are objects of charity. Teste: Andrew Downey, J. Mathews.

Page 462.—John Archer's agreement to above. Teste: Jno. Gardner, Thos. Bradshaw.

Page 463.—20th February, 1792. Robert Armstrong to Richard Mathews to prosecute a chancery suit in county court against John and Thomas Poage, executors of John Poage, deceased, who was executor with Robert of John Archer.

Page 464.—26th April, 1791. Joseph Henderson's will—To wife, Sarah, for taking care of the children; to daughter, Jean, wife of Alex. Buchanan; to four sons, John, Robert, Joseph, William, property left testator by will of his father-in-law, John Miller, deceased; to daughters, Polly and Sally Henderson. Executors, wife Sarah and son John. Teste: Elijah McClenachan, David Buchanan, Gabriel Pendel. Proved, January Court, 1792, by David Buchanan and Gabriel Pendleton. Executors qualify.

WILL BOOK No. VIII.

Page 1.—21st August, 1792. Jacob Kinney's bond as Clerk of the County Court.

Page 2.—James Lessley, Jr.'s, estate in account with James Kerr and Robt. Kinney, executors—1775, November —, paid James Culbertson for cheese for Mrs. Lessley's funeral; October —, expenditures and work done supplies of grain, &c., about the time of their death; 1776, November 20, paid Geo. Craig for making Lessley's and his wife's coffin; 1779, paid Samuel Henry for 5 gallons whiskey for Betsy Lessley's funeral.

Page 5.—John Crawford's appraisement taken 18th June, 1792, by John Givens, Jas. Rankin, Wm. Craig.

Page 7.—25th April, 1792. Francis Alexander's will, of the Long Meadow—To wife, Elizabeth; to son, Gabriel, home plantation; to son, John, 100 acres on Christie's Creek, either joining Robert Russell or John Graham; to daughter, Janet Alexander; to son, William; to daughter, Dorcas Alexander, unmarried; to son, Francis, 100 acres on Christian's Creek, to be schooled by son Gabriel, 1760 acres in Caintuckey in care of Benj. Logan. Executors, brother Gabriel Alexander and sons Gabriel and John. Teste: John Ballard, John Alexander, James Ross. Proved, 19th June, 1792, by all witnesses. Executors qualify.

Page 10.—John Francis' estate in account with John Gardner, executor—Paid legatees Jno. Hogset, Martha Francis, Samuel Hinds, Mary Francis, Wm. Francis, Jane Francis.

Page 12.—Alexander McConnell's appraisement by James Peary, Alex. Craig, Joanes Henderson—Thomas Therspy's note; Jno. Cavanough's note; Benj. Norton's note. Recorded, 19th June, 1792.

Page 14.—11th May, 1792. George Rankin's will—To brothers, Joseph and Samuel, executors, house and lot in suburbs of city of Alexandria conveyed to him by Beal Howard and wife; to younger brother, Armstrong Rankin. Teste: Isaac and Ann Rankin. Proved, 19th June, 1792, by the witnesses.

Page 16.—William Johnson's estate in account with executors—John Garvin's receipt, who married one of the legatees; Reuben Shackelford's receipt, who married one of the legatees; Elenor and Margaret Johnson's receipts.

Page 18.—26th April, 1792. Alex. Nelson's commission as Coroner; 23d August, 1792, Alex. Nelson's bond as Coroner.

Page 20.—23d November, 1791. John Gratton's will—To daughter, Margaret. unmarried; to "my poor daughter, Jane"; to son, Robert, lands at the Kentucky, and the lands that were allotted to the heirs of his brother, John Gratton, deceased, given by the Commonwealth of Virginia and to be located on the western side of Okehiow River on Waters of the Meomey; to Elijah Poug and my dear Agness, his wife—1,000 acres in Kentucky surveyed by George Mays on the Waters of Salt River, on Harden's and Ralewing Creek; to Elijah Poug and Col. Robt. Gamble jointly, 1.600 acres that Col. Daniel Boone received land warrants; to Col. Samuel Brown and wife Betey Brown, the 500 acres he surveyed for testator "that my Jackey purchased of him"; to son, Robert, lot in Fincastle; to daughter, Elizabeth Brown; to Samuel Brown's daughter, Betey, if she die without heirs, then to her brother, John Brown. Executors, son Robert, Robt. Gamble, Samuel Brown. Teste: Jacob Sanger, James Allen, Jr., Robt. McGriffin. Proved, December Court, 1792, by Sanger and McGriffin. Robert Gratton qualifies.

Page 23.—2d October, 1792. William Crawford's will—To wife, Rachel, land adjoining Robert Rennock's line, James Elliot's line, Samuel Gardner's line; to son, Alexander, land above, and to give George Crawford learning; to sons, James, John, and William; to son, George; to daughter, Polly Armstrong, £5; to Nancy Tolman, £5; to daughters, Jenny and Rachel; house to be finished and painted. Executors, wife Rachel, John Crawford, Samuel Crawford, Alex. Craig, and son Alexander. Teste: Joseph Thompson, Hannah Sawyers, Rachel Crawford, Rebecca Sawyers. Proved, December Court, 1792, by Hannah and Rebecca Sawyers and Joseph Thompson. Alexander and Rachel Crawford qualified. Alex. Craig expressly refused to qualify. Other executors have leave to qualify hereafter.

Page 25.—1st March, 1788. Richard Rankin's will—To sons, Isaac, Joseph, and George Rankin, home plantation, 1,300 acres adjoining John Gratton, John Oliver, William Blair, plantation where Hugh Donaghe now lives, commonly called the Widdow Watsai's place, on mouth of Naked Creek; to 4 sons, Richard, Isaac, Joseph, and George; to younger sons, Samuel and Armstrong, infants; to 2 sons, John and James Rankin, already provided for; to 2 daughters, Rachel Gilston and Mary Johnston, already provided for. Executors, sons Richard and Isaac. Teste: William Richardson, Isaac Waugh. Proved, December Court, 1792, by William Richardson. Waugh is dead. Richard Rankin refuses to execute. Isaac qualifies.

Page 27.—23d November, 1789. Sarah Lessley's will—To sons, Samuel, John, and daughters, Isabella, Agness, Elizabeth, and son, Robert, 1 shilling each; to niece, Agness Lessley, daughter of James Lessley; to nieces, Mary, Isabella, Elizabeth, Margaret Robertson, daughters of John Robertson, deceased; to daughter, Margaret Rodgers; to daughter, Sarah. Executor, Joseph Bell. Teste: Alex. Nelson, Jr.; Suckey Bell. Proved, December Court, 1792, by the witnesses. Executor refuses. Administration granted Joseph Wilson.

Page 28.—12th October, 1792. Joseph Jewell's bond as contractor to build a stone bridge over the creek on Beverley street in Staunton, near Sampson Mathews' lot, to be seven feet clear between the pillars, to extend down stream 23 feet.

Page 29.—5th April, 1787. James Bell's will, Sr., of South River—To son, Joseph, home tract, 300 acres, bounded by James Long, Jno. Bell, also an adjoining tract called Trimble's survey; to daughter, Sarah Bell, to be paid by his sons, John and Joseph; to son, John; to daughter, Agness Gamble; son, James Bell; son, Wm. Bell; son, Thomas Bell; son, Samuel Bell, and grandson, Robert Love; to sons, John and Joseph, and daughter, Sarah. Executors, sons John, Thomas, Joseph Bell, Walter Davis. Teste: David and Samuel Long, Gabriel Alexander. Proved, October Court, 1792, by all witnesses. John Bell refuses to qualify or to join in the probate. Other executors qualify.

Page 30.—15th January, 1790. John Stuart's will—To wife, Frances; when youngest child shall come of age of 18 years; to children, Mary Stuart, Margaret Stuart, Samuel Stuart, and child wife is now big with. Executors, wife Frances, David Stephenson, Robt. Kinney. Teste: George Crawford, James Crawford, Mary Stuart. Proved, 16th February, 1792, by Geo. Crawford, Mary Stuart. Executrix Frances qualifies.

Page 32.—Dr. the estate of James Blair in account with Jane Blair, acting executrix; 1790, February —, paid Z. Taliaferro, Hugh Danchea.

Page 34.—25th February, 1792. Dennis Burns' estate appraised by Wm. Young, Jno. Gamble, Abraham Griffith.

Page 35.—Estate of Jacob Lamir (Lamor, Lanier?) in account with Mary Lamer, executrix; paid John Unroo, Michael Wilhelm.

Page 36.—4th December, 1792. James Bell's estate appraised by Wm. Blake, David Long, James Beard, Jr.

Page 39.—15th January, 1793. Joseph Bell's bond for collection of county levy; 15th January, 1793, Joseph Bell's bond as Sheriff.

Page 43.—Account of the sale of the estate of Robert Reed—Paid Tobias Markle; received judgment vs. Hugh Tafney; John Selham's bill of £3, run away and never been heard of.

Page 47.—Robert Burgess' estate appraisement recorded December, 1792, by James Rankin, James Gwin, James Crawford.

Page 49.—26th December, 1793. Sarah Lessley's estate appraised— Paper currancy, James River Bank notes in 15 bills, £74.0.0.

Page 53.—26th October, 1792. George Pierson's estate appraised by John Gamble, William Young, John Blair.

Page 54.—7th March, 1793. Robert Young's will—To wife, Margaret, to be maintained by son Andrew; to daughter, Jean, unmarried; to daughter, Margaret Glenn; to son, James, infant (?); to son, Robert, infant (?); to son, William, infant (?); to daughter, Sarah Curry; to daughter, Lydia, unmarried; to son, Andrew, all land. Executors, son William and George Glenn. Teste: John Denson, Samuel Curry, Robert Curry. Proved, 16th April, 1793, by John Dennison and the Currys. Executors qualify.

Page 56.—11th April, 1793. James Lyle, Jr.'s, will, of Staunton—To wife, Margaret, and daughter, Julia (Juliet), estate to be kept for wife's support and Julia's education, infant. Executors, wife Margaret, friends Wm. Lyle, Archibald Stuart. Teste: J. Beal, Smith Thompson, Jinney Stuart, Mary Humphreys. Proved, June Court, 1793, by Stuart and Humphreys. Executors qualify.

Page 58.—13th June, 1793. Elizabeth Blair's will, of Staunton—To grandson, Robert Hartgrove; to Mrs. Jane Hall, as compensation for services and kindness in last illness. Executors, Alex. Humphreys and Archibald Stuart. Teste: G. Christian, John Bowyer, Robt. Douthat. Proved, June Court, 1793, by Christian and Bowyer. Executors qualify.

Page 59.—Poll of election for two trustees for the town of Staunton, taken 1st January, 1793—For Michael Garber, 18, viz: Jacob Geiger, Robt Gratton, Andrew Cutler, Jno. Boys, Phillip Dyre, Robt. Bailey, Anthony Ingleton, Michael Syford, Jno. Gates, Geo. Weifford, Jno. Gunn, Jno. Backinster, Wm. Heginbotham, Wm. Brieze, Michael Cawley, Jno. Moore, Jno. Price, John Diddy. For Robert Douthat, 22, viz: Jacob Kinney, Daniel Donavan, Robt. McDowell, Peter Heiskell, Jno. Grates, Jos. Dickey,

Jas. Barry, Samuel Merrila, Jas. Cochran, Jno. Gardner, Jas. McLaughlan, Jas. Mathews, Alex. Mason, Smith Thompson, Michael Cawley, Wm. Chambers, G. Christian, Jno. Price, Jno. McDowell, Alex. Humphreys. For James McGonegal, 4, viz: Michael Syford, Jno. Gunn, Jno. Backinston, Jno. Diddy. For Peter Heiskell, 25, viz: Jacob Geiger, Andrew Cutler, Jacob Kinney, Jos. Dickey, Jas. Barry, James Cochran, Wm. Heginbotham.

Page 60.—12th June, 1783. Catherine Clemon's will—To son, John, all estate; to daughter, Catherine. Executors, sons John and Jacob Berryer. Teste: Joseph Hannah, Frederick Stull, David Trout. Proved, June Court, 1793, by Trout (Joseph Hannah is dead), and at July Court, 1793, by Shull. John Clements qualified.

Page 61.—5th October, 1791. James Crawford's will—To wife, Jean; to son, James; to son, George, plantation on Round Oak; to son Alexander, plantation at South River, to be educated and bound; to daughters, Mary, Elizabeth, Jenet, Martha, Anne. Executors, wife Jean and cousins Alexander Robertson and James Crawford. Proved, July Court, 1793, by James Anderson, Wm. Crawford. Executors refuse. Widow Jean renounces the will. Administration c. t. a. granted the widow.

Page 62.—July Court, 1793. Recorded that Patrick Ready had lost part of his ear in a fight with Dennis Mehoney.

Page 63.—Robert Young's appraisement by John Dennison, James Young, Jno. Laur.

Page 66.—2d August, 1793. James Meteer's will—To wife, Elizabeth; to 3 sons, William, James, Samuel. Executors, wife Elizabeth and son William. Teste: Samuel McCutchen, David Doak, James Mitchell, John Walce, Samuel Doak. Proved, September Court, 1793, by the Doaks and James Mitchell, Jr. Executors qualify.

Page 67.—8th December, 1792. John Boyd's will—To Thomas Boyd, 10 shillings; to the lawful begotten heir of John White, deceased, 10 shillings; to wife, Elizabeth, lands for life and then to ——— ———; to John Varnum; to Hannah Varnum, to be paid by John Varnum at his mother's decease; to Rebecca Varnum; to Julian Varnum. Executors, Elizabeth Boyd and John Varnum. Teste: David Steele, Samuel Forsythe, John Purris. Proved, September Court, 1793, by Forsythe and Purris. Executors qualify.

Page 69.—9th September, 1793. James· Crawford's estate appraised by Alex. Nelson, Andrew Anderson, Thomas Patterson, Mathew Kenney, Ro. Kenney.

Page 73.—Appraisement of Dominick Barrett by Samuel Hays, James Moffett, Peter Fauber. Appraised 5th October, 1793.

Page 73.—Estate of Adam Painter, deceased, to his administratrix, debtor.

Page 74.—8th February, 1777. Margaret Cawby's estate appraised.

Page 77.—John McKemey's appraisement taken 22d September, 1792, by Robert Cooper, Robt. Harris, John Berry.

Page 79.—27th June, 1782. Robert Armstrong's will, cloathier—To wife, Elizabeth; to son, Samuel; to daughter, Mary; to daughter, Nancy Armstrong, unmarried, to be paid by Samuel Armstrong. Executor, Samuel Armstrong. To daughter, Jane Shields. Teste: Alexander Long, William McDavitt. Proved, 20th September, 1788, by Alex. Long, and at December

Court, 1793, commission awarded to take deposition of Wm. McDavitt.

Page 81.—20th August, 1788. Robert Campbell's will, hatter—To brother, George, all estate, and executor; to sister, Jennitt Campbell. Teste: Thomas Fulton, Thos. Boyd, Wm. Vernum. Proved, December Court, 1793, by Fulton and Boyd. Executor qualifies.

Page 82.—16th November, 1793. Jacob Clements' estate—Partial appraisement by Jacob Barger, Jas. Kerr, Alex. Robertson, Jas. Robertson.

Page 82.—20th July, 1787. Archibald Hamilton's will—To wife, Francis; to daughter, Lettice; to son, William; to son, John, plantation on Christian's Creek; to son, Audley, 5 shillings; to son, Andrew, 5 shillings; to son, Archibald, 5 shillings. Executors, son William, son-in-law John Cunningham. Teste: Robert, Mathew, and Phebe Kinney. Proved, January Court, 1794, by Ro. and Mathew Kinney. Executors qualify.

Page 84.—1st October, 1793. Thos. Poage's will, Jr.—To wife, Jean, ½ mill plantation on Falling Spring, which ½ was willed to testator by his father; to brother, John. Executors, Rev. John Campbell and brother, John Poage. Teste: Alex. Humphreys, Richard Trother (Strother?), Philip Sholl. Proved, January Court, 1794, by Stother and Sholl. Executors qualify; 3d October, 1793, John Poage, legatee above, relinquishes to widow Jean all claim under the will to any property which came to Thomas through the widow Jean, who was Jane Watkins.

Page 86.—9th November, 1793. Mary Poage's will—To son, John; to daughter, Elizabeth Hoge; to daughter, Ann Kinkaid. Executors, friend Thos. Poage and son John Poage. Teste: Thos. Poage, Margaret Allen, Polly Poage, Philip Sholl. Proved, January Court, 1794, by Thos. Poage (who refuses to act as administrator) and Sholl. Jno. Poage qualifies.

Page 88.—26th July, 1793. Hugh McDowell's will—To be sold, viz: 1 lot in Staunton bought of Sampson Mathews, adjoining Robert Gamble and John Bosang, deceased; also, ½ acre in "New Town" whereon a stable stands; to wife, Sarah, plantation until my two sons come of age; to 3 children, John, infant; Robert, infant; Mary; Mary is under 18. Executors, Alex. St. Clair and Jacob Kinney. Teste: John McDowell, Mary Robertson, Morris Austin. Proved, January Court, 1794, by McDowell and Austin. Executors qualify.

Page 92.—22d January, 1794. John Tate's bond as Sheriff.

Page 95.—26th January, 1792. Robert Reed's will—To son, Alexander, $1; to daughter, Jean Hall, $1; to the 3 boys, the land they bought from Jno. Poage, i. e., Robert, John, Thomas; to son, Robert; to son, John, land adjoining Andrew Jameson; to son, Thomas, to keep his mother and the rest of the girls; to daughter, Elizabeth. Executors, sons Robert and John. Teste: Samuel Somervil, John Walker, Wm. Johnson. Proved, 18th February, 1794, by all the witnesses.

Page 97.—28th September, 1790. Power of attorney by John Gardner, executor of John Francis, to John Hogshead to sell a tract on Middle River, 200 acres.

Page 97.—Appraisement of David Bell's estate by Andrew Anderson, Thomas Poage, Thos. Patterson, James Crawford, taken 30th March, 1780—Note on Thomas Oliver, insolvent, went a soldier, never returned.

Page 101.—3d April, 1780. Above estate sold at vendue.

Page 105.—9th April, 1794. Archibald Hamilton's estate appraised.

Page 105.—11th March, 1794. John Harrison's estate appraised by Benj. Fausset (Fansset), Benj. Talman, Jno. Bright, Geo. Henton.

Page 106.—John Crawford's estate in account with Rachel Poage, late Rachel Crawford, executrix—Balance of a bond due James Crawford, executor of Elizabeth Crawford.

Page 107.—Hugh Green's estate in account with Wm. Wilson and Robert Reed, executors.

Page 108.—Jean McCombe's estate in account with James Young, executor.

Page 110.—Andrew McComb's estate in account with James Young and Ro. Curry, executors.

Page 111.—John Boyd's estate appraisement, taken 29th March, 1794, by Jno. Purris, James Henry, George Campbell.

Page 112.—25th April, 1786. David Caile's will, Sr., farmer—To wife, Alberdina; to sons, Peter, David, Jacob, John, William, each 1 shilling; to daughters, Elizabeth Bryan, Mary Branson, Christiana Ford, Keziah Handley. Executors, wife Alberdina and son Jacob. Teste: James Peerey, Borvell Pulliam, Wm. Mitchell. Proved, 17th July, 1787, by James Peery, and on 17th June, 1794, by Mitchell.

Page 114.—27th August, 1792. William Anderson's will—To wife, Elizabeth; to son, John, tract whereon James Black lives, 244 acres; to son, George, tract known as Burnt Cabbin whereon George now lives, adjoining John, Robert, and Jacob Baylor; to son, Robert, 149 acres whereon Ro. now lives; to son, Alexander, home plantation, 290 acres; to sons-in-law and their wives, viz: James Clendenning and wife Margaret, Wm. Skillings and wife Mary, James Grigsby and wife Rebecca, Samuel Anderson and wife Elizabeth; to daughter, Jean Anderson. Executors, son John and David McNare. Teste: Edward Breadin, Sr. and Jr.; George Breaden. Proved, June Court, 1794, by all the witnesses.

Page 117.—7th January, 1794. David Caldwell's will—To sister Mary; to brothers, William and Robert. Executors, Capt. Robt. Thompson and Patterson Thompson. Teste: James Steele, Martha and Agnes Thompson. Proved, June Court, 1794, by Martha and Agnes Thompson. Patterson Thompson refuses to execute. The other executor qualifies.

Page 118.—John Harrison's estate in account with Robert Harrison, surviving executor.

Page 120.—2d October, 1780. Michael Coiner's will, soldier under Major Posey—To wife, Margaret; to daughter, Margaret Counner, remainder of pay for services in present war. Executors, wife Margaret and Robert Scott. Teste: Walter Davis, Francis Best, Jas. Davis, Chas. Doneley. Should daughter Margaret die before coming of age or before marriage, her estate to be divided between John and Wm. Griffin, my stepsons. Proved, October Court, 1792, by Walter Davis. Scott refuses to execute, and 15th July, 1794, proved by James Davis.

Page 121.—Auleric Fulwider, administrator to estate of Jacob Fulwider, deceased.

Page 122.—13th February, 1790. John Burnside's will—To wife Martha; to daughter, Frances; to 3 grandchildren, Polly, Margaret Summers, Burnside Stuart; to child my daughter is now with; to Francis Marrah, $1; to nephew, Jno. Burnside, $1; to granddaughter, Margaret; to

Jennet Treasure; to Peations Ritchey. Executors, wife Martha and John Mills. Teste: Wm. Willson, John Campbell, J. Hooks. Codicil, 17th April, 1793. To daughter, Frances Stuart. Teste: Willson and Campbell as above. Proved, September Court, 1794, by Willson, Campbell, and George Hooks. John Mills qualifies.

Page 124.—20th January, 1794. Martha Burnside's will—Widow of John Burnside; to nephew, John Mills; to Jennett Frazer; to Ann Henderson; "If daughter Frances should marry again and have children, then to such children, but if not, then to Frances' present children, viz: Polly, Sommorrison (Samuel Morrison) Burnside, and Margaret. Executors, John Mills and John Campbell. Teste: H. King, Joseph Peck, Geo. Hook. Proved, September Court, 1794, by Henry King and Joseph Peck. Executors qualify.

Page 126.—17th May, 1794. Robert Stephen's will—To son, John; son, James; daughter, Isabella; son, Robert; daughter, Mary (infant); daughter, Nancy (infant); Stephen; to son, William (infant); to wife, Agness. Youngest children are William, Mary, and Nancy. Executors, James Crawford, Robert Craig. Teste: James Patterson, George Craig, John Clemons. Proved, October Court, 1794, by George Craig, John Clemans. Robert Craig qualified.

Page 128.—20th October, 1794. Receipt by Richard Mathews to Andrew Nickle for pay of a bond.

Page 128.—1st November, 1794. Bond by Andrew Scott, Sr., to Andrew Scott, Jr.—In consideration that senior has taken junior to live with him and natural affection agrees to convey 240 acres. Teste: John, Andrew, Thomas Scott.

Page 129.—5th November, 1794. John Lowry's estate appraised by Jno. Erwin, Jno. Dennison, Jno. Gamble.

Page 131.—25th November, 1794. Above estate sold to, viz: Joseph Lowry, Mary Lowry, Christly Nave, Malven Lowrey.

Page 132.—2d December, 1794. Robert Stephen's estate appraised by Geo. Craig, James and Wm. Patterson—Account vs. his son James Stephen; Geo. Craig, son to the Rev. John Craig, by assumpsit.

Page 133.—6th November, 1794. David Caldwell's estate appraised by James Frazer, Jas. Steele, Ben Stuart.

Page 134.—6th November, 1794. Jacob Barrier's estate appraised by Robert Porterfield, Jas. Kerr, James Kennerley, Geo. Craig, Valentine Shirly.

Page 137.—2d June, 1789. Robert Christian's will—To son, John, plantation he lives on; to son, Robert, home plantation; to granddaughter, Isabellay Christian, daughter to John; to son, Jacob, in case he is living; to daughter, Mary Patterson, and her daughter, Ezabellew; to daughter, Margaret Anderson; to granddaughter, Isabella Bratton; to daughter-in-law, Rachel Christian. Executors, John and Robert. Teste: Patrick, William, and G. Christian, Jr. Proved, 16th December, 1794, by Patrick and Gilbert Christian. Executors qualify.

Page 140.—17th December, 1794. Sampson Mathews' bond as contractor on Rockfish Road.

Page 141.—John George Weaver's estate in account with John and Christian weaver, administrators.

Page 142.—20th January, 1795. John Tate's bond as Sheriff.

Page 145.—8th January, 1794. Anne Braford's (Bradford) will—To daughter, Elizabeth; to granddaughter, Elizabeth Christian; to daughter, Rachel; to daughter, Mary; to daughter, Anne; to granddaughter, Mary Braford, daughter to John Braford; to granddaughter, Anne Bradford, daughter to Samuel Bradford. Executors, Patrick Christian. Teste: John Christian, Cornelius Ruddle, Jacob Vanlear. Proved, 20th January, 1795, by Christian and Ruddle. Executor qualifies.

Page 146.—4th February, 1791. William Scott's will—Aged about 70 years; to son, Robert, to minten Saley as long as she lives; to doughter, Saley, the wan halif of my house hold furniture; to sons, William, James, John; to daughter, Fany; to son, Robert, whole of estate of sister Sarah Hutchingson. Executor, Walter Davis. Teste: William Davis, David Caldwell, Jno. Davis. Proved, 20th January, 1795, by William and John Davis.

Page 147.—28th July, 1794. Thomas Connely's will—To wife, Margaret; to 3 sons, Thomas, Alexander, Robert; to each of my daughters, viz: Martha, Mary, Elizabeth, Barbara, Jean, Isable; to son, Arthur, 200 acres in Caintucky; to son, Thomas, 240 acres in Caintucky; to son, Alexander, 200 acres in Caintucky; to son, Robert, 200 acres in Caintucky. Executors, wife Margaret and son Thomas. Teste: John Campbell, John Connely, John Hooke. Proved, 20th January, 1795 (presented by Thomas Connely, surviving executor) by Connely and Hooke. Thomas qualifies.

Page 148.—27th June, 1782. Robert Armstrong's will, cloathier—To wife, Elizabeth; to son, Samuel, executor; to daughter, Mary Armstrong, unmarried; to daughter, Nancy Armstrong; to daughter, Gean Shields. Teste: Alex. Long, Wm. Davitt. Proved, 20th September, 1788, by Long. And on 17th ———, 1792, it appears to Court that William Davit resides in State of South Carolina. On motion of Robert Stuart, commission awarded; addresses to John Henderson and John Blaingame, presiding judge of the Court of Union County. Executed 18th November, 1793, before John Henderson and Jno. Blasingame, and fully proved and recorded December Court, 1793.

Page 152.—15th March, 1794. Thomas Poage, Jr.'s, estate appraised in Charlotte County by Richard Ganes, Jr., Wm. Penticost, Thos. Rice; 16th June, 1794, appraised in Rockbridge County by William Graham, William McKee, William Lyle.

Page 155.—13th September, 1790. John Brooks' will—To wife, Martha, £20 a year to be paid by Samuel Brooks; to daughter, Elizabeth; to son, John (when he demands it); to son, Giles; to son, William; to son, Jonathan; to daughter, Sarah; to son-in-law, William Christian; to Samuel, executor, all lands except 3 poles square where there are three walnut trees grow out of one Root towards Ruddle where I desire to be buried and any friend that chooses. Teste: Daniel Rea, William Davis, Andrew Hunter, Jno. Davis. Proved, April Court, 1795, by William Davis and Hunter. Executor qualifies.

Page 157.—22d January, 1795. William Hamilton's will—To wife, Patience, plantation on Lewis Creek between Alex. Nelson's and James Johnson's; to sons, John and Hugh; wife and all children; to each of daughters; to youngest son, Andrew, home plantation; Charles Baskin to make John

Johnson deed to lot in Staunton. Executors, brother John Hamilton and Charles Baskin. Teste: Robert Graham, James Frazer, Mary Baskin. Proved, April Court, 1795, by all witnesses. Executors qualify.

Page 159.—7th March, 1795. George Hansel's estate appraised by John Kirk, James Elliott, William Sterrett; 10th March, 1795, sale of above at vendue to, viz:

Page 160.—To Miss Hansel, Thomas Tumelson, Jacob Polis, Geo. Phifer, John Broker.

Page 162.—20th August, 1789. Valentine Fauber's will, farmer—To son, John, home plantation, 180 acres, joining Wm. Kennerley, T. Dock; to other children, to wit: Eldest son Christian, son Valentine, son Jacob, son. Peter, daughter Susannah Sieg, daughter Magdalena Weitzel. Executor, son John. Teste: Evan Jones, Jacob Hoffer, Paul Seig, Jacob Stiegel. Proved, April Court, 1795, by Jones and Hoffer.

Page 164.—22d July, 1794. Thomas Patterson's estate appraised by Andrew Anderson, Robert Kinney, William and Jno. Crawford.

Page 165.—Agness Meeck's estate appraisement taken 8th October, 1794, by James Peery, James Berry, Wm. Armstrong.

Page 167.—26th January, 1795. James Brand's will, Sr.—To wife, Ann, home plantation on South River bounded by Gabriel Jones, Jacob Bear, 200 acres; to son, James; to son, George; to son, David; to sons, John and Thomas, lands in Kentucky; to son, Richard Brand, my phisical books; to daughter, Sarah Breize; daughter, Margaret. Executors, wife Ann and son James. Teste: Joseph Bell, George Andrews, Elizabeth Andrews. Proved, 16th June, 1795, by George and Elizabeth Andrews.

Page 169.—12th April, 1794. James McCune's will—To eldest sister, Rachel Bell; to sister, Anne; to eldest brother, John McCune; to brother, Samuel; to brother, Wm. McCune; to brother, Archibald; to sister's daughter, Mary Beele; to brother William's son, James A. McCune, tract on Tennessee River; to sister Elizabeth's son, Alexander M. Henry, tract on Tennessee River. Executors, brothers Samuel and Archibald. Teste: John Guthray, David McClure, John Trimble. Proved, 16th June, 1795, by Guthrey and McClure. Executor qualified.

Page 170.—6th April, 1795. John Black's will—To dear and tender daughter, Margaret Black; to brother, Joseph Black. Executors, John McCutchen, Joseph Black. Teste: John Valiaub (Vahaub), James Berry, Hannah McCutchen. Proved, 16th June, 1795, by John Vachub and Joseph Black. Executors qualify.

Page 171.—6th September, 1794. Alexander Gibson's will—To wife, Mary; to children, viz: Elizabeth, Christian, Mary Mowrey, Margaret; to grandson, Daniel Gibson, who is to make deed to Daniel McFarling for his tract on Christian's Creek; to John McFarling; to grandson Edward Atkins; to granddaughter, Sarah Allen (I believe is her name, but Mrs. Haladay knows her); to granddaughter, Ann McFarling; to granddaughter, Elizabeth Congo (Cargo?); to grandson, Samuel Cargo; to Daniel McFarling. Executors, Robert Porterfield, Henry Mowrey. Teste: Jas. Hill, Daniel McFarland, Christian Gibson. Proved, 16th June, 1795, by James Hill, Daniel McFarlin. Executors refuse to execute, widow also. Administration granted Alexander Gibson, son to decedent.

Page 174.—9th June, 1795. John Brooks' estate appraised by Walter Davis, David Henderson, James Best.

Page 176.—19th August, 1790. Elizabeth Armstrong's will—To daughter, Mary Armstrong, 30 acres left testatrix by her son Samuel. Executrix, said daughter Mary. Teste: Alex. Long, Sarah Brand, John Shields. Proved, July Court, 1795, by Alex. Long, and ——— Breeze, late Brand.

Page 176.—14th February, 1795. Samuel Crawford's will—To wife, Elizabeth, until son comes of age; to son, William; brother James Crawford empowered to sell a tract in Cumberland granted to John Sawyers by Wm. Griffith and assigned to me. Executors to sell a lot in town of Nashville in Cumberland. Executors, Wm. McPheeters, Jno. Crawford, wife Elizabeth. Teste: Jno. Young, Robert Wallace, Daniel Friel. Proved, July Court, 1795, by all witnesses. All executors qualify.

Page 178.—15th July, 1782. Alexander Gibson's will—Executor, son Alexander; to wife, Mary, to be maintained by son Alexander; to daughter, Christian, unmarried; to daughter, Mary, unmarried; to daughter, Margaret, unmarried; to grandson, Daniel Gibson; to grandchildren, Elenor McFarland, Daniel McFarland, John McFarland, Ann McFarland; to grandchildren, Isabella, Alexander, James, and Mary McFarland. Teste: John Elliot, Elizabeth Elliot, Elizabeth Gibson. Proved, July Court, 1795 (purporting to be a former will), by John and Elizabeth Elliott and recorded on motion of Alex. Gibson, Jr.

Page 179.—25th August, 1790. John Caldwell's will, planter—To son, James; to daughters, Sarah, Mary, Fenny, Annas; to wife, Jane; to sons, John, Thomas, Samuel. Executors, wife Jane and son John. Teste: Abraham Larew, Peter and Elizabeth Larew. Proved, July Court, 1795, by Abraham and Peter. Presented in court by Jane.

Page 180.—27th September, 1794. John Faries' estate appraised by Joseph and James Waddell, Wm. King.

Page 181.—12th March, 1793. William Lockridge's will—To wife, Agness; to son-in-law, John Eakin; to daughter, Elizabeth Eakin; to sons, 71—Augusta Records ffiB.U(laRecorded(Goflg7z, 2405 William, John; to daughter, Eleanor Cunningham; to William Lockridge, son of John Lockridge; to son, Samuel, home plantation. Teste: John Montgomery, Wm. Youel, James Guy, Samuel Neil. Proved, September Court, 1795, by the affirmation of John Montgomery and William Youell. Samuel Lockridge qualifies.

Page 182.—John Burnside's estate appraisement taken 10th October, 1794, by Alex. Robertson, John Gamble, A. Anderson.

Page 188.—14th October, 1794. Vendue bill of John and Martha Burnsides' estates—Recorded, September Court, 1795, sold to, viz: Thos. Dickon, Michael Acre, James Hodgson, Jno. Kinode, Peter Paul, Negro Jeam, Rose Kether.

Page 193.—11th October, 1794. Ann Henderson deposes that she heard John and Martha Burnside give to their granddaughter, Peggy Stuart, certain articles, and also to Patience Richey, also that certain bags belonged to Gemm, a negro, also a cow to Jennet Frazer. Elizabeth Blakely deposes ditto, 11th October, 1794.

Page 194.—Frances Stuart deposes ditto, that Samuel Burnside Mills, son to John Mills, was to have a colt.

Page 195.—14th February, 1795. James Bell's will—To wife, Martha; to sons, James and William, tract purchased of James Trimble on Middle River; to Frances Bell; to son, Robert; to sons, John and Samuel Bell, home plantation; to eldest daughter, Agnes, 1,000 acres in Kentucky; to daughter, Rachel, 1,000 acres in Kentucky; to son, Robert, 500 acres in Kentucky; to son, Francis, 1,000 acres in Kentucky; to daughter, Mary An, 1,000 acres in Kentucky. Executors, wife Martha, brother William Bell, brother John Kirk. Teste: William Sterrett, Francis Gardiner, Jas. Brown. Proved, October Court, 1795, by the witnesses. Widow qualifies.

Page 197.—23d September, 1795. Samuel Crawford's estate appraised by Wm. Moffett, Benj. Brown, Samuel Bell.

Page 198.—13th March, 1795. Robert McKittrick's will, Sr.—To son, Robert, the gap plantation in Gemonse's Gap; to sons, John, William, James; to son-in-law, William Metaire; to son-in-law, John Wright; to son-in-law, John Montgomery; to son-in-law, James Guye; to. granddaughter, Jenny Guy; to daughters, Sarah, Isbell, Margaret. Executors, sons Robert and John. Teste: John Hutcheson, Moses McCleur, Wm. Schoolar. Recorded in Harrison County, Kentucky, 10th July, 1795 (W. Moore, C. H. C.), and at December Court, 1795, in Augusta.

Page 199.—Joseph Wright's estate in account with Thos. Dixon and Elizabeth Wright.

Page 201.—22d August, 1794. John King's will—To wife, Margaret; five daughters and two sons (Robert and John) are married; to sons, Samuel and James. Executors, sons-in-law James Lard, Jno. Denison. Teste: Jno. Gibson, Samuel Gibson, Catren Cloverfield. Proved, October Court, 1795, by all witnesses.

Page 202.—Michael Ott, guardian of Margaret Fulwider, orphan of Jacob Fulwider.

Page 203.—14th October, 1793. William Vasteen's estate appraised by A. McClenachan, Joshua Parry, Alex. Wasan.

Page 204.—Above estate in account with Joseph Mathews.

Page 205.—Ann Brawford's estate appraisement by Samuel Hunter, Jas. Shields.

Page 206.—19th May, 1795. Thomas Dixon's bond of Counter security as administrator (with Elizabeth Wright) of Joseph Wright.

Page 207.—James Steele's settlement as Sheriff, depositum of 1790.

Page 208.—Joseph Bell's ditto, depositum of 1791. Paid Robert Douthat for a stove for Courthouse.

Page 209.—John Tate's settlement as Sheriff, depositum of 1793.

Page 210.—19th January, 1796. Alex. St. Clair's bond as Sheriff.

Page 213.—28th June, 1790. Mathew Edmiston's will, farmer—To son, James; to son, William; to son, David; to grandson, Mathew Kirk; to daughter, Mary Kirk; to granddaughter, Margaret Jones; to grandson, Matha Edmonson, Maagill; to daughter, Ann Jones; to daughter, Jean Magill. Executors, sons James and William Edmiston. Teste: David McNair, John Kirk, Jean Kirk. Proved, January Court, 1796, by McNair and Jno. Kirk.

Page 215.—25th September, 179—. Samuel Steele's will—To wife, Margaret; to daughter, Mary; to grandson, Samuel Steele Cunningham, infant; to daughters, Jenny, Kitty, Nancy; to grandson, Samuel Steele

Rankin, infant; to son, William, home plantation. Executors, wife Margaret, son William. Teste: John Cungham, David Cuningham, Robt. Hanna. Proved, 16th February, 1796, by the Cunninghams. William Steele qualified.

Page 216.—25th February, 1796. John Alexander's estate appraised by Samuel Pilson, James Frazer, Jno. Hamilton, Mathew Smith.

Page 218.—1st July, 1795. John Black's estate appraised by James Peerey, Joans Henderson, Alex. Craig, Alex. Stuart.

Page 219.—14th April, 1796. James Brown's estate appraised by John Young, William Bell, Augustine Argenbright.

Page 220.—13th October, 1795. Nathaniel Steele's will—To wife, Rosannah; to son, Nathaniel, all lands in Augusta County; to grandson, Moses McClure, son of David; to grandson, Moses McClure, son of Halberd; to grandson, Nathaniel Blackburn; to daughter, Martha Cooper, and her daughter, Elizabeth Cooper; to daughter, Rosannah; to grandson, Nathaniel McClure, son of Samuel. Executors, wife Rosannah, son Nathaniel, and son-in-law Robert Cooper. Teste: John and Samuel Steele, Jno. Fulton. Proved, 21st June, 1796, by Fulton and Samuel Steel. Executors qualified except Rosannah, and leave reserved for her.

Page 221.—22d February, 1793. Elijah McClenachan's will—To wife, Margaret, for her use and two youngest daughters till they marry, also the weaver shop; to son, Elijah; to daughters, Elizabeth and Letucann; son Elijah to take care of apprentice John Foster. Teste: David Williams, Alex. Buchanan, David Buchanan.

Page 223.—2d May, 1794. Codicil to above—To daughter, Elizabeth, now married to Jno. Tate; to wife, Margaret; to son, Elijah; to daughter, Letucann; to daughter, Margaret Mays. Executor, son Elijah. Teste: Alex. Buchanan, David, and Jean Buchanan. Proved, June Court, 1796, by David and Alex. Buchanan. Elijah qualifies.

Page 224.—20th April, 1796. William McKemey's will, Sr., farmer—To wife, Isabella; to son, John; to son, William, infant; to son, James, infant; to daughter, Peggy McKemey; to daughter, Polly McKemey; to daughters, Nancy McKemey, ———— McKemey, Ellenor McKemey, Isabella McKemey, Elizabeth McKemey. Executors, Isabella McKemey, son John and brother James McKemey. Teste: Christopher Perey, Joseph Waddell, Nancy McKemey, John McKemy. (No certificate of probate.)

Page 225.—25th November, 1795. William Hamilton's estate appraised by James Frazer, Jas. Johnston, Jos. Bell.

Page 228.—4th February, 1796. James Bell's estate appraised by Daniel Friel, Francis Gardner, Jas. Cunningham, Robert Renick.

Page 230.—4th May, 1796. Bill of sale of negro girl by Sampson Mathews to Jacob Kinney. Teste: A. Humphreys, Jno. Dickenson, R. Gratton.

Page 231.—George Pierson's estate in account with James Anderson, administrator.

Page 232.—Alex. McConnell's estate in account with James Ramsey, and Benjamin Brown—Paid Alex. Dodds.

Page 233.—15th June, 1796. John Carlile's will—Negro Ned set free; to wife, Margaret; to Robert Carlile, son of Robert Carlile, of the Bullpasture; to John and William Carlile, sons of brother James Carlile. Executors, Rev. John Montgomery, and Robert Carlile, son of Robert of B. P. Teste: Thomas Layton, John Fernnill, Nelly King. Proved, July Court, 1796, by Thos. Clayton and John Fennell. Executors qualify.

Page 234.—18th December, 1795. William Mitchell's estate appraised by James Moffett, Jacob Bowngarner, Patrick Hays.

Page 236.—Mathew Willson, administrator to the legatees of Col. John Wilson, deceased, estate Dr.—A statement of the whole; 1773, paid, 18th April, to Patrick Crawford, legatee; 1772, paid, 14th December, to James Ewing, legatee; 1774, paid, 20th April, to Wm. McKennan, legatee.

Page 237.—29th June, 1796. Elijah McClenachan's estate appraised by David Buchanan, John Hamilton, Thos. Marshall.

Page 238.—15th October, 1790. Edward Hall's will—To wife, Eleanor; to son, Alexander; to son, Benjamin; to children, viz: Isaac Hall, Sarah Fulton, Thomas Hall, Elizabeth Fulton, already provided for; to son, John. Executors, friends Benj. Stuart, Andrew Fulton, Archibald Stuart. Teste: Archibald Stuart, Wm. Kenedy, Alex. Stewart, Eleanor Stuart, Elizabeth Stuart. Proved, 20th September, 1796, by Alex. Stuart and Wm. Kennedy.

Page 240.—21st July, 1796. Moses Hays' will—To wife, Sarah, and her children, proceeds of sale of land in Harrison County, also of tract on mountain called the timber land; to daughter, Elizabeth Luce; to daughter, Hannah Halsey; to son, James Hayes; to daughter, Mary Stockdale; to son, Isaac; to son, Richard; to son, Winsted; to son, William. Executors, William McPheeters and John Tate. Teste: George Berry, Wm. (mark) McKane, Patrick Keenan. Proved, 20th September, 1796, by Berry and Kenan. Tate refuses to execute, also McPheeters. Sarah refuses to administrate. Administration granted John Tate, Jacob Kinney.

Page 241.—26th February, 1795. George Hood's estate sold at vendue.

Page 243.—28th June, 1796. William Armstrong's will—To wife, Elizabeth; to daughter, Elizabeth Armstrong; executor, John Christian. Teste: Thos. Frazer, William Blackwood. Proved, 18th October, 1796, by the witnesses. Executors personally refused to execute. Administration granted widow Elizabeth.

Page 244.—3d February, 1795. James Ewing's will—To wife, Martha, and children; after the two boys have received their part; to son, James, lands conveyed by William Scott adjoining Philip Osinger and James Hathorn, also 200 acres joining James Hathorn and Mathew Wilson in Beverley Manor; to son, Joseph, tract purchased of William Deen; to daughter, Martha; to daughter, Nancy Ewing. Executors, wife Martha, John Wilson, Mathew Willson, Jr. Teste: Robert Hanna, John McCutchen, Wm. Willson. Proved, 18th October, 1796, by the witnesses. Mathew Willson refuses in writing, others personally refused. Administration granted Martha Ewing, John Wellson, James Ewing.

Page 247.—11th August, 1796. George Lewis' will—To wife, Mary; to son, James; to daughter, Rebecka; to grandson, George Dadridge. Executor, James Lues. Teste: Alex. Reed, John Reed. Proved, 18th October, 1796, by the witness. Executor qualified.

Page 248.—Dr. the estate of John Stuart in account with executors—One spinning wheel, property of Mary Stuart, sister to deceased. Note on Thomas Gennet proved insolvent.

Page 252.—14th June, 1796. Samuel Blackburn makes oath that his removal into State of Virginia was not made with purpose of evading the law for preventing importation of slaves, nor has he brought any slaves with intention of selling them, nor has any of the slaves been imported from Africa since 1st November, 1778. (Follow) names of slaves.

Page 253.—5th November, 1796. John Gardiner's will—To John Gardiner, executor, son; to wife, Margaret; to four sons, viz: John Gardiner, James, Thomas, and William. Teste: Jacob van Fossen, Richard Trotter. Proved, 20th December, 1796, by the witnesses. Executor qualified.

Page 254.—25th October, 1796. George Lewis' estate appraised by John Poage, Marcus Cupp, Ludwig Mowry, Charles Yorehous.

Page 255.—18th April, 1796. Thomas Frame's will—To wife, Jane, tract purchased of Samuel McKee; to son, Samuel; to grandson, John Craig Frame, infant; to son, Samuel's next oldest son or daughter (after Jno. C., *supra*). Executors, wife Jane and son Samuel. Teste: D. Stephenson, James Hodgson, Thos. Connelly. Codicil, 8th September, 1796. To son, Samuel; to grandson, John Craig Frame; to Augusta Church. Teste: William Wilson, Samuel Steele, Joseph Peck. Proved, 20th December, 1790, by Connelly and Irwin. Codicil by Steele and Peck. Executors qualified.

Page 257.—19th October, 1796. John King's estate appraised; 16th January, 1797, John King's estate appraised by James Young, John Dickey, John Bell.

Page 260.—James Ewing's appraisement taken 17th November, 1796, by John Cunningham, David Cunningham, Wm. McCutchan.

Page 262.—Dr. estate of Archibald Rhea in account with Wm. Rhea, guardian—1792, paid Wm. Rhea; 1791, paid Hugh Rhea, Jno. Rhea; by rent of the farm, 1778, 1779, to Thomas Caldwell.

Page 263.—Above estate in account with Archibald Rhea, executor—1778, Shingles and nails to repair house; 1783, board and schooling Jno. Rhea 1 year.

Page 265.—27th December, 1796. Thomas Frame's estate appraised by Robert Kinney, John Campbell, Wm. Robertson.

Page 266.—18th July, 1797. Alex. St. Clair's bond as Sheriff.

Page 268.—16th January, 1797. John Shiver's (Shiry) to George Phifer—George has promised to support John for life and John conveys to George all interest in an agreement between sons Daniel and Martin Shirer, dated 7th May, 1787, by which they bind themselves to pay to John £130. Proved, February Court, 1797, by Michael Shirey and Peter Paul.

Page 269.—Nathaniel Steel's appraisement taken 30th June, 1796, by Robt. Harris, Robt. Cooper, Samuel Carson—John Alphin's bond; David Isaac's account.

Page 272.—Inventory of Francis Erwin, deceased, at time of death of his son John entitled by his father's will to a portion

Page 274.—20th June, 1797. John Erwin, Jr.'s, estate appraised by David and John Bell, John Hogset.

Page 274.—21st June, 1786. Elizabeth (mark) Caldwell's will, aged about sixty-seven years—To 3 daughters, Margrit and Catrin Caldwell, and Elibeth Sayers. Executor, John Caldwell. Teste: Walter Davis, Francis Long, Wm. Caldwell. Proved, 20th June, 1797, by Davis and

Caldwell. Executor is dead. Administration granted widow Catherine Caldwell, widow of said executor.

Page 275.—9th January, 1797. William (mark) Creaber's (?) will—To wife, Anna Maria; to eldest son, Philip, who is to pay to each of his brethren. Executors, wife Anna Maria and son Philip. Teste: Paul and Solomon Hinkle and Peter Eagle. Proved, 20th June, 1797, by Paul Hinkle and Eagle.

Page 276.—William McKemey's estate appraised 6th September, 1796, by Jno. Nicoll. John Woodell, Chas. Hogshead.

Page 278.—26th March, 1790. William Palmer's will—To sons, Robert, William, executors; to daughters, Mary, executrix, Ann, Martha; to son-in-law, James Spence. Teste: Samuel Henry, Wm. Spence, Mary (mark) Dunlap. Proved, 18th July, 1797, by Henry and Spence.

Page 279.—28th February, 1797. Edward Goeland Terrel's nuncupative will, made at home of Valentine Miller, in Staunton, where he had boarded three weeks, in presence of James Shepherd and Ann Hunter, wife of Nat Hunter; left everything to Mrs. Sibil Miller, wife of Valentine Miller, and died 28th February, 1797, at 5 o'clock p. m. Proved, 18th July, 1797. Administration granted Valentine Miller.

Page 280.—24th July, 1797. David Fulton's will—To brother, Thomas Fulton, executor; to sister, Jean. Teste: John McCarty, Robert and John Fulton. Proved, 19th September, 1797, by the Fultons. Executor Thomas qualifies.

Page 281.—8th December, 1796. William Moore's will—To wife, Mary Ann; to son, John; to son, Robert; to son, James, infant. Executors, wife Mary Ann, James Henry. Teste: Robert McCormick, Samuel Carson, Thos. Beard. Proved, 19th September, 1797, by Ro. McCormick, Samuel Carson, Thos. Beard. Executors qualify.

Page 283.—5th July, 1797. John Price's will, of Staunton, cabinet maker—To wife, Judith; to apprentice, James Wilson, cabinet maker's tools. Executors, wife Judith and Robert Douthat. Teste: Chesley Kinney, Henry Mowrey, W. Chambers, Richard S. Ellis. Proved, 19th September, 1797, by Mowrey and Ellis. Judith qualifies.

Page 284.—11th February, 1797. John Bell's will, of South River—To brothers Thomas and Joseph, lands on South River joining Gabriel Alexander; to sister, Sarah Bell; to brother James Bell's son, Samuel, and brother William's two sons, John and Stephenson Bell, lands in Kentucky; to brother, Joseph. Executors, brothers Thomas and Joseph. Teste: Gabriel Alexander, Samuel Long. Proved, 19th September, 1797. Joseph qualifies.

Page 286.—15th July, 1796. Michael (mark) Coiner's will—To wife, Margaret, house to be built by son Christian. Division among sons, except Frederick (lunatick). To sons, George, Conrad, George Michael, Gasper, John, Martin, Jacob, Christian, Philip; to daughters, Elizabeth Palsley, Mary Edebaugh, Cathrine Slagle. Executors, sons George and Kasper. Teste: Robt. Porterfield, Benj. Kennerley, John Conner. Proved, 20th June, 1797 (having been heretofore proved by witnesses) recorded, to which Christian Balsley appeals. At a District Court 7th September, 1797, affirmed except to codicil, which is rejected. And now County Court, 19th September, 1797, Gasper Coiner qualifies. George refuses.

Page 289.—15th June, 1797. John Hodge's will—To wife, Jane, and children; to sons, James and William; to daughter, Sarah Hodge; to daughter, Margaret; to son, Andrew; son, John H. Hodge; to each of daughters, Martha, and Elizabeth Mucklewains; to daughter, Jane Hodge| Executors, wife Jane, brother James Hodge, William Youll. Teste: Thomas Hughart, Samuel Lockridge, Jno. Montgomery. Proved, 19th September, 1797, by Hughart and Lockridge. Jane and James qualified.

Page 291.—25th January, 1795. John Caldwell's will—To wife, Catherine, and children. Teste: Wm. Caldwell, Bishop Humphreys. Proved, 17th October, 1797.

Page 292.—15th October, 1797. David Fulton's estate appraised by John McCarty, Alex. Brownlee, John Fulton.

Page 293.—16th October, 1797. Elizabeth Caldwell's estate appraised by Samuel Brooks.

Page 294.—16th January, 1798. David Stephenson's bond as Sheriff.

Page 296.—8th January, 1798. Michael Coyner's estate appraised.

Page 298.—30th June, 1797. John Reburn's will—To daughters, Isabella, Sarah, Margaret; to son, Robert, and his son, which has his leg cut off; to daughter Isabella's oldest son; to daughter Sarah's oldest son; to daughter Margaret's oldest son; to Robert Campbell, executor, ½ of movable property; to John Danaghe, executor, ½ of movable property. Teste: Robert Campbell, Jno. Danaghe, Margaret (mark) Donaghe. Proved, 20th February, 1798, by John Danaghe (who relinquished rights as legatee), and Margaret R. Campbell qualified.

Page 300.—25th January, 1798. James Crawford's will—To wife, Mary, land joining John Poage, Samuel Bell, George Poff, Wm. Craig for life, then to youngest son, John Crawford; to 3 sons, George, James, William; to 3 sons, George, James, William, John, lands in Kentucky; to daughters, Sarah and Elizabeth Crawford. Executors, brother William and brother-in-law Wm. Robertson. Teste: Robert Craig, George Crawford, Robert Crawford. Proved, 21st February, 1798, by George and Robt. Crawford. Executors qualified.

Page 303.—Dr. estate of Robt. Hogshead in account with James Hogshead.

Page 305.—Dr. estate of James Brown in account with David Mathews—Brown was administrator of Mathews and now Brown's administratrix, Jane Brown, settles.

Page 306.—18th November, 1794. Thomas Graham's will—To son, Robert, and all children, viz: John, Thomas, James, Joseph, Alexander, Cateran, Mary. Executors, Alexander Robertson and son Robert Graham Teste: James Young, Hugh Brown, Wm. Young, Jr. Proved, 19th June, 1798, by James Young and Brown. Graham qualifies.

Page 307.—19th June, 1798. James Tate's estate distributed by Benj Stuart and Jno. Tate, executors, to, viz: Wife Sarah, sons John and Isaac, daughters Polly, Patsey, Sally.

Page 308.—19th June, 1798. John and Isaac Tate above, being of age, manumit a slave.

Page 308.—27th March, 1798. John Price's estate appraised by Vincent Tapp, Henry Mowrey, Joseph Dickey.

Page 310.—John Murphy, Dr., to William Murphy's estate—Raising and schooling two of William's children, viz: Nancy and John Murphy.

Page 313.—Estate of Thomas Gregg in account with Benj. Smith, executor of Daniel Smith, who was executor of Thos. Gregg—1790, 17th May, paid James Reece (?) as legatee, ditto Samuel Redman, ditto Elizabeth Gregg; to recording the inventory in 1773 (1793?).

Page 314.—Hugh Green's estate in account with Wm. Wilson, Robert Reed.

Page 315.—29th May, 1798. Frederick Michael's will—To wife, Elizabeth, to live with son Christian; to six sons, viz: John Michael, Christian, George, Jacob, Frederick, William, 100 acres each; saw mill on John's tract; to daughters. Executors, son John and son-in-law Henry Simman (?). Teste: C. Percy, John Percy. Proved, 18th September, 1798, by the Percys and Jacob Hoffer.

Page 317.—2d April, 1790. Daniel Frieel's will—To wife, Agness, and her children (except John); to sons, John, Maurice (Daniel, William, lands in Kentucky). (George Sisson requested to relinquish bargain to purchase.) William Moffett, Samuel Bell, executors. Teste: Jno. Young, Jas. Cunningham, Robert Wallace. Proved, 16th October, 1798. Executors qualify.

Page 318.—13th January, 1798. John (mark) Davidson's will, plantationer—To son, John (infant); to wife, Sarah; to children, viz: Agnes Daugherty, Elizabeth Tankers (Tankersey), Sarah Davidson, Mary Davidson, Margaret Davidson; to son, Daniel; to granddaughter, Margaret Daugherty. Executors, wife Sarah and son-in-law Obadiah Tankersley. Teste: Robert Shaw, Thomas Boyd, John Hall. Proved, 16th October, 1798, by Shaw and Boyd. Executors qualify.

Page 320.—James Crawford's estate appraisement taken 13th March, 1798, by Jas. Rankin, John Givens, William Craig, George Craig.

Page 325.—John Carlile's (of Calf Pasture) estate appraised by Adam Bratton, Samuel Lockridge, Thos. Phillips—18th August, 1796, vendue bill of above estate dated 15th August, 1796, sold, viz: To Lindsay Marshall, Thos. Layton, Peter Fitch, Leroy Newman, Jacob Acord, Jno. Fennell, Thos. Ricket, Elizabeth Smith.

Page 331.—James Bell's estate appraisement by John Brown, David McNair, Wm. Sterrett. Recorded, 16th October, 1798.

Page 332.—29th October, 1789. Samuel Carlile's estate sold at vendue to, viz: Hugh Morrison, Andrew Jordan.

Page 334.—23d October, 1798. Daniel Friel's estate appraised by Jas. Cunningham, Benjamin and John Brown.

Page 336.—30th June, 1798. Alexander McPheeters' will—Executors, wife (Jane) and son Robert; to wife; to son Alexander, son John, daughter Martha, daughters Jean and Ann, daughter Rebeccah, son Robert, son James. Teste: James McPheeters, John Rab——, Kety (X) Spence. Executors qualified, and proved, 18th December, 1798, by John Rabb and Catherine Spence.

Page 337.—2d December, 1798. Peter Wiseman's (in German) will, farmer—To wife, Elizabeth Margaret. (If before son Peter comes of age.) To children, viz: Lodwick, Ana Mary (wife of Philip Hawn), Susanna, John Goerge, Christena (wife of Jacob Smith), Catherena (wife of George Doll), Mary Eve Weiseman, Margaret, Magdalena, Peter Weiseman. Executors, wife and son Lodwick. Teste: Frederick Henger, George Doll. Proved, 18th December, 1798, by Fred. Hanger and George Dull. Executors qualify.

Page 339.—17th July, 1798. Subscribers form themselves into a fire company—James Edmonson, Wm. Breckinridge, J. Bowyer, Michael Garber, Sr.; Peter Elliott, Joseph Dickey, John Gorden, Robt. McCullock, Geo. Grant McIntosh, John McCausland, Vincent Tapp, Abraham Teebo, Jacob Leas, Philip Hopkins, David Griener, John Moore, John Fackler, Alex. St. Clair, H. Paul, Jacob Swoope, Samuel Clarke, W. Herren, W. Chambers, Geo. Mitchell, Thos. Barry, David Parry, Joseph Cowan, Hamp Keyes, Cornelius Baldwin, Smith Thompson, John Backenstoe, Jno. Wayt, Jno. Johnston, Robt. McDowell, Jno. Wise, James McGongal, Joseph Points, Ro. B. St. Clair, Andrew Haveouf, Jno. McDowell, Jacob Kinney.

Page 340.—William Creever's estate appraised 18th July, 1797, by Augustin Argenbrite, Wm. Handly, James Campbell, and vendue bill, sold to, viz: Jno. Harlowe, Philip Creever, widow Creever, widow Greever, widow Greeber.

Page 342.—John Price's estate to Judith Price, executrix, Dr.

Page 343.—Alex. McPheeters, Sr.'s, estate appraised 15th January, 1799, by Wm. Brown, Samuel Gibson, John Hamilton.

Page 345.—8th September, 1798. Samuel Blackwood's will, of Christian's Creek—To wife, Sarah; to son, Samuel; son, Joseph (infant); to grandson, Samuel McAdan; to daughters, Mary, Florence, Sarah, Genet, Margaret (already provided for). Executors, son Samuel and Jno. Thompson. Teste: Samuel Long, Joseph Bell. Proved, 19th February, 1799. Executors qualify.

Page 347.—22d October, 1793. John (mark) Hogshead's will—To wife, Rebecca; son, William; son, John; daughter, Agness; daughter, Jean; daughter, Mary; daughter, Rebecca; daughter, Martha; son, Gordon. Executors, brother Michael Hogshead and friend James Hogshead. Teste: David Hogsett, Francis Gilkison, Thos. Hogsitt. Proved, 19th February, 1799, by all witnesses. Executors refuse, also widow. Eldest son William is not a resident of Virginia. Administration granted to son John.

Page 348.—19th February, 1799. David Stephenson's bond as Sheriff.

WILL BOOK No. IX.

Page 1.—19th February, 1799. David Stephenson's bond as Sheriff.

Page 4.—21st June, 1799. Adam Bickle's estate appraised by Peter Elliott, David Greiner, James McGonegal.

Page 5.—Samuel Blackwood's estate appraisement by Jno. Christian, Jno. Black, Wm. Shields, recorded 24th June, 1799.

Page 7.—7th October, 1790. Charles Berry's estate appraised by John McKemy, Robert Harris, Jacob Patton.

Page 8.—4th December, 1798. John Louchridge's will—To wife, Anna, and children; to son, James (his schooling); to 3 oldest sons, viz: Andrew, William, John; to daughter, Betsy; to daughter, Sarah; to daughter, Anna. Executors, brother Andrew and James Berry. Teste: James Peery, Samuel Tagart, Jean Shields, Sr.; Mary McKnight, Samuel Black. Proved, 24th June, 1799, by Perry and Tagart. Executors qualify.

Page 10.—28th January, 1799. Charles Depreest's nuncupative will, declared at house of John Trimble, Jr., in presence of John Trimble, Sr., and James (mark) Ross—All estate to sister Polly Trimble, wife of John Trimble, except books to Uncle Walter Trimble. Proved, 24th June, 1799. Administration granted Jno. Trimble, Jr.

Page 11.—Elizabeth Armstrong, administratrix of William Armstrong, deceased, of estate of Samuel Armstrong, deceased, Dr.

Page 12.—5th January, 1799. William Spence's estate appraised by Joseph, William, Jr., and James Bell.

Page 13.—21st March, 1799. Isabell (mark) Robinson, of Jessamine County, Ky., spinster, to brother-in-law, Adin Webb, of same place, house carpenter, power attorney to recover anything coming to Isabell by means of her grandmother, Sarah Leslie; also whatever is coming to her from John Henry, of Rockingham County. Acknowledged before Thos. Bodley at Lexington, Ky.

Page 15.—19th April, 1799. Adin Webb, of Jessamine County, Ky., in right of wife Mary, who was Mary Robertson, a devisee of Sarah Lessley, and as attorney for Isabella (above) conveys to Samuel Lessley all interests of Mary and Sarah. Teste: J. Monroe, Wm. Sterrett, C. Kinney. But above agreement does not affect John Henry, of Rockingham, who married Jane Robertson.

Page 16.—3d March, 1792. John Bosang's estate appraised by A. McClenachan, Michael Fackler, Robert McDowell, Robt. McCullock.

Page 19.—24th June, 1799. Robert Wilson's bond, authorized to solemnize matrimony.

Page 20.—Hugh Green's estate in account with William Wilson (Willson) and Ro. Reed, executors—1779, paid Hugh McCafferty attorney for Mary Gentry; paid Hugh McCafferty, attorney for Jane McCafferty.

Page 20.—26th September, 1781. Archibald Henderson's estate appraised by Hugh Brown, John Hind, James Dickey, James Young.

Page 23.—Daniel Meek, administrator of Agnes Meek, deceased, to the legatees, Dr.

Page 25.—28th October, 1789. Samuel Carlile's estate appraised by John Kinkead, John Peebles, Andrew Lockridge.

Page 28.—2d June, 1799. Frederick Hanger's will—To wife, Eve; to sons, Charles and Peter; to son-in-law, Augustine Argenbright, ½ acre where his smith shop stands; daughter, Eve, wife of Daniel Joseph. Executors, Augustine Argenbright, Peter Ingleman. Teste: John Young, George Kellar, Christian Baylor. Proved, 22d July, 1799, by all witnesses. Argenbright qualifies.

Page 29.—23d November, 1793. Robert Wilson's will, farmer—To wife, Jean; to son, Robert; to son, John; to daughter, Elizabeth; to daughter-in-law, Margaret; daughter, Rachel; son, Thomas, and his son Robert; to daughter-in-law, Elizabeth. Executors, William Brown, Thos. Wilson, my son; John Wilson, son-in-law. Teste: Thomas, Samuel, John Brown. Proved, 22d July, 1799, by Samuel and Jno. Brown. Executors refuse. Administration granted Robert Wilson. Widow is aged, infirm, and incompetent.

Page 30.—4th July, 1799. Gilbert Christian conveys to Wm. Donaldson,

Jno. McClenachan, Thomas Ray (personal property) to indemnify them for becoming his security for personal bounds.

Page 31.—September, 1799. Charles Depriest's estate appraised.

Page 32.—1st February, 1799. William (X) Poage's will—To wife, Sarah; eldest son, Robert (land joining James Henry, John Moore); to son, James; son, William; son, John; to daughter, Elizabeth Poage, 150 acres joining Hugh Beard, Jno. Cunningham, Andrew Purris (youngest daughter Elizabeth); to eldest daughters, Agnes, Sarah, and Isabel Poage. Executors, wife and sons Robert and James. Teste: Robert McCormick, James Henry, Robert Moore. Proved, 23d September, 1799, by Moore and McCormick. Sarah and Robert qualify. James Poage refused to execute.

Page 34.—Frederick Michael's estate appraisement by John Stephenson, James Snap, James Miller. Recorded, 23d September, 1799.

Page 36.—12th October, 1795. Samuel Steele's will—To son, Samuel; son, Robert; son, James; daughter, Mary; daughter, Catherine; daughter, Jenny; daughter, Sally. Executors, sons Samuel, Robert, James. Teste: John Steele, James and John Steele, John Shultz. Proved, 28th October, 1799, by James Steele, and 23d December, 1799, by John Shoultz.

Page 37.—22d May, 1799. Rosanna Rutledge's will—To mother, Sarah; brother, George (executor). Teste: D. Stephenson, Benj. Eagle. Proved, 28th October, 1799, by Stephenson, and 23d December, 1799, by Benjamin Eage.

Page 37.—John Davidson's estate appraisement taken 19th October, 1799, by David Steele, Geo. Campbell, Jno. McFadden.

Page 39.—20th May, 1799. John Wead's bill of sale of all his effects to Martha and Elizabeth Wead. Teste: Andrew (X) and Samuel (X) Weaver.

Page 39.—14th August, 1799. Robert Wilson's estate appraised by William Brown, William Shields, Mathew Thompson.

Page 41.—10th October, 1799. Frederick Hanger's estate appraised by Wm. Peery, Philip Ingleman, Jacob Shyrigh.

Page 42.—24th October, 1799. David Hogshead's will—To daughter, Jane Hogshead; son, David. Teste: David Stephenson, Robt. Gilkison, Francis Gilkison. Proved, 27th January, 1800, by all witnesses. David qualifies.

Page 43.—23d January, 1800. William Guthrey's, of Shenandoah, revocation of power of attorney given 20th March, 1795, to Isaiah Roberts to transact his business in Virginia. William is late of York County, Penna., has now returned to Virginia.

Page 43.—11th November, 1799. Uphemia (X) Hughes' will, of Staunton—To mother, Euphemia Hughes; to Euphemia Hughes Bickle; to nieces, Mary Owens and Margaret Bickle. Executor, Jacob Kinney. Teste: W. Chambers, Wm. Forbes, Vincent Tapp. Proved, 27th January, 1800. Executor qualifies.

Page 45.—Estate of Thomas Adams in account with Wm. A. Fry, executor, Dr.—1788, paid to William Britt.

Page 48.—12th September, 1799. Abner Tuttle conditional bill sale to Wm. Wilson. Teste: George and James Willson.

Page 49.—24th March, 1800. Robert Porterfield's bond as Sheriff.

Page 51.—16th February, 1788. John Gibsan's will—To wife, Mary, and children; to granddaughter, Sarah. Teste: Wm. Willson, Jno. Hamilton, John Thompson. Executors, Samuel and David Gibson, Samuel Casner (Carson?). Proved, 28th April, 1800, by Wilson and Hamilton. Executors qualify.

Page 52.—14th June, 1800. John Mills' will—To wife and children; to son, Robert; to daughter, Elizabeth. Executors, brother-in-law Andrew Allison and John Allison. Teste: Alex. Robertson, H. King, Esther Gamble. Proved, 23d June, 1800, by Robertson and Gamble. Executors qualify.

Page 54.—15th November, 1799. James McClure's estate appraised.

Page 55.—18th November, 1799. James McClure's estate sold at vendue.

Page 57.—David Hogshead's appraisement taken 14th February, 1800, by James Hogshead, James McKemy, Francis Gilkison.

Page 60.—3d May, 1800. Henry Hawk to sons John and Abraham Hawk—Bill of sale to personal property. Teste: John Coalter, Jacob Swallow.

Page 61.—24th May, 1800. John Gibson's estate appraised—English and Portugese gold, 15 oz., 4 drd., 17 grn., at 5/4, £81.15.1; Spanish and French gold, 6 oz., 8 drd., 0 grn., at 5/3, £33.12.0; in silver, 248 dollars and 20 crowns, £81.0.0.

Page 62.—15th October, 1799. Hugh Danaghe to Robert Bailey—Bill sale.

Page 63.—Archibald Henderson's estate in account with Joseph Patterson and John Dickey, executors—Paid John Crawny; paid Elizabeth Henderson, alias Gray.

Page 64.—26th September, 1781. Above estate appraised.

Page 67.—10th April, 1800. Robert Steele, Sr.'s, will—To wife, Mary; daughter, Mary Steele; to grandson John Steele, son of son John, deceased, infant; to son, David; daughters, Aliner Allen, Martha Paxton; to orphans of deceased son William. Executors, son David Steele and Thomas Paxton. Teste: John Tate, Hugh Fulton, Henry Miller. Proved, 28th July, 1800, by Tate and Fulton; on motion of Mary Steele, ordered that David Steele and Thos. Paxton, of Rockbridge, be summoned. They relinquish.

Page 68.—21st July, 1799. Thomas Barry's will, of Staunton, merchant—To John McKim, Jr., and Andrew Barry, all land in trust; to Agness Barry, daughter, infant; to mother, Sarah Barry; sister, Elenor Barry; brother, Andrew Barry. Executors, trustees above. Teste: Wm. S. Moore, N. Owings, J. Patterson. Proved, 29th April, 1800. Owings and Moore live in Baltimore. Commission awarded.

Page 72.—14th September, 1799. James Lamme's estate appraised.

Page 73.—John Mills' estate appraisement taken 22d September, 1800, by John Emmitty et als.

Page 77.—List of bonds taken by John Campbell and John Mills, who were executors of Martha Burnside.

Page 79.—6th September, 1800. John Brownlee, Sr.'s, will—To son, James Brownlee; son, Alexander; to son John's orphans; son, William; to daughter, Isabella; daughter, Rachel, and her son, John; to granddaughter, Sarah Brownlee, daughter to son James; to daughter, Margaret; to son-in-law, James Mitchell. Executors, sons James and William. Teste: James Mitchell, Sr.; Jno. Christian, Jno. Mitchell. Proved, 27th October, 1800, by all witnesses.

Page 80.—29th April, 1800. John Brownlee, Jr.'s, will—To wife, Mary; to youngest son, Moffett Brownlee; to children, son William, son John. Executors, James Mitchel, James Moffett. Teste: John Christian, James Brownlee. Proved, 27th October, 1800. Executors qualify.

Page 82.—3d May, 1800. George Campbell's will—To wife and family until youngest child is 21; to wife, Agness, and 5 children; title to be made to William Moore; live children, viz: Robert, Mary, Jenny, Betsy, Joseph Campbell. Executors, wife Agness, John Purris, Thomas Fulton. Teste: Geo. Reid, David Shoultz, Samuel Brown. Codicil, 9th June, 1800, provision for possible unborn child. Teste: Same as before. Proved, 27th October, 1800, by all witnesses. Wife Agness and John Purrer qualify.

Page 84.—16th July, 1800. Adam Bratton's will—To wife, Elizabeth, child she is big with; son, Robert Bratton, infant; to son, Robert, plantation on Jackson's River; to daughters, Peggy A. Branton, Betsy, Nancy, Susy F., Patsy W., Sally. Executors, brother John Bratton and wife Elizabeth. Teste: John Bell, Andrew Lockridge, Jane Stewart, John (X) Clayton; 28th July, 1800, codicil—wife has been delivered of a daughter. Teste: Jean Stuart, Susanna Feemster. Proved, 22d December, 1800, by Andrew Lockridge and Jean Stuart. Executors qualify.

Page 87.—January, 1800. Andrew Crist's (in German) will—To wife, Elizabeth, to live with son John; to sons, Jacob and Andrew, John, Henry, (infants), Abraham; to daughters, Polly, Betsy, Nancy, Mary, Fanny, Heddy. Executor, son John. Teste: Samuel Brown, Thos. Brown, Robt. Wilson. Proved, 22d December, 1800, by Samuel Brown, Ro. Wilson. Executor qualifies.

Page 88.—24th May, 1798. Jean (mark) Henderson's will, of Middle River—To daughter, Rebeckah; daughter, Sarah; daughter, Florence; son, David; son, Andrew; son, Alexander; sons, James and William; son, Samuel. Executors, sons Andrew and Alexander. Teste: Samuel Long, Jas. Rankin, Henry Kelly. Proved, 22d December, 1800, by Rankin and Kelly.

Page 90.—23d August, 1800. Robert McCutchen's will—To daughter, Mary; to son, James; son, Robert; son, Jones, land on Little River; daughter, Hanna Henderson; daughter, Margaret Moore (son John?); other children. Executors, son John, James Berry, Joseph Henderson. Teste: Jesse Davis, Joseph McCutchen, Mary and Jno. McCutchen. Proved, 26th January, 1801, by Davis and Joseph McCutchen. James Berry refuses to execute. Jno. McCutchen and Joseph Henderson qualify.

Page 92.—Jacob Woods' estate appraisement taken 7th March, 1800, by Jno. Gamble, Jno. Bell, Wm. Young.

Page 93.—26th January, 1801. John Tate's bond as executor of estate of Abraham Belew pending a contest of his will.

Page 93.—14th January, 1800. Archibald Armstrong's will—To wife, Margaret, tract purchased of Samuel McChesney on which Samuel now lives; to son, Robert; daughter, Ann Elliot; son-in-law, James Elliot; to heirs of deceased son, Thomas; heirs, of deceased daughter, Isabella; to son, William, and his little son, Archibald Armstong; to grandson, Thomas Armstrong, son to William; to grandson, Archibald Armstrong McCray; to grandson, Margaret McCray; to daughter, Jean McCray; to daughter-in-law, Peggy Armstrong (William's wife). Executors, son William Armstrong and James Berry. Teste: Samuel Black, Joseph Black, James,

Jennet, and Ann Peery. Proved, February Court, 1801, by Joseph Black and James Peery. Executors qualify.

Page 96.—19th August, 1797. Abraham Belew's will—To wife, Ann; to Jenny Tate, daughter to John Tate; to David Fulwider, son to John Fulwider. Executors, John Tate and John Fulwider. Teste: C. Berry, Thos. Burns, George Fullwider. Presented 26th January, 1801, and proved by Berry and Burns. Recording is contested and continued to next Court. And at February Court, 1801, objection is withdrawn and ordered recorded. John Tate qualifies.

Page 97.—6th February, 1801. William Hunter's estate appraisement by Samuel Bell, Thomas Martin, Jacob Miller.

Page 98.—21st April, 1801. Alex. Robertson's will—To wife, Jane; to sons, William and George; to daughters, Lettice and Ann Robertson. Executors, Brothers James and Mathew Robertson. Teste: Wm. Robertson, James Anderson, Andrew Russell. Proved, 27th April, 1801. Executors qualify.

Page 100.—28th January, 1801. John Kirk's will—To wife, Mary Ann Kirk; to daughter, Rachel; daughter, Jane; to daughters that are married; to daughter, Agnes Bratton; to son, James; son, John; son, William; to daughters, Rachel Cunningham, ———. Executors, wife Mary Ann, nephew William Bell, son James. Teste: John and Francis Bell, Lindsey Marshall. Proved, 27th April, 1801, by the Bells. Executors qualify.

Page 102.—10th August, 1790. Abraham Larew's will—To son, Jacob; to daughter, Mary; daughter, Anna; to Philip Drake; to son, Reuben; son Peter's 3 children; to daughter Mary's son, John Standlee. Teste: John Caldwell, Thomas, Mary, Anson Caldwell. Proved, 27th April, 1801, by John and Thos. Caldwell.

Page 103.—25th April, 1801. Andrew Crist's estate appraised by Mathew Thomson, William Brown, Thomas Willson.

Page 104.—14th September, 1799. James Lamme's estate appraised.

Page 112.—22d May, 1799. Hugh (mark) Doherty's will—To wife, Susanna, and Daniel, Polly, Margaret, Sarah, Susanna, Kitty; to son, John; son, Hugh; to granddaughter, Rosanah Dougherty; to grandson, Hugh Doherty. Executors, wife Susannah, son John. Teste: Wm. McKee, Mary Lester, Hugh Dougherty.

Page 113.—James Todd's estate in account with George Todd, administrator—Paid James Todd, Jr., for attending Pendleton Court; paid Nathan Todd, ditto.

Page 114.—James Sawyer's estate in account with Hannah Sawyers.

Page 116.—27th November, 1800. Laurence Swink's will—Executors, Henry and Mathias Swink; to wife, Margaret; sons, Henry and Mathias; to 3 daughters, Betsey Russell, Peggy Fix, Barbara Fix. Executors, wife Margaret and sons Henry and Mathias. Teste: Jno. Buchanan, Wm. Willson. Proved, 22d June, 1801. Executors qualify.

Page 117.—7th March, 1801. Joanes Henderson's will—To wife, Isabell; sons, John, Joseph, Jones. Executors, wife Isabell, son Joseph, Alex. Craig; to (son James?), daughter Becky, daughter Sarah, daughter Margaret; to grandchildren, children of daughter Jean Grey. Teste: Edward Walsh, William Seel, John Risk, Jr. Proved, 22d June, 1801. Isabella refuses to execute. Others qualify.

Page 119.—13th February, 1800. Andrew Steele's will—To wife and children; to son, Andrew; to daughter, Sarah; to daughter, Mary; son, John (land in Kentucky); daughter, Jean; to son, James (lands on Tence with Andrew). Executors, wife Mary, son John, Andrew Ramsey, Robt. Finley. Teste: Andrew Steele, Jr.; Jno. McClure, Jno. Ramsey. Proved, 22d June, 1801. Finley refuses to execute. Others qualify.

Page 123.—6th February, 1800. Thomas Barry's estate appraised.

Page 168.—7th November, 1797. Robert Donalson's will—To sons, William and Robert; to daughter, Margaret Cox; to wife, Jean; to sons, John and David; daughters, Jean and Rebecca. Executors, wife Jean and Maj. Wm. Wilson. Teste: Henry Swink, Wm. Willson, John Shields. Proved, 27th July, 1801, by Swink and Willson. Willson refuses to execute. Jean qualifies.

Page 170.—25th July, 1801. Settlement by Samuel Long, guardian for Peggy Kilkny, late Peggy Coiner (Comer?).

Page 175. 9th April, 1801. Anthony Öhler's (Ahlar) will—To deceased daughter Margaret's three children, Molly, Barbara, and Catherine; to son, John; to daughter, Barbary; to daughter, Catherine; to son, George; to daughter, Elizabeth; daughter, Susannah; daughter, Mary; daughter, Madelena. Executors, friend George Ahlar and Teater Fishburn. Teste: Tobias Danner, Hennery Benter. Proved, 29th September, 1801. Executors qualify.

Page 176.—Thomas Caldbreath's estate settled, 26th September, 1801—List of legatees' receipts produced by Margaret Caldbreath, executrix: Thomas Mitchell and Ann, his wife; Andrew Wallace and Margaret, his wife; John Gold and Elizabeth, his wife; George Rutledge and Mary, his wife; Thomas Caldbreath, Jene Caldbreath, Sally Caldbreath, Margret Caldbreath, executrix.

Page 181.—Hugh McAllery's estate appraisement.

Page 182.—24th July, 1799. Catherine (X) Merritt's will—To good friend and relation, Augustine Argenbright, executor, part of estate left her by her late husband, Valentine Cloninger. Teste: Jacob Swoope, Alex. St. Clair, Jenny Stuart. Proved, 23d September, 1799, presented and proved, but record objected to by Samuel Merritt, and continued, and at 28th April, 1800, record refused and appeal, and 29th September, 1801, recorded.

Page 183.—18th August, 1801. Parthenia Cale's nuncupative will made at house of Wm. Cale before Stophel and John Palmer—To William Cale, son of William, a cow she had sold to son William; to Madlin Cale. Proved, 29th September, 1801.

Page 186.—16th July, 1801. William Jones' estate appraised.

Page 190.—15th August, 1799. Benjamin Kennerley's will—To brother, Reuben Kennerley, all estate. Teste: Samuel (X) Crawsby, Thos. Turk, Jol. Rapp, Jacob Lymes. Proved, 28th December, 1801.

Page 190.—5th February, 1795. George Craig's will—To wife, Elizabeth and children. Executors, wife Elizabeth, James and William Craig. Teste: Peggy Evans, Mary Craig. Codicil, 16th November, 1801—Appoints James Craig, Jr., son of William Craig, executor, in room of wife Elizabeth, deceased; to sister, Sarah Thorp; sisters-in-law, Peggy Evans and Polly

Evans. Teste: Wm. Wilson, John Poage. Proved, 28th December, 1801. James and William Craig qualified.

Page 195.—16th November, 1801. James Shields' will—To wife, Rachel; to eldest daughter, Ally Shields; to youngest daughters, Margaret Shields; to son, James. Executors, wife Rachel and Samuel Torbit. Teste: Joseph Coalter, Wm. Shields. Proved, 22d February, 1802. Executors qualify.

Page 196.—24th September, 1801. John Hall's will—To wife, Elizabeth; to daughter, Fanny, and her nine children; to Fanny's son, John; to daughter, Elizabeth, and her son, John Hall Allison; to son-in-law, Andrew Allison; to daughter, Nancy, and her son, John Hall van Lear; to brother's son, John Hall; to Benjamin Harrison, $1 ———. Executors, John Bell, John Gamble. Teste: John Emmitt, Joseph Mathews, John Blair. Proved, 22d February, 1802. Executors qualify.

Page 198.—Martha Bell's estate appraisement recorded 23d February, 1802.

Page 202.—10th December, 1801. James Hogshead, Sr.'s, will, farmer—To wife, Sarah; to sons, Thomas and James; to 3 daughters, Rebekah, Gray, and Sally. Executors, wife Sarah and son Thomas. Teste: James Cooper, Francis Gilkison, Wm. Hogsett. Proved, 26th April, 1802, by James McKemy, &c. Executors qualify.

Page 204.—8th June, 1798. Samuel (mark) McCune's will, Sr.—Son, John; wife, Elizabeth; to daughter, Rachel Bell; to daughter, Ann; to friend, James Steele; to grandson, Alex. Henry; to granddaughter, Sarah Henderson; to grandchildren by daughter Mary, except Granddaughter, Mary Bell, whom I raised and to whom I give £10 more; to daughter-in-law, Margaret McCune, wife to John; to grandson, Samuel, son to son William; to grandson, Samuel, son to son John; to son, Archibald; to son, Samuel. Executors, James Steele, Benj. Stuart, James Frazer. Teste: William and John Thompson, Archibald Stuart. Proved, 26th April, 1802. Executors refuse. Administration granted John and Samuel McCune.

Page 206.—15th September, 1801. Receipt to William Black, executor of Samuel Black, by the legatees, viz: John Black, Mathew Alexander and wife Jane, Samuel Price and wife Margaret, William Black and wife Mary, William Black, Jr.; Martha Black, Samuel Black, Nancy Black, James Black.

Page 215.—26th June, 1799. David Doak's will—To wife, Jennet; to sons, Samuel and David; to daughter, Jenny Berry; daughter, Rosannah Doak; to daughter, Betsy; to 5 daughters, viz: Aggy, Fanny, Darcos, Polly, Elly; to son, Hugh. Executors, wife Jennet, sons Samuel and David. Guardian, James Berry. Teste: Thos. Mitchell, James and Samuel Meteer. Proved, 28th June, 1802. Jennet refuses. Others qualify.

Page 231.—Dr. estate of George Hood, deceased, in account with James Young, guardian to the heirs of said George Hood—August 22, 1795, by cash lent Elijah Hood by his grandfather, Robert Curry.

Page 236.—5th June, 1802. James Steele's will—To wife, Sarah; to son, Andrew; son, Samuel; to daughters, Sally Steele and Martha Henderson; to son, John, son-in-law, Daniel Henderson; to granddaughter, Polly Tate Steele. Executors, wife Sarah and sons Andrew, Samuel, and John. Teste: Andrew Ramsey, Samuel Finley, Samuel Steele. Proved, 26th July, 1802. Andrew, Samuel, and John qualify.

Page 240.—2d May, 1799. Elenor Hall's will—To daughter, Elizabeth Fulton; to son, Benjamin; to son, Alexander. Executors, Andrew Fulton, Alex. Hall, Benj. Hall. Teste: Benj. Stuart, Alex. Brown, Archibald Stuart. Proved, 25th October, 1802. Alex. Hall qualifies.

Page 242.—2d February, 1802. John Finley's will—Patsey Dicktom already provided for; daughters, Esther and Polly; daughters, Ann Shannon, Esther Finley, Polly Finley; son, James; land in Kentucky left to testator by Daddy Reid. Executors, nephew John Caldwell, Samuel Steele Finley. Teste: Samuel Finley, Wm. Ramsey, Wm. Finley. Proved, 25th October, 1802. Executors qualify.

Page 246.—8th April, 1793. James Bell's will—Children, Elizabeth, Samuel, Ann, James, Sarah, already provided for; to remainder of children, viz: Mary and Francis. Executors, sons Samuel and Francis. Teste: J. Bell, Francis Gardiner. James Bell's deposition as witness before Samuel Blair in Fayette County, Ky. Proved, October 26th, 1801, and 27th December, 1802.

Page 248.—2d January, 1802. Peter Hanger's will, Sr.—To son, Peter; to Peter Rush, who married daughter Barbara; to son, John; son, George; son, Frederick; to Frederick Fultz, who married daughter Hannah; to daughter, Catharine; son, David (infant); tract whereon King, the Schoolmaster, formerly lived, to be sold. Nine children. Executors, sons Peter and Jacob and Peter Rush. Teste: Jacob Swoope, S. Blackburn. Addendum says: Have sold the King plantation to Peter Rush and he has conveyed to me the plantation on the Winchester Road occupied now by John Fleiger, which is to be sold. To Caty Dillenger, who now lives with testator, under 18. Proved, 27th December, 1802. Peter Rush refuses to execute. Others qualify.

Page 252.—18th April, 1801. John Tate's will—To wife and children, whole estate to be kept together for their benefit. Executors, wife Jinney, friends Robert Tate, Samuel Finley, Isaac Tate. Teste: John Tate, 3d; James Henry, Wm. Fulton, Geo. Berry. Proved, 27th December, 1802. Jinney, Robert, and Sam. qualify.

Page 257.—22d November, 1802. Thomas Poage's will—To daughter, Elizabeth; son, Elijah; son, Robert; to son, John; daughter, Ann; daughter, Polly; son, William; to daughter, Agness (single). Executors, son William and John Poage, Sr. Teste: Robert Campbell, John Kerr, Moses Gresham. Proved, 24th January, 1803. Executors qualify.

Page 258.—30th September, 1801. Thomas Reed's estate appraised.

Page 271.—24th January, 1803. Philip Kennerley's bond to solemnize matrimony.

Page 271.—17th January, 1797. William (mark) Armstrong's will—To wife, Jean; to daughter, Jean Trimble (£30, to be paid by son John); to son, John; son, William; son, Robert; daughter, Margaret; son, James. Executors, sons John and James. Teste: D. McNair, D. Sawyers, Nancy Sawyers. Codicil, 5th April, 1802—If son Robert should die before his wife; to son, James. 10 acres off Robert's tract. Teste: David McNair, Lindsey Marshall. Proved, 25th October, 1802, by David Sawyers, and 24th January, 1803, by David McNair, and 28th February, 1803, by Lindsey Marshall. John Armstrong refuses to execute. James Armstrong qualifies.

Page 279.—8th May, 1800. Samuel Bell's will—To wife, Jane; sons, William, Samuel, David, George; to son, Joseph; son, John; sons, James and Thomas; to daughter, Elizabeth Glaves; daughters, Margaret and Martha Bell. Executors, wife Jane and sons David and James. Teste: D. Stephenson, Wm. Beard, Thomas Givens. Proved, 27th June, 1803. Executors qualify.

Page 281.—26th April, 1803. John Summers (German) will—To wife, Elizabeth; son, John (already provided for); daughters, Mary Doame, Barbara Hull, Elizabeth Peck, ditto; to sons, David, Henry, Jacob; to children not before named, viz: Margaret, Catharine, Eve. Executors, Daniel Peck, Daniel Hull. Teste: Jno. Young, Frederick Henger, Christian (mark) Baird. Proved, 27th June, 1803. Executors qualify.

Page 295.—3d October, 1802. John Edmondson's will—To wife, Lucy, the carriage and pair of horses, and 3 children, house servants; son, John, to be educated in the Upper Country under direction of friend John Coalter; to brother, James, owns property in Staunton; to niece, Sally Cooke; to sister, Elizabeth; brothers, William, Benjamin, George. Executors, wife Lucy, brother James, John Coalter. Teste: George G. McIntosh, Jno. Monroe, Edward B. Smith. Proved, 26th April, 1803, by McIntosh, and 25th July, 1803, by John Monroe. James Edmondson qualifies.

Page 299.—4th July, 1799. Thomas Steele's will—To wife, Jane; daughter, Rosanah; daughter, Sally; daughter, Catharine; daughter, Jane Moore; son, William; sons, William and Robert; to James Smith. Executors, wife Jane, son William. Teste: Adam Hawpe, Michael Appell, Godlieb Stone. Proved, 25th July, 1803. William qualifies.

Page 303.—19th May, 1798. Samuel (mark) Frazier's will, living on waters of Christian's Creek—To wife, Mary; to 2 daughters, Jean and Ann (land adjoining Nicholas Spring); son, William; son, James. Proved, 26th September, 1803.

Page 305.—29th April, 1802. George Peery's (Pierie) will—To son, James; son, John; son, William; to daughter, Margaret Owens; daughter, Jean Johnson; to daughter, Mary Hays; daughter, Sarah; daughter, Elizabeth Andrews; daughter, Martha; granddaughter, Esther (Easter); daughter to daughter Jean. Executors, son James Peery, James Berry. Teste: James Berry, Frederick Henger, Maria (mark) Henger. Proved, 26th September, 1803. Berry qualifies.

Page 311.—6th March, 1803. David Jackson's will—To wife, Margaret; to son, John; son, Samuel; daughter, Margaret; daughter, Elizabeth Corothers; daughter, Jane Phillips; son, David; son, Thomas. Executors, sons David Carothers, John Jackson. Teste: William Bell, William and Joseph Wilson. Proved, 28th November, 1803, and executors qualify.

Page 313.—5th May, 1803. Andrew Russell's will (proved in Knox County, Tenn., July Term, 1803)—To wife, Elizabeth; son, Mathew; son, William; to daughter, Ann; son, John; daughter, Elizabeth; daughter, Jean; to son, James; son-in-law, James Robertson; to sons, Andrew and Alexander; son, Mathew; to grandson, son Andrew. Executors, sons Mathew, Andrew, Alexander Russell. Teste: Wm. Gillespie, Wm. Henderson, Jas. Gillespie. Proved in Augusta, 29th November, 1803.

Page 315.—19th July, 1803. James Scott's will—To wife Rebecca; son, William; son, Alexander; to daughter, Sally Trotter; sons, John, Thomas,

James; to daughter, Gibly (Ibby); daughters, Rebecca, Julianna, Jean. Executors, wife Rebecca, son John, Wm. Wilson. Teste: Wm. Burgess, George Berry. Proved, 26th December, 1803. Wilson refuses to execute. Others qualify.

Page 350.—23d January, 1801. Alexander Thompson's will—To son, Alexander; son, Patterson, executors; to daughters, Agnes, Martha, Margaret, Sarah, Polly. Overseer, brother Robert. Teste: John Henry, Patterson W. Thompson, Wm. Thompson. Proved, 24th January, 1804.

Page 359.—3d May, 1800, Henry Hawk's will (Hawp?)—To wife, Catharine; to sons, John and Abraham; to son, Jacob; son, Frederick; daughter, Elizabeth Fogus; to daughter, Catharine Shoultz; son, Andrew; daughter, Rachel Gregory; to daughter, Polly Gregory; daughter, Catherine Wintermaker (Winters) by a former wife. Teste: Michael Garber, Jr.; Jacob Swallow, Jno. Coalter. Executors, sons John and Abraham. Proved, 26th March, 1804. Executors qualify.

Page 360.—24th June, 1803. Samuel Meteer's will—To brother, James (tract devised to testator by father, and tract falling to testator by brother William); to sister, Betsey; brother, James; sister Sally's son, William. Executors, sister Betsey and brother James. Teste: Thomas Mitchell, Samuel and David Doak. Proved, 26th March, 1804. Executors qualify.

Page 362.—3d September, 1798. John King's will—To wife, Isabella; son, John; son, William; daughter, Margaret; daughter, Charity; friend, Wm. Anderson; friend, James Anderson; friend, Ezekiel Cooper. Executors, wife Isabella, sons John and William. Teste: John Didell, Jno. Cook. Proved, 26th March, 1804. Executors qualify.

Page 363.— ———, ———. John Steele's will—To mother, Sarah; brother, Samuel; sister, Sally; to Andrew and Sally Steel and sister, Matty Henderson. Executors, brother Samuel, and Andrew Fulton. Teste: Robert and Jenny Stuart, Wm. McCutchen, Samuel Steele. Proved, 26th March, 1804. Executors qualify.

Page 368.—5th May, 1804. Jacob Grove's (German) will, of Walker's Company—To wife, Mary; son, Christian; son, Frederick; son, George. Executors, wife Mary and son Christian. Teste: Wm. Buchanan, James Buchanan, Peter Troxal, David Buchanan. Proved, 25th June, 1804. Christian qualifies.

Page 369.—13th August, 1802. Rudolph Hawpe's will—To wife, Catharine; son, Henry; to Mary Sights, Betsey Mummer, Susannah Coiner, Emanual Hawpe; to son, John; son, Adam Hawpe, deceased; to grandchildren, children of Adam, deceased, viz: Elizabeth, Rudolph, and George Hawpe; to daughter-in-law, Catherine, widow of Adam. Executors, sons Henry and John. Teste: Wm. Steele, Peter Halseman, Wm. Lyons. Proved, 25th June, 1804.

Page 370.—26th March, 1804. Agness Poage's will—Father, Thomas Poage, land bequeathed to her by him; to Elizabeth and Thomas Poage, infant children of brother Robt. Poage, of Fayette County, Ky.; brother Elijah Poage to be trustee; to 3 sisters, Elizabeth Wilson, Anne Wood, Polly Wilson; to niece, Nancy Wilson, daughter to Rev. Wm. Willson; to brother, John Poage, of Rockbridge; brother, Elijah, of Kentucky; to brother, William; to my four brothers. Executors, brothers John and William Poage. Teste: John and Rebecca Poage. Proved, 25th June, 1804. Executors qualify.

Page 371.—14th April, 1804. George Adam Bright's will—To sons, John and George Bright, land adjoining Steele, Tate, Hufman, and Shultz; to five daughters, daughter Rebecka, son Windle, son David. Executors, sons John and George. Teste: William and Robert Steele, James Fulton. Proved, 25th June, 1804. Executors qualify.

Page 373.—20th December, 1799. Mathew Willson's will—To wife, Heloner; to sons, William and Mathew; to 3 daughters, Martha, Sarah, Eleanor; to son, John; to daughters, Elizabeth and Mary; to son, William, lands on Little Back Creek adjoining John and Thos. Sharp, and James Hathorn. Executors, wife Heloner, son John, James Mitchell; to two grandsons, both named Mathew Willson. Teste: Isaac Gray, Jno. Risk, Jr.; Henry Grove. Proved, 25th June, 1804. All executors refuse. Administration granted sons John and Mathew.

Page 375.—8th April, 1803. George Berry's will—To son, George, land on Middle River joining the Glabe; to son, John, James Henry, son-in-law, nine children. Executors, James Berry, James Henry. Teste: David Bratton, Wm. Thompson, Robt. Mayes. Proved, 25th June, 1804, and 27th November, 1804. Executors qualify.

Page 376.—4th April, 1801. John Askins' will—To Darby Halbert; to brother Philip Askins' only son. Executors, John Buchanan and William Brown, Sr. Teste: John Buchanan, Robt. Bailey. Proved, 23d July, 1804. Executors refuse. Administration granted Mark Hatton.

Page 377.—11th February, 1799. John Hunter's will—To eldest daughter, Frances; daughter, Martha; to nephew, John Hunter, son to Robert Hunter; to Thomas Frazer, land in Greenbrier; to nephew, Henry Hunter, Samuel Hunter's son; to David Braun, suit clothes; bound boy Wm. McCormick; Wm. Roger and wife Peggy to have use of the cabbin. Executors. Andrew and Mathew Hunter. Teste: John Cunningham, Robt. Hunter, Samuel Hunter, Wm. Bean. Proved, 23d July, 1804, and executors qualify.

Page 380.—23d January, 1804. Robert (X) Cummins' will—To wife, Margaret; son, John; to Agnes Miller; to children, Jean, Robert, Margaret, Martha; to Phoeby Alford; to grandchildren, Robt. Gray and Jno. Rutherford. Executors, wife Margaret and son John. Teste: Jas. Cunningham, Wm. Bell. Proved, 26th November, 1804. John Cummins refused. Margaret is dead. Administration granted son John and daughter Margaret.

Page 382.—15th October, 1804. William Johnson about to leave Virginia for an uncertain time empowers brother Chapman Johnson to attend to his affairs.

Page 417.—29th December, 1803. Robert Curry's will—To wife, Ann; to son, Samuel; daughter, Margaret Nickel; to daughter, Mary Erwin; daughter, Ann Glenn; to six sons, viz: Samuel, William, James, Robert, Alexander and Isah. Executors, sons Robert and Samuel. Teste: James Young, Sr.; Hugh Brown, Andrew Young. Proved, 24th December, 1804. Samuel qualifies.

Page 418.—18th November, 1804. James Young's will—To son, William, land on Naked Creek; to son, James; to son, Robert; son, James; son, Thomas; daughter, Peggy; to daughter, Margaret; daughter, Jean Allison;

daughter, Elenbeth Garvin; daughter, Mary Brown; daughter, Agnes Graham; son, Andrew; to grandson, John, son to son Robert. Executors, Robert and Thomas. Teste: Wm. Young, James Allison, John Dickey. Proved, 24th December, 1804. Thomas Young qualifies.

WILL BOOK No. X.

Page 3.—12th September, 1804. Arthur Connely's will—To wife, Jean; son, Arthur, land on Eagle Creek in Kentucky; to son, James; sons, John and David; daughter, Jean; daughter, Mary; son, Robert; daughter, Sarah; to grandson, Arthur Williamson. Executors, sons John and David. Teste: Wm. Johnston, Alex. Carns, Thos. Connely. Proved, 25th March, 1805. Executors qualify.

Page 7.—22d March, 1805. John Graham's deed of gift to sons William and Robert.

Page 21.—22d April, 1799. Michael Dickey's will—To sons, John and William; to son, James, in Kentucky; to daughter, Mary Greer; to daughters, Margaret Kirkpatrick, Mary Greer, and Elizabeth Beard; to grandchildren, Mary and James Oliver, whose father lives in Georgia; to daughter, Jean Oliver. Executors, Wm. Young, Sr., of Augusta, and son-in-law David Beard, of Rockbridge. Teste: Wm. Wilson, James Young, Hugh Brown. Proved, 25th November, 1805, by Wilson and Brown. Beard is dead and Young refuses. And at 27th January, 1806, John Dickey and Dickey Beard apply for administration. Elizabeth Beard also applies. Administration granted John Dickey and Elizabeth Beard. John refuses to act in conjunction with any one else, and Elizabeth qualifies.

Page 22.—10th February, 1802. John Moffett's will, Sr.—To wife, Jane; son, John; son, William; daughter, Esther Beard, wife of Charles Beard; son, James; daughter, Eleanor Moffett; daughter, Mary Brownlee, widow of John Brownlee; to grandson, Wm. McClenachan, son to daughter Nancy, deceased; granddaughter, Esther McClenachan, daughter to said Nancy; granddaughter, Esther Woods, wife of Michael Woods; son William has but one child and no probability of having more. Executors, sons William, James, John. Proved, 25th November, 1805.

Page 28.—26th December, 1805. Martha Davis' will—To daughter, Martha Rives, heirs of son James; daughter, Euphora Donley, heirs of daughter Sally Ewin; son, Wm. Davis; daughter, Elizabeth Parks; son, John Davis. Executors, William and Jno. Davis. Teste: Jno. Caldwell, Jno. Brown, Walter Davis. Proved, 24th March, 1806.

Page 40.—7th June, 1800. William McDowell's will, of Staunton—To wife, Alice, children and grandchildren; to son, John; grandson, William McDowell; daughter, Mary Swoope; grandson, Wm. Swoope; daughter, Jane Leybourn; son, William; daughter, Elizabeth; daughter, Margaret, lands in Rockingham and Shenandoah to be sold. Executors, son John and Archibald Stuart. Proved, 25th March, 1806. Archibald refuses; John qualifies.

Page 42.—4th January, 1804. Robert Kinney's will—To wife, Pheby; daughters, Agnes, Patience, Elizabeth; to son, James; son, John (to be liberally educated in order to take a profession); son, Robert; daughter, Rebecca, now married to James Brown; sword to son John. Executors, wife Phebe, sons James and Robert. Proved, 28th April, 1806. Executors qualify.

Page 44.—3d February, 1806. Hugh Gilkerson's will—To wife, Elizabeth; daughter, Margaret; daughter, Anna; daughter, Elizabeth; son, James; sons, David and William. Executors, sons David and William. Teste: Jacob Larew, Thos. Marshall, Joseph and Benj. Larew. Proved, 28th April, 1806. Executors qualify.

Page 45.—8th June, 1802. William Chesnutt's will—To wife, Jean; daughters, Elly, Isable, Sarah; sons, John and William; to 5 married daughters, Elizabeth Patten, Nancy Harloe (Horloe), Jean Palmer, Martha Hiden, Mary Smith. Executors, wife Jean, Thos. Patten, Andrew Fulton. Teste: James and Wm. Brown, Wm. Spence. Proved, 28th April, 1806. Jane refused; Fulton qualifies.

Page 50.—7th April, 1805. Christenah Teaford's will—To son, George; granddaughter, Elizabeth Teaford, daughter to George; to Polly Teaford, wife to George; to Peggy Cook, wife to Paul Cook, and Elizabeth Haup, wife to Henry Haup (her daughters); to Catherniah, wife to John Teaford. Legatees, Jacob, John, Henry, George Teaford, Elizabeth Haup, Peggy Cook. Executor, son George. Proved, 30th April, 1806. Executor qualifies.

Page 52.—12th June, 1806. Michael Coleman's will, coachmaker, late of City of Dublin, Earl Street, now of Staunton—To wife, Ann, executrix, with friend Joseph Bamford, attorney-at-law of Dublin, Mecklenburg St.; to children. Teste: Jno. Brown, Jno. C. Sowers. Phill North.

Page 52.—13th January, 1806. Edward Beard's will—To son, William; son, Charles; son, Samuel; son, John; to daughter, Elizabeth Craige (of Kentucky); daughter, Mary Henderson (of Kentucky); grandson, James Beard, son to son William; son, Charles (of Rockingham). Executor, son William. Teste: James Rankin, Thos. Givens, John Wade, Alex. Gardner. Proved, 23d June, 1806. Executor qualified.

Page 53.—21st March, 1804. John Doak's will—To son, John; sons, Samuel and Thomas Mitchell Doak; to daughter, Julia; daughter, Nancy; daughter, Rosannah; daughter, Betsey Wilson Doak; son, Washington; son, David. Executors, brothers Vory (?), Robert, Samuel, Sr., and David Doak. Teste: Samuel Brown, James Mitchell, Sr. and Jr. Proved, 23d June, 1806. Executors qualified.

Page 55.— —— ———, 1797. Arthur Hamilton's will—To wife, Barbara; daughters, Margaret, Mary, Sarah; sons, John and James; daughter, Martha; sons, David and Alexander. Executors, wife Barbara and son John. Teste: Wm. Blair, Patrick Hays, John Cunningham. Proved, 23d June, 1906. John qualifies.

Page 56.—5th January, 1801. John Wallace's will—To grandson, Frederick Wallace; grandson, Jno. Wallace; to son, James; son, Thomas. Executors, Robt. Cooper, Ro. Harris. Teste: Wm. Cooper, John and Joseph Cooper, James Harris. Proved, 23d June, 1806.

Page 63.—12th December, 1803. Christian Zimmerman's (German) will—To son, Stophel; son, Christian; son, John (the elder, being by first wife); son, Jacob; son, Lawrence; son, Henry; son, John (the younger, by present wife); daughter, Catherine Jones; daughter, Ann Elizabeth Lukeback (who lives to the northward); daughter, Sophia Creever; wife Executors, John McDowell and David Greiner, of Staunton. Teste: Jacob Swoope, Wm. Morris. Proved, 28th July, 1806. Executors qualify.

Page 65.—9th May, 1806. John Summers, Sr.'s, will (German)—To sons, Samuel and George; son, Andrew; daughter, Christiana Sinck; son, Philip Summers; daughter, Julianna Fawver (Fawner); daughter, Sarah Summers; son, John, deceased (his son and daughter); daughter, Elizabeth Grass's children. Executors, sons Andrew and Philip, and Philip Sink. Teste: Hugh Dougherty, George Franger, John Porter. Proved, 28th July, 1806. Andrew Summers and Philip Sink qualify.

Page 73.— — ———, 1806. William Sproull's will—To wife, Susanna; son, James; son, Alexander; daughter, Margaret McCutchen; daughter Nemsey's children; son, William; son, Joseph; son, Oliver; daughter, Jane Weir; daughter, Sidney Beard; sons, John and Charles; daughters, Mary, Martha, Fanny; son, Samuel (to take profession). Executors, wife Susanna, sons William and John. Teste: Joseph and Samuel Beard, Michael Koonts. Proved, 22d July, 1806. Executors qualify.

Page 74.—21st August, 1806. Robert Craig's will, of South River—To wife, Susannah; sons, Robert and William; son, John Johnston Craig (land in Albemarle in Woods Gap); daughters, Rebecca, Agnes, Susannah, Jenny, Elizabeth Craig. Executors, friends Andrew Ramsey, Wm. Patrick, Wm. Craig. Teste: Andrew Ramsey, Wm. Finley, Ann Harvey, Sarah Finley. Proved, 23d September, 1806. Craig refuses; others qualify.

Page 89.—28th July, 1806. Enos Jones' will—To wife, Sarah; sons, Isiah and Enos; son, Peter; son, Robert; daughter, Hannah Swink; daughter. Elizabeth Koontz; daughter, Prusella Silling; daughter, Ann Silling; daughter, Jemima; daughter, Lydia; grandson, Robert Jones, son to Isiah; granddaughters. Elizabeth and Ledia Patterson. Executors, sons Isiah and Peter. Teste: Samuel Clarke, Ed. Christian, Wm. Kinney. Proved, 24th November, 1806. Executors qualify.

Page 91.—9th October, 1805. Elizabeth Stuart's will—To daughter, Jenny; son. Robert; daughter, Elizabeth; daughter, Mary; granddaughter, Elizabeth Paxton; granddaughter, Elizabeth Alexander; granddaughter, Elizabeth Moffett; daughter, Mary Moffett; son, James; to Wm. Lyle, son James' son Thomas; to William Paxton, heir to Stuart Paxton. Executors, Andrew Fulton, Ro. Stuart, Wm. Davis. Teste: Joseph Faver, Henry Sinder, Jenny Stuart, Elizabeth Paxton. Proved, 24th November, 1806. Davis refuses to execute; others qualify.

Page 93.—John Crawford's estate in account with James Crawford, who guardian to John Crawford, infant, who was son of John—20th May, 1797, paid funeral charges of John Crawford, infant, deceased.

Page 108.—Rev. Archibald Scott's estate appraisement recorded 23d March, 1807.

Page 116.—6th August, 1806. Thomas Mitchell, Sr.'s, will—To son, William; son, Thomas; daughter, Elizabeth Mitchell; daughter, Ibby Mitchell; daughter, Jenny Meteer; granddaughter, Betty McClure; grandson, Thomas McClure; granddaughter, Polly McClure. Executors, friend Thomas Mitchell and John Wilson. Teste: W. Wilson, Robt. Doak, John, James, and Thos. Mitchell. Proved, 23d March, 1807. Jno. Wilson refused; Thomas qualified.

Page 117.—11th December, 1804. Jane Erwin's will, widow—To daughter. Elizabeth Nichol; daughter, Jane Erwin; to daughter, Fanny Allen; sons, William and Francis; daughter, Susanna Erwin. Executor, friend

Wm. Miller. Teste: Samuel, Nancy, and Wm. Miller. Proved, 26th January, 1807. Executor qualifies.

Page 119.—15th January, 1807. Alexander Scott's will—To brothers, John and Andrew, all carpenter shop tools; to brother, Thomas; brother, William; to Hugh Nelson, who married my sister Mary; to sisters, Catherine, Elizabeth, Rebecca Scott; to brother, Thomas, lot 57 in Chilicothe, bought of Nathaniel Massie. Executors, brothers John and Thomas. Teste: Joseph Wright, John B. Moses. Proved, 23d March, 1807. Executors qualify.

Page 121.—7th April, 1800. Sampson Mathew's will, Sr., of Bath County—Has executed deed to John Coalter as trustee for wife Catherine, and another to Samuel Clarke as trustee for self, both recorded in General Court. Suit in Federal Court in Chancery to set aside those deeds. To four children, viz: John and Sampson Mathews, Ann Nelson, Jane Clarke. Executors, Samuel Clarke, Jacob Kinney. Teste: Andrew Barry, W. Herron. 7th April, 1800, Codicil—Makes daughter Jane residuary legatee. Proved, 24th March, 1807.

Page 125.—17th April, 1807. Receipt of heirs of James Bell to John Bell, administrator, viz: William Bell and wife Mary; Samuel Bell and wife Jane; Israel Patterson and wife Rachel.

Page 126.—22d June, 1807. Michael Garber's, Sr., deed of trust—Conveys nail works on his place on Middle River.

Page 130.—28th January, 1807. Abby Ciplinger's will, widow—Executor, Abraham Lamb; to sons, Philip, John, Peter; to daughters, Catherine and Mary; son-in-law and daughter, John Lamb and wife Elizabeth. Proved, 22d June, 1807. Executor qualifies.

Page 131.—3d February, 1807. Margaret King's will—All estate to be divided between sons and daughters. Executors, son-in-law John Denison and James Allison. Teste: John Denison, Jr., and Patsy Philip. Proved, 23d June, 1807.

Page 132.—19th April, 1807. James Craig's will—To wife, Jane; to son, John; to sons, James, Samuel, George, William, Elijah, Robert; to daughters, Sarah, Betsy, Agness, Jane; daughter, Mary McGill. Executors, son-in-law Robt. McGill, son Jno. Craig. Teste: James Rankin, Archibald Dickson, Jno. Shields. Proved, 22d June, 1807.

Page 133.—20th April, 1807. John Wilson's will—To son, Samuel, William, James, John; daughter, Agness. Executors, James Henderson, Wm. Davis. Teste: Jas. Lynch, Alex. Boyd, Jno. Caldwell. Proved, 23d June, 1807.

Page 140.—18th June, 1806. Rebekah Sawyers' will—To nephew, Alex. Crawford; to niece, Nancy Tolman (for to school her children); to niece, Mary Armstrong (for to school her children); to David Sawyers; to niece, Nancy Crawford (to school her children). To niece, Jean Crawford; to Rebecca, daughter of Alex. Crawford; to Polly, daughter to Alex. Crawford; to Rebecca Ann Tolman. Executor, friend, Alex. Crawford. Teste: Francis Gardner, Wm. Bell, Ann Gardner. Proved, 28th September, 1807.

Page 142.—22d November, 1805. Ann McCune's will—To sister Elizabeth's son, Alex. McCune Henry, horse left to Ann in her father's will; to Rebecca Gay; to James Frazer and his wife Ann; to brother, Samuel McCune; to brother, John McCune; brother, Archibald; to heirs of brother

William; to sister Mary Lessley's heirs. Teste: James Paul, John W. Frazer, Archibald Gay (Gray?). Proved, 28th September, 1807.

Page 150.—26th February, 1793. James Patterson's will—To sons, Joseph and Mathew; daughter, Elizabeth Gray; to granddaughter, Elin Henderson, daughter to Archibald Henderson; to Ellin Dickey, her grandmother's chest; to daughter, Isbald Dickey (legacy to Isbold Dickey provided Jno. Hickey provide a slave in lieu); to son Joseph's sons, Joseph and James. Executors, Jno. Dickey, Jno. Bell. Teste: James Young, Francis Brown, Robert Young. Proved, 29th September, 1807. Executors qualify.

Page 153.—26th January, 1807. William Brown's (son of James Brown, deceased) receipt (now being above 21 years) to his uncle, John Brown, his guardian.

Page 155.— — ———, ——. Martin Miller's will—To son, Henry's children, viz: Martin and others; to son-in-law, Luke Collins, executor. Teste: Robt. Doak, David Shultz, Godlieb Stone. Proved, 23d November, 1807. Executor qualifies.

Page 156.—26th August, 1807. William McPheeters' will—To wife, Rachel; daughter Rebecca Gamble, wife to Jno. Gamble; to daughter, Polly Kelso, wife to Charles Kelso, daughter, Patsey Walker, wife to Joseph Walker; daughter, Rachel Logan, wife to John Logan; son, William; daughter, Elizabeth Campbell, wife to William Campbell (to be paid to Rev. Samuel Brown, Jacob Kinney, Wm. McPheeters as trustees); to Sophronia McPheeters, daughter to son James, deceased; to Philander McPheeters, son to son James, deceased; to Theophilus McPheeters, son to son James, deceased; to Jas. Augustus McPheeters, son to son James, deceased. Executors, wife Rachel, Jacob Kinney, Wm. McPheeters, Jr. Teste: Jno. Young, Jno. Moffett, Jr.; James and Robt. Trimble. Proved, 23d November, 1807. Jacob and William qualify.

Page 157.—Rev. Archibald Scott's estate settled by Executor James Ramsey, 2d February, 1807—Principal and interest of a debt due the late Mrs. Scott by the will of her father, which is in the hands of the executor, James Ramsey.

Page 172.—6th July, 1807. John Finley's will—To wife, Sarah; to sons, John and William; to daughter, Sally Finley; daughter, Peggy Hutchinson; daughter, Jinny Frasor; son, Samuel; to Peggy Mooney, something to be done for her. Executors, Wm. Finley, Andrew Ramsey. Teste: Andrew Ramsey, Isaac McClure, Adam Russell, David McClure. Proved, 28th December, 1807.

Page 173.—Daniel Friel's estate in account with executors—2d October, 1799, paid Wm. Burgess for schooling.

Page 175.—John Kilkeney's estate in account with Sarah Jones (late Sarah Kilkenny) and Andrew Horouff (Harouff), administrators.

Page 179.—1st May, 1802. William Caldwell's will—To wife, Ann; to sons, John and David; to daughter, Jean Caldwell, living in Carter's Valley; to daughter, Mary Young; daughter, Ann Henderson; daughter, Annis Davis. Executors, son John Caldwell, son-in-law Wm. Davis. Teste: James Frazer, David Caruthers. Proved, 28th March, 1808. Executors qualify.

Page 180.—27th July, 1802. William Curry's will—To wife, Frances; son, James; son, Alexander; son, Robert; son, Benjamin; daughter, Jean; daughter, Mary; daughter, Elizabeth; to daughter, Margaret. Executors, sons Alexander and Benjamin. Teste: Samuel and Robt. Erwin, Robt. Usher. Proved, 28th March, 1808.

Page 189.—5th April, 1808. Casper Snider to son, Henry Snider—Deed of gift of personalty.

Page 190.—1st February, 1806. Francis Hull's will—To sons, Henry and Daniel; to daughters, Elizabeth Fulwider, Molly Hanger, Barbara Cook; son, Frederick; daughter, Catherine Wiseman; son, John; daughter, Susanna; windmill to son John. Executors, Daniel Hull, James Harris. Teste: John and Hugh Daugherty (affirmed); David Byers (sworn). Proved, 28th March, 1808, by Jno. Daugherty, and 26th April, 1808, by others. Executors refuse. Administration granted Jno. Hull.

Page 193.—George Craige's estate in account with Wm. Craig, surviving executor—17th November, 1807, paid James Collins, taylor; sundries to James Craig, Jr., orphan; ditto to Nancy Craige, ditto; ditto Peggy Craig, ditto; ditto to George Craig, ditto; ditto Polly Craig, ditto; paid James Boyle, schoolmaster; paid Sarah Thorp, account of a legacy left her by her father.

Page 197.—10th May, 1808. William Johnston's will—To wife, Jane; to brother-in-law, Wm. McKnob, living on Watago, North Carolina; to Katherine Kerns, wife to Alexander Kerns; to half-sister, Jane Shields, wife to Patrick Shields, living near mouth of Missouri River; to Hugh, Ruery, and Lilah Dreddan, children of Wm. Dreddan, of Madison County, Kentucky; to sons and daughters of David Dreddan, living on South Fork of Holston River; to tenant, Henry Hartman. Executors, James and Robert Rankin. Teste: Michael Cline, Henry Hartman, Jr.; Henry Hartman, Sr. Proved, 27th June, 1808. 27th March, 1809, James Rankin qualifies.

Page 207.—1st June, 1807. Frederick Hanger, of Boone County, Ky., to William Mathews, Jr.—Power of attorney to settle his affairs.

Page 216.—17th July, 1808. John Black's will—To brother, William, and sisters, Peggy and Sally; to brother Anthony Black's five sons, John, Hugh, William, Samuel, James; to sister Eleanor Shields's two sons, Robert and Thomas Shields. Executors, brother Anthony, Samuel Long and Samuel Blackwood. Teste: Joseph Long, Samuel Black, Samuel Black. Proved, 26th September, 1808.

Page 218.—6th May, 1808. Jas. Cunningham's will—To wife, Margaret; to sons, John, Robert, James, William; to daughter, Sarah Bell; daughter, Rebecca (unmarried). Executors, wife Margaret, son Robert, and son-in-law Samuel Bell. Teste: John Young, Ester Ralland, Margaret Armstrong. Proved, 26th September, 1808.

Page 219.—19th October, 1807. Rosanna Steele's will—To son-in-law, Halbert McClure; son-in-law, Archibald Blackburn; son-in-law, Samuel McClure; son-in-law, Robert Cooper; grandson, Nathaniel Steele (infant), and his sister, Sally; granddaughter, Rosana Blackburn; granddaughter, Elizabeth Cooper. Executor, Halbert McClure. Teste: Pleasant Ware Thomas Love, Jacob Bare. Proved, 26th September, 1808.

Page 220.—16th February, 1808. Mary Ann Kirk's will—To daughter, Rachel Cunningham; daughter, Jane Kirk (unmarried); son, James, who is to pay John and William; to son, John; son, William, legatee; (daughter?) Agnes Bratton. Executors, son James. Proved, 26th September, 1808.

Page 221.—11th October, 1808. John Ott's will—To wife, Mary; to son, John (Jack horse and Allen Mare); to each of three daughters and granddaughter; son, David; to daughter, Sally (unmarried). Executors, wife Mary; son, John, and Alexander Berryhill. Teste: Thos. Young, John Cooper, Wm. Cooper, Samuel Young. Proved, 28th November, 1808. John and Alexander qualify.

Page 222.—3d December, 1808. Benjamin Stuart's will—To son, Archibald; son, John (lot in Waynesboro); son-in-law, George Hutcheson; son, Benjamin (infant); to daughter, Nancy (land in Tazewell County on head of Loral Fork of Wolf Creek); to daughters, Polly, Betsy, Sally, Nancy; to three married daughters, Polly McClung, Betsy Hutcheson, Sally Diddle. Executors, Robert Stuart, Andrew Fulton, son Archibald Stuart, son-in-law Geo. Hutcheson. Teste: Alex. Hall, James Diddle, James McCord, Jno. Alexander. Proved, 26th December, 1808. Executors qualify (except George).

Page 224.—2d August, 1808. Samuel Curry's will—To sons, William, Samuel, Isaiah; daughter, Mary. Teste: Alex. Robertson, Samuel Forsythe, Jno. Keith. Proved, 26th December, 1808. Samuel and Isaiah qualify.

Page 226.—25th November, 1808. John Blair's will—To wife, Jane; daughter, Polly Blair (unmarried); to son, Mathew; daughters, Margaret Ewin and Rachel Young; to son, Alexander; to daughters, Jean Curry and Rachel Kirkland. Executors, Col. Alex. Robertson and eldest son, Alex. Blair. Teste: Wm. Wilson, Jno. Gamble, Jno. Bell. Proved, 26th December, 1808. Executors qualify.

Page 240.—John Brown's estate further settled—Paid Edward Taylor, one of the heirs; paid Daniel Brown, an heir; paid James Brown, an heir; paid Sarah Brown, an heir; paid Jane Risk, an heir.

Page 242.—Jane Blair's estate in account with James Allen, administrator, and James Ligget, and Jane, his wife, late Jane Blair, administratrix.

Page 261.—26th July, 1805. Geoge Kice (German) to Polly and Betsy Kice (Rice), his granddaughter—Deed of gift of personalty.

Page 268.—23d January, 1809. John McCausland's will—To Mary McCausland, $1; son, James, $1; daughter, Patsy Frame; to daughter, Elizabeth Glenn, all property either in Pennsylvania or Virginia, except miniature set in gold, which he leaves to granddaughter, Patsey Glenn; to friend, Mr. George Haller; executor, son-in-law Hugh Glenn. Teste: James Allison, Samuel Curry, Jno. Gibson. Proved, 26th April, 1809. Executor qualifies.

Page 269.—26th February, 1790. James Patterson's will, far advanced in years—To sons, Joseph and Mathew; daughter, Elizabeth Gray; to granddaughter, Elin Henderson, daughter to Archibald Henderson. (This will recorded p. 150, *supra*) recorded there as to personal estate. Now, 26th April, 1809, proved by deposition of Robert Young, taken in Montgomery County, Ohio, corporation of Dayton, before William McClure, president of the corporation, 13th August, 1808.

Page 274.—7th February, 1809. John Patrick's will, old and infirm—To wife, Jane; sons, William and Charles; to grandchildren, Robert, Margaret, Samuel, Jenny, John, Mary, and Rebecca Downey; daughter, Isabella McCutchen; grandson, John Patrick McCutchen. Executors, sons William and Charles. Teste: Robt. Porterfield, Andrew Ramsey, David Bell. Proved, 22d May, 1809. Executors qualify.

Page 276.—24th May, 1809. Johin Frazier's will—To nephew, Samuel C. Frazer, son to deceased brother, Samuel, adjoining testator's brother, James; to brother, James; to nephew, Jno. W. Frazer, and his brother, James. Teste: James Paul, Ezekiel Cooper, Archibald Gay. Proved, 26th June, 1809. Administration granted James Frazer.

Page 278.—19th April, 1809. William Brown, Sr.'s, will—To wife, Jean; son, Thomas; grandson, John Brown, son to Thomas; son, Samuel, and his son, William; son, John (infirm); son, William, and his son, William (under 18); daughter, Jean Hays, wife to Patrick Hays; daughter, Mary Mitchell, wife to James Mitchell, Jr.; youngest son, Robert (tract called Cross Keys tract); five sons. Executors, son Robert and son-in-law Pat. Hays. Teste: James Asten, John Asten, Sr. and Jr. Proved, 26th June, 1809. Executors qualify.

Page 280.—18th June, 1806. James Alexander's will, of Long Meadow—"Son, John Alexander, and William Alexander, and Gabriel Alexander"; son, Andrew; son, James; daughter, Mary Alexander; daughter, Dorcas Pilson; daughter, Martha Alexander; daughter, Margaret Alexander; daughter, Elisebeth Alexander. Executors, sons John, Andrew, William, Gabriel. Teste: John Thompson, Geo. Pilson, Jno. Brady, Gabriel Alexander. Proved, 26th June, 1809. Executors qualify except Andrew. Sureties, Gabriel Alexander, Sr. and Jr.

Page 283.—18th May, 1808. Christian Hess' will—To wife, Elizabeth; daughter, Elizabeth Noll; son, Joseph (to be paid by son Christian); son, John; son, Christian. Executors, Jacob Swoope, Barnet Lowman. Teste: Joseph Ewing, Jacob Lowman. Proved, 26th June, 1809.

Page 294.—13th July, 1803. Jacob Sheetz's (German) will, advanced in years—To daughter, Margaret, wife to Garrett Daulton; granddaughter, Elizabeth Miller; son, Jacob (infant by second wife); son, John; son, Philip; son, Daniel; son, Peter; son, Andrew; son, Henry; wife. Executors, sons John, Daniel, Peter. Teste: Jacob Kinney, Jno. Fackler, W. Chambers, M. Garber, Jr; Geo. Fackler. Codicil, 27th June, 1808—Son Jacob has so behaved as to forfeit respect and benevolence; bequest revoked, and to be divided between other six sons, viz: John, Philip, Daniel, Peter, Andrew, Henry. Teste: Samuel Frame, Adam Link, Jas. Crawford, Vincent Tapp, Joseph Smith. Proved, 24th July, 1809. Executor Daniel refused to qualify. John and Peter qualify.

Page 298.—Plats accompanying said will above recorded.

Page 301.—24th July, 1809. Agreement between Elizabeth Sheetz, widow and relict of Jacob Sheetz and John, Peter, Philip, Daniel, Andrew, Henry Sheetz. She releases dower.

Page 306.—3d August, 1808. Thomas Turk's will—To wife, Mary; wife's mother, Easther Woolman; grandson, Thos. Turk McCullough, infant; grandson, Thos. Turk Rhea (Reah), infant; daughters, Esther Johnston, Betsey Coger; Rebecca Anderson; son, James Turk; daughters,

Jane Allen, Betty Glave; son, Thomas. Executors, Andrew Ramsey, Wm. Patrick, Robt. Porterfield. Teste: Paley (her (X) mark) Belew, Wm. Patrick, John and Christian Fauber. Proved, 24th July, 1809.

Page 309.—31st October, 1806. James Henry, Sr.'s, will—To wife, Mary; daughters, Sarah and Nancy; son, John; son, James; to Sarah Alexander, wife of Wm. Alexander; to granddaughter, Matilda; children, viz: James, Robert, Sarah, Nancy, Mary, John. Executors, sons James and Robert. Teste: Jno. McFaddin, Samuel Eakin, James McClung, James Poage. Proved, 28th August, 1809. Executors qualify.

Page 312.—10th July, 1809. John Dickey's will—To five daughters, viz: Jean Young, Elin Lamb, Mary Johnston, Margaret Rankin, Beckey Dickey, lands in Kentucky. Executors, sons-in-law Richard Johnston, Abraham Lamb, Thos. Rankin. Teste: James Allison, Francis Brown, Thomas Young. Proved, 28th August, 1809. Executors qualify.

Page 315.—6th August, 1806. Francis Acord's (German) will—To wife, Dorothy; children. Executors, Philip Hains and Jacob Eccord. Teste: Daniel Fall, Jno. Roberts. Proved, 23d October, 1809. Executors qualify.

Page 317.—25th February, 1804. Ulrich Fulwider's will—To wife, Margaret; son, George (two entrys made in Beverly's lands); to five daughters, Margaret Cline, Susanna Bright, Mary Wearly, Betsy Hanger, Catherine Hefner (Margaret and Susanna are dead); son, Henry (?); to Margaret Gaul; son, John (?). Executors, Robert Harris and Margaret Fulwider. Teste: James and Thomas Harris. Proved, November Term, 1809. Margaret qualifies.

Page 325.—25th June, 1805. Hugh Donaghe's will—To wife, Anne; son, William W. Donaghe, infant; daughter, Elisabeth Campbell, wife to Robert Campbell; to son, John; grandson, Hugh Donaghe, son to son James, deceased, and sisters of said grandson Hugh; to children, Sarah and James. Executors, Archibald Stuart and son, Jno. Donaghe. 26th February, 1807, Codicil—Wife Anne is dead, their children were three, viz: William W., Sarah, and James. Robert Campbell and family have conducted themselves improperly towards testator. Teste: Eleanor Stuart, Mary P. Hall. Proved, 25th December, 1809. Executors qualify.

Page 349.—12th February, 1810. Francis Long's will, of South River— To nephew, William Long, son to David Long; to brother David Long's daughters, viz: Jane, Elizabeth, Dorcas, Rebecca Long, and niece, Alex. Lang, lands descended to testator from brother, Dr. Alexander Long; to niece, Alex. Long, daughter to brother David; to brother, Samuel; to nephew, Wm. Lang, son to brother David. Executors, brother Samuel Long and nephew Wm. Long. Teste: Gabriel Alexander and Joseph Bell. Proved, 26th February, 1810. Executors qualify.

Page 361.—30th May, 1809. James Allen's will—To wife, Margaret; son, James; daughter, Polly Lewis; to grandsons, Allen Trimble, Allen Page, Allen McCue; has heretofore deeded land to his children. Executors, sons William and James. Teste: James Allen, Peter Hanger, James Kinney. Proved, 28th May, 1810. James qualifies.

Page 362.—4th June, 1808. Thos. Hughart's will—To grandson, Thomas Montgomery, home plantation in Calfpasture, joining Thomas Phillips; to granddaughter, Easter Montgomery; to grandson, Jno. Montgomery; to grandson, Wm. Montgomery; grandson, Hughart Montgomery. Executor,

Rev. John Montgomery; to daughter, Agnes Montgomery; to brother, James Hughart; to Patsey Hughart and her mother. Teste: J. Ramsey, Jno. Ramsey, Wm. Ramsey. Proved, 23d May, 1810. Executor qualifies.

Page 364.—22d May, 1809. William Chambers' will—To wife; son, Thomas; daughter, Catherine H. Levier (Lewin); to son, Mustoe Chambers; daughter, Margaret; daughter, Ann; to son, Jacob Kinney Chambers; daughter, Jean; son, William; to young daughter, Harriet Maria; wife's mother to be provided for for life. Executors, wife, Ann; sons, Thomas and Mustoe. Teste: Samuel Clarke, Geo. G. McIntosh, Wm. Boys, Joseph Cowan. Proved, 30th May, 1801. Widow and Mustoe qualify.

Page 389.—11th March, 1810. John Perey's will, aged and infirm—To wife, Hannah; son, Joseph; to George Deanmor, or his next brother; daughter, Rebecca. Executors, son Joseph and John Waddle. Teste: Henry M. Smith, Peter Waggoner, Frederick Carrew. Proved, 23d July, 1810. Executors qualify.

Page 390.—16th July, 1809. Nicholas Hope's will, of Greenville in Augusta County—To wife, Rachel; to Joseph and Benj. Huston, provided they will each name a child Nicholas Hope; to Sally Huston and Adam Gains; to Thomas McKirgan. Executors, wife Rachel and Joseph Huston. Teste: Wm. Steele, N. Torbet, Ballard Smith. Proved, 27th August, 1810. Rachel qualifies.

Page 390.— — ———, 1808. Joseph Parks' will—To son, James; grandsons, Joseph, Thomas, and John Parks; children of son, Thomas, deceased, infants; to son, Joseph; son, William; son, David; daughter, Ann Wilson; daughter, Rebecca Finley. Executors, (son) Joseph Parks and Joseph Cowan. Teste: Richard, Reuben, Fanny Holt, Jas. Kennerley, Jr.; Andrew Barry. Proved, 24th September, 1810. Cowan refuses. Parks qualifies.

Page 392.—1st December, 1807. George Shultz's will—To wife, Christiana; son, David; daughter, Margaret, married to David Grove; son, Adam, infant; to son, Henry; grandchildren, John and Geo. Teaford; to Betty Teaford; son, George. Executors, wife and son, David. Teste: Samuel Finley, Job. Hart, Jno. McFadden. Proved, 24th September, 1810. Executors qualify.

Page 401.—26th September, 1810. Robert Crawford's will—To wife, Sarah; daughter, Elizabeth; sons, Hugh and James; to son, George; to John Poage (one-eighth of estate); to daughter, Jane; son, Robert; son, William; son, John. Executors, John and William Poage. Teste: William and Jas. Craig, Jas. D. Kayser. Proved, 22d October, 1810. Executors qualify.

Page 404.—25th September, 1810. James Moffett's will—To daughter, Mary McCallim; to heirs of daughter Martha McGill; to daughter, Jane Culton; daughter, Sarah Aston; son, James, Jr.; to daughters, Elizabeth and Ann. Executors, son James, daughter Elizabeth. Teste: Robt. Calleson, David and James Hamilton. Proved, 26th November, 1810. James Moffett qualifies.

Page 411.—15th June, 1810. Jacob Sheetz's heirs (see his will, p. 294, *supra*) agree to give their brother Jacob the $1,000 left him in the original will. Heirs are, viz: Daniel, Philip, Andrew, Henry, John, Peter.

Page 435.—15th April, 1810. Cornelius Adair's will—To sons, William and John, now living in Pennsylvania; to sons, Francis and James; to wife, Elizabeth; to all children, viz: John, James, William, Benjamin, Francis, Polly (wife to Peyton Shumate). Executors, son William and friend Robert Stuart. Teste: Richard Holt, Robt. Hunter, Daniel Swisher. Proved, 29th January, 1811, and 20th February, 1811, Robert Stuart refuses, and 24th February, 1812, administration heretofore granted Andrew Hunter is repealed, and administration granted to William Adair.

WILL BOOK No. XI.

Page 25.—22d October, 1810. William Young's will—To wife, Elizabeth; to son, James; son, William; to son and daughter, Robert and Margaret Anderson; to "Him who was my son-in-law, Robert Harrison"; to grandson, Robert Harrison; grandson, William Harrison; grandson, James Harrison; niece, Polly Burgess. Executors, sons William and James. Teste: John Gamble, Jos. Snapp, Jacob van Lear. Proved, 27th May, 1811. Executors qualify.

Page 32.—19th March, 1810. William Ralston's will—"Infirmities natural to old age"; to wife; daughter, Betsey, and sons, William and David; to daughter, Eleanor; sons, James and Mathew; daughter, Sally; to son, George; to Betsey Williams and David; daughter, Betsey. Teste: James A. McCue, Samuel Ralston. Executors, wife; sons, James, William, David. Proved, 24th June, 1811. William and David qualified.

Page 34.—1st January, 1811. George Moffett's will—To wife, Sarah; to daughter, Margaret, to school her two youngest children, Clarissa and Joseph; to son, James (900 acres of Glen Creek, Ky., land); son, George (South Elkhorn Survey in Kentucky); son, William; to five married daughters; daughter, Sally; daughter, Margaret (Glen Creek Survey where she now lives); to deceased daughter Martha's daughter, Sally, and son, George (Glen Creek); Martha was wife of Capt. Robert Kirk; to daughter, Mary (Glen Creek); to daughter Mary's children by her first husband; to deceased daughter Magdalene's children, viz: George, John, Henry, Addison, Samuel, Magdalene; to daughter, Elizabeth, and her son, George; to daughter, Sally; to brother William's widow and children, John, Thomas, Mary; to son George's Maria; to sister, Mary; to Charles Patrick's son, George; to sister, Hannah, and her son, George; to nephew John Patrick's oldest son; to nephew, John M. Estill, and Benj. Estill's oldest daughter. Executors, son James and nephew Jno. M. Estill. Teste: George Crosby, Wm. Young, Jno. A. Sheets. Proved, 26th August, 1811. Executors qualify.

Page 39.—7th November, 1810. Reuben Larew's will—To brother Peter's three children, viz: Abraham Larew, Sarah Felts, Elizabeth Bodine; to sister, Anne Drake, and two children; to brother Jacob's children, viz: Peter Larew, Elizabeth Allen, John Larew, Benj. Larue, Joseph Larew, Sally Best, Polly Larew, Jacob Larew, Amy Larew. Executors, Benjamin and Joseph Larew, Wm. Davis, Geo. Zumbro, Walter Davis. Proved, 27th August, 1811. Executors qualified.

Page 43.— — September, 1802. William Robertson's will (in form of a letter addressed to his son, Mathew)—Mathew is engaged to Miss Catren

Kennerley, and father advises him to fulfil the engagement; daughter, Mary; son, James. Proved, 26th August, 1811.

Page 50.—3d September, 1811. Valentine Shirley's will—To son, Henry; daughter, Betsey; daughter, Anna; wife, Catherine; to John and Jacob Rush, on account of son Charles, who owes them; to daughter, Barbara Baker, wife of Samuel Baker; to son, Adam; son Jacob Sherley and Jacob Bear, executors. Teste: John Barnett, Wm. Craig, Adam Bear, Jas. Craig. Proved, 23d September, 1811. Executors qualify.

Page 53.—12th June, 1807. James Willson's will—To sons, William and Joseph; son, George; daughters, Joanna Hogshead, Mary Erwin, Peggy Trimble; daughter, Olive McFaul. Executors, son Joseph and son-in-law Jas Hogshead. Teste: Wm. Bell, Samuel Jackson, John Jackson. Proved, 23d September, 1811. Executors qualify.

Page 57.—5th September, 1811. William Knowles' will—To wife, Mary; children now at home (those married having been already provided for), viz: Sarah, Polly, Catherine, Susan, Archibald, Daniel, William, John. Executors, Sampson Eagor and Wright Burgess. Proved, 28th October, 1811, by Geo. Brooks and Geo. Gordon. Executors qualify.

Page 63.—10th January, 1799. William Mathews' will—To wife and son; daughter, Jane Fulton; daughter, Catherine; to son, Richard; son, Joseph; son, James; daughter, Mary Rankin; son, William; daughter, Elizabeth Gains; daughter, Margaret; son, John (executor). Teste: Alex. Robertson, Wm. Curry, Elj. Robertson. Proved, 23d December, 1811. Executor qualifies.

Page 81.—2d December, 1811. James Kear's will—To wife, Jean; grandson, James, son to son John; to daughters, viz: Elizabeth Givens, Margaret Ramsey, Jane Leard; to each grandson named for testator. Executors, son John Kear, Alex. Kear, John Johnston. Teste: Mathew Robertson, Jno. Trotter, Sally Trotter. Proved, 24th February, 1812. John and Alexander qualify.

Page 91.—14th January, 1811. Jacob Bushong's will—Estate to be divided into eleven shares, one share to each child; executors, sons-in-law Philip Hains and Peter Nicholas. Teste: Daniel Fall, Jacob Smith, Peter Hill. Proved, 23d March, 1812. Peter refuses to execute. Philip qualifies.

Page 118.—17th March, 1812. John McCune's will—To wife, Marget; son, Allen McCune; son, John; sons, Samuel and James; daughter, Peggy; to daughters; daughter, Deborah Harris. Executors, sons James and Allen. Teste: Claudius Buster, Jacob Wine, George Pilson. Proved, 28th April, 1812, by Claudius Buster, and 25th May, 1812, by Geo. Pilson. Executors qualify.

Page 121.—25th March, 1809. John Givens' will—To wife, Jean; son, Alexander (to provide for son John); to daughter, Margaret Fulton; daughter (?), Ann Robertson. Executors, son Alexander and Joseph D. Kizer. Teste: James Allison, Wm. Craig, Ralf A. Loftus. Proved, 25th May, 1812. Alexander qualifies.

Page 139.—17th April, 1812. Agreement between widow Margaret McNutt, sons and daughters, James, Jane, Robert, Samuel McNutt (part of the children), heirs of James McNutt, deceased, who died 6th September, 1811, having been insane some years, for assignment of dower and division of estate. There were also children, Alex. McNutt and Wm. Beard, and wife.

Page 153.—6th July, 1812. In Fleming County Court, Kentucky—Isaac S. Keith is appointed guardian to William and Mathew Thompson. infant orphans of Mathew Thompson.

Page 165.—29th May, 1809. William Robertson's will—To son, Mathew; son-in-law, Robt. Givens; to son, James; son-in-law, Thos. Downey; estate to be divided into equal shares, and one share to each, viz: son, James; daughter, Jane, wife to John Givens; daughter, Isabella, wife to George Givens; daughter, Elizabeth, wife to Robt. Douglass; daughter, Lettice, wife to William Rankin; grandson, Edward Downing, son to Thomas; daughter, Rebecca, wife to David White; to Lettice and Ann Robertson, daughters; to son, Alexander; to Dorcas and Phoebe Allison, daughters; to William Allison. Executors, son James, Alex. Givens, Wm. Patrick. Teste: Wm. Patrick, John Porterfield, Chas. Patrick. Proved, 26th October, 1812. Givens and Robertson qualify. Patrick refuses.

Page 168.—12th December, 1811. Adam McChesney's will—To daughter, Jane Eliza McChesney; brother, James (plantation his father bought of Wm. Rhea); brother, Robert; sister, Sally (now Sally Moffett), the legacy she fell heir to by her grandfather's (Patrick Crawford's) will; father and family to live on the land for life; brother Robert's son, Adam McChesney. Executors, brothers Robert and James. Teste: John and Rebecca McChesney, Henry Miller. Proved, 29th October, 1812. Robert qualifies.

Page 169.—Distributers of Rev. Archibald Scott, viz: Jane Scott, William Wilson, James Scott, Wm. Scott, Jas. McKnight, Archibald Scott, Andrew Scott, Matilda Scott. 24th September, 1812.

Page 171.—3d June, 1812. Elizabeth Graham's will—To granddaughter, Elizabeth Redenhouse; grandson, James Nelson Bell; granddaughter, Rebecca Burgess; grandson, Lancelot Graham Bell; grandson, John Hamilton Bell. Executors, Rev. Jno. Montgomery. Teste: Ro. Dunlap, Andrew Kinkead, Jno. Clayton, Jno. Montgomery. Proved, November Term, 1812. Rev. Jno. Montgomery, refuses and admintration granted John Montgomery, Jr.

Page 173.—22d July, 1812. Jean Givens' will—To son, Alex. Givens; daughter, Margaret Fulton; to granddaughter, Jane Fulton; niece, Ann Robertson; to daughter Margaret Fulton's children. Executors, son Alexander and Jas. Allison. Teste: James Allison, Ralph A. Lofftus, Mathew Givens. Proved, November Term, 1812. Alex. R. Givens qualifies.

Page 180.—2d May, 1811. Abel Griffith's will—To wife, Magdalene; sons, Isaac and Elijah (land on Green River, Henderson County, Ky.); to son, William; to son, Abner's two children; daughter, Catherine Carson's children; daughter, Jane Evilsizer's children; daughter, Agness Wood's (deceased) children; to four youngest daughters, Elizabeth, Ruth, Hanna, Rebecca; to four youngest sons, Robert, David, Caleb, Hiram (land on Long Glade). Executors, wife Magdalene and Martin Coiner. Teste: Alex. Robertson, John Bell, Robt. Curry. Codicil—28th July, 1812, the land he bought of son James he has exchanged with Jno. M. Estill, but has no deed; devised to four youngest sons. Proved, December Term, 1812. Executors qualify.

Page 182.—25th October, 1812. James Mateer's will—To wife, Jane McTeer; to four children, William McTeer, Mitchel McTeer, Eliza Mc-

Teer, Isabella McTeer; brother, William. Executors, wife Jane, Thos. Mitchell, Jr.; Daniel Henderson. Teste: Thos. Jackson, Robt. Doake, Dorcas M. Doake, Nancy Doake. Proved, December Court, 1812. Jane and Thomas qualify.

Page 190.—29th September, 1808. William King's will—To wife, Mary; daughter, Sarah; son, Adam; son, Robert; to daughter, Margaret Smith; daughter, Elizabeth Mynes. Executors, Wm. Fowler, Samuel Ervin. Teste: John Vigors, Thos. King. Proved, 25th February, 1811, by Vigors, and December Court, 1812, recorded by order of Superior Court of Law. Administration granted John Michael (executors had refused at a former court), and at June Court, 1818, presented and having been ordered recorded by the Superior Court of Law is now recorded.

Page 200.—5th July, 1811. Frederick Hanger's will (signed in German)—To wife and infant and unmarried daughters; son, Frederick, infant; daughter, Betsey Steele, wife to Wm. Steele; daughters, Caty Shuey (Sliney), Polly Engleman, Hannah Ott; daughters, Barbara, Rebecca, Elizabeth, Eve, Sarah, Christiana. Executors, wife, Barnard Lowman, and Geo. Baylor. Teste: G. Washington Swoope, Jacob Swoope, Christian Beard. Proved, January Court, 1813. Widow Maria and others qualify.

Page 202.—2d August, 1811. John Kirkpatrick, Sr.'s, will—To wife, Martha; son, Thomas (who is to pay son, James); to son, James; daughter, Anny; sons and daughters now living; to children of deceased daughters, Nancy and Polly; to grandson, John Gillaspie. Executors, son Thomas and James McCutchen. Teste: Thomas Nelson, William Hanna, John Nelson. Proved, January Court, 1813. Executors qualify.

Page 210.—9th September, 1812. Robert Wallace's estate divided among the distributees, viz: James Wallace, Robt. P. Wallace, Moses Wallace, Betsy Wallace, Esther Wallace, Benj. Ervine.

Page 221.—30th June, 1812. Benjamin Brown's will—To wife, Elizabeth; son, Joseph; to the children of daughter, Sally Brown, being six in number. Executors, son Joseph. Teste: Hugh Young, Wm. Calhoon, Samuel Clarke. Proved, March Court, 1813. Executor qualifies.

Page 229.—Dr. James McCausland, guardian of Hugh Donaghe, orphan of James Donaghe—By James Bobkins, paid him in part of his wife's legacy bequeathed her by her grandfather, Hugh Donaghe.

Page 265.—10th December, 1812. William Ross' will—To wife, Jane; daughter, Elizabeth Gleave; son and daughter, Daniel and Margaret Green; son and daughter, Adam and Mary Russell; son, John; son and daughter, Moses and Jane Russell; daughter, Letty Ross; son and daughter, Samuel and Margret Ross; nephew, Wm. Ross; son, William. Teste: David Leonard, Benj. Greve. Executors, wife Jane and William Ross, Jr. Proved, 24th May, 1813. Executors qualify.

Page 283.—6th February, 1804. Samuel Hunter's will—To son, John; son, Samuel; younger sons, Henry and William; to four grandchildren, children of Andrew and Mathew Hunter (each having son named Samuel and daughter named Susannah). Executors, William Steele and sons Samuel and Andrew Hunter. Teste: Robt. Steele, Wm. Beard, Jno. Shields. Proved, July, 1813. Jno. Shields is dead. Wm. Steele refuses. Others qualify.

Page 285.—24th October, 1806. George Mathews' will, Sr., of Mississippi Territory—To daughters, Rebecca Meriwether and Jane Telfair, land in Kentucky on Green River; to son, John Mathews' three sons, George, Archer, and John Mathews, 1,000 acres on Ohio River four miles below mouth of Sciota; to son William's four sons, George, Francis Meriwether, Charles L., and Samuel B. Mathews, land on Dice Creek in Ohio; to wife, Mary; to Miss Sarah Carpenter Nelson. Executors, sons George and Charles L. Mathews. Teste: Lawrence Lewis, Archibald Lewis, John Cavit. Certified true copy from Adams County, Mississippi Territory. Proved in Scott County, Ky., September Court, 1813. Recorded in Augusta County, 27th September, 1813.

Page 309.—5th December, 1805. Samuel Long's will, of South River—To brother, James (who went to Kentucky), land in Kentucky; to brother, Francis, slave which went to Kentucky with my mother; to brother, David, brother, Joseph, the money he received of me when going to Kentucky; to brother, Alexander; to brother David's daughter, Elizabeth; brother David's son, Samuel; to brother David's son, William. Executors, Joseph Bell, Wm. Long, Samuel Long. Teste: Joseph Bell, Sarah Bell. Proved, 24th January, 1814. Joseph Bell refused to qualify. Wm. Long qualified, and 28th February, 1814, Samuel qualified.

Page 316.—3d March, 1813. William Bell, Sr.'s, will—To nephew, William B. Kirk, land on Middle River adjoining land testator lives on; to nephew, Wm. Bell; to Jane, wife to Robt. Cunningham; Rachel, wife to John Cunningham; Rachel, wife to Israel Patterson; William Bell, son to nephew John Bell; Margaret Jameson, each one share; nephew, William Bell (is this grandnephew above?), and his brother, Samuel; to Rachel Bell Kirk, daughter to Wm. B. Kirk. Executor, Robert Cunningham. Teste: Samuel Bell, Wm. Cunningham, Francis Bell. Proved, 28th February, 1814. Executor qualified.

Page 318.—7th January, 1814. Christian Shelly's will—To wife, Fany; son, John; daughter, Anny Rusmessel; other children that are married; daughter, Mary; daughter, Betsy; son, Daniel; son, Jacob (under 18). Executors, sons-in-law David Stover, Christian Rusmessel. Teste: Michael Shiry, David Hogshead. Executors qualify. Proved, 28th February, 1814.

Page 332.—8th January, 1814. Ann Moffett's will—To Sister, Sally Aston; brother, James Moffett; cousin, Elizabeth Morris, wife to George Morris of Bath County; niece, Evelina Asten. Executor, brother James Moffett. Teste: David Hamilton, James Aston, John Aston, Jr. Proved, 28th March, 1814. Executor qualified.

Page 336.—25th July, 1786. Joseph Mays, Sr.'s, will—To wife, Rebekah; son, James; daughter, Ester. deceased, and daughter, Rebekah, are provided for; to son, Joseph; son, Isaac (cabin where Michael Francisco formerly lived); daughter, Nancy; sister, Sarah; to Archibald. Executors, Col. John Dickinson, Richard Mays. 4th April, 1787, receipt by the legatees, viz: Rebecca Maze, Joseph Maze, Nancy Shad (Shields?), Isaac Maze. Teste: Jno. Dickinson, Richard Maise, Samuel Shrewsberry (bury). Proved, 21st June, 1791, by Ro. Hall, 26th August, 1812, commission to Woodford County, Ky., to take deposition of witness Samuel Shannon. Executed, 5th April, 1813. Fully proved and recorded 28th March, 1814.

Page 340.—9th January, 1811. David Byers' will—To son, John; wife, Rosannah; daughter, Mary Coiner; to daughter, Betsey Daugherty. Executors, wife and son John. Teste: Wm. Sproul, David and Hugh Fulton Proved, 24th March, 1814. Executor qualified. 14th March, 1805. John Erwin's will—To wife, Mary; son, Edward, and daughter, Margaret Herrin, and daughter, Mary Bell; son, Thos. Ervin; to daughter, Jean; son, James. Executors, sons Edward and Thomas. Teste: Wm. Erwin, Francis Erwin, Benj. Curry. 28th March, 1814, Edward qualifies.

Page 357.—28th March, 1814. Colonel James Allen's bond (with Jno. Poage) as guardian to Thomas Frame, orphan of Samuel Frame, under age and out of this State; estate devised to him by his grandmother, and which was in possession of his father as guardian at the time of his death.

Page 368.—19th June, 1810. James Frazer's will—To wife, Ann; to Archibald Guy and wife, Rebecca, and their son, James F. Guy, infant; Nathan Pugh is to be supported as long as he lives; to Archibald and Rebecca's son, John Guy (land in possession of Ezekiel Cooper); said James F. Guy's brother, Thomas Guy; said John Guy's brother, Robert Guy; to brother, Samuel Frazer's children, viz: John W., James, Samuel C., Bella Frazer. Executor, Ezekiel Cooper. Teste: Richard Holt, Ezekiel Cooper, Andrew Russell. Proved, 23d May, 1814. Executor refuses.

Page 395.—21st August, 1814. John Parris' will, in advanced age—To wife, Hannah; to sons, Thomas and George (has heretofore given military lands in Ohio); daughter, Jane Hudson; daughter, Margaret Henderson; daughters, Hannah and Elizabeth Parris; other daughters have been provided for at marriage; daughters, Mary Hudson, Martha Dennison, Jane Hudson, Margaret Henderson, Hannah and Elizabeth Parris; testator's land in Stokes County, N. C., to be sold; to son, John; son, Alexander; to each grandchild named after testator, i. e., John, son of Thomas; John, son of George; John, son of Charles Hudson. Executors, son John and wife Hannah. Teste: Vincent Tapp, Robt. Henderson. Proved, 26th September, 1814. Executors qualify.

Page 398.—15th March, 1814. Jane Black's will, of South River—To son, Samuel; daughter, Jane Alexander; daughter, Martha Black; daughters, Margaret Price and Mary Black; daughter, Nancy Gillespee; son, James; sons, John and William. Executors, sons James and Samuel. Teste: Joseph Bell, Moses Hughes, Elizabeth Hughes, Elizabeth Long. Proved, 24th October, 1814. Samuel qualifies.

Page 415.—22d November, 1814. Patrick Hall's will—To son, Robert; daughter, Patsey; daughter, Joanna; daughter, Polly McCormack. Executors, James Alexander and Jno. McChesney. Teste: Adam Weaver, Jeorah Davis, George Palmer. Proved, 28th November, 1814. Executors qualify.

Page 420.—10th August, 1814. Peter Cail's will—To wife, Mary Cale; to brother William Cale's children; to brother John Cale's children; brother David Cale's children; to brother, Wm. Cale; brother, Jacob; brother, John Cail's son, Isaac Cail. Executor, Mathias Link, Jr. Teste: W. Clarke, Barbara Palmer. Proved, 26th December, 1814, and 27th February, 1815, executor qualifies.

Page 430.—3d October, 1812. Mathias Link, Sr.'s, will (signed in German), of advanced age—To wife, Mary, to be paid by son, John; to sons,

Peter, Mathias, Christian; son, David; son, Adam; to daughters, Catherine Hanger, Elizabeth Wayland, Mary Grisham; to granddaughter, Sarah Link, daughter to John Link; to son, John. Executors, sons John and Peter. Teste: Wm. Wilson, Daniel Stover, Jr.; James Crawford. Proved, 27th February, 1815. John qualifies.

Page 432.—16th February, 1815. James Patterson's will—To wife, Deborah; sons, James, William, John, Samuel; to granddaughters, Deborah and Jane; granddaughter, Deborah Wynes; to grandsons, James Craige, Patterson Craige, James Wynes (Wymes); daughter, Jane, deceased, to her children; division to "Deborah Patterson any my nine children, or their lawful heirs, Martha Beard, Wm. Patterson, James Patterson, Sarah Craige, Deborah Wilson, the children of Jane Wyms (?) (Wynn?), John Patterson, Samuel Patterson, Nancy McCullough. Executors, sons James, John, Samuel. Teste: Jo. Williams, James and Samuel Patterson, John Craig. Proved, 27th February, 1815. James and John qualify.

Page 436.—29th November, 1814. William White's estate appraised.

Page 443.—20th January, 1815. Edward Burke's will—To sister, Elizabeth Bailey; brother, Joseph Burke's children; to Robert and William, infants, sons of Frederick Grass; to John Grass. Executors, Erasmus Stribling and Robert Grass. Teste: Joseph Wright, Elizabeth Argabright. Proved, 27th February, 1815. Executors qualify.

Page 456.—20th December, 1807. Michael Ocheltree's will, Sr.—To wife, Mary Eliot, otherwise Ocheltree; to son-in-law, Wm. Young; son-in-law, Joseph Lowery. Executors, Wm. Young and wife, Mary Eliot, alias Ocheltree. Teste: James Allison, John Dickey, Francis Brown. Proved, 27th February, 1815, by Francis Brown, and 27th March, 1815, by Allison. Wm. Young qualifies.

Page 458.—22d December, 1801. George Glenn's will—To son, Hugh; son, James; son, William; son-in-law, Wert Miller, and daughter, Nancy; son-in-law, Robert Young and daughter, Sarah; son-in-law, Samuel Curry, and daughter, Mary; son-in-law, John Mead. Executor, son Hugh. Teste: John Anderson, James and Geo. Anderson. 11th March, 1815, commission to Justices of Augusta County to take deposition of George Anderson, an aged and infirm witness, returned executed 14th March, 1815. Proved, 27th March, 1815 (George Anderson is dead since above deposition; James (and John?) Anderson are also dead). Executor qualifies.

Page 461.—25th May, 1813. Gasper Clemant's will—To wife, Mary; division to, viz: Christopher Clemens, John Clements, Nancy, wife to George Crawford; Catren Clements, Polly Clements, grandson, Casper Clements; to son, James. Executors, Chas. Patrick, James Craig, Jr. Teste: John Conner, Sr. and Jr.; Thos. Ellet Conner. Proved, 27th February, 1815. Craig qualifies, and 27th March, 1815, Patrick qualifies.

WILL BOOK No. XII.

Page 23.—26th May, 1814. Mary Woods' will—To son, John; son, William; daughter, Elizabeth Donovan; daughter, Mary Brown; son, Joseph; granddaughter, Jemima Woods, daughter to son Joseph; grandson, Jacob, son to son Joseph. Executors, Isaac Jones and Wm. Sillings.

Teste: Lawrence Swink, John Gamble, John Woods. Proved, 26th June, 1815. Sillings refuses. John qualifies.

Page 37.—4th December, 1810. William Thomsen's will—To son, John, and his son, William; to son, William; to daughter, Margaret; daughter, Elizabeth Willson; daughter, Mary Willson; daughter, Martha Torbet; daughter, Rachel Berryhill; daughter, Jane Brown, and her husband, Thos. Brown. Executors, son John and Samuel Blackwood. Teste: Geo. Crowbarger, Adam Shields. Proved, 26th June, 1815, and 24th July, 1815, executors refused. Administration granted William ———.

Page 39.—5th May, 1815. Mary Erwin's will—To Thomas and Edward; daughters, Peggy Herrin and Polly Bell; to son, John; son, James; granddaughter, Polly Stuart Erwin; to daughter, Jenny Ervin. Executors, sons Edward and William. Teste: Paul Roller, Beverley Staunton, Sayee (Gayee?) Staunton. Proved, 24th July, 1815. Executors, Edward Ervin and Wm. Ervin, Sr., qualify.

Page 72.—4th April, 1813. John Grayham's will, of Calf Pasture, far advanced in years—To daughter, Margret; son, James; son, Robert; son, William; son, Lanty; daughter, Elizabeth Bratton; daughter, Martha Dunlap; son, John (already provided for). Executors, son James and Rev Jno. Montgomery. Teste: Jno. Montgomery, Wm. Bratton, Jno. Montgomery. Proved, 25th September, 1815. Jno. Montgomery refused. James qualifies.

Page 88.—5th September, 1811. Samuel Irvin's will—To wife, Mary; son, Joseph; youngest daughter, Sarah Irvin; to son, William; division among ten daughters, viz: Jane, Margret, Agnes, Elizabeth, Mary, Martha, Ann, Rebecca, Sally, Nickle. Executor, son William. Teste: John Poage, Hugh Green (Glenn), Jas. Hogshead.

Page 94.—2d December, 1813. Isaac Glass' will—To son, John, and to his son and my son, Isaac Glass; to daughter, Fany King, and her son, Isaac King; to grandson, Harry King; to daughter, Margret Young; grandson, Isaac Young; to granddaughter, Margaret Young; grandson, Robert Young. Executors, son-in-law Andrew Young, James Allison, Samuel Gerry. Teste: Andrew Young, Hugh Glenn, Benj. Bryan. Proved, 23d October, 1815. Andrew and James qualify.

Page 98.—23d September, 1814. Alexander Stuart's will—To children of son James, proceeds of lot in Wythe County; to all children, already provided for; to son, Archibald; to son, James Darnely. Executor, son Archibald. Teste: Alex. Hall, Eleanor Hall, Archibald A. Hall, Polly Reede. Proved, 27th November, 1815, by Alexander and Archibald Hall. 28th January, 1817, executor qualifies.

Page 101.—24th November, 1798. David Stephenson's will—To wife, Mary, whole estate and executrix. Teste: John Smith, Alex. Robertson, Wm. Robertson. Proved, 27th November, 1815. Holograph (?) will.

Page 129.—26th January, 1815. Elizabeth Heizer's will—To sons, Joshua and Edward, executors; to daughter, Polly; to daughter, Betsy Hare (Ware? Mare?); to sons, John, Nathaniel, and Samuel; daughter, Rebekah Smith. Teste: Wm. Abney, Mathias Swink. 2d May, 1815. Codicil—She is widow of Samuel Heizer, deceased. Proved, 26th February, 1816. Executors qualify.

Page 131.—23d January, 1813. Edward Erwin's will—To Benj. Erwin; heirs of Andrew Erwin; heirs of son John; to son, James; son, William; daughter, Mary; daughter, Jane; daughter, ————; to wife and small children; to daughter, Betsy. Executors, wife; her brother, Christian Perey, and son, Edward. Teste: James Miller, Thomas Ralston. Proved, 26th February, 1816. Widow Sarah qualifies.

Page 132.—12th February, 1812. John Thomas' will—To wife, Catherine; son, Thomas; daughter, Catherine Snyder; daughter, Barbara Eckard; to daughter, Rebecca Roberts (Probeck?); son, John; daughter, Elizabeth Thomas; daughter, Rebecca, is wife of Joseph Probeck; daughter, Catherine, is wife of Martin Snider; daughter, Barbara, is wife of Christian Echard; to grandsons, Peter, John, and Conrad, children of son, Jacob; to grandson, David Simmerman, son to daughter, Mary, deceased. Executors, son John and John C. Sours. Teste: Jacob Leas, Andrew Haroff, Samuel Clark. Proved, 26th February, 1816. John Thomas refuses, Souers qualifies.

Page 164.—25th May, 1810. David Caruthers' will—To wife, Elizabeth; sons, James and John; oldest daughter, Jean; daughters. Executors, wife, Samuel Jackson, James Best. Teste: Robert Scott, Wm. Engart, Peggy Jackson, Samuel Jackson. Proved, 27th May, 1816. Best refuses to qualify. Others qualify.

Page 178.—16th May, 1816. Anny Kirkpatrick's will—Executors, Thomas Nelson and James Hanna; to mother, Martha Kirkpatrick; brother, Thomas; to brother, James, and living sisters; sister, Jane Mickamy; to James Mickamy's oldest son; sister, Peggy Armstrong; brother, George Kirkpatrick. Teste: Jacob Crist (Creek), Jno. Crick, Jno. Nelson. Proved, 26th August, 1816. Executors qualify.

Page 179.—Samuel Clarke and John Poage, contract to make an accurate chart of the County according to the provisions of Act of Assembly, 27th February, 1816.

Page 208.—17th January, 1809. Sarah Scott's will—To sisters, Frances; brother, Robert, and his wife, Mary, and all Mary's daughters. Executor, brother Robert. Teste: Jacob F. Hatton, Edward Sowell, Philip Gregory, Watts D. Ervin, Walter Davis. Proved, 25th November, 1816.

Page 209.—14th April, 1814. Robert Scott's will—To wife, Mary, and schooling children; sister Sally to be supported according to will of father; to son, Robert, infant; to daughters, Polly, Ann, Jennette, Rebecca, Martha; to sons, William Joseph and Robert; to daughter, Elizabeth Larew; daughter, Eleanor Caldwell; daughter, Sally Sowell. Executrix, wife Mary. Teste: Wm. Davis, Wm. E. Davis, Sally Davis, Martha Ann Davis, Annis Davis. Proved, 25th November, 1816. Executrix qualifies.

Page 225.—26th September, 1816. John Russell's will—To wife, Elizabeth; sons, James and Robert; daughters, Ruth Robertson, Nancy Russell; to granddaughter, Elizabeth; to daughter, Nancy, and granddaughter, Elizabeth, their maintenance; to daughter, Jammianes' heirs; to Elizabeth; son, John; to Joseph; to Samuel; to Henry; daughter, Hanna; to Anne's heirs; to Sally; to Nancy; to Nancy and Ruth; other children not here named. Executors, wife Elizabeth and sons James and Robert. Teste: W. Wilson, Jr.; Joseph Brobeck (Brucet), Mathew Robertson, David Cunningham Proved, 27th January, 1817. Executors qualify.

Page 227.—2d July, 1816. John Sharpe's will—To son, Joseph; sons, John and Robert; son, Thomas; daughter, Ann Henry; daughter, Jane Black; daughter, Letitia Clarke; daughter, Peggy Weir; daughter, Fanny Porter; son James died intestate seized of considerable lands in Georgia. Executors, sons-in-law John Henry, James Black. Teste: Aaron Beaty, Elijah Carson, George Shultz. Proved, 27th January, 1817. Executors qualify.

Page 229.—19th November, 1816. Jean Craig's will—To daughter, Mary Magill; daughters, Elizabeth and Jane; to daughter, Nancy Hamilton; son, Robert Craig; to daughter, Sarah Hamilton; son, Elijah Craig. Executors, son Elijah Craig and James Craig. Teste: James Stewart, James Craig, Sr.; Wm. Craig. Proved, 27th January, 1817. Executors qualify.

Page 230.—1st January, 1817. James Moffett's will—To sister Astin's two children, Evalina and John (Askin), both infants; to wife, Rachel; to Alexander McCrea, son of my wife's sister, Mary McCrea. Executors, William Kenneday, of Rockbridge, Jno. Astin, of Greenville. Teste: James and David Hamilton, Walter Herron. Proved, 27th January, 1817. Executors qualify.

Page 246.—26th February, 1817. Charles Sproul's will—To brother, John; sister, Jean Weir; sister, Mary Sproul; to brother, Joseph; brother, Oliver; sister, Martha Hutcheson; to sister, Fanny Thomson; sister Sidney Beard's children, viz: Polly, William, Susannah, Jeanatte, and John; to half-brother, James Sproul; to children of half-brother, Alexander Sproul; to half-sister, Margaret McCutchen; to Alexander Beard; to Wm. Beard; to Thomas Beard; to half-brother, William Sproul. Executors, brother John Sproul, Thos. Thomson. Teste: Joseph Beard, Hugh Dougherty, Ro. Hutchison. Proved, 28th April, 1817. Executors qualify.

Page 250.—26th June, 1813. William Beard's will—To all children; to grandson, Thomas Beard; to grandson, Thomas Beard; to son Samuel Beard's son William. Executors, Joseph Beard, Wm. Sproul. Teste: James Hay, John McKee, Samuel H. McNutt. Proved, 26th May, 1817. Executors qualify.

Page 265.—31st March, 1817. Benjamin Roberts' will—To wife; to son, John; granddaughter, Patsey Roberts; to grandson, John Roberts Executor, Daniel Fall, Alex. Malcom. Teste: Wm. Hodge, Peter Laporte, Daniel Fall. Proved, 23d June, 1817.

Page 267.—24th July, 1817. Robert H. Chapman certifies that he moved from North Carolina on first of present month bringing a negro slave with intention of keeping her.

Page 287.—2d March, 1796. Jacob Swallow's will—To brother, Peter Kountz, tract whereon Philip Dull lives; to brother Peter Kountz's eldest son; to Mary that was formerly my wife, but now absconded and left my bed and board without any provocation; to sister, Mary Smith; to brothers and sisters, viz: Paul Koontz, John Kountz, Wm. Kountz, Polly Smith, and Sarah Kerler. Executors, John and Wm. Koontz. Teste: J. Ray, Wm. Willson, Samuel McCorkell. Proved, 27th October, 1817, by William Wilson; Joseph Ray is since dead; Samuel McCorkle is out of Commonwealth. John Krountz qualifies.

Page 292.—2d May, 1817. Paul Seig's will—To oldest son, John, the plantation he now lives on in Shenandoah; to son, Jacob; to daughter,

Susannah Bear; to sons, Paul and David; to wife, Susannah. Executors, sons Paul and David and Daniel Fall. Teste: Emanuel Randerbush, Jonathan Hains, David Seig, Wm. Boys. Proved, November Court, 1817. Daniel and Paul qualify.

Page 299.—11th May, 1816. Sarah Finley's will—To daughters, Jean Frazier, Peggy Hutchison, Sally Finley; to son, William Finley, executor. Teste: Andrew Ramsey, James and Patsey Finley. Proved, January Court, 1818. Executor qualifies.

Page 304.—15th March, 1814. John Jamison, Sr.'s, will—To son, James; son, Mathew; to son, William's children in Kentucky (probably William's oldest son Samuel is dead; if he is, then his part to go to his brother John); to daughters, Ellen Berry, Jane Cochran, Polly Templeton; to grandson, Jamison Cochran; to son, John; to grandson, John McCormick; to son James' son John; to son Mathew's daughter Sally. Executors, Jacob Swoope, John Willson, James Jamison. Teste: James Evans, Jesse Evans, W. Willson, Samuel Black. Proved, 26th January, 1818. April 24, 1818, Jacob Swoope qualifies (the other surviving executor having refused.)

Page 307.—5th March, 1816. Mary Stephenson's will, widow of Major D. Stephenson—All slaves to be liberated and transported to some free State; all estate to be divided into two equal parts, one to David's relations and one to Mary's; 1st, to Adam Stephenson's (deceased) children, to James Stephenson's (deceased) family, to William Stephenson's (deceased) family (all three brothers to David), and to Elizabeth Herring (sister to David), and to Robert Shanklin (son to David's sister); 2d, to Catherine Gordon (Mary's sister), Mrs. Ruth Davis (Mary's sister), James Davis, Walter Davis; and the children of Robert Davis (all Mary's brothers). Executors, Charles A. Stuart. Proved, February Court, 1818. Executor qualifies.

Page 342.—16th October, 1817. James McKemey, Sr.'s, will, aged—To wife, Agnes, $15 yearly, to be paid by son James; to son, James; to daughter, Jane; to daughter, Nancy Hogshead; to son, John; to daughter, Polly Herdman (Hendman). Executors, wife Agness and son James. Teste: Wm. Wilson, Peter Hanger, James Crawford, Jr. Proved, 24th March, 1818, by Crawford, and 27th March, 1818, by Peter Hanger. James qualifies.

Page 353.—25th January, 1818. Samuel Kulpatrick's will—To son, Michael; to son-in-law, John Armstrong, and his son, Samuel Armstrong; to orphan children of son-in-law, Samuel Armstrong; to daughter, Peggy Cunningham, and her children. Executor, son-in-law, John Cunningham Teste: John McChesney, Robert McChesney, Wm. McChesney. Proved, 25th May, 1818. Executor qualifies.

Page 354.—22d April, 1817. William Sterrett's will—Wife, Isabella, to be supported by his sons, James and Josiah Baskins; to son, Samuel; to my son, Alexander Boyd; to son, John; son, Henry; to son, William Bell, and William's brother, David; to son, David; daughter, Nancy Ritchie (under age, unmarried); Henry McCormick, of Dauphin (?) Co., Penna., is indebted to testator the amount of a legacy left testator by testator's brother-in-law, Wm. McCormick, of said county; this is devised to Joseph Sterrett, who served his time as an apprentice with said Henry McCormick. Executors, wife Isabella and son Samuel. Teste: Jonathan

Sherley, W. Clarke. (Plots of Samuel Sterret's land, John Sterret's land, David Sterrett's land.) Proved, 25th March, 1818. Executors refuse; and July Court, 1818, James Sterrett qualifies.

Page 369.—26th June, 1810. Michael Hogshead's will—To wife, Martha, to be maintained by sons Thomas and William; to sons, Thomas and William and John and David; to daughters, Rebekah, Peggy Armstrong, Agnes, Sarah, Polly, Jean, Anny; to grandson, Michael Hogshead. Executors, sons John and Thomas, and son-in-law David Hogshead. Teste: Richard Rankin, James Hogshead, Francis Gilkison. Proved, 28th September, 1818. Thomas qualifies.

Page 375.—25th June, 1769. John Buchanan's will—Lands on Reed Creek called Anchor and Hope, and 500 acres on New River where Adam Harman lived; to sons, James, William, and John (all under 30); to wife and children, tract where Walter Stewart lives; to daughter, Mary Boyd, wife to Andrew Boyd; to three youngest daughters; to George Wilson; to relative, James Buchanan, merchant in this county. Executors, Col. Andrew Lewis, Col. Wm. Preston, and nephew Wm. Campbell. Teste: John Smith, Robt. Breckinridge, Wm. Thompson, Jno. McClellan. Proved, 16th August, 1769. Preston and Campbell qualify; and 23d February, 1818, the will not having been recorded a certified copy is now ordered to be spread on record.

Page 389.—15th February, 1817. Jane McClure's will—To sister Margaret Lackie's children; to my brothers' Dauter and Dauter, and dauter to John Johnson, deceased, and wife, one to me unknown and also deceased, to her child if she comes to the age of maturity, thirty pounds to her and her heirs; to Isaac McClure and David McClure, all estate, after paying the legacy left to the orphan child of Jean Johnston, deceased. Executor, David McClure. Teste: Daniel Bell, Hugh McClure, Jr.; Samuel McClure. Proved, 24th August, 1818. Executor qualifies.

Page 390.—15th February, 1814. Henry King's will, aged and infirm—To wife, Susannah; to daughter, Mary; step-daughter, Martha Cochran; to wife's grandson, John Cochran; to wife's grandson, Henry King Cochran; to William King Patterson; to grandson, Henry Thornton, who has lately intermarried with my wife's granddaughter, Susanna Patterson; to granddaughter, Nancy Thornton; to grandson, Joseph Thornton; granddaughter, Mary Thornton. Executors, Col. Andrew Anderson, James Cochran, John Cochran. Teste: Samuel Miller, Lewis Wayland, Sr.; Peter Hanger. Proved, 24th August, 1818. Cochrans qualify.

Page 398.—22d July, 1818. George Springer's will—To Henry Painter, who married daughter Catherine, executor; to children of George Springer, deceased; to children of Esther Simmerman. Teste: Daniel Gibson, David Parry, Rice Tilman. Proved, 25th August, 1818. Executor qualifies.

Page 399.—List of all established roads in the County compiled by order of Court, dated 23d June, 1818.

Page 417.—6th October, 1818. William Crawford's will—To brother, James Crawford, tracts purchased by my father, James Crawford, deceased, from Jacob Eversole and James Givens; to sister, Elizabeth McClung; to sister, Mary Allen; to brother, John Crawford; to mother, Mary Crawford. Executors, brother James Crawford and brother-in-law John Allen. Teste: James Crawford, Jr.; Ch. A. Stuart. 23d November, 1818, executors qualify.

Page 419.—13th March, 1815. David Buchanan's will—To wife, Susannah; youngest daughter, Betsey; to daughter, Polly Hanna; son, James; son, Hugh; to daughter, Peggy Walker; daughter, Betsey Buchanan; to son, George, executor. Teste: James Clarke, James Buchanan, Sr.; Archibald Smiley, Samuel Armstrong. 2d May, 1817. Codicil—Wife Susanna is dead. Teste: Wm. Walker, Alex. Buchanan. Proved, 23d November, 1818. Executor qualifies.

CIRCUIT COURT WILLS.

Will Book No. 1.

Page 8.—James Moore's will, dated 31st March, 1785, of Rockbridge—Wife, Jinet; sons, John and James; son, Joseph; daughters, Mary, Rachel, and Jean; son, John and Hugh Kelso, executors. Probated, 1st September, 1791.

Page 10.—Guardianship bond of James Wallace, orphan of Samuel Wallace, 2d April, 1792.

Page 11.—William Patton's will, dated 31st March, 1793; proved, 5th April, 1793. About 1740 he was married to Mary Beaty, daughter of Alex. Beaty, of the parish of Donnagh, County Dunnigall Ireland, by whom he had one son, John, which wife and son he left in Ireland about one year after marriage; informed Mary is now dead; to Mathew Patton, of Staunton, £50, remainder to son John, if alive, and, if not, to be divided among his lawful children; otherwise to the children of Thomas Fulton, deceased, and the children of Mathew Patton, of Staunton. Signed.

Page 13.—Administrator's bond for estate of George Hudson, 6th April, 1793.

Page 16.—Guardianship bond for John Steele, son of James Steele, 1st September, 1794.

Page 17.—1st September, 1794. James Buchanan's administrator's bond.

Page 20.—Martin Witzel's will—9th February, 1795. Proved, 8th April, 1795. Grandson, John McClure.

Page 23.—Henry Miller's will—Dated, 9th March, 1796; proved, April, 1796. Wife, Hannah; son, Samuel; son, James; son, William; children are Rachel Lewis, Samuel Miller, James Miller, William Miller, Hannah Miller, Martha Miller, Henry Miller; sons, Samuel and James, and John Lewis, executors.

Page 27.—Col. Alexander McClenachan's appraisement. 6th May, 1797

Page 33.—24th September, 1797. David Buster's inventory.

Page 38.—David Laird's will, dated 5th October, 1799—Wife and son Samuel, executors; wife, Ann; daughter, Jean Coughran; son, James, tract located for David by Benj. Logan; son, David, tract assigned to David by Robert Lamme, of Kentucky; son, Samuel.

Page 41.—John Tate's will; dated 21st November, 1792; proved, 1st April, 1801—Third son, John; oldest son, Thomas, tract to John and Isaac Tate, sons of James, deceased, his grandsons; daughter, Eleanor Stuart; son, Robert Tate; son Robert and son-in-law Benj. Stewart, executors.

Page 43.—Rebekah Black's will, widow of Samuel Black, dated 8th February, 1794—Son, Samuel; daughter, Mary Black; son, John, 5 shillings birthright; daughter, Margaret Roberts; son, Joseph. Proved, 7th April, 1802.

Page 44.—Christian Eakle's will, of Washington County, Maryland—Children, John, Benjamin, Christian, Jonathan, Elizabeth, Katy, Mattena, and Rosa Eakle. Dated, 1st February, 1802; proved, 23d March, 1802.

Page 51.—Walter Davis's will, dated, 15th March, 1803; proved, 7th April, 1803—Wife, Martha; daughter, Agness; son, John; daughter, Euphemia Donnelly; daughter, Elizabeth Parks; grandchildren, Patsey Donelly, Wats Ewin, Walter Davis, Martha Ann Davis, Patsey Davis, and Patsey Davis Herin, Martha Rivers.

Page 55.—9th April, 1803—Robert Shaw's appraisement.

Page 61.—Jacob Baylor's will, 10th May, 1800; proved, 5th April, 1804—Son, George; wife? daughter? Anna Maria; son, Jacob; daughter, Mary Fisher; daughter, Elizabeth Neidner; daughter, Christinia Zimmerman; daughter, Barbara Kella; son, Martin; son, Christian.

Page 63.—Alexander Gibson's will, 13th July, 1804; proved, 3d September, 1804—Sister, Christiana Gibson; sister, Mary, wife of Henry Mowry; nephew, Daniel Gibson; niece, Elizabeth Cargo; James Creswell, who married his sister Margaret, mother of Elizabeth Cargo; nephew, Samuel Alexander Corgo; nephew, Daniel Gibson; niece, Harriet Cresswell, daughter of Margaret.

Page 69.—Hugh Alexander's will, dated, 15th March, 1805; proved, 2d April, 1805—Robert and William Alexander, sons of his brother William, under age.

Page 70.—John Surface, Sr.'s, will, dated, 27th January, 1805; proved, 8th April, 1805—Wife, Mary, children; son, Jacob Surface, executor.

Page 73.—Wm. Abney's bond, administrator of Alex. McClenachan, 5th April, 1797.

Page 74.—6th September, 1797. Claudius Buster's bond as administrator of David Buster.

Page 76.—1st September, 1797. John Scott and James Leech, bond as administrator of Andrew Scott.

Page 78.—1st September, 1797. Guardianship bond for Sally, John, and Thomas Scott, orphans of Andrew Scott, deceased.

Page 78.—4th April, 1800. Administration bond of estate of Robert Shaw.

Page 81.—2d September, 1800. Executrix' bond for estate of David Laird.

Page 81.—1st April, 1801. Robert Tate, executor of John Tate, bond.

Page 88.—8th April, 1805. Mortin Surface, administrator c. t. a. of John Surface, bond.

Page 92.—William Buchanan's will (farmer), dated, 1st October, 1804—Wife, Isabella; son, James; son, Alexander; son, John; William Caldwell and his heirs; Martha Beard, Rebekah Hanna. Proved, 2d September, 1805.

Page 100.—4th September, 1806. David McNair's appraisement.

Page 101.—James Kennerley, Sr.'s, will, dated, 23d June, 1797—Sons, Reuben, William, and Benjamin, James, Thomas, and Samuel; daughters, Mary Lockhart, Elizabeth Poindexter, Kitty Craig. Proved, 3d April, 1807.

Page 108.—24th April, 1810. George Blakeley to Peter Hanger, deed trust for Joseph Wayland, wagon and horses.

Page 109.—John Nickle's will, dated, 17th June, 1805—Wife, Sarah; son, John; granddaughter, Peggy Hall; daughter, Martha Richey; four daughters, Martha Richey, Polly Cravens, Betty Blair, Nancy Nickle; son, John, and son-in-law, Joseph Blair, executors. Proved, 20th April, 1810.

Page 118.—6th August, 1813. John Steele, of Natchez, in Mississippi Territory, appoints William Steele, of Rockbridge, attorney, to release and convey to John's brother, Robert Steel, the estate of John's brother, Samuel Steele.

Page 120.—22d April, 1818. Sarah Thompson and Lewis Wayland, Jr.'s, bond as administrators of William Thompson.

Page 121.—September, 1819. Jacob Humbert, Jr.'s, bond as administrator of Jacob Humbert, Sr.

Page 122.—20th April, 1820. Joshua Jones, administrator of Eleanor Jones, late Eleanor Thomas, bond.

Page 154.—Isaac McClure's, Sr.'s, will, dated, 5th February, 1828—brother, David McClure; brother, Hugh McClure, a person of unsound mind.

Page 164.—Thomas Sharp's will, 12th February, 1825—Oldest sister, Lettis Clark; sister, Peggy Weir, and her son, Hugh; brother, John; sister, Fanny Porter; brother, Joseph Sharp; brother, Robert Sharp; sister, Ann Henry; sister, Jean Black; Lettis Clark's son, John; James Black's son, Sam; Alexander Sharp, son of Robert Sharp, sister Lettis' first husband; wife, Mary.

CIRCUIT COURT WILL BOOK No. 2.

Page 1.—John Searight's will, dated, 17th February, 1784—Wife, Sarah; son, James; daughter, Anne Seawright; nephew, John Seawright; niece, Margaret Seawright.

Page 4.—Will of Joseph Borden, of Iredell County, N. C., dated, 29th April, 1803.—Wife, Jane; son, Levi, all land in Green River in Kentucky; son, Benj. Joseph Borden; granddaughter, Sally Lasnet, daughter of Richard Lasnett and Rebecca; grandson, Joseph Lasnett; granddaughter, Mary Lasnett; grandchildren, children of William Saunders and Mary; brother-in-law, Thomas Bromson; sister, Deborah Henry.

Page 11.—James Bell's will, 9th May, 1829—Natural daughters, Lucinda Bell, daughter of Rachel Western, wife of Richard Western, and the late Rachel Slaton, and to James Western, son of said Richard Western, by his wife Rachel, late Rachel Slaton; father, Samuel Bell; brother, Thomas Bell; James and Cyrus Western.

DEED BOOK No. 1.

Page 1.—John Madison, Gent., appointed Clerk of the Court by Thos. Nelson, Governor, 4th November, 1745.

Page 1.—9th December, 1745. Andrew Pickens to William McFeeters, £6 12½ acres Wm. McFeeters' old survey. Witnesses, Thos. Chew, James Trimble, Jno. Madison. Acknowledged, 10th December, 1745.

Page 3.—Williamsburg, October 30, 1745. Gentlemen: Whereas the Governor and Council have been pleased to order that the Court of your

County should be held in the Court House built for that purpose at my mill place; notifies them that he will make a deed for the house and two acres, for user only, of public buildings; writes because he doesn't wish any trouble in case of his death.—W. Beverley. To: The Court of Augusta County.

Page 5.—10th February, 1745 (1746). Alexander Thompson to Henry Downs, Sr., of Orange, £60.8.4; 300 acres on both sides South River, Shanando; part of 400 acres of land Alexander now lives on, granted to Alexander 8th July, 1742. Witnesses, Thomas Lewis, Jno. Beanham, Jr,; John Nicholas. Acknowledged, 10th February, 1745.

Page 7.—18th November, 1745. Nathan Underwood, of County of Orange, planter, to Christian Clymant, of Augusta. Whereas, on 13th January, 1741 (1742), was granted to Henry Dowly, of Orange County, 236 acres in Augusta, part of which Henry conveyed to Nathan Underwood by deed recorded in Orange; £18; part of the tract on South River of Shanando, 100 acres. Witnesses, Robert Turk, George Anderson, Eastham Franklyn. Proved, 10th February, 1745-6, by all the witnesses.

Page 12.—8th February, 1745-6. George and Robert Brackenridge to Samuel Wilson, £50, 461 acres in Beverley Manor, part of 761 acres deeded to vendors by Beverley 26th day November, 1742; to George, 300 acres, and Robert, the remainder. Deed recorded in Orange. Corner to George's land. Witnesses, John Smith, John Branham, Jr.; John McMaster. Acknowledged by grantors, 10th February, 1745.

Page 15.—10th February, 1745-6. James Gibbons (order book says James Givens) to Hugh Ross, £10 Pennsylvania money, 170 acres on west side Cathey's River called Walker's Run, Benjamin Allen's road. Acknowledged, 10th February, 1745.

Page 17.—10th February, 1745-6. James Cumberford apprentices himself to John McMaster, mason for 4 years and 5 months, to be taught art and mystery of a mason and plasterer. Acknowledged, 10th February, 1745-6.

Page 18.—Same signed and acknowledged by McMasters.

Page 20.—31st December, 1745. Daniel McEnaire (McNare)), Gent., to James Trimble, surveyor, £22, 10 shillings Virginia money; 400 acres on a branch of James River called Burden's Creek. Witnesses, James Sayers, David Trimble, Silas Hart. Acknowledged by Daniel McNare and Hannah, his wife, 11th February, 1745-6.

Page 23.—10th February, 1745-6. George and Robert Brackenridge to David Doack, £42, Virginia money; 300 acres in Beverley Manor, being the tract George now lives on. Acknowledged by both, 10th February, 1745-6.

Page 27.—11th February, 1745-6. Daniel McEnair, Gent., to Thomas Gardiner, "Sawer," £18 current money of Virginia; 165 acres on Jennings Creek, part of 400 acres granted to Daniel by patent. Witnesses, Silas Hart, Matt Edmiston, James Trimble. Acknowledged by Daniel and Hannah, his wife, 11th February, 1745-6.

Page 29.—6th February, 1745-6. John Patteet, of Frederick County, yeoman. Whereas, James Greenlee, of County of Augusta, yeoman, is bound to John Pateet by covenant relating to two tracts of land lying on South Branch of James River containing 550 acres, purchased by John from James to Charles Sinckler, laborer. Assignment to Charles of John's rights under the covenant with Greenlee.

Page 31.—11th February, 1745-6. William Thompson to James Craig, £30 Virginia currency; 305 acres on north side Middle River, Shanandoe, Hugh Thompson's land. Witnesses, Thomas Lewis, Robert Craig, Wm. Thompson. Acknowledged, 11th February, 1745-6.

Page 35.—14th April, 1746. James Patton and John Lewis to John Graham, £23.9.6 currency money, Virginia; 606 acres on Great River of Calfpasture, on east side, corner to James Lockridge, corner to Given's land. Witnesses, Thomas Chew and James Carter. Acknowledged by both, 14th April, 1746.

Page 39.—27th March, 1746 (not 7, but 1745-6). Timothy Crosthwaite, of County Orange, to James Patton, —— consideration; 400 acres in fork of James River granted by patent to William Crosthwaite, deceased, 12th February, 1742, and now in possession of Timothy, eldest son and heir of William. Witnesses, Thomas Chew, Henry Downs, Sr. and Jr. Proved by all the witnesses, 14th February, 1746, and 23d May, 1747.

Page 43.—12th December, 1745. Moses Thom(p)son, of Province of South Carolina, to John Madison, of Augusta, £110 current money; 731 acres, part of 1,041 acres sold to Thomson by Wm. Beverley out of 118,491 acres known as Beverley Manor; corner to Adam Thomson's land; corner to John Ramsey. Witnesses, James Patton, Thos. Chew, Mary Patton, Rebecca Vickers, Henry Downs, Jr. Proved by James Patton, Thos. Chew, and H. Downs, Jr., 14th April, 1746.

Page 46.—Moses Thomson, late of Augusta County, now an inhabitant of South Carolina, and James Patton, to John Madison, 12th December, 1745. Bond conditioned to defend D. B. 1, p. 43, against the right of dower in said land of Jane Thomson, wife of Moses. Land adjoins James Armstrong and John Ramsey.

Page 48.—11th April, 1746. Francis McCeon (McCune, McCewn), yeoman, to Hugh Martin, yeoman, £15 current money; 227 acres, part of a large tract of 728 acres belonging to McCewn patented to him 13th August, 1743, on Tee's Creek. Witnesses, J. Buchanan, John Hawkins, Henry Downs, Jr. Acknowledged, 14th April, 1746, when Margaret, wife of Francis, relinquished her right of dower.

Page 52.—9th March, 1745-6. Francis McCewn, yeoman, to Robert Erwin, yeoman, £12 current money; 200 acres, part of 728 acres (vid. 1, p. 48, for description). Witnesses, Charles Wilson, Samuel Norwood, Thomas Taylor. Acknowledged by Francis and Margaret, his wife, 14th April, 1746.

Page 55.—9th April, 1746. Francis McCewn, yeoman, to Samuel Norwood, yeoman, £90 current money of Virginia; 500 acres, part of same patent as D. B. 1, p. 48, on Tees Creek. Witnesses, J. Buchanan, Henry Downs, Jr.; James Robertson. Acknowledged by Francis and wife Margaret, 14th April, 1746.

Page 58.—11th April, 1746. Peter Ruffnaugh (Ruftner), of County Orange, to Christopher Comber, £40 current money Virginia; on Hawksbill Run, formerly belonging to Francis Thornton. Witnesses, John Newport, Richard Price, Isaac Strickler. Acknowledged, 14th April, 1746.

Page 61.—11th April, 1746. Peter Rufnaugh (Rufnedt) to Daniel Stover, £10 current money Virginia; on South River, Shanando, at mouth of Hawksbill Creek, part of 250 acres granted to John Landrum purchased by Rufnaught from Landrum containing 196 acres. Witnesses, same as p. 58. Acknowledged, 14th April, 1746.

Page 64.—6th ———, 1746. Robert Poage, farmer, to Robert Gamble, weaver, £15 current money Virginia; 306 acres on west side Blue Ridge; corner to Alexander Blair; John Young's line. Witnesses, John Nuckens (Pickens), James Trimble, Silas Hart. Acknowledged, and dower released by Elizabeth, wife of Robert, 15th April, 1746.

Page 65.—18th February, 1743. John Lewis, of County Augusta, to James Robertson, £30 current money Virginia; 274 acres in Beverley Manor, part of 2,071 acres deeded to John by Wm. Beverley, 21st February, 1738, recorded in Orange; on Lewis Creek, Daniel Deniston's line; James Trimble's line; John Craig's line. Witnesses, William Henderson, Wm. Johnstone, Thomas Lewis. Acknowledged in Orange County, 23d February, 1743. Acknowledged in Augusta by John Lewis, 15th April, 1746, and Margaret, his wife, released dower.

Page 69.—20th February, 1745. Moses Thomson, late of County Augusta, to James Edmiston, £13.17 current money Virginia; 100 acres patented 20th August, 1745, to Moses, on east side South River, Shanandoe, on the Red Banks. Witnesses, Thos. Lewis, John Preston, David Edmiston. 15th April, 1746, proved by Lewis and Edmiston. 12th May, 1746, proved by John Preston.

Page 73.—12th May, 1746. John Mitchell, farmer, to Wm. Mitchell, farmer, £40 current money Virginia; 400 acres in Augusta; Benj. Borden's line, part of land patented to John, 15th March, 1744. Acknowledged, 12th May, 1746, by John Mitchell and Mary, his wife.

Page 77.—13th May, 1746. George Robinson to John Finley, £100 current money Virginia; 892 acres, part of Beverley Manor, and granted by Beverley to George 21st February, 1738, on Shannandore River; lines of the Manor. Witnesses, Robert Rennick, Jno. Trimble, James Price, Silas Hart. Acknowledged, 13th May, 1746, and Martha, wife of George, released dower.

Page 81.—13th June, 1746. George Hutchinson to Samuel Henderson, £8 current money Virginia; 265 acres in Beverley Manor, part of 530 acres conveyed by Beverly to George 21st February, 1738, in Orange County, on Long Meadow Run; corner to Alexander Henderson. Witnesses, Thos. Lewis, Silas Hart, John Kerr. Acknowledged, 13th May, 1746, and Eleanor, his wife, releases dower.

Page 79.—13th June, 1746. George Hutchison to Alexander Henderson, £8 current money Virginia; 265 acres in Beverley Manor, part of 530 acres granted by Beverley to George 21st February, 1738, in Orange County, on east side Long Meadow, Samuel Henderson's land. Witnesses, Thos. Lewis, Silas Hart, Jno. Kerr. Acknowledged, 13th May, 1746, and Eleanor, his wife, released dower.

Page 84.—14th May, 1746. George Hutchinson, of Augusta, yeoman, to James Clarke, wheelwright, £24.10.0; 380 acres in Beverley Manor, corner to land surveyed for John Brown. Witnesses, John Risk, James Brown, James Trimble. Acknowledged, 13th May, 1746, and Eleanor, his wife, relinquishes dower.

Page 88.—8th May, 1746. Lewis Neal (Neil) and Lydia, his wife; John Neal (Neil) and Ann, his wife, of the County of Frederick, to William

Burk, £22 current money Virginia; 400 acres on west side Blue Ridge, on a branch of South River called Boon Run. Signed by all. Ann's mark. Witnesses, W. Russell, James Porteus, John Newport. Proved, 3d May, 1746, by all witnesses.

Page 90.—19th April, 1746. Francis McCowen (mark), farmer, to Wm. Bell, farmer, £55 current money Virginia; 196½ acres in Beverley Manor; Seth Poag's line; John Lewis' line. Witnesses, Jno. Buchanan, Joseph Culton, Silas Hart, James Trimble. Acknowledged, 18th June, 1746. Francis (his mark) McCown.

Page 93.—Commission to John Anderson, Andrew Pickens, and Richard Woods to take deposition of Margaret, wife of Francis McCown.

Page 94.—Francis McCune's wife Margaret releases her dower 18th June, 1746.

Page 96.—18th June, 1746. Adam Thomson, farmer, to James Armstrong, malster, £63 current money Virginia; 310 acres on north branch of Cleristee's Creek, a small island in said creek; corner to James Caldwell; corner to John Madison. Witnesses, Andrew Lewis, Thos. Chew, James Trimble. Acknowledged, 18th June, 1746, and Elizabeth releases dower.

Page 100.—17th June, 1746. George Brackenridge, yeoman, to Samuel Lusk, farmer, £18 current money Virginia; 200 acres on south side Middle River of Shanando; William Anderson's line; corner to Jno. Finley. Witnesses, John and Robert Christian, James Trimble. Acknowledged, 18th June, 1746, and Ann released dower.

Page 102.—Robert Green, of Orange County, to Robert McCay, of Augusta, and Jost Hite, of Frederick. Bond in £3000 dated 18th June, 1746. Whereas, Robert McCay, Jost Hite, Robert Green, and Wm. Duff, deceased, did in lifetime of Duff obtain order of Council for one tract of 3,060 acres on north branch of Shanando; one tract of 9,860 acres in a hollow of the mountains in the fork of Shanando; one tract of 2,200 acres on north branch of Shanando; one tract of 7,000 acres on south branch of Shanando; one tract of 891 acres on north branch of Shanando; one tract of 310 acres on south branch of Shanando (in order for the more speedy conveying same to purchasers). Parties agree that patent should be made to Robert Green. Condition that Robert make proper conveyances to purchasers and one moiety of the residue to the other parties. Witnesses, Jno. Smith, Thos. Stevenson, Jno. Hite. Acknowledged, 18th June, 1746.

Page 104.—18th June, 1746. Robert McKay, Josh Hite, Robert Green, and Robert Green, executor and heir-at-law of Wm. Duff, deceased, to William Linwell, £62.10.0 current money Virginia; 1,500 acres, part of 7,009 acres patented to grantors 26th March, 1739. Witnesses, Gabriel Jones, Jno. Madison. Acknowledged, 19th June, 1746.

Page 107.—18th February, 1747. Commission to Robert Coningham, John Wilson, and Robert Campbell, to examine Ann, wife of George Brackenridge, who is unable to travel to the Court House. She releases dower in D. B. 1, p. 11, 5th May, 1748.

Page 110.—Jost Hite, Robert Green, and Robert Green, executor and heir of Wm. Duff to Robert McKay, £119 current money Virginia; 1,190 acres on west side Blue Ridge part of 7,009 acres patented to grantors and grantee, 26th March, 1739; north side Linwell's Creek, including the 9th and 10th lots. Acknowledged, 19th June, 1746.

Page 112.—Commission to Robert Slaughter, ——— (Finlass?), and Francis Slaughter, of Orange County, to examine Elenor, wife of Robert Green, unable to travel, and her relinquishment of dower in D. B. 1, p. 110, 3d May, 1747.

Page 115.—18th June, 1746. Hite, McKay, Robert Green, sole heir and executor of Wm. Duff, to Robert Craven, £40.4.0 current money Virginia; 670 acres on north side Linville's Creek, part of 7,009 acres patented 26th March, 1739. Witnesses, Thomas Chew, Gabriel Jones, Thos. Slaughter. Acknowledged by all, 19th June, 1746.

Page 20.—19th June, 1746. Zeruiah Borden, widow, of Frederick County and Benj. Borden, of Augusta, executors of Benj. Borden, late of Orange, to Francis McCune, £3 current money Virginia; 328 acres, part of 92,100 acres patented to Benjamin, Sr. 6th November, 1739, the Barrens on the south side of the creek; corner to Joseph Kennedy. Witnesses, Jno. Smith, Samson Archee, Repentance Townsend. Acknowledged by Benjamin in person and for Zeruiah, 19th June, 1746.

Page 123.—19th June, 1746. Zeruiah Borden (as in p. 120) to James Montgomery, £20 current money Virginia; 654 acres, part of 3,553 acres patented to Benjamin, Sr., 9th March, 1740.

Page 125.—18th June, 1746. The Bordens as above to John Hays. Testator in his lifetime had agreed to sell to Hays; 318 acres, 2 roods, 38 p., part of 92,100 acres patented to Benjamin 6th ———, 1739, on bank of Hays Creek, Moxbett Creek, where Maxbett and Hays Creek come together. Con., 5 shillings. Acknowledged as above.

Page 128.—18th June, 1746. The Bordens to William Berry, Con. 5 shillings current money Virginia. Testator in his lifetime had agreed to convey to William 145 acres, part of 92,100 acres on Moffett's Creek; Elizabeth Hunter's Corner. Acknowledged as above.

Page 131.—Same to Ezekiel Clements, 5 shillings current money Virginia. Benjamin in his lifetime had agreed to convey 400 acres patented to Benjamin 24th March, 1740, on a Jame River branch called the Mary on southwest side.

Page 135.—18th June, 1746. Samuel Wilkins to Robert McKay et als., £126.8.11; 1,264 acres in Orange County on west side Blue Ridge on Naked Creek where the Irish path crosses, part of 7,009 acres patented to McKay et als., 26th March, 1739, and by them sold to Samuel Wilkins by deeds, 29th June, 1744. Witnesses, James Porteus and John Hawkins Acknowledged by Samuel Wilkins, 20th June, 1746, and Sarah, his wife, relinquished dower.

Page 139.—18th June, 1746. Robert McKay et als. to Samuel Wilkins, £126.8.11; 1,264 acres on Naked Creek; conveys D. B. 1, p. 135. Acknowledged.

Page 143.—15th August, 1746. William Linwell and Elenor, his wife, to George Bowman, of County Frederick, £100 Pennsylvania currency; 500 acres purchased of Jost Hite & Co. on Linwell's Creek; line of Joseph Bryan (in his possession); Wm. Linwell's mark ( ); Elinor Linwell's mark ( ). Witnesses, Gabriel Jones and Benj. Johnston. Acknowledged, 20th August, 1746.

Page 148.—5th August, 1746. Robert McCay, of Augusta, and Jost Hite, of Frederick, to Robert Green, of Orange, surveying partners of a certain tract patented 26th March, 1739, to McCay, Hite, Duff and Green, 7,009 acres, £100 current money; 1,000 acres including lots 2 and 3. Witnesses, Thomas ( ) Linwell, Valentine Sevier, Gabriel Jones. Proved by all witnesses, 20th August, 1746.

Page 152.—20th August, 1746. William Linwell to Thomas Linwell, £12; 500 acres on Linwell's Creek, part of 1,500 acres granted to William by McCay & Co.; land in possession of Joseph Bryant. William ( ) Linwell. Acknowledged by William, and Eleanor releases dower, 20th August, 1746.

Page 135.—20th August, 1746. William Linwell to Joseph Bryan, £12; 500 acres on Linwell's Creek between William, and land in possession of Thomas Linwell, part of 1,500 acres granted by McCay & Co. Acknowledged, and dower released by Eleanor, 20th August, 1746.

Page 159.—21st August, 1746. Samuel McCutchen and Francis, his wife, to James Shields, cordwinder, £18.5.0; 298½ acres, part of 600 acres on Moffetts Creek bought from Borden; corner to Nathan Lusk, adjoining patent line of Beverley Manor. Witnesses, William Adair, Rob. Graham, James Trimble. Frances ( ) McCouchen. Acknowledged by both, 21st August, 1746.

Page 161.—20th November, 1746. John Moffett, mason, to Mathew Robertson, of the Province of Pennsylvania. Whereas, by patent 6th September, 1736, to Beverley & Co., and Beverley bought out the other partners 17th September, 1736, and Beverley by deed 29th February, 1739, granted to John Moffett 396 acres, part of Beverley Manor, £110 current money Virginia; 396 acres above on a branch of Shanando called Cathey's Run. Witnesses, Robert King and Silas Hart. Acknowledged by John, and dower released by Mary, his wife, 20th November, 1746.

Page 165.—14th November, 1746. Thomas Linwell and Hannah, his wife, to Jacob Christman, of Frederick County, £100 currency; 500 acres, part of 1,500 acres purchased of Jost Hite on Linwell's Creek. Witnesses, Wat Ellice, G. Jones. Acknowledged, 20th November, 1746.

Page 169.—21st November, 1746. James Carter, millwright, to Robert Gay; 300 acres, part of tract granted to James Patton and John Lewis, and sold to Carter by Patton and Lewis 2d April, 1745, on Calfpasture River; corner to John Campbell's land. Witnesses, Jno. Buchanan, Thomas Gillham, Thomas Wood. Acknowledged by James, and dower released by Dinah, his wife, 21st November, 1746.

Page 171.—22d November, 1746. Benj. Borden, Jr., late of Orange County, executor, etc., to James Davice, £18.15.7 current money Virginia. Benjamin, Sr., in his lifetime had agreed to sell to James; 626 acres, part of 8,100 acres patented to Benjamin, Sr., 6th November, 1739; corner to tract No. 2 on Cataba Creek. Witnesses, Wat Ellice, James Patton, Jno. Madison. Acknowledged, 22d November, 1746.

Page 173.—22d November, 1744. £3.3.3; Benjamin Borden, &c., to Thomas McSpeadon; 106 acres, part of 92,100 acres; corner to Alexander McCleary. Acknowledged, 22d November, 1746.

Page 177.—18th February, 1746. John Buchanan, yeoman, to James Cowan, £18.10.0 current money Virginia; 374 acres in B. M. in Patrick Campbell's line; Reed and Moor's land; Col. Patton's land. Witnesses, Andrew Cowen, Robert Foyle, James Trimble. Acknowledged, 18th February, 1746.

Page 180.—19th February, 1746. Alexander Thompson to William Beard, £15 current money Virginia; on south branch Shanando, known by the name of Cave Bottom; Alexander Thompson's ford; next to the Great Mountain; Cave Hill; 100 acres, part of tract patented to Alexander, 13th July, 1742. Witnesses, Alexander Thompson, James Beard, John Edwards. Acknowledged, 19th February, 1746.

Page 182.—18th February, 1746. James Davice to James Campbell, £64 current money Virginia; 570 acres in B. M. deed to Davice by Beverley, 21st February, 1738. James ( ) Davis. Witnesses, Samuel Gay, Wm. Henderson. Acknowledged, 19th February, 1746.

Page 185.—9th February, 1747. Robert Turk, planter, to Robert Patrick, £62 current money Virginia; 437 acres in Beverley Manor, crossing South River of Shanando. Witnesses, John Preston, Robert Scott. Acknowledged by Robert Turk, and dower released by Margaret, his wife, 18th March, 1746.

Page 188.—26th February, 1746. Thomas Linwell, yeoman, to Morgan Bryant, £16 current money Virginia; 3 cows, a set of Smith's tools. Trust to secure to Capt. Robert Green & Co., £16. Witnesses, Edward Hughes, Abraham Croson (Creeson). Proved by both witnesses.

Page 190.—18th March, 1747. Robert McClenachan to David Stuart, £32; 331 acres in Beverley Manor; corner to land of heirs of Alexander Brackenridge. Witnesses, Thos. Lewis, Jno. Buchanan, John Pickins. Acknowledged by Robert, and dower released by Sarah, 18th March, 1746.

Page 193.—11th December, 1746. James Gill and Eleanor, his wife, late of Orange County, to Edward Hughes, £25 current money Pennsylvania; on a branch of North River of Shanando called Wallings Creek, 186 acres. Witnesses, Samuel Bryan, Morgan Bryan, Jr.; John Ellis, Eleanor ( ) Gill. Proved by all witnesses, 18th March, 1746.

Page 196.—19th March, 1747. Benj. Borden, heir, executor, &c., to Col. Jno. Buchanan. Testator agreed in his lifetime to sell to J. B. £3; part of 92,100 acres, beginning on the creek corner to Jno. Edmiston; 100 acres. Witnesses, John Buchanan, Humberstone Lyon, William Sayers. Acknowledged, 19th March, 1746.

Page 198.—19th March, 1747. Benj. Borden to Henry Myrtian, £16.8.0 current money Virginia; 674 acres (bought in lifetime of Benj. Borden, Sr.); corner to John and James McDowel's land. Witnesses and acknowledged as above.

Page 200.—19th March, 1747. Benj. Borden, &c., &c., to Alexander McClure (sold to Alexander in lifetime of Benjamin); 266 acres for £7.13.0, part of 92,100 acres on Mill Creek corner to Isaac Taylor. Witnessed and acknowledged as above.

Page 203.—19th March, 1746. Benj. Borden to Halbert McClure (sold in lifetime of Benjamin, Sr.); 203 acres for £6.1.6 current money Virginia, part of 92,100 acres on north branch of James River; corner to William Hall's land; corner to Samuel McClure. Witnessed and acknowledged as above.

Page 205.—19th March, 1746. Benj. Borden to John Lyle (sold in lifetime of Benjamin); 734 acres for £22.5.0 current money Virginia, part of 92,100; corner to Mathew Lyle, John McDowell's line. Witnessed and acknowledged as above.

Page 207.—19th March, 1746. Benj. Borden to William McClung (sold in lifetime of Benjamin); 314 acres, 3 R., 25 P., for £9.7.0, part of 92,100 acres; John Stevenson's line; Andrew Baxter's stake. Witnessed and acknowledged as above.

Page 209.—19th March, 1746. Benj. Borden & Co. to Mathew Gyle (Lyle). Testator agreed to sell in his lifetime, 451 acres, 2 R., 17 P., for £13.10.0 current money Virginia, part of 92,100, grantee's old survey; Thomas McSpadon's line; John Mathews' line; John Gray's corner. Witnessed and acknowledged as above.

Page 211.—19th March, 1746. Benj. Borden to Isaac Taylor, Sr. (sold in testator's lifetime); 600 acres, £18 current money Virginia, part of 92,100, in Mill Creek, by a scollopy hill. Witnessed and acknowledged as above.

Page 213.—20th November, 1746. James Davis (Device) to John Black, £———— current money Virginia; 375 acres in Beverley Manor sold by George Home, of Orange County, to Gibbins Jennings, of Shanando. 14th March, 1740, and recorded in Orange, and afterwards sold at auction by Richard Winslow to satisfy execution vs. Gibbins Jennings; on 21st March, 1742, to satisfy Isaac Smith. Deed by Winslow to Davis in Orange, 24th June, 1743; on South River Shanando in Robert Turk's line; Samuel Gay's line; Beverley Manor line.—James S. Davis. Witnesses, Thos. Lewis, Wm. Wright, Plineeas Griffiths. Acknowledged, 21st May, 1747.

Page 217.—8th January, 1746. Thomas Gillespy to James Bell and John Rutledge, £100; 400 acres on Long Glade, a draft of North River of Janendo; head of a draft of Naked Creek. Witnesses, Robert McClenachan. James Irwin, Thomas Rutlidge. Proved by all witnesses, 21st May, 1747.

Page 222.—22d November, 1746. Samuel Norwood to John Gilmer, yeoman, £130; 500 acres, part of a large tract formerly Francis McCown's land and sold to Samuel by Francis. 9th April, 1746, recorded in Augusta on Tees Creek. Witnesses, Robt. Erwin, John Carr, Hugh Martin. Acknowledged, 21st May, 1747.

Page 225.—21st May, 1747. William Burk to Henry Downs, Gent., £85 current money Virginia; 350 acres on Shenandoe River at the upper end of 2,000 acres that did belong to Richard Malden near Peaked Mountain; corner to Paul Long; Selsor's line. Witnesses, Adam Müller, Barbary Miller, Jno. Edwards. Acknowledged, 21st May, 1747.

Page 228.—20th May, 1747. John Pickens, Gent., to William Baskins, £10 current money Virginia; 212 acres; corner to James Lesley. Teste: Jno. Buchanan, Thos. Chew, 212; Charles Campbell. Acknowledged, and dower released by Eleanor, his wife, 21st May, 1747.

Page 231.—20th May, 1747. William Porter, yeoman, to Thomas Hill, £28 current money Virginia; 395½ acres on Middle Creek; John McDowell's line; Patrick Hays' line. Teste: David Mitchell, Nathaniel Evins, Alexander Moore. Acknowledged by William, and dower released by Jane, his wife, 21st May, 1747.

Page 234.—11th February, 1746-7. Robert McCay to John James and Moses Green, £100; 500 acres on Linwell's Creek being lot No. 5, part of tract of 7,009 acres patented, 26th March, 1736, to Jost Hite & Co. and conveyed to Robert by Hite & Co., 24th June, 1744. Teste: W. Russell, James Porteus, Jno. Newport, Gab Jones. Proved, 21st May, 1747, by all but Newport.

Page 238.—10th February, 1746-7. Jost Hite, Ro. McCay, and Robert Green to John, James and Moses Green, £100; 500 acres on Linwell's Creek being lot 4, part of 7,009 acres patented, &c., 1739. Witnessed and proved as above.

Page 243.—3d October, 1746. Same parties as above, £100; 708 acres patented to grantors, 26th March, 1739; on side of Limestone Hill, near easternmost branch of Linwell's Cerek. Teste: W. Russell, G. Jones, Wm. Green. Proved, 21st May, 1747, by Russell and Jones.

Page 247.—5th August, 1746. Robert McCay and Robert Green to Jost Hite, £100; 545 acres, part of 7,009 acres including lot 8. Witnessed and proved as above.

Page 251.—7th August, 1746. Same parties as above, £100; 500 acres, part of 7,009 acres including lot 6. Witnessed and acknowledge as above.

Page 255.—11th February, 1746-7. Robert McCay to James Robinson, £40; 400 acres on Linwell's Creek, whereon the said Robinson lives being lot No. 1, part of 7,009 acres, &c.; mouth of Linwell's Creek and North River. Teste: G. Jones, Peter Scholl, Thomas T. Milseph (Milsaps). Poved by all, 21st May, 1747.

Page 259.—1st May, 1747. James Rentfroe, of Lunenburg County, to Archibald Graem (Gream), of Augusta, £——— current money Virginia; 148 acres patented to ———, 28th September, 1745; near Buffalo Creek.— James Rentfro, Esther Rentfro. Teste: Robert Mountgomery, Patrick Shirkey, James Mountgomery. Proved by first two witnesses, 21st May, 1747, and by last 18th May, 1749.

Page 263.—21st May, 1747. James Bell to Thomas Armstrong, £20 current money Virginia; 400 acres on a branch of Cathey's River called Jennings Branch. Teste: Andrew Cowen, James Bell, Jr.; Thos. Rutlidge. Acknowledged, 21st May, 1747. Rachel releases dower.

Page 265.—21st May, 1747. Benj. Borden, &c., to Nathaniel McClure (sold in testator's lifetime); 180 acres, £5.7.6, part of 92,100 acres patented, &c., on North River, Worm Run; corner to Moses McClure, on east branch of Mill Creek. Teste: Jno. Bramham, Jr.; Thos. Gorden, John Finley. Acknowledged, 21st May, 1747.

Page 267.—21st May, 1747. Benj. Bordin, &c., to John McKay (sold in testator's lifetime); 390 acres, £19 current money Virginia, part of 92,100; north side Mill Creek; corner to Baptist McNabb. Witnessed and acknowledged as above.

Page 269.—21st May, 1747. Benj. Bordin, &c., to Robert Allison (sold in testator's lifetime); 279 acres, 2 R., 36 P., £8.5.0 current money Virginia, part of 92,100; north branch of James; corner to Halbert McClure, James Thompson's land. Witnessed and acknowledged as above.

Page 272.—21st May, 1747. Benjamin Bordin, &c., to David Dryden, tailor (sold in testator's lifetime); 130 acres, 2 R., 14 P., £3.16.0 current money Virginia, part of 92,100; line of John Pattison's land; corner to Wm. Baskins. Witnessed and acknowledged as above.

Page 275.—26th May, 1747. Robert Renick, of Augusta, yeoman, to James Miles, farmer, £10; 201 acres on Buffalo's branch, part of the land Robert now lives on. Teste: James Sayers, Francis ( ) Gardner, James Trimble. Acknowleged, 17th June, 1747, by Robert, and dower released by Elizabeth.

Page 278.—19th August, 1747. Henry Downs, Gent., of Orange County, to Henry Downs, Jr., of Augusta, £60.8.4; 300 acres on South River, Shanando, part of tract Henry, Jr., now lives on; patented to Alexander Thompson for 400 acres, 30th July, 1742. Teste: John Harvie, Jno. Ruddle, Jr.; G. Jones. Acknowledged, 19th August, 1747.

Page 280.—12th August, 1747. Wm. Beverley, of Essex, to James Lynn, £———; 538 acres in Beverley Manor on South River, Shanando; Samuel Doah's land; Patrick Campbell's land; Brownlee's land; George Brackenridge's land. Teste: Robt. Davis, Jno. Mitchell, W. Russell. Proved by all witnesses, 19th August, 1747.

Page 283.—13th August, 1747. William Beverley to James Crawford, £———; 401 acres in Beverley Manor; Robert Patterson's line on south side Cathey's River; corner to McDowell's land; crossing Lewis Creek; corner to George Anderson. Teste: Wm. Henderson, Archibald Hamilton, Robt. Davies. Proved by all witnesses, 19th August, 1747.

Page 287.—13th August, 1747. William Beverley to Archibald Hamilton, £9.1.3; 302 acres in Beverley Manor, where William Smith's line crosses Christian's Creek; corner to James Crawford. Teste: Wm. Henderson, Robt. Davies, James Crawford. Proved by all witnesses, 19th August, 1747.

Page 291.—13th August, 1747. Wm. Beverley to Andrew Cowan, farmer, £8.4.8; 243 acres, near Borden's Path. Proved, 19th August, 1747, as above.

Page 294.—13th August, 1747. William Beverley to Robert Alexander, £9.9.0; 314 acres in Beverley Manor; Patrick Hays' line; corner Robert Ramsey. Witnessed and proved as above.

Page 298.—13th August, 1747. William Beverley to Robert Davies, £8.9.3 farthings current money Virginia; 145 acres in Beverley Manor; corner to Capt. Brown, on Back Creek; the patent line. Witnessed and proved as above.

Page 302.—13th August, 1747. William Beverley to James McCorkle, £16.4.11; 370 acres in Beverley Manor; graveyard in William Nutt's line; Brackenridge's line; James Brackenridge's line. Witnessed and proved as above.

Page 305.—19th August, 1747. John Anderson to John Hogshead, £9 current money Virginia; 270 acres patented, 1st December, 1740, to Jno Anderson. Teste: Thos. Lewis, John Maxwell, James Hogshead. Acknowledged by John, and dower released by Jane, his wife, 19th August, 1747.

Page 308.—4th August, 1747. Adam Caruth to John King, £7.10.0 current money Virginia; 8 acres, 3 R., on a branch of Naked Creek; corner to John Seawright's land. Teste: John Anderson, John Seawright, John Stevenson. Proved by all, 19th August, 1747.

Page 311.—13th August, 1747. Wm. Beverley to Wm. Henderson, £72.9.0 current money Virginia; 1,415 acres in Beverley Manor on a branch of Black's Creek; corner to Robt. Cunningham; corner to George Caldwell's land; corner to Wm. Thompson's land; on Christian's Creek; George Rutlidge's line; Thomas Black's land. Teste: James Crawford, John Linn, John Mitchell. Proved by all, 19th August, 1747.

Page 314.—13th August, 1747. Wm. Beverley to Samuel Brawford, farmer, £6 current money Virginia; 200 acres in Beverley Manor; corner

John Buchanan; corner John Mitchell and Samuel Doage. Witnessed and proved as above.

Page 317.—13th August, 1747. Wm. Beverley to John Mitchell, £20; 609 acres in Beverley Manor; corner to Samuel Brafford; John Buchanan's land; Patrick Campbell's land; crossing South River; Samuel Doak's land. Witnessed and proved as above.

Page 319.—13th August, 1747. Wm. Beverley to Wm. Nutt, of Orange. Whereas, Wm. Beverley, on 14th April, 1738, did agree to convey to Gibbons Jennings, late of Orange County, 650 acres in Beverley Manor, which said 650 acres were laid off by Ro. Brooke, Gent., on Christy's Creek, at Moses Thompsons; a red oak by John Brackenridge's grove, who was murdered by the Indians; in consideration of which and other, 510 acres conveyed by said Beverley to the said Gibbons Jennings, he was to pay William £38.7.2. Jennings paid all but £10 and entered on the land and built a water grist mill thereon, and afterwards, on 2d September, 1740, agreed to convey the same land to Wm. Nutt in consideration of one gray mare. Mr. Jno. Lewis's bond for 350 acres, either in the Cow or Calf Pasture, 5 shillings cash and 1,000 yards of linen. Jennings left the colony without taking any conveyance for the land from Beverley or making any conveyance to Nutt. Nutt brought suit in County Court, Orange, vs. Jennings and Beverley, to compel a conveyance, and it was decreed, 27th July, 1744, that Beverley convey to Nutt. Deed to Nutt. Teste: Robt. Davies, W. Russell, John Lin. Proved by all, 19th August, 1747.

Page 323.—13th August, 1747. Wm. Beverley to John Henderson, £25.9.9; 520 acres in Beverley Manor on a branch of Lewis Creek; line of James McCurkle's land. Witnessed and proved as above.

Page 325.—13th August, 1747. Wm. Beverley to James Gilmore, farmer, £8 current money Virginia; 204 acres in Beverley Manor; corner James Moody; corner to a place surveyed for David Davis; Bell's land. Witnessed and proved as above.

Page 330.—13th August, 1747. Wm. Beverley to Helen Mitchell, widow, £6.8.6; 200 acres in Beverley Manor; Brackenridge's line; corner to Teat's line; corner to David Doak; John Lockhart's corner; John Teat's land. Witnessed and proved as above.

Page 333.—13th August, 1747. William Beverley to John Miller, £10.2.2; 210 acres in Beverley Manor on a branch of Lewis Creek; corner David Stuart; corner to James Miller. Witnessed and proved as above.

Page 337.—13th August, 1747. William Beverley to Alexander McPheeters, farmer, £10 current money Virginia; 303 acres in Beverley Manor on north branch of Christy's Creek; corner to Samuel Downey and John Turk; McNabb's line. Teste: As above, and Archibald Hamilton. Proved by all as above.

Page 340.—13th August, 1747. Wm. Beverley to David Moore, £10.16.4; 189 acres in Beverley Manor; Joseph Reed's line; corner to Col. Patton. Teste: Robert Davies, James Crawford, John Lin. Proved by all, 19th August, 1747.

Page 343.—13th August, 1747. Wm. Beverley to Edward Hall, £10 current money Virginia; 220 acres in Beverley Manor on South Fork of Shanandore; corner to Samuel Davison's land on the river; on Col. Patton's line; the patent line. Teste: James Crawford, John Mitchell, John Linn. Proved by all as above.

Page 346.—18th August, 1747. Francis Beaty to Andrew Alexander, £25 current money Virginia; 158 acres in Beverley Manor; corner to Robert Wilson's land; corner to Thomas Shield's land; Thomas Brown's line Teste: John Maxwell, James Hamilton, Michael Dickey. Acknowledged by Francis, 19th August, 1747, and wife Martha releases dower.

Page 349.—18th August, 1747. Francis Beaty to Robert Wilson, £20; 230 acres in Beverley Manor; corner to Joseph Reed; Thomas Brown's line. Teste: John Maxwell, James Hamilton, James Mafet. Acknowledged by Francis, and Martha releases dower, 19th August, 1747.

Page 351.—28th May, 1747. John Trimble to John Ellote, £10; 200 acres on head of South Fork of Jennings Branch, North Fork of Buffilo Lick Brance. Teste: Jno. Harvey, James Porteus, John Madison. Acknowledged, 19th August, 1747.

Page 354.—20th August, 1747. Edward Hughes, yeoman, to Thomas West, farmer, £22.10.0; on a branch of North River of Shanandore called Walling's Creek; 186 acres, being the land granted to James Gill by patent, 30th June, 1743, and sold by Gill to Hughes, 11th December, 1746. Teste: John Harvie, James Porteus, Benj. Johnston. Acknowledged, 20th August, 1747.

Page 357.—20th August, 1747. Patrick Hay to Charles Mullican (Milican). £22 current money Virginia; 297 acres granted to Patrick by patent, 30th June, 1743; on James River on east side Looney's Mill Creek. Teste: William Lusk, John Wilson, Charles Hays. Acknowledged, 20th August, 1747.

Page 359.—20th August, 1747. William McMachan, Gent., of Frederick County, to Robert Young, £15.16.7; 400 acres patented to William, 12th September, 1746, on the head of a north branch of Buffilo Creek adjoining Benj. Bordin's land. Acknowledged, 20th August, 1747.

Page 361.—20th August, 1747. Benj. Bordin's eldest son, &c., to John Mountgomery (sold in testator's lifetime); 247½, £7.8.0 current money Virginia, part of 92,100 acres, &c.; corner to Beverley Manor and Borden; corner to John Huston; Samuel Dunlap's line. Teste: Benj. Johnston, James McDowell. Acknowledged, 21st August, 1747.

Page 363.—21st August, 1747. Benj. Borden, &c., to John McCroskey (sold in testator's lifetime); 306 acres, £9.9.2, part of 92,100, &c., on North Fork of the Creek; corner to William Buchanan; Isaac Anderson's line; James McDowell's land. Teste: Jno. Buchanan, Benj. Johnston, James McDowell. Acknowledgement, 21st August, 1747.

Page 365.—27th March, 1747. Benj. Borden, &c., to Ephraim McDowell (sold in testator's lifetime); 300 acres for 5 shillings, part of 92,100; John McDowell's land. Witnessed and acknowledged as above.

Page 367.—27th March, 1747. Benj. Borden, &c., to John Moore (sold in testator's lifetime); 504 acres, 1 R., 26 P., £12 current money Virginia, part of 92,100; corner to Joseph Lapsley's land; corner to Gilbert Campbell. Witnessed and acknowledged as above.

Page 369.—27th March, 1747. Benj. Borden to James Greenlee (sold in testator's lifetime); 200 acres, 5 shillings current money Virginia, part of 92,100, &c.; corner to John McDowell; Ephraim McDowell's line. Tested and acknowledged as above.

Page 372.—22d August, 1747. George and Ann, his wife, Brackenridge to Mary Cunningham, widow, £8.16.0 current money Virginia; 112 acres in Beverley Manor. Teste: J. (S.?) Bramham, Valentine Sevier, Robt. McClenachan.

Page 375.—15th September, 1747. James Patton and John Lewis to John Preston, £15; 520 acres on Great River of Calfpasture; corner to Kingcade's land; crossing Ramsey's Creek; to land of one Locherage. Teste: Thos. Lewis, Robert King, Will Henderson. Acknowledged, 16th September, 1747.

Page 377.—7th September, 1747. Benj. Borden, &c., to Robert Edmiston (sold in testator's lifetime); 244 acres, £7.6.7, part of 92,100 acres; corner to Col. John Buchanan's land; crossing Moffett's Creek; the Barrens. Teste: John Lyle, John Miller, Josiah Linn. Acknowledged, 16th September, 1747.

Page 380.—17th September, 1747. John Anderson and Jane, his wife, to Charles Campbell, farmer, £50 current money Virginia; 400 acres on a branch of North River of Shanando, called Anderson's Branch, granted to John, 10th June, 1740. Teste: James Porteus and Benj. Johnston. Acknowledged, 17th September, 1747.

Page 383.—17th October, 1747. Wm. Beverley to Samuel Steel, £17.14.0; 590 acres in Beverley Manor; corner to James Huston; David Steel's land; corner to Robert Alexander; corner to Patrick Hayes. Teste: Robert Alexander, Robert Ramsey, John Fulton. Proved by two Roberts, 18th November, 1747. Proved by John, 22d August, 1766.

Page 386.—17th October, 1747. Wm. Beverley to Robert Ramsey, £10.4.0; 340 acres in Beverley Manor; corner to Wm. Roberson; to Robt. Alexander and Patrick Hays; to Wm. Robinson. Teste: Robert Alexander, Jno. Fulton, Robt. Baird. Proved by Ro. Alexander and Ro. Beard, 18th November, 1747.

Page 389.—17th October, 1747. Wm. Beverley to George Brackenridge, £15.12.0; 540 acres in Beverley Manor; corner to Alexander Brackenridge; corner to David Mitchell. Teste: Robert Alexander, John Fulton, Robert Ramsey. Proved by Alexander and Ramsey, 18th November, 1747.

Page 393.—5th November, 1747. £8.10.0 current money Virginia. Robert Green, of Orange, to John Patton, Jr., of Augusta, 210 acres on the southermost branch of the south branch of Potomac, part of 2,643 acres patented to Rob. Green, 12th January, 1746; corner to a tract sold to Roger Dyer. Teste: James Porteus and Gabriel Jones, Wm. Russell. Proved by all, 18th November, 1747.

Page 396.—5th November, 1747. £8 current money Virginia. Robert Green, of Orange, to Roger Dyer, 190 acres, same as above; corner to John Patton, Sr. Tested and proved as above.

Page 400.—5th November, 1747. £14 current money Virginia. Robert Green to Wm. Dyer, 350 acres, same as above. Tested and proved as above.

Page 404.—5th November, 1747. £8 current money Virginia. Robert Green to Wm. Stephenson, 200 acres, same as above. Tested and proved as above.

Page 408.—5th November, 1747. £6 current money Virginia. Robert Green to Mathew Patton, 157 acres, same as above. Tested and proved as above.

Page 412.—5th November, 1747. £25 current money Virginia. Robert Green to Roger Dyer, 620 acres, same as above. Tested and proved as above.

Page 416.—5th November, 1747. £12 current money Virginia. Robert Green to John Smith, 300 acres as above. Tested and proved as above.

Page 420.—5th November, 1747. Robert Green to John Patton, Sr. £18 current money Virginia, 453 acres adjoining Wm. Stephenson as above. Tested and proved as above.

Page 423.—19th October, 1747. £50. John Fewbaker to Abraham Fewbaker, 2 parcels of land on Shanando River, 300 acres adjoining Jacob Nahale, 200 acres adjoining Jacob Nahale. Teste: Samuel Newman, Wm. Scholl, Mathias Selzer. Proved by Scholl and Selzer, 18th November, 1747.

Page 428.—18th November, 1747. £62 current money Virginia. Robert Turk and Margret, his wife, to Robert Patrick. On 6th September, 1736, was patented to Wm. Beverley, &c., &c., and Wm. Beverley on —— day —— conveyed to Robert Turk 1,313 acres thereof in Orange; 437 acres, part of 1,313 in Beverley Manor, crossing Shanandore.—Robt. Turk, Margret Turk. Teste: John Madison, Patrick Hayes, David Stuart. Acknowledged, 18th November, 1747, and Margret releases dower.

Page 432.—19th November, 1747. £27 current money Virginia. George Brackenridge to Thomas Beard, 309½ acres in Beverley Manor; corner to James Lynn and John Tate; corner to David Steel. Teste: James Fulton, Samuel Wilson, Samuel Steel. Acknowledged by George, 18th November, 1747, and Ann releases dower.

Page 434.—18th November, 1747. £11 current money Virginia. Benj. Borden, &c., to Moses Trimble (sold in testator's lifetime), 345½ acres, part of 92,100, adjoining John Huston on the Timber Ridge; corner to Samuel Gray; corner to David Edmiston; corner to Daniel Lyle. Teste: Joseph Lapsley, Alexander Douglass, Abraham Brown. Acknowledged, 18th November, 1747.

Page 436.—18th November, 1747. £5. Benj. Borden to Samuel Gray (sold in testator's lifetime), 175 acres, part of 92,100; corner to Jno. Mathews on the timber ridge; corner to Moses Trimble; John Huston's line. Teste and acknowledged as above.

Page 438.—18th November, 1747. £12.10.0. Benj. Borden to John Moore (sold in testator's lifetime), 428 acres, 26 p., part of 92,100. Teste: Robt. Alexander, James Glasgow, William Robinson. Acknowledged, 18th November, 1747.

Page 440.—18th November, 1747. £30. John Moore to Samuel Anderson, 304 acres, 3 R., 15 P., adjoining George Henderson. Tested as above and acknowledged by John, 18th November, 1747.

Page 444.— ——January, 1747. £15. William Thompson and wife Jean to the inhabitants of the Presbyterian congregation of Tinkling Spring, viz., James Patton, John Christian, John Finley, James Alexander, William Wright chose commissioners and trustees for the congregation, 110 acres called and known by the name of Tinkling Spring in Beverley Manor, and part of 944 acres (deed by Beverley to Thompson, 1744, in Orange) adjoining George Caldwell. Acknowledged, 19th November, 1747, by William.

Page 448.—6th October, 1747. £30. John Nealands, of Frederick County, to John Hite, of Frederick, 330 acres on a branch of Goose Creek.—John ( ) Nealands. Teste: James Rutledge, W. Cocks, Robert Calvert, Gab. Jones. Proved, 19th November, 1747, by Rutledge and Jones.

Page 451.—19th November, 1747. £41. John Doage, farmer, to Richard Burton, farmer, 400 acres on James River on west side Blue Ridge patented to John, 12th January, 1746. Teste: James Porteus, Benj. Johnston. Acknowledged, 19th November, 1747.

Page 453.—20th November, 1747. £5. Henry Downs, Sr., of Orange, to Ludwick Francisco, 470 acres on south side Shanado patented to Henry Downs, 25th June, 1747; corner of the 800 tract near lower end of the great island. Acknowledged, 19th November, 1747.

Page 456.—29th September, 1747. £30. James Wood, of Frederick, to Ephraim, of Augusta, 245 acres on Goose Creek patented to James Wood, 12th January, 1746, adjoining Francis Betty. Teste: James Patton, Jno. Buchanan, Charles Campbell. Proved, 19th November, 1747, by James Patton and Chas. Camell.

Page 459.—5th October, 1747. £91.5.0. Samuel Gay to Israel Christian, 323 acres on branches of Shanado River; corner to George Robinson; line of Beverley Manor. Teste: James Patton, John Graham, Chas. Dalhouse. Acknowledged, 17th February, 1747.

Page 461.—22d January, 1747. £11. Benj. Borden, &c., to Rev. William Dean, of Brandywine Manor and Chester County in Pennsylvania (sold in testator's lifetime), 265 acres, part of 92,100; corner to Robert Huston and John Gray, on Mill Creek. Teste: John Lyle, Samuel Gray, Samuel Lyle. Acknowledged, 18th February, 1747.

Page 463.—18th February, 1747. £29. Benj. Borden, &c., to Archibald Alexander (sold in testator's lifetime), 980 acres, part of 92,100; corner Thomas McSpaden; corner Alexander McCleary, near a sink hole called the Punch Bowl. Teste: None. Acknowledged as above.

Page 466.—18th February, 1747-8. £30. John Davison, farmer to Wm. Henderson, farmer, 350 acres on north branch of James River at mouth of Buffalo Creek. Teste: Jno. Christian, Robt. Christian, W. Christian. Acknowledged by John, 18th February, 1747, and Jean, his wife, releases dower.

Page 469.—18th February, 1747-8. £120. John Davison, farmer, to James Armstrong, farmer, 485 acres in Beverley Manor; Christian's corner. Tested, acknowledged, and dower released as above.

Page 472.—22d January, 1747-8. £75. William Anderson to Robt. Gilkeson, 400 acres on a branch of Cathey's River called Anderson's branch granted to Wm. Anderson by patent, 1st December, 1740; corner to James and John Hogshead. Teste: Samson Archer, John Francis, George Anderson. Acknowledged by William, 16th March, 1747, and dower released by Elizabeth.

Page 475.—16th February, 1747. £40 and divers other good considerations. Samuel Gay to Wm. Bell, Jr., and David Bell, planters, 567 acres in Beverley Manor; corner to Robt. Turk and lot No. 1; corner to Finley; corner to Samuel Gay; corner to George Homes; to Robert Turk's line. Teste: None. Acknowledged by Samuel, 16th March, 1747, and dower released by Margaret, his wife.

Page 477.—22d February, 1747. £11.5.0. David Davis to Wm. McFetters, 400 acres patented to David, 12th February, 1742, on head of a branch of North River of Shanado called Mossey Creek. Teste: John Madison, Andrew Lewis, David Stuart. Proved by all, 16th March, 1747.

479.—18th March, 1747. £15 current money Virginia. Benj. Borden, &c., to James Young (sold in testator's lifetime), 440 acres, part of 92,100; corner to John Allison on the banks of the river at the mouth of Whistle Creek. Teste: John Pickens, Wm. Lusk, Robt. Brakenridge. Acknowledged, 18th March, 1747.

Page 482.—21st April, 1748. £20. Francis Kirkley, of Orange County, to Jno. Anderson, farmer, 400 acres on a draft of North River of Shanandoe called the Long Glade joining James Anderson's and James Cathey's. Teste: Silas Hart, John Anderson, Geo. Anderson, James Anderson, Francis Kirkley. Acknowledged, 18th May, 1748.

Page 485.—8th May, 1748. £20. James Moody and Rebecca, his wife, to Robert Wilson, 185 acres, part of the land James now lives on; corner to James Wilson, a Spanish oak; corner Nicholas Leeper. Teste: Andrew Cowen, James Leeper, Chas. Dalhouse. Acknowledged, and dower released, 18th May, 1748.

Page 488.—18th May, 1748. £15. James Moody to James Wilson, 200 acres in Beverley Manor, part of 510 acres sold by Beverley to James Moody, 24th July, 1740, recorded in Orange. Tested, acknowledged, and dower released as above.

Page 491.—2d April, 1748. £19.18.4. James Patton and John Lewis to James Corolile, 600 acres on Great River of Calfpasture; corner to Jacob Clemens; corner to Wm. Worwick's land; black birch; black oak and thorn. Teste: James Carter, Robert ( ) Bratton, Robert Crockett. Acknowledged, 18th May, 1748.

Page 493.—16th May, 1748. £30. Benj. Borden, &c., to Thomas Paxton, Sr. (sold in testator's lifetime); 500 acres, part of 92,100, a post in Thomas Paxton, Jr.'s, line; patent line; Archibald Alexander's corner; crossing the river; the Punch Bowle; said Alexander's line. Teste: Mathew Lile, James Trimble, Archibald Alexander. Acknowledged, 18th May, 1748.

Page 495.—16th May, 1748. £10. Benj. Borden, &c. to John McCroskey, Jr. (sold in testator's lifetime), 284 acres, part of 92,100; corner to James Glascow. Tested and acknowledged as above.

Page 497.—16th May, 1748. £18. Benj. Borden, &c., to Thomas Paxton, Jr. (sold in testator's lifetime), 670 acres, part of 92,100; corner to John Lowry; corner to Lowry and McKy, crossing northeast branch of James River to two pines in Borden's patent line; Spanish oak on south side of river. Tested and acknowledged as above.

Page 500.—18th May, 1748. £7.10.0. Benj. Borden, &c., to John Huston (sold in testator's lifetime), 228 acres, part of 92,100 acres; corner to James Eikins and Richard Consard; corner to Consard and Samuel Dunlap. Teste: Robt. Davis, Jas. Caldwell, George Gardner. Acknowledged as above.

Page 502.—18th May, 1748. £8.10.0. Benj. Borden to John Allison (sold in testator's lifetime, 291 acres, part of 92,100; white oak on southwest side of river; corner to Gilbert Campbell; corner to said Campbell and John Moore. Tested and acknowledged as above.

Page 505.—18th May, 1748. £65. John Mathews, yeoman, to William Carruthers, yeoman, 297 acres, 2 R., 10 P., part of Borden's 92,100, and conveyed by Borden to John, 11th June, 1742, on a hill called the Timber Ridge; corner to John Gray. Teste: Benj. Borden, Richard Wood, Alexander McCoskey. Acknowledged, 19th May, 1748.

Page 509.—19th May, 1748. £35. Robert Poage to James Thompson, 378 acres, 1 R., 20 P., on a branch called Poage's Run. Teste: Peter Scholl, Jno. Buchanan, Silas Hart. Acknowledged by Robert, and dower released by Elizabeth, 19th May, 1748.

Page 512.—19th May, 1748. £18.6.7. James Patton and Jno. Lewis to Thomas Weems (Weams), —— acres on both sides Great River, Calfpasture; corner to Henry Gay; corner to Jno. Harry. Teste: Acknowledged, 19th May, 1748.

Page 515.—29th February, 1747-8. £77. John Holmes to William Wright, 260 acres in Beverley Manor, part of a large tract conveyed to James Mills and sold to Robert Wilson and John Holmes, patent line of Beverley Manor; Anthony Black's land; Wm. Robinson's line; John Wilson's line. Teste: Wm. Henderson, John Black, John Cunningham. Proved by all and dower released by Jane, 19th May, 1748.

Page 517.—19th May, 1748. £23. Robert Black to John Miller, 200 acres, part of Beverley Manor, conveyed by Beverley to Robert, 25th September, 1741; corner to William Skillern; Manor line. Teste: Wm. Preston, Wm. Jameson, Wm. Kerr. Acknowledged, 19th May, 1748.

Page 520.—22d April, 1748. £14.10.6. Finla McClure to William Bewes, 400 acres; a Spanish oak; on north side of Goose Creek; corner to George Home. Teste: Jno. Buchanan, Gent.; John Buchanan, Francis Beaty. Proved by all, 19th May, 1748.

Page 523.—12th April, 1748. £20. John Mills to David Cloyd, 400 acres on a branch of James River called Persimona Branch. Teste: James Patton, Thomas Lewis, Arther ( ) Watts. Proved by all, 20th May, 1748.

Page 525.—20th May, 1748. 40 shillings. Benj. Borden, &c., to Moses McClure (sold in testator's lifetime), 180 acres, part of 92,100; Spanish oak on east side Mill Creek; corner to Nathaniel McClure, crossing the Warar Run. Acknowledged, 20th May, 1748.

in testator's lifetime), 200 acres, part of 92,100; corner to Thomas Paxton; corner to Mathews; corner to Edmiston, near Moses Trimble's line, the barren hill. Acknowledged, 2d May, 1748.

Page 529.—20th May, 1748. £12. Benj. Borden to John Moore (sold in testator's life), 504 acres, 1 R., 20 P., part of 92,100; corner Joseph Lapsley; corner to Gilbert Campbell. Acknowledged, 20th May, 1748.

Page 532.—20th May, 1747. 20 shillings. Benj. Borden to James Brandles (sold in Benjamin's lifetime), 2,000 acres, part of 92,100; corner to Samuel McClure; James Thompsons line, bunch of box wood on Mill Creek, and to North River. Acknowledged, 20th May, 1748.

Page 535.—21st May, 1748. £30. Alexander Duglas, heir-at-law to Roger Duglas, late of Augusta County, deceased, to Alexander Ritchey, blacksmith, 400 acres on James River above mouth Craig's Creek. Teste: Robt. Renick, Mathew Edmiston, Wm. Syers. Acknowledged, 21st May, 1748.

ERRATA.

Omitted: "Page 527—20th May 1748. Benjamin Borden to John Lowery (sold," etc.

Page 538.—21st May, 1748. £5. William Nutt to James McCorkal, 24½ acres in Beverley Manor; line of McCorkal's former survey; Spanish oak. Teste: James Trimble, John Rutledge, Robert Davis. Acknowledged by William, and dower released by Elinor, 21st May, 1748.

Page 540.—Commission to Thomas Waring, James Garnet, Benj. Winslow and Francis Waring, Gent., Justices of Essex County, to privately examine Elizabeth, wife of Wm. Beverley, as to release of dower in land conveyed, 12th and 13th August, 1747, to James Lynn, 500 acres on head branches of Shanando, 21st September, 1748. Executed, and dower released, 6th February, 1749.

Page 541.—Same to same. Deed to James Crawford, 12th and 13th August, 1747. Executed as above.

Page 541.—Same as to Archibald Hamilton's deed.
Page 542.—Same as to Andrew Cowen's deed.
Page 543.—Same as to Robert Alexander's deed.
Page 543.—Same as to Robert Davis' deed.
Page 544.—Same as to James McCorkle's deed.
Page 544.—Same as to William Henderson's deed.
Page 545.—Same as to Samuel Brawford's deed.
Page 546.—Same as to John Mitchell's deed.
Page 546.—Same as to William Nutt's deed.
Page 547.—Same as to John Henderson's deed.
Page 547.—Same as to James Gilmore's deed.
Page 548.—Same as to Helen Mitchell's deed.
Page 549.—Same as to John Miller's deed.
Page 549.—Same as to Alexander McFeater's deed.
Page 550.—Same as to David Moore's deed.
Page 550.—Same as to Edward Hall's deed.
Page 551.—Same as to Samuel Steel's deed.
Page 551.—Same as to Robert Ramsey's deed.
Page 552.—Same as to George Breckinridge's deed.

DEED BOOK NO. 2.

Page 1.—Adam Miller to Jacob Miller, 16th August, 1748, on Shanandoe. Witnesses, Jno. Cormichel, Wm. Burk, Henry Downs. Delivered: Henry Miller, 24th July, 1756.

Page 5.—6th August, 1748. George Forbush, farmer, and wife Olive, farmer, to Jno. Miller, weaver, Beaver Dam Run, Barnard McHenry's line. Delivered: Jno. Miller, Jr., 3d February, 1755.

Page 9.—9th August, 1748. Wm. Walling to Jno. States. Teste: Peter Schall, Samuel Newman, David Stewart. William's wife was Mary Catharine.

Page 13.—4th September, 1747. John Millar (Millan) and wife Hannah to Francis Hughes, late of Lancaster County, Penna., part of 400 acres patented to Thomas Rutherford, of Frederick County, and by him sold to James Gill, late of Augusta; other part in possession of Thomas Moore Teste: Mathew Skeen, Thos. Milsap. Delivered to Abra. (?) Bird, January, 1754.

Page 16.—29th July, 1748. Jacob Dye and wife Mary, farmer, to Ephraim Love, late of Lancaster County, Penna. Delivered: Wm. Hopkins, 5th March, 1753. Muddy Creek; corner Daniel Harrison, Wm. White, Wm. Carroll.

Page 21.—4th June, 1748. James Wood, of Frederick, to Daniel Davison, Smith's Creek. Teste: Thos. How, south side of wagon road; patented to James Wood, 12th January, 1746. Teste: Jno. Hopes, Thos. Wood, Thos. Story, Morgan Bryan, Jno. Harrison, Jr. Delivered: Jno. Harrison, Jr., November, 1756.

Page 24.—Wm. Beverley to Nathaniel Steel, Beverley Manor; corner John Teat and Geo. Brackenridge, Jno. Lockhart and Ramsey, David Steel, James Fulton, 17th June, 1748.

Page 28.—Wm. Beverley to James Lockhart, farmer, Beverley Manor, tract surveyed for ye congregation; corner David Campbell. Teste: James Patton, W. Russell, Jno. Madison, Thos. Lewis, Jno. Buchanan, 17th June, 1748.

Page 32.—17th August, 1748. Archibald Hamilton to Thomas Storey, one Givins, land; patented to Archibald, 5th March, 1747. Archibald's wife was Frances.

Page 35.—Joseph Reed, Taylor to David Hayes, yeoman, bought by Joseph from Beverley, 24th July, 1740, and deeded, 25th September, 1741; Wm. Beverley, corner Jno. Buchanan, James Robinson, Charles Campbell. Teste: Patrick Campbell.

Page 37.—Elizabeth Reed's private examination as to above, 10th September, 1748.

Page 41.—Robert King to James Wallace and Wm. Wallace, Jr. Wm. Beverley, corner Robert Poag, Daniel Deniston, Catherine, wife of Robert. Part of 750 acres granted to Robert by Beverley, 25th March, 1742. Teste: David Stuart and Robert Patterson, 18th August, 1748.

Page 44.—18th August, 1748. Robert King to William Wallace, part of above 750 acres. Wm. Beverley.

Page 48.—18th August, 1748. Rev. John Craige to Joshua Hadley, 400 acres in fork of Craig's Creek and James River. Isabella Hellena, wife of John. Teste: Thos. Lewis, Silas Hart, Robt. McClenachan.

Page 50.—28th May, 1748. John Smith to Silas Hart, mortgage; corner James Wood patented to John, 25th June, 1747. Teste: Jno. Cunningham.

Page 53.—16th August, 1748. Benj. Borden to John Gilmer, in 92,100; John Carr's line. Delivered: James Gilmore, 10th August, 1750.

Page 55.—18th August, 1748. Benj. Borden to James Gilmer. Hugh Cunningham, Jno. Carr.

Page 58.—14th August, 1748. Benj. Borden to John Lyle, part of 92,100; corner Mathew Lyle; corner John McDowel. This same land acknowledged to John, but deed found to be insufficient.

Page 61.—19th August, 1748. Andrew Mitchell and wife Mary to James Miller, Beverley Manor.

Page 65.—19th August, 1748. James Patton and Jno. Lewis to James Lockridge; corner Robert Givins, John Preston; 520 acres on Calfpasture. Teste: Robt. Christian.

Page 68.—20th August, 1748. Henry Downs, Gent., and Jane, to John

McKemey, farmer, 388 acres on north branch Shanando at end of Buckhill. (See infra, last entry from this book.) Teste: Ro. Rennick.

Page 71.—20th August, 1748. David Steward to James Miller, 57 acres in Beverley Manor; Beverley Manor; corner John Henderson. Margaret, wife of David. Teste: Robert Davies, John Hutchinson.

Page 74.—21st September, 1748. Isaac McCullagh to John Coulter, 230 acres in Beverley Manor; corner ye Christians, James Caldwell, John Davidson. Teste: Wm. Henderson, Thos. Gordon, Margaret, wife of Isaac.

Page 78.—17th June, 1748. Wm. Beverley to Robert McClenachan, 340 acres in Beverley Manor; Lewis Creek, Brackenridge, crossing Ramsey's Branch.

Page 80.—Henry Downs, Sr., to Wm. Downs, 400 acres on Smith's Creek, patented to Henry 1st October, 1747.

Page 83.—25th May, 1748. George Robinson, gent., to Stephen Rentfrow; cor. John Buchanan. Teste: Jno. Ramsey, James Miller, Jr., Jno. Maxwell.

Page 85.—27th October, 1748. George Scott to Samuel Henderson; Sharrendoe River. Teste: Joshua Hickman.

Page 89.—15th February, 1748. Robert Rennock to Silas Hart, mason, part of 400 acres patented to Robt., 10th June, 1740; Buffilo Lick Branch. Elizabeth, wife of Robert.

Page 92.—15th February, 1748. Samuel Lusk, farmer, to William Anderson, yeoman; Middle River of Shannadoe; John Finley. Teste: George Rennick.

Page 95.—15th February, 1748. Robert Allison to Joseph Paxton; James River; the Narrows on No. Branch of James. Teste: Thomas Sheals, Robert Alexander.

Page 98.—4th February, 1748. Wm. Beverley to John Brown, 300 acres in Beverley Manor; Beverley Manor patent line, Robert Young. Teste: Moses Mann, Robt. Graham, Wm. Elliote.

Page 102.—Wm. Beverley to Moses Mann, planter. Beverley Manor patent line; Wm. McCutchen's line; Grassy Lich Run. Teste: Jno. Brown.

Page 108.—William Beverley to Robert Graham, planter. On Little Calfpasture; Beverley Manor patent line; Grassy Lick tract. Delivered: Humphrey Madison, 1753.

Page 113.—4th February, 1748. Wm. Beverley to William Eliott, Jr., planter. Corner James Carlisle; patent line.

Page 117.—4th February, 1748. Wm. Beverley to John McLeary, planter.

Page 120.—12th February, 1748. Benj. Borden to Robert Huston. Timber Ridge. Teste: Elijah McClenachan, Josiah Linn. Hugh Cunningham.

Page 122.—12th November, 1748. Benj. Borden to Hugh Cunningham. Teas Creek; corner John Carr. Teste: Josias Linn, Roger Keys, Robert Erwin.

Page 125.—6th February, 1748-9. Benj. Borden to Robert Erwin. Corner John Carr.

Page 129.—28th January, 1748-9. John and Mary McNabb (his wife) to Arthur McClure. Mille Creek; corner James Thompson; corner Robert Galloway. Teste: Andrew McNabb, Wm. Hall, Gilbert Campbell. Delivered to John Wilson, 30th April, 1751.

Page 132.—15th February, 1748-9. William Mitchell and Margaret (his wife) to James McClure. Branch of James River called the Mary, 200 acres patented to William, 25th September, 1746.

Page 135.—15th February, 1748. George Brackenridge to Mathew Erwin. Corner Samuel Lusk. Teste: John Francis, James Patterson, Robt. Alexander.

Page 138.—15th September, 1748. Joseph Reed, Taylor to David Sayers, Jr. Bought by Joseph from Wm. Beverley, 24th July, 1740, and 26th September, 1741. Corner James Robinson; Christian's Creek; corner Francis Beaty. Teste: John Buchanan, Charles and Pat. Campbell.

Page 141.—15th February, 1748-9. John Wilson, Gent., to Mathew Wilson. Delivered: Capt. Wilson, February, 1752. Beverley Manor. Corner widow Cooks, widow of Patrick Cook, part of Beverley Manor. Teste: Pat. Martin, Robt. Wilson, Francis Beaty.

Page 144.—20th August, 1748. Samuel Harrison to Mary, his wife, to Jno. Wright. Cooks Creek. Teste: Daniel Harrison, Samuel Newman.

Page 149.—4th February, 1749. John Hodge, farmer, and Elizabeth, his wife, to Jacob Woodley. Smith's Creek; Daniel James' branch; Valentine Sevear's Mill; the mill tract, ½ acre, is to return to heirs of Jacob Woodley. Teste: Wm. Rambo.

Page 153.—14th February, 1748. Wm. Bewes (Bews) to Wm. Bryan. Delivered: Ro. Breckinridge, May, 1765. On Goose Creek. Corner Joseph Love.

Page 158.—16th February, 1748. David Logan, farmer, to Wm. Craig, farmer. Corner Wm. Thompson; Samuel Givens; Cathey's River; Jane, wife of David.

Page 160.—17th February, 1748. Benj. Borden to Hugh Martin. Corner John Buchanan.

Page 163.—17th February, 1748, farmer. Robert Poage to James McAfee, farmer. On Catapa, a branch of James River opposite to mouth of Holstein's Branch at a place called Indian Camp. Elizabeth, wife of Robert. Teste: George Anderson.

Page 167.—17th February, 1748-9. Walter Trimble and Rosa, his wife, to David Trimble. Plumb Tree Bottom Branch.

Page 171.—24th October, 1748. Wm. Sayers to John Pattison, weaver, part of 1,546 acres sold by Wm. Beverley to Patrick Campbell in 1738 and by him to Wm. Sayers in 1745. Patrick Campbell. On South Branch Shanandoah. Teste: Wm. Smith, Pat. Campbell, James Mitchell, Andrew Duncan.

Page 175.—24th October, 1748. Wm. Sayers to Andrew Duncan, part of 1,546 acres above. Wm. Beverley, Patrick Campbell. Beverley Manor.

Page 179.—17th May, 1749. George Brackenridge to Robert Brackenridge.

Page 182.—17th May, 1749. Robert Scott to Mathew Thompson, Jr. Stormy Lick Branch, Jacob Thomas. Patented to Robert, 5th March, 1747. Teste: George Scott, Robt. Hook, Wm. Lamb, Ann, wife of Robert.

Page 185.—3d May, 1749. John Moore and Margaret, his wife, to Robert Moore. Woods Creek, a branch of James River; corner John Moore. Gilbert Campbell.

Page 189.—Hugh Campbell to John Young. Naked Creek, part of 400 acres patented to Hugh, 25th September, 1746. Teste: John Francis, Alexander Blair, Wm. Preston, Esther, wife of Hugh.

Page 193.—George Henderson and Elizabeth, his wife, to Wm. Moore, 320 acres in Borden tract. Teste: Nathaniel Evins, Wm. Mitchell, Samuel Moore.

Page 196.—17th May, 1749. James Bell and Rachel to James Kirk, 400 acres Cathey's River; Jennings Branch. Teste: Andrew Boyd, Alexander Crafford. Delivered Ro. Armstrong 5th March, 1753.

Page 200.—18th May, 1749. William Smith and Jacie, his wife, to Joseph Kennedy, 711 acres in Borden's tract. Corner Samuel Huston, Greenlee's line. Teste: Samuel Huston, James Trumble, Jas. Trimble.

Page 204.—17th May, 1749. William Smith to Samuel Huston, 283 acres in Borden's tract. Corner Joseph Kennedy's corner, Greenlee's line. Teste: Alexander Moore, James Trimble, James McKown.

Page 207.—5th April, 1749. William Beverley to John Cowan, 202 acres in Beverley Manor. Thomas Shield's corner in Co. Co., James Patton's line, Francis Beaty's line, Robert Christian's line. Teste: John Wilson.

Page 212.—5th April, 1749. Wm. Beverley to Thomas Shields, 202 acres in Beverley Manor. Corner Wm. Robinson and Col. James Patton's mill place. Place surveyed for Maj. Brooks. Francis Beaty's line. Corner John Cowan.

Page 217.—5th April, 1749. Wm. Beverley to John Teat, 344 acres in Beverley Manor. Corner James Linn, Steel's land. Corner Jno. Lockhart, Brackenridge's line.

Page 221.—8th May, 1749. Benjamin Borden to James Randolph, 200 acres part of 92100. Corner Samuel McClure, James Thompson's line. Mill Creek.

Page 223.—17th May, 1749. Benjamin Borden to Alexander Miller, blacksmith, 248 acres part of 92100. Corner tract surveyed for McDowell.

Page 226.—18th May, 1749. Benjamin Borden to John Harragar. Delivered: Wm. Preston 30th March, 1754. 400 acres patented to Benjamin, Sr., 5th November, 1739.

Page 229.—18th April, 1749. Wm. Beverley to Wm. Russell, Gent., 205 acres on Lewis Creek in Beverley Manor. Lewis Creek; corner Lewis.

Page 235.—20th April, 1749. Wm. Russell to Wm. Beverley, 2050 acres. Lewis Creek. Same as above.

Page 237.—5th April, 1749. Wm. Beverley to Thomas Brown of Beverley Manor. Corner Robert Wilson. Corner Andrew Alexander and John Cowan's lines. Corner John Shields. 225 acres in Beverley Manor.

Page 243.—5th April, 1749. William Beverley to John Maxwell. Patented to Beverley, et als. (Beverley Manor grant, 6th Sept., 1736). Conveyed to Beverley by deed recorded in Secretary's office of Colony. Borden's Road. 439 acres.

Page 246.—21st April, 1749. William Beverley to James Patton and other justices, John Lews, John Buchanan, George Robinson, Peter Scholl, James Bell, Robert Campbell, Robert Cunningham, John Wilson, Thomas Lewis, James Mountgomery, Silas Hart, Henry Downs, William Jameson, Rich. Burton, John Christian, Samuel Gay, William Thompson. Courthouse. 25 acres.

Page 250.—5th June, 1749. John Smith, Gent., to Silas Hart, mason, 400 acres on South Fork of North River of Shannadore. James Wood's line. Patented to John, 25th June, 1747. Margaret, John's wife, releases dower. Teste: John Thompson, John Poage, John Archer.

Page 253.—22d August, 1749. Daniel Davison, yeoman, and Phoebe, to Zebulon Harrison, yeoman. Daniel James's branch. Delivered: John Harrison, November, 1756. 46 acres patented to Daniel Davison, 25th September, 1746. Witnesses: John Denton and John Phillips. Teste: John Denton, Jr., Robert Breckenridge, John Phillips.

Page 258.—22nd August, 1749. Same as above. Phoebe, wife of Daniel, on Smith's Creek. Stephen Howorth's line. 156 acres, patented to Daniel, 25th September, 1746.

Page 262.—22d August, 1749. John Hopes (Hays?) (Hope?) of Frederick, and Mary to Patrick Quin. On Naked Creek. Corner Jost Hite, Robert McKay, William Duff, Robert Green's line. 200 acres, patented to said John Hopes, 12th January, 1746. Teste: David Logan, John Homes.

Page 265.—22d August, 1749. William Lamb to John Lynd, Gent. Shannadore. 320 acres on No. Br. No. Riv. Robert Scott's land. Stoney-Lick Branch. Teste: Gabriel Pickins and Robert Scott.

Page 269.—3rd July, 1749. William Thomptson, Sr., to William Thomptson, Jr. 400 acres on Middle River, opposite mouth of No. Br. of Shannado. James Craig. Patented to William, Sr., 22nd September, 1739. Teste: James Patton, John Buchanan, Robert and George Scott.

Page 271.—18th August, 1749. Richard Harald, Sr., planter, to son, Richard Harrald, Jr., planter of Culpepper, Cave Branch, joining John Harrald, Capt. Russell's line. Teste: Leonard Burton, Judith Hurst.

Page 272.—18th August, 1749. Richard Harrald to son, William Harrald, planter, and to son, John, and to son, Moses Harrald, and to son, James Harrald. Duggully Branch; also to son, Aaron Harrald. On condition that the sons stay with him until they are of age. Delivered to John Harrald, March, 1758.

Page 275.—31st May, 1749. William Beverley to John Black, of Beverley Manor. 738 acres in Beverley Manor. Corner William Long. Beverley Manor line. Teste: James Alexander, William Long, James Bell.

Page 278.—22nd August, 1749. Silas Hart, mason, to William Anderson, farmer. Delivered: Benjamin Morgan, August, 1762. 460 acres on North Branch James. Patented to Silas, 12th January, 1746. Teste: Alexander Wright, Andrew Johnston, James Edmiston.

Page 280.—Benjamin Borden to James Lusk, 170 acres of 92100. Corner Samuel McCutchan. Beverley Manor line.

Page 283.—23rd August, 1749. B. Borden to David Hays. Delivered: Samuel Buchanan, 21st June, 1753. 124 acres of 92100.

Page 287.—1749. John Harrison, yeoman, to James Letherdal, blacksmith. Luney's Mill Creek. 366 acres. Patented to John, 12th February, 1742. Teste: William Harbeson, James Magill, William Preston. See infra. p. 871.

Page 290.—19th May, 1749. Benjamin Borden to Arthur McClure. 153½ acres of 92100. Corner Robert Poage. Corner Israel Pickins. Corner John Pattison. Delivered: John Wilson, 30th April, 1751.

Page 294.—17th August, 1749. James Wood, Gent. of Frederick, to William Burk, 4000 acres. Patented to James, 22nd September, 1739. On South River, near Peaked Mountain, Boon's Run. Delivered: Nicholas Null, 25th May, 1753. Teste: Isaac Perkins, John Neill, James Porteus, Valentine Sevier.

Page 298.—18th August, 1749. James Wood, above, to James Trotter On Naked Creek, 268 acres. Michael Dickey's line. Patented to James, 12th January, 1746. Teste: William Burk.

Page 302.—19th August, 1749. James Wood, above, to Samuel McRoberts, 287 acres on Middle Branch of Catapo Creek. Patented to James, 12th January, 1746. Teste: James Porteus, William Burk, Valentine Sevier.

Page 304.—25th August, 1749. Benjamin Borden to John McClure 205 acres of 92100, on No. Branch James. Corner Moses McClure. Delivered: John Stevenson, 26th March, 1753.

Page 307.—21st August, 1749. B. Borden to Moses McClure. 380 acres of 92100, crossing South River. Corner John McClure. Corner Thomas Paxton. Delivered: as above.

Page 310.—29th November, 1749. George Robinson, Gent., to David Robinson, 400 acres Buffiloe Creek. Patented to George, 25th July, 1746.

Page 314.—23d September, 1749. Henry Ayler (Ehler) and Clev. Danner, of Culpeper, to Jacob Harmon. Corner Jacob Stover. Teste: Isaac Smith, Casper Vought, Jacob Harman, Jr. Delivered to Mrs. Harmon, 24th July, 1758.

Page 317.—11th August, 1749. Michael Lawler and Mary, his wife, Thomas of St. Mark's Parrish, Culpeper Co., to Thomas Kennerley, Joseph Bloodworth, Mary Bloodworth, Mary Margaret Kennerley, William Russell. Devised to his wife, Mary, after her death to Mary Margaret Kennerly, wife of Thomas. Mary Bloodworth, widow, has married Michael. 100 acres purchased by Joseph from Russell, 27th May, 1742. 300 acres patented to Joseph, 1st August, 1745. Teste: John Roberts, Jr., William Duncan, Archibald, William and Susanna Woods, James Kennerley.

Page 321.—28th November, 1749. Francis McCown, yeoman, to Andrew Steel, yeoman, Benjamin Borden, Kennedy's Creek. Teste: John Smith, Alexander Gibson, James McCowan.

Page 324.—27th November, 1749. John Stephenson to Henry Kirkham Buffalo Creek. Teste: Andrew Cowan, William Hall.

Page 327.—28th November, 1749. John Coulter to John Lusk, 230 acres in Beverley Manor. Corner Christian. Corner James Caldwell, William Armstrong's line. Isabell, wife of Jno. Coulter. Teste: James Henderson, Andrew Alexander.

Page 330.—13th October, 1749. William Beverley to John Shields, 225 acres in Beverley Manor. Corner Thomas Brown, John Cowan's line. Corner Robert Christian. Corner Moffett's land. Teste: Thomas Shields, John Cowan, Samuel Brawford.

Page 333.—13th October, 1749. William Beverley to Robert McCorkal, 269 acres in Beverley Manor. Branch of Christy's Creek known as Nutt's Mill Creek. James Caldwell's line. Teste: Thomas Sheels. Delivered to James McCorkle, 6th May, 1752.

Page 336.—29th November, 1749. Hugh Dever to Daniel Smith, 80 acres on North River, Shannado. Corner Charles Dever. Teste: Jas. Smith.

Page 339.—28th November, 1749. Hugh Dever to Charles Dever, 119 acres. Corner to above. Corner Daniel Smith. Corner John Davis, Beaver Creek.

Page 342.—29th September, 1749. James Wood, of Frederick, to Robert Shankland, of Lancaster, Penna. Muddy Creek. Corner Jacob Dye. Patented to James, 12th January, 1746, 300 acres. Teste: William Dobbin, James Carroll, Thomas Wood, Valentine Sevier, Edward Shanklin.

Page 345.—29th November, 1749. Morgan Bryan to David Johnson, 400 acres on Linwell's Creek. Corner: Jost Hite.

Page 348.—29th November, 1749. William Robinson to John Robinson, 188 acres on Christian's Creek, John Wilson's line. Corner Thomas Shields; corner Col. James Patton.

Page 350.—28th November, 1749. Thomas Stephenson and wife, Jane, to William Erwin. Walker's Run, a branch of Cathey's River, 241 acres. Delivered: Edward Beard, 17th October, 1755.

Page 354.—28th November, 1749. William Nutt, miller, to Dennis Dyer, tailor, 181 acres in Beverley Manor. Mill Creek. Corner Andrew Nutt.

Page 357.—28th November, 1749. John Smith, Gent., to William Mathews, weaver, Moffett's branch, a branch of Cathey's River. Patented to John Smith, 10th February, 1748. Delivered: John Archer, November, 1753. Teste: Samson and John Archer and Robert Renick.

Page 360.—28th November, 1749. William Logan, blacksmith, to Silas Hart, mason, John Smith's land. Robert Brackenridge, Elizabeth, wife of William, 400 acres on North River, Shannadore. Corner land formerly John Smith's; now Silas Hart's. Patented to Robert Breckenridge, 1st December, 1740, and conveyed by him to William Logan, 22nd July, 1745. Teste: James Brown, Robert Renick, William Anderson, James Sayers.

Page 362.—28th November, 1749. John Archer and Rebecca, his wife, to James Sayers (Sawyers), 225 acres; Buffalo Lick Creek, a branch of Cathey's River. Corner Ro. Renick. Delivered: Samson Archer, March, 1759.

Page 366.—28th November, 1749. John Finley to Alexander Gardner, 183 acres on Finley's Branch of Cathey's River, William Anderson's line. Delivered: John Archer, November, 1753. Teste: Robert Scott, James McCorkall, Francis Beaty.

Page 369.—Jost Hite (Heid?) to George Bowman, 4th October, 1749, Linwell's Creek, lot No. 8, 545 acres. Teste: John Hite.

Page 373.—Jost Hite (Heid?) to Paul Froman, 4th October, 1749, 500 acres; lot No. 6 on Linwell's Creek.

Page 376.—29th November, 1749. Henry Martin, of East Jersey, to B. Borden, 674 acres. Corner John and James McDowell. Teste: John and Mathew Lyle, Roger Keys, Robert Losk.

Page 379.—29th November, 1749. Robert Turk, and Margaret, to James Hamilton, 284 acres in Beverley Manor, Robert Patrick's line. On South River Shannadore. Margaret, wife of Robert Turk. Delivered: Joseph Teas, November, 1754. Teste: George Breckenridge, Daniel Davison, Francis Beaty.

Page 381.—30th November, 1749. B. Borden to John McFarrin (Pharrin?), 319 acres of 2880 acres. Patented to Benjamin, 9th March, 1740. On Catabo Creek, a branch of James River.

Page 384.—30th November, 1749. William Russell, of Culpeper, to John Ramsey, 400 acres in ———, forks of James. Adam Breckenridge, Daniel McAnaire. Not delivered.

Page 287.—18th September, 1749. James Armstrong (Malster) and Jane to Robert McClenachan, Gent. Corner James Caldwell. Corner John Madison, Gent. Jane, wife of James. 310 acres on Christian's Creek. Teste: John Madison, Da. Stewart.

Page 389.—14th July, 1749. Borden to James McCewn, 400 acres of 92100, on a Timber Ridge.

Page 393.—29th November, 1749. William Henderson to William Hudson and John Clyde, of Penna. Above the mouth of Buffalo Creek, 350 acres on the North Branch of James River. Susanna, wife of William Henderson.

Page 395.—28th November, 17—, William King, blacksmith, to John Nickoll, 400 acres on Moffett's branch of Cathey's River. Ralston's Path. Patented to William King, 10th February, 1748. Teste: Robert Ralstone. Delivered: Alexander Gibson.

Page 399.—27th February, 1749. John Maxwell to Andrew Johnston, merchant, 218½ acres in Beverley Manor. Corner John Madison. Corner John Maxwell. Teste: Alexander Wright, William Hamilton, Adam Breckenridge.

Page 402.—28th February, 1749. John McCutchan to James McCutchan Corner David Coningham, in David Campbell's line; widow Cook's line; Patrick Coningham's line. Teste: Francis Beaty, Hugh H. Young, William McCutchan.

Page 405.—26th February, 1749. John Kerr to John Hind, 100 acres in a loop neck of Cathey's River; Thomas Storey's line. Dower released by Lucy, wife of John Kerr. Delivered: William Hinds, December, 1754. Teste: Francis Beaty, John Pickens.

Page 408.—28th February, 1749. Ephraim Vause to Joseph Love, 200 acres on Goose Creek. Corner William Bewes. Teste: Francis Beaty, William Dunlapp, George Anderson.

Page 410.—Plan of City Staunton. Each lot ½ acre, except 41, 42, 43, 44. Cont. 9, one acre each. Lot 16 contains ¾ acre. No. 22 contains 8-10ths of acre. No. 29, 9-10ths acre. All laid out in 1748 and confirmed by last General Assembly. Thomas Lewis, surveyor, 27th February, 1749. Courthouse is placed on Augusta Street, first opposite the southeast corner of lot 2.

Page 411.—Survey for William Beverley of 2050 acres adjoining Staunton. Corner Lewis. Laid out in 1748.

Page 413.—27th February, 1749. William Beverley to David Campbell, 110 acres in Beverley Manor. Teste: James Alexander, Israel Christian, William Gay.

Page 416.—27th February, 1749. To John Johnson, 213 acres on Little Calfpasture patent line. Teste: William Long, John Gay. Delivered: Humphrey Madison, 30th August, 1753.

(Many of these deeds delivered to Francis Beaty.)

Page 418.—27th February, 1749. William Beverley to Morris O'Friel, planter, 40 acres on Middle River. William King's line. Corner Samuel Wallace. Teste: William Robison.

Page 421.—23rd February, 1749. William Beverley to Samuel McCune, 176 acres in Beverley Manor. Said McCune's old plantation. David Edmiston's line. Teste: William Johnston, John Lin, James Frame.

Page 424.—28th February, 1749. William Beverley to Arthur Hamilton, 270 acres in Beverley Manor. Corner Nathanial Davis. Corner James Gilmer's line; James Woody's land. Corner James Leeper. Corner said Hamilton's old plantation.

Page 427.—27th February, 1749. Same to James Gillespe, 210 acres in Beverley Manor. Corner to place formerly surveyed for James and marked, No. 3. Corner lot No. 1, No. 2, and No. 10.

Page 429.—William Beverley to William King, farmer, 251 acres in Beverley Manor. Corner John Trimble. Corner Morrice O'Friel. Teste: David Cunningham, James Alexander, Arthur Hamilton.

Page 432.—27th February, 1749. Same to William Johnstone, 100 acres in Beverley Manor on Cathey's River. George Anderson's corner.

Page 435.—27th February, 1749. Same to Gabriel Alexander, 423 acres in Beverley Manor. Line of Beverley Manor crossing South River; James Bell's line. Corner William Long. Teste: James Gilaspey, James Bell.

Page 438.—27th February, 1749. Same to James Alexander, 819 acres in Beverley Manor. Corner George Hutchison. Teste: John Bigham, James Bell.

Page 441.—17th February, 1749. Same to James Miller, 44 acres in Beverley Manor. Corner John Henderson. Corner James McCurtle. Corner James Breckenridge. Stuart's old survey. Delivered: George Bigham, 24th March, 1757.

Page 443.—27th February, 1749. Same of Parrish of St. Anne, Essex Co., to James Vance, 305 acres in Beverley Manor. Corner Martin's land. Teste: Daniel Kidney, William King.

Page 447.—26th February, 1749. Same to Jacob Martin, farmer, 141 acres on branch of Little Calfpasture, called Hall's Branch. Teste: William and James Gay.

Page 450.—27th February, 1749. Same to John Jamison, 104 acres on Back Creek in Beverley Manor. Corner Ro. Davis. Samuel Wallace's line. Hugh Young's land. Teste: John Henderson.

Page 453.—27th February, 1749. Same to Robert McClanachan, Gent., Christie's Creek, Beverley Manor. Corner William Nutt. Tract for Andrew Cowan, James Caldwell's line. Another tract called Elk Meadow, 216 acres, 190 acres. Teste: George Anderson, Arthur Hamilton.

Page 455.—27th February, 1749. Deed. Same to Robert McClenachan. ½ A. lot in Staunton, Lot No. 5. Corner Preston's land. Livery by turf and twig.

Page 458.—27th February, 1749. Same to William Currey, 360 acres Beverley Manor. Corner tract first surveyed for James Bell, now in possession of Andrew Cowin. Corner William Nutt. Tract surveyed for Adam Thompson, now belonging to Robert McClenachan. Corner Samuel McCorkall's land. Corner to James Moody; Cowin's line. Teste: Arthur Hamilton, John Linn, George Anderson.

Page 461.—22nd February, 1749. Same to Robert Moody, 473 acres in Beverley Manor, head of Long Meadow. Corner John Frazier. Delivered: Samuel Frazier, 11th November, 1773. Teste: Thomas Stewart and John Brown.

Page 464.—22nd February, 1749. Same to John Frazier, 472 acres in head of Long Meadow Run, Beverley Manor. Corner John Thompson. Corner Robert Moody.

Page 466.—27th February, 1749. Same to John Cunningham, of Town of Staunton, 2 lots in Staunton, Nos. 1 and 7; also woodland lots Nos. 2 and 3, 50A each. Delivered Francis Beaty, 1752. Livery by a latch of the door.

Page 469.—25th February, 1749. Same to John Bigham, farmer, where John now lives, 302 acres. Corner lot 16. Teste: George Bigham.

Page 470.—22nd February, 1749. Deed. Beverley to Alexander Wright, March —, Lots 8 and 9 in Staunton; also two 50A woodland lots Nos. 6 and 7. Teste: Charles Dick, John Reynolds, James Cowley.

Page 473.—23rd February, 1749. Same to William Johnston. Delivered: Zachariah Johnston, 1st June, 1773. 156 acres and 269 acres in Beverley Manor. Corner to William Wright. Corner John Thompson, Alexander Henderson's line. The Barrens. Platt. Teste: Alexander Wright, Samuel McCune.

Page 477.—27th February, 1749. Same to William Gay, of Calfpasture, 490 acres in Col. Beverley's part of Calfpasture. Little Calfpasture. Corner Samuel Gay. Corner James Stephenson; line of the patent. Teste: William Long, John Alexander, William Robinson.

Page 480.—27th February, 1749. Same to William Long, 400 acres in Beverley Manor, patent line. Corner John Wilson, crossing South River; Col. James Patton and William Robinson. Corner James Bell. Col Patton's mill place. Teste: James Alexander, Andrew McClure, John Black.

Page 483.—27th February, 1749. Same to same, 433½ acres in Beverley Manor on South River. Corner Gabriel Alexander. Corner John Black.

Page 486.—27th February, 1749. Same to James Bell, 600 acres in Beverley Manor. Corner James Alexander, patent line. Corner William Long, crossing South River. Teste: William Gay.

Page 489.—27th February, 1749. Same to William Hamilton, farmer, 578 acres in Calfpasture. Teste: James Caldwell. Delivered: Hum. Madison, 30th August, 1753.

Page 492.—27th February, 1749. Same to William Robinson, 380 acres in Beverley Manor. Corner Robert Ramsey, patent line. Corner Patrick Hays. Teste: Andrew McCord, William Robison, Andrew Duncan.

Page 494.—28th February, 1749. Same to Thomas Kirkpatrick, 282½ acres in Beverley Manor, Back Creek. Corner to his old plantation. John Wilson's line.

Page 497.—28th February, 1749. Same to James Frame, 220 acres in Beverley Manor. Corner Christian-John Lusk's line. Samuel McCorkle's corner; John Glass corner.

Page 499.—1st January, 1749-50. William Thompson, yeoman, to George Crawford, Gentleman, 200 acres on Middle River, above mouth of Littler's Creek. 400 acres patented to William, 22nd September, 1739. Teste: Patrick Crawford, John Givens.

Page 501.—1st January, 1749-50. Joshua Hickman, yeoman, to George Crawford, North River below the fork. 100 acres patented to Joshua, 5th April, 1748. Teste: Samuel Henderson, Patrick Crawford, John Givens.

Page 503.—28th February, 1749. Ephraim Vause to William McCurry, 248 acres on South Branch Roanoke. Teste: Nathanial Evins, Adam Breckenridge, Tobias Smith.

Page 505.—27th February, 1749. Deed for the Glebe. Robert Campbell, Gent., to James Lockhart and John Madison, Church Wardens, and the other vestrymen, viz: James Patton, John Buchanan, Patrick Hays, John Christian, John Buchanan, Robert Alexander, Thomas Gordon, John Archer, John Mathews, John Smith, 200 acres in Beverley Manor. Corner James Clarke. 350 acres conveyed to Robert by Beverley, 24th July, 1740. Teste: Patrick Cook, John Risk, Matthew Wilson, Nathan Patterson, Samuel Walker.

Page 509.—20th February, 1749. Cornelius Murley and Austas, his wife, to Daniel Murley, their son, half of 400 acres. Patented to Cornelius in Gap of North Mountain, next to James Baggs, on North Fork North River Shanando. Teste: Charles Harr, Robert Hook.

Page 512.—28th February, 1749. William Thompson, Jr., to William Baskins (William Lamb?), 232 acres on Branch of Buffalo Run. Corner James Beard. Patented to William, 1st June, 1741. Teste: Silas Hart, Henry Downs, Jr., William Lamb.

Page 515.—28th February, 1749. George Anderson, of Orange County, to William Lamb, 330 acres on South Branch Shannando. Patented to George, 30th January, 1741. Teste: Henry Downs, Jr., William Thompson.

Page 518.—28th February, 1749-50. Robert Poage to John Poage, 305 acres. William Beverley. Corner Lewis land. Wallace's land. Corner Daniel Dennison. Part of 773 acres conveyed to Robert by Beverley 28th April, 1739. Teste: William Jameson, Erwin Patterson.

Page 521.—28th February, 1749. James Patton and John Lewis to James Poage, 290 acres in Great Calfpasture. Corner Crockett. Corner Weems. Teste: Alexander Rose.

Page 524.—22nd February, 1749. William Beverley to James Patton, Gent., 1398 acres in Beverley Manor. Corner Beverley Manor line. Teste: Alexander Wright, Thomas Stewart.

Page 526.—22nd February, 1749. Same to same, 432 acres in Beverley Manor. Corner to the Christies, William Long's line. Joseph Mills' line. William Robinson's line. Teste: James Lockhart.

Page 529.—28th February, 1749. Same to John Lynn, Jr., 383½ acres in Beverley Manor. Corner John Bigham. Corner William Nutt, John Henderson's line. John Linn, Sr. Teste: James and Andrew Linn, James Henderson.

Page 532.—28th February, 1749. Same to James Rosebrough, 240 acres in Beverley Manor. Patent line of Beverley Manor. Teste: Arthur Hamilton, William Campbell.

Page 535.—28th February, 1749. Same to Mathew Armstrong, 190 acres in Beverley Manor. Robert King's old place. Corner Robert Patterson. Corner John Anderson. Teste: John and William Gay, John King.

Page 538.—27th February, 1749. Same to William McClintock, 360 acres in Beverley Manor, cor. Robert Young, a branch under the Sugar Loaf. Delivered to William McClintock August, 1775. Teste: Thomas Henderson, Thomas Rutledge, Robert Ramsey.

Page 541.—28th February, 1749. Same to William McNabb, 300 acres in Beverley Manor. Corner Samuel Downey, Adam Thompson's line; corner John Campbell; corner James Callison; Alexander McFeeter's line. Teste: John Lin, John Linn, Andrew McClure.

Page 544.—27th February, 1749. Same to Thomas Peerie, planter, 375 acres in Augusta County, Shennadore in Beverley Manor. Corner John Campbell; corner Robert Young; corner William McClintock. Delivered: Thomas Kirkpatrick, January, 1752. Teste: Jacob Lockhart, Nathaniel Davis.

Page 547.—28th February, 1749. Same to Hugh Young, farmer, 200 acres in Beverley Manor, joining his former survey. Pat. Martin's line. Corner Pickin's old place; William McClintock's line. Teste: John Brown.

Page 549.—28th February, 1749-50. Same to Andrew McClure, 300 acres in Beverley Manor. Corner tract surveyed for Samuel Templeton. William McClintock's line; Adam Thompson's line. Teste: James Peare, John Linn, William Wright.

Page 552.—28th February, 1749-50. Same to William Smith, 400 acres at foot of Brown Hill; Smith's Creek of Calfpasture; the Brown Hill; William McCutchin's land. Delivered: Samuel Henderson, March, 1756. Teste: John Brown, William Elliott.

Page 556.—28th February, 1749. Same to David Henderson, 580 acres on South Branch Shannandoe, in Beverley Manor on South River. William Patterson's line. Teste: William Wright, Alexander Henderson.

Page 559.—28th February, 1749. Same to John Campbell, 247 acres on Beverley Manor on South River. Manor line. Corner William Patterson; Joseph Tees' line. Teste: William Petterson and Richard Pillson, William Johnston.

Page 562.—28th February, 1749. Same to William Patterson, 347 acres in Beverley Manor on South River. Corner John Campbell in Manor line; Joseph Tees' line; McClure's land; Archibald Stuart's line. Delivered: Isabella Gibson August, 1761. Teste: John Cabell, James Hamilton.

Page 565.—28th February, 1749. Same to James Peevie, planter, 220 acres in Beverley Manor; formerly James Montgomery's; former survey of said Montgomery and Thomas Peevie's land; John Campbell's line; William McNabb's line; John Lynn's land. Teste: Thomas Henderson, Thomas Rutlidge, Robert Ramsey. Delivered: Thomas Kirkpatrick January 1st, 1752.

Page 568.—28th February, 1749. Same to Robert Steel, 309 acres in Beverley Manor; corner Robert Alexander and Robert Ramsey; corner Nathaniel Steel; James Fulton's line; corner Samuel Steel. Teste: Samuel Steel, John McClure.

Page 570.—27th February, 1749. Same to James Brown, of Staunton, Lot No. 3 in Staunton; Lot No. 8 woodland. Teste: William Ledgewood, John Jameson.

Page 573.—27th February, 1749. Same to Robert Campbell, 53 acres in Beverley Manor; corner to Manor and patent line; John Rusk's line; delivered: Joseph Tees, November, 1754.

Page 576.—28th February, 1749. Same to James Hamilton, 230 acres in Beverley Manor; Rich. Pilson's. Corner Robert Turk. Teste: Robert Turk, R. Pillson, William Johnston.

Page 579.—28th February, 1749. Same to John Glass, 236 acres in Beverley Manor. Corner to James Frame; Christian's land; passes Wilson's line. Teste: John Campbell.

Page 582.—28th February, 1749. Samuel Wilkins to Daniel Harrison, 190 acres near head of Cook's Creek. Delivered: Alexander Herron, March, 1762.

Page 586.—28th February, 1749. Daniel Harrison, Gent., to Arthur Johnston, 190 acres; 10 acres; Cook's Creek (Harrison's stonehouse).

Page 589.—1st March, 1749. Samuel Wilkins and Sarah (dower released 23rd May, 1750) to Alexander Herrin, 365 acres on Cook's Creek. Corner Danuel Harris (son?). Sarah, wife of Samuel, released dower. Delivered: Benjamin Kinley, January, 1754. Teste: William Lusk.

Page 592.—14th February, 1749. Hugh Douglas, laborer, and Margaret, to James Downing and Mary, his wife, relict of Peter Dyer (deceased), spinteres, 130 acres on Stover's Mill Creek. John Stephenson's line. Teste: Archibald Huston, John Stephenson.

Page 596.—28th February, 1749. John Pickens, Gent., to Robert Chiney (Cluney?), 220 acres in Beverley Manor; Middle River. Teste: Andrew Lewis, Archibald Huston, David Logan.

Page 599.—1st March, 1749. Ephraim Vause to James Nealey, 245 acres. Corner Francis Beaty.

Page 602.—1st March, 1749. Samuel Hughes to William Caldwell, 440 acres in Beverley Manor. Corner to survey made for Pearson and Anderson and another survey for William Russell. Corner William Palmer; corner John Hutchison; the poison (Prison) field. Teste: Robert Cunningham, W. Christian, Israel Christian.

Page 605.—1749. Samuel Wilkins to John Wilkins, 200 acres; part of 1265 acres. Teste: John Flood.

Page 608.—27th February, 1749. William Wright to William Beverley, 413 acres. Corner John Seawright, George Hutchison's line. Teste: James Henderson, Andrew McClure.

Page 611.—1st March, 1749. William Beverley to William Wright, 155 acres, 270 acres—425 acres—in Beverley Manor. Alexander Henderson's line. Corner William Johnston, John Thompson's line. Teste: James Henderson, Andrew McClure.

Page 614.—28th February, 1749. Same to James Callison, 276 acres in Beverley Manor. Corner William Ledgerwood. Teste: Nathanial Davies.

Page 617.—Same to same, 230 acres on Nutt's Creek in Beverley Manor. Corner John Linn; McNabb's corner; Bigham's line.

Page 621.—28th February, 1749. Same to George Rodger (Rodgers), 540 acres in Beverley Manor. Corner George Anderson; Cathey's River; Christie's Creek; Hamilton's corner; James Crawford's corner. Consideration paid 28th February, 1741. Teste: George Pirie, James Moffett.

Page 625.—28th February, 17—. William Beverley to David Cunningham, 226 acres in Beverley Manor. Land formerly belonging to John McCutchin but is since divided between him and his sons. James McCutchan's line (son of John); corner Patrick Cunningham; Alexander Campbell's line; David Campbell's line. Teste: Patrick Martin, John Trimble.

Page 628.—28th February, 1749. Same to George Perry, 360 acres in Beverley Manor. Corner George Vance; James Lockhart's line. Teste: Robert and David Conningham.

Page 632.—28th February, 1749. Same to David Campbell, 106 acres in Beverley Manor. Corner Alexander Campbell; corner David Cunningham. Teste: William Christian, Samuel Steel, John Christian.

Page 635.—28th February, 1749. Same to Nathaniel Davise, 150 acres in Beverley Manor. Corner Arthur Hamilton; corner Samuel Downey and James Gilmore. Teste: George Pirie, James Henderson.

Page 638.—27th February, 1749. Same to Robert Young, planter (farmer) part of John Young's land in Beverley Manor (234 acres) on Back Creek. Corner to Hugh Young and John Trimble; corner William McPheeters; corner James Young. Teste: Thomas Stewart and Charles Dalhouse.

Page 642.—28th February, 1749. Same to same, 550 acres whereon he now lives. In Beverley Manor whereon Robert now lives. Corner in his former survey; corner William McClintock; corner Hugh Young; John Browne's line.

Page 645.—28th February, 1749. Same to James Young, planter, 436 acres in Beverley Manor on Back Creek. Corner Robert Young; McFeeter's line; corner Andrew Pickens; corner Robert Campbell; corner Patrick Martin. Teste: John Wilson, John Gay.

Page 648.—Same to John Trimble, Patrick Martin and William McFeeters, planters, 140 acres in Beverley Manor. Adam Thompson's line; corner Samuel Templeton; Samuel Downey's line. Teste: Samuel Downey, John and Robert Wilson.

Page 650.—Same to Robert Craig, 178 acres in Beverley Manor; Cathey's River. Adley Maxwell, Robert Patterson's line. Delivered: Grizel Craig 4th July, 1755. Teste: William Thompson, Charles Campbell, Adam Thomson.

Page 654.—28th February, 1749. Same to John Campbell, 325 acres in Beverley Manor. Corner Adam Thomson and Andrew McClure; corner Thomas Peevy; William McNabb's line; Adam Thompson's line. Teste: Robert Wilson, William Baskins, John Lin.

Page 656.—28th February, 1749. Same to John Wilson, Gent., 306 acres, at North Mountain Meeting House in Beverley Manor. James Lockhart's line; corner William Buntine and Nathaniel Davise. Teste: Charles Campbell.

Page 659.—28th February, 1749. Same to Jacob Lockhart, planter, 210 acres in Beverley Manor. Teste: William Christian, Samuel Steel, William Campbell.

Page 662.—28th February, 1749. Same to William Dunlap, 100 acres on Middle River in Beverley Manor. Corner Robert Kenney; James Henderson's corner. Teste: John McClure, Patrick Martin.

Page 665.—28th February, 1749. Same to James Henderson, 157 acres in Beverley Manor. Corner Mathew Robertson; on Cathey's River; corner Robert Kenny. Teste: William Palmer, Robert Cunningham.

Page 668.—28th February, 1749. Thomas Stewart to William Beverley, on South Fork Shannandoe, 353 acres in Beverley Manor on South River. Corner Capt. James Patton; Beverley Manor line. Teste: Cha. Dick.

Page 670.—2nd March, 1749. William Beverley to Thomas Stewart, 353 acres. Above. Corner Col. James Patton.

Page 673.—28th February, 1749. Same to Charles Dalhouse, 414 acres in Beverley Manor. Samuel Gay's corner; James McClure's line; corner George Robinson. Teste: Francis Beaty, Thomas Stewart.

Page 677.—2d March, 1749. Same to Adam Thompson, 287 acres in Beverley Manor. In Beverley Manor, corner Samuel Downey, Wm. McNabb's and John Campbell's line; corner Andrew McClure, Sr. Teste: Chas. Dick, Thos. Wood.

Page 680.—2d March, 1749. Same to Wm. Preston, 334 acres in Beverley Manor. In Beverley Manor, John Maxwell's line; Col. Lewis' line.

Page 683.—2d March, 1749. Same to same, 365 acres. In Beverley Manor, on Lewis Creek, above Court House; Col. Beverley's Mill Place line.

Page 686.—1st March, 1749. Same to Jean Cook, widow, and John and Mary Cook, minors (the whole contains 802 acres), ⅔ of 2 tracts in one place, and to John Cook the remainder of the other third sold to Jane Cook, widow, during her life, according to will of Patrick Cook, her late husband. 1748, in Augusta—Nathan Lusk's line; John McCutchin's line. Teste: James Lockhart, Robt. Young.

Page 690.—28th February, 1749. Same to John Pickins, Gent., 300 acres in Beverley Manor. Christie's Creek, Corner to Kerr; Fork of Long Meadow Run and Christies Creek supposed to be a corner in the patent line; corner Geo. Rodgers; widow Baskins line. Teste: Jno. McClure, Chas. Campbell.

Page 693.—2d March, 1749-50. Same to Jno. McClure, farmer. In Beverley Manor, corner Edward Hall, 359 acres. Teste: W. Russell, Jno. Brown, Chas. Campbell.

Page 695.—28th February, 1749. Same to John Brown, Gent., lot No. 4 in Staunton and 50 acres in Beverley Manor, lot No. 1, Wm. Lewis's land. Teste: W. Russell, Jno. Pickins, Jno. McClure.

Page 698.—2d March, 1749. Same to Robert Robison, 82 acres in Beverley Manor; in Beverley Manor, patent line; corner James Lusk; corner Widow Cook; corner Benj. Borden's great tract. Teste: John Brown, Adam Thompson, John Shields.

Page 699.—1st February, 1749-50. Benj. Borden to Thomas Paxton, joyner; corner Wm. McClung in John Stevenson's old line; corner George Stevenson, John Paul's corner; corner Andrew Stevenson, William McLung's line, 410 acres. Delivered: Wm. McClung for Thos. Paxton, June, 1752.

Page 702.—22d February, 1749-50. Same to John McCoskery, 440 acres of 92100; corner Daniel Lyle, John Lowry, Sen's. line, Moses Trimble's line. Teste: Wm. McCoskery, Jacob Gray, Francis Beatey.

Page 706.—21st May, 1750. Thomas Black to Wm. Johnston, 269 acres in Beverley Manor, on Black's Run of Christian's Creek, Wm. Henderson's line, George Rutlidge's line; corner James Armstrong's iron mine, Margaret, wife of Thomas. Teste: Hugh Martin, George Douglass, Robert Conningham.

Page 709.— —— ——, 1750. John Finley, Gent., to William Finley, Gent., 298 acres on So. River in Beverley Manor; corner Robert Finley (his house), Charles Dolway's line, Mary, wife of John. Teste: Wm. Henderson, Robert Patrick, John Black.

Page 713.— —— ——, 1750. John Finley, Gent., to Robert Finley, Gent., 297 acres. In Beverley Manor on South River, corner Israel Christian; Charles Dolway's line; corner Wm. Finley; Manor line, near Robert's houses.

Page 716.—6th February, 1749-50. Christopher Franciscus, Sr., of Lancaster County, Penna., to Jacob Thomas, 185 acres. On Shannadore and Cub Run, part of Christopher's 3,000-acre tract, mouth of Cub Run. Teste: Christopher Franciscus, der Junger. Teste: Nicholas Moll (mark). Signed also Anna Margaret Franciscus. Delivered: Jacob Miller, February, 1753.

Page 718.—22d May, 1750. James Moore to Wm. Horbingson, Gent., chattel and mortgage. Teste: James Sloane.

Page 720.—7th February, 1749. Christopher Franciscus, Sr., of Lancaster County, Pa. (and Anna Margaret), to Henry Duly (Dewly, Dowly), 225 acres in Cub Run, part of 3,000-acre tract. Teste: Stophel Francisco, Christopher Franciscus der Junger.

Page 723.—8th February, 1749-50. Same to John Craig, 225 acres, part of same, hiccory near Null's house.

Page 726.—27th November, 1749. Christopher Franciscus, Jr., of Augusta, to Jacob and Valentine Pence, 210 acres, part of 3,000 acres on Cub Run; corner Nicholas Null. Delivered: H. Dowley (See page 720, supra.), 20th August, 1751.

Page 729.—23d May, 1750. John Collier and Sisely to William Hall. Delivered: Jos. Hall, February, 1755. 212 acres on Buffalo Creek whereon John now lives. The Shipp Rock; corner Arthur Brown. Teste: Tobias Smith, William Lusk, Patrick Deavis.

Page 731.—7th March, 1749. Morgan Bryant, farmer, of Antson Co., No. Carolina, to John Madison. Pow. att'y to collect debts in Augusta and Frederick. Teste: Thomas Bowyer.

Page 732.—22d May, 1750. Benj. Borden to John McCown, 437 acres of 92100.

Page 735.—23d May, 1750. James Patton, Gent., to William Logan. Delivered: Thos. Logan, 10th February, 1774, 400 acres, Forks of James River, patent to Wm. Crosthwaite. 12th February, 1742, Timothy Crosthwaite to Patton, 27th March, 1746. Conveyed by Timothy, eldest son, etc.

Page 738.—Same to James Carre, late of Lancaster Co., Penna., 474 acres, conveyed by Beverley to Patton, 29th May, 1741, in Beverley Manor from Wm. Bev; corner James Leper.

Page 741.—18th May, 1750. John Buchanan, Gent., to Humphrey Baker, 100 acres on Woods River. Teste: James Patton, Alexander Wright, James Porteus.

Page 744.—James Young, miller, to Lou Todd, carpenter. Delivered: William Todd, 16th May, 1756, 251 acres Fork of James, on Whistle Creek where Todd now liveth; corner Mathew Young. Teste: Arthur and Abraham Brown, James McCown.

Page 749.—18th May, 1750. James Young, miller, to Matthew Young, farmer, 150½ acres, where Mathew lives on Whistle Creek of James; corner Lou Todd. Teste: Arthur and Abraham Brown, James McCown.

Page 749.—31st March, 1750. Robert Young to Wm. Todd, 400 acres on North Br. of Buffalo Creek, Benj. Borden's line.

Page 751.—17th May, 1750. Benj. Borden to William Reagh, 230 acres on Hays Creek. Delivered: R. Breckinridge, 23d August, 1751.

Page 754.—23d May, 1750. William Wright to William Logan. Delivered: Saml. Logan, May, 1765. 155 acres in Beverley Manor, Wm. Bev, Alexn. Henderson' line; corner Wm. Johnson, Margaret, wife of Wm. Wright.

Page 757.—22d May, 1750. James Lynn to Andrew Lynn, 269 acres in Beverley Manor, Saml. Doak's line, Buffler Hill; corner Jno. Teat and Saml. Wilson. Teste: Andrew Cowan, Elijah McClenachan, John Ramsey.

Page 760.—23d May, 1750. John Harrison, Jr., to Richard Hall, on Meadow Creek of Woods River, patent to John, 5th September, 1746. Teste: James Campbell, John McFarron. Delivered: Wm. Hall, July, 1763, 400 acres.

Page 762.—23d May, 1750. Benj. Borden to Robert McElhany, 280 acres, Kerr's Creek; corner John Weyley, North River.

Page 764.—23d May, 1750. Benj. Borden to John Wiley. Kerr's Creek; corner Robert McElhenny, 280 acres. Delivered: John Stuart, February, 1758.

Page 767.—John Patterson, weaver, to John Ward, yeoman, 231 acres in Beverley Manor, Wm. Bev, Patrick Campbell, Wm. Sayers, So. River. Part of 1546 acres conveyed by Beverley to Pat. Campbell, 1738, and this part sold by Pat to Wm. Sayers, 1745. Teste: John Piery and Jno. Peery, the same, Elizabeth, wife of John Patterson. Teste: James Kerr, Jno. O. Peery.

Page 769.—22d May, 1750. Borden to David Carr (Kerr) 368 acres, survey of James McNutt, late deceased, Kennedy's Mill Creek; corner John Kerr. Delivered: Francis Beaty, 29th May, 1753.

Page 771—24th May, 1750. Same to Jacob Anderson, 350 acres.

Page 774.—24th May, 1750. Same to Moses Whiteside, 270 acres; corner David Edmiston, Paxton's line.

Page 776.—May, 1750. Same to John McClenachan, Cutapo Creek, 359 acres, part of 3530 on Catabo, patented 9th March, 1740.

Page 779.—21st May, 1750. Robert McClenachan, Gent., and Sarah, to Joseph Bell, in Beverley Manor, Sarah, wife of Robert. Delivered: Zachariah Bell, November, 1753, 216 acres in Beverley Manor.

Page 782.—24th May, 1750. Dennis Dyer, tailor, and Abigail, to William Nutt, miller, in Beverley Manor, said Nutt's mill on Mill Creek; corner Andrew Nutt, Abigail, wife of Dennis, 181 acres in Beverley Manor. Teste: Wm. Hamilton, Jno. Willson, Francis Beatey.

Page 785.—24th May, 1750. Matthew Robertson to Wm. Robertson, 137 acres on Cathey's River in Beverley Manor, part of 396 acres sold by Beverley to John Moffet, late deceased, by Wm. Beverley, 29th February, 1739, Martha, wife of Mathew. Teste: James Robertson, James Brown.

Page 787.—8th August, 1750. Robert Martin, of St. Thomas Parrish, Orange Co., and Ann, to Jeremiah Early, of St. Thomas Parrish, Culpeper Co., Gilgo Run, Hawkbill, 400 acres patented to Robert, 20th September.

1745. Delivered: Francis Kirkley, February, 1755. Teste: Johnny Scott, Haniry Trover (?), Richard Martin.

Page 790.—28th August, 1750. John Maxwell to Robert Breckinridge, in Beverley Manor, Wm. Bev; corner Andrew Johnston, 28th August, 1750, 219½ acres in Beverley Manor, part of 439 conveyed to John by Beverley.

Page 793.—10th August, 1750. John Neglee, yeoman (Nägle), of the Northern Liberties of Philadelphia, and Jacob Neglee, tanner, of same, executors of Jacob Neglee, shopkeeper, of Philadelphia, to Ladwick Haunsdone, taylor, of Lancaster Co., Pennsylvania. Mathias Elser, the Massanutting tract; corner to Propeckers. John Neglee was uncle of Jacob, deceased, and Jacob was cousin of Jacob, deceased. Proved by oath of Saml. and John Wilkins and affirmation of Jacob Strickler and recorded on motion of Daniel Stover. Teste: Saml. and John Wilkins, Jno. Reiley, Saml. Bähm, Jacob Burner, Jacob Strickler. Whereas, by deed 24th July, 1740, by Mathias Elias of Orange Co., to Jacob Neglee (deceased) of Lancaster Co., Pennsylvania, conveys part of tract called the Massanutting tract, 1200 acres, Jacob died leaving will dated 27th May, 1747, appointing his uncle, Jno. Neglee, and cousin, Jacob Neglee, executors. Will recorded in Register's office in Philadelphia. Delivered: Jacob Burner, 17th August, 1756.

Page 797.—20th August, 1750. William Burk to Nicholas Null of Co. Lancaster, Peaked Mountain, Boon's Run, 400 acres. Teste: Wm. Williams, John McGuiness, Jacob Nichols.

Page 799.—28th August, 1750. Benj. Borden to Samuel Norwood, 243 acres, Teas Creek; corner Hugh Cunningham; James Gillmor's corner.

Page 801.—28th August, 1750. Same to John Beaty, 118 acres.

Page 805.—25th August, 1750. John Mathews, Gent., and Ann, 296 acres, to John Berrisford, farmer, James River, North Branch of James; Philip Weaver's Bottom; McDowell's Meadow Creek; corner McDowell. Teste: Edward Boyle, Joshua and Richard Mathews.

Page 808.—26th August, 1750. Andrew McConnell, of Lunenburg Co., planter, to John Anderson, farmer, 400 acres, in Mill Creek of South River; corner Robert Hook; corner Wm. Williams. Teste: Henry Downs, Jr., and John Poage, Jas. Porteus.

Page 812.—22d May, 1750. John Moore, wheelwright, to John Houston, Jr., 198 acres, part of Moore's Survey; corner Robert Kirkpatrick. Teste: Robert and Samuel Houston, David Sayers.

Page 813.—29th August, 1750. Benj. Borden to Wm. Buchanan, 480 acres; corner John McCroskey and Isaac Anderson. Teste: John Buchanan.

Page 817.—21st August, 1750. Paul Whitley and Sarah to Jonathan Whitley, 200 acres on Buffalo Creek where Paul now lives. Teste: James Hemphill, Jno. Gallbrath, Pat. McKendrick.

Page 819.—9th June, 1750. Benj. Borden to John Karr, 336 acres, David Karr's line; corner Francis Beatty. Teste: Jno. Paul, Wm. Whitesides, Robt. Cilpatrick, Saml. Woods.

Page 823.—31st March, 1750. Thomas Henderson, planter, of Albemarle, to Wm. Beverley, 391 acres, in Beverley Manor; corner Jno. Davison, Christie's Creek, Thos. Black's line. Teste: Richard Pringle, Jno. Rutlidge.

Page 826.—3d April, 1750. Wm. Beverley to George Rutledge, planter, 440 acres in Beverley Manor; corner James Armstrong, Christie's Creek; corner Thos. Black and Wm. Henderson. Teste: As above.

Page 828.—3d April, 1750. Wm. Beverley to John Madison and James Lockhart, Gents., Church Wardens, hill above a spring, joining lots X and XI. 2⅜ acres, as a place to erect and build a church, adjacent to Staunton. Teste: Wm. Russell, Jno. Rutlidge, Thos. Henderson.

Page 831.—18th August, 1750. James Wood, Gent., of Frederick, to Thos. Shankland, North Mountain, 400 acres on Muddy Creek, patented to James, 12th January, 1746. Teste: Thos. Storey, David Ne(e)lson, Jno. Hopes, Thos. Wood.

Page 833.—13th June, 1750. Wm. Beverley to Thos. Lewis and John Madison, power attorney to sell land in Beverley Manor, except the Mill tract, also lots in Staunton, except lots 2, 10, 11. Attorneys required to account with Jno. Robinson, Richard Tunstall and Jas. Mills.

Page 836.—29th August, 1750. Wm. Thompson to Saml. Hines(s). Delivered: Wm. Hinds, December, 1754. South River, 139 acres.

Page 839.—29th August, 1750. John Bomgardner (signed Hans Baumgartner) to Patrick Frazier, in Stoney Lick Branch; corner Andrew McConnald, 400 acres, patented 25th September, 1746. John Lynn, Jno. Stevenson, Robt. Hook.

Page 842.—29th August, 1750. John McNabb to Baptist McNabb, 218 acres in Borden's tract, sold by Borden to John Patterson, and by Patterson to Jno. McNabb, 25th September, 1742, on Mill Cr.; corner David Dryden; corner Arthur McClure. Teste: David Dryden, Chas. Campbell, Francis Beatey.

Page 845.—James Patton, Gent., to John Poage, farmer, 238 acres on James River branches.

Page 849.—10th July, 1750. Henry Kirkham and Margaret to John Paxton, lots of Lancaster Co., Pennsylvania; Benj. Borden; on James River; on Wood's Creek; corner Joseph Lapsley; 198 A, 3 R, 36 P, conveyed to Henry by Borden, 27th July, 1742. Teste: Richard Woods, Jno. McKey.

Page 851.—29th August, 1750. Benj. Borden, Jr., Gent., to John Marshall, 182 acres, patented to Benj., 20th August, 1745; on James River; on Catabo Creek, Cedar Spring Br.

Page 854.—29th August, 1750. Benj. Borden, etc., to Joshua Hedley, 345 acres, part of 2880 acres on Catabo Creek; patented to Benj., Sr., 19th March, 1740.

Page (863) 857.—Same to John Marshell, on Catuba Creek, 259 acres of 3553; patented to Benj. Lee, 9th March, 1740.

Page (866) 860.—28th August, 1750. Same to Thomas Hadley, on Catuba Creek, 334 acres, part of above patent.

Page (869) 863.—28th August, 1750. Same to John Marshell, on Catuba Creek, 19 acres, part of 2880 acres on Catuba; patented to Benj. Sr., 9th March, 1740.

Page (874) 868.—28th August, 1750. James Letherdale, blacksmith, to John Harrison, yeoman, on Luney's Mill Creek of James, 366 acres; patented to John, 12th February, 1742. The object of this conveyance is to correct certain conveyances by Harrison to Letherdale and thereby enable Harrison to make good deeds. Teste: John Lynn, Patrick Campbell, Francis Beaty.

Page 871.—John Harrison, yeoman, to James Letherdale, blacksmith, same as above. As to above deeds, see former deed, Harrison to Letherdale, 1749, supra, p. 287.

Page 876.—30th August, 1750. Erwin Patterson to John Maxwell, 381 acres between Mill Creek and Ann Sally Hill.

Page (884) 878.—1st June, 1750. Saml. Wilkins, purposing to leave the Colony and go to settle in Carolina with his family, and great many people are indebted to him, to son, John Wilkins, power attorney to collect debts, 1st June, 1750. Teste: John Lewis, Robt. McClenachan, James Porteus.

Page 2.—Last .deed recorded 8d September, 1750.

DEED BOOK No. 3.

Page 2.—Back of book reversed. Henry Downs to John McKearney, 20th August, 1748, conveyed to Thos. Chew, George Taylor, Benj. Cave, Justices of Orange, to take privy examination of Jane, wife of Henry, 25th May, 1749. Executed 15th August, 1749. See supra, p. 69.

Page 2.—7th June, 1749. John Hamilton of New Castle Co., Pennsylvania, to Jno. Lowrey, north fork of James, 200 acres. Teste: Robert Coningham, Wm. Henderson, Wm. Johnston, Thos. Black.

Page 3.—Bond by John to have his wife execute release of dower in above. Proved, 27th November, 1750.

Page 5.—John Hopes to Randolph McDonell (McDowell), on Cook's Crek, 200 acres; patented to John Hopes, 5th September, 1479. Teste: Andrew Erwin, Thomas Stevenson.

Page 7.—27th November, 1750. John Cunningham to John Davis, lot 7 in Staunton, also woodland lot No. 3. Livery by latch of the door.

Page 10.—2d October, 1750. James Boyd, of Lunenburg Co., to James Hughey, 12th February, 1742, 340 acres; patented to James, Looney's Mill Creek. Teste: Wm. Dulaney, Jno. Michelsneler, Robert Tate.

Page 13.—13th September, 1750. James Patton, Gent., to James Coyl, 410 acres sold to Patton by Moses Thompson, 25th July, 1744, on Christian's Creek where Coyl now lives; Moses Thompson; corner Wm. Palmer; corner George Robinson (now Wm. Henderson's land), Wm. Russell's survey. Teste: Mathew Campbell, Edward Hall. Teste: Pat. McCullom, Christopher Phinney.

Page 16.—11th October, 1750. James Coyl to Patrick McCollom, 205 acres (see p. 13, supra), on Christian's Creek where Pat now lives. James Patton, Wm. Palmer, Alexander Thompson's and Jno. Thompson's lands. Teste: Mathew Campbell, Edward Hall.

Page 19.—2d November, 1750. Andrew Pickins to John McPheeters, 400 acres in Beverley Manor; corner Rob. Campbell. Delivered: Wm. McPheeters, 1752. Signed, Anne Pickings. Teste: Pat Martin, Robt. Wilson.

Page 22.—21st November, 1750. Richard Harrald, planter, to Wm. Harrald, planter, 180 acres, Shanandore River; corner John Harrald; corner Moses Harrald. Teste: John Fuich (Funk ?) Jr., Henry Nelson (Netherton), James Macay (McKay).

Page 25.—Richard Harrald to John Harrald, planter, 131 acres, Shanandoe River; corner Richard Harrald, Jr. Teste: Henry Netherton, James McKay. See above.

Page 27.—Same to James Harrald, 126 acres, Shannadoe River; corner Aaron Harrald; corner Moses Harrald.

Page 30.—Richard Harrald to Moses Harrald, planter, on **Shannandoe**; corner James Harrald and Wm. Harrald.

Page 33.—Same to Aaron Harrald, planter, 78 acres; corner James Harrald above.

Page 35.—27th November, 1750, etc. Borden to Gabriel Jones, on Cautaper Creek, now in possession of John McPharring, 190 acres of 2880 acres; patented to Benj., Sr., 9th March, 1740, being lowest lot on said Creek, and numbered 8.

Page 38.—28th November, 1750. Borden, etc., to George Henderson, 282 acres; corner John Pattison; corner Donely, Moffett's Creek.

Page 40.—28th November, 1750. Same to Alexander McCoskery, 200 acres; corner Wm. Buchanan and Isaac Anderson.

Page 43.—28th November, 1750. Same to John Stevenson, 149 acres; corner John Boyd; corner Greenlee.

Page 45.—28th November, 1750. Same to Wm. Porter, 112 acres, on North Br. of James, at said Porter's patent.

Page 47.—28th November, 1750. Same to Robert Kirkpatrick, 612 acres, John Moore's line. Delivered: Thomas Kirkpatrick, January, 1751.

Page 50.—28th November, 1750. Same to Andrew Steel, 463½ acres on Joseph Kennady's Mill Creek, adjoining Francis McCune.

Page 54.—28th November, 1750. William Thompson, Gent., to George Scott, 278 acres, part of William's 2 tracts, Cathey's River, otherwise called Middle River, Hugh Thompson's corner. Teste: Mathew Campbell, Jno. Anderson, James Craig.

Page 55.—26th November, 1750. James Davice to Benj. Borden, 626 acres on Catuba Creek of James River, part of 8,100 acres; patented to B. Borden, Sr., 6th November, 1739, conveyed by Borden to James, 22d November, 1746.

Page 57.—28th November, 1750. Borden to James Davice, 626 acres of 2888 acres; patented to B. B., Sr., 9th March, 1740. Same as above.

Page 60.—16th August, 1749. George Bowman, son of Cornelius, deceased, and Ann Bowman to his mother, Ann Bowman, chattels and slave. Teste: Martin Shoemaker, Wm. Rogers.

Page 61.—20th November, 1750. Wm. Hutchison and Ann to Wm. Henderson, 200 acres where grantor lives, Christian's Creek; Andrew Russell's line; Ann, wife of Wm. Hutchison. Teste: Charles Dalhouse, Thos. Scott, John Hutchison.

Page 65.—29th November, 1750. Robert Campbell, Gent., to James Barrey, 149 acres in Beverley Manor, adjoining Glebe land; Wm. Martin's corner, Middle Br. Shanandoe; corner James Young; corner to a graveyard. Teste: David Stewart, Andrew Cowan, John Mitchell.

Page 69.—28th November, 1750. Wm. Nutt to John Buchanan, 416½ acres dated 27th July, 1744, part of 650 acres conveyed by Beverley by decree of Orange Co. Same land involved in suit in Orange, Nutt vs. Gibbins Jennings and Wm. Beverley, conveyed by Beverley to Nutt, 13th August, 1745; corner John Coulter, Mill Creek; corner James McCorkals, etc., water grist mill. Eleanor, wife of Wm. Nutt. Teste: Andrew Cowan, John Rutledge, Francis Beatey.

Page 72.—28th November, 1750. Wm. Nutt to John Coulter, 210 **acres**, part of 650, above; part of above, Robert McClenachan's line; corner to graveyard of John Breckinridge, who was murdered by the Indians.

Page 74.—29th November, 1750. James Carolile to James Callison, 275 acres L. C. P., granted 10th April, 1745, to James by Beverley, recorded in Secretary's office; corner Wm. Hamilton; corner Wm. Elliott, on the Laurel Hill.

Page 77.—24th November, 1750. James Trimble and Sarah to Alexander Beggs, 250 acres, Buffalo Creek of James; corner Silas Hart. Teste: **James** Campbell, John Alison, Michael (?) Johnson.

Page 79.—29th November, 1750. William Crittenden of Orange, to John Frogg, Gent., of Prince William, 200 acres on Shenandoe, bought of Henry Downs by deed recorded in Orange, part of Jacob Stover's grant, 5000 acres.

Page 81.—28th November, 1750. John Harrison to Cornelius Brown, 350 acres, patented to John, 25th September, 1746, on Woods River; patented to John, Neck Creek.

Page 82.—29th November, 1750. Andrew Lewis and David Stewart, trustees of that part of Staunton belonging to Augusta Co., to Robert McClenaghan. Court ordered trustees to rent all the lots in Staunton (30th August, 1750) for 21 years. Lot No. 1 containing 48 poles, on south by creek; on W. by Augusta St.; on N. by Main St., without a name, and by No. 10. No. 2, containing half an acre; on W. by Augusta St. By lot No. 3, by lot No. 9, on So. by the main street without a name. Lease for 21 years and yearly rent of 11 sh. 6/. Teste: John Hopes, John Lewis.

Page 83.—22d February 1750-51. Swain Rambo and Jane to Andrew Bird, 400 acres by patent on Smith's Creek; corner to Andrew Bird, John Philip's line. (See infra, p. 222). Delivered: Andrew Bird, January, 1754. Teste: Peter Scholl, Saml. Newman.

Page 86.—14th February, 1750-51. Thomas Milsaps, weaver, to Wm. McGee, farmer, where Wm. now lives, Lime Stone Ridge, to a cornerstone planted for that purpose. Teste: Suen Rambo.

Page 90.—8th February, 1750-1. David Magert and Daniel Weitreith of Frederick, to John Fudge. Delivered: to Geo. Zimmerman, June, 1754. 300 acres on Shanando joining Wm. Philips. Teste: John Hopes, John Funk, Jr., Mathias Seltzer.

Page 93.—21st February, 1751. Robert Cravens and Mary to John Wright, Irish Road, 400 acres as appears by the patent.

Page 97.—21st February 1750-51. John Wright and Lydia to John Cravens, farmer, 200 acres on Cooks Creek, bought from Samuel Herrison and Mary, his wife, recorded in Augusta.

Page 101.—31st January, 1750. Richard Harrald, Sr., planter, to Richard Harrald, Jr., planter, 51 acres on So. River, Shannando; corner to Moses Harrald. Teste: James McKeey, Jacob Harrel, Wm. Hurst.

Page 105.—Hugh Martin to Francis McKown, yeoman, 227 acres, part of a large tract sold by McKown to Martin, 1751, in Tees Creek; corner Robert Erwin's.

Page 109.—12th February, 1750-1. Andrew McNab to John Gilmer (ore), 138 acres, Back Creek of Tees Creek. Line of Borden's great tract. Teste: John McKown, Moses McKown, Francis McKown.

Page 113.—28th January, 1751. Nicholas Null of Lancaster Co., Pennsylvania, to Jacob Miller, Jr., 400 acres, on So. River Shanandoe, Peaked Mountain, Boon's Run. Teste: Jacob Nicholas, Valintine Pence, Henry **Dooley**.

Page 118.—Samuel Wilkins of No. Ca., to Alexander Herring, 133 acres Cooks Creek of No. River Shanando. Delivered: Benj. Kinley, January, 1754. Teste: Robt. Rallstone, John Wilkins, Morgan Bryan.

Page 121.—15th February, 1750. William Russell and Wm. Green of Culpeper Co., to James Wood of Frederick. All interest of grantors in 2400 acres, patented to all three in 1750 on So. Fork of So. Br. of Potomac, Partition. Teste: Thomas Wood, John Sturman.

Page 123.—13th February, 1750. James Wood, Wm. Russell and Wm. Green to Peter Horse, 750 acres South Fork of So. Branch of Potomac; patented to grantors 3d October, 1750.

Page 131.—16th February, 1750. Same to Henry Lanciscus, 310 acres on North and South Forks of North Branch of South Branch of Potomac, part of 660 acres; patented to grantors. Teste: John Sturman, 23d October, 1750. Fairfax's line.

Page 136.—William King, farmer, of Mariyan, to John Trimble, farmer, 251 acres in Beverley Manor; corner John Trimble, Beverley Manor line; corner Moses Offiriel. Teste: John McKeu, Hugh Young, Wm. McFeeters.

Page 139.—27th February, 1750. Wm. Beverley (by Thomas Lewis and John Madison to John Lewis), 520 acres in Beverley Manor, part of Mill tract; corner Beverley's old line; corner James Brown; corner James Brown and joining the 50 acre lots; corner Wm. Lewis; term, 91 years.

Page 142.—27th February, 1750-51. William Preston to George Campbell and Saml. Tencher, 215 acres on head of Gr. Calfpasture. Teste: James Caldwell, John Bigham, John Maxwell.

Page 148.—26th February, 1750-51. John Cowan, yeoman, to Saml. Lusk, farmer, 202 acres; Thomas Shield's corner in Col. Patton's line; Andrew Alexander's line; corner Robert Christian, Jennet, wife of John. Teste: Edward Erwin, Hugh Campbell, George Anderson.

Note: There are two classes of Borden deeds. No. 1. Conveying lands already sold by Benjamin, Sr., in his lifetime. No. 2. Conveying lands of Benjamin, Sr., by contract with Benjamin, Jr.

Page 151.—25th February, 1750. Benjamin Borden &c., to Robert Stuart, 200 acres.

Page 155.—27th February, 1750. Roger Dyer to Matthew Patton, 190 acres on South Fork South Branch Potomac. Cor. John Patton.

Page 160.—4th January, 1750. Mathew Young and Agness to Peter Wallace, 150½ acres. Bought by James Young from Borden, recorded in Orange and conveyed by James to Mathew. On Whistle Creek of James River; corner to Low Todd. Teste: Joseph Lapsley, Richard Woods.

Page 165.—25th February, 1750. Samuel Woods and Wm. Woods of Augusta to Peter Wallace, 120 acres in Fork of James, part of Wm. Wood's land, where Peter now liveth; Joseph Lapsley's line; Richard Wood's line. Teste: John Mathews, Jr., Joseph Lapsley.

Page 169.—18th February, 1750-1751. James Moore and Jean, his wife, to Alex. McClure, 163 acres on North Br. of James where Francis Allison lives. Teste: Wm. Hall and Robert Allison. James Thompson.

Page 172.—26th February, 1750-1751. Benjamin Borden to Alexander Moor, 200 acres, cor. Widow Cowden.

Page 175.—27th February, 1750-1751. Same to George Stevenson, 200 acres of 92100. Greenlee's line, cor. to McMarray; John Stephenson's line, cor. Thos. Paxton; cor. James Greenlee.

Page 179.—27th February, 1750-1751. Same to Thomas McMurray, 250 acres, cor. John Patton in Borden's great tract; Geo. Stevenson's and James Greenlee's lines.

Page 183.—27th February, 1750-51. Same to John Patton, 200 acres, corner Thomas McMurray.

Page 187.—26th February, 1750-1751, &c. Same to John Buntin, 225 acres on Back Creek.

Page 192.—9th November, 1750. Repentance Townsend to James Brown, 227 acres on No. River of Shanado on a branch called the Second Fork of Thorney Branch. Cor. Smith's land. Mary wife of Repentance. Teste: John Brown, John Coningham, Alexander Richey.

Page 194.—2nd March, 1750-1751. Robert McClenachan, gent., and Alex. Fullerton, yeoman. Alex apprentices himself to Robert in business of bookkeeping or school keeping for four years.

Page 197.—22d September, 1750. Francis Beaty to William Martin, 359 acres on Mud Lick Run on a branch of Roanoke called Goose Creek, near an iron mine. Teste: Wm. Harbison, Erwin Patterson Francis McCune.

Page 202.—22d September, 1750. Same to Hugh Martin, 112 acres same place as above. Teste: Robert Backenridge.

Page 204.—28th February, 1750-1751. Wm. Beverley (by Lewis Madison), to James Brown, ordinary keeper. In Beverley Manor, part of Mill tract (1550 acres), whereon the Court House stands. Beverley's line; James Miller's line. Term 61 years, 260 acres.

Page 209.—20th May, 1751. Henry Downes, Sr., of Orange Co., Gent., to Philip Lung ,350 acres on Shanadore adjoining Richard Mouldin's 2000 acre tract, near Peaked Mountain. Cor. Paul Lung, Sealer (Scaler) Hill.

Page 214.—3d April, 1751. Same to John Madison, gent., 330 acres, part of Jacob Stover's 800 acre patent, 13th December, 1738, which Stover failed to improve and Downs got patent for 5th June, 1747; on South and Shanadoe River. Corner Ludwick Francisco, Upper Red Banks; Lower Red Banks. Teste: John Lewis, Mathew Edmiston, Wm. Armstrong, James Porteus.

Page 218.—24th May, 1751. Archibald Ruddle to Stephen Ruddel. Patented by Fairfax, 21st July, 1749, on Holman's Creek, land surveyed for John Dobkin, 406 acres. Teste: Peter Scholl, Jno. Dobekins, Andrew Bird.

Page 222.—18th May, 1751. Andrew Bird to Jacob Rambo, 50 acres, part of land bought of Swain Rambo and Jane. (See supra, p. 83).

Page 226.—28th May, 1751. Francis Reiley to James Skeegs, farmer, 100 acres on Little River of Wood's River.

Page 230.—25th May, 1751. Abraham Vanderpool and Rebecca to George Yoccum (Yoccomb), No. 10 held by patent of Lord Fairfax, 19th October, 1748, on ye south fork of ye Wappaconee (or) Great South Branch of Potomac, 430 acres. Endorsed and delivered to James Machir for George Harnost, Sr., one of the heirs of the grantee, 16th July, 1806. Teste: Wm. White, Thomas Moore.

Page 233.—29th May, 1751. Thomas Paxton, Jr., to John Robison, 160 acres, where Thomas lives on So. River, John Lowry's line; corner Moses Whiteside. Teste: Alexander McMullen, Richard Woods, Thos. Paxton.

Page 239.—28th May, 1751. Thomas Hadley to John Marshel, 184 acres, on Catuba Creek of James River; Borden's tract, top of Mount Hadley. Teste: James Alexander, Robt. Grey.

Page 243.—11th April, 1751. Hugh Campbell, yeoman, to William Alexander, farmer, 400 acres, on Naked Creek; corner Michael Dickey, Esther, wife of Hugh. Teste: Wm. Brown, Michael Dickey, John Hear (Ker?), John Alexander.

Page 247.—24th May, 1751. Reuben Paget and Elizabeth to Jacob Harril, 100 acres, on a branch of Flint Run; patented by Fairfax, 19th Septembre, 1749; corner John Calfee. Teste: John Sollers, Wm. Hurst, James McKay.

Page 253.—12th July, 1750. Samuel Newman, farmer, and Martha to Thomas Moore, farmer, 200 acres, where Newman now lives; patented from Fairfax, on Smith Creek. Teste: Michael Warren and Wm. Carril.

Page 259.—11th March, 1751. David Johnson, farmer, and Rebeccah, to Michael Warren, 400 acres, bought of Morgan Briant, on Linville's Creek adjoining Just Hite. Teste: Thomas Moor, Wm. Carryl.

Page 263.—28th May, 1751. Erwin Patterson, Gent., to William Harbison, Gent., 400 acres on a branch of Luney's Mill Creek. Teste: Robt. Poage, Robt. Rennick.

Page 267. 11th April, 1751. James Montgomery to Benj. Borden, 654 acres on Cataba Creek.

Page 271.—28th May, 1751. Benj. Borden to Robert Montgomery, on Cataba Creek, same 654 acres as above.

Page 276.—28th May, 1751. Wm. Beverley (by Lewis and Madison) to James Miller, taylor, 300 acres in Beverley Manor, Mill Place.

Page 280.—28th May, 1751. Borden, etc., to Mathew Edmiston, 238 acres, tract surveyed for John Allen and for Wm. Smith; corner Wm. Cowdon.

Page 284.—3d May, 1751. Andrew McClure, planter, and Eleanor, to Alexander Richey, blacksmith, 300 acres in Beverley Manor, tract surveyed for Saml. Templeton; Wm. McClintock's line; Adam Thompson's line. Teste: Michael Realy, Robert Gray.

Page 288.—23d May, 1751. Robert Rallstone and Martha, to Thomas Bradshaw, 364 acres, Moffett's branch of Cathey's River; corner John Smith; patented to Robert, 15th December, 1749. Teste: William Snadon, Alex. Gardner.

Page 292.—18th May, 1750. John Davice and Ann, to John Jones, Yayers Branch of Smith's Creek, 159 acres. Delivered: Christophall Amentrout, August, 1759.

Page 296.—18th May, 1750. John Davis and Ann, to John Jones, 166 acres, Yayers Branch of Smith's Creek; corner Adam Yayers.

Page 300.—28th May, 1751. Alexander Campbell to Michael Raily, 166 acres in Beverley Manor; corner Wm. Campbell in James Moffett's line; Widow Mitchell's corner; James Patton's corner. Delivered: Jas. Mitchell, 18th May, 1773. Teste: Walter Davis, William Campbell.

Page 304.—28th May, 1751. Alexander Campbell, wheelwright, to David

Campbell, Jr., 80 acres in Beverley Manor; corner tract surveyed for Wm. Campbell; corner David Campbell's other survey.

Page 307.—28th May, 1751. Gabriel Jones to Wm. Richey, 190 acres lately purchased by grantor from grantee and conveyed to him by Borden, 1750; conveyed by Borden; on Caturba Creek; John McFerring's corner.

Page 310.—31st January, 1750. John Miller to Robert McClenachan, Gent., 200 acres in Beverley Manor, bought of Robert Black, 1748; corner Wm. Skellern.

Page 315.—27th May, 1751. John Fowler and Margaret, to John Hope, on Naked Creek, Hite's, etc., line. Teste: Joseph Bryan, James Bell.

Page 318.—17th May, 1751. Samuel Harrison and Mary, to Alexander Herren, 265 acres on Linvell's Creek, part of 400 acres; patented to Saml., 5th September, 1749. Delivered: Benj. Kinley, January, 1754.

Page 321.—27th May, 1751. Borden, etc., to Samuel Lyle, 235 acres on Mill Creek; corner to James McClung; corner Jno. McNabb. Teste: Richard Woods, Alexander McMullan, John Lyle.

Page 325.—12th February, 1751. James Carr to John Betty, yeoman, 325 acres, Broad Creek, a branch of Buffalo. Teste: John McKown, Francis McCown, Samuel Norwood.

Page 329.—28th May, 1751. John McNabb to Samuel Lyle, 101 acres, part of Benj. Borden's great tract; on Mill Creek; corner Isaac Taylor. Teste: Richard Woods, Alexander McMullan, John Lyle.

Page 332.—29th May, 1751. Patrick Frazier to Abraham Estes of Caroline, 140 acres, Henry Down's Mill; Robert Scott's land. Patented to Patrick, 20th June, 1749.

Page 336.—28th November, 1750. Samuel Dunlap to David Dunlap, 170 acres, part of 559½ acres, conveyed by Benj. Borden in Orange, 27th August, 1742; Richard Cousart's line; corner Wm. Loughridge. Teste: Wm. McCaules, Wm. McClung, David Moore, Jno. Lowrey.

Page 340.—23d May, 1751. John Francis and Mary, to John Hogshead, 217 acres on Anderson's Branch of Cathey's River; corner Wm. Anderson. Teste: James Bell, John Anderson, Jno. Rutledge. Delivered to Gordon Hogshead, 23d August, 1802.

Page 342.—29th May, 1751. John Mills to Wm. Young, Francis Reiley's line, 400 acres on Woods River; patented to John, 20th September, 1748. Teste: James McKeachey, Robert Gray.

Page 348.—29th May, 1751. John Mills to Samuel Akerling, 100 acres on Little River of Woods River; patented to John, 15th September, 1749. Teste: Andrew Cowan.

Page 351.—27th February, 1750. William Wright (Right) and Margaret, to William Johnston, 270 acres in Beverley Manor; corner Wm. Logan; corner John Thomson. Teste: Thomas Tosh, Robert Gray.

Page 355.—28th May, 1751. Tasker Tosh to Thomas Tosh, 120 acres on North Bank of Roanoke River, commonly called Goose Creek, Goose Creek of Roanoke. Teste: Robert Grey, James McKeachey, Francis Beatey.

Page 359.—29th May, 1751. Jeremiah Chamberlain (ane) of York Co., Pennsylvania, to Francis Rich, on branches of James; corner Jeremiah's other tract. Teste: Thomas Tosh.

Page 363.—28th May, 1751. John Trimble, Pat. Martin and Wm. McPeetters, planters, 140 acres to Samuel Downey, planter, in Beverley Manor,

Adam Thomson's line; corner Saml. Tempelton. Teste: James Magill, Jno. Brown, John McPeetters.

Page 365.—30th May, 1750. Eleanor Tyler to grandson, William Downen. B. Sole. Deed gift.

Page 365.—30th May, 1751. Borden & Co., to Isaac Gray, 270 acres on Mill Creek; corner James McClung, Deavis line?; Robert Husten's line; corner Wm. Lusk, Acres Falls on Mill Creek.

Page 368.—16th March, 1751. Robert Edge to John Ramsey. This is really an apprenticeship. First recorded sale of a servant. John Lynn, aged 7 years old, 14th September, 1750, to same until of age. Teste: Mathew Campbell.

Page 371.—29th May, 1751. William Thompson, Gent., and Jane, to Alexander Thompson, 337 acres in Beverley Manor, part of 947 acres from Wm. Beverley, 22d November, 1744; corner Wm. Palmer, John Thompson and Patrick McCollum, James Coyle's line; William Henderson's line; corner George Caldwell. Teste: John Smith.

Page 376.—29th May, 1751. Same to John Thompson, 300 acres, part of 947 above, same; Robert Moody's line; corner Wm. Palmer; corner Alexander Thompson. Delivered: Wm. Thompson, ye father, June, 1756.

Page 379.—5th April, 1750. Wm. Beverley (by Lewis and Madison) to John Coningham of Staunton, ordinary keeper, 107 acres, part of Mill tract; 1550 acres joining the town whereon Court House stands; corner James Brown's leased land; James Miller's line; Col. Lewis's lot, 99-year term, 1750. Teste: John Hutchison, Jno. Hutchison, John B. Thompson.

Page 384.—1st June, 1751. William Preston to Alexander Wright, merchant, 334 acres in Beverley Manor; John Lewis's line; Maxwell's line. Teste: Henry Murray, Robert Scott.

Page 388.—1st June, 1751. John Madison, Gent., and Agatha, to Robert McClenachan, Gent, 731 acres; part of 1041 acres sold by Beverley in Beverley Manor, to Moses Thompson, 12th December, 1745; corner Adam Thompson; corner John Ramsey. Teste: Jno. Harvie.

Page 391.—1st June, 1751. Beverley (by Lewis and Madison) to John David Welppert (Wilpper), 467 acres; part of 1550 acres Mill tract in Beverley Manor; corner John Coningham; also lots 2, 10 and 11 in Staunton; lease 99 years (1751).

Page 396.—15th June, 1751. John McClure and Catherine, to Nathan McClure, 4½ acres, North Br. of James, where Jno. now lives, Pessimmon tree. Teste: James Thompson, David Dryden, Alexander McClure.

Page 400.—15th June, 1751. James Moore and Jean, to Nathan McClure, 160 acres, No. Br. James; corner Francis Allison. Teste: James Thompson, David Dryden, Alexander McClure.

Page 404.—28th May, 1751. Arthur McClure and Frances, to Robert Allison. 254 acres of Benj. Borden's 92,100; John McNabb, on Mill Creek; corner John McNabb, James Thompson's land; corner David Dryden; corner John Stevenson.

Page 409.—16th August, 1751. Asabel Hodge and Jane, to William Carryl, 176 acres. From Fairfax to John Hodgh late of Augusta, deceased, and Asabel is eldest son and heir; Crown lands, Northern Neck Grants, Smith's Creek. Teste: Thomas Bragg, Saml. Newman, Thos. Bragg.

Page 414.—3d August, 1751. William Williams and Sarah, to John Wilson, 388 acres on So. Riv. Shannandore, on a branch called Mill Creek; corner Christofell Franciscus. Teste: Henry Dickins and Evan Evans.

Page 417.—Same to Henry Beevey, 550 acres, a branch of So. Riv. Shan., called Mill Creek; corner Robert Hooks. Teste: Jacob Nicols (?), Henry Dickins.

Page 421.—27th August, 1751. John Lynn and Naomie, to Robert Shanklin. 320 acres on No, River Shan, joining Robert Scott, Stoney Lick Branch. Teste: Robt. Hook, Patrick Wilson.

Page 425.—27th August, 1751. Joseph Love and Margaret, to Baptist McNabb, 171 acres on Rentfroe's br. of Goose Creek, Rentfrow's line; corner George Robinson. Also 137 acres on Robinson's Br. of Roanoke; corner Bryan Cuff; corner Stephen Rentfroe.

Page 430.—24th August, 1751. Andrew Johnston to David Stewart, Gent., 218½ acres. From John Maxwell; corner Robert McClenachan (formerly John Madison's land); corner Robert Breckinridge (formerly John Maxwell's land). Teste: John Harman, Audley Paul, Pat. McCluskey, Mary Paul.

Page 434.—27th August, 1751. Daniel McNare to David Sayers, 23 acres Mid. Riv. Shanandore; patented to Daniel, 20th September, 1748.

Page 438.—27th August, 1751. Jacob Clemence and Mary, to John Campbell, 202 acres on Calf Pasture where Jacob lives; corner Wm. Campbell. Teste: Thomas Gillham, Loftes Pullin.

Page 442.—21st August, 1751. John Lockhart and Rebecca, to David Hayes, 202½ acres in Beverley Manor; Robert Ramsey's line.

Page 445.—27th August, 1751. Borden & Co. to John Davison, 353½ acres of 92100, Isaac Taylor's line.

Page 448.—28th August, 1751. Wm. Campbell and Sarah, and Robert Grey and Margaret, to Thomas Gillam (Gillham), 200 acres, Calfpasture where Wm. and Robert live. Delivered: Thomas Adam, 2d September, 1774.

Page 453.—27th August, 1751. David Hay, yeoman, and Jane, to William Thompson, weaver, 306 acres, Christian's Creek, sold by Beverley to Joseph Reed, taylor, 23d July, 1740; 25th September, 1741. Corner John Buchanan; David Moor's land; James Robinson's line; Charles Campbell's line; Patrick Campbell's corner.

Page 457.— — August, 1751. Andrew Pickens to William McPheetters. Power attorney to convey 211 acres to John McPheetters.

Page 460.—27th August, 1751. William Smith and Jane, to Daniel Kidney, 135 acres in Beverley Manor, Christie's Creek; George Hutcheson's line. Teste: Robt. Turk, John Anderson, Saml. Henderson. Delivered: Daniel Kidd, 16th June, 1756.

Page 464.—30th May, 1751. Joseph Teas to Archibald Stewart, contracting, mauling and laying 6700 rails, building a log house, clearing and plowing 20 acres, from Beverley to Teas, 5th June, 1739. Beverley Manor, 469 acres. Teste: Edward Hall, Thomas Stewart, William Patterson.

Page 466.—27th August, 1751. Borden, etc., to Francis Beaty, 265 acres of 92100; corner John Kerr, Beverley Manor line, including Flatt Spring, otherwise called Beaty Spring (Spring Beatey).

Page 469.—15th August, 1751. Christophel Francisco, farmer, of Lancaster Co., Pennsylvania, to son, Stophel Francisco, of same place. Power attorney to sell tract of 3000 acres on Shanandore. Teste: Ludwick Franciscus, Maurice Pound, John Lightner.

Page 472.—James Leeper, blacksmith, to Nicholas Leeper, farmer, 227 acres in Beverley Manor; corner James Moody.
Notice that many deeds are delivered to Fr. Beatey, 1753.

Page 477.—27th August, 1751. William Robinson to Thomas Blackwood, 215 acres, Christian's Creek in Beverley Manor, by Beverley to Wm., 4th September, 1741; corner Wm. Kerr; Thomas Shield's line; William Wright's line; John Willson's line. Teste: Chas. Dalhouse, Jno. Christian.

Page 482.—27th August, 1751. John Robinson to Jean, to Wm. Kerr, 188 acres in Beverley Manor, part of above. By Beverley to Wm., and by Wm. to Jno. Robinson; Col. James Patton's line.

Page 485.—Commonwealth to Robert Eastham, James Pendelton and Wm. Green of Culpeper, to take privy executio nof Mary, wife of Michael Lawyer as to deed Michael Lawler to Thomas Kennerley of Culpeper, for land where Joseph Bloodworth lives. Executed May 11th, 1751.

Page 488.—27th August, 1751. William Alexander to Martha Alexander, widow, 200 acres, part of William's 400-acre patent, near Long Glade; corner Michael Dickey. Delivered: James Alexander, May, 1768.

Page 492.—21st November, 1751. Thomas West and Christian (tiana) to Adam Rider, 1751, 186 acres on Willing's Creek of North River of Shanandore. Delivered: George Rider, 26th April, 1755.

Page 496.—25th November, 1751. John Peter Salling and Ann, to Henry Fuller and Catharine, 130 acres on No. Br. James.

Page 500.—5th October, 1751. William Williams and Sarah, to Henry Perkey, 550 acres; corner Jacob Stover's 5000 acres. Teste: Felty Pence, Jacob Nicholas.

Page 505.—19th August, 1751. James Lynn, architectus, to Samuel Braford, 269 acres in Beverley Manor; corner Andrew Lynn; corner Brownlee; corner George Breckinridge (Sarah, wife of James). Teste: Jno. Mitchell, Saml. Doack, Andrew Lynn.

Page 509.—14th August, 1751. Rev. Alexander McDowel of New Castle Co., to Wm. McRorey (Korey ?) (McCreary ?), Br. of James called the Mary, Evans Run. Teste: James Welch, Mathew Linsey, Agnes Welch.

Page 514.—26th November, 1751. Beverley (by Lewis and Madison) to Wm. Ledgerwood, Jr., 300 acres in Beverley Manor on Buchanan's Mill Creek, formerly Nutt Creek; John Bigham line; John Buchanan land; James McCorkal's line; corner John Henderson; corner John Lynn.

Page 521.—11th July, 1751. Daniel Evans to Peter Evans, 400 acres on Waters of Roanoke called Cedar Springs, at a place called Naked Farm. Teste: James Neelly, Robt. Breckinridge, James Porteus. Delivered: Wm. Preston.

Page 525.—11th July, 1751. Same to same, 400 acres same, by house of Mark Evans. Proved as to James Porteus, deceased, by the other witnesses, 26th November, 1751.

Page 529.—Same to same, 400 acres; same, Carravins Creek, Clearland or Barrens.

Page 3.—Ends 26th November, 1751.

DEED BOOK No. 4.

First Deed Recorded 26th November, 1751; Last Deed Recorded 15th November, 1752.

Page 3.—26th November, 1751. Robert Remick and Elizabeth, to Francis McCewn, yeoman, 300 acres on Cedar Creek of James River, at a place called Timber Plain; corner John Poack. Teste: Jno. Archer, Wm. Lusk, Joseph Lang. Delivered: Francis McKown, 19th May, 1752.

Page 7.—Richard Burton (Bortoo), Gent., and Ann, to James Davis, 400 acres on Buffalo Creek, joining Borden; corner Richard Wood. Teste: James McAfee, James Neelly.

Page 12.—14th October, 1751. Wm. Sayers of Craven Co., S. Ca., to David Miller, 290 acres, Buffalo Creek. Teste: Michael Finney, Geo. Wilson, William Carlile.

Page 16.—5th October, 1751. John Lynn to Robert Shanklin, 320 acres on No. River Shanandoe, joining Robert Scott, Stony Lick Br. Teste: Thomas Shanklin, Robert Hook, Thos. Shanklin, Jno. Stephenson.

Page 20.—24th September, 1751. William King, blacksmith, and Mary Ann, to John Nichol, 400 acres on Moffet's Branch of Cathey's River, Ralston's Path; patented to William, 10th February, 1748. Teste: Silas Hart, Sam Wallace, Alexander Gibson.

Page 25.—27th November, 1757. John Harrison, farmer, to Robert Renick, farmer, 241 acres. Teste: Andrew Woods, John Poage, George Crawford.

Page 29.—27th November, 1751. Daniel Harrison and Margaret, to John McCluer, 387 acres, Muddy Creek, on north side North River. Teste: James Kilburn, Ro. Renick. Patented to Daniel, 5th September, 1746.

Page 33.—27th November, 1751. John McCluer and Mary, to Silas Hart, 400 acres, South Fork of Shanandore; patented to John, 15th December, 1749. The order book says wife Margaret.

Page 37.—2 September, 1751. James Patton to John Ralston, 435 acres by patent 3d November, 1750, Looney's Mill Creek; corner James Moore. Teste: Wm. Ralston, John Flood, James Moor.

Page 41.—22d November, 1751. Jeremiah Chamberlain of York Co., Pennsylvania, to John Neeley, 400 arres, branches of James; patented to Jeremiah, 12th February, 1742. Teste: James Ewing.

Page 45.—27th November, 1751. Adam Dickinson to John Stanley and David Stanley, 546 acres on Falling Spring of Jackson River, Sinking Spring; patented to Adam, 1st June, 1750.

Page 48.—26th November, 1751. Borden, etc., to John Stephenson, 290 acres of 92100, Mill Creek; corner Moses McClure, Warm Run; corner Alexander McClure; corner Robert Allison; corner James Thompson. Teste: John Lyle, Joseph Kenedey, Baptist McNabb.

Page 53.—26th November, 1751. Beverley by Lewis and Madison to Archibald Stuart, 500 acres in Beverley Manor; corner James Campbel; Widow Edmiston's line.

Page 59.—29th August, 1751. Christophel Francisco of Borough of Lancaster (by Stofleel Francisco), and Ludwick Francisco to Thomas Lewis, Gent., Great Island, 478 acres, part of 800 acres, granted to Stover,

12th December, 1738, and by Stover to Christophel, deed recorded in Orange, on Shannandore, opposite land formerly John Bumgardner's.

Page 64.—1st September, 1751. Christophel Francisco by (as above) to same, 60 acres. The Island in Shanandore called Great Island, opposite above. £2, sh. 3 = 2 Pistoles.

Page 70.—29th August, 1751. Same to Gabriel Jones of Frederick, 244 acres, part of Jacob Stover's 5000 acres conveyed by Stover to Chrl., opposite Gr. Island of Shanandore, joining tract formerly John Bumgardner's land.

Page 76.—28th November, 1751. James Patton to John Carmichael, 100 acres by patent, 3d November, 1750; James River; corner Wm. Russell, James Trimble. Teste: John Flood, Wm. Preston.

Page 80.—28th November, 1751. Same to John Bowin, 70 acres by patent, 3d November, 1750. Br. of James. Teste as above.

Page 84.—28th November, 1751. Same to George Wilson, 173 acres on head of Broad Creek in Forks of James, land where Mary Doughort (Douchart) lives.

Page 88.—28th November, 1751. Same to James Bean, 190 acres by patent as above. Branch of Peters Creek. All these deeds witnessed by the same. Flood and Preston.

Page 92.—28th November, 1751. Same to Joshua Hadley, 186 acres by patent as above, a placed called the Long Bottom. South side of James.

Page 95.—28th November, 1751. Same o same, 50 acres, patented as above, at a place called the Pound Bottom, on James River.

Page 99.—28th November, 1751. Same to John Peter Sally, 100 acres, patented as above, on James River. James Trimble.

Page 104.—28th November, 1751. Same to Michael Dougherty, 207 acres by patent as above, Cedar Creek in Forks of James, where Mary Douchort lives. McDowell's line.

Page 108.—28th November, 1751. James Patton to John Ruckman, 280 acres by patent as above. Buffalo Creek of James.

Page 112.—Same date. Same to John Ledford, 142 acres patented 3d September, 1750. Roanoke.

Page 116.—Same date. Same to Isaac Taylor, 200 acres patented 3d November, 1750. On Roanoke.

Page 120.—Same date. Same to Joshua Hadley, 115 acres by patent as above. On James.

Page 124.—Same date. Same to George Burdwell, 140 acres ditto. Bend of James.

Page 127.—Same to John Bowin, 380 acres ditto. On James at Buck Eye Bottom.

Page 131.—Same to Thomas Ramsey, 130 acres ditto. Branch of Catawba (first time so spelt).

Page 135.—Same to John Collier, 81 acres ditto. Collier's line.

Page 139.—Same to John Sprout, 320 acres ditto. Broad Spring of James.

Page 142.—Same to Capt. John Smith, 195 acres ditto. On Craig's Creek.

Page 146.—28th November, 1751. James Patton to John and Alexander Walker, 800 acres by patent as above. Broad Creek. Corner James Carr.

Page 150.—Same date. Same to Mary Douchort, 170 acres by patent as above. Mill Creek in Forks of James. Corner Samuel Walker.

Page 153.—Same date. Same to John Wilson, 100 acres by patent as above. On a branch of Roanoke at a place called Devil's Den.

Page 157.—Same date. Same to James Moore, 197 acres by patent as above. A branch of James. Corner John Harris' land.

Page 160.—Same date. Same to Joseph Long, 50 acres on Buffalo Creek by patent as above. Buffalo Creek of James.

Page 165.—Same date. Same to John Berrisford, 120 acres by patent as above. McDowells Meadow run in Forks of James. Survey of John Mathews; McDowell's line.

Page 169.—Same date. Same to John Douchort, 94 acres by patent as above. At Indian Camp on Craigs Creek.

Page 173.—John Lynn, Jr., and Jean, to Nathan Gilliland, 383½ acres. In Beverley Manor; John Bigham's line; corner Jno. Buchanan; Jno. Henderson's line; John Lynn, Sr.'s, land. Teste: Arthur Hamilton, Samuel Wallace.

Page 177.—Israel Christian and Eliabeth, to John Ramsey, 323 acres. In Beverley Manor; corner Robert Finley, formerly said to be; Geo. Robinson's corner; line of Beverley Manor. Delivered: William Ramsey, 5th October, 1772. Teste: Robt. Davis, James McCorkall, John Crockett.

Page 179.—Beverley, late, &c., but now (28th November, 1751) of Great Britain, by Lewis and Madison to Alexander Wright, Gent., lot 12 in Staunton, 50 acres of Woodland No. 5. Livery of seisin by a latch of the door of house on the premises.

Page 182.—9th October, 1751. William Mills, of Loonenburg, to John Mills (trusty and loving friend). Power of attorney to convey land and attend to business, 1751. Teste: Erwin Patterson, Alexander Ingram.

Page 183.—26th November, 1751. Borden, etc., to John Hanley, 257 acres of 92,100. Broad Spring Run, otherwise called Back Creek, joining Joseph Kennedy's 300-acre tract surveyed.

Page 187.—25th November, 1751. Same to James Hammilton, farmer, 250 acres. Between Hays Creek and North Branch of James, by a Warm Spring.

Page 190.—28th November, 1751. Same to Samuel Wilson, farmer, 400 acres patented to Benjamin, 9th March, 1740. Broad Spring Branch of James; corner James Wood.

Page 195.—Beverley of Essex County (26th November, 1751; see p. 179 supra) by Lewis & Madison to James Wilson, 101 acres. In Beverley Manor; corner said Wilson's old survey.

Page 201.—27th November, 1751. William and Robert Brown to Robert Campel, 220 acres. Corner Jno. Anderson; corner John Erwin; Thos. Erwin's line. Elizabeth, wife of William. Teste: Andrew Erwin, Hugh Cample.

Page 205.—20th May, 1752. Hugh Campbel to William Brown, 10 acres. On Brown's or Culton's Branch of North River of Shanando; corner Robert Brown. Part of 333 acres patented to Hugh, 20th September, 1748. Teste: John Trumble.

Page 209.—20th May, 1752. Samuel Wilkins of Anson County, North Carolina, to Edward and Robert Shankland, 400 acres. Where said Wilkins lately dwelt, sold to Samuel by Robert McKay et als. Cooks Creek. Part of 1,265 acres sold to Wilkins by McKay. Teste: Peter Scholl, Will Brown, Andrew Erwin.

Page 214.—20th May, 1752. Robert McCorkal to William Marshall, 269 acres. Wm. Nutt's Mill Creek of Christian's Creek in Beverley Manor; James Caldwell's line. Teste: Edward Hall, Andrew Cowan, James McCorkall.

Page 218.—19th May, 1752. Thomas Haldman and Mary to Robert Stapleton, 428 acres, 3d February, 1749. On South Fork of Haldman's Creek, patent from Fairfax; corner George Brock; Peter Gartezer's survey; Mary Hill's line; Ruddle's line. Delivered: Chas. Stapleton, October, 1763. Teste: Mathias Selzer, Wm. Newman.

Page 223.—20th May, 1752. Patrick Campbell, Sr., and Elizabeth, to Patrick Campbell, Jr., 212 acres. From Beverley to Patrick, Sr., 21st February, 1738; Wm. Thompson's line; Samuel Braford's and John Mitchel's lines; corner John Ward; corner Charles Campbell. Crossing Christian's Creek and South River. Teste: David Hay, Arthur Hamilton.

Page 226.—20th May, 1752. Borden & Co. to Charles Berry, 326 acres of 92,100. Joseph Kennedy's Mill Creek; James Roseboro's line being Beverley Manor line.

Page 239.—20th May, 1752. John Lowry to Patrick Lowry, 200 acres North Fork of James. Teste: David Stewart, John Trimble, Robert McClenachan.

Page 234.—20th May, 1752. John McCreery and Agness to John Justice, 224 acres on Newfoundland Creek; land in possession of Samuel Delamontane. Corner land in pessession of Carlile. Delivered: Jno. Archer, November, 1753. Teste: Robert Cravens, Andrew Hamilton.

Page 239.—20th May, 1752. Arthur Hammilton and Barbara to James Moffett, 200 acres. In Beverley Manor; corner Wm. Ledgerwood; Col. Patton's, alias James Kerr's, line. Teste: Robt. Cunningham, David Hay.

Page 244.—27th December, 1751. John Cathey and Jaen, lately come from Ireland, now in the County of Augusta, intending to travel and settle in Carolina, to Samuel Wallace, 300 acres. In Beverley Manor, on Cathey's Creek, a middle branch of Shanando, part of 466 acres sold by Beverley to Wm. Cathey, 28th September, 1738, and by death of William (died intestate) descended to John, his oldest brother; corner John Trimble (formerly Wm. King); Hugh Young's and John Jamison's lines; Beverley Manor line; corner Morris O'Friel. Teste: Alexander Blear, Patrick Martin, Wm. McPhetters, James Scott, Morris O'Friel, James Berry.

Page 248.—9th May, 1752. Esther Campbell to Alexander Walker, farmer, 287 acres on a branch of Little's Creek; corner John Campbell. Teste: Robert Patrick, James Hamilton.

Page 250.—20th May, 1752. Borden, &c., to John Stewart, 313 acres of 92,100; corner Stewart's old survey.

Page 253.—20th May, 1752. Same to Thomas Hadley, 399 acres of 2,880 acres patented 9th March, 1750. Catuba Creek of James.

Page 256.—20th May, 1752. Same to Samuel McClure, 282 acres of 92,100. Woods Creek; corner tract formerly belonging to Henry Kerkham.

Page 261.—20th May, 1752. Samuel Braford and Ann to William Smith, 269 acres. In Beverley Manor on head branch of Shanando, purchased by

Braford from James Lynn and by Lynn from Beverley; corner Andrew Lynn; corner Brownlee's land. Teste: Walter Steel, Samuel Davis.

Page 264.—6th February, 1752. James McCewn (McKown) to Francis McCewn (McKown), conveyed to James, 14th July, 1749, 400 acres. On a Timber Ridge on North Branch of James. Teste: Archibald (Richard) Brush, James McCord, Charles Wilson.

Page 268.—20th May, 1752. Alexander Campbell, farmer, to William Campbell, 200 acres. In Beverley Manor, at his father's and Wm. Ledgerwood's corner; his father's and his brother David's corner; his brother Robert's corner; James Moffet's line. Teste: Arthur Hamilton, Samuel Henderson.

Page 272.—20th March, 1752. John Buchanan, miller, to Samuel Braford, planter, 410 acres. In Beverley Manor on head Christian's Creek; corner James Cowan. Patrick Campbell's line; John Mitchel's corner Teste: Charles Campbell, John Kerr.

Page 277.—29th November, 1751. Edward Erwin, Sr., yeoman, and Frances, to Edward Erwin, Jr., yeoman, 206 acres, part of 2 patents to Edward, 5th April, 1748, and March, 1747; Long Glade; corner Wm. Brown and John Anderson; Wm. Alexander's corner; John Erwin's line. Teste: Robert, Francis and Benjamin Erwin. Delivered: Benjamin Erwin, May, 1754.

Page 281.—29th November, 1751. Same to Benjamin Erwin, yeoman, 70 acres, part of patent, 5th April, 1748. Long Glade; Kern of Stones. Teste: Edward Erwin.

Page 285.—Same to same, 141 acres, patented 20th September, 1748. Same.

Page 289.—20th May, 1752. Benj. Capland and Ann to Joseph Wright, 400 acres on Buffilo Spring of North Fork Shanando. Teste: Charles Baley, Samuel Gray. Delivered: Thomas Waddell, 29th June, 1755.

Page 294.—20th May, 1752. Beverley by Lewis & Madison to Wm. Christian, 180 acres. In Beverley Manor on Christian's Creek; corner Wm. Armstrong; corner Robert Cunningham; Robert Moffett's line.

Page 300.—20th May, 1752. Beverley, &c., to John Trimble, 200 acres. In Beverley Manor; corner tract formerly Jno. Madison's, now Robt. McClenachan's line; formerly James Armstrong's line, now Ro. McClenachan's.

Page 305.—16th June, 1752. Robert Frazer to James Beard, 228 acres by patent, 5th April, 1748. Collins' branch; Beard's land.

Page 308.—16th June, 1752. Jacob Miller, Jr., to Nicholas Null, 400 acres on S. R. Shanando. Between Peaked Mountain and South River; Boon's Run.

Page 312.—17th June, 1752. David Henderson and Mary to Alexander Henderson, 326 acres on South River; corner David Henderson; Great Spring; corner John McConnolly; corner another tract belonging to Alexander Henderson. Delivered: Samuel Henderson, 29th November, 1754. Teste: Will Henderson, William Palmer.

Page 315.—17th June, 1752. Andrew Lewis and Robt. McClenachan to Joseph Kennedy. By order of County Court, 28th November, 1751, grantors ordered to convey to purchasers of lots in the 25 acres conveyed to Augusta County by Beverley. Livery by handful of earth. Lot No. 5 in Staunton. Teste: Elijah McClenachan, John Melcomb, Ro. McCorkell.

Page 318.—17th June, 1752. Same to Thomas Paxton. Lot No. 11, No. 8, No. 14, in Staunton. Livery by handfull of earth.

Page 321.—Andrew Lewis and Robt. Breckinridge (as above) to Robt. McClenachan. Lots No. 9 and 7 in Staunton. Livery as above.

Page 326.—17th May, 1752. Edward Watts and Elizabeth, of Culpeper, to John Magret, 125 acres. Mouth of Hawksbill of Shanando; 200 acres sold by Jacob Stover to Jacob Castle; Castle sold 75 acres to Jacob Coger, 26th June, 1740, and 125 acres to Elizabeth Downs, present wife of Edward Whats, 23d September, 1742.

Page 331.—17th June, 1752. Beverley by &c. to Robert Moffet, planter, 490 acres. In Beverley Manor; corner James Patton's Mill place; William Long's line; James Bell's line; Wm. Christian's line; John Christian's line.

Page 336.—17th June, 1752. John Lynn and Margaret to John Black, planter, tract No. 15 by Beverley to Lynn, 300 acres in Beverley Manor. Teste: John Blackley, Jno. Ramsey.

Page 340.—19th June, 1752. James McDowell to Joseph Lapsley, 400 acres. In Forks of James; Woods Creek; Benjamin Borden's line. Teste: William Armstrong, James Lockhart.

Page 342.—17th June, 1752. Borden, &c., to Wm. Wardlaw, planter, 343 acres; Joseph Kennedy's line; Mill Creek.

Page 345.—7th June, 1752. Borden, &c., to John Fulton, planter, 200 acres of 92,100. Moffet's Creek; Thos. Beard's line; James Trimble's corner.

Page 348.—17th June, 1752. Borden, &c., to Joseph Kennedy. 1. Mill Creek, 414 acres. 2. Broad Spring, 300 acres.

Page 354.—4th June, 1752. Isaac Gray and Mary to Jacob Gray, 270 acres, part of Benjamin Borden's large tract conveyed to Isaac by Benjamin. On Mill Creek; corner James McClung; McDean's line; Robert Houston's line; corner Wm. Lusk; Mill Creek by Acres Falls. Teste: B. Borden, Hugh Lusk, Andrew Stephenson, Samuel Gray.

Page 358.—14th February, 1752. Jackson Allen, beneficiary and administrator, Mary Allen to Jefry Beak (Beck). On Mill Creek joining Charles Dotson, 400 acres. Bought by Mary Allen from Fairfax. Teste: John Frazer, John Clark.

Page 362.—20th May, 1752. William Robinson and Martha to Samuel Houston, 380 acres. In Beverley Manor; corner Robert Ramsey; corner Patrick Hays. Teste: John Huston, John Pery, John Huston.

Page 365.—20th August, 1752. James Hamilton and Jane to Joseph Teas, 514 acres in Beverley Manor. on South River Shanando; corner Robert Turk; corner Robert Patrick. Two tracts. Teste: Joseph Bell, Wm. Robertson, Wm. Wright.

Page 369.—20th May, 1752. John Huston and Sarah to Wm. Robinson, 198 acres. In Borden's tract; corner Robert Kirkpatrick; corner John Moore. Teste: John Huston, John Perry, Samuel Huston.

Page 373.—19th August, 1752. Alexander Walker, planter, to Alexander Walker, wheelwright, 7½ acres on Hays Creek; James Walker's line; Wililam Wilson.

Page 376.—4th February, 1752. Jacob Bare and Barbara to John Bare. Little Fork Run of North River Shanando; corner Charles Robinson. Teste: Peter Scholl, Robert (X) Caldwell, Samuel Newman.

Page 380.—24th June, 1752. Cornelius Murley and Austas to Jacob Trumbo, 400 acres. On North Fork, North River Shanando, above gap in mountain.

Page 385.—4th February, 1752. Christian Funkhouser (Funkhousar) and Christianah and Henry Brock and Mary to Jacob Bare. South Fork North River, Shanando.

Page 390.—19th August, 1752. Richard Cousart and Martha to Jno. Cunningham and Robert Weir, 333 acres. In Borden's tract; corner James Eckins, Samuel Dunlap's line; corner Wm. McCanless, Robert Dunlap's line. Teste: Samuel Huston, James Eakin, Andrew Lockridge.

Page 392,—19th August, 1752. Rebecca Hays, widow and executrix of John Hays, plantationer, to Charles Hays, tract laid off and surveyed by Francis Beatey and James McCoskery, their son, planter, 318 acres. On Moffets and Hays Creek. From Zerinah Borden and Benjamin to John Hays, 18th June, 1746. Son, Andrew Hays. Fork of Walker's (otherwise called Hays' Creek) and Moffet's Creek.

Page 396.—19th August, 1752. Same to son, Andrew Hays. Same.

Page 401.—16th May, 1752. Andrew Fought, yeoman, to Casper (Gasper) Fought, 112 acres. Teste: Robert McMahan (?), (Menehan?), (McHan?). Patented to Andrew, 1st June, 1750.

Page 406.—2d July, 1752. Christophel Francisco by Stophel Francisco, his son and attorney, to Peter Hull, 230 acres. Part of Jacob Stover's 5,000 acres, on Shanandore; corner Nicholas Trout's line, on Cub Run; Morris Pound's line; corner Patrick Wilson; Val. Pence's line; the 3,100-acre lines. These Francisco conveyances are part of Stover's 5,000-acre tract. Teste: Robert Hooks, Nicholas Trout, Val. Pence. Delivered: Nicholas Trout, 3d January, 1753.

Page 411.—2d July, 1752. Same to Patrick Wilson, 380 acres as above; land Morrise Pound lives on.

Page 416.—2d July, 1752. Same to Ludwick Francisco, 180 acres as above on Cub Run; Bruster's land.

Page 421.—2d July, 1752. Same to Nicholas Nutt (Futt), Null?), 415 acres. Same; corner Wm. Peirce and Henry Dooley.

Page 426.—2d July, 1752. Same to Valentine Pence, 210 acres as above. Corner Nicholas Null, Cub Run.

Page 431.—2d July, 1752. Same to same, 168 acres. As above. Cub Run, corner John Craige; corner land said Pence lives on. Teste: Patrick Wilson.

Page 435.—2d July, 1752. Same to Nicholas Trout, 145 acres. As above. Corner Ludwick Francisco; Morrice Pound's line.

Page 440.—2d July, 1752. Same to Morrice Pound, 360 acres. As above. John Stevenson's line; corner Ludwick Francisco.

Page 444.—Same to same, 320 acres. As above. Cub Run; Pence's land.

Page 448.—19th August, 1752. James McCarral (McCarrol) to Morrice Pound, 130 acres. Between Cub Run and Peaked Mountain; Crosswait's line.

Page 450.—14th April, 1752. James Cole of Lunenburgh County, planter, to George Robinson, 400 acres joining Mark Coles, patented to James. 20th

September, 1745. Teste: Tobias Smith, Frederick Smith, John Marcs (?). Livery by a branch of a hiccory. Proved by Fred. Smith, 1766.

Page 452.—18th August, 1752. John Dunbarr, farmer, to Wm. Miller, farmer, of Frederick Country. On Lost River of Calaphon, from Fairfax, 412 acres. Delivered: Francis McBride, January, 1754. Teste: Robert Renick, John Erwin.

Page 456.—19th August, 1752. Joseph Kennedy to John Roseman, 380 acres, 20 poles. Moffett's Creek. Teste: Wm. Wilson, James Walker, Fr. Beatey.

Page 459.—20th August, 1752. James Edmiston, son and heir and administrator of David Edmiston and Isabella Edmiston, relict and heir and administrator of David Edmiston to Hugh McClure, 350 acres in Beverley Manor, from Beverley to David, 24th July, 1740. Teste: Anrdew Kerr. Teste: John Henderson, Adam Thompson.

Page 462.—19th August, 1752. James Patton to Wm. Hutchison, 185 acres by patent, 3d November, 1750. McRobert's Run on Cataba Creek; McRobert's land. Teste: Pat Shockey.

Page 466.—Beverley by &c. to John Kerr, 275 acres in Beverley Manor on Cathey's River; corner to Beverley Manor. Delivered: James Kerr, 18th November, 1794.

Page 470.—19th August, 1752. William Lewis, Gent., to Thomas Fleemster (Feemster), wheelwright, 390 acres on Cow Pasture; corner land in possession of John McCreery; Clover Creek. Teste: Andrew Lewis, Silas Heet, Jno. Poage.

Page 473.—20th August, 1752. Wm. Mitchell (son of John Mitchell) and Margaret, his wife, to Thomas Wilson, 400 acres, patented to John. 15th March, 1744. Broad Spring Branch of James; Benjamin Borden's line.

Page 476.—20th August, 1752. Thomas Williams and Jane to John Mathews, Jr., 129 acres. Poplor Spring of North Branch of James between Mill Creek and the river; Michael Dougherty's line. Teste: Mathew Campbell, Wm. Wilson, Robt. Renick.

Page 480.—20th August, 1752. Thomas Gilham (Gilham) and Margaret to James Lockridge, 168 acres in Great Calfpasture; corner Wm. Jameson; Mill Creek. Teste: George Vance, Robt. Renick.

Page 483.—17th August, 1752. Mary Doughart to John Mackee, 170 acres on head branch of Mill Creek in Forkes of James; corner Samuel Walker. Teste: Jacob Gray.

Page 485.—20th August, 1752. Thos. Singleton to Mathew Patton. Deed of apprenticeship. Teste: John Patton.

Page 487.—20th August, 1752. Thomas and Jane Williams to James Greenlee, 400 acres in Fork of James; Erwin Patterson's survey. Teste: Mathew Campbell, Jno. Mathews, Jr., Wm. Elliot.

Page 489.—19th August, 1752. John Brown, Gent., and Margaret, to Samuel Wilson, lot 4. Lot 4 in Town of Staunton and lot No. 1 of wood land; William Lewis' land. Livery by key of house on ½ acre, lot 4. Teste: John Buchanan, James McCorkall.

Page 492.—20th August, 1752. Borden, &c., to John Shields, eldest son and heir of James Shields, deceased. Consideration paid by John Shields, Sr., guardian of John, Jr. 193 acres Moffett's Creek; corner John Shields,

Sr.; Samuel McCutchan's corner; Robert Robinson's line; James Loosk's corner.

Page 496.—20th August, 1752. Edward Hogan, farmer, and Sarah, to Francis McBride, Lost River of Cacaphout (Caccaphon), 330 acres. Teste: Philip Chittam, John Dunbar, John Lewis.

Page 499.—15th August, 1752. Henry Purkey and Margaret to Abraham Eastes, of Caroline County, 110 acres on South River, Shanando; corner George Boon; corner James Barton. Teste: Nicholas Trout, Nicholas (X) Null.

Page 502.—17th July, 1752. Robert Green, Gent., of Culpeper County, son and residuary legatee of Ro. Green, of Orange, to John Miller, 500 acres Linville's Creek, being lot No. 3. Sold in lifetime of Robert, Sr. Teste: G. Hume.

Page 505.—17th July, 1752. William Green, of Culpeper, son and heir-at-law of Robt. Green, to John Miller, lot No. 3 on Linville's Creek where John now lives. Same as above.

Page 510.—29th August, 1752. Joseph Culton, Gent., to John Walker, 100 acres in Borden's tract. Moffett's Creek; Back Creek; Robert Culton's corner. Teste: Robert Coulton, Alexander Walker. Delivered: Andrew Hays, July, 1757.

Page 513.—15th November, 1752. Timothy Croswaite, of Orange, to George Zimerman, 400 acres; Cub Run. Teste: Alexander Fulerton, Wm. Thompson.

Page 516.—2d May, 1752. Joseph Powel to John Wright, 400 acres on head of Dry Fork of Smith's Creek on Irish Road. Teste: Thomas Harrison and Daniel Harrison.

Page 520.—16th June, 1752. James Leeper, blacksmith, and Margaret, to Andrew Leeper, planter, 299 acres in Beverley Manor, part of 525 acres from Beverley to James; corner Nicholas Leeper.

Page 523.—10th November, 1752. James Wood, of Frederick, to James Gillmer, 400 acres patented to Wood, 12th January, 1746. Buffalo Creek of North Fork of James. Teste: James Hemphill, Neal Cassaty.

Page 527.—15th November, 1752. James Downing and Mary to James Wait, 120 acres patented to Hugh Douglas, 25th June, 1747, and conveyed by him to Downing; John Stevenson's line. Teste: Edward Shanklin, Thomas Harrison, Daniel Harrison.

Page 530.—25th August, 1752. John Wilson to Joseph Tees, 400 acres on South River, Shanandore; Beverley Manor line, part of 660 acres deeded to John's father by Joseph Mills, 24th June, 1742. Teste: James Patton, Mary Thompson, Michael O'Donnel, Wm. Thompson, Joseph Love, Wm. Preston.

Page 533.—15th November, 1752. Borden, &c., to Wm. Berry, 130 acres of 92,100; James Trimble's line, near Moffett's Creek; Thomas Berry's line; David Hay's run. Delivered: Wm. Martin, July, 1760.

Deed Book No. 5.

First Deed Recorded 15th November, 1752; Last Deed Record 20th March, 1754.

Page 2.—14th November, 1752. William McRory (McKory?) and Margaret to Adam Reed, 175 acres on the Mary Creek, part of 350 patented to Rev. Alexander McDowel, 10th July, 1745; Evans' run. Teste: David and Samuel Moore, Nathaniel Evans.

Page 5.—16th November, 1752. James Nealey to Alexander Ingram, 245 acres; corner Francis Beatey. Delivered 1797 to Wm. Ingram, attorney-in-fact for John Ingram, to whom the land was devised.

Page 8.—4th November, 1752. Samuel McClure and Mary to John Paxton, 50 acres, Forks of James where Samuel now liveth, on Wood's Creek; corner Abraham Brown; corner Samuel McClure. Teste: Petty Wallace. Corner Paxton's old survey. Teste: Richard Woods, Petty Wallace.

Page 11.—16th November, 1752. John Poage and Mary to Wm. Cleghorn, blacksmith, 214 acres on Cedar Creek of James; Francis McCown's land. Teste: John Smith, John Anderson, Daniel Harrison.

Page 14.—27th August, 1752. Hugh Martin to Charles Hays, 250 acres on Back Creek in Borden's grant; corner Andrew Hays; John Buchanan's land. Teste: Andrew Scott, Andrew Hays, Major Scot. Delivered: Andrew Hays, July, 1757.

Page 17.—22d August, 1754 (this deed was recorded 16th November, 1752, and 2 has been erased and 4 inserted). Same to Andrew Hays, 250 acres as above. Corner Charles Hays; Thomas Paxton's line.

Page 20.—16th November, 1752. William Armstrong to John Askins, 85 acres. Corner Daniel Monation; Smith's Creek.

Page 23.—17th November, 1752. Silas Hart and Jane to Alexander Gibson, 199 acres, part of 400 acres granted Robert Rennock, 10th June, 1740. Buffalo Lick Branch. Teste: Alexander Richey, John Richey.

Page 26.—17th November, 1752. Daniel McAnore and Hannah to Alexander Gibson, 115 acres. Middle River of Shanando joining land where McAnore dwells. Corner John Trimble; Thomas Gardner's line. Teste: David Trimble, John Walker.

Page 30.—17th November, 1752. Benjamin Borden to Andrew Bird, 174 acres, Brock's Gap, on North Shanado; the Chimney Rock. Delivered to Abraham Bird, 27th January, 1754.

Page 33.—17th November, 1752. James Brown and Agness to Wm. Preston, 277 acres on second Fork of Thorney Branch of North River of Shanandore; Smith's land. From Repentance Townsend, who patented it in 1749, 5th September. Teste: John Walter and James Trimble.

Page 36.—18th November, 1752. James Patton to Hugh Mills, 208 acres by patent, 3d November, 1750, on a branch of Roanoke; Welsh Run; corner John Mills; Glead Creek.

Page 38.—18th November, 1752. Same to William Armstrong, 245 acres on Wolf Creek of Roanoke.

Page 41.—18th November, 1752. Same to John Mills, 845 acres by patent as above. Buffilo Creek of Roanoke; Corrovan's Creek.

Page 44.—18th November, 1752. James Patton to Wm. Graham, 160 acres by patent as above, Lees Creek of Catawba.

Page 46.—Same date. Same to Wm. Hall, 100 acres by patent as above. Buffalo Creek of James; corner Wm. Hall.

Page 49.—Ditto. Same to Richard Carr (Kerr), 240 acres by patent as above. Welsh Run of Roanoke.

Page 52.—Ditto. Same to Adam Looney, 271 acres by patent as above. Meadow Run or Bryan's Creek.

Page 54.—Ditto. Same to Charles Melligan, 60 acres by patent as above, on head of Looney's Creek.

Page 58.—Ditto. Same to John and Alexander Walker, 185 acres by patent as above. Broad Creek in Forks of James; James Carr's line.

Page 61.—Ditto. Same to Robert Poage, 104 acres by patent as above, on Cedar Creek in Forks of James; corner Thomas Taylor's line; McDowell's land; corner Wm. Mills.

Page 64.—21st March, 1753. Same to John Robinson, Sr., 300 acres, part of large tract patented 10th April, 1751. North Fork of Goose Creek; corner John Robinson, Jr.

Page 67.—Ditto. Same to John Robinson, Jr., 872 acres patent, as above; corner John Robinson. Sr.; corner James Gorrel.

Page 70.—21st March, 1753. James Patton to William and James Gorrel, 620 acres part of patent as above; North Fork of Goose Creek; corner John Robinson; corner Tobias (Bright).

Page 73.—Ditto. Same to Tobias Bright, 590 acres part of patent above; Goose Creek; corner James Gorrell; corner George Paris.

Page 76.—Ditto. Same to Elijah Isaac, 378 acres as above. As above, corner Errick Bright; corner Thomas Hill.

Page 79.—Ditto. Same to Thomas Hill, 70 acres as above. As above, corner to above; corner Benjamin Ogle.

Page 81.—Ditto. Same to Benjamin Ogle, 290 acres part as above. As above, corner above; corner Elijah Isaacs.

Page 84.—Ditto. Same to William Pepper, 580 acres as above. As above, corner Francis Cyphers.

Page 87.—Ditto. Same to Francis Cyphers, 400 acres by patent 10th April, 1751. As above, corner to above, The Barrens.

Page 90.—Ditto. Same to Henry Brown, Sr., 50 acres by patent 3d November, 1750. Lick Run of Roanoke; corner James Burk.

Page 92.—Ditto. Same to William Scot, 100 A. by patent, 3d November, 1750. Middle Lick Run of Catawba.

Page 95.—21st March, 1753. James Patton to Jacob Brown, 1753. W. Fork Roanoke, 100 A. by patent 3d November, 1750. Teste: John Robinson, Wm. Preston, James Gorrell, George Paris, John Robinson.

Page 98.—23d February, 1753. Same to John Mills of Lunenburg, 150 acres by patent 3d November, 1750. Murre's Run of Roanoke. Teste: Wm. Carravin, Erwin Patterson, Alexander Ingram.

Page 101.—21st March, 1753. Same to John Peteet, 40 acres by patent dated as above. James River; corner James Greenlee.

Page 103.—Ditto. Same to Robert Kirkum, 33 acres by patent dated as above. James River.

Page 106.—Ditto. Same to William Daubne Cawthon (Cauthorn), 180 acres by patent as above. Bradshaw's Creek. Teste: George and Rebecca Wilson, Wm. Preston.

Page 109.—8th December, 1752. Same to George Stevenson, 220 acres by patent as above. Poag's Draft of James River; Borden's Patent line. Teste: John and James Greenlee.

Page 111.—21st March, 1753. Same to George Peoris, 271 acres part of large patent 10th April, 1750. Goose Creek, corner Tobias Bright and Errick Bright.

Page 114.—Ditto. Same to Errick Bright, 207 acres part of above patent. Goose Creek; corner George Pearis; corner Elijah Isaacs.

Page 117.—21st March, 1753. Robert McClenachan to Robert Breckinridge. Buffalo Creek, opposite the Long Bent, Whiskey Hill, 242 acres by patent to McClenachan, 19th October, 1753. Delivered: James Lockhart, 9th February, 1758.

Page 120.—21st March, 1753. Samuel Anderson of W. Nottingham Township, Chester County, Pennsylvania, to John Moore, Gent., in Borden's tract; sold by said Moore to said Anderson; corner tract, formerly said to be George Henderson's, 304 A.. 3 R.. 15 P., in Borden's 92100, formerly sold by said Moore to said Anderson. Teste: Wm. Purris, Wm. Robinson, Francis Beatey. Delivered: David McCroskey, 14th June, 1759.

Page 122.—21st March, 1753. Alexander Gibson to James Reburn, 1753, 79½ acres on Moffet's Creek of Cathey's River, below John Davison's land. Teste: John King, John Archer, David Trimble.

Page 125.—1st March, 1753. William Berry and Jane, to Thomas Berry, 65 acres Moffet's Creek; corner David Hays; part of 145 acres conveyed by Borden to Wm., 23d June, 1746.

Page 128.—1st March, 1753. Wm. Beverley by Lewis Madison to James Gillespy, 200 acres; corner in his old survey in Beverley Manor; corner Charles Dalhouse and Wm. Bell. Delivered Thomas Stuart, 22d June, 1754.

Page 132.—20th March, 1753. John Crockett, son and heir of Robert Crockett, deceased, to James Moore. Delivered to order of William Taylor, attorney for Daniel Broughf, 21st August, 1816. Lunie's Mill Creek, 350 acres. Teste: Robert and Mildred Davis and Archibald Crockett. Delivered 1816 to Wm. Taylor, attorney for Danl. Broughf.

Page 135.—22d February, 1753. Peter Reed and Cathern of So. Fork of So. Br. of Potomac to Peter Hoos, of same. Trace No. 1 on So. Fork of the Wappacomo or Gr. So. Br. of Potomac, 680 acres. Teste: Hendrick Cortreght, Peter Thorn, Tobias Decker.

Page 139.—20th March, 1753. James McCorkle and Jane, to Elijah McClenachan, 1753, 370 acres in Beverley Manor; the graveyard in Wm. Nutt's line; corner Breckinridge; corner Wm. Nut; also 23½ acres part of tract formerly Wm. Nut in Beverley Manor; line of McCorckle's former survey. Teste: Wm. Lusk, Ro. Breckinridge.

Page 142.—21st March, 1753. Robert Davis to John Brown, 300 acres; corner James Cathey, now Samuel Wallace; Beverley Manor line.

Page 144.—22d March, 1753. Same to John Brown, 145 acres Beverley Manor; Patent Line; corner Cap. Brown, Back Creek.

Page 146.—13th March, 1753. Borden, etc., to Wm. McCandless, 37 acres of 92100. Robert Dunlap's line; said McCandless's old corner. Teste: Archibald Reoack, Wm. Reoarck, Robert Henry, Ro. Lowry.

Page 148.—12th March, 1753. Borden, etc., to James Glasgow of Cecil County, Maryland; corner Alexander Miller, 427 acres of 92100. Teste: David Moore, Wm. McCandless, Wm. Purris, Samuel Anderson.

Page 152.—21st March, 1753. James Glasgow of Susquehanna Hundred & Co. Cecil in Maryland, to Wm. Purris. Above. Teste: John Moore, Wm. Robinson.

Page 154.—19th March, 1753. Borden, etc., to John Walker, Jr., 302 acres of 92100. (Back Creek ?); corner Joseph Culton, Moffets Cr., Robert Culton. Delivered: Alexander Walker, October 2d, 1775, Archibald Buchanan. Teste: James and Wm. McCoskry, Alexander McMullen.

Page 157.—24th November, 1751. David Sayer to Robert Sayer, 247 acres, 3 R., 6 P. Sold by Wm. Beverley to Joseph Reed, 2d July, 1740, and 26th September, 1741, and by Reed to Sayer; James Robinson's line, Christian's Creek; Brooks line; Robert Wilson (formerly Francis Beaty); corner Wm. Thompson's corner. Teste: Danl. Gove, David Sayer.

Page 159.—19th March, 1753. Borden, etc., to John Buchanan, 370 acres of 92100, 1753. Walker's Creek; corner James Buchanan, said Buchanan's Run; Rutherford's line.

Page 161.—19th March, 1753. Same to William Caruthers, 340 acres of 92100; Mathew Lyle's corner; McSpadden's line; Alexander McCleery's line.

Page 164.—5th December, 1752. William Miller and Christian, to John Miller. Delivered: Jno. Miller, Jr., 3d February, 1755, on Lost River, alias Caccapheton, from Fairfax; corner Edward Hogan, 380 acres. Teste: Samuel Newman, Jacob Woodley, William Caryl.

Page 167.—21st March, 1753. David Kerr and Kathrine, to Robert Gray, 200 acres of 92100, in Borden's tract; Joseph Kennedy's Mill Creek; McNut's line; John Kerr's line.

Page 169.—12th January, 1753. Borden, etc., to Alexander McNutt, eldest son and heir-at-law of Alexander McNutt, deceased; Kennedy's Mill Creek of James River, 301 acres. Teste: Saml. Dunlop, John Brownlee, Ro. Ramsey, Wm. Lusk.

Page 171.—12th February, 1753. Same to James McNutt, son of Alexander McNutt, deceased, adjoining above, 185 acres.

Page 173.—10th February, 1753. Same to Thomas Beard, 605 acres of 92100; Moffett's Creek of James; corner John Roseman. Delivered: Saml. Buchanan, 21st June, 1758.

Page 176.—8th March, 1753. Same to John Winston; A, 448 acres; B, 609 acres; 1 on Moffett's Creek; Buchanan's line; corner Stewart; corner Robert Stewart. Teste: Mathew Lyle, John Loggan, Robt. Lowrey.

Page 178.—15th February, 1753. Borden, etc., to John Logan, 262 acres of 92100, 1753. Joseph Kennedy's Mill Creek of James; corner Joseph Kennedy and John Hanley; McNut's land, his old survey; Thomas Beard's line.

Page 181.—Same to Robert Lowry. Delivered: Jno. Murphy, 19th December, 1795. Corner tract, formerly known as William Smith's land, 412 acres of 92100.

Page 183.—13th March, 1753. Same to James Coalter. Delivered: Wm. Martin, July, 1760, 212 acres of 92100. Hay's Creek; corner Wm. Reagh.

Page 185.—13th March, 1753. Same to Archibald Reagh. Delivered: Wm. Feeters, 27th July, 1757, 200 acres of 92100. Walker's Creek; William Reagh's corner, old survey.

Page 189.—13th March, 1753. Benj. Borden to Charles Dayley, 76 acres on No. Shanando, North Shanando, Brock's Gap. Delivered: Jno. Thomas, August Ct., 1777.

Page 192.—2d September, 1752. Opattis Brock to Jacob Bare, 400 acres, So. Fork No. Riv. Shan. Teste: Jacob Trombar, Peter Scholl, Saml. Newman, John Bare.

Page 195.—22d June, 1752. Daniel Murley and Judith, to Cornelius Murley, 200 acres in Gap of North Mountain, half of 400 acres. Patented to Cornelius and conveyed by him to Daniel, next to James Baggs' land in No. Fork River of Shanado.

Page 199.—John Pickens and Ellinor, to Anthony Strother, of King George, from Beverley, 27th February, 1740; Robert Poag's, now Gorden's; corner on Lewis Creek; corner land sold by Jno. Pickens to Wm. Baskins, 552 acres, part of 764 acres, conveyed by Beverley to John, 27th February, 1740. Teste: Danl. Richeson, Thos. and Andrew Lewis, Robert Bratton.

Page 201.—22d December, 1752. Joseph Lane to wife, Margaret, care and feeding of infant by Dr. Holt, 1752. Power Attorney General. Teste: James Bratton, James Campbell, Wm. Preston.

Page 203.—Gabriel Jones and Lewis Neil, of Frederick, executors of Wm. McMachen, late of same place, Gent., to William Beard, 400 acres on Cub Run of So. River Shanando, west side Peaked Mountain, patent to Wm., 12th January, 1746. Wm. died testate.

Page 207.—21st March, 1753. Beverley by Lewis and Madison, 1753, to Thomas Teat, blacksmith, 170 acres on head of a branch of So., in Beverley Manor; David Hays's line.

Page 212.—22d March, 1753. Same to William McCutchan, 100 acres in Beverley Manor; John McCutchon's line; tract surveyed for Wm. Coningham. Delivered: Saml. McCutchan, 3th March, 1755.

Page 217.—22d March, 1753. Same to Francis Beaty, 160 acres; corner tract surveyed for James Lockhart, Gent., in Beverley Manor; Francis Lockhart, Beverley Manor line.

Page 221.—16th January, 1753. John Frogg, of Prince William, to John Madison, 200 acres on Shanando, adjoining Wm. Frazer, and purchased by Frogg from Wm. Crittenden. Teste: John Jones, Henry Murray.

Page 224.—22d March, 1753. John Trimble to Andrew Scott, 200 acres in Beverley Manor; corner Moses Thompson, James Armstrong's line. Teste: Wm. Lusk, George Wilson, James Trimble.

Page 228.—Robert Poage and Elizabeth, to James McCown, on Catawba of James. Teste: Robert Poage, James McAfee, John Poage. Delivered: Jno. Buchanan, weaver, 19th September, 1755.

Page 232.—22d March, 1753. Beverley, by, &c., to Richard Pilson, 330 acres, 1753. M. B. M. Bloodworth's line.

Page 235.— —— 175—. Same to Frederick Jacob Lipham, of Staunton, lot 18 in Staunton. Seisin by turf and twig.

Page 238.— —— 175—. Jacob Lockhart and Mary to Samuel Sprowl, 210 acres in Beverley Manor.

Page 242.—15th May, 1753. Robert Poage, Sr., and Elizabeth, to Robert, Jr., 104 acres, Cedar Creek in Forks of James; cor. Thomas Taylor, McDowell's line; cor. Wm. Mills. Teste: Wm. White, Peter Scholl, Samuel Newman. Delivered, Jno. Poage, March, 1761.

Page 245.—8th May, 1753. George Scott to Andrew Leeper, 278 acres Cathey's alias Middle River, Wm. Thompson's land; Hugh Thompson's cor. Teste: Hugh Thompson, Samuel Henderson, Henry Downes.

Page 247.—27th March, 1753. Borden to John Robinson, 300 acres, part of 92100. Mathew Robinson's survey; Wm. Reagh's cor., Back Creek. Teste: Alex. Walker, James Robinson, Mathew Robinson.

Page 251.—16th May, 1753. James Miles, farmer, to William Morrow (Murray), 201 acres on Buffalo Branch, sold by Robert Rennick to James Miles, 1747. Teste: John Risk, Andrew Hays, Joseph Love.

Page 255.—16th May, 1753. John Stephenson and Jane James to William Ramsey, 290 acres on Mill Creek in Borden's tract; cor. Moses McClure, Worm Run; Alexander McClure; cor. Rob. Allison; cor James Thompson. Teste: Walter Davis, Wm. Gay, Wm. Kerr. Delivered: John Davis, May, 1757

Page 257.—8th March, 1753. Borden, &c., to Alexander Craighead, late of Lancaster County, Pennsylvania, 1753. Cor. Richard Woods; cor Peter Wallace, 553 acres of 92100 sold in testator's lifetime. Cap. Lapsley's line. Teste: Roger and John Keyes, Nathaniel Evins.

Page 262.—6th March, 1753. Samuel and William Woods to Benjamin Borden, 263 acres on Woods Creek of James. Cor. Richard Woods; cor. Peter Wallace, Cap. Lapsley's line.

Page 264.—27th March, 1753. Borden, &c., to Mathew Robinson, 400 acres of 92100. Joseph Culton's cor., Back Creek; John Robinson's survey. Teste: John and James Robinson, Alex. Walker.

Page 268.—16th May, 1753. Thomas Blackwood and Ann to Samuel Blackwood, 105 acres in Beverley Manor, Christian's Creek, William Wright's line, Thomas Shield's line. Teste: Wm. Kerr, Wm. Wright.

Page 272.—Samuel Braford and Ann to Elizabeth Mateer (McAttore), alias Wright, widow. Sold by Beverley to Samuel Brawford in Beverley Manor. Cor. Samuel's tract purchased of John Buchanon; lines of John Mitchell and Samuel Doack. Delivered to James Mateer, 1774. Teste: Wm. Finley, Wm. Wright.

Page 275.—12th May 1753. Moses McClure and Isable to Samuel Paxton, 165 acres on North Branch James on a place called Spreading Springs Teste: Thomas Paxton, Thomas Paxton, Andrew Stephenson.

Page 279.—6th April, 1753. James Downing and Mary to John Love, 1753, on Smith Creek; corner John Love's land near land of John Davison, 175 acres. Teste: Thomas Millsaps.

Page 282.—16th May, 1753. Robert Poage and Elizabeth to James Mitchell, 263 acres on Calape Creek at the end of Cross Mountain at a place called the Fork Bottom. Teste: Robt. Renick, George Anderson.

Page 285.—15th May, 1753. John Trimble and Ann to Robert Philips. 159 acres, part of 251 acres, sold by Beverley to Wm. King, 27th February, 1749, the Beverley Manor; corner Moses Offreel.

Page 289.—17th May, 1753. Samuel Lockhart and Catherine to Edward Beard (Mason), 200 acres on North River Shanando, part of 400 acres patented to Samuel, April, 1751; corner Samuel Losk; corner James Beard.

Page 292.—15th May, 1753. Samuel Houston to John Sprowl, 194 acres in Beverley Manor on Beverley Manor and Borden's lines; John Montgomery's line; corner Patrick Hays; corner Robert Ramsey, part of 380 acres purchased by Samuel from Wm. Robinson. Teste: Thomas Paxton, James Edmiston, Francis Beatey.

Page 296.—21st March, 1753. John Stephenson, farmer, and Sarah to Archibald Houston, farmer, granted to John, 1743, 367 acres. Teste: Robert Cravens, John Pickens, Andrew Baskins. Acknowledged by Sarah, 17th August, 1753.

Page 299.—17th May, 1753. Col. James Patton to John Sproul, 285 acres patented 3d November, 1750. Drafts of James.

Page 303.—17th May, 1753. James Patton to Capt. John Smith, 1753, on Craig's Creek, 213 acres patented 3d November, 1750.

Page 306.—17th May, 1753. Same to William Armstrong, 80 acres by patent as above. Glade Creek of Roanoke; corner Wm. Armstrong. Teste: Wm. Preston.

Page 309.—17th May, 1753. Same to James Campbell, 100 acres by patent as above, on Crooked Creek of Roanoak.

Page 312.—17th May, 1753. Same to Edward McDonald, 140 acres by patent, ditto, on a branch of Buffalo Creek; corner survey of Edward McDonald.

Page 316.—18th May, 1753. William Daubnee Cawthon (Dabne Cowthon) and Ursula (Ursley) to Thomas Breneger, 50 acres, part of tract conveyed to Cawthon, 21st March, 1753, on Bradshaw's Creek of Roanoak. Teste: Esther Robinson and Wm. Robinson, Wm. Preston, Ephram Vorse.

Page 319.—18th May, 1753. James Burk to James Bane, 117 acres, part of tract patented to Burk, 20th September, 1748, on Goose Creek. Teste: George McSwine, George Robinson.

Page 323.— —— ——, 1753. John Wilson to John McCurry (McMurrey), 100 acres, at the Devil's Den.

Page 326.—20th April, 1753. Robert Green, Gent., and Mary, of Culpeper, to John Miller, farmer, 200 acres, part of 500 acres, part of greater tract patented to Hite, Green, &c., and devised by Robert Green, Sr., to grantor; Linville's Creek. Teste: Alexander Bright. Delivered: Jonathan Douglass by your order, April, 1760. Teste: Alex. Bright.

Page 330.—20th April, 1753. Same to Thomas Moore, 300 acres, part of 500. Above being part of lot 2. As above. Corner John Miller. Teste: Alexander Wright.

Page 330.—20th April, 1753. Same to Thomas Moore, 300 acres, part of 500. Above being part of lot 2. As above. Corner John Miller. Teste: Alexander Wright.

Page 333.—3d August, 1753. John Mills and Ann, of Lunenburg, to Wm. Graham, 1753. Buffalo Creek of Roanoke. The Barrens; corner Joshua McCormick; Corraven's Creek. 600 acres by patent, 3d November, 1750. Teste: Humphrey Madison. Delivered: Benj. Estell, November, 1762.

Page 337.—23d June, 1753. John Dobikin and Elizabeth to Thomas Moore; from Fairfax, 7th August, 1750, on Haldman's Creek (a pyson field), 400 acres. Teste: Griffith Thomas.

Page 340.—David Mitchel, yeoman, to Thomas McFerran, yeoman, 220 acres on Percimmon Branch of James, granted to David, 15th March, 1744; Joseph Lapsley's line. Teste: Edward McDonald and Pat. Shockey, Jno. Neelley.

Page 343.—10th August, 1753. Jacob Pousel and Barbara to Griffith Thomas. From Fairfax, 30th August, 1753, John Pennywite cor; cor. survey for Michael Henten; Jumping Run, 314 acres. Teste: Thomas Moore.

Page 346.—22d June, 1753. Jeofry Beck and Lydia to Michael Skellishner, 400 acres, on Mill Creek joining Charles Dalson's. Teste: Mathios Selzer, Samuel Newman, Peter Scholl.

Page 349.—26th July, 1753. Thomas Moore and Mary to Samuel Newman, Smith Creek. From Fairfax to Newman and by Newman to Moore, 200 acres. Teste: Wm. Carrel and John Hughes.

Page 353.—13th November, 1753. Wm. Rutledge, of Granville County, North Carolina, to Cornelius Ruddle, 237 acres, Brock's Creek, patented to Wm. 20th August, 1745. Teste: Stephen Ruddle, Thomas Lonetally, Erwin Patterson, Isaac Ruddle. Acknowledged before Thomas Lonetally, a J. P. for Granville County.

Page 357.—8th October, 1751. Cornelius Cook and Ann of Granville Co. No. Ca., late of Augusta, to Rees Thomas, 1751. Patented to Cornelius 20th September, 1748, Brock's Creek, 350 acres. Acknowledged 12th July, 1753 before Erwin Patterson. Teste: Stephen and Isaac Ruddle.

Page 360.—14th July, 1753. William Beard and Mary to Robert Frazer, South Branch Shanando, known as Cave Bottom, part of large tract patented to Alex. Thompson, 13th July, 1742, and sold to Beard; Alex. Thompson's Ford, Cave Hill, 100 acres. Teste: Robert Hoop, Robert Ralstone, James Beard.

Page 364.—14th August, 1753. Robert Shankland, Sr., to John Fulton, 1753. Cor. Jacob Dye, North Mountain, patented 1746, 300 acres. Teste: Ro. Ralstone, Ephraim Love, Jno. Thomas.

Page 367.—10th August, 1753. Stephen Ruddle and Mary to Philip Harper, 1753. Haldman's Creek adjoining Peter Gartner, Cap. Jno. Dobkins, 460 acres. From Fairfax to Archibald Ruddle and by him to Stephen. Delivered: Chas. Hyleton (Styleton), October, 1763.

Page 370.—15th August, 1753. Charles Campbell, gent., to David Bryan, 400 acres on Goose Creek, patented 24th October, 1752. Teste: Alex Wright, Wm. Lusk, John Buchanan.

Page 373.—12th May, 1753. Valentine Sevier and Joanna to Andrew Bird, 1753. Between Limestone Ridge and Smith Creek; cor. Andrew Bird's survey, Robert Milsap's survey, 184 acres. Teste: Wm. Bethel. Delivered to John Speare, 1758.

Page 376.—17th August, 1753. James Patton to Nathaniel Evans, 120 acres, Branch of Looney's Creek by patent 3d November, 1750. Teste: Margret Preston, Wm. Thompson, Geo. Robinson.

Page 379.—10th August, 1753. James Young and Sarah to Patrick Young, 340 acres on Whistle Creek in Forks of James, cor. Joseph Walker, North Branch James; cor. tract surveyed for Sarah Young. Teste: John Low, Francis McCown.

Page 381.—13th August, 1753. John Kerr (Carr) and Ann to Francis Beaty, 336 acres. From Borden to John, 1750, joining above Francis. Robert Gray and David Kerr, Joseph Kennerley's Mill Creek. Teste: Robert Robinson, David Kerr, Robert Wilson. Livery by a key of the door of the Mansion House.

Page 385.—15th August, 1753. Sarah Ramsey, widow, to John Fulton. 309 acres in Beverley Manor, cor. Robert Ramsey. Teste: Hugh Fulton, David Hay, Robert Ramsey, Jno. Kerr.

Page 388.—12th April, 1753. John Mathews and Ann to James Huston 140 acres on Back Creek of Roanoke; place called Turkey Bottom. Teste: John Mathews, Jr., and Joshua Mathews.

Page 391.—6th August, 1753. James Coningham and Margaret to Jacob

Conningham, 100 acres, part of 400 acres patented to James, 20th August, 1745. On Tees Crick of James, cor. Moses Coningham. Teste: Chas. Daugherty, Isaac Coningham, Henry (X) Campbell.

Page 394.—7th February, 1753. James Wood, of Frederick; Wm. Russell and Wm. Green, of Culpeper, to John Davis, 330 acres on South Forks of South Branch Potomac, patented 1750. Teste: Roger Dyer and Samuel (X) Patton. Delivered to Charles Smith, 1773.

Page 397.—2d August, 1753. James Hamilton and Jane to Robert Christian, 1753, 250 acres on North Branch James in Borden's tract; from Borden, 1751, by a warm spring, Hays Creek. Teste: Alexander McNutt, David Moore. Delivered to Israel Christian, 1757.

Page 401.—2d August, 1753. William Martin to John Walker, Sr., 359 acres on Mudlick Run on Roanoke, otherwise called Goose Creek. Iron mine. Delivered: Mr. Hayes, 1757. Teste: Hugh Martin, Charles and Andrew Hayes. See page 409, supra.

Page 402.—15th August, 1753. County Court, by Lewis McClenachan to Robert Finley, merchant. By order County Court, 28th November, 1751, lots 4, 3, and 13 in Staunton. Teste: Walter Patterson, John Brown, Samuel Brown. Livery by handful of earth.

Page 405.—15th August, 1753. Same to Alexander McNutt. 1753, same as above, lot No. 10. When prison stands on lot 1. Teste: George Crawford. Livery by a logg of the house.

Page 409.—2d August, 1753. Hugh Martin to John Walker, Sr., 112 acres on Mudlick Run and joining on a branch of Roanoke called Goose Creek. See page 401 above.

Page 412.—14th August, 1753. Thomas Waterson and Mary to John Fowler, 120 acres patented to Thomas 12th January, 1746, on North River Shannando, crossing Cook's Creek. Teste: Robert Wilson, Samuel McKune.

Page 415.—14th August, 1753. Samuel Dunlop to Thomas Beard, 389½ acres in Borden's tract. Cor. John Huston and Robert Wier. Teste: Jno. Edmiston, Robert Dunlap, Thomas Mitchell.

Page 418.—15th August, 1753. George Hutcheson, farmer, and Ellinor to John Hutcheson, Christian's Creek. Teste: Samuel Henderson, James Allen. 277 acres. Delivered same to Henderson, 29th November, 1754. Part of tract surveyed for George Hutcheson.

Page 421.—18th May, 1753. James Corlile to John Corlile, 250 acres in Calfpasture, from Patton and Lewis, 1748. Cor. to Clemons; cor. Warrick; cor. James Corlile.

Page 423.—16th August, 1753. Thomas Lewis to Samuel Gay, 489 acres. Jackson's River, cor. tract in possession of John Lewis.

Page 426.—17th August, 1753. John Risk to Samuel Hays, 100 acres on James River in Borden's tract, John Edmonson's line.

Page 429.—14th May, 1753. John Robinson, Sr., to William Robinson, 200 acres, part of two tracts. Patented to John, 25th July, 1746. South Fork Goose Creek. Cor. Joseph Robinson. Teste: Charles Brookin, John, Thomas, Joseph and Esther Robinson.

Page 432.—7th August, 1753. John Robinson and Mary to James Robinson, son and heir of James Robinson, deceased, 150 acres same as above Teste: James Gorrell, Wm. McCrab, Jacob Brown, Elizabeth Robinson.

Page 434.—12th June, 1753. Power attorney, Beverley to Thomas Lewis and John Madison to convey lands in Calfpasture, 1753. Teste: John O'Neal and John (his mark) Furnish, Peter Scholl, Wm. Lusk, Wm. Burk, Wm. Frazer.

Page 436.—15th May, 1753. Andrew Duncan and Jane to John Wilson, cordwainer, 1753, 232 acres, part of 1546 acres sold by Beverley to Patrick Campbell in Beverley Manor, and 232 acres, 1 rood, sold by Campbell to Wm. Syers, and by Sayers to Andrew Duncan; on South River Shannando. Cor. Charles Campbell and John Ward, John Brownlee's line; Manor line.

Page 439.—16th August, 1753. John Maxwell and Mary to John Mathews, Jr., 381 acres on a branch of Mill Creek; Ann Salling's hill. Sold to John by Ewin Patterson, 1750. Delivered: James Lockhart, June, 1757.

Page 441.—16th August. Thomas Paxton to Francis Beaty, 1750. In Staunton, lot 11 conveyed to Thomas by Andrew Lewis and Robert McClenachan on behalf of County Court, 17th June, 1752. Teste: John Archer, W. Christian, Thomas Boyd, John Shield.

Page 443.—16th August, 1753. Same to Wm. Christian. Lot 8 in Staunton, conveyed to Thomas as above. Delivered: Israel Christian, 17th February, 1757. Livery by key of the house.

Page 445.—10th August, 1753. Margaret Love (alias Bryan) to James Mitchell, mortgage or personalty to indemnify Mitchell against a judgment vs. him in County Court, Augusta, as surety (special bail) for Joseph Lane, absuit of James Dean, merchant. Teste: James Campbell and Wm. Bryan, Wm. Beard.

Page 448.—9th June, 1753. Robert Coningham, Esq., and Martha to Walter Davis, 322 acres in Beverley Manor on Cedar Spring. Teste: Pat Cunningham, Wm. Johnston, Walter Coningham.

Page 451.—17th August, 1753. Adam Dickinson to James Dunlap, 875 acres on Meadow Creek of Jackson's River near the Indian Path. Patented to Adam 1st June, 1750. Teste: Charles Dunlap, John Robison.

Page 454.—17th August, 1753. John and David Standley (Handley) to John Dickinson, 546 acres on Falling Spring of Jackson River, lower end of the Sinking Spring. Teste: John Wardlaw.

Page 456.—10th August, 1753. David Henderson for Wm. Hudson and Jno. Cloyd, both of Chester County, Pennsylvania, to Wm. Henderson. 1753, 350 acres on North Branch of James, Buffilo Creek. Livery by a branch of an oak and a handful of earth. Delivered: Walter Davis, January, 1756. Teste: Wm. Lusk.

Page 458.—17th August, 1753. David McComas to Jno. Trimble. 1753, power attorney to recover all debts, sell personalty. Teste: Andrew and Wm. Lewis.

Page 460.—18th August, 1753. James Patton to Morris O'Freel, 400 acres by patent 3d November, 1750, in Forks of James, Samuel Walker's land. Road.

Page 462.—17th August, 1753. County Court, by Lewis and McClenachan to Wm. Murray, carpenter and joiner, lot 12 in Staunton. Livery by a key of the house. Teste: John Lewis, Wm. Hamilton, Wm. Lewis.

Page 466.—14th August, 1753. William Thompson and Mary to John Madison, 1753, 363 acres, part of 400 patented to Wm. Thompson, Sr., and conveyed by him to Wm., Jr. Middle River, George Scot's line; North River, Wm. Baskins' land, Buffalo Run.

Page 469.—26th July, 1753. Francis Puicer (Puison, Puiser) and Sarah, of Rowan County, North Carolina, to John Hinton, 1753, 236 acres on Muddy Creek. Teste: Joseph and John Bryan and Paul Kuster.

Page 472.—22d November, 1753. Captain Robert Armstrong and Lydia to James Armstrong, 1753, 70 acres, part of tract patented to Robert on Middle River where he now lives. Delivered: Sampson Archer, March, 1759.

Page 475.—21st November, 1753. Charles Berry to Robert Gamwell, 140 acres, part of tract 326 acres sold by Borden to Charles.

Page 477.—7th September, 1753. Samuel McMahon to Samuel Henderson, 165 acres on Dry River between Daniel Smith's and Shifman's lands. Teste: Robert McMahon, George Crawford, Henry Reburn.

Page 479.— —— 1753. Edward McDonnald, farmer, to David Clyde, yeoman, 200 acres on Roanoke where Edward lives, patented to him 1753. 140 acres joining above and where Joseph McDonald lives. Conveyed to Edward by James Patton, mortgage.

Page 483.—21st November, 1753. William Purris, weaver, to John McMachan, of Frederick County, 427 acres in Borden's grant. Cor. Alex. Miller. Conveyed by Borden to James Glasgow and by Glasgow to Purris, 1753. Teste: Wm. Christian, Pat. Cunningham.

Page 486.— ——1753. James Wood, gent., of Frederick, to Thomas Shankland, 400 acres on Muddy Creek granted to James, 12th January, 1746. Teste: John Harrison, Walter Patterson, Wm. Russell, Joseph Rutherford.

Page 490.—John Doughert (signed Jocort) to Alex. Walker, 1753, 94 acres. From Patton, 1751, Craig's Creek at Indian Camp. Teste: John Smith, Adam Lewnis, Richard Borton, Jno. Sproul, Ro. Rennix, Samuel Walker.

Page 493.—21st November, 1753. Thomas Williams to John Mathews, Jr., 65 acres on North Branch James opposite Ann Sally's land. Delivered to John Mathews, son of Richard, 6th March,1773. Teste: John Maxwell, Jno. Sprott, Joshua Mathews.

Page 496.—25th August. Alex. Ritchie, blacksmith, and Mary to Gabriel Jones, of Frederick County, attorney, 1753, 400 acres, James River above Craig's Creek. Purchased of Alex. Douglass, heir-at-law of his brother, Roger Douglass, to whom it was patented. Teste: James Donalson (Donelson).

Page 499.—22d November, 1753. Adam Thompson, planter, and Elizabeth to John Richey, blacksmith, 100 acres in Beverley Manor. Cor. Alex. Richey, Wm. McNabb's land. Teste: Wm. Ackery, Andrew Scott, James Sayers.

Page 502.—21st November, 1753. Wm. Coruthers to John White, 187 acres in Borden's tract. Tract of John Gray, deceased, McCreary's line, McSpeden's line, Nathan People's cor.

Page 505.—21st November, 1753. Same to Nathan Peoples, 187½ acres. Borden's land; James Greenlee's and John Gray's, deceased, line; cor. above, McSpeadin's line; Mathew Lyle's cor.

Page 509.—23d November, 1753. James Patton to Daniel McAnare, 1753, 390 acres on a branch of Woods River; cor. Wm. Syers.

Page 511.—22d November, 1753. Same to John Potts, 124 acres by patent 3d November, 1750. Craig's Creek.

Page 514.—22d November, 1753. Same to Patrick Downey, 1753. As above.

Pabe 517.—22d November, 1753. Same to Henry Holdston, Sr., 1753, 181 acres. As above.

Page 520.— —— 1753. William Kerr to Edward Rutlidge. Flag Spring on Middle River. Teste: John Hind, Andrew Kerr, John Pickens, Wm. Kerr.

Page 522.— —— 1753. John Shield, an orphan child under 21, son and heir of James Shield, deceased, by his guardian and uncle, John Shield, to Robert Robinson. Borden's tract sold by James to Robert Snodon; Beverley Manor line. Robert sold to Robinson. James Shield died April, 1749. Delivered by decree of County Court. James Losk's line, cor. Samuel McCutchan.

Page 525.—Patrick Young to Sarah Young, bond 1753. Condition that be allowed to use and enjoy part of the profits of the mill and appurtenances for her lifetime, which were conveyed to Patrick by James Young. Teste: Wm. Walker and John Low.

Page 527.—Rev. John Craig and Isabella Hellena to John Crawford, 1753, Craig's Creek. Teste: Thomas Gordon and Wm. Basken. Delivered: Wm. Ritchey, 7th April, 1778.

Page 530.—Same to same, 1753. Forks of Craig's Creek and Patterson's Branch.

Page 533.— —— 1753. James Patton to James Gowthrie, Roanoke. Cor. Archibald Graham. Teste: Wm. Carravan and Neal McNeal.

Page 554.— —— 1753. Francis McCown to Robert Hamilton, late of Augusta. Delivered: Jno. Hamilton, 17th October, 1786. Part of 720 acres patented to Francis, 1743, on Tees Creek, cor. Robert Erwin. Delivered to John Hamilton.

Page 557.—Wm. Mills, late of Augusta, 1753, by attorney John Mills, of Lunenburg, to Wm. Graham; patented to William, 1752. Buffalo Creek, a branch of Roanoke.

Page 560.—John Mills and Anne of Lunenburg, to David Robinson. Patented to James Patton and by him deeded to John. Buffalo Creek of Roanoke. Conavan's Creek. Cor. Wm. Graham.

DEED BOOK No. 6.

Page 1.—15th March, 1754. Robert Robinson and Isabella, his wife, of Augusta, to Thomas Berry, of Augusta, two tracts adjoining and joining Beverley Manor and Borden's tract. 1st.—82 acres in Beverley Manor, conveyed by Beverley to Ro. Robinson. Beverley Manor line, cor. James Lusk (Loosk); cor. Patrick Cook, deceased; cor. Burden's tract and Beverley Manor. 2d.—In Borden's land, 218 acres conveyed by Borden to James Shields, cordwainer, and conveyed (vid chancery cause, County Court) by James Shields, guardian of John Shields, son and heir-at-law and orphan child of said James Shields to Ro. Robinson; James Loosk's line; Beverley Manor line, cor. Samuel McCutcheon. Robert Robinson. Isabella (her mark) Robinson. Teste: John Shields, James Welch, Thos Branan.

Page 4.—20th March, 1754. William McPheetters to John McPheeters, 212 acres between North Mountain and Cathey's River. Teste: Jno. Trimble, Jno. Speer, Robert Campbell.

Page 7.—2d February, 1754. Andrew Bird to Moses Bird, on Smith's Creek. Andrew Bird's line; Jno. Phillips' line, 350 acres, part of 400, 50 of which were surveyed for Jacob Rambo by deed. Teste: Abraham Bird. Delivered to Jno. Skean, February, 1758.

Page 10.—2d February, 1754. Andrew Bird to Abraham Bird, 174 acres in Brock's Gap on North Sharrando River, the patent line to the Chimney Rock.

Page 13.— — 1754. Jno. Mills and Ann, of Lunenburg, to Erwin Patterson, 300 acres patented 5th April, 1748, on Buffalo Creek, west side Blue Ridge.

Page 16.—21st March, 1754. James Lusk and Eleanor to James Trotter. Cor. Samuel McCutcheon, Beverley Manor line, conveyed by Borden to James 16th August, 1749.

Page 19.—16th March, 1750. Robert Stapleton and Catherine to Charles Stapleton, 200 acres, part of tract granted to Thos. Holdman by Fairfax 3d February, 1749, and by Holdman to Stapleton. Cor. George Brock and Peter Gartner, Ruddle's line. Robert (his mark) Stapleton. Catherine (her mark) Stapleton.

Page 22.—12th December, 1753. Joshua Hadley and Patience to Thomas Hadley, 400 acres in Fork of James River and Craig's Creek. Teste: Edward McDonald. Delivered to Wm. Preston.

Page 24.—21st March, 1754. William Cleghorn to Mary Chittem, relict of Philip Chittem, deceased, 214 acres on West Branch of Cedar Creek, a branch of James River at a place called Poage Farm. Robert Renix land.

Page 28.—20th March, 1754. Beverley by Lewis and Madison to Robert Wilson, 130 acres in Beverley Manor. Said Wilson's old survey cor. to Thomas Brown's land near Col. James Patton's alias James Carr's line.

Page 32.—10th February, 1754. Col. James Patton to Wm. Englis, 255 acres, part of Patton's patent on Tom's Creek, a branch of New River. Cor. John Draper's land; Lingell's line; Barrier's line.

Page 35.—10th February, 1754. Col. James Patton to John Draper, 315 acres, part of Patton's patent on Tom's Creek, a branch of New River. Cor. Wm. Englis' land; Lingell's line.

Page 38.—9th February, 1744. Same to John Draper and Wm. Engles, 440 acres, part, &c., as above. Cor. to land on which William Engles lives, estate in the Barrens. Cor. Barrier's land.

Page 41.—21st March, 1754. Same to Abraham Smith, 86 acres by patent 3d November, 1750, on Craig's Creek at Mulberry Bottom.

Page 45.—2d February, 1754. Same to Harness Sharp, 320 acres on Tom's Creek as page 35, supra. Cor. George Sharp's land.

Page 48.—21st March, 1754. Same to William Lipperd, 620 acres on Tom's Creek as page 32, supra. Cor. Captain Barrier's land.

Page 51.—2d February, 1754. Same to John Adams, 210 acres on Tom's

Creek as above. Cor. land of Michael Kinder; cor. Price's land, Lorton's line, Jacob Harmon's line.

Page 55.—2d February, 1754. Same to Michael Kinder, 200 acres on Tom's Creek as above. Cor. John Adams, white oak in the Naked Land; cor. Jacob Lingell.

Page 58.—2d January, 1754. Same to Jacob Lorton, 560 acres on Tom's Creek as above, a pine by the Beverdams; cor. Jacob Harmon; cor. Price's land. Teste: Samuel Ross.

Page 61.—10th February, 1754. Same to Jacob Lingell, 280 acres on Tom's Creek as above. Cor. Casper Bonier, Draper's lines.

Page 64.—13th January, 1754. Same to Palzer Smalzer (Smelzer), 440 acres, part of a patent to Patton on Crabb Creek, a branch of New River. Cor. Ebenezer Westcott.

Page 67.—2d February, 1754. Patton to Augustine, Henry and Daniel Price, 1130 acres on Tom's Creek, a branch of New River. Cor. Jacob Lorton, line of John Adams' land.

Page 70.—2d February, 1754. Same to Jacob Harmon, Jr., 625 acres on Tom's Creek as above, estate in the Barrens. Cor. Jacob Lorton, pine by the Beaver Dams.

Page 73.—7th February, 1754. Same to John Cook, 190 acres on Tom's Creek as above. Cor. Wm. Byer's land; cor. Conrad Kinder.

Page 16.—7th February, 1754. Same to William Byers, 160 acres on Tom's Creek. Cor. John Cook; cor. to another tract belonging to Byers: Conrad Kinder's line.

Page 79.—8th March, 1754. Same to Peter Looney, 250 acres patented 3d November, 1750, on head of Meadow Creek, a branch of Craig's Creek.

Page 82.—14th January, 1754. Same to Ebenezer Westcott, 656 acres on Crabb Creek (seep. 64, supra). Cor. Palser Smelser.

Page 85.—2d February, 1754. Same to Martin Loy, 230 acres on Tom's Creek. Cor. George Sharp's land.

Page 88.—11th February, 1754. Same to Conrad Kinder, 290 acres on Tom's Creek. Cor. Michael Kinder; cor. Wm. Byers, John Cook's line; Jacob Lingel's line.

Page 91.—2d February, 1754. Same to George Sharp 285 acres on Tom's Creek, supra. Cor. Martin Loy's land.

Page 94.—10th February, 1754. Same to Casper Barrier, 507 acres on Tom's Creek as above. Cor. Wm. Ingles, Lepard's line; Martin Loy's line.

Page 97.—10th February, 1754. Jacob Harmon to Wm. Byers, 170 acres conveyed to Harmon by Patton 1st February, 1754, on Tom's Creek. Cor. John Adams.

Page 100.—11th January, 1754. Daniel Ratcliff to James Scags, 104 acres patented to Samuel 22d August, 1753, on Meadow Creek of New River.

Page 103.—11th January, 1754. William Pellum to James Scags, 134 acres patented to William 22d August, 1753, on Meadow Creek of New River.

Page 105.—2d February, 1754. John Miller to Wm. Stroup, 124 acres patented 22d August, 1753, on Puck Creek of New River.

Page 108.—13th January, 1754. Peter Shover to John Miller, 37 acres patented 22d August, 1753, on southwest side New River on head of Mill Creek.

Page 110.—2d February, 1754. John Miller to Reuben Ratcliff, 65 acres patented 22d August, 1753, on Little River.

Page 113.—15th January, 1754. Garrett Zinn to Manuel Ekerling, 125 acres, part of 900 acres patented to Garrett 20th June, 1753, on Woods River. Cor. John Miller.

Page 116.—1st day of —— 17—. John Draper to John Die, 275 acres at a place called the hand (?) Draft on the waters of the New River. Cor. James Patton. Recorded 20th March, 1754.

Page 118.—16th January, 1754. Garrett Zinn to John Miller, 380 acres being part of a 900 acre tract patented (see p. 113). On Woods River. Cor. Manuel Ekerling, opposite a long island. Teste: Ebenezer West.

Page 121.—Daniel Stringer and Elizabeth, his wife, 21st November, 1753, to Thomas Gorden, 278 acres. Line of James Wood's land on west side of a branch of Muddy Creek. Daniel (his mark) Stringer. Eliza (her mark) Stringer.

Page 123.—George Wilson to Benjamin Watson, 21st March, 1754, 173 acres conveyed to George by Patton, 8th November, 1751, on the head of Broad Creek in the Forks of James River, adjoining land where Mary Doughert lives. George (his mark) Wilson.

Page 126.—4th January, 1754. John McCoskery, Sr., to Samuel McCoskery, 440 acres conveyed by Borden to McCoskery 22d February, 1749. Cor. Daniel Lyle; John Lowry Sr.'s, line; Moses Trimble's line. Teste: Alex., John and David McCoskery, Francis Beaty, Samuel Huston.

Page 129.—4th January, 1754. John McCoskery, Sr., to David McCoskery, 300 acres conveyed by Borden to John 21st August, 1747. Cor. Wm. Buchanan, Isaac Anderson's line on Back Creek.

Page 132.—20th March, 1754. John Hutcheson and Margaret Hutcheson, his wife, to John Craig, 292 acres in Beverley Manor. Cor. John Searight, stump in a poison field. Rev. Mr. Anderson's line.

Page 133.—21st March, 1754. Francis McBride and Mary McBride, his wife, to Jacob Gum on Lost River of Cacaphore, 330 acres, all rights, Royal Mines excepted and a full third part of all lead, coffee, tinn, coals, iron mines and iron ore that shall be found there on Fairfax's land.

Page 134.—19th August, 1752. John Dunbar, Wm. Miller of Frederick County, 412 acres on Lost River of Cacaphore. Consideration is " good causes and composition to me paid and annual rent hereafter reserved to Lord Fairfax." Same exceptions and provisions as above.

Page 136.—4th January, 1754. Patton to Thomas Luttenton (Littleton), 120 acres, part of tract patented to Patton 3d November, 1750, on South Fork of Roanoke, also West Fork. Cor. to John Brunegar. Teste: Theodosia and Ephraim Vause.

Page 139.—4th January, 1754. Same to John Brinnegar, 80 acres, part of a tract patented to Patton 3d November, 1750. Cor. Thomas Luttenton, crossing West Fork of Roanoke, crossing Roanoke River. Cor. Henry Lidford.

Page 141.—4th January, 1754. Same to Henry Ledford, 75 acres, part of a tract patented to Patton 3d November, 1750, on West Fork of Roanoke. Cor. John Brinnegar.

Page 144.—3d January, 1753. Same to William Ledford, 90 acres patented 3d November, 1750, on West Fork of Roanoke, crossing Bradshaw's Creek.

Page 147.—17th December, 1753. Same to John Stedham, 190 acres by patent 3d November, 1750, east side of the creek. (?) Teste: Jacob Patton, Sarah (her mark) Patton.

Page 150.—18th Deember, 1753. Same to Frederick Hartsough, 130 acres by patent 3d November, 1750, on Craig's Creek, a branch of James River.

Page 152.—17th December, 1753. Same to Mathew Patton, 266 acres by patent 3d November, 1750, on Craig's Creek. Teste: Robert Williams.

Page 155.—20th December, 1753. Same to Charles Nutts, 64 acres by patent 3d November, 1750, in a bent of Craig's Creek. Teste: Jacob and Mathew Patton.

Page 158.—17th December, 1753. Patton to Robert Williams, 275 acres patented 3d November, 1750, on Craig's Creek. Teste: Henry Halstone.

Page 160.—20th December, 1753. Same to Haunce Maurice, 246 acres patented 3d November, 1750, on Craig's Creek.

Page 163.—18th December, 1753. Same to Plackard Scilar, 162 acres patented 3d November, 1750, on Craig's Creek.

Page 166.—20th December, 1753. Same to George Fridley, 100 acres patented as supra, on Craig's Creek.

Page 168.—18th December, 1753. Same to William Plummer, 218 acres patented, supra, on Craig's Creek.

Page 172.—21st March, 1754. Beverley by Lewis and Madison to Geo. Rodgers, 170 acres in Beverley Manor. Cor. Robert Wilson and Robert Sayers; cor. land of David Moore, deceased.

Page 174.—21st March, 1754. Beverley to Robert McClenachan, lot 13 in Town of Staunton containing ½ acre. Livery of seisin.

Page 176.—21st March, 1754. Beverley to John Harman, of Staunton, 91 acres in Beverley Manor in the Plumtree Draft above Robert Poage's, lot No. 6 in Staunton, lot No. 4 of Woodland. Livery of seisin.

Page 179.—23d March, 1754. John McPheeters to Wm. Martin, 198 acres, part of land Jno. now possesses. Cor. John McPheeters in James Young's line; cor. Robert Campbell's land, now James Berry's.

Page 181.— — March, 1753. Jno. Brown, planter, to Haunce Harper, planter, 175 acres on Newfoundland Creek, cor. to land in possession of Haunce Harper, also of Mathew Harper. Margaret, wife of John, releases dower.

Page 182.—20th March, 1754. Frances Beatey to Israel Christian, merchant of Augusta, lot 11 in Beverley Manor in the town commonly called and known by the name of the town of Staunton, conveyed by Lewis & McClenachan on behalf of the County to Thomas Paxton 17th June, 1752 and sold by Paxton to Beaty. Livery of seisin by handful of earth.

Page 185.—2d March, 1754. Patrick Downey (Downing) to William Miller, 155 acres on Craig's Creek, conveyed to Downey by Patton. Teste: David Miller, Wm. Carravin.

Page 188.—16th March, 1754. Beverley to Samuel Downey, 80 acres in Beverley Manor. Cor. Alex. McFeeters, Wm. McNabb's line; cor. said Downey's old survey.

Page 191.—19th March, 1754. Beverley to Robert Finley, of Town of Staunton, merchant, 155 acres on a chestnut ridge in Beverley Manor. Cor. Wm. Preston's land near Staunton.

Page 194.—16th January, 1754. James Brown to Robert Finley, of Town of Staunton, merchant, lease formerly made to Brown by Beverley, adjoining the widow Preston's land. Cor. said Brown and James Miller.

Page 197.—21st March, 1754. Robert Moffet, planter, to Jacob van Lear, farmer, 490 acres in Beverley Manor. Cor. to James Patton, Co. Lieut., his mill tract on Christian's Creek; Wm. Long's line; James Bell's line; Wm. Christian's line; John Christian's line. Teste: James Price.

Page 198.—25th March, 1754. Israel Christian and Patrick Clinch, breeches maker. Indenture of apprenticeship 3 years and 6 months.

Page 200.—26th March, 1754. James Miller and Catherine, his wife, to Israel Christian, 300 acres in Beverley Manor, conveyed by Beverley to Miller — May, 1751. Col. Beverley's Mill Place line.

Page 202.—27th March, 1754. James Campbell to William Lusk, 267 acres on Roanoke at Arthur Bottom. Mortgage.

Page 205.—15th May, 1754. George Anderson and Elizabeth, his wife, to Robert McKitrick, 200 acres on Jennings Branch of Cathey's River, patented to George 25th November, 1743. Elizabeth (X) Anderson.

Page 207.—3d May, 1754. Cornelius Ruddle and Ingabo, his wife, to James Claypool. On Beach's Creek patented to Wm. Rutledge 20th August, 1754, and conveyed by Rutledge to Ruddle, 237 acres. Cornelius Ruddle. Ingebo Ruddle.

Page 210.—14th May, 1754. John Wilkins, of Province of Carolina, to Wm. Snoden, 200 acres, part of 1265 acres. Acknowledged in open court.

Page 212.—15th May, 1754. Jacob Gray to Edward Tarr, 270 acres in Borden's tract and conveyed to Gray by Borden — 1754, on Mill Creek. Cor. James McClung, McDean's line; Robert Huston's line, cor. Wm. Lusk.

Page 215.—15th May, 1754. Beverley to Robert Gibson, 370 acres in Beverley Manor. Cor. George Caldwell; cor. Wm. Henderson.

Page 218.—15th May, 1754. Beverley to Thomas Thompson, 230 acres in Beverley Manor, cor. to tract surveyed for Robert Caldwell, line of Samuel McCune's new survey; Robert Moody's line, north side of the Indian Road.

Page 223.—15th May, 1754. Beverley to Samuel McCune, 104 acres in Beverley Manor, cor. McCune' old survey; Hugh McClure's line; line of Thos. Thompson's survey.

Page 227.—15th May, 1754. Beverley to Joseph Vachub, 378 acres in Calfpasture, on the head of Meeting Branch, cor. to meeting house land; Thomas Smith's land; William McCutcheon's land.

Page 230.—14th May, 1754. Nicholas Null and Margaret, his wife, to John Craig, 415 acres on Cub Run, a branch of Shanando, part of Stover's large tract of 5,000 acres, cor. William Pierce and Henry Dooley; line of Nicholas Null's land; line of Stover's 5,000 acre tract.

Page 233.—10th May, 1754. Humphrey Baker to John Bingamon, Sr., 100 acres conveyed by Col. Jno. Buchanan, 18th May, 1750, on north side Wood's River. To lie for further proof.

Page 235.—16th May, 1754. James McCarroll to Valentine Pence, 275 acres by patent 5th July, 1751, on a branch of North River of Shanando. Cor. David Lojo.

Page 238.—15th May, 1754. Beverley to Wm. Scott, 125 acres in Beverley Manor. Cor. Ro. Coningham, John Black's line.

Page 242.—14th May, 1754. Beverley to Wm. Ramsey, 582 acres in Calf Pasture on Little River. Cor. Alex Dunlap.

Page 244.—10th April, 1754. Borden's executors to John Paul, 400 acres in Borden's tract. Cor. to patent line on the northeast end of a hill by a small run that descends from the house where the said John McDowell and Benj. Borden the younger, dwelt at the time of their decease.

Page 249.—15th May, 1754. Same to John Montgomerie, 150 acres in Borden's tract. John Montgomerie's old corner in patent line of Beverley Manor and Borden's tract.

Page 252.—15th May, 1754. Same to Andrew Moore, orphan infant, only son of Samuel Moore, late of Augusta, plantationer, who was one of the sons of Andrew Moore, late of Augusta County, deceased plantationer. by his uncle and guardian David Moore. Contract by Borden to sell a large tract to Jno. McDowell and Jno. sold this 700 acres to Andrew Moore, the Elder. Deed in pursuance of a chancery suit in County Court. Cor. to Wm. Moore, Wm. Lougbridge's line; cor. David Moore; cor. David and Alex. Moore.

Page 256.—15th May, 1754. Same to David Moore, son of Andrew Moore. See above. 200 acres cor. Nathaniel Evans in Borden's patent line; cor. Andrew Moore above; cor. Alex Moore. Delivered to Wm., son of David, 4th January, 1788.

Page 261.—20th April, 1754. Same to Abraham Brown. Benj., in his lifetime convenanted to sell 400 acres to Abraham. 480 acres. cor. John Paxton's old and new survey; cor. Alex. McCorkel; cor. Samuel McClure.

Page 264.— —day, 1754. Same to Robert Reagh, carpenter and joyner Covenant as above. 118 acres on Hay's Creek. Cor. Widow Smiley.

Page 267.—15th May, 1754. Same to Alexander Moore, son of Andrew Moore as above. 250 acres as above. Cor. Wm. Moore, Andrew Moore, David Moore's line; cor. Wm. Loughridge. Delivered: Wm. Moore September, 21, 1798.

Page 271.—15th May, 1754. Same to William Porter, planter, 200 acres in Borden's tract on North Branch of James River, John McKown's line. Delivered to Thos. Hill, January, 1757.

Page 274.—15th May, 1754. Same to Thomas Hill, 50 acres in Borden's tract, cor. to a tract which Thos. Beard purchased of Samuel Donlop; cor. said Thomas Baird and Patrick Hays; cor. said Thos. Hill's old survey. Delivered to Thos. Hill, January, 1757.

Page 277.—25th April, 1754. John Peter Salling and Ann to Sampson Mathews, 180 acres on North Branch, James River; corner Henry Fullers land; corner William Henderson's land. Teste: Henry Fuller.

Page 281.—15th May, 1754. Beverley to Wm. Gay, 410 acres in Calf Pasture on both sides Little River; corner Wm. Gay's land; lines of Rev. Mr. Hindman's land.

Page 285.—15th May, 1754. Same to Samuel Gay, 354 acres in Calf Pasture on Little River; corner Wm. Elliot's land; corner Wm. Gay.

Page 289.—16th May, 1754. Same to John Ward, 246 acres in Calf Pasture on head of Grassey Lick Run; corner Wm. McCutchin's and Johnson's land; Meeting House Run; corner John Johnson.

Page 293.—15th May, 1754. Beverley to John McNutt, £6, 200 acres on north side Christian's Creek in Beverley Manor; Geo. Rutledge's line above mouth John Buchanan's Mill Creek; corner Wm. Marshal on said Mill Creek; James Colewell's line.

Page 295.—15th May, 1754. John Paul to Roger Keys. Benjamin Borden, Sr., had agreed to convey to John McDowell several parcels or tracts of land in Borden's tract to John McDowel and McDowell had covenanted to sell 400 acres to John Paul. Borden and McDowell both died, and Paul brought suit to compel a conveyance, which was decreed, but Benjamin, Jr., died before conveyance; but Archibald Alexander and Magdalen did convey to Paul, 10th April, 1754, now, $12, 400 acres where Benjamin Borden, Jr., and John McDowell lived on a small branch of Mary Creek at a corner in patent line; corner to said John Paul's land; corner to said John Paul and Thomas Paxton, joyner.

Page 300.—17th May, 1754. John (his mark) Justess (Justice) to Michael Harper, £30, 224 acres conveyed to Justice 22d May. 1752, on Newfoundland Creek; corner to a tract in possession of Samuel Delamounthony; corner to land in possession of Carrolile.

Page 304.—2d May, 1754. John Richey, blacksmith, to Adam Thompson, planter, £40, 100 acres in Beverley Manor; corner Alexander Richey's land; Wm. McNabb's line.

Page 307.—16th May, 1754. Adam Thompson, planter, to Samuel Kinkead (Kingkead), £6, 100 acres in Beverley Manor; corner Alexander Richey; Wm. McNabb's line. Delivered to Jno. Buchanan January, 1756.

Page 308.—15th May. 1754. Patrick Campbell, Sr., and Elinor to son John Campbell. Patrick had purchased from Beverley 1,546 acres in Beverley Manor by deed 21st February, 1738. recorded in Orange; conveyance paternal love. good will and affection; 270 acres of the 1,546 acres. corner Patrick Campbell. Jr., in Wm. Thompson's line; Charles Campbell's line.

Page 312.—10th April, 1754. Robert Sayer and Hannah to Geo. Rogers, £9.5.0. 50 acres in Beverley Manor, part of 2 tracts conveyed in fee by Beverley to Joseph Reed and by Joseph Reed to David Sayer and by David to Robert Sayer; corner Ro. Sayer in Wm. Thompson's line; corner in said Roger's old line; Robert Wilson's line.

Page 315.—19th May, 1754. Adam Dickinson to James Boreland, £75, 327 acres. part of a large tract patented to Adam 1st June, 1750, on Jackson's River, west side of River; corner John Bordon (Bardon), the patent line.

Page 318.—19th May, 1754. Adam Dickinson to William Dean, £75, 327 acres, part of 820 acres patented to Adam as above on Jackson River; corner James Boreland on Indian Camp Creek. Teste: Archibald Boreland. Delivered to John Dean, 1765.

Page 321.—18th May, 1754. Adam Dickinson to John Bird, £25, 215 acres, part of above patent; corner Wm. Jackson. Delivered to John Dean June, 1765.

Page 324.—21st August, 1754. Beverley to James Hamilton, £6, 200 acres on Elk Run in Beverley Manor; corner to tract surveyed for David Edmiston, deceased; James Alexander's line. Delivered to James Hamilton 24th July, 1765.

Page 327.—25th April, 1754. Samuel Henderson and Jane, yeoman, to Andrew McClure, yeoman, £116, 265 acres in Beverley Manor, part of 530 acres conveyed by Beverley 21st February, 1738, to George Hutchison, recorded in Orange and 265 acres conveyed by Hutchison to Samuel 13th June, 1746, recorded in Augusta on Long Meadow Run; corner to Alexander Henderson's line; livery of seizin by a branch of a growing white oak and a handful of earth. Delivered to Andrew McClure 18th February, 1757.

Page 329.—29th July, 1754. Timothy Crosthwait, of Parish St. Thomas in County Orange, to Jeremiah Early, in Parish of Bramfield and County of Culpeper, £25, 400 acres on Elk Run of Shanando. Livery of seisin. Teste: Francis Kirtley, Jeremiah Early (Jr.), John Early, Thos. Kirtley, Thos. Stanton. Delivered to Francis Kirkey February, 1755.

Page 331.—21st August, 1754. Joseph Kennedy (his mark), Gent., and Elizabeth, to Samuel Buchanan, James Walker, Robert Reagh, John Logan, Alexander Miller and William Kennedy, trustees appointed and chosen by the Presbyterian Congregation of New Providence in Augusta County for and on behalf of themselves and the rest of the said Congregation and their successors adherents to the Squad of New York of the other part. Consideration: The sincere regard, good will and affectionate love which he beareth unto the said Congregation, and with an eye to encourage the worshipers of the most Blessed and Glorious Trinity, the Father, Son and Holy Spirit, who is God over all, and Blessed forever, Amen; and for and in consideration of the sum of six pence sterling; for public use and benefit of the said Congregation for a Presbyterian Meeting House to worship Almighty God in and for a burying place and graveyard to them and such as shall hereafter joyn with them the said Congregation of New Providence a certain moiety piece or parcel of land whereon the said Congregation hath already began to prepare and build a meeting house containing 3 A., 1 R., 27 P., on west side Moffet's Creek in Borden's tract; said Kennedy's and Francis McCown's line being a line of land now in possession of Andrew Duncan. Delivered to Samuel Buchanan, 21st June, 1758.

Page 335.—21st August, 1754. Joseph Kenedy, Gent., and Elizabeth, to Edward McColgan, cordwinder, £60, 300 acres at Broad Spring in Borden's tract; crossing Broad Spring Run with John Handly's line. Signed without mark (see Deed Book No. 6, page 331). Delivered to Samuel Buchanan, 21st June, 1758.

Page 339.—20th August, 1754. David Kerr and Catherine, plantationer, to Arthur Kennedy, taylor, £57, 168 acres on Joseph Kennedy's Mill Creek, part of 368 acres purchased by David from Kerr; corner to Robt. Gray, who possesses the other part of the tract; McNut's line; corner Francis Beaty. Teste: John Wardlaw, William Gray.

Page 344.—2d August, 1754. James Trimble and Grace, plantationer, to Joseph Kennedy, Gent., £132.10.0, 402 acres which James purchased of Borden, 1742, recorded in Orange on Moffet's Creek; corner John Fulton.

Page 347.—20th August, 1754. James ( ) Roseborough and Margaret to John Buchanan, £63, 240 acres purchased from Wm. Beverley 28th February, 1749, in Beverley Manor, in patent line. Teste: Moses Whiteside.

Page 350.—21st August, 1754. Beverley to Robert Gibson, 190 acres in Beverley Manor on the Back Draft.

Page 354.—4th July, 1754. William Murray, of Rowan County, North

Carolina, to John Pickens, Gent., 5 shillings, lot No. 12 in Staunton. Teste: John Nealy, Jese ( ) Harris, James Huey, Jane ( ) Huey, James Gattire.

Page 357.—21st August, 1754. Alexander (his mark) Brownlee and Sarah to Jno. Trimble, 400 acres by patent, dated 8th November, 1752, on the southermost fork of the North River of Shanando on Stoney Lick Branch, near a Stony Lick.

Page 360.—21st August, 1750. Beverley to Thomas Stewart, 100 acres in Beverley Manor; John Black's line; corner Thomas Stewart's old survey; Col. Patton's line. Delivered to Thos. Stewart, 15th June, 1772.

Page 364.—21st August, 1750. Same to Adam Murray, 200 acres in Beverley Manor, 2 pines on the Barrons; John McClure's line.

Page 369.—21st August, 1754. Beverley to Edward Hall, £4, 125 acres; oaks in Col. Patton's line. Delivered to Benj. Hall, son of Edward Hall, 6th April, 1792.

Page 373.—21st August, 1754. Henry Purkey and Margaret M. to Abraham Eastus, of the County of Carolina of the Colony aforesaid, £100, 150 acres on south of the South Branch of Shanando, a sycamore about half a mile below the plantation whereon Jacob Stoner formerly lived.

Page 376.—19th August, 1754. John Kerr, yeoman, and Margaret (her mark) to John McKee, yeoman (signed Carr), £200, 280 acres conveyed to John Carr by Borden, 8th July, 1743, part of 92,100 acres, on Tees Creek. Teste: Samuel Norwood, James Goodfellow, Wm. Woods. Delivered to James Lockart, 17th May, 1757.

Page 379.—16th July, 1754. Peter Cue (his mark) and Mary Cue, his wife, to Mathias Selzer, of Frederick County, £35, 120 acres on southeast side Shanando River. Delivered to Mathias Selzer, 6th October, 1760.

Page 383.—22d August, 1754. Francis Kirkley (mark R and P) to Henry Null, £55. 345 acres by patent, dated 6th December, 1753, on Naked Creek; corner Charles Crossen. Delivered to N. Null, 10th September, 1755.

Page 385.—21st August, 1754. James Miller, taylor, and Cathorine, to Jones Henderson, farmer, £35, 3 tracts—first containing 112 acres purchased by said Miller of Andrew Mitchell and Mary which was conveyed to Mary before her marriage with Andrew by George Breckenridge and Ann, by the name of Mary Coningham; the second containing 57 acres purchased by James of David Stewart; the third containing 43 acres purchased by James of Beverley. Delivered to George Bigham, March, 1757.

Page 389.—22d August, 1754. Robert Poage and Elizabeth to John Allison, £50, 195 acres on Mill Creek of James River joining Samuel Walker and John Poage; corner Samuel Walker; corner John Poage; Elizabeth Page.

Page 391.—21st August, 1754. Borden's executors to Wm. McClung, £5, 165 acres joining William's old plantation, part of 92,100 acres.; corner said McClung and Andrew Stevenson; Nathaniel Ervin's line.

Page 394.—21st August, 1754. Borden's executors to Samuel Gray, 40 shillings, 66 acres, part of 92,100; William Caruther's and Samuel Gray's old corner; Moses Trimble's line; corner William Caruther's new survey.

Page 397.—21st August, 1754. Same to James McClung, plantationer, £6, 200 acres, part of 92,100; John Mackey's corner on Mill Creek; corner to Ned, the blacksmith; McDean's line. Delivered to Wm. Lusk, June, 1757.

Page 400.—21st August, 1754. Same to Moses Whiteside, £4, 145 acres, part of 92,100; corner Moses Whiteside's old place; Samuel McCoskery's line; John Davison's line. Delivered to Wm. Edmondson, 2d June, 1758.

Page 403.—21st August, 1754. Same to Joseph Lapsley, Gent. Benjamin Borden, Jr., had sold to Joseph in his lifetime one acre adjoining said Lapsley's old survey where he now lives; Joseph Lapsley's and John Paxton's old corner by a branch of Wood's Creek.

Page 406.—21st August, 1754. Same to William Caruthers, £3, 96 acres, part of 92,100; corner Wm. Caruthers and Samuel Gray. Delivered to Wm. Bowyer, May, 1758.

Page 409.—21st August, 1754. Same to William Porter, plantationer, £3, 110 acres, part of 92,100 on west bank of North Branch of James River; corner to said Porter's old survey; John McCown's line; James Mile's line. Delivered to Jno. Mitchell, January, 1758.

Page 413.—21st August, 1754. Same to William Gray, £9, 300 acres, part of 92,100; corner Moses Whiteside's new survey; Moses McClure's line and new survey, adjoining Moses' old land. Delivered to Benjamin Gray, 26th September, 1773.

Page 416.—21st August, 1754. Same to Andrew Hays, £14, 717 acres in three separate surveys, joining the lines of said Andrew's old plantation, part of 92,100 acres. First tract, John Walker's line by north edge of Moffet's Creek; Back Creek to Forks of Walker's Creek; Andrew Hays' old line passing by the dwelling house, grist mill and fulling mill, 307 acres. Second tract, on Hays' Creek; corner to his old survey, 250 acres. Third tract; corner Charles Hays; Andrew Hays' corner; line of Charles Hays' new survey. Delivered to Andrew Hays, March, 1757.

Page 420.—21st August, 1754. Same to Robert Wire (Weir), 240 acres, part of 92,100, both sides of Halfway Creek; corner to Patrick Hays. Delivered to James Telford, October, 1763.

Page 425.—22d August, 1754. James Gatlive to James Nealy, 350 acres by deed from James Patton, 22d November, 1753, on a branch of Roanoke; corner Archibald Graham.

Page 427.—13th February, 1754. Jacob Stover, Jr., of Lunenburg County, son and heir of Jacob Stover, late of Orange County, deceased, to William Russell of Culpeper, Gent., £85, 4,000 acres, the reversion of a patent granted to Jacob, Sr., for 5,000 acres on west side of Blue Ridge of mountains on the waters of the Sherondoe, then Spottsylvania County, now Augusta, dated 15th December, 1733, which descended to Jacob, Jr., son and heir of Jacob, Sr. Teste: Thomas West.

Page 429.—22d August, 1754. Archibald Alexander to John Bowyer, power of attorney to act for Archibald in the sale of the Borden lands.

Page 432.—23d August, 1754. Jacob Stover, Jr., of Lunenburg, and William Russell, of Culpeper, to John Madison, £6, 200 acres of Shanando River, part of 5,000 acres patented to Jacob Stover, Sr.; corner to Francisco's land; line of land formerly belonging to John Bumgardner.

Page 435.—21st March, 1754. Robert Graham to John Graham, £20, 307 acres on Little River in the Calf Pasture, part of 600 conveyed by Beverley to Robert.

Page 438.—9th August, 1754. James Patton to James Willey, £87, 2,050 acres on a branch of Woods River called Criple Creek. Teste: Alexander Noble, William and Patrick Callhoun.

Page 442.—6th August, 1754. Robert McForland to John Downing, £20.14.0, 248 acres on Stoney Fork of Re(e)d Creek. Teste: Abraham Dunckleberry, Nathaniel Wilshire.

Page 444.—Joseph Lane to John Mountgomerie, mortgage, £30, 200 acres on Roanoke whereon he now dwells, for term of 500 years for one peffer corn on feast of St. Michael, dated 5th July, 1754.

Page 447.—21st November, 1754. Robert Poage and Elizabeth to John Poage, £25, 300 acres on Mill Creek of James River; corner John Mathews; corner Joseph Walker.

Page 450.—20th November, 1754. Samuel Lusk, farmer, and Agness, to Alexander Thompson, taylor, £55.10.0, 202 acres in Beverley Manor; Thomas Shields' corner in James Patten's line; Andrew Alexander's line; corner Rob. Christian. Delivered to Mat. Thompson, May, 1761.

Page 453.—20th November, 1754. Wm. Bell, Jr., and David Bell, to Ro. Patrick, £30, 283 acres, part of a tract conveyed by Samuel Gay to William and David, 16th February, 1747, in Beverley Manor; corner said Patrick; corner Samuel Givens, Finley's land; corner John Ramsey; corner Black's land. Teste: William and Zachariah Bell.

Page 455.—5th September, 1754. Commission to take privy examination of Lettice wife of William Cleghorn, as to her release of dower in a tract conveyed by William to Mary Chittam on 20th March, 1754. Executed 12th November, 1754.

Page 457.—1st November, 1754. Abraham Estis, of Carroline County, to John Madison, £1.1.6, 2 acres lying between the main road and Madison's land.

Page 458.—1st November, 1754. William Johnston and Ann to Zachariah Smith, £5, 160 acres in Beverley Manor; Alexander Henderson's line; oaks in the Barrens.

Page 462.—16th November, 1754. Col. James Patton to Henry Holston, £7.6.0, 146 acres by patent, dated 3d November, 1750, on Craig's Creek; sycamore in the fork of John's Creek. Teste: Thos. Cobune, Henry Holston, Jr.

Page 465.—18th November, 1754. Col. James Patton to Alexander Wright, merchant, £5, 35 acres by patent 3d November, 1750; corner Peter Kinder on west side Roanoke.

Page 468.—17th October, 1754. John Kinkead, Clerk, of the County of Chester in Pennsylvania, to John Kinkead, weaver, of Augusta County, £54, 530 acres, part of 1,061 acres conveyed to John Kinkead, clerk, by James Patton and John Lewis, 17th July, 1745, recorded in Orange on Calf Pasture; corner William Preston's land. Teste: John Kinkead. Delivered: Thos. Kinkead, August, 1770.

Page 471.—8th October, 1754. Henry Holston to John Lowry, £———, 181 acres conveyed to Henry by Col. James Patton, 22d November, 1753, on Craig's Creek; Henry (his mark) Holston. Teste: Thos. Weems, Mary Preston.

Page 474.—18th September, 1754. Daniel (his mark) Luney (Looney) to Abraham Looney, £100, 180 acres by patent, 20th August, 1748, on the

Long Run, a branch of James River; corner Robert Looney, Sr. Teste: Wm. Harbison. Delivered to Abraham, August, 1762.

Page 477.—26th September, 1754. James Davise to William Preston, £215, 626 acres by deed from Benjamin Borden, Jr., 28th November, 1750, on Catawbo Creek of James River. Teste: James Donelson and Thos. Lloyd.

Page 480.—8th October, 1754. John Sprout to John Bowen, £———, 320 acres by deed from Col. Patton, 28th November, 1751, on Broad Spring, a branch of James River. Signed John Sprott.

Page 483.—9th October, 1754. Erick Bright to Joseph McDonald, £45, 207 acres by deed from Col. Patton, 20th March, 1753, on North Fork of Goose Creek; corner George Pearis; corner Elijah Isaac. Signed Earick Bright.

Page 487.—22d November, 1754. Sampson Mathews, farmer, to John Mathews, Jr., farmer, £5, 180 acres on North Branch of James; corner Henry Fuller; corner Wm. Henderson; conveyed to Sampson in May, 1754, by John Peter Salling. Delivered: James Lockhart, June, 1757.

Page 488.—22d August, 1754. Alexander Wright, merchant, to John Madison, £9, paid by Mary McDonald, to the use of Mary McDonald, lot in Staunton, No. 12, whereon Mary now lives, and also lot No. 5, containing 50 acres, also in possession of Mary.

Page 491.—20th April, 1754. Robt. Breckinridge and Mary to David Stewart and Robt. McClenachan, £9, 300 acres by patent to Robt. Breckinridge, 6th February, 1754; corner to a survey by James Bartone in Forks of Shanando, near Peaked Mountain.

Page 493.—9th October, 1754. James Brown, of Staunton, to Alexander Wright, of Staunton. Whereas Beverley by &c., 28th February, 1750, demised to James, 260 acres, part of mill tract for 61 years, conveys for 57 years and 6 months; £20, 173 acres, part of 260; Beverley's line; James Miller's line; corner to part leased to Robert Finley. Teste: Newman McGonegal.

Page 495.—7th March, 1755. Hugh (his mark) Young, plantationer, to John Young, son of Hugh. Consideration, paternal love, 250 acres in Beverley Manor, part of land on which Hugh now lives on Back Creek; corner to Robt. Young on Back Creek; corner both of Hugh's old surveys; Wm. McClintock's line; corner Capt. Patrick Mortin's line. Teste: John and Samuel Young. Livery of seisin before Hugh (his mark) Young. Delivered: Hugh Young, May, 1759. Livery of seisin signed by Robt. Young.

Page 497.—15th March, 1755. Robert Young, plantationer, to John Young, plantationer, £40, 234 acres in Beverley Manor purchased by Robert of Beverley, 27th February, 1749, on Back Creek; corner Hugh Young; John Trimble's corner; corner Wm. McFeeters; James Young's corner. Delivered: James Young, March, 1758.

Page 499.—18th March, 1755. Robert Young, plantationer, to James Young, his son, paternal regard and affectionate love, £25, paid by Samuel Young, brother said James Young, 150 acres in Beverley Manor, part of land where Robert now dwells, and part of 550 acres conveyed to Robert by Beverley; corner Samuel Young; Wm. McClintock's line. Livery, &c., by branches of a white oak and hicory. Teste: John Sims, &c. Delivered: James Young, March, 1758.

Page 501.—17th March, 1755. Robert Young, plantationer, to Samuel Young, his son. Same consideration as above. £30, 295 acres in Beverley Manor, part of 550 acres as above. Beginning at 2 oaks above the bridge on east side of Meadow; Robert Young, Jr.'s, corner; Maj. Brown's old line. Delivered: James Young, 1758.

Page 503.—18th March, 1755. Robert Young Sr., plantationer, to Robert Young, Jr., son of Robert, Sr., affection and £25 paid by John Young. brother of Robert, Jr.; 105 acres in Beverley Manor, part of where Robert, Sr., dwells, and part of 550 acres; Wm. McClintock's line; corner James Young's part; Samuel Young's line. Livery by a key in door of mansion house. Delivered: James Young.

Page 506.—18th March, 1755. Robert Young, plantationer, to William, Hugh and Joseph Young, his sons, for their better preferment and advancement. Conveys his personal estate. Duncan McFarland, weaver; Thomas Bradshaw, weaver; (Robert called distiller). Teste: Francis Dame. Delivered: James Young.

Page 507,—13th March, 1755. Alexander Blair to James Blair, his son, 144 acres on Middle River, crossing the Bould Hill. Signed Alexander Blear. Delivered: James Blair, April, 1763.

Page 508.—12th March, 1755. John McLeary, yeoman, to James McLeary, his son, plantationer, love and affection and £10; 200 acres, part of 420 acres, conveyed by Beverley, 4th February, 1748, in Beverley Manor; Thos. Kirkpatrick's line, a head branch of Middle River of Shanandoe; James Clerk's line. Livery, &c., John McLeary. Delivered: James McLeary, November, 1758.

Page 512.—19th March, 1755. James Trotter and Mary to Hugh Campbell, £50, 268 acres on Naked Creek; Michael Dickey's line; conveyed to Trotter by James Wood, 18th August, 1749.

Page 515.—19th March, 1755. Robert Poage and Elizabeth to John Mathews, Gent., £30, 194 acres on Mill Creek joining John Poage. Delivered: John Mathews, son of Richard, March 6, 1773.

Page 516.—17th March, 1755. Wm. McPhatters (McFeeters), Sr., to William, Jr., his son, natural love and affection, 322 acres where William, Sr., now lives, in Beverley Manor; John Trimble's corner; corner Wm. Vance, now John McPheeters.

Page 518.—10th February, 1755. John Buchanan, Jr., weaver, to James McCown, £95, 370 acres in Borden's tract, conveyed by Borden to Buchanan by deed recorded; James Buchanan's corner, crossing Walker's Creek; John Walker's line. Livery by key of mansion house.

Page 521.—21st December, 1754. John Peter Salling to Joseph Benton and Mary Elizabeth, his wife, of Albemarle County, £100, 200 acres on North Branch of James; Henry Fooler's corner. Teste: Wm. Burt, Wm. Green ( ), Joseph ( ) Ryan, Sarah C. Ryan.

Page 523.—12th March, 1755. Borden's executors to John Logan, £5.15.0, 195 acres, part of 92,100; Thos. Baird's line; John Logan's old survey; McNut's line; Wm. Berry's line; corner to land Joseph Kendy purchased of James Trimble; John Fulton's line.

Page 526.—19th March, 1755. John Logan, farmer, to Alexander Logan, his son, paternal love, &c., and £10, 237 acres in Borden's tract on Capt. Joseph Kennedy's Mill Creek of James River; corner McNutt's land;

Wm. Berry's line; corner Capt. Joseph Kennedy; Thomas Baird's corner. Livery, &c. Delivered: Alexander McNut, September, 1765.

Page 528.—15th March, 1755. Borden's executors to John Wallace, plantationer, 895 acres in two tracts, part of 92,100, 645 acres on Walker's Creek; corner Wm. Reagh; corner Archibald Reagh, 250 acres adjoining above, including the Pond Spring, the Barrons. Delivered: John Buchanan, weaver, 19th September, 1755.

Page 531.—17th March, 1755. Same to Alexander Walker, wheelwright, 170 acres on Walker's Creek; corner James Robinson. Delivered: Andrew Hays, March, 1757.

Page 535.—21st Setember, 1754. Same to John Walker. Sr., plantationer, 190 acres, part of 92,100, on Walker's Creek; corner Alexander Walker, plantationer; corner James Moore. Delivered: Andrew Hays, March, 1757.

Page 538.—18th March, 1755. John Wallace, plantationer, to James Rutherford, plantationer, £20, 322½ acres of Borden's tract on Walker's Creek; corner Wm. Reagh; Archibald Reagh's corner. Livery, &c. Delivered: John Buchanan, weaver, September, 1755.

Page 541.—26th September, 1754. Adam Dickinson and Catherine to Alexander Craighead, clerk, £150, 310 acres in Cowpasture, part of land where Adam now lives.

Page 544.—15th February, 1755. Andrew Leeper and Jane to Gawin Leeper, £120, 299 in Beverley Manor, part of 526 acres sold by Beverley to James Leeper and by James to Andrew; corner Nicholas Leeper.

Page 547.—19th March, 1755. Robert Bratton to Wm. Smith. Consideration, 361 acres, made over to Ro. by Beverley by deed, dated herewith, and 24 shillings; 400 acres granted by Beverley to Robert, 14th October, 1748, recorded in secretary's office, foot of the Brown hill in Wm. McCutchen's land.

Page 549.—18th March, 1755. Joseph Kennedy to his son Wm. Kennedy, 402 acres purchased by Joseph from James Trimble, farmer, and by James from Borden on Moffett's Creek in Borden's tract; corner John Fulton; corner Alexander Logan; corner Wm. Berry.

Page 552.—19th March, 1755. Beverley to Robert Bratton, £10.16.0, 361 acres on Little River of Calf Pasture called Hall's Branch.

DEED BOOK No. 7.

Page 2.—August, 1754. William Bell, Jr., and David Bell to Saml. Givens, £80, 283 acres conveyed to grantors by Saml. Gay, 16th February, 1747, in Beverley Manor; corner Ro. Patrick; corner Finla.

Page 3.—1st November, 1754. John Paunton and Charles McNally, wheelwright. John apprentices himself to Charles, to learn wheelwright

Page 6.—2d January, 1755. John Love and Johanna, to Philip Arrantrout, £18, 175 acres bought by Love from James Downing, who patented it 5th February, 1753, corner said Love's other patent near John Davis's land on the head waters of Smith Creek. Teste: Frederick Anantrout. John (his mark) Love. Johanna (her mark) Love.

Page 9.—18th March, 1755. Joseph Kennedy and Elizabeth, to Mathew Buchanan, of the Province of Pennsylvania, £80; 711 acres in Borden's tract; Saml. Huston's line; Greenlee's line. Delivered: Saml. Buchanan, June, 1758. Teste: Alexander Patton, Elizabeth Kennedy.

Page 11.—9th October, 1754. James Brown and Agnes, of Staunton, to

John Madison, John Brown and John Lewis, £60, Lot No. 3 and Lot 8 of woodland. Ann (her mark) Brown. William Lusk, Newman McGouneig. Livery by a latchet of the door of the house.

Page 13.—20th March, 1755. John Madison, John Brown and John Lewis to Joseph Mays. Conveyances above.

Page 16.—15th March, 1755. John Wilson, Gent., to James McClery, James Mitchell, James McCutcheon, Robert Wilson, William Thompson, Alexander McPheeters, Saml. McCutchon, trustees chosen by the Presbyterian Congregation of the North Mountain Meeting House. £12, 10, 6; 306½ acres in Beverley Manor being the tract of land whereon the house now stands commonly known by the name of North Mountain Meeting House; Cap. James Lockhart's line; for the use of the members of said congregation adhering and continuing to adhere to the Synod of Philadelphia as it stands now constituted provided that if any member or members of the said Congregation who have paid any of the purchase money of said land shall or do change or turn to any other denomination or Religion, then their part of said money be repaid them and they to have no further demands on the same. Provided that surviving trustees may elect trustees to fill vacancies, and sell the land except 20 acres to be kept for the church and graveyard.

Page 20.—20th March, 1755. John Hutcheson, farmer, and Mary, to Saml. Henderson, £5; 277 acres on Christian's Creek, part of a tract surveyed for George Hutcheson.

Page 23.—1st February, 1755. Henry (his mark) Dooley and Martha (her mark) Dooley, his wife, to Frederick Hermontrout, £20; 54 acres on Cubb Run. Teste:Phillip Hermontrout.

Page 25.—1st February, 1755. Abraham Hite, of Hamshire Co., and Parish, to Charles Dick and Fielding Lewis, of Fredericksburg, £400, 1,200 acres on Linville's Creek, conveyed to Abraham by McCoy, Duff, Hite and Green, recorded in Orange. Mortgage to secure £400.

Page 28.—20th March, 1755. Thomas Lewis and John Madison for Beverley to Alexander Wright, £10, 4 lots in Staunton numbered 14, 15, 20, 21.

Page 31.—10th October, 1754. John Pickens and Ellioner, to Wm. Williams, £20, lot 12 in Staunton fronting the New Court House Street on South. Teste: Wm. Bell, Wm. (his mark) Baskins, Saml. Bell, William Bell.

Page 35.—9th October, 1754. John Pickins and Elioner, to Wm. Bell, one shilling, 300 acres on Christian's Creek, bought by John from Beverley; corner Carr's land; fork of Long Meadow Run and Christian's Creek, supposed to be a corner of the patent line thence with patent line due south; corner Geo. Rogers; widow Baskins's line. Teste: Wm. Baskins (his mark).

Page 38.—21st March, 1755. Robert Poage and Elizabeth (her mark), to James Gilmore, £30, 285 acres in Fork of James on head of Mill Creek; corner Joseph Walker; corner Mary Doughert. Delivered to James Gilmore, November, 1766.

Page 41.—22d March, 1755. George Robinson to Joseph McDonald, £245 acres, part of 2 tracts belonging to George, on a branch of Buffalo Creek, a branch of Roanoak; Renfroe's lines; Tobias Smith's line.

Page 46.——— day, ———. 1754. Beverley to Joseph Bell, £8, 8, 280 acres in Beverley Manor; corner James Hamilton's land; the Long Meadow lines; said Bell's old line.

Page 50.—22d March, 1755. John Buchanan, of Beverley Manor, and Margret, to Charles Campbell, of said Manor, £50, 1,000 acres on the Indian Creek, Margret (her mark) B———.

Page 54.—22d March, 1755. John Buchanan, yeoman, and Margret, of Beverley Manor, to John Buchanan, gentleman, of Reed Creek, £60, 684 acres by patent, 22d August, 1753, on Chestnut Creek, a branch of New River on So. side thereof.

Page 57.—22d March, 1755. Same to same, £10, 10, 2, 130 acres on the waters of Mississippi on a branch called Indian River, opposite a small island, a great sink hole. Sent to Col. Wm. Preston, May, 1771.

Page 61.—20th March, 1755. Same to same, £60, 880 acres by patent, 22d August, 1753, on Indian River.

Page 63.—24th ———, 1755. Daniel McBride puts himself apprentice and servant to John Roseman, cordwainer or shoemaker, for 2 years. Teste: Ro. Armstrong (mark), and James Goodly.

Page 64.—24th March, 1755. John Culbert, of Co. Donegal, Ireland, to his trusty and well beloved friend, Andrew Erwin, power attorney to sue for debts ,especially to recover from James Lockhart, executor of Wm. Buchanan, £139, Cur. Money Pennsylvania. Teste: Thomas Lloyd.

Page 65.—8th May, 1755. Borden's executors to William Loughridge (Lockridge), £4.2.4, 250 acres, part of 92,100 on Halfway Creek; corner Thomas Hill; said Wm. Loughridge's corner; Moore's corner; David Moore's corner, east side of the Great Road in the patent line; corner Robt Weir.

Page 68.—8th May, 1755. Same to Andrew Steel, plantationer, 40 acres adjoining said Andrew Steel; corner John Lowry's new survey; Andrew Steel's old line; corner survey made for Robert Henry. Delivered to James McDowell, August, 1758.

Page 72.—21st May, 1755. John ( ) Johnston and Mary (mark) to Archibald Elliott, £70, 213 acres on Little River in Calfpasture. Teste: Charles Knight, Wm. Elliot. Delivered: Benjamin Estill, August, 1762.

Page 75.—21st May, 1755. Ephraim Love to Wm. Hopkin, £50, 258 acres, part of 307 acres patented to Jacob Dye, 21st June, 1748, and sold by Dye to Love; corner said Love. Delivered: Thomas Poage, April, 1780.

Page 79.—19th May, 1755. John Vance, of Bedford County, to Robert Alleson, £20, 192 acres on North Fork Reed Creek patented to said John Vance. Teste: Wm. Scott, Geo. Wilson, Peter Scott.

Page 82.—21st May, 1755. George Stevenson and Rebecca (mark), his wife, to Andrew Brown, £35, 220 acres conveyed to George from James Patton, 8th December, 1752, on Poage's Draft of James River; line of Borden's patent line.

Page 85.—21st May, 1755. Thomas McMurray to Rev. John Brown, 250 acres conveyed to Thomas by Borden, 27th February, 1750; corner John Patton in Borden's tract; corner George Stevenson in James Greenlee's line. Teste: George Stinson. Delivered: Thos. Bowyer, December, 1756.

Page 87.—3d May, 1755. Arthur Kennedy and Jane, taylor, to Thomas Berry, plantationer, £56.12.6, 168 acres purchased by Arthur from David Kerr on Capt. Joseph Kennedy's Mill Creek, part of Borden's tract; corner

Robert Gray's line; McNut's new line; corner Francis Beatey. Jeane (mark) Kennedy. Livery by a rail in the fence.

Page 91.—10th April, 1755. Jacob Green, farmer, and Sarah ( ) Green to Thomas Gorden, farmer, £22, 165 acres on head springs of Linwell's Mill Cerek. Teste: Ephraim Love, Thomas Shanklan, Isaiah Shipman. "Sent by P. Grant, August, 1760."

Page 93.—1st April, 1755. Jacob Lockhart, plantationer, to James Clerk, wheelwright, £17, 436 acres on which Jacob now lives in Beverley Manor, on Back Creek; said James Clerk's line; corner Glebe land; James Berry's line; James Young's line. Mortgage. Teste: James Goodly, John Jones, William Clerk. Delivered: John Clerk, March, 1758.

Page 97.—3d May, 1755. Ephraim McDowell to James McDowell, £5, 300 acres; John McDowell's line, part of Borden's 92,100. Ephraim ( ) McDowell. Teste: John Bowyer, Samuel McDowell, Magdalen Bowyer.

Page 100.—17th May, 1755. James McDowell, farmer, to John Bowyer, £175, 300 acres above. Delivered: J. Bowyer, May, 1761.

Page 102.—20th May, 1755. Borden's executors (Magdalen Bowyer, relict and administratrix of John McDowell, late of Orange County, and mother of Samuel McDowell, an orphan under 21 years, being eldest son and heir-at-law of said John McDowell to said Samuel McDowell under the tuition of his guardian, Richard Woods, Gent.). Benjamin, Sr., had agreed to sell in his lifetime to Jno. McDowell. John entered the land under the agreement. John was killed by Indians. John had had the land surveyed by. Borden's surveyor, John Hart; contained 1,359 acres; of this, John McDowell had covenanted to sell to John Paul 400 acres, whereupon Paul and others brought suit, vs. Samuel, for title. Decree, 22d August, 1752. Conveys all residue of the 1,359 acres whereon John lived; Roger Key's land; John Lyle's line; Mathew Lyle's corner, 959 acres. Delivered: Samuel McDowell, March, 1764.

Page 109.—21st May, 1755. John Smith and Rebecca (mark) to Nicholas Havener, £107.10.0, 300 acres conveyed to John by Robert Green, of Orange, 5th November, 1747, on southermost branch of South Branch of Potomac; corner to tract surveyed for Mathew Patton. Delivered to Nicholas Havener, 1765.

Page 112.—21st May, 1755. John Patton, Jr., to Jacob Sybert, 210 acres conveyed by Ro. Green to John Patton, 5th November, 17xlii (1752?), recorded in Augusta on same stream as above; corner to tract sold to Roger Dyer. Teste: Thomas Fulton, John Mills.

Page 114.—13th March, 1755. John White, yeoman, to Wm. Caruthers, yeoman, 10 acres adjoining said Wm. Caruthers in Borden's land; corner John White's little survey. Teste: Moses Whiteside, Jacob Gray. Livery by branches of an oak and hiccory.

Page 117.—12th March, 1755. Wm. Caruthers, yeoman, to Jno. White, yeoman, 20 shillings. 10 acres in Borden's tract as above. Livery as above.

Page 120.—20th May, 1755. Wm. Beard and Mary (signature) Beard to Robert Bellsher, £30. 220 acres on the Island Draft of North River, Shanando, by patent, 10th February, 1748. Mary (signature) Beard. Teste: Samuel Lockhart and James and Edward Beard.

Page 123.—21st May, 1755. Joseph Bell and Margret, to Zachariah Bell, £20, 10, 238 acres on head of Elk Run in Beverley Manor, part of Joseph's two surveys, Andrew McClure's line, the Barrons. Delivered: Z. Bell, May, 1762.

Page 127.—20th May, 1755. Beverley to John Kirkpatrick, £3, 200 acres in Beverley Manor; Thomas Kirkpatrick's old line by the Back Creek; Saml. Sprouls line.

Page 132.—— —— day, ———, 1755. Same to David Doak, £3, 100 acres in Beverley Manor; corner said Doak's old survey. Delivered: Robert Doak, March, 1768.

Page 135.—21st May, 1755. John Kirkpatrick to John Parry (Peery), plantationer, £3, 100 acres in Beverley Manor on Back Creek in Thos. Kirkpatrick's old line (see p. 127, supra). Delivered: Jno. Kilpatrick, 1760.

Lot 139.—21st May, 1755. John Campbell and Elizabeth (her mark) Campbell to Joseph Coulton, Gent, £130, 400 acres on Cathey's River on the Sinking Spring Branch at the head of Little's Run (?), patented to said John, 12th January, 1742. Teste: Joseph Hanna.

Page 141.—22d May, 1755. Robert ( ) Allen to Robert Beatton, £41, 4, conveys 15 head black cattle and other cattle and personal property. Teste: Jno. Semple.

Page 142.—22d May, 1755. Thomas Gorden and Sarah, to Rev. Jno. Craig, £125, 265 acres in Beverley Manor on So. Side Lewis Creek; Robert King's line; John Smith's corner. Delivered: George Craig, 6th March, 1788.

Page 146.—22d May, 1753. Saml. Lockhart and Catherine, to Edwd. Beard, £60, 179 acres patented 20th August, 1747, on No. Riv. Shanandoe; Alexander Thompson's land. Teste: Robt. Hook, Robt. Ralstone.

Page 147.—18th April, 1755. Humphrey Madison to John Madison, £82, conveys two bay mares that run at the Falling Spring, one bay mare purchased at sale of Moffett's estate, and 2 colts that run at George Moffett's, 1 bay mare purchased of James Means, one mare purchased of Joseph England, and other various personal property; mortgage. Teste: Francis Tyler.

Page 150.—22d May, 1755. John Patton, Sr., to Jno. Dunkle and Ludwick Waggoner, £100, 453 acres granted to Patton by Ro. Green, 5th November, 1748, west side of said (?) river; corner tract sold to Wm. Stephenson. Delivered to grantees, June, 1765.

Page 153.—7th March, 1755. Joseph Bell to William and David Bell, £20, 108 acres on Elk River in Beverley Manor; corner Zachry Bell; Hamilton's line

Page 156.—28th May, 1755. William McCutchen to Thos. Meek, plantationer, £40, 310 acres on Little River in Calf Pasture, part of William's 895 acre tract; corner Ro. McCutchon. Teste: David and Walter Coningham.

Page 160.—20th August, 1755. Thomas Watterson and Mary (her mark), to Saml. Black, £25, 200 acres, part of two joining surveys, viz., 1st, 185 acres granted to Thos. by patent, 12th January, 1746; 2d, another survey, etc., on Naked Creek; James McConnell's line. Teste: John Henderson and Jno. Anderson.

Page 162.—5th April, 1755. Jeremiah Early, of Culpeper, to Francis Kirtley, Jr., £100, 200 acres, part of 400 acres patented to Ro. Martin, 20th September, 1745, on Jilgo run, Elk Run; Livery, etc. Teste: Francis Kirtley, Sr., Jeremiah Earley, Jr., Wm. and Thos. Kirtley, Jno. Earley and Thos. Staunton.

Page 165.—3d June, 1755. Saml. Wilson, plantationer, to Robt. Wilson, farmer, £55, 461 acres in Beverley Manor, part of 761 acres granted by Beverley to Geo. and Rob. Breckinridge, 26th November, 1742, and said 461 acres were sold by Geo. and Ro. to Saml., 8th February, 1745; corner David Doak.

Page 168.—20th August, 1755. Saml. Lockhart and Catherine, to Edward Beard, £ 50, 200 acres on No. Riv. Shanandoe, part of 400 acre granted by patent to Saml., 10th April, 1751; corner said Edward's land.

Page 171.—12th August, 1753. James Wood and Mary, of Frederick, to Ro. Rollstone, £64, 10, 350 acres on Muddy Creek patented to James, 12th January, 1746. Teste: David Ralston, Arthur, army trader.

Page 174.—20th August, 1755. Robt. Rallstone and Martha (her mark) to Wm. Castleberry, £110, 350 acres on Muddy Creek. Teste: Ephraim Love and Arthur, army trader. Delivered: Grantee, March, 1757.

Page 178.—20th August, 1753. Alexander Brownlee ( ) and Sarah ( ), to John Cozbey, £14, 5, 400 acres patented to Alexander, 20th June, 1749, on No. Side Southermost Branch of No. River of Shanando. Teste: John Brownlee, Pat. Campbell, Mathew Thompson.

Page 180.—21st July, 1755. James Willey, Gent., and Martha (her mark), to Alexander Noble, Gent, £47, 1,132 acres. Teste: James Maley.

Page 183.—24th January, 1755. Robert Ewing and Mary, of Lunenburg County, to Benj. Starrat, £38, 10, 160 acres on Glade Creek, of Roanoke, patented to Robert, 15th December, 1749. Teste: James Callhoun, Hugh and Pat. Callhoun, Jos. Long, Wm. Sayers.

Page 185.—Commission to Zachary Isbell, Saml. Horstone and Richard Calloway, from Bedford Co. Ct. to take acknowledgement of Mary as to above; returned 26th May, 1755.

Page 186.—1st July, 1755. Robert Finley, of Staunton, to Alexander Wright, of Staunton, by virtue of a lease to him by James Brown, conveys 6 acres of meadow adjoining widow Preston, Alexander Wright, and Ro. Finley's woodland, for 7 years. Teste: Ro. Brown, Patrick ( ) McCluskey.

Page 190.—28th June, 1755. Francis Beatey, surveyor, to Jno. Teat, plantationer, £25. 160 acres in Beverley Manor on Beverley Manor and Borden's lines, cor. survey for James Lockhart, gent., being the place known as Beatey's well place. Teste: David Hay, Jno. and Pat. Campbell, Thos. Teat.

Page 192.—20th August, 1755. James Berry to George Beery, £53, 149 acres joining the Glebe land in Beverley Manor, cor. Wm. Martin's line, crossing Middle Branch of Shanando to James Young's corner, and with his line to between a white oak and a black oak saplin, So. 30°, w. 32 poles to a post, corner to a graveyard. Teste: James Gillmor, James Bower (Bouu?).

Page 195.—23d September. 1755. John Hopes and Mary ( ), of Frederick County, to Ann and Richard Vare, £45, 200 acres on Naked Creek patented to John Fowler and conveyed by Fowler to Hopes 27th May, 1751. Hite's, &c., line. Teste: Charles Lewis, Jno. Archer, Robert Reed, Jno. Craven. Delivered: Jno. Davis, January, 1761.

Page 198.— —— April, 1755. Valentine Pence and Catherine ( ) to Christian Crup, £20, 100 acres on branch of Cub Run, part of 3100 acres formerly Christopher Francisco's. Cor. said Valentine and John Craig. Delivered Jacob Auchenbright, 31st July, 1764.

Page 201.—19th November, 1755. John Lusk to John Cafferton (Capebriton), £4, 230 acres in Beverley Manor; cor. to the Christians; cor. James Calwell, John Davison's line. Delivered Wm. Armstrong 2d March, 1758.

Page 203.—8th August, 1755. John Carmichael, of Rowan County, North Carolina, yeoman, to friend Wm. Buchanan, planter, power attorney to sell land on James River on South Fork of said river, between a survey of Thos. Lewis and Richard Burton, 100 acres purchased of James Patton November, 1751. Teste: James Goodfellow and Samuel Norwood.

Page 205.—15th October, 1755. Archibald ( ) Elliott and Sarah ( ) to Archibald Armstrong, £55, 213 acres on Little River in Calfpasture. Teste: Wm. French, John and James Clark. Delivered: Jno. Graham, September, 1762.

Page 207.—19th November, 1755. Wm. Cunningham and Gennet ( ) to Chas. Killpatrick, £14, 90 acres on head of Moffett's Branch, patented to William 12th February, 1755. Teste: John Davis, James Hogshead, John Malkem. Delivered: James Lockhart, 17th May, 1757.

Page 210.—2d July, 1755. Thomas Beall, of Frederick County, Maryland, planter, to Jonathan Douglass, weaver, 400 acres on a branch of Broad Run on a draft of Brock's Creek. Teste: Silas Hart, Gabriel Pickens, Daniel Smith. Delivered: grantee, 1760.

Page 213.—11th October, 1755. George ( ) Lewis to John Lewis, £120, 215 acres on the Cowpasture, part of the tract where George now lives. Cor. Benjamin Lewis. Teste: Jno. Paxton, Samuel McCluer. Delivered: George Lewis, November, 1757.

Page 216.—11th October, 1755. Same to Benj. Lewis, £90, 215 acres on Cowpasture. Cor. John Lewis; cor. John McCreery's line.

Page 219.—3d June, 1755. Joseph Bryan and Alice to Jacob Chrisman, of Frederick, £150, 500 acres purchased by Joseph from Wm. Linvil and part of 1500 acres purchased by Linvil from Hite, &c., on Linvil's Creek, cor. to land in possession of Thomas Linvil.

Page 221.—Commission to examine Alice above at house of Joseph. Executed, 4th June, 1755.

Page 222.—21st May, 1755. Borden's executors to Moses McClure, plantationer, £3. 6, 110 acres, part of 92100, Moses McClure's old line, cor. Moses Whitesides, Thos. Paxton's line.

Page 227.—24th November, 1755. David Robinson to Thomas Moor, £40, 100 acres, part of 400 conveyed to David by George Robinson, 29th November, 1769 (1749 ?), on Buffalo Creek of Roan Oak. Teste: Henry Murray.

Page 229.—12th November, 1755. Same to William Graham, £122, 100 acres, part of 400 above, adjoining above. Teste: Robt. Martin, James Neelly.

Page 232.—18th November, 1755. John Stevenson to Samuel Henderson, £16, 149 acres cor. John Boyd's land; cor. Greenlee's land.

Page 235.—19th April, 1755. Robert Box to Ephraim Vause, 5 sh., 179 acres by patent 22d August, 1753, on a branch on the north side the Little River. Teste: Hugh Means. Proved, 1755 by James Neelly and James Campbell, and 20th November, 1771 by Hugh Means.

Page 237.—15th September, 1755. Alexander Ingrem to Jacob Reed, £31, 373 acres on south side said creek (?). Teste: Audly Paul, James Donelson.

Page 240.—3d October, 1755. John ( ) Alison (Aliceson) and Jean ( ) to Joseph Walker, £100, 291 acres on North Branch James; cor. Gilbert Campbell; cor. said Campbell's and John Moore's lines. Teste: Andrew Uall, Wm. Buyers. Delivered: Thos. Stewart, February, 1758.

Page 242.—20th November, 1755. Stephen and Jane Arnold to John Poage, £5, 335 acres on Taylor's branch of Buffalo Creek. Not signed nor acknowledged by Jane. Teste: Richard Borton, John Macuell.

Page 245.—20th November, 1755. William Hutchison and Agness ( ) (signed Ann) to John Hutchison, £5, 240 acres in Beverley Manor on Christian's Creek, part of 572 acres surveyed for Wm. Hutchison, cor. Wm. and George Hutchison. Acknowledgement certificate says Ann.

Page 248.—20th November, 1755. Wm. Russell, gent., of Culpeper, to John Wilson, £40, 388 acres on Mill Creek, a branch of Shanando, part of a patent to William, 14th December, 1753, for 3100 acres, cor. Perky's land.

Page 250.— — November, 1755. Joseph Long to Samuel Gibson, 50 acres on Buffalo Creek, a branch of James.

Page 252.—7th May, 1751. James Young, miller and plantationer, to Sarah McMurtry, £400, marriage contract. To be married according to rules of Church of Scotland. Sarah was a widow with children. Patrick, son of James. Teste: John Collyer, Wm. Brown. Proved and recorded, 20th Novembtr, 1755. Delivered: John Low, May, 1758.

Page 254.—9th August, 1755. Jacob ( ) Brown to John Wilson, £20, 91 acres on North Fork of Roanoke. Teste: George Elliott, Jas. Cull.

Page 257.—9th August, 1755. James Campbell to Matthias Yoakham (Yocam), £40, 261 acres on north side Roan Oak above Arthur's Bottom.

Page 258.—18th November, 1755. Borden's executors to Jacob Gray, £15. 10, 450 acres, part of 92100. Cor. Rev. Jno. Brown, Houston's line.

Page 262.—20th May, 1755. William Russell, Wm. Green, of Culpeper, and James Wood, of Frederick, to Henry Lanciscus, £70, 350 acres remaining part of 660 acres granted, patented to grantors, west side South Branch, Lord Fairfax's line at mouth of North Fork. Delivered: Valentine Power, November, 1771.

Page 265.—21st November, 1755. John Harrison, yeoman, to Jeremiah Harrison, £38, 272 acres (one line supposed to interfere with Ro. Craven's land) on Crab's Creek, cor. John Hopes.

Page 267.—27th September, 1753. Commission to Edward Hughs, Squire Boone and James Carter of Roan County, North Carolina, to take acknowledgement of Martha, wife of Morgan Brian, as to deed Brian to David Johnston, then of Augusta County, dated 29th November, 1749. Executed and returned, 20th May, 1754.

Page 269.—5th July, 1755. Joseph Wright to Thomas Weddel (Waddell), £74, 400 acres on a branch of North Fork Shannando called Buffalo Spring, conveyed to Joseph by Benj. Copeland, 20th May, 1752. Teste: Joseph ( ) Reburn. Delivered: Thomas, December, 1763.

Page 271.—15th March, 175 Samuel Huston to John Huston, £30, 283 acres (woodland), part of Borden's tract, cor. Joseph Kennedy, Greenlee's line. Teste: James Wardlaw. Delivered: Wm. Bowyer, May, 1758.

Page 273.—13th February, 1756. James ( ) Cunningham, yeoman, to Isaac Cunningham, £10, 128 acres, part of 400 acres by patent 20th August, 1745, on Tees Creek, cor. Wm. Gillmer. Signed by Margrit Cunningham, but certificates say wife Mary. Teste: Jacob Cunningham, Charly Dougherty, Jno. Gillmer, John Coler, James Simson (Coler, Collier ?).

Page 275.—17th March, 1756. John ( ) Sproul, weaver, to William Purris, weaver, £45, 194 acres in Beverley Manor conveyed to John by Samuel Houston, a stony timber hill in John Montgomerey's and Beverley Manor's and Borden's patents line, Pat. Hays' cor.

Page 278.—6th March, 1756. John ( ) Robison and Margrey ( ) to Wm. Carruthers, £43, 160 acres, part of Borden's 92100 and conveyed to John by Thos. Paxton, Jr., 29th May, 1751, on South River. John Lowry's line, cor. Thos. Paxton; cor. Moses Whiteside. Teste: James McKee, John Makey.

Page 280.—13th March, 1756. William Coruthers and Margaret ( ) to John Macky, £115, 361 acres, part of Borden's 92,100 and conveyed to William by John Mathews, gent., 18th June, 1748. Cor. John White in James Greenlee's line; cor. Samuel Gray's new survey; said Coruthers' old survey.

Page 282.—11th February, 1756. James Bartley and Jean ( ) to Christopher Thompson, £20, 95 acres on Cook's Creek, cor. to McDonal's and one Fisher's survey. Teste: David Weelson, David Crighton. Delivered: Christopher Thompson, 1764.

Page 284.—16th March, 1756. William Loughridge to Thos. Hill, 5 sh. ½ d., 6 acres in Borden's 92100, opposite said Hill's old survey, on Halfway Creek, Robert Weir's line. Teste: Robert Wiear, Wm. Buchanan, Nathaniel Steel. Livery.

Page 286.— —— March, 1756. Joseph Culton, gent., and Mary to John Campbell, £130, 400 acres on north side Cathey's River on the Sinking Spring Branch at the head of Little Run, patented 12th January, 1746.

Page 287.—16th December, 1755. Samuel Givens to Patrick Crawford, mortgage. £36.4.2, 311 acres where Samuel now lives on Middle River of Shannandore, cor. John Givens. Teste: Michael Null. Delivered: Pat. Crawford. 12th November, 1757.

Page 289.—3d March, 1756. Paul Froman, of Frederick, to George Speece, £50, 500 acres being lot No. 6 on Linnvell's Creek, conveyed to Paul by Jost Hite, 4th October, 1749. Delivered: Jos. How by order Speace, March, 1758.

Page 290.—16th January in 29th year of reign (1756 ?). Commission to take acknowledgement of Elizabeth, wife of Adam Thompson, as to deed, Thompson to Samuel Kingkade, 16th May, 1754., Executed 17th March, 1756.

Page 292. — —— 1756. William Buchanan, attorney-in-fact for Jno. Carmichael, to William Burks. Jno. Carmichael, yeoman, of Roan County, Province North Carolina, on 28th August, 1755, appointed William his attorney, &c., 100 acres on north side James River, cor. Wm. Russell.

Page 295.—3d July, 1755. Humberston Lyon to Allexander Sayers (Sawyers), £50, 650 acres on Wood's River. Teste: James Harress, Christopher Hicks, Eabreham Dunckleberry, Wm. Sayers, J. Buchanan, gent.—

Page 296.—20th February, 1756. Beverley to William Long, lease 467 acres, part of the Mill tract in Beverley Manor. Beverley's line, cor. Jno.

Cunningham, near the old bridge. Also 3 lots in Staunton, Nos. 2, 10, 11, all granted to Jno. David Wilpert, 1st June, 1751, and forfeited to Beverley for non-payment of rent. Term, 96 years from date.

Page 299.—20th March, 1756. David Hays and Jean to Nathaniel Steel, £77, 202½ acres in Beverley Manor. Jno. Fulton's line. Teste: Samuel and Robert Steel.

Page 301.—13th March, 1756. John ( ) Miller to David Stuart (Stewart), £50, 210 acres in Beverley Manor and sold to John by Beverley, 13th August, 1747. Cor. David Steward's land; cor. James Miller.

Page 303.—18th May, 1756. Hugh Thompson to Bryce Russell, £20, 150 acres on Shanandore River. Cor. James Craig, George Crawford's four small wild chiri tree corner. Teste: Samuel Henderson, James Thomson. Delivered: Bryce Russell, January, 1763.

Page 305.—20th May, 1756. Nathaniel Evans to James Hay, £4, 100 acres on the South River alias the River Mary. Cor. Borden's tract. Delivered: Wm. Edmondson, 21st June, 1758.

Page 307.—8th May, 1756. John Smith and Margaret ( ) to Mathew Campbell, £30, 250 acres on North Branch of South River of Shanando. Teste: Joshua and John Mathews, Jr.

Page 309.—15th May, 1756. James Young and Sarah, Patrick Young and Isabell to Andrew Hall, £50, 110 acres being the tract where James Young now liveth, including James Young's mill in the Fork of James River, crossing Whistle Creek, cor. Patrick Young. Teste: Jno. Lapesley, Samuel McCluer. Delivered: Wm. Bowyer, August, 1758.

Page 310.—17th May, 1756. Borden's executors to James Campbell, £5.10, 434 acres, part of 92100 on North Branch James joining to James Young's land, mouth of Whistle Creek. Cor. James Young; cor. James Campbell's land. Teste: Joseph Lapesley (Lapsley ?), Wm. Hall.

Page 313.—18th May, 1756. James Campbell and Elizabeth ( ) to James Crawford, £18. 181 acres, part of tract where James Campbell now liveth in Fork of James. Cor. Ro. McElheney, John Wiley's line; cor. James Campbell.

Page 315.—15th May, 1756. James Gilmor, yeoman, and Marthow to James Todd, yeoman, £77, 185 acres upon Buffelo Creek, part of James Gilmor's tract. Delivered, Francis McBride, August, 1769.

Page 317.—19th February, 1756. Nathan McClure to Alexander McClure, £38, 166½ acres on North Branch of James. Cor. Jno. McClure; cor. Francis Allison. Teste: David Dryden. Delivered: Alexander McClure, June, 1778.

Page 320.—8th December, 1755. Thos. Waterson and Mary ( ), farmer, to Israel Christian, merchant, £155, 300 acres on a branch of Naked Creek, James Wood's line. Teste: Thomas ( ) Kirkpatrick.

Page 323.—6th January, 1756. Andrew Lewis to Thomas Hicklin, £60, 348 acres on a branch of Cowpasture River called Newfoundland Creek, patented to Andrew, 11th June, 1750, cor. Jno. Willson.

Page 324.—10th April, 1756. Samuel Black, farmer, and Maxwell McCormick, late of Augusta County. Maxwell, in consideraiton of his being freed from the service as soldier in the Virginia Regiment by the exchange of Thos. Lane, an indented servant of said Samuel Black, binds himself to Black for five years as labourer. Teste: Thos. ( ) Black.

Page 326.—18th May, 1755. John Berrisford and Mary ( ) to James Edmiston, £115, 416 acres on North Branch of James, Samuel McDowell's line.

Page 327.—21st May, 1756. Wm. Rutlidge, Thos. Rutledge, Wm. Marshall, Jean ( ) Rutledge, heirs and legatees of Jno. Rutledge, to James Bell. Receipt for £60 which Bell was required to pay in lieu of land held by Jno. Rutledge and James Bell from Thos. Gilespy.

Page 328.—20th May, 1756. John Buchanan, gent., late of Reed Creek, to Samuel Buchanan, £132, 393 acres in 2 surveys: 1st containing 293 acres conveyed to John by Borden and recorded in Orange; 2d containing 100 acres conveyed to John by Borden and recorded in Augusta, on Moffet's Creek, cor. Jno. Edmiston.

Page 330.—20th May, 1756. William Hinson (Hanson) and Margaret ( ) Hinson, his wife, having been adjudged to serve a certain Wilson and not being able to support their two children, Mary, aged 4 and William, aged 1, bind them to Wm. Burt..

Page 331.—8th April, 1756. Commission to Augusta to take acknowledgement of Elizabeth, wife of James Berry, in deed to George Berry, 20th August, 1755. Executed, May, 1756.

Page 332.—17th August, 1756. Jacob ( ) Anderson and Esther to Isaac Anderson, £9, 350 acres.

Page 335.—16th August, 1756. John Mathews Sr. (Jr ?), and Anne ( ) to Richard Mathews ,£10, 300 acres in Forks of James upon Mill Creek, joining George Mathews. Jno. Maxwell's line, cor. Jno. Mathews, Sr. Teste: Jno. Mathews, Jr., Geo. Trout, Ann Mathews, Jr. Delivered: James Lockhart, June, 1757.

Page 337.—16th August, 1756. John Mathews, Sr., gent., and Ann to George Mathews, £10, 300 acres in Forks of James on Mill Creek, joining Jno. Poage. John Maxwell's line, cor. Richard Mathews.

Page 339.—17th August, 1756. John Shields and Mary to John Davis, £9, 320 acres, part of Borden's 92100, cor. Jno. Pattison's land, crossing Morphet Creek. Delivered: Jno. Davis, February, 1759.

Page 341.—1st June, 1756. Silas Hart, gent., and Jane to John Smith, Jr., 230 acres, part of 400 acres patented to Jno. McClure, 15th December, 1749, and conveyed by McClure to Hart, on South Fork of North River of Shannandore. Teste: Jno. Malkem, Alexander Herring, Robert Gragg. Recorded on motion of Daniel Smith on behalf of John. Delivered: Henry Smith, 28th July, 1764.

Page 343.—1st June, 1756. Silas Hart, gent, and Jane to Henry Smith, £50, 170 acres on South Fork of North River Shanando, part of 400 acres above.

Page 345.—20th August, 1756. John Brownlee and Sarah to Alexander Brownlee, £15, 222 acres, part of 444 acres conveyed by Phinley McCluer to Brownlee, 27th May, 1742, recorded in Orange, in Beverley Manor, cor. said Jno. Brownlee's land on Pine Run, line of Fulton's land.

Page 347.—18th August, 1756. Henry Smith and Amie (Emie) ( ) to John Poage, £45, 135 acres on Howell Branch patented to Henry, 3d November, 1750, cor. Abraham Smith. Teste: Sampson Archer, Daniel ( ) Callachan.

Page 348.—18th August, 1756. Borden's executors to Samuel Dunlop,

150 acres, part of 92100, on North Branch of James River opposite an island. Mount Miserable to Hays Creek . Delivered: Andrew Hays, January, 1760.

Page 351.—18th August, 17—. Daniel Smith and Jean to James Ramsey, 80 acres on North River Shanandore, cor. Charles Divir's land. Teste: John Henton (Heaton ?). Delivered: Jno. McCoy, 9th November, 1767.

Page 353.—29th May, 1756. Daniel McAnaire and Hannah to James Sayers, £80, 147 acres, part of 400 patented to Daniel, 10th June, 1740 and bounded by a tract laid off for Thos. Gardner on west and one for Alex Gibson on east. Teste: Jean ( ) Beard, William Christell. Delivered: Sampson Archer, November, 1759.

Page 354.—26th October, 1756. Alex. Thompson, Captain, to William Thompson, yeoman, £20. Bill sale of horses and cattle. Teste: Samuel McKune, John Gray.

Page 355.—26th October, 1756. Same to John Thompson, farmer, £15, bill sale of one feather bed with the furniture, two other beds with their furniture, one woman's saddle and bridal, one putter dish, two basions, one dozian of plates, two pots with all ye other veshals and furniture belonging to my house at this present, one chist of cloaths of wooling and linning, one loom and all the takelings and utensils to her belonging, one plough and irons with the takelings thereto belonging with all the crape that is now on my plantation of wheat, ray, coran, oats, flex, hay and fodder, two axes and two mattocks.

Page 356.—11th November, 1756.: Alex. McClure and Susanna ( ) to Thomas Dredin, £38, 163 acres on North Branch of James, cor. James Moor. Teste: John Lapslie, Wm. Lapslie, Moses McCluer, James Thompson.

Page 359.—17th November, 1756. James Lockridge and Isabela ( ) to Wm. Kinkade, £24, 260 acres on Great River of Calfpasture, cor. Ro. Guin's land; cor .Robert Lockridge, Preston's line. Teste: Samuel Tencher. Delivered: Jno. Kincaid per order, 19th April, 1819. Recorded on motion Margret Kinkade for William.

Page 361.—16th November, 1756. Godfrey Bombgardner and Cortrought ( ) (she signs Anglice) to Valentine Smith, £24, 190 acres on headwaters of Smith's Creek, granted to Godfrey, 16th August, 1756, Jno. Davis's line.

Page 363.—15th June, 1754. George Henderson to John Roseman, £50. Bill sale conveys all horses and cows, sheep and hogs, all movable goods and chattels. Teste: Wm. Wardlaw, Robert Henry. Acknowledged, 17th November, 1756.

Page 364.—16th November, 1756. Borden's executors to Samuel Hazard, gent., 220 acres of 92100, cor. Jno. Lusk; cor. Jno. Montgomerie's new survey, line of Beverley Manor. Delivered: Jno. Cunningham, 14th February, 1774.

Page 366.—17th November, 175—. Bordens executors to Andrew Buchanan, £7.10, 250 acres, part of 92100, cor. Alex. McCoskery, Robert Cultons line.

Page 370.—17th November, 1756. George Breckinridge, of Albemarle, to John Steel, £55, 230 acres in Beverley Manor, cor. Thos. Beard. Teste: Samuel Steel, Wm. Read, John Erwin.

Page 372.—18th November, 1756. Samuel ( ) Temple (Sample) and Anne ( ) to Rev. Alex. Miller, £41.10, 300 acres by patent dated 2d March, 1756, on Hunters Spring Draft. Delivered: Jos. Craven by your order, March, 1759.

Page 374.—19th November, 1756. John Walker and Ann ( ) to Andrew Duncan, £100, 190 acres of Bordens land on Walkers Creek, cor. Alex. Walker; Alexander's cor.; James Moor's cor.

Page 375.—1st May, 1756. John Black, plantationer, to John Black, his son, natural love, &c., and £5, 210 acres on South River Shanando in Beverley Manor, part of 375 acres conveyed by Beverley to Geo. Home and by Home to Gibbons Jennings, 14th March, 1740, and by Jennings having afterwards absconded, said land was sold at public auction to James Davise by Richard Winston, sheriff of Orange, to satisfy Isaac Smith's judgment on Jennings by deed in Orange dated 24th June, 1743, and conveyed by Davise to Black, 21st November, 1746, patent line of Beverley Manor, William Bell's line; John Ramsey's line. Teste: Jno. Morten. Livery, &c. Delivered: Jno. Black, May, 1763.

Page 377.—1st May, 1756. Same to son James Black. Same consideration. 165 acres in Beverley Manor on South River Shanando, part of 375 acres above Beverley Manor patent line; cor. Ro. Patrick, Wm. Bell's line. Delivered: James Black, May, 1763.

Page 381.—1st February, 1757. John (Jacob) Gardner to Jno. Craven and Jno. Wright, £100, 310 acres on East Fork of Cook's Creek and a draft of Smith's Creek, Daniel Harrison's land, granted to Jacob, 16th August, 1756. Teste: Ro. Craven ( ), Samuel Hemphill, Matt. and Robert Black. Delivered: Jno. Wright, August, 1758.

Page 383.—10th February, 1757. Jno. Bumgardner, Jr., heir to Jno. Bumgardner, deceased, to Robert Ellet (Elliot), £15, 250 acres on a branch of Cub Run. Teste: Uriah Humble, Adam Reder. Delivered: Robert Elliot, November, 1758.

Page 385.—15th March, 1757. James Givens and Martha to Geo. Crawford, £—, 311 acres on Middle River patented to Givens, 30th August, 1743. Teste: Wm. Givens.

Page 388.—14th March, 1757. Wm. Givens and Jean to James Givens, £— tract on Middle River patented to Sarah Givens and Wm. Givens, 30th August, 1743. Delivered: James Givens, August, 1758.

Page 390.—16th March, 1757. William ( ) Castleberry and Margaret ( ), his wife, to Ersbald Hopkins (delivered Archibald Hopkins, May, 1763), £130, 350 acres on Muddy Creek.

Page 393.—15th March, 1757. Robert Phillips and Mary ( ) to Walter Trimble, £110, 159 acres, part of 251 conveyed by Beverley to Wm. King, 27th February, 1749, and by King to Jno. Trimble, 23d February, 1751, in Beverley Manor; cor. Morris O'Freels; cor. Jno. Trimble, Beverley Manor patent line. Teste: Wm. Read, Samuel Henderson, Walter ( ) Trimble. Delivered: Walter Trimble, 7th December, 1762.

Page 395.—16th March, 1757. John ( ) Wilson and Mary to Henry Perky, £11, 30 acres on Mill Creek, a branch of Shanando, part of 380 acres belonging to John, cor. Henry's own land.

Page 398.—16th March, 1757. Thomas Berry and Esther ( ) to James Trotter £60, two tracts adjoining each other and the line of Beverley Manor and Borden's tract: 1st, 82 acres in Beverley Manor, cor. James Loosk, patent line; cor. lines of Patrick Cook; cor. Borden's tract and Beverley Manor; 2d, 218 acres in James Loosk's line; Beverley Manor patent line and Borden's tract; cor. Samuel McCutchen; cor. James Shields, both conveyed to Thomas, 15th March, 1754, by Ro. Robinson and Isabella. Teste: Wm. Frame, James Bell, Jno. McPheetters. Delivered: Jno. Davis, 1758.

Page 400.—26th November, 1755. Francis ( ) McCown and Margret ( ) to Jno. Maxwell (delivered Wm. McGee, May, 1764), £65, 250 acres on a branch of Cedar Creek, a branch of James River, at a place called the Timber Plain; cor. Jno. Poage's land; cor. Francis McCown. Teste: Hugh McConwell, Ro. Renick.

Page 403.—18th March, 1757. Samuel McDowell and Mary to James McGavock, £60, 400 acres by patent dated 25th June, 1747, in Forks of James on branches of Cedar Creek. Delivered: McGaffock, February, 1760.

Page 406.—8th March, 1757. Same to James McDowell, £100, 400 acres by patent 1st June, 1741, on Big Spring Branch, running into the North Branch James. Delivered: James McDowell, August, 1758.

Page 408.—8th March, 1757. Samuel McDowell and Mary to James McDowell, £100, 400 acres by patent, 10th November, 1742, in Fork of James River.

Page 410.—13th March, 1757. Borden's executors to Jno. Lowrey (delivered Wm. Bowyer, August, 1758), £3, 170 acres, part of 92100, said Lowrey's cor, Steel's old line; Steel's new survey; cor. survey made for Robert Henry; cor. Ro. Lowrey; cor. Wm. McCanless, Ro. Dunlop's line.

Page 413.—15th March, 1757. Richard Woods, gent., and Elizabeth, of Augusta, to Richard Wood, son-in-law of Richard, £25, 195 acres in Fork of James River and part of tract where Richard, grantor, now liveth; cor. in Borden's patent line by James Davis's field; cor. Peter Wallace; cor. Richard Wood.

Page 416.—10th March, 1757. Cornelius Robinson, of Anson County and Province North Carolina, to Adam Reider (Rider), £60, 400 acres on North River Shannando on both sides Fort Run. Teste: Michael Warren.

Page 418.—10th March, 1757. Same to same. Whereas Cornelius empowered to make deed for this land by will of his father, Charles Robinson, which will is recorded in Anson County Court in North Carolina, as appears by the copy certified by the Clerk, Jno. Frohock, £60, 400 acres on a branch of North River of Shanando called Fort Run.

Page 421.—15th March, 1757. William Hutchison and Agness ( ) to Ro. Graham and John Graham, £140, 172 acres formerly surveyed for Wm. Hutchison; cor. John Hutchison; cor. Wm. Henderson. Teste: Ro. Montgomery. Delivered: Jno. Graham, 17th October, 1768.

Page 422.—1st December, 1756. John Scot to Jno. Pickin, mortgage of 400 acres adjoining Cub Run, Col. Woods on one side and James Buseter on the other, £37.15 secured. Teste: Arnold Kuster ( ), Wm. ( ) Pickin, Uriah Humble.

Page 423.—17th March, 1757. Joseph ( ) Mays and Rebeckah ( ) to Jno. Stewart, £59, lot 3 in Staunton, woodland lot 8. Livery by a latch of door of house on the premises. Teste: Wm. Lusk, Jno. Cochran. Delivered: Jno. Stewart, June, 1759.

Page 425.—15th March, 1757. James Trimble and Sarah to Geroge Wilson, £55, 364 acres on heard of Newfoundland, near water of Potomac.

Page 428.—15th March, 1757. Mathew Edmiston and Margaret to Jno. Richey, £32, 76 acres on a draft of Jenning's Branch. Teste: Wm. Wallace, Samuel Colwell.

Page 430.—17th March, 1757. James Edmonson (Edmiston) to Alex. Henderson ,£—, 100 acres conveyed by Moses Thomson to James, recorded in Orange, on South River Shanando on the Red Banks. Delivered: Bryan Russell, September, 1761.

Page 432.—3d March, 1757. Ro. Dunlap and Elizabeth to John Wardlaw, £20, 188 acres, 3 rods and 16 perch, cor. Wm. McCanlis; cor. Jno. Lowrey. Delivered: James McDowell, August, 1758.

Page 434.—8th March, 1757. Jno. Lyle and Samuel Gray, executors of John Gray, late of Augusta, yeoman, deceased, to James Greenlee, yeoman, 203 acres devised to be divided be his executors between his wife and children, but not being susceptible of division, they, with consent of wife and as many children as are of age, decide to sell the land and divide the money. The 203 acres is part of Borden's 92100 and conveyed by Borden to Jno. Gray, 27th July, 1742. £94, on northwest side Timber Ridge. Delivered: Samuel Greenlee, 17th June, 1779.

Page 437.—15th March, 1757. Wm. Stephenson and Sarah ( ) to Mathias Tise, £90, 200 acres on southernmost Fork of South Branch Potomac, part of 2640 acres patented to Ro. Green, 12th January, 1746, and conveyed by Green to William, 5th November, 1747; cor. tract sold to Jno. Patton, Jr. Delivered: Mathias Tice, March, 1769.

Page 440.—18th March, 1757. Mathew Patton to Wm. Dyer, £30, 157 acres on southernmost branch of South Branch of Potomac, part of 2643 acres granted to Mathew; cor. tract sold to Wm. Dyer. Delivered: Joseph Cravens, 17th November, 1788.

Page 442.— — —, 1757. Adam Rader and Barbara (signed in German, Adam Räder, Bora ( ) Rädjiou) to Mathias Rader (Rider), £50, 100 acres, part of 400 acres on North River of Shanando, patented to Cornelius Robinson, 15th March, 1744, and conveyed by him to Adam.

Page 445.— — — 1757. Same to Alex. Painter, £50, 250 acres, part of 480 acres above, a corner made for the division of Mathias Rader's part. Delivered: George Skiliron, 13th March, 1761.

Page 448.—6th April, 1757. Jno. Nicholls, of Frederick, by Jno. Harden, his attorney in fact, to Robert, Alexander and David Tedford. Nicholls, by letter of attorney recorded in Frederick, appointed Harden his attorney to sell lands he might be entitled to by the will of Borden or otherwise. £30, 500 acres in Forks of James, part of Borden's 92100, North Branch of James. Teste: Valentine Sevier, Wm. Magee. Delivered, Andrew Hays, January, 1760.

Page 450.—16th April, 1757. Cap. Richard Pearis to Sarah Paris and Margaret Pearis, £, love and goodwill; his daughters, slaves and other personalty; to Sarah in case she marries with father's consent; to Margaret, same condition (conveys one Indian wench named Pratchey. Delivered: Cap. Peter Hog, December, 1770.

Page 451.—14th June, 1757. John Taylor and Esther ( ) to Thomas Gordon, £20, 120 acres cor. Wood's and Green's land on head Muddy Creek;

cor. Jno. O'Neal's land. Teste: Geo. Bigham, Elijah Clery. Delivered: Thos. Gordon, April, 1771.

Page 453.—10th June, 1757. Peter Wallace and Martha to Francis McCown, yeoman, £56, 150½ acres on Whistle Creek in Forks of James; cor. Low Todd. Teste: Alex. Creaghead, Richard Woods, Ro. McElheney. Delivered: Samuel Wilson, Augusct, 1769.

Page 456.—27th January, 1757. Edward Erwin, Sr., yeoman, to Francis Erwin, yeoman, £200, 184 acres, part of 350 acres patented to Edward, 5th April, 1748; cor. Edward Erwin, Jr., kern of stones; cor. Benj. Erwin. Also 100 acres, part of 220 acres patented to Edward, — March, 1747; cor. Wm. Brown and Wm. Alexander. Teste: John, Andrew, Edward Erwin. Sent to Francis Erwin by order 28th September, 1774.

Page 459.—18th June, 1757. William Caldwell and Anne ( ) to Jno. Caldwell, £18, 440 acres in Beverley Manor on survey for Pearson Anderson and another survey for Wm. Russell; cor. Wm. Palmer; cor. Jno. Hutchison in the Poison Field.

Page 461.—1st June, 1757. James Hamilton, farmer, to Jno. Hamilton, farmer, £2, 100 acres, part of 200 acres surveyed for Andrew McClure and Alex. Henderson and known by name of Elk Run and now seated by said Jno. in Beverley Manor, cor. tract surveyed for David Edmiston, James Alexander's line. Delivered: Jno. Hamilton, 24th July, 1765.

Page 463.—15th June, 1757. Samuel Givens and Martha to Jno. Williams, £40, 283 acres, part of a tract conveyed to Samuel, August, 1754. Cor. Ro. Patrick; cor. Finla. Teste: Patrick Crawford, Geo. Wilson, Wm. Lamb. Delivered: Jno. Williams, April, 1783.

Page 465.—17th August, 1757. Hugh Campbell and Esther ( ) to Jno. Hair, Sr., £10, 160 acres on Fowler's Branch of North River Shanando, between Naked Creek and North River, patented 16th August, 1757. Teste: Andrew Alexander, Michael Dickey, James Allen. Delivered: Jno. Hare, January, 1763.

Page 467.—18th August, 1757. Alexander (Alexter) Henderson to John Hutchison, 265 acres in Beverley Manor, part of 530 acres conveyed by Beverley to Geo. Hutchison, 21st February, 1738, and sold by George to Alexander, 13th June, 1746; cor. Samuel Henderson's land, on Long Meadow. Teste: Wm. Logan, Andrew McClure.

Page 468.—Commission from Augusta to Wm. Harris, Wm. Cabell, Jr., and Wm. Dinguid to take acknowledgment of Anne, wife of Geo. Breckinridge, of Albemarle, to deed, 17th November, 1756, George to Jno. Steel, dated 10th June, 1757. Executed 11th August, 1757.

Page 469.—16th August, 1757. William Williams to Joseph Bell, £20, lot 12 in Staunton.

Page 471.—15th March, 1757. John Buchanan, gent., and Margaret to Robert Allison, £25, 83 acres on North Branch James, part of 634 acres, part of Borden's 92100; cor. Jacob Anderson (bought by John from Borden).

Page 473.—18th August, 1756. Same to William Young, £20, 100 acres part of 634 above, like description.

Page 476.—9th March, 1757. Same to James Anderson, £75, 200 acres, part of 634 above. Cor. Hugh Martin's old survey on Back Creek.

Page 478.—19th August, 1757. Same to Jacob Anderson, farmer, £40,

232 acres, part of 634 above. Cor. Wm. Young; cor. Ro. Allison. Delivered; Jacob Anderson, 27th July, 1772.

Page 479.—16th August, 1757. Borden's executors to Conord Lamb, £10, 212 acres, part of 800 patented to Borden, 1746. Delivered: Geo. Kinder, 1767.

Page 481.—17th August, 1757. Borden's executors to John Camplin, £10, 156 acres, part of 800 acres above.

Page 484.—16th November, 1757. Francis ( ) McCown and Margaret to Andrew Duncan, £140, 317 acres conveyed to Francis by Benj. Jr., south side Moffett's Creek, cor. Joseph Kennedy's land; cor. Samuel Steel's land, Wilson's corner. Teste: Robert Brown, Petter Wallace. Delivered: Wm Edmondson, June, 1758.

Page 486.—16th November, 1757. Hugh Campbell, wheelwright, and Esther ( ) to James Patterson, sadler. Teste: Francis Brown, James Allen. Delivered: James Patterson, January, 1763.

Page 489.—16th March, 1755. Thomas Watterson and Mary ( ) to James McConell, £10, 100 acres, part of a large tract. Teste: John Seawright, Robert Curry, Robert Brown, James Jackson, Samuel Black, Mary Jackson. Delivered: James McConald, May, 1759.

Page 491.—8th November, 1757. Robert Ralstone (Rollstone) and Martha (Matherew) to David Ralston, £50, 350 acres by patent, 16th August, 1756, on Mossey Creek, cor. Wm. McReeters. Teste: John Edwards, Ephraim Love, Reuben Rutherford. Delivered: Ralston, August, 1758.

Page 494.—27th September, 1757. David ( ) Dunlap to Hugh Beard, £29, 170 acres in Borden's tract; Jno. Cunningham's line; cor. Wm. Lockridge. Teste: Wm. Lockridge, Jno. Lowry, Thos. Hill, Wm. Beard. Delivered: Hugh Beard, February, 1779.

Page 496.—12th November, 1757. Andrew Steel to his son, Samuel Steel, £60, 240 acres, part of the tract where Andrew now lives, containing 463 acres, conveyed to Andrew by Borden; cor. Ro. Henry and Andrew Steel, Wilsons line; cor. Andrew Duncan; cor. Joseph Kennedy. Teste: Jno. Tat. Delivered: Samuel Steel, August, 1770.

Page 499.—15th November, 1757. John Bowen, Sr., and Lilly ( ) to John Bowen, Jr., 10 acres by patent, 3d November, 1750, on a branch of James. Teste: Jno. Mathews, John Poage, Mathew Campbell. Delivered: Jno. Bowen, October, 1761.

Page 500.—14th November, 1757. Borden's executors to James Buchanan, £10, 415 acres, part of 92100; James McKown's cor., crossing Hay's Creek, the patent line. Teste: Wm. Caruthers, Samuel McCosky, Alexander Buchanan. Delivered: Wm. Buchanan, November, 1762.

Page 503.—14th November, 1757. Borden's executors to David Wallace, £3.10, 200 acres, part of 92100; cor. James McNabb's. Teste: Jno. Mills, Wm. Hall. Delivered: David Wallace, November, 1763.

Page 505.—15th November, 1757. Same to Robert Erwin, £6, 100 acres, part of 92100; cor. Ro. Erwin's former tract in Jno. McKee's line; Hugh Cunningham's line.

Page 508.—13th November, 1757. Same to James Henry, £3, 408 acres, part of 92100; Andrew Steel's cor.; Robt. Lowrey's line. Delivered: Robert Buchanan, April, 1765.

Page 510.—17th November, 1757. Joseph Lapsley, as guardian of Hannah, Jean and Elizabeth Kirkham, to Jonathan Whitley. Robert Kirkham, formerly of Augusta, had bargained to Wm. Cleghorn, and Cleghorn to Jonathan, but Robert died without making deed and Jonathan has brought suit. Conveys 30 acres on James River. Teste: Jno Semple, Jno. Gilmer. Delivered: Samuel Hunter, 1763.

Page 512.—17th November, 1757. Jno. Poage to Jno. Maxwell, £100, 238 acres on James River. Delivered: Wm. McKee, May, 1764.

Page 514.—16th November, 1757. James Davies to Wm. Preston, £50, 200 acres on northwest side of the Catawbo on Davies Branch, patented to Davies, 10th September, 1755; signed James (mark) Davies. Teste: James Dunlap. Delivered: McGilbert by your order, 3d October, 1759.

Page 516.—17th November, 1757. William Christian and Mary to George Willson, £30, lot 8 in Staunton, sold by County Court to Thomas Paxton and by Paxton to William, 16th August, 1753. Delivered: George, August, 1758.

Page 518.—17th November, 1757. Francis Gardiner ( ) to Robert Shaw, £5, 95 acres.

Page 520.—17th November, 1757. James ( ) Coyle to Wm. Preston, £15, 145 acres by patent, 16th August, 1756, on North River Shanando; cor. Benj. Copeland. Teste: Jno. McNeill.

Page 522.—15th March, 1758. Richard Woods and Elizabeth to George Gibson, 200 acres on North Branch Colyer's Creek.

Page 524.—29th December, 1757. Patrick Crawford, yeoman, to Samuel Givens. Release of lease, 16th December, 1755. Teste: Wm. Poage, James Henderson.

Page 525.— — — 1758. Henry ( ) Duley, of Bedford, yeoman, and Martha to John Craige, yeoman, £30, 171 acres, part of 225 acres bought by Henry from Christopher Francisco, and part of Christopher's 3000 acres on Cub Run, cor. Frederick Harmantrout.

Page 529.—18th February, 1758. William Downs to John Madison, £15, 200 acres patented to William, 5th November, 1747; Stover's Mill Creek; land of Wm. Lamb. Teste: Henry Downs, Abraham Miller.

Page 531.—17th March, 1758. John Mills to William Graham, £—, 600 acres, part of a tract deeded to John by James Patton, 17th December, 1752, on Buffelo Creek, a branch of Roanoke; cor. David Robinson, Caravan's Creek.

Page 534.—15th March, 1758. Jno. Lyle to James McKee, £35, 210 acres, part of Borden's 92100; cor. Mathew Lyle; cor. Jno. Gray. Teste: Wm. Todd, Mathew Lyle, Robert Huston. Delivered: Jno. Lyle, 16th August, 1774.

Page 535.—15th March, 1758. Borden's executors to James McKee, £5, 310 acres, part of 92100; cor. Samuel Norwood on Kerr's Creek, Jno. Wiley's line. Delivered: Wm. McKee, April, 1764.

Page 539.—16th March, 1758. Daniel Harrison to Robert Harrison, £40, 400 acres on head of Dry Fork of Smith's Creek. Delivered: Captain Daniel Smith, January, 1763.

Page 541.—18th August, 1756. James Trimble and Sarah to Hanse Harper, £13, 180 acres on Black Thorn, a branch of South Branch of Potomac. Delivered: Harper, November, 1760.

Page 543.—15th March, 1758. Borden's executors to Michael Bowyer, of Hanover, £1, 226 acres, part of 92100. Delivered: Michael Bowyer, 30th April, 1762.

Page 546.—14th March, 1758. Sampson and George Mathews, executors of John Mathews, Jr., £8.12, 291 acres on Mill Creek in Fork of James; Thos. Williams line, cor. Joshua Mathews; cor. Wm. Bradshaw. Teste: Audly Paul, Wm. Mathews.

Page 548.—20th February, 1758. Archibald ( ) Eliot (Elet), of Anton County, North Carolina, to James Clark, Sr., and Wm. Eliot, power attorney to convey 163 acres to John Johnston on Jackson River. Teste: Jno. Mophet, Patrick Jack.

Page 550.—16th March, 1758. Wm. Smith to Thomas Meek, £10, 200 acres, foot of Brown Hill in line of Wm. McCutchen. Teste: Jno. Clark, Adam Dickenson. Delivered: George Wilson, August, 1758.

DEED BOOK No. 8.

Page 2.—18th March, 1758. Thomas Walker, of Louisa County, to Alex. Sayers, £15, 504 acres on a branch of Reed Creek where the Buffelo lick is, part of a tract patented to Thomas, 4th July, 1752; cor. Montgomery, the Barrens. Sent to Col. Wm. Preston, October, 1773.

Page 4.—15th March, 1758. James Davis to sons Henry, William and Samuel Davies, love and affection, 1,300 acres known as Davies' Fancy on the Indian River. 1st, to Henry,a portion on the South Fork known as the Beaver Dam, down the said Fork to where the two Forks meet; 2d, to son William, 350 acres; 3d, to son Samuel, 350 acres. Signed, James ( ) Davies. Delivered: Wm. Davis, May, 1765.

Page 6.—17th March, 1758. John Young to Robert Allen, £100, 234 acres in Beverley Manor, on Back Creek; corner Hugh Young; John Trimble's corner; corner Wm. McFeeters, James Young's corner. Delivered: Hugh Young, August, 1762.

Page 8.—18th March, 1758. Robt. Breckinridge to James Simpson, £35, 242 acres by patent, 19th October, 1753, on south side Buffelo Creek, opposite Long Berch, top of the Whiskey Hill. Delivered: Jno. Mathews, son of Richard, March 6, 1773.

Page 10.—2d May, 1758. Robert Reagh (Reah, Reaoh), carpenter and joiner, and Sara to Archibald Reah, Jr., yeoman, £60, 118 acres on Hays Creek; corner widow Smyley. Teste: Wm. Reah. Delivered: Archibald Reah, 23d March, 1768.

Page 12.—17th May, 1758. Joseph Hanna and Ann to Rob McCutchon, £67, 273 acres on a Sinking Branch of the south side Naked Creek.

Page 14.—14th November, 1758. Borden's executors to Wm. Buchanan, £10, 280 acres, part of 92,100; corner James Miles, on North Branch of James; several corners of the very crooked river.

Page 17.—13th May, 1758. John Wilson ( ) and Mary ( ) to Henry Perkey, £80, 388 acres on Mill Creek of Shanando purchased by Jno. from Wm. Russell; corner said Perkey's line. Teste: Robt. Hook, Jacob ( ) Persenor (Persinger, Parchinger), Charles Rush.

Page 20.—13th May, 1758. Peter Hull and Susanna ( ) to Charles Rush, £32, 210 acres, part of larger tract purchased by Peter from Francisco; corner to Trout's land, on Cub Run, line of Pence's land. Some witnesses as above. Delivered: Charles Rush, February, 1765.

Page 23.—16th August, 1758. John Lusk and Elizabeth ( ) to Alexander Kyle (Kile), £5, 90 acres on North River, Shanando, at a place called the Long Neck, patented to John, 13th June, 1755. Teste: Wm. Lusk, Robt. ( ) Delshe, Alexander ( ) Walker. Delivered to Alexander Kyle, January, 1761.

Page 26.—14th August, 1758. John Richey and Margaret (signed Margret ( ) Wales) to Robert Armstrong, Jr., £14.10.0, 76 acres on a draft of Jennings Branch.

Page 27.—14th November, 1757. Borden's executors to William Adams, £4, 336 acres, part of 92,100, on Moffets Creek; David Hays' line (ivery sapline?); Jas. Trimble's line. Teste: James Simpson.

Page 31.—16th August, 1758. Thomas Turk and Margaret to James Turk, £50, 320 acres on South River, Shanando; corner to land formerly Bloodworth's, crossing the Cranberry Swamps, Christian Clemance's land. Delivered: Robert Turk, 20th April, 1759.

Page 34.—16th May, 1758. John Gilmor, Sr., and Agness ( ) to Wm. Gilmore, yeoman, £10, 250 acres on Tees Creek in Fork of James, part of the tract John now lives on containing 500 acres. Teste: Wm. McKemey, Jno. Gilmer. Sent to Wm. Gilmore, May, 1769.

Page 37.—15th August, 1758. George Wilson and Elisebeth to Samuel Wilson, £40, 200 acres, part of tract deeded to George by James Trimble, on the Bullpasture River. Delivered: Wm. Elliott, October, 1759.

Page 40.—16th August, 1758. John Fulton, farmer, and Mary, to Wm. Fulton, £40, 200 acres in Borden's tract, Thomas Beard's line, on Moffet's Creek; Wm. Kennedy's corner. Teste: Hugh Fulton.

Page 43.—17th August, 1758. Peter Haaz to Hanah Haaz, £25, 370 acres, on South Fork Potomac, being part of No. G., surveyed for Col. Wood, Capt. Green, Capt. Russell. Delivered: Robt. Davis, November, 1763.

Page 45.—15th November, 1758. David Hogshead, farmer, and heir of Wm. Hogshead and Margrit to Charles Stewart, shoemaker, £7, 54 acres on head drafts of Moffet's Creek patented to William, 16th August, 1756. Teste: James Bell, Sampson Archer, Jno. McKemey.

Page 48.—15th November, 1758. John Mountgomery to Samuel Huston, 30 shillings; a piece of meadow 2 A., 1 R., 3. P., in Borden tract. Teste: Mathew Huston, James Henry.

Page 50.—15th November, 1758. Thomas Thompson, farmer, and Mary ( ) to Robt. Thompson, £30, 200 acres, part of tract on which John Thompson, deceased, formerly lived on Long Meadow; corner Wm. Wright's land. Teste: Jno. Poage, Geo. Crawford, Alexander McDonnall.

Page 51.—15th November, 1758. John (signed Thomas) Thompson to Robert Thompson. Good consideration, lease 3¾ acres of meadow on Long Meadow on the upper end of the meadow formerly belonging to my father, now deceased, 999 years. Teste: Samuel Caldwell.

Page 53.—29th October, 1758. James ( ) Coyle to John and Robt. Thompson, £49.5.0, tract on Christian's Creek where Coyle now lives bought by Coyle from James Patton, 12th September, 1750, 310 acres; corner Wm. Palmer; corner Geo. Robinson (now Wm. Henderson's land; corner tract surveyed for Wm. Russell (now Alexander Thompson's land). Teste: Alexander Thompson, Wm. Tohmpson, Jno. Henderson. Delivered: Rob. Thompson, August, 1762.

Page 56.— —— day ——, 1757. John Miller and Ann to John Ramsey.

£———, 316 acres on Gr. River, Calf Pasture; corner Samuel Hodges. Delivered Ro. Bratton, May, 1762.

Page 58.—11th November, 1758. William ( ) Hall and Jane ( ) to Andrew Hall, £100, 280 acres on North Branch James in Borden's tract, and conveyed by Borden, 8th April, 1743. Teste: Geo. Campbell, Robt. Cowan. Delivered: Wm. Hall, 1762.

Page 65.—11th November, 1758. Andrew Hall to Wm. Hall, £50, 110 acres, the tract where James Young formerly lived, including James Young's mill in Fork of James, crossing Whistle Creek; corner Patrick Young.

Page 63.—6th October, 1758. Hendry Downs and Francis to Joseph Hanna, £100, 300 acres on South River, Shanando, lower end of tract Joseph now lives on, and part of 400 patented to Alexander Thompson, 30th July, 1742. Teste: Andrew Leeper. Delivered: Joseph Hanna, June, 1772.

Page 65.—18th November, 1758. John King and Mary to David Bell, £104, 400 acres in Beverley Manor on Branch Middle River, Wm. Wallace's land; corner James and Wm. Wallace, Jr.; corner Mathew Armstrong. Delivered: David Bell, January, 1767.

Page 67.—18th November, 1758. Jno. Madison to Thos. Lewis, £50, 260 acres on Shanando, part of 1,000 patented to John, 10th March, 1756; end of the Great Island; corner to said Thos. Lewis.

Page 69.—21st March, 1759. Jno. Scott to Robt. Hook, £18. Bill sale of a negro woman. Teste: Robt. Breckinridge.

Page 70.—20th March, 1759. Archibald Alexander to Wm. Alexander, £8, 208 acres; corner Mrs. Cummins, Thos. McSpeden's corner. Teste: Jno. McClung, Joseph Alexander, James ( ) Edmeston.

Page 72.—21st March, 1759. Alexander Gibson, farmer, and Mary ( ) to Thomas Gardner, blacksmith, £100, 199 acres, part of 400 acres patented to Robt. Rennock, 10th June, 1740, and conveyed by Robert to Silas Hart, 15th February, 1748, and by Hart to Gibson, 17th November, 1752, on Buffalo Lick Branch. Teste: James Kirk.

Page 75.—20th March, 1759. Wm. McClung to Jno. McClung, £10, 26 acres; corner Stephenson's land. Teste: James Wellch, Andrew Crop.

Page 77.—21st March, 1759. James Henery, blacksmith, to Robert Telford (Tedford), joiner, £50, 200 acres, part of 408 acres in Borden's tract surveyed for Robt. Henery, deceased; corner James Henery. Teste: Andrew Hays, Alexander Miller. Delivered: Andrew Hays, January, 1760.

Page 80.—21st March, 1759. Gawen Leeper to Thos. Tate, £130, 299 acres in Beverley Manor; corner Nicholas Leeper. Teste: Randal Lockhart, Walter Davis, Robt. Steel.

Page 82.—20th March, 1759. Robert Ralston and Martha (her mark) to Thomas Campbell, £6, 40 acres on a branch of North River called Muddy Creek. Teste: Ephraim Love, James Bruster, Jno. Davison. Delivered: Archibald Hopkins, March, 1763.

Page 83.—21st March, 1759. James Gay to Jno. Warrick, £4 yearly for three years; lease, 149 acres in Calf Pasture bounded by Jno. Gay and Wm. Eliot. Teste: Pat. Cunningham and Thos. Rutledge.

Page 84.—24th April, 1758. Alexander Ritchey, late of Augusta County, in Virginia, blacksmith, but now of Augusta in the Province of Georgia, to Robt. Campbell, of Augusta County, planter, power attorney to deed 300 acres and joining Adam Thompson and George Perry and a Little Mount called the Sugar Loaf. Teste: Dugald Campbell, John Clark. Executed in Georgia and proved here by Jno. Clark.

Page 85.—21st March, 1759. Thos. Shields to Robt. Douglass, £19, 129 acres on Pine Run on south side Beverley Manor; line of Charles Campbell; line of James Robinson. Teste: Hugh McClure, Andrew McClure, Thos. Shields.

Page 87.—21st March, 1759. John Scot and Ann ( ) to James Bruster, £20, 100 acres on a branch of Cub Run, part of 400 acres whereon Scot now lives; line of said Brewster's own land. Delivered: James Bruster, 24th December, 1762.

Page 90.—12th February, 1759. Stephen ( ) Rentfro to Wm. Preston, £100, 191 acres; corner Jno. Buchanan, conveyed to Stephen by Geo. Robinson, Gent., 25th May, 1748. Teste: Jno. Dickinson, Wm. Ward, Wm. Davis, Edward McMullin, Jno. Shields, Henry Earnest. Delivered: Mr. Gilbert by your order, 3d October, 1759.

Page 92.—21st March, 1759. John Anderson and Jane ( ) to Mathew Thompson, £107, 400 acres on Mill Creek of Shanando, patented to Andrew McConnall, 30th August, 1743, conveyed by Andrew to John in Augusta; corner Robt. Hook; corner William Williams. Delivered: Thompson, November, 1760.

Page 95.—21st March, 1759. George Rutledge to Thomas Rutledge, £5, 220 acres in Beverley Manor; corner old survey and Wm. Johnston's land; corner Wm. Henderson on a branch of Christian's Creek. Signed, George Rutlage. Teste: Walter Davis and Wm. Rutledge. Delivered: Thos. Rutledge, November, 1763.

Page 96.—10th March, 1759. James McCowen and Margaret (her mark), weaver, to William Buchanan, farmer, £90, 370 acres in Borden's tract, conveyed by Borden to James and Margaret, recorded in Augusta, James Buchanan's corner, crossing Walker's Creek to said McCoven's run; Jno. Wallace's line. Teste: Alexander Archibald and Robt. Buchanan. Livery by keyl in the door of mansion house on the premises. Certificate says McCown. Delivered: Wm. Buchanan, November, 1762.

Page 99.—21st March, 1759. William Bell to Samuel Bell, £40, 300 acres in Christian's Creek in Beverley Manor; corner Carr's land, point or end of a hill in Fork of Long Meadow Run and Christian's Creek, supposed to be a corner in the patent line; corner Geo. Roger; widow Baskin's line.

Page 101.—21st March, 1759. William Henderson and Susanna ( ) to James Henderson, £15, 430 acres, part of 1,415 acres whereon said William now lives, on a branch of Christian's Creek; line of Thos. Black; corner said Black and Robt. Cunningham; George Caldwell's line. Teste: James Mitchell, James Hutchinson. Delivered: James Henderson, November, 1768.

Page 104.—21st March, 1759. Wm. Henderson and Susanna ( ) to Jno. Henderson, £20, 200 acres, part of 1,415 as above; Thos. Rutledge's crossing Black's Branch. Teste: James Mitchell. Delivered: Jno. Henderson, March, 1760.

Page 106.—21st March, 1759. Same to same, £20, 200 acres, part of a tract surveyed for William Hutchinson on Christian's Creek; line of Andrew Russell.

Page 108.—2d January, 1759. William Lusk to James Lockhart, late sheriff, £166.13.0; mortgage of land where William lives, 200 acres, bounded by lands of Isaac Taylor, Daniel Lyle, James McClung, in Borden's tract; also thirds of 400 acres on James River, formerly belonging to Andrew Gahagan; Wm. Lusk, James Lockhart, Robt. Breckinridge obtained a judgment in General Court for lapsed law; also third of one other tract of 400 acres on Roanoke, formerly belonging to James Burk; also obtained by a like judgment in General Court. Teste: Jno. McCampbell, Wm. Tamson, Ronald and William Lockhart. Tomson (Thompson).

Page 109.—2d January, 1759. William Lusk to James Lockhart, £47.7.0, cattle, horses and other personalty.

Page 112.—16th May, 1759. Jacob ( ) Hermon to John and Adam Shaup, heirs of Mathew Shaup, £40, 350 acres devised to John and Adam by Mathew's will, their father, near upper end of Peaked Mountain Teste: Jno. Couts, Jacob Parsinger, Jacob Goodman.

Page 115.—16th May, 1759. James Leeper to his son, James Leeper, £5, on Naked Creek of North River patented to James, Sr., one patent 12th July, 1746, part of patent 26th April, 1746, containing 230 acres. Teste: Michael Dickey. Delivered Wm. McMullin, July, 1761.

Page 118.—16th May, 1759. Same to son, Gawen Leeper, £5, on Naked Creek, part of two patents dated June 5, 1747, and April 26, 1742, 352 acres. Delivered: D. Laird by your order, July, 1763.

Page 122.—16th May, 1759. John Young and Elizabeth ( ) to James Young, £30, 2 tracts containing 335 acres on a branch of Naked Creek, 200 acres conveyed to John by Hugh Campbell, 18th May, 1749, and 135 acres patented to John, 12th July, 1750, near corner of James Bell and John Rutledge, Erwin's land. Teste: James Gambel.

Page 125.—16th May, 1759. Robt. Cravens to his son, Joseph Cravens, £5, 59 acres, part of 200 on a branch of Cook's Creek patented to Robert, 10th February, 1748. Signed, Robt. ( ) Cravens. Teste: Samuel Downey. Delivered: Robt. Cravens, 14th August, 1772.

Page 127.—4th April, 1759. Robt. Cravens to Joseph Cravens, £50, 300 acres on a branch of Cook's Creek; corner Samuel Harrison. Teste: Samuel Hemphill, John ( ) Jones.

Page 130.—16th May, 1759. John Young to his son, Robert Young, £5, 265 acres in a branch of Middle River, Shanandore, part of two patents granted to John, one of four hundred acres dated 25th November, 1743, the other 200 acres dated 10th September, 1755.

Page 133.—16th May, 1759. James Caldwell and Mary to Samuel Caldwell, £5, 300 acres in Beverley Manor on Christian's Creek, part of 600 surveyed for said James, Moses Thomson's line. Teste: Alexander Reid, Abraham Smith. Delivered: Samuel Caldwell, November, 1762.

Page 136.—16th May, 1759. James McConall (McConnald) to Wm. McMullen (McMillin), £10, 100 acres, part of a large tract. Teste: James Leeper, Josua Russell. Delivered: Wm. McMullen, January, 1762.

Page 138.—16th May, 1759. George Wilson and Elizabeth to Wm. Stewart, £20, 105 acres on Cowpasture River; corner Carlile's land.

Page 140.—28th March, 1759. John Erwin and Jean to Wm. Curry, £20, 200 acres, part of 400 patented to John, 16th August, 1756, on Long Glade, a branch of North River, Shanando; corner Francis Erwin. Teste:

Andrew Francis, Edward Erwin. Delivered: Executor of grantee, 17 June, 1812.

Page 144.—16th August, 1759. Robt. Poage (Poock) to his son, Thos. Poage, £5, 262 acres, part of 772 acres in Beverley Manor where Robert now lives; John Poage's line; corner Williams, joining Lewis; corner Wm. Lewis; Wm. Poage's line. Teste: Francis Brown, Jno. Anderson. Delivered: Jno. Poage, 27th October, 1762.

Page 147.—16th August, 1759. Robt. Poage to Wm. Poage, £5, 205 acres, part of 772 acres in Beverley Manor as above; corner John Poage; corner Thos. Poage.

Page 149.—15th August, 1759. John Caperton and Mary, yeoman, to Henry Wilson, £25, 115 acres on a branch of Christian's Creek in Beverley Manor; corner James Caldwell. Teste: James Allen.

Page 152.—13th August, 1759. James ( ) Baggs and Elizabeth ( ) to Uriah Humble, £25, 220 acres in Brock's Gap of North Mountain patented to James and lies on side of Third Hill upon Dry River, a branch of Shanando. Teste: James Johnson, Johannis Keplinger. Delivered: Uriah, April, 1765.

Page 155.—15th August, 1759. Jacob Gillespy ( ) and Hannah ( ) to Jacob and Christian Rollman, £30, 280 acres on a branch of Beaver Creek called Howell's Branch; corner to land formerly belonging to Henry Smith. Teste: Thos. ( ) Shankland. Delivered: Jno. Shankland, May, 1762.

Page 158.—15th August, 1758. Robert Lowry to Wm. Edmiston, £34.13.4, 130 acres in Borden's tract. Delivered: Mary Edmiston, 10th December, 1771.

Page 161.—15th August, 1759. Jno. Davis ( ) and Judith ( ) to Wm Sprowle, £100, 320 acres on Moffet's Creek of James River in Borden's tract; corner Jno. Patterson. Delivered: Wm. Sprowl, 15th May, 1771.

Page 164.—14th August, 1759. Michael Finney and Catherine to John Colier (Collier), £5, 106 acres in Forks of James. Delivered: James Davis, September, 1762.

Page 167.—13th April, 1759. William ( ) Hall and Margaret ( ) of ———— County, North Carolina, to James Davis, £40, 212 acres on a branch of Buffelo Creek joining Jno. Collier's land; 3 white oaks by the Ship Rock; corner Arthur Brown. Teste: Wm. Davis, Henry H. Kerkham, James Campbell. Delivered: Jno. Low by your order, September, 1761. (Above conveyed to Wm. Hill by John Collier and Sisely, his wife, 22d May, 1750.)

Page 170.—15th August, 1759. James Trimble and Sarah to Wm. Burnet, of Pennsylvania, £35, 450 acres called the Limestone Spring on the head of the Branches of Black Thorne, a branch of the South Branch of Potomac, through the Laurel Gap. Teste: Wm. Bibb.

Page 173.—10th August, 1759. James Trimble and Sarah to Thos. Lorimer, £7.10.0, 100 acres at a place called the Oyl Trough on a branch of Black Thorne; corner Wm. Burnet. Delivered: Thos. Lorimer, May, 1760.

Page 176.—13th August, 1759. John Marshall, of Orange County, North Carolina, to Wm. Preston, £50, 203 acres in two surveys on Catawba Creek of James River; corner Burden's patent line, top of Mount Hadley. Teste: Jno. Hughes.

Page 177.—May, 1759. Alexander and John Buchanan, agreement. In 1755 they jointly purchased a tract of land from Humberstone Lyon for £50, of which Buchanan paid £38 and £12 by Sayers, but deed made to Sayers; contract by Sayers to convey to Buchanan one-half interest, and appoint Gabriel Jones, his attorney to make conveyance in case of death or absence of Sayers.

Page 179.—17th August, 1759. Thomas Black and Margaret (Margreat) to Samuel Love, £150, 300 acres on Christian's Creek in Beverley Manor; corner Wm. Johnston.

Page 181.—16th August, 1759. Robert Finley to Felix Gilbert, merchant. Beverley in 1749 conveyed to County Court 25 acres. County Court conveyed to Robert, 1753, lots 4, 3, 13, in Staunton, £30, lot 4 and 50 acres; corner Thos. Stewart, Wm. Preston's line. Teste: Audley Hamilton.

Page 184.—16th August, 1759. Geo. Wilson and Elizabeth to James Shaw, £10, 100 acres on Cowpasture River. Delivered: Jno. Bodkin, October, 1765.

Page 185.—15th August, 1759. Robert McClenachan to Jno. Buchanan and Wm. Preston, Justices. Lease, consideration yearly rent. Lots No. 1 and 2 (except the old courthouse, the old prison, and another house known by the name of McClenachan's tent and the ground whereon they stand) until 28th November, 1771, rental of £6. The justices shall not build or erect any buildings or houses on the above leased land nor suffer or permit any person to erect any booth stalls or arbours on the same, but Robert may build outside chimneys to the houses excepted out of this lease.

Page 187.—21st November, 1759. Wm. Preston to Thomas Waddel, £15, 145 acres on North River, Shanando; corner Benjamin Copeland. Delivered: Thos. Waddel, December, 1763.

190.—17th November, 1759. Patrick Hays and Frank (Frances) to Wm. Hays, £100, 255 acres on both sides of patent line of Beverley Manor and Burden's great tract, part of 854 acres held by patent of Beverley and Borden; corner Dunlape. Teste: Samuel Gallt, Hugh Hays.

Page 193.—21st November, 1759. Nicholas Null and Margaret to Henry Tack, £————, 225 acres on Boones Creek, near Shenandore River, part of 400 patented to Nicholas, 1739. Delivered to Henry, November, 1766.

Page 195.—21st November, 1759. Nicholas Null and Margaret to Chas. Foy, £————, 84 acres, part of 400 surveyed for Nicholas on Boon's Run, a branch of main River Shanandore; corner Henry Tack. Signed Nich ( ) Null, Margret ( ) Null. Delivered: Charles, November, 1766.

Page 198.—20th November, 1759. Helenor (Helander) ( ) Mitchell to Robt. Mitchell, £5, 200 acres in Beverley Manor, Robt. Wilson's line; corner Jno. Teate (Tate), David Doack's land; Jno. Lockart's corner. Teste: James Kowan.

Page 200.—21st November, 1759. John Burk to John McDonald, of Orange County, North Carolina, £35, 108 acres on Boon's Run, part of 400 acres surveyed for Jno. Burk. Delivered: Jno. Burk, May, 1760.

Page 203.—18th August, 1759. John Ker, of Rowan County, North Carolina, to James Hamilton, £25, 180 acres on Middle River at mouth of Christian's Creek, hill between Long Meadow Run and Christian's Creek; corner Beverley Manor. Teste: James Kerr, Jno. Gillespie, Jno. Hamilton. Proved by witnesses.

Page 205.—7th November, 1759. Samuel Steel and Sarah to Robert Steel, £20, 330 acres in Beverley Manor, part of 590 acres granted Samuel by Beverley; corner Robt. Alexander and Patrick Hays. Teste: Wm. Peerviance, Patrick McCorkle. Delivered: Samuel Steel, June, 1766.

Page 208.—10th October, 1759. Alexander Gibson and Mary ( ) to Anthony Black, £89, 115 acres on Middle River, joining Daniel McNeer where he now dwells; corner John Trimble; Thos. Gardner's line.

Page 211.—21st November, 1759. John ( ) Cozby (Cosby) and Elizabeth ( ) to Edward Erwin, Jr., £25, 400 acres on north side southermost branch of North River, Shanando, conveyed to John by Alexander Brownlee, 20th August, 1755. Delivered: Edward Erwin, May, 1767.

Page 212.—21st November, 1759. Robert Houston to Samuel McDowell, John McClung, John Lyle (Lisle) Wm. Alexander and John Thomson, trustees, appointed in name of trustees of Presbyterian Congregation of Timber Ridge, 5 shillings, 1 acre and 9 perches, part of Robert's plantation upon which acre, &c., the Presbyterian Meeting House is erected. Teste: Archibald Alexander, Mathew Lyle, John McClung, Jr.

Page 215.—18th September, 1759. John ( ) Coyler (Coyler, Collier, Colyer) and Sisely ( ) to Robert Huston, £25, 95 acres on a branch of Bufflow Creek called Colyer's Creek patented to John, 16th June, 1756, on creek; corner Jno. Summers. Teste: Wm. Lusk, John ( ) Alleson, John McClung.

Page 218.—21st November, 1759. Aaron Oliver, late of Augusta County, and Elizabeth ( ), to Thomas Shankland, £31.10.0, 196 acres on Muddy Creek below James Wood's land. Teste: Robert Shanklin, Richard Shanklin, Jno. Davidson.

Page 220.—26th September, 1759. Elnathan Davies (Davis), of Orange County, North Carolina, to John Smith, Gent. Benjamin Davies, of Orange County, North Carolina, on 15th June, 1759, gave power attorney to Elnathan to convey this land, 100 acres on south side James River; £50; corner Rob Looney. Teste: Thomas Lloyd.

Page 223.—21st November, 1759. Thomas ( ) Armstrong to son Wm, Armstrong, £5, 200 acres on Jennings' Branch, part of 400 surveyed for Thomas. Teste: John Finley, Jno. Burnside. Delivered: Wm. Armstrong, January, 1769.

Page 225.—22d November, 1759. Samuel McCutchin (McCotshin) to William McCutchin, £50, 112 acres on head branches of Cathew's River, a line of Burden's great tract, near said McCutchen's house.

Page 227.—20th November, 1759. Charles ( )Diver to John Divir, £47, 119 acres on North River, Shanando; corner James Ramsey; corner John Davis, opposite mouth of Bear Creek.

Page 229.—13th August, 1759. Borden's executors to Samuel and John McMurtrey. Benjamin, Jr., agreed to sell to grantees 292 acres for £3, part of 92,100; corner to place surveyed for Wm. Hall, but now Bordin's, Young's line; corner James Young and the Brisley Hill place. Teste: James McDowell.

Page 231.—November, 1759. Wm. Long, of Staunton, to Samuel Wilson, of same place. Lease. 50 acres on Lewis Creek, part of tract leased by Beverley to Long for 99 years, now leased for 94 years, £2 yearly. Delivered: Wm. Crow, September, 1767.

Page 233.—24th November, 1759. Robt. Finley to Felix Gilbert. County Court conveyed lots 3, 4, and 13 to Robert, 1753, now Robert conveys to Felix, £30, half lot No. 4, parallel with Samuel Wilson's lot to Sampson Mathews; also 50 acres, part of a large tract belonging to Robert in Beverley Manor; corner Thos. Stewart, Wm. Preston's line. Livery, &c., by handful of earth.

Page 235.—24th November, 1759. Robert Finley to Thomas Stewart (conveyed to Robert by County Court, 1753), £30, half of lot 3; also 40 acres, part as above, near Felix Gilbert's land. Livery, &c., by handful of earth. Delivered: Thomas, July, 1766.

Page 238.—21st November, 1759. John Smith, Gent., to Malcom Campbell, £———, 400 acres on Goose Creek of Roanoke, including the Great Lick, on side Smith's Creek, near mouth of Lick Branch. Sent to Wm. Campbell, the heir-at-law, by his order October, 1773.

Page 240.—18th March, 1760. John Moore to Robt. Alexander, £95.10.0, 304 A., 3 R., 15 P., in Borden's tract; corner Wm. Moore. Teste: Arwaker Johnston.

Page 243.—19th March, 1760. Andrew Foster and Margaret M. to James Bell, £20, 45 acres, part of 300 acres patented to Andrew, 5th September, 1749. Delivered: James Bell, 14th November, 1774.

Page 246.—18th March, 1760. Same to William Hodge, £10, 35 acres, part of 300 above. James Bell's line. Teste: James Phillips, James Bell. Delivered: James Bell as above.

Page 249.—18th March, 1760. Thomas ( ) Beard and Margaret to William Beard, £100, 605 A., 1 R., 28 P., in Borden's tract, on side Moffet's Creek; corner Jno. Roseman's land. Delivered: Wm. Beard, August 12, 1791.

Page 252.—18th March, 1760. Same, Baird to John Tate, £67.10.0, 309½ acres in Beverley Manor; corner James Lynn; corner David Steel. Teste: Thomas Teat.

Page 255.—21st September, 1759. John ( ) Colyer and Sisely ( ) to Jno. Summers, £8.10.0, 44 acres on Colyer's Creek of Buffelow, part of 277 acres patented to Collier, 16th June, 1756; corner John Colyer; corner Robert Huston. Teste: Alexander Collyer, James ( ) Davis, James McBride. Delivered: T. Smith, April, 1768.

Page 258.— —— day ———, 1760. John Henderson to Mathew Harper, £40, 200 acres, part of 1,415 formerly surveyed for Wm. Henderson, on Christian's Creek, Thomas Rutledge's land, Black's Branch. Teste: Pat. Martin, Wm. Henderson, David Bell. Delivered: Wm. Shannon, December, 1764.

Page 261.—Nathaniel Davise and Sarah to Francis McDonnall, £34, 150 acres in Beverley Manor; corner Arthur Hamilton; corner Samuel Downey; corner James Gilmer. Teste: Andrew Cowan, Arthur Hamilton.

Page 264.—March, 1760. Robt. Armstrong to Samuel Wilson, £50, 76 acres deeded to John Ritchie by Mathew Edmiston and by Ritchie to Robert, on a draft of Jennings' Creek.

Page 267.—18th March, 1760. Wm. and James Bell and Sarah ( ), wife of James, to William Magill, £85, 400 acres on Buffalo Lick Branch of Cathey's River granted to James Bell, deceased, of Augusta, by patent, 1st December, 1740, and bequeathed to said Wm. and James. Teste:

James Callison, Samuel Wallace. Delivered: Wm. McGill, 30th November, 1768.

Page 270.—14th March, 1760. John Trimble and Ann ( ) to Robt Phillips, £24, 100 acres on Cathey's River; line of Robert Davis; oak on McClure's Run. Teste: Hugh ( ) Young, Morris ( ) Ofreal, Samuel Wallace, Wm. Stewart. Delivered: April Court, 1778.

Page 273.—19th March, 1760. John Graham to Joseph Vauchub (Wauchub), £87, 307 acres on Little River in Calfpasture, part of 614 acres conveyed to John by Beverley. Delivered: 22d July, 1784.

Page 276.—27th January, 1760. Michael ( ) Harper and Isabel ( ) to Wm. Shannon, £35, 224 acres conveyed to Michael by Jno. Justice, 16th May, 1754, in Newfoundland Creek; corner Jno. Botkin; corner land in possession of Carlile. Teste: Wm. Stewart, Patt Martin, Jno. Jameson. Delivered: Wm. Shannon, December, 1764.

Page 279.—19th March, 1760. John Campbell, yeoman, to Thomas Sheals, yeoman, £33, 270 acres in Beverley Manor; corner Patrick Campbell in Wm. Thompson's line; Charles Campbell's line. Delivered: Shields, August, 1761.

Page 283.—19th March, 1760. John Hutcheson, farmer, to Francis Alexander, £5, 265 acres on Long Meadow, part of tract granted to George Hutcheson, 21st February, 1738; corner Samuel Henderson. Teste: James Alexander, James Alexander, Lazarus Inman. Delivered: Francis Alexander, February, 1773.

Page 286.—19th March, 1760. John Caldwell to Samuel Frazier, £5, current money of Augusta, 440 acres in Beverley Manor; corner to a survey made for Mr. Andrews, a minister, and corner to survey for Wm. Russell; corner Wm. Palmer's; line of Jno. Hutchison in the Poison Field.

Page 289.—26th November, 1759. Mathew Campbell to Adam Stephenson, £27.10.0, 250 acres on North Branch of South River, Shanando. Teste: Abraham Smith, Thos. Gordon, Ephraim Love, Wm. Cravens.

Page 292.—2d May, 1760. John McDaniel, of Orange County, North Carolina, to Stephen Greerrod, £30, 180 acres on Boon's Run of Shanando, part of 400 acres surveyed for Lewis and Jno. Neal and transferred to Burk. Acknowledged by John, 2d May, 1765. Delivered: Stephen, 20th January, 1761.

Page 295.—20th May, 1760. Samuel Henderson, farmer, and Jean ( ) to Jno. Hutchison, £5. 277 acres on Christian's Creek, part of tract surveyed for George Hutchison; corner George Hutcheson. Delivered: Samuel Pilson, October, 1765.

Page 297.—16th May, 1760. Borden's executors to James Wilson (Wittson), £5, 382 acres, part of 92,100; corner to his tract where widow Patterson dwells, crossing Kennedy's Mill Creek; corner plantation of Robert Edmiston; corner Samuel Buchanan on side Buffler draft. Teste: James McDowel, Jno. Paxton, Richard (his mark) Brown.

Page 301.—16th May, 1760. Same to William Wilson, £5, 377 acres, part of 92,100; corner Andrew Steel, crossing James Kenneday's Mill Creek; corner Hugh Marten; corner land where Jno. Wilson dwells.

Page 305.—14th May, 1760. Thomas ( ) Meek, farmer, to James Risk, £10, 200 acres at foot of the Brown Hill, Wm. McCutchen's land. Teste: Jno. Clark, Jno. Kirkpatrick, James Hunter. Delivered: Samuel Craig, 12th May, 1785.

Page 309.—4th October, 1760. Robert Brooke and Mary, of Essex County, to John Hunter, £40, 500 acres conveyed to Robert by Beverley, 26th November, 1741; corner Wm. Campbell; James Miles' line; Wm. Robinson's corner; Robt. Moffet's line. Teste: Robert ( ) Hunter, Wm. Palmer, Samuel Hunter, John ( ) McCallam.

Page 312.—5th April, 1760. Ephraim Vause to John Madison, £300, 1 parcel containing 360 acres and 1 parcel containing 320 acres adjoining and lying on Meadow Creek, a branch of Roanoke, whereon Vause formerly dwelt, patented to him 15th December, 1749.

Page 315.—21st May, 1760. Alvanis Byor and Barbara ( ) to Jno. Couts, £20, 140 acres, part of 280 patented to Alvanis, 10th August, 1759, on a branch between Shanando and Peaked Mountain. Delivered: Jno. Counts, March, 1762.

Page 319.—21st May, 1760. James Moody to Robt. Wilson, £60, 125 acres in Beverley Manor; corner Nicholas Leeper and said Robt. Wilson; corner James Wilson.

Page 322.—20th May, 1760. James Gilmore, eldest son and heir-at-law of John Gilmore, deceased, and Martha, to Thomas Gilmore, £5, 250 acres on Tees', alias Carr's, Creek; corner Jno. and Wm. Gilmore, part of 500 acres conveyed to John Gilmore, deceased, by Samuel Norwood. Sent to Thomas Gilmore, December, 1760.

Page 328.—19th May, 1760. Low Todd, of Bedford, to Hugh Cunningham, £78, 251 acres on Whistle Run in Forks of James; corner Mathew Young. Teste: Alexander Miller and Alexander Tallford, Jno. Huston. Delivered: Hugh Cunningham, May, 1773.

Page 332.—21st May, 1760. James ( ) Callison to James Boreland, £30, 175 acres on Jackson's River. Teste: James Ward, James Lockridge.

Page 335.—24th February, 1760. Alexander Ritchey and Mary M. to Joseph Kenaday, £66, 300 acres in Beverley Manor; corner tract surveyed for Samuel Templeton; Wm. McClintock's line; Adam Thompson's line. Teste: Hugh ( ) Young, Robt. ( ) Allen, Wm. Stewart.

Page 339.—20th May, 1760. Joseph ( ) Kennedy to John Handley, Jr., £80, 300 acres in Beverley Manor, above. Delivered: Jno. Handly, 1766.

Page 343.—27th February, 1760. Hugh Carothers, of Orange County, North Carolina, to Margaret Clerk, £35, 158 acres on James River, on Loonie's Creek; corner Robt. Sloan's. Teste: David Luney. Delivered: Benjamin Estill, December, 1761.

Page 346.—22d May, 1760. Robt. McClenachan and Sara to James Hughes, of Staunton, 32 acres Woodland, part of No. 10 surveyed for Mr. McClenachan, Joseph Gamble's lot, Wm. Preston's land; also lot 7 in Staunton. Teste: Wm. Givens.

Page 348.—26th February, 1760. Hugh Carothers, of Orange County, North Carolina, to Jno. Buchanan, power attorney to convey by deed to Margaret Clerk, 86 acres, joining land on which Margaret now lives.

Page 348.—26th February, 1760. Same to James Lawderdale, power attorney to convey to John Vaunce, 300 acres on a branch of Loonie's Creek, joining Wm. Harbinson.

Page 350.—12th May, 1760. Robert McClenachan and Sara to Margaret and Joseph Gamble, of Staunton, 28 acres Woodland, northeast of Staunton, part in lot 9 and part in lot 10, between James Hughes' lot and John Kess' lot; also lot 5 in Staunton.

Page 352.—22d May, 1760. Same to David Stewart and Samuel Cowden, £27, 30 acres, lot No. 9, Woodland, near Staunton; also No. 13 in Staunton. Teste: John McNulty.

Page 355.—18th March, 1760. Wm. Curry to John Buchanan, £21, 63 acres on Christian's Creek; corner said Buchanan's land; corner Cowan's land. Delivered: Pat. Buchanan, December 1770.

Page 359.—March, 1760. Hugh Carothers by Jno. Buchanan by power attorney, p. 348, supra., to Margaret Clerk, £12, 86 acres on a branch of James River; corner James Louderdale.

Page 364.—13th May, 1760. Tobias Smith to Wm. Preston, £60, 330 acres on waters of Roanoke.

Page 367.—22d March, 1760. Alexander Wright, merchant, in Fredericksburg, to James Bratton, blacksmith, £75, 334 acres in Beverley Manor; Mr. Lewis' corner; Maxwell's line. Teste: Patt. Couts, Wm. Long, Chas. Lewis, Wm. Preston, Thos. Bowyer, John Neil.

Page 371.— — day ———, 1760. John Hunter to Robt. Hunter, £———, 255 acres on Christian's Creek; corner Thos. Shields, Sayer's land; corner Robt. Wilson; Alexander's corner. Teste: James Logan. Delivered: Jno. Hunter, November, 1764.

Page 373.—10th June, 1760. James Laird, yeoman, to James Craig, yeoman, £60, 400 acres purchased by James from Wm. Downs, Smith's Creek; 500 years; mortgage. Signed David ( ) Laird. Recital of deed and acknowledgment says James Laird. Teste: Isaiah Curry. Delivered: Craig, May, '61.

Page 378.—30th May, 1760. William Downs to James Laird, £40, 400 acres, glade of Smith's Creek above (?). Teste: Joseph Hannah, James Craig, Samuel Henderson, James Laird. Delivered: James Laird, 27th June, 1761.

Page 382.—19th August, 1760. Jonathan Douglas and Jemima ( ) to Nicholas Mase, £15, 160 acres on Broad Run near Linvell's Creek, part of 400 surveyed for Thos. Beal and conveyed to Jonathan, 1755; cor. to that part of tract surveyed to Henry Mace; cor. John Fare. Teste: Michael Hogshead, Margaret Woods. Delivered: Geo. Skelerom, 25th April, 1761.

Page 386.—19th August, 1760. Same to Henry Mace, £5, 34 acres, art of 400 above; cor. Robert Poage. Delivered: Geo. Skileron, 1761.

Page 392.—19th August, 1760. Andrew Duncan and Jane ( ) to Samuel Lindsay, £100.10, 190 acres on Walker's Creek in Borden's 92100; cor. Alex. Walker; James Moore's cor. Acknowledged, 19th August.

Page 394.—19th August, 1760. Loftus Pullen to James Shaw, £9, 240 acres on Great River Calfpasture, conveyed to Pullen by James Patton and Lewis, 17th July, 1745; cor. land formerly in possession of John Miller and now in posession of Jno. Ramsey; cor. Robert Bratton. Delivered: Jno. Bodkin by your order, October, 1765.

Page 399.—19th August, 1760. James ( ) Hall and Susanna ( ) to Robert Hall, £10, 212 acres on Cowpasture River; cor. to tract formerly in possession of Michael Rainey, but now Charles Gillum.

Page 403.—20th August, 1760. Henry Brown and Alice, of Bedford, to Thomas Walker, of Louisa, £100, 200 acres on Goose Creek. Teste: Archibald Brycers. Delivered: Thomas Madison, 11th March, 1763.

Page 405.—17th September, 1760. Commission to Joseph Rentfrow and

Turner Hunt Christian, of Bedford, to take privy execution of Alice to above. Executed, 22d September, 1760.

Page 408.—20th August, 1760. Henry Brown and Alice to Esther Brown, £5, 54 acres by patent, 3d November, 1750, on a branch of Roanoke called Lick Run; cor. James Burke.

Page 410. Commission as before.

Page 413.—20th August, 1760. Henry Brown and Alice to Thomas Brown, £5, 87 acres on Goose Creek.

Page 415.—Commission as before.

Page 418.— — — 1760. Anthony Strother and Mary, of Spottsylvania, to Randal Lockhart, £325, 552 acres purchased by Anthony of John Pickens, 22d March, 1753, beginning at patent Thomas Gordon's, now Rev. Jno. Craig's on Lewis Creek, Wm. Baskin's lines. Delivered: Randal Lockhart, August, 1762.

Page 422.—4th July, 1760. Joseph ( ) Kennedey to Wm. Kennedey, £100, 414 acres in Borden's tract; cor. Andrew Steel, crossing the Mill Creek; cor. Andrew Duncan. Delivered: Jno. Handley by your order.

Page 426.—18th August, 1760. Robert ( ) Craven and Mary to John Halpe, £35, 165 acres on North River Shanando opposite mouth of Fort Run, purchased by Robert of Elisha Fowler, and title confirmed by decree of County Court and patented to Fowler, 10th February, 1758. Delivered: John Halpe, July, 1765.

Page 429.—21st August, 1760. Robert Breckinridge and Lettice to Alexander Gibson, £160, 219½ acres in Beverley Manor, part of 439 granted to John Maxwell and 219½ conveyed to Robert by John; cor. Andrew Johnson. Delivered: Alex. Gibson, May, 1761.

Page 432.—6th June, 1760. Thomas Lewis and Jean to Andrew Lewis, £300, 740 acres in Beverley Manor on Lewis Creek; Alex. Wright's field.

Page 436.—21st August, 1760. Steven ( ) Arnold to John Poage, Sr., £44, 120 acres; cor. Hugh Mares. Delivered: Jno. Poage, March, 1769.

Page 439.—20th August, 1760. John McCreery and Agness to Jno. Bodkin, £15, 200 acres on Newfound Creek, patented to grantor 10th August, 1759; cor. Archibald Elliot.

Page 442.—19th August, 1760. Wm. Marten and Janet ( ) to John Davis, £110, 198 acres purchased by Wm. from John McPheeters, 23d March, 1754, and part of a tract he now possesses, line of James Young, deceased; cor. Robert Campbell, now James Berry's. Delivered: Felix Gilbert, February, 1762.

Page 446.—19th August, 1760. James Campbell and Lettice ( ) to Alex. Boyd, Lieutenant and paymaster to the Virginia Regiment, £430, 400 acres on waters of Roanoke, patented to James, 12th February, 1752, on Goose Creek. Delivered: Alex. Love, October, 1762.

Page 450.—21st August, 1760. Same to same, £20, 100 acres on Crooked Run, a branch of Roanoke, conveyed to James by Patton, 1753.

Page 453.—21st August, 1760. James Trimble and Sarah to Thomas Parsons, of Hampshire, £15, 200 acres on South Branch Potomac.

DEED BOOK No. 9.

Page 2.—18th November, 1760. John Capbritton and Mary to Christian

Dedor (signed Caperton), £15, 275 acres between Shanandore and Picked Mountain, patented to John, 2d June, 1760; cor. to survey of Peter Sellars Delivered: Andrew Lewis, 11th July, 1785.

Page 5.—16th October, 1760. Maurice Poutz (signed Pound), of Fairfax, to John Peter Gully, £—, 130 acres patented to James McCarroll, 20th September, 1748, on Cub Run, Crosswait's line. Teste: Jno. Kurtz, Jacob Curtnes, Anna Curtnes, Peter Hog, Henry Pirgy, Henry Sellar, Philip Horless. Delivered: John Peter Gally.

Page 9.—16th October, 1760. Same to Henry Pirgy, £154, 360 acres, part of Jacob Steven's great tract, formerly conveyed to Christopher Francisco, the elder, and by Stophel Francisco, his attorney in fact, to Maurice Pound, 2d July, 1752, on north side Shenandore; John Stevenson's meadow; cor. Ludwick Francisco. Delivered: Jacob Pirkey, February, 1767.

Page 13.—18th November, 1760. David Cloyd and Margaret ( ) to James Cloyd, £20, 400 acres on North Branch James joining Wm. Mills, patented to David Cloyd, 20th September, 1748. Delivered: Jno. Thompson by Cloyd's order, 5th May, 1777.

Page 15.—18th August, 1760. Joshua Hadley (Hedley) and Patience, of Orange County, North Carolina, to Robert Kyle, of Albemarle, £90, 345 acres on Catawba of James River, part of 2,880 acres granted to Benj. Borden, 9th March, 1740. Teste: James Rowland, Joshua Hadley, Jr., David Irvine. Livery of seisin. Delivered: Rev. Alex. Miller, 21st May, 1770.

Page 17.—9th November, 1760. John Wright and Lydde and John Cravens and Margaret ( ) to Daniel Pouder, £40, 510 acres on head of east fork of Cook's Creek and a draft of Smith's Creek; Daniel Harrison's land, patented to Jacob Gardner, 16th August, 1756. Teste: Daniel Harrison, Jonathan Douglass.

Page 21.—18th November, 1760. James Alexander to John and Wm. Long, heirs of Frances Long, deceased, of Chester County, Pennsylvania, £5, 400 acres, part of 800 on Long Meadow of Middle River; cor. Andrew McClure's; cor. James Alexander. Delivered: John Long, 23d October, 1766.

Page 25.—26th September, 1760. George Adam Salling, of Cumberland County, North Carolina, and John Salling, of Orange County, North Carolina, to John Paxton, £120, 200 acres, part of 400 patented to John Peter Salling, deceased, 6th July, 1741, and bequeathed in his will to grantors in the first fork of James, cor. Geo. Adam Salling. Delivered: John Paxton, December, 1762.

Page 33.—18th November, 1760. John Rodes, of County Frederick, to Henry Price, of Frederick County, £15, 400 acres at foot of Peaked Mountain. Delivered to grantee's son, Adam Price, 20th March, 1815.

Page 36.—18th November, 1760. Same to Daniel Sinks, £10, 400 acres in Forks of Shenandore near Picked Mountain.

Page 39.—18th November, 1760. George Crawford to Henry Reburn, £50, 100 acres on North River Shanandore below the Fork; land now Henry lives on, patented to Josia Hickman, 5th April, 1748. Delivered: Henry Reburn, August, 1762.

Page 41.—10th November, 1760. Borden's executors to James Robinson, £5, 416 acres, part of 92100, on Hays Creek; cor. Samuel Walker; cor. Joseph Culton. Delivered: James Wallace, 1767.

Page 45.—10th November, 1760. Same to Wm. Robinson, £—, 124 acres, part of 92100, on Hays Creek; cor. James Robinson. Delivered: James Wallace, August, 1767.

Page 50.—19th November, 1760. Samuel McClure and Mary ( ) to James Campbell, £160, 232 acres in Forks of James on Woods Creek; cor. Jno. Paxton. Delivered: Benj. Estill, November, 1763.

Page 54.—19th November, 1760. Same to James Gilmore, £100, 190 acres in Forks of James on Cedar Creek; cor. Rob. Poage's land, Thomas Hatton's line, John Darrick's line; cor. Samuel Walker and John Allison. Delivered: James Gilmore, November Court, 1766.

Page 58.—19th November, 1759. Edward Beard and Mary to Thomas Lorimer, £30, 159 acres, part of 179 acres patented to ——, 30th August, 1748, on North River Shanandore. Delivered: Lorrimer, June, 1762.

Page 60.—16th May, 1760. Alex. Wright, merchant in Fredericksburg, to Thomas Fulton, of Staunton, £200; lots 8 and 9 in Staunton, also lots 6 and 7 of woodland. Livery by key of door. Delivered: Thomas Fulton, 29th January, 1762.

Page 62.—16th June, 1760. Same to same, £100, lote 14, 15, 20 and 21, conveyed to grantor by Wm. Beverley, 1755. Livery by one fence rail. Executed and delivered, 29th January, 1762.

Page 65.—22d October, 1760. Robert Abercromby, of North Carolina, to Robert Gay, £—, 5 sh., 664 (646 ?) acres on West Fork of Jackson's River, patented to Robert Abercromby, 10th August, 1759. Delivered Benj. Estill, November, 1762.

Page 68.—19th November, 1760. Samuel Carr (Kerr) and Margaret ( ) to James Hughes and Andrew Greer, £120, 224 acres on Big Meadow Run by patent, 16th August, 1756, Beverley Manor line.

Page 72.—19th November 1760. John Black to Samuel Black, his son, £5, 369 acres on South River of Shanandore in Beverley Manor, part of 738 acres on which said Jno. and Samuel now live; cor. Thos. Stewart. Delivered: Samuel Black, 3d August, 1772.

Page 76.—19th November, 1760. James Anderson to Wm. McMillen, £70, 120 acres on Woods Creek of north branch of North River of Shanandore. Teste: John, John and Robert Anderson. Delivered: McMillen, November, 1762.

Page 79.—15th November, 1760. Thos. ( ) West and Christina ( ) to Marten Witsell, £45, 120 acres patented to Thos., 16th August, 1756, on North Branch Shanandore above Brock's Gap; cor. Jno. McDonel's survey. Teste: Wm. ( ) Glasgoro (Glasgow ?).

Page 84.—19th November, 1760. James Reburn and Elizabeth ( ) to son Joseph Reburn, £5, 93 acres on Moffets Branch of Middle River, part of 130 acre sand also a small part of a survey of —— acres on which said James now lives; cor. Wm. Mathews. Delivered: Joseph Reaburn, August, 1762.

Page 88.—15th September, 1760. James Huston and Agness to Alex. Boyd, £50, 140 acres on Back Creek of Roanoke at Turkey Bottom. Teste: John Neill, Archibald Brycers. Delivered: Alex. Love, October, 1762.

Page 104.—22d December, 1760. Charles Dick and Fielding Lewis, of

Fredericksburg, to Abraham Hite, of Hampshire, release of deed, 1st February, 1755, by grantee here to grantor; Hite's Mill tract. Teste: David Ralstone, Jere Herreson, John and Abraham Wright.

Page 108.—31st December, 1760. Alex. Hite and Rebecca, of Hampshire, to John Wright, £150, 550 acres on Linvel's Creek, part of 1200 acres patented to McCoy, Hite & Co. and by them conveyed to Abraham by deed recorded in Orange; cor. to portion of said tract belonging to Jeremiah Harrison. Delivered: John Johnston by order of Cap. Daniel Smith, August, 1766.

Page 112.—31st December, 1760. Same to David Ralstone, £150, 250 acres on Linvel's Creek, part of 1200 above, adjoining 550 above.

Page 115.—31st Decemebr, 1760. Same to Jeremiah Harrison, £150, 400 acres on Linvel's Creek, part of 1200 above, adjoining Wright and Ralstone above. Delivered: Jeremiah Harrison, 14th October, 1765.

Page 119.—17th February, 1761. John Camplin (Johannes Keplinger) and Lydia ( ) Camplin (Keplinger), his wife, to John Gratton, £50, on the River, 156 acres, part of 800 acres taken up by Benj. Borden, Jr., and by his executors conveyed to John Camplin, 7th August, 1757. Teste: John Camplin. Delivered.

Page 123.—22d January. 1761. David Miller to Robert Brackenridge, £105, 307 acres on Buffelo Creek, a branch of Roanoke, including said David Miller's improvements, joining lands of said David Miller, David Robinson, William Graham, Baptist McNab and Andrew Hays, part of two surveys: A, conveyed to David by Wm. Syers; B, patented to David, 10th March, 1756. Teste: Geo. Paris.

Page 126.—14th February, 1761. John Dunlupe (Dunlap, Dunlop, Dunlape) to Robert Dunlape, £100, 295 acres on Calfpasture, part of 625 acres on Mill Creek, the river where the Creek empties. Teste: Arwaker Johnston, James Beard, Jas. Trimble.

Page 129.—17th February, 1761. Jeremiah (Jere) Harrison and Catherine to Samuel Semple, £22, 19 acres by patent, 10th April, 1759, at the great Spring on head of South Branch of Linvell's Creek; cor. Samuel Stewart's land. Teste: William Preston, George Skillern, William Anderson.

Page 133.—10th February, 1761. William Sprowl and Jean to William Stewart, £30, 168 acres on Cowpasture River. Teste: William Marten, Hugh ( ) Young, James ( ) Trotter. Delivered, October, 1761.

Page 137.—3d February. 1760. George Speece and Christina to Michael Hober, £35, on east side Linvell's Creek, 150 acres, part of 500 surveyed for Paul Froman and afterward conveyed to said George Speece; cor. John Miller's land. Teste: Henry Maese and Nicolas ( ) Mase. Delivered: Francis Morisey, April, 1763.

Page 141.—17th February, 1761. Samuel Bell and Margaret ( ) to James Ker, blacksmith, £40, 300 acres in Beverley Manor, at mouth of Christian's Creek on Middle River; cor. James Hamilton's land, formerly Ker's, fork of Long Meadow Run and said Creek, suposed to be a corner in the patent line; cor. George Roger, Thomas Baskin's line, formerly Widow Baskin's. Delivered: James Ker, 10th June, 1771.

Page 144.— — February, 1761. George ( ) Patterson and Margaret to Philip Horless (Horlish), £50, 110 acres on head of a draft running into one Givens' land, patented to said Archebell Hamilton, said Givens' line. Teste: George Drout. Delivered: Philip Horless, May, 1764. Acknowledged by Margaret.

Page 148.—17th February, 1761. William Lusk to Hugh Lusk, £—, 5 sh., 220 acres patented, 10th August, 1759, on north side Buffalo Creek. Delivered: Hugh Lusk, 15th August, 1771.

Page 151.—18th February, 1761. Jeremiah (Jerre) Harrison and Catherine ( ) to Thomas Harrison, £20, 120 acres by patent, — ——,1760, on east draft of Cook's Creek, a branch of Shannandoe River, joining Robert Cravens.

Page 155.—29th January, 1761. John Madison and Agatha to William Lamb, £300, 363 acres purchased of William Thompson, south bank of Middle River; cor. Andrew Leeper, fork of the river; cor. William Baskins, Buffelow Run. Delivered: Wm. Lamb, September, 1768.

Page 158.—17th February, 1761. Jeremiah (Jere) Harrison and Catherine ( ) to Samuel Semple, £22, 270 acres patented, — ——, 1760, on head waters of Linvel's Creek, whereon Samuel now dwells, joining Jost Hite, Samuel Stewart, Thomas Harrison.

Page 162.—29th November, 1760. Robert Gibson to William Caldwell, £30, 186 acres on a branch of Christian's Creek; cor. George Caldwell; cor. land belonging to the heir of Robert Gibson, deceased. Teste: Wm. Armstrong, Wm. Palmer, George Caldwell, George Caldwell. Delivered: Philip Dold by written order from David Caldwell, 20th May, 1803.

Page 165.—29th January, 1761. Borden's executors to David Gray, £—, 100 acres of 92100; Moses Whiteside's cor. on John Davidson, Samuel McCosky's line..

Page 168.—29th January, 1761. Same to David Gray, £—, 100 acres of 92100, James Greenlee's cor. on John Davidson's line; Moses Whiteside's line, William Gray's cor.

Page 172.—10th February, 1761. Same to William Hall, £—, 150 acres of 92100; cor. Halbert McClure, Samuel McMurtry's line, Mary Anne Crawford's line. Delivered: William Hall, August, 1762.

Page 176.—7th February, 1761. Same to Samuel Davis, £—, 200 acres of 92100; cor. James Anderson in a line of a tract of 636, said to be sold by John Buchanan, gent., unto Robert Allison, side of Mount Atlas; cor. tract surveyed for Mr. James Greenlee, William Davis' Cor.

Page 180.—13th February, 1761. Same to William Davis, £—, 100 acres of 92100; cor. John Scot; cor. said Scot's and Samuel Davise's line; cor. Francis Reynolds, Scot's and Anderson's line.

Page 184.—11th February, 1761. Same to John Scot, £—, 100 acres of 92100; cor Francis Reynolds and James Anderson; cor. Hays' land; cor. Paxton's land, Davison's line, said Rundal's line.

Page 189.—12th February, 1761. Same to Francis Reynolds, £—, 100 acres of 92100; James Anderson's line, cor. survey for Samuel Davis.

Page 193.—8th November, 1760. Same to Samuel Norwood, £—, 400 acres of 92100; cor. Francis McCown, bank of Kerr's Creek; cor. William Hamilton. Delivered: Wm. McKee, May, 1764.

Page 197.—11th February, 1761. Same to Alexander McCorkle, £—, 300 acres of 92100; cor. John Smiley on west side North Branch of James River; Abraham Brown's cor., including a large island. Delivered: Alex. McCorkle, 9th January, 1796.

Page 203.—13th February, 1761. Nathaniel Evins and Mary to John Keys, £15, 161 acres on west side of the South River alias the River Mary, a branch of James River, patented to Nathaniel, 1759; cor. tract belonging to heirs of John McDowell, the low ground of Reverend Alexander McDowell. Teste: Thomas Bowyer, Samuel and James McDowell.

Page 208.—18th February, 1760. Thomas ( ) Shanklin and Eleanor ( ) to John Shanklin, their son, £10, 220 acres on a branch of Muddy Creek, a branch of North River of Shanandoe, part of 400 acres where Thomas now lives; cor. Green's land. Teste: Robert Shanklin, William ( ) Pickens. Delivered: Thomas Shanklin, 27th August, 1763.

Page 213.—18th February, 1761. John Ward to Joseph Waughub, £—, 246 acres in Calfpasture on head of Grassy Lick Run, top of Black Oak Hill; cor. Wm. McCutchin's and Johnson's land, Meeting House Run; cor. John Johnson's land.

Page 217.—17th February, 1761. Jeremiah (Jere) Harrison and Catherine ( ) to John Stewart, £95, 272 acres on Cooke's Creek; cor. John Hope's. Teste: Robert Breckenridge, Geo. Skillem, William Preston.

Page 221.—17th February, 1761. John Mountgomery to James Montgomery, £40, — acres in Borden's tract, the patent line, cor. Mathew Huston, Beverley Manor line. Delivered: John Cunningham, 1st August, 1779.

Page 225.—9th December, 1760. John Black to his son William Black, £10, 369 acres on South River of Shanandoe, part of 738 acres whereon John now lives; cor. William Long, Samuel Black's part of said tract. Teste: Thomas Stewart, James and Gabriel Alexander, Samuel Black. Delivered: William Black, 19th July, 1787.

Page 230.—18th February, 1761. William Thompson, of Spring Hill, to Alexander Boyd, gentleman, paymaster to the Virginia Regiment. Whereas, Mathias Yoackum, of Bedford County, yeoman, on — November, 1760, constituted William his attorney to convey to Alexander 267 acres, £100, 267 acres on the river. Delivered: Alex. Love, October, 1762.

Page 235.—18th February, 1761. William McCutcheon (Cutchin) to Joans Henderson, £80, 314 acres, part of 585 acres conveyed to William by Beverley, 10th November, MDCCLXVI (1746 ?) recorded in the Secretary's office, on Smith's Creek, a branch of little Calfpasture; cor. Francis Fulton; cor. John Johnston. Delivered: John King, August, 1764.

Page 239.—18th February, 1761. William McCutchin to Francis Fulton, £62.10, 271 acres, part of 585 acres conveyed to William by Beverley, 10th November, 1746, recorded in Secretary's office, as above, on Smith's Creek; cor. Robert McCutchin.

Page 244.—19th May, 1761. William Kennedy and Martha to William Clarke, £120, 402 acres of Borden's large tract, on Moffet's Creek; cor. William Fulton (except two acres sold to William Adams). Teste: Hugh Wardlaw, Ro. Lusk. Delivered: Robert Clarke, March, 1763.

Page 247.—19th May, 1761. John Mitchel to Thomas Mitchel, £10, 234 acres in Beverley Manor, part of 609 acres conveyed to John by Beverley, 13th August, 1747; cor. Samuel Braford. Teste: John Finley, Robert Wilson, David Doack. Delivered: Thos. Mitchell, 3d November, 1764.

Page 251.—16th May, 1761. James Lockhart to his son William Lockhart, £5, 324 acres, part of 624 conveyed to James by Beverley, 17th June, 1748; cor. to part of tract belonging to Patrick Lockhart; cor. David Campbell. Teste: James Hughes, Ranl. Lockhart. Delivered: William Lockhart, April, 1767.

Page 256.—16th May, 1761. James Lockhart to his son Patrick Lockhart, £5, 300 acres of 624 preceding on head branch of Middle River of Shannandoe; line of the Meeting House land; cor. Perrey's land; cor. William Lockart's part of said tract. Delivered: Pat. Lockhart, April, 1767.

Page 260.—19th May, 1761. Robert Turk and Marget ( ) Turk, his wife, to Adam Dean, £140, 160 acres on southeast side South River, part of tract patented to Robert, 6th September, 1736. Teste: Robert and Thomas Turk, James Davison.

Page 264.— — ——, 1761. Robert Hook to William Hook, £60, 150 acres on Mill Creek, a branch of South River of Shannando, Steven's line. Teste: Archibald Brycers. Delivered: Wm. Hook, March, 1764.

Page 267.—19th May, 1761. John Ker and Lucie ( ) to Hugh Botkin, £13.10, 174 acres on a draft of North River of Shanando; cor. Robert McMahan. Teste: John Botkin, William Kerr, William ( ) Mathers, John Reburn. Delivered: John Botkin, 5th June, 1762.

Page 270.—19th May, 1761. Same to Willam Mathers, £10, 112 acres, part of a survey of 275 acres surveyed for John Kerr in Beverley Manor on a branch of Middle River; Manor line. Teste: William and Jes. Kerr, John Hind. Delivered: Henry King per order of Wm. Mathers, 29th December, 1774.

Page 274.—21st April, 1761. Alexander Craighead, of North Carolina, to John Bowyer, £300, 533 acres of Borden's 92100; cor. Richard Woods; cor. Peter Wallace, Cap. Lapsley's line. Teste: John Dickenson.

Page 277.—6th May, 1761. Charles Milliken (Mellegan, Millegan), of Orange County, North Carolina, to John Buchanan, gent., power of attorney to convey 297 acres patented to Patrick Hays, 30th June, 1743, and since conveyed to Charles by said Hay. Teste: Jno. Smith, David Robinson, David Luney, John Luney.

Page 279.—5th May, 1761. Charles Milligan, of Orange County, North Carolina, to John McClalan, of Bedford County, Virginia, £65, 60 acres by patent 3d November, 1750, and conveyed to Charles by James Patton, 18th November, 1752, on head of Lunie's Creek. Delivered: Francis Smith, 1st October, 1767.

Page 283.—19th May, 1761. James Hughs and Euphie (Euphemia), of Staunton, to William Willson, of Staunton, £15, part of two lots: A, in Staunton, part of lot —; B, 2½ acres, part of a lot of 30 acres woodland betwixt Col. Preston's and Joseph Gamble's woodland lot about ½ mile northwest of Staunton, part of lot No. 10. Delivered: Edward Long, August Court, 1765.

Page 286.— — —— 1761. Samuel Givens and Martha to Samuel Bell, £90, 159 acres, part of 311 acres patented to said Givens, on southeast side Middle River of Shanando betwixt lands of John and James Givens; cor. said James Givens. Teste: William Lamb, Wm. Walters. Delivered: Samuel Bell, 10th August, 1786.

Page 290.—19th April, 1761. Samuel Givens and Martha to Samuel Henderson, £110, 151 acres, part of 311 acres on Middle River Shanando; cor. John Givens; cor. Samuel Bell's part of same tract. Teste: George Crawford, John Ritchey, Samuel Bell.

Page 294.—31st December, 1760. Mary Wood, of Frederick, to Joseph Rutherford, £100, 400 acres on a branch of South River of Shanando, called Cub Run, spur of Peaked Mountain, patented to James Wood, deceased, 12th January, 1746, and devised to Mary by his will in Frederick. Teste: Thomas Rutherford. Delivered: Reuben Rutherford, May, 1768.

Page 297.—3d May, 1761. James Claypool, Jr., and Margaret ( ), of Hampshire County, to James Thomas, £40, patented to said James Claypool, 15th December, 1757, at head of Cedar Branch, 240 acres. Delivered: James Claypole, 1st August, 1764.

Page 302.—15th May, 1761. Same to Jacob Gum. £30, patented to William Rutledge, 20th August, 1745, and by him conveyed to Cornelius Ruddle an dby him to said James, on a branch of Brock's Creek, 237 acres. Delivered: Jacob Gum, 6th August, 1764.

Page 306.—15th May, 1761. Same to same, £20, patented to said James, 10th September, 1755, on a branch of Linvel's Creek; William Mark's land; John Bryan's land; 48 acres. Delivered.

Page 311.—17th May, 1761. Mathew Wilson, eldest brother and heir-at-law of William Wilson, deceased, and Eleanor ( ) to Robert Graham, £67.10, 281 acres on a branch of the Cowpasture River called Newfoundland; line of land in possession of the Caroliles; cor. land in possession of Andrew Lewis.

Page 315.—27th March, 1761. James McCarrell to John Joans (Jones), £12, 260 acres at a place called Snoden's Spring. Teste: William and Joseph Cravens, James Robertson. Delivered: John Jones, November, 1764.

Page 318.—15th May, 1761. Michael Finney and Catherine ( ) to Samuel Moore, £38 ,335 acres in Fork of James River, part of a tract of 700 whereon Michael now lives; cor. McDowel's and MichaelFinney's land; cor. William Holman. Teste: James Bailey, Abram Goodding. Delivered: Wm. Foster by your order, February, 1768.

Page 322.—11th March, 1761. Robert ( ) Patterson, yeoman, to Thomas Patterson, his son, £10, 167 acres more or less in Beverley Manor, part of 331 acres conveyed to Robert by Beverley, 27th February, 1741, on Middle River; cor. that part of the tract belonging to John Patterson. Teste: William Baskian, Mathew Armstrong, David Bell. Delivered: Thomas Patterson, 24th June, 1765.

Page 326.—11th March, 1761. Same to his son John Patterson, £10, 164 acres, part of 331 acres (see above); cor. John Anderson. Delivered: Thos. Patterson, 24th June, 1765.

Page 329.— — — 1761. Jno. Buchanan and William Thompson, executors of James Patton, to James Lecock, of the city of Limerick, Ireland. Power of attorney to sue and recover all debts due James Patton in Kingdom of Ireland, either by hand, bill, book account, or in trust from any person, but particularly from Mr. Campbell, of City of ——. Teste: Wm. Preston, John Brown.

Page 331.—17th April, 1761. Robert Cunningham (Coningham) to Walter Davies, £—, 5 sh., in Beverley Manor, on Cedar Spring Run; cor. Thomas Black and James Armstrong, 160 acres. Teste: John Cuningham, William Scot, John Davies. Delivered: W. Davis, 9th April, 1796.

Page 335.—18th May, 1761. Thomas Lewis to James and Robert Allen, £80, 560 acres on West Fork of Jackson's River.

Page 339.—10th April, 1761. William Johnston to John Davies (Davis), £—, 5 sh., 269 acres in Beverley Manor on Black's Run, a branch of Christian's Creek; cor. said Black's land, William Henderson's line, George Rutledge's line; cor. said Rutledges and James Armstrong's; said Black's cor., two white oaks at an iron mine. Teste: Walter Davies, Thomas Rutlidge, John Cunningham.

Page 343.—20th May, 1761. David Cloyd to Michael Cloyd, £10, 400 acres on Pecimmon Branch of James River. Teste: Joseph Robinson, James Cloyd, George Alexander. Delivered: William McClenachan, November, 1766.

Page 346.—20th May, 1761. David Cloyd to Michael Cloyd, £5, 262 acres on Percimmon Branch of James River, adjoining David Mitchel and William Mills; cor. Mills' former survey. Delivered.

Page 349.—29th May, 1761. David Cloyd, Sr., to David Cloyd, Jr., £20, 400 acres on a south branch of Cedar Creek. Teste: Joseph Robinson, James Cloyd, George Alexander.

Page 351.—4th April, 1761. David Cloyd to Edward McDonald, release of mortgage by Edward to David, 21st November, 1753, for 340 acres. Teste: James Cloyd, David Cloyd, Jr. Delivered.

Page 353.—20th May, 1761. John Kerr and Lucie ( ) to John Allison, £2, 10 acres on east side Shanandoe betwixt land of said Ker and Allison, part of 400 acres; Andrew Ker's line. Teste: Andrew Russell, Edward Rutledge, William Ker. Delivered: John Allison, February, 1768.

Page 357.—19th May, 1761. John Hind and Jean ( ) to Hugh Allen, £130, 100 acres in a loop neck or turn of Cathey's River; William Ker's line; Thomas Story's line, small island cor. Story. Delivered: James Allen, administrator Hugh Allen, 11th March, 1794.

Page 360.—20th May, 1761. Thomas Stewart to Thomas Jones, £2, 145 acres in Forke of James; cor. John Mathews, the barrens. Teste: Sampson Archer, John Mathews, John Miller. Delivered: Nathaniel Evins, September, 1763.

Page 363.—20th May, 1761. Robert Poage to John Baidie (Bailey, Bailie), £50, 250 acres on Cedar Run, a branch of North River, patented to Robert, 3d March, 1760; also 40 acres adjoining above. Teste: John Poage. Delivered: Jno. Baile, October, 1765.

Page 366.—20th May, 1761. Sampson Archer and Rebecka to John Archer, gent., £100, 380 acres on a branch of Middle River called Elk Meadow. Delivered: Jno. Archer, September, 1765.

Page 369.—5th May, 1761. Jacob Chrisman and Magdalina ( ), of Frederick County, to George Chrisman, of Frederick, £100, 376 acres on Linville's Creek, part of greater tract; cor. John Chrisman. Teste: Jno. D. Wilper.

Page 373.—5th May, 1761. Same to John Chrisman, £100, 300 acres on Linvel's Creek, Francis McBride's land; cor. George Chrisman. Delivered: Francis McBride, January, 1763.

Page 376.—5th April, 1761. Same to Francis McBride, £150, 300 acres on Linvel's Creek, part of 500 acres purchased of Joseph Bryan, which is part of 1500 acres surveyed for William Linvells. Teste: Cuthbert Bullett Delivered: Francis McBride, June, 1762.

Page 379.—19th May, 1761. John Draper and Elisabeth ( ) to Richard

Doggett, of Bedford County, £75, 315 acres on Tom's Creek; cor. William Inglese's land, Lingell's line. Delivered by your order, September, 1762.

Page 382.—19th May, 1761. Same to same, £75, 220 acres, part of 440 acres conveyed to John Draper and William Inglis by Patton, 8th February, 1754 (220 to be laid off next to the land where said John formerly dwelt), cor. land whereon Wm. Inglis lived, stake in the Barrens; cor. Casper Barrier. Delivered.

Page 385.—29th April, 1761. Edward McGarry (McGeary) to John McGarry, Andrew Grear and Robert McGarry, £12 (odd) to be paid to Wm. Preston and £100. Furniture and house and cattle. 12 head cattle at South Fork of Pertomock and all other horses too tedius to mention. Teste: Robert Shanklen, David Bell, to secure grantees as bail for grantor, who is deilvered up and Edward conveys above to Robert Shankland, his security in a bond.

Page 387.—2d January, 1761. Erwin Patterson, of Lunenberg, to Erwin Wood, of Lunenburg (?) (Augusta ?), £—, 5 sh., 108 acres by patent, 10th September, 1755, on Roanoke. Teste: John and Jane Mills, John Wood.

Page 390.—22d May, 1761. John Mills and Mary, of Lunenburg, to Leonard Huff (Hooff), of Halifax County, £25, 400 acres, part of 580 patented to John, 22d April, 1760, at Bent Mountain, on Huff's Creek, a branch of Roanoke. Delivered: Samuel Lewis, December, 1777.

Page 392.—20th May, 1761. John Cunningham and Sarah, of Staunton, to Walter Cunningham, of Staunton, £50, lot No. 1 in Staunton; also lot 2, of Woodland, 50 acres. Delivered.

Page 394.—23d May, 1761. John Cunningham and Walter Cunningham, covenants, 107 acres in Beverley Manor, part of 1550 acres called Mill tract whereon Court House stands; cor. James Brown, adjoining Staunton, James Miller's line; cor. Beverley; cor. Col. Lewis' lot. Lease, 89 years. Delivered: Walter, June, 1762.

Page 397.—26th May, 1761. John Madison and Agatha to Peachey Gilmore, £30, 300 acres on south side Shanando River, patented to John, 2d June, 1758, Frazier's land. Teste: Geo. Gray, Henry ( ) Reburn.

Page 400.—20th August, 1760. Henry Brown and Alice to Thomas Walker, of Louisa. Commission to Joseph Rentfro and Turner Hunt Christian, of Bedford County, to take privy examination of Alice. Executed, 22d September, 1760.

Page 402.—18th May, 1761. Robert McMahon and ——, his wife, to John McMahon, his son, £10, 140 acres on a branch of North River of Shanandoe, part of 300 acres patented to Robert, 12th May, 1759; cor. Conolley's land.

Page 406.—19th May, 1761. Robert McMahon to Robert Rebourn, £30, 380 acres on the Buffalo Draft on south side North River, patented Robert Smith, 16th August, 1756; cor. James Beard's land.

Page 408.—20th May, 1761. James Hamilton to George Skillern, £30, 180 acres on Middle River of Shanando between Christian's Creek and Long Meadow Run; cor. Beverley Manor.

Page 411.—10th August, 1761. Jacob Bear (Bare, Bair) and Barbary ( ) to John Bare, £20, on Fort Run; cor, Raider's land, 130 acres. Teste: Burr Harrison, Adam Reder, Mathias Reder. Dleivered: Jas. Craig, February, 1763.

Page 415.—18th August, 1761. Henry Seller to son John Seller, £5, 130 acres on Price Run between Shanandoe River and the mountain.

Page 421.—18th August, 1761. Henry Seller to Peter Seller, £30, 123 acres, 100 acres whereof patented to Henry, 10th March, 1756; 23 acres part of tract whereon Henry now lives, on Shanando River. Delivered: Jno. Seller, August Court, 1776.

Page 424.—15th August, 1761. Moses Bird and Clair, of Frederick County, to John Blizard, £140, on Smith's Creek; cor. Andrew Bird's land, John Phillip's line, 400 acres except 50 acres surveyed for Jacob Rambo, bounded, viz: cor. Jno. Phillips. Teste: Archible Ruddle (Ruddell), Thomas Beggs, Abraham Bird. Delivered: John Blizard, 25th March, 1762.

Page 427.—18th August, 1760. John ( ) Nicolas (Nickle) and Barbra ( ) to his son John Nicolas, £5, 250 acres on Moffett's Branch of Middle River, part of 400 acres patented to William King, 10th February, 1748, and conveyed to said Nicolas. Delivered: John Nickel, February, 1767.

Page 431.—19th August, 1761. John Megill (Magill, McGill) and Mary to Samuel Brigs, £24, 120 acres, part of 300 acres patented to said John, 12th May, 1759, on North River of Shanandoe; John McClure's land, opposite James Megill's. Teste: Will Brown, Frances ( ) Brown.

Page 434.—9th August, 1761. John Bear and Caterean ( ) to Eve Sircle, £20, 130 acres at a place called the Bair Glade. Delivered: Lud Zirkle, May, 1770.

Page 437.—2d August, 1761. Adam Reder and Barbary ( ) to Alexander Painter, £5, adjoining land said Paitner lives on, Raider's old patent, 20 acres. Teste: Burr Harrison, Robert Peyton, Andrew ( ) Trumboer.

Page 439.—10th August, 1761. Adam Raider and Barbary to Matthios Raider, £20, 100 acres adjoining land Matthios lives on; cor. Alex. Painter. Teste: Burr Harrison, Robert Peyton, Andrew ( ) Trumboer.

Page 442.—10th August, 1761. Same to George Rader, £20, adjoining land Adam lives on, 200 acres.

Page 446.—5th August, 1761. Same to Teter Couts, £10, on Walnut Creek, branch of North River of Shanando, James Gill's old patent, being same 186 acres taken up by said James. Teste: John Thomas, Robert Williams, Frederick ( ) Benter. Delivered: Teter Couts, February, 1779.

Page 449.—23d May, 1761. Samuel Young to John Brown, £71, mortgage, 225 acres whereon Samuel now dwells, adjoining said John Brown, James Robert and Hugh Young. Teste: David Stewart, John Niell, Charles Lewis.

Page 452.—18th August, 1761. Thomas Hicklen to John Hicklen, £50, 217 acres, part of 348 acres on Bull Pasture patented to Andrew Lewis. 1st June, 1750, and since conveyed to said Thomas. Delivered: Jno. Hicklen, August, 1768.

Page 455.—18th August, 1761. Joseph Harman and Anna ( ) to Robert McCutheon, 68 acres on a branch of Naked Creek, half of 136 acres below said Robert's line, patented to Joseph, 12th May, 1759. Delivered: Benj. Estill, November Court, 1762.

Page 456.—29th May, 1761. Mary Wood, of Frederick, James and Moses Green, of Culpeper, to Joseph Skidmore, Jr., £50.15, on North Fork of South Branch of Potowmack, 203 acres, part of 660 acres patented to Robert Green, 25th June, 1747. Teste. Mathew Patton, Michael Prop

(Propps), Frederick Easter (Hister). Delivered: Andrew Johnston, June, 1767.

Page 458.—29th May, 1760. Same to George Hammer, £19.17, at same place, cor. tract sold to Jonas Friend; cor. tract sold Jacob Harper, 114 acres, part of 350 acres patented to Robert Green, 12th January, 1746. Delivered to same.

Page 460.—29th May, 1761. Same to Jacob Harper, £16.6.4, at same place, 96 acres, part of 350 acres, supra. Delivered to same.

Page 462.—29th May, 1761. Same to Uldrick Conrod, £55.12, 278 acres at same place, part of 370 acres patented to Robert Green, 12th January, 1746. Delivered to same.

Page 465.—29th May, 1761. Same to Henry Penniger, £11.15.2, at same place, 168 acres, part of 370 acres, supra. Teste: Frederick Hister (as above). Delivered to same.

Page 467.—29th May, 1761. Same to Jonas Friend, £8.15, at same place, 44 acres, part of 350 acres above. Delivered as above.

Page 469.—29th May, 1761. Same to George Kaplinger, £19.7, at same place, cor. George Hammer, 114 acres, part of 350 acres patented as above. Delivered to same. Teste: Gabriel Coil.

Page 471.—29th May, 1761. Same to Geoge Bush, £40, on South Fork of South Branch of Potowmock, 116 acres, part of 470 acres patented to Robert Green, 25th June, 1747. Delivered: Bastian Hover, September, 1763.

Page 473.—29th May, 1761. Same to Andrew Smith, £17.10, on North Fork of South Branch of Potowmack, 131 acres, part of 370 acres patented to Robert Green, 12th January, 1746. Delivered.

Page 475.—29th May, 1761. William Green, surviving joint tenant of James Wood, William Green and William Russell (by consent of Mary Wood, devisee of James Wood and William Russell, son and heir-at-law of said William) and Ann, his wife, to Jeremiah Ozburn (Osburn), £41.16, on South Fork of South Branch of Potowmack; cor. tract surveyed for Charles Willson, 220 acres, part of tract patented to James, William and William above, 23d October, 1750. Teste: Frederick Kister (see Easter, Hister, &c., above). Delivered: Andrew Johnston, June, 1767.

Page 477.—29th May, 1761. Mary Wood, of Frederick, and James and Moses Green, of Culpeper, to Michael Proops, £30, on South Fork of South Branch of Potowmack; cor. tract sold to Mark Swadley, 415 acres, part of 1470 acres patented to Robert Green, 25th June 1747. Teste: Mark ( ) Swately. Delivered as above.

Page 479.—29th May, 1761. Same to Mathew Patton, £75.4.2, on South Fork of South Branch of Potowmack; cor. in the bank of a lick; cor. to Frederick Kester (see this name as witness *ubi supra,* Easter, Hister), 327 acres, part of patent to Robert Green, 25th June, 1747. Delivered: Mathew Patton, March Court, 1764.

Page 481.—29th May, 1761. Same to Frederick Kester, £64, on South Fork of South Branch of Potowmack, 256 acres, part of 1470 acres above. Delivered: A. J. above.

Page 485.—29th May, 1761. William Green, surviving joint tenant, &c., &c., and Anna as above, to Charles Willson, £19.13, on South Fork of South Branch of Potowmack, on Kettle River, 131 acres, part of tract patented to Wood, Green and Russell, 23d October, 1750. Delivered: A. J. as above.

Page 487.—29th May, 1761. Mary Wood, &c. (as above), to Mark Swatley, £27.10, on South Fork, &c., as above, 426 acres, part of 1470 acres patented to Robert Green, 25th June, 1747. Delivered: A. J. as above

Page 490.—29th May, 1761. William Green, surviving joint tenant, &c., and Ann to Adam Rutherback, £48, on South Fork, &c., cor. tract laid off for Jeremiah Osburn, 240 acres; also another tract adjoining above, belonging to Mary Wood, containing 200 acres, together part of 2400 acres patented to Wood, Green and Russell, 23d October, 1750. Delivered: A. J. June, 1767.

Page 492.—29th May, 1761. William Green, surviving joint tenant, &c., and Ann to John Rouback, £50, on South Fork of South Branch of Potowmack, between lands of Mary Wood and heir of Christian Tosher, deeased, 400 acres, part of 2400 acres patented to Wood, Green and Russell, 23d October, 1750. Delivered: A. J. as above.

Page 495.—14th February, 1761. John ( ) McFall, of Bedford, to David Miller, £25, 141 acres on Glade Creek, branch of Roanoke; cor. John Bowin's land. Teste: John Smith, John Miller, John Thomson, David Luney, Francis Liber. Delivered: Israel Christian, January, 1767.

Page 497.—9th June, 1761. Same to George Paris, £39, 220 acres on Roanoke on Glade Creek, by patent, 10th March, 1756; John Boens line. Delivered: Robert Paris, 27th August, 1787.

Page 503.—18th August, 1761. William ( ) Patterson (Petterson) and Agness ( ) to James Bell, £120, 247 acres in Beverley Manor on South River of Shanandoe, conveyed to William by Beverley, 26th February, 1749; cor. John Campbell in the Manor line, Joseph Teas' line; cor. said Teas and McClure; cor. Archibald Stuart. Delivered: Jas. Bell, 1768.

Page 507.—18th August, 1761. Alexander McClure, farmer, to John Allison, £130, 370 acres on North Branch of James River; cor. William Hall; Robert Poage's corner; cor. tract surveyed for Robert Hutson. Delivered: John Allison, September, 1769.

Page 511.—18th August, 1761. Wallace (Walliss, Wallos) Estill and Ann to Bandy Estill, £40, 133 acres on Bull Pasture. Delivered: John Estill, November, Court, 1773.

Page 515.—17th February, 1761. Elizabeth Thomas, infant, only daughter and heir-at-law of Jacob Thomas, deceased, by John Madison, her guardian, to Jacob Miller, Jr. Whereas Jacob, in 1751, purchased of Nicholas Null 185 acres on Cub Run on Shanandoe River for £25 sometime prior being purchased by Null from Jacob Thomas and it was agreed that Jacob Thomas should convey to Jacob Miller, but Thomas died intestate, leaving Elizabeth, only child and heir; chancery suit brought, and on — May, 1755, decree for conveyance by Elizabeth, 185 acres, part of Francisco's 3000 acres, and whereon said Miller now lives. Delivered: Jacob Miller, May, 1769.

Page 518.—1st April, 1761. Martha Givens, wife of Samuel Givens, release of dower in tract sold to Samuel Henderson. Teste: George Woolridge, Samuel Bell, John Ritchey.

Page 520.—18th August, 1761. Hugh Corruthers, of Orange County, North Carolina, by James Ledderdale, to Andrew McNeilly, £25, 300 acres on a branch of Lunie's Mill Creek. Delivered: John Buchanan by your order, July 1766.

Page 523.—19th August, 1761. Charles Millican, of Orange County, North Carolina, by John Buchanan, to John McClellon, £—, 297 acres on a branch of James River, on Looney's Mill Creek. Delivered: Francis Smith, 1st October, 1767.

Page 525.—18th August, 1761. James Neilly to Robert Neilly, £50, 350 acres on a branch of Roanoke; cor. Archabald Graham. Sent to Israel Christian, January, 1767.

Page 528.—15th August, 1761. James Todd to Joseph McBride, £5, 185 acres on Buffelo Creek. It is agreed between the parties that Joseph shall not enter into possession during natural life of said James and his wife Susanna Todd, but James and Susanna to have full possession during their natural lives, and after their decease, then Joseph to enter.

Page 529.—14th August, 1761. Thomas Walker, of Albemarle, to James Patton's executors, £100, releases all interest in 4500 acres on waters of New River known by name of Birk's Garden, patented to James Patton. Teste: Israel Christian, John Mills, John Miller.

Page 531.—20th August, 1761. Ephraim Love to William Hopkins, £20, on head branch of Muddy Creek above John Hopkins' land patented to said Love and William Hopkins, 5th September, 1749, the Aspe Bottom Branch, 204 acres. Teste: John Poage, Daniel Love, John Hopkins.

Page 533.—20th August, 1761. William Hopkins and Elizabeth to John Hopkins, £20, 200 acres, part of 258 acres conveyed to William by Cap. Ephraim Love, on a branch of Muddy Creek; cor. between William and John Hopkins; cor. Ephraim Love. Teste: Daniel and Ephraim Love.

Page 536.—20th August, 1761. Joseph ( ) Skidmore, Jr., to his brother John Skidmore, £25, 101 acres on South Branch of Potowmack, part of one of the lots formerly surveyed for Robert Green, gent., No. 16, cor. with part of said tract belongin gto Gabriel Coil. Delivered: John Skidmore, February, 1764.

Page 539.—20th August, 1761. Joseph ( ) Skidmore, Jr., to Gabriel Coil, £25, 102 acres, part of lot No. 16 above. Delivered: Andrew Johnston, June, 1767.

Page 542.—20th August, 1761. Matthew Harper and Margaret to John Henderson, shoemaker, £40, 200, part of 1415 acres in Beverley Manor, formerly surveyed for William Henderson, on Christian's Creek; cor. Thomas Rutledge, crossing Black's Branch. Teste: Alex. Gibson, Francis Smith, George Skillern.

Page 544.—18th August, 1761. James Trimble and Sarah to Mary Cunningham, of Hampshire, £12.5, 160 acres on North Fork of South Branch of Potowmack, above John Cunningham's Walnut Bottom. Teste: John McFerran, Malcolm Allen, Samuel ( ) Luisey.

Page 547.—18th August, 1761. James Trimble and Sarah to Robert Cunningham, on South Branch in Hampshire County, £22.10, 300 acres in the Crab Apple Bottom, on a branch of South Branch of Potowmack.

Last deed recorded, 19th August, 1761.

Page 92.—18th November, 1760. Erwin Patterson and Eleanor, of Lunenburg, to Israel Christian, £100, 200 acres on Buffalo Creek of Roanoke; corner Wm. Graham. Delivered: Wm. Thompson per order 30th August, 1762.

Page 96.—17th November, 1760. Same to same, £130, 300 acres on Buffalo Creek.

Page 98.—20th March, 1760. Joseph Kennedy to Sampson and Geo. Mathews, £30, lot 5 in Staunton, conveyed to Joseph by the County. Delivered: Samuel Mathews, January, 1770.

Page 102.—20th November, 1760. Robert McClenachan and Sarah to William and Andrew Russell, £60, 200 acres in Beverley Manor bought by Robert from John Miller, 3d January, 1750, and purchased by Miller from Robt. Black; corner to land formerly William Skellern's, Manor line to Wm. Skellern's corner. Delivered: Andrew Russell, August, 1762.

DEED BOOK No. 10.

Page 2—19th August, 1761. Robert McClenachan and Sarah, David Stewart and Margaret to Peter Braminer, of Augusta, £63, 300 acres granted to Robert Breckinridge by patent, 27th February, 1754, survey made by James Barton, in the Forks of James's River. Delivered: Peter Braminer, 18th December, 1783.

Page 5.—17th August, 1761. William Henderson and Susanna to Nathaniel Evans, £—, 350 acres on North Branch of James, above mouth of Buffalo Creek. Delivered: Nathaniel Evans, 1761.

Page 8.—19th August, 1761. John Mills, of Lunenburg County, to Israel Christian. Whereas Wm. Mills, of Augusta, on 9th October, 1751, constituted John Mills his attorney to sell his lands in Augusta, £—, 117 acres on Roanoke; Jno. Mill's line.

Page 11.—17th August, 1761. James Armstrong and Jean ( ) to Wm. Armstrong, £100, 485 acres in Beverley Manor, beginning at the Christian's White Oak Stake.

Page 14.—20th August, 1761. James Hamilton and Jean to James Ker, blacksmith, £2, 1 acre, 3 rods, 10 perch, part of 180 acres patented James Ker, 5th September, 1749, conveyed to James Hamilton, in the Fork of Christian's Creek and Middle River.

Page 17.—16th May, 1761. Jno. White and Katharine ( ) to Wm. Peoples, £48, 187½ acres; cor. to Corruthers in James Greenlee's line; Nathaniel People's cor.

Page 20.—17th November, 1761. Peter Miller, executor of Valentine Pence, to Valentine Malchier, £25, 275 acres on North River of Shanandore, first granted to James McCarrel by patent, 5th July, 1751, and conveyed to Valentine Pence and devised by Pence; cor. David Logan. Delivered to Valentine Melchior, October, 1786.

Page 23.—17th September, 1761. Thomas Lewis to Wm. Crawford, £48, 370 acres patented to Thomas, 9th October, 1753, in Forks of James on First and Second Run, George Rutledge's land. Delivered to George Crawford, devisee of Wm. Crawford, 13th January, 1784.

Page 27.—3d September, 1761. Robert Abercromby, of Orange County, South Carolina, to John Stewart, £150, 320 acres on east side of Jackson's River and mouth of Falling Spring.

Page 30.—17th November, 1761. Thomas Shields and Alice to Mathew Thomson, £131, 202 acres in Beverley Manor; cor. Thos. Blackwood and Robert Armstrong; cor. said Blackwood and Jno. Hunter; cor. Andrew Alexander's land; cor. Wm. Dean; Dean's cor. in Robert Armstrong's line. Delivered: Mathew Thomson, November, 1766.

Page 34.—17th November, 1761. Baptist ( ) McNabb and Catherine to John Nealey, £155, 171 acres on Rentfroe's Branch of Goose Creek; Rentfroe's line, cor. George Robinson; also 137 acres on Robinson's Branch of Roanoke; cor. Bryan Cuff; cor. Stephen Rentfroe; cor. George Robinson's and Rentfroe's tract.

Page 38.— — day —. 1760. Edward Beard and Mary ( ) to James Beard, £30, 36 acres on North River of Shanandoe, part of 400 acres patented to Samuel Lockhart, 10th April, 1751; also 20 acres, part of 179 acres patented to Samuel Lockhart, 30th August, 1748, adjoining above. Teste: Robert Homes, Joseph ( ) Homes.

Page 41.—18th November, 1760. Richard Woods, of Albemarle, merchant, to Peter Wallace, of Augusta, farmer, £60, 195 acres in Forks of James River; cor. in Borden's patent by James Devises Field; cor. Peter Wallace's other land; cor. Richard Woods, gent. Delivered: Cap. Samuel Lapsley, 17th August, 1784.

Page 45.—18th November, 1761. Jonathan Douglass and Jemima ( ) to Patrick Quin, £20, 350 acres on head of Broad Run, a branch of North River of Shanandoe, part of two tracts, one of 400 acres patented to Jonathan, 11th July, 1761, the other of 400 acres also patented to Jonathan, adjoining above; cor. Nicholas Mace.

Page 47.—Commission for privy examination of Jane, wife of William Sproul, deed to William Stewart dated 9th/10th February, 1761, executed, 3d November, 1761.

Page 50.—18th November, 1761. Jonathan Robinson to David Robinson, £25, 110 acres on North Branch of Shanandoe, part of 400 acres devised to Jonathan by his father James Robinson, 9th April, 1760, recorded in Augusta; cor. David Robinson's land.

Page 54.—25th September, 1761. Henry Fuller, of Orange County, North Carolina, to John Paxton, £125, 190 acres on North Branch James River, being the farm where Henry formerly lived. Delivered: John Paxton, December, 1762.

Page 57.—16th November, 1761. James Armstrong and Jane ( ) to Samuel and Mirian Cloyd, £200, 300 acres in Beverley Manor on Christian's Creek. Delivered: Cloyd, June, 1763.

Page 61.—17th November, 1761. James Trimble and Sarah to Samuel Bright, £7.10, 100 acres on sontheast branch of Black Thorn, a branch of the South Branch of Potowmack. Delivered to James Gamble by your order, 23d June, 1765.

Page 65.—14th November, 1761. James Bailey (Baley, Bailly) to Benj. Bennett, blacksmith, £40, 175 acres in Fork of James River, joining Samuel McDowell's tract.

Page 69.—21st November, 1759. James Clerk and Wm. Elliote to Wm. Johnson, assignee of John Johnson. Whereas Archbald Elliote, of Anson County, North Carolina, on 20th February, 1758, by power attorney constituted James Clark and Wm. Elliott his attorney to make this conveyance, 163 acres on Jackson's River, £60.

Page 72.—13th October, 1761. Patrick McDonald, talour, to Stephen Herd (Heard), of Albemarle County, £70, lot No. 12 in Staunton (one dwelling house and two office houses) and also 50 acres woodland belonging to it, one negro boy. Teste: Thomas Heard, Thos. Fitzpatrick, Michael Daugherty.

Page 75.—17th November, 1761. James Trimble and Sarah to Valentine Goyle, £16, two tracts 230 acres on South Branch Potowmack above the Front Rock: 1st, containing 100 acres; 2d, containing 130 acres adjoining. Delivered: Jacob Goyle, 7th October, 1772.

Page 78.—27th June, 1761. Zachary Lewis, of Spottsylvania, to John Buchanan and Wm. Thompson, release of all rights in an order of Council for 100,000 on the waters of James River and Roanoke, granted to Zachary Lewis, Wm. Waller, Benj. Waller and Robert Green, 3d November, 1740. renewed, May, 1745, for 50,000 acres and since renewed for 30,000 acres in which grant James Patton was a partner.

Page 80.—17th November, 1761. John ( ) Miller and Morthew ( ) to John Kinkead, £80, 286 acres on Cowpasture. Delivered: Patrick Miller, 4th May, 1771.

Page 84.—19th November, 1761. James Beard to John Davidson, Sr., and John Davidson, Jr., £14.5, 228 acres on Collins Branch by patent dated 5th April, 1748; cor. to one Beard's land. Delivered: Jno. Sr., August, 1765.

Page 87.—16th November, 1761. James Patton's executors to Robert Armstrong, £60, 432 acres on Beverley Manor; cor. to the Christian's land, Wm. Long's line, Joseph Mill's line, Wm. Robinson's line. Delivered: Wm. Armstrong, September, 1765.

Page 91.—20th November, 1761. Silas Hart and Jane to John Robertson, £45, 184 acres on North River Shanando, part of 400 acres patented to Robert Breckinridge, 1st December, 1740, and conveyed to Wm. Logan, 22d July, 1745, and to Silas Hart, 28th November, 1749, recorded at Williamsburg, Orange and Augusta. Delivered: Alex. Robertson, 20th January.

Page 94.—21st November, 1761. William Skillern to James Anderson, £50, 100 acres on Long Meadow; cor. to Wm. Skillern, Carr's line. Delivered: Benj. Tudor, March, 1768.

Page 96.—19th November, 1761. James Anderson and Elizabeth ( ) formerly Elizabeth Skilleron, widow of Wm. Skilleron, to George and William Skilleron, sons and devisees of said William Skilleron: 1. A tract on Linvel's Creek, 343 acres; 2. A tract on Long Meadow, 635 acres; £—, 20 shillings; except 100 acres of second tract bounded viz: cor. Wm. Skilleron, Care's line.

Page 99.—16th February, 1762. Henry Gay to Ann Gay and Martha Gay, £100, 216 acres on a branch of Cowpasture. Delivered: Henry Gay, May, 1773.

Page 103.—9th February, 1762. John ( ) Davies and Judith ( ) to George Berry, £135, 198 acres. part of the land formerly belonging to Andrew Pickens; cor. John McPheeters in James Young's line, deceased; cor. to said George Berry's line. Teste: W. Ward, Jno. McPheeters, Joseph Ward Delivered: George Berry, April, 1774.

Page 107.—20th November, 1761. William Todd, of Bedford, to Samuel Todd, of Augusta, £40, 400 acres on the head of North Branch of Buffalo Creek, Benj. Borden's line. Teste: James Hutton. Delivered: Wm. Lusk, January, 1765.

Page 110.—16th February, 1762. Alex. ( ) Kile (Kyle) and Elizabeth ( ) to Jno. Hare, £40, 90 acres on North River Shanando, at a place called the Long Neck, conveyed to Alex. by Jno. Lusk, 16th August, 1758. Teste: Andrew Alexander, Charles Kelso.

Page 114A.—16th February, 1762. George Wilson and Elizabeth to James Clemons, £15.2.6, 100 acres, part of a tract patented to George Wilson, 15th December, 1758, on the Cowpasture River. Delivered: John Bodkin, October, 1765.

Page 115B.—16th February, 1762. Samuel ( ) Hinds and Isabella ( ) to Patrick Miller, £25, two tracts on South River Shanandoe: 1st, 139 acres patented to Wm. Thompson, 20th August, 1748, and conveyed to Samuel, 29th August, 1750; 2d, six acres patented to Samuel, 14th February, 1761, joining Turk's land.

Page 119.—16th November, 1761. James Knox to Edward Thompson, £31.10, 93 acres on Cowpasture opposite land in possession of John Moore.

Page 122.—16th February, 1762. John Madison and Agatha to Peachy Ridgway Gilmore, £200, 490 acres on Shanando, patented to John, 7th August, 1761. Delivered: Robert Grattan, 23d June, 1801.

Page 126.—1st October, 1761. John Roberts and Margaret (Margate) to Robert Williams, £41.1, 166 acres on a branch of Smith's Creek called Yayer's Branch; cor. Adam Yayer;also 159 acres on same. Delivered: Robert Williams, October, 1766.

Page 131.—18th November, 1761. John, James and Moses Green, of Culpeper, to John Miller, £180, two tracts, 500 acres each, on Linvell's Creek known as lots No. 4 and 5, lot No. 4 conveyed to grantors by Jose Hite, et als, 5th February, 1746; lot 5 conveyed to Robert McCay, 11th February, 1746, both part of 7,009 acres patented to Hite, et als, MDCCXLXXXIX.

Page 135.—17th November, 1761. Same to William Ewing, £140, 708 acres on easternmost branch of Linvel's Creek, conveyed by Hite, et als, 3d October, 1746. Delivered: Andrew Ewin, October, 1769.

Page 139.—18th February, 1762. William Bell to Samuel Morra, £5, 216 acres patented to John Bell, 1st December, 1740. John Bell died intestate the property is invested in William Bell by hereditary right. On Jenning's Branch near North Mountain; cor. Thomas Armstrong's land.

Page 143.—17th November, 1761. Joseph ( ) Kennedy to James Wardlaw, £100, 236 acres in Borden's tract, crossing Andrew Duncan's mill dam, George Henderson's land. Teste. Wm., James, Andrew Kennedy, Hugh Wardlaw. Delivered to Andrew Wardlaw, son of James, 2d February, 1791.

Page 146.—26th January, 1762. William Preston and Susanna to Mary Preston, £100, 520 acres on Great River of the Calfpasture; cor. to Kinkead's land, crossing the river and Ramsey's Creek, the land of Lockridge. Teste: Robert and Lettice Breckinridge (Brackenridge). Delivered: Wm. Preston, February, 1763.

Page 150.— — February, 1762. Andrew Kerr (Carr) and Rachel ( ) to John Allison, £45, 77 acres, part of 230 acres patented to Andrew, 5th September, 1749, on Middle River Shanando; cor. said Allison's other land. Delivered: Jno. Allison, February, 1768.

Page 154.— —day ——, 176—. John Anderson to James Anderson, £—, 200 acres on Long Glade, a branch of North River of Shanandoe, part of 400 acres on which Jno. now lives, line of James Anderson's land. Teste: Robert Anderson. Delivered: James Anderson, March, 1765.

Page 159.—8th December, 1761. William Patrick and Mary ( ), late Mary Chittam, to William McElhenney, farmer, £53, 214 acres, line of

Robert Renick's land, conveyed by Wm. Cleghorn to Mary Patrick, then Mary Chittam, March, 1754. Delivered: Wm. McElhenney, 14th August, 1788.

Page 162.—16th February, 1762. William Lusk and Elizabeth to Robert Breckinridge, £100, 400 acres on James River, an island, patented to William, 7th August, 1761. Sent to Maj. Robert Breckinridge, 9th February, 1771.

Page 165.—13th February, 1762. James Hamilton and Jean ( ) to Wm. Skillern, £40, 180 acres on Middle River of Shanandoe, point of a hill between Christian's Creek and Long Meadow, Beverley Manor. Teste: John Robert and Margaret Poage. Delivered: George Skillern, January, 1770.

Page 169.—14th April, 1760. Ephraim Vause to John Stewart and John Given, £40, 179 acres on the Little River (description omitted).

Page 173.—17th February, 1762. William Johnson to Thomas Hamilton, £16.10, 215 acres on a small branch of Bull Pasture. Delivered: Thomas Hamilton, January, 1773.

Page 176.—7th February, 1762. John Stewart and Sarah to William Mann, £152.10, 320 acres on Jackson's River and mouth of Falling Spring.

Page 181.—16th February, 1762. George Rodgers, Jr., to Nathaniel Lyon, £40 two tracts: 1st, 170 acres in Beverley Manor; cor. Robert Wilson and Joseph Reed's old place; cor. David Moore. 2d, 50 acres in Beverley Manor; cor. Robert Syer's land in Wm. Thomuson's line, Robert Wilson's line. Teste: Samuel and Jos. Moore. Delivered: Thomas Bowyer, April, 1765.

Page 183.—1st July, 1760. Jomes ( ) Birk and Lucretia, of Cumberland County, North Carolina, to Thomas Walker, of Albemarle, £40, 100 acres on Goose Creek, William Campbell's line. Teste: Wm. Ingles, James Bane, Jno. Hawkins. Delivered: Thomas Madison, 11th March, 1763.

Page 188.—25th November, 1761. Robert (Robin) ( ) Reburn and Jean to Hugh Donachy, £60, 380 acres on the Buffalo Draft on the south side of the North River, cor. James Beard's land. Teste: John Lowrie, Jno. Burk, Robert McMechen. Delivered: Hugh Donaho, December, 1771.

Page 190.—9th October, 1760. James Hamilton to Thomas and William Stevenson, £14, household goods. Teste: David, James and Mary Stevenson.

Page 191.—Robert ( ) Dare (Adair) to Israel Christian, 24th January, 1762, £6, personalty.

Page 193.—17th February, 1762. Alex. Thompson by William Thompson, attorney to William Dean. Alex. Thompson, of Mill Creek Hundred, County of New Castle, on Delaware, taylor, on 7th October, 1761, gave power to William. £58, 202 acres in Beverley Manor, Mathew Thompson's cor. in a line of Robert Armstrong's land; Alexander's land, cor. to Thompson's; cor. Robert Christian's land. Delivered: Jno. Dean, June, 1765.

Page 197.—18th May, 1762. Andrew Alexander and Catherine to Wm. Brown, £50.5, 158 acres in Beverley Manor; cor. Robert Wilson's land; cor. Mathew Thompson's land, Thomas Brown's line. Delivered: Wm. Brown, March 1774.

Page 201.—18th May 1762. Robert Givin, Sr., and his wife ,to their son, Robert Givin, Jr., £—, a certain piece of work done, £241 acres, part of 544 acres on Great River Calfpasture conveyed to Robert, Sr., by James Patton and Jno. Lewis; cor. John Grame's land, John Graham's land.

Page 205.—17th May, 1762. George Stevenson, of Louisa, and Rebecca

( ) to Samuel Henderson, of Albemarle, £4, 200 acres in Borden's tract, Greenlee's line; cor. McMurray, John' Stevenson's line; cor. Thos. Paxton; cor. James Greenlee. Teste: Wm. Graham, James Hollis, Marget ( ) Luney.

Page 209.—17th April, 1762. Richard Borton, of Cumberland County, North Carolina, and Ann ( ) to Samson Mathews, £47, 400 acres on James River. Teste: Joh. Bower, Arter ( ) Bowen.

Page 212.—19th May, 1762. Sampson Mathews to John Bowen, £47, 400 acres, conveyed as above.

Page 215.—12th May, 1762. Charles Crosson and Christina (signed Corous, Croson) to Jacob Mayer, £70, 380 acres on east side of Shanadore on Naked Creek. Teste: Augustin ( ) Price, Henery ( ) Price, Thomas Burk. Delivered: Jacob Mayer, March, 1770.

Page 219.—16th March, 1762. James Thompson and Jean ( ) to Samuel Henderson, £200, 250 acres on Middle River of Shanadore, part of 400 acres granted to William Thompson and made over to Hugh Thompson, deceased, 23d May, 1744, and now James Thompson's by hereditary right; cor. George Crawford, Bryce Russell's land; also another tract adjoining above, 60 acres patented to Hugh Thompson, 10th December, 1757. Delivered: Samuel Henderson, May, 1769.

Page 223.—18th May, 1762. Thomas Turk and Margaret ( ) to Frederick Stull, £30, 226 acres on South River of Shannando, William Lamb's line by an island, Robert Ellot's cor. Delivered: Frederick Stull, May, 1766.

Page 227.—18th May, 1762. John ( ) Miller and Hannah to Jonathan Robison, £45, 230 acres on Linvel's Creek, cor. John Miller's part of same tract; cor. William Mynter's part of same tract, Spiece's line, being parts of lote 4 and 5 conveyed by Green to John Miller, 18th November, 1761.

Page 231.—18th May, 1762. John Miller and Hannah to Wm. Mynter, £45, 270 acres on Linvel's Creek; cor. Jonathan Robinson, part of same tract; cor. George Speice's land as above. Delivered: John Scott by your order.

Page 236.—18th May, 1762. Henry ( ) Price to Augustine Price, £30, 121 acres patented to John Roads, 15th March, 1744, and conveyed by John to Henry, between Shanando River and Peaked Mountain; cor. Daniel Sinks. Delivered to A. Price. 8th January, 1789.

Page 240.—18th May, 1762. Henry ( ) Price to Daniel Price, £30, 112 acres, part of 400 acres patented to John Roads, 15th March, 1764, between Shanando River and Peaked Mountain. Delivered: Adam Price, the present owner, 20th March, 1815.

Page 243.—18th May 1762. John McMachen and Isabella, of Frederick County, to John Berry, £105, 427 acres in Borden's tract purchased by John McMachen from Wm. Purris, and he from James Glasgow, who purchased from Benj. Borden; cor. Alex. Miller.

Page 247.—8th May, 1762. James, Henery and Mary ( ) to Robert Buchanan, £32.10, 208 acres in Borden's tract; cor. Robert Telford; cor. Andrew Steel. Delivered: Robert Buchanan, April, 1765.

Page 251.—8th May, 1762. James Moore and Jane ( ) to John Moore, £50, 136 acres, part of James' plantation on Hay's Creek, where John now lives; cor. James Moore. Delivered: John Moore, 21st April, 1785.

Page 255.—16th May, 1762. Thomas Moore and Mary, of Frederick, to Aaron Huse, £50, 90 acres on Long Meadow of Shanando, part of tract patented to James Gill and surveyed by James Wood; cor. Thomas Rutherford. Delivered: March, 1782.

Page 259.—16th May, 1762. Daniel ( ) Johnson and Mary ( ) to James Johnson, £23, 320 acres on head of Fort Run.

Page 263.—18th May, 1762. John McCutchan, of Augusta, to Wm. McCutchan, £15, 200 acres in Beverley Manor.

Page 266.—15th May, 1762. William ( ) Frazier to John Heterick, £10, 28 acres on Shanando patented to Wm., 10th March, 1756; Stover's line, Haine's Bottom. Teste: Jacob Nicolas, Peter Miller, Peter Brisler (Treslar).

Page 270.—8th May, 1762. John Heterick and Susannah ( ) to Peter Tresler, £10, 134 acres on Stony Run on north side Shanando River, part of 285 acres patented to John 2d June, 1760; cor. Jacob Man and land of said Hetrick. Delivered: Gabriel Jones, November Court, 1778.

Page 274.—12th May, 1762. Moses Whitesides and Margaret to David Gray, £10, 109 acres, part of Bordin's tract; cor. said Whitesides.

Page 278.—5th February, 1762. George ( ) Henderson to Hugh Wardlaw, £60, 284 acres in Bordin's tract, on Moffett's Creek; cor. John Roseman; cor. Wm. Wardlaw, James Wardlaw's line. Teste: Henry Long.

Page 282.—19th May, 1762. James Davis, gent., and Jean ( ) to John Davis, £5 paid by John Davis, his eldest son, 350 acres on head of a branch of Buffalo Creek; Borden's line.

Page 286.—20th March, 1762. Richard Fields (Faields) and Ales ( ) to Zebulon Harrison, £30, 220 acres on Daniel James' Branch, patented to Richard, 16th August, 1730; cor. Wm. Carrell's survey; cor. Zebulon Harrison's land.

Page 289.—18th May, 1762. Zachariah Bell, of Craven County, South Carolina, to Samuel Logan, £30.1.3, 238 acres at head of Elk Run in Beverley Manor; Andrew McClure's line, ye Barrens; Joseph Bell's cor. Teste: Zechariah Smith, Zechariah Johnston, Hugh McClure. Delivered: Samuel Bell, May, 1763.

Page 293.—10th February, 1762. James McKay (McAkay) and Mary, of Frederick, to Thomas Bryan, £80, 300 acres on Linvell's Creek, part of 1200 acres patented to McKay, Green and Hite, 26th March, 1739, and by them conveyed to Robert McKay, 19th June, 1746, and by Robert devised to James by will in Augusta; John Bryan's line. Teste: Samuel Moncy, Robert Semples, Francis ( ) McBroid. Delivered: Thomas Bryan, July, 1766.

Page 298.—18th May, 1762. Samuel Fraizer to James Fraizer, his brother, £5, 234 acres, part of 472 on Long Meadow of Middle River of Shannandoe in Beverley Manor between said Fraizer and Robert Moody.

Page 302.—16th February, 1762. James Mitchel and Elizabeth to Walter Smiley, £60, 263 acres on Catapo Creek at the end of the Cross Mountain, at a place called the Fork Bottom. Teste: Hugh Allen, Robert Shields. Delivered: W. Smiley, 10th February, 1786.

Page 306.—18th May, 1762. John Duncle to Ludwick Wagoner, £20, 151 acres on South Fork of Potomac (Patowmack), part of 2643 acres patented to Robert Green, 12th January, 1746, part of which was conveyed to

John Patton, and by Patton 453 acres were conveyed to John, and 151 is now laid off for Wagoner. Delivered: Ludwick Wagoner, 19th June, 1765.

Page 310.— 27th August, 1761. James McClure, of Craven County, South Carolina, to John Ramsey, £56.12, 408 acres devised to James and his brother Samuel by will of father James McClure and descended to grantor by survivorship, being the same that James the father bought of Wm. Beverley, 6th June, 1739, in Beverley Manor, Geo. Robinson's line. Delivered: Wm. Ramsey, 5th October, 1772.

Page 314.—17th May, 1762. Richard ( ) Botkin and Elizabeth ( ) to Samuel Given, £158, 339 acres on Clover Creek now called the Bull Pasture River, a branch of Cow Pasture; cor. to land in possession of Loftus Pullen. Teste: Wm. Stewart, James Boadkin, George Woolridge. Delivered: Samuel Givens, August, 1768.

Page 318.—19th May, 1762. Thomas Hugart and Rebeckah to John Davis, £5, 65 acres on Jackson's River.

Page 322.—18th May, 1762. Nathaniel Evins to William Ward, £90, 279 acres, 249 part of Bordin's tract, and 30 acres part of an entry of King's land adjoining the same; cor. Thomas Wilson. Teste: George Wilson, Benj. Estill, Wm. Haddin. Delivered: James Trotter by your order, May, 1769.

Page 326A.— — May, 1762. Samuel Crockett to Alex. Hamilton, £40, 283 acres on Jackson's River above mouth of Falling Spring.

Page 326.—1st June, 1761 (1760 ?). James Pritchard and Abigail ( ), of Orange County, North Carolina (Abigail was one of the daughters and devisees of Benj. Borden), to Joseph Borden, of Frederick County (Abigail was Abigail Worthington), £90, 1000 acres given to Abigail (then Worthington). Teste: John McDaniel, Jacob Layton, Levi Branson, John ( ) Alexander. Commission for privy examination of Abigail executed, 1st June, 1761. Delivered: Joseph, 10th March, 1763.

Page 331.—18th May, 1762. Gabriel Pickens to Abram Smith, £50, 200 acres on a branch of Bever Creek; cor. Henry Smith; cor. Jacob Gillespy's land. Delivered: Col. Abraham Smith, March, 1772.

Page 335.—18th May, 1762. Andrew Russell and Florence ( ) to Joshua Russell, their son, £5, 150 acres on Christian's Creek in Beverley Manor, part of 496 acres conveyed by Beverley to Andrew, 24th September, 1741; John Henderson's line. Delivered: Joshua Russell, March, 1767.

Page 339.—13th May, 1762. Honorius Powell and Jannet, of Orange County, to John David Wilper, £35, 270 acres on Hawk's Bill, a branch of Shanandore, patented to Honorius, 15th December, 1757. Teste: James and Francis Kirtley, Frances Slaughter. Delivered: Francis Kirtley, Esq., of Rockingham, 27th May, 1789.

Page 342.—10th May, 1762. Borden's executors to William Taylor, £12, 200 acres, part of 92100; cor. Isaac Taylor, William Lusk's line; Daniel Lyle's line, white oak on the Warm Run. Bought of Benj., the younger.

Page 347.—5th May, 1761. Samuel McDowell and Mary to Walter Smiley, £5, 200 acres by patent 6th July, 1741, on the Mary, a branch of James River. Teste: John, Michael and William Bowyer. Delivered: W. Smiley, 10th February, 1786.

Page 351.—5th May, 1761. Samuel McDowell and Mary to James

Welsh, £10, 200 acres by patent 6th July, 1741, on the Mary, a branch of James; cor. Walter Smiley. Delivered: James Welsh, 20th July, 1765.

Page 354.—12th May, 1762. Samuel McDowell and Mary to Samuel McClure, £45, 400 acres by patent 1st June, 1741, on the Poak Hill Branch. Delivered: Wm. Foster by your order, February, 1768.

Page 358.—19th May, 1762. Alex. Henderson to Alex. Campbell, £20, 100 acres granted to Henderson by James Edmiston, 17th March, 1757, on the Red Bank on South River of Shanando. Acknowledged. Delivered: Alex. Campbell, May, 1765.

Page 362.—19th May, 1762. John Trimble and Mary ( ) to Henry Criswell, 400 acres on southemost branch of North River of Shanando, on Stony Lick Branch. Acknowledged and privy examination of Mary.

Page 366.—18th May, 1762. William Armstrong and Mary ( ) to Joseph Kincaid, £100, 242½ acres on South Fork of Christian's Creek, part of 485 acres, on which Wm. now lives, Wm. Christian's line. Acknowledged and privy examination. Delivered to Wm. Kinkaid, June, 1777.

Page 368.—2d September, 1761. Charles ( ) Diver to Robert Shanklin.

Page 370.—12th May, 1762. Andrew Hays and Margret to Henry Miller (Dutchman), £40, 231 acres, part of Borden's 92100, on Moffett's Creek, on John Walker's line, on Back Creek, Fork of Walker's Creek. Acknowledged and privy examination.

Page 373.—17th May, 1762. Borden's executors to James Davis, husbandman, £165, 436 acres, part of 92100; cor. to patent line and William Todd; Todd's, Robert Young's and the patent line, Buffalow Creek, Low Todd's line; cor. Peter Wallace. Teste: George Pearis, John Neily, Joseph Gray.

Page 379.—6th January, 1762. John Snelson, of Hanover, merchant, and Robert Donald, late of County of Hanover, merchant, by Thos. Buchanan, John McDowell, of Hanover, Peter Belshus, of Louisa, merchants, to Robert Breckinridge, 265 acres conveyed by mortgage by John Hays, of Albemarle, 4th April, 1751, mortgage foreclosed by decree of General Court, 15th October, 1756, £40 paid for use of Snelson and Donald, on Roanoke; cor. to survey made by John Smith. Teste: Francis Smith, Stephen Willis, Francis Smith, Jr., Wm. Anderson. Proved by witnesses. Delivered: Maj. Robert Breckinridge, 9th February, 1771.

Page 387.—17th August, 1762. John McClerey, Sr., ( ) to John McClerey, Jr., his son, £5, in Beverley Manor on head branch of Middle River of Shanandoah, conveyed to John, 4th February, 1748, part of 420 acres, containing 100 acres. Acknowledged. Delivered to John McClerey, May Court, 1767.

Page 391.—17th August, 1762. Andrew Ker and Rachel ( ) to Timothy Coll (Coul), £42, 153 acres on Middle River, patented to Andrew, 5th September, 1749, Wm. Ker's line. Acknowledged and privy examination. Delivered: Timothy Coll, November, 1764.

Page 395.—16th August, 1762. Jane Teas ( ), relict of Joseph Teas, deceased, to Joseph Love, £50, 400 acres on South River Shanando, line of Beverley Manor. Acknowledged. Teste: Adam Dean, Samuel Love.

Page 398.—17th August, 1762. William Sprowle and Jean to Alex. McElroy, £200, 320 acres on Moffet's Creek; cor. John Patterson, part of

Borden's 92100. Acknowledged and privy examination. Teste: James Trotter, W. Ward, Jas. Ward. Delivered: McElroy, December, 1768.

Page 403.—17th August, 1762. Alex. McElroy and Agness to Wm. Sprowle, £200, 200 acres patented to Alexander, 10th April, 1751; John Dickenson's line on Cowpasture; cor. John Donely's land. Acknowledged and privy examination.

Page 405.—13th May, 1762. John Smith to William Bowyer, £100, two slaves and 600 acres on Craig's Creek, joining Col. James Patton's lands; mortgage for £100. James ( ) Cloyd. Wilton ( ) Walton.

Page 406.—16th August, 1762. James Turk and Mary to Thomas Turk, £40, 250 acres on South River of Shanandoe below Humble's land. Acknowledged and privy examination. Delivered: Thos. Turk, July, 1769.

Page 410.—29th June, 1762. Thomas Ruckman, eldest brother and heir-at-law of John Ruckman, late of Augusta County, deceased, of the County of Northampton, in Pennsylvania, to William Davies, of Philadelphia, £43.10, 280 acres on head of Buffalo Creek of James River. Proved by witnesses.

Page 414.—16th August, 1762. William Davies, of Philadelphia, to John Wiley, Jr., £43.15, 280 acres on head of Buffalo Creek of James. Acknowledged. Delivered: Joseph McBride, 1st September, 1769.

Page 416.—12th May. 1762. Borden's executors to Samuel Todd, £12, 200 acres, part of 92100; cor. Wm. Hall; cor. to the Meeting House; cor. James Campbell's new survey, Samuel McMurtry's line. Teste: Benj. Hawkins, Alex. Collyer, Samuel McMurtry. Delivered: Richard Williamson, 26th May, 1774.

Page 422.—18th May, 1762. Isaiah Shipman and Elizabeth ( ) to Aaron Oliver, £22.10, 150 acres on Beaver Creek of North River of Shanando, part of 380 acres patented to Isaiah, 10th March, 1756. Teste: Robert Brown, Samuel Moor, Thos. ( ) Turk. Acknowledged and privy examination. Delivered: Col. Abraham Smith, May, 1769.

Page 425.—10th February, 1762. Jeremiah Hadley, of Orange County, North Carolina, to John Reid, of Amherst, £42.10, 115 acres patented to James Patton, 3d November, 1750, and conveyed to Joshua Hadley and devised by Joshua to Jeremiah, on James River. Teste: Alex Reid, Thos. Henderson, Alexander Reid, Jr., John Lyon. Proved by witnesses. Delivered: Thomas Reed, May, 1765.

Page 429.—17th August, 1762. John Botkin and Mary to Robert Duffield, £21.10, 200 acres on the New Found Creek, patented to John McCreery and assigned to said John Botkin, dated 10th August, 1759; cor. to tract surveyed for Archibald Elliot. Teste: Mathew Harper. Acknowledged and privy examination.

Page 433.—17th August, 1762. James Kerr, of Roanoke County, North Carolina, to Patrick Hays in Derry Township, Lancaster County, Pennsylvania, £250, 474 acres in Beverley Manor, conveyed to Jame Patton, 18th May, 1750; cor. James Leeper. Teste: Elax. ( ) Brownlee. Acknowledge. Delivered: Pat. Hays, March Court, 1769.

Page 436.—17th August, 1762. James Leeper, Jr., to his father, James Leeper, Cr., £100, on Naked Creek of North River Shanandore, patented to James Leeper, Sr., 12th July, 1746, part of a patent, 26th April, 1742, 230 acres. Teste: Hugh Ross, Isaiah Curry, John Hind. Delivered: John Henderson, September, 1765.

Page 440.—27th May, 1762. Isaac ( ) Taylor and Isabel ( ) to George Taylor, £5, 200 acres in Borden's tract, on Mill Creek; cor. said Isaac Taylor. Delivered: Samuel Lyle, June, 1783.

Page 442.—17th August, 1762. John ( ) Edwards and William Hyde, indenture of apprenticeship. John Edwards apprentices his son, Griffy Edwards, to William Hyde to be taught "his art, trade and mistery" of a carpenter for four years. Delivered: Thomas Bowyer, April, 1764, by Wm. Hides' order.

Page 445.—17th June, 1762. Philip Haws, of Lancaster County, Pennsylvania, to Jacob Passenger, £30, 125 acres between Cub Run and Picked Mountain, patented to Haws, 14th February, 1761. Cor. Nicholas Trout, Jacob Pence's line. Teste: Jacob ( ) Pence, Adam Pence. Delivered: Jacob Argenbright, November, 1764.

Page 450.—27th July, 1762. Benjamin Bennett to John McNutt, £43, 175 acres in Fork of James, joining Samuel McDowel. Teste: Patrick ( ) McCollam, Patrick McCorkle. Delivered: James Trimble, 12th November, 1772.

Page 454.—20th March, 1762. John McNutt, weaver, and Catren ( ) to John Attkins, coardwaner, £26, 200 acres on Christian's Creek in Beverley Manor, George Rutledge's line, John Buchanan's Mill Creek; cor. Wm. Marchal, James Caldwell's line.

Page 458.—10th July, 1762. John ( ) O'Bryan and Mary and Cornelius ( ) O'Bryan and Ann ( ), surviving joint tenants of Cornelius, John and Cornelius O'Bryan, Jr., to Thomas O'Bryan, £20, 150 acres, part of 500 acres conveyed by Hite & Co. to Cornelius, John and Cornelius, Jr., 24th June, 1744, on Linvel's Creek, beginning at kern of stones; cor. John O'Bryan; cor. Cornelius O'Bryan, on the side of the Bald Hill, Watering Spring Run. Delivered: Thomas O'Bryan, July, 1766.

Page 463.—10th August, 1762. Thomas O'Bryan (signed Bran and Bryan) and Elizabeth ( ) to John O'Bryan, £5, 200 acres on Linvel's Creek, Hite & Co.'s patent line. Delivered: Thomas O'Bryan, July, 1766.

Page 465.—9th August, 1762. John O'Bryan and Mary and Cornelius O'Bryan and Ann, partition. Cornelius O'Bryan was in his lifetime seised jointly with John and Cornelius O'Bryan in 500 acres on Linvel's Creek, conveyed to them by Hite & Co., 24th June, 1744. By the death of Cornelius, the father, John and Cornelius, his sons, became by survivorship, joint tenants, and they conveyed to their brother Thomas O'Bryan, 150 acres, 10th July, 1762. Now John and Cornelius partition the remaining 350 acres, John to have as follows, cor. McCay's crossing, Linvel's Creek, kern of stones; cor. Thomas O'Bryan, Watering Spring, 200 acres. Cornelius to have as follows: 150 acres, cor. George Bowman near a graveyard; cor. Thos O'Bryan, Bald Hill. Proved by witnesses. Delivered to Thomas O'Bryan, July, 1766.

Page 472.—3d June, 1762. George Bigham, late of Augusta, to Robert Erwin, yeoman, £32.5, 251 acres on Muddy Creek of Shanando. Teste: Andrew Cowan, Robert Hamilton and James ( ) McNabb. Acknowledged, 17th August, 1762. Delivered: Francis Erwin, 9th July, 1773.

Page 475.—16th August, 1762. Jacob Reed, of Hampshire, to Alex. Love, £100, 373 acres on Goose Creek. Teste: James Reily and Mathew Read. Acknowledged, 18th August, 1762.

Page 479.—13th August, 1762. Jacob Coger, of Hallifax County, to Michael Coger, £100, 455 acres on Shanando, part of 930 acres patented to Jacob, 24th April, 1753. Cor. Thomas McCready (conveyed from Jacob), the patent lines. Teste: Felta Kop (Valentine Cope), Stephen Conrad. Delivered: M. Coger, 26th April, 1763.

Page 483.—17th August, 1762. Patrick ( ) McCallam to Alex. Gibson, £70, 205 acres in Beverley Manor conveyed by James Coyle to Patrick, 11th October, 1750, on Christian's Creek, cor. William Palmer, Alex. Thompson and Jno. Thompson. Cor. James Coyle. Acknowledged. Delivered: Samuel Frazier by your order, 5th September, 1765.

Page 487.—17th August, 1762. Joseph Carpenter to John Mann, £70, 230 acres on Jackson's River.

Page 490.—18th August, 1762. Isaac Taylor and Esabella to Isaac Taylor, Jr., £50, 181 acres on the waters of James River. Acknowledgement and privy examination, 18th August, 1762. Delivered: Francis Smith, May Court, 1767.

Page 494.—18th May, 1762. Alex. Craig and Margrett ( ) to James Patterson, £5, 47 acres, part of 144 acres patented to Alexander, March, 1756, on Middle River of Shanandoe.

Page 498.—18th May, 1762. Alex. Craig and Margrett ( ) to Alex. Craig, his son, £5, 132 acres on a small branch of Middle River of Shanandoe, part of 335 acres patented to Alex., 10th September, 1755; cor. James Gamble's land. Delivered: Alex. Craig, — January, 1764.

Page 502.—11th August, 1762. Abram Smith to Israel Christian, £20, 86 acres by deed, 11th August, 1762, at Mulberry Bottom, on Craig's Creek. Teste: Thomas Barnes.

Page 506.—18th August, 1762. Robert Ramsey and Margaret, of Anson County in North Carolina, to James Henry, £70, 340 acres in Beverley Manor, cor. Samuel Huston; cor. Robert Alexander and Patrick Hays; cor. Wm. Purris. Acknowledged and privy examination. Delivered: Samuel Henry, 21st June, 1771.

Page 510.—14th May, 1762. John Macky, farmer, to James McClung, Sr., £120, 390 acres on Mill Creek of James River, cor. Baptist McNabb. Proved by witnesses. Delivered to John McClung, May, 1773.

Page 514.—17th August, 1762. William Wilson and Agness ( ) to David Williams, £—, 200 acres, part of 400 acres patented on North Fork of North River of Shanando, an island of said river.

Page 516.—14th June, 1762. Samuel ( ) Gay, of Anson County, North Carolina, and Jean ( ) to James Gay, £70, 354 acres on Little River of Calfpasture in Beverley's patent. Cor. William Elliott; cor. William Gay. Teste: Samuel Crockett, Alex. Hamilton, Jno. Stinson. Proved by witnesses.

Page 521.—8th February, 1762. James ( ) Sloan to John Mills, £5, 178 acres by patent, 20th September, 1745, on a branch of James River, on a branch of Lunie's Mill Run. Delivered to John Craig by your order, May, 1764.

Page 524.—18th August, 1762. Richard ( ) Kerr to Israel Christian, £54, 240 acres by patent deed from Col. James Patton to Richard Kerr, 18th November, 1752, on Welsh Run, a branch of Roan Oak. Teste: Wm. Christian, Thomas Barnes, Archibald Handley.

Page 528.—18th August, 1762. William Johnson and Mary to John Bollor (also Wm. Johnson and Rose), £50, 163 acres on Jackson's River. Acknowledged by William.

Page 532.—18th August, 1762. James Hughes and Euphemia, and Andrew Greer and Ruth ( ) to John Cochran, £122, 224 acres on Big Meadow Run, a branch of Cathey's River, line of Beverley Manor. Acknowledged and privy examination, 19th August, 1762. Delivered: Henry King, September, 1775.

Page 536.—18th August, 1762. John Dickinson, gent., to James Fitzpatrick, £30, 195 acres on Cedar Creek of Jackson's River. Delivered: John Fitzpatrick, 29th June, 1792.

Page 540.—2d July, 1762. John Given and John Stewart and Sarah ( ) to Hugh Lenox and William Scott, merchants of Spottsylvania, £120, 179 acres on a branch on north side of the Little River of New River, patented, 22d August, 1753, to Robert Box and conveyed by Ephraim Vause to said John Given and John Stewart, 14th April, 1760. Teste: James Ward. Acknowledged and privy examination.

Deed Book No. 11.

Page 2.—18th August, 1762. Hugh Martin to William Martin, £100, 310 acres on Christian's Creek; cor. Wm. Palmer; George Robinson's cor., now Wm. Henderson's land; cor. Alex. Thompson. Signed by John and Robert Thompson and acknowledged by them, 19th August, 1762.

Page 5.—10th August, 1761. John Crockett and Margaret ( ) and Archibald Crockett and Mary ( ), of Anson County, North Carolina, to James Beard, £120, 246 acres on Cowpasture, cor. James Mease. Teste: Samuel Crockett. Delivered: Mrs. Beard, June, 1784.

Page 8.—18th May, 1762. Johannes ( ) Miller, of Anson County, North Carolina, to John Smith, of Augusta, and Richard Pearis, of Frederick County, £52.15, 380 acres, part of 900 patented to Garret Zinn, 20th June, 1754, on Woods River, opposite an island; cor. Imanuel Eberling.

Page 10.—29th March, 1762. Thomas Neal (O'Neal, Peel) to John Hamilton, £30, tract between Thomas Gordon and John Megery that John Neel formerly lived on, now the property of Thomas Neal, his only son. Mortgage.

Page 12.—20th August, 1762. Robert ( ) Allen and Martha ( ) to John Moffet, £181, 234 acres in Beverley Manor; cor. Hugh Young; cor. Jno. Trimble; cor. Wm. McPheeters; cor. James Young, Back Creek. Delivered: Mr. Moffett, 15th April, 1786.

Page 15.—20th August, 1762. Randal Lockhart to Sampson and George Mathews, merchants, £410, 550 acres purchased by Randal of Anthony Strother, 1760; cor. Thos. Gordon, now Rev. John Craig's; cor. on Lewis' Creek; cor. land sold by John Pickens to William Baskins.

Page 18, 1762. £100, John Smith to Alex. Sayers, ½ of a tract held jointly by John and Richard Pearis, containing 380 acres, part of 900 patented to Garrett Zinn, 20th June, 1753, and conveyed to us by John Miller, 18th May, 1762. described as in above conveyance. Sent to Col. Preston by his order, October, 1773.

Page 20.—23d August, 1762. Israel Christian and Felix Gilbert to John

Stewart. Part of the 25 acres conveyed by Beverley to the County, and now conveyed under the order of the County Court, 20th November, 1760. £4, lot No. 17, fronting lot 16, belonging to Col. Christian, and joining a lot belonging to James Hughes. Teste: Ann Christian, Thos. Barnes, Priscilla Christian. Livery and seizin. Delivered: Michael Bowyer, March, 1774.

Page 22.—24th August, 1762. Same to Michael Bowyer, £7.10, lot 21 in Staunton, 1¼ acres. Teste: Charles Lewis, Will Cabeen, Jas. Ward. Livery of seizin.

Page 25.—22d August, 1762. David Frame to Margaret Frame, £50, horses and other personal property. Teste: James Hamilton, James Stephenson, James Blear.

Page 25.—26th February, 1762. Francis Tyler to Israel Christian, £40, a negro slave Hanna. Teste: W. Christian, Charles Donelly.

Page 27.—16th November, 1762. Samuel Henderson and Jean to Charles Smith, £40, two tracts on Dry River, a branch of North River of Shanandoe. 1st tract of 165 acres conveyed to Samuel by Samuel McMahon, 7th September, 1753. 2d tract, containing 117 acres patented to Samuel, 14th February, 1761; cor. Daniel Smith. Teste: Pat. Lockhart, Jno. Henderson, Alexander McDonnall. Delivered: Charles Smith, February, 1765.

Page 30.—28th August, 1762. Samuel Young and Jannet ( ) to John Brown. £108, 295 acres in Beverley Manor on Young's Mill Creek, conveyed by Robert Young to Samuel Young, adjoining land of said John Brown, John Young, Wm. McClintig, James Young; cor. Robet Young, Jr., Major Brown's old line. Delivered: Jno. Brown, 1764.

Page 34.—24th September, 1762. George Adam Salling, of Orange County, North Carolina, to George Salling, £170, 200 acres in first fork of James River; cor. John Paxton's land. Teste: Andrew Evins, Christopher Vingard. Delivered: Jacob Hickman, 1st June, 1789, by written order from Peter Salling.

Page 37.—16th November, 1762. Henry Maese and Ann ( ) to Michael and George Kinder, £10, 34 acres on a branch of Broad Run near Linvell's Creek, part of 400 acres surveyed for Thomas Beal and conveyed to Jonathan Douglas, 3d July, 1750, and conveyed to Henry, 19th August, 1760. Cor. Nicholas Mase's part of said land; cor. Robert Poage's land. Teste: Benj. Kinley, Wm. Wilson. Delivered: Michael Kinder, February, 1767.

Page 40.—12th November, 1762. James Johnston to Abraham Bess, £30, 108 acres on waters of Catawba, part of 230 patented to James, 7th August, 1761.

Page 42.—15th November, 1762. Lillie ( ) Bowin, executor of John Bowin, to Reice (Rees) Bowin, son of said John, £20, 230 acres on Glade Creek of Roanoke.

Page 45.—8th November, 1762. James McDowell and Elizabeth to John Bowyer, £300, 400 acres on main branch of James River, conveyed by Samuel McDowell and Mary. Delivered: Jno. Bowyer, 1765.

Page 47.—13th November, 1762. Robert ( ) Luney and Elisabeth to John Bowyer, £300, 250 acres on James River patented to Robert, 30th July, 1742.

Page 50.—22d July, 1762. Joseph Hanna and Anna ( ) to David Frame, £10, 68 acres, part of a moiety of 136 acres patented, 12th May,

1759, on a draft of Naked Creek, east side the Pennsylvania Road. Teste: Samuel Henderson, William Lamme, James Frame. Delivered: Hugh Donaho, 29th September, 1767.

Page 52.—30th January, 1761. Mathias Celzar and Renamia ( ), of Frederick County, to George Cutlip, £40, conveyed to Mathias Celsar by Peter Carr and Mary, 1th July, 1754, on Shanando, 120 acres.

Page 55.—22d April, 1763. George Rodgers and Elisabeth to Robert Rodgers, of Augusta, and Robert Wallace, of Lancaster County, Pennsylvania, £200, two tracts in Beverley Manor: 1st, containing 540 acres conveyed by Beverley to George, 28th February, 1749; cor. George Anderson, Cathies River, Christian's Creek; Jacob Carr's cor.; James Crawford's cor; 2d tract, 135 acres conveyed to George by Daniel Kidd, 20th September, 1763; Christie's Creek, George Hutcheson's line.

Page 58.—15th November, 1762. Samuel ( ) Lindsey and Margrett ( ) to William Kelly, £130, 130 acres on Walker's Creek of James River, cor. Alex. Walker; James Moore's cor. Delivered: John McCown, November, 1766.

Page 61.—Mathew Armstrong and Lillie ( ) to Jno. Patterson, £117.10, 190 acres in Beverley Manor on a branch of Middle River, line of Robert King's place, cor. said Patterson; cor. Jno. Anderson's line; cor. said King's old place. Teste: John and George Anderson, Charles Baskin. Delivered: Thos. Patterson. 25th June, 1765.

Page 63.—8th September, 1762. John David Wilper and Anna Christina ( ) to Francis Kirkley, Jr., £35, 270 acres on Hawksbill, branch of Shanandore, conveyed to John David by Honorius Powell, 13th May, 1762. Delivered: Francis Kirtley, Esq., 27th May, 1789.

Page 66.—8th September, 1762. Mary Wood, of Frederick, James and Moses Green, of Culpeper, to George Dill, £60, 348 acres on South Branch of Potomac, part of 800 acres patented to Robert Green, 12th July, 1746.

Page 69.—15th November, 1762. James Simpson and Jane ( ) to John Handey, £150, 300 acres on Cowpasture. Delivered: Jno. Handley, 19th November, 1770.

Page 72.—16th November, 1762. William Poage and Ann to John Poage, £100, 205 acres, part of 772 acres surveyed for Robert Poage, Sr., in Beverley Manor where said Poage lives; line of Wallaces land, cor. said John Poages land; cor. Thomas Poages land.

Page 75.—16th November, 1762. Robert Poage and Jean to William Poage, 104 acres on Cedar Creek in Forks of James; cor. Thomas Taylor, McDowell's land; cor. William Mull's land. Delivered: Robert Poage, Sr., 3d March. 1768.

Page 77.—15th November, 1762. John Poage and Mary to Robert Poage. Sr., £50, 135 acres on Howell's Branch of North River of Shanandoe joining lands of Abraham Smith.

Page 79.—18th October, 1762. Samuel Harrison and Mary ( ), of Craven County, South Carolina, to Wiliam Minter, millwright, £125, 245 acres on South Branch of Linvel's Creek, Abraham Hill's line. Teste: Daniel Smith, Daniel Pouder, John ( ) Eubanks, Gasper ( ) Fought. Delivered: John Curry, September, 1767.

Page 82.—26th May, 1761. Peter Horse to Adam Stroud, £20, 275 acres on South Fork of Potomac, part of 700 acres of Postle Hover's, Michael

Kynes' cor. Teste: Mathew Patton, Robert Ralston, Postle ( ) Horse. Delivered: Adam Stroud, March, 1769.

Page 85.—8th October, 1762. Thomas Story and Mary ( ) to John Stuart, £200, 200 acres, part of 675 acres patented to — and granted by Andrew Cathey to Thomas, 20th July, 1745, on Middle River of Shanando. Delivered to Maj. D. Stephenson.

Page 87.—16th November, 1762. Richard Pearis and Rhoda, of Frederick County, to Alexander Boyd, of the Virginia Regiment, £50, ½ of a tract containing — acres in upper part of Dunger Bottom, conveyed by John Miller to said Richard Pearis and a certain John Smith, August, 1762. Delivered: Alex. Love, November, 1763.

Page 90.—16th November, 1762. John Carlile and Mary ( ) to Thomas Hugart, £50, 250 acres in the Calfpasture, part of 600 acres formerly surveyed for James Carolile and by him conveyed to said John; James Carolile's land; Rev. Mr. John Kinkead's land; James Campbell''s land; land of Jacob Clemons, deceased. Delivered to Wm. Hugheart, 21st December, 1790.

Page 92.—18th November, 1762. John Henderson and Mary ( ) to Hugh Martin, £75, 200 acres on Christian's Creek, cor. Thomas Rutledge's land. Teste: James Hughes, Wm. Shannon, Moses Thomsen.

Page 95.—20th November, 1762. Nicholas Green, of Culpeper, to Wm. Chesnut, £132, 400 acres, part of 1700 acres granted to Robert Green, deceased, 15th March, 1744, on head branches of Muddy Creek, Daniel Callacahn's Meadow. Delivered: Gawin Hamilton, March Court, 1774.

Page 98.—20th November, 1762. Same to Daniel Callachan, £40, 100 acres, part of same; cor. to above, a sasifrage by Dry River. Delivered: as above.

Page 99.—6th Setpember, 1762, John Stewart and Sarah ( ) to Thomas and Andrew Lewis and William Preston, £170, ¼ acre lot, being part of lot 3 in Staunton, lower end of Francisco's house in the Main Street, Robert Read's lot; lot on which John Stewart now dwells; and 25 acres of woodland, part of 50-acres lot No. 8, bounded by lot No. 7, 9, by William Beverley's land. Teste: Peter Grant, James Crawford, John Murray. Delivered: Jno. Frogg, March Court, 1773.

Page 101.—16th November, 1762. Charles Patrick and John Patrick, division of estate of their father Robert. John is to have 283 acres conveyed to Robert by Wm. and David Bell, also all the land lying on north side of South River in the tract whereon the said Robert lately dwelt, and to have a waggon way over the ford of the river opposite a pond and so up the river on the south side. Charles to have that on the north side, John to pay Charles £30. Delivered: J. Patrick, February, 1767.

Page 101.—Report of commission of privy examination of Jane, wife of James Thompson, deed to Samuel Henderson, 16th March, 1762. Executed, 28th September, 1762.

Page 102.—Ditto of Rebecca, wife of Abraham Hite, of Hampshire County, deed to Jeremiah Harrison, 31st December, 1760. Executed, 10th December, 1762.

Page 103.—Ditto of ditto, deed to David Ralston, 31st December, 1761. Executed 10th ——, 1761.

Page 104.—Ditto of ditto, deed to John Wright. Executed, 10th December, 1761.

Page 107.—12th February, 1763. Andrew ( ) Balfaut and Elizabeth ( ) (Faut) to Christian Clemans, £5, 266 acres, part of 400 acres patented to John Balfaut, 20th February, 1745. Pat. Frazier's line. Teste: George Faut. Delivered: Christian Clemmons, May, 1766.

Page 109.—15th February, 1763. Same to Gasper Balfaut, his brother, £2, 67 acres, art of 400 acres patented to John Balfaut, 20th February, 1745, on a small branch of Shanando; cor. Christian Clemmon's land. Teste: Jacob Lingell. Delivered: Casper Fought, April, 1779.

Page 111.—15th February, 1763. John Hair (Hear), Sr., and Mary (Marry) to Isaiah Curry, £5, 90 acres on North River Shanando at a place called the Long Neck, formerly sold to John by Alex. Keyla, was patented to John Lusk, 13th June, 1755. Delivered: Isaiah Curry, January, 1766.

Page 114.—15th February, 1763. John Lusk (Lisk) and Elisabeth to Henry Wilson, £20, 230 acres in Beverley Manor on Christians Creek; cor. to the Christian's lands; cor. James Caldwell, William Armstrong's line. Delivered: Henry Wilson, January, 1764.

Page 116.—11th December, 1762. William Lockridge and Agness ( ) to David Steel, £100, 244 acres on Halfway Creek in Borden's tract; cor. Thomas Hill; Moore's cor.; David Moore's cor. Teste: Samuel and Robert Steel, Patt. Campbell. Delivered: Samuel Steel, June, 1766.

Page 119.—15th February, 1763. Robert Alexander to William Alexander, £100, 304 acres, 3 roods and 15 perches; cor. George Henderson. Delivered: William Alexander, May Court, 1765.

Page 121.—15th February, 1763. Samuel Wilson and Mary to John Kirk, £80, 76 acres on a draft of Jenning's Creek. Teste: Robert Armstrong, Wm. Magill, James Bell.

Page 123.—11th February, 1763. Robert ( ) Fletcher and Christian ( ) to James Stevenson, £50, 200 acres on Little Calfpasture, part of 460 acres conveyed by Beverley to John Hindman, 9th-10th April, 1745, and recorded in General Court, which descended to Robert and Christian as nephew and heir-at-law of Hindman; cor. James Stevenson. Teste: James Lockridge, Samuel Crockett, Edward Thompson. Delivered: Mr. Stevenson, 31st August, 1787.

Page 126.—10th February, 1763. Andrew () Brown and Jane ( ) to Joseph Ward, £55.10, 220 acres conveyed to George Stevenson by James Patton, 8th December, 1752, on Poage's Draft of James River, line of Burden's patent. Teste: W. Ward, Adam ( ) Reed, Jno. Parks.

Page 128.—10th February, 1763. Adam ( ) Reed and Barbara ( ) to John Parks, £100, 175 acres on the Mary Creek, part of 350 acres granted to Rev. Alex. McDowell by patent, 10th July, 1745, crossing Evans's Run.

Page 130.—20th October, 1762. Borden's executors to Andrew and John Kenady, £20, 341 acres, part of 92100; cor. Andrew Steel, crossing Mill Creek; cor. Hugh Martin. Delivered to Andrew Kenady.

Page 133.—27th May, 1762. William Bell, David Bell and Florence, his wife, to Samuel Logan, £30, 108 acres on Elk Run in Beverley Manor; cor. said Logan's other land, Hamilton's line. Delivered: Samuel Logan, May, 1765.

Page 134.—7th November, 1762. Borden's executors, to Archibald Buchanan, £5, 406 acres, part of 92,100, crossing McCowns Run; Robert Christian's corner; white oak by a warm spring, on Hays' (Nays?) Creek.

Teste: Robert King, John Lawrance, John Lawrance, Jr. Delivered: Wm. Buchanan, August, 1769.

Page 137.—14th February, 1763. Same to Andrew Hays, £50, 200 acres. part of 92,100; corner Samuel McDowell; corner James McDowell. Delivered: John Hays, January, 1770.

Page 140.—30th November, 1762. Samuel Lawrence to Gabriel Jones, £215, 400 acres on James River above mouth of Craig's Creek, which Lawrence lately purchased of said Jones; mortgage for £215. Delivered: Gabriel Jones, March, —64.

Page 142.—6th September, 1762. John Bingeman and Elizabeth ( ) of Broomfield in Culpeper Co. to Thomas Stanton, Jr., of same parish and county, £70, 184 acres patented to John Bingeman, Sr., 20th June, 1753. Livery and seisin. Teste: James Kirtley, Jonathan Cowhard, Thomas Kirtley, Richard Stanton, Thomas Stanton, Sr. Delivered: Thomas Madison, February, 1770.

Page 144.—6th September, 1762. Same to same, £50, 100 acres by patent to John Buchanan, 5th April, 1748, on Wood's River, known by the name of Bufflo Pond. Teste: Jno. Hume, Thos. Stanton, Joseph Ham, Richard Stanton, Simon Tomison. Delivered: Thos. Madison, 1770.

Page 146.—16th October, 1762. Same to Thomas Stanton, £61, 460 acres by patent to John, 20th June, 1753, on Woods River at Poplar Camp. Teste: Nicholas ( ) Null, Thomas Stanton, Jr.; Richard Stanton, Jno. Hume. Delivered: Thomas Madison, 1770.

Page 149.—4th February, 1763. John Thompson and Susanna to Henry Ferguson, £70, 109 acres on a branch of Glade Creek. Teste: Wm. Preston, Jno. Buchanan, Jno. Smith, Robt. Breckinridge.

Page 152.—11th January, 1763. David Miller and Hannah ( ) to Robt. Breckinridge, £97.10, two tracts, 1st containing 190 acres, part of 2,900 acres formerly possessed by said David Miller on Buffelo Creek of Roanoke; corner land of said Robt. Breckinridge. 2d containing 35 acres adjoining above by patent, 7th August, 1761, on Buffelo Creek. Teste: Wm. Preston, Jno. Miller, Wm. Anderson, Pat. Sharkey, Francis Smith, Wm. Davis, Thos. McFarren. Delivered: Israel Christian, March, 1764.

Page 155.—11th February, 1763. James ( ) McAfee, Sr., to George McAfee, £100, 190 acres, part of 300 acres patented to James, 15th December, 1749, on Catawbo, a branch of James River; corner James McAfee, Jr. Delivered: James McAfee, Jr., February, 1765.

Page 157.—11th February, 1763. Same to James McAfee, Jr., £100, 110 acres (other part of 300 above); corner James McCown.

Page 158.—3d February, 1763. David ( ) Harman to Peter Harman and Geo. Man, £15.10, horses, cows, pigs, beds, &c. Teste: Robt. Shanklin, Jacob Nicolas. "Received of Peter Harman and George Man, £15.10, in full satisfaction for all legacies that shall be left me by my father at his death, dated 3d February, 1763. N. B.—If the said David Harmon shall pay said Harmon or Man the above sum, then this receipt shall be void."

Page 160.—9th February, 1763. William ( ) Ledgewood and Rebecca ( ) to Moses Williams, £27, 300 acres in Beverley Manor on Buchanan's Mill Creek; John Begam's line; corner John Buchanan's land; Elijah McClenachan's land, formerly James McCorkle's; corner John Henderson;

Nathan Gillilan's land, formerly John Lynn's. Teste: Abraham Biss. Delivered: Moses Williams, 5th August, 1783.

Page 162.—27th November, 1762. Gabriel Jones and Margaret to Samuel Lawrance, yeoman, £215, 400 acres on James River above mouth of Craig's Creek, purchased by Jones from Alexander Richey and he from Alexander Douglass, eldest son and heir-at-law of Roger Douglass, deceased, original patentee. Delivered: Samuel Lawrance, March Court, 1769.

Page 164.—15th February, 1763. David Frame to Margaret Frame, £5, 150 acres on south branch of Naked Creek. Teste: James and William Frame and John Botkin. Delivered: Margaret Frame, 28th October, 1768.

Page 166.—16th February, 1763. William Wilson and Agness to Robt. Gragg, £20, 200 acres, part of 400 acres on North Fork of North River of Shanandoe patented to William, 25th March, 1752; David Williams' land. Delivered: Frederick Michael, 7th March, 1792.

Page 168.—15th February, 1763. Thomas ( ) Thompson to Joseph McClung, £30, 93 acres on Cowpasture river, opposite land of John Moore.

Page 170.—14th February, 1763. Mary Preston to Robert Lockridge, £110, 520 acres on Great River of Calfpasture; corner Kinkead's land, crossing Ramsey's Creek. Teste: Jno. Brown, Thos. Gillham. Delivered: Robt. Lockridge, November, 1764.

Page 173.—19th February, 1763. Sampson Mathews and Mary to Patrick McCollom, £130, 350 acres by patent to John Mathews and willed to Sampson on Burden's Creek of James River; Benj. Borden's line. Also 18 acres, line of above tract; corner James Trimble. Delivered: James McClure, 2d March, 1772.

Page 174.—21st August, 1762. Thomas Fulton to Wm. Preston and Robt. Bratton, £50, conveys one negro boy named Murray.

Page 175.—15th February, 1763. David Steuert and Margaret to John Miller, £130, 331 acres in Beverley Manor; corner land of heirs of Alexander Breckinridge. Teste: Robt. Gorrell. Delivered: John Miller, 1776.

Page 177.—19th February, 1763. Robert McClenachan and Sarah to Alexander McClenachan, £300, 731 acres in Beverley Manor conveyed to Robert by John Madison, 1st June, 1751; corner Adam Thompson's land; corner John Ramsey. Teste: Jane, John, Lettice McClenachan. Delivered: Alexander McClenachan, February, 1767.

Page 180.—19th February, 1763. Robert McClenachan and Sarah to John McClenachan, £250, 310 acres by deed from James Armstrong on North Branch Christians Creek, small island in said creek; corner James Caldwell; corner Alexander McClenachan. Also 190 acres from Beverley on Christian's Creek; corner Wm. Nut's land; corner tract surveyed for Andrew Cowen, James Caldwell's line. Delivered: Alexander Sinclair per order, 13th December, 1773.

Page 182.—28th March, 1763. Samuel Wilkins, of Anson County, North Carolina, to William Snodden, £15, 70 acres, part of 1,264 acres patented to Robt. McCoy and Co., 26th March, 1739, and conveyed to Samuel by McCoy & Co., on west branch of Cook's Creek; coroner Alexander Heron's land; corner said Snodden's land. Delivered: Wm. Snodon, March, 1769.

Page 183.—9th April, 1763. John Smith to Abraham Smith, £36, 100 acres on James River joining Robt. Looney's, term 500 years; mortgage.

Page 185.—19th April, 1763. Charles Gillham annd Elisabeth ( ) to

James Bodkin, £41, 216 acres on the Cowpasture; corner tract formerly in possession of James Hall, now Robt. Hall. Teste: George Skillem, Ezekiel Gillham, John Carlile.

Page 187.—19th April, 1763. William McCutchan to James Risk, £50, 169 acres at mouth of Cedar Creek on Jackson's River, an island of the river. Teste: Adam and William Dean.

Page 189.—19th April, 1763. John Greenlee to James Greenlee, £25, 250 acres in forks of James River, granted to James Greenlee, Sr., Gent., deceased, who was father to said John Greenlee, who is eldest son and heir-at-law by patent, 20th September, 1745. Delivered: Samuel Greenlee, 1780.

Page 192.—19th April, 1763. John Greenlee to David Greenlee, £10, 400 acres on a branch in forks of James River patented to Thomas Williams, 20th June, 1749, and made over by William to James Greenlee, Sr., Gent., deceased, father of John, who is eldest son and heir-at-law by deed prior to this; corner survey of Erwin Patterson's. Delivered: Samuel Greenlee, March, 1780.

Page 194.—19th April, 1763. Same to Samuel Greenlee, £50, 200 acres; corner James McDowell; corner Ephraim McDowell, purchased by James Greenlee, Sr., from Borden, part of Borden's tract. Delivered: Samuel Greenlee, 31st March, 1780.

Page 196.—20th April, 1763. Isaiah Curry to George Martin, £31, 100 acres on South River Shannando, Christian Clemmans' land. Teste: Samuel Eastlake, John Henderson, George Trout.

Page 198.—2d April, 1762. Mathew Lyle and Esther to John Lyle, £10, 451 acres, part of Borden's 92,100 and conveyed by Borden to Mathew; corner Thomas McSpadin, John Mathews' line; corner John Gray. Delivered: Jno. Lyle, 4th March, 1774.

Page 201.—26th March, 1763. Mathew ( ) Robinson to Henry Campbell and James Culton, £40, 200 acres, part of Borden's 92,100; corner said Campbell, crossing Back Creek; corner John Robinson.

Page 203.—25th March, 1763. Same to Henry Campbell, £25, 200 acres, part of 92,100; corner Joseph Cultan, crossing Back Creek.

Page 206.—26th March, 1763. Alexander Logan and Rachel ( ) to James Kenedy, £35, 237 acres in Borden's tract, Capt. Kenedy's Mill Creek; corner McNuts land; William Berry's line; William Kennedy's corner; John Fulton's line; to Thos. Baird, to Thomas Loggan, John Logan's line. Teste: Wm. Alexander, Hugh Wardlaw, Arthur Graham, William Kenedy. Proved by Archibald Grymes.

Page 208.—20th April, 1763. William Armstrong and Mary ( ) to William Bell, £150, 242 acres, part of 485 acres in Beverley Manor on Christian's Creek purchased by William Armstrong by deed, 18th February, 1747-8. Division line made for Joseph Kinkead's land. Teste: Samuel Caldwell, Samuel Love.

Page 211.—18th April, 1763. Samuel Henderson and Jean to James Givens, £3, 4½ acres on Middle River Shanandoe adjoining land said Givens lives on. Teste: Thos. Baskin.

Page 213.—18th April, 1763. James Givens and Martha to Samuel Henderson, £3, 7¾ acres on Middle River Shanandoe, part of 311 acres on which said Givens lives. Delivered: Samuel Henderson, May, 1769.

Page 215.—8th February, 1763. Joseph McDonald and Elisabeth to William Preston, £180, 142 acres on Tinker's Creek; line Geo. Robinson's land; line of land of heirs of Edward McDonald; corner land said Preston now dwells on; Capt. Robinson's line. Teste: Samuel McKnab. Delivered: William Preston, December, 1763.

Page 217.—22d December, 1762. William Monger, blacksmith, to Augustine Price and Jacob Persinger, £28, household goods, iron stove, smith tools,; mortgage. Teste: Jacob Nicolos, Archibald Huston.

Page 218.—4th December, 1762. John ( ) Ledford, of Carolina and late of Virginia, appoints Isaac Taylor, yeoman, to convey, 142 acre. Teste: Alexander Love, James Fairlee. Proved by James Fairlee.

Page 218.—18th April, 1763. Valentine Sevire, of Frederick, farmer, to Andrew Bird, miller, £42.10.7, all his household goods, cattle, &c. Teste: Nicholas Jeehon, Jno. Phillips. Proved by Jno. Phillips. Delivered: Jno. Phillips, February, 1764.

Page 219.—14th July, 1760. David Robinson to Wm. Graham. Whereas John Mills of Augusta County did on 9th February, 1752, agree to convey to Joshua McCormick title for 245 acres, part of 845 acres on a branch of Round Oak called Buffler's Creek. Joshua, on 23d February, 1753, assigned his right to David Robinson, late of Augusta County, now of New Gorden Township, County of Chester, Province of Pennsylvania, and David obtained a deed. Power attorney to Wm. Grahames to bring suit against John Mills to recover the title and to make conveyance to Daniel McCormick. Teste: Elizabeth Young, Andrew Treper, John Armstrong, Bryan McDonald, Robert McGee, Benjamin Reelson.

Page 221.—Privy examination of Martha, wife of George Robinson, deed to Joseph McDonald, taken 10th April.

Page 222.—19th May, 1761. John Stephenson to James Hartgrove, of Staunton, £7, ½ acre lot 6, joining Sampson Mathews and James Hughes. Teste: Wm. Hyde, James Means.

Page 225.—21st May, 1763. James Bratton and Elisabeth to Robert Kinkead, £140, 334 acres in Beverley Manor; Mr. Lewis' two white oaks; Maxwell's line.

Page 226.—13th April, 1763. David Frame to George Patterson, horses, cattle and clothing. Teste: James Rowland, James Abbot, John Haynes. Bill sale to pay debts.

Page 227.—22d April, 1763. James Hartgrove, yeoman, to John Anderson, yeoman, £40, mortgage of ½ acre, p. 222 above.

Page 229.—22d June, 1763. Ann Vare ( ) to Richard Shankling, £45, 200 acres on Naked Creek, patented to John Fowler and conveyed by John to John Hope, and by John Hope to Ann and Richard Vare, and by said Ann Vare, 22d June, 1763.

Page 231.—24th June, 1763. Relinquishment of dower by Elizabeth, wife of Thomas Fulton, in land conveyed by Thomas to William Preston and Robt. Bratton, 24th June, 1763.

Page 231.—24th June, 1763. Thomas Fulton to Robt. Bratton and Wm. Preston, £26, household furniture, &c. Teste: Preston and Robt. Bratton.

Page 232.—3d June, 1763. Alexander Sayers to John Buchanan, £200, slaves.

Page 232.—23d June, 1763. Caleb Worley to Malcome Allen, £89, personal property.

Page 233.—20th December, 1762. Samuel Newman and Martha ( ), of Frederick County, to Mathias Celser, of same place, 10 shillings, 1757 acres on Smith's Creek patented to Samuel, 29th August, 1757 (conveys 105 acres). Teste: Wm. Minter, Isaac Carr, Samuel ( ) Newman, Jr. Delivered: Henry Selzer, March, 1770.

Page 236.—21st June, 1763. Same to Jacob Hodge (Hodgh), 10 shillings, 105 acres as above. Delivered to Christopher Vicker, 9th November, 1772.

Page 238.—22d June, 1763. James McCowen and Margarett ( ) to Gabriel Jones, £57.6, 380 acres on Catawpa of James River, whereon James now lives, purchased of Robert Poage. Teste: Daniel Smith, Felix Gilbert, Daniel Harrison.

Page 241.—19th April, 1763. James Gay to David Martin, £116.10, 354 acres on Little River of Calf Pasture; corner William Elliot's land; corner Wm. Gay; same purchased by said James from Samuel Gay, who purchased from William Beverley.

Page 242.—21st June, 1763 . Thomas Berry and Esther to James Berry, son of Thomas, £25, 168 acres purchased by Thomas from Arthur Kenedy on Capt. Joseph Kennedy's Mill Creek, in Burden's tract; corner Robert Gray; McNutt's new line; corner Francis Beaty. Teste: Alexander McNutt, Jas. McNutt. Thomas Berry, Jr. Delivered: James Berry, April, 1765.

Page 244.—22d June, 1763. Thomas Campbell to Archibald Hopkins, £7, on Muddy Creek of North River, 40 acres; corner to land now or formerly Robt. Raulston's. Teste: John Poage, Richard Shanklin, James Hughes.

Page 247.—22d June, 1763. Thomas Stevenson and Jean ( ) to Robert Black, £15, 230 acres on a branch of Cook's Creek.

Page 249.—10th June, 1763. Nathaniel Evins and Mary ( ) to Thos. Paxton, £100, 190 acres on North Branch of James, part of the tract where Nathaniel now lives, mouth of Buffalo Creek; corner Alexander Baggs. Teste: James Trimble, Sarah Trimble, Mary Preston. Delivered: Thomas Paxton, June, 1766.

Page 251.—21st June, 1763. James Lockridge and Isabella ( ) to Moses McElvain, £50, on Great River, Calf Pasture between said Lockridges and Robert Givens' lands, 260 acres. Teste: Samuel Hodge. Delivered: Moses McElvain, April, 1770.

Page 253.—21st June, 1763. Thomas Weems and Elinor to William Givens, £217, 552 acres on Great Calve Pasture; corner Henry Gay; corner John Harvey. Teste: James Lockridge, John Stewart, John Handley.

Page 256.—5th June, 1763. Robert Patterson and Elisabeth ( ) to Robert Young. £70, 60 acres on Falling Spring, a branch of Middle River of Shanando, part of 90 acres patented to Robert King, 1st August, 1745, and descended by hereditary right by will of Robert King to Robert Patterson, joining that part of the patent belonging to John King. Teste: James Anderson, Samuel Caldwell. Delivered: Robt. Young, August, 1768.

Page 258.—21st June, 1763. William Mintors to Skidmore Monsly, £105, 270 acres on Linvel's Creek, part of lots No. 4 and 5 conveyed by the Givens and Miller to William Myntors, November, 1751; corner Jonathan Robinson's, part of the same tract; corner George Speer's land. Delivered: Geo. Speer, November, 1764.

Page 261.—21st June, 1763. Jacob (mark) and Margaret (mark) Rollman and Christian (mark) Rollman to Henry Black, £60, 280 acres on Howell's branch of Bever Creek; corner Robt. Poage. Delivered: George McVey, 31st June, 1774. (Margaret, wife of Jacob.)

Page 263.—28th June, 1763. Walreck Conrad, planter, and Margaret (signed in German) to Samuel Morral, Jr., of Amherst Co., planter, £40, 240 acres on the Mountain between South Fork and South Branch of Potomac, on Switcher's branch, now in possession of said Samuel Morrall. Delivered: Samuel Morrall, 25th June, 1787.

Page 265.—10th June, 1763. Samuel Paxton's executors to James Allison, £52, 165 acres on North Branch of James River called the Spreading Springs. Teste: Nathan Evins, Mary Evins, Mary Paxton. Delivered: Samuel McCorkle, 5th June, 1770.

Page 267.—17th June, 1763. James Trimble and Sarah to Arthur McClure, £30, 206 acres in Fork of James River; corner James Trimble; corner Samuel McClure. Delivered: A. McClure, November, 1775.

Page 270.— — day ———, 1763. Robert Rowland and Martha to William Rowland, £50, 113 acres by patent, 10th September, 1755, on waters of James River. Delivered: Pat. Lockhart, September, 1772.

Page 274.—21st June, 1763. Robert Rowland and Martha to George Rowland, £50, 244 acres by patent, 10th September, 1755, on west side James River.

Page 274.—15th April, 1763. Borden's executors to Dominick Morin (Morrin), £10, 150 acres, part of 92,100; corner Samuel Davison; Jacob Anderson's line; another of Davis' line; corner Andrew Fitzpatrick.

Page 276.—7th June, 1763. Borden's executors to Alexander Govouck (McGuffy), £3, 100 acres, part of 92,100 on Walker's Creek opposite James Coulter's lower corner; corner Wm. Robinson. Teste: Wm. Hall, Richard Crump. Delivered to James McGuffey, one of the heirs of the said McGuffy this 16th October, 1806.

Page 278.—10th June, 1763. Borden's executors to John Smyley, £5, 44 acres, part of 92,100 on North Branch of James, the patent line; corner Alexander McCorkle's survey. Delivered: John Smyley, June, 1770.

Page 281.—11th June, 1763. Borden's executors to William Hall, £26, 346 acres, part of 92,100; line of said Hall's old survey; corner said Hall's old land called Crawfords.

Page 284.—20th June, 1763. Archibald Alexander to Samuel Cummins, of Chester County, Pennsylvania, £20, 250 acres on South River; Thomas McSpeden's line; corner Archibald Alexander. Teste: William and Joseph Alexander. Delivered: Capt. Samuel McDowell, November, 1768.

Page 286.—7th January, 1763. Alexander Miller and Hannah to Alexander Telford, £120, 248 acres, part of 92,100, and conveyed by Borden to Miller; corner tract surveyed for James McDowell. Teste: James McCampbell. David McCoskry. Delivered: James McCampbell, November, 1773.

Page 289.—22d June, 1763. William Brown and Isble to Benjamin Logan, £30, 160 acres on North River Shanando, close to mouth of Cook's Creek, patented to William, 11th July, 1761.

Page 291.—18th June, 1763. John Ramsey to Charles Floyd, £7, 90 acres near Jennings' Gap. Deceased, Charles Floyd, 25th January, 1775.

Page 293.—22d June, 1763. Thomas Fulton, of Stanton, to William Howard, of Albemarle County, £45.10, lot 9 in Staunton and 13 acres of woodland laid off at the south corner of one of the said Thomas Fulton's lots numbered 6 bought by Thomas from Alexander Wright, 16th May, 1760. Delivered: Wm. Howard, March, 1765.

Page 295.—19th April, 1763. William McMullin and Mary ( ) to John Hinds, £65, 120 acres on North Branch North River Shanando called Woods Creek. Teste: Jonathan Douglass. Delivered: John Hinds, May 11, 1764.

Page 298.—21st June, 1763. William Skillem and Mary ( ) to George Skillem, £50, 180 acres on Middle River of Shanandoe, beginning at a point of the hill between Christian's Creek and the Long Meadow Run; corner Beverley Manner.

Page 300.—21st June, 1763. Samuel Caldwell and Ann to Abram Smith, £106.10, 300 acres on Christian's Creek in Beverley Manor, part of 600 acres surveyed for James Caldwell; Moses Thompson's line. Teste: James Reed. Delivered: Col. Abraham Smith, March, 1772.

Page 303.—21st June, 1763. Daniel Harrison to Charles Man, £25, 120 acres patented to Daniel, 15th December, 1755, on North River of Shanando above the Gap in the mountain including the third fork of said river, an island below the fork.

Page 305.—22d June, 1763. Daniel Harrison and Sarah to James Green, £9, 100 acres in north fork of Linwell's Creek. Teste: James Gamwill, Charles Donnelly.

Page 307.—22d June, 1763. Same to same, £23, 250 acres on a draft of Linvell's Creek joining on west the land Bryan and Linvel lived on; line of survey of Joseph Bryan.

Page 310.—15th February, 1763. William Chesnut, farmer, to Henry Henry, £5, 80 acres on Muddy Creek, a branch of the North River of Shanandoe, part of 400 acres on which Chesnut now lives. Daniel Callachan's land on Green's old line; line of Wood's land. Delivered: Andrew Johnston by your order, March, 1770.

Page 312.—15th February, 1763. William Chesnutt, farmer, to Daniel Callachan, £10, 40 acres as above. Delivered: Gawin Hamilton, March, 1774.

Page 314.—22d June, 1763. Thomas Lorimer to John Richey, £55.10, 159 acres, part of 179 acres patented to John Richey, 30th August, 1748, on North River Shanandore. Teste: George Wooldridge, David Erwin, James Hargrave. Delivered: Jno. Richey, May, 1766.

Page 317.—21st June, 1763. John Graham to James Graham, his son, £5, 150 acres, part of 696 acres on which said Graham, Sr., now lives, on Great Calfpasture; corner Robert Givens's land. Teste: Bryce Russell, Jas. Graham.

Page 319.—21st June, 1763. John Graham to Robert Graham, his son, £5, 128 acres, part of above 696; corner John Graham. Delivered: Wm. Clayton, December, 1818.

Page 321.—20th June, 1763. Same to John Graham, his son, £5, 128 acres, part of 696 above, on which said John Graham, Sr., now lives. Delivered: Jno. Graham, 19th April, 1775.

Page 324.—20th May, 1763. John Marshall, of Orange County, North

Carolina, to Israel Christian, £20, 259 acres on Catawbo Creek of James River. Teste: George Robinson, Francis and Anne Smith. Proved by Francis and Anne, George being dead.

Page 326.—8th March, 1763. Ludwick Ipsher, eldest son and heir of Peter Ipsher, deceased, to Israel Christian, £50, 200 acres by patent to Peter, 29th May, 1760, on John's Creek of Craig's Creek. Teste: Wm. Carvin, Thos. Barnes. Ludwick ( ) Ipsher.

Page 329.—4th May, 1763. John McFarland and Mary ( ), of Bedford County, to Hugh Montgomery, £52.10, 106 acres by patent, 30th October, 1752, on a branch of Reed Creek. Teste: Robert Mountgomery Delivered: H. Montgomerie, May, 1765.

Page 331.—2d August, 1762. Robert Orr, of Johnson County, North Carolina, to John Thomson, £50, 179 acres on Glade Creek of Roan Oak, by patent, 10th March, 1756; corner John Boen's land. Teste: John Mills.

Page 334.—11th June, 1763. Baptist Armstrong to Thomas Akers, £37.10, 245 acres on Wolf Creek of Roanoke. Teste: Robert Neelley. Delivered: Francis Smith, March, 1768.

Page 336.—23d June, 1763. Jonathan Douglas to Daniel Harrison, £40, 306 acres, part of two tracts of 400 acres each, whereof Nicholas and Henry Mace and Patrick Quin possess the other part, the one tract granted to Jonathan by Thomas Beal, of Frederick County, Maryland, 1755; the other patented to Jonathan, 11th July, 1761, on head of Broad Run, a branch of North River of Shanandoe, whereon said Douglas now lives. Mortgage.

Page 338.—6th April, 1763. William Moore to Francis Smith, £30, 275 acres patented to William, 15th March, 1744, on branches of James River; corner John Scott, now Samuel McRobert's land. Teste: Samuel McKnab, Samuel Robinson, Martha Robinson. Delivered: James Anderson by your order, 5th March, 1771.

Page 340.—8th March, 1763. Paul ( ) Garrison, of Roan County, North Carolina, to John Donilly, £20, 68 acres, said Garrison's part of 137 acres patented to John Donelly, Sr., and Paul Garrison, 29th May, 1760, on waters of Catawbo at a place called the Knob; corner land of John Donilly, Sr.

Page 343.—24th June, 1763. Thomas Fulton and Elisabeth to William Preston and Robert Bratton, £200, lots 8, 15 and 21 in Staunton, and two lots of woodland, Nos. 6 and 7, 50 acres each, all conveyed to Thomas by Alex. Wright, 1760.

Page 346.—7th April, 1763. David Looney and Mary to Amos Potts and John Potts, Jr., £25, 204 acres by patent dated August, 1761, on waters of Craig's Creek of James River. Teste: Steven ( )Rentfroe, Margret ( ) Looney. Sent to Pat. Lockhart by your order, 8th October, 1773.

Page 348.—19th April, 1763. William Hutcheson and Anne ( ) to John Graham, £140, 196 acres on Christian's (Christee's) Creek between lands of John Hutcheson and John Henderson, 172 acres of which were formerly conveyed by said Hutcheson to said John Graham and Robert Graham; corner Jno. Henderson. Teste: Abraham Biss. Delivered: John Graham, March Court, 1767.

Page 350.—5th June, 1762. John McGarry and Sarah ( ) to James Greer, farmer, power of attorney to recover a patent for the land John now lives on and convey same to Archibald Hopkins. Teste: Ephraim Love and John Hopkins.

Page 352.—17th September, 1763. John Megarry and Sarah by James Greer, attorney, to Archibald Hopkins (John, formerly of Augusta, but now of North Carolina), £40, 170 acres on Muddy Creek on a line of Pincher's old place. Teste: John Archer, Wm. Hyde. Delivered to Thomas Hopkins, the grandson of grantee, who produced the original patent for the same lands in testimony of his right to have the same as per receipt filed with the deeds of this same date, 19th January, 1814. (Receipt says Thomas is entitled to the land by devise from Archibald, his grandfather.)

Page 354.—21st June, 1763. Jacob Gum and Sarah to Thomas Gordon, £20, 165 acres patented to Jacob. 16th August, 1756, on head spring of Linville's Creek. Teste: Ephraim Love, James Green, John Hopkins.

Page 357.—17th September, 1763. Thomas ( ) Shanklin, Sr., to Thomas Shanklin, Jr., his son, £20, two tracts, one containing 100 acres, 80 acres of which is part of 400 patented to James Wood, 12th January, 1746, on branch of Muddy Creek; corner John Shanklin's land; the other tract containing 80 acres patented to Thomas Shanklin, Sr., June, 1755, on branches of Muddy Creek; O'Neal's land, John Fulton's line. Delivered: Thomas Shanklin, 30th August, 1790.

Page 359.—20th September, 1763. John ( ) Davis and Judith to William Clark, £65, 65 acres on Jackson's River, formerly conveyed by Thomas Hughart to John, May, 1762. Delivered to William Clark, September, 1765.

Page 362.—20th September, 1763. Robert Allen to John Young, £45, 280 acres on Back Creek, west fork of James River. Teste: Andrew Greer, Robert Shanklin. Delivered: John Young, 2d May, 1766.

Page 364.—18th June, 1763. John Cunningham and Robert Weir to Hugh Weir, £100, 333 acres in Borden's tract; corner James Eckins, Samuel Dunlap's line; corner William McCanless, Robert Dunlap's land. Teste: John Neill, Robert Reed, Samuel ( ) Loge, John Mountgomerey, Samuel and Mathew Huston.

Page 367.—20th September, 1763. Daniel Kidd and Anne ( ) to George Rodgers, £90, 135 acres in Beverley Manor on Christian's Creek, George Hutcheson's line. Teste: Samuel Moore, Jno. Hunter.

Page 369.— — day ——, 1763. Richard ( ) Hall, of Halifax, to Abraham Chrisman, of Frederick County, £175, 400 acres on a branch of Woods's River, alias New River, called Meadow Creek, conveyed by John Harrison, Jr., to Richard, 23d May, 1750. Teste: William Hall, Preston Hampton, John ( ) Done. Delivered: Abraham Chrisman, 4th September, 1773.

Page 373.—14th September, 1763. John ( ) Coulter and Isbell ( ) to John Brown and Thomas Gardner, £140, 210 acres in Beverley Manor, purchased by John Coulter from William Nutt, 28th November, 1750, on Mill Creek; Robert McClenachan's line, corner James McCorkle; corner to graveyard of John Breckinridge, who was murdered by the Indians; corner John Buchanan's land. Delivered: Thos. Brown, May, 1771.

Page 376.—20th September, 1763. Charles ( ) Stuart and Grizel ( ) to Robert Mountgomery, £32, 54 acres on head of Moffet's Creek, patented to William Hogshead, deceased, 16th August, 1756, and conveyed to Charles by David Hogshead, heir-at-law to the said William Hogshead. Teste: Robert Willey. Delivered: Robert Montgomery, 16th March, 1774.

Page 379.—20th September, 1763. John Cunningham and Margrett ( ) to Robert Law, £40, 200 acres, part of 400 acres patented to John, 5th April, 1749, on Thorney Branch. Teste: John Poage, James Fowler, John Cunningham. Delivered: Robert Law, 26th November, 1783.

Page 382.—10th September, 1763. Daniel Pouder and Jemiah ( ) to Joseph Rutherford, £150, 310 acres on head of East Fork of Cook's Creek, and a draft of Smith's Creek, black oak near Daniel Harrison's land, patented to Jacob Garner, 16th August, 1756, conveyed by Garner to John Cravens and John Wright, and by Cravens and Wright to Daniel. Teste: Daniel Smith, Felix Shellman, Patrick ( ) Fraysher, John Scott. Delivered: Reuben Rutherford, May, 1768.

Page 383.—10th May, 1763. Samuel Moore, tavernkeeper, to John Hunter, Sr., yeoman, £62, personal property, one hair trunk. Teste: Wm. Rodgers and Samuel Hunter. Delivered: Jno. Hunter, 1765.

Page 385.—17th September, 1763. William Hays and Frances to Hugh Hayes, £98, 255 acres on line of Beverley Manor and Borden's tract; corner Patrick Hayes; corner Dunlap. Delivered: Francis Smith, 1st October, 1767. Teste: John McMahon, Thomas Hill, James ( ) Telford.

Page 387.—12th January, 1763. John Law to Samuel Tod, bill of sale of horse to secure payment to James Davice of £8.8. Teste: John Lowrey.

Page 389.—21st September, 1763. John McCreery and Agness ( ) to Richard Bodkin, £45, 280 acres on Newfoundland Creek; corner land in possession of the Caroliles. Delivered: Hugh Bodkin, 15th October, 1772.

Page 391.—1st June, 1763. James Black, plantationer, and Sarah ( ) to John Ramsey, £107.10, 165 acres in Beverley Manor on both sides South River of Shanando, part of 375 acres conveyed by Beverley to George Home, and by George Home to Gibbons Jennings, 1750, and said Jennings having afterwards absconded, the land was sold to highest bidder, viz., James Davise, by Richard Winston, sheriff of Orange County, to satisfy judgment against Jennings in favor of Isaac Smith, 21st April, 1752, and Winston conveyed the land to Davise in Orange County, 24th June, 1753, and land was conveyed by Davise to John Black, 1756; corner Robert Patrick, William Bell's line. Teste: Robert Brown, Andrew Greer, Samuel Black. Livery of seisin. Delivered: Jos. Black, January, 1773.

Page 395.—20th September, 1763. John Bowyer and Magdalen to James McDowell, £200, Rogers Keys' line, James Greenlee's line, Samuel McDowell's line. Delivered: Samuel McDowell, May, 1773.

Page 397.—21st September, 1763. Robert Allen to John Davis, £100, 280 acres on West Fork of James River called Back Creek; corner John Young's part of said tract. Delivered: Jno. Davis, 14th April, 1777.

Page 399.—21st September, 1763. Robert Allen to John Davis, bond to secure title to above.

Page 400.—15th February, 1763. William Young, of Kingsoss, County of Philadelphia, Pennsylvania, cordwainer, to John Madison, power of attorney to convey to William Davis, of Philadelphia, Pennsylvania, skinner, 400 acres on east side of New River or Woods' River, formerly patented to John Mills, and conveyed by him to William Young, £65. Teste: Paul Isaac Vato, John Kirke, David Robinson, John Boller. Acknowledged by

Vato and Kirke, both of Philadelphia, before Henry Harrison, Mayor of Philadelphia.

Page 402.—21st September, 1763. William Young, of, &c., as above, to William Davis above, £65, 400 acres above Francis Ryley's line on east side New River.

Page 405.—30th June, 1763. John Scott and Anne ( ) to Felix Gilbert, £243, 300 acres, part of 400 acres patented to Samuel Scott, 30th August, 1744, on Cub Run of Shenando; corner to land sold by said Scott to James Banister (Bruister).

Page 408.—21st September, 1763. John Cunningham and Margaret ( ) to John Cunningham, Jr., their son, £20, 200 acres on a thorny branch, part of 400 acres; corner Robert Law's land. Teste: Charles Kirkpatrick, Alex. Kirkpatrick. Delivered: Patrick Cunningham, 30th August, 1770.

Page 410.—22d September, 1763. William Davis, of Philadelphia, to Jno. Wiley, £120, 400 acres on east side New River, Francis Riley's line. Acknowledged by William. Delivered to John Wiley, August, 1765.

Page 413.—13th September, 1763. James Humpheries, of Rowan County, North Carolina, to Henry Smith, £30, 400 acres on Free Mason's Branch of North River Shanando, David Davis' line, pine on top Castle Hill on south side North River, patented to James, 20th June, 1747. Teste: Jno. Malcolm.

Page 415.—18th September, 1763. William Sharp to John King, £30, 115 acres on both sides Middle River Shanando, patented to William, 10th March, 1756; Robert Craig's land, crossing the Falling Springs; corner said King's land. Teste: John, Robert and Anne Poage.

Page 418.—15th January, 1763. James and Kitrin ( ) Blair to Hugh Doneghe, £65, 144 acres on south side Middle River Shanando, crossing the Bald Hill. Teste: John King, Thos. Stevenson, John ( ) Dowell.

Page 420.—1st July, 1762. William Judd, of Northampton County, North Carolina, to Rev. John Craig, £75, conveys slaves. Teste: Charles Mahafey and Maray Craig.

Page 421.—22d September, 1763. Thomas Fulton and Elisabeth to William Galloway, £65, 115 acres on west side Jackson's River, beginning about ¾ mile above mouth of Cowpasture. Delivered: William Galloway, September, 1765.

Page 424.—24th September, 1763. Israel Christian and Elisabeth ( ) to William Fleming, gent., £100, 300 acres, Beverley's Mill Place, crossing the Meadow Branch, part of Beverley Manor granted to James Miller, 28th May, 1751, and by Miller to Israel Christian, 26th March, 1754.

Page 426.—24th September, 1763. Israel Christian, of Staunton, and Elisabeth to Wm. Fleming, gent., of same place, £50, 48 poles in lot 11, part of 25 acres conveyed by Beverley to the county, conveyed by Francis Beaty to Israel Christian, 20th March, 1754. Livery of seisin.

Page 429.—23d September, 1763. Thomas Fulton and Elisabeth to Rosannah Maus, £50, ½ acre, lot 14 in Staunton, one of the lots conveyed to Thomas, 7th July, 1783.

Page 430.—Return of commission for privy examination of Elisabeth, 26th September, 1763.

Page 432.—12th November, 1763. Hugh Donaghey and Elisabeth ( ) to Alexander Blair, £63, 144 acres on south side Middle River Shanando, crossing the Bald Hill. Teste: John Blear, Robert Stevenson, John Anderson. Delivered: Alex. Blair, Jr., January, 1766.

Page 435.—16th November, 1763. George Bush ( ) and Susannah ( ) to Sebastian Hover, £94, 116 acres on South Fork of South Branch of Potowmack, conveyed to George by Mary Woods and Green, 29th May, 1761. Delivered: Andrew Johnston, June, 1767.

Page 437.—24th May, 1763. James Green and Moses Green, of Culpeper, and Mary Wood, of Frederick, to Jacob Conrod, £90, 457 acres on South Branch Potomac, part of 660 acres patented to Robert Green, who devised the same to grantors, 203 acres being sold to Joseph Skidmore and Gabriel Coyle. Teste: Mathew Patton, Postel ( ) Hover and Henry ( ) Pickles. Delivered: Jacob Conrad, January, 1765.

Page 440.—24th May, 1763. William Green, of Culpeper, to Jacob Rollman and Catherine Zorn, £—, 200 acres on South Fork of Potomac, part of 600 acres patented to James Wood and William Russell, deceased, and said William Green; corner Boston Hover. Teste: Boston Hover ( ). Delivered: Andrew Johnston, June, 1767.

Page 443.—24th May, 1763. Same to Henry Rule, £10, 176 acres on Mill Creek, a branch of South Branch of Potomac, patented to Wm. Green, 25th March, 1762. Lord Fairfax's line, Timothy Holoway's line.

Page 445.—25th May, 1763. Same to Nicholas Semon, £11, 145 acres near head of South Fork of Potomac, patented to William, 5th March, 1762. Delivered: Andrew Johnston, June, 1767.

Page 448.—24th May, 1763. William Green, &c., to Jacob Rollman, £15, 200 acres on South Fork of Potomac, part of 600 acres patented to Wood, Russell and Green; corner Jacob Rollman and Catherine Zorn's land. Delivered: Henry Stone, March, 1764.

Page 450.—24th May, 1763. Same to Mathew Patton, £30, 407 acres on Mill Creek, a branch of South Branch of Potomac, part of 1650 acres patented to Green, 25th March, 1762. Delivered to Mathew Patton, March, 1764.

Page 453.—24th May, 1763. Same to John Wyse, £20, 283 acres on Mill Creek, a branch of South Branch of Potomac, part of 1650 acres. Delivered: Andrew Johnston, June, 1767.

Page 455.—24th May, 1763. Same to Martin Judy, £27.10, 367 acres as above. Delivered: Andrew Johnston, June, 1767.

Page 458.—24th May, 1763. Same to Nicholas Harpole, £15, 195 acres, on Mill Creek as above, &c. Delivered: Nicholas Harpole, October, 1766.

Page 460.—25th May, 1763. Same to Henry Pickle, £18, 190 acres on South Fork of Potomac near head. Delivered: Andrew Johnston, 1767.

Page 463.—25th May, 1763. Same to Boston Hugler, £30, 400 acres on Mill Creek, part of 1650 acres above. Delivered: Andrew Johnston, 1767.

Page 465.—24th May, 1763. Same to Boston Hover, £15, 200 acres part of 600 patented to Wood, Russell and Green. Delivered to Andrew Johnston.

Page 468.—17th June, 1763. Thomas Paxton and Rebeka ( ) to Mathew Robertson, £40, 210 acres on Southeast Branch of James River, part of the tract where Thomas now lives; corner Moses McClure. Teste: Benj. Benit, Stephen ( ) and Margaret ( ) Rentfroe.

Page 470.—14th November, 1763. Joseph Dictom and Rachell to Conrad

Custard, £130, 160 acres on North Branch of Shannandore, near the Clover Lick. Delivered: Uriah Humble, April, 1765.

Page 472.—16th November, 1763. William ( ) Smith and Mary ( ) to Jonathan Davis, of Culpeper County, £40, 170 acres on branches of the Hawksbill on the north side of top of Blue Ridge. Livery of seisin.

Page 475.—17th November, 1763. James Walker and Mary ( ) to Hugh Kelso, £5, 74 acres, 1 rood, 3 poles, in Borden's tract, patent line. Teste: David Scott, Alex. Walker, Anthony Kelly.

Page 477.—14th October, 1763. John ( ) Harger and Agness ( ), of Louisa County, to Andrew Brown, £60, 260 acres in Fork of James, on North Branch of James. Teste: William ( ) Hollman.

Page 480.—20th October, 1763. Same to Christian Godfrey Miliron, £35, 140 acres, part of 400 acres formerly belonging to John in Forks of James, Andrew Brown's line. Teste: Andrew ( ) Brown, Wm. Holman ( ). Delivered: Wm. Foster by your order, February, 1768.

Page 483.—30th September, 1763. Israel Christian, merchant, to Thomas Watterson, farmer, £155, 300 acres on a branch of Naked Creek, James Wood's line. Teste: John Stuart, James McRoy, Thomas Doran.

Page 484.—Report of privy examination of Margaret, wife of James McCown, deed 21st-22d June, 1763, to Gabriel Jones, taken 6th July, 1763.

Page 485.—Privy examination of Ann, wife of Jacob Reed, of Hampshire County, deed 15th-16th August, to Alex Love, 375 acres, taken 12th October, 1763, by Benj. Kuykendale and Felix Seymore.

Page 486.—27th October, 1763. John Davis, of Bucks County, Pennsylvania, to Robert Reed, of Staunton, £24, lot 7 iin Staunton, and woodland lot No. 3. Teste: Edward McGarry, James Magavock, Wm. Read, James Buchanan and David Miller. Livery of seisin in presence of Hugh Johnston, John Taylor, Joseph Scott, James Buchanan. Delivered: Mrs. Reed, 5th June, 1781.

Page 488.—18th November, 1763. David Ralston (Rollstone) and Ann ( ) to Samuel Ralston, £70, 350 acres on Morssey Creek; corner Wm. McKeters. Teste: Moses Sample.

Page 491.—25th February, 1764. Robert Rodgers to John Johnson, £20, 62 acres on Middle River of Shanandoe, alias Cathey's River, part of 540 acres in Beverley Manor, originally surveyed for Nathan McClure and conveyed by Beverley to George Rodgers and by George to his son Robert, September, 1763. Teste: Robert, John and Thomas Poage. Delivered: Wm. Johnston, September, 1765.

Page 493.—12th December, 1763. James Kain to Samuel Paxton, £6.7, one sorrel horse.

Page 494.—20th March, 1764. Philip Long, eldest son and heir-at-law of Paul Long, deceased, who was eldest son and heir-at-law of Philip Long, deceased, of Frederick County, Virginia, to Jacob Campbell, £20, 150 acres purchased by Philip, the elder, of Richard Mauldin, and deed recorded in Orange; corner Jacob Coger. Delivered: Jacob Campbell, February, 1768.

Page 496.—8th March, 1764. Thomas Paxton and Rebecca to Samuel Paxton, £200, 500 acres in Borden's tract; corner Archibald Alexander, black oak by the Punch Bowl. Teste: Mathew Robertson, John J. Jarvis, John ( ) Robertson, James Edmunston.

Page 499.—20th March, 1764. Alex. Blair and Jean (Jany to John Blair, his son, £10, 102 acres on Long Glade, part of 400 acres on which Alex. lives; corner James Blair's land, joining James Anderson. Teste: John Hogshead, Isaac Carson.

Page 502.—28th February, 1764. Alex. Craig, Jr., ( ) and Elizabeth ( ) to James Gamble, £25, 132 acres on a small branch of Middle River of Shanandoe, part of 335 acres patented to Alex Craig, Sr., and conveyed by him to Alex. Craig, Jr., 18th May, 1762; corner James Gamble. Teste: Alex. and Jno. Blair. Delivered: Jas. Raeburn by your order, April, 1766.

Page 504.—18th September, 1763. Samuel and Mirian Cloyd and Elisabeth ( ) and Mary ( ), their wives, to William Armstrong, £209, 300 acres in Beverley Manor on Christian's Creek. Teste: Walter Davis, George Rutledge, Samuel Love, Robert Cunningham, James Bell.

Page 507.—21st March, 1764. John King, miller, and Mary ( ) to James Allen, Jr., wheelwright, £24, 85 acres, part of 115 acres patented to William Sharp, 10th March, 1756; the river, Hamilton's land. Teste: William ( ) Hamilton, Pat. Hamilton.

Page 509.—24th January, 1764. Richard ( ) Pilson to John Williams, £20, 45 acres on Gilespie's Run in Beverley Manor, part of Richard's survey of 320 acres. Delivered: Jno. Williams, April, 1783.

Page 512.—16th March, 1764. John Mitchell to John McCollom, £10, 119 acres in Forks of James, on Buffalo Creek. Teste: Henry Kirkam, Jas. Lapsley, Alex. Collier.

Page 514.—21st November, 1763. James Kennedy to James McNutt, £20, 118 acres in Borden's grant on Kennedy's Mill Creek; William Fulton's line, Wm. Beard's and John Loggan's corner. Delivered: Alex. McNutt, 10th September, 1765.

Page 517 (518).—20th March, 1764. James Arbuckle and Rachel to James Gilmore, £60, on James River below the Island Ford, 400 acres patented to James, 5th September, 1749 (this is a mortgage of lease and release). Delivered: James Gilmore, August, 1765.

Page 520.—3d March, 1764. James Gilmore and Martha to Andrew Misscampbell, £111, 328 acres on Carr's Creek of James River in Borden's grant, and conveyed to James by Borden; corner Hugh Cunningham; corner John Kerr.

Page 523.—18th September, 1763. Samuel Hays and Elisabeth ( ) to Wm. Thomson, £45, 100 acres in a line of Borden's great tract, near land of John Edmiston. Teste: Wm. Buchanan, Archibald Reaugh, David Wilson, George Buchanan.

Page 525.—20th March, 1764. Daniel Love and Jean ( ) to Joseph Dictom, £115, 255 acres on Cook's Creek, part of 280 acres granted to Daniel, 16th August, 1756; corner John Craven's land. Delivered: Joseph Dictom, April, 1770.

Page 527.—2d January, 1764. Borden's executors to John Paxton, £3, 32 acres in Forks of James, part of 92100; corner said Paxton and to Joseph Lapsley; Abraham Brown's land, branch of Woods' Creek. Teste: Wm. McKee. Delivered: John Paxton, August, 1766.

Page 529.—10th March, 1764. Same to Alexander Moore, £10, 120 acres, part of 92100; corner William McClung's new survey; Widow Cowden's corner. Delivered: Samuel Hight, 28th September, 1796, by order M. Coalter.

Page 532.—15th March, 1764. Same to Henry McClung, £11, 70 acres, part of 92100; corner Samuel Lyle; old corner to said McClung. Delivered: Henry McClung, 17th September, 1800.

Page 535.—19th March, 1764. Robert Douglas to William Tincher, £50, 129 acres on the Pine Run on the south side of Beverley Manor in a line of Charles Campbell, and of James Robinson. Teste: John Bigham, George Campbell.

Page 536.—9th March, 1764. Honorias Powell and Jannet, of Orange County, to William Buchanan, of the County aforesaid, £15 (paid by Wm. Bohannon), 200 acres; corner Cap. Francis Kertley's. Teste: Francis Kirtley, John Early, Wm. ( ) Smith. Delivered: Francis Kirtley, April, 1767.

Page 537.—9th March, 1764. Same to Valentine Cook, £18.10, 118 acres on Hawksbill. Delivered: Val. Cook, October, 1775..

Page 539.— — March, 1764. Jeremiah ( ) Early and Elisabeth ( ), of Culpeper County to William Smith, £56, 400 acres on Elke Run. Teste: Jonathan Couherd, John Early, Will ( ) Bohannon. Delivered: Jeremiah Smith, son of Burton Smith, heir to Wm. Smith, deceased, 12th October, 1798.

Page 541.—8th March, 1764. Michael Fenney and Cathrine ( ) to William Foster, £120, 365 acres in Fork of James on which Michael now liveth; corner Samuel Moore and Samuel McClure, Holman's line, McDowell's land. Teste: John Eger, Christian Godfrey Milliron. Delivered: Wm. Foster, 1768.

Page 544.—22d February, 1764. Henry Willson and Mary to John Taylor, £55, 230 acres in Beverley Manor on a branch of Christian's Creek; corner to the Christians' land; James Caldwell's corner, William Armstrong's line. Delivered: John Taylor, 1766. Teste: W. Christian, P. Christian, Wm. Means.

Page 545.—21st May, 1764. Mathew Patton to Robert Davis, £75, on South Fork of South Branch of Potomac; corner Frederick Kiester. Teste: John Smith, John Poage, Robert Armstrong. Delivered: Samuel Morrel, 25th June, 1787.

Page 546.—3d May, 1763. Benjamin Kinley to Martin Humble, £16, 215 acres adjoining Rees Thomas and Daniel Harrison, and a survey of said Benjamin Kinley commonly called the Sinking Spring. Teste: Robert Morris, Conrad Humble, A. Hamilton.

Page 549.—15th November, 1763. Jean Graham, only acting executor of Robert Graham, to Lanty Graham, £82, 307 acres on Little Calf Pasture, corner land formerly Jno. Graham's. Delivered: Lanty Graham, November Court, 1777.

Page 550.—30th October, 1763. James Gorrell, of Baltimore County, Maryland, to William Robinson, of Augusta, power of attorney to convey to David Robinson, quantity as may be laid off by William and David, part of 620 acres on North Branch Roanoke, joining lands of Jno. Robinson and Tobias Bright, £79.10. Teste: Wm. Davis, Edward Thorp.

Page 551.—20th March, 1764. William Preston and Susannah and Robert Bratton and Ann, to Daniel Kidd, £260, 3 half-acre lots in Staunton, Nos. 8, 6, 7, and two lots of woodland containing 87 acres, conveyed to Preston and Bratton, August, 1760. Teste: Wm. Brown, Daniel Pouder, Jno. Cunningham. Delivered: Daniel Kidd, April, 1769.

Page 553.—14th November, 1763. Daniel Harrison and Sarah to Daniel and Jesse Harrison, his grandchildren, sons of Jesse Harrison, £20, 400 acres on head Linville's Creek, Jos. Hite's line. Delivered: Benj. Bowman, by order of Jesse Harrison, 18th February, 1793.

Page 556.—22d March, 1764. Same to Jesse Harrison, his son, £40, two tracts, one containing 200 acres on a branch of Muddy Creek, patented to Daniel, 5th September, 1749; corner said Daniel, the other containing 200 joining the former, being part of 400 acres patented to Daniel, 25th September, 1746; Love's line, corner with Daniel Harrison's part of said tract. Delivered: Jessey Harrison, March, 1783.

Page 559.—24th November, 1763. Henry Smith and Cemey ( ) to Wm. Shannon, £62.10, on Free Mason's Branch of North River Shanando, 400 acres; David Davis's line, a pine on top of Castle Hill, patented to James Humphries, 25th June, 1747, and sold by James to Henry Smith, 1763.

Page 561.— — March, 1764. Francis Kirtley and Elisabeth to Jacob Peters, £40, 270 acres on head branches of Elk Run at the foot of the Blue Ridge; corner to Early's land.

Page 563.—10th December, 1763. James Parsons and Huldah ( ), of Hampshire County, to Ephraim Richardson, £30, 200 acres at the mouth of the dry branch on the South Branch of Potomac, patented 2d September, 1757, to James. Delivered: 15th October, 1765, to Ephraim Richardson.

Page 564.—20th July, 1763. John Sallord, in Augusta County, and late Lieutenant in the Virginia Regiment, to Alex. Boyd, late of the Virginia Regiment, £90, slave and horses. Teste: Jas. Facler, John Bowman. Delivered to Mr. Boyd, June, 1765.

Page 566.—24th March, 1764. Robert Christian to Israel Christian, £70, 250 acres on North Branch of James in Borden's tract, conveyed to Robert 25th November, 1751, oak by a warm spring, on north side Hais Creek. Delivered: Andrew Hays, November Court, 1773.

Page 568.—26th March, 1764. John Stewart and Sarah to Israel Christian, £150, part of lot No. 3 adjoining the lot whereon Wm. Crow now lives, also ½ woodland lot No. 8. Livery by a latch of the door of the house on the premises. Delivered: Thomas Madison, March Court, 1773.

Page 570.—17th September, 1763. Pat. Martin and Jane to Samuel Cowden and Andrew Greer, £200, 321 acres on Back Creek of Middle River in Beverley Manor, land formerly belonging to Jno. Young, on an island of said creek.

Page 572.—16th May, 1764. John ( ) McClure and Mary ( ) to Moses McClure, £250, 325 acres on Northeast Branch of James. Delivered: John McClure, June, 1766.

Page 574.—16th May, 1764. Same to Alexander McClure, £10, 11 acres, 3 rods, on Northeast Branch of James River, beginning at a pysimon. Delivered: Alex. McClure, June, 1778.

Page 576.—10th May, 1764. Hannah ( ) Kirkum to John McClure, £35, 100 acres in Forks of James River, part of 200 acres formerly belonging to Robert Armstrong, deceased. Delivered: John McClure, June, 1766.

Page 578.—12th April, 1764. William Minter to Adam Stephen, of Frederick, £125, 212 acres patented to William, 26th September, 1760, on

Mossey Creek; line of Edward Erwin's land. Delivered: Robert Stephen, 29th September, 1767.

Page 581.—5th May, 1764. John Stephenson and Jane to James Trimble, of Green Spring, Gent., of the same county, £50, 180 acres in Fork of James River upon Borden's Creek; corner James Trimble's, Mathew line. Teste: Richard Woods, Michael Finney, Wm. Foster, Wm. Hale.

Page 583.—10th May, 1764. George Adam Salling, of Orange County, North Carolina, and Joseph Burton and Margaret Elizabeth ( ), of Saint Mathew's Parish and upper district of Abenezer in the Province of Georgie, to Thomas Paxton, millwright, £180, 200 acres on east side North Branch of James River; Henry Fuller's corner. Teste: Nathaniel Evins. Delixered: Thos. Paxton, June, 1766.

Page 586.—15th May, 1764. John Park and Rebecka to William Kennedy, £100, 143 acres on Mary's Creek. Teste: William Crow, John Thompson, John Stewart.

Page 588.—15th April, 1764. John Collier and Sicilly to Moses Collier, £5, 106 acres in Fork of James.

Page 590.—9th May, 1764. Hugh Cunningham to Jonathan Cunningham, £5, the plantation the said Hugh now lives on, 281 acres, 1 rood, 10 perch, on Carr's Creek; corner John Carr, Jno. McKee, Robert Hamilton, Robert Erwin.

Page 593.—15th May, 1764. David ( ) Frazer, of Albemarle County, to James Frazer, £40.10, 220 acres, southeast side Shanando River, the lower corner to Frazer's line. Teste: Wm. Patterson, Robert Frazer, Jno. Reburn.

Page 595.—23d May, 1764. Joseph Love and Mary to Samuel Caldwell, £150, 400 acres on South River Shanando, Beverley Manor line, part of 660 acres deeded to John Willson's father by Joseph Mills, 24th June, 1742. Teste: Pat. Cunningham, Samuel Love, Walter Davis, Robert ( ) Crawford. Delivered to Samuel Culwell.

Page 596.—15th June, 1764. Wm. Berry, planter, and Jane to John Trotter, planter, £—, 210 acres on Moffet's Creek in Borden's tract; Wm. Clark's line, Thomas Berry's line. Teste: George Berry. Delivered: John Cunningham by order, 11th August, 1781.

Page 598.—19th June, 1764. William Teas to Robert Allen, bond conditioned upon making title to Robert for half of a tract of 200 acres joining land of said Allen and Teas, equally the property of both, but the patent issued in name of Teas. Teste: John Poage, James Hughes. Delivered: Robert Allen, March, 1765.

Page 600.—18th June, 1764. Charles Teas to Robert Allen, £250, 600 acres, part of 900 acres formerly belonging to Joseph Teas, deceased, and devised to Charles, on South River in Beverley Manor. Teste: Francis Alexander. Delivered: Robert Allen, Jr., March, 1765.

Page 602.—17th May, 1764. John Cunningham and Margret to Patrick Cunningham, his son, £20, 230 acres on Thorny Branch; corner William Cunningham's land. Teste: Daniel Kidd, John King, George Anderson. Delivered: Edward Erwin, Jr., May, 1767.

Page 603.—17th May, 1764. John Cunningham to son Patrick, bill sale personalty, consideration of a competent and reasonable maintenance for me and my wife Margret during life if we shall have necessity for the same. Delivered: Edward Erwin, Jr., May, 1767. Teste: William Cunningham.

Page 605.—19th May, 1762. William Lamma (Lamb) and Anna to William Patterson, £250, 330 acres on South River Shanandoe. Teste: James Lamme, Thomas Raferty. Delivered: Wm. Patterson, February, 1768.

Page 608.—17th May, 1764. James Carr (Kerr) to William Robertson, £300, three tracts joining each other on Long Meadow of Middle River of Shanandoe. "A" contains 473 acres in Beverley Manor, old line of said Manor. "B," 350 acres adjoining "A." "C" corner aforesaid tract. Teste: Mathew and Robert Kenney. Delivered: Wm. Robinson, May, 1767.

Page 611.—12th May, 1764. John Davis and Jane to Joshua and Mirian Cloyd, £30, 269 acres in Beverley Manor; corner Thomas Black's land, William Henderson's line, George Rutledge's line; corner James Armstrong's line, oaks at an iron mine.

Page 613.—2d June, 1764. Robert ( ) Kinney to Mathew and Robert Knney, Jr., two tracts in the bent of Middle River, 196 acres there lying in Beverley Manor, and 24 acres patented to Robert, 2d July, 1755. Teste: Daniel McNare. Delivered: Thomas Baskins by your order, 14th May, 1765.

Page 616.—5th June, 1764. Silas Hart and Jane to William Ramsey, £3, 120 acres on North River of Shanando; corner said Hart's and Hugh Diver's patent land, pine on the Oak Draft, near Hugh Diver's corner, part of 280 acres patented to Silas, 7th July, 1763. Delivered: John McCoy, 9th November, 1767.

Page 618.—4th May, 1764. William ( ) Patterson to Thomas Rafferty, £12, 18 acres on South River Shanando, part of 330 acres patented to —, 30th January, 1741. Delivered: Thomas Rafferty, January, 1765.

Page 620.—17th November, 1763. William Adims (Adams) to George Jemison, £50, 336 acres in Borden's tract on Moffet's Creek; David Hays' line, James Trimble's line. Teste: Wm. McCutchan, Wm. Kennedy, Samuel Steel, Jno. Handly, Andrew Kennady, Wm. Edmiston. Delivered: George Jamison, 17th January, 1787.

Page 623.—21st May, 1764. John Handley and Grizel ( ) to William Reah, £50, 257 acres corner tract of 300 acres surveyed to Joseph Kennedy, on Broad Spring Run, otherwise called Back Creek. Teste: James Wardlaw, Wm. Edmiston, Jas. Pollock, Mathew Morehead.

Page 626.—15th May, 1764. Hugh Martin to Mathew Harper, £80, 200 acres, part of 1415 surveyed for William Henderson and conveyed to John Henderson, and from him to Mathew Harper, Mathew to John Henderson, from Henderson to Hugh Martin, on Christian's Creek; corner Thomas Rutledge's land, crossing Black's Branch. Teste: John Handley and Archibald Handley.

Page 628.—15th May, 1764. Mathew Harper and Margret to Hugh Martin, £80, 220 acres on the Bullpasture, branch of Cowpasture, or Newfoundland Creek. Delivered: Wm. Martin, August Court, 1768.

Page 631.—20th June, 1764. Jacob ( ) Rollman and Margret ( ) to Christian Rollman, £50, 200 acres, part of 600 acres patented to James Wood, Wm. Russell and Wm. Green, conveyed by them to Jacob, 23d May, 1763; corner Catherine Zorn's land. Teste: Mark ( ) Swadley,

Joseph Gamwell. Delivered: Moses Hinckle, Esq., 3d July, 1793, by order of Rollman.

Page 633.—20th July, 1764. Andrew Russell, Sr., to Andrew Russell, Jr., his son, £10, 150 acres in Beverley Manor on Christian's Creek, part of 496 acres whereon said Russell now lives. Teste: Alex. McDonnall. Delivered: Andrew Russell, March Court, 1767.

Page 635.—10th June, 1764. Alex Reid, of Amherst County, to his brother Thomas Reid, of the same County, £50, 115 acres formerly conveyed by Joshua Hoadley to Jno. Reid, 1760, and since the death of said John, descended to the aforesaid Alexander as eldest son and heir-at-law of John, on north side James River. Delivered: Thomas Reid, 1765.

Page 638.—17th March, 1764. George Skillern and Elisabeth to James Kerr, £1.10, 1 acre, 3 roods, 10 perches, in fork of Christian's Creek and Middle River of Shanandore, part of 180 acres patented to John Kerr, 5th September, 1749, and by John to James Hamilton, and conveyed to George, on Christian's Creek. Teste: Jno. Anderson, Robert Wilson, William Kerr. Delivered: James Kerr, 10th June, 1771.

Page 640.—9th June, 1764. Peter Hull and Susanna to Jacob Passenger, £60, receipt whereof, &c., and discharge the said George Lewis Hockheimer, 240 acres in southwest side of Cub Run, a branch of Shanandoe; corner Charles Rusk's land, line of Curby's land; corner Patrick Wilson; corner Pouley's land, line of Russell's land, part of tract patented to Jacob Stover and conveyed to Christophell Francisco, the elder, and by him to Peter Hull. Delivered: Nicholas Mildebarger, March, 1769.

Page 643.—16th May, 1758. Robert ( ) Finley and Martha ( ) to William Finley, £20, 100 acres on South River Shanandore, part of the land on which Robert now lives, and joining south side, John Ramsey's land; corner between William and Robert Finley; corner Charles Dalhoss; corner William's old survey. Delivered: Robert Finley, son of Wm. Finley, 13th April, 1798.

Page 645.—20th June, 1764. Hugh Ross and Sarah ( ) to John Campbell, £—, 170 acres on west side of Cartley's River called Walker's Run, side of Benj. Allen's Road. Delivered: John Campbell, December, 1765.

Page 647.—9th April, 1764. Samuel Harrison to Daniel Smith, £100, 100 acres on South Branch of Linville's Creek, patented to Samuel, 5th September, 1749. Teste: Walter Crow, Peter ( ) Kinder, Felix Shelman (Sheltman), Joseph Rutherford. Delivered: Daniel Smith, November, 1765.

Page 650.—20th June, 1764. Mathew ( ) Edmiston and Margret to Samuel Patterson, £55, 238 acres in Borden's tract, and conveyed to Mathew, 28th May, 1751; corner tract surveyed for William Smith; corner Wm. Cowden's land. Teste: Pat. Martin, James McCleerey, Jno. Mophet.

Page 651.—20th March, 1764. James Craig, yeoman, to James Leard, yeoman, deed of surrender of mortgage by James Laird to James Craig, dated 10th June, 1760, for 400 acres purchased by Laird of William Downs on Smith's Creek.

Page 654.—16th May, 1764. James Bane (Bean) and Rebecca to Thomas Walker, gent., £250, two tracts: A, 190 acres on Peters' Creek, conveyed by James Patton, gent., to Bean, 28th November, 1751; B, 117 acres on Goose Creek, a branch of Roanoke, part of 400 acres conveyed by James

Burk to Bean, 18th May, 1753. Delivered: Col. Andrew Lewis, August, 1766.

Page 655.—18th June, 1764. Thomas Fulton, of Staunton, to Samuel Cowden, of Staunton, £59.41, beds, furniture, &c.

Page 656.—28th June, 1764. Same to Joseph Gamble, £65, conveys a slave.

Page 657.—14th August, 1764. Jacob Gum and Sarah ( ) to Samuel Nicholas, 237 acres patented to William Rutledge, 20th August, 1745, and conveyed by Rutledge to Ruddle and by Ruddle to James Claypool, and by Claypool to Jacob, 14th May, 1761, on a branch of Brock's Creek.

Page 659.—11th August, 1764. Jonathan Roberson to William Dunlap. £100, 230 acres on Linville's Creek, purchased by Jonathan of John Miller, between said Miller's land and George Spears'; corner John Miller's part of same tract; corner William Bean's land. Teste: Alex Herring, Joseph Rutherford. Delivered: George Speirs, Decemmber, 1766.

Page 661.—10th August, 1764. James Bailey and Anne ( ) to Edmund Crump, £20, 142 acres in Forks of James, John Taylor's line; corner James Bailey. Teste: James Edmiston, John ( ) Taylor, Patrick ( ) McCollom.

Page 663.—10th August, 1764. James Edmundson and Agness to James Welch, £53.15, 140 acres on North Branch of James, part of the tract whereon James Edmundson now lives; corner McClung. Delivered: James Welsh, September, 1783.

Page 665.—19th June, 1764. Phillip Long, eldest son and heir-at-law of Paul Long, who was eldest son and heir-at-law of Phillip Long, of Frederick County, to Stephen Hemsburger, £40, 176 acres purchased by Phillip, Sr., of Joseph Phillips (deed recorded in Orange) on Shannando River. Teste: George Carpenter. Delivered: Stephen Hansberger, November, 1766.

Page 667.—21st August, 1764. Christopher ( ) Thompson and Mary ( ) to Jacob Conrod, £30, 95 acres on Cook's Creek; corner McDonald's line and one Fisher's survey. Teste: Archibald Huston, Daniel Love, James Thompson.

Page 668.—21st August, 1764. Archibald Huston, of Augusta, farmer, appoints Hugh Huston, of New Providence in North Carolina, farmer, attorney to recover Archibald's interest in the estate of David Huston, deceased testate. Teste: Felix Gilbert, James Thompson.

Page 670.—23d January, 1764. James Carlile and Rachel ( ) to Thomas Hugart, £130, 350 acres, part of a tract deeded by Col. James Patton and John Lewis, 2d April, 1758, iin the Calfpasture; corner Jacob Clemonses orphants; corner Rev. John Kinkade. Teste: Benj. Estill, Robert Knox, Wm. Kinkead, John Carlile, Samuel Campbell.

Page 672.—20th March, 1764. Thomas Paxton to James Hughes, of Staunton, £20, lot 14 in Staunton. Teste: John King, Joshua Russell, George Skillern. Delivered: Mr. Owen Owens, 4th May, 1787.

Page 673.—2d August, 1764. John Robinson and Sarah ( ) to Daniel Harvey, £25, 150 acres in Borden's tract, Mathew Robinson's line. Teste: John and Samuel Edmiston and John Stewart. Delivered: Daniel Harvey, April, 1768. Conveyed by Borden to Robinson.

Page 675.—21st July, 1764. Joshua Hadley, executor of Joshua Hedley, late of Augusta County, gent., to John McClure, £46, 186 acres by patent

3d November, 1750, in the Long Bottom, south side James River. Teste: Hugh Martin, Malcolm, Martha and Hugh Allen.

Page 677.—10th August, 1764. Michael Finney and Catherine ( ) to James Bailey, £31, 330 acres in Fork of James River; corner Wm. Holman; corner John Taylor; William Foster's line. Teste: Edmund ( ) Crump, John ( ) Taylor. Delivered: Wm. Lyle per order 1st January, 1796.

Page 679.—10th August, 1764. Same to John Taylor, £35, 320 acres in Forks of James River; corner Michael's former survey. Teste: James Bailey, Joseph Reed.

Page 681.—21st August, 1764. David Stevenson and Annos ( ) to Jno. Burnside, £170, 400 acres on Cathey's River and on North Branch of the Great Meadow, east side Walker's Run; corner Thomas Stevenson, patented to said David, 16th June, 1744. Teste: James Bell, Hugh Hamilton, John King.

Page 682.—15th April, 1764. Borden's executors to Samuel Lyle, £11, 100 acres, part of 92,100, said Lyle's old line. Teste: Arthur Woods. Delivered: Samuel Lyle, August Court, 1773.

Page 684.—9th May, 1764. Same to James McCalister, £———, 150 acres, part of 92,100; corner Robert Ervin. Delivered: William McClenachan, March, 1766.

Page 687.—17th August, 1764. Samuel Davis and Mary to Samuel Lyle, £55, 200 acres of Borden's tract; corner James Anderson, north side of Mount Atlas, tract surveyed for James Greenlee; Wm. Davis' corner. Teste: James McDowell. Delivered: Samuel Lyle, August Court, 1773.

Page 689.—17th August, 1764. Frederick Kister and Hannah ( ) to George Fults, £20, 35 acres at a place called the Little Walnut Bottom on the mountain between the South Fork and the South Branch of Potowmack.

Page 691.—28th March, 1764. John Dickinson to Samuel Hamilton, £120, 195 acres in the Cowpasture on the river. Teste: Ben. Estill, Samuel Crockett, Samuel Clark, Jas. Hmailton. Delivered: Samuel Hamilton, 18th May, 1774.

Page 693.—18th August, 1764. Samuel McDowell and Mary to John and Robert Moffet, £20, 340 acres patented to Samuel 5th August, 1751; Laurance Morrin's line. Teste: Arthur Campbell. Delivered: Jno. Moffet, September, 1766.

Page 695.—21st August, 1764. James Loghridge to Andrew Loghridge, his son, £20, 280 ares on Great River of Calf Pasture below ye Graham's land; corner Bratton's land; corner John Graham's land. Teste: Thos. Teat, Wm. King.

Page 697.—21st August, 1764. William Beard and Mary ( ) to James Bellshie, £30, 219½ acres on the island draft of North River Shanando by patent, 10th February, 1748. Teste: Joseph Bell, John Ralstone, Mathew McDowell.

Page 699.—21st August, 1764. Daniel Harrison and Sarah ( ) to Daniel Harrison, his son, £20, 200 acres, part of 400 patented to Daniel, 25th September, 1746; corner Jesse Harrison's part of same tract. Teste: Joseph Gamwell.

Page 701.—20th August, 1764. Isaiah Shipman and Elizabeth ( ) to Wm. McNeill, £17, 265 acres on Dry River. Teste: Jno. Dickinson, Abner Smith.

Page 702.—May, 1764. Alexander Wright, merchant of Fredericksburg, to Daniel Kidd. Whereas James Brown on 9th October, 1754, leased 173 acres, part of 1550 acres known by the name of the Mill tract on which the Court House now stands, for 57 years 6 months to said Alexander Wright, for £20. This lease witnesseth. £20 paid by said Thomas Fulton, and 40 shillings yearly rent. Alexander leases to said Daniel 173 acres; James Millers' line; Beverley's line; corner Robt. Finley's land, crossing the Creek; 47 years term; reenter if said Thomas Fulton fails to pay. Teste: James Hargrove, Is. Christian, Thos. Fulton. Delivered: Daniel Kidd, April, 1769.

Page 704.—7th June, 1764. David Robinson and Annabale (Annabell) to Israel Christian, £80, 245 acres on Buffalo Creek of Roanoke, near Carvin's Creek, Wm. Graham's, about 20-24 acres is overlapped by Wm. Graham's patent and is excepted. Teste: Wm. Davis, James Robinson, David Bryan, Wm. Christian.

Page 706.—21st June, 1764. George and William Skillem to Walter Crow, £———. 343 acres patented to William Skillem, deceased, 30th August, 1743, and devised by William that his sons, George and William, should dispose of same on head of a draft of Linville's Creek on Daniel Harrison's road. Teste: James Hughes, James Huston, Robt. Russell. Delivered: Walter Crow, October, 1766. Acknowledged by George.

Page 708.—25th August, 1764. Thomas Gillham and Margaret to John Corolile, £45, 200 acres in Calfpasture bounded by lands now in possession of Robert Gay's orphants, and Samuel Campbell's lands and William Wills' lands.

Page 709.—20th July, 1764. William McPheeters, Cenor, to Samuel McPheeters, his son, £———, natural love and affection and for better maintenance, 400 acres on Mossey Creek, branch of North River of Shanando. Delivered: Samuel, March, 1768.

Page 711.—11th August, 1764. James McDowell and Francis, of the County of James City, Virginia, to Thomas Paxton, £250, 400 acres patented to James, 1st March, 1743, said river. Delivered: Thomas Paxton, June, 1766.

Page 712.—20th November, 1764. Mathew Buchanan and Martha, of the Province of Pennsylvania, to James Wilson of the same Province, £161.5. 711 acres in Borden's tract; Samuel Huston's line; Greenlee's line. Teste: Samuel Buchanan, Robert and Thomas Wilson. Delivered: James Wilson, 28th October, 1773.

Page 714.—10th November, 1764. John Berry to William Berry, £100, 427 acres in Borden's tract; corner Alexander Miller. Delivered: Wm. Berry, May, 1772.

Page 715.—4th November, 17—. Samuel Long to John Long, £100, 15 acres on Buffalo Creek of James River. Teste: Wm. Davis, James Young, Edward Faris.

Page 717.—6th November, 1764. Same to Henry Long, £100, 200 acres on Buffalo Creek of James River. Teste: Joseph Long. Delivered: David Scott, July, 1768, by your order.

Page 719.—15th November, 1764. Same to James Young, 5 shillings and his maintenance during Samuel's life, 185 acres on Buffalo Creek of James

River, part of a patent to Samuel. Teste: Peter Wylie, Edward Faris, Joseph Robinson. Delivered: Robert Young, August, 1766.

Page 719.—18th November, 1764. Edward ( ) Gill to Solomon Whitley, £13, farming implements and household furniture. Teste: Christopher ( ) Best.

Page 720.—Relinquishment of dower by Mary, wife of Christopher Thompson, to deed to Jacob Conrad (ninety-five acres on Cook's Creek) acknowledged by Mary, 29th August, 1764.

Page 721.—16th November, 1764. John ( ) Jones and Elizabeth ( ) to Daniel Young, £11.5, 260 acres at Snodon's Springs.

Page 723.—1st August, 1764. Christian Curp and Catherine ( ) to Jacob Archenbright, labourer, £90, 100 acres on a branch of Cub Run purchased by Christian of Valentine Pence, and his part of Francisco's tract of 3,100 acres; corner lands of Valentine Pence and John Craig. Teste: Jacob Nicolas, Jacob ( ) Passinger, Burr Harrison. Delivered: Jacob Archenbright, August, 1769.

Page 725.—20th November, 1764. Jacob ( ) Passinger and Catherine ( ) to Jacob Archenbright, £————, 125 acres between Cub Run and the Peaked Mountain the same that Jacob purchased of Phillip Haws, to whom it was patented 14th February, 1761; corner a survey of Nicolas Trout, Jacob Pence's line. Delivered: Jacob Archenbright, August, 1769.

Page 727.—19th November, 1764. Robert ( ) Hunter, late of Augusta County, to William Doherty, £87.10, 255 acres on Christian's Creek; corner Thomas Shields' land; line of Sawyers' land; corner Robert William's land, Alexander's line. Teste: John Hunter, John ( ) Shield, Sr., Jno. Shields, Jr. Delivered: Wm. Dougherty, August, 1766.

Page 728.—10th November, 1764. William Preston and Susannah to Peter Cockran, £7.10, 32 acres on James River; Givens' corner. Delivered to Ephraim Richardson, 15th October, 1765.

Page 730.—12th November, 1764. Thomas Hadley and Mary of Cumberland Co., N. C., to George Poage, £140, 400 acres in Forks of James River and Craig's Creek. Teste: Henry Carter.

Page 731.—13th November, 1764. Same to James Boreland (Rowland), £130, 549 acres on Catawbo Creek; corner in the Great Patent line and a small tract belonging to William Preston, Mount Hadley (first surveyed in two tracts and conveyed to Thomas Hadley by Borden. Delivered: Francis Smith, March Court, 1762.

Page 734.—14th November, 1764. James Young to Samuel Long, 185 acres, bond to make title to 185 acres. See deed, p. 719, supra.

Page 735.—10th September, 1763. John Mann and Damis to Thomas Meek, £73.15, 254 acres conveyed by Beverley to Moses Mann, 4th February, 1748, and descended to John as eldest brother and heir-at-law of Moses; corner Wm. McCutchen's land, Grassy Lick Run. Teste: Hugh Johnston, Robert Reed, Wm. Mann, John Smith, James Graham. Delivered: Thos. Meek, March, 1773.

Page 736.—Damis Mann's relinquishment of dower, 9th July, 1764. Delivered: John Meek, 10th January, 1787.

Page 738.—21st November, 1764. Zebulon ( ) Harrison and Reubin Harrison, executors of John Harrison, deceased, to Jacob Peters, £90, 400 acres on a branch of South Branch of Potomac called West Fork of Mill Creek. Delivered: Moses Hinkle, 31st July, 1793.

Page 740.—20th November, 1764. Robert ( ) Looney to Joseph Looney, £20, 160 acres at the Sinking Springs on west side James River.

Page 742.—21st November, 1764. Stephen Conrad and Catherine ( ) to George Huffman, Jr., £25, 220 acres; corner Wood's land on Boon's Run. Delivered: Geo. Huffman, 21st May, 1771.

Page 744.—11th November, 1764. Francis ( ) Randles to John Scott, £33.10, 100 acres in Borden's tract; corner Samuel Davis, James Anderson's line. Teste: David Cloyd, Jr., Lanty Armstrong, James McDowell.

Page 746.—21st November, 1764. Robert Lockridge and Rebecca to David and Jno. Kinkead of Albemarle, £90, 520 acres on Great Calfpasture; corner Kinkead's land, crossing Ramse's Creek, said Lockridge's land. Teste: Francis Tincher, Wm. Wills, George Campbell. Delivered: David Kinkead, November, 1768.

Page 748.—22d August, 1764. John Mills to John Thompson, £———, 213 acres on Glade Creek of Roanoke; corner said Jno. Mills' land Delivered: Israel Christian, November, 1768.

Page 750.—19th November, 176(4), Nathaniel Lyon (and Margaret) to James Cotton, £51.10, 220 acres in Beverley Manor; corner Robert Sawyer's land in Wm. Thompson's line, line of land formerly belonging to George Rodgers and sold to Nathaniel. Teste: Wm. Brown, Wm. Hyde, Robt. Rodgers. Delivered: Thos. Bowyer, April, 1765.

Page 752.—19th November, 1764. Thomas Harrison and Sarah to Jeremiah Harrison, £———, 212 acres on Dry Fork of Smith's Creek.

Page 754.—19th November, 1764. Same to John Harrison, £———, 150 acres on a Sinking Spring Branch of Linvel's Creek; corner Mary Adams.

Page 756.—22d November, 1764. Thomas ( ) Harrison and Sarah ( ) to David Berry, £100, two tracts, 429 acres on Muddy Creek—A, 22 acres on Muddy Creek; B, 195 acres.

Page 759.—22d November, 1764. Abraham Smith and Sarah to Daniel Smith, £243, two tracts adjoining each other, on head of Dry Fork of Smith's Creek: A, 400 acres patented to Daniel Harrison, 20th August, 1741 and conveyed by him to his son Robert, 16th March, 1748, and purchased by Abraham from executors of Robert, end of the Timber Bottom; B, 260 acres patented to said Robert Harrison, 20th August, 1741, and sold to Abraham by his executors, end of Timber Bottom; corner Daniel Harrison, Robert Cravens's line. Delivered: Daniel, May, 1765.

Page 761.—16th November, 1764. Daniel Smith and Jesse Harrison, executors of Robert Harrison, to Abraham Smith, £243, conveys two tracts above. Delivered: John Poage, May, 1765.

Page 763.—10th January, 1764. John Buchanan and Wm. Thompson executors of James Patton, £215, 400 acres on north side James River. Teste: Henry Field, Wm. Simpson, Thomas ( ) Garraway, Jno. Frazer, Wm. and Alex. Ingles

Page 764.—18th June, 1764. Thomas Fulton and Elisabeth, of Staunton, to Stephen Loye, £25, lot in Staunton, leased by Beverley to Alex. Wright, 22d February, 1749, who conveyed to Thomas. Delivered: Stephen Loy, April, 1767.

Page 765.—19th November, 1764. Margret Woods and Joseph Gamble (signed Gamwell) to Archer Mathews, £10, A, 14 acres, a part of No. 9 (woodland adjoining Staunton), joining Jno. Kerr's lot; corner said Gamble's part of said lot; also B, part of lot 5 in Staunton.

Page 767.—18th March, 1765. Robert Hook to James Hook, £5, 200 acres on south side the land said Hook now lives on, patented, 1st October, 1747. Teste: Wm. Hook, Mathew McDowel, Samuel Scott. Delivered to James Scot, August Court, 1773.

Page 768.—19th March, 1765. Patrick Fraizer and Mary to John Fraizer, his son, £10, 110 acres, part of 400 acres patented to John Baumgardner, 25th September, 1746, and conveyed by him to Patrick, 19th August, 1750, on head branches of Stony Lick, a branch of Shanandore. Teste: William Christian, Jr. Delivered: John Frazier, August, 1768.

Page 770.—21st July, 1764. Joshua Hedley, executor of Joshua Hedley, deceased, to Malcome Allen, of Prince Edward County, Virginia, £15, 50 acres by patent, 3d November, 1750, called the Pound Bottoms, beginning south side James River, at the lower end of the Bottom, a hill opposite an island. Teste: Hugh Martin, Martha Allen, Hugh Allen, Robert ( ) Martin, Mary ( ) McElheny. Delivered: Francis Smith, 1st October, 1767.

Page 772.—4th September, 1764. Thomas O'Neal to Archibald (Ersbald) Hopkins, £4, 27 acres on a branch of Muddy Creek; corner Wood's land. Teste: Ephraim Love, Jno. Hopkins, Geo. Baxter.

Page 773.—18th March, 1765. Hance Harper and Elizabeth ( ) to William Martin, £24, 180 acres on Blackthorn, a branch of South Branch of Potomac. Teste: Thos. Stuart, Elizabeth Stuart, Wm. Jameson. Delivered: Wm. Martin, August, 1768.

Page 775.—19th March, 1765. Adam Dean and Eleanor, his wife, to Charles Teas, 5 sh., 310 acres on South River, part of a tract patented to Robert Turk, 6th September, 1736; corner to Robert Turk's land; corner John Patrick's line. Teste: Wm. Teas, Jno. Dean, Samuel Kinkade. Delivered: Charles Teas, September, 1766.

Page 776.—19th March, 1765. Same to same. Bond to make above conveyance.

Page 778.—12th March, 1765. James Trimble, of Green Spring, and Sarah, to John Berryhill, £60, 180 acres on Borden's Creek in Forks of James; corner James Trimble, Patrick McCollom's line.

Page 780.—5th March, 1765. Isaac ( ) Taylor to Andrew Taylor, £40, 250 acres; corner George Taylor, oak on Mill Creek; corner Wm. Taylor. Teste: Wm. Taylor. Delivered: Andrew Taylor, 10th March, 1772.

Page 782.—20th March, 1765. Isaac Taylor, Sr., to Isaac Taylor, Jr., £10, 70 acres on Purgatory Creek of James River. Teste: David Fulton. Delivered: Francis Smith, May Court, 1767.

Page 783.—5th March, 1765. Isaac Taylor, Sr., and Isabell ( ) to William Taylor, £5, 150 acres in Borden's tract; corner Andrew Taylor, on Mill Creek. Teste: Wm. Lusk, Samuel Lyle, Andrew Taylor. Delivered: Samuel Lyle, June, 1783.

Page 785.—14th March, 1765. William Graham and Priscilla to David Robinson, £100, 100 acres (by lease and release from said David, 12th November, 1755), on Buffalo Creek of Roanoke. Teste: James Cartey and Samuel Scott.

Page 787.—2d March, 1765. Same to Joseph Robinson, £100, 236 acres, part of 600 acres conveyed to William by Jno. Mills, 3d August, 1753, on Buffalo Creek; corner Israel Christian, formerly Daniel McCormick's. Delivered: Cap. Thos. Madison, 22d October, 1770.

Page 789.—19th May, 1765. James Anderson, blacksmith, to his son James Anderson, £4, 200 acres on head of Long Glade Branch of North River of Shanandoe, part of 400 acres patented to James Anderson, Sr. Teste: George and Wm. Anderson and John Frazer. Delivered: Joseph Redburn, September, 1768.

Page 791.—25th December, 1764. John Sharp and Ann ( ) and Adam Sharp, of Bedford, to Jacob Persinger, £140, 350 acres devised to John and Adam by their father Mathew Sharp, who purchased it from Jacob Harmon and it was conveyed to John and Adam since the death of Mathew, 16th May, 1759, near upper end of the Peaked Mountain. Teste: Michael Prinder, Christopher ( ) Persinger, Mikell ( ) Barnett. Delivered: Anthony Ailer, April, 1772.

Page 793.—18th March, 1765. George Caldwell to William Caldwell, his son, £10, 130 acres, part of 405 acres in Beverley Manor on a branch of Christian's Creek, branch near said William Caldwell's house. Teste: Walter Davis, Alex. Stewart, Jas. Caldwell. Delivered: Mr. John Caldwell, 21st May, 1808.

Page 795.—19th March, 1765. Jacob Pence, eldest son and heir-at-law of Jacob Pence, late of Augusta, deceased, and Adam Pence, ditto of Valentine Pence, ditto to Jacob Nicholas. Whereas Jacob, Sr., and Valentine owned in common 164 acres near the Peeked Mountain, the patent being issued in the name of Jacob. Jacob Nicholas purchased Valentine's moiety, but before title was made Jacob devised the whole to Valentine to enable him to make conveyance to said Jacob Nicholas and to Adam Hetrick, who had bought Jacob Pence's half. Valentine died without making conveyance, and Nicholas brought suit in chancery and the grantors here were decreed, on 21st August, 1762, within three months after they come of age, to make conveyance, £14, 75 acres, part of 164 acres, patented to Jacob, 20th August, 1747, at end of Peaked Mountain; Jacob Nicholas's field, corner land formerly John Lawrence's. Delivered: Col. Jno. Rusk.

Page 797.—18th March, 1765. Adam Pence, eldest son, &c, as above, to Jacob Nicholas, £10, 31 acres, part of 166 acres which Valentine purchased of Christopher Francisco on Cub Run. Delivered: Col. Jno. Rusk.

Page 798.—16th March, 1765. Jacob ( ) Pence, eldest son, &c., of Jacob Pence, to Adam Hetrick, yeoman, £22, 89 acres, part of 164 acres patented to Jacob Pence, father of grantor; corner land formerly Jno. Lawrence's; corner Jacob Nicholas. Delivered: Adam Hetrick, July, 1767.

Page 800.—27th February, 1765. Jacob ( ) Persinger and Catrina ( ) to Augustine Price, £80, tract conveyed to Jacob by Sharp, 16th May, 1759, 167 acres; corner Harmon and Peter Miller; also 65 acres joining aforesaid tract, part of 130 acres granted Jacob by patent, 30th August, 1763. Teste. Delivered: Anthony Ailer, April, 1772.

Page 802.—9th March, 1765. Teawalt ( ) Harman and Sarah ( ) to George Mallow, £30, 50 acres between Peeked Mountain and Shanandore, devised to Teawalt by his father Jacob, Price's line. Teste: John Madison, John Madison, Jr., Peter Miller. Delivered: George Mallow, May, 1776.

Page 804.—9th March, 1765. Peter ( ) Harmon and Margaret ( ) to George Mallow, £60, 104 acres between Peeked Mountain and Shanandore River, devised to Peter by his father Jacob by will dated 18th September, 1761; corner Peter Harmon, Jr.; corner Teawalt Harmon; corner Augustine Price; corner Jacob Harman's line. Delivered: George Mallow, May, 1776.

Page 807.—2d March, 1765. George Dougherty to William Robinson, £40.15, 80 acres on Carr's Creek of James River, between House Mountain and North Mountain. Delivered: Wm. Robinson, April, 1767.

Page 809.—18th March, 1765. John Finley, gent., to Wm. Finley, gent., £160, 297 acres in Beverley Manor on South River, Manor line; corner Wm. Finley, Charles Dalloway's line, John Ramsey's line. Teste: John Dividson, Francis Alexander, William Caldwell.

Page 811.—19th March, 1765. William Bell and Rachel to Samuel Craig, £15, two tracts: A, 30 acres, part of 400 whereon Bell now lives, on McClure's Run, a branch of Middle River of Shanandore; B, 60 acres adjoining above, and between it and Morris O'Friel's and Andrew Foster's lands. Delivered: Samuel Craig, 26th May, 1773.

Page 813.—27th September, 1764. Henry Smith, farmer, and Amelia, to Adam Stephen, of Frederick County, £136, 170 acres conveyed to Henry by Silas Hart, 1st June, 1756, on South Fork of North River of Shanandoe. Delivered: Robert Stephen, 29th September, 1767. Teste: William Teas and William Stuart.

Page 815.—27th September, 1764. Same to same, £100.10, 400 acres by patent, 27th June, 1764, to Henry Smith on North River of Shanandoe, Hickory in the Barrens.

Page 817.—19th March, 1765. William ( ) Martin and Agness ( ) to William Jameson, £100, 310 acres on Christian's Creek whereon Martin now lives, conveyed to Martin by Jno. and Robert Thomson, 12th September, 1750; corner Wm. Palmer; George Robinson's corner (now Wm. Henderson's land), plat surveyed for Wm. Russell (now Alex. Thomson's land). Teste: Hugh Martin, Mathew Harper, Wm. Doherty. Delivered: Wm. Jameson, 8th November, 1769.

Page 819.—14th March, 1765. Robert McKetrick and Jane ( ) to Wm. Wills, 110 acres on a branch of Great Calfpasture; corner Robert Gay, line of Wm. Campbell's land, patented to Robert, May, 1759.

Page 821.—20th March, 1764. Adam Miller to Henry Miller, £50, 600 acres on Shanando River and Elk Run; corner Adam Miller, Jr.; line of Jacob Miller. Delivered: Henry Miller, May, 1769.

Page 823.—28th September 1764. Adam Miller to Jacob Bear, £300, 280 acres whereon Adam now lives, purchased by him from Joseph Bloodworth and he from Jacob Stover, part of tract of 820 acres, on Shanandore River; corner Eastes land; corner Henry Miller's land, including an island in river. Delivered: Jacob Bear, May, 1769.

Page 824.—29th April, 1764. Jacob Bear, yeoman, to Adam Miller, mortgage, £200, conveys above.

Page 826.—28th September, 1764. Bond by same to same conditioned upon payment of the £200 above and also during Adam's life yearly 25 bushels of wheat ground, 10 bushels of barley, 33 gallons of whiskey, 400 weight of meat, ½ of pork and ½ of beef; 1/3 of orchard or profits of it;

Adam and his family to dwell in the new house now a-building on said plantation, and to have a garden, two cows and a horse.

Page 827.—18th March, 1765. Adam ( ) Murray to John Coulter, £75, 200 acres in Beverley Manor, pines in the Barrons, Jno. McClure's line. Delivered: Joseph Coulton, July, 1772.

Page 828.—8th February, 1765. Valentine Metcher (Matcher) to Ludwick Francisco and Charles Rush, mortgage, £25, 275 acres on a branch of North River of Shanandoe, purchased by Valentine from Peter Miller; corner David Logan's land. Delivered: Charles Rush, May, 1766.

Page 829.—10th March, 1765. Justices of Augusa County, by Israel Christian and Felix Gilbert, to William Fleming, gent., order of 24th November, 1760, £5, lot 16 fronting a lot belonging to John Stewart and joining a lot whereon the said William now dwells. Livery of seisin by handful of earth. Delivered: Wm. Fleming, May Court, 1765.

Page 831.—20th March, 1765. William Shannon to Edward Erwin, mortgage, £29, 400 acres on North River of Shanandore, David Davies' line, top of Castle Hill. Teste: Charles Lewis, Hugh Donaghe. Delivered: Ed. Erwin, May, 1767.

Page 833.—15th March, 1765. Peter Horse to Bastian Hover, £5, 100 acres, part of 750 acres on South Fork of Potomac, between the lands of Postle Hover and Adam Strowd. Teste: Mathew Patton, John Davis, James Dyer. Delivered to Mr. Hover, March, 1786.

Page 835.—17th March, 1765. John Trimble to Walter Trimble, his son, £5, 30 acres, part of 541 acres in Beverley Manor on head branches of Middle River. Delivered, 13th November, 1792.

Page 836.—20th March, 1765. John Brown, gent., and Margret to Thomas Brown, £100, 145 acres. Delivered to Thomas Brown, 29th May, 1771.

Page 838.—19th March, 1765. John Brown and Margret to same, £100, 300 acres; corner James Cathey's, now Samuel Wallace's, Beverley Manor line.

Page 840.—21st March, 1765. John Robertson and Mary to Thomas Tosh, £40, 560 acres on Mason's Creek, branch of Roanoke; corner John Mason's land. Teste: Alex. Stuart, James Lessley. Delivered: Jas. Crawford, June, 1769.

Page 842.—10th December, 1764. Daniel ( ) Young to Samuel Beard, £12, 260 acres at Snodon's Spring. Teste: Thomas Harrison, Egeniah Virden. Jeremiah Harrison.

Page 843.—20th March, 1765. Thomas Fulton, of Staunton, tavernkeeper, appoints John Jeremiah, merchant in Frederick Town, Maryland, his attorney to recover from George Larderson, of Lancaster Town in Pennsylvania, £18. Delivered: James Telford, June, 1765.

Page 844.—21st March, 1765. James Huston and Agness to Henry Larken, £30, 120 acres in Fork of James River, John Harger's line.

Page 847.—23d January, 1765. Israel Christian to his son William Christian, £200, two tracts on James River: A, 400 acres at Locust Bottom, point of an island; B, 54 acres joining above, both patented to Israel, 7th June, 1764. Teste: Thomas Barnes.

Page 849.—22d February, 1765. William Shannon and Jean ( ) to Robert Scott, £29, 224 acres conveyed to William by Michael Harper, 26th January, 1760, on the New Foundland Creek; corner John Botkin; corner land in possession of Carlile. Teste: Wm. and John McPheeters, John Jameson, William McClintock. Delivered: Robert Scott, November, 1767.

Page 851.—22d March, 1765. Alex. Herring (Heron) and Abigail to Samuel Samples, £5, 38 acres on East Fork of Linville's Creek, between David Ralstone's and Samuel Harrison's land, Hite's land.

Page 853.—22d March, 1765. Same to Walter Crow, £25, 200 acres on South Fork Linville's Creek; corner Samuel Harrison's land. Delivered: Walter Crow, October, 1766.

Page 855.—19th March, 1765. John Moore to Charles Campbell, £60, 230 acres in Borden's tract; corner John Houston's land. Teste: Wm. Mann, Archibald Reaugh, Samuel Downey. Delivered to C. Campbell's executors, 23d March, 1827.

Page 857.—19th March, 1765. Samuel Norwood and Elisabeth to Robert McElhemy, blacksmith, £150, 400 acres in Borden's tract; corner Francis McCoun's (McCown), bank of Kerr's Creek, Wm. Hamilton's land. Teste: Hugh Cunningham, John McKee, Wm. Napier. Delivered: Cap. James McDowell, February, 1769.

Page 859.—Release of dower by Mary Ann Moore, wife of John Moore, as to deed, p. 855, supra.

Page 859.—Tripartrite—21st May, 1765. John Madison, of 1st, Mary McDonald, of Frederick, of 2d, and Agnes Walsh, of Spottsylvania County. Whereas Alex. Wright, merchant, 22d August, 1754, conveyed to John Madison in trust for Mary, lot 12 in Stanton whereon Mary then dwelt, and lot 5 laid off contiguous to said town, £9, conveys to Agness Walsh the two lots above. John Madison. Mary ( ) McDonald. Teste: John Anderson, John Anderson, Jr., George Anderson. Delivered: Agness Walsh, September, **1765.**

Page 861.—20th May, 1765. (John ( ) Edmiston and Margret ( ) to John Stewart, £50, 132 acres in Borden's tract; corner John Stewart; corner Wm. Edmiston. Teste: Samuel Buchanan, Wm. and Samuel Edmiston. Delivered: Jno. Stuart, 10th December, 1790.

Page 863.—19th March, 1765. Samuel Wallace and Elis (Elizabeth) to Robert Wallace, his son, £10, two tracts: A, 110 acres, part of 300 acres conveyed by Beverley to John Cathey, 7th December, 1757, and by Cathey to Samuel, corner said O'Friel; B, 50 acres joining above.

Page 865.—22d May, 1762. Robert Beverley to James Lesley, Jr., £11.14, 160 acres in Beverley Manor on Christian's Creek, George Rogers' line; **John Pickens' corner, in the Manor line.** Delivered: James Lesley, Jr., June. 1770.

Page 867.—20th May, 1765. William ( ) Ervine to Henry Ervine, his son. £15, 225 acres on a branch of Linville's Creek, part of 707 acres whereon **William now lives.** Teste: John Grattan. Delivered: Thos. Bell, 16th May, **1772.**

Page 869.—19th May, 1765. Same to Andrew Ervin, his son, £15, 200 acres, part of 707 acres above. Delivered: Thos. Woodrow, September, 1778.

Page 871.—20th May, 1765. Joseph Carpenter, Sr., to Joseph Carpenter, Jr., £10, 232 acres.

Page 873.—20th May, 1765. Same to Solomon Carpenter, planter, £10, 160 acres, John Man's line. Delivered: Wm. Huggart, 4th November, 1772.

Page 875.—21st May, 1765. Robert Beverley to Samuel Hodge, £35, 700 acres patented to Wm. Beverley, 1743, and descended to Robert as eldest son and heir, on Great River of Calf Pasture; corner John Preston.

Page 877.—17th May, 1765. Samuel Gray and Agnes to Joseph Reed £70, 241 acres in Borden's tract; Moses Trimble's line, corner Wm. Caruthers.

Page 879.—21st May, 1765. John Poage and Mary to Peter Hog, £220, 305 acres conveyed by Robert Poage to John, February, 1749, part of 772 acres granted to Robert by Beverley, 9th April, 1739, and recorded in general court, in Beverley Manor; corner Lewis's land; Wallace's land; corner Daniel Dennison.

Page 881.—20th May, 1765. John Cloyd and Margret ( ) and Mirian Cloyd and Mary to Joseph Love, £100, 269 acres in Beverley Manor on a branch of Christian's Creek (by virtue of a lease by said Wm. Johnston) called Black's Run; William Henderson's line; Rutledge's line; corner Armstrong's line; corner Samuel Love.

Page 883.—21st May, 1765. Robert Beverley to James Graham, £25, on South River of Calfpasture; corner Christopher Graham's land, by the Black Lick.

Page 885.—22d May, 1765. Same to Alexander Stewart, £60, 100 acres, on South River in Beverley Manor, joining former survey of Alexander Henderson; corner his old survey; corner John McConnolay.

Page 886.—22d May, 1765. Bond by same to same to secure release of dower by Maria, wife of Robert, to above.

Page 887.—20th May, 1765. Michael Hover and Barbara to Samuel Monsey, £25, 75 acres, part of 150 acres conveyed by George Speece, 3d February, 1760, on Linvell's Creek; corner Miller's land (part of said tract). Teste: Wm. Woods, Jno. Grattan. Delivered: Samuel Monsey, November, 1766.

Page 889.—20th May, 1765. Same to John Miller, £50, 75 acres, part of 150 above; corner said Miller's other land.

Page 890.—22d May, 1765. Samuel Wallace and Elizabeth ( ) to Jannet and Rachel Wallace, his daughters, deed of gift, 100 acres in Beverley Manor, part of 300 acres conveyed by John Cathey, 7th December, 1751; corner Jamison's land, branch of Middle River; corner John Trimble's land.

Page 892.—Release of dower by Elizabeth Norwood, wife of Samuel, in deed to Robert McElhenny, 13th May, 1765.

Page 893.—3d March, 1763. Elijah ( ) Isaac, of Roan County, North Carolina, to Robert Magee, £60, 200 acres, part of 378 acres conveyed by Col. James Patton to Elijah, 21st March, 1753, on North Branch Roanoke; corner land of Errick Bright; corner Thomas Hill. Teste: Wm. Preston, Francis Smith, Bryand McDonald, David Frame. Delivered: Robert Magee, August, 1773.

Page 895.—22d May, 1765. Robert Beverley to Felix Gilbert, £14.8 480 acres in Beverley Manor; corner to a 50-acres lot No. 1 in line of the Mill Tract; Anderson's road, the Plum Tree Draft; corner survey for John Harmon. Delivered: grantee, November, 1770.

Page 897.—22d May, 1765. Same to same, £10, four lots in Staunton, Nos. 37, 38, 39, 40. Livery by Twig and Turff. Teste: Wm. Fleming, Jno. Brown.

Page 898.—22d May, 1765. Same to Andrew Lewis, £5, 185 acres in Beverley Manor, his and James Bratton's line. Delivered: Andrew Lewis, 13th March, 1776.

Page 900.—18th March, 1765. Henry Long and Catrina ( ) to George Fridley, £20, 120 acres between Picked Mountain and Shenandore River, part of 250 acres patented to Henry, 20th August, 1760; Jacob Harmon's line, corner Peter (?) Miller's land. Delivered: Jacob Pence, 16th April, 1779.

Page 902.—25th April, 1765. James and Moses Green to Steven Conrad, £60, 234 acres, part of 2000 acres patented to James Wood and Robert Green, on Boon's Run between Picked Mountain and Shanandore River, between John Burke's and Runkle's land. Teste: Henry Long, Jacob ( ) Parshinger, George Conrad. Delivered: George Conrad, August Court, 1776.

Page 904.—22d May, 1765. Hugh ( ) Davor (Dever) (Diver) and Anne ( ) to Robert Williams, £40, 100 acres on headwaters of Cub Run. Teste: Hugh Hamilton, John Frezer. Delivered: Robert Williams, October, 1776.

Page 905.—Caleb Worley to Malcom Allen, heretofore recorded. Delivered: Francis Smith, October, 1767.

DEED BOOK NO. 12.

Page 2.—22d May, 1765. William Baskins and Mary to George Crawford, £200, 212 acres on Lewis Creek; corner James Lessley; corner Pickens; corner Mathews. Delivered: George Crawford, 4th October, 1772.

Page 4.—22d May, 1765. Samuel Love and Dorcas to Joseph Love, £10, 44 acres on Black's Run of Christian's Creek, part of 300 acres conveyed by Thos. Black to Samuel, in Beverley Manor; corner James Henderson; corner Joseph's other land. Teste: John Dailey, Wm. Teas, George Francisco

Page 6.—5th October, 1764. William McMillen ( ) to James Blair, £10, 100 acres, part of a larger tract. Teste: Francis Brown, Samuel Black, James Patterson. Delivered: James Blair, August, 1766.

Page 8.—22d May, 1765. Robert Beverley to John Poage, £6, 190 acres in Beverley Manor adjoining the land John now lives on; corner Poage and Wallace. Delivered: Mr. Poage, May, 1776.

Page 10.—23d May, 1765. Robert Beverley to William Fleming, £3, 152 poles, beginning at upper corner of William's lot in Staunton on the Creek. Livery of seisin by turf and twig.

Page 11.—23d May, 1765. Thomas ( ) Harrison, farmer, to John Sheltman, £50, 61 acres on head spring of Cook's Creek, part of 250 acres patented to Thomas, 1744, 15th March. Teste: Felix Sheltman, Jeremiah Harrison. Delivered: Richard Regan, by written order from John Sheltman, 25th July, 1788.

Page 14.—24th May, 1765. Robert Beverley to William Lewis, gent., £40, in Beverley Manor; corner James Brown, joining the 50-acres lots, the Creek, 520 acres. Delivered: Thomas Lewis, December, 1777.

Page 16.—22d May, 1765. Same to William Lewis, £3.12, 120 acres in

Beverley Manor between his, Thomas Poage's, John Harmon's and Felix Gilbert's lands, 50-acres lot No. 1. Delivered as above.

Page 17.—23d May, 1765. Same to Thomas Lewis, power attorney to sell and convey Robert's lands in Augusta. Delivered: Jno. Lewis, March, 1766.

Page 19.—23d May, 1765. Robert Beverley to William Fleming, £17, two tracts: A, 440 acres; B, 120 acres in Beverley Manor. A, line of said Fleming's own land; corner David Stuart and John Miller; corner John Henderson. B, corner said Fleming; corner Preston's land in line of Beverley Mill Tract. Delivered: Wm. Fleming, gent., 12th September, 1765.

Page 21.—23d May, 1765. Same to Sampson and George Mathews, £20, 560 acres in Beverley Manor, including two hills called and known by the name of Betsey Bell and Mary Gray, Alexander Gibson's line; corner Col. Stewart's; McClanahan's corner. Delivered: Sampson, October, 1768.

Page 24.—23d May, 1765. Same to same, £220, 1200 acres in Calfpasture on a branch of Calf Pasture called Elk Branch (Elk Run).

Page 26.—23d May, 1765. Same to Ephraim Wilson, £6, 200 acres in Beverley Manor on a branch of Christian's Creek; John Hutchinson's line; John Henderson's line; John Graham's corner.

Page 28.—23d May, 1765.—Same to John Brown, £4.5.6, 100 acres in Beverley Manor. Delivered: Joseph Trotter, 2d December, 1785.

Page 30.—22d May, 1765. William Anderson and Elizabeth ( ) to John Daily (Dealey), £200, 400 acres on North Branch of James, opposite an island. Sent to John Dailey by his order, September, 1770.

Page 32.—23d May, 1765. Robert Beverley to John Thompson, £3.12, 120 acres in Beverley Manor; corner to tract entered by Alexander Thompson, near Meeting House line. Teste: Archer Mathews. Delivered: Alex. Thompson, June, 1771.

Page 34.—23d May, 1765. Same to Alex. Thompson, £3.6, 110 acres in Beverley Manor.

Page 36.—23d May, 1765. Same to Sarah Thompson, £10.16, 360 acres in Beverley Manor, James Campbell's line; corner Robert Caldwell.

Page 38.—22d May, 1765. Same to Robert Thompson, £6, 200 acres in Beverley Manor, called McCord's Draught; corner Wm. Henderson.

Page 40.—28th November, 1764. Alex. Boyd, merchant in Augusta County, to Alex. Baine, merchant in Virginia, to secure payment of £1092.-9.5, and to secure him as surety for Boyd, to James Lyle, merchant of Chesterfield, on account of Boyd, on North Fork of Roanoke called Stanton River, and sometimes by name of Roanoke River, 1200 acres, 400 acres thereof purchased from James Campbell and Lettes, his wife, oaks on Goose Creek, 100 acres more thereof purchased from same, crossing Crooked Run, 98 acres patented to Alexander Boyd, 30 acres more, part thereof, on Roanoke, patented to Alexander Boyd, 14th February, 1761; corner James Campbell, 267 acres, part thereof purchased from Mathias Yoakam, 305 acres thereof, entered on Augusta surveyor's book, and surveyed by Wm. Preston, one of the surveyors of said County. The aforesaid tracts adjoin and the plantation thereon, well known by the name of Fort Lewis. Conveys also 5 negroes. Mortgage. Teste: Wm. Watts, Alex. Love, David Ross, Charles McPherson.

Page 44.—19th August, 1765. John Willey (Wiley) to Peter and Alex.

Wiley, sons of John, £200, 400 acres on New River, Francis Riley's line. Delivered: Pat. Lockhart, September, 1772.

Page 46.—14th August, 1765. George Campbell, Agness ( ) Campbell, his wife, and Prudence Campbell, his mother, to Andrew McClure, £130, 194 acres in Forks of James and in the fork of Wood's Creek and North Branch of James; corner Joseph Walker. Teste: Jno. McCampbell, Charles Campbell. Delivered: grantee, September, 1770.

Page 48.—10th August, 1765. John Dailey and Mary to John Porter, £60, 130 acres in Forks of James, part of 400 acres known as Hart's Bottom, whereon said John now liveth, smal lisland in the river. Teste: John Mitchell.

Page 50.—20th June, 1765. Borden's executors to Thomas Vance, £64, 800 acres on North Branch James. Delivered: Robert McKemy, February, 1785.

Page 53.—20th August, 1765. George Trout and Mary ( ) to Margaret Barger, £30, on a branch of South River of Shanando on west side of Christian Clemon's land, 324 acres, patented to George, 14th February, 1761. Delivered: Casper Barrier, 3d April, 1769.

Page 55.—20th August, 1765. James Robinson and Hannah ( ) to Arthur Graham, £75, 200 acres in Borden's tract on Hays Creek; corner John Walker's land. Teste: David Scott, Andrew Hays, Charles Hays. Delivered: Wm. Buchanan, August, 1769.

Page 58.—20th August, 1765. Robert Turk and Margret and Thomas Turk to George Trout, £40, on South River Shanando, mouth of Pain's Run, 100 acres patented to said Turk, 10th September, 1755. Delivered: James Craig, May, 1766.

Page 60.—20th August, 1765. Patrick Hays and Frances to Hugh Hays, £100, 400 acres corner Robert Alexander, Halfway Creek. Teste: John Taylor Wm. Robertson, Robert Alexander. Delivered: Francis Smith, 1st October, 1767.

Page 62.—20th June, 1765. James Hamilton, farmer, to John Hamilton, farmer, £2, 100 acres, part of 200 acres formerly surveyed for Andrew McClure and Alex. Henderson, and known by name of Elk Run, now seated by said John Hamilton, in Beverley Manor; corner tract surveyed for David Edmiston, James Alexander's line. Teste: Francis and John Alexander, Andrew McClure.

Page 64.—11th August, 1765. James Kennedy and Alex. McNutt to Robert McNutt, £37, 158 acres, 2 roods woodland ground (viz., 118 acres. 2 roods, bought of said James Kennedy and 140 acres bought of said Alex. McNutt), in Borden's tract, on Kennedy's Mill Creek; corner Alex. McNutt, James Berry's line; Wm. Berry's line, corner Wm. Clarke, Wm. Fulton's line. Delivered: Robert McNutt, 17th October, 1774.

Page 66.—19th August, 1765. Joseph Dictum and Rachel to James Marshall, £20, 100 acres patented to Richard Tictom, 25th June, 1747, on North River Shanadoe; corner Bernard McKenny, mouth of Beaver Run. Delivered: Francis Stewart, 2d March, 1767.

Page 69.—20th August, 1765. John Edmiston and Margaret to Samuel Steel, £150, 440 acres in Borden's tract on Moffett's Creek, Buchanan's line. Teste: David Syer, James Kennedy, Wm. and Samuel Edmiston. Delivered: Samuel Steel, August Court, 1770.

Page 71.—20th August, 1765. Samuel Steel and Mary ( ) to Robert Steele, £17, 34 acres in Borden's tract, courses of the Creek. Delivered: Robert Steel, August Court, 1770.

Page 73.—5th August, 1765. James Welsh and Agness ( ) to James Richey, £100, 200 acres on a branch of James River, formerly called Mary, now known by the name South River; corner Walter Smiley.

Page 75.—2d March, 1764. Thomas Feemster and Elizabeth to John Mountgomery, £48, 100 acres on Cowpasture, part of Thomas' plantation, up said River and Clover Creek. Teste: Robert Knox, Wm. Jackson, Wm. Black. Delivered: Alex. Black, 17th May, 1790, per order.

Page 78.—20th August, 1765. John ( ) Stewart and Mary ( ) to Samuel Steel, £50, 148 acres in Borden's tract; corner John Stewart; corner Robert Stewart. Teste: John Stewart, William, Samuel and Jno. Edmiston.

Page 80.—20th August, 1765. Hugh ( ) Botkin and Easter (Esther) to Henry Pickett, £20, 174 acres on a draft of North River Shanandoe, corner Robert McMahon. Delivered: Hugh Donaho, 1st June, 1769.

Page 82.—16th August, 1765. James Knox and Jane to Robert Knox. £20, 100 acres on Cowpasture; corner to land in possession of said James. Teste: Wm. Black, Francis Jackson, Wm. Jackson. Delivered: Robert Knox, August, 1765.

Page 84.—20th August, 1765. John McCreery, Sr., to John McCreery, Jr., £120, 260 acres on Cowpasture, part of tract whereon John, Sr., now lives, great spring, corner George Lewis. Teste: Thomas Feemster, Robert Knox, Wm. Black. Delivered: John McCreery, 2d December, 1786.

Page 86.—16th August, 1765. William Black and Sarah ( ) to Alex. Black, £40, 125 acres in Forks of Cowpasture River; corner to land in possession of said William Black; corner James Knox. Delivered: Alex. Black, 17th May, 1792.

Page 88.—16th August, 1765. William Jackson to Francis Jackson, £90, 170 acres in Cowpasture; corner to land in possession of Wm. Jackson, opposite land in possession of Alex Black. Teste: Robert Knox. Delivered: Francis Jackson, October Court, 1769.

Page 90.—20th August, 1765. Robert Campbell and Margret ( ) to Charles Campbell, £20, 220 acres; corner Charles Campbell; corner John Erwin. Teste: James ( ) Trotter, John ( ) Craney, Jno. Trimble.

Page 93.—20th August, 1765. Robert ( ) Brown, plantationer, and Mary ( ) to James Trotter, £250, 300 acres on Culton's Branch of North River of Shanandoe, south side Anderson's Branch. Teste: Charles ( ) Campbell, John ( ) Craney.

Page 94.—20th August, 1765. James Trotter, plantationer, and Mary ( ) to Wm. Sprowle, £60, 170 acres in Borden's tract; corner Samuel McCutchen's land, line of Beverley Manor. Deed of feoffment. Delivered: Wm. Sprowl, 15th May, 1771.

Page 95.—20th August, 1765. Same to same, £90, two tracts joining each other and Beverley Manor and Borden's tracts lines: A, 82 acres in Beverley Manor, adjoining above, corner Wm. Dean's land; B, 218 acres in Borden's tract, corner Samuel McCutchen's land; corner James Shields, deceased. Deed of feoffment.

Page 98.—8th June, 1765. Andrew Hays and Margaret ( ) to William Miller, £30, 337 acres on branches of James.

Page 100.—17th August, 1765. Henry ( ) Campbell and Sarah ( ) and James Culton and Marray to David Scott, £55, 200 acres in Borden's tract; corner said Campbell's, crossing Back Creek; corner John Robinson. Delivered: David Scott, 1768.

Page 102.—20th August, 1765. Hugh Hays and Mary to William Walker, £73.16, 176 acres in Beverley Manor; corner said Hays, Henry's line, Henry's and Purris's line. Teste: Mathew Huston, James Henry, John Weir. Delivered: Wm. Walker, August, 1767.

Page 105.—David Robinson and Anneble (Annable) to Israel Christian, 10th August, 1765, £40, 167 acres by patent, 10th March, 1756, on Buffalo of Roanoke. Teste: David Robinson, Thos. Ramsey, Robert Buchanan, Daniel McNeil, James Robertson.

Page 107.—18th May, 1765. Alexander Henderson and Jane ( ) to James Bratton, £80.10, 320 acres granted to Alex. by David Henderson, 18th June, 1752, on South River; corner David Henderson's line, crossing the Great Spring; corner John McConnolly. Delivered: James Bratton, 1st March, 1768.

Page 109.—2d January, 1761. James Clark, Sr., to John Clark, £50, 80 acres in Beverley Manor, on Back Creek, a branch of Middle River, and part of 380 acres belonging to James Clerk. Teste: Wm. and Samuel Clark. Delivered: Samuel Clark, 19th November, 1770.

Page 111.—20th August, 1765. John Poage to Robert Poage, £100, 190 acres in Forks of James on a branch of Buffalo Creek. Teste: John Poage, George Givens, Hugh Allen. Delivered: John Poage, December, 1778.

Page 113.—20th August, 1765. Same to John Poage, Jr., £100, 270 acres lying as above; corner Robert Poage; corner Hugh Mair's land.

Page 116.—17th August 1765. Samuel Porter, of Dromore township, County of Lancaster, Pennsylvania, schoolmaster, by John Mitchel, of Augusta County, to James Dryden, £25, 300 acres below the Fork of Buffalo Creek. Teste: David Dryden, Arthur McClure. Delivered: David Dryden, son of James, 1st April, 1791.

Page 118.—19th August, 1765. Samuel Todd and Jane to William and John McKee, £170, 400 on head of North Branch of Buffalo Creek, Borden's line. Teste: Benj. Hawkins, Joseph Robinson, Alex. Evans. Delivered: Wm. McKee, September, 1775.

Page 121.—6th August, 1765. William Preston and Susanna to Edward Hinds, £20, 130 acres by patent, 3d May, 1763, on a small branch of the Bull Pasture. Delivered: Thos. Hamilton, January, 1772.

Page 123.—6th August, 1765. William Preston and Susanna to Daniel McCormick, £40, 204 acres on North Fork of Roanoke, Shirkey's line, walnut in Cupher's line.

Page 126.—6th August, 1765. Same to Michael Cloyd, £20, 50 acres on Roanoke, William Armstrong's line, patented to William, 23d May, 1763. Sent to said Cloyd by hands of Chas. Lofland, 2d January, 1794.

Page 129.—9th September, 1764. Plackerd Scilor, of Orange County, North Carolina, to Nicholas Welsh, of Bedford County, £40, 162 acres patented to James Patton, deceased, 3d November, 1750, by him conveyed to said Scilor, 8th December, 1763, on Craig's Creek. Teste: Anthony Bledsoe, Jno. Buchanan, John and Mary Mills.

Page 131.—10th December, 1764. John Mills and Mary (Mearey) to

William Carvin, £50, 325 acres on Little Bottom Creek, a branch of Roanoke, corner Huff's land. Delivered: Thos. Madison, 10th January, 1769.

Page 134.—5th December, 1764. Same to same, £30, 180 acres, part of 500 acres patented to said John, on the Bent Mountain, waters of Roanoke; corner Alex. Ingram; corner Leonard Huff.

Page 136.—10th December, 1764. Same to same, £50, 341 acres on Carvin's Creek, a branch of Roanoke, called the Cove.

Page 139.—20th August, 1765. Archibald Alexander to Joseph Alexander, £30, 256 acres, crossing the South River. Teste: John Lowrey, John Peoples, Nathaniel McClure.

Page 141.—21st August, 1765. Samuel Hodge and Elizabeth ( ) to William Kinkead, £20, 350 acres on Calfpasture, part of 700 acres patented to William Beverley, 13th August, 1743. Teste: Thos. Hugart. Delivered: Wm. Kinkead, July, 1769.

Page 143.—20th August, 1765. Philip Lung, eldest son and heir of Paul Long, deceased, who was eldest son and heir of Philip Lung, deceased, of Frederick County, to Henry Lung, of Augusta, £200, 350 acres on Shanandore River, at the upper end of Richard Mauding's 2,000-acre tract, purchased bq Philip, Sr., from Henry Downs, pine near Peaked Mountain, Paul Lung's line, Scaler's line. Delivered: Henry Lung, October, 1766.

Page 146.—15th May, 1765. Same (Long) and Kathrine ( ) to Henry Long, brother of said Paul, and uncle to said Philip, Jr., £100, 240 acres sold by Richard Mauldin to Philip, Sr., 22d September, 1743, descended to Paul and from Paul to Philip Jr., on Shanandore River, Henry Long's other land.

Page 149.—21st August, 1765. Andrew and Margret Hays to John Misscampble. £50, 250 acres in Borden's grant; corner Andrew Fitzpatrick's line on Back Creek; Thomas Paxton's corner. Delivered: James Misscampble. November Court, 1773.

Page 150.—17th August, 1765. Borden's executors to William Pollock, £30. 190 acres, part of 92100; corner Thomas Beard in John Montgomery's line; corner Patrick Hays, Beverley Manor line, James and Samuel McDowell, and Wm. McKee.

Page 153.—9th August, 1765. Borden's executors to Joseph Weir, £35, 199 acres, part of 92100; corner John Weir, Cowden's line.

Page 156.—17th August, 1765. Same to John Weir, £35, 201 acres, part of 92100; Wm. McCandless' corner. Delivered: Jno. Weir, February, 1783.

Page 159.—21st August, 1765. William McFeeters and Mary ( ) alias Mary Perey, executors of Thomas Peary (Peery), to Samuel McNab (Mary was widow of Thomas but is now married to William), £42, 225 acres on Middle River of Shanandore; corner John Campbell's land. Teste: John Malcom, John Jameson, David Frame.

Page 162.—21st August, 1765. Same to John Perey, £12.10, 50 acres on a branch of Middle River of Shanandore; corner Samuel McNab.

Page 165.—19th August, 1765. Margret ( ) Risk. Jr., relict to James Risk. deceased, to John Risk, Jr., £—, 200 acres at foot of Brown Hill in line of Wm. McCutchen's land. Teste: John Risk, John Worick, Moses Moore. Delivered: Jno. Risk, Jr., 19th November, 1770.

Page 167.—16th July, 1765. James Pollock to James Pollock, Jr., (the name is in the deed "Poage" but is signed and indexed "Pollock"), £50, 290 acres on Great Calfpasture; corner Crocket's land; corner Weem's land. Delivered: Jas. Pollock, 1784.

Page 169.—18th August, 1765. John Mills and Mary to Israel Christian, £50, 122 acres on a branch of James River, line of Sloan's land. Delivered: Wm. Fleming, August, 1766.

Page 171.—19th August, 1765. Same to same, £50, 150 acres on waters of James River, Adam Looney's line.

Page 174.—17th August, 1765. Same to same, £50, 178 acres by patent, 20th September, 1745, on a branch of James River, beginning on a branch of Looney's Mill Run.

Page 177.—8th July, 1763. Robert Williams, of Orange County, North Carolina, to William Walker, of Bedford County, £33.18.3, 275 acres conveyed to Robert by James Patton, 17th December, 1753, on Craig's Creek. Teste: John Mills, David Looney. Delivered: William Walker, March, 1766.

Page 179.—21st August, 1765. Robert Poage, of Albemarle, to Jared Erwin, £70, 135 acres on a branch of North River called Nowls Branch; corner Abraham Smith's survey.

Page 181.—5th September, 1764. Joseph Steps, of Orange County, to Daniel Smith, gent., £45, bill sale for a negro slave. Teste: Alex. West, John Boucher.

Page 182.—20th August, 1765. James Patton's executors to Patrick Calhoon, late of Augusta, but now of Province of South Carolina, yeoman, £14.10, on Reed Creek whereon Patrick formerly lived, 322 acres by a survey made by said John Buchanan, 9th April, 1752, John Vance's line.

Page 185.—15th March, 1765. Absolum ( ) Luney and Margret to Peter Luney, heir-at-law of Peter Luney, deceased, £80, 180 acres on Long Run, a branch of James; corner another tract belonging to Peter, formerly in possession of Robert Luney, Sr. Teste: David Looney. Delivered: Peter Looney, 26th September, 1783.

Page 189.—2d February, 1765. James Gorrell by William Robinson, to David Robinson. James Gorrell, of Baltimore County, Maryland, constituted William his attorney on 30th October, 1763. £79.10, 215 acres on North Branch Roanoke, part of 620 acres conveyed by Patton to William and James Gorrell, Tobias Bright's line, now in possession of Dr. Thomas Walker, John Robinson's land. Teste. Thomas Barnes.

Page 191.—21st August, 1765. Robert McClenachan and Andrew Lewis to Samuel Furguson (Farguson), £2.10, ¼ acre in Staunton, part of County lot 15, of which James Shaw is now possessed. Delivered: Samuel Farguson, 17th August, 1772.

Page 193.—22d August, 1765. Nicholas Leeper, of Mecklenburg County, North Carolina, to John Leeper, of Augusta, £20, 200 acres on Naked Creek whereon James Leeper, deecased, formerly lived. Delivered: John Leeper, June, 1777.

Page 195.—17th July, 1765. William ( ) Dean and Sarah ( ) to John Dean, £100, 327 acres, part of 820 acres patented to Adam Dickenson, 1st June, 1751, on Jackson's River; corner James Borelan, white oaks on Indian Camp Branch. Teste: John Shields, Thos. ( ) Brown, Mathew Thomson. Delivered: Jno. Dean, 16th March, 1772.

Page 198.—20th August, 1765. John Bowyer to Peter Looney, eldest son of Peter Looney, deceased. Whereas Peter, Sr., and his brother David Looney, on 11th October, 1759, purchased of Robert Looney, father of Peter, Sr., and David, the tract Robert was living on, situated on James River and —— Creek, excepting the part on the south side the Creek, which Robert had some time before exchanged for a place called the Draper place, with Daniel Looney, another son of Robert's, notwithstanding which, said Robert under pretence that Peter and David had not complied with their contract, refused to make conveyance, but sold the same to said John Bowyer. Peter, Sr., soon after making the purchase, died, leaving Peter, his eldest son, infant, who, with said David, brought suit against Robert Looney and John Bowyer, in which it was decreed that John reconvey to Peter, Jr. 80 acres on James River.

Page 200.—20th August, 1765. Same to David Looney. Similar deed as above, 140 acres; corner Col. John Smith; corner to above tract.

Page 202.—8th March, 1765. John Davidson to William Finley, £33.10, conveys household goods and horses. Mortgage.

Page 203.—22d August, 1765. County of Augusta by Patrick Martin and Felix Gilbert to James Hill, £11, lot 18 in Staunton, joining the lot whereon James Huston now dwells, on southwest, ½ acres. Teste: Geo. Wilson and John Stuart. Livery by handful of earth. Delivered: James Hill, July, 1772.

Page 206.—23d August, 1765. James Hughes and Euphie (Euphemia) and William Wilson and Mary, of Albemarle County, to John Hunter, of Staunton, £40, part of lot 14 excluding a house on northwest corner where Edward Long now lives; lot faces James Huston's front on the south and James Hughes on the west. Delivered: Jno. Hunter, May, 1770.

Page 208.—18th August, 1765. James Finley, heir-at-law and administrator of estate of Robert Finley, and Agness ( ) to James Huston, £28, 37 acres woodland in Beverley Manor on the Chesnut Ridge, part of 155 acres of woodland surveyed to Robert, 22d February, 1753, joining Felix Gilbert and William Preston; also ¼ of an acre lot in Staunton, No. 13, opposite the lots of George Wilson and Samuel Moor. Delivered: Thos. Smith, 25th September, 1772.

Page 210.—23d August, 1765. Joshua ( ) McCormack to Israel Christian £—, 1 bay horse. Teste: Samuel Robinson, Wm. Christian, Andrew Johnston.

Page 211.—20th August, 1765. Alex. ( ) Campbell and Frances ( ) to Alex. Stewart, £62, 100 acres on South River, on Red Banks, conveyed to Campbell by Alex. Henderson, 19th May, 1762, who purchased it from James Edmondson, 17th March, 1757.

Page 213.—14th October, 1765. John Willey (Wiley) to Thomas Wilson, £100, on Buffalo Creek in Forks of James, 170 acres patented to John 15th June, 1760. Delivered: Thomas Wilson, March Court, 1769.

Page 216.—10th October, 1765. George Poage and Rachel ( ) to William Logan, £115, 210 acres conveyed to George by Thomas Hadley, in Forks of James River and Craigs Creek, opposite John Crawford, land of George Poage. Teste: Andrew ( ) Crawford, Jonathan ( ) Richeson, John Kirkland.

Page 218.—11th October, 1765. David Campbell to John Campbell, £5,

232 acres woodland ground. Teste: John Buchanan, Robert McNutt, Arthur Campbell. Delivered: John Campbell, March, 1769.

Page 220.—21st May, 1765. John Dunlap to Alexander Dunlap, his brother, £10, 100 acres patented to William Dunlap, father to said John, 1st June, 1750, and descended to John, eldeste son and heir-at-law, on Jackson's River, at the mouth of Meadow Creek. Delivered: Robert Bratton, May, 1773.

Page 222.—15th October, 1765. Robert Young and Jean ( ) to Isaac Carson, £90, 265 acres on a branch of Middle River of Shanandoe conveyed by John Young to Robert, 16th May, 1759. Teste: James Henderson, John Burnsides, John Young, Jr. Delivered: John Francis, March, 1768.

Page 225.—7th March, 1765. James Hollis and Anne to George Patterson, £70, 395 acres by patent, 7th August, 1761, on waters of Catawba; corner Burden's land, Thomas Ramsey's line. Teste: Wm. Davis.

Page 228.—23d September, 1765. William Baskin and Mary ( ) to Hugh Donaghe (Donaho), 232 acres on a branch of Buffelo Run; corner James Beard, patented to William, 8th February, 1749. Teste: Edward Sampson, James Gamwell, Thos. Patterson. Delivered: Grantee, 9th Dec., 1803.

Page 230.—16th October, 1765. John Hutcheson and Isabella ( ) to Samuel McCune, £20, 277 acres on Christian's Creek, part of a tract surveyed for George Hutcheson. Teste: John Hunter, George Rodgers, William Wallas.

Page 233.—7th August, 1765. John Scott and Catherine, William Davis and Mary, to William McCutchen, £105, 200 acres in Borden's tract; corner Francis Randolson, James Anderson's line; corner said Anderson's and Andrew Hays'; corner Thomas Paxton; corner Samuel Daviss. Teste: Andrew Hays, Samuel McDowell, Samuel Henderson, William Patton. Delivered to John McCutchen, executor of William, 3d June, 1793.

Page 236.—5th October, 1765. Nicholas Leeper to Margaret Leeper, £105, 227 acres in Beverley Manor; corner James Moody, said James Leeper's line. Teste: Andrew, Gawin and John Leeper. Delivered: Margaret Leeper, May, 1767.

Page 239.—9th August, 1765. John ( ) Allison and Janet ( ) to Charles Allison, £25, 195 acres on Mill Creek of James River; corner James Gilmore; corner John Poage. Delivered: Charles Allison, 31st January, 1771.

Page 241.—15th October, 1765. Edward McColgen and Marion (Mary Ann) to Hugh McFadden, £68, 300 acres in Borden's tract, on Broad Spring Run, Jno. Hanley's line. Delivered: Robert Henderson. Delivered: 1769.

Page 244.—4th September, 1765. John McMahan and Isabella of Frederick County, to Benj. Logan, £100, 400 acres on North River of Shanandow on the next spring branch below the mouth of Cooks Creek. Delivered: George Mallo, March, 1773.

Page 247.—15th October, 1765. Henry ( ) Miller and Elenor ( ) to Andrew Hays, Gent., £55, 231 acres in Borden's tract, John Walker's line by edge of Moffett's Creek, Oak on Back Creek, the forks of Walker's Creek. Teste: Andrew and Wm. McCampbell, Andrew Hayes.

Page 249.—15th October, 1765. Andrew Hays and Margaret to John

Kelley, £46, 231 acres in Borden's tract, John Walker's line by north edge of Moffet's Creek; ash on Back Creek as above. Delivered: John Kelley, 10th August, 1773.

Page 251.—11th October, 1765. Borden's executors to Andrew McCampbell, 73 acres, £6, in 92,100; oak on Teas Creek; corner said McCampbell's, Hugh Cunningham's line; Samuel Norwood's corner. Teste: John Wardlaw, Andrew Hays, Andrew Hays.

Page 253.—19th August, 1765. Same to Halbert McClure, 300 acres, part of 92,100; corner Robt. Faris; corner Moses Trimble. Teste: Wm. Lusk, Charles Campbell, Robt. Gay.

Page 255.—14th October, 1765. Same to Robert Gay, 100 acres, part of 92,100, oak on Moffet's opposite John Rosemand's old survey, opposite George Henderson's land, post in the Barrens. Delivered to Robert and Archibald Rhea, devisees, 17th January, 1803.

Page 259.—9th October, 1765. Charles Hays and Barbara to Andrew Hays, Jr., £10, 90 acres in Borden's tract; corner John Miss Campbell's on James Anderson's line; walnut on the bank of Back Creek. Teste: Andrew Hays, Sr., John Hays, Wm. McCampbell.

Page 261.—8th October, 1765. Same to John Hays, £20, 160 acres in Borden's tract; corner Andrew Hays' in John Miss Campbell's line; corner James Anderson. Delivered: Jacob Anderson, 27th July, 1772.

Page 264.—15th October, 1765. William Robinson to Patrick Denny, £51, 80 acres on Cunningham's Creek of James River between House Mountain and North Mountain.

Page 267.—1st October, 1765. Samuel McDowell and Mary to Christopher Vingard, £60, 300 acres patented to his father, John McDowell, 10th November, 1742, and said Samuel is eldest son and heir-at-law, whereon said Vingard now lives, on James River. Delivered: Christopher Vingard, 6th July, 1793.

Page 269.—4th October, 1765. Same to James McDowell, £30, 60 acres in Borden's tract; corner James McDowell. Delivered: Samuel McDowell, May Court, 1773.

Page 271.—8th October, 1765. James McKee and Lydia ( ) to Thomas Kilpatrick, £68.10, 300 acres on Kerr's Creek; corner Samuel Norwood on Kerr's Creek, John Wiley's line. Delivered: Thomas Kilpatrick, 4th January, 1772.

Page 274.—20th May, 1765. James Thomas and Sarah to Evan Thomas, £15, 165 acres, part of 350 acres patented to Cornelius Cook, 20th September, 1748, and conveyed by him to Reece Thomas, deceased, father to said James Thomas, on Brock's Creek. Delivered: Evan Thomas, June, 1770. Teste: John Thomas.

Page 277.—20th May, 1765. Same to Reece Thomas, £15, 185 acres, part of 350 above patented to Reece Thomas, father of said James and Reece Thomas, as above. Teste: James Marshall, Jonathan Douglass. Conrod ( ) Kuster, John Thomas.

Page 280.—12th October, 1765. William Smith and Mary, of Hampshire County, to James Thomas, £67, on south side of Timber Ridge, on a draft of Linvil's Creek, patented to William Smith, deceased, father of said William, 10th March, 1756, 154 acres. Teste: John Dunbar, Rülen May, Jacob ( ) Trumbo, John Thomas, Conrad Humble. Delivered: Nicholas Mose, December, 1768.

283.—15th October, 1765. Patrick ( ) Willson to George Weaver, £130, 380 acres, art of 5,000 acres patented to Jacob Stover, 3,100 acres thereof being conveyed by Jacob to Christopher Francisco and recorded in Orange County, on Shanando River; corner Morris Pound whereon he lives. Delivered: Geo. Weaver, 20th December, —94.

Page 286.—15th October, 1765. John Jameson and Mary ( ), late of the County of Augusta, to Archibald Armstrong, £50, 280 acres on Jackson's River; corner land in possession of James Ewing patented to John Jamison, 26th September, 1760. Teste: Charles Teas, David Bell, John Ward.

Page 289.—9th October, 1765. John Edmiston and Margaret to John Berry, £43, 170 acres, part of Borden's 92,100; corner John Stewart ( ). Teste: Samuel Buchanan, George Dougherty, Robt. Buchanan, Samuel Edmiston.

Page 292.—18th May, 1765. Robert Buchanan and Mary ( ) to William Alexander, £100, 208 acres, part of Borden's 92,100; corner Robert Telford; corner Robert Steel. Teste: James Henry.

Page 295.—15th October, 1765. John Davis, son and heir of Nathaniel Davis, deceased, and Sarah Davis, relict of Nathaniel to Moses Cavet, £35, 115 acres by patent, 30th August, 1763, on Bufflo Creek. Teste: John Maxwell, Audly Paul, George Wilson. Delivered: Samuel McNabb, June, 1779, by order.

Page 298.—27th Setember, 1765. John McCoy and James McCoy to Joseph Malcom, £30, 160 acres on Mossey Creek, the lower end of the place this said John and James McCoy lives on; David Ralstone's land. patented to John and James, 25th September, 1762. Teste: Jacob Gallespie, John and Alexander Malcom. Delivered: Joseph Malcom, 14th November, 1772.

Page 301.—15th October, 1765. Robert Beverley by Thomas Lewis to Walter Cunningham, of Town of Staunton, Gent., £45, 107 acres, part of 1,550 acres part of the Mill tract in Beverley Manor adjoining the lots of the Town of Staunton; corner James Brown's lease land, James Miller's line; corner William Beverley's land; corner Col. Lewis' lot.

Page 304.—15th October, 1765. Jeremiah Harrison and Catherine to John Hinton, of County of Berks, Province Pennsylvania, £267.10, 400 acres on Linvel's Creek; corner John Wright, David Ralstone; corner conveyed by Abraham Hite to Jeremiah, 31st December, 1760, part of 1,200 acres conveyed to Abraham by McCoy et als., to whom it was originally granted. Delivered: John Hinton, August, 1768.

Page 307.—3d September, 1765. William Graham and Priscilla to Philip Watkins, £65, 160 acres on Lee's Creek, a branch of Catawba. Teste: Wm. Davis, Francis Smith, Robt. Breckinridge, Is. Christian. Delivered: Martin McFerrin per receipt 2d September, 1799.

Page 310.—2d October, 1765. George Patterson, eldest son and heir of John Patterson, to John Roseman, £30, 380 acres on Moffet's Creek. David Mitchell.

Page 313.—11th October, 1765. William Bryan, Sr., to William Bryan, Jr., son of William, Sr., £5.5, 133 acres on Roanoke River adjoining Joseph Love. Delivered: Thos. Madison, January, 1771.

Page 315.—16th October, 1765. John Maxwell and Mary to Benj. Estill,

£250, 238 acres on main branch of James River. Delivered: Jas. Poage, per order, December, 1775.

Page 318.—15th October, 1765. James Hutton (Hatton) and Ally ( ) to David Wallace, £61.10, 84 acres on a north branch of Buffalo Creek in Forks of James joining land formerly William Todd's, now the property of Wm. McKee. Teste: Wm. McKee.

Page 320.—6th September, 1765. Lilley Bowin, widow and executrix of John Bowen to Henry Bowen, son of said John and Lilley, £55, 197 acres, part of 380 acres whereon John formerly dwelt on James River.

Page 323.—15th October, 1765. Nathaniel Evins and Mary to John Alcorn, £30, 120 acres on a branch of Looney's Creek. Delivered: Robert Doage, October Court, 1769.

Page 326.—2d October, 1765. Henry Bowin and Anne to William Mc-Alhany, £50, 197 acres by deed from Lilley Brown, p. 320, supra.

Page 328.—11th October, 1765. William ( ) Kelley and Margaret ( ) to Anthony Keely, £5, 95 acres in Borden's grant; corner James Moore; corner Alexander Walker. Teste: Alexander Walker, James and John Moore.

Page 330.—30th May, 1765. Borden's executors to Andrew Fitzpatrick, £20, 150 acres, part of 92,100; corner Domnick Morren, on John Kirk's line. Teste: Samuel and James McDowell, Wm. Davis.

Page 334.—15th October, 1765. Robert ( ) Armstrong and Elizabeth ( ) to William Armstrong, £100, 200 acres in Beverley Manor on a branch of Christian's Creek; William Robinson's corner, Joseph Mills' land. Delivered: Wm. Armstrong, October, 1766.

Page 336.—14th October, 1765. Archibald Alexander, executor of Benj. Borden and Magdalene Bowyer, administratrix of John McDowell and mother of Samuel McDowell, orphan and heir-at-law of John McDowell, to William Lusk (contracted by Benj., Sr., to John McDowell). John covenanted to convey to Wm. Armstrong 300 acres for £9 in two tracts. Armstrong entered into possession, 200 acres thereof on Mill Creek in Borden's grant, and 100 acres on a west branch of James River called Catawbo Creek and made improvements on both places. John McDowell died 1742 without making conveyance. Armstrong brought suit in chancery, in which in 1752 it was ordered that conveyance be made to Armstrong, but Armstrong has covenanted to convey to Wm. Lusk the 200-acre tract for £26.10, beginning at a black oak; corner Isaac Taylor on Mill Creek, Daniel Lyle's line; corner Daniel Lyle and Edward Tarr. Teste: James and Samuel McDowell, Christopher Vinyard. Delivered: Wm. Lusk, November, 1766.

Page 342.—16th October, 1765. Alexander Hamilton and Margaret to Wm. Hamilton, £100, 238 acres on Jackson's River. Teste: A. Thompson, Andrew Hays. Delivered: Richard Morris, November Court, 1773.

Page 345.—14th September, 1765. James McClung and Mary ( ) to Henry McClung, £60, 150 acres, part of 390 acres whereon James now liveth; corner tract belonging to Henry McClung. Teste: James Dryden, Samuel McClung. Delivered: James McClung, Jr., 7th April, 1796.

Page 348.—14th September, 1765. Same to William McClung, £50, 212 acres on Mill Creek; corner Henry McClung; corner Jacob Gray, Wm. Dean's line; corner survey intended for James Greenlee. Delivered: James McClung, 10th June, 1789.

Page 351.—15th October, 1765. James Dryden to David Dryden, Jr., £50, 144 acres in Forks of James below fork of Buffelo Creek. Delivered: D. Dryden, Jr., October, 1775.

Page 352.— — October, 1765. John ( ) Roseman and Gabriel Jones to George Patterson, £150. Bond conditioned, whereas John Patterson, late of Augusta, deceased, father of George Patterson, was seised of 380 acres which he sold to Joseph Kenedy, but never made title, and Joseph sold to John Roseman for £45.10, and either mistake or design the said Kennedy conveyed to John Roseman, 19th August, 1752, though the title was in Patterson and devolved upon the above named Geo. Patterson as eldest son of John, and George has conveyed to John Roseman; if John and Gabriel keep said George safe of law suits, troubles, &c., then to be void.

Page 355.—16th October, 1765. Ephraim Richardson, of Hampshire, to Adam Harper, £32, 200 acres on South Branch Potomac at mouth of Dry Branch patented 22d September, 1757, to James Parsons. Delivered: Adam Harper, May Court, 1774.

Page 357.—9th October, 1765. Thomas Parsons, Jr., of Hampshire, and Mary ( ) to Leonard Seaman, £31, 200 acres on South Branch Potomac patented 22d September, 1757.

Page 360.—26th September, 1765. Thomas Parsons and Esther ( ) of Hampshire to Peter Flesher, £50, 200 acres on South Branch Potomac. Delivered: Wm. Flesher, 14th May, 1787.

Page 363.—3rd October, 1765. Peter Cockran and Margaret to James McAfee, £40, 32 acres on James River.

Page 366.—25th May, 1765. Col. Andrew Lewis and Mr. Robt. McClenachan to James Shaw, £20, lot 15 in Staunton being that half of the lot joining the lot in Staunton now in the possession of Samuel Moore, containing ¼ acre. Teste: Wm. Crow, Alexander Gibson, Wm. Kinkead.

Page 369.—12th October, 1765. John ( ) McCleland to Edward Sharp, £30, 60 acres by patent 3d November, 1750, and conveyed by Patton to Charles Milligan, 17th November, 1752, and conveyed by Milligan to McClelan, on head of Looney's Creek.

Page 372.—12th October, 1765. Same to Same, £45, 84 acres by patent, 23d May, 1763, at the Big Meadows, part of Zachary Lewis' order of Council.

Page 375.—10th October, 1765. John ( ) Roseman and Sarah to Robert Gay, £120, 380 acres, 20 p., on Moffet's Creek. Teste: Francis ( ) Railey. Delivered: Robt. Rhea, one of the devisees, 17th January, 1803.

Page 378.—16th October, 1765. Robert Gay and Sarah ( ) to Samuel Vance and Wm. Hutcheson, £60, 364 acres on Back River, to Back Creek to Back River.

Page 381.—16th October, 1765. James Trimble and Sarah of Green Spring, Augusta County, to Peter Haall, £114, two tracts containing 630 acres on a branch of South Branch of Potomac above Crab Bottom, and a tract containing 300 acres. Delivered: Capt. Peter Hull, 23d December, 1786.

Page 383.—21st August, 1765. Robert Breckenridge and Lettice to Stephen Loy, £230 (paid by said Martin Loy), 245 acres in Beverley Manor conveyed to Robert, 17th May, 1749.

Page 386.—10th October, 1765. James Patton's executors to Wm.

Preston, £5.13.4, 80 acres by patent 3d November, 1750, on Daily Branch of Catawba. Teste: David Mitchell.

Page 389.—16th October, 1765. Thomas Lewis, eldest son and heir-at-law of John Lewis, Gent., deceased, who was surviving patentee of James Patton, Gent., deceased, to Andrew Hamilton, £50, 600 acres patented to Patton and Lewis, 30th August, 1743, lying on Elk Creek, a branch of Calfpasture.

Page 392.—15th October, 1765. John Smith to William and Thomas Crow, £50, two several tracts of 195 acres and 213 acres on Craig's Creek, patented to James Patton, 3d November, 1750, and conveyed by Patton to Smith, 195 acres.

Page 395.—15th October, 1765. William Clark and Margret to Wm. Reah, £60, 65 acres on Jackson's River, purchased by Wm. Clark from John Davis and he from Thos. Hugart, the original patentee.

Page 398.—14th October, 1765. Daniel Harrison to Daniel Smith, £50, 200 acres on Muddy Creek and Dry River, high bank of rocks opposite an island. Delivered: Daniel Smith, March Court, 1772.

Page 400.—15th October, 1765. John Finley acknowledges receipt from his father ,James Finley, one bond of John Frows; one account of Cap. Israel Christian, which John takes as his full part of his uncle Robert Finley's estate. Delivered: James Finley, May, 1766.

Page 402.—4th March, 1763. Thomas Hill, of Roan County, North Carolina, to David Miller, £20, 70 acres conveyed to Thomas by Col. James Patton, 21st March, 1753, on Goose Creek, or North Branch of Roanoke; corner Elijah Isaac; corner Benj. Ogle's land, now the property of said David Miller. Teste: David Mitchell, Daniel ( ) McCormick. Delivered: Andrew Miller, son of David, 2d April, 1789.

Page 405.—17th October, 1765. James Sawyers (Sayers) and Rachel ( ) to Sampson Sawyers, £100, 355 acres; corner Robert Rennick; corner one Crawford's land.

Page 408.—13th October, 1765. Samuel McDowell, eldest son and heir of John McDowell, deceased, and Mary to George Skillern, £300, 400 acres on James River.

Page 411.—14th October, 1765. John Stewart and Mary to Francis Stewart, £130, 240 acres on Cook's Creek, pine in Thompson's line; corner McDonald's land; corner Hafe's land. Delivered: Francis Stewart, 2d March, 1767.

Page 414.—2d October, 1765. David Wallace and his wife to Henry Black, £40, 210 acres on waters of Carr's Creek, part of Borden's 92100; corner James McNabb. Teste: James anr Samuel McDowell, James Greenlee, John McKee.

Page 417.—7th October, 1765. Samuel Givens to James Burnsides, £40, 100 acres, part of 339 acres conveyed to Samuel by Richard Bodkin, on Bullpasture. Delivered: James Burnsides, August Court, 1768.

Page 418.—17th October, 1765. John Stewart to David Stewart, £100, one negro woman and child, four feather beds and furniture. Teste: James Ray. Delivered: John Stewart, April, 1766.

Page 420.—15th October, 1765. James Arbuckle to Mathew Arbuckle, £70, on James River below Island Ford, 400 acres patented to James, 5th September, 1744. Teste: Randal Lockhart. Delivered: George Mathews, 6th December, 1772.

Page 423.—20th May, 1765. Walter Trimble and Rosanna ( ) to their son, Robert Trimble, £95, 370 acres on Free Mason's Run, a branch of North River Shanandore. Teste: George Moffet, William Shanan, Robert Gragg.

Page 426.—20th September, 1765. John Harrison, Sr., to Reuben Harrison, his son, £10, part of two tracts: 1st contains 117 acres, part of 234 acres patented to John, 25th June, 1747, on Smith's Creek; the other tract contains 83 acres, part of 166 acres patented to John, 25th June, 1747, on Smith's Creek. Teste: Daniel Smith, Jos. Rutherford, Wm. Kavanaugh, Jane ( ) Smith. Delivered: Reuben Harrison, November, 1766.

Page 429.—16th June, 1765. Patrick Duffy to Elizabeth Hartgrove, £5. one mare. Teste: Francis Hargrove.

Page 430.—21st October, 1765. Daniel McAnare and Hannah ( ) to Buchanan and Thompson, executors of Col. James Patton, £100, 390 acres on a branch of Woods River, part of a large tract patented to Col. James Patton; corner land of Wm. Sayers; corner Harman's land. Delivered: William Campbell, December, 1770.

Page 433.—21st October, 1765. James Sayers and Rachel to Daniel McAnare, £200, 140 acres, part of 400 patented to Daniel, 10th June, 1740, and conveyed to James, 29th May, 1756, bounded by tract laid off for Thomas Gardner, also a tract laid off for Alex. Gibson. Delivered: Daniel McAnare, 4th January, 1773.

Page 436.—22d October, 1765. John ( ) Taylor and Mary ( ) to Benj. Bennet, £45, 320 acres in Forks of James; corner Michael Finney's old survey. Teste: John Leo.

Page 439.—5th October, 1765. Patton's executors to Andrew Woods, of Albemarle County, £100, 275 acres on North Fork of Roanoke, part of large tract patented to James Patton, 3d November, 1750, on Goose Creek, now called the Nort Fork of Roanoke, line of Pepper's land, David Miller's land. Teste: Wm. Christian, Edward Carvin, John Neelley, Dr.

Page 442.—19th October, 1765. John Bowyer to Margaret Looney, only child and heiress of Daniel Looney, deceased. Whereas Robert Looney was seised of a tract on James River and Looney's Creek, and sold so much as lay on south side of the Creek to his son Daniel, in consideration of a tract called Draper's place, but conveyed the whole tract to John Bowyer, and Daniel dying soon after, left Margaret, his only daughter and heir, who brought suit against John Bowyer and Robert Looney (decree, 24th May, 1765), and this conveyance in accordance therewith, conveys the land conveyed to him by Robert Looney.

Page 445.—20th May, 1766. William Watterson to John King, £17, 200 acers on southeast side Naked Creek, beginning John King's land above a mill pond. Teste: Wm. Frame, James Gambell, Samuel McCutchan. Delivered: John King, 22d May, 1769.

Page 446.—20th November, 1765. James Gilmore to James Arbuckle, Release of mortgage, 20th March, 1764.

Page 448.—15th October, 1765. Alex. Craighead and Jeane ( ), of Mecklenburg County, North Carolina (paster), to Archibald Alexander, power attorney to convey a tract of land containing by survey 310 acres. Teste: Pat. Calhoun, John and Thomas Poage. (Name signed Cragehead.)

Page 450.—28th October, 1765. Charles Crosson and Martha to William

Harshman, £200, 230 acres on Shanandore River. Teste: Conrad Bloss, Wm. Owler, Michael Coker (Coger).

Page 452.—William Owler died before 20th May, 1766, date of recording.

Page 453.—15th May, 1766. John Young and Mary to John Davis, £67, 280 acres on West Fork of James River called Back Creek. Teste: James Hughes, Samuel Moor and Samuel Cowden.

Page 456.—20th May, 1765. Thomas Beard and Jean to John Beard, their son, £40, 183 acres on a branch of Cathey's River called Jenning's Branch; corner Daniel McNare. Delivered: John Beard, January, 1769.

Page 459.—20th May, 1766. Samuel Craig and Margrett to James Gamble, £—, 97 acres, part of 144 acres patented to Alex. Craig, 10th March, 1756, corner James Patterson; corner Young's line. Delivered: John Archer, Esq., January, 1768.

Page 461.—21st May, 1766. Joseph Love and Mary, one of the daughters of Joseph Tees, deceased, and William Tees, eldest son and heir of Joseph Tees, to Samuel Caldwell, late of the Province of Pennsylvania, but now of County of Augusta. Joseph Tees devised to his daughter Mary Love, by the name of Mary, the place he bought of John Wilson during her life, &c., if she lived thereon, but she revomed, and the wdow, thinking the title descended to her, conveyed it to said Joseph Love, her son-in-law, and he to Samuel Caldwell, now then is in doubt whether the widow could convey. To remove that doubt this conveyance is made. £5 to Joseph and £10 to William, 400 acres in Beverley Manor on Shenandoah River. Teste: William Wright, Robert Thomson, William Karr. Delivered: Caldwell, November, 1767.

Page 469.—21st May, 1766. Barnet Man and Margret ( ) to George Man, £20, 100 acres, part of tract patented to Barnet, 12th May, 1759, on Stoney Run, corner Jacob Man's land. Teste: Jacob Parsinger, Steven Conrod, John Man.

Page 472.—21st May, 1766. Same to Jacob Man, £20, 100 acres, part of above patented tract on Stoney Run.

Page 475.—15th October, 1765. Joseph ( ) Cannady (Kennedy) to James Wardlaw, £100, 231 acres in Borden's tract; corner Hugh Wardlaw. Teste: David Moore, John Parks, William ( ) McCandls, William Kennedy. Delivered: James Wardlaw, November, 1793.

Page 476.—Relinquishemtn of dower by Mary, wife of Samuel McDowell, in land conveyed by Samuel to George Skellorn, 12th-13th October, 1765. Relinquishment, 7th December, 1765.

Page 478.—21st May, 1766. George Trout and Mary ( ) (spelled Troat) to James Craig, £38, 100 acres granted to George by deed, 20th August, 1755, on both side South River Shanando, mouth of Pear's Run. Delivered: James Craig, 30th September, 1774.

Page 481.—10th April, 1766. Ephraim Wilson and Isabella to Sampson and George Mathews, £25, 200 acres in Beverley Manor; oaks in John Hutcheson's line, John Henderson's line, John Graham's corner, conveyed to Ephraim by Robert Beverley.

Page 483.—15th July, 1766. Randal Lockhart to Mathew Reed and Hugh Johnston, merchants in Staunton, power attorney to sue for, &c., all sums of money, debts, rents, goods, wares, dues, accounts and other demands from Hugh Allen, Hugh Donahoe, James McDowell, James Ward, John

Robertson, Daniel Harrison, John Brown, Walter Daviss and Michael Waring; above claims asigned to secure indebtedness to Reed and Johnston. Teste: William, Jacob, Anthony Rodgers.

Page 484.—15th July, 1766. Randal Lockhart to Reed and Johnston, £133, slaves and horses.

Page 485.—23d October, 1765. William Lockridge and Agness ( ) to Jno. Wier, £131, 266 acres in Borden's tract; corner Beard, Wm. Moore's line; corner Alexander's land, McCanlees line. Teste: Benj. ( ) Blackburn, Samuel ( ) Wier, Robert Alexander, Thos. Bowyer, William Crow, David Stewart. Delivered: Robert Steel, 15th March, 1813, by order of John Wier.

Page 487.—Release of dower as to above, 29th July, 1766.

Page 489.—19th August, 1766. Alexander ( ) Walker and Elisabeth to Alexander Walker, his son, £10, 287 acres on a branch of Little's Creek, patented to Esther Campbell, 3d November, 1760, and conveyed by her to Alexander, Sr., 19th May, 1752; corner John Campbell. Delivered: Alex. Walker, Jr., April, 1769.

Page 491.—17th May, 1766. Rudolph Mauk and Cathrine ( ) to Michael Hauber (Hober), £70, 335 acres on head of Fort Run at foot of North Mountain, patented to Rudolph, 30th August, 1763, oak in Johnson's line. Teste: Joseph Dictum, Andrew Trumbo, John Cain, George ( ) Shoomaker. Delivered: Michael Hober, 16th June, 1772.

Page 493.—21st October, 1765. Robert McMahon and Margaret ( ) to Hugh Donehge, £30.18, 300 acres on a draft of North River of Shanando, patented to Robert, 12th May, 1759. Teste: John Reburn, John Ritchey, Andrew Ralston. Delivered: Hugh Donaho, January, 1768.

Page 495.—17th July, 1766. Alexander Blair and Jean ( ) to Robert Reed, £78, 144 acres on Middle River Shanando, crossing the bald hill. Delivered: Robert Reed, March, 1766.

Page 498.—19th August, 1766. Patrick Cunningham to Edward Erwin, £80, 230 acres on Thorney Branch; corner William Cunningham's land. Delivered: Edward Erwin, Jr., May, 1767.

Page 500.—19th August, 1766. William Doherty and Elizabeth ( ) to John Thomson, £110, 255 acres on Christian's Creek; corner Mathew Thomson's land, Sawyer's land; corner Robert Willson; corner William Brown. Teste: Andrew Alexander, James Cotton, William Brown. Delivered: Andrew Alexander, March, 1770 by your order.

Page 503.—15th August, 1766. Nicholas ( ) Cain and Catherine ( ), of Albemarle County, to Andrew Trumboe, £32, 100 acres on North River of Shanand and within the gap of the mountain, patented to Nicholas, 20th August, 1747; corner Bernerd McHenry. Teste: Rudy Mauk, John Cain, Joseph Dictum, George ( ) Shoomaker. Delivered: Andrew Trumbo, 8th November, 1774.

Page 505.—19th August, 1766. Robert Beverley to Nathaniel Steel, £10, 180 acres; corner John Tate, Thomas Tate's line. Delivered: Nathaniel Steel, April, 1773.

Page 507.—18th August, 1766. Release of dower in deed, 15th February, 1763, by Andrew Balfaut to Christian Clemons, by Elizabeth, wife of Andrew.

Page 509.—9th January, 1766. John King to Robert Sleven, £12, 180 acres on South River Shanando, oak below Christian Clemon's land; corner Woodruff's (Woodroof) land, patented to John King, 5th October, 1765. Teste: John and Robert Anderson. Delivered: Robert Sleven, February, 1769.

Page 511.— — day ——, 1766. John King and Mary ( ) to John Poage, £335, 169 acres on a branch of Middle River, Young's line. Teste: Joseph ( ) Reaburn, John Francis, John Gillespy, Samuel Young. Delivered: John Poage, 21st May, 1798.

Page 513.—27th July, 1766. Thomas Nicholas (Nickels) and Jean ( ) to John Francis, £41.7, 200 acres on Middle River of Shanandore, oaks in the Naked Land at the foot of a ridge; Wiley's corner, George Moffet's line. Teste: Jno. Poage, Jno. Gillespy. Delivered: Jno. Francis, March, 1768.

Page 516.—20th August, 1766. Robert Knox to Thomas Nickle, £31, 100 acres on Cowpasture River; corner land in possession of James Knox, part of his patent land, this tract formerly conveyed by James Knox to Robert Knox, 16th August, 1765. Delivered: Thomas Nickle, February, 1767.

Page 519.—4th June, 1766. Thomas Tosh and Mary ( ) to Andrew Lewis, £100, 269 acres on south side Roanoke or Goose Creek. Teste: David Stewart.

Page 520.—4th June, 1766. Release by Mary of dower in above.

Page 522.—19th August, 1766. John Reaburn and Jean ( ) to Jacob Campbell, £—, 317 acres on Buffelo Draft, a branch of North River of Shanandore; corner Henry Leaburn. Delivered: Jacob Campbell, February, 1768.

Page 523.—7th January, 1766. Articles of vendue by Mary ( ) McClure, James and Nathaniel McCluer, for sale of the plantation on which they live, and sundry other moveables. The chattels, purchases under 10 shillings, ready money; above that, credit till 1st November, next. The plantation, £30, cash, remainder in three payments. Purchaser required, if the stamp act is in force, to renew bonds. Subscribers to live on the place until May next.

Page 525.—19th August, 1766. John Ritchey and Margret to Hugh Donagha, £55, 159 acres, part of 179 acres patented to Samuel Lockhart, 30th August, 1748, and conveyed to him to Ritchie, 1763, by North River of Shanandore. Delivered: Hugh Donaho, February, 1773.

Page 527.—19th August, 1766. Thomas ( ) Kirkpatrick to John Kirkpatrick, his son, £20, 200 acres in Beverley Manor on head branch of Middle River of Shanandore, part of 390 acres conveyed to Thomas, 25th March, 1741, patent line, McCleerey's line. Teste: Wm. Christell. Delivered: Jno. Kirkpatrick, May Court, 1767.

Page 529.— — October, 1765. Valentine Sevier and Joanna ( ) to George Shumaker, £30, 310 acres on which George now lives, on North River Shanando; corner Benj. Burden's lands. Teste: John Gratton, Martin Humble, Jacob Woodle (Woodley), Nicholas Zeburnn (Zeborn, Seehorn ?).

Page 532.—18th August, 1766. Same to Jacob Woodley, £41, 200 acres on Smith's Creek, crossing Daniel James' Branch. Teste: Nicholas Zeburn. George ( ) Shoemaker.

Page 534.—15th August, 1766. Stephen ( ) Arnold and Jane ( ) to George Campbell, £40, 120 acres at the Cove on south side James River, crossing Elk Creek. Teste: Daniel Evans, Samuel McCluer (?).

Page 537.—19th August, 1766. John Willey to Thomas Wilson, £25, £70, on Buffelo Creek in Forks of James. Delivered: Thomas Wilson, March, 1769.

Page 539.—19th August, 1766. William Given(s) and Agness to Robert Lockridge, £172, 552 acres on both sides Great River Calfpasture; corner Henry Gay's; corner David Davis. Teste: Robert Bratton, Andrew Lockridge. Delivered: Mr. Lockridge, 18th November, 1788.

Page 542.—19th August, 1766. Robert Beverley to John Johnston, £10, 65 acres in Beverley Manor in a bent of Middle River of Shanandore called the Brushey Neck; corner William Johnston, George Anderson's line. Delivered: John Johnston, April, 1770.

Page 545.—16th August, 1766. Adam Stephenson and Rebeka ( ) to James Douglass, £17, 355 acres patented to Adam, 5th June, 1765; corner Daniel Henderson's survey; corner Daniel Smith, Henderson's former survey. Teste: Samuel Patterson, Samuel Colwell, Jno. Douglass. Delivered: John Stephenson, 9th November, 1768.

Deed Book No. 13.

The first deed recorded in this book was 19th August, 1766; the last deed recorded in this book was 17th November, 1767.

Page 2.—29th October, 1765. Joseph Wardlaw and Agness to William Wardlaw, £45, 171½ acres in Borden's 92100; corner Joseph Kenady; corner Hugh Martain. Teste: James Kennedy, John Taylor, John and James Wardlaw.

Page 4.—19th August, 1766. John McCoy and Sarah ( ) to John Campbell, £100, 130 acres, part of 320 acres patented to John and his brother James McCoy, 25th September 1762, on Mossey Creek, Ralstone's line. Teste: John Malcom, John Archer, John Davidson. Delivered: John McCoy, 9th November, 1767.

Page 7.—19th August, 1766. James Trimble, of Greenspring, and Sarah, his wife, of Augusta County, to Abraham Haplenstall, £10.15, 140 acres on head of South Fork of Black Thorn, a branch of South Branch of Potomac, corner George Wilson's land. Teste: John Paxton, Wm. Mathews, Wm. Alexander. Delivered: Abraham Heplenstall, March Court, 1774.

Page 8.—12th August, 1766. William Ritchie, farmer, to John Buchanan, gent., certain horses and cows in consideration of the payment of certain debts due the estate of Col. James Patton, and mortgaged to Buchanan for that purpose. Teste: John McFerson, Mary ( ) Ritchie, Wm. Preston.

Page 10.—19th August, 1766. Robert Beverley to Joseph Mays, £10, 205 acres in Beverley Manor, Alexander Campbell's line, Samuel Braford's line; corner James Mitchell, to the beginning by Francis Beatey. Delivered: Jos. Mays, May, 1767.

Page 13.—21st August, 1766. James ( ) Coulter to Michael Coulter, £40, 212 acres on Hays Creek; corner Wm. Reagh (Raigh, Reaigh). Teste: Alex. Stewart, Alex. Walker. Delivered: Michael Coulter, 31st June, 1773.

Page 15.—20th August, 1766. Joseph Ward and Janet ( ) to John Hays and Elizabeth Ray, £37, 220 acres conveyed to Joseph by Andrew Brown, 21st May, 1755, on Poage's Draft of James River, Borden's patent line. Teste: Archibald Alexander, John Greenlee, Andrew Wilson.

Page 18.—2d August, 1766. John Wardlaw and Margret to Alex. Grier (Greer), £137, 188 acres, 3 roods, 16 perches; corner William McCandless; corner John Lowry. Delivered: Alex. Greer, 13th March, 1772.

Page 20.—8th August, 1766. Borden's executors to John Dunlap, £11, 150 acres, part of 92100, on Hays Creek, Samuel Dunlap's line, chesnut on Mount Miserable (Missorable). Teste: Benj. Hawkins, James Cowden.

Page 23.—2d May, 1766. Same to Charles Hays, £4, 165 acres agreed by Benj., Jr., to be sold to John Kirk, part of 92100, beginning his old corner in James Moore's line, spur of North Mountain. Delivered: Chas. Hays, 16th August, 1773.

Page 25.—2d August, 1766. Same to Charles Hays, £6, 200 acres in 92100 on river side, Hays' Creek, Robert Christian's corner on said Creek.

Page 28.—2d October, 1766. Same to Andrew Hays, £20, 100 acres, part of 92100, beginning on Back Creek in John McCoskry's line, corner Isaac Anderson; John Buntin's corner. Delivered: Robert Risk per order, 20th December, 1773.

Page 30.—23d January, 1766. James Shaw to George Wilson and Wm. Crow, certain horses and cattle, £16. Teste: Archibald Mathews, James Huston. Delivered: David Bell, February, 1770.

Page 31.—7th August, 1766. James Shaw to John Botkin, £26, 100 acres on both sides Cowpasture River. Teste: Charles Lewis, John McCreery, Thos. Feemster, Jno. Montgomery. Delivered: Jno. Lewis, 7th June, 1770.

Page 34.—19th August, 1766. Robert Kinkead and Anna Helena ( ) to Mathew Kinkead, £72.10, 174½ acres, part of 334 acres conveyed to Robert by James Bratton, 20th April, 1763, on a draft of Christian's Creek; corner Mr. Lewis' land. Delivered: Thos. Kinkead, August, 1770.

Page 35.—2d August, 1766. Borden's executors to James McKee, gent., £50, 301 acres, part of 92100, on northwest branch of Mill Creek, in line of a tract surveyed for the Rev. Mr. Dean; John Gray's line, corner John Lyle; corner Greenlee's survey.

Page 38.—3d June, 1766. John Thompson, Sr., to Joseph Lapsley, John Moore, Andrew Hall, John Thompson, Jr., £250, bill sale of cattle and other personalty. Condition is such that whereas John Thompson, Sr., at a court for this county was lately convicted of felony and then bailed to grand jury, and the grantees became surety on the bail bond, now if John makes his appearance this bill to be void. Teste: Pat. Lockhart, Wm. Howard.

Page 39.—19th August, 1766. George Mathews and Ann to John and James Wilson, £130, 300 acres, part of 1600 acres patented to John Mathews, on Mill Creek in Forks of James River, joining John Poage's land, Mr. Mathews' patent line; John Maxwell's line; corner Richard Mathews. Delivered: John Anderson by order of James Wilson.

Page 41.—11th August, 1766. Peter ( ) Caley to Joseph Dennis, mortgage of personal property for £10. Teste: James Berton, Caleb May.

Page 43.—5th June, 1766. Andrew Stevenson and Sarah and John Paul and Mary to Robert Carruthers, £57, 200 acres formerly belonging to Andrew Baxter and bequeathed by him to Andrew Stevenson, his grandson, after the death of Margaret, his wife, by will dated 15th September, 1748, recorded in Augusta, but John Paul and Mary were the true proper heirs of said Andrew Baxter; corner Borden's tract. Teste: Walter Smiley, Joseph Ward.

Page 46.—19th August, 1766. James Clarke to Samuel Clarke, his son, £10, 84 acres on a branch of Middle River, part of 384 acres conveyed to James by Beverley, 15th May, 1746; corner Robert Clarke's part of same tract; corner John Clarke's land. Teste: George Carpenter. Delivered: Samuel Clarke, 19th November, 1770.

Page 48.—19th August, 1766. James Clarke to Robert Clarke, his son, £20, 216 acres in Beverley Manor on head branch of Middle River, part of 380 acres above; corner McCleerey's land. Delivered: R. Clarke, July, 1784.

Page 49.—18th August, 1766. John Williams to Adam Dean, of Albemarle, £10, horse and hogs on John's plantation, condition to abide by result of an arbitration. Teste: William Teas, Robert Allen.

Page 51.—23d April, 1766. James Robinson and Sarah (James being eldest son and heir of George Robinson and one of the executors of said George) to William Preston, £50, 191 acres by patent to George, — day ——, 1740; corner John Buchanans land, now in possession of David Cloyd, on a branch of Buffelo Creek, a branch of Roanoke. Teste: John Neally, Robert Breckinridge, Francis Smith, Ann Smith, Michael Cloyd. James Thompson.

Page 54.—22d August, 1766. John Carlile and Mary ( ) to Thomas Adams, of the County of New Kent, £117.10, on both sides of Great River of Calfpasture, 200 acres, bounded according to the ancient known and reputed bounds, purchased by John of ——— Gilliam. Delivered: Sampson Mathews, 19th March, 1772.

Page 56.—11th August, 1766. Samuel Stuart and Lydia ( ), of North Carolina, yeoman, to Jacob Caplin, £25, 153 acres on South Fork of Linvell's Creek, patented to Samuel, 5th September, 1749; Ralston's line; Patterson's line. Teste: Wm. Cravens, Robert Black, Magey ( ) Black.

Page 59.—21st August, 1766. John Dickinson, Gent., and Martha, to William Hugart, £80, 490 acres on Meadow Creek of Jackson's River, at a place called Great Meadows.

Page 62.—19th August, 1766. Gabriel Jones and Margaret to James, George and Robert McAfee, £107.10, tract purchased by Gabriel of James McCown, and he from Robert Poage, on Catawpa, a branch of James River. Delivered: Francis Smith, 1st October, 1767.

Page 64.—21st August, 1766. Robert McClanachan and Sarah to George Willson, of Hampshire County, £31, lot in Staunton, ¼ acre of the County lot, joining No. 8, a part of the lot No. 9, on east side of the Court House lot.

Page 66.—22d August, 1766. Nicholas Green, of Culpeper, to James Davidson, £154.10, 400 acres on the Dry River, part of 1700 acres patented to James Wood and Robert Green, joining Daniel Callachan's and Wm. **Chesnut's lands.**

Page 67.—9th August, 1766. Relinquishment by Abigail, wife of Alex. Herron, of dower in tract sold by Alexander to Walter Crow, 22d March, 1765.

Page 69.—Ditto in deed Alex. Herron to Samuel Samples.
Page 69.—6th June, 1766. John Dailey to David Stewart and Samuel Cowdon, mortgage, consideration is grantees going bail for grantor in a suit in general court brought by Keppen & Co. for £250; conveys the land Dailey now lives on called Hart's Bottom, 270 acres, part of 400 acres patented to Silas Hart, and by Hart sold to one William Anderson, and by Anderson to Dailey. Teste: Andrew Lewis, Jno. Madison, Jos. Ray.
Page 71.—13th June, 1766. Samuel Cowden, of Staunton, to David Stewart. Consideration, David's going Samuel's security on several occasions. Tract which Samuel and Andrew Greer bought of Patrick Martin, 321 acres. Mortgage. Teste: Wm. Crow, John Stewart.
Page 73.—19th August, 1766. James Henderson and Martha ( ) to John Stuart, £119.15, 157 acres in Beverley Manor; corner Mathew Robertson on Cathey's River; corner Robert Kenney's. Teste: Walter Cunningham, William Brown. Delivered: Archibald Dixon, 8th September, 1785. Teste: Samuel McConkey, deputy clerk.
Page 75.—23d August, 1766. William Brown and Isabella ( ) to James Henderson, £200, 400 acres on head of Culton's Branch of North River of Shannandor; corner James Trotter; also ten acres on same branch below same and between James Trotter and Hugh Campbell, part of Hugh Campbell's tract of 333 acres.
Page 77.—23d May, 1766. Samuel Cloyd, britches maker, to Nyrian (Narnan) Cloyd, £25, beds, bolsters, blankets, quilts, mares. Teste: Walter and John Davis.
Page 79.—23d August, 1766. William ( ) Hall, Sr., to William Hall, his son, £20, 175 acres, part of two tracts of land, one containing 390 acres, and the other containing 500 acres, both patented to William, 16th September, 1761, on Cedar Creek in forks of James River; corner John Hall, David Cloyd's line. Delivered: John Buchanan, 13th March, 1772.
Page 81.—18th August, 1766. Executors of John Wright (Daniel Smith and Lydia Wright) to John Johnston, £200, 300 acres on Linvel's Creek, part of 550 acres granted to John by Abraham Hite, 31st December, 1760; corner Green and Harrison's lands. Delivered: Josiah Davidson, November, 1769.
Page 84.—23d August, 1766. Andrew Greer and Ruth to David Stuart, £100, one moiety of 321 acres on Back Creek originally surveyed for Alexander Walker and sold by him to Patrick Martin, and by Martin to Andrew Greer and Samuel Cowden, the same tract whereon Patrick lately lived, joining John Moffet and Samuel Young, the other moiety being lately mortgaged by Samuel Cowden to David Stuart.
Page 85.—7th June, 1766. Samuel Cowden to Sampson Mathews on account of Wm. McClure, of Pennsylvania. £19, bill sale of personal property conditioned to pay £19. Teste: Walter Cunningham and Jno. Murray.
Page 86.—10th June, 1766. Same to John Murray, £10.2.4, bill sale of personal property conditioned for payment of above sum.
Page 87.—14th November, 1766. Francis Fulten and Eleanor to Alex. Hamilton, £90.5, 271 acres on Little River of Calfpasture, James Henderson's line; corner Robert McCutchin. Teste: Mathew Moorehead, Robert McCutchen, Thos. Meek. (This name looks like Fullen.)
Page 89.—4th August, 1766. James McAllister and Mary to Patrick

McConnel, £47, 150 acres on a branch of Carrs Creek in the Fork of James River, oak in Borden's patent line; corner Robert Erwin. Delivered: P. McConnell, 21st April, 1781.

Page 92.—2d October, 1765. Adam Looney and Hanna, of Mecklenburg County, North Carolina, to Alex. Evans,£40, 140 acres by patent, 10th March, 1756, on a branch of Looney's Creek. Teste: John Looney, Moses Luney, Christian ( ) Epshear (Apshear Upshur ?).

Page 94.—18th November, 1766. Robert ( ) Finley, gent., and Martha to John Ramsey, £65, 88 acres in Beverley Manor on both side South River of Shanando, William Finley's line. Delivered: William Ramsey, 5th October, 1772.

Page 96.—8th November, 1766. John ( ) McClure and Mary ( ) to John Davis, £43, 100 acres in Forks of James and his part of a tract of 200 acres formerly belonging to Robert Armstrong, deceased. Teste: James Crow, John and James Berry. Delivered: Jno. Davis, November, 1775.

Page 99.—28th October, 1766. John and Wm. Long, of Chester County, Pennsylvania, to William Long, Sr., of Augusta County, £10, 400 acres, part of 800 acres in Beverley Manor on Long Meadow, a branch of Middle River; corner tract now Andrew McClure's; corner James Alexander's part of this said tract. Teste: James and Wm. Bell, John and Wm. Long. Delivered: Samuel Long, 29th May, 1783.

Page 101.—19th November, 1766. Benj. Logan to Jacob Hornbarrier, £40, 160 acres on North River Shanandore, patented to Wm. Brown, 11th July, 1761, and by him conveyed to Benj., below mouth of Cook's Creek. Delivered: Jacob Hornberry (Hornberger), November, 1768.

Page 104.—15th November, 1766. Alex. ( ) McKorkle and Mary ( ) to Patrick McKorkle, £25, 150 acres on North Branch of James, part of 300 acres whereon Alex. now lives; corner Abraham Brown's land. Teste: James McCluer, James Trimble, James Crow.

Page 106.—11th November, 1766. Hugh Hicklin and Elizabeth to James Bratchey, £50, 100 acres on a draft of Newfoundland Creek, now called the Bullpasture. Wallis Estill and Robert and John Carlile. Delivered: James Bratchey, November, 1767. This name is Bradshaw.

Page 109.—19th August, 1766. William ( ) Hall and Jannet ( ) to James Hall, their son, £5, 150 acres in Forks of James; corner James Todd, Samuel McMurtree's line. Maryan Crafford's line. Teste: John Milliken. John Moore, Nathaniel Hall.

Page 111.—16th November, 1766. Samuel Patterson and Martha ( ) to James Patterson, £21.16.8, 80 acres whereon said James now lives; corner James Cowdon. Delivered: J. Patterson. 16th October, 1786.

Page 114.—19th November, 1766. John Pearey (Peerie) and Sarah to his brother James Pearey, £30, 150 acres in Beverley Manor, part of 375 acres first made over to Thomas Pearey, deceased (father of John), by deed, 1749, on a branch of Middle River of Shanandore.

Page 116.— — day ——, 1766. Richard ( ) Pillson, of Albemarle, to George Caldwell, Jr., £33, 285 acres in Beverley Manor, on a branch of South River of Shanandore, Kennerley's line. Teste: John Poage, Robert Rodgers, John Caldwell. Delivered: John Kennerley, April, 1773.

Page 119.—19th November, 1766. Robert Gay and Sarah ( ) to John Vance, £50, 133 acres, part of 664 acres conveyed to Robert by Robert

Abercrombie, 23d October, 1760, on Back Creek, a branch of Jackson's River; corner Samuel Vance's part. Delivered: Samuel Vance, devisee, 7th November, 1797.

Page 121.—19th November, 1766. Same to Samuel Vance, £50 to the said Henry and —— Gay paid, 180 acres, part of 664 acres above, mouth of Naps Creek.

Page 123.—20th November, 1766. William ( ) Hall to Nathaniel Hall, his son, £40, 246 acres. Teste: James Simson, Wm. Gillespy. Delivered: Nathaniel Hall, 27th December, 1785.

Page 125.—11th February, 1766. John Mills and Mary to James Huston. £40, 150 acres on Murrie's Run, a branch of Roanoke. Delivered: Samuel Lewis, 8th April, 1775.

Page 127.—19th November, 1766. Robert Trimble and Hannah to Roger Kilpatrick, of Albemarle, planter. By patent, 20th May, 1759, there was granted to Walter Trimble 370 acres on North Branch of Shanandore, which was purchased by Walter's son Robert from Walter, £95. Delivered: Alex. Kilpatrick, 4th November, 1771.

Page 129.—30th October, 1766. John ( ) Wilkins, of Mecklenburg County, North Carolina, to Alexander Herron, £80, 400 acres on Naked Creek, part of 1264 acres patented to McCoy, Hite & Co., and by them conveyed to Samuel Wilkins, deceased, father to said John, Daniel Harrison's line. Teste: John Poage, Hugh Johnston, Mathew McCullagh, Agness Poage. Delivered: Alex. Herron, June, 1767.

Page 131.—13th March, 1764. Jeremiah ( ) Early and Elisabeth ( ), of Culpeper, to Francis Kirtley, £80, 240 acres on Elk Run. "Beginning confirmed unto Jeremiah Early a tract containing 40 acres between Elk Run and the Hawk's Bill; corner said Jeremiah Early; corner survey of Francis Kirtley's to the beginning, thence the several courses of Martin's patent, on the south side Elk Run, being the remainder of Martin's patent the said Francis Kirtley purchased before, &c." Teste: James Kirtley, John Earley, William ( ) Bohanon, William ( ) Smith.

Page 133.—11th November, 1765. Sampson Archer and Rebekah, of York County, Pennsylvania, to John Archer, £20, 75 acres on a draft of Anderson's Branch, patented to Sampson, 26th September, 1760. Teste: Robert Armstrong, John Gardner, Robert Archer, Samuel Shinan (Shanan).

Page 136.—19th November, 1766. Thomas Craige, of Charlotte County, to John Craig, his brother, of Augusta, £27, 178 acres in Beverley Manor, by the Middle River of Shanandore, Kenney's low grounds, Patterson's line. Teste: John Patterson, Robert and Seth Rodgers.

Page 138.—9th September, 1766. John Moffete, Robert Moffette and Jean to John Buchanan, gent., £40, 170 acres, part of 340 acres made over to John and Robert by Samuel McDowell, 18th August, 1764; corner Robert Moffette in Samuel Walker's line, corner Robert Moffette in James McGavock's line. Teste: John Maxwell, John Taylor, Alex. Walker.

Page 140.—18th November, 1766. James Phillips and Mary to John Phillips, £250, 171 acres on a branch of Shannando, patented to James, 29th May, 1760. Teste: J. Ray, John Davis, James Hogsead. Delivered: April Court, 1778.

Page 143.—3d September, 1766. Robert Black and Magey ( ), of Mecklenburg County, North Carolina, to Martin Archenbright, £65, 232 acres on Cook's, patented to Thomas Stevenson, 25th June, 1747, and conveyed to Robert, 22d June, 1763. Teste: Hugh Johnson.

Page 145.—20th November, 1766. James Shaw to Robert Hall, of Orange County, North Carolina, £4, ¼ acre, part of Samuel Furguson's lot No. 15 in Staunton. Teste: Robert Martin, Thomas Brown and James Crow.

Page 147.—21st November, 1766. Thomas Bullett, of Fauquier County, of 1st part; Thomas and Andrew Lewis, of 2d part. The parties had taken up 300 acres including the Little Warm Springs, and entered into agreement in regard to a division thereof and managment. This is a deed of partition. Delivered: Hon. Cuthbert Bullitt, 10th September, 1789.

Page 152.—18th August, 1766. Borden's executors to John Grattan, £120, lots Nos. 1 and 2. No. 1 containing 235 acres on a small branch of Shanando; No. 2, contains 185 acres on North Branch of Shanando, the Mill Creek, both Nos. 1 and 2 being parts of Borden's tract. Teste: Archer Mathews and John Cowardin.

Page 156.—19th August, 1766. Borden's executors to John Grattan, £25, tract known as the Mill Place on Shanando and the lot No. 4 containing 300 acres, Mill Creek below the fall.

Page 160.—19th August, 1766. Same to John Dunbar, £50, lot No. 3, 180 acres on Mill Creek, a branch of North Shanando. Delivered: John Dunbar, November, 1769.

Page 165.—18th November, 1766. Same to Rodolph Maught (Mauck), £80, lot No. 2, 163 acres on North Shannando, forks of said river where the two branches meet. Delivered: John Dunbar, November, 1769.

Page 168.—23d November, 1766. John Kinkead to Gabriel Jones, £100, mortgage, 530 acres, part of 1061 acres, one moiety of which John sold to John Kinkead, of Albemarle, the moiety hereby conveyed being whereon John now lives, on the Calfpasture. Teste:Andrew Lewis, Alex. Miller, M. A., Thos. Madison.

Page 170.—8th November, 1766. Samuel Logan and Mary ( ) to Thomas Hutcheson, £30, 238 acres at head of Elk Run in Beverley Manor; Andrew McCluer's line, grub in the Barrens, new corner of Joseph Bell's. Delivered: Sarah Hutchison, 14th October, 1773.

Page 173.—20th May, 1766. James Finley, of Staunton, farmer, and Agness to Sampson and George Mathews, merchants and partners in Staunton, mortgage, £110, three half lots of land in County lots, lot No. 3, lot No. 4, lot No. 13; also the residue of tract conveyed to James by Beverley, 19th March, 1754, containing 155 acres, part of which was formerly granted to Felix Gilbert, Thomas Stewart and James Huston; also remainder of a lease for 87 acres in Beverley Manor, and described in a lease from James Brown to the saiid Robert Finley, 16th January, 1754, for the term of 57 years; all which land was conveyed to Robert Finley, late of Augusta County, deceased, and descended to James Finley as his brother and heir-at-law.

Page 176.—15th January, 1767. Samuel Moor to John Hunter, £62, beds, tables, trunks, and other personalty. Teste: Wat. Cunningham, Robert Brown, Jno. Patterson.

Page 177.—2d December, 1766. William Green, of Culpeper, son and heir of Robert Green, late of Orange County, deceased, to John Miller. There was a contract by Robert to sell to John for £75, lot now and then occupied by said Miller, being lot No. 3 on Linville's Creek, 500 acres, but Robert died before making conveyance, testate, but making no devise of this tract, whereby same descended to William (will recorded in Orange). Now conveys same. Memorandum—This tract is the same this day conveyed to Miller by Robert Green, the reason for which double conveyance may be seen by Robert's deed and is the same tract for which William and Robert formerly passed deeds to John Miller, but same was not properly proved. Teste: Francis ( ) McBride, James Wright, Daniel ( ) Murley.

Page 181.—2d December, 1766. Robert Green, of Culpeper, residuary legatee of Robert Green, of Orange County, deceased, to John Miller. Recites contract of sale above and conveys same tract.

Page 184.— — March, 1767. John ( ) Miller and Hannah ( ) to Cornelius Ruddle, £600, 500 acres, being lot No. 3 above, and also 200 acres, part of lot No. 2, lying on Linvel's Creek, part of 7009 acres patented to Hite, Green & Co., 26th March, 1739, and by McCoy and Hite conveyed to Robert Green, 5th August, 1746, who devised said 200 acres to son Robert, who conveyed same to John Miller, 20th April, 1753. Delivered: Cornelius Ruddle, July, 1775.

Page 188.—17th March, 1767. Francis ( ) McBride, farmer, and Mary ( ) to John Bear, farmer, £270, 300 acres on Linvel's Creek, part of 500 acres which Jacob Chrisman purchased of Joseph Bryan; also part of 1500 acres surveyed for William Linvell, being the same 300 acres conveyed by Jacob Chrisman to Francis McBride, 5th April, 1761. Delivered: Obediah Monsey.

Page 190.—26th January, 1767. Brice (Bryce) Hanna to Patrick Campbell, one horse. Teste: Jno. Taylor, Thomas Steel. Delivered: Wm. Hay, December, 1767.

Page 191.—24th January, 1767. Thomas Watterson and Mary ( ) to Abraham Smith, £47.15, 540 acres patented to Thomas, 12th May, 1759, line of Francis Brown's land. Teste: James Bell, Robert Currey, Jarrod Erwin, Benj. Logan. Delivered: Col. Abraham Smith, March, 1772.

Page 194.—13th March, 1767. Robert Miller and Margret ( ), of Albemarle, to George Skillern, £100, 150 acres on Jackson's River patented to Robert, 25th September, 1762; corner to his own land. Teste: Robert Hooke, Thos. Miller, John and Wm. Elliot.

Page 196.—21st June, 1763. Robert ( ) Given, Jr., and Jean ( ) to his brother Joseph Given, £5, 120 acres, part of 544 acres on Great River of Calfpasture between Moses McElvain's and John Graham's. Delivered: Robert Carlile, June, 1770.

Page 199.—10th March, 1767. Malcom Allen and Mary ( ) to Martin Kayser (Kaysay), £33, 54 acres by patent, 16th September, 1765, on James River. Teste: Gabriel Smither, Hugh and Moses Allen. Sent to Kayser, February, 1776.

Page 201.—17th March, 1767. Stephen ( ) Hernsberger and Arsley ( ) to John Miller, £53, 200 acres on Shanand River, part thereof being a tract of 176 acres sold to Stephen by Phillip Long, 19th June, 1764, the other part being part of 304 acres patented to Stephen, 31st October, 1765, line of Henry Sellers. Teste: Jacob Pirkey.

Page 204.—4th February, 1763. John Sloan, of Roan County, North Carolina, to John Adams, £35, 300 acres on Loonie's Mill Creek. Teste:

John Buchanan, David Luney, Benj. Davis, Abraham McClelan, George Adams, Hugh ( ) McNelle.

Page 206.— — March, 1767. John ( ) Davis and Judey ( ) to Samuel McKee, £45, 230 acres on Walker's Run, a branch of Middle River, between William and Robert Stevenson's lands.

Page 208.—17th March, 1767. John ( ) Davis and Judey ( ) to David Tate,£17, 85 acres on Jackson's River. Delivered: David Tate, June, 1770.

Page 211.—5th March, 1767. James ( ) McAffee and Jannet ( ) to Archibald Fisher, £55, 150 acres on Catawbo of James River, joining John Bryan's land, opposite mouth of Holeston's Branch. Teste: James Curry, William Fleming, Andrew Woods. Delivered: Archibald Fisher, March, 1773.

Page 213.—18th March, 1767. Thomas Bradshaw ( ) and Margrit ( ) to James Hogshead, Jr., £59, 150 acres on Moffet's branch, part of 364 acres patented to Robert Ralstone, 15th December, 1749, and by him conveyed to Thomas; corner James Hogshead.

Page 215.—20th February, 1767. David ( ) Rule, £7.9.8 by Charles Rush, £3.9.1 by Henry Tack, £3.4.2 by Mathias Corse. Bill of sale to above parties, conditioned to pay the several persons the several sums.

Page 217.—3d February, 1767. Patrick ( ) McCalm (McCollom) to John McCalm (McCollom), £20, 168 acres, part of tract on which Patrick now lives; corner John Berryhill, James Trimble's line. Delivered: John McCollom, June, 1769.

Page 219.—17th March, 1767. Robert Young and Mary to John Young, both of Forks of James River, 5 shillings, 112 acres in Forks of James. Delivered: John Young, March, 1776.

Page 222.—9th March, 1767. Malcom Allen and Mary ( ) to Patrick Willson, £45, 80 acres by patent dated 16th September, 1765, on James River, George Poage's land. Teste: Gabriel Smithers, Hugh and Moses Allen. Delivered: Wm. McClenachan, July, 1769.

Page 223.—4th November, 1766. Cornelius Brown, of Congras in South Carolina, taylor, power attorney to Abraham Brown, his brother, planter, of Augusta County, to make deed to William Davis, of County Philadelphia, Pennsylvania, to 175 acres on Woods River, otherwise called New River, part of 350 acres conveyed by John Harrison to Cornelius. Teste: John Paxton, James Trimble, John Hickman, John Trimble.

Page 225.—17th March, 1767. James ( )Hays and Agness ( )to John Lusk, £90, 100 acres on the Mary or South River of James River; corner Borden's great tract. Teste: William Scott, William Kennady, Malcom Allen. Delivered: Jno. Lyle, May Court, 1778.

Page 227.—18th March, 1767. Wm. Willson and Barbara to Duncan McFarland, £30, 100 acres on Jackson's River.

Page 230.—16th March, 1767. Valentine Sevier and Joannah ( ) to Lawrence Bell, £47, 280 acres near a survey of John Harrson's. Teste: Andrew Bird, William Magee (McGee), Valentine Sevier, Jr. Delivered: Lawrence Bell, April, 1773.

Page 234.—3d February, 1767. Samuel McRoberts ( ) to James Wood, gent., of Frederick, £48, 287 acres by deed of James Wood, gent., deceased, of Frederick, 19th August, 1749, on head of Middle Branch of Catawbo Creek.

Page 235.—18th March, 1767. David Frame to John Bodkin, £15, 66 acres joining Robert McCutchin's land, on Naked Creek. Mortgage.

Page 237.—6th December, 1766. Adam Rider to Jacob Hite, gent., of Frederick, covenant and yearly rent. Lease of tract known as Rider's hundred acres tract, northwest of tract whereon Adam now lives, 100 acres, for ten years, at yearly rental of £200; said mine or mines which are now opened or any other thtat may be hereafter opened, lease may be extended if the mines prove profitable.

Page 240.—10th March, 1767. David Miller and Hannah to Israel Christian, merchant, £15, 120 acres on a branch of Buffalo, a branch of Roan Oak, Baptist McNabb's line Edward McDonald's line. Teste: Francis Smith, Wm. Christian, Wm. Preston, Robert Breckenridge, Ben. Hawkins, Wm. Fleming, Edward Carvin, Stephen Trigg, Nathan ( ) Gillilan, Wm. Christian. Delivered: Israel Christian, 9th February, 1773.

Page 243.—10th March, 1767. Same to Israel Christian, £50, 141 acres on Glade Creek of Roanoke; corner John Bowing's land.

Page 246.—21st November, 1766. David Looney and Mary to William Crow, of Staunton, £290, 140 acres, art of 250 acres patented to Robert Looney, 1742, whereon David lately lived, and which he recovered from John Bowyer, on James River; corner Col. Smith's land.

Page 249.—13th May, 1767. Joseph Robinson to Edward Springer, £200, 190 acres by patent to said Joseph, 20th September, 1748, on the waters of Rone Oak, joining land formerly George Robinson's, on Buffalo Creek; corner Coleses land. Teste: Samuel Pepper, Thomas Lloyd.

Page 252.—15th May, 1767. Benjamin Bennet and Catherine to Isaac Ward, taylor, £48, 320 acres in Forks of James River; corner William Foster's land.

Page 255.—16th May, 1767. James Botkin and Dinah ( ) to Robert Carlile, £50, 216 acres on Cowpasture River; corner a tract in possession of Robert Hall. Teste: John Carlile, Jas. Bradshaw, Wm. Black.

Page 258.—19th May, 1767. William Shannon and Jean ( ) to Robert Gragg, £35, 100 acres, part of 400 patented to William Humphrey, 25th June, 1747, and by him conveyed to Henry Smith, and by him to Wm. Shannon, on North River Shanando, white oak on Castle Hill. Teste: Samuel McFeeters, Moses Hall, John ( ) Cozby. Delivered: Frederick Michael, 7th March, 1792.

Page 261.—17th May, 1767. Robert ( ) Allison to Andrew McCampbell, £80, horses and house furnishings and clothes. Teste: Wm McKemey, Wm. McCampbell.

Page 261.—1st November, 1766. John Davis, of Mecklenburg County, North Carolina, to James Davis, of Augusta County, power of attorney to collect all sums of money due John in Augusta County, and to convey to purchasers all tracts of land belonging to John. Teste: Joseph Davis, Hugh Hays.

Page 262.—17th May, 1767. Ebenezer ( ) Wascoat, of South Carolina, and Jacob Shell, of Augusta, to Jacob Lorton. Ebenezer Wastcoat, late of Augusta County, but now of Berkeley County, South Carolina, sometime before his removal from Augusta County agreed to sell to Jacob a tract of 656 acres on Crab Creek, a branch of New River and received from Jacob £40, and afterwards (on 9th February, 1767) he gave a power of attorney to Jacob Shell to execute deeds to Jacob Lorton, purchased by Ebenezer James Patton, 14th January, 1754; corner Palser Smallser. Delivered: Thos. Dunn by your order, October, 1767.

Page 265.—17th May, 1767. Same by Jacob Miller, Jr., his attorney, to Jacob Shell, same recital, 200 acres on New River, patented to Ebenezer, 7th November, 1752. Delivered: John Burk, June, 1768.

Page 270.—15th May, 1767. Richard Raynolds (Randels, Randals) and Elizabeth to William Ramsey, £130, 300 acres on North Branch of James; corner John Daley's land. Teste: William and Alexander Moore, Moses Trimble.

Page 273.— —— ———, 1767. John Miller and Ann, of Albemarle County, to George Skillern, Gent., £250, 244 acres on Jackson's River, patented to John Miller, 20th August, 1760; red oak in the Barrens.

Page 276.—19th May, 1767. Henry Cresswell and Rebecca R. to John Faris, £47, 400 acres in southermost fork of North River Shanando on Stoney Lick Branch; oak near Stony Lick. Teste: Elijah McClenachan and John Buchanan.

Page 279.— —— ———, 1767. George Skillern and Elizabeth to Thomas Miller, £300, 270 acres on Long Meadow in Beverley Manor. Delivered: Thos. Miller, 20th April, 1772, £300.

Page 283.—19th May, 1767. James Sayers to James Sayers, his son, £150, 2 tracts on Middle River of Shanando—A containing 230 acres, corner John Trimble, crossing the Buffelow branch; B containing 100 acres adjoining the former, corner Thomas Gardner. Teste: George Elliot. Delivered: David Sawyers, devisee of James Sawyers, the grantee, 6th December, 1805.

Page 287.—6th January, 1767. Robert Neelley (Neally, Neilly, Nealy) (and Anna), of Halifax County, to William Christian, £78, 350 acres on a branch of Roan Oak, adjoining Robert Breckenridge and Archibald Graham. Teste: Isaac Christian, Stephen Trigg, Arthur Campbell, James McCorkle, John Crocket.

Page 289.—21st February, 1767. John Neelley (Neilly) Dr. (doctor?), of Augusta County, to William Graham, of Hallifax County, Gent., £30, 2 feather beds, all his pewter and household furniture, one sorrel mare natural pacer, one bay mare natural trotter, one white mare, one gray stallion, one sorrel stallion, conditioned for payment of £30. Teste: James Neilly, Edward Carvin, Stephen Trigg.

Page 291.—16th May, 1767. William Carvin, son and heir-at-law of William Carvin, to Edward Carvin, £100, 174 acres by patent to William. Sr., 1st April, 1748, on Roan Oak. Teste: William Christian, Stephen Trigg, Nathan ( ) Gillilen, Wm. Simpson. Delivered: Stephen May, October, 1775.

Page 294.—24th February, 1767. James Patton's executors to Joseph McMurtery, £21.18, 197 acres by patent 3d November, 1750, on Craig's Creek, on John's Creek, crossing Bryan's Creek. Delivered: Martin Baker, January, 1770.

Page 298.—15th May, 1767. Christian Godfrey Miliron and Mary ( ) to James Bailey, £5.10, 16 acres, part of the tract whereon Miliron now lives; Wm. Halman's line; corner James Bailey's former survey. Teste: Thomas Ratlif. Delivered to William? per order, 1st January, 1796.

Page 302.—4th May, 1767. Sampson and George Mathews, executors of John Mathews, to William McBride. John in his lifetime sold to William Bradshaw 306 acres in forks of James River and by his will directed his executors to make deed for same, and Bradshaw relinquishes his purchase in favor of William McBride. £70 paid to John and £80 paid to executors. 306 acres, corner John Mathews.

Page 305.—9th December, 1766. Robert Rogers, of Augusta County, and Robert Wallace, cf Hanover Township, Lancaster County, Pennsylvania, and Mary ( ) to Seth Rogers, of the same County and Colony, £200, 135 acres in Beverley Manor conveyed from Daniel Kidd to George Rogers, 20th September, 1763, and by George to Robert Rogers and Robert Wallace above, on 22d September, 1763, oak in George Hutcheson's line at Christie's Creek. Teste: James Cooper, Thomas McNeal. Delivered: Seth Rodgers, 5th April, 1774.

Page 307.—20th May, 1767. John Dickenson to Benj. Estill, £100, 546 acres on a branch of Jacksons River called the Falling Spring, patented to Adam Dickenson on 1st June, 1750, and conveyed by Adam to John and David Stanley and by them conveyed to John Dickenson; also a survey adjoining above containing 250 acres. Mortgage for payment of £100. Teste: William Hugart, Wm. McClenachan, Jas. McDowell.

Page 311.—18th May, 1767. Thomas Teat (Tate) and Ann to George Bright. £28, 170 acres in Beverley Manor on the head of a branch of South River; David Hays line. Teste: James Tate, Wm. Campbell, Robert Doak. Delivered: George Bright, November, 1770.

Page 315.—15th May, 1767. John Ramsey and Mary ( ) to John Gilmer, Jr., £145 paid to Andrew Evans, 220 acres, part of 400 acres which did belong to John Ramsey upon main branch of James River, corner Carmickel's land. Delivered: Robert Thompson, 24th May, 1784.

Page 318.—19th March, 1767. Andrew Leeper and Jean to John King, £180, 278 acres on Middle River of Shanando; corner Hugh Thompson. Teste: Gilbert Christian, John Ramsey, Wm. Black. Delivered: John King, March, 1768.

Page 320.—27th April, 1767. Jesse ( ) Jackson to George Anderson, £5.10, horses.

Page 322.—20th May, 1767. James Loghridge, of Long Cove Settlement in Granville County in South Carolina, by John Poage, attorney in fact, to John Dickenson. £50, 168 acres on Calf Pasture River, corner William Jameson's land, crossing Davis's Mill Creek, Dunlap's line.

Page 326.—20th May, 1767. John Dickenson, gent., and Martha to William Thompson, 24th June, 1784.

Page 330.—20th May, 1767. Archibald Armstrong, Sr., and Margaret to Robert Armstrong, Sr., £100, 280 acres on Jackson's River, corner land in possession of James Ewing.

Page 333.— — day —— 1767. William Hamilton, Sr., and Else (Alice) to Alex. Hamilton, £100, 507 acres in the Calfpasture. Teste: Jas. Callison, Wm. Mann, Robert Armstrong.

Page 336.—9th February, 1767. John Kirk (Kerk) to John Beaty, £10, horses. Mortgage to pay £12. Teste: David Beaty.

Page 337.—7th October, 1765. James Lockridge, of Long Cove Settlement, Granville County, South Carolina, planter, to John Poage, power attorney to make conveyance, p. 322. supra. Teste: Robert Anderson, Thomas Poage. Acknowledged by James before Pat. Calhoun, J. P.

Page 339.—22d May, 1767. John Willson, Gent., to William Reah, £245, 600 acres on Elk Creek of Calfpasture. Delivered: Wm. Buchanan, August, 1769.

Page 341.—20th April, 1767. James Findley, brother and heir of Robert Findley, deceased, and Agnes to Sampson and George Mathews, £30, lots 3, 4 and 13 in Staunton, part of the County lots, and 155 acres in Beverley Manor. This indenture conveys one-half of lot 4, the other half having been sold to Felix Gilbert; also one-half lot 13, the other half being sold to James Houston; also 16 acres, part of 155 above, corner George Wilson. Teste: John Redpath.

Page 345.—17th April, 1767. Same to George Willson, of Hampshire County, £90, ¼ acre, one-half of lot 3, the other half being sold to Thomas Stuart: also 16 acres, part of 155 above.

Page 351.—19th May, 1767. James Donaldson and Elizabeth, of Montjoy Township, York County, Pennsylvania, by Robert Reed, his attorney, to Mathew Reed, of Staunton, shopkeeper, £40, Pennsylvania money, 100 acres on Tinker's Creek of Roan Oke. Delivered: Mathew Reed, 7th March, 1772.

Page 355.—13th May, 1767. Privy examination of Elizabeth above.

Page 356.—20th December, 1766. William Rodgers, of Staunton, to Mathew Reed and Hugh Johnston, merchants in Staunton, £2.6.3, cow, beds, pots, &c. Mortgage.

Page 357.—19th January, 1767. Daniel Brown, of Orange County, North Carolina, to Isaac Taylor, £30, 103 acres on Little River, a branch of New River, mouth of Old Field Creek. Teste: William Ingles, Samuel Adams, Henry Brown. Delivered: John Reaburn by your order, October, 1768.

Page 359.—11th August, 1767. James Trimble, of Green Spring, and Sarah to Peter Holle, of Hampshire, £15, 85 acres on the Crab Apple Fork, a branch of South Branch of Potomac; corner survey formerly made for James, but now belonging to Peter; corner Peter Holle. Teste: Thos. Ratlif, John and Jean Trimble.

Page 362.—14th August, 1767. John ( ) Taylor to Thomas Ratliff. 75 acres on James River. Teste: James Trimble, James Allison, John McNutt, John Allison. Delivered: (?) John Trimble, 12th September, 1755 (possibly his own signature).

Page 364.—19th August, 1767. John ( ) McCloward (McClure) and Mary ( ) to Andrew Johnston, £50, 50 acres on the Mole Hill Draft.

Page 366.—14th May, 1767. Thomas Batts, farmer (Beats), to Jonathan Whitley, weaver, (Whitlow), £19, horses and cows. Mortgage. Teste: Joseph Long.

Page 367.—14th May, 1767. Robert Shannon, weaver, to Jonathan Whitlow (Whitley), weaver, £16, horses, &c. Teste: Solomon Whitley, Archibald Graham.

Page 368.—18th August, 1767. Stephen ( ) Arnold (Arnel) and Jean ( ) to John Hall, £60, 130 acres by patent, 11th July, 1761, on Love Run and Elk Creek, a branch of James River.

Page 371.—15th August, 1767. John and Robert Armstrong, of Granville County, South Carolina, to John Moore, £77, two tracts containing together 180 acres, on Broad Creek in Fork of James, A containing 100 acres; B containg 80 acres; crossing Lick Run. Delivered: John Moore, May Court, 1774.

Page 373.—8th August, 1767. John Cravens, eldest son and heir and executor of Robert Cravens, farmer, deceased, and Mary Cravens, widow and executrix of Robert, to Archibald Huston, farmer, £170, 470 acres, corner to tracts devised to Zebulon and Robert Harrison, part of 7009 acres patented to McCoy, Hite, &c., 26th March, 1739. Teste: John Wilson, Joseph Dictum, John Guin.

Page 377.—17th August, 1767. Adam Stephenson and Rebeckah ( ) to Mark Riggs, £20, 80 acres patented to Adam, 5th June, 1765. Teste. James Divier, Mathew Patton, Samuel Patterson.

Page 380.—14th August, 1767. William Carruthers and Margret ( ) and Mathew Robertson and Elizabeth ( ) to Moses McClure, £1.5, 3½ acres on South River, a branch of North Branch of James River, Moses McClures line. Teste: Joseph Walker.

Page 383.—18th August, 1767. Archibald Huston, farmer, and Mary to John Cravens, farmer, £171, 470 acres, part of 7009 acres patented to McCoy, Hite, &c., on Linvelle's Creek, corner that part devised by Robert Cravens to Zebulon and Robert Harrison, conveyed to Archibald by deed dated 8th of this inst. Teste: John Wilson, Joseph Dictum, John Guin. Delivered: Michael McMullin, March, 1770.

Page 386.—19th August, 1767. Zebulon ( ) Harrison and Margaret ( ) to Thomas Looker, £70, two tracts, A containing 220 acres patented to Richard Fields, 16th August, 1730, corner Wm. Carroll's land; corner said Harrison's land; B, containing 46 acres joining above on Daniel James' branch, patented to Daniel Davison, 25th September, 1746, conveyed by him to Zebulon. Teste: Joseph Skidmore. Delivered: James Lookey, November, 1768.

Page 389.—18th August, 1767. Robert ( ) Patterson, farmer, and Ann ( ) to Alexander Stuart, £40, on South River Shanando, a woodland of George Anderson, 193½ acres patented to Robert, 16th August, 1756. Delivered: Alex. Stewart, March Court, 1773.

Page 392.—6th August, 1766. James Crocket and Martha ( ), of Augusta County, and Robert Crocket and Jennet, of Mecklenburg County, North Carolina, to William Thompson, £60, 370 acres on Great River of Calfpasture, corner Thomas Gillam's land, crossing Mill Creek; corner John Harry's land. Teste: Benj. Lowry, Thos. Stevenson, John Coffey. Delivered: Wm. Thompson, 24th June, 1784.

Page 396.—18th August, 1767. John Campbell, Sr., and Elisabeth to Robert Campbell, his son, 200 acres on Sinking Spring, a branch of Middle River of Shanando, part of 400 acres patented to said John, 12th June, 1746, corner John Campbell, Jr.; corner John Campbell. Delivered: Thomas Frame by your order, 25th January, 1773.

Page 399.—10th May, 1767. Thomas Walker, gent., of Albemarle County, and Mildred to Andrew Lewis, £200, two tracts, A containing 190 acres on Peters Creek, conveyed by James Patton to James Bean, 28th November, 1751, and by him to Thomas Walker, 16th May, 1764 and B lying on Goose Creek, a branch of Roan Oke River, part of 400 acres formerly in the seisin of James Burk and by him conveyed to James Bean, 18th May, 1758, and by him to Thomas Walker, 16th May, 1764, 117 acres. Teste: Robert Erwin, Henry Fry, James McCallister, John Neely, George ( ) Gibson, Robert McClenachan, James Madison.

Page 403.—10th June, 1767. Same to same, £5, two tracts, A containing 200 acres conveyed by Henry Brown to Thomas Walker, 20th August, 1760, on Goose Creek; B conveyed by James Burk to Thomas Walker, 100 acres, William Campbells line.

Page 407.—18th August, 1767. Alexander Hamilton and Margaret to John Stephenson, £90.5, 271 acres on the little river in the Calfpasture, Henderson's line; corner Robert McCutcheon's land; corner said Jones Henderson's land. Teste: John Hays, Jr., James Moore, Jr.

Page 411.—19th August, 1767. John Stevenson (Stenson, Steenson) and Margret (Margey, Marget) to John Galespy, £30, 190 acres on a branch of Stuart's Creek. Delivered: —— 18th October, 1785.

Page 415.—24th March, 1767. James ( ) McCoy, of Roan County, North Carolina, to John McCoy, of Augusta County, £30, 160 acres on Mossey Creek, part of 320 acres patented to said James and John McCoy, 25th September, 1762, David Ralstones line. Teste: John Campbell, Joseph Malcome, Elizabeth Campbell, Elizabeth McNight. Delivered: John McCoy, 9th November, 1767.

Page 417.—18th August, 1767. Edwad Erwin to William Shannon, release deed for 400 acres mortgaged by grantee to grantor, 20th March, 1765. Moses Hall, Samuel McFeeters, Robert Gragg. Delivered: Col. Abraham Smith, 25th October, 1768.

Page 419.—18th May, 1767. William Shannon to Abraham Smith, £35.9.5, mortgage of 300 acres on North River of Shanandore, corner David Davis.

Page 424.—18th August, 1767. Jacob Woodley (Woodle) and Grace ( ) yeoman, to Thomas Moore, blacksmith, 200 acres conveyed to Jacob by Valentine Sevior, on Smith's Creek, crossing Daniel James' branch.

Page 426.—29th July, 1767. Charles Patrick and Mary, of Albemarle. to John Patrick. Whereas Robert Patrick by will, 10th August, 1761, devised to sons Charles and John 720 acres and Charles and John agreed to divide said land by deed of partition, 16th November, 1762, and recorded in Augusta, viz, John to have tract 283 acres formerly conveyed to Robert by Wm. and David Bell, 20th August, 1754, and to Wm. and David by Samuel Gay, 21st February, 1747; also the land on North of South River whereon said Robert lately dwelt, &c., &c., £200, all the land on south side of the river above.

Page 428.—Return of privy examination of Lettice, wife of Robert Breckinridge, dated 5th August, 1767, as to deed dated 21st August, 1765. to Stephen Loy.

Page 431.—6th August, 1767. William Graham to his son Francis Graham, £100, 364 acres on Buffelo Creek of Rone Oak and in a fork of same adjoining Israel Christian, William Carvin and Joseph Robinson, part of 845 acres patented to James Patton, 3d November, 1750, oak in the Barrens; corner said Israel Christian, formerly Joshua McCormick's; oak on Carvin's Creek, fork of Buffelo Creek; corner 236 acres deeded to Joseph Robinson. Teste: Donald Campbell.

Page 435.—19th July, 1767. James McDowell and Elizabeth, of Augusta, to James Templeton, £250, 300 acres on Big Spring, a branch of North Branch of James. Teste: James Greenlee. Delivered: Jas. Templeton, 7th November, 1770.

Page 439.—19th August, 1767. Thomas ( ) Burk and Clerey ( ) to David McCaumus, £20, 100 acres on Shanandore, part of 320 acres patented to said Thomas, 17th July, 1763, oak below mouth of Dry Run. Delivered: John Burk, March, 1773.

Page 443.—19th August, 1767. Same to Francis Kerkley gent., £350, two tracts, A containing 220 acres on Shanandore, oak by mouth of Dry Run, McCoumus's corner; B containg 200 acres adjoining former, deeded to Wm. Burk, 23d February, 1743. Delivered: Francis Kirtley, 20th March, 1786.

Page 446.—10th June, 1767. Peachy Ridgway Gilmore to Thomas Burke, £85, 300 acres on Shanando River, patented to John Madison, 2d June, 1758, and sold by John to grantor, a gum near Frazer's land. Delivered: Robert Grattan, Esq., 15th October, 1808.

Page 449.—18th August, 1767. William Ramsey and Jane ( ) to Moses Moore, £210, 582 acres on Little River of Calfpasture, corner Alex. Dunlop's land. Teste: John Cunningham, Joseph Walker, James Trimble.

Page 453.—18th August, 1767. Michal Neice (Niece) and Margret (Margaret) to Adam Painter, £215, 360 acres patented to Michael, 10th August, 1759.

Page 457.—14th August, 1767. Andrew ( ) Brown and Jean to David Lyttle, £125, 260 acres in Fork of James River, on North Branch of James. Delivered: David Lyttle, July, 1769.

Page 461.—30th June, 1767. Robert Kinkade, farmer, and Leona (Lena) ( ) to Andrew Lockridge, £40, 159½ acres, part of 334 acres conveyed by James Bratton to Robert, 21st May, 1763, hereby conveyed all the residue of said 334 acres after conveyance heretofore by Robert to Mathew Kinkead, — August, 1766. Mortgage. Corner Lewis's tract. Teste: Thomas Smith, John Ridpath, Pat. Lockhart.

Page 464.—18th August, 1767. William Fleming and Anne (Anna) to Robert Reed, tavernkeeper, of Staunton, £200, two tracts, A containing 300 acres purchased by William of Israel Christian, 24th September, 1763, Beverley's Mill Place line; also B containing 440 acres purchased by William of Robert Beverley, 23d May, 1765, Israel Christian's line, corner David Stuart and John Miller; corner John Henderson. Delivered to Mrs. Reid, 5th June, 1781.

Page 468.—19th August, 1767. Andrew Hamilton to Thomas Lewis, eldest son and heir of John Lewis, gent., deceased, who was surviving patentee of James Patton, gent., £50, 600 acres patented to Patton and Lewis, 30th August, 1743, and conveyed to Andrew by Thomas Lewis, heir, &c., 16th October, 1765, but since found not to be the land intended to be conveyed, the intent hereof being to reconvey the same to Thomas, lying on Elk Creek. Teste: Andrew Lewis, John Grattan.

Page 472.—19th August, 1767. John Kelly to William Hill, £27, 105 acres in the Forks of Hayse's Creek, corner John Walker's line. Delivered to John Hays, January, 1770.

Page 475.—20th May, 1767. Daniel ( ) Oharra and Elizabeth to Alexander Miller, £24.10, 125 acres on south branch of the Cowpasture River.

Teste: Wm. Crow, Henry Key, Jno. Mills. Delivered: Alex. Miller, September, 1769.

Page 479.—19th August, 1767. William Thompson and Jean to James Crocket, £50, 295 acres, part of 370 acres first surveyed for Robert Crocket, deceased, on the Calfpasture above Jameson's land, pines on Mill Creek, Davise's land, said Thompson's corner. Delivered: James Crockett, 14th October, 1773.

Page 483.—26th May, 1767. William ( ) McCurry, of Roan County, North Carolina, to Samuel Crocket, £130, 248 acres on south branch of Rone Oak. Teste: Walter and Joseph Crocket, Andrew Boyd.

Page 487.—26th May, 1767. Same to Thomas Goodson, £50, 80 acres on south branch of Roan Oak.

Page 489.—17th January, 1767. John King and Mary ( ) to David Bell, £5, 10 acres between his and John Patterson's land, William Wallace's corner. Teste: John Burnsides. Delivered: David Bell, heir of the grantee, 20th February, 1806.

Page 491.—2d April, 1766. Margret Cameron to sons Charles and George Cameron, love and goodwill, household goods. Teste: George Francisco and John Murray.

Page 492.—21st May, 1767. Thomas Watterson to Abraham Smith, £47.15, horses and cattle. Teste: James Divier, Daniel Henderson, Jacob ( ) Gilespy.

Page 493.—13th August, 1767. Joshua McCormick ( ) to Israel Christian, £25, horses and cattle. Teste: Wm. Christian, Wm. Fleming, Daniel McNeal, John Smith.

Page 495.—21st August, 1767. Ruben Moore ( ) and Ann, of Frederick County, to Rubin Harrison, £100, 400 acres on the Dry Fork of Smith's Creek, patented to John Harrison, deceased, 10th February, 1748 who devised the same to said Ann. Delivered: Thomas Patterson by your order, January, 1773.

Page 497.—21st August, 1767. John Hutcheson to George Skillern, £32.13.4, 240 acres whereon John now lives, part of 573 acres surveyed for William Hutcheson on Christian's Creek in Beverley Manor; corner Wm. Hutchison and George Hutchison. Delivered: George Skillern, 19th June, 1773.

Page 502.—25th April, 1767. Mathew Patton, of Johnson County, North Carolina, to William Rowland, £63, 266 acres by deed from Col. James Patton, 17th December, 1753, on Craig's Creek. Teste: Patt Sharkey. Sent to Wm. Rowland, 1793 (1773 ?).

Page 505.—22d August, 1767. Israel Christian and Elisabeth to William Bowyer, £150, one-half of lot No. 3, in Staunton, whereon William now lives and keeps store, purchased by Israel from John Stewart, he from Joseph Mais,and he from John Madison, Jno. Brown and Jno. Lewis, and they from James Brown, who purchased from Beverley; also one-half undivided moiety of 50 acres adjoining said town, now held by Israel Christian, Andrew Lewis, Wm. Preston and Thomas Lewis.

Page 508.—22d January, 1767. Account of slaves purchased by John Buchanan, gent., executor of James Patton. Six slaves cost £337.10.0, purchased for Buchanan's oldest daughter Mary Buchanan and annexed to her lands on James River.

Page 510.—22d August, 1767. William Cunningham and Jane to Ralph Lofftus, £90, 350 acres patented to William, 10th August, 1759, on Thorny Branch of North River of Shanandoah, corner Benj. Copeland's land, John Crosby's land. Teste: Edward Erwin, John Cozbe.

Page 513.—22d August, 1767. Peter Hog, attorney at law, to Gabriel Jones, gentleman, £150, on Paage's (Poage's ?) Run, between Thomas and John Poage and Daniel Denniston, being part of tract formerly in possession of Robert Poage and by him granted to John Poage, 1750, and by John conveyed to Peter, 1761, whereon said Peter Hog now dwells, containing 350 acres. Mortgage.

Page 518.—22d August, 1767. John Coffey, eldest son and heir of Hugh Coffey, deceased, and Susannah, of the Province of South Carolina. to John Ramsey, £40, 220 acres by patent, 3d November, 1750, to Hugh Coffey, father of John, corner John Donoly, crossing Cowpasture River.

Page 521.—16th May, 1767. Cormick ( ) McKeachvy to Thomas Stevenson, £10, cows, bed clothes and household goods.

Page 522.—29th April, 1767. George Lewis to Thomas Stevenson, £5.10, cows and horses. Teste: Robert Williams.

Page 523.—29th July, 1767. William Howard, of Albemarle County, to Sampson and George Mathews, £45, lot 9 in Staunton; also 13 acres of woodland at south corner of one of Thomas Fulton's lots, numbered 6, conveyed by Thomas to William, and to Thomas by Alex. Wright, 16th May, 1760. Teste: Archer Mathews, Thomas Smith, Thomas Rennick, John Ridpath.

Page 526.—15th July, 1767. William Watterson to Michael Bowyer, one negro wench, £60. Teste: Mathew Reed, Daniel Kidd.

Page 526.—24th August, 1767. John Cowardin, sadler, to William Bowyer, merchant, £40, slaves and horses. Teste: Michael Bowyer, Chas. Cameron.

Page 527.—19th August, 1767. John Cunningham to William Bowyer. £9, cattle. Teste: Andrew Johnston, Wm ( ) McFarling.

Page 530.—7th July, 1767. Conrad Lamb, farmer, and Catherine ( ) (Cathrina) to John Thomas, £150, in Brock's Gap, 212 acres conveyed to Conrod, 16th August, 1756, by executors of Benj. Borden, Jr., part of 800 acres patented to Benj. 1747. Teste: Adam ( ) Haverstick, Mathias House, Michael ( ) Ginder, George ( ) Ginder. Delivered to Jno. Dunbarr, November, 1769.

Page 535.—17th November, 1767. John Hutchison and Isable ( ), wheelwright, to William Hutchison, farmer, £5, 242 acres on Christian's Creek in Beverley Manor, granted to George Hutchison by Wm. Beverley, 21st February, 1738. George died intestate and the land descended to John, his oldest son, to make a title to William, 242 acres on Christian's Creek; corner Samuel Pilson's land. Teste: John Henderson, Samuel Pilson, Zechariah Johnston, John Thomson. Delivered: Wm. Hutchison, 24th December, 1771.

Page 541.—17th November, 1767. Same to Samuel Pilson, farmer, £5, 148 acres in Beverley Manor on Christian's Creek, conveyed to George as above, &c., as above. Delivered: Samuel Pillson, 1st May, 1775.

Page 546.—7th October, 1767. John ( ) Huchens (Hutchens) and Martha( ), of Johnson County, North Carolina, to John Hickman, £20,

309 acres in Fork of James River, oak corner to Michael Dockerty's in Erwin Pattersons line; corner Thomas Williams. Teste: James Edmuston, Abram Brown, Samuel McClure. Delivered: John Hickman, September, 1782.

DEED BOOK No. 14.

Page 2.—17th October, 1765. Patrick Calhoun, Jr., of Long Cane Settlement, Granville County, South Carolina, to Hugh Montgomery, late of Augusta County, £300, 610 acres on Reed Creek, opposite John Buchanan's land. Memorandum: that the name is written Patrick Colhoun, but Patrick Calhoun, Jr., acknowledges he is the person meant. Teste: Robert Anderson. Delivered: Col. James Stuart, June, 1793.

Page 8.—4th September, 1767. William Minter, of Craven County, South Carolina, to John Curry, £75, 245 acres on South Branch of Linvel's Creek, line of Abraham Hills, being tract conveyed to said Minter from Samuel Harrison and Mary, 19th October, 1762. Teste: Francis, Edward and Samuel Erwin, Joseph Curry, William Curry, Robert Dunwody. Delivered to James Curry, 23d December, 1783.

Page 13.—10th November, 1767. John Lowry to James Robinson, £120, 260 acres on North Branch of James, John Dailey's line, crossing the river into Fork of James. Delivered: James Edmiston, July, 1777.

Page 18.—17th November, 1767. John ( ) Ferrill and Margaret ( ) to Daniel Price, £20, 47 acres patented to John, 5th June, 1755, between the Picked Mountain and Shanando; corner said Price's land.

Page 21.—25th August, 1767. Samuel Cowdon to Mathew Willson and James Cowdon, chairs and beds in trust to secure payment of £20 to Samp and George Mathews for which Mathew and James are security for Samuel. Teste: Susanna ( ) Cockran, John Murray, Pat. Lockhart.

Page 22.—16th November, 1767. John Canterberry to Francis Kirtley, 5 shillings 9/, a slave that the said Kirtley bought of Jeremiah Brent that married my sister Margaret. Teste: William ( ) Buchanan, Michael Coger.

Page 23.—27th September, 1767. William Russell, of Culpeper, to Francis Kirtley, power of attorney to convey tract adjoining Margaret Perkey, Robert Hooks and John Stinson, being part of 5,000 acres patented to Jacob Stover. Teste: Michael Coger, Wm. Bohannon, Robert Eastham, Jr.

Page 27.—17th November, 1767. William Russell, late of Culpeper County, by Francis Kirkley to John Stevenson, yeoman, £32.10, 700 acres on Mill Creek, part of Stover's 5,000 acres, part whereof being lapsed and forfeited was granted to William Russell, Gent., father of said William Russell and contains 250 acres whereon John now lives as by survey made by Thomas Lewis, crossing Hooks' Branch; corner Perkey's land, Weaver's line; another tract of Perkey's; corner Francisco's land. Delivered: John Stevenson, October, 1769.

Page 34.—17th November, 1767. Cornelius Brown of the Congres in South Carolina, taylor, by Abraham Brown, of Augusta County, brother of Cornelius, to William Davis, of Philadelphia, Penna., skinner. Cornelius gave Abraham power of attorney, 24th November, 1766; £43, 175 acres, one-half of 350 acres on south side of Woods' river, commonly called New River. Conveyed to Cornelius 28th November, 1750, and was patented to John Harrison 25th September, 1746, on side of Neck Creek. Delivered: Wm. Davis, 31st July, 1770.

Page 42.—12th November, 1767. William Ramsey and Agness, eldest son and heir of James Ramsey, to Margaret Ramsey, £18, two tracts on North River of Shanando—A containing 120 acres, corner Silas Hart and Hugh Diver, side of a small meadow called the Elk Draft, being tract conveyed to said Ramsey by Silas and Jane Hart, 5th June, 1764; B containing 80 acres conveyed by Daniel and Jane Smith to James Ramsey, father of said William, 18th August, 1756, on North River of Shanando; corner Charles Diver's land. Teste: Daniel Henderson, John Douglass, Nathaniel Douglass. Delivered: Thomas Reed, 21st May, 1770.

Page 48.—22d August, 1767. John Dickenson and Martha to Gabriel Jones, £250, 546 acres on Falling Spring, a branch of Jackson's river, bought by John from John and David Stanleys, who bought it from Adam Dickenson to whom it was patented 1st June, 1750.

Page 53.—17th June, 1767. John Adams and Elizabeth ( ) to Andrew Woods, £70, 300 acres on a branch of Looney's Mill Creek. Teste: Robert Finley, Stephen Trigg.

Page 59.—17th November, 1767. John Campbell and Elizabeth to John McCay, £100, 130 acres, part of 320 acres patented to John and James McCay and afterwards conveyed by John McCay to John Campbell 19th August, 1766, on Mossey Creek, Ralestone's line. Teste: James Stevenson, James Campbell, Elizabeth McKnight. Delivered: Joseph Malcom, 14th November, 1772.

Page 64.—18th November, 1767. Jacob Hornberrier and Elizabeth M. to Jacob Friend, £17, on a branch of the South Fork called Richardson's Run on west side of Dyche's land, 229 acres patented to Jacob Hornberrier, 10th July, 1767.

Page 68.—17th November, 1767. John Sproul to Samuel Lyle, £14, one horse and eight cows.

Page 69.—10th August, 1767. Borden's executors to Benjamin Gray, £25, 260 acres, part of 92,100; corner widow Davison and William Taylor, poplar in Daniel Lyle's line, David Gray's corner. Delivered: Benjamin Gray, 26th September, 1773.

Page 75.—17th August, 1767. Same to James Lecky, £30, 200 acres, part of 92,100 acres, side of North River on or near Mathew Robinson's line; corner James Campbell; widow McClure's line. Delivered: James Lackey, August, 1770.

Page 80.—17th August, 1767. Borden's executors to James Harris, £14, 200 acres, part of 92,100; corner Francis Wilson. Sent to James Harris, per order, February, 1776.

Page 88.—29th October, 1767. John McFarland and Mary, of Bedford County, to James Holles, £40, 98 acres on a branch of Reed Creek, a branch of New River, betwixt the land of the said John and the Cove, patented to John 20th June, 1753. Teste: Israel and William Christian, Daniel McNeill, Robert Breckenridge, Samuel Black, William Wright, William Bates, George Dair.

Page 93.—15th September, 1767. Israel Christian, to his daughter Rosanna Christian, £200, 148 acres, hill near the Buffalo Creek. Teste: Jno Mills. Delivered: Rosanna Christian, February, 1773.

Page 96.—17th November, 1767. Abraham Smith (and Sarra) to James Hanna, £5. (This is a deed of B. and S., but recites a lease prior which does not appear of record at this place.) 150 acres; corner Hugh Diver's land. Teste: William Crow, James Hill, Benj. Keys.

Page 100.—18th November, 1767. William Bowyer to John Smith, Release and surrender of mortgage dated 13th May, 1762, and recorded.

Page 102.—21st May, 1767. William Teas to Hugh Walker, of Gloucester County, mortgage of slaves for £40. Teste: Wm. Watterson. Pat. Lockhart, Jno. Murray. Sent to Mr. Walker by his order, March, 1768.

Page 106.—17th November, 1767. John Finley and Thankful to George Finley, 5 shillings, 176 acres, part of the tract John now lives on. Teste: Thos. Brown, Ro. Finley. Delivered: George Findley, November, 1771.

Page 109.—19th November, 1767. John Shelton, of Hanover County, to Patrick Henry, Jr., of Louisa County, £200, mortgage of the following tracts patented to John, 16th August, 1756: A, 650 acres on the waters of Clinch River; B, 1,400 acres on a branch of Clinch called Mockison Creek; C, 940 acres on the Middle Fork of Indian River; D, 995 acres on the Indian River; E, 155 acres on south side of the Indian River; F, 1,000 acres on two branches of Clinch River; also one undivided share of a patent to Col. James Patton and Others, of which the above lands are a part. Teste: Thomas Jefferson, &c. Delivered: Ephraim Dunlap, 30th September, 1772.

Page 112.—14th September, 1767. William Crow, storekeeper, £81.12.11, to James Richey & Co. of Glasgow, mortgage of two negro slaves.

Page 113.—2d June, 1767. James Hill to S. and G. Mathews, merchants, £62.19.5½, mortgage of horses, cows and one silver watch, maker's name, Charlson Landon, No. 263; household goods, coffey pot, one horse head, 1 brick iron, 200 lbs. old copper, 100 lbs. old pewter, 60 lbs. lead. Teste: Thomas Renick.

Page 115.—24th November, 1767. John Cowarden to S. and G. Mathews, £45.11, mortgage of negro slaves.

Page 117.—24th November, 1767. James Findley, brother and heir of Robert Findley, deceased, late of Staunton, to S. and G. Mathews. On 28th February, 1750, Beverley leased to James Brown, of Staunton, 260 acres, part of 1,550 acres known as the Mill tract and where the Court now stands for term of 61 years at a rental of £3. James leased to Robert, 87 acres, part of 200. This indenture, £30, and yearly rent of £1, 87 acres, part of 260 above. Term of 44 years and 4 months.

Page 123.—15th March, 1767. Robert Poage to Robert Poage, his son, £20, 150 acres on Back Creek, a branch of Roanoke, at a place called the Forks, patented to Robert 20th June, 1749. Teste: John Buchanan, William ( ) Hall, Robert Bellshe. Delivered: Robert Poage, May, 1770.

Page 127.—15th March, 1767. John Cravens and Margaret ( ) to Robert Belshie, Jr., £50, 230 acres, part of 670 acres devised by Robert Cravens, whose executor John is, on Linvel's Creek, George Speece's line; corner part of said tract belonging to Zebulon and Robert Harrison. Teste: Isaac Robinson. Delivered: Robert Belshire, June, 1783.

Page 132.—8th March, 1768. Edward Sharp to Robert Whitely (Whitly),

£5, 335 acres patented to Edward, 15th July, 1760, on Cedar Creek in fork of James, Samuel McDowel's line. Sent William Berkeley, 9th February, 1771.

Page 135.—12th March, 1768. David Frame and Mary to Hugh Donaho, 5 shillings, 68 acres a moiety of 136 acres patented 12th May, 1759, on a draft of Naked Creek, east side of the Pennsylvania road. Teste: **Edward Womer**, Thomas Smith, Joseph Dickenson, Samuel Cowdan. Delivered: Hugh Donaho, December, 1771.

Page 138.—16th March, 1767. John Fares and Nance ( ) (name is signed Nance on the lease; Agness in recital of the release, and Margaret in the certificate of record of release) to Robert Edgar, £20, 100 acres, part of 400 acres patented to John Brownlee, 8th November, 1752, on the Lick Run, a branch of North River of Shanando. Teste: John Hogshead. Delivered: Ro. Edgar, 5th November, 1784.

Page 142.—16th March, 1768. David Hogshead and Margaret ( ) to John Hogshead, Jr., £25, 172 acres on Moffet's Branch, part of 285 acres patented to John Hogshead David 16th June, 1744, hiccory at the foot of the Little Mountain. Teste: George Moffett, Roger and Alexander Kilpatrick. Delivered: James Hogshead, 25th July, 1770.

Page 145.—24th February, 1768. Elizabeth Erwin ( ) to Edward Braden, £45, 200 acres formerly conveyed from George Breckenridge to Mathew Erwin, 15th February, 1748, and devised to Elizabeth by Mathew; corner Samuel Lusk. Teste: James Bell, John Francis. Delivered: Elizabeth Erwin, 27th July, 1772.

Page 148.—14th May, 1767. William Stewart and Margaret ( ) to James Bodkin, £27, 105 acres on the Cowpasture; corner land in possession of James Clemons. Teste: John Carlile, Hugh Hicklin, Francis Jackson, William Black. Delivered by James Bodkin, order 7th March, 1793.

Page 152.—15th March, 1768. Hugh Donaho, farmer, and Elizabeth to James Anderson, son of John Anderson, £68.15, on a draft of North River of Shanando; corner Charles Campbell's land on northwest side of the Pennsylvania road, field of Robert McMahon's, being 300 acres patented to Robert McMahon 12th May, 1759, and conveyed by Robert to Hugh 21st October, 1765. Delivered: John Anderson, November, 1767.

Page 155.—2d March, 1768. James ( ) Carr and Mary ( ), of Bedford County, to Henry Cartmill, £60, 120 acres patented to James 10th September, 1767, on Purgatory Creek. Teste: Walter Stewart. Sent to Henry Cartmill, October, 1773.

Page 158.—15th March, 1768. John Scott and Ann ( ) to Abraham Miller, £35, 150 acres on McCoy's draft of Linvell's Creek, east of Cravens' land; corner George Speer's land patented to John 1st October, 1765. Delivered: Abraham Miller, December, 1768.

Page 160.—15th March, 1768. John Bodkin to David Frame. Release of mortgage dated 18th March, 1767. Teste: John Wattkins, Hugh Donaho.

Page 162.—10th March, 1768. Borden's executors to Mary Boyles, Boyle, widow, £20, 200 acres, part of 92,100; corner Robert Telford, oak on North River. Delivered: James Boyles, September, 1779.

Page 165.—16th March, 1768. Same to Robert McElwrath, £40, 230 acres of 92,100, cedar and sugar trees on Walker's Creek; corner Alexander Walker. Delivered: Robert Hamilton, March, 1773.

Page 69.—17th March, 1768. Same to John Summers, £40, 440 acres of

92,100, William McKee's corner in the patent line; corner James Davis; corner Samuel Willson and Hugh Cunningham; corner Samuel McMurty. Teste: James and Samuel McDowell, Moses Trimble.

Page 173.—1st March, 1768. Same to John Allison, £30, 190 acres of 92,100; corner Andrew Hays near his mill; corner Samuel McDowell.

Page 177.—2d March, 1768. Same to John Lusk, £12, 259 acres (no part of 92,100); corner Robert Lusk on Hugh McFaden's line; corner John Montgomery's new survey; corner John Huston; corner Walter Eaken.

Page 180.—2d March, 1768. Same to Robert Lusk, £10, 241 acres, part of 92,100; corner John Lusk, Walter Eakins' line; corner John Handly; corner Hugh McFaden.

Page 184.—10th March, 1768. Same to David Quin, £———, 210 acres, part of 92,100; corner John Bunton, North River, mouth of Back Creek.

Page 189.—6th February, 1768. James Patton's executors to John Craig, £65, 400 acres patented to James 22d August, 1753, on Crab Creek, a branch of New River.

Page 192.—16th March, 1768. David Steel to Nathaniel Steel, £———, 3½ acres in Beverley Manor. Teste: William McAdow, Robert Doak, Thomas Steel. Delivered: Nathaniel Steel, April, 1773.

Page 195.—17th March, 1768. William Wilson and Mary ( ) of Albemarle County to Abraham Haptonstall (Hoplenstall), £46, 112 acres on a branch of New Found Creek. Delivered: James Thomas, April, 1773.

Page 199.—16th March, 1768. James ( ) Scott and Easter to Patrick Corrigon, £20, 24 acres on Jackson's River. Delivered: Mathias Kessenger, July, 1769.

Page 203.—19th March, 1768. Stephen Loy and Mary ( ) to John Sharp Watkins, 5 shillings, half lot No. 14 in Staunton, formerly leased by Beverley, 22d February, 1749, to Alexander Wright, who conveyed it to said Thomas Fulton, and now conveyed by Stephen Loy. Teste: Randal Lockhart, Michael Weaver, John Cawley. Delivered: Jno. Sharp Watkins, 4th August, 1773.

Page 207.—16th March, 1767. Robert Scott to Hugh Donaho, £50, 170 acres on Shanando River opposite mouth of South River, patented to Robert Scott 16th August, 1756; corner Thomas Lewis' land. Delivered: Hugh Donaho, December, 1771.

Page 210.—16th October, 1767. Samuel Ekerling, eldest brother and heir-at-law of Emanuel Ekerling, deceased, of County of Philadelphia, Penna., to William Davis, of Philadelphia City, £60, 125 acres on New River, part of 900 acres patented to Garret Zinn 20th June, 1753, and by him conveyed to Emanuel, 15th January, 1754; corner John Miller opposite a small island. Teste: Alexander McClenachan, John King, William Christian. Delivered: Wm. Davis, 31st July, 1770.

Page 214.—9th December, 1767. William Bell and Rachel to Rev. Charles Cummins, £120, 164 acres, part of 400 acres patented to James Bell, deceased, father of said William, on a branch of Middle River of Shanando near the North Mountain, Samuel Craig's corner. Teste: Samuel Craig, James Bell, Henry Cresswell, James Bell. Delivered: Cumings, December, 1768.

Page 218.—16th March, 1768. John Montgomerie to Mathew Huston, £10, on James River in Borden's tract, 1 acre, 2 roods, 27 perches; corner

Jno. Montgomerie and Mathew Huston. Delivered to Mr. Rowan, 14th December, 1790.

Page 222.—10th March, 1768. Thomas Vance (and Jennet) to John Kirk, £40, 400 acres at mouth of Andrew Fitchpatrick's Run on North River.

Page 226.—17th March, 1768. William Hugart to Andrew and Thomas Lewis, £120, 490 acres on Meadow Creek, a branch of Jackson's River at a place known as the Great Meadow, patented to John Dickenson, 26th ———, 1760, conveyed by John to William 21st August, 1766.

Page 229.—28th February, 1767. John Smith to Jonathan Smith, £90, slaves. Teste: John Mills, Joseph Luney, James McKair (McKain?), William Bowen.

Page 231.— ———, 1767. James Kirk and Agness to Alexander Kirk, their son, £20, 200 acres, part of 400 acres patented to James Bell 12th January, 1746, on a small fork of Jennings' Branch. Delivered: Alexander Kirk, March, 1774.

Page 236.—16th March, 1768. Nathaniel ( ) Steel and Rosana to David Steel, £12, 201½ acres in Beverley Manor, part of the tract Nathaniel formerly lived on; corner John Tate's land; corner John Fulton. Delivered: David Steel, 16th November, 1771.

Page 241.—16th March, 1768. Robert Scott to James Scott, £30, 196 acres (100 acres patented to said Robert, 16th August, 1756); corner Mathew Thompson's land on Collins' branch; oak near William Beard's land), 96 acres, the other part thereof part of his other parcel of land, the one containing 200 acres patented to said Robert 30th July, 1742, the other containing 85 acres patented to Robert 15th August, 1764, on Stoney Lick Run. Delivered: James Scott, August, 1773.

Page 244.—10th November, 1767. Alexander to James Stewart, £3, hay and other articles now on the plantation of Francis Smith, mortgage. Teste: Thomas McIlhany, Gordon Potter.

Page 246.—7th November, 1767. Josiah Davidson, eldest son and heir of Daniel Davidson, deceased, to Thomas Moore, blacksmith, £160, 370 acres on Smith's Creek, the same that was conveyed to Daniel 4th June, 1748, by James Wood, to whom it was patented 12th January, 1766 (1756). Delivered: Thos. Moore, 14th June, 1770.

Page 251.—22d February, 1768. Jacob ( ) Lorton and Lydia ( ) to George Taylor, £85, 656 acres on Crab Creek of New River by a deed by Jacob Schull as attorney for Ebenezer Westcoat to said Jacob; corner Poulson Smelser. Delivered to Jno. King's letter, July, 1795.

Page 256.—2d February, 1768. Jacob ( ) Lorton and Lydia ( ) to James Bane, £100, 560 acres by deed from James Patton 2d February, 1754, on Toms Creek, a pine by the Beaver Dams; corner Jacob Harmon's land; corner to the Price's land. Teste: William Preston, Robert Lusk, George Dair, Thomas Tosh, Daniel McNeill, Robert Cowan, John Buchanan, Francis Smith, Robert Breckinridge, Thomas Loyd, Peter Wright. Delivered: Jacob Sciler, 29th March, 1773.

Page 261.—23d February, 1768. Jacob Harmon and Sarah ( ) to Joseph McDonald, £145, 455 acres, part of a tract conveyed to said Jacob by Col. James Patton, 2d February, 1754, on Toms Creek of New River; corner William Byers, a stake in the Barrens; corner Lorton's land, now James Bane's, pine by the Beaver Dams. Delivered: Jacob Scilor by your order, 29th March, 1773.

Page 266.—5th March, 1768. Daniel ( ) McCormick and Anne ( ) to Joshua McCormick, £30, 110 acres, part of a tract conveyed to Daniel by William Preston on North Branch of Roanoke, Frederick Smith's line; corner said Daniel McCormick. Teste: William Preston, Robert Breckinridge, Arthur Campbell, Joseph Cloyd, Is. Christian, Wm. Crow.

Page 271.—14th March, 1768. William Bryan to James Bryan, £100, 267 acres on Roanoke, alias Goose Creek; corner William Bryans, Jr., James Burk's line. Teste: William Ingles, William Tutt, Samuel Woods, William Preston. Delivered: Mr. Samuel Lewis, 16th January, 1772.

Page 275.—9th August, 1767. Archibald Graham and Margaret, of Pittsylvania County, to Israel Christian, £200, 148 acres, hill near the Buffalo Creek. Teste: Edward Carvin.

Page 280.—8th August, 1767. Same to same, £150, 280 acres on a branch of Buffalo Creek; corner Christian Rutlishberger (Rutlishber).

Page 284.—10th October, 1766. John ( ) Mitchell and Sarah ( ), of Orange County, N. C., to George Wilson, of Hamshire County, £80, 234 acres by patent 10th August, 1759, on Stewart's Creek; corner James McCoy. Teste: William and Susanna Preston, Samuel McNabb, Nicholas Smith, Francis Smith, Anne Smith, Francis Smith, Thomas Smith.

Page 289.—18th March, 1768. George Wilson and Elizabeth, of Hampshire, to Charles Donnelly, £90, 234 acres by patent 10th August, 1759, on Stewart's Creek above. Delivered to Charles Donnelly, March, 1778.

Page 292.—22d February, 1768. William Crow, of Staunton, ordinary keeper to James Crow, yeoman, £800, 140 acres on James River purchased by William from David Looney by deed recorded; corner Col. Smith's land.

Page 295.—14th March, 1768. William Crow to Col. Andrew Lewis, mortgage, £55, 1 stoned horse, 1 bay horse, 1 sorrel mare, 1 black mare, 9 head cow kine.

Page 297.—17th November, 1767. Benj. Estill to Gabriel Jones, surrender of mortgage of 20th May, 1767, by John Dickinson to Benj. Estill, 546 acres, also 250 acres. Gabriel has contracted with John for the purchase of said tracts for $250. Gabriel pays $100 to Benjamin and Benjamin conveys to Gabriel.

Page 301.—17th March, 1767. George Wilson, Gent., and Elizabeth, of Hampshire County, to David Bell, £15, 74 acres patented to said George 16th September, 1765, on head branch of Cowpasture. Delivered: 26th October, 1778.

Page 303.—20th March, 1768. James Crow to Alexander McCaul and Andrew Edmiston of Henrico County, £360.6, 140 acres, part of 250 acres patented to Robert Loney, 30th July, 1742, whereon said David Looney lately lived, on James River, and conveyed to William Crow 21st November, 1766 ( ), on ——, near ——, to James Crow. Mortgage.

Page 307.—24th November, 1767. William and Thomas Crow to John Ellis and Company, of Leeds in Yorkshire, £100.11.1, 213 acres on Craig's Creek conveyed by Col. Jno. Smith to said William and Thomas. Mortgage. Delivered: William Bowyer, February, 1772.

Page 310.—14th December, 1767. James Ewing (Ervin) to Israel Christian, £10, spotted cow bought from Wm. Davis in Forks of James River, one bay horse called Terrible bought from Edward Sharp, one bay mare bought of Abraham McClellon, 1 rifle with brass mountings.

Page 311.—4th December, 1767. Joshua ( ) McCormick to Israel Christian, £10, cow, calf and mare. Teste: James Cloyd.

Page 312.—28th January, 1768. Robert Brown, tanner, £8, to Israel Christian, a black mare bought of a Dutchman at New River and another black mare.

Page 312.—19th March, 1768. Is. Christian to his son, Wm. Christian, £———, natural love and affection and 5 shillings, and in consideration of his marriage with his wife Annie, seven negro slaves. Teste: William Bowyer, P. Henry, Jr., William Christian, Elisabeth Bowyer.

Page 315.—7th October, 1766. Jacob ( ) Brown and Agness ( ) to Thomas Tosh, £20, 100 acres by deed from James Patton, deceased, on West Fork of Roan Oak. Teste: John Buchanan Robert Breckinridge, David Robinson, Thomas Barnes, William Preston.

Page 319.—11th March, 1768. David Robinson and Annable to Francis Smith, £440, 300 acres (two hundred of which is part of 400 conveyed to David by George Robinson 29th November, 1749, and the remaining 100 acres known by name of the Saw Mill place was reconveyed by William Graham to said David Robinson, on Buffelow Creek, branch of Roan Oak; corner Robert Breckinridge; corner Thomas Moore. Teste: Mathew Ralston, Wm. McMullen, James Hutcheson. Delivered: Thos. Madison, by Francis Smith's order, March, 1772.

Page 324.—16th March, 1768. William Poage (and Ann) to William McClenachan, £260; two tracts,—A containing 104 acres in Forks of James River on a branch called Cedar Creek, corner Robt. Whitlow's land, James McGuffey's line, corner (supposed) William Mill's land; B containing 100 acres patented to William 23d May, 1763, on said creek. Teste: John Frogg. Delivered: William McClenachan, June, 1769.

Page 326.—29th January, 1768. John Henry Eastminger, blacksmith, to Mathias Gabert, £40, blacksmith's tools, cows, iron stove and all the articles in the house belonging to me; mortgage. Teste: Simon Robinson, Margaret ( ) Clotzhine, Elizabeth ( ) Sasinger.

Page 327.—10th February, 1768. Thomas Breden (Batton) to Michael Weaver, £20, 1 waggon, 4 horses, and 2 cows. Teste: William Johnson.

Page 328.—4th November, 1767. James McCutchan, planter, to William McCutchan, £15.19.8, one still and furniture. Teste: Samuel and John McCutchan.

Page 329.—14th October, 1766. Commission directed to Thomas Hinds and Robert Lyle to take privy examination of Sarah, wife of John Mitchell of Orange County, N. C., as to conveyance by John to George Wilson dated 10th October, 1766. Executed, 14th October, 1766.

Page 331.—18th May, 1768. John Kerr and Lucy ( ) and William Kerr and Martha ( ) to James Laird, £50, 124 acres on Middle River of Shanando, 100 of which is part of 400 joining Beverley Manor and patented to said John 30th July, 1742, the other 24 acres patented to said William 2d June, 1760, joining the former tract; corner John Allison. Teste: Edward Rutledge, Alexander Walker, Wm. ( ) Mathers. Delivered: James Laird, February, 1770.

Page 335.—17th May, 1768. Samuel Muncy and Mary ( ) Mousie

(Monsey) to John Miller, Sr., £50, 75 acres, part of 150 acres conveyed by George Speere to Michael Hober, 3d February, 1760, and by Hober to Samuel Monsey, 20th May, 1765, on Linvell's Creek; corner Riddel's land, a part of same original tract. Delivered: John Miller, August, 1773.

Page 339.—17th May, 1768. John Tate to Thomas Tate, £1, 200 acres; corner James Lynn and John Tate. Teste: Thomas Paxton, Finley McClure. Delivered: Pat. Campbell, 4th August, 1773.

Page 342.—18th May, 1768. William Carr and Martha ( ) to Andrew McClure, £40, 164 acres, part of 188 acres patented to William 2d June, 1760, on Middle River of Shanando; corner Beverley Manor. Teste: Alex. Kelly ( ), John Gillespie, Wm. Robertson. Delivered: Andrew McClure, March, 1779.

Page 345.—17th May, 1768. James ( ) Alexander, eldest son and heir-at-law of William Alexander, deceased, to John Alexander, 20 shillings, part of 400 acres patented by William Alexander, deceased, containing 200 acres, being tract conveyed by William Alexander, deceased, to Martha Alexander, 27th August, 1751, and after decease of Martha, who died intestate, descended to said William as heir-at-law to Martha, and after decease of William, who died intestate, descended to James Alexander as eldest son and heir, lying near the Long Glade; corner said William; corner Michael Dickey. Delivered: John Alexander, 23d June, 1786 (?).

Page 348.—10th May, 1768. David Gray and Ruth (mark) to James McCrosky, £18, 100 acres; James Greenlee's corner on John Davidson's line; Moses Whiteside's line; William Gray's corner. Teste: Moses Whitesides, John Carouthers, Benj. Gray. Delivered: Jas. McCoskry, son to James, 27th March, 1788.

Page 351.—18th May, 1768. Michael Dickey and Mary to James Dickey, his son, £40, 160 acres, part of two tracts surveyed for Michael, one containing 350 acres, the other 170 acres on head branches of Naked Creek. Delivered: James Dickey, June, 1771.

Page 355.—2d April, 1768. William Ledgerwood and Agness ( ) to Robert Braford, £103.15, in Beverley Manor, part of tract on which William now lives, containing 200 acres. Teste: James Mitchell, James Moffet, Samuel Braford, Fras. McDonald.

Page 359.—12th May, 1768. Samuel McCutchan, Sr., and Frances ( ) to Samuel McCutchon, Jr., son of said Samuel 5 shillings, and diverse and good causes done to me; tract Samuel, Sr., now lives on, 150 acres; corner Borden's patent line; William Sproul's line; also all properties. Teste: Robert Patterson, Chas. Campbell, Arter Hamilton. Delivered: Jno. McCutcheon, March Court, 1774.

Page 362.—16th May, 1768. William ( ) McCandless to Andrew Moore, £60, 150 acres; corner Hugh Weir and Alexander Greer; corner William McCandless and Alexander Greer; William Alexander's line; corner Hugh Beard and John Weir. Teste: Thomas Wilson, Samuel Wilson, William Moore.

Page 366.—31st March, 1768. James Shaw to John Ramsey, £45, 240 acres on Great Calfpasture, conveyed to Loftus Pullen by James Patton and Jno. Lewis, 17th July, 1745, and to James Shaw by Loftus, 19th August, 1760; corner land formerly in possession of John Miller, now in possession of Jno. Ramsey; corner Robert Bratton. Teste: James Crockett, John Stewart. Delivered: John Ramsey, August, 1770.

Page 370.—15th March, 1768. William ( ) Hall and Jean ( ) to William Logan, £50, 300 acres in Forks of James River; corner William Hall and David Cloyd. Teste: Samuel Kirkham, Daniel Evans, Hugh Logan.

Page 373.—12th May, 1768. Samuel McCutchan, Sr., and Frances ( ) to John McCutchan, Jr., £———, divers reasons and good causes done to me, Samuel, by son John, 150 acres; Borden's patent line on northwest; William Sproul's line; Samuel McCutcheon, Jr.'s, line. Delivered: John McCutchon, March, 1774.

Page 375.—15th March, 1768. Samuel McCutchan, Jr., binds himself in £200 to take care of his father Samuel and his mother. Samuel, Sr., agrees to convey 20 acres to Samuel, Jr., when he is no longer able to do for himself. Delivered: Jno. McCutchan, July, 1775.

Page 377.—15th March, 1768. Barnet Man and Ann Margret ( ) to John Man, £10, 120 acres, part of 320 acres patented to Barnet, 12th May, 1759, on Stoney Run; corner George Mann's land. Teste: George Mallow, Jacob ( ) Man. Delivered: Jno. Mann, 31st May, 1773.

Page 380.—17th May, 1768. John ( ) Davis and Judith ( ) to James Gregory, £75, 280 acres on West Fork of James River called Back Creek conveyed by John Young to said John Davis, 15th May, 1766. Delivered: Arther Hickens (Kichens), May, 1773.

Page 385.—10th May, 1768. John Ramsey and Mary ( ) to John White, £100, 180 acres on James River; corner John Gilmore.

Page 389.—4th May, 1768. William Robinson and Martha to James Crawford, £68, 198 acres; corner Robert Kirkpatrick; corner Charles Campbell. Teste: James McDowell, Wm. McCandless, Charles Campbell.

Page 393.—15th March, 1768. John Hall and Mary to James McGavock and John Maxwell, £50, 45 acres of Cedar Creek in Forks of James; corner William Hall, Jr., William Poage's line; corner David Cloyd. Delivered: Hugh Brawford, May, 1778.

Page 396.—18th May, 1768. James Hogshead and Elizabeth ( ) to John Hogshead, Jr., 20 shillings, 45 acres on Moffet's branch being part of his father's tract of 400 acres bearing date 1st June, 1746,; corner said John's line. Delivered: George Moffett, Michael Hogshead, James Allen Delivered: James Hogshead, 25th July, 1770.

Page 401.—17th May, 1768. James Hogshead, Sr., and Elizabeth ( ) to James Hogshead, Jr., £10 shillings, 31 acres on Moffet's Branch, part of 400 acres patented to James Hogshead, 5th June, 1746; also 29 acres adjoining above patent to James, 16th August, 1756.

Page 406.—17th May, 1768. Borden's executors to James Campbell, husbandman, £30, 175 acres in 92.100 acres on North Branch of James; said Campbell's old corner; Wood's Creek, Abraham Brown's line. Delivered: James Campbell, January, 1772.

Page 411.—10th May, 1768. 'Same to Robert McElhenny. £9, 100 acres, part of 92,100, Car's Creek; corner said McElhenny. Delivered to son, July, 1777.

Page 414.—12th May, 1768. Same to John McKee, £15, 150 acres, part of 92.100; corner Jonathan Cunningham. Delivered: John McKee, April, 1773.

Page 418.—10th May, 1768. Same to Robert Talford, £40, 250 acres, part of 92,100, bank of the North River in the patent line; corner Charles Hays. Delivered: Robert Tedford.

Page 424.—28th March, 1767. Richard Stanton and Charity ( ) to William Herbert, £105, tract that Thomas Stanton, Sr., purchased from John Bengamon, Sr., to whom it was patented, 20th June, 1753, containing 460 acres on a branch of Woods River at place called Poplar Camp. Teste: Is. Christian, Anthony Bledsoe, W. Ingles, John Hanna, Jacob Lorton ( ), Edmund Vausell, James Hodge, Andrew Miller. Delivered: Thomas Madison.

Page 429.—17th May, 1768. Hance Harper and Elizabeth ( ) to Samuel Black, £100, 175 acres on Bull Pasture patented to John Brown, 3d November, 1750, and since conveyed to Hance; corner land in possession of John Brown; corner land now in possession of Mathew Harper, now William Martin's. Delivered: Samuel Black, 3d August, 1772.

Page 433.—6th April, 1768. George Skellern and Elizabeth to Daniel McNeill, £55, 100 acres patented to George, 10th July, 1766, on Smith's Creek, otherwise called Tinker Creek, a branch of Rone Oak. Teste: Benj. Rice, Wm. Preston, Granville Smith, Francis Smith, Pat Buchanan. Delivered: Capt. Thomas Madison, 22d October, 1770.

Page 437.—16th May, 1768. Charles Smith and Margarett to Alexander Henderson, of Albemarle County, £40, two tracts on Dry River, a branch of North River of Shanandore—A, containing 165 acres conveyed to Charles by Samuel Henderson, 17th November, 1762; B, containing 117 acres conveyed to same by same; corner Daniel Smith's land. Delivered: Samuel Henderson. February, 1774.

Page 442.—10th May, 1768. James Trimble of Green Spring and Sarah to James Robison, £40, 95 acres on a branch of James River on west side of Camp Mountain.

Page 445.—30th March, 1768. William Watterson to John Stevenson (distiller), one house. Delivered: Jno. Stevenson, November, 1770.

Page 445.—18th May, 1768. James McKain to Jonathan Smith, Robert Faris and James Latherdale, £30, 1 waggon, 2 black horses, 1 bay mare, 1 bay horse. Teste: Margaret ( ) McKain.

Page 447.—5th November, 1767. Robert Sloan, of Rowan County, N. C., weaver, to Andrew Woods, £40, on Looney's Mill Creek next above, Hugh Carother's land containing 264 acres. Teste: James Young, Samuel ( ) Lindsey, Walter Lindsey, George Gillespie. Delivered: Thos. Madison.

Page 450.— —— March, 1768. John Brown and Margaret to John Trimble, John Finley, William McFetters, Jr., George Berry and Hugh Young, representatives or commissioners appointed by the congregation of the meeting house lately called by the name of Brown's by the approbation and under the conduct or the incumbency of the Rev. Charles Cummins, £1.5, 2 acres and a stone meeting house by a branch of the Meadow Run, a branch of Middle River of Shanandore, stone in the Glebe Road. Teste: James Brown, James Crow, Pat. Martin. Delivered: Wm. Moffett, 11th September, 1807.

Page 453.—18th May, 1767. (Sons of John.) George ( ) Windlecoit and Mary ( ) to William Windlecoit, £20, 79 acres patented to John

Windlecoit, their father, in a larger tract of 316 acres, 10th February, 1748. Delivered: Martin Coite, per order, 12th May, 1795.

Page 457.—18th May, 1767. (Sons of John.) Same to John Windlekite, £20, 79 acres, part of 316 acres above, on Shanandore River; corner Philip Windlecoit's part of said tract. Delivered: Martin Coite, per order, 12th May, 1795.

Page 461.—18th May, 1767. (Sons of John.) Same to Philip Windlecoit, £20, 79 acres, part of 316 above. Delivered: Michael Coger, August Court, 1781.

Page 464.—17th May, 1768. Patrick ( ) Denny and Elizabeth ( ) of Forks of James River, to John McKee, of said Forks, £44, at head of Kerr's Creek in the abovesaid Forks of James, branch of Kerr's Creek called Cunningham's Creek, 80 acres. Teste: John Gilmer, Robert McElhenny, David Tate ( ). Delivered: John McKee, April, 1773.

Page 468.—17th May, 1768. Robert Scot to his son Jacob Scot, £50, 175 acres on north side of Shanando, part of 350 acres patented to Robert Scott, 30th July, 1742. Teste: Samuel Henderson, William Robertson. Delivered: Jacob Scott, 15th November, 1771.

Page 472.—7th May, 1768. Elizabeth ( ) Rea to Henry Larkin, £30, 98 acres on the south side of North Branch of James River; corner John Harger; corner Alexander Baggs and William Henderson. Teste: John Bowyer, Joseph Cloyd, James McDowell.

Page 476.—27th September, 1767. Adam Looney of Craven County, S. C., to John Looney, £30, 271 acres by deed from Col. James Patton, 18th November, 1752, on head of Meadow Run or Bryan's Creek, a branch of Craig's Creek. Teste: Wm. Preston, Pat. Buchanan, James Crow.

Page 481.—16th May, 1768. Michael Mallo to William Mountgomery, £50, 470 acres on the mountain between South Fork of South Branch of Potowmac, line of Jacob Sybert's survey.

Page 486.—11th May, 1768. William Buchanan and Isbelah to James McCampbell, £50, 280 acres; corner James Miles on North Branch of James River, opposite to an island. Delivered: James McCampbell, November, 1773.

Page 488.—18th May, 1768. John Wamsley to William Gragg, £———, security for going bail, 10 cows, 3 cows, 3 horses. Teste: Henry Erwin, Benj. Harrison.

Page 489.—17th May, 1768. Antony Ealer to Jacob Archenbright and Augustine Price, £24.4, 2 stills and all the tubs, 6 cows. Teste: J. Maury, Jr.

Page 491.—16th May, 1768. Joseph Rediford (Redeford, Rutherford) to Joseph Rutherford, Jr., £50, 134 acres on Cub Run, part of 400 acres patented to James Wood, 12th January, 1746, and by him bequeathed to Mary Wood by will recorded in Frederick and by Mary conveyed to Joseph Rutherford, 31st December, 1760; corner Thomas Rutherford in line of Felix Gilbert's land on spur of Peaked Mountain. Teste: John Dickenson, Ralph Lafferty, Daniel Kidd. Delivered: Jas. Rutherford, 23d February, 1773.

Page 496.—16th May, 1768. Joseph Rutherford to Reuben Rutherford, £50, 134 acres on Cub Run. part of 400 above; Gilbert's line. Delivered: Felix Gilbert, 26th July, 1774.

Page 501.—16th May, 1768. Joseph Rediford (Rutherford) to Thomas Rutherford, £50, 134 acres, part of 400 above on Cub Run; corner Reuben Rutherford in Gilbert's line.

Page 504.—18th May, 1768. Robert ( ) Allen (and Martha) to John McClenachan, £30; two tracts—A, 34 acres, and B, 10 acres patented to Robert 14th February, 1761. Delivered: Alexander Sinclair, per order, 13th December, 1773.

Page 508.—18th May, 1768. Robert Reed and Barbara to John Poage, £54, 170 acres on Linvel's Run, a small branch of Middle River of Shanandore patented to Robert 30th August, 1763; corner James Allen's land. Teste: Geo. Moffett, William Lusk, John Young.

Page 513.—16th May, 1768. Alexander McDonald and Margaret ( ) and Jean ( ) McClelland, his mother, to John Ramsey, £100, 141 acres in Beverley Manor; corner Andrew Russell on branches of Christie's Creek; oak on Maxwell's branch; Andrew Russell's line. Teste: Hugh Ross, Andrew Russell. Delivered: William Ramsey, 5th October, 1772.

Page 515.—16th May, 1768. Alexander McDonald, John Gray and William Hutcheson to John Ramsey, bond in £200 conditioned to make secure title to 141 acres for £100 in Beverley Manor, excepting mines and minerals, if any (mentions deeds of lease and where as having been made on same date as this).

Page 518.—17th May, 1768. John ( ) Blizard and Ruth to Andrew Hulings, £20, between Bird land and Smith's Creek, part of 400 acres patented to Swan Rambo; corner old patent and John Philips; Andrew Bird's line; 30 acres. Teste: Andrew Bird, John Phillips, Edward Sampson. Delivered: Andrew Huling, May, 1773.

Page 524.—3d May, 1768. John Blizard ( ) and Ruth to Frederick Zircle of Frederick County, £250, on Smith's Creek; corner Andrew Bird; line of John Phillips, 400 acres (except 50 acres surveyed off for Jacob Rambo, the plat whereof followeth John Phillips' land, which is conveyed by Andrew Bird to Jacob) as also said Blizard doth, except a parcel bounded, viz: Patent line and Bird's line; 30 acres conveyed to Andrew Hulings above. Teste: Andrew Bird, Phillip Herbern, Edward Sampson Delivered: Ludwick Zircle, May, 1770.

Page 529.—16th May, 1768. Andrew Bird and Mary ( ) to Andrew Hulings, £35, between Smith's Creek and the mountain; corner John Phillips and Swain Rambo, 186 acres. Teste: John ( ) Blizard, Jno. Philips. Delivered: Andrew Huling, May, 1773.

Page 533.—23d May, 1768. Chas. Frederick Severt to John Coworden and John Murray, £5, 1 small bay horse, 1 iron pot, 5 pewter plates, 1 pewter dish, 1 duffle blanket. Mortgage.

Last order of record is 23d May, 1768.

Deed Book No. 15.

First order of Court admitting to record is 16th August, 1768, the last is 15th August, 1769.

Page 2.— ——— day of May, 1768. George Reader and Margaret ( ) to Jacob Kiblinger, £———, a certain tract of land in Frederick which said Kiblinger formerly lived on that he purchased of Peter Cotten's heirs,

200 acres at a place called Sinking Spring; corner land Adam Reader lives on. Delivered: Daniel Rose, June, 1779.

Page 5.—16th August, 1768. John Carr (Ceer, Keer) and Lucy ( ) to William McClure, £40, 150 acres, part of 275 acres in Beverley Manor on a small branch of Middle River joining Cohorn's land; Beverley's line. Teste: John Stuart, Hugh Allen, Andrew McClure. Delivered: Wm. McClure, August Court, 1779.

Page 9.—2d December, 1767. William ( ) Hall to John Hall, £10, 415 acres on Cedar Creek in Forks of James; corner William Hall, Jr., William Poage's line; corner David Cloyd; corner William Hall. Teste: Richard Woods, James Campbell, William McKee.

Page 11.—17th May, 1768. Thomas Stanton, of Orange County, N. C., to Henry Paulin, of Bedford County, Va., £85, on Woods River, 100 acres. Teste: John Pearey, Richard Davis, Nicholas Welch.

Page 14.—17th August, 1768. John Bear and Kartharine ( ) to Francis McBride, £190, 200 acres on Linvell's Creek, part of 500 acres patented to William Linwell and by him conveyed to Joseph Bryant, 20th August, 1746, and by him to Jacob Crisman, who conveyed 300 acres thereof to said Francis McBride and by him to said John Bear, 17th March, 1746, 200 acres whereof is bounded, viz., corner Josiah Boon's part. Delivered: Jacob Miller, 7th August, 1771.

Page 17.—17th August, 1768. Same to Josiah Boon, £90, 100 acres on Linvell's Creek, part of 200 acres as above; corner Francis McBride; Chrisman's line. Receipt for £90 is signed by Jacob Bear. Delivered: Jacob Bear, 7th August, 1771.

Page 21.—16th May, 1768. Francis Green and Margaret ( ) to Evan Thomas, 5 shillings, 240 acres on Middle Branch of Linvel's Creek joining one Hite and near a survey of Daniel Harrison patented to Francis, 29th May, 1760; also a tract containing 20 acres joining his own land patented to Francis, 10th November, 1757, Daniel Harrison's line; Hite's line. Teste: Robert Culwell, Thomas Pickens, Thomas Bowen. Delivered: Evan Thomas, 24th November, 1787.

Page 26.—17th May, 1768. Same to same, 5 shillings, 22 acres on a branch of Linvel's Creek near foot of Round Hill joining George Bowman, patented to Francis 10th November, 1757. Delivered: As above.

Page 29.—6th April, 1768. Samuel McNabb and Isabell ( ) to Jacob Gabhart, 10 shillings, 225 acres, part of a larger tract surveyed for Thomas Perey, deceased, in Beverley Manor conveyed to him, 28th February, 1749, this part being bounded, viz., joining John Campbell, William McClintick and James Perey. Teste: Mathias Gabert, William Jamison, Andrew Thompson. Delivered: Jacob Gabbert, August Court, 1769.

Page 35.—16th August, 1768. Mathew Harper and Margaret to Samuel Black, £100, 200 acres, part of 1415 acres formerly surveyed for William Henderson on a branch of Christian's Creek, and on said creek; corner Thomas Ruttchledge's land, crossing Black's Branch. Delivered: Samuel Black, 3d August, 1772.

Page 39.—6th August, 1768. Francis Reiley to Joseph Cloyd, £135, 400 acres on branches of James River; corner Jeremiah Chamberlain's tract Teste: Benjamin Hawkins, Patrick Sharkey, Samuel ( ) McRoberts.

Page 42.—7th July, 1768. David ( ) Stuart and Margaret to Alexander Stuart, their son, £50, 200 acres on a small branch of Middle River of Shanandore, James Sayers' line, oak near Buffalo Branch. Teste: John Poage, James Sayers, Andrew Moody. Delivered: Alexander Stuart (Stewart), November Court, 1773.

Page 45.—7th July, 1768. David Stuart to son Alexander Stewart, all his horses, 4 cows, 5 steers, 4 calves, sheep, hogs and tools for plantation, household furniture, £———. Alexander agrees to let his father and mother, David and Margaret Stuart have quiet possession of the plantation where he now lives to maintain themselves and family.

Page 47.—11th August, 1768. William Tincher and Mary ( ) to Moses Eagar, £60, 129 acres on the Pine Run on south side of Beverley Manor; Charles Campbell's line; James Robinson's line, South River Teste: John Hunter, Thomas Teat.

Page 52.—22d June, 1768. Zechoriah McKay (and Lydia), Moses McKay (and Mary), Robert and James McKay, of Frederick County, to John Lincon (Linkhorn), £250, 600 acres on Linvel's Creek, part of 1,200 acres patented to McKay, Green and Hite, 26th March, 1739, and by them conveyed to Robert McKay, 20th June, 1746, and by Robert devised to grantors here; corner Tunis Vanpeet's land; Boman's line. Teste: Michael Waren, John ( ) Jackson. Delivered: John Linkhorn, December, 1768.

Page 57.—22d June, 1768. Robert, James, Zachoriah and Moses McKay, of Frederick County, to Tunis Vanpeet, £———, 300 acres on Linvel's Creek, part of 1,200 acres above; corner Thomas Bryant's; corner John Lincon. Delivered: Tunis Vanpeet, December, 1768.

Page 61.— ——— ———, 1768. Same to Thomas Bryan, £80, 300 acres on Linvel's Creek, part of 1,200 above; John Bryan's line. Delivered: Thomas Bryant, December, 1768.

Page 66.—6th July, 1768. John Mills and Mary to James Alcorn, £50, 143 acres patented to John Mills, 4th June, 1764, on waters of James River, a branch of Looney's Creek; corner land in possession of Adam Looney.

Page 68.—19th February, 1768. Andrew Miller, heir-at-law of John Miller, deceased, to Israel Christian, £100, 81 acres on a South Branch of Catawba Creek; corner survey of Samuel McRoberts, crossing the Mill dam. Teste: John Bowman, Daniel McNutt, Wm. Simpson. Release only; lease follows the above.)

Page 73.—15th August, 1768. William ( ) Hall and Jenny ( ), of Fork of James, to John Millican, of ditto, £10, 100 acres in Forks of James; corner another survey of William Hall's; Crawford's corner. Teste: Nathaniel McClure, James and Andrew Hall, Wm. McKee. Delivered: Jno. McElhany, 23d May, 1784.

Page 78.—16th August, 1768. Michael Weron (Warren, Waring) and Catherine to Joshua Hudson, £150, 310 acres, parts of 2 tracts—A, of 400 acres, patented to Morgan Bryant, 20th September, 1745, and conveyed to Michael, May, 1751; B, of 365 acres patented to Waron, 10th July, 1767. Teste: Peter Vaneman, Patt. Cunningham. Delivered: Michael Waring, June, 1769.

Page 81.—12th February, 1768. Frederick Starn (Stern) to George Teetar, £10, 85 acres by patent 22d August, 1753, on Crab Creek, a branch of New River. Teste: W. Ingles, William Davis, John Taylor, John and Wm. Buchanan. Sent to George Teeter by his order, April, 1769.

Page 85.—16th August, 1768. John Campbell ( ) and Ann ( ) (the name is also written Mary, but signed Ann) to John Carlisle, £75, 202 acres on the Calf Pasture, part of tract Jacob Clemons formerly lived on; corner William Campbell; also 50 acres joining said land, the way the Big Creek runs, if divided. Teste: J. Murray, William Hamilton, Robt. Brown.

Page 89.—10th August, 1768. Henry Long to William Logan, £250, 200 acres on Buffalo Creek of James River. Teste: Patrick Brown, Wm. McClenachan, Wm. Hall. Delivered: John Logan, 28th May, 1788.

Page 92.—18th August, 1768. John Paxton, Sr., to John Paxton, Jr., £100, 200 acres in the first fork of James River; corner George Adam Salling. Teste: Archibald Alexander, James Paxton, Joseph Walker.

Page 95.—5th July, 1768. William Davis, of Mecklenburg County, N. C., to Morris Ofreil, planter, 5 shillings, 160 acres, Bell's Spring Run, adjoining James Bell, William Bell and Charles Phillips patented to William Davis 16th August, 1756. Teste: John Stuart, Robert Wallace, William Blear.

Page 98.—10th August, 1768. Samuel McDowell and Mary to James Edmiston, £10, 170 acres; corner James Richey (on) the Mary; Archibald Alexander's line. Delivered: Moses McSpadden by order James Edmiston, 26th July, 1774.

Page 102.—2d August, 1768. James Campbell and Elizabeth ( ) to Charles Kirkpatrick, £92, 253 acres on Whistle Creek in Forks of James, mouth of said Creek; corner Patrick Young, Hall's Mill; corner James Crawford. Teste: John Bowyer, R. Alexander, Jr., Pat. ( ) Doney, John Paxton. Delivered: John Kirkpatrick, 4th January, 1772.

Page 104.—12th August, 1768. Elizabeth Inzer to Capt. Ephraim Love. Recantation of slander, that she said Ephraim was father of her bastard child. Teste: Geo. Skillern, Daniel Love, Samuel Montgomery, Jesse Harrison.

Page 106.—5th July, 1768. Christian Godfrey Milliron and Mary to Joseph Cooper, £50, 124 acres on North Branch of James River in Forks of James, corner James Bailey; David Little's corner. Teste: Isaac Ward.

Page 109.—23d March, 1768. John ( ) McClure and Mary ( ) McClure to Samuel Briggs, Benj. Harrison, Francis Erwin, cows, sheep, hogs, horses, 8 reads for use of weavers, £27, mortgage. Teste: Benj .Logan, Edward Erwin, Elizabeth McClure, Jas. Campbell. Delivered: James Trimble, 14th December, 1773.

Page 111.—17th August, 1768. Robert ( ) Shaw to John Woods, Jr., £40, 95 acres, corner Francis Gardner's land. Teste: Patt. Cunningham. Delivered: Mary Woods, 13th August, 1773.

Page 115.—17th August, 1768. Jean ( ) Craighead and John Davis, of Mecklenburg County, North Carolina, executors of Alex. Craighead, deceased, whose will was proved and recorded in North Carolina, to Andrew Sitlington, £200, 1 moiety of lands mentioned in said will, on Cowpasture, corner tract of Adam Dickinson, 310 acres. Teste: Robert Harris, Jr., David Caldwell, Robert Harris, Robert Creaghead, Jas. Alexander, John

McClure. Acknowledged in Mecklenburg County, North Carolina, before David Rees and Abraham Alexander, Justices, and Robert Harris, clerk.

Page 120.—11th August, 1768. Isabella ( ) Robinson and John ( ) Robinson, her son, to Alexander Hindman, £60, 124 acres on Hays's Creek, part of Borden's 92100, the patent line corner James Robinson. Teste: Andrew Hays, Sr., Samuel Buchanan, Arthur Graham, John Hays, Jr.

Page 124.—15th August, 1768. John Brown and Margaaret to James Brown, £100, 295 acres in Beverley Manor on both sides of the Creek on which Gabert's Mill stands, conveyed by Samuel Young to John, adjudging William McCintage and others. Delivered: James Brown, June, 1769.

Page 127.—16th June, 1768. Thomas Smith, yeoman, to Alexander Walker, cow, calf, mare. Bill sale. Teste: Robert Patterson, John Hind.

Page 129.—15th August, 1768. James Todd, of Forks of James River, to Joseph McBride, of the Forks, £80, 185 acres on Buffalo Creek in Forks of James. Teste: William McBride, Wm. McKee.

Page 133.—18th August, 1768. James Frame and Martha ( ) to Thomas Frame, their son, £100, 220 acres in Beverley Manor, corner Christian's lands, in a line of land once belonging to Lusk; McCorkale's corner; John Glasse's corner. Teste: John Stuart, John ( ) Vance. Delivered: Thomas Frame, 14th June, 1770.

Page 137.—17th May, 1768. Robert Scott to James Burnsides and Isabella, his wife, £42, 224 acres made over to said Robert by Wm. Shannin, 22d February, 1765, on Newfoundland Creek, corner tract of John Botkins, Carlile's land. Delivered: James Burnsides, October, 1769.

Page 140.—10th August, 1768. Joseph Gamwell to John Cawley, £20, grantor's part of one- half lot woodland northwest of Staunton, 14 acres, being half of a lot of 28 acres, part of No. 9 of part in No. 10, surveyed for Robert McClenachan, between lots of James Hughes and John Kerr, conveyed from Robert to Margaret and Joseph Gamwell, 22d May, 1760, the other half being since sold to Archer Mathews; also ¼ acres in Staunton, part of lot 5, being the part John Cawley now lives on.

Page 142.—18th August, 1768. John Wilson, by Sampson Mathews, to William Morrice, Mathews has obtained a pardon for Morrice and paid £5, to attorney-general therefor, also his expenses in bringing him from Williamsburg (£1), now William Morrice, late servant of John Wilson, agrees to serve John one year additional time. Teste: Richard Mathews, Jas. Campbell.

Page 143.—12th April, 1768. William Watterson to James McCarty, of City of Williamsburg, £150, 600 acres bounded by the lands of John Anderson and James Allen, Jr., on Middle River, in County aforesaid, called Shanando. Mortgage. Teste: William Goodall, Lewis Tyler, John Warburton, Daniel Kidd, Malcom Allen, William Bowen, William Crow.

Page 145.—23d August, 1768. Leonard ( ) Simmons to Adam Harper, £40, 104 acres on North Fork of South Branch of Potomac. Teste: Thomas Smith, Andrew Johnston. Delivered: Adam Harper, March, 1770.

Page 148.—22d August, 1768. John Madison to son John Madison, deed of gift, natural love and affection, 141 acres commonly called the Great Meadow, upon a branch of Cook's Creek, between lands of John and Joseph Cravens, purchased of William Cravens, 19th March, 1764, and recorded in the secretary's office; also a tract patented to John, 10th July,

1767, containing 200 acres, on Cook's Creek, Joseph Craven's corner. Delivered: Wm. Lambe, February, 1780.

Page 151.—1st July, 1768. John Bowman to Abraham Miller, £180, 545 acres known as lot No. 8, on Linvel's Creek, devised to John by his father, George Bowman.

Page 153.—1st September, 1768. Commission to take privy examination of Susannah, wife of William Preston, as to deed to Peter Cochrane, dated 10th November, 1764. Executed, 21st September, 1768.

Page 156.—15th November, 1768. John Davison and Martha to James Dunn, £33, 225 acres on a branch of Dry River of Shanandore; Abraham Smith's line, corner on Stevenson's land. Delivered: Ben. Forsythe, April, 1777.

Page 158.—26th August, 1768. David ( ) Frazeir, eldest son and heir of William Frazier, deceased, and Barbara, ( ) to Gabriel Jones, attorney at law, £45, a certain island called the Great Island, 54 acres in Shanandore River, nearly opposite the plantation whereon Jones lives, patented to William Frazier, 20th June, 1753. Delivered: Jacob Kinney per order, 6th April, 1804.

Page 161.—15th November, 1768. Jacob Bowman, late of Frederick County, but now of South Carolina, yeoman, to Josiah Davidson, £180, 500 acres on Linwell's Creek, sold by William Linwell to George Bowman, father of Jacob and devised to Jacob by George.

Page 163.—2d November, 1768. Thomas ( ) Burk and Clearey ( ) to Conrad Peterfish, £14, 177 acres on Dry River, branch of Shanandore, patented to said Burk, line of land patented for John and Lewis Neall. Teste: Joseph Hannah, Robert ( ) Frazor, David Frazor.

Page 168.—11th November, 1768. James Douglass and Hannah to John Stevenson, £50, 355 acres patented to Adam Stephenson, 5th June, 1765, and conveyed same to James, 16th August, 1766, corner Daniel Henderson, Daniel Smith's corner. Delivered: Jno. Stephenson, October, 1769.

Page 171.—11th November, 1768. Commission to take privy examination of Hannah as to foregoing deed. Executed 11th November, 1768.

Page 174.—20th November, 1768. James ( ) Anderson, Jr., and Elizabeth to James Anderson, Sr., his father, £70, 200 acres, part of 400 acres patented to said James Anderson, Sr., and by him conveyed to James Jr., 19th May, 1765, on head of Long Glade. Teste: James Bell, John and William Anderson. Delivered: James Anderson, 15th August, 1771.

Page 179.—2d November, 1768. John Eakin and Elizabeth, his wife, and James Eakin and Anne Eakin, of Bedford, £120, 261 acres, part of Borden's 92100 acres, corner Andrew and Samuel Eakin. Teste: John, James and Mathew Lyle.

Page 183.—21st May, 1768. James ( ) Peerie and Katharine to Thomas Scot, £5, 220 acres, corner former survey of Thomac Peerie, John Campbell's line, William McNabb's line, corner John Lynn. Teste: John Handly, Patrick Buchanan, William Bell. Delivered: Thomas Scott, 30th December, 1773.

Page 186.—15th November, 1768. William Dean and Mary to Hugh Davis, of York County, Pennsylvania, £5, 550 acres in Beverley Manor, part of 800 acres formerly belonging to Patrick Cook; corner William Dean;

Corner David Campbell. Teste: Patt. Cunningham, David Doack. Delivered: Hugh Davis, March, 1770.

Page 190.—16th November, 1768. Archer Mathews to William Mathews, £100, his part of 299 acres willed to William and Archer by John Mathews, Sr., deceased, in Forks of James, on Mill Creek, corner Richard Mathews, William McBride's line; corner John Murry; corner tract belonging to John Mathews, Jr.'s heirs. Delivered: William Mathews, 18th March, 1771.

Page 194.—16th November, 1768. Peter ( ) Kinder (Ginder) to James Neelly, £100, 150 acres on Goose Creek. Delivered: James Neelly, October, 1774.

Page 197.—8th November, 1768. Thomas Paxton and Elizabeth ( ) to John Paxton, their son, £100, 230 acres on James River, corner another tract of Thomas Paxton. Teste: William Paxton. Delivered: Thomas Paxton, your father, 31st June, 1773.

Page 200.—17th August, 1768. Borden's executors to John Sproul, £10, 250 acres, part of 92100, corner Andrew Steel and Wm. Alexander; corner Robert Telford, Robert Lowry's line.

Page 204.—2d November, 1768. Same to James Cooper, £5, 112 acres, part of 92100, corner Cap. Joseph Kenady, Andrew Steel's line; John Lowry's old corner; James Akin's corner; corner John Lusk. Delivered: James Cooper, April, 1773.

Page 209.—14th November, 1768. Col. Abraham Smith and Sarrah to Thomas Fulton, £110, 200 acres patented to Gabriel Pickens, 12th May, 1759, on a branch of Bever Creek; corner Hennery Smith's land; corner Jacob Gallespy. Teste: John Grattan, Ralph Lofftus, Jese Harrison. Delivered: Ezekiel Loagan, per James Magill's order, executor of said estate, 10th July, 1806.

Page 212.—3d August, 1768. John Shelton, of Hanover County, to Patrick Henry, Sr., all equity of redemption in three tracts, A 940 acres on Middle Fork of Indian River; B 995 acres on Indian River, C 1400 acres on Mockeson's Creek of Clinch River, which Patrick is to sell or otherwise dispose of. Teste: Wm. Parks Shelton. John Shelton, Jr. Delivered: Ephraim Dunlap, 30th September, 1772.

Page 212.—17th November, 1768. John Dickinson to David Martin, of Roan County, North Carolina, £205.12.6, 400 acres whereon John now lives, patented to Richard Fields, 16th August, 1730, James McDowell and Francis, of James City County.

Page 216.—17th November, 1768. Thomas ( ) Looker (Loker) to James Looker, his son, £20, two tracts on Daniel James' Branch, A 220 acres patented to Richard Fields, 16th August, 1730, and by him conveyed to Zebulon Harrison and by him to said Thomas, 19th August, 1767, corner William Carrell; corner Zebulon Harrison; B 46 acres patented to Daniel Davidson, 25th September, 1746, and conveyed to Zeb. Harrison, and by him to said Thomas, 19th August, 1767. Delivered: Abraham Bowens, a son-in-law of the grantee, 18th September, 1813.

Page 220.—5th November, 1768. John Hughes and Sarah ( ) to Joseph Lear (Lair), £80, 224 acres at the Watering Spring of Linvel's Creek, by patent. Teste: Andrew Bird. Matthias Lair, Edward Sampson. Delivered: your father Mathias Lair, 25th June, 1771.

Page 223.—18th September, 1768. Henry Long and Catharine ( ) to Jacob Arkinbright, £31.10, 125 acres, remainder of 250 acres patented 12th August, 1760, to said Henry, the other moiety being sold to George Fridley, on a branch between the Peaked Mountain and Shanandoah River. Teste: Adam Pence, Jacob Pence, John Archenbright. Delivered: Jacob Archembright, August, 1769.

Page 227.—17th November, 1768. George ( ) Gibson and Isabella ( ) to James Gilmore, Jr., £150, 200 acres on North Branch of Collier's Creek. Teste: Moses Collyer, John Collier.

Page 230.—11th June, 1768. James McDowell and Frances, of James City County, to John Berry, £52.10, 120 acres on James River, opposite mouth of Cedar Creek. Teste: John Craig, James Gambell. Delivered: Jno. Berry, 25th July, 1772.

Page 234.—24th October, 1768. James Johnson and Susanna to Charles Long, £130, 320 acres on head of Fort Run, patented to Daniel Johnson, 16th August, 1756, and by him conveyed to James. Teste: Abraham Bird, Jacob Miller, Rudy Mauck. Delivered: Jno. Bear by order, 19th December, 1774.

Page 237.—William ( ) Sallix to John Madison, bed and furniture, three head of cattle, two pots and frying pan, bore iron and two heeters, one spinning wheel and check real, three puter plates, two dishes, two water pails and a piggin. Teste: Thomas Madison.

Page 237.—18th November, 1768. Francis Beaty, of Mecklinburgh County, North Carolina, deputed collector, &c., to Joseph Alexander, £50, 265 acres, part of Borden's 92100, including the Flat Spring, where Francis Beaty formerly dwelt, corner John Ker's old place, Beverley Manor line. Teste: John Frogg, G. Madison, Luke Bowyer. Delivered: Joseph Alexander, November, 1778.

Page 241.—18th November, 1760. Robert Gray, of Rowan County, North Carolina, by John Tate, attorney, to James Craige, 5 shillings, 200 acres in Borden's tract; corner to tract sold by Francis Beaty on Flat Spring Run; corner Thomas Berry; conveyed by Borden, Jr., to David Kerr and by David and Katherine to Robert. Teste: Gabriel Madison, John Frogg, Luke Bowyer.

Page 243.—20th November, 1768. Israel Christian to his daughter Anne, wife of Cap. Wm. Fleming, natural love, &c., and marriage portion. For her natural life, a place whereon William now lives, called Bell Mount, upwards of 500 acres, at the Fording of Tinker's Creek, formerly property of John Robinson and adjoining lines with said Robinson; after her death to go to Leonard Israel Fleming, eldest son of Ann. In default of issue, to revert to grantor, in case of death of Leonard before Ann, she may designate beneficiary by will.

Page 246.—19th November, 1768. William Crow and Margaret ( ) and Thomas to Ninian Minzies & Co., of Richmond, merchants, £322.1, two tracts on Craig's Creek, patented to James Patton, 1750, and conveyed to John Smith, and by John to William and Thomas Crow, 15th October, 1765, 195 acres; also 273 acres; also slaves, household goods and furniture. mentioned in a mortgage to David Stewart and Robert Breckinridge, 1760. Teste: Archer Mathews, Sampson Mathews, Robert McClenachan. De-**livered: Ninian Minzies, 22d August, 1773.**

Page 251.—4th March, 1769. John Buchanan and Margret to Michael Dougherty (Docherty), £10, 84 acres in Forks of James, part of 170 acres purchased by John Buchanan from John Moffet; corner Michael Docherty's land; corner James McGavock's land. Teste: James Crow, James Gilmore, Jonathan Smith. Delivered, October, 1777.

Page 253.—15th March, 1769. Ezekiel Morrise, only acting executor of Daniel Morrise, late of County of Bedford, deceased, to Samuel Lindsay, £16, 33 acres by patent, 3d May, 1763, on James River below mouth of Catapa Creek. Teste: Malcom Allen, William Porter. Delivered: Walter Smiley, 20th February, 1786.

Page 255.—30th November, 1768. Gabriel Jones to Samuel Lawrence, release of mortgage, 30th November, 1762.

Page 257.—18th March, 1769. Henry ( ) Black to Nathan Peoples, £40, 210 acres, corner James McNabb. Teste: Wm. Peoples, Joseph Reed.

Page 259.—16th February, 1769. James and Moses Green, of Culpeper County, to John Burk, £10, 143 acres near Peaked Mountain, patented, 20th August, 1740, to Robert, father of James and Moses, on Boone Run. Teste: Thomas ( ) Burk, John ( ) Miller, Robert ( ) Rains.

Page 261.—21st March, 1769. John Burk to George Conrod, £30, 108 acres on Boone's Run, a branch of Shanando. Delivered: George Conrod, August, 1776.

Page 263.—20th March, 1769. John Burk to Henry Armontrout, 40 shillings, 3¼ acres, part of 400 acres patented to John and Lewis Neal, 1st December, 1740, and by them conveyed to William Burk, deceased, and descended to John by William's will, on Boon's Run of Shanandore. Teste: John Couts, George Eliot. Delivered: John Pence by Mr. Armentrout's order, 3d November, 1786.

Page 266.—25th January, 1769. Robert Rowland to Thomas Rowland, £100, 369 acres patented to Robert, 25th July, 1746, on head branch of Looney's Creek. Teste: Benj. Hawkins, Michael Woods, Jr., Thomas Arnott, Andrew Woods. Delivered: Pat. Lockhart by your order, March, 1772.

Page 267.—14th March, 1769. Jacob ( ) Parsinger and Cathrine ( ) to Nicholas Millberry, £70, 240 acres on Cub Run of Shanando, Charles Rush's line; Courtz's line; corner Patrick Wilson; corner Pound's land, part of Stevens' patent conveyed to Christophel Francisco and to Peter Hull, and to Jacob Parsenger. Delivered: Peter Rush, 20th August, 1787.

Page 272.—15th March, 1769. Peter Miller and Mary ( ) to Charles Long, £50, 248 acres on Stony Run, corner Barnet Man, Hermon's line. Delivered: Conrod Levingston, 26th April, 1785.

Page 276.—11th March, 1769. George ( ) Null, heir-at-law. Margaret ( ) Null, relict of Nicholas Null, Barbara ( ), wife of George, to Henry Armentrout, £100, 243 acres on Boon's Run, 188 acres being part of 250 acres patented to Nicholas, 25th September, 1762; the other 55 acres being part of 220 acres patented to Nicholas, 15th August, 1764, Hammer's line; Charles Ties (Teas) land; Young's corner. Teste: John Seller. Delivered: Peter Conrod, 25th April, 1784.

Page 280.—11th September, 1768. Henry Seller to Adam Seller, £60, 168 acres patented to Henry, 1st June, 1750, on Shanando, Philip Long's land; corner Peter Sellers'; also 205 acres patented to Henry, 30th August,

1763, between Peaked Mountain and Shanando River; corner Stephen Hemsberger. Teste: John Seller, Daniel ( ) Price, Jacob Hammer.

Page 282.—21st March, 1769. Jacob ( ) Shell, yeoman, to Thomas Burk, £67, 200 acres conveyed to Jacob by Ebenezer Wastcoat, 17th May, 1767, on New River, mortgage. Delivered: Jacob Shell, January, 1770.

Page 283.—18th March, 1769. Charles Tees to Benj. Yardly, £56.2, 310 acres, corner Robert Turk on South River; ocrner John Patrick, mortgage. Delivered: Benj. Yardly, February, 1770.

Page 285.—18th March, 1769. Same to same, bill sale of cattle and household furniture.

Page 286.—9th March, 1769. James Campbell and Lettis (Leths) ( ) to Moses Bennet, £28, 64 acres on North Branch James River, part of 175 acres belonging to James Campbell. Delivered: Robert Lusk, 26th July, 1774.

Page 289.—21st March, 1769. Andrew ( ) Foster, of Mecklenburg County, North Carolina, to James Bell, £80, 220 acres, part of 300 acres patented to said Andrew, 5th September, 1749, on McClure's Run of Middle River of Shanandore, Morris O'Freel's line; said Bell's corner. Delivered: James Bell, 14th November, 1774.

Page 290.—20th March, 1769. Charles Tees, £4, to William Craig, 6 acres of wheat. Teste: Benj. Yardly.

Page 291.—7th June, 1768. William Graham to David Cloyd, £100, 400 acres on a branch of Roan Oak whereon William Graham now lives. Teste. William Christian, Francis Smith, James Templeton.

Page 293.—21st March, 1760. James ( ) Turk and Mary to James Kennerley, £130, 320 acres on South River of Shanando, conveyed to James by Thomas, 16th August, 1758, corner land formerly Bloodworth's, the Cranberry Swamps, Christian Clemonts' land.

Page 296.—21st March, 1769. John McClure (McCleward) and Mary to Barney (Begney) Murray and John Huston, £60, 200 acres on Muddy Creek, patented to Daniel Harrison, and conveyed by him to said McClure.

Page 299.—21st March, 1769. John Burk to Jacob Runcle, £30, 100 acres part of 400 patented to Lewis and John Neal, 1st December, 1740, and by them to Wm. Burk, deceased, and by his will to John Burk, on Boone Run, of Shanandore, corner one Conrad. Delivered: grantee, 17th June. 1817.

Page 302.—1st March, 1769. William Magill and Jean ( ) to Charles Philips, £122, 400 acres on a branch of Cathey's River, called Buffalo Lick Branch, granted William by deed from William and James Bell, 18th March, 1760, patented to James Bell, 1st December, 1740, and bequeathed said William and James by James's will. Teste: John Young Robert Clendinen, William Hogshead. Delivered: John Philips, July, 1774.

Page 305.—21st March, 1768. James Anderson to John and James Hookes, £40, 300 acres patented to Robert McMahon, 12th May, 1759, on a branch of North River of Shanandore, Alexander Walker's corner. Delivered: James Hook, 21st March, 1775.

Page 308.—15th November, 1768. Valentine Matchier to Hugh Gibson £40, 275 acres patented to James Carrill, 5th July, 1751, and by him conveyed to Valentine Pence, by whose will Peter Miller was directed to make conveyance, who devised same to Valentine Matcheier; corner Benj. Logan's land. Delivered: Hugh Gibson, 3d March, 1772.

Page 310.—17th August, 1768. Andrew Loghridge to Robert Kinkead, deed of surrender of tract whereon Robert now lives, 159½ acres, mortgaged by deed, July, 1767, £40. Teste: William McClenachan, John Graham.

Page 313.—3d March, 1769. John Buchanan, gent., and Margret to John Campbell, £340, 740 acres on a branch of the Indian or Holston River, called the Middle Fork, said tract being known by the name of the Royal Oak. Teste: James Crow, John Mills, David Campbell, Arthur Campbell, John Howard, George Skillern. Delivered: David Campbell, May, 1771.

Page 316.—13th March, 1769. John Mills to Blany Nulls, £30, 200 acres on waters of Roan Oak, near Glade Creek, adjoining land of Thomas Acres. Delivered: John Mills, son of William, 8th October, 1773.

Page 318.—22d March, 1769. Henry Long to Gabriel Jones, £50, 350 acres purchased by Henry from his brother Philip Long, descended to Philip as eldest son of his father Philip Long, on Shanandore River at upper end of Richard Maulding's 2000 acres tract, near Peaked Mountain, Sealer's line. Mortgage.

Page 321.—22d March, 1769. Charles Lewis and Sarah to John McCastlin (McCastling), on Stewart's Creek, a branch of Cowpasture River; corner land in possession of Thomas Gillaspie.

Page 324.—21st March, 1769. William Lewis and Ann to Archibald Smathers, £15. 100 acres on a branch of James's River called Back Creek, about three miles above Allen's land below Falling Spring Run. Delivered: Archibald Smithers, March, 1778.

Page 327.—21st March, 1769. Same to same, £37.10, 172 acres on Back Creek of James River above Allen's land.

Page 330.—9th November, 1768. John Smith and Mary to Andrew Lockridge, £80, 100 acres on Little Creek in the Calfpasture, being one-half of William Smith's tract where he formerly lived. Delivered: Jno. Wilson, September, 1782.

Page 333.—21st March, 1769. John Alexander to his brother James Alexander, £20, 35 acres, part of 400 acres patented to William Alexander, deceased, on head branches of Naked Creek. Teste: William, Mathew and John Thomson. Delivered to Mr. Alexander, 18th May, 1786.

Page 336.—20th March, 1769. Zachariah Johnston and Ann to Thomas Calbreath, £5, 241 acres, part of 270 in Beverley Manor on Long Meadow of Middle River of Shanando, formerly belonging to William Johnston, who died intestate; descended to Zechariah as his eldest son and heir, joining Thompson's land. Delivered: Wm. Galbreath, 26th June, 1794.

Page 338.—27th February, 1767. John Byers (Buyers), blacksmith, to Samuel McClure, £18.9.6, mortgage of cows and smith tools. Teste: Joseph Walker, James Trimble.

Page 340.—20th March, 1769. Adam ( ) Stroud (Strowd) and Mary ( ) to Bastian Hover, £24, 275 acres, part of 700 acres above said Hover's other line on South Fork of South Branch of Potowmac. Teste: Archibald Reaugh. Delivered to Mr. Hover.

Page 342.—18th March, 1769. George Pence to Jacob Pence. Jacob Pence and Valentine Pence together purchased a tract from Stoval Francisco, and Jacob Pence died before title was made and by will devises his part to Jacob and George Pence, his sons, but after his father's death, Valentine Pence obtained title in his own name and dies and devises that moiety to Jacob Pence, brother to George, that their father never got title to during his lifetime. Now George, 20 shillings, conveys to Jacob all his part. Delivered: Henry Pence, son of Jacob, 18th March, 1805.

Page 344.—16th August, 1768. George ( ) Null and Barbara to Jacob Hamor (or Hammer), £30, 90 acres on Boon's Run, a branch of Shanandore River, patented to Nicholas Null, 15th August, 1764, and descended to George as eldest son and heir; corner Tack's land, Charles Foy's line. Teste: Daniel Smith, Thomas ( ) Burk, Jacob Nicholas, Robert Shanklin (Certified by A. McClenachan, C. A. C., for John Madison, late C. A. C. This is the first, 23d March, 1769). Delivered: Henry Hammer, 30th June, 1792.

Page 345.—21st March, 1769. John Sibert (Sciber), late of North Carolina, but now of North Carolina (?), son of Andrew Sibert, deceased, binds himself apprentice to Jacob ( ) Archenbright, to be taught the trade, occupation or science of a blacksmith, which Jacob now useth, until he is 21, John being now 16 years and 6 months. Delivered: John Siber, May, 1774.

Page 347.—12th December, 1768. Dennis ( ) Henry and Cathrine ( ) of Capefair, of Cumberland County, North Carolina, to Jacob Waring, £35, 270 acres on head of Long Meadow Draft, waters of Linvell's Creek, patented to Dennis, 7th June, 1764. Delivered: Samuel Dehart, who intermarried with Ann Warren, devisee of Jacob, 18th February, 1790.

Page 350.—12th December, 1768. Commission for privy examination of Catharine to above deed. Executed, 14th December, 1768.

Page 351.—24th March, 1769. William Simpson to Israel Christian, £40, beds, furniture, horses, plows, dishes, basons, plates, chests, trunks, &c.

Page 351.—25th March, 1769. Same to Archibald Graham, power of attorney to convey to Israel Christian a tract formerly sold by Graham to Simpson in Pittsylvania County.

Page 355.—24th January, 1769. Israel Christian to his son William Christian, £1,000, five tracts, 1095 acres, on Buffalo Creek, a branch of Roanoak, commonly called the Stone House Lands, A 300 acres whereon Locust in Little Hell; B containing 117 acres; C 200 acres, corner William Graham; D, 400 acres, Mill's Mountain; E, 78 acres on Dry Run; also two surveys adjoining said Stone House Lands, Tinker Mountain, Rosanna Christian's land, Creely's Gap.

Page 358.—25th November, 1768. Commission for privy examination of Mary, wife of William Crow, in deed of mortgage by William Crow and Mary, and Thomas Crow, to Minzies, 19th November, 1768. Executed, 8th December, 1768.

Page 361.—9th March, 1769. Jacob ( ) Boughman, eldest son and heir of Henry Boughman, deceased, to Andrew Lewis, £100, 780 acres on Greenbrier, opposite mouth of Muddy Creek, patented to Henry Boughman, 10th August, 1759, Fork of the Green Bryer River and Wolf Creek. Delivered: James McDowell per order to whom the lands now belong, 16th April, 1811(?)

Page 363.—21st December, 1768. Commission for privy examination of Mary, wife of William McIlhenny, deed dated 14th February, 1769, to Alexander Stewart. Executed, 14th February, 1769. Delivered: Wm. Moore, January, 1780.

Page 364.—14th February, 1769. William McIlhenny to Alexander Stuart, £155, 197 acres purchased by Henry Bowen from Lilly Bowen, his mother, 6th September, 1765, and conveyed by Henry Bowen and Ann to William McIlhenny, 2d October, 1765, on James River; corner tract belonging to John Bowen, deceased, of which this 197 acres is a part. Teste: Samuel Walker, James McGavock, James McElhiney, Samuel McDowell.

Page 368.—14th November, 1768. John Seawright and Sarah to Hugh Campbell, Jr., £15, 126 acres on North Branch of Naked Creek, part of 188 acres.

Page 371.—26th November, 1767. John Mitchel and Margaret ( ) to Francis Fullen, £29, 170 acres on Buffalo Creek in Forks of James; corner John McCollum. Teste: Richard Woods, John Thompson, Robert Campbell, James Davies. Delivered: Mr. J. Lyle, 18th November, 1791.

Page 374.—30th May, 1769. John Davis, of Roan County, North Carolina, to James Davis, of Forks of James, £62, 436 acres in Forks of James; corner William McKee's, formerly William Todd's land; corner Borden's tract, Robert Young's line, branch of Buffalo Creek; Hugh Cunningham's line, formerly Low Todd's; corner Peter Wallace. Teste: Samuel Wilson, James McMath, Archebeld McCurey, Samuel Davis.

Page 377.—17th April, 1769. Thomas Vance and Jenat ( ) to John Campbell, £35, 148 acres on North Branch of James; corner Mr. Thomas Vance's plantation. Teste: James Cowan, John Alison, Charles Campbell, John Shields, Jr. Delivered: Thos. Vance, 26th July, 1774.

Page 381.—24th May, 1769. John ( ) Sproul and Margaret to Alexander Wilson, £40, 250 acres of Borden's tract; corner Andrew Steel and William Alexander; corner Robert Telford, Robert Lowry's line. Teste: Charles Campbell, Thomas Alexander, Robert Wardlaw. Delivered: Alexander Wilson, March, 1772.

Page 384.—20th June, 1769. John Burk to Nicholas Alstot, £200, 163 acres, part of 400 patented to Lewis and John Neal, 1st December, 1740, and by them conveyed to William Burk, deceased, and by him devised to said John; corner Steven Conrod. Delivered: Peter Conrod, 21st April, 1784.

Page 388.—20th June, 1769. William Ward, of South Carolina, to John McClung. £52.10, 279 acres, part of Borden's 92100, and 30 acres, being part of an entry of King's land adjoining the same; corner Thomas Wilson. Teste: John Handley, Edward ( ) Thompson, Thomas ( ) McClung Delivered: Daniel Kidd, January, 1779.

Page 392.—9th June, 1769. John ( ) Summers and Isabella, of the Forks of James River, to James McMath and Susanna, his wife, of said Forks, £60, 440 acres in Forks of James; corner Wm. McKee's on Borden's patent line; corner James Davis; corner Samuel Wilson, Hugh Cunningham's line; corner Samuel McMurtry.(Teste: James Davies, John McMurtrey, John Young.

Page 395.—10th May, 1769. John Davis to Joseph Davis, £10, 350 acres on head of a branch of Buffelo Creek, oak in Borden's line. Teste: James McMath.

Page 398.—10th May, 1769. John Davis to Samuel Davis, £10, 400 acres on branches of Buffelo Creek, joining Benj. Borden's; corner Richard Woods.

Page 400.—2d February, 1769. William Ritchie, Sr., to William Ritchie, Jr., son of William, Sr., love, &c. William, Jr., covenants to cultivate the plantation whereon William, Sr., lives; within three years after death of William, Sr., William, Jr., is to give to each of his sisters then alive, £10, 195 acres whereon William Sr., now lives, on Catawbo Creek of James River, adjoining John McFerrin and Philip Watkins, conveyed by Borden to William, Sr. Teste: Thomas McFerran, Samuel and Martin McFerran.

Page 402.—6th May, 1769. Col. Andrew Lewis and George Matthews, executors of David Stewart, to Samuel Cowdon, one moiety of 321 acres conveyed by Patrick Martin and Jane, 17th September, 1763, to Samuel Cowdan and Andrew Greier, this moiety of 160½ acres conveyed to David by Andrew Greer and Ruth, 23d August, 1766, on Back Creek. Teste: Sampson Mathews, John Cawley, Pat. Lockhart, Mathew Read, Walter Cunningham.

Page 406.—1st June, 1769. Samuel Cowdon and Martha ( ) to John McPheeters, £250, 321 acres on Back Creek of Middle River in Beverley Manor, conveyed to Samuel Cowdon and Andrew Greyor by Patrick Martin and Jane, 17th September, 1763, corner land formerly John Young's on an island of said Creek. Delivered: John McFeeters, 5th January, 1773.

Page 409.—31st May, 1769. James Callison (Calleson) and Isble (Esable) ( ) to Gasper Taylor, £50, 230 acres on Nut's Mill Creek, corner John Lynn's land; McNabb's corner, Bigham's line. Delivered: Casper Tayler. April, 1773.

Page 412.—20th June, 1769. Andrew Thompson, son and heir of Adam Thompson, deceased, and Annie ( ) Thompson, widow and relict of Adam Thompson, to Peter Hanger, of Frederick County, sadler, £35, 187 acres, remainder of 287 acres conveyed by Beverley to said Adam, 2d March, 1749, the other 100 acres Adam sold to Samuel Kinkead. Delivered: Peter Hanger, 6th January, 1801.

Page 415.—15th June, 1769. Charles Campbell and Margret ( ) tc Joseph Walker, £135, 188 acres on Woods Creek in Fork of James River corner Arthur McClure; corner Arthur McClure, Joseph Walker's line, Robert Moore's line. Teste: James Hall, Joseph Walker. Delivered: Joseph Walker, June, 1783.

Page 418.—20th June, 1769. Henry Picket and Jean to Hugh Donaghoe, £10, 174 acres on a draft of North River of Shanandoe, corner Robert McMahon. Teste: John McMahon, James Coulter, Samuel Erwin. Delivered: Hugh Donaho, 8th March, 1775.

Page 421.—15th June, 1769. Samuel McClure and Mary ( ) to William McClure, £100, 274 acres in Forks of James River, corner Samuel McClure, John Poage's line. Teste: Samuel McClure, John and James Trimble.

Page 423.—15th April, 1769. Bryce Russell to Gabriel Jones, mortgage, £80, 150 acres on Shanandore whereon Bryce now lives, purchased of Hugh Thompson. Teste: John Gabriel Jones.

Page 426.— — —, 1769. William ( ) Hamilton and Margret ( ) to their son Patrick Hamilton, £10, 100 acres patented to William Hamilton,

29th May, 1760, on Middle River of Shanandore, corner Robert Reed's land. Delivered: Patrick Hamilton, 15th August, 1771.

Page 430.—3d January, 1769. John ( ) Mourie, eldest son and heir of Hance Mourie, late of Bedford County, deceased, of Bedford County, Virginia, to James Wilson, £—, 246 acres on Craig's Creek, a branch of James River, conveyed to Hance by James Patton, 20th December, 1753. Teste: Benj. Hawkins, John Crawford, Jr., Thomas Arnet, Walter Stewart. Delivered: Pat. Lockhart, September, 1772.

Page 433.—22d June, 1769. Jacob Grub and Barbara ( ) to Daniel Grub, £20, on Smith's Creek, part of 250 acres patented to Jacob Grub, 25th September, 1762. Delivered.

Page 436.—25th April, 1769. Peter Wylie and Mary ( ) and Alexander Wylie and Mary to Henry Stafford, £60, 150 acres, part of 400 acres conveyed to Peter and Alexander by John Wyley, Sr., and to John by William Davis, 22d September, 1763, on New River, corner land of John Wiley, Sr.,; corner Peter Wiley. Teste: Benj. Hawkins, Thomas and Samuel McFarran, William Curey. Delivered: Pat. Lockhart, September, 1772.

Page 440.—25th April, 1769. Same to John Wiley, Sr., £50, 100 acres on New River, part of 400 acres deeded to Peter and Alexander by said John Wiley and to John by William Davis, 22d September, 1763, Henry Stafford's line.

Page 443.—21st June, 1769. Joshua Hudson to Isaac Morris, £150, 310 acres, part of two tracts, one of 400 acres, patented to Morgan Bryan, 20th September, 1745, and by him conveyed to Michael Waring, May, 1751; the other contains 365 acres, patented to Michael Waring, 10th July, 1767, and conveyed to Joshua, 17th August, 1768. Delivered: Michael Waring, 4th August, 1773.

Page 446.—21st June, 1769. Philip ( ) Horless and Margaret to Michael Price, £26.5, 365 acres, part of 650 acres patented to Philip, 31st October, 1765, on Tom's Creek, a branch of New River. Delivered: Thomas Madison, January, 1770.

Page 448.—21st June, 1769. Michael Price binds himself in £100 to Philip Horless. Whereas Michael and Philip jointly purchased a tract from Col. James Patton, on Tom's Creek, containing 650 acres, but patent was issued in name of Philip alone, 31st October, 1765, of which Philip has conveyed 365 acres above, conditions not to hold Philip responsible of the patent fails.

Page 450.—17th June, 1769. James Patton's executors to Henry Paulin, £15, 62 acres patented to James, 3d November, 1750, on Craig's Creek. Teste: Andrew Crockett, Samuel McRoberts.

Page 456.—18th October, 1768. John Buchanan and Margaret and William Thompson and Mary, to James Skidmore, £55.5, 88 acres, part of a tract patented to John and William, 8th April, 1767, on James River, John Jones's line. Teste: Robert Campbell, Hugh Logan, David Smith. Delivered: Randolph Guin per order filed 22d June, 1798.

Page 459.—22d October, 1768. Same to Hugh Logan, £70, 125 acres, part of above patented tract on James River, corner Thomas Stevenson, crossing Jennings Creek. Teste: Robert Campbell, David Smith, Thos. Stevenson.

Page 463.—22d October, 1768. Same to Thomas Stevenson, £70, 118 acres, part of patent above, on James River, corner Logan's line. Teste: Hugh Logan, Robert Campbell, David Smith.

Page 466.—22d October, 1768. Same to David Smith, £40, 230 acres, similar deed to above. Delivered: David Smith, September, 1772.

Page 470.—21st June, 1769. William Shannon and Jane ( ) to John Lowry, £100, 300 acres on North River of Shanandore, part of 400 acres patented to James Humphreys, 25th June, 1747, and by him conveyed to Henry Smith, 13th. September, 1763, and by him to William Shannon, 24th November, 1763, David Davise's line. Teste: Andrew Campbell, Jame Byride. Delivered: John Lowrey, 5th December, 1773.

Page 474.—16th May, 1769. David Doack and Mary ( ) to John Alexander, of York County, Pennsylvania, £310, 400 acres. Teste: Randal Lockhart, John Finley, William Doack. Delivered: David Doack, November, 1771.

Page 477.—21st January, 1769. Robert Henderson to Andrew Johnston, £30, 240 acres on a branch of Dry River, patented to Robert, 25th September, 1762. Teste: Silas Hart, Daniel ( ) Henderson, John Robertson, John Paton.

Page 480.—8th February, 1769. James Hanna to John Crawford and Robert Bruster, £50, 150 acres on Briery Branch, corner Hugh Diver's land. Teste: James Divier, Charles Callahan, Robert Dunwoody, Daniel Henderson. Delivered: Samuel Dunn, 11th March, 1773.

Page 481.—Jacob ( ) Lorton to Michael Price, £19.19, negro slave. Teste: Cap. Thomas Madison, January, 1770.

Page 482.—20th June, 1769. Abraham Smith to William Shannon, surrender of mortgage, 18th May, 1767. Teste: William Hogshead, Samuel McNab, Jonathan Lowry, Jr.

Page 485.—1st May, 1769. William Reaugh (Reaoh, Reah) and Elizabeth to William Robinson, £65, 65 acres on Jackson's River, purchased by William Reaugh from William Cleark. Delivered: William Robinson, February, 1771.

Page 487.—22d May, 1769. Wallace Harrison to Richard and Peter Footman, merchants of Philadelphia, mortgage, £453.18.8, on North River Shanandoah, part of tract called the Great Plain, patented to James Wood, 12th January, 1746, 210 acres; also one tract near above, joining dividing line, between His Majesty and Lord Fairfax, and the lands of Michael Neece (Nees), 270 acres, patented to Mary Wood, 27th June, 1764; both conveyed to Mathew by Mary Wood by deed of even date herewith. Teste: William Campbell, Robert Wood, Alexander White.

Page 492.—10th April, 1769. Alex. Bohannon (Buchanan) and Isabella, of North Carolina, to Michael Bowyer, £200, the tract commonly known by the place whereon Valentine Sevier formerly lived, containing 400 acres, side of Daniel James' Branch, Absalom Hayworth's line. Teste: W. Bowyer, John Stewart, Thos. Brown, Christopher Graham.

Page 494.—17th June, 1769. Ephraim Love, farmer, and Elizabeth to George Baxter, 130 acres on head waters of Mudey Creek at foot of North Mountain, Daniel Harrison's line.

Page 498.—20th June, 1767. Daniel Harrison, Jr., and Sarah to George Baxter, £53, 106 acres on a branch of Muddy Creek, part of 400 acres patented to Daniel Harrison, Sr., 25th September, 1746, 200 of which

Daniel, Sr., conveyed to his son Daniel, Jr., of which this 106 is part, corner Jesse Harrison's part of said tract. Delivered: Jesse Harrison, 29th March, 1783.

Page 501.—23d June, 1769. Thomas Wilson and Elizabeth to Nathaniel Wilson, £100, 200 acres on Northeast Branch of James River, part of 400 belonging to Thomas Wilson, Borden's patent line, corner David Moore.

Page 504.—6th May, 1769. James and Moses Green to Jacob Lingle, £40, 200 acres, part of 2000 acres on south side of Peaked Mountain on a branch of Lick Run. Teste: Henry ( ) Miller, John ( ) Miller, Christian Miller. Delivered to Mr. Kease (?), May, 1770.

Page 507.—22d June, 1769. Joseph Watson to James Scot, £22, 200 acres on Cowpasture, corner land Hugh Coffey now lives on. Teste: Randal Lockhart, George Marshall, Geo. Rutledge. Sent James Scot by his order, October, 1773.

Page 509.—25th June, 1769. Ludwick Francisco, eldest son and heir of Christopher Francisco, of Lancaster Borough, Pennsylvania, to Jacob Nicholas, 5 shillings, 390 acres, part of 3000 acres purchased by Christopher of Jacob Stover, and still is part of a greater tract of 5000 acres patented to Stover, oak near an old cabin, Hetrick's line; corner Pence's land; corner Archembright. Delivered: Jacob Nicholas, May, 1771.

Page 511.—14th April, 1769. Commission to Charles Lewis and David Rodes, to the privy examination of Judith, wife of William Howard, of Albemarle, as to deed by William to George and Sampson Matthews, of date 29th July, 1767. Executed 29th April, 1769.

Page 513.—15th August, 1769. William McBride and Martha to Edward Erwin, £50, 152 acres in Forks of James, part of tract belonging to William. Delivered: James Todd, 22d June, 1772.

Page 517.—10th August, 1769. Jacob Lingle and Ann ( ) to Peter Gunrod and Stephen Gunrod (Conrod), £46, 280 acres on Tom's Creek of New River, conveyed to Jacob by Col. James Patton, patentee, corner Casper Barger, Draper's line.

Page 521.—15th August, 1769. Patrick Hays, in Derry Township, Lancaster County, Pennsylvania, to Samuel Hays, £250, 215 acres in Beverley Manor, by deed, 18th May, 1750, corner Thomas Yates' land; corner James Mitchell; corner William Hays. Teste: Patrick, John and Robert Buchanan, Wm. Brownlee. Delivered: Alex. Brownlee, October, 1779.

Page 524.—15th August, 1769. Same to William Hays, £250, 259 acres by deed, 18th May, 1750, in Beverley Manor, Thomas Yates' land. Delivered: James Mitchell per Mr. Hayes' order, 14th April, 1777.

Page 527.—7th August, 1769. Patrick ( ) Wilson to William McClenachan, mortgage, £36.6.2, on James River, George Poage's line, purchased by Patrick of Malcomb Allen by deed, 9th March, 1760. Teste: John Maxwell, Audly Paul, James Neelly, John Buchanan, William Hall. Delivered: William McClenachan, August, 1770.

Page 531.—8th April, 1769. Samuel Campble and Ellenor to William Lockridge, £114, 208 acres on Great River of Calfpasture, part of 308 conveyed by James Patton and John Lewis to William Campble, 100 acres being conveyed to Thomas Gilham and since conveyed to Thomas Adams, John Campbell's land (John Carlile's now); also 50 acres, part of entry of 100 acres patented to John and Samuel Campbell, and John sold to John

Carlyle, his 50 acres. Teste: Thomas Hugart, Andrew Lockridge, Wm. Kinkead.

Page 535.—12th August, 1769. William Logan and Elizabeth to John Logan, 5 shillings, 200 acres on James River, deeded to William by Timothy Croswick, 27th March, 1746. Teste: George Skillern, William McClenachan Alex. Buchanan.

Page 538.—13th August, 1769. James Knox and Jane to Patrick Miller, £70, 160 acres on Cowpasture, corner land in possession of Alexander. Teste: John Dickinson, Samuel Brown, Ralph Laverty.

Page 541.—14th August, 1769. Malcom McQuon (Malcom McCown), of Forks of James, to Samuel Wilson, of said Forks, £100, on Whistle Creek in Forks of James containing 150½ acres, corner formerly to Low Todd, now Hugh Cunningham. Teste: Jas. Hall, Joseph Walker, William Sproul.

Page 545.—16th August, 1769. Samuel Henderson, farmer, and Jean to John Henderson, £5, 120 acres on Middle River of Shanandoe, containing 120 acres, part of 250 acres patented to Jas. Thompson and conveyed to Samuel, 16th March, 1762. mouth of Littlers' Run. Teste: James Craig, James Alexander, ——— Femster. Delivered: Jno. Henderson, August, 1773. Recorded, 15th August, 1769.

DEED BOOK No. 16.

First deed recorded 15th August, 1769; last deed recorded 22d August, 1770.

Page 2.—19th August, 1767. Jacob Conrod to Joseph Skidmore, £3, 14 acres on South Branch of Potomac (Patowmack), part of 457 acres whereon Jacob lives adjoining said Skidmore's mill tract.

Page 4.—16th August, 1769. Robert ( ) Bratton and Ralph Lafferty to William Givens, £70, 244½ acres on Jackson's River. Delivered: James Bratton, 7th April, 1772.

Page 8.—16th August, 1769. Joseph McClung and Margaraet, of the Cowpasture, to Thomas McClung, planter, £—, 93 acres on Cowpasture, John Moore's land, in possession of John Moore. Teste: James Crockett, James Stevenson, John Jameson.

Page 10.—20th August, 1769. Borden's executors to Thomas Paxton, £52, 774 acres, part of 92100, the creek, Alex. Telford's line.

Page 14.—10th August, 1769. Same to John Thompson, £7, 100 acres, part of 92100, corner said James Thompson, Robert Allison's line. Delivered to John Thompson, March, 1777.

Page 17.—10th March, 1769. Same to Charles Boyl, £10, 180 acres, part of 92100, Low Todd's line.

Page 21.—16th August, 1769. John Campbell to Arthur Campbell, £100, 240 acres called the Royal Oak, on Holston or Indian River, patented to John Buchanan, gent., 22d August, 1753, and conveyed to John Campbell, 2d March, 1769. Teste: Pat. and Alex. Buchanan, James Cowan. Delivered David Campbell, May, 1771.

Page 24.—3d June, 1769. James McDowell to Gabriel Jones, mortgage, two tracts in Borden's land, whereon James now lives: A containing 300 acres conveyed to James by John Bowyer and Magdalen, 20th September,

1763; B containing 60 acres conveyed to James by his brother Samuel, 4th October, 1765.

Page 26.—16th Auugst, 1769. Jacob Gabbert and Barbara ( ) to Frederick Hanger, £60, 225 acres conveyed to Jacob by McNabb, 7th April, 1768, joining John Campbell, Wm. McClintock and James Peary. Delivered: Fred. Hanger, 25th June, 1771.

Page 27.—15th August, 1769. William Montgomery and Jean ( ) to Adam Harpole, £82, 470 acres on mountain between South Fork and South Branch of Potomac, line of Jacob Sivert's survey. Delivered: Adam Harpole, 23d May, 1785.

Page 30.—14th August, 1769. Michael Hover and Barbara ( ) to Peter Pannenger (Pennenger), all parties of Frederick County, £25, 100 acres, part of 335 acres patented to Rudolph Mauck, 30th August, 1763, and by him conveyed to Michael on North Branch of Shannandore, corner Charles Long. Teste: Daniel Smith, Adam ( ) Hoverstick, Peter Churu. Delivered: Peter Panninger, 12th August, 1771.

Page 33.—11th August, 1769. Israel Christian and Elizabeth to Edward Carvin, £110, 200 acres on John's Creek bought by Israel from Upshur. Teste: James Crawford, Uriah Humphries, James McCorkle. Delivered: Pat. Lockhart, 31st July, 1781.

Page 35.—10th August, 1769. Gasper Bramer and Catharine ( ) to Benjamin Grigsbey, £100, 72 acres on Shanando River above Lord Fairfax's line. Teste: Andrew Bird, William McDowell, William McGill.

Page 38.—19th February, 1769. William McGee and Jane ( ) to William McDowel, £60, between the Timber Ridge and Smith's Creek, corner Valentine Sevear, line of Andrew Byrd's land; Borden's line; Thomas Millsap's line, on the side of the Limestone Ridge, 158 acres by patent. Teste: Andrew Byrd, Edward Sampson, Jos. Wat. Peace.

Page 42.—17th February, 1769. Elias ( ) Bane to Alexander Armstrong, £5, mortgage, one horse, pacer and trotter.

Page 43.—3d January, 1769. Alexander Evans and Jane to James Alcorn, £17, 37½ acres on Back Creek of James River, part of tract whereon Alexander now lives. Teste: John Miller, Thomas Arnet, John Harbison, Francis Smith. Delivered to himself, November, 1773.

Page 46.—23d May, 1769. Thomas Ogle, of Roan County, N. C., to William Murphy, £40, 67 acres on Little River, a branch of New River. Teste: Wm. Fleming, Thomas Madison, Andrew Lewis, Robert Breckinridge, Is. Christian, Gent.

Page 49.—26th April, 1769. James ( ) Scaggs (Skeggs), Sr., and Rachel ( ) to James Scaggs, Jr., £100, 104 acres patented to Samuel Ratlive 22d August, 1753, and conveyed to James, Sr., on Meadow Creek, a branch of New River. Teste: William Preston, Richard Whitt, James ( ) Skggs, John ( ) Skggs, Is. Christian, James Buchanan, W. Ingles.

Page 51.—25th April, 1769. Same to Henry Scaggs, £100, 100 acres by deeds from Francis Rieley to James, 29th May, 1751, on Little River, a branch of Woods' River.

Page 35.—18th August, 1769. Archibald Buchanan and Agness to William Buchanan, £45, 406 acres, part of Borden's 92.100 acres, crossing McCason's Run; Robert Christian's Corner, oak by a Warm Spring, north branch of Hays' Creek.

Page 59.—17th October, 1769. Thomas Paxton and Rebekah ( ) to James McDowell, Samuel McDowell and James Cowdon, £52, 378 acres, part of Borden's 92,100; Alexander Telford's line; corner James McCampbell. Teste: Isaac Anderson, James McCampbell, Alexander Sinclair, James Robinson. Delivered: Samuel McDowell, 17th August, 1772.

Page 64.—17th October, 1769. Same to James Campbell, £80, 396 acres, part of Borden's 92,100; corner Alexander Telford. Delivered: James Campbell, November Court, 1773. Teste: Alexander McCroskry.

Page 68.—17th October, 1769. Henry Gay and Martha ( ) to James Frazier, £10, 100 acres on Great River of Calfpasture, joining Francis Donaley's land. Teste: Samuel Blackwood, Andrew Steel.

Page 71.—11th September, 1769. James Neelly and Jane to William McClenachan, 400 acres on Roanoke; Griffith's line; Evans' line. Teste: John Neelly, Peter ( ) Ginder, John Reaburn.

Page 75.—20th January, 1769. Henry ( ) Ferguson to Israel Christian, £50, 109 acres on a branch of Glade Creek of Roanoke whereon Henry now lives, near John Boreland's. Teste: Bryan McDonald, James McCorkle, Edward Carvin, Daniel McNeill, Thos. Madison, Arthur Campbell, William Christian.

Page 80.—28th January, 1769. John Thompson and Susanna (mark) to Israel Christian, £125, two tracts containing 392 acres on Glade Creek, a branch of Roanoke—A, containing 213 acres, corner land formerly John Mills'; B, containing 179 acres, corner John Boon's land. Teste: James Allen, Thomas McShery, George Inglebird. (The name is written Thos. McElhenny on lease, but McShery on release). Delivered.

Page 83.—Commission for privy examination of Susanna to above, executed 11th September, 1769.

Page 85.—17th October, 1769. Robert Allen, Sr., and Martha to Robert Allen, Jr., £100, 80 acres whereon Allen's mill now is on South River of Shanando, part of 600 acres as conveyed to him by Charles Teas and recorded in the secretary's office. Teste: George Eliott, John Stewart, William Teas. Delivered: Jane Allan, widow of Robert Allen, 6th October, 1790.

Page 89.—17th October, 1769. William Teas to Robert Allen, Jr., £100, 100 acres more or less; corner of Beverley Manor line. Teste: George Elliott, Thomas Crow, Archibald Armstrong. Delivered: James Allen, October 6, 1790.

Page 92.—17th October, 1769. John McClure and Mary ( ) to Samuel McClure, £80, 90 acres, part of tract whereon John now liveth on south side of James River; corner John McClure. Delivered: Samuel McClure, Jr., as per affidavit, 28th September, 1802.

Page 96.—22d October, 1768. John Mills and Mary to William Carvin, £50, patent to John Mills, 10th July, 1767, 325 acres on the Bent Mountain and Little Bottom Creek, a branch of Roanoke; corner Leonard Huff's land. Teste: Arthur Campbell, John Bowyer, Ben. Estill, Samuel McDowell, William Christian.

Page 100.—17th October, 1769. Joseph Inglish and Elizabeth ( ) to Reuben Rutherford, £50, 150 acres on Cub Run, hill near Wood's land, spur of the Peeked Mountain; patented to Joseph, 20th July, 1768.

Page 104.—24th July, 1769. William, John and Samuel Craig to James

Gamble, £45, 247 acres in 2 tracts; 202 acres is part of 335 acres patented to Alexander Craig, 10th September, 1755, the other 45 acres patented to Alexander 5th June, 1765, which he devised by will dated 1st May, 1764, to wife Margaret and sons William and John; but Margaret has since deceased, the sole property descended to William and John, on a branch of Middle River, said Gamble's old corner. Tract of 45 adjoins above, hill near Craig's old house; corner to Alexander Blays; William Frame's line. Teste: John Archer, Rebecca ( ) Archer, William Frame. Delivered: James Gamwell, December, 1770. (Signed in this order, Samuel, William, John.)

Page 109.—18th October, 1769. Francis Jackson and Elizabeth ( ) to William Renick, £42, 170 acres on cowpasture; corner land in possession of William Jackson, opposite to land in possession of Alexander Black. Teste: William Mathews, J. Murray, Pat. Lockhart, Arthur Campbell. Delivered: William Renix, August Court, 1776.

Page 111.—22d May, 1769. Mary Wood, of Frederick, to Alexander White, Gent., of Frederick, and Elizabeth, his wife, deed gift, £———, marriage between Alexander and Elizabeth, daughter of Mary; on North River of Shanandoah, part of a tract called the Great Plains patented to James Wood, deceased, 12th January, 1746; corner on line between Mathew Harrison and said Alexander White according to the division of said plain made by Robert Rutherford, Daniel Holeman and Thomas Moore; line between His Majesty and Lord Fairfax, 165 acres. Teste: Robt. Wood, William Campbell, Jno. Magill, Jno. McGill, M. Harrison. Delivered: Alexander White, Gent., 28th May, 1770.

Page 114.—17th October, 1769. William Raigh (Reigh, Reaigh, Reaoh) to Archibald Raigh, £100, 230 acres of Borden's 92,100, on Hays' Creek. Delivered: Hugh Rhea, 16th December, 1795.

Page 117.—3d October, 1769. John Kinkead of parish ———, County ———, Province of Philadelphia, to Samuel Griffin of Henrico County, Va., £250, 530½ acres bounded by lines of John Kinkade, Thomas Hagert, James Campbell, Andrew Hamilton, being ½ of tract purchased by John from Patton and Lewis (deed recorded in Orange County). Teste: Richard Adams, Samp. Mathews, Wm. Armstrong, Wm. Kinkead, Jas. Vaughan, J. Meredith. (Certificate says was proved by witness William Kimsey.) Delivered: Thos. Adams.

Page 120.—11th September, 1769. Will Gwynn to John Cawley and Daniel Kidd, of Staunton, £6.5.6, 1 horse and several cows. Teste: M. Bowyer, Christopher Graham. Delivered: Grantee, 1770.

Page 122.—7th October, 1769. Frances Smith and Anne (Agness, signed Anne) to Robert Finley, £50, 272 acres patented to Francis, 6th April, 1769, on waters of Catawbo; said Smith's line; William Hutchison's line; Riely's line. Teste: William Campbell, John Tatham, William Preston.

Page 125.—7th October, 1769. Commission for privy examination of Anne to above deed. Executed 7th October, 1769.

Page 126.— ———, 1769. Sampson and Geo. Mathews to William Bowyer, £15, lot No. 9 in Staunton; also 13 acres of wood land at south corner of one of Thomas Fulton's lots numbered 6 and conveyed by Thomas Fulton to William Howard and by him to S. and G. Mathews; conveyed to Thomas Fulton by Alexander Wright, 17th May, 1760. Teste:

Wat. Cunningham, Pat. Lockhart. Delivered: Wliliam Bowyer, Esq., 25th April, 1775.

Page 132.—27th September, 1769. John Askins, of Fairfax County, to John McIlhany, of Loudoun County, Gent., £65. Two tracts—A, containing 85 acres purchased by John from Wm. Armstrong, 16th November, 1752, corner Daniel Manahon, Smith's Creek; B, containing 75 acres patented to John, 10th September, 1755, on waters of Roanoke. Teste: Wm. Hyde. Enclosed to William Fleming, Esq., Botr., by order of Mr. McElhenny, 4th June, 1791.

Page 136.—18th October, 1769. James Blair and Jean ( ) to John Graham, mortgage, £44, 220 acres; Hugh Campbell's line; corner Alexander Blair. Teste: Randal Lockhart, Archibald Armstrong, Jos. Ray. Delivered: Wm. Young, 6th March, 1772.

Page 139.—17th October, 1769. James Young to Mathias Gabert, £———, 150 acres in Beverley Manor, transferred to James by his father Robert by deed of gift; corner Samuel Young, William McClintock's line. Agness ( ) Young, widow of Robert, release dower in above. Delivered: Mathias Gabbert, 1780.

Page 144.—11th April, 1769. Alexander Buchanan, of Cumberland County, N. C., to Valintine Severe, £———, 375 acres on Long Meadow of Shanando, patented to Valentine, 5th September, 1749, and by him conveyed in mortgage to George Buchanan and William Hamilton, merchants of Loudon, together with several other tracts, being one of the tracts conveyed to said Alexander Buchanan by Francis Jordone, of Louisa County, merchant and attorney for Samuel Richards, William Cook and Archibald McLain, assignees in bankruptcy of Buchanan and Hamilton, 31st October, 1763, and recorded in the secretary's office. Delivered to ———, 15th October, 1777.

Page 149.—9th September, 1769. Mathew Harrison, of Augusta, Alexander White and Elizabeth, of Frederick, to Mathias Kersh (Kerse), £62.10, near Peaked Mountain, part of 2,000 acres patented to Robert Green, 20th August, 1740, 290 acres. Delivered: Mr. Kerse, May, 1776.

Page 152.—22d May, 1769. Mary Wood, of Frederick, to Mathew Harrison, £———, marriage heretofore celebrated between Mathew and Mary's daughter, Mary, deceased, on North River of Shanandoah, part of a tract called the Great Plain, patented to James Wood, deceased, 12th January, 1746, 210 acres; also one tract adjoining Fairfax's line and the lands of Michael Nees, 270 acres, patented to Mary Wood, 27th June, 1764. Teste: Robt. Wood, William Campbell, Alexander White, Jno. Magill. Delivered: William McDowell, August, 1780.

Page 156.—6th November, 1769. William Jameson and Margaret to John Jameson, £55, on Christian's Creek, whereon William now lives, conveyed to William by William Martin, 19th March, 1765, 310 acres; corner William Palmer; corner George Robinson, now Samuel Black's land, plot surveyed for Mr. William Russell now Alexander Thompson's land. Teste: William Palmer, Jean ( ) Palmer, William ( ) Calin. Delivered: Samuel Ferguson, 17th August, 1772.

Page 160.—22d November, 1769. William Beard and Mary ( ) to Jacob Bowyer, £400, 2 tracts on Cub Run on west side Peaked Mountain Delivered: Geo. Keesle, 16th March, 1781.

Page 164.—22d November, 1769. Samuel Black and Rebecca ( ) to James Young, of Sissel County, Maryland, £90, 200 acres on a branch of Naked Creek conveyed to Samuel by Thomas Watterson, James McConnal's land.

Page 167.—2d August, 1769. Mary ( ) Williams and Wm. Fleming, £25. Indenture to serve 5 years. Delivered: Wm. Fleming, Gent., March Court, 1770. Condition that William is to pay Thomas Huff £8.12, Mary's debt, for which Mary is to serve William at rate of £5 per annum; £15 is to be allowed for the curing of a disorder Mary suffers with.

Page 170.—15th March, 1770. Jacob Trout and Barbara ( ) to George Shaver, £65, 145 acres, part of Jacob Stover's great tract formerly conveyed to Christopher Francisco, Sr., then to Nicholas Trout, 2d July, 1752, and inherited by Jacob as heir-at-law of Nicholas, on Shanando River, beginning on side of Cub Run; corner Ludwick Francisco; corner Morris Pond. Teste: John Peter Tresler, Nicholas ( ) Millbery, Volintine ( ) Trout Delivered: Geo. Shaver, 2d June, 1770.

Page 174.—15th March, 1770. Nicholas ( ) Millberry, farmer, and Barbara ( ), to Peter Tresler, farmer. £20, 130 acres patented to Nicholas, 14th July, 1769; corner Samuel Thornhill, Stony Run. Delivered: Henry Tresler, 13th May, 1786.

Page 178.—19th March, 1770. Benjamin Kinley to William Hopkins, £70, on a branch of Brock's Creek, 215 acres; Rees Thomas' line.

Page 182.—4th January, 1770. Francis Kirtley and Elizabeth to John Futch, £50, 210 acres, lower fork of Elk Run in a line of Earley's land. Teste: Jacob Bear, Conrad Futch, David Magert. Delivered: John Futch, November, 1776.

Page 184.—3d May, 1769. Nicholas Sybert (Seybert), eldest son and heir-at-law of Jacob Sybert, deceased, of Frederick County, Maryland, to John Blizard, £200, 210 acres on southernmost branch of South Branch of Potowmack, part of 2,643 acres patented to Robert Green, 12th January, 1746, and by him conveyed to John Patton, Jr., 5th November, 1747, and by him conveyed to said Jacob Seybert, 21st May, 1755; corner Rodger Dyer. Teste: Mathew Patton, James Dyer, Adam Lock, Robert Minnis. Delivered: Daniel Smith, September, 1770.

Page 187.—3d May, 1769. Same to Adam Lock, £10, 88 acres on the mountain between the South Fork and South Branch of Potowmac patented to Jacob Sybert, 10th November, 1757; Michael Mallow's line. Teste: John ( ) Blizard. Delivered: Grantee, 15th April, 1814.

Page 190.—20th March, 1770. James Laird to John Hinds, £50, mortgage, 124 acres on Middle River of Shanando, part of 400 acres formerly John Kerr's; corner John Allison's land. Teste: Jno. Poage, Samuel Erwin, Alexander Walker.

Page 194.—20th March, 1770. John Young and Margret to William Young, £10, 53 acres on Middle River of Shanando; Alexander Craig's line; John Hall's line; patented to John Young, 20th July, 1768. Teste: Robt. Young, Francis Brown. Delivered: William Young, 25th June, 1773.

Page 198.—20th March, 1770. James Trotter and Mary to Samuel Trotter, their son, £5, 100 acres, part of 380 acres patented to Robert Brown, 10th June, 1740, and by him conveyed to said Trotter. Delivered: Samuel Trotter, 21st October, 1772.

Page 203.—18th August, 1767. James Robinson and Hanah ( ) (also written Esebello) to James Wallace (Wallis), £137, 216 acres on Hayes' Creek, part of Borden's tract; corner Walker's land; corner Joseph Culton's land. Teste: John Hays, Jr.; James Moore, Jr.; Andrew Hays, Jr.; James Culton, Jr.; Arthur Graham. Delivered: H. (Hugh) Kelso (Kelsey, 30th August, 1785.

Page 207.—18th December, 1769. Samuel ( ) Dunlap and Margaret ( ) to Patrick Woods, of Albemarle County, £10, 150 acres on North Fork of James River at mouth of Hays' Creek, beginning on the last branch of North Fork of James River opposite an island, Mount Miserable. Teste: John Hays, Alexander Walker, Andrew Hays, James Wallace, John Kelly, Henry ( ) Campbell, Samuel Kelly. Delivered: Wm. Hamilton, 11th May, 1771.

Page 211.—18th December, 1769. John ( ) Dunlap and Jennet ( ) to Joseph Woods, of Albemarle, £10, 150 acres on Hays' Creek, beginning at a Beetch by a post, being James Miles' daughter-in-law; corner on southeast side of Hays' Creek; Samuel Dunlap's line, Mount Miserable. Delivered: Wm. Hamiliton, 11th May, 1772.

Page 215.—20th March, 1770. William ( ) Logan and Isabella ( ) to Samuel Wright, £130, 155 (C L V) acres in Beverley Manor, part of a tract sold by Beverley to William Wright and by William to said Logan, 23d May, 1750; Alexander Henderson's line; corner William Johnson. Teste: Elijah McClenachan, Patrick Campbell, William Meteer.

Page 219.—24th February, 1770. Patrick Davis and Esther to James Millican, £30, 44 acres by patent dated 10th September, 1767, on Cowpasture River. Teste: Charles Lewis, Charles and Andrew Donnelly. Delivered: Andrew Donnelly, December, 1775.

Page 223.—20th March, 1770. Hugh Cunningham and Sarah ( ) of Forks of James River in Botetourt County to John McKee, of Kerr's Creek, £300, tract whereon Jonathan Cunningham, deceased, son of Hugh, formerly dwelt, 281 acres on Kerr's Creek, formerly called Teaze's Creek, partly in Botetourt and part in Augusta. Teste: Hugh Weir, Nathan Peoples, William McKee. Delivered: John McKee, April, 1773.

Page 227.—20th March, 1770. Benjamin ( ) Scot and Mary ( ) to Philip Harper, £100. Two tracts on North Fork of South Branch of Potowmack—A, 200 acres; B, 70 acres below A; both A and B patented to Benjamin 14th February, 1761. Delivered: Moses Hinckle, 3d April, 1793.

Page 230.—20th March, 1770. Joseph Poindexter and Elizabeth to Thomas Rodgers, £50, 143 acres on north side Shanandore; John Patrick's line; Thomas Turk's line. Teste: John Rodgers, James Kennerly, Jr., Samuel Woods.

Page 234.—19th May, 1770. Martin Judy (Juddy, Juda) and Rosanna to Henry Judey (Juda), their son, £20, 204 acres on North Mill Creek, a branch of South Branch of Potowmack, part of 367 conveyed to Martin by William Green, Gent., 24th May, 1763. Teste: William Lamme. Delivered: Nicholas Judy, December, 1778.

Page 238.—10th March, 1770. William Skillem and Mary to Isaac White, £300, 265 acres in Long Meadow, part of 535 acres in Beverley Manor; corner Thomas Miller's land; James Anderson's line. Delivered: Isaac White, 26th May, 1772.

Page 241.—20th March, 1770. George Martin and Mary ( ) to James Rodgers, £50, 100 acres on South River of Shanando; Christian Clemons' land. Teste: John and James Rodgers, Alexander Campbell.

Page 244.—21st March, 1770. Daniel Harrison and Sarah to Felix Gilbert. On 23d June, 1763, Jonathan Douglass mortgaged to Daniel 306 acres on head of Broad Run, a branch of North River of Shanandore being parts of two tracts of 400 acres each, one patented to Jonathan 11th July, 1761, the other purchased by Jonathan from one Thomas Beal of Maryland, the remainder now in possession of Nicholas and Henry Mace and Patrick Quin, being the land whereon Jonathan then lived. Jonathan failed to pay the debt, wherefore Daniel brought bill in Augusta County Court; decree rendered 25th March, 1769. Now, £55. Teste: James McDowell, Wm. Patton. Delivered: Felix Gilbert, March, 1773.

Page 247.—1st March, 1770. George Lewis, distiller, to John Poage, £5, several horses. Teste: George Eliot, William Hambleton.

Page 249.—21st March, 1770. James Pearey to John Archenbright, £———, 150 acres on a branch of Middle River of Shanando conveyed to James, 19th November, 1766. Delivered: John Archenbright, 12th March, 1773.

Page 252.— ———, 1770. John ( ) Allison and Janet ( ) to William Ramsey, £130, 204 acres on North Branch of James; corner Andrew Hall; John Thomson's line; corner widow Alison. Delivered: John Ellison August, 1773.

Page 256.—21st March, 1770. John ( ) Elliot, Sr., to his son, John Elliot, Jr., £10, 24 acres on a small branch of Middle River of Shanandore, part of 200 acres. Delivered: October, 1779.

Page 260.—20th June, 1769. Francis Kirtley and Elizabeth to Boston (Bostian) Ostler (Osler), £20, 70 acres between Stony and Dry Run; corner Jacob Runkle's land. Delivered: Bosten Osler, 30th August, 1771.

Page 262.—22d March, 1770. James Divier (Dever) and Betty to Reuben Daniel, £50, 400 acres patented to James Dever, 20th May, 1763. Delivered: William Walker, 4th April, 1771.

Page 265.—12th August, 1769. Timothy ( ) Solovane of Calfpasture to daughter, Catherine Solovane, £———, her being a dutiful child; horses and furniture. Teste: Michael Reiney, Sam Campbell, Thomas Campbell.

Page 266.—12th August, 1769. Same to daughter Margaret Solovane, £———, same as above; cows, horses and furniture.

Page 266.—6th January, 1770. Samuel Cowden and Mathew Cowden to John Graham and Daniel Kidd, £80, mortgage, ¼ acre in Staunton, part of a lot formerly James Hughes' and purchased by Col. David Stewart and Samuel Cowden and 15 acres of wood land belonging to the same and bounded by Sampson Mathews, Archer Mathews, James Hartgrove, Euphram Hughes, widow; being the same whereon Randal Lockhart and John Readpath now lives; also ½ acre lot lying above Daniel Kidd's and joining Water Street and divided by one street from a lot belonging to Doctor John Mathews, and 30 acres of woodland thereto belonging; also ½ acre lot in Staunton, formerly property of Joseph Bell bounded by Robert Reed and Doctor William Fleming's lots. Teste: John Virner.

Page 268.—17th October, 1769. Volintine Sevear to Thomas Reeves, £160. Two tracts containing 679—A, containing 375 acres; B, containing

304 acres on northwest side of Long Meadow. Teste: Thomas Moore, Jacob Woodley, Brewer Reeves.

Page 271.—24th February, 1770. Stephen Loy, tanner, to Sampson and Geo. Mathews, £45, negro slave, condition that Stephen Loy and Doctor John Watkins on 20th February, 1769, executed a bond to S. and G. Mathews for £60; now if Stephen make payment. Teste: William Robertson and Cathorine Loy.

Page 272.—27th September, 1769. John Cawley and Margaret, of Staunton, to Sampson and George Mathews, £40, ½ lot of woodland on northwest of Staunton, 14 acres, part in No. 9 and part in No. 10, surveyed for Robert McClenachan lying between lots of James Hughes and John Kerr, see deed McClenachan to Margaret and Joseph Gamwell, 22d May, 1760; also ½ of a half-acre lot in Staunton; half of lot No. 5 also conveyed by McClenachan in above deed; both which pieces since sold by Gamwell to Archer Mathews, the remainder being conveyed by Joseph Gamwell to said John Cawley, now husband of the late said Margaret Gamwell. August, 1768. Teste: Pat. Lockhart, William Mitchell, Euphemia Hughes, John Walsh.

Page 275.—23d October, 1769. Jacob ( ) Archenbright, yeoman, to George Conrad, blacksmith, £40, mortgage, on Cub Run, purchased by Jacob from Christian Grub, whereon Jacob lately lived, containing 100 acres. Teste: John Gabriel Jones, William Roebuck. Delivered: George Conrod, 11th November, 1771.

Page 277.—27th September, 1769. John Cawley, of Staunton, innkepeer, to Sampson and George Mathews, £50.9.2, 5 horses, 1 iron kettle fixed in the kitchen, and all household furniture, mortgage; if this is not sufficient, then Mathews are to sell a ½ lot in Staunton whereon John now lives, and 13 acres of wood land belonging thereto conveyed to Mathews this day.

Page 281.—15th May, 1770. James Beard and Jean ( ) to David Laird, £40, on north side of North River of Shanando, 95 acres; corner land formerly Samuel Lockhart's; also 20 acres, part of 179 acres patented to Samuel Lockhart, 30th August, 1748, adjoining above. Delivered to Mr. Laird, 18th April, 1786.

Page 285.—15th May, 1770. John Cravens and Margaret ( ) to John Bear, £130, on Linvel's Creek, part of 7,009 acres patented to Hite, McCoy et als., 28th March, 1739, and sold by several intermediate conveyances to Cravens, 8th August, 1767, containing 240 acres. Delivered: John Bear, November, 1772.

Page 287.—15th May, 1775. John, James and William Gillespy to Thomas McCollock, £5, 80 acres in Beverley Manor, part of 3 tracts conveyed to James Gillespy, deceased—A, 210 acres from Wm. Beverley, 27th February, 1749; B, 208 acres; C, 200 acres, all adjoining the 80 acres bounded; John Williams' corner, land formerly Charles Dalhouse's; corner James and William Gillespie; corner John Gillespie.

Page 291.—15th May, 1770. John ( ) Adam (Adams) and Agness ( ) to Joseph Foard, £32, 90 acres in South Mountain on west side of the main ridge.

Page 295.—15th May, 1770. Hugh ( ) Wier and Margrate ( ) to Samuel Wier, £50, 120 acres in Bordens 92,100; corner Alexander Greer and William McCanless; corner Hugh Beard; corner in Eakin line. Teste: William and Alexander Moore, James Mitchell.

Page 297.—14th May, 1770. Christian Clemons and Catharine ( ) to John Maharfey, 5 shillings, 266 acres, part of 400 acres patented to John Balfort, 20th February, 1745, and conveyed to Christian by said Belfort, 14th February, 1763; Patrick Fraziers line. Delivered: John Maharfey, 18th December, 1771. (Maharphy.)

Page 300.—15th May, 1770. Same to Henry Liner, £10.55 acres, part of 236 acres patented to Henry Dooling, 30th January, 1741, and by him conveyed to Christian, on South River of Shanandore. Delivered: Henry Liner, August Court, 1784. (Quaere? Is this Laneor?)

Page 304.—15th May, 1770. William Samples and Sarah ( ) to the Rev. Thomas Jackson, £75, 230 acres patented to William, 27th June, 1764, on drafts of Linvell's and Muddy Creek. Delivered: Thomas Jackson, 29th December, 1770.

Page 308.—24th January, 1770. Ralph ( ) Lafferty (Laverty) and Jean and Robert Bratton (mark) and Ann to Adam Bratton, £150, 244½ acres on Jackson's River; corner William Wilson's land; corner William Givens. Delivered: James Bratton, 7th April, 1772.

Page 312.—15th May, 1770. Robert Beverley, of Essex, to Henry Black, £16, 200 acres in Beverley Manor; corner Duncan McFarland, George Peary's line; Alexander Reachey's line. Delivered: H'y Black, August, 178—.

Page 315.—15th May, 1770. Samuel Adams, of North Carolina, to Joseph Dictum, power of attorney to convey 340 acres on Linvel's Creek, devised by Margaret Adams and from him descended to Samuel as eldest son and heir, having been patented in the name of Mary Adams. Title yet to be made to Samuel.

Page 316.—22d March, 1770. John King to John Poage, £21.6, a negro slave. Teste: Abrm. Smith, Alexander Miller, M. A. Delivered.

Page 318.—14th May, 1770. Mathias Gabbert and Christian ( ) to James Brown, £35, 7½ acres, part of a tract bought of James Young. Delivered: Jas. Brown, April, 1783.

Page 322.—18th June, 1770. Uriah Humble and Charity ( ) to his son, Conrad Humble, £30, 220 acres in Brock's Gap on Dry River patented to James Baggs, 12th January, 1746, and by him conveyed to Uriah. Teste: Jacob Miller, Conrad Custer, John Thomas. Delivered: Jno. Ruddle, 10th May, 1784.

Page 325.—19th June, 1770. Hugh ( ) McFadden and Elisabeth ( ), of Botetourt, to Robert Cooper, £70, 150 acres on Bordens 92,100; corner Lusk's land; corner Robert Wason. Teste: Elijah McClenachan, William and Alexander Moore.

Page 329.—19th June, 1770. Same to Robert Wason, £60, 150 acres in Borden's 92,100; corner Robert Cooper, John Handley's line. Delivered: Grantee, 29th September, 1801.

Page 332.—1st January, 1770. Borden's executors to John Wiley, £30, 236 acres, part of 92,100; corner Robert McElhenny on Carr's Creek; corner William McCampbell. Teste: Lew Bowyer. Delivered: John Wiley, 18th October, 1785.

Page 336.—1st March, 1770. Same to Samuel Nusbit (Nesbit), £17, 100

acres of 92,100; John Berry's line. Delivered: Samuel Neizbit, 11th May, 1787.
Page 339.—1st March, 1770. Same to Andrew Buchanan, £25, 200 acres of 92,100; corner Robert Kilpatrick; corner James Wardlaw; corner Samuel Buchanan, Moffet's Creek; corner Moses Buchanan; Joseph Culton's line; Andrew Buchanan's old corner. Delivered: Andrew Buchanan, March, 1773.
Page 343.—1st March, 1770. Same to Alexander Telford, £7, 40 acres of 92,100; corner William Berry and said Telford; corner David McCosky and James Buchanan. Delivered: James Telford, 14th June, 1805.
Page 347.—1st March, 1770. Same to Samuel Buchanan, £37, 240 acres of 92,100, Buffalo Draft, said Buchanan's old line; Samuel Steel's line; corner James Stewart. Delivered: James Huston, May, 1772.
Page 353.—15th June, 1770. Moses McElvain and Margaret to Thomas Kinkead, £70, on Great Calfpasture between William Kinkead and Robert Givin, 26 acres conveyed to Moses by James Loughridge, 21st June, 1763. Teste: John and William Kinkead.
Page 356.—17th June, 1770. John Hunter and Frances ( ) to Samuel Hunter, 40 pence, 128 acres conveyed to John by Robert Brookes, conveyed by Beverley, 26th November, 1751, in Beverley Manor; John Thompson's line; corner Robert Hunter, now John Thompson; corner Anthony Black, a cabin by the road between John Hunter's and his son, Samuel Hunter's. Teste: W. Christian, David Carson.
Page 360.—20th June, 1770. William Milsap (Milsaps) and Anne ( ) to William McDowell, £120, 186 acres on a branch of Smith's Creek, part of 400 acres patented to Thomas Milsaps, 100 acres having been conveyed to William McGee, 114 acres for John Dilling; Benj. Bordens' line; Fairfax's line.
Page 364.—23d April, 1770. William ( ) McNabb and Martha ( ) to Jacob Gebhard (Gabhard, Gabherd, Gabhert, Gebhort), £10, 150 acres in Beverley Manor on North Branch of Christian's Creek; corner James McNab's, part of same tract; corner Samuel Downey; Adam Thompson's line; corner James McNab's, part of same tract. Delivered: Jacob Gabbert, February, 1779.
Page 367.—14th May, 1770. William ( ) McCandless to George Campbell, £119, 183 acres of Borden's 92,100; corner William Alexander; corner Alexander Greer. Teste: Wm. Alexander, Andrew Moore, Alexander Greer, Thomas Wilson.
Page 369.—24th May, 1770. Robert Mitchell to Thomas Shields, 1 horse branded, 1 Dand Flower of de luce, cattle, furniture and crops. Teste: Wm. Thompson, Patt. Campbell. Delivered: Thos. Shields, 27th March, 1772.
Page 372.—20th April, 1770. John Lowry and Jane ( ) to John Carruthers, £200, 200 acres; corner Thomas Paxton; corner Mackey; corner Edmiston; Moses Trimble's line, the Barren Hills. Teste: Archibald Alexander, Halbert McClure, Moses Whitesides. Delivered: John Carruthers, 15th November, 1774.
Page 376.—7th April, 1770. David Kinkead and Winnifred and John Kinkead and Elizabeth ( ) to William Meeteer, £215, 520 acres on Great Calfpasture; corner Kinkead, crossing the river and Ramsey's Creek,

Lockridge's land. Teste: Thos. (his mark) Armstrong, Robert McKittrick, John Kirk. Delivered: William Meteer, 8th August, 1791.

Page 380.—15th June, 1770. Ralph Laferty and Jane to William Laverty, £25, 224 acres; corner Adam Dickinson, on Cowpasture River.

Page 382.—20th March, 1770. Robert Patterson to John Patterson, £7.3.9, cows, beds and furniture. Teste: Robert Young, Robert Williams.

Page 383.—20th March, 1770. Same to John King, £6.5, 1 mare and cows.

Page 385.—25th January, 1770. Robert Hall and Isbaella ( ), of Orange County, North Carolina, to Andrew Donnaly, £70, 150 acres by patent, 3d November, 1750, to James Hall, deceased, father to Robert, on Stewart's Mill Creek. Teste: Richard Holeman, James Faris, Edward ( ) Long, Chas. Lewis, Hugh Hicklin, James Bodkin. Delivered: Andrew Donnerly, December, 1775.

Page 388.—6th June, 1770. Randal Lockhart to Joseph Kinkead, £4.15.4, 1 feather bed and furniture, viz., bolster, sheets, blanket and rug and one bedstead, 1 pine table, 1 corner cubbard, 4 chairs, 1 large trunk, 3 pewter dishes, 1 doz. plates, 1 pot and hooks, 1 frying pan. Delivered: Joseph Kinkead, August Court, 1770.

Page 389.—20th June, 1770. Nathaniel Lyon to Joseph Kinkead and William Brown, £30, cows, horses, furniture. Teste: J. Rae.

Page 391.—23d April, 1770. William ( ) McNabb and Martha ( ) to son, James McNabb, £10, 150 acres on North Fork of Christian's Creek in Beverley Manor; corner Alexander McFeeters; corner Samuel McNab's part of the tract. Teste: Jas. Ewing, Alexander McFeeters, Samuel McNabb, John ( ) Campbell. Delivered: James McNab, June, 1780.

Page 393.—18th December, 1769. Daniel ( ) Henderson to Abraham Smith, £30.4.10, mortgage, 675 acres on Bever Creek and Spring Creek; corner Hugh Devers land. Teste: James and Hugh Divier, John Craford, James Dunn. Delivered: Abraham Smith, September, 1770.

Page 398.—19th June, 1770. John ( ) McCutchon to Samuel McCutchon, £200, 442 acres in Beverley Manor; corner William McCutchon's land; corner James McCutchon's. Teste: David Fulton. Delivered: Samuel McCutchon, May Court, 1774.

Page 402.—20th June, 1770. Joseph Mays and Rebecca to Robert Jamison, £45, 205 acres in Beverley Manor on head branches of Christian's Creek; Alexander Campbell's line; Samuel Brafford's line; corner James Mitchel.

Page 404.—23d September, 1769. Richard Williamson to wife Abby. Abby refuses to be reconciled and to return to Richard, who renounces all claim to her, returns her property, refuses to pay her debts, &c. Teste: William Tees, David Burger.

Page 406.—20th June, 1770. Robert Kinkead and Annaheleney (Belina) ( ) to Andrew Kinkead, £———, 159 acres in Beverley Manor, part of 334 acres conveyed to Robert by James Bratton and Elizabeth, 1st May, 1763; corner Col. Lewis' land; corner Gibson's land. Delivered: Andrew Kinkead, November, 1771.

Page 409.—2d June, 1770. Commission to Silas Hart and James Lockhart for privy examination of Barbara, wife of Jacob Trout; deed, 15th March, 1770, to George Shaver. Executed, 15th June, 1770.

Page 410.—26th October, 1769. John Craig and Sarah ( ) to George Null, eldest son and heir of Nicholas Null, deceased, £15, 400 acres on Shanandore between river and Peaked Mountain patented to said John Craige, 16th May, 1765, Boone's Run; this tract was formerly patented to James Wood, but was forfeited for non-payment of quit rents and cultivation.

Page 413.—26th October, 1769. Commission for privy examination of Sarah to above. Executed 17th March, 1770.

Page 416.—20th June, 1770. Abraham Smith to James Fowler, of Lowdon County, £100, 142 acres on a branch of South Branch of Potowmack called Licking Creek, above Paul Shavers' Run. Delivered: James Fowler, 10th August, 1771.

Page 419.—18th August, 1770. Evan Thomas and Rebekah to Rees Thomas, £55, 165 acres, part of 350 acres patented to Cornelius Cook, 20th September, 1748, and by him conveyed to Rees Thomas, deceased, father to James Thomas, who conveyed to Evan Thomas, on Brock's Creek. Teste: Daniel Smith, Jacob Bear, John George Kipp.

Page 424.—18th August, 1770. Adam ( ) Hovestick and Margrett to William Sampson, £80, on Brock's Creek; corner Rees Thomas, 235 acres patented to Adam 7th July, 1763. Delivered: George Hevener, 8th October, 1773.

Page 429.—18th August, 1770. George ( ) Shooemaker and Elizabeth ( ) to Conrad Weavell, £15, 31 acres on North Branch of Shanadore, part of 310 acres patented to Valentine Sevear, 27th June, 1764, and conveyed to George; Bordens line. Teste: Jacob Bear, Robert Balshee, Jno. Geo. Kipp. Delivered: Geo. Hevener, 8th October, 1773.

Page 431.—16th July, 1770. George Conrad (and Catherine ( )), eldest son and heir of Stephen Conrad to Stephen Conrad, brother of said George, £———, natural love and affection. Two tracts 125 acres, 106 acres of which is part of 108 acres conveyed to said George by John Burk and 19 acres, part of tract whereon George now lives, on Boon's Run, a branch of Shanandore; also 24 acres patented to Stephen Conrad, father to Stephen, 30th August, 1763, and descended to George as eldest son and heir, lying between Lusk and Boon's Runs; corner John Sellers; corner Nutt's land; corner Wood's land; Kipling's (Kisling's, Rifling's) corner.

Page 433.—20th August, 1770. John Lewis, of Albemarle, to William Glaves, £40, on South River of Shanando, Joseph Hannah's land, Robert Frazer's survey, 164 acres patented to said Lewis, 21st September, 1762. Teste: Thomas Rodgers, James Kennerley, Jr., Thos. Turk. Delivered: Wm. Glaves, March, 1771.

Page 437.—10th October, 1769. Francis Beaty, of Mecklenburg County, North Carolina, Gent., to his brother-in-law, John Tate, power of attorney to sell all lands belonging to Francis, including land bought of John Keer, on Flat Spring Branch, joining the other land where I last lived; also 200 acres joining Charles Berry. Teste: Robert Gay, John and James Beaty.

Page 438.—16th August, 1770. Margrett Smith, wife of John Smith, of Augusta County, to Samuel McCutchon, Sr., £12, and divers good reasons, horses, crops. Teste: James Crow and William Berry.

Page 439.—17th August, 1770. John Smith to James and Samuel Clark, £3.10.10, cows. Teste: John Clark, William McCutchan, Jr.

Page 441.—17th August, 1770. William Owler to Michael D(a)ufflemire, £17.10, 181 acres, part of 1900 acres patented to William Owler, deceased, 16th September, 1765, on north side of Shanandore, said Owler's line, corner David Louderback's land. Delivered: Michael Roreck for Dauflemire, 11th June, 1790.

Page 444.— ——, 1770. William Owler to Adam Bowyer, £———, 200 acres on north side Shanandore, part of 1,900 acres patented to William Owler, deceased, 16th September, 1765, pond near Strickler's convey; corner David Lowderback; corner William Mungar. Delivered: Adam Bowyer, August, 1781.

Page 449.—15th June, 1770. Joseph Gwin and Mary to his brother, Robert Gwin, £70, 120 acres, part of 544 acres belonging to Robert Gwin, Sr., by patent on Great Calfpasture between tract where Moses McElvain now dwells and John Graham's land, conveyed by Robert Gwin, Jr., to said Joseph Gwin, 21st June, 1763, and now conveyed back to said Robert; corner John Graham. Delivered: Joseph Reaburn, March, 1775.

Page 455.—22d March, 1770. Thomas Hicklen, Sr., to Thomas Hicklin, Jr., £100, 131 acres on Newfound Creek of the Cowpasture and now known by the name of the Bullpasture, part of 348 acres patented to Andrew Lewis, 1st June, 1750, and coneyed by him to Thomas, Sr.; corner land formerly in possession of John Wilson; corner land in possession of Samuel Givens. Teste: John Carlile, Robert ( ) Carlile, William Black.

Page 458.—30th December, 1767. William Craige to James Hamilton, £30, 108 acres on Elk Run in Beverley Manor; corner said Logan's other land. Delivered: John Hamilton, March, 1779.

Page 460.—1st May, 1770. John Hite, of Frederick County, eldest son, &c., of Jost Hite to George Speers, £20, 35 acres on Linvell's Creek, patented to Hite et als.; corner said Speer; corner widow Smith. Delivered: Doctor Michael Archdeacon, November, 1771.

Page 465.—21st August, 1770. Charles Campbell to James Campbell, £30, 220 acres; corner John Anderson; corner John Erwin. Teste: John Lowry, Hugh Campbell (Camble).

Page 471.—20th August, 1770. James Davidson and Jean ( ) (Gen) to James Rolstone, £86, 200 acres, part of 1,700 acres patented to Robert Green, 15th March, 1744; corner said Davidson. Teste: John Gratton, Benjamin Harrison, James Carry. Delivered: James Ralstone, 13th May, 1788.

Page 475.—20th August, 1770. Robert Davis and Sarah to Frederick Havoner, £10, 33 acres on South Fork of South Branch of Potowmack, part of 327 acres whereon said Davis lives; said Hevener's corner. Delivered: David Steel, per order, 28th September, 1817.

Page 477.—18th December, 1769. Michael Proops and Cathorine to Henry Stone, Ludwick Wagoner, Mark Swadley and Christian Roleman commissioners for the members of the congregation of the Lutheran Church at the South Fork of Potowmack, 5 shillings, 3½ acres, part of 415 acres whereon Michael now lives for use of the congregation forever. Teste: Leonard ( ) Proopst, Robert Davis, Ludwig Adam Wagener, William Davis.

Page 479.—9th August, 1770. John Madison and Agatha to John Denniston, £25, 200 acres on north side Shanando River patented to William

Downs, 5th March, 1747, and by him conveyed to John Madison, 18th February, 1758, mouth of Stover's Mill Creek; corner William Lamb and Robert Shanklin. Delivered: John Denniston, 3d August, 1772.

Page 484.—20th August, 1770. George (Michael) Kiff and Barberry ( ) to Phillip Dailey, £23, 200 acres, the river, Isaac Robinson's line. Delivered: John Thomas, 7th August, 1772. On north side of North River of Shannando.

Page 488.—14th May, 1770. John Miller and Ann, of Albemarle, to David Gum (name is probably Givin, written also Grim, Gwin). Delivered: David Gwin, April, 1793, £100, 243 acres on Jackson's River patented to said Miller, 20th August, 1760. Teste: Thomas and John Miller.

Page 491.—18th August, 1770. Andrew Kinkead and Jean to Thomas Kinkead, £40, 45 acres on Calfpasture River; corner said Thomas. Teste: John Finley, William Tincher. Delivered: Tully Davitt, 1776.

Page 495.—21st August, 1770. John ( ) Kinkead and Elizabeth ( ) to Andrew Kinkead, £40, 106 acres on Great Calfpasture, part of 530 acres conveyed to John Kinkead by John Kinkead, clerk, 17th October, 1754. Delivered: Jno. Kinkead, 21st February, 1776.

Page 498.—17th August, 1770. John Smith to James Clark, Jr., £27, cows and horses. Teste: John Clark. Delivered: Wm. McPheeters, Gent., 3d September, 1787.

Page 500.—22d August, 1770. John and James Hooks to John McMahon, £16, 100 acres on a draft of North River of Shanando patented to said Robert McMahon, 12th May, 1759. Teste: Robert Hook, John Gabriel Jones. Delivered: John McMahon, January, 1773.

Page 503.—15th May, 1770. Commission to Daniel Smith and Felix Gilbert to take privy examination of Mary, wife of Benjamin Grigsby, as to deed to Henry Null, dated 12th May, 1770. Executed 16th August, 1770.

Page 506.—21st August, 1770. Joseph Culton to James Culton, £———, 300 acres on Moffett's Creek, branch of Hayse's Creek; corner James Wallace; corner Hindry Campbell; Samuel Steel's line; John Walker's corner. Delivered: James Moffett, 10th September, 1778.

Page 509.—21st May, 1770. John Heagons (Hagens) to William Brown, £5, mortgage. Teste: John King, John Canterberry. Assigned by Brown to David Laird, £2.17.7½, 11th August, 1770.

Page 511.—21st August, 1770. Samuel ( ) Briggs and Mary ( ) to John Logan, £45, 120 acres, part of 380 acres patented to John Megill, 12th May, 1759, and conveyed to Samuel, 19th August, 1761, on north side of North River of Shannadore; corner John McClure, opposite James McGill's. Teste: Samuel Patterson, George Rutledge. Delivered: John Logan, June, 1773.

Page 516.—21st August, 1770. James Bratton (Bratin) and Elizabeth to Peter Kinder, £70, 900 acres on Bratton's Run, branch of Calfpasture, patented to James Bratton 6th April, 1769; Dunlap's corner. Delivered: Matain Sea, 25th April, 1772.

Page 519.—23d June, 1770. Stephen Loy and Mary ( ) to William Bowyer, £150, 245 acres whereon Stephen now lives, which he purchased of Robert Breckinridge and joining Alexander McClenachan, Andrew Scott,

Robert McClenachan, David Stuart and Elisha McClenachan. Teste: G. Jones, Lew Bowyer, Wm. Madison, Michael Bowyer.

Page 524.—23d August, 1770. William Finley to son, John Finley, £53.6.8, 215 acres in Beverley Manor, part of 297 acres laid off for John Finley, Sr., part of 892 acres on Shannandore surveyed for John Finley, Jr., manor line; William Finley's line; Ramsey's line. Teste: Wm. Marshal, Wm. Armstrong. Delivered: John Finley, 15th December, 1773.

Page 528.—23d August, 1770. James Burnsides to William McCanlos, £42, 224 acres conveyed to James by Robert Scot on the Newfoundland Creek; corner John Botkin; corner land in possession of Carlile. Teste: Jno. Gabriel Jones, John Hays, John Botkin.

Page 530.—8th March, 1770. Matthew Harrison to John Ashburner, of Baltimore, mortgage, £287; corner tract called the Plains, 210 acres.

Page 536.—20th August, 1770. John ( ) Kinkead, Sr., and Elizabeth ( ) to John Kinkead, Jr., £40, 88 acres, part of 530 acres conveyed to John Kinkead by John Kinkead, clerk, 17th October, 1754, on Calfpasture River; corner Mathew Kinkead.

DEED BOOK No. XVII.

First Deed Recorded 24th August, 1770; Last Deed Recorded 20th November, 1771.

Page 1.—25th August, 1770. William Wilson and Mary ( ), of Albemarle, and John Hunter, Sr., and Frances, of Augusta, to Francis Hartgrove, of Staunton, £40. In Staunton, part of lot No. 14, 5 poles north and south and 4 poles east and west, only excluding a house on northwest corner wherein Edward Long lived, of 18 by 22 feet in length and breadth. Lot faces James Hustons front on south and James Huse on west, containing 20 square perches, only reserving said house; also 2½ acres wood land on south end of lot of 30 acres between (betwixt) Col. William Preston's land and Joseph Gamble's wood land, about ½ mile northwest of Staunton, bounded according to courses of Staunton, lot No. 10. Delivered: Francis Hartgrove, 9th September, 1773.

Page 5.—25th August, 1770. John Johns(t)on and Mary to William Bowyer, £30, 124 acres, part of 200 acres left by Arthur Johnston, deceased, to his two sons, John and Andrew, bounded as by decree of Augusta County Court; corner Daniel Harrison; also 18½ acres, part of 37 acres adjoining above tract also left by said Arthur to said two sons by will. Delivered: Wm. Bowyer, 8th April, 1771.

Page 8.—27th August, 1770. Martin Gryder to Daniel Zink and Lewis Runkle, £27.10.5, for which amount grantees have become security for grantor to Francis Sanderson, coppersmith of Pennsylvania, to secure said grantee; 1 still holding 50 gallons with all utensils, horses, cows, beds and furniture; one English ironpipe stove. Teste: John Sevier, Edward Sampson.

Page 9.—26th June, 1770. John Stuart (Stewart), taylor, to William Bowyer, £80, mortgage, negro slave. Teste: Michael Bowyer John Frogg. Jas. Ray.

Page 11.—8th September, 1770. Samuel Lusk and Agness ( ) to John

Hare, £20, 150 acres patented to Samuel, 20th July, 1768, river bank; corner John Lusk. Teste: John Hare. Delivered: John Hare, March Court, 1778.

Page 16.—17th November, 1770. George Adam ( ) Bright and Mary ( ) to James and Samuel Gilliland, of County of York, £80, 170 acres in Beverley Manor at head of a branch of South River, David Hays line. Teste: Joseph Moore, James and John Tate.

Page 20.—18th November, 1770. George Campbell and Samuel Tincher and Margaret, of Albemarle County, to Thomas Kinkead, £75, 215 acres on Great Calfpasture, patented to William Preston, 1st June, 1750. Teste: John Bigham, Andrew and Joseph Kinkead. Delivered: Tully Davit, 1776.

Page 24.—20th March, 1770. Hugh Campbell to James Campbell, £5, 5 acres on Andersons Branch of North River of Shanandore, part of a larger tract, Robert Fowler's line. Teste: John and William Campbell, John McPheetters.

Page 28.—20th November, 1770. James Young and Mary ( ) to William Jordon, £10, 98 acres on head branch of Cowpasture, a branch of James River, patented to James, 14th July, 1769. Teste: Thomas Fimster, William Young, James Gambel. Delivered: Anthony Johnston, 15th April, 1777.

Page 31.—2d April, 1768. William ( ) Bohannon (Buchanan) and Ruth ( ) to Francis Kirtley, £30, 200 acres, corner said Kirtley, foot of Blue Ridge. Teste: Jacob Nicholas, Henry Tamewood, John Fudge.

Page 35.—9th November, 1768. John Hicklin and Jane ( ) to Samuel Givens, £150, 217 acres, part of 348 acres conveyed by Andrew Lewis to John Hicklin, 18th August, 1761. Delivered: Samuel Givens, 15th June, 1772.

Page 40.—9th November, 1768. Samuel Givens and Martha to John Hicklin. £150, 239 acres on Clover Creek, now commonly called the Bull Pasture, a branch of Cowpasture, part of 339 acres patented to Richard Botkin, and by him conveyed to John, 17th May, 1762, corner land in possesion of Loftus Pullin, part of said tract in possession of James Burnsides.

Page 42.—8th November, 1770. Commission to Daniel Smith and Felix Gilbert to take privy examination of Catherine, wife of George Conrad, deed to Stephen Conrad, dated 16th July, 1770. Executed, 17th November, 1770.

Page 45.—20th November, 1770. John Searight (Sewright) to James Seawright, his son, 5 shillings, 294 acres on Naked Creek, part of 400 acres. Delivered: James Leeper, March, 1773.

Page 49.—20th November, 1770. John Leeper to John Seawright, 40 shillings, 43 acres on Naked Creek, part of 400 acres patented to Joseph Stover, 1st December, 1740, part of tract on which Seawright now lives; corner John Seawright. Delivered: Jno. Seawright, March, 1773.

Page 51.—20th October, 1770. John Anderson, of Middle River, farmer, and James Allen, Jr., wheelwright, articles of agreement. A joint trade and partnership has existed for some time and by the permission of God, is intended to be carried on between above parties in trade act or calling as miller, for the term the water grist mill now erected shall stand; began, 1st January, 1768, now John Anderson, for love and affection he bear John Allen, Jr., his son-in-law. Partnership contract. John furnishes mill site and James to act miller.

Page 54.—20th November, 1770. John Anderson, farmer, to James Allen, Jr., wheelwright, bond in penalty of £100, conditioned that John provide the land, millrace and dam for the mill.

Page 57.—19th November, 1770. James Green and Mary ( ) to Benjamin Kinley, £50, 260 acres on a branch of Muddy Creek, near John O'Neal's lands, Harrison's lands. Teste: John Hinton, Michael Waren, John Gordon. Delivered: Benj. Kinley, 31st September, 1771.

Page 62.—20th November, 1770. William Fleming, gent., of Botetourt, and Ann to John Frogg, sadler, £120, three lots in Staunton, No. 11, joining a hillside, formerly conveyed by Israel Christian to said William, 24th September, 1763; No. 16, fronting a lot belonging to John Stewart; also 152 poles conveyed by Beverley to William, 23d May, 1765. Delivered: John Frogg, 2d March, 1771.

Page 66.— — November, 1770. William Fleming and Ann, of Botetourt, to John Frogg, £120, 120 acres in Beverley Manor, corner Robert Reed; corner Prestons land in line of Beverley's Mill tract.

Page 69.—7th July, 1770. Archer Mathews and Lettice to Sampson and George Mathews, £20, one-half lot woodland northwest of Staunton, 15 acres; also one-half of lot 5 in Staunton; the former is one-half of lot No. 10, and both conveyed by Robert McClenachan to Margaret and Joseph Gamble, 22d March, 1760, and since conveyed to Archer Mathews. Teste: Pat. Lockhart, John Cowley and John Walsh.

Page 71.—3d November, 1770. Stephen Loy to Michael and William Bowyer, £250, horses, cows, furniture, one blue rug, one desk and bookcase of walnut,six setting cheers, pewter plates and dishes, four copper sase pans, one coffy and one peper mill, three pus flatirons, three tea kittles, churns, 200 sides leather now in the tan vats, sundry doctor's medisens and other articles conveyed to Stephen by Dr. John Watkins by bill sale recorded. Delivered: Luke Bowyer, 31st August, 1771.

Page 75.—23d November, 1770. John Clark and Frances to Robert Clark, £57.10, 80 acres on Back Creek in Beverley Manor of Middle River, part of 300 acres belonging to James Clark. Delivered: Robert Clark, 21st July, 1784.

Page 79.—23d November, 1770. Samuel Clark to Robert Clark, £70, 84 acres on a branch of Middle River of Shanadore, part of 380 acres conveyed to Samuel by James Clerk, corner Robert Clerk's part of said tract; corner John Clerk's land.

Page 83.—21st November, 1770. John Anderson to Robert Hamilton, £30, 360 acres on a branch of Shanandore (Shanando).

Page 87.—John ( ) Miller (the signature is recorded Hen.) and Barbara ( ) to Adam Sellers, £6, 6 acres on north side Shanando, part of tract whereon John now lives. Delivered: Adam Sellers, 17th July, 1794.

Page 93.— — ——, 1771. John Futch, Sr., and Katharine ( ) to John Futch, Jr., their son, £10, 140 acres, part of tract whereon John now lives, on Shanando River, patented to David Magart (Magot) and Daniel Weitreith, 1st June, 1741 and by them conveyed to John, Sr.; also 96 acres, part of a patent for 290 acres on north side Shanando, to John, Sr., 15th August, 1764; corner Hemburger's survey. Teste: Conrad Futch, Jacob Bare, David Magett. Delivered: John Futch, November Court, 1776.

Page 98.— — ——, 1771. Same to Conrod Futch, £10, 140 acres on

Shanando, part of patent to Magot and Weitreith, corner John Futch, Jr.; also 96 acres on Shanando, part of 290 acres above. Teste: Conrod Futch, Jacob Bare, David Magott.

Page 101.—9th August, 1770. Mathew Harrison to Benjamin Marshall, of Philadelphia, mortgage, £233, one-half undivided of 840 acres between Shenandoah River and Peaked Mountain, by plats made by Lewis, 28th September, 1768, part of upwards of 1100 acres conveyed to said Harrison and Alexander White by Mary Wood, et als., 6th September, 1769; also negro slaves.

Page 106.—15th March, 1771. Andrew ( ) Fitzpatrick and Mary ( ) to David McNeelley, £5, 150 acres of Borden's 92100. Teste: James Buchanan, Samuel Lyle, Andrew Campbell.

Page 110.—19th March, 1771. Robert ( ) Bratton to son James Bratton, £40, 400 acres, part of 834 acres on Great Calfpasture. Delivered: James Bratton, 7th April, 1772.

Page 115.—19th March, 1771. David Campbell and Mary ( ) to James Trotter, £282.10, 234 acres, part of his old survey in Beverley Manor, conveyed to David by Beverley, 28th May, 1741, Pat. Cook's line; also 110 acres conveyed by same to David, 27th February, 1749, corner said Campbell. Teste: William Campbell, Wm. Lockhart. Delivered: Samuel Trotter, 21st October, 1772.

Page 120.—17th November, 1770. James Lackey and Elizabeth to Moses Bennet, £33, 110 acres, part of 200 acres on northeast side of North Branch of James River; McClure's line, corner Moses Bennets old survey. Teste: Pat. McCorkle. Delivered: Robert Lusk, 26th July, 1774.

Page 123.—8th December, 1770. Rev. John Jones, Rector of Parish of Augusta, to Patrick Lockhart, power of attorney to recover from members of the parish all that may be due him from levy of 1769. Teste: Thos. and George Smith, John James Kennerley.

Page 126.—28th March, 1771. John Buchanan and Margret ( ) to Patrick Buchanan, £300. 176 acres in Beverley Manor, corner John Coulter; corner John Buchanan; corner William Curry. Delivered: Pat. Buchanan, 16th February, 1773.

Page 130.—18th March, 1771. William Currey to James Currey, £20, 130 acres in Beverley Manor; corner McCorkel's land; corner James Moody, Andrew Cowan's line; corner William Curry. Teste: George McAfee. Wliliam Cowan. Delivered: James Curry, 1st June, 1773.

Page 135.—20th March, 1771. Daniel Denison (Danston) and Elizabeth ( ) to Joseph Bell. £220, 300 acres conveyed to Daniel Denison, deceased, by Beverley, 10th April, 1739, and devised to grantor, Daniel, by Daniel, deceased. on a branch of Lewis Creek. corner Petter Hog, Andrew Lewis' line. Delivered: Joseph Bell, December, 1777.

Page 138.—9th December, 1770. John Carlile. of the Calfpasture, to Thomas Adams, gent., of St. Peter's Parish, New Kent County, £100, 250 acres purchased by John from John Campbell, on Great Calfpasture. Delivered: Sampson Mathews, 19th March, 1772.

Page 143.—19th March, 1771. John King and Mary to John Poage, £335, four tracts on south side Middle River of Shanandore and on both sides of the Falling Spring Branch: A, 44 acres, part of 90 acres patented to Robert King, 1st August, 1745 and by his will devised to his two daughters, Elizabeth and Catharine, and on division this 44 acres became the property of Katharine, wife to James Blair, who conveyed to John King, 18th September, 1763, corner Robert Patterson, now Robert Young's; also B, 30 acres adjoining above, part of 115 acres patented to William Sharp, 10th March, 1756, and coneyed to John, July, 17—; also C, 95 acres adjoining, patented to John, 20th July, 1768; D, 148 acres, patented to said John, 20th July, 1768. Teste: Michael Dickey, John King, Robert Young. Delivered: John Poage, devisee of John Poage, deceased, 1st October, 1799.

Page 148.—15th November, 1770. Andrew Hays to John Hays, £5, 300 acres of Borden's 92100, below forks of Hays and Moffet's Creeks, corner Charles Hays. Teste: Andrew McCampbell, John Walker, John Walker, Joseph Moore.

Page 153.—22d February, 1771. Arthur Graham (Grimes) and Mary to John Walker, £20, 61 acres, part of tract whereon Arthur now lives. Teste: Alexander, John, James and Joseph Walker. Delivered: Alex. Walker, October, 1775.

Page 157.—19th February, 1771. James Walker and Mary ( ) to Hugh Kelso, £10, 26 acres adjoining land Hugh now lives on, Borden's patent line. Teste: John Hay, Joseph Walker, Michael Coulter, John Walker. Delivered: Hugh Kelso, 30th August, 1785.

Page 159.—21st March, 1771. Thomas Doyle binds himself to Thomas Stewart as servant, £20, from 9th January, 1771, for 4½ years. Delivered: Thomas Stuart, 23d May, 1771.

Page 160.—1st March, 1771. Henry Davis to Benj. Logan, binds himself servant for 1 year and 10 months, £15. Teste: Benj. Yardly. Delivered: James Magill, July, 1771.

Page 163.—9th January, 1771. William Robertson and Letis to John Stewart, £200, on north side of Middle River of Shanandore, part of two tracts: A, sold to John Moffett by Beverley, 24th May, 1750; B, patented to Mathew and William Robertson, 10th July, 1755, 196 acres; corner Mathew Robertson. Delivered: Jas. Robertson, 5th April, 1797.

Page 166.—2d March, 1771. Commission to William Christian and John Bowman, of Botetourt, to take privy examination of Ann, wife of William Fleming, as to deed to John Frogg, dated 21st November, 1770. Executed, 20th March, 1771.

Page 167.—2d March, 1771. Ditto as to deed dated 20th November, 1770.

Page 172.—27th December, 1770. James Anderson and Elizabeth ( ) to Joseph Reaburn, £125, 100 acres on Long Meadow, corner land formerly belonging to William Skillern and now Isaac White's, William Robertson's. Teste: Samuel McKee. Delivered: Jos. Reaburn, 20th May, 1771.

Page 175.—20th November, 1770. Henry Pickett to Hugh Donaghe (Donaho), £28, slaves and furniture, conditioned for payment of £28. Teste: Benj. Morgan and Audley Hamilton. Delivered: Hugh Donaho, 10th August, 1772.

Page 178.—20th March, 1770. Andrew Johnston to Joseph Bennet, £38, on North Fork of South Branch of Potomac, near the Great Clover Lick, patented to said Andrew, 20th July, 1768. Teste: John Madison, Jr., William Crow, William Long.

Page 182.—22d May, 1771. George Huffman ( ) to John Herdman, £60, 220 acres conveyed to George by Stephen Conrad, 21st November,

1764, corner Wood's land, on Boon's Run. Teste: Thos. Bowyer and Wm S. Madison.

Page 187.—21st May, 1771. Zebulon ( ) and Reuben Harrison to Robert Dickey, £30, 18 acres patented to John Harrison, deceased, 26th July, 1765, and by him devised to grantors, said Harrison's land. Delivered: Robert Dickey, April, 1773.

Page 191.—22d May, 1771. Benjamin Kinley to Jacob Guin, £9, 80 acres on Brock's Creek at foot of North Mountain, at a place called Bear Wallow.

Page 193.—20th May, 1771. Thomas Rodgers and Betty to James Kennerley, £100, 143 acres, north side Shanandore River, John Patrick's lines; corner Poindexter's land, Thomas Turk's line. Teste: Richard Poindexter Delivered to Mr. Kennerley, March, 1777.

Page 198.—21st May, 1771. John Henderson and Jean ( ) to Joseph Henderson, £200, 520 acres in Beverley Manor on a branch of Lewis Creek, James McCorkle's line. Delivered: Joseph Henderson, 18th January, 1773. Teste: John Hind.

Page 202.—21st May, 1771. Alexander Campbell and Jean ( ) to Thomas Steel, £107, 113 acres in Beverley Manor, corner David Campbell, William Ledgerwood and William Campbell's corner; corner William and David Campbell. Teste: William Has. Delivered: Thomas Steel, 17th August, 1772.

Page 208.—21st May, 1771. John Kirk and Margret to Blackly (Blakely) Brush, £25, 100 acres of Borden's 92100, John Kirk's line.

Page 213.—14th May, 1771. Alexander Painter and Margaret ( ) to Christly Painter, £100, parts of several tracts patented to said Alexander, on waters of North River of Shanandoah, Thomas Moore's survey, crossing Fort Run, corner land purchased by Alexander from Adam Raider, containing 279 acres. Delivered: Christly Painter, November Court, 1773.

Page 218.—14th May, 1771. Alexander Painter and Margaret ( ) to John Painter, £100, parts of several tracts patented as above; Michael Nees land, now Adam Painter's; corner Mathias Reader's land, 341 acres. Teste: John Painter, November, Court, 1773.

Page 221.—2d May, 1771. Gabriel ( ) Powel to Archibald Hopkins, £15, cows and horses, horses and cows. Mortgage to secure £15.

Page 223.—1st March, 1771. Borden's executors to Mathew Morehead, £5, 32 acres of Borden's 921700, corner his old survey. Delivered: September, 1778.

Page 227.—1st March, 1771. Same to Robert Allison, £30, 200 acres of 92100, on North River.

Page 234.—19th March, 1771. John King and Mary ( ) to John Givens, £265, 278 acres on Middle River of Shanadore, Hugh Thompson's corner. Delivered: John Givens, November, 1775.

Page 237.—26th May, 1771. Jacob Argabright ( ) and Susanna Marrett ( ) to Conrat Smither, £35, 125 acres, remainder of 250 acres patented to Jacob, 20th August, 1760, the other half of which Jacob sold to Election George Fridley, between Peaked Mountain and Shanandoh River. Teste: Archibald Huston, Valentine Cloninger.

Page 241.—20th May, 1771. Alexander Kirk to his father James Kirk,

£20, 200 acres, part of 400 acres which James formerly conveyed to Alexander Kirk. Delivered: Alexander Kirk, March Court, 1774.

Page 245.—21st May, 1771. James Kirk and Jean ( ) to his son Alexander Kirk, £40, 185 acres, part of 400 acres where said Kirk now lives. Delivered: Alex. Kirk, March Court, 1774.

Page 251.—20th May, 1771. James Hind (Hinds), of Albemarle, to his father William Hind (Hinds), £40, 295 acres, Turk's line, corner Bloodworth. Teste: James Allen, Charles ( ) Clendenen.

Page 256.—29th December, 1770. Joseph Reaburn and Margaret to William Robertson, £125, 100 acres on Long Meadow, corner land formerly belonging to William Skillern, and now Isaac White's, William Robertson's line. Teste: Samuel McKee, Hugh Donaghe, James Kerr.

Page 260.—25th May, 1771. John Campbell, of Botetourt, to James Trotter, £150, 232 acres, part of his father's survey in Beverley Manor. Teste: James Lockhart, James Hargrave, Sampson Archer. Delivered: Samuel Trotter, 21st October, 1772.

Page 265.—25th May, 1771. Mathew Thompson, Sr., and Rachel to Robert Hill, £400, 400 acres on Mill Creek of Shannando, patented to Andrew McConnal, 30th August, 1743, and by them conveyed to John Anderson and by him to Mathew, Sr., corner Robert Hook; corner William Williams. Delivered: Samuel Hill, May Court, 1778.

Page 270.—25th May, 1771. Same to Samuel Beaty, of York County, Pennsylvania, £90, 210 acres patented to grantor here, 12th May, 1759, on Collin's Branch, Robert Scott's line, Patrick Frazier's line. Delivered.

Page 275.—11th April, 1770. Elizabeth ( ) Ray and John ( ) Haye to John Parks, £36, 220 acres, Borden's patent line. Teste: William and James Ray, Colbert and James Blair, James Buntin.

Page 278.—17th August, 1771. Thomas Slaughter and Ann to Robert Slaughter, Jr., of Frederick County, 5 sihllinngs, on Shanandoe River, 465 acres which Jacob Cogar sold to Thomas McCredie, late of Fredericksburg, merchant, deceased, 24th May, 1753, recorded in General Court, pursuant to decree of the General Court upon a bill in equity, Wm. McCredie vs. Jacob Cogar, right descending to William, as brother and heir of Thomas McCredie, and purchased by Thomas Slaughter of Alexander Cunningham late merchant of Falmouth, Virginia, as attorney for William McCredie, 4th May, 1768. Teste :Michael Cogar, Daniel Lusk, William Kite. Deliered: Thomas Slaughter, November, 1771.

Page 282.—20th August, 1771. John Buchanan and Martha to Charles Berry, £90, 240 acres in Beverley Manor, said patent line. Teste: John Handly, Robert Buchanan, Robert Gamel. Delivered: Charles Berry, 31st June, 1773.

Page 287.—17th August, 1771. Jacob Bair (Bear) and Barbara Miller ( ) Bear, his wife, and Jacob Mayer (Moyer, Meirs) and Christenah ( ) to Mishael and George Huffman, £64, 276 acres on Shanando River, patented to Jacob Moyer and Jacob Bair, 20th July, 1768, Daniel Link's line. Teste: Daniel Link, Thos. Slaughter, Robert Slaughter, Jr. Delivered: Geo. Huston.

Page 292.—3d July, 1771. Robert ( ) Frazor and Frances ( ) to Benjamin Yardly (Yearly), £125, on south branches of Shanando, known by the name of Cave Bottom, part of 400 acres patented to Alex. Thompson, 12th May, 1742, and conveyed by Alexander to Wm. Beard, 100 acres, Alex. Thompson's Ford, the Cave Hill. Teste: Joseph Hannah, Robert Scott, Wm. Hook. Delivered to Benj. Yardley, January, 1773.

Page 297.—20th August, 1771. Robert ( ) Allison and Ann ( ) to William Sprowl, £104, part of Borden's tract conveyed to Robert by Borden's executors in two deeds: A, containing 108 acres of which 25 acres have been conveyed by Robert to Jacob Anderson; B, containing 240 acres; corner Jacob Anderson, North Fork of James River. Teste: John Thompson, Daniel Lile, John McKee, William Sprowl. Delivered: William Sprowl, August Court, 1774.

Page 301.—19th August, 1771. William Logan and Elizabeth ( ), of Botetourt, to Samuel Gibson, £180, 386 acres patented to William, 10th March, 1756, Terrence Kelly's line. Teste: Richard, Edward and Robert Shanklin. Delivered: Samuel Gibson, November, 1775.

Page 306.—19th August, 1771. Robert ( ) Jameson and Sarah to John Alexander, £45, part of 400 lying along Beverley Manor line; corner James Bell; 200 acres. Teste: Walter Davis, John Cunningham, Samuel Blackwood.

Page 311.—20th August, 1771. James Berry and Elizabeth ( ) to James McKemy, £115, 168 acres purchased by James Berry from Thomas Berry, his father, on Cap. Joseph Kennedy's Mill Creek, in Borden's 92100; corner Robert Gray's land, McNutt's new line; corner Francis Beatie's land. Teste: James Cooper, John McCutchen, John Malcom. Delivered: Wm. McKemy, 19th June, 1772.

Page 316.—20th August, 1771. John Hind and Jean ( ), of Augusta, to Daniel Denison, £148, 330 acres patented to John Hind, 6th April, 1769, on Muddy Creek of North River of Shanandore, on Dry River. Teste: Elijah McClenachan, John King, John Mophet. Delivered: George Eyry, of Rockingham County, present owner, 13th March, 1821.

Page 320.—21st August, 1771. William Lewis and Ann to William Cunningham, of Hampshire, £32.10, 110 acres on Back Creek, patented to William Lewis, 13th August, 1763.

Page 324.—22d August, 1771. Robert Beverley to John Ramsey, Jr., £13.10, 110 acres in Beverley Manor., Hugh McClure's corner, Samuel McCunes line. Delivered: William Ramsey, 5th October, 1772.

Page 328.—2d August, 1771. Same to Patrick Campbel, £40, 234 acres in Beverley Manor, on south side of Timber Ridge, James Leeper's line, John Shield's line; corner Robert Christian and John Shields; corner James Hamilton, James Wilson's line. Delivered: Patrick Campbell, 11th March, 1772.

Page 330.—6th May, 1771. Mathew Harrison to Thomas Carson, of Fairfax County, and Henry Mitchell, of Spottsylvania, merchants, mortgage, £748, tract whereon Mathew now lives, known as the Great Plains, 210 acres conveyed to him by Mrs. Mary Woods; also 965 acres, three surveys for Mathew, 2d December, 1768, not yet patented, on North River of Shanandoe, corner Wood's land. Teste: John Tyler, Jr., Robert Rutherford.

Page 336.—25th May, 1771. John Campbell and Elizabeth to Thomas Frame, £130, 288 acres on Middle River of Shanandore on Walter's Run, Robert Campbell's line. Teste: Robert and John Campbell, Andrew McClure. Delivered: Thomas Frame, 25th January, 1773.

Page 340.—29th June, 1771. John Buntain to John Wilson, £20, 225 acres of Bordens 92100, on Back Creek. Teste: John, Andrew and James Hays, Alex. Wilson, James Colter. Delivered: Mr. Wilson, August Court, 1777.

Page 345.—20th August, 1771. William ( ) Hamilton and Margaret ( ) to Samuel Erwin, £37, two tracts: A, 50 acres patented to William, 20th July, 1768, on Middle River of Shanandore known by name of Bald Rock survey; B, 47 acres joining former, part of 235 acres. Delivered: S. Erwin, May, 1778.

Page 347.—22d August, 1771. George Mathews, High Sheriff of Augusta, and Ursilla Long, wife of Charles Longe, late of Augusta, to John Bear, farmer. On 25th June, 1770, John Thomas brought bill in chancery in County Court Augusta, against Charge Longe, clerk, to subject Charles's lands to payment of a debt in which decree was entered, 29th November, 1770, £90.1, on head of Fort Run, 320 acres patented to Daniel Johnston, 16th August, 1756, and by him conveyed to James Johnston, 16th May, 1762, and by him conveyed to said Charles Longe, 24th October, 1768. Delivered: Jno. Bear, December, 1771.

Page 351.—20th August, 1771. Thomas Steel and Isabel to Windel Grove, £125, 114 acres in Beverley Manor, John Steel's line, Andrew Lynn devised to Thomas by will of William Smith, deceased, dated 3d December, 1754. Delivered: Windle Grove, 17th June, 1793.

Page 356.—20th August, 1771. Thomas Steel and Isabel to Windel Bright, £125, 155 acres in Beverley Manor, corner Brownlee; corner John Steel, devised to Thomas by will of William Smith, dated 3d December, 1756. Delivered: Windle Bright, 30th September, 1773.

Page 360.—20th August, 1771. James Blair, Jr., farmer, to Samuel Curry, £30, 100 acres. Teste: William Young, John Hare, James Searight. Delivered: Samuel Curry, March Court, 1773.

Page 365.—11th May, 1771. Mary Wood, executrix and devisee of James Wood, late of Frederick, to Andrew Trumbo, £240, on south fork of South Branch of Potowmac, 600 acres, part of 2400 acres patented to James Wood, William Russell and William Green, 23d October, 1750, and conveyed to Wood by partition. Delivered:Andrew Trumbo, 8th November, 1774.

Page 369.—20th August, 1771. Patrick Hamilton and Agness (signed Ann) to William Oldham, £20, 90 acres on Middle River of Shanandore, joining George Lewis, corner to that small piece of said tract laid off for said Lewis; corner Robert Reed. Delivered: Alexander Reed, August, 1779.

Page 373.—20th August, 1771. Daniel Love to John Quin (Guin), £10, two tracts: A, 53 acres on Fork of Cook's Creek, patented to Daniel Love, 20th July, 1768, corner his other land, Cravens' line; B, 255 acres, part of 280 acres patented to Daniel, 16th August, 1746, joining the 53 acres; corner Joseph Dicktum; corner John Craven's land. Delivered: John Guin (Gwin), March, 1776.

Page 378.—15th August, 1771. Peter Penigar (Pannenger, see Deed Book 16, p. 30) and Magdalene ( ) to Frederick Wolfaart, £29, 100 acres, part of 335 acres patented to Rudolph Mauk, 30th August, 1763, and by him conveyed to Michael Hower (Hover), and by Michael and Barbara to Peter Penigar, 14th August, 1769 (Deed Book 16, p. 30), on North Branch

Shanandore, corner Charles Long. Teste: John Thomas. Delivered: Michael Hober, 16th June, 1772.

Page 383.—20th August, 1771. John ( )Kinkead and Elizabeth ( ) to Mathew Kinkead, his son, £40, 230 acres on Great Calfpasture, said Andrew's corner. Delivered: David Kinkead, August, 1784.

Page 387.—20th August, 1771. Same to James Kinkead, their son, £40, 106 acres on Great Calfpasture, part of 530 acres; corner Andrew Kinkead's part of said tract.

Page 391.—20th August, 1771. Matthew Kinkead and Elizabeth ( ) to John Kinkead, his father, £80. 174½ acres, part of 334 acres in Beverley Manor, on draft of Christian's Creek, corner Lewis' land.

Page 395.—20th August, 1771. John Poage and Mary to Barbara Smith, £60, on branch of Middle River of Shanandore, 170 acres, corner James Allen's land. Delivered: John Poage, 6th July, 1772.

Page 401.—17th August, 1771. Francis ( ) McBride and Mary ( ) to Thomas Hood, of Frederick County, £248, 200 acres on Linwill's Creek, between Josiah Boon and Josiah Davison, part of 1500 acres patented to McCay, Hite & Co., and by them conveyed to William Linvil, and by him to Jos. Bryant, and by him to Jacob Chrisman, Sr., by him to Francis McBride, by him to John Bear, by him to Francis again, 17th August, 1768, corner Josiah Boone's part of same tract. Teste: Abraham Miller, Michael Warren, Daniel Smith, John Thomas. Proved by oaths of some and by affirmation of Abraham Miller. Delivered: John Thomas, 7th August, 1772.

Page 404.—21st August, 1771. John McKemey and Agness to William McKemey, son to said John, £100, 107 acres, part of tract conveyed to John by Henry Downs, on branch of North River of Shanando, at end of Buckhill. Teste: Thomas Woddall, John Hogshead, Alex. Kilpatrick. Delivered: William McKemy, 19th June, 1772.

Page 410.—17th August, 1771. Thomas West ( ) to Jno. Fitzwater, £20, 130 acres on North River Shanando, above West's Gap, at a place called the Slippery Ford, patented to West, 10th June, 1760. Delivered: John Fitzwater, November Court, 1773.

Page 414.—19th August, 1771. Robert Beverley to Mathew Kenny and Robert Kenny, £12, on Middle River in Beverley Manor, corner Wm. Dunlap, 63 acres; corner their old survey. Teste: David Corson. Delivered: Mathew and Robert Kenny, June, 1772.

Page 419.—22d August, 1771. Same to Robert Bratton, £50, 340 acres in the Calfpasture, called the Meeting House land, Meeting House Branch. Delivered: James Bratton, 7th April, 1772.

Page 424.—12th January, 1771. James Lakey (Leky, Lacky) to John Bowyer, £50, 100 acres, part of 200 purchased from Borden's executors, whereon James now lives, the other part having been sold to Moses Bennet. Delivered: John Bowyer, November Court, 1773.

Page 426.—22d August, 1771. Thomas Moore to Michael Bowyer, £10, 145 acres, part of 190 acres patented to said Moore, 12th May, 1770, on Smith's Creek, said Bowyer's line, Thomas Lookie's land. Delivered: Boston March by Mr. Bowyer's order, March Court, 1777.

Page 429.—28th March, 1771. Johnathan Davis and Lucy ( ), of Orange County, to Philip and Joshua Bush, of county aforesaid, £50, 170 acres on northwest side of the Blue Ridge on the branches of Hawk's Bill. Teste: James Dever, John Patterson, Robert Rodgers.

Page 434.—20th March, 1771. Thomas Frame and Jean to John Campbell, 296 acres conveyed to him, 25th May, 1771; 220 acres in Beverley Manor conveyed to Thomas by James Frame, 18th August, 1768, corner the Christians' land, land belonging to one Lusk; one McCorkle's corner; John Glass's corner. Teste: William Young, Andrew McClure, Chas. Campbell.

Page 437.—22d August, 1771. John Campbell and Elizabeth, 25th May, 1771, to Thomas Frame. Privy examination returned 23d August, 1771. Delivered: Thomas Frame, 25th January, 1773.

Page 438.—18th November, 1771. John Alexander to Nathaniel Steel, mortgage, £120, tract whereon John now lives, 400 acres conveyed to him by David Doage and whereon he formerly lived. Teste: Francis Patton, David Doage. Delivered: Nathaniel Steel, April, 1773.

Page 443.—19th November, 1771. William Oaler to William Munger, £4, 250 acres, part of 1900 acres patented 16th September, 1765, one Windleverley's corner; Adam Boyer's corner; one Strickler's corner. Delivered to order of grantee's heirs, 6th September, 1804.

Page 447.— — —, 1771. Same to Andrew Bartell (Bartill), £5, 230 acres, part of 1900 acres above, on west side of Shanandore River, corner Windlecoit's land. Delivered.

Page 451.—21st August, 1771. Robert Beverley to James Gillespy, £12.1.4, 130 acres in Beverley Manor, corner James Gillespy, deceased, McClure's corner. Teste: John Davidson, William Finley, Hugh McClure, Samuel Pilson.

Page 455.—17th November, 1771. Boston ( ) Hostler and Susannah ( ) to John Cooke, £32, 70 acres between Stony and Dry Runs, corner Jacob Runkle. Teste: Daniel Sink, Henry Lung, Barbara Lung Jacob Runkles. Delivered: John Cooke, March, 1773.

Page 458.—10th October, 1771. Lodowick Francisco and Elizabeth ( ), of Botetourt, to John Young, £124, 180 acres conveyed to Lodowick by Christophel Francisco, 2d July, 1752, on north side Shanandore River, on Cub Run, near Bruster's land. Teste: Hugh Johnston. Delivered: Wm. Young, March, 1773.

Page 461.—10th October, 1771. Commission for privy examination of Elizabeth above, returned 10th October, 1771.

Page 465.—19th November, 1771. Robert Beverley to David Cunningham, £15, 150 acres in Beverley Manor, corner Wm. Bunton and Alex. Campbell. Delivered Pat. Buchanan, 16th February, 1773.

Page 470.—19th October, 1771. Thomas Rafferty and Esther (Easter) ( ) to Andrew Moody, £32, 18 acres on north side South River of Shanidore, part of 330 acres patented to George Anderson, 1741. Delivered: **Andrew Moody, 18th April, 1775.**

Page 474.— — November, 1771. John Elliot (Elliote), Sr., to James Elliote, £10, 200 acres on head of south fork of Jennings Branch, north fork of Buffaloes Lick Branch. Delivered, October, 1779.

Page 478.—19th November, 1771. David Frame and Elizabeth to Robert Dinwiddie, £5, 50 acres on Jackson's River above Vanderpool's Gap. De**livered: William Denwiddie, 25th September, 1797.**

Page 482.—19th November, 1771. John Cunningham to John Lewis

Piercey (Purcy), £78, 200 acres on Thorney Branch, part of 400 acres, corner Robert Laws. Delivered: Jno. L. Piercy, 19th July, 1796.

Page 486.—4th May, 1771. Alexander ( ) Deal and Isabel ( ), yeoman, to Robert Deal, yeoman, £10, 80 acres on Cas Creek.

Page 491.—20th November, 1771. Joseph Carroll, only surviving son and heir of William Carroll, deceased, late of Frederick County, and Mary ( ) to John Alderson, Jr., £25, on Stroud's branch between Smith's Creek and the Peaked Mountain, corner another survey of William Carroll's; being 158 acres patented to William 16th August, 1756; also at same place, a tract called Carroll's Meadow; corner survey belonging to Zebulon Harrison, crossing Daniel James' Branch, containing 265 acres patented to Wm. Carroll, 10th September, 1752. Delivered: John Alderson, 27th November, 1774.

Page 497.—20th November, 1771. William Lowrie and Isabel and Robert Lowrey, Sr., to James Henry, 170 acres of Borden's 92100, 160 acres of which was devised to Wm. Lowrie by his father John Lowrie, by will in Augusta, the remaining 10 acres sold by said Robert Lowry, John Weir's line, Edmiston's corner. Teste: Samuel Huston, William Walker, Robert Lowrey, Samuel Henry. Delivered: James Henry, 26th July, 1774.

Page 500.—16th November, 1771. Henry Long and Barbara to Michael Coagar, £35, 100 acres on Shanando, between Philip Long and Jacob Coagor. Delivered: Michael Cogor, 26th April, 1785.

Page 506.—20th November, 1771. Robert Beverley to William Cowen, £20, 200 acres in Beverley Manor joining his own land, corner Buckhanon Mrs. Teeteer's corner. Delivered: Wm. Cowen, March Court, 1774.

Page 511.—20th November, 1771. Same to Alex. Kelly, £17, 150 acres in Beverley Manor, whereon he now lives. Delivered: Alex. Kelly, 28th July, 1774.

Page 516.—20th November, 1771. Same to James Coulter, £45, 300 acres in Beverley Manor, corner Andrew Campbel, Stuarts line. Delivered: Joseph Coulter, July, 1772.

Page 522.—21st November, 1771. Same to James Hamilton, £5, 35 acres in Beverley Manor, corner John Hamilton. Delivered: John Hamilton, March, 1779.

Page 528—20th November, 1771. Same to John Hamilton, £10, 100 acres in Beverley Manor, near Indian Road.

Last deed recorded, 20th November, 1771.

DEED BOOK No. 18.

From No. 18 to No. 25, historical purposes only; not complete.

First deed recorded 20th November, 1771; last deed recorded 17th November, 1772.

In this book, I only note such records as seem to have matter of historical value.

Page 2.—19th November, 1771. Hugh Donaghe (Donoho) and Eliazbeth to Thomas Rankin, £100, on head of Buffalo and Diver's Lick Drafts, patented to Hugh, 7th July, 1763, corner John Strain's survey. Teste: John Reaburn, James Henderson, Andrew Ralston. Delivered: James Neal, 10th March, 1772.

Page 22.—19th November, 1771. William Reah (Reaoh) and Elizabeth ( ) to Mathew Moorehead, £85, 257 acres in Borden's land conveyed to

William by John Handly and Grizel, 22d May, 1764, corner 300 acres surveyed for Joseph Kennedy on Broad Spring Run, otherwise called Back Creek. Delivered, September, 1778. Teste: John Rusk, Daniel Kidd, Archibald Reaugh.

Page 26.—19th November, 1771. John Madison, Jr., to John Black. Delivered: James Black, January, 1773.

Page 28.—19th November, 1771. Same to John Ramsey. Delivered: William Ramsey, 5th October, 1772.

Page 30.—20th November, 1771. Warranty bond for title deed, p. 26 above, signed by John Madison, Jr., Thomas Madison; mentions two plantations belonging to John Ramsey, Sr. Teste: Samuel Price, Richard Mathews. Delivered.

Page 34.—19th November, 1771. Rudolph ( ) Eurabough and Mary ( ) to William Stolp, £45, 195 acres, part of 221 acres patented to said Rudolph, 14th July, 1769, corner Adam Eurabough. Teste: Michael Archdeacon, John Hogshead. Delivered: Adam Eurabough, June, 1780.

Page 38.—19th November, 1771. Same to Adam Eurebough, £4, 26 acres, part of 221 acres above patented, corner Jacob Rivellner's line; corner Andrew Hudloe. Delivered.

Page 42.—18th November, 1770. George Skillern and Elizabeth, of Botetourt, to John Wilson, £155, 244 acres on Jackson's River, patented to John Miller, 20th August, 1760. The Barrens. Teste: Mary and William Skillern, Benj. Estill. Delivered: John Wilson, May, 1773.

Page 46.—20th November, 1771. David Steel and Mary to George Bright, £120, 199 acres in Beverley Manor whereon David formerly lived, corner John Tate, corner John Fulton.

Page 48.—2d October, 1771. Borden's executors to Archibald Reah, Jr., corner Archibald Reah, part of 92100. Delivered: Hugh Rhea, 16th December, 1795. Teste: Alexander and Halbert McCluer, William Leakey.

Page 53.—19th November, 1771. Robert Beverley to Edward Hall. Delivered: Benjamin Hall, son of Edward, 3d September, 1792.

Page 61.—19th November, 1771. Beverley to John Anderson, in Beverley Manor. Delivered to grantee, 17th March, 1806.

Page 65.—19th November, 1771. Same to James Cameron, in Beverley Manor, whereon said James now lives.

Page 69.—22d November, 1771. Thomas Langdon, of Granville County, in Province of South Carolina, by his attorney, William Bole, of the same place, to Isaiah Shipman, £40, 200 acres, corner Isaiah Shipman.

Page 71.—28th September, 1771. Benj. Marshall, of Philadelphia, to Alex. White, of Frederick County, power attorney to sell land and slaves mortgaged by Mathew Harrison to said Benjamin. Teste: Peter Bruin, John Magill.

Page 72.—26th November, 1771. Robert Young, formerly of Augusta County, but now of South Carolina, yeoman, to Mathias Gabbert, 105 acres in Beverley Manor, conveyed to Robert by his father, and part of 550 purchased by Robert's father from Beverley, corner Wm. McClintock in James Young's part of said 550 acres, Samuel Young's line .

Page 75.—18th March, 1772. John Tate and Mary to James Tate. Teste: William Campbell, Wm. Livingston, Thomas Tate.

Page 78.—18th March, 1772. Joseph Alexander and Abigail ( ) to

James and Oliver Alexander, £60. Teste: William Livingston, Alexander Mountgomery.

Page 81.—18th March, 1772. Same to Alexander Mountgomery. Teste: William Livingston, Oliver Alexander.

Page 83.—17th March, 1772. Francis Beaty, of Rowan County, North Carolina, public register, &c., to Joseph Alexander, tract purchased by Francis from John Kerr. Delivered, November 1778.

Page 85.—26th February 1771. Alexander McNutt and Sarah to James McNutt. Teste: Arthur Campbell, Robert McNutt.

Page 88.—6th November, 1771. Robert Hamilton and Margaret to David Caldwell, on Back Creek. Teste: George, John and William Caldwell. Delivered: David, June, 1779.

Page 90.—Delivered: John Sellers, April, 1773. Teste: Michael Can, John Kiss, Peter Conrod.

Page 93.—17th March, 1772. Tract whereon John Finley now lives.

Page 96.—16th March, 1772. Robert Gamell and Mary (Gamwell) to James Harris, 140 acres, part of 326 sold by Borden to Charles Berry, 16th March, 1752. Delivered: Wm. Markley, October, 1780.

Page 99.—12th March, 1772. James Phillips, Jr., and Mary to James Trimble, £46.

Page 101.— — February, 1772. William Dean and Mary (?) to James Ewing, part of 802 acres conveyed to said Mary Dean, late Mary Cook and to Jean and John Cook by Wm. Beverley, all which land descended to the said Mary Dean, she being the only surviving heir.

Page 105.—20th March, 1772. Oliver Alexander, teste.

Page 108.—28th November, 1771. Henry Lancisco, Sr., to Henry Lancisco, Jr., son of said Henry, 194 acres, part of the plantation whereon said Henry now lives and part of 350 acres conveyed to said Henry Lancisco, Sr., by Wood, Russell and Green, 20th May, 1753, and part of 660 acres patented to said Wood, Russell and Green, 23d October, 1750, on South Branch of Potomac. Teste: Henry Judy, Necolaus ( ) Herbould, Martain ( ) Juty, Bastain ( ) Hackley. Delivered: Samuel Millar per order 25th February, 1788.

Page 111.—28th November, 1771. Same to Zichman Harman, £20, on North Fork of South Branch of Potomac, 130 acres, part of 310 acres conveyed by Wood, Russell and Green, to Henry, 16th February, 1750, and part of greater tract patented to James Wood, 23d October, 1750. Delivered: Samuel Miller as above.

Page 114.—28th November, 1771. Same to Valentine Power, part of 310 acres above. Teste: Henry Judy, Nicholaus ( ) Herbould, Martain ( ) Juty, Bastain ( ) Hackley.

Page 117.—3d March, 1772. Same to Michael, Henry, Daniel, William, Magdalen and Mary Miller, North Fork of South Branch of Potomac, 144 acres, part of 350 acres conveyed to Henry in 1755.

Page 125.—17th March, 1772. Mark Riggs and Margaret to Samuel Dunn, on Howel's Creek, a branch of North River. Delivered: Samuel Dunn, 17th August, 1774.

Page 128.—23d March, 1772. Benjamin Lewis and Susanna ( ) to Davis Frame, £190, 215 acres on Cowpasture, corner John Lewis, part of original tract, corner John McCreerey. Delivered: David Frame, 17th August, 1784.

Page 130.—18th March, 1772. William Lusk's executors (Andrew Hays and Samuel Lyle) to Thomas Stewart, merchant, of said county, tract on which William lived. Delivered: A. Reed, March Court, 1779.

Page 132.— — ——, 1772. David Moore and Mary ( ) to Samuel Moore. Patent to David, 7th July, 1763, on Thomas Wilson's Spring Branch. Teste: Walter Power, Thomas ( ) Steaton, William Moore. Delivered: William Moore, 1780.

Page 135.—17th March, 1772. Same to Thomas Steaton, Sr., £30, on Mary's Creek, a branch of James River, patented to David, 16th July, 1768, corner James Richey, John Slown, Walter Smiley's line. Teste: Walter Power, William and Samuel Moore.

Page 138.—18th March, 1772. Samuel Black, son and heir-at-law of John Black, deceased, and Rebecca ( ) to John Black, 180 acres in Beverley Manor on a branch of Lewis' Creek, corner David Black's land. Delivered: Patrick Buchanan, 30th June, 1774.

Page 147.—18th March, 1772. Benjamin Logan to James Donnald, 110 acres, part of 268 acres patented to Benjamin, 16th February, 1771, on North River, corner Samuel Gibson, David Nelson's part of said tract, Delivered: Benj. Logan, 17th March, 1773.

Page 149.—Delivered to John Dixon, June, 1777.

Page 149.—23d August, 1771. William Wilson and Mary, of Albemarle County, to John Ridpath, £14, part of lot 14 in Staunton, joining the house where Edward Long forerly lived, facing Mrs. Huse's new house; also the land whereon the house stands wherein Edward Long lived. Teste: John Rodgers, James Brown, Mathew Morehead, James Culbertson.

Page 151.—Hugh Donachey and Elisabeth. Delivered: Robert Campbell, 31st June, 1773.

Page 153.—17th March, 1772. Benjamin Logan to David Nelson, Sr., part of 268 acres patented to Benjamin, 16th February, 1771.

Page 156.—3d February, 1772. Abraham Wright and Susannah ( ) to Daniel Smith, gent., £200, 400 acres, 300 thereof devised to Abraham by his father, John Wright, the remaining 100 descended to Abraham by death of his sister, infant of very tender years, unborn at time of his father's death, as heir-at-law of his father, conveyed to John by Joseph Powell, to whom it was patented, 3d July, 1753, on head of Dry Fork of Smith's Creek, west side of the Irish Road. Delivered: Smith Lofland, who intermarried with a daughter of said Smith, 20th July, 1791.

Page 158.—12th December, 1772. George Mathews and Ursilla Lange, wife of Charles Lange. Privy examination of Ursilla to deed, 22d October, 1771, to John Bear. Taken, 12th December, 1772.

Page 159.—7th December, 1771. John ( ) Kinkead and Elisabeth ( ) to John Kinkhead, Jr., £40, 174½ acres, part of 334 acres in Beverley Manor, on some draughts of Christian's Creek, corner Lewis' land. Delivered: John Kinkead, 24th August, 1772.

Page 160.—17th March, 1772. James ( ) Kinkead to John Kinkead, £—, on Great River of Calfpasture, 106 acres granted to James by John Kinkhead and Elizabeth, 20th August, 1771, part of 530 acres, corner Andrew Kinkhead's part of said tract. Delivered to Mathew Kinkhead, 16th November, 1774.

Page 164.—20th March, 1772. Robert Beverley to Alexander and William Robertson. Delivered: Alexander Robertson, Esq., 29th March, 1788.

Page 169.—16th March, 1772. Jacob ( ) Argen(Archen)bright and Susannah ( ) to Henry Sturtsnocker, £33.10, 125 acres between Cub Run and the Peaked Mountain patented to Philip Haws 14th February, 1761, and by him conveyed to Jacob Parsenger 17th June, 1762, and by him to grantor here 20th November, 1764; corner Nicholas Trout; corner Jacob Pence. Teste: Samuel and James Craig, Jacob Nicolas, Valentine Cloninger. Not delivered.

Page 171.—19th March, 1772. John Carlisle and Mary ( ) of the Calf Pasture to Thomas Adams of Parish of Saint Peter and County of New Kent, £100, tract purchased by said John Carlisle of John Campbell, 250 acres on Great Calfpasture.

Page 174.—18th March, 1772. John Clements (Clemens) and Elizabeth ( ) to John Lyle, Sr. Delivered: Jno. Lyle, 4th March, 1774.

Page 175.—20th March, 1772. Lanty Graham, son and heir of John Graham, deceased, to James Blayr (taylor), John Graham in his lifetime had obtained a mortgage of 220 acres whereon said Blair now lives according to the patent. Release of the mortgage. Not delivered.

Page 177.—21st March, 1772. James Blayr (taylor) and Jean ( ) to Wililam Young, £65, 220 acres patented to James 10th March, 1756; corner John Blayr. Teste: John Blair, James Young, William Young. Not delivered.

Page 179.—17th March, 1772. Abraham Smith to Daniel Henderson. Release of mortgage dated 18th December, 1769, on Beaver and Spring Creek. Not delivered.

Page 183.—Teste: George Berry, James Brown, 21st March, 1772.

Page 185.—10 acres, part of 89 acres patented to Robert Reed, 16th March, 1771. Teste: Patrick Hamilton, Alexander Waddell, Wm. Poage, Robert Reed and Barbara (mark), Patrick Hamilton and Agness (signed Ann).

Page 190.—110 acres patented to Robert McKittrick, 12th May, 1759.

Page 192.—19th November, 1771. Hugh Donaho and Elizabeth to Thomas Rankin. Privy examination of Elizabeth 12th March, 1772.

Page 197.—21st March, 1772. Robert McClenachan and Sarah to Alexander Sinclair (St. Clair), part of lot No. 9 in Staunton, adjoining George Wilson's lot, ¼ acre. Delivered: Alexander St. Clair, 14th May, 1781.

Page 197.—275 acres patented to James Carrell 5th July, 1751, and by him conveyed to Valintine Pence and by him devised to Peter Miller, his executor, who devised same to said Valintine, and by him to Hugh Gibson ( ).

Page 200.—11th May, 1772. Baptist ( ) McNabb and Kathren ( ) to Moses Cunningham, of Botetourt County. Teste: Andrew Hays, Robert Tedford, Andrew McCampbell.

Page 204.—20th May, 1772. George Caldwell to John Caldwell, tract whereon George now lives; William Caldwell's part of said tract. Teste: Walter Davis, William Caldwell.

Page 206.—Delivered Mr. William Woodlaw, 18th June, 1787.

Page 215.—John Glasses' corner. Delivered: Hugh Johnston, September, 1773.

Page 219.—Andrew Hudlow and Mary ( ), of Frederick County, at a place called the Forest, between Jacob Sword's land and Fairfax's line; Michael Niece's line. Delivered: Jacob Moyle, August Court, 1774.

Page 224.—24th January, 1772. William Christall and Anne ( ) to Henry Reaburn and Charles Harris, their sons-in-law, £150; William divides 320 acres whereon he now lives between Henry and Charles equally. Teste: William and Margaret Edmiston.

Page 226.—19th December, 1771. Samuel Henderson and Jean to Michael Law, £60, 200 acres whereon said Law now lives; James Greenlee's line; corner to Rev. John Brown; John Stephenson's line; corner Thomas Paxton. Teste: Samuel Patterson, William Patton, James Patterson.

Page 230.—19th May, 1772. Beverley to John Bunton, £48, 320 acres in Beverley Manor; corner Wm. Ledgerwood, William Campbell, Thomas Steele; line of the Meeting House Place. Delivered: John Bunton, August Court, 1773.

Page 234.—18th May, 1772. John Duncle and Margaret to George Duncle, his son, part of 302 acres whereon said John now lives; corner Mathew Patton. Delivered: Jacob Hoover, 17th April, 1787, for Mr. Duncle.

Page 241.—137 acres on Canoe Run, a branch of South Branch of Potowmack.

Page 243.—4th April, 1772. John Caldwell, Junior, farmer, to John Caldwell, Sr., £12, cows, mortgage. Teste: James Armstrong, William Scott.

Page 245.—Corner land Carliles lived on.

Page 253.—14th November, 1771. James Wardlaw and Martha to James Logan, Samuel Buchanan, Alexander Walker, Sr., Andrew Hays, James Henry, James McCampbell, Thomas Hill, John Huston, Alexander Walker, Jr., elders of the Congregation of Presbyterian Dissenters of New Providence, £50, 8½ acres whereon New Providence Meeting House now stands; Andrew Duncan's line; trust for purpose of a meeting house for public worship, and a grave yard. Teste: Alexander Sinclair, Samuel Bell, George Weir. Delivered: Joseph Moore, 1st April, 1796.

Page 256.—McClure to Morris Morris. Delivered: Morris Morris, Jr., 16th August, 1800. Teste: John Malcom, Thomas Reed. Patented to Daniel Harrison, 25th September, 1746.

Page 261.—13th January, 1772. David McCoskry and Grisel ( ) to Samuel Kirkpatrick, £10, 100 acres on Mill Creek in Timber Grove, part of Borden's 92,100. Teste: Alexander McCoskry. Delivered: Michael Dickey, 28th July, 1774.

Page 265.—20th May, 1772. Beverley to James Meteer, in Beverley Manor at Cave Hill, 36 acres. Delivered: James Meteer, 11th March, 1796.

Page 267.—Delivered: Joseph Mayze, 18th February, 1794.

Page 272.—9th May, 1772. William and John Shelton, of Hanover, to John Poage, £22, 35 acres, part of 464 acres patented to Robert Green, 12th January, 1772, on South Branch of Potomac.

Page 274.—Delivered: Arthur Connerly, 9th May, 1773, 35 acres, part of 230 acres patented to William Johnston, 12th May, 1770.

Page 277.—28th March, 1770. Alexander Walker to Thomas Connerly, bond to make title ½ of a tract surveyed for said Alexander and to be made as soon as the patent can be obtained. Delivered: Thomas Connerly, 9th May, 1773.

Page 278.—21st May, 1772. William Dean, of Augusta, one of the children and devisee of the late Rev. William Dean, of Province of Pennsylvania, and lawful attorney for Joseph Dean, merchant of City of Philadelphia; John Dean, sadler of said city; Benjamin Dean, merchant of said city; the Rev. John Slemmon, of Marsh Creek in County of York, Pennsylvania, and Sarah (Slemmons), his wife, to Hugh Kelso. Delivered: Hugh Kelsey, 30th August, 1785. Whereas William Dean, late of Pennsylvania, was seized of 265 acres, and on 7th July, 1748, and devised said land to said Joseph, John (Benjamin?), Sarah, now wife of John Slemmon, and William. Teste.

Page 282.—16th May, 1772. Daniel Smith to Joseph and Hennery and Lawens. Teste: Silas Hart, Felix Gilbert, Abraham Smith.

Page 285.—21st September, 1771. William Young, of Botetourt, to Thomas Lacky. Teste: James McDowell, Lew Bowyer, John Bowyer Proved, 20th May, 1772, by Lew and John Bowyer, who swore they saw James McDowell, Gent., who is since dead, sign it.

Page 289.—20th May, 1772. Hugh Hicklin, son and heir by descent of Thomas Hicklen, deceased, to Samuel Givens, on waters of Newfoundland known by name of Bulpasture. Teste: Ralph Lofftus, John Malcom, Robert Stewart.

Page 291.—20th May, 1772. Patent has issued for 500 acres on Jackson's River in Augusta County, in which is included the Great Warm Spring jointly to John Lewis, son of Thomas Lewis, and to John Lewis, son of Andrew Lewis. Waiver of survivorship. Teste: Gabriel Jones, John Harvie, Thomas Lewis, Peachy R. Gilmer.

Page 292.—25th May, 1771. Mary ( ) Edmiston, of Philadelphia, Penna., widow, one of the devisees named in will of David Moore, of Virginia, deceased, to Samuel Hunter, yeoman, £17, on head waters of Christie's Creek in Beverley Manor adjoining lands of William Thompson, James Cowan, William Hays and Robert Wilson, 94½ acres. Teste: William Hutcheson, John Adudell, James Alexander, Benjamin McMechan, Alexander ( ) Thompson.

Page 295.—15th May, 1772. Eleanor Green, widow and executrix of Robert Green, late of Culpeper; Robert Green, surviving executor of Robert Green; Mary Wood, widow and executrix of Col. James Wood, of Frederick, to Patrick Crawford. Teste: Gerald Hooe and Aaron Lane et als. Delivered to Patrick Crawford, 9th August, 1772.

Page 299.—Delivered to John Dean, 18th November, 1774.

Page 308.—14th February, 1772. Robert Hall and Isabella to Joseph Gwinn (Gween). Delivered: Grantee Joseph Gwinn, 29th April, 1806.

Page 314.—17th August, 1772. William ( ) Hamilton and Margret to James Kirkpatrick. Delivered to John Sharp, the now proprietor, 25th March, 1795.

Page 314.—17th August, 1772. William ( ) Hamilton and Margaret to John Poage, 6 acres, part of 235 acres where said Hamilton formerly lived on south side of Middle River.

Page 318.—Patent to John McDaniel, 10th July, 1767. Teste: John Smith, David ( ) McDonald, Isaac McDonald.

Page 319.—Delivered to Samuel McCune, 22d August, 1794.
Page 322.—Delivered: William Walker, farmer, November Court, 1775.
Page 327.—18th August, 1772. Jeremiah Harrison and Katharine ( ) to Nehemiah and Josias (Josiah) Harrison.
Page 330.—Patent to Robert Cravens, 10th September, 1755. Teste: William Fowler, Andrew Thompson, John (mark) Campbell. Delivered: John Magill, 3d July, 1782. (This conveyance by Joseph Cravens and Neomi (Emie).
Page 333.—3d August, 1772. Michael ( ) Hover and Barbere ( ) to Nicholas Karin (Kearn), 335 acres patented to Rudolph Mack 30th August, 1763, on north side of the North Fork of Shenandore, on head of Fort Run; corner Frederick Woolfort.
Page 335.—Delivered: Peter Conrad, 1st November, 1788.
Page 340.—18th August, 1772. Jacob Runkle to John Cooke, consideration paid by said John Kislinger. Delivered: Jno. Cooke, March Court, 1774.
Page 344.—18th August, 1772. Charles Campbell to Joseph Campbell, his son, on small branch of North River of Shanandore, part of 400 acres where said Campbell now lives; corner John Campbell; also 50 acres adjoining, patented to Charles, 1766; corner John Hinds; corner James McGill. Delivered: Joseph Campbell, 27th June, 1783.
Page 347.—18th August, 1772. Charles Campbell to son John Campbell, similar to above, part of 400 acres patented to John Anderson 10th June, 1740, and conveyed to Charles 17th March, 1747. Delivered: John Campbell, 21st April, 1785.
Page 354.—17th August, 1772. Beverley to Walter Davis. Delivered to William Davis, one of W. Davis' executors, 2d July, 1804.
Page 363.—18th August, 1772. William Campbell to David Steel, £112; corner Alexander Campbell; corner David Cunningham (the 80 acres that David Campbell got from his father. Delivered: David Steel, 22d February, 1774.
Page 365.—Delivered to Mr. George Marshall, 8th September, 1790.
Page 369.—17th August, 1772. David ( ) Fraizer and Barbara ( ) to George Conrad, £90, 157 acres patented to William Frazier, deceased, father to said David, 25th September, 1746, on south side of Shanandore, 2 mile run. Delivered: Geo. Conrod, August Court, 1776.
Page 372.—Delivered: Samuel Carson, 18th May, 1784.
Page 377.—Patent to Robert Jameson, 1771. Teste: Patrick Buchanan, Jacob Lockhart, Gilbert Christian.
Page 381.—On South Branch Potomac, patent to Joseph Skidmore 10th September, 1767. Sent as per order 22d January, 1802.
Page 387.—26th August, 1772. Joseph Skidmore, Sr., and Agness to Samuel Skidmore, their son, £45, patent to said Joseph, 1767, 10th September, on South Branch of Potowmack where said Skidmore formerly lived. Teste: John Skidmore, Jonas Friend, John ( ) Caplinger. Delivered: Felix Gilbert, August Court, 1773.
Page 391.—17th August, 1772. Same to their son Thomas Skidmore. At a place called the Little Walnut Bottom, on North Fork of South Branch of Potomac. Delivered: Jno. Skidmore, August, 1773.
Page 395.—Patent to John Malcom, 25th September, 1762.

Page 398.—18th August, 1772. George ( ) Shaver, eldest son and heir apparent of Paul Shaver, deceased, and Elizabeth ( ) Shevar, widow of Paul, to Michael Mallow, 200 acres lately the property of Paul on Licking Creek, a branch of South Branch of Potowmac, opposite Shelton's land.

Page 402.—Patent to Samuel Lusk, 20th July, 1768. Teste: Archibald Huston, John Carlile.

Page 404.—18th May, 1772. Jacob ( ) Persinger (Passenger) and Catherine, of Botetourt, to Anthony Elar (Aler. Ayler), near Peaked Mountain, whereon Jacob lately lived ½ of tract patented to Jacob 13th August, 1763; tract purchased by Jacob of John and Adam Sharp, devisees of their father Matthew. Delivered: Anthony Ayler, August, 1773.

Page 407.—20th March, 1772. Patrick Lockhart and Mary, of Botetourt, to Peter and Jacob Cails, £150, part of 624 acres conveyed by Beverley to James Lockhart, 17th June, 1748; line of Meeting House land; corner Perry's land; corner William Lockhart's part of said tract. Delivered: David Cale, June, 1780.

Page 410.—Privy examination of Mary to above taken, 18th April, 1772.

Page 411.—13th June, 1772. Peter and Jacob Cail, farmers, to Patrick Lockhart, merchant of Botetourt, mortgage. Teste: John Madison, Jr., Richard Madison, Peter Hanger, Sampson Mathews.

Page 417.—Patent to John Harrison, deceased, 10th July, 1755, and was devised to Feby Harrison, wife of said James Dyer. Teste: Daniel Smith, Felix Gilbert, Andrew Shanklin, Andrew Greer.

Page 423.—1st May, 1772. Marriages heretofore had between Mathew Harrison and Mary, daughter of Mary Wood, and Alexander White and Elizabeth, daughter of Mary. Teste: Cornelius Thompson, Robert Macky, Aron Lane, Patrick ( ) Kirk.

Page 426.—18th August, 1772. Michael Warron (Waren, Warren) to Felix Gilbert, £32, mortgage, on Linvel's Creek, being part of tract whereon said Warren lives; Hudson's corner.

Page 430.—19th August, 1772. Adam Painter and Elizabeth ( ) to Jacob Myer, of Dunmore, patent to Michael Neice, 10th August, 1759, on north side of Alexander Painter's line. Delivered: Michael Hover, November Court, 1773.

Page 433.—18th August, 1772. Samuel Forgason and Mary to John Readpath, part of lot 15 in Staunton, the other part belonging to James Shaw.

Page 435.—20th August, 1772. John Allison and Lucie ( ) to Wliliam Allison, his son, 92 acres, part of 245 acres patented to said John, 12th May, 1770. Delivered: John Allison, 25th February, 1773.

Page 439.—Patent to John Poage, 27th August, 1770. Teste: John Bodkin, James Brown, George Berry.

Page 442.—19th May, 1772. Robert ( ) Gwynn (Gween) to Thomas Kinkead, blacksmith, land conveyed to Robert, 17th July, 1745, adjoining a tract now in possession of William Kinkead and said Thomas Kinkead. Delivered: Grantee, 25th November, 1815.

Page 445.—Patent to Thomas ( ) Dooley, 3d August, 1771, part heretofore conveyed to William Smith, tract whereon Thomas now lives.

Page 449.—19th August, 1772. Beverley to John Coulter. Delivered to

David Coalter, 19th May, 1803, which said land was willed to him by said John Coalter, his father, signed David ( ) Coalter. Teste: Samuel Crutchfield.

Page 459.—91 acres patented to Robert King 1st August, 1745; devised by Robert's will 23d August, 1749, to 3 daughters, Sarah, Elizabeth and Catherine. Sarah died without issue; Elizabeth has married Robert Patterson, and Cathorine has married James Blair (grantor here).

Page 461.—19th August, 1772. William McNiece and Jane to James Dollzil (Dallzell). Patent to Isaiah Shipman 10th June, 1760.

Page 465.—Patent to Daniel Smith (wife Jean), 16th August, 1756 Delivered: November Court, 1782.

Page 473.—18th August, 1772. Beverley to James Porterfield. Delivered to James Porterfield 17th February, 1775.

Page 478.—19th August, 1771. Same to Francis Patton; corner William Reid, Robert Terrol.

Page 482.—18th August, 1772. John ( ) Sloan, of Botetourt, and Margaret ( ) to Thomas Steaton. Delivered to Gasper Bottorph, 16th December, 1786.

Page 487.—10th August, 1772. Reuben Harrison and Lydia ( ) to Christopher Waggoner, tract patented to John Harrison, deceased, 20th September, 1751, and devised to Reuben by John, his father. Teste: Abraham Lincoln.

Page 491.—18th August, 1772. David Scott and Catherine ( ), of Botetourt, to Andrew Kennedy; corner Henry Campbell.

Page 494.—Mill Creek by Aciers Fall; Borden's tract.

Page 496.—19th August, 1772. William Edmiston (Admenston) to Samuel McChesney and James Wilson. Delivered: McChesney, 21st January, 1789.

Page 499.—20th August, 1772. George ( ) Gindner and Susanna ( ) to Francis McBride, part of 350 acres patented to Cornelius Cook and conveyed by him to Reece Thomas and by him willed to his son, Reece Thomas, and by him to Geo. Gindner; also tract patented to George Gindner, 20th July, 1768. Delivered: John Thomas, August Court, 1773.

Page 503.—Felix Gilbert and Ann to Mathews, lot purchased by Felix from Robert Finley, whereon Gilbert lately lived and commonly known as Gilbert's, on a corner and bounded on south by Beverley St., on west by Augusta. Teste: Thomas Posey, George Alger.

Page 505.—21st July, 1772. Nicholas Leeper, of Tryon County, Province North Carolina, planter, to his son, James Leeper. Attorney to execute deed to Hugh Donaghough. Teste: Ezekiel Polk, Nicholas Corry. Proved by Nicholas Corry.

Page 507.—Part of 200 acres on Cook's Creek patented to Robert Cravens 10th February, 1748, and by him conveyed to Joseph Cravens (grantor here).

Page 509.—21st August, 1772. John Caldwell to Thomas Stuart, yeoman, tract conveyed by Joseph Lane and William Teas to Samuel Caldwell, father to John, in whom the property is become invested by being heir-at-law to devise the said land, and joining that part of said tract belonging to William Long; mortgage. Delivered to John Caldwell by Stuart's order, March Court, 1778.

Page 512.—Patent to John Madison, Jr., 22d March, 1775.

Page 517.—27th October, 1772. William Preston and Susannah, of Botetourt, to John McDougall, on a branch of North River of Shanandoe called the second Fork of Thorny Branch. Delivered: John McDougall, 7th February, 1775.

Page 520.—19th March, 1769. Gabriel Goyle, eldest son and heir of Volintine Goyle, deceased, to Jacob Goyle, on South Branch of Potowmack above Trout Rock, patented to James Trimble MDCCL, and by him conveyed to Volintine Goyle, 1761. Delivered to Jacob Coyle, 16th May, 1774.

Page 522.—The Hunters Spring Draft. Patent to Thomas Campbell, 10th June, 1760.

Page 527.—14th November, 1772. John McCoy and Sarah ( ) to Abel Griffith, on Mossey Creek, part of 320 acres patented to John McCoy and James McCoy, 25th September, 1762, and since conveyed by James to John, 24th March, 1767. Teste: David Stephenson, Evan Griffith, Joseph Malcom.

Page 530.—Delivered to Joshua Humphreys, February, 1777.

Page 535.—Delivered to John Ramsey, Jr., 22d June, 1798.

Page 539.—3d March, 1772. Patrick ( ) Denny and Elizabeth ( ), of Botetourt, to Hugh McFawden (McFaddon), 2 leases, not followed by releases.

Page 541.—12th October, 1772. Thomas Turk, Sr., to Thomas Turk, Jr. (his son), bond to convey lower half of tract Thomas, Sr., now lives on. Delivered: Thomas, Jr., November, 1783. Last deed recorded, 17th November, 1772.

DEED BOOK No. 19.

First Deed Recorded 17th November, 1772; Last Deed Recorded 16th November, 1773.

Page 2.—21st October, 1772. Robert, John and William Christian to Gilbert Christian. Teste: William Anderson, Jacob Van Lear, John Abney. Delivered: Wm. Anderson, 9th April, 1774.

Page 5.—17th November, 1772. John Alexander and Mary to David Humphress in Beverley Manor. First sold by Beverley to George Breckinridge and by him transferred to David Doak. Delivered: David Humphries, 24th November, 1774.

Page 8.—15th November, 1773 (acknowledged 17th November, 1772). William Chestnut, Sr., to William Chestnut, Jr., on the War branch, a branch of Dry River; Daniel Calahan's line; corner Harry Henry; John Chesnut's line. Delivered: Wm. Chesnutt, Jr., 18th March, 1783.

Page 11.—18th November, 1772. William Chesnutt to son John Chesnutt, part of 400 acres conveyed to said William by Nicholas Green, on Muddy Creek; Wood's corner. Delivered: Jno. Chesnutt, 5th April, 1779.

Page 14.—12th November, 1772. George Skillern and Elizabeth, of Botetourt, to James Kerr, blacksmith, patent to John Kerr, 5th April, 1749 (1 acre, 1 R., 10 P., formerly conveyed by George to said James, 17th March, 1764. Teste: Nicholas Salles (Sollas, Sally, Sallas), John Cox, George Eliot. Delivered: James Cochran, 3d January, 1788.

Page 17.—18th May, 1772. James Trotter and Mary to William Trotter. Delivered: William Trotter, 18th March, 1780.

Page 20.—21st August, 1772. Patrick ( ) Gwenn (Gween, Gwinn) and Jean (Jeanet) ( ) to Phelix Gilbert, on head of Broad Run, a branch of North River of Shanandore, part of two tracts patented to Jonathan Douglass; corner Nicholas Mace. Teste: Daniel Smith. Delivered.

Page 22.—17th November, 1772. Adam Bratton, son of Robert Bratton, to George Bratton, his brother. Delivered: Geo. Bratton, 8th October, 1774.

Page 26.—Patent to William ( ) Callan (wife Elizabeth ( )), 1770; corner Henry Dawson. Teste: John Cunningham, Patrick Buchanan.

Page 30.—Delivered to Archibald Blackburn.

Page 32.—17th November, 1772. Robert Hall and Isbel (Elesbet) ( ) to John Readpath, of Staunton, ¼ acre, one of County lots conveyed to James Shaw and by Shaw to Robert, north of Samuel Moore's lot, and part of Samuel Forgason's lot No. 15.

Page 37.—8th May, 1772. Mathew Harrison, late of Augusta County, now of Dumfries, in County of Prince William, and Alexander White, of Frederick County, and Elizabeth, to Frederick Haines, £420, and other good causes and considerations, on Branches of Lick Run, part of patent to Robert Green, deceased, 20th August, 1740, and divided between representatives of Robert Green and Mary Wood, widow and devisee of Col. James Wood. Delivered: Christopher Armentrout, 25th October, 1774.

Page 40.—9th October, 1772. Privy examination of Elizabeth to above, by John Hite and Isaac Zane, justices of Frederick County.

Page 41.—17th November, 1772. William Lewis to William Gregory, on a branch of Jameses River, called Back Creek, known by the name of the Sugar Tree Bottom, opposite to John Millar's. Delivered: Joe Gregory, October, 1779.

Page 45.—Joshua, Andrew and Robert Russell.

Page 51.—Delivered: James Hill, April, 1778.

Page 54.—Delivered: A. Gibson, 24th Ouctober, 1786.

Page 64.—18th November, 1772. Beverley to Joseph Colter. Delivered: John Coalter, son of deceased grantee, 18th October, 1815, corner Edward Holland, Spring Hill line, Edward Hall's line.

Page 69.—Patent to Bryce Russell, wife Rachel, 3d August, 1771. Teste: Samuel Henderson, John Craig, Thomas Renkin.

Page 75.—10th September, 1772. James Shannon and Martha to John Wilson. Patent to John Malkem, 25th September, 1762, and by him conveyed to James Shannon. Teste: William Shannon, John Magill, John Logan.

Page 78.—19th November, 1772. Thomas Nicholas (Nickle, Nichels) and Jean ( ), of Botetourt County, to John Hinds. Delivered: William Dickey by Hind's order.

Page 81.—26th August, 1771. Nicholas Leeper, eldest son and heir-at-law of James Leeper, deceased, of Tryon County, North Carolina, by his son and attorney, James Leeper, to Hugh Donaghe. Patents to James Leeper, Sr., 12th July, 1746, and 26th April, 1742. Teste: Mathew and William Robertson. Delivered.

Page 84.—17th November, 1772. John Poage to Rev. John Craig, John

Anderson, Robert Poage, Alexander Blair, James Allen, Sr., Alexander Walker, Michael Dickey, James Henderson, Andrew McComb, James Allen, Jr., George Moffett, being the session and regularly chosen for the Congregation of Augusta or Stone Meeting House and appointed as Commissioners to act in behalf of said congregation and to accept and take a title for a tract of 27 acres for the sole use of a Dissenting Presbyterian Congregation as a place of Public Worship. Patent to John Poage, 14th July, 1769, corner old brick kiln.

Page 86.—21st November, 1772. Mathew Patton to John Likens. Whereas John Reager in his lifetime had purchased of James Wood and Robert Green a tract of land on North Mill Creek, a branch of South Branch of Potowmack, 407 acres, but before conveyance was made, John was murdered by the enemy, Indians, and his son and two daughters carried into captivity; said Mathew administered on the personal estate and obtained a title from Green in his own name, 24th May, 1763, but on condition if the heirs of John should return from captivity Mathew should reconvey the land as by a bond in the hands of James Wood, of Frederick; Dorothy Reager and Barbara Reager, daughters of said John, did some years ago return from captivity, but John Reager, son and heir of John, deceased, has never returned nor has been heard of since he was taken and it is doubtful if he is alive. Dorothy has, since her return, intermarried with said John Likens. Delivered: Jacob Coil per order filed 15th March, 1798.

Page 88.—Similar deed to above. Same to John Caplenger, Jr. Barbara has, since her return, intermarried with John Caplenger, Jr. Both deeds contain condition to reconvey to John Reager, Jr., if he should return.

Page 90.—21st November, 1772. Bond by John ( ) Likens and Jacob Harper, John Caplinger, Jr., and Henry Stone to Mathew Patton, to reconvey above if John Reager, Jr., should return.

Page 92.—21st November, 1772. John Caplenger, Jr., and Henry Stone to Mathew Patton, to reconvey above if John Reager, Jr., should return.

Page 94.—20th November, 1772. Christopher Vickrey and Hannah, of Guilford County, North Carolina, to Andrew Bird, part of 210 acres patented to Samuel Newman, 29th August, 1757, sold by Samuel to Jacob Hodgh, 21st June, 1763, on Smith's Creek. Teste: John Lilly, John ( ) Benson, James West. Certificate of release of dower by Hannah in Guilford County, North Carolina, 29th October, 1772, tract formerly belonging to Jacob Hodgh, brother to said Hannah Vickery. Christopher Nation and William Gosset swear they saw Hannah sign.

Page 97.—8th July, 1772. John Frogg and Agatha to John Abney, £300, lots 11, No. 16 and another joining No. 11; also 120 acres in Beverley Manor. Delivered: John Abney, May Court, 1774.

Page 99.—21st November, 1772. Wm. Bowyer, merchant in Staunton, to Alex. Sinclair, merchant in Staunton, £700, tenement in Staunton whereon William now lives, which William bought of Israel Christian, and all buildings which William has erected thereon.

Page 102.—21st November, 1772. Thomas Bell, son and heir of Joseph Bell, deceased, to Andrew McClure, on Long Meadow adjoining land on which Joseph formerly lived. Teste: John Patrick, Tully Davitt, Thomas Bell. Delivered: Samuel McClure, February, 1778.

Page 106.—10th November, 1772. William Jackson, of Orange County,

North Carolina, to Robert Hall. Patent to William Jackson, deceased, 1st June, 1750, on Jackson's River, and conveyed by his son and heir, William Jackson, aforesaid. Teste: George Rutledge, Charles ( ) Hay, Lew Bowyer.

Page 110.—25th November, 1772. Robert Hill, only son and heir apparent at law to the estate of Jonson Hill, deceased, to Abraham Smith, joining a survey formerly John O'Neal's; two tracts on Dry River, patented to Jonson Hill. Teste: Henry Black, Jared Erwine, Samuel Dunn, John Reynolds.

Page 113.—25th November, 1772. Abraham Smith to Robert Hill, on head branches of Dry Run, a branch of the North Branch of the South Branch, Potowmack, above a tract of Joseph Skidmore's. Same witnesses as to above.

Page 115.—On Moffet's Creek, corner Wm. Mathews, patent to Joseph Reaburn, 26th September, 1760, land Wm. Mathews lives on. Delivered: William Mathews, 24th March, 1774.

Page 116.—Lands of Robert Slaughter, Jr., and Michael Coagar, purchased by Jacob Campbell (wife Jane), son and heir of Paul Long, deed recorded in Orange. Delivered to Kite's order, 24th May, 1817.

Page 118.—9th September, 1772. John Hays and Mary to John Tedford. Teste: Robert Tedford, John McCampbell, Samuel McDowell. Delivered: John Tedford, 31st May, 1794.

Page 121.—16th March, 1773. Oliver Alexander and Margaret ( ), James Alexander and Martha ( ) to Robert Thomson, corner Francis Beatty's other tract, the great road. Teste: James ( ) Trotter, Jacob ( ) Patton. Borden's 92100.

Page 124.—13th March, 1773. Henry Sellers to Adam Sellers. Teste: Jacob Nicholas, Augustine ( ) Price, Jacob ( ) Argabrite. Delivered: Jno. Sellers, August Court, 1776.

Page 126.—16th March, 1773. John Burk to Nicholas Allstot, part of 400 acres patented to Lewis and John Neill, 1st December, 1740, and by them conveyed to William Burk, deceased, father of said John Burk. Delivered: Peter Conrod, 21st April, 1784.

Page 129.—21st November, 1772. John Keys and Agness ( ) to Walter Smelly (Smiley), on west side of the South River, alias the River Mary, a branch of James River, corner tract belonging to the heirs of the late John McDowell, low ground of the Rev. Alex. McDowell. Teste: Archibald Alexander, Andrew Bird, William Alexander, Robert Fearis, Joseph Alexander. Delivered to Mr. Smiley, 10th February, 1786.

Page 130.—15th February, 1773. John Greenlee, of Botetourt, to Adam Reid, lease. Teste: William McKemy, David Tedford. Delivered: Ab. Wilson, 4th June, 1779.

Page 131.—Release of above (?). John Greenlee and Hannah and Mary Greenlee, widow and relict of James Greenlee, deceased, to John Reid (recorded as to Adam Reid).

Page 133.—5th March, 1773. Borden's executors to Andrew Kismer (Kinner). Delivered: Andrew Kinner, 7th April, 1782.

Page 139.—21st November, 1772. Jacob Lockhart, Sr., to Windle Bright, part of tract Jacob now lives on in Beverley Manor, corner John Kirkpatrick; corner Robert Clark. Delivered: Windle Bright, 18th May, 1775.

Page 140.—23d November, 1772. Privy examination of Mary, wife of Jacob Lockhart above, before James Lockhart and Sampson Mathews.

Page 145.—18th June, 1770. Charles Hays, Sr., and Margaret ( ) to Charles Hays, Jr., 10 acres devised to Charles, Sr., by his father John Hays, by will dated 5th December, 1750. Teste: Andrew and John Hays, Ericus Smith. Delivered, October Court, 1784.

Page 146.—16th December, 1772. John Dennison (Denniston) to Gabriel Jones, on Shanandore, whereon John now lives.

Page 149.—John Davis and Jane ( ) to John Summers. Delivered, 3d February, 1786.

Page 151.—20th October, 1772. William Hill and Jean to Samuel McChesney, in forks of Hays' Creek. Teste: James Buchanan, John Hays, Samuel and John Kelly, James, Walter and Robert McChesney, Samuel Steel.

Page 155.—16th March, 1773. Benj. Logan, of Fincastle County, to Windle Butts. Delivered: Anthony Ayler, August, 1776.

Page 156.—16th March, 1773. Robert Thompson and Agness, James Thompson and Rebecca ( ), to Zachariah Johnston, 400 acres in Beverley Manor, conveyed by Beverley to John Seawright, and by him to John Thompson, 24th November, 1743; John Thompson dying intestate, land descended to his son Thomas, his heir-at-law, who conveyed 200 acres to his brother Robert, and devised 200 acres by his will, 25th March, 1760, to said James Thompson.

Page 158.—17th March, 1773. Margaret ( )Thompson, widow, late wife of John Thompson, deceased, releases dower in above. Teste: John Davidson.

Page 159.—10th April, 1751. Patent to Samuel Lockhart. Delivered: David Laird, 8th May, 1784.

Page 162.—17th March, 1773. Beverley to Thomas Stuart. Delivered: Robert Stuart, 7th December, 1801.

Page 164.—17th March, 1773. Same to Andrew McClure. Delivered: Samuel McClure, February, 1778.

Page 166.—Corner Zachary Smith.

Page 169.—17th March, 1773. Beverley to Andrew Campbell. Delivered to Mr. Campbell, 5th January, 1787.

Page 172.—16th March, 1772. Same to Robert Hannah. Delivered to R. Hannah, 2d January, 1793.

Page 176.—Ditto. Same to Walter Davis. Delivered to James Davis, gent., 19th November, 1785.

Page 182.—Corner Francis Patton.

Page 184.—17th March, 1773. Beverley to William Hughes. Delivered: William Hughes, 24th March, 1775.

Page 189.—17th March, 1771. Beverley to Mathew Reed. Delivered: John Reed, August, 1773.

Page 191.—11th September, 1772. John Lewis and Mary to Charles Lewis, £100, part of land on Cowpasture whereon George Lewis lived. Teste: Margaraet McClenachan, Felix Gilbert, John McClenachan, Matthew Matthewson.

Page 193.—Privy examination of Mary as to above, 11th September, 1772.

Page 194.—2d March, 1772. Samuel McDowell and Mary, and James Cowdon, surviving joint tenants (James McDowell, the other joint tenant being dead), to Alexander Stuart, part of Borden's 92100. Teste: Samuel and James Lyle, William Alexander, John McDowell.

Page 197.—17th March, 1773. Beverley to Jacob Sallas, Dutchman.

Page 204.—18th March, 1773. Benj. Logan, of Fincastle County, to Windle Butt, part of 268 acres patented to Benjamin, 16th February, 1772. Delivered: Anthony Ayler, August, 1776.

Page 208.—14th November, 1772. Joseph Malcom to Abel Griffith. Privy examination of Dorothy, wife of Joseph, 25th December, 1772.

Page 209.—14th November, 1772. John McCoy to Abel Griffith. Privy examination of Sarah, wife of John, 25th December, 1772.

Page 211.—18th March, 1773. Robert Williams and Margret ( ) to Elijah McCollister, patent to John Davis, 5th September, 1749, and by him conveyed to Jane Jones, and by John Roberts to Robert Williams, 2nd October, 1761, on Yeager's Branch of Smith Creek, corner Adam Yeager. Delivered to Robert Williams, 4th November, 1776, but returned and then delivered to James McCalister, 19th January, 1791.

Page 213.—27th November, 1773. Thomas Bell, heir of Joseph Bell, of Botetourt County, to Thomas Smith, No. 12 in Staunton. Teste: Christopher Graham, William Bowyer, James Hill, John Graham, Daniel Kidd.

Page 215.—27th November, 1773. Same to John Griffen, lot 12 in Staunton.

Page 216.—Corner Philip Fogel in Beverley Manor.

Page 220.—17th March, 1773. Andrew Kinkead, Jr., to Thomas Hugart, Andrew Lockridge, William Kinkead, Andrew Hamilton, Lanty Graham. James Bratton, trustees of a congregation of Dissenters, on the Calfpasture River, for use of a burying ground and meeting house.

Page 223.—Patent to William Pickens (wife Ann), 20th September, 1748.

Page 225.—16th November, 1772. Jacob Runkle and Annamarie ( ) to Peter Runkle, his son, part of 225 acres patented to Jacob, 30th August, 1763, part of which he conveyed to——

Page 227.—20th May, 1765. Adam Reider and Anna, and Alexander Painter (Peinter) and Margret, to Peter Schol and Michael Neice, divers good causes and considerations thereunto moving, but more especially for the Glory of God and the Preaching his Precious Gospel, lease, small quantity of land for the building of a church house or proper place to meet tc worship God in, to Peter Scholl in behalf of the Presbyterian Church and to Michael Neice in behalf of the church called the Lutherine Church, back of said meeting house where it now stands, three acres. Delivered: 16th February, 1785.

Page 229.—27th May, 1773. Michael Nease and Margaret ( ), of Dunmore, to Frederick Kaylor, land where Michael formerly lived and sold to Adam Bainter and Thomas Moores, patented to Michael, 20th September, 1768. Delivered: George Kipp, 16th September, 1777.

Page 231.—18th May, 1773. James Patterson to Joseph Patterson, his son, part of 344 acres inclusive survey to James on head of Naked Creek. Delivered: Joseph Patterson, 9th September, 1793.

Page 234.—18th May, 1773. Jacob ( ) Trumbo and Mary ( ) tc

Michael Hover, patent to Cornelius Murley, 16th June, 1744, and by him conveyed to Jacob, 24th June, 1752.

Page 237.—17th May, 1773. John ( ) Stephenson, farmer, and Sarah ( ) to Archibald Huston, farmer. Delivered: Jno. Huston, 7th February, 1785. Teste: John McMaster, James and George Huston. Patented to the Stevens, 1st June, 1741.

Page 239.—Patented to John Stephenson, 16th August, 1756.

Page 243.—Patented to same, 16th March, 1771.

Page 247.—Richard Moulding's two hundred acre tract.

Page 250.—18th May, 1773. Charles Rush and Marchius, his wife, to Philip Ermantrout. Patent to Charles, 1st August, 1772, corner John Davis, deceased. Delivered: George Harmon, 5th March, 1776.

Page 252.—18th May, 1773. Jacob Eberman and Barbara ( ) to Daniel Mouse, on North Fork of South Branch of Potomac, about one mile from Suicea Creek. Teste: Ephraim Dunlop.

Page 255.—17th May, 1773. Robert Scott, Sr., to Robert Scott, Jr., part of 200 acres patented to Robert, Sr., 30th July, 1742, and of 85 acres patented 15th April, 1764, on Collins Lick Run. Delivered to Scott, 4th October, 1777.

Page 259.—18th May, 1770. George ( ) Null and Barbara ( ) to Conrod Young, part of three tracts belonging to Nicholas Null, deceased, and now by descent vested in said George, corner Charles Foy. Teste: Calem Price. Delivered: Mr. Young, 28th May, 1785.

Page 261.—2,000 acres patented to Richard Malden, 30th June, 1743, on Picked Mountain, Henry Lung and Barbara to Henry Julias (Julius). Delivered: Jacob Julius, 13th June, 1788.

Page 263.—Corner Perkey's land; corner Ann Perkey.

Page 267.—130 acres on head of South Branch of Potowmack, patented to Michael Arbocust.

Page 268.—17th May, 1773. James McCleerey, James Mitchell, Robert Wilson, William Thompson, Alexander McFeeters, Samuel McCutchen, trustees of the North Mountain Meeting House (James McCutchen, another trustee, being dead), to Joseph Blair, surrounding the North Mountain Meeting House, joining Peter Keyl.

Page 273.—18th May, 1773. Joseph Gregory, heir-at-law of James Gregory, deceased, to Arthur Hickman, on West Fork of James River, called Back Creek. Delivered: Robert Clark, June, 1783.

Page 276.—Part of 335 acres patented to Rudolph Mauck, 30th August, 1763.

Page 279.—18th May, 1773. George ( ) Adam Bright and Mary to James Tate. Delivered: Isaac Tate, 7th April, 1802.

Page 281.—139 acres patented to William Thompson, 20th August, 1748; 6 acres patented to Samuel Hinds, 14th February, 1761. Delivered: Michael Kern, March Court, 1777.

Page 284.—16th March, 1773. Ann ( ) Acken to George Weir, in Borden's 92100, corner Andrew and Samuel Eakins. "The above name of Ann Acker was inserted in the room of John Lyles before this deed was executed."

Page 291.—19th May, 1773. John Shields, eldest son and heir of James Shields, deceased, and Margaret ( ) of Amherst County, to James Sproul, part of 298 acres conveyed to James Shields by McCutcheon, 21st August, 1746, and descended to John, eldest son; another tract conveyed to John as eldest son of James by Borden, 20th August, 1752, corner James Loosk. Delivered: Wm. Sprowl, 19th January, 1782.

Page 293.—24th April, 1773. Robert Boyd, of Botetourt, to Robert Young. Patented to Robert Boyd, father of Robert, 10th March, 1756 and descended to grantor by descent.

Page 296.—18th May, 1773. Beverley to Archibald Hamilton. Delivered: John Hamilton, 20th June, 1795.

Page 303.—18th May, 1778. Same to Philip Creever. Delivered: Philip Greever, 25th March, 1774.

Page 309.—18th May, 1773. Alexander Walker and Elizabeth ( ) to Arthur Connly, part of 430 acres patented by inclusive patent to said Alexander, 6th April, 1769.

Page 312.—19th May, 1773. Beverley to James Lessley, Jr. Delivered: Robert Kenny, November Court, 1776.

Page 321.—9th March, 1773. Thomas and James Parsons, of Hampshire, to Jacob Wice. Teste: George Wilson, John Wood.

Page 323.—Patent to Robert Patterson, 16th August, 1756.

Page 324.—14th April, 1773. John Caldwell, South River, and Sarah to Mathews, part of 400 acres conveyed to Samuel Caldwell by Love and wife, and Tease, 20th May, 1766, and descended to John as son and heir of Samuel, the other two hundred acres being made over to his brother, Robert Caldwell, since his father's decease. This 200 acres have a saw mill and oyle mill thereon.

Page 328.—Mill Creek, otherwise known as Brock's Creek, a branch of Shanandore.

Page 329.—18th May, 1773. William Hinds to John Hinds, mortgage. 195 acres whereon William now lives, devised to William by his father, William.

Page 331.—22d May. 1773. Daniel Smith, High Sheriff of Augusta, to John and Mathew Thompson. Sale under decree of County Court, 23d May, 1772, Felix Gilbert vs. James Cotton.

Page 333.—24th May, 1773. Colonel George Wilson, of Hampshire, to Valentine Cloninger, lot 3 in Staunton.

Page 335.—Privy examination of Elizabeth, wife of Col. George Wilson, to above deed. Certified by Joseph Neavill and Abraham Hite.

Page 338.—13th August, 1773. Daniel Smith and Jean ( ) to Daniel Stover. Patented to Samuel Harrison, 5th September, 1749, and conveyed to Daniel. Teste: John Henton, Joseph Smith, Daniel Smith, Jr.

Page 341.—13th August, 1773. Samuel Samples and Hannah ( ) to Daniel Stover, 38 acres patented to Alexander Herring, 30th August, 1763.

Page 344.—13th August, 1773. part of 196 acres patented to Alex. Herring, 10th September, 1755.

Page 347.—Patent to Samuel Harrison, 5th September, 1749 (see p. 338, supra).

Page 349.—Patent to Thomas Gragg (wife Elizabeth), 1st March, 1773. Teste: Joseph Smith, John Waren, Thomas ( ) Harrison, Henry Ewin.

Page 354.—John Davis and Elizabeth ( ) to Josiah Davis (Davison ?), part of patent to Wood, Green, &c., 23d October, 1750.

Page 357.—17th August, 1773. Cornelius ( ) O'Bryan and Anne ( ) to Thomas O'Bryan, part of 500 acres conveyed to Cornelius O'Bryan, deceased, and John O'Bryan and said Cornelius O'Bryan, by Hite, McCoy & Co., 24th June, 1744. Cornelius, Sr., died before any partition. John and Cornelius, Jr., made partition by deed, 1762. Teste: Michael Waren.

Page 361.—12th August, 1773. John Lincoln and Rebecca ( ) to Abraham Lincoln, on Linvel's Creek, part of 1200 acres patented to Duff, Green, Hite, 26th March, 1739, conveyed to Robert McKay, devised to Zachariah, Moses, Robert and James McKay, corner Isaac Lincoln. Teste: Josiah Davidson, Corneliays ( ) Briant, Ann ( ) Briant.

Page 364.—12th August, 1773. Same to Isaac Lincoln, part of same tract as above, corner to his brother Abraham's land. Delivered: Jacob Lincoln, February, 1779.

Page 367.—On North Fork of South Branch of Potowmack, patented to Jacob Eberman, 1st August, 1772.

Page 372.—Patent to George Welsh, 16th February, 1771, on North Fork of South Branch Potomac.

Page 374.—17th August, 1773. Edward ( ) Breden and Elisabeth ( ) to George Breakinridge, of Fincastle County, tract formerly conveyed by George to Mathew Erwin.

Page 376.—16th August, 1773. William Curry to Robert Buchanan. Delivered: James Buchanan, September, 1778.

Page 381.—Patent to Barnet Man, 12th May, 1759, corner George Man.

Page 382.—11th August, 1773. Dawson Wade and Rachel ( ), of Botetourt, to William Stewart, on a branch of Bull Pasture, corner Alex. McCandles, formerly patented to Dawson Wade.

Page 387.—Patent to Morgan Bryan, 20th September, 1746; patent to Michael Warren, 10th July, 1767.

Page 390.—18th August, 1773. John Guin and Alise ( ) to Henry Bear, of Frederick County, Maryland, patent to John Gum, 12th May, 1759, on Cedar Branch, corner James Claypool. Delivered: Joseph Lemon, May Court, 1779.

Page 394.—— ——, 1773. Same to Isaac Gum, patent to John, 14th July, 1769, in gap of North Mountain.

Page 397.—11th August, 1773. Thomas ( ) Hamilton and Jean ( ), of Botetourt, to Joseph Beeth, on Bullpasture.

Page 400.—10th August, 1773. Martin ( ) Whitzel and Elizabeth ( ) to John Rhuble, above Brock's Gap, adjoining land formerly belonging to Thomas West, patented to Martin, 10th July, 1767. Teste: Ben. Forsythe, Joseph Goare, John Fitzwater.

Page 403.—On a branch of Linvel's Creek called McKoy's Draft, containing 190 acres granted by patent to Francis McBride, 1st March, 1773. Teste: Christopher ( ) Wagoner, Skidmore Munsey, Jno. Thomas.

Page 406.—17th August, 1773. William Samples and Sarah ( ) to George Kersner, on Brock's Creek, 235 acres patented to Adam Hoverstick, 7th July, 1763. Teste: Henry Runyon, Obediah ( ) Muncy.

Page 409.—18th August, 1773. Skidmore Munsey and Mary ( ) to John Kring, late of Lancaster County, Pennsylvania, corner Jonathan Robinson's part of same tract. Delivered: George Speare, 17th August, 1774.

Page 411.—18th August, 1773. James Gay, son and heir-at-law of Robert Gay, deceased, to Robert Gay and John Gay, his brothers.

Page 415.—Teste: William Lewis, Patrick Buchanan.

Page 418.—17th August, 1773. Daniel Henderson to John Henderson, patented to the said Daniel Henderson (by distinction "Junior"), 25th September, 1762. Teste: Joseph Malcom, John Malcom, Sr., John Malcom, Jr.

Page 421.—Patent to John McCreery, 21st September, 1760, on Newfoundland Creek.

Page 423.—90 acres on Bratton's Run of Calfpasture, patented to James Bratton, 6th April, 1769.

Page 429.—200 acres on the Bare Spring, a branch of the Dry River, at a place called the Maple Swamp, patented to William Stephenson, deceased, 16th June, 1756, 10th November, 1757, and devised to son Mathew. Teste: Robert Davis and John Stephenson.

Page 433.—On Pudding Spring Draft, patented to Moses Hall (wife Honore), 16th August, 1756, 12th February, 1755. Delivered: John McDougal, 25th March, 1791, for Mr. Hogshead.

Page 435.—18th August, 1773. James McKemy to William Leviston, part of a large tract called "Bird Tract." Teste: Ebenezer Alexander, John Hogshead, Jr., John McKemy, Jr. (See following deed, p. 437, whether Bird's tract is Burden's tract.)

Page 443.—17th June, 1771. Ephraim Love to John Hopkins, on head branches of Muddy Creek, part of tract whereon said Love now lives. Teste: Silas Hart, Daniel Smith, Jno. Grattan, Jno. Steed, Jno. Gorden.

Page 448.—Teste: Archibald and William Alexander, Walter Smiley.

Page 449.—Patent to James Dever, 23d May, 1773. Teste: John Davies, John Devir, Hugh Devir.

Page 451.—11th August, 1773. William McClenachan and Sarah, of Botetourt, to William Hutcheson, patent to William McClenachan on Jackson's River, 14th July, 1769, 12th May, 1770. Teste: John and Alexander McClenachan, Mathew Arbuckle, James Byrnside.

Page 454.— — ——, 1773. Valentine Sevior and Joanna ( ) Sevior to Michael and David Holesinger. Teste: M. Harrison, Robert Rutherford, Mary Rutherford, Margaret ( ) Benson.

Page 458.—Patent to Thomas Hog, 1st March, 1773.

Page 472.—21st July, 1773. John Hamilton, late of Augusta, to Thomas O'Neal, surrender of mortgage and quit claim, tract surveyed for John O'Neal, deceased, under the North Mountain, which descended to Thomas as only son of John. Teste: John McClenachan, William Elliott, Margaret ( ) Elliott.

Page 474.—Patent to Robert Reed, adjoining William Oldham. Mortgage.

Page 476.—17th August, 1773. John Henderson, farmer, and Ann ( ) to Jacob Bear, part of 250 acres patented to James Thompson and conveyed to Samuel Henderson and by him to John, his son, mouth of Little Is Run. Delivered: Valentine Shirley, February, 1779.

Page 482.—Patent to John Magill, 12th May, 1759. Teste: Alex. Sinclair, W. Cunningham, Richard Madison.

Page 482.—Lot 18 in Staunton, adjoining the lot whereon James Herston formerly dwelt and Thomas Smith now dwells.

Page 486.—James Hill to Mathews, bill sale and conveys the house and lot whereon James now lives.
Page 487.—Henry Seller to Henry Munger, between Shanando River and Peaked Mountain. Delivered: grantee, 3d April, 1812.
Page 489.—Part of 2464 acres patented to Robert Green, 12th January, 1746, on South Branch of Potowmack. Teste: James Dobbins, Samuel Bell.
Page 499.—Part of 310 acres patented to Valentine Seviear, 27th June, 1764.
Page 502.—15th November, 1773. Joel Robinson and Margarett, of Hampshire County, to John Bear, patented to Joel, 31st October, 1765, corner James Robinson.
Page 506.—Part of patent to Robert Jameson, 1770.
Page 509.—15th October (?) November (?), 1773. Windle Bright and Elizabeth ( ) to Joseph Thompson, tract bequeathed to Thomas Steel by William Smith, 3d December, 1754.
Page 516.—Teste: Archibald McSpeden.
Page 516.—On the Straight Fork of South Branch of Potowmack, patented to Barnet Linch, 3d August, 1771.
Page 518.—4th October, 1773. William Gray and Katharin to Moses Whitesides. Delivered to James Love, June, 1780.
Page 524.—5th May, 1773. Samuel Wilson and Mary to John McCay, on Bullpasture River, part of tract whereon Samuel now liveth, corner Robert Duffell. Delivered: Oliver McCoy, 2d September, 1802. Teste: John Rice.
Last deed recorded, 16th November, 1773.

Deed Book No. 20.

First deed recorded, 16th November, 1773; last deed recorded, 21st March, 1775.
Page 2.—11th October, 1773. Joseph Cravens to John Cravens, on Cook's Creek, part of tract patented to Robert Cravens, 10th September, 1755. Teste: William Lamm, Daniel Guin, Michael Mullan. (This deed is again recorded infra, p. 180, of date, 15th March, 1774.)
Page 5.—6th September, 1773. Matthew Thompson, late of Augusta County, now of County of Granville, South Carolina, to Felix Gilbert. Pattent to Mathew Thompson and Mathew Thompson, Jr., 5th March, 1747, on Honey (Stoney ?) Lick Branch. Teste: Gasper ( ) Goodenburgh, Joseph Haynes. Delivered: George Kissel, 4th May, 1774, for Mr. Gilbert.
Page 10.—16th November, 1773. John McCutcheon, and Elizabeth and Patrick McCutcheon, of Fincastle County, to John McCutcheon, tract on Little Calfpasture, conveyed by Beverley to James McCutcheon, deceased, 26th November, 1747, and devised by James to sons John and Patrick.
Page 14.—11th March, 1773. John Carlile, Sr., and Elizabeth ( ), and Robert ( ) Carlile and Nancy ( ), to John Carlile, Jr., tract, 300 acres, on Bullpasture, patented to John and Robert, 10th August, 1759. Teste: John Hicklen, Bond Estill, Thomas Hicklen, east side of the Indian Draft.
Page 17.—11th November, 1773. Same to George Carlile.

Page 20.—11th November, 1773. John Carlile and Elizabeth ( ) to Robert Carlile, on Clover Creek, now called Bull Pasture, being one-half of tract, 10th August, 1759.

Page 23.—11th November, 1773. Robert ( ) Carlile and Nancy ( ) to John Carlile, one-half of above tract.

Page 25.—11th March, 1773. John Carlile, Jr., of Bullpasture, to Robert Carlile, Jr., his brother, of said pasture, conveys above, p. 23.

Page 28.—28th April, 1773. Henry ( ) Dawson and Mary ( ) to Neil Adair, on South Mountain at Reed's Gap, patented to Henry, 1770. Teste: Walter Davis, James Best, Samuel Love, John ( ) Wiley.

Page 30.—16th November, 1773. Thomas Stevenson and Elizabeth to Thomas Dixon, 330 acres patented to Robert Stevenson, 16th August, 1756, and devised to his son Thomas. Teste: Thomas Stevenson.

Page 33.—17th November, 1773. David Cunningham and Ann ( ) to Alexander Cunningham. Delivered: James Cunningham, 30th June, 1787.

Page 37.—6th June, 1772. Robert Henderson, eldest son and heir of Daniel Henderson, deceased, to John Henderson, his brother, on Bever Creek and Spring Creek, patented to said Daniel, 7th August, 1769.

Page 57.—Corner James Anderson—on north side of Mount Atlas.

Page 77.—2d May, 1772. William Arn (Arwen) (signed Erwin) to Hugh Donaghe. mortgage of chattels. Teste: Edward Warner, Minian ( ) Curry.

Page 78.—1st October, 1773. William Mitchell and Rebecca ( ), of 1st part; Margaret ( ) Sprowl, widow and relict of Samuel Sprowl, deceased, of 2d part; James Patterson and Sarah ( ) and Alex. Thompson and Martha ( ) of 3d part; George Peerey of 4th part. Samuel Sproul devised one-half of 210 acres to Mitchell with remainder in other half after death of widow; died leaving three daughters, who are women above. Mitchell has sold his interest to George Peerey. Delivered: George Peerey's son, February, 1782.

Page 83.—Tract whereon John Logan now lives, patented to John Magill, 12th May, 1759. Delivered: Jno. Breeden, January, 1783.

Page 87.—9th September, 1773. Francis Hardgrove and Sarah, of Surry County, North Carolina, to John David Griner, part of lot 14 in Staunton, house wherein Edward Long lived, faces James Huston and James Hughes.

Page 91.—21st September, 1773. George ( ) Gutlip and Susanna ( ), of Dunmore County, to John Breeden. Teste: John Schoon, Jacob Woodle

Page 97.—18th November, 1773. Israel Christian, of Botetourt County, to John Hays. Delivered: James Hays, 26th November, 1799.

Page 99.—Delivered to Wm. Rice, per order, 1st October, 1823.

Page 107.—18th August, 1773. Beverley to David Karethers, corner James Karithers.

Page 111.—95 acres patented to John Hanna, 3d August, 1771, at a place called the Flat Gap. Delivered: George Keezell, November Court, 1779.

Page 116.— — ——, 1773. John Dunlap to William Dunlap, part of tract in Beverley Manor conveyed to William Dunlap, deceased, 28th February, 1749, and descended to said John. Delivered: Matt. Kinney, 10th May, 1784.

Page 121.—Teste: Francis, Jean and Elizabeth Erwin.

Page 129.—17th November, 1773. Archibald Hamilton to his son Audley Hamilton.

Page 134.—Patent to Thomas Campbell, 10th September, 1755. Delivered: John Ewing, November Court, 1783. Teste: Michael Mullan, Thomas Smith, Josiah Harrison.

Page 135.—15th March, 1774. Robert Steel and Mary to Robert's son, David Steel. Teste: William Moore, Thomas Hill, Hugh Torbet.

Page 138.—Delivered: Peter Shoemaker, 19th April, 1791, part of 335 acres patented to Rudolph Mack, 30th August, 1763, conveyed by Michael Hober to Nicholas Kairn, 3d August, 1772, but as Michael was not then naturalized, the conveyance was void, corner Frederick Wollfort's part of same tract.

Page 145.—George Speece and Hichael Hober being not then naturalized. Teste: John Miller, George McNeall, Samuel ( ) Conrod.

Page 148.—15th March, 1774. John McKee and Rosanna ( ), of Kerr's Creek, to James McKee, their son, on Kerr's Creek, part in Augusta and part in Botetourt, corner plantation whereon said John McKee now lives.

Page 152.—Jacob Miller, Sr., to Christian Miller.

Page 154.—Delivered: William Steel, April, 1776.

Page 169.—Tract whereon Thomas Shields now lives in Beverley Manor Delivered: John Shields, October, 1780.

Page 172.—Patent to Jacob Runkle, 13th August, 1763. Teste: Archibald Dickison, John Lowry.

Page 174.—Part of 2,000 acres patented to Richard Malden, 30th June, 1743, corner Henry Eulia. Teste: George and Michael Huffman ( ).

Page 178.—15th March, 1774. John Jackson and Martha ( ) to John Hunter, on a branch of North River of Shanando, called Valls Spring, joining lands of Borden and Shoemaker, patented to said John Jackson, 16th February, 1771.

Page 182.—11th October, 1773.—Joseph Cravens to John Cravens, Patented to Robert Cravens, 10th September, 1755, on Cook's Creek. Teste: William Lamme, Daniel Guin, Michael Mullen.

Page 185.—Daniel ( ) Calaihan to Charles Calaihan, on Dry River near land Daniel lives on.

Page 187.—William Alexander to John McClung. 304 acres whereon said Alexander now lives. Teste: Samuel Lyle, Samuel McDowell, Wm. Alexander.

Page 191.—Patents to Robert Fowler (wife, Ann).

Page 197.—17th September, 1773. David ( ) Guin to Mary Greenlee, 210 acres in Borden's tract on North Branch of James at mouth of Back Creek. Teste: Samuel McDowell, John Letcher, Margaret Greenlee, William Stewart, Grace and David Greenlee.

Page 199.— — October, 1773. William Christall (Christal) and Ann ( ) to Charles Harris and Henry Reaburn, 320 acres on Jennings Creek, patented to William, 10th July, 1767. Teste: John Madison, Jr., George Mathews, Thomas Patterson, Richard Madison.

Page 202.—Henry Reaburn and Margaret ( ) and Charles Harris and Jean, to James Campbell, conveys above.

Page 205.—Delivered to John Moore, heir-at-law of William Moore, 29th November, 1806.

Page 209.—15th March, 1774. Hugh Hays and Mary to William Pullock. Teste: James Henry, Patrick Hay, William Moore.
Page 212.—Tract on which William Oldham now lives.
Page 213.—Tract where John Rice now lives, on Dry River.
Page 217.—Lot in Staunton whereon Mathew Ried now lives.
Page 220.—19th March, 1774. Mathews to John Cawley. John Cawley now husband of the late Margaret Gamwell, who was wife of Joseph Gamwell.
Page 223.—11th October, 1773. Privy examination of Ann, wife of John Anderson.
Page 227.—16th October, 1773. Privy examination of Margaret, wife of Henry Reaburn, and Jean, wife of Chas. Harris.
Page 229.—16th October, 1773. Same as to Ann Christall, wife of William.
Page 240.—16th May, 1774. Henry Long (signed Emmaniel Henrich Lung), and Barberry ( ) to Henry Tamewood.
Page 242.—Teste: Michael Coger, Martin Nalle, Jr., Wm. Nall.
Page 243.—16th May, 1774. George ( ) Goile and Hannah ( ) to Jacob Goile, 131 acres on north side of South Branch of Potowmack, patented to George, 14th July, 1769. Teste: Thomas Jones.
Page 248.—Patent to John Harrison, Jr., 10th February, 1748, bequeathed to Phebe Davis, now wife of John Ewins, by said John's will.
Page 252.—Patent to Valentine Sevear, 15th December, 1757.
Page 255.—17th May, 1774. Daniel ( ) Mouse and Eve ( ) to George Millar, on south side of North Fork of South Branch of Potomack, patented to Daniel, 12th May, 1770.
Page 259.—On above stream about three miles below mouth of Seneca Creek, patented to Daniel, 6th April, 1769.
Page 260.—Joseph Rutherford to Arthur (Archer) Rutherford, of Frederick County, 310 acres patented to Jacob Gardner, 16th August, 1756; patented to Joseph, 25th July, 1765. Teste: Daniel Smith, Robert Rutherford.
Page 265.—18th November, 1773. John Madison and Aggathy, of Botetourt, to George Boswell, tract whereon George now dwells, part of 1000 acres patented to John, 10th March, 1756; patented to John, 2d June, 1758, corner Abraham Estis; patented to John, 16th August, 1756.
Page 271.—Line of Swetzer's land on Canne Run, a branch of South Branch of Potomac.
Page 276.—Teste: Joseph Hayne.
Page 277.—Two tracts patented to Daniel Henderson. John Henderson to Abraham Henderson. Delivered: Robert Henderson, 2d June, 1785. Teste: Samuel McConkey, D. A. C.
Page 279.—Same to Joseph Henderson. Delivered: B. Forsythe, February, 1776. Patented to Daniel Henderson, Jr., 25th September, 1762, and conveyed to said John Henderson by letter deeds.
Page 284.—Patent to Joseph Hanna, 12th May. 1759. Patent to Hugh Donaho.
Page 286.—Patent to David Frame, 15th June, 1773.
Page 289.—John Lyle, Sr., to Mathew Donald. Delivered to Alex. Campbell, June, 1780.

Page 291.—22d October, 1773. John Stewart, of Botetourt, son and heir-at-law of David Stewart, deceased, to Harmon Lovingood.

Page 296.—19th May, 1774. Sarah ( ) Hutcheson, widow of Thomas Hutcheson, deceased, to Andrew McClure, assignee of John Williams, carpenter. Thomas had sold to William 100 acres known as the Strawberry Draft (Thomas died on or about month of April, 1772). Delivered: Samuel McClure, February, 1778.

Page 300.—Patent to Mathew Thompson and Mathew Thompson, Jr., 5th March, 1757.

Page 302.—2nd May, 1774. John Griffen, silversmith, and Elizabeth, to Alexander Sinclair, merchant, lot 12 in Staunton. Teste: Thomas Jones, Samuel Bell, Thomas Poage.

Page 305.—On the Rough Run, a branch of South Fork above Sweedland Hill.

Page 307.—Patent to Andrew Faut. 5th September, 1752, patent to John Balfaut, 20th September, 1754, and by John devised to Andrew.

Page 311.—Patent to James Parsons, 22d September, 1757.

Page 315.—Starr Lick on head of Benj. Allin's River, crossing the North Fork, pine on South Fork, patented to Thomas West, 20th June, 1749. Teste: John Dunbarr, Sarah ( ) Dunbarr, Paul Custard, John Caplenger.

Page 317.—10th April, 1774. Conrad Custer (Custard), eldest son and heir of Arnold Custard, deceased, who was eldest son and heir of Conrad Custard, lately deceased, and Elizabeth ( ) to Paul Custard.

Page 321.—16th August, 1774. John Dunbarr and Sarah ( ) to Henry Wister, on Mill Creek of North Shanando, known as lot No. 3, part of tract patented to Benj. Borden. Delivered: Jno. Thomas, April Court, 1777.

Page 325.—17th August, 1774. John Kirkpatrick and Martha ( ), of Augusta, and John Peerie and Sarah ( ) of Botetourt, to Robert Hanna.

Page 335.—Patent to John Trotter, 20th September, 1768. Delivered· Nathaniel Kelly per order, 8th December, 1800.

Page 337.—Delivered to William Wardlaw, 2d April, 1796.

Page 342.—14th August, 1774. Reuben Rutherford and Eliner ( ) to Felix Gilbert, part of 134 acres conveyed to Reuben by his father Joseph Rutherford, part of 400 acres patented to James Wood, 12th January, 1746, and by him devised to Mary by will recorded in Frederick. Teste: John Brownlow, Jacob Woodle, William West.

Page 344.—Delivered: John Cummings, 1st April, 1794.

Page 347.—Delivered: Peter Weaver, January, 1776.

Page 352.—7th April, 1774. Adam Stephen, of Berkeley County, Virginia, to Mark Bird and Henry Miller, of Berks County, Pennsylvania.

Page 366.—Part of tract in Beverley Manor whereon Alexander McClenachan now lives.

Page 371.—Teste: Samuel McDowell, David Stephenson, Robert ( ) Feris.

Page 371.—17th August, 1774. Abraham Smith to John Smith, son of Daniel Smith. Whereas John Smith, brother of said Abraham Smith, about 1753 did agree with Silas Hart for the purchase of a tract on South Fork of North River of Shanandoah; John died in year 1757, having will wherein he devised to above John, son of his brother Daniel Smith; Daniel paid the consideration to Hart, 1st June, 1756, and received deed to John, 1st

June, 1756. John Smith's will was proved by only one witness and may be called in question by the heirs of said Abraham, who was eldest brother and heir-at-law of John, deceased.

Page 375.—The Meeting House line. Teste: James Steel, William Scott. Samuel Henry.

Page 380.—Teste: John Burnside, Jacob Nicolas.

Page 380.—Henry Pickle to Casper Eager. Delivered to Philip Ekert, January, 1783.

Page 391.—Patent to Mathew Thompson and Mathew Thompson, Jr., 5th March, 1747.

Page 394.—Part of plantation whereon John Campbell now lives Teste: James Foster.

Page 397.—14th September, 1773. Joaken Vauferson (Jefferson) to Daniel Smith and Felix Gilbert, power of attorney to sell 1000 acres whereon Joaken now lives, patented to him, 3d August, 1771.

Page 401.—14th November, 1774. Thomas Paxton and Mary, of Botetourt, to William Paxton, son of Thomas. Teste: Nathaniel Evans, Joseph Snodgrass, James Alexander.

Page 405.—11th November, 1774. Bowd (Bondy) Estill and Jane, of Botetourt, to James Carlyle.

Page 409.—11th November, 1774. Wallas Estill and Ann, of Botetourt, to John Peoples, on Clover Creek, now called Bullpasture, patented to Wallas, 3d November, 1750.

Page 411.—Part of a patent to Andrew Foster, 5th September, 1749.

Page 416.—Teste: William Frogg.

Page 417.—24th May, 1774. Elisha Estis, of Caroline County, and Gabriel Long, of Culpeper, to Cap. Francis Kirtley, Sr.

Page 418.—Teste: William, John and Francis Kirtley, William Kirtley, Jr., Thomas Fortson.

Page 421.—Delivered to William Alexander, February, 1778.

Page 424.—6th September, 1774. Marthew ( ) Wilson, widow and devisee of Samuel Wilson, late of Staunton, 1st part; John Griffin, of Staunton, and Elizabeth, late Elizabeth Wilson, one of the daughters and devisees of Samuel, of 2d part. Samuel died seised if lot 4 in Staunton and lot 1, outlot of woodland, and made will, 28th May, 1760, devising one-third to each: wife Martha, daughter Elizabeth and daughter Martha. Martha is under age and her mother enters into agreement for her. Deed of partition. Teste: Robert and Margaret Reed, Samuel Coleman, Daniel Kidd.

Page 435.—At a place called Snoddon's Spring, patented to James McCarrell, 10th August, 1769.

Page 437.—15th November, 1774. Daniel Kidd and John Graham to Theobald, alias Devault, Bosang. James Hughes seised of ot 7 in Staunton and 30 acres of woodland purchased by James from Robert McClenachan and bargained to sell part of each to James Leister, deceased, trader. Leister died before deed made, and James agreed with Leister's administrators and surviving partners to convey to them in consideration of their paying him the remainder of the purchase money; James died before conveyance; through several transfers and suit in chancery, property was conveyed in trust to Daniel Kidd and John Graham to secure them as securities for

Samuel Cowdon, by decree in chancery foreclosing the equity of redemption. Delivered: John Bosang, February, 1776.

Page 442.—16th November, 1774. Immanuel Herliss to Henry Herless, formerly the property of Philip Herless, deceased. Delivered: Samuel Bell, August, 1782.

Page 446.—12th November, 1774. William Laverty and Jane, of Botetourt, to John Sitlington.

Page 448.—16th November, 1774. William Patterson and Mary ( ), of Cumberland County, Pennsylvania, to Patrick Quin, a tract joint property of four sisters, heirs of Randal McDonald, deceased, patented to John Hope, 5th September, 1749, and by him conveyed to Randal McDonald, who died intestate, and Mary, wife of Wm. Patterson became invested in the ¼ part on Cook's Creek.

Page 452.—16th November, 1774. Nicholas Mace ( ) and Ann ( ) to Michael and George Kintner, part of patent to Thomas Beal. Teste: John Dunbar, John ( ) Bailey, John Thomas.

Page 456.—16th November, 1774. Abraham Smith to Gawin Hamilton, £100, two tracts on Dry River and Muddy Creek, patented to Johnson Hill and by Robert Hill, only son and heir of Johnson, to Abraham Smith. Delivered: Col. Guy Hamilton, 10th October, 1785.

Page 459.—16th November, 1774. Abraham Smith to Benijah Rice, of Culpeper County, on Dry River in the North Mountain above a place called Craig's Hole.

Page 464.—Patent to John Peartree.

Page 471.—17th January, 1775. Robert Young and Jean ( ) to William and Samuel Anderson. Patent to Robert Boyd, 10th March, 1756, and by his decease intestate, became invested in his son Robert Boyd, who conveyed to Robert Young.

Page 473.—Delivered: R. Stuart, January, 1781.

Page 480.—Patent to John Sheltman (wife Cecily), 12th May, 1770. Delivered to Wm. Staen (or Stone) 28th July, 1787. Teste: Jno. Johnson.

Page 485.—Land which Samuel Cartmill is in possession of, the Indian Draft. Teste: Robert Stewart, Ralph Laverty ( ), William Young.

Page 489.—Patent to the Rev. Alexander McDowel 10th July, 1745. Delivered: A. Alexander, A. Court, 1777.

Page 495.—Corner to land now in possession of heirs of Samuel Wilson.

Page 503.—Part of tract in Beverley Manor whereon Samuel Hays now lives.

Page 507.—10th September, 1774. Matthew Thompson and Rachel ( ), of Granville County, South Carolina, to Michael Leese. Patent to Robert Scott 5th March, 1747, and by him conveyed to Matthew. Patent to Mathew Thomson 16th March, 1771.

Page 511.—6th March, 1775. John Stephenson and Stephen(son) Huston, agreement—John gives Stephen(son) Huston charge oversight of all his concerns and the management of his whole plantation from 26th August last past and allow him 4 grown slaves, &c., &c. In consideration of Huston's faithful oversight of John's affairs until his death, John gives grants and bequeaths to Huston 250 acres where his dwelling house is. Delivered: Jno. Stephenson by order of Stephenson Huston in presence of James Codington (Ronoak), 12th February, 1776.

Page 521.—Teste: William Brown, William Wilson, Matthew Thompson.

Page 523.—Part of tract that Samuel Steel now lives on on South River of Shanando. Delivered: John Ramsey, Jr., December, 1777.

Page 526.—Tract John Risk now lives on.

Page 530.—Delivered: Terrance Falls, 17th February, 1789.

Page 536.—10th January, 1775. Margaret ( ) Borger (Bergen) to Jacob Borger, her son, patented to Margaret 14th February, 1761. Teste: David McNeelly, John Davidson, William McNeelly.

Last deed recorded 21st March, 1775.

Deed Book No. 21.

First Deed Recorded 21st March, 1775; Last Deed Recorded 19th August, 1777.

Page 3.—231 acres in Beverley Manor, part of 1,546 acres sold by Beverley to Patrick Campbell in 1748, by Campbell to Wm. Sawyers, 1745; by him to John Patterson, 1748; by Patterson to Ward, 19th May, 1750.

Page 7.—Teste: John Clark, John Reagh, corner James Reagh.

Page 15.—16th March, 1775. William Reagh, Sr., and Elizabeth ( ) to John Reagh, son to said William, on Mill Creek, a branch of Calfpasture, west side of Cabin Creek.

Page 20.—Part of the tract John Finley now lives on.

Page 22.—18th May, 1775. Privy examination of Mary, wife of Robert Clendenin.

Page 25.—Patent to Felix Gilbert, 5th June, 1765.

Page 29.—Patent to John Bomgardner 10th September, 1755. Teste: John Johnson, John Smith, John I. Sheltman, Daniel Smith, Robert Maitland, Lachlan Campbell, James Maury.

Page 35.—Patent to George Moffett 1st March, 1773.

Page 42.—11th March, 1775. John Davidson, Sr., and Sarah and John Davidson, Jr., and Mary to William Campbell, 228 acres by patent 5th April, 1748. Teste: John Peden.

Page 44.—Lot in Staunton owned by Agatha Welsh.

Page 51.—15th March, 1775. James and William Cowdon, of Pittsylvania County, Va., to Thomas Steel, conveyed by Borden to William Cowdon 11th July, 1742, and devised by William's will to James and William. Teste: Ch. Simms, Patrick Lockhart, John Todd, Jr., Geo. Rutledge.

Page 54.—Corner Robert Cooper.

Page 58.—18th November, 1774. William Lockhart, of Fincastle County, to Philip Olinger, late of Frederick County, Maryland, conveyed by Beverley to James Lockhart, 17th June, 1748, and sold by James to William, that part of said tract belonging to Patrick Lockhart. Acknowledged in Staunton in pursuance of writ adjoining the Court from Fort Dunmore.

Page 64.—Teste: John William Leo.

Page 64.—21st March, 1775. Robert Reed and Barbara to Alexander Reed, their son, tract on Middle River where Robert lives.

Page 68.—14th August, 1775. Francis ( ) Allison and Hannah ( ) Allison, his mother, to Alexander McCluer, Sr. Delivered: Halbert McClure, son of Alexander McCluer, 10th October, 1793.

Page 78.—Delivered: John Thompson, 25th April, 1786.
Page 86.—Teste: William Rinken, James Corson.
Page 87.—August, 1775. Thomas Dryden and Agness, of Botetourt, and Nathaniel Dryden and Mary, of Augusta, to William Dryden, of Augusta.
Page 92.—Patent to Nicholas Cain, 20th August, 1747; corner Bernard McHenry, on North River of Shanando within the Gap of the Mountains. Delivered: Jno. Thomas, August Court, 1777.
Page 96.—On a branch of the Straight Fork of Patowmack, at a place called Frame's Cabbin patented to Samuel Black, 1st August, 1775. Teste: Patrick Buchanan, John King, Jr., Samuel Givens.
Page 100.—14th May, 1774. Agness Welsh, of the Province of Maryland, daughter of Mary McDonald, late of Augusta County, to Sampson Matthews, lot 12 in Staunton where Mary, formerly lived. Delivered to John, son of Sampson Mathews, 12th October, 1787.
Page 107.—28th July, 1775. Robert Young and Jean ( ) to Ludwick Murra. Inclusive patented to said Robert, 5th July, 1774, at head of the Falling Spring.
Page 112.—Teste: Walter Cunnningham, John Todd, Jr., Thomas Smith, Samp, Mathews, Thomas Jones, Joseph Love, Thomas Douglass, Lawrence Van Hook, Timothy Hughes. Privy Examination of Rachel, wife of Samuel Love before Thomas Douglass, Lawrence Van Hook, and John See in North Carolina, 6th February, 1775.
Page 115.—Property of John Henderson conveyed to John by Robert Henderson, son and heir apparent at law of Daniel Henderson, deceased, on Bever Creek.
Page 135.—Teste: John William Leo, William Christian.
Page 136.—15th May, 1775. Wallis Estill and Ann ( ) to Mathew Patton, £60, on Jackson's River at Vanderpole's Gap, patented to Wallis 1st March, 1773.
Page 139.—August, 1775. Samuel Glass, John Glass and Martha ( ), William Glass, of Botetourt to John Sansabough.
Page 145.—Borden's executors to Walter McChesney. Delivered: Samuel McChesney, June, 1783.
Page 154.—Patent to John Keenon (Keening), 1774.
Page 156.—17th Augusta, 1775. Philip ( ) Nicholas, eldest son of Samuel Nicholas and John Thomas, executors of Samuel Nicholas to Jacob Brunk, of Frederick County, Maryland, on Brock's Creek, patented to William Rutledge, 20th August, 1745, and by him conveyed to Cornelius Ruddle. Teste: Caspar Karsnar, George Ruddle.
Page 161.— —— ——, 1775. Valentine Cook and Susanna to John Jones, of Orange County, 180 acres on the Hawksbill.
Page 164.—215 acres on Cedar Run, a branch of the North Branch below James Thomas' land patented to John Jackson, 16th March, 1771. George Shoemaker's line. Teste: John Thomas.
Page 167.—25th September, 1775. Jacob Gillaspy to John Casner, on Briery Branch, patented to Jacob Gillaspey, deceased, and by his decease vested in said Jacob Gillaspey (grantor) as eldest son and heir.
Page 170.—The land said Callahan now lives on, patented to Daniel Callahan.
Page 174.—5th August, 1775. Joseph Sawin (Sawings) and Katherine

and Henry Sawin and Jennet to Abraham Smith. Patented to Daniel Harrison and by him conveyed to Daniel Smith, 14th October, 1765.

Page 177.—15th November, 1775. Tully Davitt and Jane to John Hiner, of Dunmore County, 140 acres on South Fork of Blackthorn, a branch of South Branch of Potomac. Delivered: John Heslin, February, 1777.

Page 182.—16th November, 1775. William McCandless ( ) of Green Brier and Botetourt to Jacob Hestent, of Dunmore County, known by name of Burdy House on Bullpasture.

Page 184.—8th August, 1775. John Patton, of Tryon County in the Province of North Carolina to James Dyer, on South Fork of Potowmack between Sweedeland Hill at Six Mile Lick.

Page 188.—5th July, 1773. William Moffett, farmer, to George Moffett, on Jenning's Creek, part of 400 acres patented to Daniel McNare and by him conveyed to Thomas Gardner, now dect., and is since become the property of said William Moffett by marrying the daughter of said Gardner who was heir-at-law to said land.

Page 192.—17th August, 1774. Charles Philips to John Crawford, on Buffelo Lick Branch, a branch of Cathey's River, part of tract patented to James Bell, deceased, 1st December, 1740, and devised to William and James Bell by will of James Bell. Delivered: Hugh Brown, August, 1779.

Page 194.—14th November, 1775. James Dalzell, of Botetourt, to Mark Riggs.

Page 196.—6th October, 1775. James Robinson, Jr., of Roane County, North Carolina, to David Robinson; James Robinson, Sr., in his lifetime was seized of 400 acres, part of Hite and Co.'s patent of 7,900 dated 26th March, 1739, on North River and Linville's Creek. Devised same to David, Isaac and Jonathan, his sons, now James Robinson, Jr., son and heir of James, Sr. Teste: John Fulton, Jr., John McNees, Samuel Johnston, John Thomas, John Gratton, Sr., John Gratton, Jr.

Page 199.—Patent to John Skidmore, 1st March, 1773, on Mud Lick Branch on south side of North Fork of South Branch of Potowmack. Teste: Jos. Haynes, Benjamin Jones, Charles Powers.

Page 201.—21st November, 1775. Charles Powers and Hannah ( ) to George Peter Bosett, on South Fork of Richardson Rich Run, a branch of South Branch of Potowmack. Teste: John William Leo, George ( ) Dunkle, Martha Leo. Delivered: Mr. James Allen, attorney, 16th March, 1791.

Page 206.—17th November, 1775. Augustine ( ) Price and Elizabeth ( ) to Augustine Pyper (Fyper?); corner Henry Eulia. Delivered: John Wise, son-in-law of Fyper (?), 5tn April, 1790.

Page 208.—Survey for Mathew Sceleher. Delivered: Peter Conrad, April, 1784.

Page 210.— —— August, 1775. Nicholas ( ) Simmons to George Simmons, on South Fork of South Branch of Potowmack, part of 145 acres patented to Nicholas Simmons, 5th March, 1762. Delivered to Jacob Simmons, heir of grantee, 30th November, 1811.

Page 212.—19th June, 1775. William and John Shelton to George Coil, part of patent to Robert Green, 12th January, 1746, on South Branch of Potowmack. Proved, 20th June, 1775, court being adjourned from Fort Dunmore.

Page 215.—21st November, 1775. Andrew Johnson, of Culpeper, and Michael Erreman (Ebermann), of Augusta, to William Gragg. Patented to Andrew and Michael 16th, 1771, on Senecar Creek, a branch of North Branch of South Branch of Potowmack.

Page 217.—On North Fork of South Branch, part of 156 acres patented to Daniel Mouse, 6th April, 1769. Delivered: Leonard Miller by order of George Mills, 1st April, 1794.

Page 219.—Patent to Morgan Bryant, 20th September, 1775; corner John Benedeck, Right to use of water for irrigation.

Page 224.—18th November, 1774. Philip Olinger, late of Frederick, Maryland, to William Lockhart, of Fincastle County. Delivered to Jacob Olinger, 8th February, 1785.

Page 226.—23d November, 1775. John Hiner, of Dunmore County, to Sebastian Hover and Gasper Taylor, on head of South Fork of Blackthorne, a branch of South Branch of Pattomack; corner tract belonging to heirs of Samuel Wilson, deceased.

Page 229.—23d November, 1775. Alexander Sinclair, merchant, and Jane, to Joshua Humphries, watch and clockmaker, part of lot 12 in Staunton. Teste: William Halliday, Seraiah Stratton. Delivered: T. Smith, October, 1780.

Page 230.—20th March, 1776. William Anderson and Rebecca ( ) and Samuel Anderson to Casper Siller (Silling), part of 195 acres patented to Robert Boyd, 10th March, 1756, and conveyed by Robert Boyd, heir of Robert, to Robert Young.

Page 233.—22d November, 1775. John Kennerley and Mary, of Craven County, Camden District, South Carolina, to James Kennerley. Patented to Wm. Russell, 1st December, 1740. Patented to Joseph Bloodworth, 1st August, 1745. Teste: John Strother, William Kennerley, Joseph Strother. Certificate that the other witnesses that Joseph Strother, the other witness who came with them from South Carolina to prove this deed, died since his arrival. Privy examination of Mary as to above certified by Robert Goodwin, David Hopkins and Richard Brown.

Page 242.—20th November, 1775. Patt. Campbell and Ann ( ) to Thomas Stevenson, of Amherst County.

Page 248.—21st November, 1775. John Givens and Margaret ( ) to John Givens, Jr., and George Givens.

Page 251.—Patent to John McKinney, Sr., deceased, 10th March, 1756, and bequeathed by John, Sr., to John Jr. Teste: George ( ) Burwell, James Phillips, George Here, John Philips.

Page 253.—144 acres patented to Alexander Craig 10th March, 1756. Delivered: R. Young. August, 1777.

Page 255.—20th September, 1775. Daniel Smith, late sheriff of Augusta County, to John Ashburner and Thomas Place, Merchants in Baltimore. Whereas Mathew Harrison, late of Augusta County, 22d May, 1769, sold to Richard and Peter Footman by mortgage. The Footmans foreclosed by suit in County Court and sheriff ordered to sell. Delivered: Mr. Lickton, 27th March, 1776.

Page 258.—Patent to Robert Poage, Sr.

Page 261.—19th March, 1776. John Young and Margaret to Jacob Trace, on South Branch of Potowmack below Hoals land.

Note: This was spelled Hoal, Hale and Hull.

Page 267.—26th February, 1776. Jacob Miller and Elizabeth ( ) to Conrad Futch. Delivered: John Futch, November Court, 1776.

Page 271.—9th July, 1772. Joshua Wright and Charity to Handel Vence (Vance), late of Lancaster County, Penna., but now of Augusta. Delivered: William Vance, June, 1776, part of patent of 1,200 acres to McCay Hite, &c., and conveyed to John Wright, deceased, who devised it to Joshua, his son.

Page 274.—7th February, 1776. Privy examination of Elizabeth, wife of Thomas Stephenson. Deed to Thomas Dixon.

Page 275.—Delivered: Thomas Smith, 4th January, 1785.

Page 279.—11th March, 1776. Privy examination of Hannah, wife of Thomas Kinkead.

Page 281.—2d March, 1775. Thomas and William Lewis to John Cowordin, contract of rental to Cowordin of the lower plantation on the Cowpasture belonging to the estate of Col. Charles Lewis, deceased.

Page 283.—21st May, 1776. John Hutchison and Margaret ( ) to Charles Baskin, part of 572 acres surveyed for William Hutchison. Delivered: John C. Baskins, per order, 16th October, 1812. Acknowledged 20th August, 1776, at a Court by authority of Commonwealth.

Page 287.—20th August, 1776. William Black and Rachel to Alexander Thompson, part of plantation whereon said William now lives on South River.

Page 291.—20th August, 1776. John Walker to his son, Alexander Walker.

Page 295.—17th May, 1776. James Frazier and Ann, John Gillespy and Martha to Henry Gay. Teste: A. Thompson, Robert Thompson, James Trimble.

Page 298.—Tract on Great Cowpasture conveyed to John Kinkead, weaver, by John Kinkead, clerk, 17th October, 1754, and by said John, weaver, and Elizabeth to Andrew Kinkead, 21st August, 1770.

Page 303.—Teste: A. Thompson, Robert Thompson, James Trimble.

Page 305.—8th May, 1776. John Boyd, formerly of Augusta County, to Joseph Douglass, tract patented to Robert Boyd 20th September, 1768, and vested in John as son and right heir of Robert on head of Fisher's Creek, a branch of North River of Shanando; corner Hugh Douglass. Teste: Hugh Donaghe, Thomas Patterson, John Reaburn, William Magill, John Huston, Nathaniel Douglass.

Page 308.—20th August, 1776. David Mathew. of Tygar's Valley, to Jacob Roote, on North Fork of South Branch of Potowmack below Deep Spring.

Page 312.—— —— ——, 1775. Beverley to Isaac White. Delivered to James White, 15th March, 1779.

Page 315.—30th September, 1775. Mary Moffett, widow of William Moffett, deceased, late of County of Fincastle, to George Moffett. Mary Moffett, late Mary Gardner, only daughter and heir-at-law of Thomas Gardner, deceased, was seised of tract on Jennings' Branch, and during her coverture conveyed same to George Moffett, and William executed deed to George; now Mary executes deed to George; part of 400 acres patented to Daniel McNare and by him conveyed to Thomas Gardner, 11th February,

1745. Teste: George Blackburn, James and Joseph Douglass, Henry Crisswell, James Trimble, John Bierey.

Page 319.—On Tees Creek in Forks of James River.

Page 322.—March, 1776. Jacob Lingle and Elizabeth ( ) (heir-at-law of John Lingle, deceased, to James Archer), tract patented to John Lingle, deceased, 3d August, 1771, on Quails Run, a branch of Shanando.

Page 324.—20th August, 1774. Thomas Smith and Elizabeth, of Staunton, to Sampson Mathews, mortgage, part of lot 12 conveyed to said Thomas by Thomas Bell, heir-at-law of Joseph Bell, 7th November, 1773, in trust for benefit of said Isabella Lockhart until said Sally Lockhart shall arrive to age of 21 or is married (then certain remainders); after death of Isabella the whole to remain to use of said Sally and her heirs on the part of her mother. Teste: Chas. Simms, Sam. Coleman, Jas. Thomas. Delivered to Mrs. Burns.

Page 331.—Teste: Andrew Kinnear.

Page 337.—22d April, 1776. Borden's executors to Samuel Patterson. Delivered to James Patterson, one of the heirs of Samuel, 11th October, 1806. Teste: William Robertson, Abraham Goodpasture, William Smith.

Page 343.—20th March, 1776. James Armstrong and Mary to Michael Comber. Teste: Roger North, Valentine Hamm, Thomas Rhoads.

Page 344.—21st August, 1776. Jacob Pence and Kathorine to Adam Pence, on both sides of Cub Run where he lives.

Page 347.—20th November, 1776. Samuel Givens, of Botetourt, and Martha to Andrew Lockridge.

Page 351.—2d September, 1773. James Gay and Jane to John Gay, on Cromby's Run, a branch of the Cowpasture. Teste: John Dunlap, Robert Dunlap, James Elliott.

Page 353.—4th September, 1775. Privy examination of Elizabeth, wife of Tunis Hood, deed to Abraham Brandiman.

Page 356.—26th March, 1776. Andrew Duncan to John Brown. Teste: Charles Campbell, John Brown, John Marshall, Robert Wardlaw, Alexander Wilson.

Page 359.—Patent to James Wright, the elder, 16th August, 1756, who died intestate, and tract descended to said John Wright, the surviving heir of James, and was devised to James Wright, Jr., by John Wright, deceased. Teste: Kathorine Fish.

Page 362.—185 acres patented to Thomas Waterson 12th January, 1746. Teste: James Anderson, James Gambel, Jno. Christian.

Page 365.—16th November, 1776. John Kisling to Martin Finder, part of 225 acres patented to Jacob Runkle 30th August, 1773 (1763?), west of land where said Runkle lives. Teste: Peter Runkle, George Hoffman, Lewis Rinehart.

Page 368.—19th November, 1776. John Bratton, eldest son and heir of James Bratton, deceased, and Ann ( ) to Elizabeth Bratton, widow and relict of James, part of 320 acres whereon James formerly lived.

Page 372.—17th June, 1776. Richard Rowland and Bridgett ( ) to Conrad Hartingen, part of 190 acres patented to Richard 16th March, 1771, on a branch of Daniel Holeman's Creek. Teste: John Thomas, George ( ) Kersner, Josiah Boone, Daniel Smith, Elizabeth ( ) Miller.

Page 376.—20th May, 1776. Hugh Young and Agness to their son, John Young. Teste: James Hughes.

Page 379.—19th November, 1776. Alexander Kilpatrick and Mary to Geo. Moffett, 90 acres patented to William Cunningham 12th February, 1755; 30 acres patented 1st August, 1772.

Page 382.—Patented to Thomas Watterson 12th January, 1746.

Page 386.—Teste: James Anderson, Robert Kinney, Gawin Leeper.

Page 387.—12th November, 1776. Privy examination of Margaret, wife John Hutchison, late of Augusta, deed to Charles Baskins, before William Fleming and Andrew Woods.

Page 390.—10th September, 1773. Charles Hays and Margaret to William Tedford. Teste: John and Charles Hays, James McCampbell, John Tedford.

Page 392.—19th November, 1776. Hugh McClure to John Ramsey. Delivered: Samuel Ramsey, one of legatees of grantee, deceased, 1st October, 1813.

Page 394.—20th November, 1777. Andrew ( ) Fowler and Margaret ( ) to Jno. Poage, 400 acres being the proportion to which the said Andrew was entitled as an adventurer in the Virginia Regiment under Governor Dinwiddie's Proclamation, which was laid off for him in a larger tract of 28,400 patented in the name of Captain Stoboes' heirs, Vanbran, and others, on the branches of the Ohio.

Page 396.—19th November, 1776. Andrew Lockridge to Samuel Givens, of Botetourt, and John Hicklen, deed to correct a mistake as to tract conveyed by Givens to Montgomerie, and deeds dated 8 and 9, November, 1768

Page 404.—20th November, 1776. James Henderson and Sarah, of Botetourt County, to John Hunton, tract where James Formerly lived. Teste: David Henderson, James Crow.

Page 413.—Patent to William Hamilton, wife Margaret, 29th May, 1760.

Page 416.—14th January, 1777. Richard Randels (Randall) and Eilzabeth and John Randall and Winnifor to William Alexander, of Botetourt.

Page 419.—Inclusive patent to Barbara Smith, 1st March, 1773. Barbara Smith to David Taylor. Delivered: A. Moody, July, 1777.

Page 422.—21st February, 1777. James Brownlow and Katherine ( ) to John McCullock. Teste: William Walker, Samuel Wier, Alexander Tedford.

Page 426.—18th March, 1777. John Yancey and Susanna to Michael Kern, 139 acres patented to William Thompson, 20th August, 1748; 6 acres patented to Samuel Hinds 14th February, 1761.

Page 429.—16th March, 1777. Joseph Vachob (Vahub) to Jean Graham, on head of Grassey Lick Run in the Calspasture, formerly surveyed for Thomas Smith, on Black Oak Hill, between Grassy Lick Run and Meeting House Run.

Page 432.—18th March, 1777. Samuel Lisk to John Grattan, on Naked Creek, patented to Samuel 16th March, 1771.

Page 435.—15th March, 1777. Josiah Boone, Sr., and Hannah H. to Michael Shank, 100 acres, part of 12,009 acres patented to Hite, Green and Duff and conveyed to William Linvil. Deliverd: Jno. Shank, 21st October, 1778.

Page 438.—18th March, 1777. Robert Shanklin and Rebecca ( ) to George Weaver, patented to Robert 20th July, 1768.

Page 440.—18th March, 1770. Thomas Dixon and Elizabeth ( ) to John Lowry, 330 acres patented to Robert Stevenson 16th August, 1756, and by his will devised to son Thomas Stevenson.

Page 444.—18th March, 1777. Beverley to Windle Bright. Delivered: Peter Hanger, May Court, 1778.

Page 446.—Edwin Erwin ( ) to Errowmous Dike, 230 acres patented to John Cunningham 12th May, 1759, and by him conveyed to his son Patrick Teste: John McKemy, Jr., John Hogshead, Edward Erwin.

Page 449.—170 acres on Thorny Branch joining the plantation whereon Thomas Waddle now (18th March, 1777) lives, formerly possessed by Benj. Copeland, and the plantation of Ralph Lofftus, formerly possessed by William Cunningham. Teste: James Curry, Jr.

Page 453.—10th March, 1777. John Sharp Watkins and Louis Christiana (Cristena) to Frederick Conrad, of Frederick County, lot 14 in Staunton. Delivered: R. P. Bell, attorney for U. S. Government 30th October, 1891.

Page 456.—Jonas Friend and Sarah ( ) to Charles Powers, on North Fork of South Branch of Potowmack, part of patent to Robert Green 21st January, 1756. Teste: Robert McClenachan, John Sharp Watkins, Valentine Cloninger, Robert Poage.

Page 458.—15th June, 1776. Thomas Lewis and Jane, Andrew Lewis and Elizabeth, of Botetourt, William Preston and Susanna, of Fincastle County, to William McDowell, merchant in Staunton, part of lot No. 3 in Staunton to be half the length of John Stewart's lot or square off from lower end of Francisco's house on the main street, joining lot Jno. Stewart formerly lived on. Teste: Samuel McDowell, Pat. Lockhart, William Nalle, William Robertson, Samp. Mathews, Stephen May, Richard Thomas, Ad. Smyth, James Hill.

Page 462.—18th March, 1777. Ulrick Conrad, Sr., to Ulrick Conrad, Jr., his son, at mouth of Black Thorn on South Branch of Potowmack, 6 acres with mill seat thereon erected, patented to Ulrick 12th May, 1770.

Page 264.—19th March, 1777. Michael Bowyer and Eupheme (Phraney) to Sebastian March (delivered: Reuben Moore, November, 1779), tract patented to Valentine Sevior 12th January, 1746, on Smith's Creek, Daniel James' Branch, Abssolom Hayworth's line.

Page 471.—19th May, 1777. William Porter, Sr., to his son, William Porter, Jr., tract purchased by William, Sr., from Borden, Sr., and conveyed to him by Borden, Jr., 1750.

Page 475.—20th May, 1777. Patrick Campbell and Agness to John Burk, of Philadelphia, Penna., tract bought by Patrick Campbell, deceased, from Beverley 21st February, 1738, and deed recorded in Orange.

Page 478.—80 acres patented to John Couts 1st March, 1773. Teste: George Malloa, Jacob Nicolas, Gasper Haines.

Page 480.—20th May, 1777. Jacob ( ) Goyle and Margaret ( ) to Christian Pickle, 100 acres on South Branch of Potowmack above Trout Rock patented to James Trimble ———, and by him conveyed to Valentine Goyle, deceased 17th November, 1761, and descended to Gabriel Goyie as eldest son and heir. Teste: Valentine Cloninger, Valentine White.

Page 482.—20th May, 1777. David Bell and Florence to William Jordane, Jr., patented to David 16th March, 1771.

Page 486.—167 acres on a branch of the Straight Fork of Potowmack at a place called Frame's Cabbin patented to Samuel Black.

Page 488.—29th April, 1777. Sampson Mathews and Mary and George Mathews and Ann to John Caldwell, 4 tracts—A, on head South River with saw mill and Oyle mill, part of 400 acres conveyed to Samuel Caldwell by Love and Tease 20th May, 1766, and descended to John as eldest son and heir, who conveyed one-half to his brother Robert; B. C. D. patented to Sampson and George 5th July, 1774. Delivered: Daniel Kidd, January, 1779.

Page 490.—Plantation whereon John Caldwell (South River) now lives.

Page 493.—20th May, 1777. James Blair, son and heir of Joseph Blair, deceased, to Joseph Blair (excepting 4½ acres around North Mountain Meeting House).

Page 496.—15th April, 1777. William Hays, of Cumberland County, Peters Township, Pennsylvania, to James Mitchell.

Page 499.—20th May, 1777. Thomas Waddle and Alese (Elise) to their son, James Waddle, part of 400 acres on which said Thomas now lives.

Page 501.—20th May, 1777. Same to son Joseph Waddle. Patented to James Coyle, 16th August, 1756.

Page 505.—20th May, 1777. Zechoriah Johnston and Ann to Thomas Galbraith. Delivered: William Galbraith, 26th June, 1794.

Page 512.—James Patton to William Patton. Whereon James Patton formerly lived being the land willed to James by his father, John Patton, and ½ of 250 acres willed by said John to his 2 sons, William and James.

Page 519.—Patent to Stephen Hancebarger 31st October, 1765.

Page 521.—11th March, 1777. Privy examination of Martha Givens, wife of Samuel, deed, to Andrew Lockbridge 20th November, 1776, before William Fleming and Richard May.

Page 538.—Land conveyed by Beverley to Alexander Breckinridge, recorded in Orange, and by Alexander's decease intestate became vested in his eldest son and heir, George Breckinridge, who conveyed same to Robert **Breckenridge 17th May, 1749, and by Robert and Lettice, his wife, to** Stephen Loy, 21st October, 1765.

Page 542.—10th August, 1777. George Robertson and Jane, of Botetourt, to Alexander Robertson, of Montgomery County, 274 acres in Beverley Manor purchased by their father, James Robertson, of John Lewis, Gent., and bequeathed to said George and Alexander. Teste: Hugh Crockett, John Barnet, Stephen ( ) Childers.

Page 544.—10th August, 1777. Privy examination of Jane before Hugh Crockett and John Barnett.

Page 546.—Patent to William Sharp 10th March, 1756.

Page 549.—7th July, 1777. John Faris and Agnes to Barnabas Johnston. Delivered: William Johnston, July, 1779.

Page 553.—19th August, 1777. George Boswell and Judith to John Corthrae, 150 acres whereon John lives.

Page 557.—19th August, 1777. William Gibson and Ann to Charles Yarrass, part of 235 acres patented to William Hamilton 29th May, 1760. Delivered: Joseph Bogle, 2d **May, 1780.**

Last deed recorded 19th August, 1777.

Deed Book No. 22.

First Deed Recorded 19th August, 1777; Last Deed Recorded 18th May, 1779.

Page 1.—4th November, 1768. Abraham, a Mohawk Chief; Sennghors. an Oneida Chief; Sagnarisera, a Tuscarora Chief; Chenangheata, an Onondaga Chief; Tagaaia, a Cayuga Chief, and Gaustrax, a Seneca Chief, chiefs and sachems of the six united nations, to George Croghan. Recorded in Philadelphia 12th January, 1769; recorded at Augusta County Court at Pittsburg 23d September, 1775; recorded at Staunton August 19, 1777.

Page 10.—9th August, 1777. Joseph Love and Mary, of Montgomery County, to Richard Payne, conveyed to Joseph by John Clide. Teste: Walter Davis, John Hunton, Chas. Hunt, Martin Shearman.

Page 15.—Patent to John Stephenson, farmer, 16th August, 1756 (wife Ester). Teste: George and John Huston, Jacob Pirkey.

Page 19.—Tract on Christian Creek whereon Andrew Russell now lives.

Page 21.—20th August, 1776. Mary Henderson, relict and executrix of Halbert McClure, deceased, to James Patton. Teste: Archibald and Joseph Alexander, James Lyle and Robert Shaw.

Page 24.—Corner John Michael Brooks' land, patented to James Baggs 10th June, 1760. Teste: John Ruddell, Thomas Baggs, Conrad Humble.

Page 27.—Patent to Robert Scott.

Page 29.—Patent of 144 acres patented to Alexander Craig 10th March, 1756.

Page 32.—Patent to James Blair 10th March, 1756.

Page 33.—386 acres patented to William Logan 10th March, 1756, on Curteys' Run.

Page 35.—19th August, 1777. Samuel Gibson and Elizabeth ( ) to his son, Robert Gibson.

Page 38.—15th August, 1777. James Thomas and Sarah, of Hampshire County, to Stuffle Brunk, head of cedar branch patented to James Claypol, Jr., 15th December, 1757, patented to James Thomas 27th August, 1770, between his and Samuel Nicholas' land. Teste: John Thomas, Charles Daley, John Brown.

Page 41.—19th August, 1777. Thomas O'Neal to Henry Henry. Delivered: Jesse Harrison, March, 1783.

Page 44.—Patent to John Fudge 3d August, 1771; corner to Old Fudge.

Page 46.—Patent to Thomas West 20th June, 1749, at Stair Lick, on head of Benjamin Allen's River.

Page 50.—18th August, 1777. Gilbert Christian and Margaret, of Washington County, to Leonard Miller.

Page 63.—Teste: John Thomas, John ( ) Davis, James Poage.

Page 72.—19th May, 1777. Jacob Nicholas to John Rush, on Cub Run, at foot of Peacked Mountain, part of 460 acres patented to Jacob 1st August, 1772; corner Anthony Ayler. Delivered: Peter Rush.

Page 91.—Patent to Charles Dailly 16th August, 1756, on Johnston's Branch of North River of Shanando. Teste: Daniel Smith, John Thomas, Henry ( ) Easters (Etters).

Page 95.—17th July, 1777. William Hutchinson, of Greenbrier, in Botetourt, to John Fudge (delivered to your son, Conrad), 667 acres first surveyed for George Hutcheson and conveyed to him by Beverley 21st February, 1738, on Christian's Creek.

Page 98.—10th June, 1777. Joseph Poindexter and Elizabeth, of Bedford, to William Foster (delivered: William Foster, Jr., 13th August, 1782), 500 acres, part of 643 acres conveyed to Joseph by Adam Dean, deed recorded in General Court.

Page 101.—15th August, 1777. John Bailey, of Botetourt, and Mercey, to Joseph Lemon, on Cedar Run, a branch of North River. patented to Robert Poage 3d March, 1760.

Page 105.—On North River of ———, patented to Joel Robinson 31st October, 1765. Teste: John Thomas, Charles and Elinor ( ) Dailey.

Page 107.—16th November, 1776. Michael Sircle and Cathorine ( ), of Dunmore County, to Ludwick Fulmor (delivered: John Separs, 20th August, 1793), 130 acres patented to John Bair 10th March, 1755, and conveyed by him to Eve Sircle; also 54 acres patented to my mother, Eve Sircle, now deceased, 10th September, 1755, and descended to Michael as eldest son and heir of Eve.

Page 111.—16th November, 1776. Same to John Chrisman Pap, 130 acres patented to John Bear 10th March, 1755, and conveyed by John to Eve Sircle August, 1761, and descended to Michael as eldest son.

Page 117.—Teste: Anthony Reader, Conrad Humble.

Page 117.—18th August, 1777. Francis ( ) McBride and Mary ( ) to Margaret Marks, widow and devisee of Jacob Marks, late of Augusta.

Page 124.—Part of 350 acres patented to Cornelius Cook 20th September, 1748, conveyed to Rees Thomas and by him devised to his youngest son, Rees Thomas, and conveyed by James Thomas, son and heir of Rees Thomas, deceased, to his said father, Rees Thomas, deceased, and afterwards conveyed by said Rees Thomas to George Gindner 28th December, 1770; also 90 acres patented to George Gindner 20th July, 1768. In trust according to the directions of Jacob Marks.

Page 127.—On Fort Run, patented to Daniel Johnson 16th August, 1756.

Page 130.—21st March, 1774. Adam Hoverstick, of Culpeper, to George Kersner, patent to Adam 7th July, 1763, and conveyed by him to William Samples 18th August, 1770, and William Samples to George Kersner 17th August, 1773. Adam was an alien and foreigner when he conveyed to William Samples and continued so until 16th March, 1774, when he was naturalized. Teste: John Dunbarr, Francis ( ) McBride, John Thomas, Benjamin Kinley.

Page 138.—10th July, 1777. Robert Henderson and Mary ( ) and John Henderson, and Mary ( ) to Henry Miller, ironman. On 6th June, 1772, Robert conveyed to his brother, John, above, 675 acres hereafter conveyed, but before deed was fully proven the time expired in which it could be proved and title remains in Robert, although, but John has in the meantime sold 100 acres to Abraham Smith and Abraham Henderson; now convey 550 acres on Bever Creek and Spring Creek. The 650 acres were patented to Daniel Henderson, father of said Robert, and John, 7th August, 1761. Teste: Stephen and Abraham ( ) Harding, Alexander, Thomas and John Wade.

Page 142.—Teste: Stephen and Daniel Trigg.

Page 147.—27th May, 1777. Robert Williams and Margaret to Bartholomew Older, of Lancaster County, Penna., on Yeager's Branch of Smith's Creek. Teste: John Thomas, Abraham Raiff, Tom Raiff, Martin Bowman.

Page 153.—22d January, 1776. Abraham Miller and Elizabeth to John Kring, lot 8 on Linvel's Creek, devised to John Bowman by his father, George Bowman, patent to John Scott 31st November, 1765, on McKay's draft, a branch of Linvel's Creek, patented to Abram Miller 1st March, 1773. Teste: Daniel, Joseph and Robert Smith, John Thomas, Cornelius Ruddle.

Page 157.—144 acres patented to Alexander Craig 10th March, 1756.

Page 167.—Teste: Archibald Alexander and Joshua Humphreys.

Page 167.—21st September, 1777. Adam Bratton to James Kailor. Delivered: George Keller, 5th January, 1791, on Meadow Run in Beverley Manor, a branch of Middle River. Teste: John Heaning.

Page 172.—17th November, 1777. Robert Shanklin and Rebecca to Andrew Hutton, of Dunmore County, patent to Robert 20th July, 1768. Delivered: Henry Black, November, 1778.

Page 175.—In Beverley Manor on McCord's Draft.

Page 179.—17th November, 1777. James Carruthers to James Brent, tract Carithers now lives on known by name of McCord's Draft and on waters of Christian's Creek. Delivered: Daniel Ray, 15th September, 1784.

Page 184.—Patent to Robert Sample, 1771.

Page 187.—18th November, 1777. James Hunter and Isabella ( ) to Lois Usher, widow and William Usher, her son, in spurs of the North Mountain patented to said James 20th September, 1751.

Page 190.—18th November, 1777. Francis Berry and Isabel ( ) to Andrew Haysaw. Teste: John and Rebekah McPheeters, William Berry.

Page 194.—6th September, 1777. William ( ) Jordane, Sr., to Anthony Johnston, 90 acres patented to James Young 14th July, 1769, on head of Cowpasture, 90 acres adjoining, patented to William Jordan 1st March, 1773. Delivered: Mr. Readman by your order, 26th June, 1792. Teste: John ( ) Jordan.

Page 197.—16th August, 1774. Joseph Lair to Andrew Lair, his brother, 224 acres patented to John Hughes and by him conveyed to, 5th November, 1768; 224 acres patented to said Lair 14th July, 1769, on Linvil's Creek.

Page 200.—Patented to David, Margaret and Daniel Weitreith 1st June, 1741, and by them conveyed to John Fudge, Sr., on Shanandore River. (Named spelled Futch.)

Page 202.—Walter Cunningham and Jane to Alexander Sinclair, lot 1 in Staunton conveyed to Walter by his father, John Cunningham, 30th May, 1761. Teste: Owen Owens.

Page 205.—Patented to John Frame 29th May, 1760, and conveyed by him to Margaret.

Page 209.—15th November, 1777. James Morrow, of Botetourt, to John Slaven, on Jackson's River; corner Robert Dinwiddie.

Page 213.—Inclusive patent to Robert McClenachan 16th September, 1765.

Page 215.—16th December, 1777. Rev. John Brown and Margaret to George Gall, of Washington County, Maryland.

Page 221.—16th March, 1778. Beverley to John Allen. Delivered to William Allen, October, 1780. The above is part of 725 acres sold William Allen and by him divided into 3 parcels, and separate deeds made for each.

Page 230.—17th March, 1778. Beverley to Samuel Pilson. Delivered: George Pilson, son of Samuel.

Page 238.—11th March, 1778. John Smith and Margaret to Nicholas Seybert, on a branch of the Straight Fork of Potowmack, at a place called Frame's Cabbin.

Page 241.—29th January, 1778. William McNees, of Westmoreland County, Pennsylvania, and Jane, to John Miller, Mason. Delivered: Benj. Forsythe, February, 1779. Patent to William, on west branch of Cook's Creek joining Cravens and Hemphill. Teste: James McVey.

Page 244.—15th December, 1777. Edward Erwin and Mary to Mark Bird, of Pennsylvania, and Henry Miller, of Augusta, partners and iron men, on Mossey Creek, patented to Edward, 12th May, 1770, by name of Edward Erwin, Jr.

Page 246.—17th March, 1778. David Bell and Florence to Eness Jones, of Lowden County.

Page 250.—In Borden's tract on Flat Spring Run.

Page 254.—17th March, 1778. Ronimus Teck (Tick), of Rockingham, and Margaret, to John Stuneard, of Rockingham, on Thorny Branch, patented to John Cunningham, 12th May, 1759.

Page 259.—17th March, 1778. Alexander Montgomery and Sarah and Robert Thompson and Agness, all of Augusta County, to Cutlip Black, late of same place, in Borden's tract on head of James River. Delivered to Francis Hull, 21st May, 1781.

Page 260.—12th February, 1778. Ralph Lofftus and Sarah to Adam and John Stephenson and Samuel Anderson. Patented to William Cunningham, 10th August, 1759, on Thorny Branch. Delivered: John Bing, August, 1778. Teste: Thomas, Joseph and James Waddle.

Page 263.—Patent to John McDougall, 1st August, 1772, on the Straight Forg of the Bullpasture.

Page 267.—Line formerly surveyed for James Lockhart, but now claimed by Richard Burns.

Page 269.—268 acres patented to Barbara Smith by inclusive patent, 1st March, 1773.

Page 273.—Tract on Lewis Creek whereon William now lives.

Page 275.—17th March, 1778. John Leeper and Susanna, and Gawin Leeper, to Anthony Aylor, 150 acres patented to James Leeper; 100 acres patented to John Leeper, 20th July, 1768, corner land he lives on.

Page 287.—19th May, 1778. Henry Waterson and Ann ( ), of Botetourt, to Samuel Woods, of Amherst. Delivered: Claudius Bustard, August, 1780.

Page 289.—19th May, 1777. Privy examination of Ann to above before Joseph, James and John Reaburn.

Page 295.—Patent to Robert Stevenson, 16th August, 1756, and by him devised to his son Thomas Stevenson, and by Thomas to Thomas Dixon.

Page 298.—Patent to James Humphrys, 25th June, 1747.

Page 300.—Delivered: Francis Hull, August Court, 1781.

Page 307.—18th May, 1778. James Trimble's executors (John, Isaac and James Trimble), of Rockbridge County, to Woolderick Conrod, Jr. Delivered: Jacob Conrod, son of Wooldruck Conrod, 23d May, ——, on South Branch of Potomac.

Page 309.—19th May, 1778. James McCutchen, of Washington County, Virginia, to Doctor John Johnston, devised to him by his father, James McCutcheon, 1st February, 1759, in tail cites statutes converting estates tail into fee simple, corner Widow Cook.

Page 312.—19th May, 1778. Leonard ( ) Miller and Katherine ( ), of Rockingham County, to Henry Mowyer.

Page 317.—18th March, 1778. Alex. McClenachan and John Poage, executors of John Cawley, to Henry Miller.

Page 319.—Patent to Robert Wiley, 29th May, 1760.

Page 322.—In Beverley Manor on waters of North River, part of plantation Thomas Nelson now lives on. Delivered: Joseph Nelson, 12th September, 1787.

Page 325.—13th July, 1774. John Bowyer and Magdalene, of Botetourt, and Moses Bennett and Mary to Robert Lusk. Teste: Samuel Lapsley, John Lyle, Robert Stuart, Moses Whitesides.

Page 328.—18th July, 1778. Privy examination of Sarah, wife of Francis Hartgrove (deed to John David Greiner, 9th September, 1773), before Charles Gordon, John Grier, John Brown, justices of Wilks County, North Carolina.

Page 334.—18th August, 1778. William Cowan and Elizabeth ( ), of Rockbridge County, to Andrew Cowan, Sr.

Page 342.—On Back Creek of James River, above Hickman's land, below Falling Spring Run, Archabald ( ) Smithers and Cecilia to Alexander Hamilton. Teste: Samuel Vance, Charles Hamilton, John ( ) Daivs.

Page 347.—7th July, 1778. John Hunton and Frances to John Brooks, of the County of Bartly, 430 acres (except 3 acres sold to Richard Payne) on north side of the main road that leads from Richard Payne's to Walter Davis's. Teste: Walter Davis, John Hunton, Jr., John Brooks, Jr.

Page 350.—Part of the plantation James Gilliland lives on.

Page 352.—Teste: John Bell, Samuel Long, Gabriel Alexander.

Page 357.—17th August, 1778. John Anderson to Francis Hartgrove, only son and heir-at-law of James Hartgrove, deceased, of Wilks County, North Carolina, contract, 22d April, 1763, between John and James; lot 6 in Staunton. Release of mortgage. Teste: William Anderson.

Page 360.—3d November, 1777. Andrew Kinkead and Mary to Rebecca Black, widow. Delivered: Jones Henderson, 21st February, 1794.

Page 363.—Teste: Peter Weaver, Benjamin Odell, Allen Fox.

Page 365.—18th November, 1777. Thomas Wilmuth and Ann to Conrod Good, on branches of Skidmore's Run, waters of South Branch of Potomac, patented to said Wilmuth, 20th July, 1768.

Page 366.—26th August, 1777. Privy examination of Rebecca, wife of Joseph Kinkead, of Washington County (deed to Martin Shearman, 24th June, 1777) before Arthur Campbell and William Edmiston.

Page 369.—Above deed, 242 acres, part of 485 acres formerly belonging to William Armstrong, whereon said Martin now liveth. Teste: Charles Hunt.

Page 372.—18th August, 1778. William, John and Robert Christian and their wives, to Patrick Christian.

Page 376.—On the Wet Stone Draft of Mossey Creek. Teste: Jas. McVey, Moses Sample, William Ralston.

Page 378.—18th August, 1778. David Kail (Cail) and Bethemia to Peter Cail (Cale).

Page 381.—18th August, 1778. Peter and Jacob Kail (Cail) and Grizzel to David Cail, plantation in Beverley Manor whereon Peter and Jacob now live. Delivered: Wm. Cale by order of Barthemia, his mother, 21st April.

Page 384.—16th June, 1778. Privy examination of Mary, wife of Joseph Love, of Montgomery County (deed, 9th August, 1777, to Richard Payne), before Wm. Davis and Wm. Doack.

Page 386.—Teste: William Livingston, William Morrow.

Page 387.—15th September, 1778. Richard Payne and Ailer (Ailie) to Cornelius Riddle (Ruddle), of Albemarle County, on Black Run, a branch of Christian's Creek.

Page 391.—20th November, 1778. Andrew ( ) Cowan, Sr., and Mary ( ) to David Kerr and Robert Donaldson, plantation that Andrew and William Cowan lived on.

Page 396.—Teste: Joseph and William Alexander, John Alley.

Page 397.—17th November, 1778. Christopher Harris and Agness ( ), of Albemarle, to John Collins. Delivered: Thos. Turk, August, 1779.

Page 398.—17th November, 1778. James Trotter and Mary to David Trotter, part of plantation on which James lives, with a tub mill thereon.

Page 400.—Same to James Trotter, Jr.

Page 403.—17th November, 1778. David Kerr to Robert Donaldson, 230 acres, part of the tract that Andrew Cowan lived on in Beverley Manor. (See deed Donaldson to Kerr next succeedinng.)

Page 412.—Delivered to Valetine White, May Court, 1779.

Page 416.—Delivered to Miles Hunter, March Court, 1782.

Page 417.—26th August, 1778. Privy examination of Margaret, wife of Samuel McFeeters (deed to John McDougall, 20th March, 1778).

Page 423.—14th November, 1778. John Hunton, of Albemarle, to Cornelius Riddle. Teste: Walter and James Davis, Martin Shearman, Mary Donly.

Page 426.—15th September, 1778. John Meclure to Andrew Alexander, part of the plantation said John now lives on, on South River. Delivered: John Alexander, one of the heirs of the grantor (grantee ?). Teste: James Best.

Page 428.—Part of the plantation on the Long Meadow whereon William Robertson now lives, corner Isaac White.

Page 430.—19th January, 1779. Nicholas Leeper by George Seawright, his attorney, to John Oliver. Gawin Leaper, late of Augusta, sold to John Oliver 66 acres patented to James Leeper, father to said Gawen, 5th June, 1747. James died intestate and land became vested in Nicholas Leeper as heir (?).

Page 435.—Patent to John Trimble, Sr., 10th March, 1756, on Cathey's River.

Page 435.—16th March, 1779. Robert Buchanan and Jean, of Washington County, to Philip Saylor. Delivered: James Buchanan, March, 1779.

Page 437.—18th November, 1778. Alexander Stewart and Jean, late Jean Graham, to Alexander McGinney, in Calfpasture on head of Grassey Lick, purchased by Jane in her widowhood, of Joseph Vahub, 17th March, 1777.

Page 442.—16th March, 1779. Henry Black and Catherine ( ), of Rockingham County, to Stephen Beck, of Shanandore.

Page 444.—23d November, 1770. Reverend Charles Cummins and Mille, his wife, of Washington County, to Robert Cummins, of Augusta, part of 400 acres patented to James Bell, deceased, father to the said William Bell, of whom said Charles purchased on Middle River near the North Mountain.

Page 449.—16th March, 1779. James Cameron and Jean, of Washington County, to Thomas Caruthers. Delivered. Teste: Joseph Nelson, James, David, Alexander, John Cunningham.

Page 451.—On waters of Long Meadow, joining survey known by name of Strawberry Bottom.

Page 453.—16th March, 1779. William ( ) Russell and Sarah ( ), of Rockbridge, to Henry Vernon.

Page 455.—20th November, 1778. Hugh Johnston, of Washington County, to John Chapman.

Page 457.—16th March, 1778. Robert Buchanan, of Washington County, to Patrick Buchanan.

Page 465.—16th March, 1779. William Bell and Mary ( ) to William Richards, of Orange County.

Page 466.—Lines of Abraham Lene and Philip Drake.

Page 467.—3d October, 1778. Daniel Smith and Gaw'th. Hamilton. take privy examination of Judith, wife of George Boswell, deed to John Carthrea, 19th August, 1777.

Page 469.—16th March, 1779. James Rhea and Elizabeth ( ) to James Bratton, on Mill Creek, a branch of Calfpasture, by patent, 27th August, 1770. Line of William Rhea, Jr. Delivered to Samuel Clarke, Esq., for Andrew Bratton, heir of James Bratton, 23d February, 1836.

Page 472.—Patent to Robert Ralston and conveyed to David Ralston. Teste: Alex. Robertson, Thomas Hughart, Robert Poage.

Page 476.—Teste: Moses Sample.

Page 478.—21st May, 1778. James Thompson and William Thompson, of Washington and Montgomery Counties, to Rev. James Waddell (Waddls), Spring Hill tract of which Thompson is seized in fee-tail and of which William Thompson is entitled to the use.

Page 482.—16th March, 1779. Andrew Linn, Benjamin Lowrey and Sarah, of Mecklinburg County, North Carolina, to Robert Doack, on South River, a hill called the bufler (Buffalo ?) hill.

Page 485.—19th November, 1778. James Cowan, of Rockingham, to Anthony Gholston. Delivered: Stephen Beck, May, 1780.

Page 487.—6th March, 1779. Patrick Lockhart, of Botetourt, to Peter and Jacob Cale, part of 624 acres conveyed by Beverley to James Lockhart. 17th June, 1748. Release of mortgage. Teste: William Allen, Stephen Woods, James Thomas.

Page 494.—Teste: William Patton.

Page 498.—On Back Creek above Sugar Bottom.
Page 501.—On both sides of Elk Run in Beverley Manor, 5th April, 1779, James Hamilton to James Gallespie. Teste: James Gallespie.
Page 504.—19th May, 1779. Martin Shearman and Mary, of Albemarle County, to William Richards, of Orange.
Page 508.—Part of the plantation whereon James Bell now lives.
Page 510.—18th May, 1779. James Trimble and Jean to James Bell, part of the plantation whereon Trimble now lives.
Page 515.—363 acres patented to Jacob Bear, 5th July, 1774. Teste: Thomas Bradshaw, John Sterling.
Page 517.—On Maxwell's Branch near Christian's Creek.
Page 518.—Teste: Jacob Patton.
Page 520.—15th May, 1779. John Tate and Mary to Hance Patton.
Page 524.—Tract whereon William Oldham now lives.
Page 525.—Teste: Joseph Patterson, John Campbell, Samuel Erwin.
Page 526.—120 acres on South Branch of Potomac below Crab Apple Bottom, Peter Hool to Nicholas Seybert, corner to his father's land.
Page 527.—18th May, 1779. David Kerr and Margaret to Robert Tate. Delivered to William Tate, July, 1782.
Page 533.— — May, 1779. William Kerr to Ulrick Followider. Delivered to John Folowider, 12th March, 1782.
Page 538.—Teste: John Dixon, Thomas Myns.
Last deed recorded, 18th May, 1779.

DEED BOOK No. 23.

First deed recorded, 18th May, 1779; last deed recorded, 19th August, 1783.
Page 6.—18th May, 1779. Beverley to William Shields. Delivered to William Shields, Jr., and John Russell, 18th November, 1795.
Page 10.—Same to Abraham Larew. Delivered: Jacob Larew.
Page 19.—26th April, 1773. Privy examination of Sarah, wife of John Davidson, deed to William Campbell, 12th March, 1779, before George Boswell and Thomas Hewitt.
Page 20.—In Beverley Manor, part of the plantation William McClintiic lives on, corner Jacob Helford.
Page 23.—26th April 1779. Mark Bird and Mary, of Union Township, County of Berkshire, Pennsylvania, to Henry Miller. Whereas Adam Stephen, of Berkeley County, sold to Mark and Henry, 7th April, 1774, 400 acres purchased by Adam from Henry Smith; also another tract conveyed to Adam by William Minter on Mossey Creek; also another tract purchased from Henry Smith on South Fork of North River of Shenandoah; afterwards Mark and Henry entered into partnership, 1st June, 1774, as ironmasters and to build necessary forges, furnaces and mills. Teste: Jesse Potts, David Davis, Sarah Lincoln.
Page 29.—19th May, 1779. James Moffett and John Campbell, trustees, to John Scott, 452 acres on Middle River, patented to John Spear, deceased, 10th September, 1755, and bequeathed by him to his children, and grantors here are trustees for the legatees of said estate.
Page 32.—Patent to John Spear, 10th March, 1756.

Page 35.—Corner to Phillips Drake.

Page 37.—6th October, 1778. Nicholas Leeper, of Tryon County, North Carolina, to George Seawright, Jr., power of attorney to convey to John Oliver land said Oliver now lives on. Teste: James Leeper and James Seawright.

Page 40.—17th August, 1779. John Handly, Sr., and Margaret ( ) to John Handly, Jr., part of the plantation whereon said John now lives in Beverley Manor.

Page 44.—Patent to Anthony Johnston, 1st March, 1773, on head branch of James River above the Stony Lick.

Page 46.—5 acres, part of the plantation whereon Jeremiah O'Friel now lives, on waters of the Middle River. Delivered to William Moffett, executor of Daniel O'Friel, 23d August, 1815.

Page 48.—17th August, 1779. Alexander ( ) Mceleroi and Agness to William Sprowl, part of the plantation Alex. now lives on, in Borden's tract.

Page 52.—Patent to James Campbell, 16th March, 1771. Teste: William Young, Samuel Anderson, Isaac Carson.

Page 53.—Privy examination of Mary, wife of John Davidson, deed to William Campbell, 12th March, 1779, before Alexander Robertson and Joseph Bell.

Page 56.—17th August, 1779. John Montgomery and Esther to David Allen. Teste: John and James Montgomery. Delivered to the son and heir of David Allen, 8th December, 1780.

Page 58.—Plantatiion David Henderson now lives on, in Beverley Manor.

Page 63.—17th August, 1779. Peter Venimon and Elizabeth ( ), of Rockingham, to John Wormsley, patent to Peter 1st March, 1773, on Dry Run of North Fork of South Branch of Potomac. Teste: Thos. Myns, Richard Barret.

Page 67.—Teste: Thomas Steel, Michael Dickey.

Page 70.—26th October, 1778. Ebenezer Alexander and Agness ( ) to Thomas Hinds and Ann, his wife, on James River above the Great Falls. Delivered to James Bridget per order Thomas Hinds, 16th April, 1769. Teste: Abraham Draper.

Page 76.—18th August, 1779. Jacob Peck and Mary (Polly) to Robert Astrop, lot 25 in Staunton.

Page 77.—Teste: John Erwin, William Gibson.

Page 79.—25th April, 1777. Charles Phillips to Alexander Simpson. Delivered to William Clendennin, October, 1779, on Buffalow Lick Branch of Cathey's River, part of tract conveyed to Charles by William Magill, 1st March, 1769, patented to James Bell, deceased, 1st December, 1740, conveyed by William and James Bell to Magill, 18th March, 1760. Teste: John Phillip.

Page 81.—10th July, 1779. James Leslie's executors to Robert Rogers. James Leslie's widow, Mary, died shortly after James, without having remarried. Teste: Mathew Kenney, John ( ) Dixon, William Donlap, John and Thomas Graham.

Page 89.—18th August, 1779. Christopher Sumwalt and Marilus to Hugh Bodkin, on Black Thorn, a branch of South Branch of Potomac. Teste: James Culbertson, Valentine Cloninger, Francis Kirtley.

Page 90.—17th August, 1779. Abraham Smith and Sarah, of Rockingham, to Michael Armingcost, on Crab Apple Waters on head of the South Branch of Potomack, Lynche's line. Teste: William Booney, Jonathan Shipman.

Page 93.—Part of the plantation William Shields now lives on.

Page 95.—23d April, 1779. Sampson and George Mathews, and Mary and Ann, to James Hill, lot 18 in Staunton, joining lot whereon Thomas Smith formerly lived.

Page 98.—Thomas Lewis, son to William.

Page 100.—16th September, 1779. James Clemons and Florah ( ) to Jared Erwin, of Rockingham County, on Cowpasture, patented to George Wilson, 15th December, 1758.

Page 104.—21st September, 1779. John Buchanan, Jr., of Washington County, to George Hudson, in Beverley Manor, conveyed to John, Jr., by his father, John and Mary, 19th November, 1773. Teste: Patrick Buchanan, Philip ( ) Saylor, Andrew Scot.

Page 106.—Jean Buchanan, wife of Robert Buchanan, deceased, relinquishes her right of dower in 260 acres in Beverley Manor, joining Patrick Buchanan's land, to Philip Saylor, as by his bargain of sale more fully appears, 4th September, 1779. Teste: Elijah McClenachan, James Buchanan, John Marshall, Walter Dunn, William Rodgers.

Page 106.—21st September, 1779. John Cunningham and Jean to Jacob Folowider. Delivered: John Folewider, 12th March, 1782.

Page 108.—On Cowpasture, patented to John Poage, 27th August, 1770.

Page 109.—21st September, 1779. Grace ( ) Shaw, widow of Robert Shaw, deceased. Receipt to John Woods and release of dower to Joseph Redmond.

Page 112.—185 acres in Beverley Manor devised to James Gibson by his father, Robert Gibson.

Page 113.—21st September, 1779. Isabella ( )Gibson to Philip Dold. Release of dower to above as widow of Robert and mother of James.

Page 120.—16th November, 1779. Andrew Donarly, of Botetourt, and Jane, to Leonard Bell, 150 acres by patent dated 3d November, 1750. Teste: Hugh Hicklin, Ralph ( ) Laferty, Robert Stuart, John ( ) McCaselon.

Page 123.—19th October, 1779. Patrick Hays, brother of Hugh Hays, deceased, late of Lancaster County, Pennsylvania, to James Buchanan, all his interest in estate of Hugh, deceased, in Pennsylvania, or of his daughter Margaret (deceased ?).

Page 124.—19th October, 1779. Hugh Hays, of Augusta, son of Patrick Hays and nephew of Hugh Hays, late of Lancaster County, Pennsylvania, deceased, to James Buchanan. Similar to above.

Page 126.—16th November, 1779. James ( ) Bell to John Bell, in Beverley Manor, on South River of Shanando, part of plantation that he now lives on.

Page 132.—16th November, 1779. John McMahon and Deborah ( ) to Jno. Harper. Patented to Robert McMahon, 12th May, 1759, whereon said Harper now lives.

Page 136.—On Bullpasture, tract known as Burdey house.

Page 138.—17th September, 1779. William ( ) Jordan, Jr., and Mary to John Kingin. Delivered to Jno. Redmon, November Court, 1781, patented to David Bell and by him conveyed to said William. Teste: Thomas Wright, Anthony Johnston, William ( ) Jordan, John Hinging, alias Kinging.

Page 144.—Teste: Hugh Tarbet, Robert and David Doak.

Page 145.—Tract whereon Thomas Kennerley now lives. Delivered: William Kennerley, 19th October, 1784.

Page 147.—Patent to Thomas Turk, 19th May, 1757, corner the Loril Swamp.

Page 152.—16th November, 1779. David Hays' executors to Robert McChestney.

Page 154.—Part of the plantation David Henderson now lives on.

Page 157.—13th September, 1779. John Montgomery and Esther ( ) to James Montgomery. Delivered: Thomas Love, June, 1780.

Page 159.—21st October, 1779. Joseph Gregory, eldest brother and heir-at-law of William Gregory, deceased, of Monengehalia, and Ann, to Samuel Gregory, tract known as Sugar Tree Bottom, on Back Creek of James River, conveyed by William Lewis to William Gregory, deceased, 17th November, 1772. Teste: Elijah Poage.

Page 164.—Teste: William Youl, Thomas ( ) Hinds.

Page 168.—15th February, 1780. William Wallace and Agness to John Ritchey, tract whereon he now lives in Beverley Manor, part of 750 acres conveyed by Beverley to Robert King, 25th March, 1742.

Page 170.—18th September, 1779. Henry McDonald and Martha, Francis McDonald and Margaret, Hugh Martin and Mary, John and James McDonald, to William Allen, in Beverely Manor on Christian's Creek. Teste: John Graham, James Brattain, Adam and John Bratton, James Fulton.

Page 172.—17th September, 1779. Part of 380 acres patented to Robert Brown, 10th June, 1740, and by him conveyed to James Trotter, and thence to said Samuel Trotter. Teste: John Lowry, William Campble, William Henderson, John ( ) Meglamery.

Page 176.—Part of the tract in Beverley Manor whereon Elijah McClenachan lives.

Page 178.—Along Ager's line. Teste: Ralph Loftus, David ( ) Gawin, Isaac ( ) Gawin.

Page 180.—22d November, 1779. Henry Ewing, of Rockingham, and Jane ( ) to Samuel Redmond, part of patent to John Poage. Delivered: John Redmon, November Court, 1781.

Page 182.—21st March, 1780. Jacob Trace, of Hampshire, to Bastain Stone, on head of South Branch of Potomac, patented to said Jacob, 5th July, 1774. Teste: James Dyer, Henry Flersher.

Page 186.—Teste: John Bosang, George Craige, Christopher Faber.

Page 187.—Part of 144 acres patented to Alex. Craige, 10th March, 1756.

Page 191.—29th November, 1779. William Preston and Susanna, of Montgomery, to Peter Hanger.

Page 196.—18th March, 1780. Michael Carn (Kearn) and Catherine (Caty) ( ) to Thomas Turk. Delivered: John Byers, 1780.

Page 200.—Teste: Wm. Gibson, Alex. Reid.

Page 200.—14th March, 1780. James Graham and Florence, of Green Brier, to John Kelly. Delivered: James Peerey by written order, 24th October, 1789.

Page 201.—21st March, 1780. Cornelius Ruddell (Riddle) and Ingabo ( ) to William Grahams, touching Davison's Branch. Delivered to Peter Sciler, 1780.

Page 204.—Part of 460 acres patented to Andrew McComb, 20th July, 1768.

Page 206.—9th September, 1778. Adam ( ) Reaburn, of Monongalia County, to Andrew and William McComb, power of attorney to convey to Robert Mathews.

Page 207.—21st March, 1780. Adam Reaburn (by Andrew McComb), of Westmoreland County, to William Mathews.

Page 213.—Teste: George Hudson, David Greiner.

Page 215.—21st March, 1780. John Davidson and Mary ( ) to William Craig. Delivered to Jos. Craig, 25th April, 1786.

Page 217.—3d February, 1780. Thomas Tate and Ann to Benj. Estill. Delivered to Wallam Estill, attorney in fact for the heir-at-law for this land, 17th February, 1790.

Page 220.—Teste: John Wright, James Potter, Robert McKittrick.

Page 223.—21st March, 1780. William Lewis and Ann to Cap. Thomas Smith, tract whereon William now lives.

Page 231.—18th February, 1780. Patrick McDavid and Martha to John Handley and Gasper Snider, two-thirds of house and half lot in Staunton where Patrick now dwells.

Page 234.—Part of the plantation Thomas Brown now lives on.

Page 236.—Daniel McNare's land where he now lives.

Page 241.—16th May, 1780. James Gamble and Agness to their son Robert Gamble.

Page 247.—On Middle River where John Brown, deceased, formerly lived, and willed to Hugh Brown by his father, John Brown.

Page 248.—20th November, 1779. Thomas Brown, son and heir of John Brown, to Hugh Brown.

Page 250.—24th April, 1780. Robert Armstrong and Jane to Benjamin Tolman, 145 acres patented to Robert, 12th May, 1759, corner James Kerk; 240 acres patented to Robert 8th July, 1752. Teste: John and Alex. Kirk, Casper Ekert.

Page 253.—11th April, 1780. Hugh Hicklin and Elizabeth to Charles Errowin. patented to Hugh, 14th July, 1769.

Page 256.—18th August, 1780. Commission of Augusta County to Hugh McDowell merchant of Staunton. Andrew Greer's share of lots in Staunton purchased by him and James Hughes, James Huston and George Wilson, which Greer gave up, being unable to pay for it; lot in possesion of John David Greiner.

Page 258.—Patent to James Bell, deceased, 1st December, 1740.

Page 260.—Patent to Robert Stevenson, deceased, 16th August, 1756.

Page 262.—235 acres patented to William Hamilton, 29th May, 1760, corner Charles Yarhass. Teste: Alex. Reed, David Gibson.

Page 268.—Tract conveyed to James Young, deceased, by William Beverley, 28th February, 1749, and descended to James Young, eldest son and heir.

Page 269.—Patent to John Bumbordner, 25th September, 1746, on head spring of Honey Lick Branch. **Patented to Patrick Frazer, 12th May, 1770.** Delivered: Hugh McCawley, 29th September, 1792.

Page 275.—27th March, 1780. Privy examination of Elizabeth, wife of Jacob Histent, of Shannando County, deed to Paul Summers, 13th July, 1779, before Jacob Holeman, Richard Branham.

Page 280.—Teste: William Moare, Peter Alexander, Thomas Boyd.

Page 281.—20th September, 1779. Robert Weir and Rebecca to William Moare. Delivered to John Moore, heir-at-law of William, 29th November, 1806.

Page 282.—19th May, 1780. Martha ( ) Cowdon, late Martha Wilson, widow and executrix of Samuel Wilson, deceased, of Staunton, to Patrick McDavid, grants a lease of which Samuel was seised by deed, 3d November, 1752, lot No. 4, by the end of the bridge. Teste: Alex. Sinclair, Jacob ( ) Grass, Valentine Cloninger.

Page 286.—18th April, 1780. John Bigham (Bingham) and Jane, and Sarah Bigham, wife of John Bigham, deceased, to Thomas Scott. Delivered to William H. Scott, 27th January, 1802. The plantation in Beverley Manor John Bigham now lives on.

Page 288.—1st May, 1780. David Keer to William Gilkison, of Frederick County, part of tract that Andrew Cowan formerly lived on in Bveerley Manor, Dr. Jackson's line.

Page 297.—16th June, 1780. Anthony Litching (Litzey) and Susanna ( ) to Andrew Jaeger (Teager, Taeger), of Shanandoah County.

Page 302.—15th August, 1780. Barbara Nickall, Joseph Nickoll and Elizabeth, Isaac Nickoll and Margaret, of Greenbrier, to Andrew Nickoll, of Augusta, part of 400 acres patented to John Nickoll, deceased, 10th February, 1748.

Page 304.—18th July, 1780. James Kirkpatrick and Agness to John Sharpe, late of Chester County, Pennsylvania, plantation James lives on.

Page 307.—15th August, 1780. John Burger and Suckey, of Albemarle, to Claudius Buster, of Augusta.

Page 309.—22d July, 1780. Philip ( ) Saylor and Christian ( ) to John Wallace, of Lancaster County, Pennsylvania.

Page 314.—John Gray and Jeane, late Jeane Craige, administrators of John Craige, deceased, and William Gullet and Jeane ( ), late Jane Craige, only child and heiress of John Craige, deceased, of Greenbrier County, to Thomas Rodgers, in Beverley Manor, conveyed to John Craige, deceased, 20th March, 1754.

Page 316.—17th March, 1780. Mathew Pattison and Jane to Robert Pattison, brother of Mathew, conveyed to Nathan Pattison, father of Mathew and Robert, by Beverley, 24th July, 1740 (recorded in Orange), part of the tract was devised to Mathew and John, elder brother of Mathew, who died without rites stan (?) and his part descended to Mathews.

Page 324.—Teste: James Brownlee, James Trotter, Jr.

Page 325.—19th September, 1780. Edward Erwin (Irvine) and Mary, to Benj. Crow, of Rockingham, part of 400 acres patented to Alex. Brownlee, 12th June, 1749. Teste: James Gauy (Guy), Francis Mara, Robert ( ) Gregg.

Page 327.—17th October, 1780. Robert Gray and Margery ( ) to

William Coffey, of Amherst County, on South Mountain near Reid's Gap on Back Creek. Teste: Robert Stewart, David Horbison.

Page 329.—Part of the plantation Major John Brown formerly lived on. Thomas Brown to John Brown.

Page 331.—3d October, 1771. John Gillespy and his brother James Gilespy. Arbitration of land dispute under will of their father.

Page 334.—Old James Trotter's line. Teste: Andrew Kenneday, Jacob Cale.

Page 337.—20th November, 1780. Joshua Russell, son and heir of Andrew Russell, Sr., deceased, to Robert Russell. Teste: Samuel and James Frazer.

Page 339.—Part of 200 acres patented to Hugh Campbell, 25th September, 1746, and by him conveyed to William Alexander and descended to James Alexander as heir-at-law, corner John Alexander, Sr. Delivered: Mrs. Gibson, 9th August, 1784.

Page 341.—Patent to John Poage, 12th January, 1780.

Page 345.—13th August, 1780. William Wilson, of Sulivan County, North Carolina, to William Wilson, Jr., of Augusta, power of attorney Teste: William Armstrong, Samuel Wilson.

Page 354.—21st November, 1780. Casper Hoffman and Margaret ( ) to Robert Alexander. Delivered to James Alexander, 1st April, 1831.

Page 355.—17th November, 1780. Thomas Adams to Moore Fauntleroy, diverse good causes and considerations, especially 5 shillings, on Calfpasture, 235 acres patented to Thomas, 6th April, 1769.

Page 358.—Teste: William McDowell, Michael Bowyer, William Alexander, Samuel McDowel, James Reed, James McDowel.

Page 359.—Delivered: Charles Baskin, 7th May, 1782.

Page 363.—Patent to Joseph Reaburn, of Botetourt, 1st February, 1781, on a branch of Mossey Creek, called Pudding Spring.

Page 370.—7th April, 1781. James Kennerley, Sr., to his son William Kennerley. Delivered. Teste: Birnis Brown, Charles B. Hunter, Cornelius Maupin, Thos. Kennerley, Kitty Kennerley, James Kennerley, Jr.

Page 381.—On a branch of Middle River of Shanandoah, on side of the Bald Hill. Teste: James Laird, David and Samuel Gibson.

Page 387.—Patent to James Armstrong, 12th May, 1757. Patented to Robert Armstrong, deceased, and conveyed by him to his son James, 22d November, 1753.

Page 390.—21st August, 1780. Samuel McClure to John McClure, four tract in Beverley Manor, joining survey of Long Meadow, part of tract Andrew McClure now lives on, tract known as the Strawberry Bottom.

Page 400.—21st August, 1781. George Gibson and Elizabeth, of Washington County, to James and Francis Best.

Page 410.—Tract first granted to William Sharp.

Page 412.—Delivered: Dr. Hugh Richie, 12th March, 1782.

Page 414.—Patent to Barbara Smith, 1st March, 1773.

Page 416.—Delivered to John Graham, January, 1783.

Page 422.—20th March, 1781. Martha ( ) Gay, widow of Henry Gay, of Rockbridge, to Andrew Moody.

Page 424.—Teste: James Sawyers, Samuel McCutchon, Jacob Patton.

Page 430.—20th March, 1781. Robert Risk, son and heir of John Risk, deceased, and Margaret Risk ( ), widow and executrix of John, deceased, to Robert Shields. Patented to John Risk, 1st March, 1773, on Smith's Creek, a branch of Little River of Calfpasture.

Page 432.—22d March, 1782. Catharine ( ) Carpenter, relict of Nicholas Carpenter, to Michael Bowyer, release of dower in 950 acres in Greenbrier County.

Page 432.—22d May, 1782. Enos Atwater and Annahellena to Moses Early, William Crawford, John Beach, one-half acre in Staunton whereon Enos now lives, formerly occupied by Wm. Gilham and Thomas Smith, fronting the house and lot of the late Rodger North, deceased, conveyed to Enos by Gilham.

Page 435.—Tract devised by James Gillespy to John Gillespy, his son, and by him conveyed to Christopher Graham; John, brother of William Gillespy.

Page 436.—15th May, 1781. John ( ) Anderson to his son James Anderson, tract conveyed by Beverley to John, 15th March, 1739; also 135 acres patented to John, on Middle River of Shanandore.

Page 437.—On head drafts of the Falling Springs, adjoining lines with William Lewis, Lodwick Moura and Eness Jones. Patented to George King, 16th March, 1771.

Page 440.—Patent to William Sharpe.

Page 441.—8th February, 1781. Robert Armstrong and Daniel Friel, executors of John Jameson, to Moses Hays. Teste: Wm. McPheeters, Wililam Allen, Wm. Handly, James Cunningham.

Page 442.—Delivered: William Kenady, son of James Kenady, 6th February, 1786.

Page 443.—Teste: Walter Davis, John Caldwell, John Brooks.

Page 444.—Teste: Daniel Ray, Jonathan Brooks.

Page 446.—Teste: John Jordon, Thomas Douglass, George Benston, David ( ) Frame, John McCreerey.

Page 448.—21st May, 1782. Claudius Bustard and Dorcas to James Hays and Braxton Easthum, on Blue Ridge Mountains in Augusta and Amherst, known as Rockfish Gap, patented to William Rodgers and John Burger.

Page 449.—Patent to William Thompson, 20th August, 1748. Patented to Samuel Hinds, 14th February, 1761.

Page 456.—16th April, 1782. John Waddle (Signed in German and apparently some other name—Null ?) and Mary ( ) Waddle, to the Cnogregation adhering to Bethel Meeting House, part of the tract John now lives on, on waters of Christian's Creek. Delivered: Robert Doack, one of the grantees.

Page 456.—Patent to Frederick Stull, 27th August, 1770.

Page 464.—Teste: John and Andrew Ramsey, Henry Luse.

Page 465.—Delivered: Frederick Hanger by order of James Peerey.

Page 466.—15th October, 1782. William Grahames and Ann (signed William Grames, Ann Grahames).

Page 471.—Patent to David Bell, deceased, 16th March, 1771, corner land now in possession of James Mathinearly.

Page 474.—Part of tract Robert Allen, Sr., now lives on.

Page 475.—Patent to William Jordan, Sr., 1st March, 1773, and by him conveyed to Anthony Johnston. Delivered to John Erwin by order of Wm. Jordan, 26th June, 1794.

Page 477.—19th August, 1782. William Thompson and Mary, heir-at-law of Thomas Thompson, deceased, to James Sloane. Teste: John Lewis, Alex. Crawford, Samuel McDanual. Patented to Thomas, 1st June, 1750.

Page 482.—20th August, 1782. William Thompson, son and heir-at-law of Thomas Thompson, deceased, and Mary, to Samuel McDonald. Teste: John Cowardin.

Page 485.—13th August, 1781. James Brooks, executor of Samuel Woods, deceased, of Albemarle, to Moses Hays. Delivered: Hugh Richey by order of Moses Hays.

Page 486.—20th August, 1782. Robert Callwell to Robert Black, of Bartley County. Elizabeth Caldwell, widdow of Samuel Caldwell, deceased, relinquished dower, conveyed to Robert by John Caldwell.

Page 488.—20th August, 1782. John McClenachan's executors to John Berry. Patented to Robert Allen.

Page 492.—Tract devised by John Jackson to his son William.

Page 499.—On Jackson's River, patented to Mathew Patton, 7th September, 1774.

Page 501.—Tract surveyed for Robert Finley, 22d January, 1753.

Page 503.—22d January, 1782. Robert Shields, eldest brother and heir-at-law of John Shields, deceased, of Botetourt, to William Shields.

Page 507.—19th February, 1782. William Christian, heir-at-law of John Christian, deceased, and Robert Christian Jr. (?), Sr. (?), to John, Gilbert and Robert Christian, Jr., brothers of William. Teste: Joseph Ray, Wm. ( ) Williams, Patrick ( ) McGonagle.

Page 509.—15th June, 1782. William ( ) Ledgerwood to his daughters Martha Patterson and Jean Moffett, gift of negroes. Teste: James and Elizabeth Moffett.

Page 511.—Delivered to Thomas Rutlidge by order from Mr. Buster, 16th July, 1787. Teste: John Brooks, Jr., George Marshall, Charles Hunt.

Page 513.—Patent to Edmond Berton, 12th January, 1780.

Page 516.—Teste: Andrew Alexander, Andrew Alexander, Jno. Hamilton.

Page 519.—Patent to Alex. Brownlee, 20th June, 1749, on north side of the southermost branch of the North River. Delivered: Robert and Samuel Gragg.

Page 522.—Ralph Willson and Margaret to Joseph Bell, 62 acres by survey, 19th February, 1768, patented 1st June, 1782, between Straight Forks of Pawtomack and the Crabb Runs.

Page 524.—19th November, 1782. John Black, son and heir-at-law of Samuel Black, deceased, to Joseph Bell, 97 acres on head springs of the Straight Fork of Jackson's River, patented to said Samuel, 7th December, 1774.

Page 527.—15th November, 1781. John Hemphill, of Baltimore County, Maryland, to Edmond Burton. Patented to said John, 12th January, 1780. Teste: James Anderson, John and Robert Campbell, Robert Connely.

Page 529.—Delivered: Samuel Bell, 20th August, 1785, part of land belonging to Philip Harless, deceased.

Page 532.—15th July, 1782. William Hinds, heir-at-law of John Hind, deceased, to John and William Dickey. Teste: Michael and James Dickey.

Page 539.—Teste: Shem Thompson, Andrew Hamilton, Ad. Smythe, John Linsey.

Page 540.—Teste: Isabella Lockhart, Elisabeth Smith.
Page 547.—Teste: Will Hamilton, James Culbertson, James Buchanan, Hugh Brown, Jno. Lewis.
Last deed recorded, 19th August, 1783.

DEED BOOK NO. 24.

First deed recorded, 21st September, 1784.
The dates of record are very irregular in this book.
Page 7.—232 acres patented to William Thompson, 1st June, 1741.
Page 10.—18th March, 1783. Benjamin Bennett, of Rockbridge, son and heir-at-law of Richard Bennett, deceased, to Rev. Archibald Scott, 245 acres gained by Benjamin from Beverley by a suit in chancery in 1780 in Augusta County Court, being the plantation where Wm. McKnab and Jacob Gabert formerly lived.
Page 12.—Plantaion in Beverley Manor on Christian's Creek, where Jacob Grass lived.
Page 14.—Part of tract on Jacksons River, patented William Jackson, deceased. Teste: John Dean, Richard Elliote, James McLean.
Page 32.—20th March, 1783. Privy examination of Jane, wife of Robert Armstrong, late of Augusta, deed to Benj. Tolman, before William Renick, Wm. Ward, justices of Greenbrier.
Page 35.—Teste: Samuel McKee, John Richey, Robert Connly, John Huddle, Daniel Joseph.
Page 42.—Patent to William Hogshead, deceased, 16th August, 1756, and conveyed to Charles Stuart by David Hogshead, heir-at-law to said William.
Page 45.—3d May, 1783. Jeremiah Frame, son and heir-at-law of William Frame, deceased, to Thomas Graham. Delivered: James Graham, son of Thomas, 14th April, 1787.
Page 48.—18th March, 1783. William Foster, Sr., to William Foster, Jr., 250 acres on South River, part of 500 acres conveyed to William, Sr., by Joseph Poindexter and Elizabeth, in the General Court. Delivered: Samuel Bell, 10th August, 1786.
Page 52.—22d April, 1783. Robert Sayers, of Montgomery County, son and heir to Robert Sawyers, deceased, to John Ramsey.
Page 55.—20th May, 1783. William Hinds and Ann ,of Rockingham, to Thomas Garvin. William conveys as heir-at-law of William Hinds, Sr.
Page 59.—Survey dated 12th November, 1773. Patent dated 1st February, 1781.
Page 62.—100 acres patented to William Jackson, 1st June, 1750, part of 1100 acres.
Page 71.—Teste: William Lane, Joseph Bell.
Page 74.—Two patents to Edward Erwin, Sr., father of Edward Erwin, Jr., 5th April, 1748, and March, 1747. Patent to Edward Erwin, Jr., 12th May, 1770. Teste: Chas. Cameron, Thos. Hughart.
Page 80.—Patent to Bryan Kenney, 1st February, 1781.
Page 86.—Patent to Samuel Turk, 7th August, 1761, on South River.
Page 90.—Patent to Mark Swadley, deceased, 14th July, 1769, and descended to Henry Swadley, of Rockingham, as son and heir, on a branch

of Black Thorn, called Winter Spring, at a place called the Lower Meadows.

Page 94.—Patent to Benj. Tolman, of Rockingham, 11th August, 1783.

Page 99.—Patent to John Young, 20th July, 1768, in Crab Bottom.

Page 104.—19th August, 1783. George Coager (Cowgar), of Hampshire, and Hannah Waaz (Haaz), tract conveyed by Peters Haaz (Waaz) to said Hannah, 16th August, 1768.

Page 113.—20th August, 1783. Lewis and William Usher and Mary, to Thomas Dorset. Delivered to Charles Yearout per order, 4th March, 1786.

Page 117.—400 acres patented to John Nickoll, deceased, 10th February, 1748, and devised by his will.

Page 120.—Teste: John Allison, William Robertson, Sr., Robert Kenney, James Kerr, George Givens.

Page 124.—18th August, 1783. James Thompson and William Thompson to Rev. James Waddell, Spring Hill tract devised to William Thompson, his son-in-law, by James Patton. William Thompson's wife Mary, died soon after her father.

Page 134.—Teste: John and Hugh Cunningham, Thomas Read, James Mitchell.

Page 144.—Patent to Henry Dooling, 30th January, 1741, and by him conveyed to Christian Clemons (now deceased), now invested in Jasper Clemons as heir-at-law. Patented to Christian Clemons, 16th March, 1771. Teste: Jno. McCune.

Page 147.—375 acres patented to John Young in Crab Apple Bottom.

Page 154.—Patent to Edward Erwin, Jr., 12th May, 1770. Delivered: John Erwin, 1st March, 1793. Teste:Francis Erwin, Sr., and Jr., Edward and Samuel Erwin.

Page 158.—Patent to John Brownlee, 20th June, 1749. Teste: Francis Erwin, Francis Erwin, Sr., John Erwin, Samuel Erwin, Sr., Samuel Erwin.

Page 165.—Patent to Samuel Hind.

Page 170.—21st June, 1783. Privy examination of Margaret, wife of John Brown, deed to George Gall, 16th December, 1777. Before Andrew Moore and Charles Campbell.

Page 175.—18th November, 1783. Sampson and George Mathews to John Brock, 100 acres in Beverley Manor on Lewis' Draft of Christian's Creek, part of the plantation purchased for the poor of Augusta Parish. Delivered: John Thomas, 8th October, 1785.

Page 182.—2d November, 1782. William Buchanan, of Augusta, Robert Buchanan and Margaret, of Montgomery, George Buchanan and Margaraet, of Washington, to David Buchanan, of Augusta. James Buchanan, father of grantors, died seised of a tract on Walker's Creek, 415 acres, and devised same to the grantors and grantee. Teste: James Weir, William Walker, Joseph Wear.

Page 185.—16th March, 1784. James Brown, son of John Brown, deceased, to Hugh and John Brown. John died seised of 210 acres in Beverley Manor, and devised same to be sold, corner to graveyard of John Breckinridge, who was murdered by the Indians; corner tract purchased of William Null. Teste: James Curry.

Page 187.—10th November, 1783. John Lewis, surviving partner of John McClenachan, deceased, and Margaret, to John McClenachan, eldest son and heir-at-law of said John, deceased, ½ of 1000 acres patented to Lewis and McClenachan 1st November, 1783, in Monongahalia County on Glady Creek at Pringle's ford, a branch of the Monogahalia River, the 1000 acres being part of 3,000 acres surveyed; Charles Scott 6th April, 1774, by virtue of a military warrant and assigned to Lewis and McClenachan. Delivered.

Page 191.—16th September, 1783. John Black, son and heir-at-law of Samuel Black, deceased, to John Black, plantation that David Black, deceased, live on in Beverley Manor. Teste: Alexander Williams, Walter Dunn.

Page 200.—Patent to William Anderson 1st March, 1781. Teste: Samuel, Andrew and James Anderson.

Page 208.—10th May, 1784. David Russell and Margaret, of Washington County, N. C., to Robert Leister, tract David formerly lived on in Borden's tract; corner Robert Mason. Teste: John McKenny, Robert Harris, Andrew Wilson.

Page 213.—16th March, 1784. Robert Thompson and Nancy, of Sullivan County, N. C., to Robert Harris. Teste: William and Mathew Wallace, James Harris.

Page 216.—26th April, 1784. Deposition of above witnesses before William Wallace, Samuel Smith, Thomas Sharpe, Jr., Justices in Sullivan County, North Carolina.

Page 218.—Plantation David Black, deceased, lived on.

Page 220.—18th May, 1784. John Waddel and Mary ( ) to Christian Bomgardner and Lewis Celamous (Childmour). Delivered: Jacob Bumgardner, 1st October, 1790.

Page 222.—18th May, 1784. John Cowman of first part, and 8½ acres of land for a church or Presbyterian Meeting House or school house in the county aforesaid and the congregation thereto belonging of the other part, part of the plantation where John now lives in Beverley Manor.

Page 228.—20th ———, 1784. Privy examination of Catharine, wife of James Thompson, deed to Rev. James Waddel 8th September, 1783, before Arthur Campbell and Aaron Lewis, of Washington County. Delivered: Wm. Kenedy 28th October, 1789.

Page 231.—On the Falling Spring, a branch of Middle River of Shanandore.

Page 234.—In a bend of Middle River of Shanandore in Beverley Manor conveyed to William Dunlap by his elder brother, John Dunlap, heir-at-law of their father, William Dunlap.

Page 241.—Delivered: Henry Hawpe, 6th August, 1785.

Page 244.—14th June, 1784. Robert McCutchan and Margaret to their son, William McCutchan. Delivered to John McCutchan, 20th July, 1787, tract surveyed by Beverley 11th November, 1746, to Robert; side of the Black Oak Hill.

Page 251.—18th May, 1784. Hugh Campbell and Margaret to Caspar Miller. Delivered to Jno. Dicky, 7th March, 1786, part of tract of 150 acres first surveyed for John Searight 2d September, 1767.

Page 254.—15th June, 1784. Daniel Joseph and Eve to John Bance. Delivered: Jno. Allison per order 19th August, 1793.

Page 265.—Patented to ———, by inclusive patent, 12th August, 1783.

Page 269.—20th July, 1784. Edward Erwin, Sr., grandson and heir-at-law of Edward Erwin, deceased, and Elizabeth, to Francis Erwin, on Long Glade patented to Edward Erwin, deceased, 12th May, 1770.

Page 281.—22d June, 1784. William Powell Riddle to Jacob Peck, power of attorney to prosecute a suit in General Court against James and Lewis Riddle, of Orange County, executor of William Riddle, deceased, for his part of said estate; also a negro that I left with my father, and all estate left by me or my father to me in Orange County.

Page 284.—6th July, 1784. John Huston, of Rockbridge, to James Rowan; James Rowan now in possession by L. and R. from Mathew Huston and Martha and descended to John as eldest son and heir of Robert Huston, deceased, who was eldest son and heir of John Huston, deceased, claims the revision after death of Mathew Huston.

Page 295.—17th August, 1784. Robert Leister and Sarah to Abraham Bellow. Teste: John McKemey, Robert McGwillan, William Anderson. William Morrow, Robert Cooper, Robert Cooper.

Page 298.—7th August, 1784. Robert Christian, Sr., and William Christian, son and heir-at-law of John Christian, deceased, to Gilbert Christian, son to William Christian, deceased, 299 acres whereon William Christian, deceased, lived. Teste: John Christian, G. Christian, Jr., Benjamin Richards.

Page 300.—Part of 200 acres patented to Hugh Campbell 25th September, 1746, and by him conveyed to William Alexander and became the property of said James Alexander, heir-at-law, and by him said James conveyed to his brother, John.

Page 306.—Tract conveyed by McCutchan to James Shields 21st August, 1746, and descended to John Shields, eldest son and heir of James; second tract conveyed to said John Shields as son and heir of James by Benjamin Borden 20th August, 1752.

Page 310.—5th June, 1784. Edward and Sarah Rutledge to their son, James Rutledge, £———, love, good will and affection; tract known as the Black Oak Spring.

Page 312.—6th July, 1784. William Haddin, of Fayette County, Va., to David Haddin, power attorney to convey to John Woneck 186 acres in Monongehala County. Teste: William McConnell, James Gay, Alexander Dunlap.

Page 313.—17th March, 1784. John Skidmore and Mary, his wife, and Sarah Smith, relict of Abraham Smith, deceased, and John Smith, heir-at-law of Abraham, all of Rockingham County, to John Gumm. Delivered: Peter Hull, by order 1st April, 1795. Abraham had made exchange with John Gumm and title was made to William Smith, recorded in Rockingham. Patent was issued in name of Smith and Skidmore. Smith purchased Skidmore's interest, title was made to him for the whole, but not recorded in time Skidmore signs this deed. Patent dated 10th June, 1780.

Page 317.—17th August, 1784. David Kinkead to Joseph Guin, David's shore of two tracts devised by Mathew Kinkead to his two sons, David and John, when they should arrive at 21 years.

Page 320.—10th July, 1784. Elesibeth ( ) Kinkead to David Kinkead, of Fayette County, Ky., to sign her name to above deed. Teste: John Tode, John Kinkead, John Wallace.

Page 323.—18th August, 1784. William Hinds, grandson and heir-at-law of William Hinds, deceased, to Joseph Moore, part of 295 acres patented to William Hinds, Sr. Teste: John Allison and Thomas Caul.

Page 327.—17th August, 1784. Robert Clarke and Agness to James Scott, late of the County of Lancaster, Penna. Delivered to William Scott, son of James, 2d February, 1789, 86 acres patented to Robert 16th February, 1771, near James Clark's old plantation, between Beverley Manor line and North Mountain.

Page 331.—17th August, 1784. Same to same, tract conveyed by Beverley to James Clarke 15th May, 1746, on head branch of Middle River of Shanandoa and Back Creek, a branch of Middle River.

Page 336.—4th July, 1784. Arthur Campbell, surviving executor of Margaret Campbell, who was sole executrix of Charles Campbell, deceased, to Rudolph Hawpe, 100 acres patented to Rudolph Hawpe, 100 acres patented to Charles Campbell 5th March, 1747; corner land Hugh Torbet lives on.

Page 341.—Patent to William Curry 1st September, 1780, on Mossey Creek, at a place called White Stone.

Page 344.—10th August, 1784. Mathew Penn and Catherine to Isaac Johns, 250 acres patented to Mathew Penn 18th February, 1783, on Shaw's Fork of Cowpasture. Delivered: Wm. Johns, executor of Isaac, 28th December, 1797.

Page 352.—18th August, 1784. Isaiah Vansant and Margaret, of Botetourt, to Zechariah Johnston. Thos. Thompson, son and heir of John Thompson, deceased, conveyed 200 acres to his brother, Robert, and 213 to his brother, James, but not to his heirs, who sold to Z. Johnston, but the title being faulty, title became invested by descent in said Margaret, daughter and only heir of Thomas Thompson.

Page 355.—On north side of the Indian Road.

Page 362.—Part of a tract whereon Wm. McClintock lives.

Page 363.—16th August, 1784. Jane Dnulap releases dower to Robert Keuny in tract sold to Robert by her son, William Dunlap.

Page 368.—Thomas Hughart and James Hughart and Margaret to Nathan Crawford, tract patented to James Hughart, Sr., 10th April, 1751, and devised to Thomas and James, his youngest son; corner John Cartmill. Teste: Andrew Sitlington, John Dean, Hugh Brown.

Page 373.—12th October, 1784. James Dobbins (Daubin) and Elizabeth, of District of Ninety-Six, South Carolina, to Jacob Shultz.

Page 378.—Patent to John Brownlee, November, 1752. Teste: Joseph Waddell, James Waddall, Joseph Waddall, John Stevenson.

Page 383.—25th October, 1784. Jane McCoy, of Greenbrier, widow and sole executrix of James McCoy, to Andrew and Charles Donnerley, patented 10th August, 1759, to said James on Stewart's Creek. Teste: Hugh Brown, Andrew Sitlington, Nathan Crawford.

Page 390.—Teste: William Willson. Robert Donaldson, Rboert Willson

Page 393.—Patent to Walter Trimble and by him conveyed to his son, Robert Trimble. Teste: James, William and John McKenney.

Page 401.—18th October, 1784. John Miller and Martha, of the Cowpasture, to William Randolph, eldest son and heir-at-law and residuary legatee of Peyton Randolph, late of Wilton, in Henrico County.

Page 403.—16th November, 1784. Janet and Rachel Wallace, of Washington County, to Benjamin Brown. Teste: Wm. Bell.

Page 409.—Patent 1st June, 1782, to Nicholas Seybert on Straight Creek of South Branch of Potomac.

Page 412.—Patent to John Spear 10th September, 1755, on waters of Middle River, bequeathed by John to his children and sold by the trustees of said estate to Hugh Brown 19th May, 1779.

Page 419.—Patent to Edward Erwin, Sr., 12th May, 1770, on Long Glade.

Page 421.—Patent to Jacob Peck 1st March, 1781, on a branch of Middle River.

Page 428.—21st December, 1783. Robert Rodgers and Elizabeth to Paulser Teverbaugh, part of 54 acres in Beverley Manor first conveyed to George Rodgers, deceased.

Page 431.—Tract willed by Valentine Cloninger to Nicholas Spring; corner Philip Rogal.

Page 433.—18th January, 1785. John Oliver and Sarah ( ) to James Oliver, his son, tract on Naked Creek where said Oliver now lives.

Page 436.—14th August, 1784. John ( ) Davis and Elizabeth ( ) to Ozburn Hamilton. Delivered: William Poage, of Bath, per order 3d April, 1807.

Page 440.—June, 1784. Moses Hays to Henry Miller. Delivered to James McCann, clerk for Mr. Miller, 5th November, 1789. Teste: Samuel Forsythe, John Gossom.

Page 446.—25th August, 1784. Immanuel ( ) Harless, of Montgomery County, to William Beard. Delivered to Isaac Darnell by a written order from William Beard and commission of privy examination 22d November, 1788, 40 acres patented to Archibald Hamilton and was finally conveyed to Philip Harless, deceased, 400 acres patented to Philip 27th August, 1770, and devised to Immanuel by Philip, his father.

Page 450.—16th November, 1784. William Burk, son and heir of William Burk, to Andrew Scott. Teste: James Curry.

Page 455.—(See certificate of Jno. Poage, surveyor to Mr. William Young, 15th July, 1784. This belongs to the following deed.) Your brother, John Young, deceased. 16th November, 1784—James Young and Mary to William Young, £———, natural love and affection. See accompanying plat of Isaac Corsons and Samuel Curry's parts of same tract.

Page 457.—Branch of Mossey Creek called Pudding Spring. Patent.

Page 460.—26th September, 1784. Privy examination of Sarah Caldwell, wife of John Caldwell, deed to Robert Black dated ———, before Gabriel Madison and George Adams. "Lincoln Lct," Lincoln County?

Last deed recorded November 15, 1785.

Deed Book No. 25.

First Deed Recorded 15th March, 1785; Last Deed Recorded 17th July, 1787.

Page 3.—295 acres patented to William Hind, to Jacob Laslea. Delivered to Jacob Leslea.

Page 6.—Test: Joseph Poythress, William Banks, John Cowordin, Andrew Donnally, Samuel Vance.

Page 7.—15th March, 1785. James Clark, son and heir-at-law of William Clark, deceased, to James Clark, Sr. Delivered: James McChesney, order, December 2, 1793, plantation William Clark, deceased, lived on on Moffet's Creek.

Page 9.—17th March, 1785. Thomas Hughes to Michael Bowyer to secure George Divers, of Albemarle.

Page 10.—Patent to William Trotter assignee of William Kerr, 1st October, 1783.

Page 13.—17th March, 1785. Moses Hays to John Bosang, power of attorney to recover tract in Orange County conveyed to Moses by George Leathers and sell same. Teste: Robert Renick, Peter Hume, Anthony Mustoe.

Page 14.—Teste: Robert McCullough.

Page 14.—11th June, 1782. Moses Estey and John Beach to William Crawford, grantors and grantee had purchased in partnership a lot and house in Staunton from Enos Attwaters. Grantors authorize grantee to sell as grantors are about to leave the State. Teste: Val. White, Thos. Smith, Enos Atwater.

Page 15.—Patent to Robert Turk on South River 6th September, 1736.

Page 28.—17th May, 1785. Thomas Edwards to James Griffith and John Gardner, on head drafts of Falling Spring. Teste: Samuel McConkey.

Page 32.—17th May, 1785. Daniel Joseph and Eve to George Hammer (Hamor), of Rockingham, tract patented to Jacob Darir 3d May, 1780, on drafts of Moffet's Branch. Teste: Moses Moore, John Johnston.

Page 36.—George Leedekey's line.

Page 43.—26th April, 1785. James Rucker and Mary to Leonard Rucker, power attorney to convey tract to Mathew Penn and a tract to William Horschings (Houchings), of Amherst County.

Page 50.—17th May, 1785. John ( ) Fudge and Christian ( ) to Joseph Bell. Teste: Joseph Bell.

Page 52.—17th May, 1785. James Rusk, Jr., to Samuel Craig, 200 acres formerly the property of James Rusk, Sr., deceased, James Rusk, Jr., being his lawful and full proper heir, on Calfpasture, at foot of the Brown Hill.

Page 58.—18th April, 1785. Robert McCutchen and Margaret to James Blayr. Delivered to John Blair 23d June, 1787.

Page 65.—17th May, 1785. Frederick Burkett and Dorothy to Samuel McKee. Delivered: David McKee (son of Samuel), 14th April, 1788. Patented to Frederick 1st February, 1781.

Page 68.—18th May, 1785. John McKnight (signed McNutt), of Rockbridge, to Thomas Smith, lot in Staunton.

Page 73.—Tract conveyed to James McLeery by his father, John McLeery, 12th March, 1755. Patent to James 27th May, 1783.

Page 77.—8th March, 1785. David Bells land whereon he lived. Division of by order of Court, with plat, according to his will—to William Bell, 240 acres; to David Bell, 174 acres; widow's dower assigned; field called Wetsal's.

Page 83.—17th May, 1785. Robert Gwinn, of Calfpasture, to his son, Joseph Given (this name is signed Given).

Page 84.—21st June, 1785. John Kinkead and Sarah and Agness Dean to John Brownlee, Jr., tract devised by John Wilson to his daughter, Sarah, now wife of John Kinkead.

Page 89.—11th March, 1785. John Taite, Sr., to Thomas Stevenson. Delivered to Jacob Swallow 1st June, 1787, 400 acres patented to said John Taite on Pine Run, a branch of South River near South Mountain. Teste: Samuel McConkey, Anthony Mustoe.

Page 92.—30th October, 1784. Hugh Brown and Rebekah and John Brown and Mary to Peter Hanger; corner John Breckenridge, who was murdered by the Indians.

Page 97.—Patented to William Preston on Great Calfpasture; patented to Andrew Kinkead; patented to Tully Davite 1st September, 1780.

Page 103.—Teste: John Gillespey, Samuel Gillespey, Wm. Connelly.

Page 106.—17th July, 1785. John Griffin to Martha Cowdon, filed in suit, Cowdon vs. Handly, 19th August, 1791. In 1775 John gave up to Martha his right to the house now occupied by her and Dennis Callahan, which he was entitled to in right of his wife, Elizabeth Griffin, and she gave up her right in lot 4 sold by John to Robert Reed.

Page 107.—25th June 1785. John Anderson to his son, Andrew Anderson. Delivered: Wm. Anderson, the present owner. 8th July, 1815.

Page 111.—Rebekah Black to Joseph Bell, £35 paid to Jones Henderson for a tract of 97 acres on head of Straight Fork of Jackson's river patented to Samuel Black 7th December, 1774, of which Samuel died seized, but Henderson has the right to dispose and has sold to Joseph and John Black, son and heir of Samuel, has already conveyed to Joseph.

Page 113.—31st March, 1785. Patrick Cunningham and Jane, of Wilks County, Georgia, to John and David Cunningham, power attorney to convey tract which belonged to Alexander Cunningham in his lifetime to James Ewing. Teste: Alexander McNutt, Wm. Hamilton, Med. Wood. Acknowledged before Wilks County Court 21st March, 1785, signed George Dalton, Chief Justice of Georgia. Attest: Benj. Catching, C. W. C.

Page 117.—26th March, 1785. Arthur Edwards and Jane ( ) to Thos. Gragg. Teste: Robert Gragg, Sr., John Hair, Robert Gragg, Jr.

Page 124.—15th August, 1785. Charles Hamilton and Margaret to Roger Hickman, 280 acres conveyed by Joseph Gregory to Arthur Hickman and by decease of Arthur descended to his son, William Hickman, heir-at-law, and by him conveyed to Charles.

Page 126.—4th July, 1785. William Hickman, son and heir of Arthur Hickman, of Montgomery County, Maryland, to Charles Hamilton, on West Fork of James River called Back Creek, tract conveyed by Davis to James Gregory, deceased, by whose death it became vested in Joseph Gregory as his heir. Teste: Roger Hickman, John ( ) Tousand, James Ellis.

Page 133.—4th July, 1785. Frederck Lipham, of Wilkes County, Georgia, to George Mathews, No. 18, in Staunton. Teste: Jas. Fontain, Jas. Grigsby, Thos. Merewether, Jno. Brown, John Gilmer, James ( ) Erwin.

Page 135.—Adjoining John Sharp, Jr.

Page 142.—9th March, 1785. Privy examination of Elizabeth, wife of John McLeery (deed to James Hawthorn, dated 21st September, 1784) before Wm. Montgomery and Gabriel Madison.

Page 145.—30th September (2d year of George III, 1761?).—Alexander McNutt, now at Hallifax, Nova Scotia, to John McNutt, of Augusta County, power of attorney to collect debts, &c. Teste: William Nesbett, John Binney. Acknowledged 30th March, 1761, before William Nisbett, Notary and Tabillion, now dwelling at Halifax. Delivered: Thos. Smith, 21st October, 1785.

Page 147.—16th August, 1785. Deed as above to Thomas Smith, lot 10 in Staunton. Delivered as above. Teste: John McElhenny.

Page 150.—Patent to David Frame 15th June, 1773.

Page 162.—27th August, 1785. Samuel Kinkead, son and heir-at-law of Samuel Kinkead, deceased, and Margaret, of Greenbrier, to Henry Eagle, of Barracks County, Penna.

Page 166.—Part of the plantation Joseph Teas, deceased, lived on and on which Robert Allen, Sr., now lives.

Page 168.—Corner Honeyman's land.

Page 171.—Tract on Cowpasture now in possession of Hugh Brown, land formerly John Cartmills.

Page 175.—10th October, 1785. John Kinkead and Margaret, of the Calfpasture, to Alexander Thompson, late of North Britain, now of Augusta County.

Page 178.—18th October, 1785. Reuben Kennerley to Archibald Boling, of Buckingham.

Page 181.—Patent to James Blayr, 17th May, 1784.

Page 183.—20th September, 1785. John Stuart and Frances, heir-at-law of William Stuart, deceased, to Archibald Dixon.

Page 185.—Teste Thomas Brown, Alex. Wiley, John Willey.

Page 187.—15th November, 1785. George Mathews and Anne to William McDowell, lot 18 in Staunton, originally conveyed by Beverley to Frederick Jacob Lepham and by Frederick, son and heir of Frederick Jacob, to George.

Page 200.—14th November, 1785. Robert Bailey to Anthony Mustoe. "Lie Bill."

Page 205.—18th October, 1785. Plat of Prison Bounds: 9 acres, 152 perches, John Abner's garden, crossing the Creek; Mr. St. Clair's Meadow; west end of Robert Reed's house; Joshua Perry's garden; John David Griner's garden; passing through the two doors of Robert Gray's house.

Page 206.—27th September, 1785. Salathiel Martin, son and heir of David Martin, deceased, of Rowan County, North Carolina, to John Dickenson. Delivered to Nathaniel Crawford by Dickinson's order. Release of mortgage.

Page 209.—23d April, 1785. Moses Easley, Crawford Black & Co., by Wm. Crawford, to Henry Miller, mortgage, lot whereon Peter Heiskell now lives, formerly occupied by Enos Atwater, by William Gilham and Thomas Smith, fronting the house of the late Roger North, deceased, and also 80 acres, as described in deed, Gibson to Atwater. Teste: Charles Cameron, Benj. Roberts, Geo. Mayberry.

Page 214.—Corner to Comber.

Page 216.—20th August, 1785. Thomas Murray, of Green County, North Carolina, to John Allison, Jr. Teste: D. Stephenson, Edward Rutledge, James Agnew, Thomas Carel.

Page 218.—To William Scott, of Lincoln County.

Page 224.—340 acres patented to Alex. Stuart, 16th February, 1771. Alex. Stuart and Mary, of Rockbridge, to Archibald Stuart. Teste: Robert Stuart, John, Andrew and James Fulton.

Page 227.—20th February, 1786. John Wright and Margaret to William Yool, of Rockbridge. Teste: Robert Campbell, Thos. Hughart, Alex. Wright.

Page 236.—21st February, 1786. Jacob Cale and Grissilla to Wm. Bryan, of Fauquier, 87 bbls. good common flour delivered at Fredericksburg. Mortgage.

Page 243.—Patent to David Stuart, 6th September, 1768.

Page 245.—9th January, 1786. Privy examination of Elizabeth, wife of Thomas Smith (deed, 18th August. 1785. to Peter Heiskell).

Page 252.—22d February, 1775. Patrick ( ) Dickson and Mary to Hugh Donaghe, tract patented to Patrick, 16th March, 1771, on Shanando. Teste: Ralph Loffius, Wm. Blair, Samuel Craige.

Page 262.—4th November, 1785. Elizabeth ( ) Hair, widow to John Hair, part of 400 acres patented to James Humphreys, 25th June, 1747. Teste: James McKemey, James Malcolm, John Alexander.

Page 267.—23d March, 1786. John Campbell, yeoman, to James Craig, yeoman, on Cathey's River on Sinking Spring Branch, the head of Little's Run where said Campbell now liveth. Mortgage. Teste: George Craig, James Eley.

Page 272.—22d March, 1786. John McDougall, of Augusta, to Henry Miller. Delivered: Samuel Miller, 15th March, 1805.

Page 273.—Teste: John Dickey, William Hind, William McPheeters.

Page 274.—22d March, 1786. Beverley to John Shields, son and heir to Thomas Shields, deceased.

Page 280.—Patent to David Hogshead, 1st June, 1782. Teste: Robert Gragg, John Davis, Jas. Hogshead.

Page 281.—Patent to John Cunningham, 12th May, 1759. Teste: Ralph Loftus, John and Christian Percy, John Stunkard to his son William Stunkard.

Page 284.—29th August, 1785. Job Gaskins, of Washington County, Samuel and Christian Carrall, of Augusta, to Robert Craig, tract patented, 6th February, 1784.

Page 286.—21st March, 1786. William Patterson, Sr., to his son William Patterson, Jr., tract patented to George Anderson, 20th January, 1741.

Page 287.—17th January, 1786. William Scott and Agness to William Scott, of Lincoln County.

Page 291.—July, 1750. Recorded. 20th June, 1786.

Page 295.—25th August, 1785. William Allen to John Handley (Henley). Delivered to William Handley, 9th August, 1793.

Page 300.—15th November. . Patrick Hays, of Lincoln County, Virginia. to John Greenlee, of Rockbridge County, power attorney to sell tract on Halfway Creek. Teste: Michael Coulter, Hugh Fulton.

Page 302.—21st February, 1786. McDonald to Andrew Scott. Teste: Andrew Scott, Sally Mathews, Margaret Dean.

Page 303.—Patented to Samuel Hind and by him conveyed to Gilbert Kerr (Karr, Carr).

Page 304.—Patented to William Hamilton ,— July, 1762.

Page 305.—Hanse Patton and Phebe ( ) to Jacob Patton, 10th March, 1786. Teste: Jno. McKemey, Samuel McCutchan, Jr., Hanah Martin (Mardin), Jesse Martin.

Page 309.—19th September, 1786. (Record very dim.) John Alexander and James Alexander and Rachel ( ) to John Long, £281, two tracts containing 200 acres, part of 400 acres granted to William Alexander, corner Wm. Alexander, Michael Dickey.

Page 310.—1st May, 1786. Sarah ( ), Jane ( ), and Agness ( ) Hutchenson, of Shenagreen, Parish Donogh Henry County of Tyrone, Ireland, daughters and devisees of Thomas Hutchinson, late of Tinkling Spring Congregation, near Virginia in America, deceased. Thomas by his will, devised all his goods and lands to his three daughters, and about August, 1784, they appointed Francis McFarland, then of Escragh, to receive the legacies and devises; now they appoint their friend and relation, John McFarland, now of Grange in Ireland, to settle with Francis McFarland. Deposition by Hugh Burns, aged 60 years, of Evaal, County Tyrone, at Stewartstown, Tyrone County, 1st May, 1786, that he was personally acquainted with Thomas who lived in Sherragrim and went from thence many years ago to America, and Sarah, Jane and Agness are his daughters, and he knows John Farland before mentioned to be son to said Sarah Hutcheson. Witnessed and proved by John Higgins.

Page 312.—19th September, 1786. James Henderson and Rebecca, and Martha Henderson, wife to James Henderson, deceased, of Fayette County, to Robert Usher.

Page 314.—31st July, 1786. Justices to Jenny Owens, late Jenny Hughes, daughter and co-heiress of James Hughes, deceased.

Page 315.—31st July, 1786. Same to Mary Bickle, late Mary Hughes, daughter and co-heiress of James Hughes, deceased.

Page 316.—31st July, 1786. Same to Euphemia Hughes, daughter and co-heiress of James Hughes, deceased.

Page 318.— — May, 1786. Samuel Williams and Sabina, his wife, daughter of David Stuart, deceased, and John Stuart, heir-at-law of David, of Greenbrier, to John Elliott. Teste: Lewis Myers, Christopher Olinger, Wm. Shires, Christian ( ) Acres.

Page 319.—18th March, 1785. John Gray and Jane, late Jane Craig, administratrix of John Craig, deceased, to William Gullett and Jane, his wife, only child of John Craig, deceased, of Greenbrier, to Nicholas Spring, stump in a poison field; Rev. Mr. Anderson's line, John Seawright's corner.

Page 321.—Patent to James Burnside, 26th September, 1760. Teste: John Handley, John Handley, Jr., Thomas Scott.

Page 325.—Teste: John Gardner, John McDugall, P. Heiskell, Wm McCay.

Page 327.—19th September, 1786. Zachariah Johnston and Ann to Samuel Guyler, tract conveyed by Beverley to Thomas Thompson, deceased, 15th May, 1754, and was left by him to his only daughter Margaret, now wife of Isaiah Vinzent, and by them conveyed to Zachariah, 18th August, 1784.

Page 329.—Teste: Joseph Trotter, Alex. Crawford, Charles McDonald, Robert Stuart, Wm. McPheeters, Geo. Berry, Jno. Wilson.

Page 331.—19th September, 1786. John Peery (Peerie) and Martha, of Caussewell County, North Carolina, to Jacob Gabbert.

Page 332.—15th August, 1786. John Poage, of Augusta, and Robert Armstrong, executors of John Archer, deceased, of Greenbrier, to George Moffett.

Page 339.—19th September, 1786. Robert Black to James Brand, Sr., of Washington County, Maryland.

Page 340.—331 acres conveyed to John Patterson by his father Robert, 11th March, 1761.

Page 341.—16th May, 1786. Philip ( ) Hansell to sons Lawrence and George Hansell, horses, cattle, chattels.

Page 347.—Teste: John Bradshaw, James Peebles, Andrew Lockridge.

Page 347.—14th September, 1786. William Foster, Sr., of Botetourt, William Foster, Jr., and Elisabeth, of Augusta, to Samuel Bell, tract conveyed by Joseph Poindexter to William Foster, Sr., and by him conveyed to his son William, 20th May, 1783. Teste: Robert Porterfield, John Patrick, John Cullen.

Page 351.—16th May, 1786. Ralph Laverty, of the Cowpasture, to his youngest daughter Rebekah Laverty, natural love and affection and for her better maintenance and livelihood, one-half to remain in possession of Ralph and his wife for their natural lives. Delivered to John Hamilton, 29th December, 1786.

Page 352.— — ——, 1786. William Long, of Greenbrier, by John Atkinson, his attorney, to Alexander St. Clair. John was appointed attorney to sell all the lands which William held as heir of his father, William Long, deceased. Lease of lot 2 in Staunton, corner Alex.'s store, for 66 years right to re-enter is in Beverley. Teste: James Buchanan, Robert McCollough, Samuel Merritt.

Page 354.—Similar deed to Michael Bowyer, part of 467 acres leased to Long by Beverley. Teste: Thomas Thackum.

Page 360.—Teste: Robert Harnsberger, Hugh Nelson.

Page 361.—4th October, 1786. Deed similar to p. 352, supra, to Thomas Thackum, of Henrico County, except 45 acres made over by William to his mother for her relinquisment of dower. Lease for 66 years. Teste: William McCay, Abraham Grover, William Chambers, William Blear, John Abney, Peter Heiskell.

Page 363.—20th September, 1786. John Brooks, Jr., and Ann ( ) to John Emmett, of Pennsylvania. Delivered: John Emmett, 21st January, 1790, part of plantation John Brooks, Sr., now lives on.

Page 367.—Teste: William Ralston, William Henry, William Houston.

Page 369.—Corner William and Charles Dalhouse. Teste: John Dalhouse.

Page 372.—25th November, 1786. Sarah, Jane and Agness Hutcheson (by John McFarland, attorney) (vid., power of attorney, &c., supra, p. 310) to Thomas Higgins, in Beverley Manor on head of Elk Run, grub in the Barrens.

Page 382.— 2d (?) September, 1786. William Long, of Greenbrier, by John Atkinson, of Spottsylvania, to Anthony Mustoe, lease of lot 2.

Page 385.—To Jacob Daughey, alias Daggy. Patented to James Humphreys, 25th June, 1747, and by him conveyed to Henry Smith.

Page 392.—Teste: Joseph Malcolm, Robert McCoy, Thos. Neal.
Page 396.—25th October, 1786. Corner Widow Inman.
Page 400.—20th February, 1787. John McCreery and Martha to John Boreland. Delivered to Wm. Robertson (Captain), 2d February, 1795. Patented to John McCreary (Sr. or Jr.), 12th July, 1770.
Page 403.—4th January, 1787. George Lemon to Paul Kook, 85 acres patented to said George, 4th November, 1785, on Naked Creek.
Page 408.—On a draft of Anderson's Branch.
Page 409.—15th December, 1786. Edward Rutledge and Sara to their son George Rutledge, place salled Flag Spring, part of 250 acres patented to William Kerr, 5th September, 1749. Delivered to David Stephenson, 20th July, 1790.
Page 410.—20th February, 1787. Samuel Anderson and Sarah to William Curry, part of 137 acres patented to James Anderson, deceased (whose heir by will Samuel is), 1st September, 1780.
Page 414.—20th September, 1786. William Scott, of Lincoln County, to James Ewing. Delivered to Joseph Ewing, son of the grantee, 4th January, 1800.
Page 420.—12th March, 1787. John Cowardine and Mary to William Jarid, formerly of Fauquier, and now of Augusta; patented to John.
Page 428.—Teste: Richard Bohannon, Francis Crutchfield, Thos Hansford.
Page 430.—Teste: John McKemy, Andrew Kannady, John McCoskry, Henry Venus, Elizabeth McCoskry, Thomas Beard, Robert Cooper.
Page 432.—26th February, 1787. John Lewis, of Warm Springs, to White, Kirk & Co., merchants at said Springs, mortgage of chattels, £38. Teste: Wm. Bell, Wm. Garrard, John Cowardine.
Page 440.—Teste: Patrick Buchanan, Samuel Gibson, David Hamilton, John Gibson.
Page 443.—9th September, 1786. David Hogshead and Catharine, of Rowan County, North Carolina, to Nicholas Tropough.
Patent to Walter Trimble on North Fork North River Shanandore. Certificate of relinquishment of dower by Catharine in Roan County, North Carolina, 9th November, 1786, before Jas. Nichols, Daniel Caldwell, Justices.
Page 449.—19th November, 1786. John Woods, of Augusta, to his mother Mary Woods, of Augusta, tract patented to John's father, John, 25th February, 1762, and by his decease intestate is invested in grantor as heir.
Page 453.—Broad Spring Branch. Teste: John Gardner, Wm. Ralson, Richard ( ) Cairn.
Page 462.—24th May, 1774. Elisha Estis, of Caroline County, and Gabriel Long, of Culpeper County, to Cap. Francis Kirtley, Sr. Teste: William, William, Jr., John, Francis Kirtley, Thos. Fortson. First proved by two witnesses and certified, 15th November, 1774; 20th February, 1787, proof compleated, but court refused to order record unntil tax of 3 shillings per 100 acres was paid, which was refused, and then on 19th June, 1787, the tax being paid, ordered recorded.
Page 470.—19th June, 1787. Peter Hall, eldest son and heir of Peter Hall, to Jacob Hall. Delivered to Nicholas Sybert, 25th August, 1787. Same to George Hall. Same to Adam Hall.

Page 482.—19th June, 1787. Henry Flesher to Conrod Flesher, conveyed to Henry Flecher, November, 1783, by Jacob Trace or Drais.

Page 484.—19th June, 1787. Frederick Burket and Rageena to John Shaver, 55 acres, part of 213 acres patented to Edmond Burton, 12th January, 1780; 18 acres patented to Frederick, 2d November, 1785.

Page 487.—Patented to David Bell, 16th May, 1771, and by him conveyed to William Jordan.

Page 493.—Tract in possession of James Makem Arley.

Page 493.—Teste: Enos Atwater, Fred. Grof, Thomas Douglass, Andrew Yegart, Edward ( ) Martin.

Page 504.—House in Staunton now occupied by William Shives, 12th January, 1787, the lot occupied by Isabella Burns.

Page 507.—Ditto occupied by John Bosang.

Page 511.—260 conveyed to said John and George Givens by their father, John Givens.

Page 514.—97 acres patented to John Givens, 1st September, 1780.

Page 516.—Valentine Shirley—Felty Shirley.

Page 522.—12th March, 1787. William Garrard to John Fowler, of Fairfax, mortgage.

Page 526.—14th May, 1787. Leonard Simmons to Peter Simmons, his son, tract patented to Leonard by the Commonwealth, joining Mark Simmons and John Somvalt, crossing Gyle's Run.

Page 528.—Tract patented to Thomas Persons, 22d September, 1757.

Page 534.—19th June, 1787. Andrew ( ) Shown to Samuel Merit, tract on Lewis' Creek where Leonard Shown, deceased, formerly lived.

Page 536.—Tract whereon George Peery now lives.

Page 551.—17th July, 1787. Samuel Anderson and Sarah to Mustoe and Chambers, 316 acres on Long Glade conveyed to Samuel by his father, corner Phersythe's land.

Page 556.—5th July, 1787. John ( ) Jordan and Ann ( ) to Andrew Jordan, part of 90 acres patented to John, 1st March, 1773; patented to John, 1st June, 1782.

Last deed recorded, 17th July, 1787.

Deed Book No. 26.

First deed recorded, 17th July, 1787; last deed recorded, 15th June, 1790.

Page 2.—5th July, 1787. John ( ) Jordan, of Bullpasture, and Ann ( ) to John Armstrong, part of patents to John, 90 acres, 1st March, 1773, and 170 acres, 1st June, 1782.

Page 7.—Patent to John Beard, 1st February, 1781.

Page 9.—Tract on Back Creek, patented to William Lewis, 30th August, 1763.

Page 11.—200 acres on Divers Lick Branch.

Page 13.—15th August, 1786. John Archer's executors to Richard Mathews, 75 acres patented to Sampson Archer and sold to his brother, John Archer, deceased, but no title ever made. Teste: James Cunningham, James McKibbin, Joseph Trotter, Daniel Friel, David Greiner, Hugh McDowell, Alex. Nelson, Jr., Stephen Smith.

Page 19.—Patent to John King, 1st February, 1781.

Page 21.—House on Beverley Street where Martha Cowdon now lives.

Page 23.—18th September, 1787. Ralph Laverty's power of attorney to his son-in-law, Mr. John Hamilton, to collect accounts and pay bills

Page 29.—24th August, 1787. Richard Mathews to Alex. St. Clair, Robert Gamble, J. Heron, mortgage. Teste: Hugh McDowell, Alex. Nelson, Jr., Stephen Smith.

Page 33.—20th August, 1787. William Gillaspie and Rose to George Adam Coynart (delivered to Gasper Coinert, 22d August, 1789), tract conveyed to William by will of James Gillaspie.

Page 37.—22d August, 1787. James Gillispie and Elizabeth to Michael Coynart, of Cumberland County, Pennsylvania.

Page 40.—16th September, 1787. Abel Griffith to James McKemy, of Augusta, and John Davis, of Rockingham, on behalf of Mossey Creek Congregation, 3½ acres on Mossey Creek and also 1 acre including the old burying ground.

Page 42.—21st August, 1787. George Stount and Mary to Henry Peninger, 131 acres on South Branch Potomac, below Trout Rock

Page 44.—3d July, 1787. James Gillespy and Sarah, of Sevier County, North Carolina, to Andrew Lecky, 143 acres on Elk Run in Beverley Manor, corner Thomas Hutcheson, deceased. Acknowledged in State of Franklni, Sevier County, 3d July, 1787, before Oliver Alexander and Thomas Gillespy, certified that they are justices by Samuel Wear, Clerk of Sevier County Court.

Page 46.—18th September, 1787. Euphemia Hughes, Sr., Euphemia Hughes, Jr., Owen Owens and Jane, Adam Bickle and Mary, to Sampson Mathews.

Page 51.—1st January, 1787. Jacob Vanfosson, John ( ) Henger, teste.

Page 52.—23d January, 1787. Privy examination of Isabella Burnsides, wife of James Burnsides (deed, 6th September, 1786, to John Hicklin), before Alexander and Hugh Caperton, Justices of Greenbrier.

Page 53.—16th October, 1787. Joseph Lance to George Lance, two tracts patented to Barnet Lance, 10th April, 1781, in Crab Bottom. Delivered: Conrod Buck, 28th August, 1788.

Page 59.—17th October, 1787. John Gardner and Elizabeth, and James Griffith and Mary, to John Poage, on head branches of Falling Spring, patented to George King, 1770.

Page 61.—27 acres patented to Peter Smith, 10th July, 1767, on Smith's Branch of Potomac. Teste: William Shires, Charles Marchle.

Page 62.—18th March, 1786. Philip Hansell to Lawrence and Geo. Hansell.

Page 65.—On Mill Creek, by Acois Falls. Delivered: Andrew McNare, 18th May, 1790.

Page 68.—28th May, 1787. Michael Coulter to Philip Dalby, of Fairfax County. Delivered to Col. Robert Gamble. Teste: Thomas Swarm, Francis Peyton, John Reynolds.

Page 73.—8th November, 1786. James Anderson and Ann (Agness) to Nathaniel Birkett (delivered: Andrew Moody, 25th October, 1788), part of 747 acres conveyed to John Anderson by Beverley, 15th March, 1739; also part of 135 acres patented to said John and since conveyed to James by said John, 15th May, 1781.

Page 76.—On Thorn Branch, patented to Robert Gragg, Jr. Teste: Thomas Greene, Wm. McKemy, Richard ( ) Cain.

Page 88.—18th September, 1787. William McCutchen and Margaret to John McCutcheon, 100 acres on Calfpasture, part of 358 acres conveyed by Beverley to Robert McCutchen and now by Robert and Margaret to their son, Wiliam.

Page 104.—19th September, 1787. David Fulton, grantee, to Sampson Mathews, grantor, of Richmond, attorney in fact for James McCutchen, eldest son and heir-at-law of William McCutchen, deceased, on head waters of Carthie's River, house of Samuel McCutchen. Sampson is mortgagee of William and debt was paid by David Fulton.

Page 106.—Tract patented 12th January, 1780, to Edmund Burton.

Page 108.—Teste: James Cunningham, William Sterrett, James and Wm. Bell.

Page 110.—Tract where William Lewis formerly lived, part of Beverley's Mill Tract.

Page 111.—14th April, 1788. William Kennerley, of Augusta, to Archibald Bowling, of Buckingham, on Laurel Run of South River.

Page 112.—9th February, 1788. James ( ) Bell, Sr., releases all his claim to the estate of Samuel Bell, his son, who died devising all his estate to be equally divided between James' other children, John, Thomas, Joseph and Sarah Bell. Teste: Robert and Esther Gamble, Samuel Long.

Page 113.—Delivered. Teste: Coats Thornton, Wm. Forbes, George Wieford.

Page 115.—Tract patented to Robert Brown, 10th June, 1740, on Culton's Branch of North River; also tract patented to James Trotter, 6th April, 1769.

Page 121.—17th April, 1787. John Black, son and heir to Samuel Black, deceased. to James Curry, tract on Carlile's Run of Bullpasture, patented to Samuel Black. Delivered Edward Erwin, per order, 19th March, 1798.

Page 122.—16th April, 1788. County Commissioners to Alex. McClenachan, lot 45, formerly sold to James Hughes; lot 46, formerly sold to George Wilson, deceased, and since sold by Samuel Kinkade, who intermarried with Elizabeth Wilson, daughter of said George Wilson, to whom lot was devised by George.

Page 123.—16th April, 1788. John Keenon to William Bell. Teste: Hugh Keenon, Samuel Bell.

Page 130.—Patent to John Adair in 1783.

Page 131.—15th June, 1788. Samuel Bell, Sr., and Jane to Samuel Bell, Jr., and David Bell, tract conveyed by William Foster, Sr., to his son William.

Page 132.—1st August, 1787. John Bell and Lettice ( ), Robert Bell, Elizabeth Bell, of Rockbridge, to James Rowland. Teste: David Wilson, Jno. Adair, Jno. Fulton.

Page 134.—13th November, 1787. John Bell and Lettice, Robert Bell, Elisabeth Bell, widow ——, deceased, to Florence Falls.

Page 139.—On Calfpasture River, patented to John Elliot, 27th August, 1783. Delivered: Samuel Bell, 25th February, 1792. Elliot to James Bell,

Page 140.—15th April, 1788. Samuel Frazer and Isabella Helena ( ) to James Frazer, tract on Long Meadow conveyed 22d February, 1749, by

Beverley to John Frazer, deceased intestate, and Samuel is eldest son and heir-at-law.

Page 146.—Patent to John Hind, 10th April, 1780.

Page 148.—17th June, 1788. William Hind, heir-at-law of John Hind, deceased, and Ann to John Dickson, part of patent to John Kerr, 30th July, 1742; also part of patent to William Kerr.

Page 151.—26th May, 1788. Robert, Jacob and James Upshur, of the County of Northampton, to John Crawford, sale of slaves.

Page 152.—Plantation Alex. Brownlee, Sr., lived on; tract patented to Alex. McClenachan, 19th June, 1787. Delivered to John McCorley, 28th December, 1791.

Page 155.—7th April, 1788. John Miller and Margret, of Rockingham, to Thomas Devericks, Sr., 125 acres, part of tract patented to Daniel O'haro, 23d May, 1763, on a south branch of the Cowpasture, adjoining tract surveyed to Mathew Penn, now in possession of Isaac Johns.

Page 158.—17th June, 1788. Thomas Poage and Nancy ( ) to William McDowell, lot 6 in Staunton, vested in Thomas by Act of Assembly, October, 1787.

Page 160.—17th June, 1788. Jacob Peck to Christian Geabill (Geable). Delivered to Henry Grable, 23d November, 1804.

Page 162.—5th May, 1788. Ann Story ( ), relict of Thomas Story, deceased, of Green County, North Carolina, to John Story, of Augusta, release of dower in tract on Middle River, devised to John by his father's will; reversion belongs to said John and Thomas Story. Proved in Washington County, North Carolina, May, 1788. Teste: J. Carter, Edm. Heron, J. Hamilton, Wm. Hamilton.

Page 163.—28th April, 1788. William Crawford, Moses Eastey, surviving partners of themselves and John Beach, deceased, who were joint tenants, to Robert McCulloch, now of the town of Staunton, part of lot 13 in Staunton, opposite George Wilson's lot, now Philip North's.

Page 165.—12th July, 1788. Hugh Campbell, of Rockbridge, heir-at-law of James Campbell, to Benjamin Erwin, of Rockingham. Teste: Ro. Gamble, Robert Astrop, Samuel Clark, James Megongal (McGongal).

Page 169.—13th June, 1788. John Handley and Margaret, of Augusta, and Gasper Snider and Margret, of Rockingham, to Anthony Mustoe and William Chambers, conveyed to Samuel Wilson by John Brown, August, 1752, and to grantors here by Patrick McDavid and Martha, his wife, daughter of Samuel Wilson, 18th February, 1780.

Page 174.—Teste: Thomas Hughart, Andrew Lockridge, Jonathan Hicklin.

Page 174.—15th June, 1787. Wm. Long and Elizabeth ( ), of Greenbrief, to William Chambers and Anthony Mustoe, lot in Staunton, leased to Wm. Long, deceased, by Beverley and now leased for remainder of term.

Page 177.—15th July, 1788. Anthony Mustoe and Dorothy, and William Chambers and Ann, to Robert Gamble.

Page 179.—7th January, 1788. John Bays, Peter Kuhn and Gustavus Risberg, of Staunton, to James and John McKibben. John and James are indebted to said Peter and Gustavus (merchants). Part of plantation whereon John Elliott now lives.

Page 183.—4th January, 1788. Robert Jones and William Forbes to John

Phillips, patent to John, 5th July, 1774. Teste: Robert Stuart, George Moore, John Patterson, John Gorden, Peter Eagle.

Page 185.—15th July, 1788. Alexander St. Clair, and Jane to Archibald Stuart, lot 31 containing ½ acre, part of 25 acres property of said St. Clair, added to Town of Staunton by Act of Assembly, October Session, 1787, corner Stuart's Alley and Church Street. (Mentions plat of said 25 acres on record. Plat is recorded, p. 192.)

Page 192.—Survey and plat of 25 acres belonging to Alex. St. Clair, and added to Staunton by Act of Assembly, October, 1787.

Page 193.—Patent to Edmund Burton, 12th January, 1780. Patent to Frederick Burket, 2d November, 1785.

Page 198.—16th July, 1788. Commission to George Clendenin and Samuel McClug, gent., Justice of Greenbrier, to take privy examination of Elizabeth, wife of William Long, deed to Anthony Mustoe, dated September, 1786. Executed and returned, 20th July, 1788.

Page 203.—1,000 acres on Jackson's River, patented to William Jackson, 1st June, 1750. Patent to Robert Hall, 7th February, 1784. Teste: A. Stuart, Joseph Jewell, Michael ( ) Cawley, J. Lyle, Jr.

Page 209.—Patent to James Campbell, 16th March, 1771. Teste: Thomas Hughart, William Yooll, Thomas Kinkead.

Page 219.—Lot No. 2 in Staunton, end of Wm. Shire's house; end of house now occupied by Wm. Forbush.

Page 221.—15th September, 1788. Hugh Donaghe to David Laird, executor of John Buts (Brits ?).

Page 231.—71 acres on Jackson's River, patented to Robert Hall, 18th March, 1784.

Page 234.—145 acres on Jackson's River, patented to Robert Hall, 7th February, 1784.

Page 237.—Patent to John and James McCoy, 5th September, 1762, 320 acres on Mossey Creek; 86 acres patented to Abel Griffith on Mossey Creek, 1st March, 1773; 316 acres on Mossey Creek, patented to Abel Griffith, 1st March, 1781, joining Thomas Reed; 160 acres patented to same on same day.

Page 240.—217 acres patented to John Frances, 5th April, 1748. 100 acres patented to John Hogshead, 16th August, 1786. Teste: Zachariah Taliaferro.

Page 242.—25th February, 1788. James Hayes, of Albemarle, Braxton Eastham, of Rockbridge, to William Greyson, Nathaniel Garland and James Brooks, of Albemarle, 333 acres at Rockfish Gap, three patents belonging to Manus Burger, deceased, and John Burger, lately in possession of Henry Lyon, and now in possession of James P. Hulse. Teste: Jesse and Thomas Stockton, John Mills.

Page 248.—16th September, 1788. William Seawright and Jane and Alexander Seawright and Sarah ( ), of Rockbridge, to Samuel Carson, tract in Borden's grant.

Page 250.—18th December, 1787. Margaret Reed, of Staunton, to Alexander Sincklair, of Staunton, tract on Calfpasture conveyed to Margaret by Thomas Smith; in trust for use and benefit of Elizabeth Smith. Delivered: M. Garber, Jr., 5th July, 1828. Teste: James Culbertson, Jon Johnston, Asher Waterman.

Page 253.—12th July, 1788. Josep Phillips and James Ware, both of Wilkes County, Georgia, to James Graham, of county and state aforesaid, power of attorney to sell land and collect and pay debts. Teste: Isaiah and Margaret Curry, Henry and Catherine Poss.

Page 254.—3d September, 1788. Robert Hall and Isabella to Jacob Warrick (deed dated 14th July, 1788). Privy examination before James Wilson and Samuel Vance.

Page 255.—The Great Road.

Page 259.—Teste: James Guy, Francis Fergus, Alex. Warner, David Hogshead, John Wilson.

Page 260.—27th October, 1788. Nathaniel Burkett and Karthrine ( ) to Andrew Moody, part of two tracts originally surveyed for John Anderson and by several conveyances came into possession of Nathaniel, on south side Middle River.

Page 261.—21st October, 1788. John and Thomas Story to Hugh Donaghe.

Page 262.—21st October, 1788. Samuel Anderson and Sarah, wife of Samuel, heir-at-law of his son, James Anderson, Jr., deceased, to Anthony Mustoe and Wm. Chambers, on Long Glade, 200 acres devised to said James by his grandfather, James Anderson, Sr., and conveyed to James, Sr., by John Anderson, 17th February, 1762; 34 acres patented to Samuel Anderson, 1st June, 1782.

Page 264.—6th October, 1788. John Lewis, of Warm Springs, to William Bowyer, of Staunton, assignee of Valentine White, two half-acre lots in a town laid off by John at Warm Springs, on the main street thereof, on a line with the large dwelling and storehouse already built.

Page 265.—16th December, 1788. William Anderson and Jane, and Samuel Anderson and Elizabeth, to Henry Dill, part of patent to James Blair, 10th March, 1756.

Page 268.—24th July, 1788. Martha Cowden (relict of Samuel Wilson, deceased), John Griffen and Elizabeth, with Robert Gamble, contract of arbitration.

Page 270.—House lately occupied by Martha Cowden on corner Beverley and Augusta Streets.

Page 271.—6 acres beginning at Sompson Matthews' lot at corner of the house that stands thereon, which was built for a public magazine.

Page 273.—20th January, 1789. John Miller and Margaret, of Rockingham, to Charles Callahan, tract granted by order of Council, 29th October, 1743, to John Robinson, James Wood, Henry Robinson, John Lewis, and by them patented to Mathew Harper, 15th December, 1758, on Newfoundland Creek of Cowpasture; 75 acres on Bullpasture, patented to said John Miller, 1st March, 1781; 232 acres patented to said John Miller, 1st June, 1784, on Bullpasture; 58 acres patented to John on last date.

Page 280.—19th August, 1788. Michael Garber, Robert Jones, William Forbes, John Phillips and Jane, to Zachariah Johnston, sale of lands deeded in trust by said John to grantors, 14th January, 1788; said John failed to comply with the conditions; tract patented to John, 5th July, 1774, and 56 acres patented to same at same time. Delivered: grantor's executors, Jno. Johnston, 9th August, 1805.

Page 282.—20th November, 1788. John ( ) King, with Samuel and

James King, agreement: John by age and infirmity has been rendered incapable of supporting himself; conveys to grantees his cattle, &c.; they agree to support him during his natural life. Teste: David Gibson, Jno. Denison.

Page 283.—Same parties on same agreement as above; conveys slaves.

Page 286.—Delivered: William Kennerley, 21st October, 1789. Teste: John Rab.

Page 291.—14th February, 1789. James Story and Sarah to George Crawford, son of the late George Crawford. Whereas Thomas Story died seized of a tract on Middle River and devised same to his eldest son, said James.

Page 293.— — November, 1788. Samuel Anderson (signed "James," but certificate says "Samuel") to Able Griffith and John Blair, certain smith's tools and other personal property. Teste: Z. Taliaferro and John Gamble.

Page 293.—20th January, 1788. Thomas Mynes and Martha to David Trust. Delivered: —— Trout, 19th September, 1792.

Page 295.—23d January, 1789. Privy examination of Elizabeth Harless, wife of Immanuel Harless (deed to William Beard, dated ——, 440 acres), taken by Daniel Howe and John Preston.

Page 297.—21st April, 1789. George Eagle and Elizabeth to Peter Genewine, part of tract whereon Wm. McClintock lived, corner George Caller; corner Jacob Helford, Morris's Draft.

Page 299.—Patent to John and James Alexander, 16th August, 1787.

Page 300.—28th December, 1788. William Kennedy, of Washington County, to Daniel Miller, of Rockbridge (Samuel Miller in body of deed). Delivered to Mary Martin, formerly widow of grantee, 16th October, 1811.

Page 302.—295 acres patented to William Hind, deceased, and devised to his son William, but not to his heirs or assigns, whereby said land became vested in William Hind, grandson and heir-at-law of William, Sr., corner Thos. Garvin's land.

Page 305.—183 acres patented by Governor Blair to John Finley, 1st December, 1740, and by him conveyed by lease to Alex. Gardner and became vested in John Gardiner, only son and heir-at-law to said Alexander, deceased, on Finley's Branch of Cathey's River.

Page 314.—Teste: James Buchanan, George Moore, James St. Clair, Robert Douthat, James Buchanan, Sr., Hugh Paul.

Page 315.—16th June, 1789. Hugh Green's executors (William Wilson and Robert Reed) to Peter Hanger, Jr. Patented to Hugh, 10th April, 1781.

Page 317.—17th June, 1788. James Long and Elizabeth to Doctor Alexander Long, part of tract William Long, deceased, lived on, and willed to James by his father, William. Delivered: Samuel Long by order of William Long, executor of Alexander, 13th May, 1814.

Page 322.—Delivered to John Cunningham, 11th January, 1791.

Page 323.—13th June, 1789. Thomas Cartmill and Mary to Abraham Ingram, 358 acres by survey 13th June, 1780, on an east branch of Greenbrier, called Deer or Warrick's Creek, the mine bank; corner Jacob Gallaspie. Delivered: John Warrick, 4th September, 1797.

Page 327.— — ——, 1789. Thomas ( ) Jarvis and Elizabeth to Jacob

Gillespy, Deer or Warrick's Creek. Teste: Thos. Cartmill, Abraham ( ) Ingraham, David Moore.

Page 328.— — ——, 1789. John Slaven and Elizabeth to John Huchin, 130 acres by survey, 9th June, 1780, on Back Creek of Greenbrier River, corner Jacob Warrick.

Page 330.—185 acres patented to Thomas Watterson, 12th January, 1746, corner George Glen.

Page 332.—31st October, 1788. Robert Gragg to Frederick Michel, of Rockingham, 513 acres patented to Robert, 6th April, 1769; 70 acres on Nores Run of North River of Shanidore, patented to Robert, 10th April, 1781; 400 acres patented to Robert, 1st June, 1782; near Castle Hill.

Page 336.—19th May, 1789. James Oliver and Mary to Hugh Donaghe, of Green County, North Carolina.

Page 343.—Tract of the late John Francis' land. Teste: John Hogset, Samuel Miller, James McCaw.

Page 344.—Patent to Robert Curry, 1st September, 1780.

Page 347.—25th June, 1771. Henry Murray and Rosannah, of Rowan County, North Carolina, to Robert McCittrick, in Jennings Gap, 90 acres patented to said Henry, 3d May, 1763. Teste: Samuel Young, Wm. Kinkead, Andrew Hamilton, Jno. McIlvaiin, Thomas Cowan, Archibald Kinkead, Thos. Kinkead. Proved, 21st July, 1789, by Hamilton and Wm. and Archibald Kinkade.

Page 352.—126 acres patented to John Risk, Sr., deceased, near the Black Spring large tract that John Risk, Sr., lived on and conveyed to his son David Risk. (This name is spelled Rusk). Teste: John Cunningham, Robert McChesney, John Barry.

Page 355.—20th July, 1789. Maj. Andrew Lockridge and Jane to John Lockridge, son of said Andrew, on Little Creek in Calfpasture, whereon William Smith formerly lived, and conveyed to Andrew by John Smith and Mary, 9th November, 1768. Teste: Thos. Hughart, Joseph Mays, Oliver McCoy.

Page 356.—20th July, 1789. Same to Andrew Lockridge, Jr., their son, tract conveyed to Maj. Andrew Lockridge by James Lockridge, his father. 21st August, 1764.

Page 357.—20th July, 1789. Same to James Lockridge, their son.

Page 359.—17th July, 1789. Daniel ( ) Munroe (Monrow) and Elizabeth ( ) to Stephen Wandless, plantation lastly occupied by said Daniel and by James Monrow, his father, on Stuart Creek, adjoining James Blake, formerly belonging to Van Swearingen.

Pane 360.—Patent to William Wilson, 25th March, 1762. Teste: Nicholas ( ) Trowerbough, John ( ) Keglan, Wm. King, Frederick Michael.

Page 362.—15th September, 1789. John Ralston, of Fayette County, Kentucky, appoints his brother William Ralston, his attorney to receive, demand and sue for debts and give receipts and sell a tract of land. Teste: Wiliam and Henry Ralston, Wm. Hind.

Page 363.—6th October, 1772. John Ridpath, of Augusta, to William Bowyer, merchant, bond to convey title to four lots in Staunton, viz: ¼ acre, formerly property of James Mair and then Daniel Kidd, of whom Ridpath purchased it; also ¼ acre purchased of Samuel Forggson; also ¼ acre he purchased of John Carlie, formerly property of Robert Hawl

(?); also ½ acre purchased of Edward Long. Teste: Ben. Forsie, Chris. Graham, Wm. Anderson. A copy, teste: Peter Tinsley, C. H. C. C.

Page 365.—15th September, 1789. Trustees of Augusta County (Alex. St. Clair and R. Gamble) to Wm. Bowyer, lot 20 in Staunton, pursuant to above, purchase money having been paid by said Ridpath.

Page 366.—Delivered: Joseph Burkley, order of Peter Grass, 1st October, 1789.

Page 368.—15th September, 1789. Gilbert Christian and John Christian and Rachel to James Moffet.

Page 370.— — ——, 1789. John Gardner and Elizabeth, his wife, heir-at-law of Alexander Gardner, deceased, to George Phypher, patent to Alexander, 1st February, 1781, adjoining George Wigel and Michael Hogshead.

Page 374.—6th August, 1788. Joseph Gregory, brother and heir-at-law of William Gregory, deceased, who was original proprietor, by his attorney, John Gregory, of Harrison County, to John Dever. Teste: William Burk, James Townsend, Zekail Townsend, Jacob Storkley.

Page 378.—Teste: Patrick Buchanan, Samuel Merrit, George Rubble.

Page 378.—Tract left to William Campbell (wife Elizabeth) by will of his father, Charles Campbell, deceased, part of 400 acres patented to John Anderson, 20th June, 1740, and conveyed to Charles, 1747.

Page 380.—7th October, 1789. Beverley to William Bowyer, release of lease to William Long, 20th February, 1756.

Page 383.—20th October, 1789. Hermon Lovingood and Ann to Ardolph Spindle. Delivered: Philip and John Lovingood, two of the heirs of Ardolph, deceased, 27th November, 1826.

Page 384.—20th September, 1788. Alexander Elliot and Ann Conway Elliot, his wife, now of Rockbridge, appoint William Anderson attorney to convey to William Brent, of Amherst, all lands in County of Lancaster, state aforesaid (Virginia?), to which they are entitled as heirs-at-law of James Campbell, late of Lancaster County, deceased, provided Brent shall convey to Anderson plantation on Back Creek whereon Brent formerly lived. Teste: John and William King, Wm. Berry.

Page 386.—James Anderson's part of same land.

Page 387.—15th December, 1789. Henry Dill (German, Düll) to Sebastian Woolf, part of 216 acres patented to John Bell, 1st December, 1740.

Page 389.—5th December, 1789. Jacob Peck to Thomas Thompson and Mary, Grant for life of mill property. Teste: Abraham Grove.

Page 390.—Part of 311 acres patented to James Givens, 30th August, 1743.

Page 400.—19th January, 1790. William Christian, Jr., to Jacob van Lear, 40 acres devised to William by William Christian, deceased, part of tract Andrew Wilson now lives on, on Christian's Creek.

Page 401.— — January, 1790. Anthony Mustoe, administrator of David Grayner (Griner), deceased, and guardian of his children, with Catherine ( ) Grinor, administratrix and relict of said David. Agreement to use and control of David's lots and houses in Staunton. Teste: Michael Bowyer and Peter Hanger.

Page 403.—9th January, 1790. Organization of Staunton Fire Company.

W. Bowyer, Michael Bowyer, Alex. St. Clair, Ro. Gamble, James Lyle, Jr., Robert Stuart, Daniel Donovan, A. Stuart, Wm. Abney, R. Douthat, W. Chambers, Jno. and Samuel Boys, P. Heiskell, Jacob Peck, Ro. McDowell, Michael Garber, Michael Sifort, Jacob Geiger, Adam Bickle, James Megongal, A. Waterman, Robert McCullough, J. Holmes for Robert Astrop, Joseph Dickey, John Gorden, Michael Garber, Jr., A. Mustoe, Alex. Humphreys, Geo. Harden, Jno. Fleiger, Sol. Wolfort, Jno. Price, Hugh McDowell, Wm. Forbes, Jno. ( ) Moore, Margt. Reed, Wm. Sharyer, Andrew Cutler, Jno. Gunn, Wm. McDowell, North and Mathews, Alex. Nelson, Jr., Jno. Bosang, Chr. Grove, James McLoughlin, Jno. ( ) Gates, Smith Thompson, Francis Huff, Michael Cawley, Christian Mummer, Nicholas Faulkler, Samuel Merrit, Daniel Kidd, Jno. Tennant, Geo. Weifford, Isaac Ong, Charles Hedrick, Joshua Parry, Henry, Spering, Anthony ( ) Ingleton, Jno. Backenst, James Kenner.

Page 405.—Teste: Samuel Vance, Jno. Dever, Peter Robinson, George Benson.

Page 408.—Tract on Jackson's River surveyed for Wm. McClenachan in 1766, and by him conveyed to William Hutchinson.

Page 409.—10th October, 1787. Sampson Mathews, of Richmond, to Alex. St. Clair and Robert Gamble, bond conditioned. Whereas Sampson has heretofore sold to Robert Gamble and Hugh McDowell, a house and lot in the City of Staunton, whereon they now live and desires to secure to his wife, Catharine, an equivalent for her release of dower, Sampson binds himself to build on a lot known as "water lot," a dwelling house 30 ft. square, two stories high, with two rooms and a passage below and three or four rooms above; also a kitchen and smoke house suitable, and all necessary outhouses, and convey same to trustees for Catharine's benefit, for her life. Teste: Archibald Stuart, W. Bowyer.

Page 410.—13th January, 1790. Teste: John Kisling ( ), Thomas Waddell, Fred. Trobuch.

Page 412.—Interest accrued to Bond Estill as heir-at-law to John Estill.

Page 414.—380 acres patented to Robert Brown, 10th June, 1740, and by him conveyed to James Trotter, by him to John Hinds, and by William Hinds, son and executor of John, to John Long; on a branch of North River of Shanandoah, formerly known by name of Culton's Branch, 250 acres patented to John Hind, 10th April, 1781.

Page 416.—7th November, 1789. John Greenlee of Rockbridge, attorney in fact for Patrick Hayse, Sr., of Lincoln, Kaintuckey, to James Hendry (Henry). Teste: James and Robert Henry.

Page 422.—Patent to James Dickey, 9th February, 1786.

Page 424.—28th March, 1789. William Blair to Henry King and James Blair, mortgage.

Page 434.—30 May, 1788. John Gillespie and Martha, James Frazer and Ann, John Frazer, Jean Frazer, Robert Gay, executors of Henry Gay, deceased, to John McRoberts.

Page 438.—21st April, 1790. John Boys to Peter Kuhn and Augustavus Resburg, of Pennsylvania, part of tract whereon John Elliot now lives.

Page 441.—Teste: Nelly King.

Page 442.—Adjoining the plantation of Robert Carlile, son of John Carlile, and joining lands of the heirs of Edward Hinds.

Page 446.—25th October, 1781. Thomas Wright and Jane to John Botkin. Teste: John Jordan, Thos. Dueglass, George Bentson, David Frame, John McCreery. Proved, 19th March, 1788.

Page 448.—150 acres on Moffett's Branch of Middle River, part of 400 acres patented to William King, 10th February, 1748; and 145 acres patented to James Rankin, 1st September, 1780.

Page 450.—400 acres on head of Mossey Creek, patented to David Davis, 12th February, 1741; 180 acres patented to Samuel McFeeters, 1st August, 1772.

Page 453.—On Sidlington's Creek. Teste: Samuel Vance, Geo. Poage, Alex. Gibson.

Page 454.—12th June, 1786. Doctor John Jackson, of Washington County, Maryland, to Cap. John and David Cunningham, power of attorney to settle all claims and demands in Augusta County. Teste: James Ewing, Lettice Cunningham.

Page 456.—On Jennings Branch and Middle River, 525 acres patented to Daniel McNare 1st February, 1781; also 96 acres patented to said Daniel 20th July, 1768. Teste: Rebekah and Hanna Sawyers, Wm. Buchanan.

Page 460.—24th April,, 1790. Joseph Erwin, son and heir to Benjamin Erwin, deceased, of North Carolina, Johnston County, to John Erwin.

Page 462.—350 acres patented to Edward Erwin, 5th ———, 1748. Teste: Cullen Earp, Nathaniel Bagwill. Acknowledged before James Shaw, a justice for Johnston County, North Carolina.

Last deed recorded 15th June, 1790.

DEED BOOK No. 27.

First Deed Recorded 15th June, 1790; Last Deed Recorded August, 1794. Deeds are the conveyances and descriptions are very unsatisfactory.

Page 5.—15th June, 1790. John Conner and Rebeckah to Jacob Barager and Nicholas Bush, trustees for the Congregation of Spindle Meeting House. on South River; corner John Conners, in a line of Michael Coyners.

Page 12.—15th June, 1790. Samuel Steele, of Rockbridge, to Robert McQuillen, 100 acres on Half Way Creek; Boyd's line; McClenachan's and Campbell's corner; Williams' corner; part of patent to Samuel 20th July, 1768.

Page 17.—20th July, 1790. William Seeright and Jean and Sharah Seeright, of Rockbridge, to William McCaslin.

Page 24.—Part of 400 acres patented to Andrew Kinkead; corner Richard Mathews.

Page 28.—20th July, 1790. Robert Armstrong, executor of John Archer, deceased, and George Moffett, to Henry Hermone, part of 2,400 acres patented to John Archer, deceased, 2d March, 1781, and George Moffett, having by mistake received a title.

Page 30.—17th September, 1790. Privy examination of Elizabeth Campbell, wife of William Campbell, deed to John Voice dated ———.

Page 31.—34 acres patented to James Dickey 30th August, 1786. Teste: James Anderson, Robert Curry, John Dickey.

Page 32.—14th November, 1787. Martha ( ) and Joseph Henderson, of Fayette County, being their part of the land divided to Martha Henderson, James and Joseph Henderson, by James Henderson, deceased, by his will. Teste: Samuel McKee, Robert and Lindsay Thompson.

Page 33.—232 acres by survey (to John Chesnut), on Bull Pasture Mountain, 15th February, 1768.

Page 35.—213 acres patented to Edmund Burton 12th January, 1780, on Walker's Run of Middle River.

Page 36.—1st May, 1790. John Ramsey, of District of Kentucky, to Andrew Steel and Andrew Ramsey, all his interest in estate of Daniel Ramsey, deceased, as heir-at-law to James Ramsey, and also devisee of Daniel Ramsey, deceased, viz., 323 acres willed to Daniel by John Ramsey, deceased, and conveyed to said John by Israel Christian, on South Branch of Shanandoah; 2 surveys to John Ramsey, deceased. Teste: Benjamin Stuart, James and John Ramsey.

Page 40.—16th April, 1794. Delivered: Adam Dickinson, son of Col. Dickinson.

Page 41.—On Brown Hill on little Calfpasture patented to Alexander Craig 16th April, 1789.

Page 43.—On Long Glade patented to John Anderson and became property of Mustoe and Chambers, 27 acres patented to Samuel Anderson 1st June, 1782.

Page 45.—Delivered to Jno. Guthrey, son of William, 1st December, 1790. Teste: William Orr.

Page 47.—19th October, 1790. Andrew Anderson and Martha and James Allen and Margaret to John Griner, part of tract patented to John Anderson, deceased, and by him conveyed in his lifetime to Andrew and James.

Page 48.—1st October, 1790. Alexander Sinclair and Robert Gamble, trustees of Augusta County, to William Hickam Bottom (Higginbothom) and John Sherman, on Beverleys Market Street, lot formerly sold to John McDanaght.

Page 53.—23d September, 1790. John Campbell, of North Carolina, to John Lowry. Delivered to Joseph Lowry, son of John, 10th August, 1791, part of 400 acres patented to John Anderson 10th June, 1740, and by him conveyed to Charles Campbell 17th March, 1747, and by him to his son, said John Campbell, 18th August, 1772. Teste: Benjamin Henkle, Jno. McPheeters, Wm. Wilson, Jos. Lowry, W. Fowler, Maurice Morris.

Page 56.—Part of plantation in Beverley Mnaor whereon John Christian, deceased, lived.

Page 60.—217 acres patented to John Francis 5th April, 1748, on Anderson's Branch.

Page 63.—Part of patent to James Bell 5th July, 1774, part patented to Andrew Foster; McClure's Run.

Page 64.—Delivered to Nancy Fisher, wife of Daniel Fisher (of Rockingham) 18th August, 1800.

Page 67.—29th November, 1790. John Sitlington to James Kelso, his son-in-law, husband to John's daughter, Elizabeth, marriage portion, plantation on Cowpasture where John now lives.

Page 70.—27th September, 1780. Mathew (mark) Edmondson to John Kirk and David McNare, power of attorney to sell land.

Page 71.— —— December, 1790. Peter Kuhn and Gustavus Risburg, of Pennsylvania (by John Swoope, attorney; power recorded in District Court), to Peter Lohr, of Maryland.

Page 73.—3d September, 1790. Hugh Campbell, of Washington County, North Carolina, appoints John Dickey, attorney to obtain grant or deed to 190 acres joining John Tanner and Hugh Brown and convey same to Robert Brown. Teste: John Donaghe, Peter Bleke, John Bernard.

Page 74.—10th October, 1774. John Ramsey and Margaret and Andrew Crockett, of Mecklenburg County, N. C., to James Crockett, of Augusta, tract on Calfpasture known by name of entry patented to Margret and Andrew Crockett 5th September, 1749.

Page 93.—On Thorny Branch, joining John Stunkard and John Bing.

Page 97.—19th May, 1789. James and Mary Griffith to Abel Griffith, 100 acres, part of 400 patented to John Fancie, deceased, 15th June, 1773, and devised to James and Mary by Johns will. Teste: James Anderson, John Hogset, John Dickey.

Page 106.—268 acres patented to Barbara Smith 1st March, 1773. Teste: George Hooke, Arthur Connely, Thos. Bleakely.

Page 111.—On Calfpasture corner to land of Clemon's orphans.

Page 117.—14th January, 1791. William Tate, of Washington County, Va., and Agness, to George Lots.

Page 120.—517 acres patented to Thomas Waterson 12th May, 1759, by Waterson to Abraham Smith, deceased, and by him devised to his son, Benjamin Smith, grantor here.

Page 123.—21st June, 1777. John Hodge to James Hodge. Whereas Samuel Hodge, late of Calfpasture, deceased, devised to his younger son, James Hodge, plantation Samuel lived on, and James is advised only a life estate passes passes; John, eldest son and heir of Samuel and brother to James, releases the reversion. Teste: Thomas Adams, Andrew Hamilton, Henry McDonnald, Elizabeth Adams.

Page 125.—18th November, 1787. John Campbell, Sr., to James Steel, part of 570 acres formerly property of James Campbell, deceased, and sold to James Steel by consent of said John Campbell, joining John Cloid's part of said tract. Teste: Geo. Hutcheson Ben. Stuart, Andrew Fulton, Robert Bell.

Page 126.—14th April, 1791. Martha Downey, wife to Samuel Downey, deceased, Samuel Downey and Rachel to John Shuye of Washington County, Maryland, tract willed by Samuel to his son. Samuel, 2d January, 1773, in Beverley Manor; corner land laid off for William Blair and John Wilson; corner William Downey. Teste:Patrick Buchanan, Robert Donaldson, Godlib Harfman, Augustine Argenbright.

Page 134.—14th November, 1787. Jean (mark) White, widow to Isaac White, deceased; David and Isaac White, executors of Isaac White, deceased; James and Gordon White, legatees of Isaac, to James Steel.

Page 36.—Teste: James McCan, Andrew Shroffe, Samuel Miller.

Page 139.—4th March, 1791. Privy examination of Eve, wife of Daniel Joseph, of Rockingham, before John Pirkey, and Peter Nicholas. Deed to Wm. Baker, dated 12th February, 1791.

Page 140.—29th July. 1788. Ditto of Elizabeth, wife of Frederick Myers, deed to Jacob Eversole, dated 25th May, 1787.

Page 141.—14th May, 1782. John Gay and Sarah and James Gay, his brother, to Henry Rockey, of Lancaster County, Penna., tract on Cromby's Creek of Cowpasture, made to said John and James by their last will and testament.

Page 329.—183 acres patented to John Finley 1st December, 1740.
Page 331.—23d November, 1791. Levi Lockhart and Hannah, of Bourbon County, Ky., to John Moffett, 144 acres, part of tract Jacob Lockhart formerly lived on.
Page 333.—26th November, 1791. Privy examination of Hanna to above before Andrew Hood, William Sudeth, Jno. Waller.
Page 341.—Note that the remainder of this book is superseded by No. XXVIII.
Last deed recorded 17th April, 1792.

CIRCUIT COURT DEEDS.

Deed Book No. 1.

Page 1.—29th March, 1789. Alexander Stuart to daughter, Elenor, gift of slave.
Page 1.—29th March, 1789. Same to daughter, Mary Hall, gift of slave.
Page 2.—2d September, 1789. Alexander St. Clair and Jane to John Price, ¼ acre in Staunton, part of 25 acres added to Staunton by Legislature October, 1787.
Page 3.—7th October, 1789. James Fleming and Ann, of South Carolina, to James McGonnigle, of Augusta, lot claimed by James as heir-at-law of William Fleming, deceased. No. 18 in Staunton, whereon Thomas Smith formerly dwelt, conveyed to William by James Hill and wife. Proved by witness, James Agnew, before Justice John Willson in Pendleton County, S. C.; also before William Baskin, Justice.
Page 12.—1st September, 1790. Francis Erwin, of Augusta, attorney for Alexander Curry, of Kentucky, to Balser Baumbardner.
Page 17.—1st September, 1790. Hugh Campbell, of Rockbridge, to John Lowry, of Augusta. Delivered: Joseph Lowry, son of John, 10th August, 1791. 130 acres, part of 200 acres conveyed by Charles Campbell to James Campbell and descended to Hugh as heir of James.
Page 35.—16th August, 1791. James Wright and Alexander Wright, sons and devisees of William Wright, deceased, and Elizabeth, wife of James, of Augusta, to Jacob Bear, 260 acres in Beverley Manor, part of tract originally surveyed for Joseph Mills, and sold to Robert Wilson and Jno. Holmes by deed which was conveyed to said William Wright, deceased, by John Holmes, February, 1748.
Page 36.—14th July, 1791. Before Andrew Kinkead, Justice of Bourbon County, Ky., appeared Margaret Wright, widow of Wm. Wright, and relinquished dower in above; also Elizabeth, wife of James, does same.
Page 40.—20th October, 1791. Robert Patterson and Martha to Michael Carr, late of Pennsylvania, conveyed by Beverley, 1740, to Nathaniel Patterson.
Page 43.—1st January, 1792. Archibald Stuart, of Augusta, to Robert Stuart, of Rockbridge, 5 shillings, 100 acres in Rockbridge conveyed to Archibald by Alexander Stuart, who purchased from 'Samuel McCampbell; corner Alexander Tedford.
Page 49.—27th June, 1791. Robert Sconce, of Bourbon County, Ky.,

appointed John Waller, of same place, attorney, to collect bond given by James Reed, of Greenbrier, to Robert, then of same County.

Page 50.—4th November, 1791. John Login, of Augusta, to Archibald Henderson, of Rockbridge, 52 acres adjoining land formerly John Login's, deceased, purchased by said John of David Russell.

Page 92.—21st May, 1792. John Wilson, of Fayette County, Penna., appoints James Lyle, his attorney, to receive from the County deeds to lots 49 and 59 in Staunton sold to John's father, George Wilson.

Page 97.—13th February, 1792. Alexander Stuart, of Rockbridge, to Robert Stuart; Alexander Tedford's line; corner James McCampbell.

Page 106.—11th July, 1792. John Tenant and Catherine ( ) to Michael Garber, Sr., recites that John has enlisted as soldier in U. S. Army and wishes to secure a livelihood to Catherine; conveys their distributive share in estate of Jacob Seilor after death of widow of Jacob; also their rights in estate of John David Greinor, late of Staunton, deceased, whose widow Catherine is.

Page 142.—22 October, 1793. William Erwin and Susanna to James Hutchinson, tract in Pendleton County.

Page 159.—6th September, 1794. John and Robert McKinney, of Bourbon County, Ky., executors of Alexander McKinney, deceased, of Fayette County.

Page 169.—2d April, 1795. William Logan and Jane, of Rockbridge, to Michael Coalter, of Amherst, tract in Rockbridge.

Page 263.—6th November, 1797. Robert Black, Jr, of Robertson County, Tenn., appoints David Buchanan attorney to collect debts and recover tract of land claimed by Robert by right of his marriage with Jane Buchanan, daughter and heiress of James Buchanan, deceased.

Page 288.—5th September, 1799. Wm. Chambers et als., to Hugh Donaghe, 50 acres on Naked Creek devised to Elizabeth Blair by her brother, John Blair, by will 15th April, 1788. Elizabeth has married Joseph Byers and he gave deed of trust to grantors here.

Page 308.—14th June, 1796. Joseph Grubb, of Peters Township, Franklin County, Penna., yeoman, by his attorney, James Irwin (Erwin), of Miersburg in same County.

Page 330.—7th April, 1800. John Bratton to John Dunlap, John Gay. John McCutcheon, James Berry, James Bratton, trustees of the Little River Congregation in the Calfpasture, 2 acres on Meeting House Branch.

Page 342.—5th August, 1800. Rosanna Walter, widow of Henry Walter, and late Rosanna Mans (otherwise Man), widow of Peter Man (otherwise called Peter Mans), of Frederick County, Maryland, to Michael Harman, conveys tract, lot 14 in Staunton, which Rosanna purchased from Thomas Fulton by deed 23d September, 1763.

Page 360.— —— ———, 1794. Peter Weaver and Elizabeth, Margaret Denton, John Stickleman and Elizabeth to John Weaver, interest in tract descended from their father, John George Weaver.

INDEX

INDEX

The spelling in the original manuscript has been followed throughout this publication.

Abbot, James, 397.
Abecost, Michael, 125.
Abercrombie, John, 447.
Abercromby, Robert, 365, 377.
Aberman, Mary, 137.
Aberman, Michael, 137.
Abner, John, 575.
Abney, Isabella (Isabel), 169, 181.
Abney, John, 134, 142, 144, 163, 166, 179, 181, 183, 193, 525, 527, 578.
Abney, William, 181, 244, 250, 589.
Abot, Benjamin, 152.
Abraham, 551.
Abrams, Henry, 39.
Absheir (Appinger), Peter, 64 .
Acker, Ann, 531.
Ackery, Wm., 318.
Acard, Dorothy, 235.
Acord, Francis, 235.
Acord, Jacob, 214.
Acre, Michael, 207.
Acres, Christian, 577.
Acres, Ruth, 12.
Acres (Akers), Simon, 9, 12, 17.
Acres, (Akers), Thomas, 12, 16, 401, 482.
Acres, Uriah, 12, 18.
Acres (Akers), William, 9, 12, 16, 19.
Adair, Benjamin, 237.
Adair, Cornelius, 237.
Adair (Adaer), Elizabeth, 176, 237.
Adair, Francis, 237.
Adair, James, 237.
Adare, John, 131, 237, 582.
Adair, Neil, 536.
Adair, Robert, 84, 102.
Adair, Wm., 6, 49, 54, 81, 82, 237, 257.
Adam, Agness, 497.
Adams, Elizabeth, 113, 182, 461, 592.
Adams, Francis, 114.
Adams, George, 64, 65, 450, 572.
Adames, James, 102.
Adams (Adam), John, 73, 114, 320, 321, 449, 461, 497.
Adams, Margaret, 9, 113, 114, 498.
Adams, Mary, 498.
Adams, Richard, 182, 492.

Adams, Samuel, 9, 10, 113, 114, 454, 498.
Adams, Thomas, 135, 173, 182, 189, 192, 217, 444, 488, 492, 507, 519, 564, 592.
Adams, Wm., 182, 352, 368, 411.
Aderson, Mary, 192.
Adkins, John, 167.
Adudell, John, 521.
Ager, John, 143.
Agnew, James, 575, 595.
Agnew, Margaret, 187.
Ahart, Michael, 44.
Aiken (Akin), James, 12, 478.
Akerling, Samuel, 295.
Akers, Mary, 9, 12.
Alcoran (Allcorn), Robert, 22, 28.
Alcorn, James, 474, 490.
Alcorn, John, 435.
Aldeman, Richard, 167.
Alderson, John, 52, 147, 515.
Alderson, Thomas, 145, 171.
Alexander, Abigail, 516.
Alexander, Abraham, 476.
Alexander, Agness, 559.
Alexander, Alexander, 135.
Alexander, Andrew, 39, 41, 67, 183, 234, 263, 273, 275, 292, 330, 348, 377, 379, 381, 440, 556, 566.
Alexander, Ann, 111, 168.
Alexander, Archibald, 23, 24, 31, 36, 43, 49, 62, 72, 76, 80, 82, 114, 119, 122, 126, 133, 137, 145, 266, 267, 326, 329, 353, 354, 358, 399, 406, 429, 435, 438, 443, 475, 499, 528, 534, 551, 553.
Alexander, Catherine, 183, 381.
Alexander, Dorcus, 153, 198.
Alexander, Ebenezer, 148, 534, 559.
Alexander, Eleanor, 168.
Alexander, Elizabeth, 198, 229, 234.
Alexander, Esther, 111, 157, 168.
Alexander, Francis, 123, 153, 198, 360, 420, 426.
Alexander, Gabriel, 151, 153, 160, 198, 199, 212, 234, 235, 278, 279, 368, 555.
Alexander, George, 371.
Alexander, Hugh, 168, 250.
Alexander, James, 5, 10, 44, 46, 60, 111,

151, 153, 160, 168, 183, 234, 242, 265,
274, 277, 278, 279, 294, 298, 326, 348,
360, 364, 368, 426, 446, 468, 475, 482,
489, 517, 521, 528, 540, 564, 570, 577,
586, 594.
Alexander, Jane, 222, 242.
Alexander, Janet, 198.
Alexander, John, 135, 143, 153, 161, 183,
198, 209, 233, 234, 279, 294, 384, 426,
468, 482, 487, 511, 514, 525, 556, 564,
570, 576, 577, 586.
Alexander, Joseph, 125, 353, 399, 429, 479,
516, 517, 528, 551, 556.
Alexander, Magdalen, 326.
Alexander, Margaret, 153, 234, 528.
Alexander, Martha, 168, 234, 298, 468, 523.
Alexander, Mary, 234, 525.
Alexander, Mathew, 165, 180, 222.
Alexander, Oliver, 517, 528, 581.
Alexander, Peter, 168, 563.
Alexander, Rachel, 577.
Alexander, Robert (R.), 8, 16, 17, 29, 30,
37, 41, 42, 53, 84, 85, 108, 168, 169,
250, 261, 264, 265, 269, 271, 272, 280,
281, 358, 359, 388, 393, 426, 440, 475,
564.
Alexander, Sarah, 168, 235.
Alexander, Thomas, 111, 157, 168, 484.
Alexander, William, 18, 19, 111, 122, 125,
137, 145, 168, 170, 198, 234, 235, 250,
294, 298, 303, 348, 353, 358, 393, 396,
399, 434, 442, 468, 478, 482, 484, 499,
520, 530, 534, 537, 540, 548, 556, 564,
570, 577, 594.
Alford, Phoeby, 226.
Alger, George, 524.
Algyre, Michael, 156.
Alkier, John, 153.
Alkeir, Michael, 141.
Allen, Aliner, 218.
Allen (Allin), Benjamin, 5, 6, 8, 192, 252,
412, 539, 551.
Allen, David, 155, 156, 179, 559.
Allen, Elizabeth, 155, 179, 237.
Allen, Fanny, 229.
Allen, Francis, 183, 196.
Allen, Hugh, 112, 113, 120, 139, 154, 184,
371, 383, 414, 418, 428, 439, 449, 450,
473.
Allen, Ingbor, 21.
Allen, Jackson, 22, 304.
Allen, James, 43, 44, 72, 89, 92, 116, 124
134, 139, 150, 151, 153, 154, 155, 172,
174, 177, 179, 183, 185, 188, 192, 196, 197,
199, 233, 235, 242, 316, 348, 349, 356
370, 371, 407, 469, 472, 476, 491, 505,
506, 510, 513, 527, 544, 591, 594.
Allen, James, J., 155.
Allen, Jane (Jean), 139, 183, 235, 491.
Allen, John, 155, 179, 192, 248, 294, 505,
554.

Allen, John C., 155.
Allen, Joseph, 22.
Allen, Malcom, 88, 97, 101, 105, 370, 376,
397, 414, 418, 424, 449, 450, 476, 480,
488.
Allen, Margaret, 202, 235, 591.
Allen, Martha, 192, 389, 414, 418, 472, 491.
Allen, Martin, 118.
Allen, Mary, 22, 25, 155, 179, 196, 248,
304, 449, 450.
Allen, Moses, 449, 450.
Allen, Mountecue, 192.
Allen, Reuben, 6, 13, 17, 21, 22, 575.
Allen, Robert, 48, 55, 67, 155, 179, 183,
184, 192, 337, 351, 361, 389, 402, 403,
410, 444, 472, 491, 565, 566.
Allen, Sarah, 206.
Allen, Thomas, 155, 179, 192.
Allen, William, 43, 192, 235, 554, 557, 561,
565, 576.
Alley, John, 556.
Allison, Agness, 109.
Allison, Andrew, 188, 192, 218, 222.
Allison, Ann, 511.
Allison, Charles, 432.
Allison, Dorcas, 239.
Allison, Elizabeth, 222
Allison, Francis, 109, 188, 292, 296, 342,
542.
Allison, Halbert, 109.
Allison, Hannah, 62, 109, 542.
Allison, James, 109, 113, 177, 227, 230, 233,
235, 238, 239, 243, 244, 399, 454.
Allison, Janet, 109, 432, 496.
Allison (Alison), Jean, 226, 340.
Allison (Alison), John, 34, 35, 36, 55, 62,
77, 82, 109, 114, 177, 188, 189, 194,
218, 267, 291, 328, 340, 358, 365, 371,
375, 380, 432, 454, 464, 467, 484, 494,
496, 523, 568, 569, 571, 575.
Allison, John H., 222.
Allison, Lucy (Lucie), 177, 188, 523.
Allison, Phoebe, 239.
Allison, Robert, 19, 20, 22, 80, 109, 117,
129, 260, 271, 292, 296, 299, 313, 335,
348, 349, 367, 451, 489, 509, 511.
Allison, William, 177, 194, 239, 523.
Allist, George, 157.
Allstot, (Alstot), Nicholas, 484, 528.
Almond, William, 153.
Alphin, John, 211.
Alvard, Will, 82.
Amone, Arnest, 146.
Anderson, Agnes (Agnis), 154, 193, 581.
Anderson, Alexander, 76, 78, 79, 203.
Anderson, Andrew, 161, 167, 172, 174, 177,
184, 185, 188, 197, 201, 202, 206, 569,
574, 591.
Anderson, Ann, 71, 538, 581.
Anderson, Elizabeth, 12, 184, 203, 266, 324,
379, 425, 477, 508, 585.

Anderson, Esther, 343.
Anderson, George, 15, 19, 23, 56, 70, 87, 154, 177, 184, 203, 206, 243, 252, 261, 266, 267, 272, 277, 278, 280, 282, 292, 313, 324, 391, 410, 419, 422, 442, 453, 455, 514, 576.
Anderson, Hannah, 83.
Anderson, Isaac, 8, 12, 14, 51, 57, 70, 80, 263, 287, 290, 322, 343, 443, 491.
Anderson, Jacob, 12, 29, 30, 44, 57, 60, 67, 70, 80, 114, 286, 343, 348, 349, 399, 433, 511.
Anderson, James, 12, 30, 51, 124, 153, 154, 156, 158, 159, 167, 176, 177, 184, 193, 201, 209, 220, 225, 243, 267, 348, 365, 367, 379, 380, 398, 401, 407, 414, 417, 419, 432, 433, 463, 477, 481, 495, 508, 536, 547, 548, 565, 566, 569, 579, 581, 585, 586, 590, 592.
Anderson, Jane (Jean), 154, 177, 184, 203, 261, 264, 354, 585.
Anderson, John, 12, 14, 15, 20, 21, 29, 38, 45, 48, 70, 75, 90, 92, 124, 127, 154, 167, 177, 184, 203, 243, 255, 261, 264, 267, 280, 287, 290, 295, 297, 301, 303, 308, 337, 354, 356, 365, 370, 380, 391, 397, 405, 412, 422, 441, 443, 463, 476, 477, 502, 505, 506, 510, 516, 522, 527, 538, 555, 565, 574, 581, 585, 588, 591.
Anderson, Margaret, 83, 157, 184, 204, 237.
Anderson, Martha, 12, 591.
Anderson, Mary, 12, 184.
Anderson, Nancy, 184.
Anderson, Pearson, 348.
Anderson, Rebecca, 234, 545.
Anderson, Robert, 177, 184, 203, 237, 365, 380, 441, 454, 460.
Anderson, Samuel, 154, 156, 168, 171, 177, 183, 203, 265, 310, 541, 545, 554, 559, 569, 579, 580, 585, 586, 591.
Anderson, Sarah, 579, 580, 585.
Anderson, Thomas, 144.
Anderson, William, 15, 30, 77, 87, 103, 115, 135, 142, 154, 156, 177, 184, 203, 225, 248, 255, 266, 271, 274, 276, 295, 366, 385, 394, 419, 425, 445, 477, 525, 541, 545, 555, 569, 570, 574, 585, 588, 594.
Andiddle, James, 184.
Andrew, Peter, 53.
Andrew, Thomas, 149.
Andrews, Elizabeth, 206, 224.
Andrews, Robert, 95, 102.
Angel, Peter, 54.
Aphinger, Eve, 61.
Apinger, Peter, 61.
Appell (Apple), Michael, 224, 593.
Arbocust, Michael, 531.
Arbuckle, James, 36, 43, 70, 407, 437, 438.
Arbuckle, Mathew, 93, 99, 164, 437, 534.
Arbuckle, Rachel, 407.

Arbuckle, Thomas, 104.
Archdeacon Michael, 502, 516.
Archenbright (Argabrite, **Argenbright**, Arkenbright), Jacob, 110, 339, 387, 416, 471, 479, 483, 497, 509, 519, 528.
Archenbright, John, 479, 496.
Archenbright, Martin, 447.
Archer, Edmond, 151.
Archer, Elizabeth, 151.
Archer, Isabella, 151.
Archer, James, 151, 547.
Archer, John, 21, 22, 23, 24, 43, 44, 72, 78, 89, 101, 102, 109, 115, 138, 151, 158, 161, 197, 274, 276, 280, 299, 302, 310, 317, 338, 371, 402, 439, 442, 447, 492, 578, 580, 590.
Archer, Rebecca, 158, 186, 276, 371, 447, 492.
Archer, Robert, 447.
Archer (Archee), Sampson, 24, 25, 44, 45, 47, 49, 54, 56, 60, 79, 158, 197, 256, 266, 276, 318, 343, 344, 352, 371, 447, 510, 580.
Archer, Samuel, 55.
Archer, William, 151.
Arehart, Michael, 65.
Arewen, Andrew, 62, 63.
Arewen, John, 63.
Argabright, Elizabeth, 243.
Argenbright, (Argabrite), **Augustine**, 177, 209, 215, 216, 221, 592.
Argenbright, Susannah, 519.
Argon, John, 158.
Arley, James M., 580.
Armengash, Michael, 195.
Armingcost, Michael, 560.
Armstrong, Abel, 143.
Armstrong, Agnes, 36.
Armstrong, Alexander, 490.
Armstrong, Alice, 36.
Armstrong, Ann, 143.
Armstrong, Archibald, 43, 51, 58, 64, 70, 119, 219, 339, 434, 453, 491, 493.
Armstrong, Baptist, 107.
Armstrong, Benjamin, 36.
Armstrong, Catherine, 45.
Armstrong, Elizabeth, 181, 195, 201, 205, 207, 210, 216, 435.
Armstrong, Isabella, 219.
Armstrong, James, 36, 37, 55, 56, 78, 79, 110, 146, 167, 223, 253, 255, 266, 277, 284, 287, 303, 312, 318, 370, 371, 377, 378, 395, 411, 520, 547, 564.
Armstrong, Jane (Jean), 55, 78, 223, 277, 377, 378, 562, 567.
Armstrong, John (Jhorn), 36, 45, 70, 79, 87, 103, 110, 118, 120, 223, 247, 397, 454, 580.
Armstrong, Lanty, 91, 110, 118, 417.
Armstrong, Lillie, 391.
Armstrong, Lydia (Liddy), 55, 79, 318.

Armstrong, Margaret (Peggy), 219, 223, 232, 245, 248, 453.
Armstrong, Martha, 36.
Armstrong, Mary (Polly), 181, 199, 201, 205, 207, 230, 385, 396, 547.
Armstrong, Mathew, 23, 24, 280, 353, 370, 391.
Armstrong, Nancy, 201, 205.
Armstrong, Robert, 19, 27, 28, 36, 38, 43, 55, 70, 78, 79, 110, 112, 118, 128, 137, 142, 143, 158, 197, 201, 205, 219, 223, 273, 318, 335, 352, 359, 377, 379, 381, 393, 401, 408, 409, 435, 446, 447, 453, 454, 562, 564, 565, 567, 578, 590.
Armstrong, Samuel, 181, 184, 201, 205, 207, 216, 247, 249.
Armstrong, Sarah, 55.
Armstrong, Susanna, 12.
Armstrong, Thomas, 21, 25, 44, 78, 143, 145, 260, 358, 380, 500.
Armstrong, William, 6, 9, 12, 15, 18, 23, 61, 74, 79, 117, 143, 171, 181, 188, 194, 206, 210, 216, 219, 223, 275, 293, 303, 304, 308, 314, 339, 358, 367, 377, 379, 385, 393, 396, 407, 408, 428, 435, 492, 493, 504, 556, 564.
Arn (Arwen) (Erwin), William, 536.
Arnet, David, 145.
Arnet (Arnott), Thomas, 480, 486, 490.
Arnold, James, 93.
Arnold, Jane (Jean), 340, 442, 454.
Arnold, Jonathan, 87.
Arnold, Samuel, 74.
Arnold, Stephen, 74, 93, 99, 340, 363, 443, 454.
Arshers, John, 66.
Artsugh, Frederick, 147.
Arvig (Awigand), Francis, 114.
Ashburner, John, 504, 545.
Ashton, Mary A., 56.
Askin (Astin), Evalina, 246.
Askin (Askins, Astin), John, 156, 226, 246, 308, 493.
Askins, Philip, 226.
Asten, Evelina, 241.
Aston (Asten), James, 234, 241.
Aston (Asten), John, 234, 241, 246.
Aston, Sarah (Salley), 236, 241.
Astrop, Elizabeth, 191.
Astrop, Henry, 191.
Astrop, Jane, 191.
Astrop, Jesse, 191.
Astrop, Polly, 191.
Astrop (Aistrap), Robert, 167, 169, 191, 559, 583, 589.
Atkins, Edward, 206.
Attkins, John, 387.
Atkinson, John, 578, 593.
Atwater, Annahellena, 565.
Atwater, Enos, 565, 573, 575, 580.
Atwaters, Annalina, 174.

Aulter, Bartholomew, 149.
Austin, Esther, 169.
Austin, Morris, 202.
Austin, William, 169.
Austner, Michael, 152.
Ayler (Aylor, Ailer, Eler), Anthony, 127, 197, 419, 523, 529, 530, 551, 554.
Ayler (Ehler), Henry, 275.
Aylett, William, 14.
Backenstoe (Backenst, Backinster, Backinston), John, 200, 201, 215, 589.
Backfish, Conrad, 69.
Baggs, Alexander, 93, 398, 471.
Baggs, Elizabeth, 356.
Bagge, James, 40.
Baggs, James, 280, 312, 356, 498, 551.
Baggs, Thomas, 133, 551.
Bagwill, Nathaniel, 590.
Bahm, Samuel, 287.
Baile (Baidie), John, 371.
Bailey, Anne, 413.
Bailey, Drury, 31.
Bailey, Elizabeth, 243.
Bailey, James, 370, 378, 413, 414, 452, 475.
Bailey (Bealey), John, 105, 125, 540, 552.
Bailey, Mercey, 552.
Bailey, Robert, 156, 200, 218, 226, 575.
Bailey, William, 138.
Baine, Alexander, 104, 425.
Bainter, Adam, 530.
Bair (Bear), Jacob, 510.
Bair (Bear), John, 552.
Baird, Adam, 106.
Baird, Christian, 224.
Baird (Beard), Robert, 264.
Baird, Sairah, 147.
Baird, Thomas, 169, 332, 333, 396.
Baith, Joseph, 181.
Baker, Barbara, 238.
Baker, Elias, 141.
Baker, Humphrey, 21, 285, 324.
Baker, Lewis, 150, 157, 162, 181.
Baker, Martin, 452.
Baker, Samuel, 238.
Baker, William, 196, 592.
Baksdal, Goodman, 169.
Baldwin, Cornelius, 215.
Balew, Abraham, 169.
Balew, Ann, 169.
Baley, Charles, 303.
Balfaut (Faut), Andrew, 393.
Balfaut, Elizabeth, 393, 440.
Balfaut, Gasper, 393.
Balfaut (Balfort), John, 393, 498, 539.
Ballard, John, 198.
Baller, John, 100, 162.
Ballinger, Gasper, 194.
Balsley, Christian, 212.
Bambridge, James, 109.
Bamford, Joseph, 228.
Bance, John, 569.

Bane, Elias, 490.
Bane, James, 54, 64, 75, 117, 314, 381, 412, 465.
Bane, Rebecca, 412.
Banener, Henry, 63.
Banister (Benister), James, 404.
Banks, William, 573.
Bannett, John, 143.
Banniger, Henry, 71.
Bannister, Mark, 147.
Barager, Jacob, 590.
Barber, Elizabeth, 16.
Barber, George, 16, 17.
Barberer, George, 9.
Barbour, James, 118.
Bare, Barbara, 304.
Bare, Jacob, 27, 103, 136, 142, 232, 304, 305, 311, 506, 507.
Bare, John, 9, 82, 304, 311, 372.
Barefield, William, 115.
Barger, Benjamin, 21.
Barger, Casper, 60, 488.
Barger, Jacob, 165, 187, 202.
Barger, Margaret, 426.
Barker, Elias, 151.
Barker, Isabel, 154.
Barkley, John, 167.
Barkley, Lazarus, 160.
Barlet, Margaret, 143.
Barnes, Thomas, 97, 98, 103, 388, 390, 401, 421, 430, 467.
Barnet, Dorcas, 160.
Barnet (Barnett), John, 238, 550.
Barnet, Patrick, 76.
Barnet, Rachel, 55.
Barnett, Mickell, 419.
Barnett, William, 189.
Barns, John, 161.
Barns, Richard, 41.
Barrenhinsell, John, 14.
Barret, Richard, 559.
Barrett, Dominick, 201.
Barrett, John, 85.
Barrey, James, 290.
Barrier, Casper, 59, 110, 321, 372, 426.
Barrier, Jacob, 164, 204.
Barrier, Margaret, 59.
Barrier, William, 151.
Barringer, Henry, 65.
Barry, Agnes, 218.
Barry, Andrew, 218, 230, 236.
Barry, David, 92.
Barry, Elenor, 218.
Barry, James, 201.
Barry, James, 587.
Barry, Sarah, 218.
Barry, Thomas, 215, 218, 221.
Barselinsmayer, John, 129.
Bartell, Andrew, 514.
Bartley, James, 70, 341.

Bartley, Jean, 341.
Barton, Edward, 159.
Barton, James, 307, 331, 377.
Basken (Baskins), Andrew, 107, 313.
Basken (Baskin, Baskins), William, 8, 18, 27, 38, 56, 72, 157, 259, 260, 280, 283, 312, 318, 319, 334, 363, 367, 370, 389, 424, 432, 595.
Baskin (Baskins), Charles, 134, 205, 206, 391, 546, 548, 564.
Baskin, John C., 546.
Baskin (Baskins), Mary, 206, 424, 432.
Baskin (Baskins), Thomas, 84, 366, 396, 411.
Baskins, James, 247.
Baskins, John, 51.
Baskins, Josiah, 247.
Baskins, Robert, 18.
Bates, Ephraim, 163.
Bates, Henry, 73.
Bates, James, 73, 189.
Bates, Thomas, 93, 188.
Bates, William, 73, 461.
Battrorff, Philip, 187.
Batts (Beats), Thomas, 454.
Baughman (Boughman), Henry, 49, 50, 483.
Baumbardner, Balser, 595.
Baumgardner (Bomgardner, Bumgardner), John, 21, 288, 300, 329, 345, 419, 542.
Baumgartner, Hans, 17, 288.
Baxter, Andrew, 29, 259, 444.
Baxter, Ann P., 82.
Baxter, George, 138, 178, 419, 487.
Baxter, Margaret, 29, 444.
Baylor, Anna Maria, 250.
Baylor, Christian, 216, 250.
Baylor, George, 240, 250.
Baylor, Jacob, 203, 250.
Baylor, John, 203.
Baylor, Martin, 250.
Baylor, Robert, 203.
Bays, John, 583.
Beach, John, 565, 573, 583.
Beak (Beck), Jefry, 304.
Beal, J., 200.
Beal (Beall), Thomas, 362, 339, 390, 401, 496, 540, 541.
Beale, Samuel, 147.
Bealey (Beaty), Francis, 36.
Bealey (Realey), Michael, 36.
Beall, Leonard, 173.
Beall, Zachariah, 188.
Bealy (Bailey), Drury, 33.
Beames, William, 10.
Bean, Ellis, 106.
Bean, Isaac, 6, 9.
Bean (Bein), James, 38, 44, 55, 70, 79, 308, 455.

Bean, Rebecca, 45.
Bean, William, 89, 171, 226, 413.
Branham, John, 252.
Bear, Adam, 238.
Bear, Barbara M., 510.
Bear, Barbary, 372.
Bear, Caterean, 373.
Bear, Henry, 533.
Bear, Jacob, 40, 110, 128, 206, 238, 372, 420, 473, 494, 501, 534, 558, 595.
Bear, John, 115, 131, 132, 373, 449, 473, 479, 497, 512, 513, 518, 535.
Bear, Kartharine, 473.
Bear, Susannah, 247.
Beard, Adam, 96.
Beard, Alexander, 246.
Beard, Charles, 227, 228.
Beard, Christian, 240.
Beard, David, 227, 593.
Beard, Dickey, 227.
Beard, Edward, 45, 228, 276, 313, 336, 337, 338, 365, 378.
Beard, Elizabeth, 227.
Beard, Esther, 227.
Beard, Fane, 111.
Beard, Hugh, 111, 217, 249, 468, 498.
Beard, James, 17, 29, 53, 56, 69, 94, 111, 118, 200, 228, 258, 280, 313, 315, 336, 366, 372, 378, 379, 381, 389, 432, 497.
Beard, Jean (Jeanatte), 246, 344, 439, 497.
Beard, John, 142, 143, 228, 246, 439, 580, 594.
Beard, Joseph, 229, 246.
Beard, Margaret, 359.
Beard, Martha, 243, 250.
Beard, Mary (Polly), 246, 315, 336, 365, 378, 414, 493.
Beard, Samuel, 228, 229, 246, 421.
Beard, Sidney, 229, 246.
Beard, Susannah, 246.
Beard, Thomas, 6, 10, 14, 17, 29, 30, 89, 111, 112, 157, 194, 212, 246, 265, 304, 311, 316, 325, 344, 352, 359, 429, 439, 579.
Beard, William, 39, 40, 57, 58, 59, 63, 64, 70, 80, 86, 89, 111, 224, 228, 238, 240, 246, 258, 312, 315, 317, 336, 349, 359, 407, 414, 465, 493, 511, 572, 586.
Beatey (Beatie, Beaty, Beatty), Francis, 18, 26, 263, 268, 272, 273, 276, 277, 279, 282, 284, 286, 288, 290, 293, 295, 297, 298, 305, 306, 308, 310, 311, 312, 313, 315, 317, 322, 323, 327, 336, 337, 338, 398, 404, 442, 479, 501, 511, 517, 528.
Beaton, Nancy, 180.
Beats, James, 46, 48, 109.
Beatton, Robert, 337.
Beaty, Aaron, 246.
Beaty, Alexander, 249.
Beaty, David, 453.
Beaty, James, 501.
Beaty, John, 117, 287, 453, 501.
Beaty, Martha, 263.
Beaty, Mary, 249.
Beaty, Samuel, 510.
Beck, Anna C., 181.
Beck, Catherine, 181.
Beck, Jeofry, 314.
Beck, Lydia, 314.
Beck, Peter, 181.
Beck, Stephen, 181, 557.
Beder, Mathias, 86.
Beéle (Bell), Mary, 206.
Beens, Jacob, 163.
Beery, George, 338.
Beeth, Joseph, 533.
Beevey, Henry, 297.
Beggs, Alexander, 48, 291.
Beggs, James, 39, 115.
Beggs, Thomas, 148, 373.
Belew, Abraham, 219, 220.
Belew, Ann, 220.
Belew, Paley, 235.
Belfaut, Andrew, 440.
Belfield, John, 171.
Bell, Agnes, 168, 208.
Bell, Ann, 223.
Bell, Catrin, 5.
Bell, Daniel, 248.
Bell, David, 45, 70, 115, 116, 126, 153, 156, 158, 168, 174, 184, 197, 202, 211, 224, 234, 247, 266, 330, 333, 337, 353, 359, 370, 372, 392, 393, 434, 456, 458, 466, 550, 554, 561, 565, 573, 580, 582.
Bell, Elizabeth (Bessy), 20, 46, 156, 159, 172, 223, 582, 594.
Bell, Florence, 156, 163, 393, 550, 554.
Bell, Francis, 165, 168, 208, 220, 223, 241.
Bell, George, 224.
Bell, James, 5, 8, 15, 20, 22, 23, 25, 29, 38, 43, 48, 54, 55, 59, 71, 72, 77, 79, 83, 86, 111, 120, 141, 145, 149, 151, 153, 156, 157, 159, 160, 165, 168, 173, 174, 177, 192, 199, 200, 208, 209, 212, 214, 216, 223, 224, 230, 251, 259, 260, 273, 274, 278, 279, 295, 304, 324, 343, 346, 352, 355, 359, 375, 393, 407, 414, 446, 449, 463, 464, 465, 475, 477, 481, 511, 544, 557, 558, 559, 560, 562, 582, 591.
Bell, James Nelson, 239.
Bell, Jane (Jean), 20, 48, 187, 224, 230, 582.
Bell, John, 46, 54, 153, 156, 160, 168, 179, 181, 189, 196, 197, 199, 208, 211, 212, 219, 220, 222, 224, 230, 231, 233, 239, 241, 380, 555, 560, 582, 588.
Bell, John H., 239.
Bell, Joseph, 45, 51, 54, 59, 116, 131, 132, 153, 156, 158, 160, 176, 178, 179, 196, 197, 199, 200, 206, 208, 209, 212, 215, 216, 224, 235, 241, 242, 286, 304, 334,

336, 337, 348, 383, 414, 448, 496, 507, 527, 530, 547, 559, 566, 567, 573, 574, 582, 593, 594.
Bell, Lancelot, 239.
Bell, Lawrence, 450.
Bell, Leonard, 151, 164, 560.
Bell, Lettice, 582.
Bell, Lucinda, 251.
Bell, Margaret, 20, 23, 123, 196, 224, 336, 366.
Bell, Martha, 208, 222, 224.
Bell, Mary (Polly), 45, 222, 223, 230, 242, 244, 557.
Bell, Mary A., 20, 48, 102, 208.
Bell, Rachel, 20, 38, 48, 206, 208, 222, 260, 273, 420, 464.
Bell, Rebecca, 168.
Bell, Robert, 39, 46, 48, 208, 582, 592.
Bell, R. P., 549.
Bell, Samuel, 21, 45, 101, 104, 112, 123, 140, 145, 149, 151, 168, 179, 185, 199, 208, 212, 213, 220, 223, 224, 230, 232, 241, 251, 334, 354, 366, 369, 375, 383, 520, 535, 539, 541, 566, 567, 578, 582.
Bell, Sarah, 168, 179, 199, 212, 223, 232, 241, 359, 582.
Bell, Stephenson, 212.
Bell, Suckey, 199.
Bell, Susannah, 156.
Bell, Thomas, 159, 168, 170, 179, 180, 181, 199, 212, 224, 251, 422, 527, 530, 547, 582.
Bell, William, 20, 23, 44, 45, 47, 86, 111, 120, 145, 151, 156, 157, 160, 170, 196, 199, 208, 209, 212, 216, 220, 224, 226, 230, 238, 241, 247, 255, 266, 310, 330, 333, 334, 337, 345, 354, 359, 380, 392, 393, 394, 396, 403, 420, 446, 456, 464, 475, 477, 481, 544, 557, 559, 572, 573, 579, 582, 593, 594.
Bell, Zachariah, 286, 330, 336, 337, 383.
Bellfaught, John, 64, 94.
Bellow, Abraham, 570.
Bellshe, (Belshire, Belshe, Bellsher), Robert, 97, 336, 462.
Bellshie, (Belshe), James, 84, 414.
Below, Solomon, 169.
Belshus, Peter, 835.
Bender, Catherine, 131.
Bender, (Painter), John, 131.
Bender, Margaret, 131.
Benedick, John, 545.
Bengamon, John, 470.
Benleven, Isaac, 160.
Bennet, Catherine, 451.
Bennet, John, 163.
Bennett (Bennet, Benit), Benjamin, 30, 93, 378, 387, 405, 438, 451, 567.
Bennett (Bennet, Benit), Joseph, 126, 139, 156, 508.
Bennett, Mary, 555.

Bennett (Bennet), Moses, 481, 507, 513, 555.
Bennett (Bennet), Richard, 19, 30, 567.
Bennett, Sarah, 19.
Bennett, William, 158.
Bennigar (Benninger), Henry, 134, 144.
Benson (Benston), George, 164, 565, 589, 590.
Benson, John, 527.
Benson, Margaret, 534.
Benston, Leven, 150.
Benston, Mathias, 164.
Benter, Frederick, 373.
Benter, Hennery, 221.
Benton, Joseph, 332.
Benton, Mary E., 332.
Bentz, Valentine, 18.
Ber, Hans, 9.
Berger, Philip, 164.
Berkley, James, 53.
Berkley (Berkeley), William, 157, 463.
Bernard, John, 592.
Berrisford, Ann, 83.
Berrisford, John, 25, 75, 83, 287, 301, 343.
Berrisford, Lydia, 83.
Berrisford, Mary, 343.
Berry, Challe, 185.
Berry, Charles, 13, 14, 31, 118, 159, 163, 185, 215, 220, 302, 318, 501, 510, 517.
Berry, David, 51, 94, 417.
Berry, Elizabeth, 118, 159, 185, 343, 511.
Berry, Elizabeth E., 14.
Berry, Ellen, 247.
Berry, Esther, 345, 398.
Berry, Francis, 118, 159, 167, 553.
Berry, George, 20, 89, 128, 144, 147, 159, 160, 167, 210, 223, 225, 226, 343, 379, 410, 470, 519, 523, 577.
Berry, Isabel, 553.
Berry, James, 14, 17, 20, 47, 118, 159, 163, 167, 179, 180, 185, 206, 215, 219, 222, 224, 226, 302, 303, 323, 336, 338, 343, 363, 398, 426, 446, 511, 596.
Berry, Jane (Jean, Jenny), 185, 222, 310, 410.
Berry, John, 20, 47, 51, 104, 118, 119, 120, 159, 185, 201, 226, 382, 415, 434, 446, 479, 499, 566.
Berry, Joseph, 115.
Berry, Mary, 118, 163, 185.
Berry, Nancy, 121.
Berry, Rebecca, 118.
Berry, Robert, 185.
Berry, Thomas, 14, 95, 114, 117, 137, 149, 307, 310, 319, 335, 345, 398, 410, 479, 511.
Berry, William, 20, 118, 120, 159, 256, 307, 310, 332, 333, 396, 410, 415, 426, 499, 501, 553, 588.
Berryer, Jacob, 201.
Berryhill, Alexander, 233.
Berryhill, James, 84.

Berryhill, John, 64, 84, 418, 450.
Berryhill, Rachel, 84, 244.
Berton, Edmond, 566.
Berton, James, 443.
Bess, Abraham, 89, 390.
Bess (Biss), Isabell, 89.
Bess (Best), James, 89, 207.
Bess, Margaret, 89.
Best, Bett (Bell), 180.
Best, Christopher, 416.
Best, Francis, 188, 203, 564.
Best, James, 166, 188, 245, 536, 556, 564.
Best, Mary, 180.
Best, Sally, 237.
Bethel, William, 315.
Bets, James, 32, 92, 97.
Betty (Beaty), Francis, 266.
Betty, John, 7, 13, 295.
Beven, Richard, 150.
Beverlcy, Elizabeth, 269.
Beverley, Maria, 423.
Beverley, Robert, 170, 422, 423, 424, 425, 434, 439, 440, 442, 457, 498, 511, 513, 514, 515, 516, 519.
Beverley, William, 252, 253, 254, 261, 262, 264, 265, 268, 269, 270, 271, 272, 273, 274, 275, 277, 278, 280, 282, 283, 284, 285, 286, 287, 288, 290, 292, 293, 294, 296, 298, 299, 300, 301, 302, 303, 310, 311, 327, 365, 384, 392, 398, 423, 429, 434, 459, 497, 517, 562.
Bewes (Bews), William, 272, 277.
Bibb, William, 356.
Bickle, Adam, 215, 581, 589.
Bickle, Euphemia H., 217.
Bickle, Margaret, 217.
Bickle, Mary, 577, 581.
Bierey, John, 547.
Bigham, George, 107, 278, 279, 328, 348, 387.
Bigham, Jane, 563.
Bigham, John, 279.
Bigham, Sarah, 563.
Bigman, John, 26.
Bing, Elizabeth, 191.
Bing, Esther, 191.
Bing, James, 191.
Bing, John, 191, 195, 554, 592.
Bing, Margaret, 191.
Bing, Martha, 191.
Bing, William, 191.
Bingaman (Bigaman), Christian, 75, 76, 110.
Bingaman, Henry, 76, 107, 113.
Bingaman (Bingeman, Bigham, Bigam), John, 41, 42, 44, 54, 55, 66, 70, 75, 76, 107, 110, 112, 134, 141, 278, 280, 292, 298, 301, 324, 394, 408, 505, 563.
Bingman, Christopher, 60.
Binney, John, 575.
Bird, Abraham (Abram), 32, 40, 52, 53, 60, 77, 105, 117, 123, 128, 269, 308, 320, 479.
Bird, Andrew, 13, 19, 22, 25, 26, 57, 78, 105, 115, 291, 293, 308, 315, 320, 373, 397, 450, 472, 478, 490, 527, 528.
Bird, Clair, 373.
Bird, John, 9, 43, 47, 49, 50, 184, 326.
Bird, Magdalene, 19.
Bird, Mark, 539, 554, 558.
Bird, Mary, 472, 558.
Bird, Moses, 32, 320, 373.
Bird, Mounce (Mount), 57, 77.
Bird, Sarah, 49.
Bird, Thomas, 167.
Bird, William, 64.
Birk, Lucretia, 381.
Birk, Thomas, 113.
Bishop, William, 29, 36, 47.
Biss, Abraham, 117, 395, 401.
Black, Alexander, 26, 86, 88, 164, 427, 492, 593.
Black, Andrew, 113.
Black, Anthony, 36, 65, 68, 120, 128, 232, 268, 358, 499.
Black, Catherine, 557.
Black, Crawford, 575.
Black, Cutlip, 187, 554.
Black, David, 48, 112, 113, 118, 518, 568.
Black, Elizabeth, 65, 112, 113.
Black, Henry, 126, 132, 167, 399, 437, 480, 498, 528, 553, 557.
Black, Hugh, 232.
Black, Isabell, 48.
Black, James, 65, 113, 128, 164, 203, 222, 232, 242, 246, 251, 345, 403, 516, 587.
Black, Jean (Jane), 165, 242, 246, 251.
Black, John, 10, 24, 29, 30, 36, 48, 50, 60, 66, 79, 112, 113, 120, 146, 164, 165, 166, 169, 170, 187, 206, 209, 215, 222, 232, 242, 250, 259, 268, 274, 279, 285, 304, 325, 328, 345, 365, 368, 403, 516, 518, 566, 569, 574, 582.
Black, Joseph, 206, 219, 220, 250, 574.
Black, Magey, 444, 447.
Black, Margaret (Peggy), 132, 165, 187, 206, 232, 284, 357.
Black, Martha, 66, 165, 170, 222, 242.
Black, Mary, 68, 143, 165, 222, 242, 250.
Black, Mathew, 71, 76, 81, 345.
Black, Nancy, 165, 222.
Black, Rachel, 546.
Black, Rebecca (Rebekab), 250, 494, 518, 555, 574.
Black, Robert, 6, 66, 81, 268, 295, 345, 377, 398, 444, 447, 566, 572, 578, 596.
Black, Samuel, 48, 54, 60, 112, 115, 118, 164, 165, 166, 170, 177, 183, 215, 219, 222, 232, 242, 247, 250, 251, 337, 342, 349, 365, 368, 403, 424, 461, 470, 473, 493, 494, 518, 543, 550, 566, 569, 574, 582.
Black, Sarah (Sally), 121, 232, 403, 427.
Black, Shusy, 187.

Black, Thomas, 40, 261, 284, 287, 289, 342, 354, 357, 370, 411, 424.
Black, William, 86, 115, 135, 152, 164, 165, 172, 183, 222, 232, 242, 368, 427, 451, 453, 463, 502, 546.
Blackburn, Archibald, 232, 526.
Blackburn, Benjamin, 440.
Blackburn, George, 547, 593.
Blackburn, Nathaniel, 209.
Blackburn, Rosanna, 232.
Blackburn, Samuel, 211, 223.
Blackfild, Isaac, 105.
Blackimore (Blackmore), John, 104, 118.
Blackley, John, 304.
Blackley, Thomas, 171.
Blackwood, Ann, 313.
Blackwood, Eleanor (Elenor, Eloner), 153, 156, 192.
Blackwood, Florence, 215.
Blackwood, Genet, 215.
Blackwood, Joseph, 153, 215.
Blackwood, Margaret, 215.
Blackwood, Mary, 167, 215.
Blackwood, Samuel, 135, 153, 215, 232, 244, 313, 491, 511.
Blackwood, Sarah, 215.
Blackwood, Thomas, 298, 313, 377.
Blackwood, William, 144, 153, 154, 156, 192, 210.
Blagg (Blag), William, 176, 181.
Blair (Blear), Alexander, 22, 48, 71, 136, 159, 193, 233, 254, 273, 302, 332, 404, 405, 407, 440, 493, 527.
Blair, Cathorine, 524.
Blair, Colbert, 510.
Blair (Blear), Elizabeth (Betty), 185, 186, 200, 251, 596.
Blair, Governor, 586.
Blair, Jacob, 148.
Blair (Blayr, Blear), James, 177, 185, 186, 193, 200, 332, 399, 404, 407, 424, 493, 508, 510, 512, 519, 524, 550, 551, 573, 575, 585, 589.
Blair (Blayr, Blear), Jane (Jean), 61, 185, 186, 200, 233, 407, 440, 493, 519.
Blair (Blayr, Blear, Bleir), John, 51, 61, 129, 131, 154, 158, 165, 168, 169, 172, 173, 176, 180, 182, 185, 186, 193, 200, 222, 233, 405, 407, 519, 573, 586, 596.
Blair, Joseph, 147, 185, 251, 531, 550.
Blair, Kitrin, 404.
Blair (Blear), Margaret, 185, 186.
Blair (Blear), Mary (Polly), 34, 185, 186, 233.
Blair, Mathew, 233.
Blair, Samuel, 193, 223.
Blair (Blear), William, 143, 153, 155, 158, 166, 174, 186, 193, 199, 200, 228, 475, 576, 578, 589, 592, 593.
Blakeley, George, 251.
Blakely, Elizabeth, 207.
Bland, Margaret, 163.

Bland, Thomas, 156, 163.
Blasingame (Blaingame), John, 205.
Blather, Anthony, 106.
Blays, Alexander, 492.
Bleake, James, 166, 172.
Bleake, Jean, 166.
Bleake, William, 138.
Bleakley, Thomas, 185, 592.
Bledsoe, Anthony, 106, 113, 428, 470.
Bleke, Peter, 592.
Bleomate, Anthony, 171.
Blizard, John, 147, 373, 472, 494.
Blizard, Ruth, 472.
Bloodworth, Joseph, 275, 298, 420, 545.
Bloodworth, Mary, 275.
Bloss, Conrad, 76, 439.
Blower, Adam, 146.
Blowes, George, 146.
Blows, Gunrod, 141.
Bloze, Conrad, 57, 136.
Bloze, Eve E., 137.
Bloze, George J., 136.
Bloze, John A., 136.
Bloze, Mary C., 136, 137.
Bloze, Valentine, 136.
Boal, John, 188.
Bobkins, James, 240.
Bodeker, William, 52.
Bodine, Elizabeth, 237.
Bodkin, Hugh, 126, 403, 559.
Bodkin (Boadkin), James, 384, 396, 463, 500.
Bodkin, John, 357, 362, 363, 380, 451, 463, 523.
Bodkin, Richard, 58, 403, 437.
Bodley, Thomas, 216.
Boen, John, 375, 401.
Bogard (Bougard), Anna, 7, 76.
Bogard, Jacob, 8, 121.
Bogard (Bougard), Johannes (John), 7, 8.
Bogard, Warner, 76.
Bogart (Bogard), Anthony (Antoine), 6, 7, 19, 76.
Bogart, Gasper, 156.
Bogert (Bugard), Sarah, 6, 7.
Boggess, Elisha, 594.
Boggess, Seth, 594.
Boggs, Jennat, 16.
Bogle, Joseph, 550.
Bogs, Francis, 188.
Bohannon, Richard, 168, 579.
Boldin, Jonathan, 182.
Bole, William, 516.
Bolle, Hugh, 8.
Boller (Bollar), John, 389, 403.
Bolling (Boling, Bowling), Archibald, 575, 582, 594.
Bolling, Elizabeth, 194.
Bolling, Jane, 594.
Bombgardner, Godfrey, 344.
Bomgardner, Christian, 569.

Bomgardner, Cortwright, 344.
Bonier, Casper, 321.
Boon, George, 307.
Boon, John, 491.
Boon (Boone), Josiah, 473, 513, 547, 548.
Boone, Daniel, 198.
Boone, Hannah H., 548.
Boone, Squire, 340.
Booney, William, 560.
Boraf, Henry, 147.
Borden, Abigail, 384.
Borden (Burden), Benjamin, 7, 28, 31, 33, 55, 77, 254, 256, 257, 258, 259, 260, 263, 264, 265, 266, 267, 268, 270, 271, 272, 273, 274, 275, 277, 284, 285, 286, 287, 288, 290, 292, 293, 294, 295, 296, 299, 301, 302, 304, 305, 306, 308, 311, 313, 325, 326, 329, 331, 336, 349, 358, 364, 366, 379, 382, 384, 395, 435, 441, 443, 459, 485, 499, 539, 570.
Borden, Benjamin Joseph, 251.
Borden, Hannah, 31.
Borden, Jane, 251.
Borden, Joseph, 31, 251, 384.
Borden, Levi, 251.
Borden, Magdalene, 7, 31.
Borden, Martha, 31, 55, 68, 77.
Borden, Jeremiah, 256, 305.
Bordon (Bardon), John, 326.
Boreland, Archibald, 37, 326.
Boreland (Borelan, Bourland), James, 37, 38, 43, 47, 50, 67, 93, 326, 361, 416, 430.
Boreland, Jinny, 37.
Boreland (Bourland), John, 194, 195, 491, 579.
Borger, Jacob, 542.
Borger (Bergen), Margaret, 542.
Borland, Richard, 38.
Borning, James, 62.
Borner, Jacob, 14.
Borton, Ann, 382.
Borton, Richard, 36, 318, 340, 382.
Bosang, Barbara, 149.
Bosang, David, 135, 149, 154.
Bosang, Elizabeth, 175.
Bosang, John, 149, 169, 170, 175, 177, 185, 202, 216, 541, 561, 573, 580, 589.
Bosang, Theobald (Devault), 540.
Bosanques, Duval, 132.
Bosett, George P., 544.
Boswell, George, 538, 550, 557, 558.
Boswell, John, 107.
Boswell, Judith, 550, 557.
Botkin, Dinah, 121, 451.
Botkin, Easter (Esther), 427.
Botkin, Elizabeth, 384.
Botkin, Hugh, 105, 369, 427.
Botkin, James, 431.
Botkin (Botkins), John, 92, 105, 360, 369, 386, 395, 421, 443, 476, 504, 590.

Botkin, Mary, 386.
Botkin, Richard, 384, **505.**
Bott, James, 167.
Bottom, Arthur, 324.
Bottorph, Gasper, 524.
Boucher, John, 430.
Boucher, Nicholas, 156.
Boughman, Jacob, 483.
Bour, Jacob, 83.
Bourke, Elizabeth, 184.
Bourland, Andrew, 130.
Bourland, Betsey, 194.
Bourland, Sarah, 130.
Bourland, William, 194.
Bovill, Edward, 60.
Bowen (Bowin), Ann, 105, 111, **435.**
Bowen, Arter, 382.
Bowen, Charles, 62.
Bowen, Elizabeth, 105, 111.
Bowen, Henry, 105, 435, 484.
Bowen (Bowin, Bowing), John, 42, **57,** 62, 64, 67, 75, 81, 86, 105, 111, **300,** 331, 349, 375, 382, 390, 435, 451, **484.**
Bowen (Bowin), Lillis (Lilley), 62, **63,** 81, 88, 105, 349, 390, 435, 484.
Bowen, Mary, 62.
Bowen, Moses, 63, 64, 81, 105, 111.
Bowen, Rachel, 105.
Bowen, Rebecca, 105, 111.
Bowen (Bowin), Rees, 81, 102, 390.
Bowen, Robert, 88, 105.
Bowen, Thomas, 473.
Bowen, William, 105, 111, 465, 476.
Bowens, Abraham, 478.
Bower, James, 338.
Bower, Joh, 382.
Bowers, Charles, 141.
Bowman, Ann, 290.
Bowman, Benjamin, 409.
Bowman, Cornelius, 290.
Bowman, George, 39, 94, 256, 276, **290,** 387, 473, 477, 553.
Bowman, Jacob, 477.
Bowman, John, 103, 409, 474, 477, 508, **553.**
Bowman, Martin, 553.
Bowman, Peter, 76.
Bowngarner, Jacob, 210.
Bourne, James, 41.
Bowyer, Adam, 502.
Bowyer, Alvanious, 113, 137.
Bowyer, Anthony, 79.
Bowyer, Elizabeth, 467.
Bowyer, Eupheme (Phraney), **549.**
Bowyer, Jacob, 137, 493.
Bowyer, James, 167.
Bowyer, John, 36, 41, 47, 50, 51, 55, **62,** 68, 73, 76, 77, 81, 82, 87, 95, 106, **107,** 111, 116, 134, 200, 329, 336, 369, **384,** 390, 403, 431, 438, 451, 471, 475, **489,** 491, 513, 521, 555.
Bowyer, Lew, 504, 521, **528.**

Bowyer, Luke, 70, 77, 479, 506.
Bowyer, Magdalen, 336, 403, 435, 489, 555.
Bowyer, Michael, 77, 89, 106, 112, 116, 154, 167, 191, 197, 350, 351, 384, 390, 459, 487, 504, 506, 513, 549, 564, 565, 573, 578, 588, 589, 593.
Bowyer, Thomas, 87, 89, 104, 105, 112, 285, 335, 362, 368, 381, 387, 417, 440, 509.
Bowyer, William, 91, 106, 112, 116, 138, 140, 169, 171, 172, 329, 340, 342, 346, 384, 386, 458, 459, 462, 466, 487, 492, 493, 503, 504, 506, 527, 530, 585, 587, 588, 589.
Box, Robert, 74, 339, 389.
Boyd, Alexander, 95, 230, 247, 363, 365, 368, 392, 409, 425.
Boyd, Andrew, 16, 17, 95, 118, 248, 273, 458.
Boyd, Eleanor, 24.
Boyd, Elizabeth, 201.
Boyd, Esther, 88.
Boyd, James, 289.
Boyd, John, 9, 16, 146, 171, 201, 203, 290, 339, 546.
Boyd, Margaret, 64, 118, 248.
Boyd, Rebecca, 16.
Boyd, Robert, 24, 33, 88, 532, 541, 545, 546.
Boyd, Thomas, 16, 161, 201, 202, 214, 317, 563.
Boyd, William, 64.
Boyer, Adam, 514.
Boyle, Edward, 287.
Boyles (Boyl), Charles, 83, 93, 489.
Boyles (Boyd), James, 232, 463.
Boyles (Boyle, Boyls), Mary, 93, 463.
Boys, John, 181, 200, 589.
Boys, Samuel, 589.
Boys, William, 236, 247.
Bozard, Ruda, 53.
Brack, Jacob, 150.
Brackenridge (Breckinridge), Alexander, 8, 258, 264, 395, 550.
Brackenridge (Breckinridge), Ann, 255, 264, 265, 328, 348.
Brackenridge (Breckinridge), George, 8, 24, 26, 28, 252, 255, 261, 264, 265, 269, 270, 272, 276, 298, 328, 338, 344, 348, 463, 525, 533, 550.
Brackenridge (Breckinridge), James, 261, 278.
Brackenridge (Breckinridge), John, 262, 291, 402, 568, 574.
Brackenridge (Breckinridge), Robert, 8, 13, 15, 22, 24, 30, 31, 35, 38, 45, 51, 55, 60, 61, 82, 87, 91, 95, 97, 98, 110, 111, 115, 248, 252, 267, 272, 274, 276, 286, 287, 293, 297, 298, 304, 310, 331, 338, 351, 353, 355, 363, 366, 368, 377, 379,

380, 381, 385, 394, 434, 436, 444, 451, 452, 456, 461, 465, 466, 467, 479, 490, 503, 550.
Brackfiel, Barbary, 105.
Brackfiel, Catherine, 105.
Brackfiel, Elizabeth, 105.
Brackfriel, Stophel, 105.
Brackfield, Christopher, 115.
Brackfield (Brackfriel), Isaac, 105, 108, 115.
Brackfield (Brackfriel), Jacob, 105, 115.
Braden (Breadin, Bredon), Edward, 53, 203, 463.
Bradley, Jemima, 171.
Bradley, John, 89.
Bradon, Thomas, 126.
Bradshaw, Agness, 121.
Bradshaw, James, 121, 122, 153, 451, 593.
Bradshaw, Jane, 153.
Bradshaw, John, 186, 194, 578.
Bradshaw, Margrit, 450, 593.
Bradshaw, Robert, 81.
Bradshaw, Thomas, 85, 115, 126, 153, 154, 197, 294, 332, 450, 558, 593.
Bradshaw, William, 46, 351, 453.
Brady, James, 189.
Brady, John, 234.
Braford (Bradford, Brawford), Anne, 183, 184, 205, 208, 302, 313.
Braford, Elizabeth, 184, 205.
Braford (Brawford), Hugh, 184, 469.
Braford, James, 184.
Braford, John, 183, 184, 205.
Braford, Mary, 183, 205.
Braford, Rachel, 184, 205.
Braford, Robert, 468.
Braford (Bradford, Brafford, Brawford), Samuel, 183, 184, 186, 205, 261, 263, 269, 275, 298, 302, 303, 313, 368, 442, 468, 500.
Bragg, Jacob, 156.
Bragg, Thomas, 296.
Brains, James, 60.
Bramer, Catherine, 490.
Bramer, Gasper, 490.
Bramham, John, 9, 260, 264.
Braminer, Peter, 377.
Branan, James, 96.
Branan, Thomas, 156, 320.
Brand, Ann, 206.
Brand, David, 206.
Brand, George, 206.
Brand, James, 181, 206, 578.
Brand, John, 206.
Brand, Margaret, 206.
Brand, Richard, 206.
Brand, Sarah, 207.
Brand, Thomas, 206.
Brandiman, Abraham, 547.
Brandles, James, 268.
Branham, Richard, 563.

Braun, David, 226.
Branson, Levi, 384.
Branson, Mary, 203.
Branston, William, 10.
Branton, Peggy A., 219.
Branum, Fras, 169.
Bratchy (Bradshaw), James, 446.
Bratton, Adam, 173, 214, 219, 498, 526, 553, 561.
Bratton, Agnes, 220, 233.
Bratton, Andrew, 557.
Bratton, Anne, 173, 408, 498, 547.
Bratton, Catherine, 125, 126.
Bratton, David, 226.
Bratton, Elizabeth (Betsy), 219, 244, 397, 500, 503, 547.
Bratton, George, 173, 526.
Bratton, Isabella, 204.
Bratton (Bratain), James, 96, 135, 173, 312, 362, 397, 424, 428, 443, 457, 489, 498, 500, 503, 507, 513, 530, 534, 547, 557, 561, 596.
Bratton, John, 173, 188, 219, 547, 561, 596.
Bratton, Mary, 173.
Bratton, Nancy, 219.
Bratton, Patsy W., 219.
Bratton, Robert, 6, 23, 24, 27, 30, 50, 56, 60, 69, 80, 97, 127, 135, 138, 176, 219, 267, 312, 333, 353, 362, 395, 401, 408, 432, 442, 469, 489, 498, 507, 513, 526.
Bratton, Sally, 219.
Bratton, Susy F., 219.
Bratton, Thomas, 125.
Bratton, William, 244.
Brawford, Jean, 185.
Brayton, Edward, 167.
Breaden, George, 203.
Break, Jacob, 121, 156.
Break, Malldlin, 121.
Breame, James, 82.
Breath (Reath), Elizabeth, 160.
Breath, Joseph, 176.
Breckenridge, Adam, 277, 280.
Breckinridge (Brackenridge), Lettice, 8, 80, 363, 380, 436, 456, 550.
Breckinridge, Mary, 331.
Breckinridge, William, 215.
Breden, Elizabeth, 533.
Breden (Bratton), John T., 125.
Breden, Thomas, 467.
Breeden, John, 536.
Breize, Sarah, 206.
Breneger (Brineger), Thomas, 75, 314.
Brent, James, 553.
Brent, Jeremiah, 460.
Brent, Margaret, 460.
Brent, William, 588.
Brett, John, 131.
Brian, Martha, 340.
Briant, Ann, 533.
Brice, James, 75.

Bridget, James, 559.
Brieze, William, 200.
Briggs, Mary, 503.
Briggs (Brigs), Samuel, 65, 373, 475, 503.
Bright, Alexander, 314.
Bright, David, 226.
Bright, Elizabeth, 535.
Bright, Errick, 74, 309, 310, 331, 423.
Bright, George, 161, 162, 226, 453, 516.
Bright, George A., 226, 505, 531.
Bright, John, 187, 203, 226.
Bright, Mary, 505, 531.
Bright, Rebecka, 226.
Bright, Samuel, 378.
Bright, Susanna, 235.
Bright, Tobias, 9, 24, 25, 34, 74, 110, 309, 408.
Bright, Windle (Windel), 226, 512, 528, 535, 549.
Brinegar, John, 74.
Brininger, Peter, 113.
Brisco, William, 169.
Brisler (Treslar), Peter, 383.
Britt, William, 217.
Broabacks (Brubaks), Adam, 171.
Broabacks, Elizabeth, 171.
Broabacks, Philip, 171.
Broabacks, Sarah, 171.
Brobeck (Brucet), Joseph, 245.
Brock, Efey, 17.
Brock, Elsye, 10.
Brock, Eve, 9.
Brock, Frederick, 9.
Brock, George, 9, 10, 17, 302, 320.
Brock, Henry, 305.
Brock, John, 568.
Brock, Julia, 10.
Brock, Julian (Julia), 9, 10.
Brock, Mary, 305.
Brock, Nicholas, 69.
Brock, Opattis, 311.
Brock, Rudal (Rudy), 9, 10, 17.
Broker, John, 206.
Bromson, Thomas, 251.
Bronomer, Peter, 149.
Brook, Nicholas, 45.
Brooke, Mary, 361.
Brooke (Brookes), Robert, 262, 499.
Brookin, Charles, 316.
Brooks, Ann, 578.
Brooks, Elizabeth, 205.
Brooks, George, 238.
Brooks, Giles, 205.
Brooks, James, 566, 584.
Brooks, Jean, 195.
Brooks, John, 72, 76, 172, 183, 205, 207, 555, 565, 566, 578.
Brooks, John M., 551.
Brooks, Jonathan, 205, 565.
Brooks, Martha, 205.
Brooks, Robert, 107.

Brooks, Samuel, 205, 213.
Brooks, Sarah, 205.
Brooks, William, 184, 205.
Broughf, Daniel, 310.
Brown, Abraham (Abram), 31, 109, 265, 285, 286, 308, 325, 367, 407, 446, 450, 460, 469.
Brown, Adam, 16.
Brown, Agness, 308, 333, 467.
Brown, Alexander, 223.
Brown, Alice, 362, 363, 372.
Brown, Andrew, 335, 393, 406, 443, 457.
Brown, Ann, 334.
Brown, Arthur, 285, 286, 356.
Brown, Benjamin, 170, 194, 208, 209, 214, 240, 572.
Brown, Birnis, 564.
Brown, Caesar, 63.
Brown, Cornelius, 291, 450, 460, 461.
Brown, Daniel, 16, 73, 110, 233, 454.
Brown, David, 16.
Brown, Elizabeth (Betey), 190, 199, 240, 301.
Brown, Esther, 46.
Brown, Frances, 122, 373.
Brown, Francis, 197, 231, 235, 243, **349**, 356, 424, 449, 494.
Brown, George, 109, 112, 116.
Brown, Henry, 9, 16, 25, 30, 38, 46, 48, 50, 51, 110, 309, 362, 363, 372, 454, 456.
Brown, Hugh, 114, 162, 166, 194, **197**, **213**, 216, 226, 227, 544, 562, 567, 568, **571**, **572**, **574**, **575**, 592.
Brown, Isabel (Isble, Isabella), 141, 399, 445.
Brown, Jacob, 75, 110, 309, 316, 340, **467**.
Brown, James, 18, 35, 37, 45, 83, 114, **140**, 161, 190, 208, 209, 213, 227, 228, **231**, 233, 254, 276, 281, 286, 292, 293, **296**, 308, 324, 331, 333, 338, 372, 415, **424**, 434, 448, 458, 462, 470, 476, 498, **518**, 519, 523, 568.
Brown, Jane (Jean), 213, 234, 244, 393, 457.
Brown, John, 5, 33, 35, 37, 38, 40, 57, **58**, 59, 67, 81, 83, 114, 115, 143, 167, **190**, 199, 214, 216, 227, **228**, **231**, 233, 234, 254, 271, 279, 281, 283, **284**, 293, 296, 306, 310, 316, 323, 334, **335**, 340, 370, 373, 390, 395, 402, 421, **423**, 425, 440, 458, 470, 476, 520, 547, **551**, 554, 555, 562, 564, 568, 574, 583.
Brown, Jonathan, 12.
Brown, Joseph, 240.
Brown, Margaret, 114, 190, 306, 323, 421, 470, 476, 554, 568.
Brown, Mary, 16, 62, 80, 83, 93, 166, **227**, 243, 427, 574.
Brown, Patrick, **475**.
Brown, Rebecca, 128, **227**, **574**.

Brown, Richard, 360, 545.
Brown, Robert, 27, 32, 84, 95, 118, **234**, 301, 349, 361, 386, 403, 427, **448**, **467**, 475, 494, 561, 582, 589, 592.
Brown, Samuel, 5, 11, 16, 20, **198**, **199**, 216, 219, 228, 231, 234, 316, **489**.
Brown, Sarah (Sally), 233, 240.
Brown, Shildrick, 45.
Brown, Thomas, 10, 41, 62, 67, 69, **83**, **114**, 148, 177, 190, 216, 219, 234, **244**, **263**, 273, 275, 320, 363, 381, 402, 421, **430**, 448, 462, 487, 562, 564, 575.
Brown, William, 48, 62, 67, 71, **106**, **123**, 184, 215, 216, 217, 220, 226, 228, **231**, 234, 294, 301, 302, 303, 340, 348, **373**, 381, 399, 409, 417, 440, 445, 446, **500**, 503, 542.
Brownfield, Robert, 81.
Brownlee, Alexander, 27, 37, 47, 167, **186**, 213, 218, 328, 338, 343, 358, 488, **563**, 566, 583, 594.
Brownlee, Florence, 196.
Brownlee, Isabella, 218.
Brownlee, James, 161, 186, 196, **218**, **219**, 563.
Brownlee, John, 29, 30, 42, 47, 101, **106**, 186, 218, 219, 227, 311, 317, 338, **343**, 463, 568, 571, 574.
Brownlee, Margaret, 218.
Brownlee, Mary, 219, 227.
Brownlee, Moffet, 219.
Brownlee, Rachel, 218.
Brownlee, Sarah, 218, 328, 338, **343**.
Brownlee, William, 128, 186, 218, **219**, **488**.
Brownlow, James, 548.
Brownlow, John, 539.
Brownlow, Katherine, 548.
Bruce, Alexander, 101, 106, 113.
Bruce, George, 180.
Bruce, Richard, 180.
Brudeback, Adam, 84.
Bruester, Elizabeth, 94.
Bruester (Bruster), James, 67, 68, **114**, 126, 131, 132, 136, 353, 354.
Bruffy, John, 182.
Bruin, Peter, 516.
Brumbly, Austin, 106.
Brunegar, John, 322.
Brunk, Jacob, 543.
Brunk, Stuffle, 551.
Brunt, John, 172.
Brush, Archibald, 303.
Brush, Blackly (Blakely), 82, **93**, **509**.
Brush, Richard, 60, 82, 85, 303.
Bruster, Robert, 487.
Bryan, Alice, 339.
Bryan, Benjamin, 244.
Bryan, David, 42, 96, 97, 103, **315**, **415**.
Bryan, Elizabeth, 97, 203.
Bryan, George, 139.

Bryan (Bryans, Bryant), James, 40, 98, 117, 466.
Bryan (Bryant), John, 11, 21, 22, 318, 370, 383, 474.
Bryan (Bryant), Joseph, 21, 35, 37, 38, 256, 257, 295, 318, 339, 371, 400, 447, 473, 513.
Bryan, Margaret, 317.
Bryan, Mary, 97.
Bryan (Bryant), Morgan, 258, 270, 276, 285, 292, 294, 340, 474, 486, 533, 545.
Bryan, Samuel, 258.
Bryan, Solomon, 26.
Bryan (Bryant), Thomas, 37, 52, 54, 76, 383, 474.
Bryan (Bryant), William, 30, 38, 87, 95, 96, 97, 109, 272, 317, 434, 466, 576.
Bryant (Briant), Cornelius, 11, 533.
Bryce (Brycers), Archibald, 67, 362, 365, 369.
Buchanan, Agnes, 62, 490.
Buchanan, Alexander, 47, 48, 62, 88, 160, 187, 197, 209, 249, 250, 349, 357, 487, 489, 493.
Buchanan, Andrew, 344, 499.
Buchanan, Archibald, 15, 59, 62, 67, 78, 88, 104, 311, 393, 490.
Buchanan, Catherine, 187.
Buchanan, David, 88, 145, 160, 187, 196, 198, 209, 210, 225, 249, 568, 593, 596.
Buchanan (Bohanon), Elizabeth (Betsey), 7, 47, 97, 196, 249.
Buchanan, George, 88, 135, 249, 407, 493, 568.
Buchanan, Hannah, 71.
Buchanan, Hugh, 249.
Buchanan (Bohanan), Isabella (Isbelah), 250, 471, 487.
Buchanan (Bohanon), James, 14, 19, 20, 30, 38, 47, 52, 54, 55, 57, 71, 88, 90, 98, 104, 105, 115, 116, 117, 145, 167, 161, 168, 187, 189, 225, 248, 249, 250, 311, 332, 349, 354, 406, 490, 499, 507, 529, 533, 557, 560, 567, 568, 578, 586, 596.
Buchanan (Bohannon, Bochanan), Jean, 7, 8, 160, 197, 209, 557, 560, 596.
Buchanan, Johanna, 144.
Buchanan (Bohannon), John, 5, 6, 7, 38, 39, 40, 41, 47, 54, 55, 58, 59, 62, 63, 67, 70, 73, 75, 83, 86, 88, 92, 95, 97, 100, 101, 110, 113, 115, 116, 117, 119, 123, 141, 187, 220, 226, 248, 250, 255, 257, 258, 259, 262, 263, 264, 266, 268, 270, 271, 272, 273, 274, 280, 285, 287, 290, 297, 298, 301, 303, 306, 308, 311, 312, 313, 315, 324, 326, 327, 332, 333, 335, 343, 348, 354, 357, 361, 362, 367, 369, 370, 375, 376, 379, 387, 394, 397, 402, 417, 428, 430, 432, 442, 444, 445, 447,
450, 452, 458, 460, 462, 465, 467, 475, 479, 482, 486, 488, 489, 507, 510, 560.
Buchanan, Joseph, 170.
Buchanan, Margaret, 40, 41, 187, 335, 348, 480, 482, 486, 507, 568.
Buchanan, Martha, 187, 415, 510.
Buchanan (Bochanan), Mary, 7, 41, 88, 100, 118, 182, 187, 196, 434, 458, 560.
Buchanan, Mathew, 333, 415.
Buchanan, Merian, 71.
Buchanan, Moses, 499.
Buchanan, Patrick, 116, 146, 173, 182, 187, 192, 195, 196, 362, 470, 471, 477, 488, 489, 507, 514, 518, 522, 526, 534, 543, 557, 560, 579, 588, 592, 593.
Buchanan, Rebecca, 19, 71, 88, 159.
Buchannan, Robert, 88, 119, 134, 187, 349, 354, 382, 428, 434, 488, 510, 533, 557, 560, 568.
Buchanan (Bohannon), Ruth, 71, 505.
Buchanan, Samuel, 16, 36, 49, 68, 70, 107, 274, 311, 327, 333, 343, 360, 415, 422, 434, 476, 499, 520.
Buchanan, Sarah, 160.
Buchanan, Susannah, 249.
Buchanan, Thomas, 385.
Buchanan (Bohannon), William, 47, 54, 59, 62, 71, 75, 80, 88, 104, 109, 119, 135, 160, 187, 192, 195, 225, 248, 250, 263, 287, 290, 322, 335, 339, 341, 349, 351, 354, 394, 407, 408, 426, 447, 454, 460, 471, 475, 490, 505, 568, 590.
Buck, Conrod, 581.
Bugard (Bougard), Johannes, 6, 7.
Buis, Thomas, 20.
Buis, William, 20.
Bukket, John, 38, 39.
Bullett (Bullitt), Cuthbert, 371, 448, 593.
Bullett, Thomas, 448.
Bumbordner, John, 562.
Bumgardner, Jacob, 569.
Bumgarner, Christian, 21.
Bumgarner, Elizabeth, 21.
Bumgarner, Madley, 21.
Bumgarner, Mary, 21.
Bumpass, William, 127.
Bunginger, Peter, 113.
Buntin (Bunting), James, 125, 510.
Buntin (Buntain, Bunton), John, 44, 293, 443, 464, 512, 520.
Buntin (Bunting, Bunton), William, 61, 93, 283, 514.
Burbeg, Maley, 121.
Burbridge, William, 189.
Burdon, George, 152.
Burdwell, George, 37, 300.
Burger, David, 500.
Burger, John, 563, 565, 584.
Burger (Burgey), Manus (Manis), 189, 584.
Burger, Suckey, 563.

Burgess, Polly, 237.
Burgess, Rebecca, 239.
Burgess, Robert, 200.
Burgess, William, 160, 225, 231.
Burgess, Wright, 238.
Burgie, Henry, 18.
Burk, Ann, 161, 175.
Burk, Bridget, 34.
Burk, Catherine, 34.
Burk, Charles, 21, 25.
Burk, Clerey, 457, 477.
Burk, Edward, 161, 175, 186, 190.
Burk (Burke, Birk), James, 6, 9, 197, 309, 314, 355, 363, 381, 455, 456, 466.
Burk (Burke), John, 34, 45, 159, 357, 424, 452, 457, 480, 481, 484, 501, 528, 544.
Burk (Burke), Joseph, 175, 243.
Burk, Judea, 34.
Burk, Thomas, 34, 382, 457, 477, 480, 481, 483.
Burk (Burke, Burks, Bourk), William, 34, 35, 38, 45, 80, 161, 163, 174, 175, 181, 186, 255, 259, 269, 275, 287, 317, 341, 457, 480, 481, 484, 528, 572, 588.
Burke, Edward, 243.
Burke, Judith, 35.
Burket (Burkett), Frederick, 573, 580, 584.
Burket, Rageena, 580.
Burkett, Dorothy, 573.
Burkett, Karthrine, 585.
Burkett (Birkett), Nathaniel, 581, 585.
Burkley, Joseph, 588.
Burner, Abram, 158.
Burner, Jacob, 7, 21, 287.
Burnes, Samuel, 112.
Burnet, Ann, 55.
Burnet, Jacob, 21.
Burnet, William, 356.
Burnley, Israel, 109.
Burns, Dennis, 196, 200.
Burns, Henry, 163.
Burns, Hugh, 577.
Burns, Isaac, 188.
Burns (Burnes), Isabella, 163, 180, 580, 593.
Burns, James, 172.
Burns, Margaret C., 163.
Burns, Mary, 163.
Burns, Peter, 144, 151.
Burns, Richard, 142, 554.
Burns, Robert, 163, 180.
Burns, Thomas, 163, 220.
Burns, William, 171.
Burnside, Francisco, 203.
Burnside, James, 99, 577.
Burnside, John, 113, 151, 203, 204, 207, 540.
Burnside, Marthia, 151, 172, 203, 204, 207, 218.
Burnsides, Isabella, 476, 581.

Burnsides, James, 12, 63, 80, 90, 94, 146, 437, 476, 504, 505, 581.
Burnsides, John, 149, 358, 414, 432, 458.
Burnsides, Matthew, 151.
Burnsides, Rachel, 12.
Burre, John, 146.
Burt, William, 332, 343.
Burtain, Richard, 80.
Burton, Ann, 299.
Burton, Edmond, 580, 582, 584, 591.
Burton, George, 188.
Burton, Joseph, 38, 410.
Burton, Leonard, 274.
Burton, Margaret E., 410.
Burton, Mary E., 38.
Burton, Richard, 266, 273, 299, 399.
Burwell, George, 545.
Buseter, James, 346.
Bush, George, 58, 83, 374, 405.
Bush, Joshua, 513.
Bush, Michael, 140.
Bush, Nicholas, 590.
Bush, Philip, 513.
Bush, Richard, 97.
Bush, Susannah, 405.
Bushberry, George, 150.
Bushong, Jacob, 238.
Bustard, Dorcas, 565.
Buster (Bustard), Claudius, 238, 250, 554, 563, 565.
Buster, David, 249, 250.
Butcher, Mary, 129.
Butcher, Nicholas, 127.
Butcher, Valentine, 57, 65, 112, 129, 134.
Butcher, Valentine M., 127.
Buts (Brits), John, 584.
Butt, William, 188.
Butt (Butts), Windle, 529, 530.
Buyers, William, 340.
Buzzard, Peter, 148.
Byar (Byor), Alvenus, 57, 361.
Byarly, Andrew, 53.
Byers, David, 232, 242.
Byers, Elizabeth, 596.
Byers (Buyers), John, 242, 482, 561.
Byers, Joseph, 596.
Byers, Rosannah, 242.
Byers, William, 73, 321, 465.
Byire, John, 146.
Byor, Barbara, 361.
Byrd, John, 194.
Byride, Jame, 487.
Byrn (Byruns), Richard, 121, 156.
Byrne, John, 158.
Byrnside (s), James, 534.
Cabeen, William, 70, 390.
Cabell, John, 281.
Cabell, William, 348.
Cadden (Caddon), Thomas, 52, 57, 60.
Cafferton, John, 339.
Cail, Bethemia, 556.

Cail (Caile, Cale), David, 180, 203, 242, 523, 556.
Cail, Isaac, 242.
Cail (Caile), John, 203, 242.
Caile, Alberdina, 203.
Caile (Cale), Peter, 203, 242, 523, 556, 557.
Cain (Carn), Catherine, 440, 561.
Cain (Kain), James, 115, 406.
Cain, John, 54, 440.
Cain (Carn), Nicholas, 39, 128, 440, 543.
Cain, Patrick, 53.
Cain (Cairn), Richard, 579, 582.
Calaihan, Charles, 537.
Calaihan, Daniel, 537.
Calbert, Will, 82.
Caldbreath, Jene, 221.
Caldbreath, Margaret, 179, 221.
Calbreath, Nathan, 25.
Caldbreath, Sally, 221.
Caldbreath, Thomas, 180, 221, 482.
Caldwell, Agness, 165.
Caldwell, Ann (Anne), 231, 348, 400.
Caldwell, Annas, 207.
Caldwell, Anson, 220.
Caldwell, Catherine (Catrin), 211, 212, 213.
Caldwell, Daniel, 579.
Caldwell, David, 165, 203, 204, 205, 231, 367, 475, 517.
Caldwell, Eleanor, 245.
Caldwell, Elizabeth, 211, 213, 566.
Caldwell, Fenny, 207.
Caldwell, George, 36, 59, 123, 261, 265, 296, 324, 354, 367, 419, 446, 517, 519.
Caldwell (Calwell), James, 39, 41, **207**, 255, 267, 271, 275, 277, 278, 279, 292, 302, 339, 355, 356, 387, 393, 395, 400, 408, 419.
Caldwell, Jane (Jean), 207, 231.
Caldwell, John, 123, 161, 189, 207, 211, 213, 220, 223, 227, 230, 231, 348, 360, 419, 446, 517, 519, 520, 524, 532, 550, 565, 566, 572.
Caldwell, Margaret (Margrit), 56, **211**
Caldwell, Mary, 165, 203, 207, 220, **355**.
Caldwell (Colwell), Robert, 7, 14, 22, 165, 166, 203, 304, 324, 425, 532, 550, 566.
Caldwell (Colwell), Samuel, 70, 189, **207**, 347, 352, 355, 396, 398, 400, 410, **439**, 442, 524, 532, 550, 566.
Caldwell, Sarah, 207, 532, 572.
Caldwell, Thomas, 207, 211, 230.
Caldwell, William, 59, 161, 165, 166, 203, 211, 213, 231, 250, 282, 348, 367, 419, 420, 517, 519.
Cale (Cail), Grissilla (Grizzel), 556, **576**.
Cale (Caile), Jacob, 177, 203, 242, 523, 556, 557, 564, **576**.
Cale, Mary, 242.
Cale, Parthenia, 221.

Cale (Caile), William, 203, 221, 242, **556**.
Caley, Peter, 443.
Calfee, John, 294.
Callin, William, 493.
Callahan, Charles, 487, 585.
Callahan (Calahan, Callachan), **Daniel**, 343, 392, 400, 444, 525, 543.
Callahan, Denis, 127, 574.
Callar, Elizabeth, 526.
Callan, William, 526.
Caller, George, 586.
Calleson, Robert, 236.
Callesone, Martha, 182.
Calley, Benjamin, 157.
Callhoun (Cahoun), Agness, 27, 46.
Callhoun, Hugh, 338.
Callhoun (Cahoon), James, 21, 27, **28**, 66, 333.
Callhoun (Calhoun, Calhoon), **Patrick**, 26, 27, 73, 330, 338, 430, 438, 454, 460.
Callhoun, William, 26, 27, 28, 240, 330.
Callison, Agnes, 185.
Callison, Dorothy, 185.
Callison, Eloner, 185.
Callison, Isabella (Isble), 185, 485.
Callison (Calleson), James, 25, 39, 40, **64**, 113, 134, 185, 281, 282, 291, 360, **361**, 453, 485.
Callison, Jean, 185.
Callison, John, 185.
Callison, Margaret, 185.
Callison, Mary, 185.
Callison, Robert, 185.
Callison, William, 185.
Calloway, James, 85, 109.
Calloway, Richard, 338.
Cally, John, 63, 71.
Calvert, Robert, 266.
Cambel, Farghagh, 100.
Camell, Martha, 6.
Cameron, Charles, 138, 144, 164, 169, **178**, 458, 459, 567, 575.
Cameron, George, 458.
Cameron, James, 516, 557.
Cameron, Jean, 557.
Cameron, Margaret, 70, 458.
Camp, Thomas, 74.
Candler, John, 107.
Campbell, Agness, 219, 426, 549.
Campbell, Alexander (Sander), 49, **50**, 189, 283, 294, 303, 385, 431, 442, **496**, 500, 509, 514, 522, 538.
Campbell, Andrew, 42, 66, 167, 487, **507**, 515, 529.
Campbell, Ann, 97, 475, 545.
Campbell, Archibald, 80.
Campbell, Arthur, 109, 414, 432, 452, **466**, 482, 489, 491, 492, 517, 555, 569, **571**.
Campbell, Charles, 8, 10, 14, 15, 19, **34**, 44, 47, 52, 55, 72, 76, 97, 104, 105, **107**, 130, 132, 140, 152, 154, 160, 259, **264**,

266, 270, 272, 283, 284, 288, 297, 302, 303, 315, 317, 326, 334, 354, 360, 408, 422, 426, 427, 433, 463, 468, 469, 474, 484, 485, 502, 514, 522, 547, 568, 571, 588, 591, 595.
Campbell, Daniel, 33, 34.
Campbell (Camell), David, 8, 30, 270, 277, 283, 295, 303, 431, 478, 482, 489, 507, 509, 522.
Campbell, Donald, 456.
Campbell, Dugald, 354.
Campbell, Elenor, 192, 326, 488.
Campbell, Elizabeth (Betsy), 19, 80, 97, 174, 219, 231, 235, 302, 337, 342, 455, 456, 461, 475, 511, 514, 588, 590.
Campbell, Esther, 140, 273, 294, 302, 348, 349, 440.
Campbell, Florence, 49.
Campbell, Frances, 431.
Campbell, George, 19, 39, 48, 161, 162, 202, 203, 217, 219, 292, 353, 408, 417, 426, 442, 499, 505.
Campbell, Gilbert, 19, 20, 22, 48, 263, 268, 271, 272, 340.
Campbell, Henry (Hindry), 49, 80, 107, 189, 316, 396, 428, 495, 503, 524.
Campbell, Hugh, 14, 48, 51, 105, 139, 140, 152, 272, 292, 294, 301, 332, 348, 349, 355, 445, 484, 493, 502, 505, 564, 569, 570, 583, 592, 594, 595.
Campbell, Isabella (Isbell), 80, 136, 192.
Campbell, Jacob, 151, 406, 441, 528.
Campbell, James, 10, 19, 28, 30, 33, 34, 52, 55, 56, 59, 62, 110, 215, 258, 286, 291, 299, 312, 314, 317, 324, 339, 340, 342, 356, 363, 365, 386, 392, 425, 461, 469, 473, 475, 476, 481, 491, 492, 502, 505, 537, 559, 583, 584, 588, 592, 595.
Campbell, Jane (Jean, Jenny), 49, 80, 97, 219, 509, 528.
Campbell (Camell), John, 6, 9, 10, 14, 34, 39, 42, 43, 56, 66, 68, 85, 114, 137, 139, 149, 151, 152, 167, 168, 170, 171, 173, 184, 185, 186, 188, 189, 190, 202, 204, 205, 211, 218, 235, 257, 281, 282, 283, 284, 297, 302, 326, 337, 338, 341, 360, 375, 412, 429, 431, 432, 440, 442, 455, 456, 461, 473, 475, 477, 482, 484, 488, 489, 490, 500, 505, 507, 510, 511, 514, 519, 522, 540, 558, 566, 576, 591, 592.
Campbell, Joseph, 161, 219, 522.
Campbell, Lachley, 542.
Campbell, Lettice (Lattise, Lettis), 19, 48, 363, 425, 481.
Campbell, Malcom, 18, 25, 59, 80, 87, 96, 106, 359.
Campbell, Margaret, 7, 33, 34, 84, 97, 105, 427, 485, 569, 571.
Campbell, Margaret R., 213.
Campbell, Marthew, 140.
Campbell, Mary, 10, 49, 80, 152, 161, 162, 219, 475, 507
Campbell, Mathew, 36, 46, 289, 290, 296, 306, 342, 349, 360.
Campbell, Patrick, 30, 41, 49, 52, 77, 87, 110, 257, 261, 262, 270, 272, 286, 288, 297, 302, 303, 317, 326, 338, 360, 393, 449, 468, 495, 499, 511, 542, 545, 549.
Campbell, Prudence, 19, 22, 102, 426.
Campbell, Rebeckah, 80, 135.
Campbell, Robert, 6, 15, 24, 30, 34, 39, 47, 49, 52, 60, 81, 85, 97, 105, 114, 129, 140, 146, 148, 152, 161, 162, 171, 183, 189, 202, 213, 219, 223, 235, 255, 273, 280, 281, 283, 289, 290, 301, 303, 320, 323, 353, 363, 427, 455, 484, 486, 487, 511, 518, 566, 576.
Campbell, Samuel, 56, 413, 415, 488, 496.
Campbell, Sarah, 19, 129, 146, 162, 297, 428.
Campbell, Thomas, 353, 398, 496, 525, 537.
Campbell, William, 49, 56, 80, 84, 97, 110, 139, 140, 146, 152, 189, 231, 248, 280, 283, 294, 295, 297, 303, 359, 361, 381, 420, 438, 453, 456, 475, 487, 488, 492, 493, 505, 507, 509, 516, 520, 522, 542, 558, 559, 561, 588, 590.
Camplin, John, 349, 366.
Camplin (Keplinger), Lydia, 366.
Can, Michael, 517.
Canon, John, 148.
Canote, John, 593.
Canterberry, John, 460, 503.
Caperton, Alexander, 581.
Caperton, Hugh, 581.
Caperton (Capbritton), John, 94, 356, 363.
Caperton (Capbritton), Mary, 356, 363.
Caphart, Peter, 141.
Caplinger, Adam, 141.
Caplinger (Ciplinger), Cathorine, 141, 230.
Caplinger, Dorothy, 114.
Caplinger, Elizabeth, 141.
Caplinger (Kaplinger), George, 63, 65, 100, 129, 141, 374.
Caplinger, Henry, 141.
Caplinger (Caplin, Cepliner), Jacob, 128, 133, 141, 156, 157, 444.
Caplinger (Caplener, Ciplinger), John, 129, 135, 141, 230, 522, 527, 539.
Caplinger, Samuel, 114, 124, 143.
Carel, Thomas, 575.
Cargo (Congo), Elizabeth, 206, 250.
Cargo, Margaret, 250.
Cargo, Samuel, 206.
Cargo, Samuel Alex., 250.
Cark (Clark), John, 60.
Carleton, William, 62.
Carlie, John, 587.
Carlile, Elizabeth, 27, 535, 536.
Carlile (Carlyle), George, 535, 593.

Carlile (Carolile, Corlile, Corolile), James, 27, 33, 56, 59, 61, 209, 267, 271, 291, 316, 392, 413, 540.
Carlile (Carlyle, Carolile, Corlile), John, 37, 50, 58, 78, 81, 88, 92, 104, 108, 116, 122, 124, 209, 214, 216, 316, 392, 396, 413, 415, 444, 446, 451, 463, 475, 488, 489, 502, 507, 519, 523, 535, 536, 589.
Carlile, Margaret, 209.
Carlile, Mary, 78, 392, 444, 519.
Carlile, Nancy, 535, 536.
Carlile, Rachel, 56, 413.
Carlile, Robert, 122, 124, 194, 209, 210, 446, 449, 451, 502, 535, 536, 589.
Carlile, William, 209, 299.
Carlock, Hunkrist, 20, 30.
Carlock, Theobald, 15.
Carmichael (Cormichael), John, 269, 300, 339, 341.
Carn, George, 18, 69.
Carn (Kearn), Michael, 18, 69, 561.
Carnes, Gasper, 167.
Carns, Alexander, 227.
Carpenter, Adam, 142.
Carpenter, Catharine, 565.
Carpenter, George, 18, 66, 86, 114, 142, 143, 146, 413, 444.
Carpenter, Jacob, 156.
Carpenter, Joseph, 24, 49, 59, 87, 388, 422.
Carpenter, Nicholas, 565.
Carpenter, Solomon, 422.
Carpenter, Zopher, 100.
Carr (Kerr, Karr), David, 17, 286, 287.
Carr, Gilbert, 177, 178.
Carr, Henry, 63.
Carr, Isaac, 398.
Carr, Jacob, 391.
Carr, James, 84, 124, 285, 295, 300, 309, 320, 411, 463.
Carr (Ceer, Keer, Karr), John, 12, 147, 259, 270, 271, 287, 410, 473.
Carr, Lucy, 473.
Carr, Margaret, 365.
Carr, Mary, 391, 463.
Carr, Martha, 468.
Carr, Michael, 595.
Carr, Peter, 391.
Carr (Kerr), Richard, 39, 308.
Carr (Keer), Samuel, 365.
Carr (Care, Karr), William, 29, 41, 55, 439, 468.
Carrall, Christian, 576.
Carrall, Samuel, 576.
Carraven (Carravin), William, 28, 38, 39, 117, 309, 319, 323
Carrew, Frederick, 236.
Carrick, Samuel, 175.
Carroll (Carrell, Carrill), James, 276, 481, 515, 519.
Carroll (Carrol, Carrel, Carrell, Carrill, Carryl, Caryl), William, 6, 9, 11, 13, 14, 20, 22, 40, 57, 96, 270, 294, 296, 311, 315, 383, 455, 478, 515.
Carruthers (Caruthers), John, 144, 156, 245, 468, 499.
Carruthers (Coruthers), Margaret, 341, 415.
Carruthers, Robert, 145, 444.
Carry, James, 502.
Carsh (Kersh), Mathias, 76.
Carson, Abraham, 168.
Carson (Corson), Agnes, 168, 180, 183.
Carson, Catherine, 239.
Carson, David, 499, 513.
Carson, Elijah, 246.
Carson, Henry, 21, 24.
Carson (Corson), Isaac, 83, 144, 154, 165, 168, 172, 180, 183, 407, 432, 559, 572.
Carson (Corson), Jane, 168, 183
Carson, Mary, 168, 183.
Carson, Rebecca, 168, 173, 180.
Carson, Samuel, 192, 193, 211, 212, 522, 584.
Carson, Simon, 163.
Carson, Susannah, 21.
Carson, Thomas, 175, 511.
Carson, William, 9, 18, 55.
Carter, Dinah, 257.
Carter, Henry, 109, 416.
Carter, James, 253, 257, 267, 340.
Cartledge, Edmond, 9.
Cartley, Frank, 63.
Carthrea (Corthrea), John, 550, 557.
Cartmill (Cartmell), Henry, 48, 76, 80, 84, 463.
Cartmill (Cartmil), John, 17, 85, 103, 123, 133, 571, 575.
Cartmill, Mary, 586.
Cartmill, Samuel, 541.
Cartmill, Thomas, 170, 586, 587.
Cartwright, Henry, 13
Carty (Cartey, Cartie), James, 97, 103, 106, 178, 418.
Caruth, Adam, 261.
Caruthers (Corothers), Elizabeth, 224, 245.
Caruthers (Corothers, Karithers), David, 224, 231, 245, 536.
Caruthers, Esther, 156.
Caruthers (Carrothers, Corruthers), Hugh, 42, 75, 117, 361, 362, 375, 470.
Caruthers (Corruthers, Karithers), James, 156, 172, 245, 536, 553.
Caruthers, Jean, 245.
Caruthers, Rebecca, 156.
Caruthers, Thomas, 557.
Caruthers (Carruthers), William, 13, 24, 26, 50, 121, 156, 268, 311, 318, 323, 329, 336, 341, 349, 423, 455.

Carvin, Edward, 99, 438, 451, 452, 466, 490, 491.
Carvin, William, 25, 44, 69, 75, 99, 110, 401, 429, 452, 456, 491.
Cary, Richard, 593.
Casedy (Casity, Cassaty, Cassedy), Neal, 98, 101, 103, 307.
Cassidy, Simon, 121, 122.
Casety, James, 101.
Casety, John, 158.
Casnaw, Benonee, 144
Casil, William, 81.
Casner, Jacob, 177.
Casner, John, 543.
Casner (Carson), Samuel, 218.
Castle, Jacob, 304.
Castleberry, Margaret, 345.
Castleberry, William, 338, 345.
Catching, Benjamin, 574.
Cathern, John, 72.
Cathey, Andrew, 392.
Cathey, Jaen, 302.
Cathey, James, 267, 310, 421.
Cathey, John, 302, 422, 423.
Cathey, William, 302.
Cauger, George, 119.
Caul, Agnes, 192.
Caul, Elizabeth, 192.
Caul, Hugh, 192
Caul, James, 192.
Caul, Margaret, 192.
Caul, Mary, 192.
Caul, Thomas, 192, 571.
Caul (Cole), Timothy, 84, 192, 194.
Caul, William, 192.
Caully, Henry, 76.
Causan, Lawrence, 156.
Cavanough, John, 198.
Cave, Benjamin, 289.
Cavet, Moses, 434.
Cavit, John, 241.
Cawby, Margaret, 201.
Cawfield, Mary, 167.
Cawley (Cowley), John, 133, 140, 145, 154, 156, 168, 464, 476, 485, 492, 497, 506, 538, 555.
Cawley, Margaret, 140, 145, 159, 497.
Cawley, Michael, 140, 200, 201, 584, 589.
Cawley, Thomas, 140.
Cawthon (Cauthorn), William D., 309, 314.
Cbaven, William, 155.
Celamous (Childmour), Lewis, 569.
Cerral, Samuel, 18.
Celzar, Renamia, 391.
Centern, William, 81.
Challe, Peter, 154.
Chamberlain, Jeremiah, 295, 299, 473.
Chambers, Ann, 236, 583.
Chambers, Harriet M., 236.
Chambers, Jacob K., 236.

Chambers, James, 178.
Chambers, Jean, 236.
Chambers, Margaret, 236.
Chambers, Mustoe, 236.
Chambers, Thomas, 236.
Chambers, William (W.), 116, 180, 181, 201, 212, 215, 217, 234, 236, 578, 583, 585, 589, 596.
Chaner (Cleaver), Benjamin, 151.
Chapman, John, 557.
Chapman, Robert H., 246.
Chapman, Sarah, 182.
Charch, Mithes, 146.
Charles, Peter, 144.
Chasm, John, 157.
Chenangheata, 551.
Cherry, Alice, 21.
Cherry, Edward, 21, 23.
Chestnut (Chesnut), John 228, 525, 591.
Chestnut, Mary S., 184.
Chestnut, William, 143, 184, 228, 392, 400, 444, 525.
Chestnutt, Elly, 228
Chestnutt, Isable, 228.
Chestnutt, Jean, 228.
Chestnutt, Sarah, 228.
Chew, Benjamin, 139.
Chew, Thomas, 251, 253, 255, 256, 259, 289.
Childers, Stephen, 550.
Chiney (Cluney), Robert, 282.
Chittam, Eleanor, 32.
Chittam, John, 32.
Chittam (Chittem), Mary, 32, 320, 330, 380, 381.
Chittam (Chittem), Philip, 15, 32, 36, 307, 320.
Chittam, William, 32.
Chrisman, Abraham, 130, 402.
Chrisman, George, 130, 371.
Chrisman, Isaac, 130.
Chrisman, Jacob, 130, 257, 339, 371, 449, 513.
Chrisman, John, 130, 132, 371.
Chrisman, Joseph, 130.
Chrisman, Magdalina, 371
Chrisman, Mary, 130.
Christall, Anne, 520, 537, 538.
Christall (Christell), William, 300, 441, 520, 537, 538.
Christian, Ann, 390, 467, 479
Christian, Edward, 229.
Christian, Elizabeth, 154, 184, 205, 301, 404, 458, 490.
Christian, Gilbert, 154, 166, 184, 194, 204, 216, 453, 522, 525, 551, 566, 570, 588.
Christian, Isaac, 452.
Christian, Isabella (Ezabellow), 197, 204.
Christian, Israel, 29, 39, 42, 47, 50, 51, 55, 67, 68, 77, 94, 95, 99, 101, 109, 165, 266, 277, 282, 285, 301, 316, 317,

323, 324, 342, 375, 376, 377, 381, 388, 390, 389, 394, 401, 404, 406, 409, 415, 417, 419, 421, 428, 430, 431, 434, 437, 451, 456, 457, 458, 461, 466, 467, 470, 474, 479, 483, 490, 491, 506, 527, 536, 591.
Christian, Jacob, 204.
Christian, John, 6, 15, 27, 29, 44, 47, 56, 77, 103, 105, 138, 142, 154, 165, 168, 169, 178, 184, 197, 204, 205, 210, 215, 218, 219, 255, 265, 266, 273, 280, 283, 298, 304, 324, 525, 547, 556, 566, 570, 588, 591.
Christian, Margaret, 154, 165, 551.
Christian, Mary, 154, 350.
Christian, Patrick, 154, 176, 184, 204, 205, 556.
Christian, Priscilla, 390.
Christian, Rachel, 197, 204, 588.
Christian, Robert, 12, 27, 29, 38, 40, 44, 66, 72, 75, 106, 131, 133, 138, 145, 154, 161, 165, 204, 255, 266, 270, 273, 275, 292, 316, 330, 381, 393, 409, 443, 490, 511, 525, 556, 566, 570, 594.
Christian, Rosanna, 462, 483.
Christian, Turner H., 363, 372.
Christian, William (W.), 12, 27, 29, 52, 83, 89, 91, 97, 98, 110, 116, 131, 138, 149, 154, 156, 165, 204, 205, 266, 282, 283, 303, 304, 317, 318, 324, 350, 385, 388, 390, 408, 415, 418, 421, 431, 438, 451, 452, 458, 461, 464, 467, 481, 483, 491, 499, 508, 525, 543, 556, 566, 570, 588.
Christy, William, 82.
Church, John, 144.
Churchill, H., 59.
Churu, Peter, 490.
Chuson (Chusour), George, 144.
Cimmerlan, Mary, 147.
Cimsey, William, 66.
Ciplinger, Abby, 230.
Ciplinger, Mary, 230.
Ciplinger, Peter, 230.
Ciplinger, Philip, 230.
Circle, Lewis, 113.
Circuit Court Wills, 249.
Claftrock, Ash, 100.
Clark, Alexander, 150, 160.
Clark, Elizabeth, 32, 150, 160.
Clark, Frances, 506.
Clark, Francis, 173.
Clark, George, 87.
Clark (Clerk), James, 26, 119, 133, 150, 160, 167, 249, 254, 280, 332, 336, 339, 351, 378, 428, 444, 501, 503, 506, 571, 573.
Clark (Clerk), John, 32, 79, 93, 136, 150, 251, 304, 336, 339, 351, 354, 360, 428, 444, 501, 503, 506, 541.

Clark (Clerk), Margaret (Margret), 54, 87, 93, 150, 361, 362, 437.
Clark, Mary, 87.
Clark, Mathew, 70.
Clark (Clerk), Samuel, 99, 150, 160, 215, 230, 236, 240, 245, 336, 414, 428, 444, 501, 506, 557, 583.
Clark, Sarah, 150
Clark, Thomas, 171.
Clark, Watson, 155.
Clark, William, 32, 35, 93, 95, 150, 153, 160, 173, 368, 402, 410, 426, 428, 437, 487, 573.
Clarke, Agness, 571.
Clarke, Jane (Jean), 150, 230.
Clarke, Letitia (Lettis), 246, 251.
Clarke, Robert, 54, 58, 79, 103, 112, 119, 145, 150, 157, 160, 164, 368, 444, 506, 528, 531, 571.
Claypole, James, 40, 321, 370, 413, 533, 551.
Claypole, Jane, 78, 103, 125.
Claypole, John, 66.
Claypole, Joseph, 66
Claypool, Margaret, 370.
Claypole, Martha, 48.
Claypole, Mary, 66.
Claypole, William, 39, 48, 66, 78, 103, 125.
Clayton, John, 219, 239.
Clayton, Thomas, 210.
Clayton, William, 400.
Cleaver, Benjamin, 153.
Cleghorn, Lettice, 330.
Cleghorn, William, 308, 320, 330, 350, 381.
Clemens, Christopher, 243.
Clements (Clemons), Elizabeth, 55, 164, 519.
Clements, Ezekiel, 81, 256.
Clements, Isabella, 55, 78.
Clements (Clemence, Clemons), Jacob, 33, 55, 56, 78, 202, 267, 297, 392, 413, 475.
Clements, Margaret, 55.
Clements (Clemence), Mary (Polly), 56, 243, 297
Clements, Rebecca, 55.
Clements, Ruth, 55, 78.
Clements, Sarah, 55.
Clemons (Clemance, Clemont, Clemons), Christian, 31, 64, 94, 164, 165, 172, 187, 352, 393, 396, 426, 440, 441, 481, 496, 498, 568.
Clemons, Andrew, 9.
Clemons (Clemonts), Catherine (Catren, Katrine), 64, 164, 201, 243, 498.
Clemons, Florah, 560.
Clemons (Clements), Gasper (Casper), 164, 243.
Clemons (Clements), James, 243, 380, 463, 560.

Clemons, Jasper, 568.
Clemons (Clements), John, 164, 201, 204, 243, 519.
Clendenin, George, 584.
Clendenin, Mary, 542.
Clendennin, Mary A., 83.
Clendennin (Clendinen), Robert, 128, 481, 542.
Clendennin, William, 559.
Clendenning, Ann, 80, 85, 100.
Clendenning, Archibald, 12, 14, 17, 80, 85, 100
Clendenning (Clendenen), Charles, 25, 89, 510.
Clendenning, Esther, 12, 14.
Clendenning, James, 203.
Clendenning, John, 12, 83, 100.
Clendenning, Margaret, 12, 83, 203.
Clenkaid, Margaret, 160.
Clerkston, David, 188.
Clery, Elijah, 348.
Click, Jacob, 93.
Clifton, John, 143.
Clinch, Patrick, 324.
Cline, Andrew, 112.
Cline, Margaret, 235.
Cline, Michael, 232.
Cloninger, Catherine, 170.
Cloninger, Philip, 170.
Cloninger, Valentine, 135, 140, 142, 149, 170, 179, 221, 509, 519, 532, 549, 559, 563, 572.
Clotzhine, Margaret, 467.
Clover, William, 152
Cloverfield, Catren, 208.
Cloyd (Cloid), David, 24, 28, 35, 48, 56, 61, 63, 77, 87, 91, 268, 364, 371, 417, 444, 445, 469, 473, 481.
Cloyd, Elizabeth, 407.
Cloyd (Cloid), James, 63, 87, 89, 99, 117, 118, 364, 371, 386, 467.
Cloyd (Cloid), John, 56, 63, 67, 77, 84, 87, 99, 104, 118, 317, 423, 592.
Cloyd, Joseph, 89, 115, 117, 466, 471, 473.
Cloyd, Joshua, 411.
Cloyd, Margaret, 91, 364, 423.
Cloyd, Mary, 77, 407, 423.
Cloyd, Michael, 371, 428, 444.
Cloyd, Ninian (Nyrian, Mirian), 79, 378, 407, 411, 423, 445.
Cloyd, Samuel, 72, 79, 102, 106, 378, 407, 445.
Clunie, William, 158.
Clyde, David, 318.
Clyde (Clide), John, 277, 551.
Clymant, Christian, 252.
Clymer, George, 139.
Clyne, Jacob, 187.
Coagar (Cowgar), George, 568
Coaler, Henry, 166.
Cobune, Thomas, 330.

Coburn, Isaac, 13.
Coburn, Jacob, 13.
Coburn (Cobourn), James, 9, 13.
Coburn (Cobourn), Jonathan, 9, 53, 58.
Coburn, Samuel, 13.
Cochran, Elizabeth, 168.
Cochran, Henry King, 248.
Cochran, James, 188, 201, 248, 525.
Cochran, Jamison, 247.
Cochran, Jane, 247.
Cochran, John, 35, 59, 91, 92, 104, 118, 168, 248, 346, 389.
Cochran, Josiah, 158.
Cochran (Cohorn), Martha, 168, 248.
Cochran (Cockran), Peter, 416, 436, 477.
Cochran, Robert, 166.
Cochran (Cockran), Susanna, 91, 460
Cock, John, 53, 189.
Cocke, James P., 594.
Cocke, William, 182.
Cockbeam (Cockburn), Robert, 169.
Cockran, Margaret, 168, 436.
Cocks, William, 103.
Codington, James, 541.
Coffee, Mary, 167.
Coffey, Hugh, 7, 17, 20, 459, 488.
Coffey, John, 455, 459.
Coffey, William, 564.
Colley, John, 96.
Coffman, Abigail, 121.
Coffman, Elizabeth, 116.
Coffman, Henry, 116, 117, 121.
Coffman, John N., 117.
Cogar, Nicholas, 40
Coger, Betsey, 234.
Coger (Coager, Cogar), Jacob, 13, 304, 388, 406, 510, 515.
Coger (Coager, Cogar, Coker), Michael, 40, 86, 95, 96, 388, 439, 460, 471, 510, 515, 528, 538.
Coil (Coyle, Cvle, Gile, Goyle, Kyle), Gabriel, 63, 65, 94, 100, 156, 374, 376, 405, 525, 549.
Coil (Goil, Goyle, Kile), Jacob, 94, 167, 379, 525, 527, 538, 549.
Coil (Gile, Goyle), Valentine, 50, 71, 99, 100, 103, 379, 525, 549.
Coile (Coyle, Goile, Kile), George, 94, 100, 126, 137, 143, 538, 544.
Coile (Coyle, Goil), Martin, 94, 100, 141.
Coiner, Christian, 212.
Coiner, Conrad, 212.
Coiner, Frederick, 212.
Coiner (Coinert), Gasper, 212, 581.
Coiner, George, 212.
Coiner, George Michael, 212.
Coiner, Jacob, 212.
Coiner, John, 212.
Coiner (Counner), Margaret (Peggy), 203, 212, 221.
Coiner, Martin, 212, 239.

Coiner, Mary, 242.
Coiner (Coinart, Coyner), Michael, 124, 203, 212, 213, 581, 590, 594.
Coiner, Philip, 212.
Coiner, Susannah, 225.
Coite, Martin, 471.
Coke, John, 100.
Cokenour, Joseph, 16.
Coker, Peter, 149.
Colar (Coler), Henry, 57, 94, 145.
Coldu, Gerd, 121.
Cole, James, 169, 305.
Cole (Coles), Mark, 9, 42, 305.
Coleman, Ann, 228.
Coleman, James, 191.
Coleman, Michael, 228.
Coleman, Samuel, 122, 540, 547.
Coleman, Wiat, 122.
Coler, John, 341.
Colewell, James, 326.
Coll, Timothy, 23, 285.
Collen, William, 167.
Colley, Barbery, 58.
Colley, Catharn, 58.
Colley (Colly), Christian, 58, 113.
Colley, Clorah, 58.
Colley (Colly), Elizabeth, 58, 112.
Colley, Hans, 92.
Colley, John, 49, 58, 59, 63, 112.
Colley, Margaret, 58.
Colley, Mary, 58, 112,
Colley, Owen, 196.
Colley, Peter, 58.
Colley, Susan, 58.
Collier (Collyer, Colyer), Alexander, 90, 109, 359, 386, 407.
Collier (Collyer), John, 31, 56, 62, 73, 75, 85, 90, 92, 110, 285, 300, 340, 356, 358, 359, 410, 479.
Collier (Collyer), Moses, 90, 98, 410, 479.
Collier, (Colyer), Sisely (Sicilly), 90, 285, 356, 358, 359, 410.
Collins, Edward, 195.
Collins, James, 232.
Collins, John, 13, 140, 556.
Collins, Luke, 231.
Colter, (Coalter, Coulter), David, 180, 182, 188, 524.
Colter, (Coalter, Coulter), James, 16, 103, 180, 188, 192, 311, 399, 442, 485, 512, 515.
Colter, (Coalter, Coulter), John, 67, 79, 126, 180, 182, 188, 218, 224, 225, 230, 271, 275, 290, 402, 421, 507, 523, 524, 526.
Colter, (Coalter, Coulter), Joseph, 180, 188, 222, 515, 526.
Colton, (Culton), James, 102, 130, 396, 428, 495, 503, 528.
Colven, Joseph, 98.

Colyer, Aaron, 90.
Colyer, Margaret, 90.
Comber, Christopher, 253.
Comber, Michael, 547.
Coningham, Martha, 317.
Connell, (Connelly), William, 188, 191, 574.
Connely, Alexander, 205.
Connely (Connly, Conaly, Coneley, Connerly), Arthur, 116, 139, 151, 171, 205, 227, 520, 532, 592.
Connely, Barbara, 205.
Connely, David, 227.
Connely, Elizabeth, 205.
Connely, Isable, 205.
Connely (Connelly, Connerly), James, 24, 28, 227.
Connely, Jean, 205, 227.
Connely, John, 205, 227.
Connely (Connelly), Margaret, 176, 205.
Connely, Martha, 205.
Connely, Mary, 205, 227.
Connely, Sarah, 227.
Connely (Connly), Robert, 205, 227, 566, 567.
Connely (Connelly, Connly, Connerly), Thomas, 114, 139, 149, 176, 205, 211, 227, 520, 521.
Conner, John, 149, 212, 243, 590.
Conner, Rebeckah, 590.
Conner, Thomas Ellet, 243.
Connly, Darby, 140, 155.
Conrad, Barbara, 143.
Conrad, Catherine, 101, 417, 501, 505.
Conrad, Elizabeth, 143.
Conrad, Frederick, 549.
Conrad, George, 101, 110, 144, 424, 480, 497, 501, 505, 522.
Conrad, Jacob, 133, 143, 146, 405, 413, 416, 489, 555.
Conrad, John, 56.
Conrad, Margaret, 399.
Conrad, Mary, 143.
Conrad (Conrod, Gunrod), Peter, 480, 484, 488, 517, 522, 528, 544.
Conrad Gunrod), Stephen, 57, 63, 86, 101, 103, 110, 144, 388, 417, 424, 439, 484, 488, 501, 505, 508.
Conrad (Conrat), Ulrick (Uldrick, Ulrunk), 122, 141, 374, 549.
Conrad, Woolrick (Woolderick, Wolric, Wolerey), 51, 65, 71, 100, 133, 143, 399, 555.
Conrod, Hance, 51.
Conrod, Samuel, 537.
Consolive, James, 169.
Consolvant (Cousalvan), Charles, 143, 175.
Convey, Timothy, 15.
Coofman, Madlin, 121.
Cook, Ann, 315.
Cook, Barbara, 232.

Cook, Cornelius, 315, 433, 501, 524, 552.
Cook, Henry, 42, 44, 169.
Cook, Jane (Jean), 10, 11, 284, 517.
Cook, John, 11, 16, 35, 73, 225, 284, 321, 514, 517, 522.
Cook, Mary, 11, 35, 42, 284, 517.
Cook, Patrick, 10, 11, 13, 35, 272, 280, 284, 319, 346, 477, 507.
Cook, Paul, 228.
Cook, Peggy, 228.
Cook, Susanna, 543.
Cook, Valentine (Kock, Felty), 57, 161, 408, 543.
Cook, William, 144, 493.
Cooke, Sally, 224.
Coombs, Ignetius, 121.
Coonby, John, 121.
Cooper, Elizabeth, 209, 232.
Cooper, Ezekiel, 225, 234, 242.
Cooper, James, 167, 222, 453, 478, 511.
Cooper, John, 186, 228, 233.
Cooper, Joseph, 228, 475.
Cooper, Martha, 209.
Cooper, Robert, 169, 181, 201, 209, 211, 228, 232, 498, 542, 570, 579.
Cooper, William, 228, 233.
Cope (Kop), Valentine (Felty), 388.
Copland (Capland) Anne, 32, 51, 303.
Copland (Capland), Benjamin, 32, 35, 37, 39, 51, 303, 340, 350, 357, 459, 549.
Copland, Hannah, 51.
Copland, Jacob, 51.
Copland, Mary, 51.
Copland, Sarah, 51.
Coraford (Craford), John, 126.
Correy (Corry), William, 55, 122.
Corrigon, Patrick, 464.
Corry, Nicholas, 524.
Corry, Samuel, 92, 122.
Corse, Mathias, 450.
Corson, James, 543.
Cortreght, Hendrick, 310.
Cotess, John, 146.
Cotner, George, 27.
Cotner, Mary, 27.
Cotner (Cottner), Peter, 27, 29.
Cotten, Peter, 472.
Cotton, James, 417, 440.
Cottrel, Thomas, 81.
Couch (Coutch), John, 57, 69, 110, 113.
Couch, Tetrach, 57.
Couchman, Henry, 53.
Cough, Valentine, 57.
Coughran, Jean, 249.
Couherd, Jonathan, 408.
Coulter, Isabella, 188, 275, 402.
Coulter (Coalter), Michael, 133, 191, 196, 442, 508, 570, 581, 596.
Coulton (Culton), Joseph, 5, 7, 15, 21, 41, 48, 69, 82, 104, 119, 130, 132, 255, 307, 310, 313, 337, 341, 365, 421, 495, 499, 503.
Coulton (Culton), Robert, 12, 96, 130, 307, 311, 344.
Countryman, Christian, 141.
Counts, John, 97.
Coursey, William, 169.
Courtsious, Jacob, 69.
Cousart, Martha, 305.
Cousart (Cousard), Richard, 267, 295, 305.
Couter, Michael, 135.
Couters, Jacob Fred, 112.
Couts (Coutts), Elizabeth, 46, 141.
Couts (Coutts, Kouts), John, 47, 58, 59, 62, 103, 152, 355, 361, 480, 549.
Couts, Patrick, 362.
Couts, Teter, 94, 373.
Coven, William, 79.
Cover, James, 94.
Cowan (Cowen, Cowin), Andrew, 48, 54, 67, 167, 257, 260, 261, 267, 269, 275, 278, 286, 290, 295, 302, 359, 387, 395, 507, 555, 556, 563.
Cowan, Elizabeth, 555.
Cowan (Cowin), James, 18, 54, 67, 146, 150, 189, 257, 303, 484, 489, 521, 557.
Cowan, Jennet, 292.
Cowan, John, 273, 275, 292.
Cowan, Joseph, 215, 236.
Cowan, Mary, 556.
Cowan, Robert, 189, 353, 465.
Cowan, Thomas, 587.
Cowan (Cowen), William, 112, 507, 515, 555, 556.
Cowarden (Cowordin), John, 95, 132, 144, 448, 459, 462, 472, 546, 566, 573, 579.
Cowardin, Margaret, 144.
Cowardine, Mary, 579.
Cowden (Cowdon), James, 10, 443, 446, 460, 491, 530, 542.
Cowden, Jane, 10.
Cowden, Mathew, 496, 585.
Cowden (Cowdon), Samuel, 67, 72, 93, 98, 362, 409, 413, 439, 445, 460, 463, 485, 496, 541.
Cowden (Cowdon), William, 10, 14, 294, 412, 542.
Cowdon, Martha, 563, 574, 581.
Cowdon, Robert, 122.
Cowdon, Walter, 67, 93.
Cowger, George, 158.
Cowhard, Jonathan, 394.
Cowley, James, 279.
Cowley, Joseph, 129.
Cowman, John, 569.
Cox, John, 525.
Cox, Margaret, 221.
Cox, William, 97.

Coyle (Coyl), James, 110, 289, 296, 350, 352, 388, 550.
Coynart, George A., 581.
Cozby, Elizabeth, 358.
Cozby (Cosby), John, 338, 358, 451.
Cradock, David, 121.
Craider, Martin, 115.
Craig, Agness, 229, 230.
Craig, Alexander, 37, 159, 191, 198, 199, 209, 220, 388, 407, 439, 492, 494, 545, 551, 553, 561, 591.
Craig, Anne, 163, 181, 193.
Craig, David, 196.
Craig, Eleanor, 167.
Craig, Elijah, 230.
Craig, Grizel, 283.
Craig, George, 134, 193, 198, 204, 214, 221, 230, 232, 337, 561, 576.
Craig, Isabella H., 134, 270, 319.
Craig, James, 36, 45, 56, 58, 71, 72, 79, 170, 172, 184, 187, 192, 193, 194, 197, 221, 222, 230, 232, 236, 238, 243, 246, 253, 274, 290, 342, 362, 372, 412, 426, 439, 479, 489, 519, 576.
Craig. Jane (Jean, Jenny), 229, 230, 246, 563, 577.
Craig, Janet (Jennet), 42, 51, 56.
Craig, John, 36, 41, 42, 51, 56, 57, 65, 69, 71, 75, 94, 97, 110, 134, 163, 165, 174, 181, 182, 187, 193, 194, 204, 230, 243, 254, 270, 285, 305, 319, 322, 324, 337, 339, 350, 363, 388, 389, 404, 416, 447, 464. 479, 491, 492, 501, 526, 563, 577.
Craig, John, 229.
Craig, Joseph, 562.
Craig, Kitty, 250.
Craig, Margaret (Peggy), 128, 192, 232, 388, 439, 492.
Craig, Mary (Maray, Polly), 193, 196, 221. 232, 404.
Craig, Rebecca, 181, 229.
Craig, Robert, 23, 56, 58, 60, 69, 174, 181, 182. 204, 213. 229, 230, 246, 253, 283, 404. 576.
Craig, Samuel, 48, 65, 120, 128, 157, 179, 192, 193, 230, 360, 420, 439, 464, 491. 492, 519, 573, 576.
Craig, Sarah, 230, 243, 501.
Craig, Susannah, 229.
Craig, Valentine, 339.
Craig, William, 53, 56, 69, 70, 71, 136, 177, 184, 193, 197, 198, 213, 214, 221. 222, 227, 229, 230, 232, 236, 238, 246, 272, 481, 491, 492, 502, 562, 594.
Craigard, Robert, 156.
Craige, Elizabeth (Betsy), 221, 228, 229, 230, 246, 407.
Craige, Nancy, 232.
Craige, Patterson, 243.
Craige, Thomas, 447.

Craighead, Alexander, 313, 333, 348, 369, 438, 475.
Craighead, Jean, 438, 475.
Crane, William, 138.
Craney, John, 102, 166, 427.
Cravens, Agnes, 68.
Cravens, Elizabeth, 68, 81.
Cravens, John, 45, 47, 56, 68, 71, 75, 76, 81, 89, 92, 109, 291, 338, 345, 403, 407, 455, 462, 476, 497, 512, 535, 537.
Cravens, Joseph, 68, 69, 106, 109, 345, 347, 355, 370, 476, 477, 522, 524, 535, 537.
Cravens, Margaret, 68, 71, 364, 462, 497.
Cravens, Mary (Polly), 68, 81, 251, 291, 363, 455.
Cravens, Neomi (Emie), 522.
Cravens, Robert, 7, 13, 14, 19, 48, 51, 54, 57, 66, 68, 70, 72, 79, 81, 82, 97, 120, 256, 291, 302, 313, 340, 345, 355, 363, 367, 417, 455, 462, 522, 524, 535, 537.
Cravens, William, 68, 70, 81, 360, 370, 444, 476.
Crawford (Crafford), Alexander, 20, 26, 59, 77, 86, 89, 103, 104, 107, 121, 123, 132, 167, 175, 178, 186, 199, 201, 230, 273, 566, 577.
Crawford, Anne, 201.
Crawford, Andrew, 431.
Crawford, Elizabeth, 19, 134, 157, 174, 194, 195, 201, 203, 207, 213, 236.
Crawford, Florence, 190.
Crawford, George, 56, 60, 79, 104, 120, 146, 157, 165, 174, 178, 187, 190, 195, 199, 200, 201, 213, 236, 243, 279, 280, 299, 316, 318, 342, 345, 352, 364, 369, 377, 382, 424, 586.
Crawford, Gilbert, 73, 74.
Crawford. Hugh, 236.
Crawford, Isabella, 146.
Crawford, James, 19, 21, 23, 118, 146, 153, 157, 158, 174, 178, 179, 182, 187, 190, 193, 194, 197, 199, 200, 201, 202, 203. 204. 207, 213, 214, 229, 234, 236, 243, 247, 248, 261, 262, 269, 282, 342, 391, 392, 421, 469, 475, 490.
Crawford, Jane (Jean), 137, 157, 194, 201, 230, 236.
Crawford, Jenet (Jenny), 199, 201.
Crawford, Joel, 157.
Crawford (Craford), John, 157, 174, 178, 179, 182, 187, 188, 194, 197, 198, 199, 203, 206, 207, 213, 229, 236, 248, 319, 431, 486, 487, 500, 544, 583.
Crawford, Josiah, 104.
Crawford, Marian, 70.
Crawford, Martha, 132, 157, 178, 194, 201.
Crawford, Mary (Polly), 103, 178, 201, 213, 230, 248.
Crawford, Mary Anne, 93, 367, 446.
Crawford, Nancy, 230, 243.

Crawford, Nathan (Nathaniel), 571, 575.
Crawford, Patrick, 19, 23, 149, 167, 178, 210, 239, 279, 280, 341, 348, 350, 521.
Crawford, Rachel, 188, 197, 199, 203.
Crawford, Rebecca, 104, 146, 230.
Crawford, Robert, 107, 157, 174, 194, 213, 236, 410.
Crawford, Samuel, 35, 128, 190, 199, 207, 208.
Crawford, Sarah, 157, 194, 213, 236.
Crawford, Thomas, 53, 70, 94.
Crawford, William, 103, 104, 132, 134, 157, 169, 174, 178, 186, 188, 190, 197, 199, 201, 206, 207, 213, 236, 248, 377, 565, 573, 575, 583.
Crawny, John, 218.
Crawsby, Samuel, 221.
Creaber, Anna M., 212.
Creaghead, Robert, 475.
Creedrick, Samuel, 158.
Creeley, Daniel, 9.
Creely, John, 188.
Creever (Creaber), Philip, 212, 215, 532.
Creever, Sophia, 228.
Creever (Creaber), William, 212, 215.
Creighton, John, 99.
Cresswell, Harriet, 250.
Cresswell (Crisswell, Cryswell), Henry, 83, 89, 107, 122, 124, 385, 452, 547.
Cresswell, Rebecca, 452.
Creswell, James, 250.
Creswell, Margaret, 250.
Crewger, John, 175.
Cribb, Adam, 167.
Crick, John, 245.
Crider, Samuel, 158.
Crighton, David, 53, 70, 341.
Crigler, Reuben, 151.
Crington, John, 106.
Crisman, Jacob, 473.
Crist, Abraham, 219.
Crist (Crists), Andrew, 219, 220.
Crist, Elizabeth (Betsy), 219.
Crist, Fanny, 219.
Crist, Heddy, 219.
Crist, Henry, 219.
Crist, Jacob, 219, 245.
Crist, John, 219.
Crist, Mary (Polly), 219.
Crist, Nancy, 219.
Critchs, Jacob, 141.
Crites, Philip, 121.
Crittenden, William, 291, 312.
Crocket, Jennet, 455.
Crockett, Agness, 16, 98.
Crockett, Alexander, 6, 38, 39, 49.
Crockett, Andrew, 38, 39, 48, 113, 486, 592.
Crockett, Archibald, 24, 310, 389.
Crockett, Asbal (Arsble), 6.
Crockett, Catherine, 16.

Crockett, Elizabeth, 98.
Crockett, Esther, 16.
Crockett, Hugh, 98, 550.
Crockett, James, 6, 38, 39, 48, 146, 147, 455, 458, 469, 489, 592.
Crockett, Jane (Jean), 6, 16, 97.
Crockett, John, 6, 16, 37, 113, 301, 310, 389, 452.
Crockett, Joseph, 16, 22, 27, 28, 97, 98, 117, 458.
Crockett, Margaret, 6, 7, 389, 592.
Crockett, Martha, 98, 455.
Crockett, Mary, 98, 389.
Crockett, Robert, 6, 7, 24, 38, 39, 48, 49, 98, 267, 310, 455, 458.
Crockett, Samuel, 6, 16, 21, 38, 39, 98, 110, 384, 388, 389, 393, 414, 458.
Crockett, Walter, 62, 97, 98, 109, 458.
Croghan, George, 551.
Crommett, Christopher, 150.
Crop, Andrew, 353.
Crosbe (Cozbe), John, 459.
Crosby, George, 237.
Crose, Christian, 53.
Croson (Creeson), Abraham, 258.
Crossen (Crosson), Charles, 328, 382, 438.
Crosson, Christina, 382.
Crosson, Martha, 438.
Crosthwaite (Croswaite), Timothy, 253, 285, 307, 327.
Crosthwaite, William, 253, 285.
Croswick, Timothy, 489.
Crotes, John, 146.
Crotingal, Peter, 38.
Crouch, John, 155.
Crouch (Croutch), Joseph, 128, 137.
Crow, Benjamin, 563.
Crow, James, 168, 171, 446, 448, 466, 470, 471, 480, 482, 501, 548.
Crow, John, 70, 92.
Crow, Margaret, 76, 479.
Crow, Mary, 483.
Crow, Thomas, 437, 466, 479, 483, 491.
Crow, Walter, 412, 415, 422, 444.
Crow, William, 67, 70, 72, 82, 89, 90, 98, 106, 358, 409, 410, 436, 437, 440, 443, 445, 451, 458, 462, 466, 476, 479, 483, 508.
Crowbarger, George, 244.
Crum, John, 25, 26.
Crum, Philip, 15.
Crump, Edmond, 86, 93, 413, 414.
Crump, Richard, 399.
Crup, Christian, 338.
Crutchfield, David, 524.
Crutchfield, Francis, 579.
Cryton (Carrington), John, 97.
Cuddy, James, 149.
Cue, Mary, 328.
Cue, Peter, 328.
Cuff, Bryan, 9, 297, 378.

Culbert, John, 334.
Culberts (Culbert), William, 81, 93, 97.
Culbertson, Anne, 181.
Culbertson, James, 140, 180, 190, 198, 518, 559, 567, 584.
Culbertson, Margaret, 181.
Culbertson, Molly, 181.
Culbertson, Robert, 181.
Cull, James, 340.
Cullen, John, 578.
Culliland, John, 52, 62.
Culton, Jane, 130, 236.
Culton, Margaret, 130.
Culton, Mary (Marray), 341, 428.
Culwell, Robert, 473.
Cumberford, James, 252.
Cumberland, Catherine, 11.
Cumberland, Jacob, 147.
Cumberland, James, 11.
Cumberland, John, 11, 13.
Cummin, Alex., 177.
Cummings, Daniel, 43.
Cummings (Cummins), John, 226, 539.
Cummings, Joseph, 42, 44.
Cummins, Charles, 464, 470, 557.
Cummins, Jean, 226.
Cummins, Margaret, 226.
Cummins, Martha, 226.
Cummins, Mille, 557.
Cummins, Robert, 226, 557.
Cummins, Samuel, 399.
Cunningham, Alexander, 99, 150, 161, 510, 536, 557, 574.
Cunningham, Ann, 150.
Cunningham, Archibald, 163.
Cunningham, Christopher, 49.
Cunningham (Coningham), David, 36, 50, 150, 171, 209, 211, 245, 277, 278, 282, 283, 337, 514, 522, 536, 557, 574, 590.
Cunningham, Eleanor, 207.
Cunningham, Elizabeth, 88, 99, 163.
Cunningham, Gennet, 339.
Cunningham, Hugh, 56, 67, 73, 76, 88, 106, 112, 270, 271, 287, 349, 361, 407, 410, 422, 433, 464, 484, 489, 495, 568.
Cunningham (Coningham), Isaac, 57, 64, 88, 316, 341.
Cunningham (Coningham), Jacob, 56, 60, 88, 316, 341.
Cunningham (Coningham), James, 88, 90, 150, 156, 177, 209, 214, 226, 232, 315, 316, 341, 536, 557, 565, 580, 582, 593.
Cunningham, Jane (Jean), 57, 81, 150, 241, 459, 553, 560, 574.
Cunningham (Coningham), John, 26, 29, 30, 38, 51, 61, 66, 68, 88, 128, 134, 150, 196, 202, 209, 211, 217, 226, 228, 232, 241, 247, 268, 270, 279, 289, 293, 296, 305, 342, 344, 349, 368, 370, 371, 372, 376, 402, 403, 404, 409, 410, 457, 459, 511, 514, 526, 549, 553, 554, 557, 560, 568, 574, 576, 586, 587, 590.
Cunningham, Jonathan, 112, 410, 469, 495.
Cunningham, Lettice, 590.
Cunningham (Coningham), Margaret (Peggy), 8, 88, 232, 247, 315, 341, 403, 404, 410, 411.
Cunningham (Coningham), Mary, 7, 88, 112, 150, 163, 264, 328, 376.
Cunningham, Moses, 88, 519.
Cunningham (Coningham), Patrick, 43, 70, 99, 150, 277, 283, 317, 318, 353, 404, 410, 440, 474, 475, 478, 549, 574.
Cunningham, Rachel, 220, 232, 241.
Cunningham, Rebecca, 232.
Cunningham (Coningham), Robert, 5, 6, 27, 34, 68, 99, 121, 232, 241, 255, 261, 273, 282, 283, 284, 289, 302, 303, 317, 325, 354, 370, 376, 407.
Cunningham, Ruth, 163.
Cunningham, Samuel, 7, 8.
Cunningham, Samuel S., 208.
Cunningham, Sarah, 150, 163, 372, 495.
Cunningham, Thomas, 129, 163, 172.
Cunningham (Coningham), Walter, 98, 100, 128, 161, 177, 181, 185, 317, 337, 372, 434, 445, 448, 485, 493, 543, 553.
Cunningham (Coningham), William, 61, 71, 90, 150, 232, 241, 312, 339, 410, 411, 440, 459, 511, 534, 548, 549, 554.
Cupp (Cupps), Marcus, 183, 211.
Curdsake, Henry, 28.
Curp, Catherine, 416.
Curp, Christian, 416.
Currance, William, 188.
Curren, Pady, 121.
Curry, Agnes, 180.
Curry, Alexander, 196, 226, 232, 595.
Curry, Andrew, 180.
Curry, Ann, 226.
Curry, Barbara, 179.
Curry, Benjamin, 232, 242.
Curry, Elizabeth, 180, 232.
Curry, Frances, 232.
Curry, Isaiah (Isah), 93, 226, 233, 362, 386, 393, 396, 585.
Curry, James, 171, 195, 226, 232, 450, 460, 507, 549, 568, 572, 582.
Curry, Jean, 179, 180, 232, 233.
Curry, John, 391, 460.
Curry, Joseph, 460.
Curry, Margaret, 180, 232, 585.
Curry, Martha, 174.
Curry, Mary, 180, 232, 233.
Curry, Minian, 536.
Curry, Robert, 122, 180, 195, 196, 200, 203, 222, 226, 232, 239, 349, 449, 587, 590.
Curry, Samuel, 200, 226, 233, 243, 512, 572.
Curry, Sarah, 200.
Curry (Currey, Correy), William, 66, 73,

180, 226, 232, 233, 238, 278, 355, 362, 460, 486, 507, 533, 571, 579.
Curtnes, Anna, 364.
Curtnes, Jacob, 364.
Curtract, Henry, 28.
Custard (Kuster), Arnold, 40, 52, 77, 346, 539.
Custard, Bridget, 52.
Custard (Custer, Couster, Kuster), 77, 121, 123, 133, 135, 406, 433, 498, 539.
Custard, Elizabeth, 539.
Custard, Morris, 133.
Custard (Kuster), Paul, 121, 133, 135, 318, 539.
Custert, Nicholas, 40.
Cutler, Andrew, 200, 201, 580.
Cutlip (Gutlip), George, 391, 536.
Cutman, Jacob, 63.
Cutwright, Peter, 119.
Cypher (Cyphers), Francis, 50, 74, 309.
Cypher, John, 167.

Dabige, William, 145.
Dache, Henry, 178.
Dadridge, George, 210.
Dailey (Daley, Dayly, Dayley), Charles, 22, 311, 551, 552.
Dailey, Elinor, 552.
Dailey (Daley, Dayley), John, 64, 67, 424, 425, 426, 445, 452, 460.
Dailey, Mary, 426.
Dailey, Phillip, 503.
Dalby, Philip, 581.
Dale, Alexander, 81, 90, 93.
Dalhouse (Dalhoss), Charles, 47, 60, 79, 266, 267, 283, 284, 290, 298, 310, 413, 491, 497, 578.
Dalhouse, George, 60.
Dalhouse, James, 60.
Dalhouse, John, 60, 578.
Dalhouse, William, 578.
Dall, Alexander, 110.
Dalloway, Charles, 420.
Dalson, Charles, 314.
Dalton, George, 574.
Dalzell, James, 524, 544.
Dame, Francis, 332.
Danaho, Joseph, 153.
Danchea, Hugh, 200.
Dandridge, William, 188.
Daniel, Hugh, 158.
Daniel, Reuben, 496.
Danner, Clev., 275.
Danner, Tobias, 221.
Dare (Dair), George, 106, 461, 465.
Dare (Adair), Robert, 381.
Darin, Jacob, 573.
Darling (Darline), William, 53, 150.
Darlington, William, 10.
Darnell, Isaac, 572.
Darnely, James, 244.

Darr, George, 93, 109, 115.
Darrick, John, 365.
Daubekins (Dobekin), John, 13.
Daufflemire, Michael, 502.
Daugherty, Agnes, 214.
Daugherty, Betsy, 242.
Daugherty, Charles, 316.
Daugherty, Hugh, 232.
Daugherty, John, 232.
Daughey (Daggy), Jacob, 578.
Daulton, Garrett, 234.
Daulton, Margaret, 234.
Davidson (Davison), Ann, 23, 82, 175.
Davidson (Davison), Daniel, 14, 19, 77, 95, 214, 270, 274, 276, 455, 465, 478.
Davidson (Davison), James, 143, 369, 444, 502.
Davidson, Jean, 502.
Davidson (Davison), John, 15, 23, 29, 34, 69, 81, 84, 95, 112, 126, 130, 143, 164, 175, 193, 214, 217, 266, 271, 287, 297, 310, 313, 329, 339, 353, 358, 367, 379, 420, 431, 442, 468, 477, 514, 529, 542, 558, 559, 562.
Davidson, Josiah, 77, 143, 445, 465, 477, 513, 533.
Davidson, Margaret, 214.
Davidson (Davison), Mary, 109, 143, 214, 542, 559, 562.
Davidson (Davison), Samuel, 51, 107, 175, 262, 399.
Davidson, Sarah, 214, 542, 558.
Davies (Davis), Elnathan, 358.
Davis, Agness, 250.
Davis, Ann, 294.
Davis, Annis, 231, 245.
Davis (Davies), Benjamin, 56, 358, 450.
Davis, Charles, 98.
Davis, Daniel, 23.
Davis, David, 262, 267, 404, 409, 421, 442, 456, 487, 558, 590.
Davis, Edward, 25.
Davis, Elizabeth, 143, 147, 532, 572.
Davis, Esther, 495.
Davis, George, 130, 593.
Davis (Davies), Henry, 46, 351, 508.
Davis, Hugh, 477, 478.
Davis (Davies), James, 9, 11, 15, 22, 54, 67, 69, 73, 87, 90, 96, 97, 98, 106, 110, 203, 247, 257, 258, 259, 290, 299, 331, 345, 346, 350, 351, 356, 359, 383, 385, 403, 451, 464, 484, 529, 556.
Davis, James S., 259.
Davis, Jane (Jean), 96, 383, 411, 529.
Davis, Jeorah, 242.
Davis, Jesse, 219.
Davis (Davise, Davies), John, 6, 7, 9, 14, 33, 37, 39, 40, 44, 52, 60, 69, 70, 77, 78, 79, 83, 87, 106, 119, 121, 126, 138, 139, 140, 143, 147, 148, 149, 163, 205, 227, 250, 276, 289, 294, 313, 316, 333, 338,

339, 343, 344, 346, 356, 358, 363, 370, 371, 379, 383, 384, 402, 403, 406, 411, 421, 434, 437, 439, 445, 446, 447, 450, 451, 469, 475, 484, 485, 529, 530, 531, 532, 534, 551, 555, 572, 576, 581.
Davis, Jonathan, 406, 513.
Davis, Joseph, 451, 484.
Davis (Davison), Josiah, 532.
Davis, Judith (Judy), 87, 356, 379, 402. 450, 469.
Davis, Lucy, 513.
Davis, Martha (Patsey), 227, 250.
Davis, Martha A., 245, 250.
Davis, Mary, 414, 432.
Davis, Mildred, 310.
Davis (Davise, Davies), Nathaniel, 57, 80, 278, 281, 282, 283, 359, 434.
Davis, Patrick, 495.
Davis, Phebe, 538.
Davis, Richard, 473.
Davis (Davies), Robert, 6, 84, 108, 127, 128, 130, 134, 147, 148, 247, 261, 262, 267, 269, 271, 278, 301, 310, 352, 360, 408, 502, 534.
Davis, Ruth, 247.
Davis (Davies), Samuel, 96, 101, 303, 351, 367, 414, 417, 432, 484, 485.
Davis, Sarah (Sally), 93, 245, 359, 434, 502.
Davis, Thomas, 89, 95.
Davis (Davies), Walter, 33, 35, 49, 68, 75, 79, 116, 117, 125, 130, 146, 162, 165, 168, 180, 183, 188, 197, 199, 203, 205, 207, 211, 227, 237, 245, 247, 250, 294, 313, 317, 353, 354, 370, 371, 407, 410, 419, 440, 445, 511, 519, 522, 529, 536, 551, 555, 556, 565.
Davis (Davies), William, 31, 37, 40, 53, 60, 93, 127, 130, 147, 205, 227, 229, 230, 231, 237, 245, 351, 354, 356, 367, 386, 394, 403, 404, 408, 414, 415, 432, 434, 435, 450, 460, 461, 464, 466, 475, 486, 502, 522, 556.
Davis, William E., 245.
Davison, Amoziah, 149.
Davison, Elizabeth, 69.
Davison, Jane, 143.
Davison, Martha, 477.
Davison, Phoebe, 19, 82, 274.
Davison, Robert, 23.
Davitt, Jane, 544.
Davitt, William, 205.
Davitt, Tully, 138, 503, 505, 527, 544, 574.
Davor (Dever, Diver), Hugh, 424.
Dawson, George, 158.
Dawson, Henry, 526, 536.
Dawson, Mary, 536.
Day, Susannah, 170.
Deal, Alexander, 117, 515.
Deal, Isabel, 515.
Deal, Robert, 515.

Deal, William, 131.
Dean, Adam, 67, 80, 95, 130, 369, 385, 396, 418, 444, 552.
Dean, Agnes, 197, 574.
Dean, Benjamin, 521.
Dean, Eleanor, 418.
Dean, Elizabeth, 130.
Dean, James, 317.
Dean, John, 43, 47, 49, 67, 115, 121, 130, 138, 139, 171, 326, 381, 418, 430, 521, 567, 571.
Dean, Joseph, 521.
Dean, Margaret, 576.
Dean, Mary, 130, 477, 517.
Dean, Samuel, 266.
Dean, Sarah, 430, 521.
Dean, William, 43, 102, 130, 131, 210, 326, 377, 381, 396, 427, 430, 435, 477, 517, 521.
Deanmor, George, 236.
Deavis, Patrick, 285.
Decker, Garrett, 13.
Decker, Tobias, 310.
Decon, Archibald, 127.
Decoson, Jacob, 101.
Dedor, Christian, 364.
Dedy, Dorby, 132.
Deed Book No. 1, 251.
Dehart, Samuel, 483.
Dehart, Simon, 100.
Delamontane, Samuel, 302.
Delamounthony, Samuel, 326.
Delany (Deleney), Francis, 96, 106.
Delap, John, 60.
Dell, Alexander, 60.
Delong (Delay), Henry, 155.
Delshe, Robert, 352.
Demat, Henry, 131.
Denison, Elizabeth, 507.
Dennis, Jeremiah, 93.
Dennis, Joseph, 443.
Dennison (Denniston), John, 200, 201, 204, 208, 230, 502, 503, 529, 586.
Dennison, Martha, 242.
Denniston (Dennison), Daniel, 15, 38, 98, 254, 270, 280, 423, 459, 507, 511.
Denniston, Sarah, 15.
Denny, Elizabeth, 471, 525.
Denny, Patrick, 93, 433, 471, 525.
Denton, John, 274.
Denton, Margaret, 596.
Denton, Robert, 40, 50.
Denton, Samuel, 15.
Depriest, Charles, 216, 217.
Depriest, William, 145.
Derret, Marshal, 169.
Devenport, John, 169.
Dever, Anne, 424.
Devier, Betty, 496.
Dever (Deavier, Diver), Charles, 63, 84, 145, 276, 344, 358, 385, 461.

Dever (Devir, Diver, Divier), Hugh, 15, 167, 276, 411, 461, 462, 487, 500, 534.
Dever (Divier), James, 455, 458, 487, 496, 500, 514, 534.
Dever (Devir, Diver, Divir), John, 358, 534, 588, 589.
Deverix (Devericks), Thomas, 156, 583.
Devoir, James, 152.
Dey, Elizabeth, 190.
Dice (Dise, Dyce), George, 99, 111, 119, 122, 129, 141.
Dice, Margaret, 141.
Dice, Mary, 119.
Dice (Dyce), Mathias, 65, 103, 111, 113, 142.
Dick, Deck, Tack, Teck, Tick, 136.
Dick, Catherine, 136.
Dick, Charles, 136, 279, 284, 334, 365.
Dick, Christian, 136.
Dick, Henry, 45, 136.
Dick, Jacob, 136.
Dick, John, 136.
Dick, Michael, 136.
Dick, Runamus, 136.
Dicken, Michael, 55.
Dickenson, Joseph, 463.
Dickey, Becky, 235.
Dickey, Ellin, 231.
Dickey, Henry, 18.
Dickey, Isbold (Isbald), 231.
Dickey, James, 154, 161, 170, 173, 216, 227, 468, 566, 589, 590.
Dickey (Dicky), John, 159, 170, 193, 211, 218, 227, 231, 235, 243, 566, 569, 576, 590, 592.
Dickey, Joseph, 200, 201, 213, 215, 589.
Dickey, Martha, 180.
Dickey, Mary, 468.
Dickey, Michael, 83, 154, 170, 227, 263, 275, 294, 298, 332, 348, 355, 468, 508, 520, 527, 559, 566, 577, 594.
Dickey, Robert, 101, 509.
Dickey, William, 182, 194, 227, 526, 566.
Dickins, Henry, 297.
Dickins, How, 28.
Dickinson, Adam, 16, 25, 28, 31, 42, 44, 45, 48, 49, 59, 61, 70, 299, 317, 326, 333, 351, 430, 453, 461, 475, 500, 591.
Dickinson, Catherine, 58, 70, 333.
Dickinson (Dickenson), John, 16, 21, 40, 42, 43, 44, 47, 50, 52, 53, 69, 80, 119, 123, 124, 138, 139, 175, 209, 241, 317, 354, 369, 386, 389, 414, 444, 453, 461, 465, 466, 471, 478, 489, 575.
Dickinson, Magey, 444.
Dickinson, Martha, 124, 453, 461.
Dickison, Archibald, 537.
Dickon, Thomas, 207.
Dickson (Dixon), Archibald, 168, 176, 184, 230, 445, 575.
Dickson (Dixon), John, 173, 518, 558, 559, 583.
Dickson, Mary, 576.
Dickson, Patrick, 113, 576.
Dickson, Robert, 51.
Dicktom, Patsy, 223.
Dictom (Dictum), Rachell, 405, 426.
Dictom (Dicton), Richard, 9, 36.
Dictum (Dictom, Dicktom), Joseph, 36, 114, 405, 407, 426, 440, 455, 498, 512.
Diddle, James, 233.
Diddle, Sally, 233.
Diddy, John, 200, 201.
Didell, John, 225.
Die, John, 73, 322.
Differ, Charles, 71, 76.
Dike, Errowmous, 549.
Dilap (Delapp), Robert, 170.
Dill, George, 391.
Dill (Dull), Henry, 585, 588.
Dillen, Elizabeth, 57.
Dillenger, Caty, 223.
Dilling, Elizabeth, 111.
Dilling, John, 111, 113, 499.
Dilling, Thomas, 111.
Dilling, William, 111.
Dillon, Mary, 167.
Dinguid, William, 348.
Dinwiddy, Elenor, 194.
Dinwiddie, Robert, 514, 553.
Dinwiddie, William, 514.
Dinwoody, Robert, 138.
Divat, Tolly, 196.
Divers, George, 180, 573.
Diveyer, Michael, 167.
Dixon, Clement, 21.
Dixon, Elizabeth, 549.
Dixon, Martin, 145.
Dixon, Thomas, 123, 208, 536, 546, 549, 554.
Doack, William, 487, 556.
Doak, Aggy, 222.
Doak, Betsey, 222.
Doak, Betsey Wilson, 228.
Doak, Darcos, 222.
Doak (Doack, Doage), David, 108, 123, 201, 222, 225, 228, 252, 262, 327, 333, 357, 368, 478, 487, 514, 525, 561.
Doak, Flinor, 123.
Doak, Elizabeth, 123.
Doak, Elly, 222.
Doak, Fanny, 222.
Doak, Hugh, 222.
Doak, Isbel, 123.
Doak, Jane, 123.
Doak, Jennet, 222.
Doak (Doage), John, 123, 228, 266.
Doak, Julia, 228.
Doak (Doack), Mary, 123, 487.
Doak, Nancy, 228, 240.

Doak, Polly, **222**.
Doak (Doack, Doake, Doage), **Robert**, 123, 161, 194, 228, **229**, 231, **240**, **337**, 435, 453, 464, 557, 561, **565**.
Doak, Rosamah, 222, 228.
Doak (Doack, Doake, Doage), **Samuel**, 8, 15, 18, 26, 30, 123, 124, 201, **222**, **225**, 228, 261, 262, 286, 298, 313.
Doak, Thomas, **228**.
Doak, Vory (?), **228**.
Doak, Washington, **228**.
Doake, Dorcas M., **240**.
Doame, Mary, 224.
Dobbin, William, 276.
Dobbins (Dobikin), Elizabeth, 314, **571**.
Dobbins (Doubin), James, 30, **535**, **571**.
Dobikin (Dobkin, Dobbins), John, 5, 6, 9, 11, 19, 21, 24, 131, 293, 314, **315**.
Dobikin, John A., 5.
Dobikin, Mary, 5.
Docherty, Cornelius, 112.
Dodds (Dods), Alexander, 192, **209**.
Doearn, James, 116.
Doggett (Doged), Richard, 103, 109, **372**.
Dogherty, John Mc., 173.
Dogherty (Dougherty, Doherty), Margaret, 173, 214, 220.
Dogherty (Doherty, Dougherty), William, 7, 12, 131, 416, 420, **440**.
Doherty, Daniel, 220.
Doherty, Elizabeth, **440**.
Doherty, Polly, 220.
Doherty, Sarah, 220.
Doherty, Susanna, 220.
Dold, Philip, 367, 560, **593**.
Doll (Dull), Catherena, **215**.
Dull, George, 215.
Dollinson, Margaret, 113.
Dolly, Thomas, 65.
Dolson, Thomas, 14.
Dolway, Charles, 285.
Donaghe, Anne, 235.
Donaghe (Donaghey, Donachey, Donaho), Elizabeth, 404, 463, 515, 518, 519.
Donaghe (Donachey, Donohy, Donaghough, Donahoe, Donotha), Hugh, **47**, 98, 111, 141, 150, 161, 171, 180, 199, 218, 235, 240, 381, 391, 404, 421, 427, 432, 439, 440, 441, 463, 464, 485, **508**, 510, 515, 518, 519, 524, 526, 536, **538**, 546, 576, 584, 585, 587, 596.
Donaghe, James, 235, 240.
Donaghe (Donaghe), John, 213, 235, **592**.
Donaghe, Margaret, 213.
Donaghe, Sarah, 235.
Donaghe, William W., 235.
Donald, Mathew, 538.
Donald, Robert, 385.
Donaldson, Elizabeth, 454.
Donaldson, James, 454.

Donaldson (Donalson), Robert, 183, 221, 556, 571, 592.
Donaldson (Donalson), William, 216, **221**.
Donalson, David, 221.
Donalson (Donelson), James, 318, 331, 340.
Donalson, Jean, 221.
Donalson, John, 221.
Donarly, Jane, 560.
Donavan (Donovan), Daniel, 200, **589**.
Done, John, 402.
Donelson, Andrew, 37.
Donelson, Margaret, 37.
Doney, Patrick, 475.
Donnald, James, 518.
Donnally (Donaley), Francis, 61, 64, **491**.
Donnally, Henry, 64.
Donnally, James, 64.
Donnally, Samuel, 64.
Donnally, Sarah, 64.
Donnally, William, 64.
Donnelly (Donally, Donanly, Donnerly), Andrew, 166, 175, 495, 500, 560, 571, 573.
Donnelly, Ann, 166.
Donnelly, Catherine, 166.
Donnelly (Donnaly, Donelly, Donerly), Charles, 70, 87, 103, 132, 160, 166, **167**, 191, 203, 390, 400, 466, 495, 571.
Donnelly (Donley), Euphemia, 227, 250.
Donnelly (Donaley, Donnaly, Donoly), John, 20, 64, 74, 91, 103, 117, 118, **386**, 401, 459.
Donnelly (Donally, Donly), Mary, **64**, 166, 188, 556.
Donnelly, Patsey, 250.
Donovan, Elizabeth, 243.
Dooley (Dooling), Henry, 69, 292, **305**, 324, 334, 498, 568.
Dooley, Martha, 334.
Dooley, Thomas, 523.
Doolin, Thomas, 149.
Doran, Jacob, 133.
Doran, Thomas, 406.
Dorset, Thomas, 568.
Doscher (Dosher, Dousher, **Dorcher**), Christian, 53, 108.
Dosian, George, 176.
Dotson, Charles, 304.
Douchort (Doughert), John, 301, 318.
Doughert (Doughort), Mary, 300, 301, 306, 322, 334.
Dougherty, Charles, 80.
Dougherty, George, 88, 420, 434.
Dougherty (Doherty), Hugh, 220, **229**, 246.
Dougherty, John, 220.
Dougherty, Kitty, 220.
Dougherty (Daugherty, Dockerty, Dougherday), Michael, 36, 39, 75, 82, 110, 117, 162, 300, 306, 378, 460, 480.

Dougherty, Rebecca, 80.
Dougherty, Rosanna, 220.
Douglass, Alexander, 265, 268, 318, 395.
Douglass, Elizabeth, 239.
Douglass, George, 284.
Douglass, Hannah, 477.
Douglass, Hugh, 7, 37, 45, 282, 307, 546.
Douglass, James, 442, 477, 547.
Douglass, Jemima, 362, 378.
Douglass, John, 66, 110, 148, 154, 175, 442, 461.
Douglass, Jonathan, 66, 82, 314, 339, 362, 364, 378, 390, 400, 401, 433, 496, 526.
Douglass, Joseph, 546, 547.
Douglass, Margaret, 45, 282.
Douglass, Nathaniel, 461, 546.
Douglass, Robert, 239, 254, 408.
Douglass (Duglas), Roger, 268, 318, 395.
Duglass (Dugless, Dueglass), Thomas, 157, 543, 565, 580, 590.
Douthat, Robert, 188, 190, 200, 208, 212, 586, 589.
Dove, Francis, 13.
Dove, Thomas, 13.
Dowell, John, 404.
Dowly, Henry, 252.
Downen, William, 296.
Downey, Andrew, 197.
Downey, Elizabeth, 130, 132.
Downey, James, 69, 70.
Downey, Janet (Jenny), 130, 234.
Downey, John, 75, 234.
Downey, Margaret, 130, 234.
Downey, Martha, 130, 592, 593.
Downey, Mary, 234.
Downey, Mary Ann., 130.
Downey (Downing), Patrick, 74, 319, 323.
Downey, Rachel, 130, 132, 592, 593.
Downey, Rebecca, 130, 234.
Downey, Robert, 234.
Downey (Downy), Samuel, 41, 68, 69, 108, 130, 132, 134, 143, 234, 262, 281, 283, 284, 295, 323, 355, 359, 422, 499, 592, 593, 594.
Downey, Thomas, 239.
Downey, William, 130, 592, 593.
Downing, Anne, 594.
Downing, Edward, 239.
Downing, James, 20, 282, 307, 313, 333.
Downing, John, 16, 330.
Downing, Mary, 282, 307, 313.
Downing, Patrick, 81.
Downing Thomas, 239.
Downs, Elizabeth, 304.
Downs, Frances, 353.
Downs, Henry (Hendry), 10, 13, 20, 33, 36, 47, 53, 252, 253, 259, 261, 266, 269, 270, 271, 273, 280, 287, 289, 291, 293, 295, 312, 350, 353, 429, 513.
Downs, Jane, 270, 289.
Downs, William, 271, 350, 362, 412, 503.

Doyle, Bridget, 140.
Doyle, Thomas, 508.
Draffors (Draffons), Robert, 180.
Drake, Abraham, 6, 7.
Drake, Anne, 237.
Drake, John, 102.
Drake, Philip, 220, 557, 559.
Drake, Samuel, 106.
Draper, Abraham, 559.
Draper, Eleanor, 11.
Draper, Elisabeth, 371.
Draper, George, 11, 17.
Draper, John, 110, 320, 322, 371, 372.
Draper, William, 22, 25, 26.
Dredan (Dryden), David, 81, 97.
Dredan (Dredin), Thomas, 59, 344.
Dreddan, David, 232.
Dreddan, Hugh, 232.
Dreddan, Lilah, 232.
Dreddan, Ruery, 232.
Dreddan, William, 232.
Drien, David, 70.
Droudy, Daniel, 75, 110.
Drout, George, 367.
Drum (Dunn), Michael, 121.
Dryden, Agness, 543.
Dryden, David, 8, 27, 34, 62, 70, 73, 80, 124, 133, 148, 260, 288, 296, 342, 428, 436.
Dryden, Dorothy, 124, 133, 148.
Dryden, Elinor (Elliner), 124, 148.
Dryden, Elizabeth, 124.
Dryden, James, 124, 148, 428, 435, 436.
Dryden, Jane, 124.
Dryden, Mary, 543.
Dryden, Nathaniel (Nathan), 124, 133, 148, 543.
Dryden, Thomas, 102, 124, 133, 148, 543.
Dryden, William, 124, 133, 148, 543.
Dryer, William, 71.
Duerson, Charles, 102.
Duff, William, 255, 257, 274.
Duffield (Duffell, Duffels), Robert, 37, 176, 386, 535.
Duffy, Patrick, 438.
Dulaney, William, 289.
Duley, Martha, 350.
Dull, Peter, 246.
Duly (Duley, Dewly, Dowly), Henry, 285, 350.
Dunbar, Ann, 33.
Dunbarr (Dunbar), John, 15, 19, 20, 39, 43, 50, 66, 125, 135, 142, 148, 306, 307, 322, 433, 449, 459, 539, 541, 552.
Dunbarr, Jonathan, 166.
Dunbarr, Sarah, 539.
Dunbarr, Thomas, 137, 142.
Duncan, Andrew, 36, 69, 70, 78, 196, 272, 279, 317, 327, 345, 349, 362, 363, 380, 520, 547.
Duncan, Elizabeth, 69.
Duncan, Florence, 69.

Duncan, James, 69, 78, 95.
Duncan, Jean (Jane), 69, 317, 362.
Duncan, Jennet (Jannet), 69, 78.
Duncan, John, 40, 78, 84, 95.
Duncan, Joseph, 78.
Duncan, Mary, 69.
Duncan, William, 100, 275
Duncell, George, 145.
Duncle, Margaret, 520.
Duncleberry, Abraham (Eabreham), 58, 330, 341.
Dunkle (Dunke), George, 103, 520, 544.
Dunkle (Duncle, Dunkell), John, 43, 51, 56, 65, 68, 83, 84, 89, 92, 103, 337, 383, 520.
Dunlap, Alexander, 79, 325, 432, 457, 570.
Dunlap, Andrew, 37.
Dunlap (Dounlap), Anne (Ane), 150, 160.
Dunlap, Charles, 37, 317.
Dunlap, David, 295, 349.
Dunlap, Elizabeth, 347.
Dunlap (Dunlop), Ephraim, 462, 478, 531.
Dunlap, James, 40, 42, 50, 58, 80, 97, 317, 350.
Dunlap, Jane, 571.
Dunlap, Jennet, 495.
Dunlap, John, 60, 79, 144, 146, 173, 366, 432, 443, 495, 536, 547, 569, 596.
Dunlap, Margaret, 495.
Dunlap, Martha, 244.
Dunlap, Mary, 111, 212.
Dunlap, Nate, 84.
Dunlap, Robert, 14, 107, 144, 147, 148, 239, 305, 310, 316, 346, 347, 366, 402, 547.
Dunlap (Dunlop), Samuel, 36, 263, 267, **295, 305, 311, 316, 325, 343, 402, 443,** 495.
Dunlap, Thomas, 111, 157.
Dunlap, William, 99, 102, 133, 170, **277,** 283, 413, 432, 513, 536, 559, 569, 571.
Dunn, Eleanor, 167.
Dunn, James, 143, 477, 500.
Dunn, Richard, 102.
Dunn, Samuel, 487, 517, 528.
Dunn, Thomas, 452.
Dunn, Walter, 560, 569.
Dunwiddy, William, 158.
Dunwoody (Dinwoody), James, 138, 152
Dunwoody (Dunwoody), John, 138, 142, 150, 152.
Dunwoody (Dunwody), Robert, 460, 487.
Duttose, David, 102.
Dwier, Michael, 196.
Dyche, Margaret, 150.
Dye, Jacob, 110, 270, 276, 315, 335.
Dye, Mary, 270.
Dyer, Abigail, 286.
Dyer, Dennis, 276, 286.
Dyer, Hanna, 52, 53, 69, 84, 96.
Dyer, James, 52, 68, 79, **125, 145, 150,** 421, 494, 521, **544, 561.**
Dyer, John, 89.
Dyer, Margaret, 50, **71.**
Dyer, Mary, 10.
Dyer, Peter, 6, 10, 13, **282.**
Dyer, Roger (Rodger), 52, 53, **54, 69, 84,** 89, 264, 265, 292, 316, 494.
Dyer, William, 50, 53, 84, 89, 150, **264,** 347.
Dyerly, Peter, 106.
Dyre, Philip, 200.

Eabrem (Abraham), Leavy (**Leary**), **593.**
Eager, Casper, 540.
Eager, Moses, 474.
Eagle (Eaga), Benjamin, 217.
Eagle, Elizabeth, 586.
Eagle, George, 586.
Eagle, Henry, 575.
Eagle, Peter, 212, 584.
Eagor, Sampson, 228.
Eakin, Agness, 88.
Eakin (Eakins), Andrew, **88, 111, 477, 531.**
Eakin, Anne, 477.
Eakin, Elizabeth, 72, 207, 477.
Eakin (Eckins, Eikins), James, **10, 34,** 35, 39, 61, 78, 88, 89, 111, 267, **305,** 402, 477.
Eakin, John, 88, 111, 157, 207, 477.
Eakin, Margaret, 88.
Eakin, Mary, 88.
Eaken, Mathew, 103.
Eakin (Eakins), Samuel, 88, 235, **477, 531.**
Eakin, Walter, 10, 34, 71, 88, 103, **464.**
Eakle, Benjamin, 250.
Eakle, Christian, 250.
Eakle, Elizabeth, 250.
Eakle, John, 250.
Eakle, Jonathan, 250.
Eakle, Katy, 250.
Eakle, Mattena, 250.
Eakle,, Rosa, 250.
Ealer, Anthony, 137, 471.
Earhart, Nicholas, 192.
Earley, Jeremiah, 45, 286, 327, **337, 408.**
Earls, William, 72.
Early, Benjamin, 116.
Early, Elizabeth, 408, 447.
Early, John, 45, 327, 337, 408, **447.**
Early, Moses, 565.
Earnest, Henry, 354.
Earp, Cullen, 590.
Earseist, Michael, 53.
Earskins, John, 188.
Easley, Moses, 575.
Easter (Kister, Hister), Frederick, **63, 74,** 374.
Easters (Etters), Henry, 551.
Eastham, Braxton, 179, 565, 584.

Eastham (Estham), Robert, 165, 298, 460.
Eastin, Philip, 59.
Eastlake, Samuel, 396.
Eastminger, John H., 467.
Eavach, Christian, 43.
Eaye, Stoufall, 127.
Eberling, Immanuel, 389.
Eberman, Barbara, 531.
Eberman, Jacob, 139, 151, 531, 533.
Eberman, Samuel, 152.
Eccles, John, 65.
Eccord, Jacob, 235.
Eckard, Barbara, 245.
Echard, Christian, 245.
Edebaugh, Mary, 212.
Edgar, Robert, 463.
Edge, Robert, 296.
Edmiston, Andrew, 466.
Edmiston (Edmondson), David, 21, 22, 208, 254, 265, 278, 286, 306, 326, 348, 426.
Edmiston, Dorothy, 16.
Edmiston, Margaret (Margret), 347, 412, 422, 426, 434, 520.
Edmiston, Eleanor, 10.
Edmiston (Edmondson), Isabella, 21, 306.
Edmiston (Edmonston), James, 16, 86, 208, 254, 274, 306, 313, 343, 353, 385, 406, 416, 460, 475.
Edmiston, Jean (Jane), 16.
Edmiston (Edmonson, Edmondson), John, 12, 16, 17, 20, 70, 224, 258, 316, 343, 407, 413, 422, 426, 427, 434.
Edmiston, Mary, 10, 356, 521.
Edmiston (Edmondson), Mathew, 16, 24, 208, 252, 268, 293, 294, 347, 359, 412, 591.
Edmiston (Edmondson), Robert, 7, 16, 17, 20, 264, 360.
Edmiston, Samuel, 413, 422, 426, 427, 434.
Edmiston (Edmondson), William, 16, 17, 41, 70, 82, 84, 107, 118, 188, 208, 224, 329, 342, 349, 356, 411, 422, 426, 427, 520, 524, 555.
Edminston, Janet, 196.
Edmondson (Edmonson), James, 21, 23, 167, 215, 224, 347, 431.
Edmondson, Benjamin, 224.
Edmondson, Elizabeth, 224.
Edmondson, George, 224.
Edmondson, Lucy, 224.
Edmund, David, 54.
Edmundson, Agnes, 161, 413.
Edwards, Arthur, 574.
Edwards, Edward, 31.
Edwards, Elizabeth, 31, 98.
Edwards, Griffy, 387.
Edwards, Hugh, 31, 35.
Edwards, Jane, 574.
Edwards, Jeremiah, 102.
Edwards, John, 98, 258, 259, 349, 387.
Edwards, Robert, 107.
Edwards, Thomas, 573.
Eger, John, 408.
Ehrhard, John, 167.
Eiford (Ayford), George, 186.
Ekerling, Emanuel (Manuel), 322, 464.
Ekerling, Samuel, 464.
Ekert (Eakert), Casper, 155, 157, 562.
Ekert (Eaker), Philip, 155, 157, 540.
Elder, Mathew, 148.
Eley, James, 576.
Elias, Mathias, 287.
Ellice, Wat., 257.
Elliot, Alexander, 189, 588.
Elliott, Ann, 175, 219.
Elliott, Ann C., 588.
Elliot (Elliott, Eliot), Archibald, 28, 37, 119, 153, 175, 335, 339, 351, 363, 378, 386.
Elliot (Ellot), Elizabeth, 175, 191, 207.
Elliot (Elliott, Ellot, Eliot), James, 119, 140, 144, 148, 175, 191, 199, 206, 219, 514, 547.
Eliot (Elliott), Jean (Jane), 119, 160, 175.
Elliot (Ellet, Ellote), John, 48, 119, 120, 121, 124, 175, 184, 207, 263, 449, 496, 514, 577, 582, 583, 589.
Eliot (Eliott), Lanty, 119, 153, 175.
Elliot, Margaret, 175, 534.
Eliot, Mary, 243.
Elliot, Sarah, 160, 175, 339.
Elliot, Thomas, 219.
Elliot (Elliott, Eliot), William, 7, 10, 14, 31, 37, 39, 43, 45, 55, 58, 70, 77, 119, 120, 175, 271, 281, 291, 306, 325, 335, 351,, 352, 353, 378, 388, 398, 449, 534, 452, 480, 491, 495, 525.
Elliott (Eliot), George, 113, 117, 189, 340, 452, 480, 491, 495, 525.
Elliott, Isabella, 121.
Elliott, Peter, 215.
Elliott Ellett, Eliot, Elliote), Richard, 124, 140, 154, 163, 567.
Elliott (Ellet, Ellot), Robert, 86, 345, 382.
Ellis, James, 574.
Ellis, John, 258, 466.
Ellis, Richard S., 212.
Ellison, James, 161.
Ellison, Robert, 6.
Ellot, Mathew, 147.
Ellwick, Thomas, 56.
Elser, Mathias, 287.
Elswick, John, 11, 18.
Elswick, Lydia, 11.
Elsworth, Moses, 99.
Ely, James, 193.
Ely, Sarah, 193.
Emmitt, John, 188, 222, 578.
Emmitty, John, 218.
Engart, William, 245.
England, Joseph, 337.

Engleman, Polly, 240.
English (Inglish), Alice (Else), 67, 72.
English (Inglish), Joseph, 86, 101, 491.
English (Englis, Ingles, Ingless), Wilham, 17, 25, 66, 71, 75, 85, 95, 101, 110, 320, 372, 381, 417, 454, 466, 470, 475, 490.
Epps, Tabitha, 182.
Epshear (Upshur, Apshear), Christian, 446.
Erreman (Ebermann), Michael, 545.
Errowin, Charles, 562.
Erskin, George, 170.
Erskin, John, 170.
Ervin, Watts D., 245.
Erwin (Irwin), Agnes, 71, 244.
Erwin (Ervin), Andrew, 15, 32, 68, 71, 73, 87, 92, 130, 132, 143, 245, 289, 301, 302, 334, 348, 356, 422.
Erwin (Irwin), Ann, 71, 92, 244.
Erwin (Ervine), Benjamin, 92, 240, 245, 303, 348, 583, 590.
Erwin (Irving), David, 364, 400.
Erwin (Ervin, Irvin), Edward, 73, 92, 122, 140, 166, 196, 242, 244, 245, 292, 303, 348, 356, 358, 410, 411, 421, 440, 456, 459, 460, 475, 488, 549, 554, 563, 567, 568, 570, 572, 582, 590.
Erwin, Edwin, 549.
Erwin (Irvin), Elizabeth (Betsy), 71, 244, 245, 463, 536, 570.
Erwin, Ellinor, 71.
Erwin, Frances, 303.
Erwin, Francis, 73, 92, 122, 141, 174, 196, 197, 211, 229, 242, 303, 348, 355, 356, 387, 460, 475, 536, 568, 570, 595.
Erwin, Gennet, 71.
Erwin (Ervine), Henry, 422, 471.
Erwin (Irwin), James, 242, 244, 245, 259, 574, 596.
Erwin (Ervin, Irwin), Jane (Jean, Jenny), 71, 73, 196, 229, 242, 244, 245, 355, 536.
Erwin, Jared (Jarod, Jarad, Jarred), 126, 134, 430, 449, 528, 560.
Erwin (Ervin), John, 15, 32, 34, 73, 76, 122, 176, 194, 195, 196, 204, 211, 242, 244, 245, 301, 303, 306, 344, 348, 355, 427, 502, 559, 565, 568, 590.
Erwin (Irvin), Joseph, 194, 244, 590.
Erwin (Irvin), Mary, 71, 177, 196, 226, 238, 242, 244, 245, 554, 563.
Erwin, Mathew, 71, 272, 463, 533.
Ervin, Nathaniel, 328.
Erwin, Polly Stuart, 244.
Erwin (Ervin), Robert, 80, 90, 232, 252, 259, 271, 291, 303, 319, 349, 387, 410, 414, 446, 456.
Erwin (Irwin), Samuel, 109, 111, 232, 240, 244, 460, 485, 494, 512, 558, 568.
Ewin (Irwin), Sarah (Sally), 244, 245.

Erwin, Susannah, 196, 229, 596.
Erwin (Ervin), Thomas, 242, 244, 301.
Erwin (Irvin), William, 177, 196, 229, 242, 244, 245, 276, 422, 596.
Estill, Ann, 375, 540, 543.
Estill, Benjamin, 81, 86, 102, 161, 237, 314, 335, 361, 365, 373, 384, 413, 414, 434, 453, 466, 491, 516, 562.
Estill, Bowd (Bond, Bandy), 63, 161, 375, 535, 540, 589.
Estill, Jane, 540.
Estill, John, 161, 175, 375, 589.
Estill, John M., 237, 239.
Estill, Rebecca, 161.
Estill, Wallace (Wallis), 26, 44, 78, 94, 375, 446, 540, 543.
Estill, Wallam, 562.
Estis, Elisha, 540, 579.
Estes (Estis, Eastes), Abraham, 293, 307, 328, 330, 538.
Estey (Eastey), Moses, 573, 583.
Eubanks (Hughbanks), John, 71, 391.
Eulia, Henry, 537, 544.
Eurabough, Adam, 516.
Eurabough, Mary, 516.
Eurabough, Rudolph, 516.
Eurman, Ezekiel, 29.
Evab, George, 128.
Evans, Andrew, 29, 73, 85, 390, 453.
Evans, Alexander, 428, 446, 490.
Evans, Catherine, 111.
Evans, Daniel, 10, 38, 42, 44, 107, 111, 298, 442, 469.
Evans, Elizabeth, 107.
Evans, Evan, 29, 69, 94, 297.
Evans, James, 247.
Evans, Jane, 490.
Evans, Jesse, 247.
Evans, Jonathan, 107.
Evans, Mark, 9, 10, 14, 298.
Evans (Evins), Mary (Polly), 109, 222, 368, 398, 399, 435.
Evans (Evins), Nathaniel, 7, 13, 29, 37, 42, 71, 75, 99, 114, 259, 273, 280, 308, 313, 315, 325, 342, 368, 371, 377, 384, 398, 399, 410, 435, 540.
Evans, Peggy, 221.
Evans, Peter, 38, 42, 298.
Evans, Rhoda, 42.
Evans, Susannah, 107.
Eve (Evo), Francis (Franc), 129.
Everman, Jacob, 92.
Everman, John, 159.
Eversole, Jacob, 248, 592.
Evick, Francis, 83, 100.
Evilsizer, Jane, 239.
Ewigh, Christian, 13.
Ewin, Andrew, 145, 380.
Ewin (Ewing), Henry, 132, 145, 532, 561.
Ewin (Ewing, Ewins), John, 132, 537, 538.

Ewin, Margaret, 233.
Ewin, Sally, 227.
Ewin, Wats, 250.
Ewing, Charles. 9.
Ewing (Ewin), James, 28, 99, 101, 106, 115, 146, 150, 158, 162, 210, 211, 299, 434, 453, 466, 500, 517, 574, 579, 590.
Ewing, Jane, 561.
Ewing, Joseph, 86, 210, 234, 579.
Ewing, Joshua, 81.
Ewing, Martha, 210.
Ewing, Mary, 338.
Ewing, Nancy, 210.
Ewing, Robert, 338.
Ewing, Samuel, 106.
Ewing, William, 380.
Eyry, George, 511.

Faber, Christopher, 561.
Facler, James, 409.
Fackler, George, 234.
Fackler, John, 215, 234.
Fackler, Michael, 216.
Fairbern, John, 107, 178.
Fairfax, Lord, 293, 487, 490.
Fall, Daniel, 235, 238, 246, 247.
Falls, Florence, 582.
Falls, Terrence, 542.
Fanow, Thornton, 125.
Fares (Faris, Feris), Agnes (Nance), 179, 463, 550.
Fares, Margaret, 463.
Faris (Fearis), Edward, 35, 60, 415, 416
Faris, James, 500.
Faris (Fare, Fares, Faries, Farris, Feris), John, 71, 158, 179, 207, 362, 452, 463, 550.
Faris (Faries, Feris, Fearis), Robert, 119, 122, 159, 433, 470, 528, 539.
Faris (Feris), William, 35, 179.
Fairlee, James, 397.
Fauber, Christian, 206, 235.
Fauber, Jacob, 206.
Fauber, John, 206, 235.
Fauber, Peter, 201, 206.
Fauber, Valentine, 206.
Faught (Faut, Fought), Andrew, 64, 70, 94, 305, 539.
Faught (Fought), Casper (Gasper), 29, 64, 69, 94, 305, 391, 393.
Faught (Fought), Catrina (Cath.), 94.
Faught (Bellfought), John, 67.
Faught (Fought), Johan Paul, 53, 64.
Faught, Mary Katrine, 64.
Faulkler, Nicholas, 589.
Fauntleroy, Joseph, 173.
Fauntleroy, Moore, 564.
Fausset, Benjamin, 203.
Faut, George, 393.
Faver, Joseph, 229.
Fawver (Fawner), Julianna, 229.

Feemster, Elizabeth, 427.
Feemster (Femster, Fimster), Thomas, 10, 65, 88, 92, 104, 150, 152, 182, 306, 427, 443, 505.
Fegley, Jacob, 152.
Felts, Sarah, 237.
Femster, Henry, 13.
Fennell, John, 214.
Feny, John, 146.
Fergason, George, 169.
Fergus, Francis, 585.
Ferguson, Henry, 394, 491.
Ferguson (Forgason, Furguson), Samuel, 37, 105, 430, 448, 493, 523, 526.
Fernnill, John, 210.
Ferill (Ferril), John, 95, 113, 460.
Ferrill, Margaret, 460.
Fewbaker, Abraham, 265.
Fewbaker, John, 265.
Fiea, Charles, 146.
Field (Fields), Henry, 94, 99, 417.
Field, James D., 378.
Field (Fields), Richard, 13, 383, 455, 478.
Fields, Ales, 383.
Fiey, John, 146.
Fillson, Florans, 104.
Fillson, Robert, 104, 112.
Finder, Martin, 547.
Finley (Findley), Agness, 431, 448, 454.
Finley, David, 195.
Finley, Esther, 223.
Finley (Findley), George, 195, 462, 594.
Finley (Findley), James, 82, 96, 223, 247, 431, 437, 448, 454.
Finley (Fienley), Jane (Jean), 187, 195.
Finley (Findley), John, 9, 27, 34, 42, 47, 56, 59, 60, 66, 67, 68, 79, 83, 86, 89, 91, 95, 111, 123, 126, 128, 161, 170, 185, 194, 195, 197, 223, 231, 254, 255, 260, 265, 271, 276, 285, 358, 368, 420, 437, 462, 470, 487, 503, 504, 517, 542, 586, 594, 595.
Finley, Martha (Patsy), 116, 247, 412, 446.
Finley, Mary (Polly), 223, 285.
Finley, Patrick, 83.
Finley, Rebecca, 236.
Finley (Findley), Robert, 82, 89, 95, 96, 185, 195, 221, 285, 301, 316, 323, 324, 331, 338, 357, 359, 412, 415, 431, 437, 446, 448, 454, 461, 462, 492, 524, 566, 594.
Finley, Samuel, 187, 222, 223, 231, 236.
Finley, Samuel S., 223.
Finley, Sarah (Sally), 185, 229, 231, 247.
Finley, Shusanna, 116.
Finley, Thankful, 128, 195, 462.
Finley, Thomas, 195.
Finley, William, 22, 34, 42, 47, 79, 95, 169, 170, 178, 185, 223, 227, 231, 247, 285, 313, 412, 420, 431, 446, 504, 514.

Finey, Christopher, 29.
Finney (Fenney), Catherine, 36, 356, 370, 408, 414.
Finney, John, 593.
Finney, Mary, 161.
Finney, Michael, 33, 74, 110, 299, 356, 370, 408, 410, 414, 438.
Finney, Robert, 161.
Firnselson, Charles, 140.
Fish, Katharine, 547.
Fishburn, Teater, 221.
Fisher, Archibald, 117, 127, 450.
Fisher, Daniel, 591.
Fisher, Elizabeth, 143.
Fisher, George, 143.
Fisher, Lewis, 110.
Fisher, Mary, 250.
Fisher, Nancy, 591.
Fitch, Peter, 214.
Fitzgeral, Daniel, 171.
Fitzgeral (Fitzjarrel), William, 81, 85, 87, 119.
Fitzpatrick, Andrew, 93, 399, 429, 435, 465, 507.
Fitzpatrick, James, 119, 389.
Fitzpatrick, John, 389.
Fitzpatrick, Mary, 108, 507.
Fitzpatrick, Thomas, 378.
Fitzwater, John, 513, 533.
Fitzwaters, Thomas, 139.
Fix, Barbara, 220.
Fix, Peggy, 220.
Flasher (Flesher), John, 155, 158.
Flasher, Mary S., 155.
Fleiger, John, 223, 589.
Fleisher (Flasher, Flesher, Flersher), Henry, 83, 89, 92, 155, 158, 561, 580.
Fleisher, Peter, 143.
Fleming, Anne, 457, 479, 506, 508, 595.
Fleming, David, 117.
Fleming, James, 595.
Fleming, Leonard I., 479.
Fleming, Margaret, 178, 195.
Fleming, Nelly, 176.
Fleming, William, 110, 178, 194, 195, 404, 421, 423, 424, 425, 430, 450, 451, 457, 458, 479, 490, 493, 494, 496, 506, 508, 548, 550, 595.
Fleming, William P., 173.
Flesher, Conrod, 580.
Flesher, Paulser, 158.
Flesher, Peter, 436.
Flesher, Susan, 158.
Flesher, William, 436.
Fletcher, Christian, 393.
Fletcher, Eleanor, 17.
Fletcher, Henry 63, 158.
Fletcher, Job, 119.
Fletcher, John, 17.
Fletcher (Flitchers), Robert, 192, 393.
Flood, John, 23, 29, 31, 47, 68, 72, 282, 299, 300.

Flowers, Samuel, 89, 106.
Floyd, Charles, 118, 170, 399.
Floyd, David, 120.
Floyd, James, 157.
Floyd, Samuel, 118.
Floyd, William, 118.
Foalke, Ludwick, 58.
Foard, Joseph, 497.
Fogas (Fogus), Elizabeth, 178, 225.
Fogel, Philip, 530.
Foger, Samuel, 172.
Fogess, Henry, 190.
Fogle, John, 195.
Foil (Foyle), Robert, 32, 34, 257.
Follin, William, 120.
Fontain, James, 574.
Footman, Peter, 487, 545.
Footman, Richard, 487, 545.
Forbes, William, 197, 217, 582, 583, 585, 589.
Forbush, George, 10, 269.
Forbush, Olive, 269.
Forbush (Forbuss), William, 190, 584.
Ford, Christiana, 203.
Ford (Foard), Francis, 153, 156.
Forelight, Martin, 28.
Forgas, William, 171.
Forgason, Mary, 162, 523.
Forgason, William, 162.
Forggson, Samuel, 587.
Fornelson, Eliah, 155.
Fornelson, John, 155.
Forsie, Benjamin, 588.
Forsythe, Benjamin, 477, 533, 538, 554.
Forsythe, Samuel, 201, 233, 572.
Fortson, Thomas, 540, 579.
Foster, Andrew, 20, 25, 26, 56, 60, 359, 420, 481, 545, 591.
Foster, Elizabeth, 90, 578.
Foster, James, 540.
Foster, John, 209.
Foster, Margaret M., 359.
Foster, Thomas, 87, 90.
Foster, William, 75, 103, 110, 370, 385, 406, 408, 410, 414, 451, 552, 567, 578, 582.
Fought, Conrad, 29.
Fought, Jacob C., 29.
Foulke, Caleb, 116.
Fowler, Andrew, 548.
Fowler, Ann, 537.
Fowler, Elisha, 363.
Fowler, James, 403, 501.
Fowler, John, 63, 295, 316, 338, 397, 580.
Fowler, Margaret, 53, 295, 548.
Fowler (Fouller), Robert, 51, 76, 140, 505, 537.
Fairler, William, 240, 522, 591.
Fox, Allen, 555.
Foy, Charles, 136, 357, 483, 531.
Frailey (Fraelich), Frederick, 17, 21.
Fraizer, George, 169, 192.

Fraizer, Joseph, 192.
Frame, David, 164, 390, 395, 397, **423**, 429, 451, 463, 514, 517, 538, 565, 575, 590.
Frame, Elizabeth, 514.
Frame (Fraim), James, 34, 36, 278, **279**, 282, 391, 395, 476, 514.
Frame (Fraim), Jane (Jean), 34, 211, 514.
Frame, Jeremiah, 164, 567.
Frame, John, 553.
Frame, John C., 211.
Frame, Margaret, 390, 395, 553.
Frame, Martha (Patsy), 233, 476.
Frame, Mary, 463.
Frame, Samuel, 211, 234, 242.
Frame, Thomas, 120, 151, 178, 183, **186**, 188, 211, 242, 455, 476, 511, 514, **594**.
Frame, William, 71, 129, 159, 346, 395, **433**, 492, 567.
Francey, George, 145.
Francis, Agnis, 175.
Francis, Ann, 175.
Francis, Elizabeth, 175.
Francis, George, 102.
Francis, Henry, 106.
Francis, Jean, 175, 198.
Francis, John, 70, 71, 83, 175, 177, **198**, 202, 266, 272, 273, 295, 432, 441, **463**, 584, 587, 591, 592.
Francis, Margaret, 175.
Francis, Martha, 175, 198.
Francis, Mary, 71, 83, 175, 198, 295.
Francis, William, 198.
Francisco, Christophell (Stophel), 65, **285**, 297, 299, 300, 305, 364, 412, 480, **482**, **514**.
Francisco, Christopher, 285, 339, 350, 364, 419, 434, 488, 494.
Francisco, Elizabeth, 514.
Francisco, George, 70, 72, 164, **424**, **453**.
Francisco (Franciscus), Ludwick, 13, **57**, **58**, 266, 293, 298, 299, 305, 364, **420**, **488**, 494, 514.
Francisco, Michael, 241.
Franciscus, Anna M., 285.
Francklin, John, 76.
Franger, George, 229.
Frank, John, 133.
Frank, Nicholas, 51.
Franklyn, Eastham, 252.
Frazer (Frasure), Bella (Isbell), 51, **242**.
Frazer, Isabella H., 582.
Frazer (Freasure), Jenet, 136, 171, **192**, 204, 207.
Frazer, John W., 231, 234, 242.
Frazer (Fraizer), Samuel, 51, 174, **177**, 224, 234, 242, 279, 360, 383, 388, **564**, **582**, 583.
Frazer, Samuel C., 234, 242.
Frazer, Thomas, 210, 226.

Frazier, Amy, 86.
Frazier (Frazer), Ann., 177, 192, 224, **230**, 242, 546, 589.
Frazier (Fraizer), Barbara, 477, 522.
Frazier (Fraizer, Frazer), David, 86, **410**, 477, 522.
Frazier (Frazer), James, 86, 95, 96, **165**, 166, 177, 180, 189, 204, 206, 209, **222**, 224, 230, 231, 234, 242, 383, 410, **491**, 546, 564, 582, 589.
Frazier (Frazer), Jean (Jinnie), 224, **231**, 247, 589.
Frazier (Frazer, Frezer), John, 28, 81, **88**, 177, 192, 234, 279, 304, 417, 418, **419**, 424, 583, 589.
Frazier (Fraizer), Mary, 224, 418.
Frazier (Frazer, Frasure, Frazsher), Patrick, 29, 55, 68, 81, 85, 88, 130, **288**, 295, 393, 403, 418, 498, **510**, 563.
Frazier (Frazer, Frazor), Robert, 86, **303**, 315, 410, 477, 501, 510.
Frazier (Frazer), William, 69, 86, 87, **95**, 192, 224, 312, 317, 383, 477, 522.
Frazor, Frances, 510.
Fredericksbore, Charles, 172.
Freedley, Ann Mary, 10.
Freedley, Ludwick (Lewis), 10, 11.
Freeholder, William, 195.
Freel, Catrine, 157.
Freeling, Frederick, 14.
French, William, 339.
Frenger, Catherine, 181.
Frenger, Peter, 181, 183, 184.
Fretwell, Alexander, 169, 176.
Frew, James, 111, 113.
Fridley, Election George, 509.
Fridley, George, 323, 424, 479.
Fridley (Fredley), Loudawick (Ludwick), 112, 120, 124, 129.
Friel, Agness, 214.
Friel, Daniel, 207, 209, 214, 231, 565, 580.
Friel, John, 214.
Friel, Maurice, 214.
Friel, William, 214.
Friend, Jacob, 122, 133, 461.
Friend, Jonas, 65, 99, 103, 143, 154, **155**, 374, 522, 549.
Friend, Sarah, 549.
Frise (Freez), Michael, 49, 50.
Frogg, Agatha, 137, 189, 527.
Frogg, Arthur, 116.
Frogg, John, 116, 133, 137, 138, 291, **312**, 392, 467, 479, 504, 506, 508, 527.
Frogg, William, 540.
Frohock, John, 346.
Froman, Paul, 276, 341, 366.
Frows, John, 437.
Fruit, Martha, 55, 57.
Fry, Charles, 113.
Fry, Henry, 456.
Fry, William A., 182, 217.

Frye, John, 146.
Fryer, Robert, 26, 28.
Fudge, Christian, 573.
Fudge (Futch), Conrad, 494, 506, 507, 546, 552.
Fudge (Fuge, Futch), John, 57, 70, 110, 149, 170, 291, 494, 505, 506, 507, 546, 551, 552, 553, 573.
Fulk, Ludwick, 51.
Fullen, Francis, 484.
Fuller (Fooler), Catherine, 38, 298.
Fuller (Fooler), Henry, 38, 298, 325, 331, 332, 378, 410.
Fuller, William, 134.
Fullerton, Alexander, 293, 307.
Fullingar, George, 110.
Fulmar, Ludwick, 552.
Fulton, Eleanor (Elliner), 29, 445.
Fulton, Alexander, 223.
Fulton, Andrew, 69, 182, 189, 190, 210, 223, 225, 228, 229, 233, 576, 592.
Fulton, Benjamin, 222.
Fulton, David, 29, 190, 212, 213, 242, 418, 500, 582.
Fulton, Elizabeth, 29, 86, 190, 210, 222, 397, 401, 404, 417.
Fulton, Francis. 368, 445.
Fulton, Hugh, 29, 37, 53, 146, 169, 171, 187, 190, 218, 242, 315, 352, 576.
Fulton, James. 8, 12, 16, 17, 29, 37, 161, 189, 226, 265, 270, 281, 561, 576.
Fulton, Jane (Jean), 29, 212, 238, 239.
Fulton, John, 29, 39, 53, 56, 85, 86, 87, 108, 160, 161, 168, 169, 189, 190, 209, 212, 213, 264, 304, 315, 327, 332, 333, 342, 352, 396, 402, 465, 516, 544, 576, 582.
Fulton, Margaret, 40, 145, 190, 238, 239.
Fulton, Mary, 189, 190, 352.
Fulton, Robert, 212.
Fulton, Samuel, 189.
Fulton, Sarah, 29, 37, 146, 190, 210.
Fulton, William, 29, 133, 145, 189, 223, 352, 368, 407.
Fulton, Thomas, 29, 30, 39, 40, 43, 54, 59, 70, 71, 79, 84, 145, 190, 202, 212, 219, 249, 336, 365, 395, 397, 400, 401, 404, 413, 415, 417, 421, 459, 464, 478, 492, 596.
Fults, Catherine B., 127.
Fults, Eave, 127.
Fults (Foltz), George, 127, 134, 141, 414.
Fults, Hanna, 127.
Fults, John, 96.
Fults, John P., 127.
Fults, Susanna, 127.
Fultz, Frederick, 223.
Fulwider, Auleric, 203.
Fulwider, Elizabeth, 232.
Fulwider, George, 220, 235.
Fulwider, Henry, 235.

Fulwider (Folowider), Jacob, 161, 203, 208, 560.
Fulwider (Folowider), John, 220, 235, 558, 560.
Fulwider, Margaret, 208, 235.
Fulwider (Folowider), Ulrich, 235, 558.
Funk, Catrine, 64.
Funk (Fuick), John, 289, 291.
Funk, Peter, 64, 67, 94.
Funkhouser, Christian, 305.
Funkhouser, Christiana, 9, 305.
Furguson, James, 100.
Furnish, John, 317.
Futch, Katherine, 506.

Gabbert, Barbara, 490.
Gabbert, Christian, 498.
Gabbert, Cutlip, 150.
Gabbert (Gabert, Gabord, Gabhart, Gebhard), Jacob, 160, 177, 473, 490, 498, 567, 578.
Gabbert (Gabert), Mathias, 467, 473, 498, 498, 516.
Gabert, Gotlove, 128.
Gabeson, Samuel, 33.
Gahagan, Andrew, 355.
Gaines (Ganes), Robert, 168, 205.
Gains, Adam, 236.
Gains, Elizabeth, 238.
Galbreath, Mathew, 87.
Galbreath, Thomas, 84, 550.
Galbreath, William, 482, 550.
Galenbe, William, 5.
Galespie, Robert, 100.
Galford, Thomas, 163, 195.
Gall, George, 554, 568.
Gallagher, Charles, 18, 19, 20.
Gallbrath, John, 287.
Gallon, Robert, 36.
Galloway, David, 70, 100.
Galloway, John, 178.
Galloway, Molly, 192.
Galloway, Robert, 75, 82, 96, 110, 271.
Galloway, William, 404.
Gallt, Samuel, 357.
Gally, Christian, 59, 63.
Gamble, Agness, 159, 171, 199, 562.
Gamble, Elizabeth, 159.
Gamble, Esther, 159, 218, 582.
Gamble, Isabella, 176, 181, 193.
Gamble (Gambel), James, 37, 117, 123, 129, 134, 144, 159, 160, 171, 355, 375, 389, 407, 433, 439, 479, 492, 505, 547, 562.
Gamble, John, 159, 169, 172, 181, 185, 193, 194, 200, 204, 207, 219, 222, 231, 233, 237, 244, 586.
Gambell, Joseph, 100, 157, 163, 176, 181, 361, 369, 413, 417, 418, 504, 506.
Gamble, Margaret, 361, 506.

Gamble, Rebecca, 231.
Gamble (Gambel), Robert, 22, 123, 159, 165, 172, 180, 181, 193, 198, 199, 202, 254, 562, 581, 582, 583, 585, 589, 591,
Gamble, Sarah, 159, 171.
Gamel, William, 145.
Gamell (Gamwell), Mary, 517.
Gamell (Gamwell), Robert, 13, 318, 510, 517.
Gammen, Carl, 90.
Gamwell, James, 79, 400, 432, 492.
Gamwell (Ganal), Joseph, 84, 120, 127, 137, 139, 145, 412, 414, 476, 497, 538.
Gamwell, Margaret, 497, 538.
Garber, Michael, 200, 215, 225, 230, 234, 584, 585, 589, 596.
Gardiner, James, 211.
Gardiner, Margaret, 211.
Gardiner, William, 211.
Gardner, Alexander, 88, 161, 228, 276, 294, 586, 588.
Gardner, Ann, 58, 59, 60, 230.
Gardner, Elizabeth, 581, 588.
Gardner, Esther, 160.
Gardner, Francis, 85, 88, 95, 101, 126, 160, 208, 209, 223, 230, 260, 350, 475.
Gardner, George, 267.
Gardner (Garner), Jacob, 345, 364, 403, 538.
Gardner (Garner, Gardiner), John, 134, 145, 160, 161, 162, 171, 175, 184, 197, 198, 201, 202, 211, 345, 447, 573, 577, 579, 581, 586, 588.
Gardner, Mary, 58, 59, 77, 91, 95, 546.
Gardner (Garner), Rebecca, 85, 128.
Gardner, Samuel, 95, 126, 160, 199.
Gardner, Sarah, 179.
Gardner (Gardiner, Garner), Thomas, 58, 59, 60, 72, 77, 85, 86, 91, 95, 126, 128, 211, 252, 308, 344, 353, 358, 402, 438, 452, 544, 546.
Gardon, Thomas, 107.
Garland, Nathaniel, 584.
Garman, Cathrine, 59.
Garnet, James, 269.
Garrard, William, 579, 580.
Garraway, Thomas, 417.
Garrison, Paul, 74, 401.
Gartezer, Peter, 302.
Garthon, Elizabeth, 141.
Gartner, Peter, 9, 10, 315, 320.
Garton, Elijah, 147.
Garton, Eliza, 142.
Garvin, Elizabeth, 227.
Garvin, John, 198.
Garvin, Thomas, 567, 586.
Gaskins, Job, 576.
Gass, David, 14.
Gates, John, 200, 589.
Gatlive, Martha M., 76.
Gatlive, James, 72, 76, 80, 328, 329.

Gatton, John, 44.
Gaughagin, Andrew, 9, 22.
Gauker, George, 141.
Gaul, Margaret, 235.
Gaurner, John, 183.
Gaustrax, 551.
Gawin, David, 561.
Gawin, Isaac, 561.
Gay, Agness, 39, 144, 147.
Gay, Ann, 62, 379.
Gay, Archibald, 231, 234.
Gay, Elizabeth, 62, 147.
Gay (Guy), Henry, 7, 57, 61, 79, 85, 92, 96, 99, 119, 268, 379, 398, 442, 491, 546, 564, 589.
Gay, Hugh, 31.
Gay, James, 32, 40, 58, 92, 96, 120, 126, 134, 139, 144, 146, 278, 353, 388, 398, 534, 547, 570, 592.
Gay, Jean (Jane), 144, 147, 388, 547.
Gay, John, 7, 10, 14, 38, 39, 42, 50, 51, 52, 55, 57, 58, 60, 63, 79, 85, 144, 147, 148, 166, 277, 280, 283, 353, 534, 547, 592, 596.
Gay, Margaret, 39, 67, 266.
Gay, Martha, 379, 491, 564.
Gay, Marthew, 144.
Gay, Mary, 39, 57, 144, 147.
Gay, Rebecca, 230.
Gay, Robert, 16, 33, 39, 56, 67, 69, 92, 95, 96, 144, 257, 365, 415, 420, 433, 436, 446, 501, 534, 589.
Gay, Samuel, 32, 144, 258, 259, 266, 273, 279, 284, 316, 325, 330, 333, 388, 398, 456.
Gay, Sarah, 436, 446, 592.
Gay, William, 39, 51, 99, 103, 277, 278, 279, 280, 313, 325, 388, 398.
Geabill (Geable)), Christian, 583.
Geiger, Jacob, 200, 201, 589.
Geighford, Anna M., 186.
Geldmaker, Lawes, 171.
Genewine, Peter, 586.
Gennet, Thomas, 210.
Gentry, John, 104.
Gentry, Mary, 182, 216.
George, Reuben, 593.
Gerry, Samuel, 244.
Gest, Samuel, 97.
Gester, Hanna, 53.
Gholston, Anthony, 557.
Ghost (Gost), George, 102, 106, 112.
Gibbs, John M., 172.
Gibson, Alexander, 25, 70, 134, 138, 139, 144, 179, 191, 194, 197, 206, 207, 250, 275, 277, 299, 308, 310, 344, 353, 358, 363, 376, 388, 425, 436, 438, 590.
Gibson, Ann, 550.
Gibson, Christian, 206, 207.
Gibson, Christiana, 250.

Gibson, Daniel, 22, 25, 26, 206, 207, 248, 250.
Gibson, David, 173, 180, 218, 562, 564, 586.
Gibson, Elizabeth, 22, 179, 206, 207, 551, 564.
Gibson, George, 57, 73, 350, 456, 479, 564.
Gibson, Hugh, 481, 482, 519.
Gibson, Isabella, 57, 281, 479, 560.
Gibson, James, 57, 560.
Gibson, John, 57, 159, 182, 208, 218, 233, 579.
Gibson, Jonathan, 53.
Gibson, Margaret, 206, 207.
Gibson, Mary, 206, 207, 218, 353, 358.
Gibson, Robert, 42, 47, 57, 59, 169, 324, 327, 367, 551, 560.
Gibson, Samuel, 140, 162, 174, 182, 208, 215, 218, 340, 511, 518, 551, 564, 579.
Gibson, Sarah, 218.
Gibson, William, 53, 68, 550, 559, 561.
Gibsons, Jordon (Jourdan), 159, 187.
Gilaspey, Jennet, 111.
Gilaspy, Agness, 111.
Gilaspy, Ann, 15, 172, 173, 188, 191.
Gilaspy (Gillaspie), Elizabeth, 111, 581.
Gilaspy, Jean, 15.
Gilaspy, Patrick, 15.
Gilaspy, Sarah, 15.
Gilbert, Ann, 524.
Gilbert, Felix, 43, 49, 50, 55, 56, 60, 63, 77, 80, 81, 84, 85, 89, 91, 92, 94, 115, 118, 126, 127, 141, 357, 359, 363, 389, 398, 404, 413, 421, 423, 425, 431, 448, 454, 471, 496, 503, 505, 521, 522, 523, 524, 526, 529, 532, 535, 539, 540, 542.
Gilchrist, Robert, 41.
Gildart, James, 123.
Gilham, William, 166, 172, 565.
Gilkerson, Ann, 228.
Gilkerson, David, 228.
Gilkerson, Margaret, 228.
Gilkeson, Archibald, 141, 162, 171, 194.
Gilkeson (Gilkerson), Elizabeth, 228, 593.
Gilkeson (Gilkerson), Hugh, 162, 197, 228, 593.
Gilkeson (Gilkerson), James, 162, 228.
Gilkeson, Rebecca, 141, 162.
Gilkeson (Gilkenson, Gilkison), Robert, 43, 141, 142, 162, 217, 266, 594.
Gilkeson, Sarah, 162.
Gilkeson (Gilkerson, Gilkison), William, 183, 228, 563.
Gilkison (Gilkenson), Francis, 215, 217, 218, 222, 248, 594.
Gill, Edward, 90, 416.
Gill, Eleanor, 258.
Gill, James, 258, 263, 269, 373, 383.
Gillaspie, Rose, 581.
Gillaspy, Rebecca, 159.
Gillespie, Nancy, 242.

Gillespie, Andrew, 55.
Gillespie, George, 470.
Gillespy (Gilespy), Alexander, 37, 48, 51, 52, 72.
Gillespy, Eleanor, 188.
Gillespy, Gene, 188.
Gillespy, Hannah, 356.
Gillespy, Hugh, 172.
Gillespy (Gallespie, Glaspy, Gillaspy), Jacob, 9, 125, 126, 168, 188, 356, 384, 434, 458, 478, 543, 586, 587.
Gillespy (Gallespie, Gilaspy), James, 29, 47, 59, 79, 111, 112, 173, 188, 191, 224, 278, 310, 497, 514, 558, 564, 565, 581.
Gillespy (Gilaspy), John, 111, 140, 143, 148, 172, 174, 188, 240, 357, 441, 456, 468, 497, 546, 564, 565, 574, 589.
Gillespy, Martha, 172, 173, 174, 546, 589.
Gillespy, Mary, 172, 173.
Gillespy, Samuel, 172, 188, 191, 574.
Gillespy, Sarah, 581.
Gillespy (Galespy, Gillespie), Thomas, 12, 23, 80, 87, 188, 259, 343, 482, 581.
Gillespy (Galespy, Gillaspie), William, 12, 54, 57, 100, 111, 112, 151, 166, 169, 170, 188, 191, 224, 447, 497, 565, 581, 594.
Gillham (Gillum), Charles, 56, 362, 395.
Gillham, Elisabeth, 395.
Gillham, Ezekiel, 396.
Gillham (Gilham), Margaret, 56, 306, 415.
Gillham (Gilham, Gillam), Thomas, 6, 27, 55, 56, 257, 297, 306, 395, 415, 488, 455.
Gilliland, James, 505, 555.
Gilliland (Gillilen), Nathan (Nathaniel), 82, 96, 301, 395, 451, 452.
Gilliland, Samuel, 505.
Gilmor, Agness, 352.
Gilmore, Alexander, 174.
Gilmore, Ann, 174.
Gilmore (Gilmer), James, 55, 56, 59, 60, 68, 70, 81, 86, 90, 106, 141, 174, 262, 269, 270, 278, 283, 287, 307, 334, 338, 342, 359, 361, 365, 407, 432, 438, 479, 480.
Gilmore, Jannet, 93.
Gilmore (Gilmer), John, 47, 55, 56, 70, 80, 81, 82, 90, 117, 125, 149, 159, 174, 259, 270, 291, 341, 350, 352, 361, 453, 469, 471, 574.
Gilmore, Martha (Marthow), 342, 361, 407.
Gilmore, Peachy, 110, 372, 521.
Gilmore, Peachy R., 380, 457.
Gilmore, Thomas, 55, 82, 125, 361.
Gilmore (Gilmer), William, 81, 93, 341, 352, 361.
Gilor, Samuel, 177.
Gilston, Rachel, 199.
Ginder, Michael, 459.
Ginder, Peter, 491.

Gindner (Ginder), George, 459, 524, 552.
Gindner, Susanna, 524.
Given, Joseph, 449, 573.
Givens (Given), Agnes, 173, 442.
Givens, Alexander, 238, 239.
Givens, Alexander R., 239.
Givens, Elizabeth, 238.
Givens, George, 187, 239, 428, 545, 568, 580.
Givens, Isabella, 239.
Givens (Gibbons), James, 59, 155, 187, 195, 248, 252, 345, 369, 396, 506, 588, 593.
Givens, Jean (Jane), 238, 239, 345, 449.
Givens, John, 104, 112, 113, 123, 157, 179, 184, 187, 197, 198, 214, 238, 239, 279. 280, 341, 369, 381, 389, 509, 545, 580.
Givens, Margaret, 187, 545.
Givens, Martha, 345, 348, 369, 375, 396, 505, 547, 550.
Givens, Mary, 187, 239, 502.
Givin, Patrick, 81.
Givens, Robert, 54, 175, 239, 381, 398, 400, 449, 499.
Givens, Samuel, 10, 163, 187, 272, 330, 333, 341, 348, 350, 369, 375, 384, 437, 502, 505, 521, 543, 547, 548, 550.
Givens, Sarah, 345.
Givens, Thomas, 187, 224, 228.
Givens, William, 64, 125, 173, 187, 345, 361, 398, 442, 489, 498.
Glasgoro (Glasgow), William, 365.
Glasgow (Glascow), James, 112, 265, 267, 310, 318, 382.
Glass, David, 38.
Glass, Elizabeth, 38.
Glass, Isaac, 244.
Glass, John, 38, 41, 244, 279, 282, 476, 514, 519, 543.
Glass, Joseph, 38.
Glass, Martha, 543.
Glass, Mary, 38.
Glass, Samuel, 38, 543.
Glass, Sarah, 38, 39.
Glass, William, 38, 543.
Glassgow, Elizabeth, 112.
Glaves, Mat, 169.
Glaves, William, 501.
Gleave (Glave, Glaves), Elizabeth (Betty), 126, 224, 235, 240.
Glenn, Ann, 226.
Glenn, Elizabeth 233.
Glenn, George, 149, 180, 191, 200, 243, 587.
Glenn, Hugh, 191, 233, 243, 244.
Glenn, James, 191, 243.
Glenn, Margaret, 200.
Glenn, Martha (Patsy), 191, 233.
Glenn, Mary, 191, 243.
Glenn, Sarah, 191, 243.
Glenn, William, 191, 243.
Gnear, Robert, 187.

Goare, Joseph, 533.
Gochenour, Henry, 9.
Godall, Richard, 160.
Gogure, Jacob, 26.
Goil, Barbary, 94.
Goil (Kile), Elizabeth, 94, 379.
Goil (Kyle, Coil, Gile), Felty, 94.
Goil (Goyle), Margaret, 94, 549.
Goile, Hannah, 538.
Gold, Elizabeth, 221.
Gold, John, 50, 221.
Gold, Priscilla, 161.
Goldbreath, Martha, 98.
Goldman, Jacob, 21, 26.
Goldman, John, 21, 26, 73.
Goldman, Mary, 21.
Gommers, Michael, 26.
Good, Conrad, 128, 555.
Goodal, Charles, 54.
Goodall, William, 476.
Goodding, Abram, 370.
Goodenburgh, Gasper, 535.
Goodfellow, James, 328, 339.
Goodly, James, 335, 336.
Goodman, Catherine, 49.
Goodman, Jacob, 49, 65, 112, 156, 355.
Goodpasture, Abraham, 547.
Goodpasture, Jacob, 95, 98, 105.
Goodson, Thomas, 118, 458.
Goodwin, Daniel, 93, 117.
Goodwin, Robert, 545.
Goose, Christian, 84.
Gorden, Sarah, 337.
Gordon, Catherine, 247.
Gordon, Charles, 555.
Gordon, George, 238.
Gordon, James, 41, 83.
Gordon (Gorden), John, 215, 506, 534, 584, 589.
Gordon (Gorden), Thomas, 21, 31, 45, 55, 138, 260, 271, 280, 319, 322, 336, 337, 347, 348, 360, 363, 389, 402.
Gore, Henry, 144.
Gorrell, James, 74, 110, 309, 316, 408, 430.
Gorrell, Ralph, 70.
Gorrell, Robert, 395.
Gorrell, William, 74, 110, 309.
Gorton (Gorthon), Francis, 141.
Gosset, William, 527.
Gossom, John, 572.
Gouger, William, 169.
Gove, Daniel, 311.
Govouck (McGuffy), Alexander, 399.
Gowthrie, James, 319.
Grable, Henry, 583.
Grace (Grad?), Christian, 103.
Grad, William, 92.
Gradner (Gardner), John, 121.
Graft, Christian, 54.
Graft, Michael, 54.
Gragg (Gregg), Elizabeth, 214, 532.

Gragg, Margaret, 72.
Gragg (Gregg), Robert, 67, 72, 343, 395, 438, 451, 456, 563, 566, 574, 576, 582, 587.
Gragg, Samuel, 566.
Gragg (Gregg), Thomas, 49, 51, 94, 132, 157, 214, 532, 574.
Gragg (Gregg), William, 65, 66, 68, 72, 137, 157, 471, 545.
Graham, Agnes, 227.
Graham, Alexander, 213.
Graham, Anne, 120, 565.
Graham (Graem), Archibald, 23, 75, 260. 319, 329, 376, 452, 454, 466, 483.
Graham, Arthur, 106, 396, 426, 476, 495. 508.
Graham, Cateran, 213.
Graham, Christopher, 6, 10, 81, 115, 180, 423, 487, 492, 530, 565, 588.
Graham, David, 23, 119, 120.
Graham, Elizabeth (Betty), 81, 120, 134, 140, 156, 239.
Graham, Florence, 61, 70, 120, 561.
Graham, Francis, 80, 456.
Graham, James, 23, 120, 156, 213, 244, 400, 416, 423, 561, 567, 585.
Graham, Jane (Jean), 81, 120, 134, 141, 408, 548, 557.
Graham, John, 10, 17, 23, 25, 37, 42, 43, 59, 69, 70, 81, 96, 120, 122, 135, 150, 156, 198, 213, 227, 244, 252, 266, 329, 339, 346, 360, 381, 400, 401, 408, 414, 425, 439, 442, 482, 493, 496, 502, 519, 530, 540, 559, 561, 564.
Graham, Joseph, 213.
Graham, Lanty, 120, 134, 148, 156, 244, 408, 519, 530.
Graham, Margaret, 81, 244, 466.
Graham, Mary, 213, 508.
Graham, Priscilla, 418, 434.
Graham, Rebbeca, 81, 120, 134, 156.
Graham, Robert, 6, 42, 43, 61, 70, 81, 92, 104, 115, 120, 124, 134, 135, 140, 141, 156, 206, 213, 227, 244, 257, 271, 329, 346, 370, 400, 401, 408.
Graham, Sarah, 134, 141, 156.
Graham, Thomas, 81, 157, 213, 559, 567.
Graham (Grahames), William, 14, 23, 28, 44, 49, 55, 74, 80, 110, 205, 227, 244, 308, 314, 319, 339, 350, 360, 376, 382, 397, 415, 418, 419, 434, 452, 456, 467, 481, 483, 562, 565.
Grant, Peter, 392.
Grass, Barbara, 185.
Grass, Elizabeth, 178, 229.
Grass, Frederick, 185, 243.
Grass, Jacob, 154, 173, 178, 185, 563, 567.
Grass, John, 243.
Grass, Mary, 175, 185.
Grass, Peter, 185, 186, 588.
Grass, Robert, 243.

Grates, John, 200.
Gratton, Jane, 198.
Gratton, John, 104, 118, 120, 125, 128, 139, 140, 198, 199, 366, 422, 423, 441, 448, 457, 578, 502, 534, 544, 548.
Gratton, Margaret, 198.
Gratton, Robert, 200, 209, 380, 457.
Gravin, David, 136.
Gray, Agness, 23, 423.
Gray, Ann, 23.
Gray, Benjamin, 23, 55, 77, 329, 461, 468.
Gray, David, 23, 69, 104, 367, 383, 461, 468.
Gray, Elizabeth, 23, 218, 231, 233.
Gray, George, 372.
Gray, Isaac, 226, 296, 304.
Gray, Jacob, 23, 29, 31, 33, 47, 284, 304, 306, 324, 336, 340, 435.
Gray, James, 71.
Gray (Grey), Jean (Jane), 220, 563, 577.
Gray, John, 23, 24, 55, 57, 72, 77, 94, 259, 266, 268, 318, 344, 347, 350, 396, 443, 472, 563, 577.
Gray, Joseph, 23, 55, 77, 385.
Gray, Katharin, 535.
Gray, Mary, 172, 304.
Gray (Grey), Robert, 226, 294, 295, 297, 311, 315, 327, 336, 398, 479, 511, 563, 575.
Gray, Ruth, 468.
Gray, Samuel, 23, 24, 55, 77, 265, 266, 303, 304, 328, 329, 341, 347, 423.
Gray, William, 23, 55, 77, 327, 329, 367, 468, 535.
Grayner (Grinor), David, 588.
Greeg, Ann, 130.
Greeg, Elizabeth, 130.
Greeg, Mary, 130.
Greeg, Thomas, 130.
Green, Agnus, 182.
Green, Ann, 374, 375.
Green, Daniel, 204.
Green, Eleanor, 256, 521.
Green, Francis, 54, 132, 473.
Green, Hugh, 131, 182, 183, 203, 214, 216, 244, 586.
Green, Jacob, 113, 336.
Green, James, 259, 260, 335, 373, 374, 380, 391, 400, 402, 405, 424, 480, 488.
Green, Jinny, 182.
Green, John, 13, 259, 260, 380.
Green, Margaret, 240, 473.
Green, Mary, 314, 506.
Green, Moses, 259, 260, 373, 374, 380, 391, 405, 424, 480, 488.
Green, Nicholas, 392, 444, 525.
Green, Robert, 255, 256, 258, 260, 264, 265, 274, 307, 314, 336, 337, 347, 373, 374, 375, 376, 379, 383, 391, 392, 405, 424, 444, 448, 449, 480, 493, 494, 502, 520, 521, 526, 527, 535, 544, 549.

Green, Sarah, 336.
Green, William, 41, 183, 260, 292, 298, 307, 316, 332, 340, 374, 375, 405, 411, 448, 449, 495, 512.
Greene, Thomas, 582.
Greenlee, David, 396, 537.
Greenlee, Grace, 537.
Greenlee, Hannah, 528.
Greenlee, James, 76, 79, 81, 252, 263, 293, 306, 309, 318, 341, 347, 367, 377, 382, 396, 403, 414, 435, 437, 457, 468, 520, 528.
Greenlee, John, 76, 79, 309, 396, 443, 528, 576, 589.
Greenlee, Margaret, 537.
Greenlee, Mary, 76, 79, 528, 537.
Greenlee, Samuel, 347, 396.
Greer (Grier), Alexander, 18, 26, 443, 468, 497, 499.
Greer, Andrew, 70, 72, 365, 372, 389, 402, 403, 409, 445, 485, 523, 562.
Greer, Arthur 61.
Greer, James, 401, 402.
Greer (Grier), John, 18, 26, 555.
Greer, Martha, 26.
Greer, Mary, 26, 227.
Greer, Rebecca, 26.
Greer, Ruth, 389, 445, 485.
Greerrod, Stephen, 360.
Greever, William, 166.
Gregory, Ann, 561.
Gregory, James. 119, 127, 133, 469, 531, 574.
Gregory, John, 70, 134, 187, 588.
Gregory, Joseph, 526, 531, 561, 574, 588.
Gregory, Mary (Polly), 71, 81, 108, 152, 225.
Gregory, Mary M., 119.
Gregory, Naphtalum (Naphtaly), 37, 71, 72, 81, 133.
Gregory, Philip, 245.
Gregory, Rachel, 225.
Gregory, Samuel, 134, 561.
Gregory, William, 133, 526, 561, 588.
Greiner, David, 154, 169, 188, 215, 228, 562, 580.
Greiner (Griner), John D., 149, 186, 536, 555, 575, 596.
Gresham, Moses, 223.
Greve, Benjamin, 240.
Grey, Margaret, 297, 563.
Greyson, William, 584.
Grider (Gryder), Martin, 131, 145, 504.
Gridle, John, 160.
Griff, Thomas, 159.
Griffey, David, 81.
Griffie, Benjamin, 16.
Griffie, Elizabeth, 16.
Griffie, Hannah, 16.
Griffie, John, 16.
Griffie, Lucretia, 16.
Griffie, Mathusalem, 16.
Griffie, Morrice, 16.
Griffin, Elizabeth, 133, 539, 540, 574, 585.
Griffin, John, 134, 141, 171, 186, 203, 530, 539, 574, 585.
Griffin, Samuel, 492.
Griffin, William, 203.
Griffith, Abel, 156, 167, 175, 177, 239, 525, 530, 581, 584, 586, 592.
Griffith, Abner, 239.
Griffith Abraham, 200.
Griffith, Benjamin, 83.
Griffith, Caleb, 239.
Griffith, David, 239.
Griffith, Elijah, 239.
Griffith, Elizabeth, 239.
Griffith, Evan, 167, 525.
Griffith, George, 50.
Griffith, Hanna, 239.
Griffith, Hiram, 239.
Griffith, Isaac, 239.
Griffith, James, 239, 573, 581, 592.
Griffith, John, 83, 190, 540.
Griffith, Lucretia, 22.
Griffith, Magdalene, 239.
Griffith, Mary, 581, 592.
Griffith, Methusalem, 9, 22, 25.
Griffith, Morris, 83.
Griffith, Rebecca, 239.
Griffith, Robert, 239.
Griffith, Ruth, 239.
Griffith, Susanna, 42.
Griffith, William, 207, 239.
Griffiths, Plineeas, 259.
Grigsbey, Benjamin, 490, 503.
Grigsby, James, 203, 574.
Grigsby, Mary, 503.
Grigsby, Rebecca, 203.
Grimes (Grymes), Archibald, 9, 10, 18, 396.
Grimes (Grymes), David, 77, 107.
Grimes (Grymes), Jane, 10. 107.
Grimes, John, 41.
Grimes (Grymes), William, 10, 77.
Griner, Anna C., 186.
Griner, John, 591.
Grinor, Catherine, 588, 596.
Grisham, Mary, 243.
Grisom, Thomas, 106.
Grod, Christian, 100.
Grof, Fred, 580.
Groob, Christian, 92.
Groone, Thomas, 593.
Grove, Abraham, 588.
Grove, Christian, 225, 589.
Grove, David, 236.
Grove, Frederick, 225.
Grove, George, 225.
Grove, Henry, 226.
Grove, Jacob, 225.
Grove, Margaret, 236.

Grove, Mary, 225.
Grover, Abraham, 578.
Grub, Barbara, 486.
Grub, Christian, 45, 497.
Grub, Daniel, 486.
Grub, Jacob, 101, 112, 142, 145, 486.
Grubb, Joseph, 596.
Grubbs, Thomas, 6, 15, 80, 83.
Gruber, Margaret, 149.
Gruber, Philip, 149.
Grumbs, John, 26.
Grutrix, Samuel, 158.
Guin, Alise, 533.
Guin, Daniel, 535, 537.
Guin, Jacob, 509.
Guin, John, 455, 533.
Guin, Randolph, 486.
Guines, Rebecky, 19.
Guinn (Gwinn), Joseph, 149, 502, 521, 570.
Gullet, Jeane (Jane), 563, 577.
Gullet, William, 563, 577.
Gully (Sally?), John P., 364.
Gum (Givin, Guin, Gwin), David, 93, 97, 503, 537.
Gum, Isaac, 533.
Gum, Jacob, 21, 33, 37, 114, 148, 322, 370, 402, 413.
Gum (Gunn), John, 92, 195, 197, 200, 201, 533, 570, 589.
Gum, Sarah, 402, 413.
Guthery, Adam, 184.
Guthray (Guthrey), John, 206, 591.
Guthrie, Daniel, 593.
Guthrie (Guthrey), William, 217, 591, 593.
Gutlip, Susanna, 536.
Guy, Agnes, 62.
Guy, Archibald, 172, 174, 242.
Guy, Elisabeth, 172, 173.
Guy, Henry, 172, 173.
Guy (Gauy), James, 207, 208, 563, 585.
Guy, James F., 242.
Guy (Gay), John, 61, 242.
Guy, Martha, 61.
Guy, Mary, 62.
Guy, Rebecca, 242.
Guy, Robert, 172, 242.
Guy, Thomas, 242.
Guy, William, 61.
Guye, Jenny, 208.
Guyler, Samuel, 577.
Gwin (Guin, Gwynn), Robert, 344, 502, 523, 573.
Gwin, Elizabeth, 194.
Gwin, James, 200.
Gwinn, Jean (Jeanet), 526.
Gwinn (Gwenn, Gween), Patrick, 526.
Gwynn, William, 122, 124, 492.

Haall (Hull), Peter, 436.
Haaz, Hannah, 352.

Haaz, Peter, 352.
Hackley, Bastain, 517.
Haddin, David, 570.
Haddon (Haddin), William, 138, 154, 384, 570.
Hadley, Jeremiah, 386.
Hadley (Hedley), Joshua, 33, 218, 270, 300, 320, 364, 386, 413, 418.
Hadley, Mary, 416.
Hadley, Patience, 320, 364.
Hadley, Thomas, 288, 294, 302, 320, 416, 431.
Hadrick, Adam, 141.
Hagarty, John, 143.
Hagert, Thomas, 492.
Hagle, John, 153.
Hagler, Benjamin, 65.
Haile, Nicholas, 12.
Haines, Abraham, 102.
Haines, Dicey, 168.
Haines, Frederick, 526.
Haines, Gasper, 549.
Haines, Sarah, 168.
Haines, Stephen, 168.
Hains, Jonathan, 247.
Hains, Peter, 169.
Hains, Philip, 235, 238.
Hair, Elizabeth, 576.
Hair (Hare, Hear), John, 348, 393, 574, 576.
Hair, Mary, 393.
Haislip, Andrew, 75, 110.
Haith, James, 98.
Halbert, Darby, 226.
Halbert, Philip, 58.
Haldman, Mary, 302.
Haldman, Thomas, 302.
Haldiman, Elizabeth, 192.
Haldiman, Jacob, 192, 194.
Hales, John, 94.
Haley, William, 106.
Haliman, William, 452.
Hall, Adam, 579.
Hall, Alexander, 182, 210, 233, 244.
Hall, Andrew, 73, 154, 342, 353, 443, 474, 496.
Hall, Archibald A., 244.
Hall, Benjamin, 210, 328, 516.
Hall, Edward, 29, 36, 40, 41, 46, 60, 65, 73, 75, 110, 111, 112, 138, 155, 180, 210, 262, 269, 284, 289, 297, 302, 328, 516, 526.
Hall, Eleanor, 111, 210, 222, 244.
Hall, Elizabeth, 222.
Hall, Fanny, 222.
Hall, George, 579.
Hall, Henry, 149.
Hall, Honore, 534.
Hall, Isaac, 210.
Hall, Isabella (Isbel), 500, 521, 526, 585.
Hall, Jacob, 579.

Hall, James, 52, 59, 85, 88, 129, 362, 396, 446, 474, 485, 489, 500.
Hall, Jane (Jean, Jenny), 200, 202, 353, 469, 474.
Hall, Jannet, 446.
Hall, Joanna, 242.
Hall, John, 73, 117, 122, 149, 210, 214, 222, 445, 454, 469, 473, 494.
Hall, Joseph, 285.
Hall, Margaret (Peggy), 129, 251, 356.
Hall, Mary, 469, 595.
Hall, Mary P., 235.
Hall, Moses, 101, 451, 456, 534.
Hall, Nancy, 222.
Hall, Nathaniel, 446, 447.
Hall, Patrick, 155. 156, 161, 242.
Hall, Patsey, 242.
Hall (Hald), Peter, 149, 156, 579.
Hall, Richard, 12, 17, 24, 26, 286, 402.
Hall, Robert, 52, 55, 59, 241, 242, 362, 396, 448, 451, 500, 521, 526, 528, 584, 585.
Hall, Sarah, 111.
Hall, Susannah, 85, 362.
Hall, Thomas, 142, 210.
Hall, William, 20, 31, 62, 65, 67, 73, 75, 110, 117, 258, 271, 285, 286, 292, 308, 342, 349, 353, 356, 358, 367, 375, 386, 399, 402, 410, 445, 446, 447, 462, 469, 473, 474, 475, 488.
Hall, William J., 275.
Haller, George, 233.
Halley, William, 103.
Halliday, William, 545.
Halpe, John, 363.
Halseman, Peter, 225.
Halsey, Hannah, 210.
Halstone, Henry, 323.
Halter, Benjamin, 25.
Halterman, Jacob, 29.
Ham Joseph, 126, 142, 158, 394.
Hamilton, Agnes (Ann), 512, 519.
Hamilton, Alexander, 51, 52, 63, 112, 146, 163, 228, 384, 388, 435, 445, 453, 456, 555.
Hamilton, Andrew, 43, 47, 55, 56, 59, 122, 138, 148, 156, 189, 202, 205, 302, 437, 457, 492, 530, 566, 587, 592, 593.
Hamilton, Archibald, 35, 56, 113, 202, 261, 262, 269, 270, 367, 532, 537, 572.
Hamilton, Arthur (Arter), 30, 41, 57, 62, 84, 85, 174, 228, 278, 280, 283, 301, 302, 303, 359, 468.
Hamilton, Audley, 202, 357, 508, 537.
Hamilton, Barbara, 228, 302.
Hamilton, Charles, 555, 574.
Hamilton, David, 228, 236, 241, 246, 579.
Hamilton, Else (Alice), 453.
Hamilton, Frances, 270.
Hamilton, Francis, 202.
Hamilton, Gawin, 149, 392, 400, 541.
Hamilton, Gaw'th, 557.
Hamilton, Guy, 541.
Hamilton, Hugh, 65, 66, 205, 414, 424.
Hamilton, Isabel, 593.
Hamilton, James, 17, 19, 37, 39, 42, 43, 45, 66, 72, 228, 236, 246, 263, 276, 281, 282, 301, 302, 304, 316, 326, 334, 348, 357, 366, 372, 377, 381, 390, 412, 414, 426, 502, 511, 515, 558.
Hamilton, Jane (Jean), 102, 304, 316, 381, 533.
Hamilton, Jesse (Jese), 154, 157.
Hamilton, Joannah, 174.
Hamilton, John, 51, 66, 67, 78, 112, 123, 125, 155, 180, 202, 205, 206, 209, 210, 215, 218, 228, 289, 319, 348, 357, 389, 426, 502, 515, 532, 534, 566, 578, 581.
Hamilton, Lettice, 202.
Hamilton, Margaret, 68, 228, 435, 456, 485, 512, 517, 521, 548, 574.
Hamilton, Martha, 189, 229.
Hamilton, Mary, 228.
Hamilton, Nancy (Nansey), 120, 246.
Hamilton, Osburn, 572.
Hamilton, Patience, 205.
Hamilton, Patrick, 140, 407, 485, 486, 512, 519.
Hamilton, Robert, 76, 106, 112, 189, 319, 387, 410, 463, 506, 517.
Hamilton, Samuel, 165, 414.
Hamilton, Sarah, 228, 246.
Hamilton, Thomas, 381, 533.
Hamilton (Hambleton), William, 17, 30, 35, 37, 152, 155, 189, 202, 205, 209, 277, 279, 286, 291, 317, 367, 407, 422, 435, 453, 475, 485, 493, 495, 512, 521, 548, 550, 562, 567, 574, 576, 583.
Hamm, Valentine, 547.
Hammer, George, 89, 94, 100, 114, 119, 129, 141, 374, 573.
Hammer, Henry, 483.
Hammer (Hamer), Jacob, 149, 481, 483.
Hampton, Preston, 402.
Hancebarger, Hance, 550.
Handley, Archibald, 388, 411.
Handley, Grizel, 411, 516.
Handley (Handly, Hanley), John, 53, 78, 85, 108, 111, 113, 134, 173, 174, 301, 311, 327, 361, 363, 391, 398, 411, 432, 464, 477, 484, 498, 510, 516, 559, 562, 576, 577, 583.
Handley, Keziah, 203.
Handley (Handly), Margaret, 559, 583.
Handley (Handly), William, 173, 215, 565, 576.
Handy, George, 41, 42, 56.
Hane, Frederick, 146.
Hanger, Barbara, 223, 240.
Hanger, Catherine, 223, 243.
Hanger, Charles, 216.

Hanger, Christian, 240.
Hanger, David, 223.
Hanger, Elizabeth (Betsy), 235, 240.
Hanger, Eve, 216, 240.
Hanger (Henger), Frederick, 129, 177, 215, 216, 217, 223, 224, 232, 240, 490, 565.
Hanger, George, 223.
Hanger, Hannah, 223.
Hanger (Henger), John, 223, 581.
Hanger (Henger), Maria, 224, 240.
Hanger, Molly, 232.
Hanger, Peter, 134, 149, 163, 170, 177, 185, 188, 216, 223, 235, 247, 248, 251, 485, 523, 549, 561, 574, 586, 588.
Hanger, Rebecca, 240.
Hanger, Sarah, 240.
Hanly, Darby, 27.
Hanna, Ann, 351, 390.
Hanna, Brice, 449.
Hanna (Hamm), Isaac, 173, 180.
Hanna, James, 245, 462, 487.
Hanna, John, 32, 46, 84, 470, 536.
Hanna, Polly, 249.
Hanna, Rebecca, 183, 250.
Hanna, Robert, 209, 210, 529, 539.
Hanna, William, 64, 240.
Hannah, Elizabeth, 160.
Hannah, Isabell, 173.
Hannah, Joseph, 139, 142, 173, 201, 337, 351, 353, 362, 390, 477, 501, 511, 535.
Hannegan, Michael, 115.
Hannet, Joseph, 78.
Hansbaig, Steen, 146.
Hansbarger, Adam, 142.
Hansbarger, Conrad, 142.
Hansbarger, Henry, 142.
Hansbarger (Hensberger, Hernsberger) Stephen, 110, 142, 413, 449, 481.
Hansbarger, Uashel (Rachel), 142.
Hansel, George, 206, 578, 581.
Hansell, Lawrence, 578, 581.
Hansell, Philip, 578, 581.
Hansford, Thomas, 579.
Haplenstall, Abraham, 442.
Haptonstall, Abraham, 464.
Harnagar, John, 273.
Harbison, David, 197.
Harbison, John, 490.
Harbison, William, 42, 274, 293, 294, 331, 361.
Harbold, Elizabeth, 141.
Harchy, Conrad, 74, 75.
Harden, George, 589.
Harden, John, 37, 347.
Hardin, Benjamin, 16.
Harding, Abraham, 552.
Harding, Stephen, 552.
Hardman, John, 92.
Hardy, John, 188.
Hare (Ware, Mare), Betsy, 244.
Hare, John, 379, 505, 512.

Harfman, Godlib, 592.
Harford, Nicholas, 9.
Hargar, John, 33, 406, 421, 471.
Harger, Agness, 406.
Hargrave, James, 510.
Harkins, Edward, 188.
Harles, David, 123.
Harles (Herless, Horless), Henry, 123, 130, 541.
Harles (Herliss, Horless), Immanuel, 123, 130, 541, 572, 586.
Harles (Horless), Margaret, 122, 123, 130, 486.
Harles, Mary, 123.
Harles (Harless, Herless, Horless), Philip, 75, 110, 122, 123, 125, 130, 364, 366, 367, 486, 541, 566, 572.
Harless (Herlis), Elizabeth, 186, 586.
Harless, Martin, 122.
Harloe (Horloe), Nancy, 228.
Harlow, Nathaniel, 169.
Harlowe, John, 215.
Harly, Philip, 116.
Harman, Adam, 26, 75, 85, 248.
Harman, Anna, 373.
Harman, Caleb, 35, 50, 77.
Harman, Catherine (Catrina), 85, 108.
Harman, Elizabeth, 85.
Harman (Herman), Jacob, 25, 69, 70, 75, 85, 106, 107, 110, 117, 275, 321, 355, 419, 420, 424, 465.
Harman (Herman), John, 35, 45, 50, 60, 62, 71, 85, 147, 297, 323, 423, 425.
Harman, Joseph, 373.
Harman, Michael, 596.
Harman (Herman), Peter, 22, 57, 69, 85, 107, 394, 420.
Harman, Teawalt, 85, 419, 420.
Harman, Zichman, 517.
Harman (Herman), Barbara, 60, 147.
Harmantrout, Barbara, 147.
Harmentrout (Armentrout, Ermantrout), Christopher, 58, 59, 65, 112, 113, 294, 526.
Harmentrout (Armentrout), Elizabeth, 140, 142, 145.
Harmentrout (Armentrout, Ermentrout), Frederick, 57, 58, 65, 85, 125, 140, 333, 334, 350.
Harmentrout (Armentrout), George, 61, 141, 145.
Harmentrout (Armentrout), Henry, 140, 141, 148, 480.
Harmentrout (Armentrout, Ermentrout) John, 46, 47, 140, 141, 148.
Harmentrout (Armentrout), Peater, 145.
Harmentrout (Armentrout, Arrantrout), Philip, 140, 145, 333, 334, 531.
Harmer (Hammer), George, 77.
Harmon, David, 159, 394.
Harmon, George, 531.

Harmon, Margaret, 420.
Harmon, Sarah, 156, 419, 465.
Harmon, Thomas, 14.
Harndon, Hannah, 131.
Harned, David, 142, 145.
Harness, Conrad, 31, 38, 52.
Harness (Harnis, Harns), Michael, 8, 15, 24, 28, 52, 121.
Harnish, Christian, 9.
Harnost, George, 293.
Harnsberger, Robert, 578.
Haroff, Andrew, 245.
Harper, Adam, 68, 436.
Harper, Elizabeth, 418, 470.
Harper, Hance (Hanse, Haunce), 323, 350, 418, 470.
Harper, Isabel, 360.
Harper, Jacob, 50, 62, 124, 374, 527.
Harper, John, 151, 152, 172, 186, 560.
Harper, Margaret, 374, 411, 473.
Harper, Mathew, 84, 99, 105, 323, 359, 374, 386, 411, 420, 470, 473, 585.
Harper, Michael, 37, 99, 100, 105, 326, 360, 421.
Harper, Nickless, 158.
Harper, Philip, 49, 65, 77, 90, 156, 315, 495.
Harper, Robert, 105.
Harper, Thomas, 476.
Harpole, Adam, 53, 127, 490.
Harpole, Nicholas, 127, 405.
Harr, Charles, 280.
Harra, Michael, 114.
Harrad, Thomas, 159.
Harrah (O'Hara), Daniel, 59.
Harrald, Aaron, 274, 289, 290.
Harrald, James, 274, 289, 290.
Harrald, John, 274, 289.
Harrald, Moses, 274, 289, 291.
Harrald, Richard, 274, 289, 290, 291.
Harrald, Wiliam, 274, 289, 290.
Harrel (Harril), Jacob, 291, 294.
Harris, Agness, 556.
Harris, Charles, 122, 520, 537, 538.
Harris, Christopher, 556.
Harris, Deborah, 238.
Harris, Frederick, 140.
Harris, George, 65.
Harris, Henry, 94.
Harris (Harress), James, 163, 228, 232, 235, 341, 461, 517, 569.
Harris, Jean, 537, 538.
Harris, Jese, 328.
Harris, John, 301.
Harris (Herris), Robert, 181, 211, 215, 228, 235, 475, 476, 569.
Harris, Thomas, 235.
Harris, William, 348.
Harrison, Abigail, 64.
Harrison, Ann, 64.

Harrison, Benjamin, 63, 64, 115, 118, 222, 471, 475, 502.
Harrison, Burr, 37, 372, 373, 416.
Harrison, Catherine, 366, 367, 368, 434, 522.
Harrison, Daniel, 16, 19, 20, 36, 38, 44, 48, 50, 54, 56, 64, 66, 71, 78, 87, 88, 115, 118, 120, 270, 272, 282, 299, 307, 308, 345, 350, 364, 398, 400, 401, 403, 408, 409, 414, 415, 417, 437, 440, 447, 473, 481, 487, 488, 496, 504, 520, 544.
Harrison, Ester, 113, 114.
Harrison, Gideon, 63, 66.
Harrison, Henry, 404.
Harison, Isaiah, 8.
Harrison, James, 237.
Harison, Jeremiah (Jeremy) (Jere), 8, 13, 15, 19, 94, 340, 366, 367, 368, 392, 417, 421, 424, 434, 522.
Harrison, Jesse (Jese), 64, 68, 141, 409, 414, 417, 475, 478, 488, 551.
Harrison, John, 19, 25, 41, 77, 82, 83, 101, 118, 121, 147, 148, 149, 171, 203, 270, 274, 286, 288, 291, 299, 318, 340, 402, 416, 417, 438, 450, 458, 461, 509, 523, 524, 538.
Harrison, Joseph, 8, 9, 15.
Harrison, Josiah (Josiah), 522, 537.
Harrison, Lydia, 524.
Harrison, Margaret, 299, 455.
Harrison (Herrison), Mary, 64, 272, 291, 295, 391, 460, 493, 523.
Harrison, Mathew, 492, 493, 504, 507, 511, 516, 523, 526, 545.
Harrison, Nehemiah, 522.
Harrison, Phebe (Feby), 118, 523.
Harrison, Phel, 82.
Harrison, Reuben, 42, 82, 115, 118, 171, 416, 438, 458, 509, 524.
Harrison, Robert, 42, 52, 64, 66, 68, 92, 201, 203, 237, 350, 417, 455, 462.
Harrison (Herrison), Samuel, 15, 272, 291, 295, 355, 391, 412, 422, 460, 532.
Harrison, Sarah, 65, 115, 118, 400, 409, 414, 417, 487, 496.
Harrison, Thomas, 13, 75, 307, 367, 417, 421, 424, 532.
Harrison, Wallace, 487.
Harrison, William, 237.
Harrison, Zebulon, 42, 68, 81, 82, 92, 118, 274, 383, 416, 455, 462, 478, 509, 515.
Harry, John, 268, 455.
Harshman, Olerick, 146.
Harshman, William, 439.
Hart, Jane, 308, 343, 379, 411, 461.
Hart, Job, 236.
Hart, John, 50, 336.
Hart, Peter, 15.
Hart, Silas, 22, 41, 42, 44, 52, 64, 66, 87, 93, 112, 120, 252, 254, 255, 257, 267, 268, 270, 271, 273, 274, 276, 280, 291,

299, 306, 308, 339, 343, 353, 379, 411, 420, 445, 461, 487, 500, 521, 534, 539.
Hart, William, 59, 60.
Hartgrove (Hardgrave), Elizabeth, 133, 154, 438.
Hartgrove (Hardgrave, Hargrove), Francis, 133, 438, 504, 536, 555.
Hartgrove (Hargrave), James, 93, 133, 134, 397, 400, 415, 496, 555.
Hartgrove (Hardgrave), Robert, 116, 133, 200.
Hartgrove (Hardgrove), Sarah, 536, 555.
Hartingen, Conrad, 547.
Hartman, Henry, 232.
Hartsook, John, 196.
Hartsough, Frederick, 37, 74, 75, 323.
Harvey, Ann, 227.
Harvey, Daniel, 413.
Harvey, Henry, 66.
Harvey (Harvie, Hervie), John, 15, 39, 45, 138, 261, 263, 296, 398, 521.
Has, William, 509.
Haslet (Heslet), Robert, 139, 178, 194.
Hass, Ben, 17.
Hass, Philip, 147.
Hastings, Robert, 35.
Hathorn (Hawthorn), James, 210, 226, 574.
Hatrick (Hettrick), Adam, 62, 137, 142, 419.
Hatthorn, John, 28.
Hatton, Jacob F., 245.
Hatton, Mark, 167, 184, 226.
Hatton, Thomas, 365.
Hauber (Hober), Michael, 440.
Haunsdone, Ladwick, 287.
Haup, Elizabeth, 228.
Haup, Henry, 228.
Hause, Hannah, 49.
Hause, Henry, 49.
Havener, Nicholas, 65, 83, 100, 108, 111, 336.
Havoner (Havener), Frederick, 108, 502.
Havenor, Catren, 100, 108.
Havenor, Elizabeth, 108.
Havenor (Heffenor), Jacob, 108, 156.
Haveouf, Andrew, 215.
Hawk, Abraham, 218, 225.
Hawk, Andrew, 225.
Hawk, Catherine, 225.
Hawk, Frederick, 225.
Hawk (Hawp), Henry, 218, 225.
Hawk, Jacob, 225.
Hawk, John, 218, 225.
Hawkins, Benjamin, 87, 95, 104, 386, 428, 443, 451, 473, 480, 486.
Hawkins, John, 253, 256, 381.
Hawl, Robert, 587.
Hawn, Ana M., 214.
Hawn, Philip, 214.
Hawpe, Adam, 224, 225.

Hawpe, Catherine, 225.
Hawpe, Elizabeth, 225.
Hawpe, Emanuel, 225.
Hawpe, George, 225.
Hawpe, Henry, 225, 569.
Hawpe, John, 181, 225.
Hawpe, Rudolph, 225, 571.
Haws, Henry, 39.
Haws, Peter, 121.
Haws, Philip, 387, 416, 519.
Haws, Sarah, 39.
Hayard, Mary, 167.
Hayes, Abigail, 19.
Hayl, George, 34.
Haynes, John, 397.
Haynes (Hayne), Joseph, 535, 538, 544.
Hays, Agness, 450.
Hays, Andrew, 12, 14, 15, 19, 20, 22, 23, 31, 36, 45, 47, 48, 51, 56, 60, 65, 71, 72, 95, 103, 114, 119, 120, 130, 305, 307, 308, 313, 316, 329, 333, 344, 347, 353, 366, 385, 394, 409, 426, 427, 429, 432, 433, 435, 443, 464, 476, 495, 508, 512, 518, 519, 520, 529.
Hays, Barbara, 433.
Hays, Charles, 15, 19, 20, 46, 52, 65, 78, 263, 305, 308, 316, 329, 426, 433, 443, 470, 508, 528, 529, 548.
Hays, David, 17, 30, 43, 52, 90, 114, 144, 145, 148, 173, 270, 274, 297, 302, 307, 310, 312, 315, 338, 342, 352, 411, 453, 505, 561.
Hays, Elizabeth, 184, 407.
Hays, Frances, 403, 426.
Hays, Frank (Frances), 357.
Hayes, George, 6, 7, 8, 41.
Hayes, Hugh, 357, 403, 426, 428, 451, 538, 560.
Hays, Isaac, 210.
Hays, Isabella, 144.
Hays (Hay), James, 19, 41, 210, 342, 450, 512, 536, 565, 584, 593.
Hays, Jean (Jane), 234, 297, 342.
Hays, John, 6, 19, 20, 21, 93, 103, 130, 144, 147, 150, 246, 256, 305, 385, 394, 433, 443, 456, 457, 476, 495, 504, 508, 510, 512, 528, 529, 548.
Hays, Joseph, 144.
Hays, Margaret, 383, 427, 429, 432, 529, 548, 560.
Hays, Mary, 147, 224, 428, 528, 538.
Hays, Moses, 210, 565, 566, 572, 573.
Hays, Patrick, 6, 12, 16, 36, 37, 54, 55, 60, 61, 77, 210, 228, 234, 259, 261, 263, 264, 265, 279, 280, 304, 313, 325, 329, 341, 357, 358, 369, 386, 388, 403, 426, 429, 488, 538, 560, 576, 589.
Hays, Prudence, 19.
Hays, Rebecca, 19, 20, 305.
Hays, Richard, 210.
Hays, Robert, 144.

Hays, Samuel, 19, 48, 52, 181, 184, 186, 189, 201, 316, 407, 488, 541.
Hays, Sarah, 6, 8, 53, 210.
Hays (Hay), William, 16, 60, 132, 144, 210, 357, 403, 449, 488, 521, 550.
Hays, Winsted, 210.
Haysaw, Andrew, 553.
Hayworth, Absalom, 487, 549.
Hazard, Samuel, 344.
Heagons (Hagens), John, 503.
Heaning, John, 553.
Heany, John, 167.
Hear (Ker), John, 294.
Heard, Thomas, 378.
Heath, Jonathan, 108.
Heath, Margaret, 111.
Heath, Peter, 53.
Hedd, Richard, 172.
Hedges, Solomon (Solom), 38, 53.
Hedrick, Barbara, 143.
Hedrick, Charles, 143, 589.
Hefner, Catherine, 235.
Heginbotham, William, 200, 201, 591.
Heiskell, Peter, 178, 188, 190, 200, 201, 575, 576, 577, 578, 589.
Heizer, Edward, 244.
Heizer, Elizabeth, 244.
Heizer, John, 182, 244.
Heizer, Joshua, 244.
Heizer, Nathaniel, 244.
Heizer, Polly, 244.
Heizer, Samuel, 183, 244.
Helford, Jacob, 558, 586.
Helveston, Philip, 70.
Hempenstall, Abram, 164.
Hemphill, James, 76, 287, 307.
Hemphill, John, 566.
Hemphill, Samuel, 54, 56, 66, 71, 81, 345, 355.
Henderson, Abraham, 538, 552.
Henderson, Alexander, 163, 182, 187, 190, 219, 279, 281, 282, 286, 303, 327, 330, 347, 348, 385, 421, 426, 428, 431, 470, 495.
Henderson, Andrew, 163, 182, 187, 219.
Henderson, Ann, 187, 195, 204, 207, 231, 534.
Henderson, Archibald, 154, 159, 170, 216, 218, 231, 233, 596.
Henderson, Daniel, 37, 51, 92, 103, 125, 126, 127, 222, 240, 442, 458, 461, 477, 487, 500, 519, 534, 536, 538, 543, 552.
Henderson, David, 103, 116, 125, 127, 130, 159, 163, 167, 170, 207, 219, 281, 303, 317, 428, 548, 559, 561.
Henderson, Eleanor, 159, 170.
Henderson, Elin, 231, 233.
Henderson, Elizabeth, 159, 160, 170, 218, 273.
Henderson, Florence, 163, 219.
Henderson, George, 13, 30, 34, 35, 265, 273, 290, 310, 344, 380, 383, 393, 433.
Henderson, Hanna, 219.
Henderson, Isabella, 220.
Henderson, James, 23, 44, 45, 95, 100, 111, 116, 154, 163, 170, 182, 187, 190, 219, 220, 230, 275, 280, 282, 283, 350, 354, 424, 432, 445, 515, 527, 548, 577, 591.
Henderson, Jane (Jean), 163, 172, 219, 327, 360, 390, 396, 428, 489, 509, 520.
Henderson, Joanes (Jones), 172, 179, 180, 198, 209, 220, 328, 368, 456, 555, 574.
Henderson, John, 15, 24, 48, 86, 95, 96, 104, 111, 112, 116, 125, 167, 172, 189, 197, 198, 205, 220, 262, 269, 271, 278, 280, 298, 301, 306, 337, 352, 354, 359, 376, 384, 386, 390, 392, 394, 396, 401, 411, 425, 439, 457, 459, 489, 509, 534, 536, 538, 543, 552.
Henderson, Jon, 117.
Henderson, Joseph, 73, 129, 134, 144, 170, 197, 219, 220, 509, 538, 590, 591.
Henderson, Margaret, 165, 194, 220, 242.
Henderson, Martha (Matty), 116, 170, 222, 225, 445, 577, 590.
Henderson, Mary (Polly), 198, 228, 303, 392, 551, 552.
Henderson, Rebecca (Beckey), 219, 220, 577.
Henderson, Robert, 172, 197, 242, 432, 487, 536, 538, 543, 552.
Henderson, Rose, 95.
Henderson, Samuel, 8, 21, 29, 36, 54, 56, 58, 60, 71, 79, 89, 93, 96, 104, 116, 119, 149, 154, 163, 219, 254, 271, 280, 281, 297, 303, 312, 316, 318, 327, 334, 339, 342, 345, 348, 360, 362, 369, 375, 382, 399, 391, 392, 396, 432, 470, 471, 489, 520, 526, 534.
Henderson, Sarah (Sally), 165, 197, 198, 219, 220, 222, 548.
Henderson, Susanna (Shusanna), 116, 183, 277, 354, 377.
Henderson, Thomas, 281, 287, 288, 386.
Henderson, William, 5, 8, 21, 22, 24, 29, 42, 60, 70, 95, 100, 116, 117, 159, 163, 170, 183, 197, 219, 224, 254, 258, 261, 264, 266, 268, 269, 271, 277, 284, 285, 287, 289, 290, 296, 303, 317, 324, 325, 331, 346, 352, 354, 359, 371, 376, 377, 389, 411, 420, 423, 425, 471, 473, 561, 594.
Henican, Michael, 150.
Henkle, Benjamin, 591.
Henry, Alexander, 222.
Henry, Alexander M., 206, 230.
Henry, Ann, 246, 251.
Henry (Kenney), Bryan, 154.
Henry, Cathrine, 483.
Henry, Deborah, 251.
Henry, Dennis, 66, 92, 483.

Henry, Elizabeth, 159, 185, 206, 230.
Henry, Henry (Harry), 400, 525, 551.
Henry (Hendry), James, 54, 88, 148, 155, 164, 168, 169, 189, 192, 203, 212, 217, 223, 226, 235, 349, 352, 353, 382, 388, 428, 434, 515, 520, 538, 589, 593.
Henry, John, 216, 225, 235, 246.
Henry (Henery), Mary, 235, 382.
Henry, Matilda, 235.
Henry, Nancy, 235.
Henry, Patrick, 462, 478.
Henry, Robert, 193, 235, 310, 335, 344, 346, 349, 353, 589, 593.
Henry, Samuel, 165, 175, 177, 189, 198, 212, 388, 515, 540.
Henry (Hendry), Sarah, 161, 165, 235.
Henry, Thomas, 110.
Henry, William, 17, 30, 73, 578.
Henton, Even, 149.
Henton (Hinton), George, 145, 147, 203.
Henton (Hinton), John, 44, 47, 115, 121, 130, 318, 344, 434, 506, 532.
Henten, Michael, 314.
Henton, Peter, 147.
Henton (Hinton), William, 121, 147, 148.
Herbern, Phillip, 472.
Herbert, Benjamin, 84.
Herbert, William, 95, 102, 113, 470.
Herbould, Necolaus, 517.
Herd (Heard), Stephen, 378.
Herdman, John, 151, 508.
Herdman (Hendman), Polly, 247.
Here, George, 545.
Herin, Patsey Davis, 250.
Herlis, Monanel, 186.
Hermone, Henry, 590.
Herndon, Joseph, 77.
Hernsberger, Arsley, 449.
Heron, Edm, 583.
Herrberrger, Jacob, 95.
Herrin, Margaret (Peggy), 242, 244.
Herring (Herron), Abigail, 422.
Herring (Harron, Herrin, Herron), Alexander (Ellick), 11, 50, 54, 142, 282, 292, 295, 343, 395, 413, 422, 444, 445, 447, 532.
Herring, Elizabeth, 247.
Herring, Leonard, 145.
Herring, William, 147.
Herrington, Charles, 144.
Herron, Walter, 246.
Hershman, Peter, 146.
Herston, James, 534.
Heslin, John, 544.
Heslip, Robert, 171.
Hess, Elizabeth, 234.
Hess, John, 234.
Hess, Joseph, 234.
Hess, Christian, 234.
Hestent (Histent), Jacob, 544, 563.
Hestin, David, 149.

Heterick, Susannah, 383.
Heterick (Hetrick), John, 69, 383.
Hevener, George, 501.
Hewit, Thomas, 141, 558.
Heyn, Peter, 169.
Hickcock, Meshick, 169.
Hickens (Kichens), Arther, 469.
Hickey, John, 231.
Hicklen, George, 535.
Hicklin, Elizabeth, 446, 562.
Hicklin, Hugh, 40, 43, 81, 115, 120, 121, 127, 138, 446, 463, 500, 521, 560, 562.
Hicklin, Jane, 505.
Hicklin, John, 92, 115, 120, 152, 190, 373, 505, 548, 581.
Hicklin, Jonathan, 583.
Hicklin, Joseph, 122.
Hicklin, Thomas, 52, 63, 81, 115, 120, 127, 152, 194, 342, 373, 502, 521, 535.
Hickman, Arthur, 531, 574.
Hickman, Jacob, 390.
Hickman, John, 73, 109, 450, 459, 460.
Hickman, Joshua, 157, 271, 280.
Hickman, Josia, 364.
Hickman, Roger, 574.
Hickman, William, 574.
Hicks, Christopher, 54, 67, 341.
Hicks, Thomas, 158.
Hiden, Martha, 228.
Hider, Adam, 53.
Hider, Michael, 87.
Higgins, John, 106, 121, 156, 175, 577.
Higgins, Thomas, 578.
Higher, Looney, 65.
Hight, Samuel, 407.
Higins, Daniel, 106.
Higins, Michael, 106.
Hill (Hills), Abraham, 391, 460.
Hill, Aney, 98.
Hill, Ann S., 289.
Hill, Elizabeth, 11.
Hill, Hannah, 11.
Hill, James, 11, 102, 126, 133, 142, 149, 154, 206, 431, 462, 526, 530, 535, 549, 560, 595.
Hill, Jean, 529.
Hill, John, 11.
Hill, Johnson (Johnston, Jonson), 55, 63, 66, 68, 70, 78, 98, 528, 541.
Hill, Joseph, 11.
Hill, Mary, 11, 302.
Hill, Naomi, 63.
Hill, Peter, 238.
Hill, Rachel, 11.
Hill, Robert, 78, 98, 162, 510, 528, 541.
Hill, Samuel, 169, 510.
Hill, Sarah, 11.
Hill, Sealer (Scaler), 293.
Hill, Thomas, 50, 74, 111, 112, 133, 148, 259, 309, 325, 335, 341, 349, 393, 403, 423, 437, 520, 537.

Hill, William, 11, 13, 107, 356, **427, 529.**
Hindman, Alexander, 476.
Hindman, John, 10, 14, 17, **393.**
Hinds (Hind), Ann, 559, 567, **583.**
Hinds, Edward, **428**, 589.
Hinds, Isabella, 380.
Hind(s), James, 510.
Hind(s), Jean, 161, 371, 511.
Hinds (Hind, Hines), John, **94, 126, 139,** 161, 163, 166, 195, 216, 277, 319, **369,** 371, 386, 400, 476, 494, 509, 511, **522,** 526, 532, 566, 583, 589.
Hinds, Samuel, 149, 198, **288**, **380**, **531,** 548, 565, 568, 576.
Hinds (Hines), Thomas, **467**, 559, **561,** 594.
Hinds (Hind, Hines), William, **43**, **161,** 195, 277, **288**, 371, 510, 532, 566, 567, 572, 576, 583, 586, 587, 589.
Hiner, John, 157, 176, 544, 545.
Hinging (Kinging), John, **561.**
Hinkle, Benjamin, 190.
Hinkle, Jacob, 142.
Hinkle (Hinckle), Moses, **412, 417, 495.**
Hinkle, Paul, 212.
Hinkle, Solomon, 212.
Hinson, Mary, 343.
Hinson, Margaret, 343.
Hinson (Hanson), William, **343.**
Hire, Lanie, 121.
Histent, Elizabeth, 563.
Histrop, Robert, 159.
Hite, Abraham, 23, 25, 334, **366**, **392**, **434,** 445, 532.
Hite, Alexander, 366.
Hite, Jacob, 128, 451.
Hite, John, 255, 266, 276, 502, **526.**
Hite, Jost (Just), 25, 255, 256, 257, **259,** 260, 274, 276, 294, 341, 367, 380, **409,** 502.
Hite, Rebecca, 366, 392.
Hive, Peter, 53.
Hix, Thomas, 158.
Hoadley, Joshua, 412.
Hobbes, Thomas, 102.
Hockheimer, George L., **412.**
Hockman, Barbara, 9.
Hockman, Johannes, 9.
Hockman, Ulrick, 9.
Hodge, Andrew, 213, 593.
Hodge, Asabel (Asabel), 19, **25**, **296.**
Hodge, David, 25.
Hodge, Eleanor, 139.
Hodge, Elizabeth, 25, **28**, 139, 272, **429.**
Hodge, Frank, 187.
Hodge, Hannah, 25.
Hodge (Hodgh), Jacob, 25, **398**, **527.**
Hodge, James, 139, 213, 470, 592.
Hodge, Jane, 213, 296.
Hodge, John, 19, 20, 22, 139, 145, 213, **272,** 296, 592.

Hodge, John H., 213.
Hodge, Jonathan, 25.
Hodge, Margaret, 213.
Hodge, Martha, 213.
Hodge, Rachel, 25.
Hodge, Ruemia, 25.
Hodge, Samuel, 14, 27, 39, 54, **127, 139,** 353, 398, 423, 429, 592.
Hodge, Sarah, 213.
Hodge, William, 213, 246, 359.
Hodges, Francis, 159.
Hodgson, James, 207, 211.
Hoffer, Jacob, 206, 214.
Hoffman, Casper, 564.
Hoffman, George, 547.
Hoffman, Margaret, 564.
Hoffman (Hofman), Nicholas **(Nichles),** 62, 116.
Hog, Peter, 56, 95, 96, 115, 122, 126, **134,** 140, 145, 347, 364, 423, 459, 507.
Hog, Thomas, 140, 534.
Hogan, Edward, 307, 311.
Hogan, Sarah, 307.
Hoge, Elizabeth, 202.
Hogg, James, 106, 127, **157, 163.**
Hoggs, Francis, 157.
Hogleer, John, 63.
Hogles, Ellis, 87.
Hogshead, Agnes, 215, **248.**
Hogshead, Anny, 248.
Hogshead, Catherine, 579.
Hogshead, Charles, 186, 212.
Hogshead (Hogsett), David, 43, 141, **161,** 162, 215, 217, 218, 241, 248, 352, **403,** 463, 567, 576, 579, 585.
Hogshead, Elizabeth, 161, 469.
Hogshead, Gordon, 215, **295.**
Hogshead, Gray, 222.
Hogshead (Hogsett), James, 43, **56**, **99,** 115, 136, 142, 161, 213, 215, 218, **222,** 238, 244, 248, 261, 266, 339, 447, **450,** 463, 469, 576.
Hogshead, Jean (Jane), 215, 217, 248.
Hogshead, Joanna, 238.
Hogshead (Hogsett), John, 24, 27, **43,** 44, 99, 141, 142, 161, 168, 197, **198,** 202, 211, 215, 248, 261, 266, 295, **407,** 463, 469, 513, 516, 534, 549, 584, **587,** 592.
Hogshead, Margaret (Margrit), **141, 162,** 352, 463.
Hogshead, Martha, 215, 248.
Hogshead, Mary (Polly), 215, **248.**
Hogshead, Michael, 43, 141, 161, 168, **215,** 248, 362, 469, 588.
Hogshead, Nancy, **247.**
Hogshead, Rebecca, 43, 215, 222, **248.**
Hogshead, Robert, 161, 175, 213.
Hogshead, Sarah (Sally), 222, 248.
Hogshead (Hogsett), Thomas, 153, **215,** 222, 248.

Hogshead (Hogsett), William, **161, 168,** 195, 215, 222, 248, 352, 402, 403, **481,** 487, 567, 593.
Hohl, Susanah M., **142.**
Holdman, Daniel, 10, 13, **16, 17, 18, 22, 25,** 27, 28.
Holdman, John, 14.
Holdman, Samuel, 27.
Holdman, Thomas, 320.
Hole, Enees, 158.
Hole, George, 158.
Hole, Leasy, 158.
Hole (Holes, Hool, Hohl), Peter, **50, 112.** 142, 143, 144, 158, **454,** 558.
Holeman, Richard, 500.
Holesinger, David, **534.**
Holesinger, Michael, **534.**
Holland, Edward, 526.
Holland, George, 187.
Holle, Conrad, 131, 132.
Holliday, William, 180.
Hollingsworth, George, 25.
Hollingsworth, Hannah, **25.**
Hollis, Anne, **432.**
Hollis, James, 74, 96, 102, 110, **382, 432,** 461.
Holloback, Ann, 29.
Holinan (Holeman), Daniel, 8, **492, 547.**
Holman (Holeman), Jacob, 115, **563.**
Holman, William, **370,** 406, **414.**
Holmes, Gabriel, 5.
Holmes, James, 191.
Holmes, Jane, 268.
Holmes, Jannet, 5.
Holmes (Homes), John, 10, **268, 274, 595.**
Holmes (Homes), Robert, 5, **378.**
Holoway. Timothy, 405.
Holston (Houlston, Holdston), **Henry,** 17, 37, 38, 74, 75, 319, 330.
Holt, Fanny, 236.
Holt, Reuben, 236.
Holt, Richard, 236, 237, **242.**
Homes (Home, Homs), **George, 50, 259,** 266, 268, 345, 403.
Homes, Joseph, 378.
Homs, Frederick, 102.
Hood, Andrew, 595.
Hood, Elijah, 222.
Hood, Elizabeth, **547.**
Hood, George, 183, 210, 222.
Hood, Thomas, 513.
Hood, Tunis, 5, 130, **547.**
Hooe, Gerald, 521.
Hoofman, Christopher, 84.
Hoofman, Honekil, 113.
Hoofman, Stophel, 53.
Hoofner, Christopher, 156.
Hooke (Hooks), George, **169, 171, 204,** 592.
Hook, Harmus, 53.
Hook, Jane, 126.
Hooke (Hooks), James, 131, 169, **192, 418,** 481, 503.
Hooke (Hookes), John, 205, 481, 503.
Hooke (Hookes), Robert, 7, 11, 14, **22,** 53, 58, 67, 68, 70, 126, 130, **192, 272,** 280, 287, 288, 297, 299, 305, 337, **351,** 353, 354, 369, 418, 449, 460, 503, **510.**
Hooke, William, 95, 151, 169, 171, **172,** 192, 369, 418, 511.
Hoop, Robert, 315.
Hoope, Randolph, 593.
Hooper, John, 166.
Hoos, Peter, 310.
Hoover, Jacob, 520.
Hope, Elizabeth, 84.
Hope, James, 51.
Hope (Hopes), John, 270, 274, **288, 289,** 291, 295, 338, 340, 368, 541.
Hope, Margaret, 51.
Hope, Nicholas, 236.
Hope, Rachel, 236.
Hopes, Mary, 274, 338.
Hophman, John N., 124.
Hopkins, Archibald, 87, 118, 138, 143, **195,** 345, 353, 398, 402, 418, 509.
Hopkins, David, 545.
Hopkins, Elizabeth, 376.
Hopkins, Ephraim, 195.
Hopkins, John, 62, 66, 82, 87, 118, **141, 143,** 376, 402, 418, 534.
Hopkins, Philip, 215.
Hopkins, Thomas, 402.
Hopkins, William, 18, 138, 270, 335, **376,** 494.
Horad, Samuel, 60.
Horbingson, William, 285.
Horbison, David, 564.
Horbush, George, 102.
Horn, Michael, 13.
Hornback, James, 53.
Hornback, Joel, 13, 28, 58.
Hornback, Simon, 53.
Hornbeck, Anthony, 112.
Hornbeck, Daniel, 141.
Hornbeck, Michael, 112.
Hornberrier, Elizabeth, 461.
Hornberrier, Jacob, 446, 461.
Horouff (Harrouff), Andrew, **231.**
Horschings (Houchings), William, **573.**
Horse, Henry, 84.
Horse, Peter, 53, 55, 391, 421.
Horse, Postle, 392.
Horse, Sarah, 84.
Horstone, Samuel, 338.
Hostler, Boston (Pouston), 113, **514.**
Hostler, Susannah, 514.
House, Mathias, 459.
Housen, Thomas, 22.
Housing, Dr., 29.
Hover (Hower), Barbara, **423, 490, 512,** 522.

Hover, Bouston (Boston), **43, 405.**
Hover, Castle, 83.
Hover (Hober, Hower), Michael, **366,** 423, 468, 490, 512, 513, 522, 523, **531,** 537.
Hover, Paslin, 57, 83.
Hover, Postle, 391, 405, 421.
Hover, Sebastian (Bastian), 67, 71, **84,** 94, 116, 125, 150, 374, 405, **421, 482,** 545.
Hoverstick (Haverstick), Adam, **459, 490,** 501, 533, 552.
Hovestick, Margrett, 501.
How, Joseph, 33, 118, 341.
How, Thomas, 270.
Howard, Beal, 198.
Howard, John, 482.
Howard, Judith, 488.
Howard, William, 79, 102, 400, **443, 459,** 488, 492.
Howe, Daniel, 586.
Howe, Madline, 116.
Howarth, Stephen, 274.
Huchens (Hutchens, Huchin), **John, 459,** 587.
Huchens, Martha, 459.
Huddle, George, 179.
Huddle, John, 567.
Hudlough (Herdlough, Hudloe, Hudlow), Andrew, 129, **516, 520.**
Hudlow, Mary, 520.
Hudson, Charles, 242.
Hudson, George, 249, 560, **562.**
Hudson, Jane, 242.
Hudson, John, 242.
Hudson, Joshua, 474, **486.**
Hudson, Mary, 242.
Hudson, Samuel, 116.
Hudson, Thomas, 104.
Hudson, William, 277, 317.
Huey (Hughey), James, 289, **328.**
Huey, Jane, 328.
Huff, Francis, 589.
Huff, Leonard, 103, 372, **429, 491.**
Huff, Thomas, 494.
Huffman, Conrad, 58.
Huffman, George, 417, 508, **510, 537.**
Huffman, Michael, 510, 537.
Huffman, Philip, 65.
Hufman, Horical, 65.
Hufman, Nicholas, 65.
Hugart (Hughart, Huggart), **James, 86,** 99, 103, 236, 571.
Hugart, Rebeccah, 384.
Hugart (Hughart, Huggart), **Thomas, 41,** 44, 49, 50, 78, 108, 110, 122, 137, **156,** 169, 175, 179, 182, 190, 213, 235, **384,** 392, 402, 413, 429, 437, 489, 530, **557,** 567, 571, 576, 583, 584, 587, 593.
Hugart (Huggart), William, 108, 392, **422,** 444, 453, 465.

Hugens, William, 44.
Huggart, Agness, 99.
Huggen, Daniel, 120.
Hughart, Patsey, 236.
Hughart, Margaret, 571.
Hughes, Barnibas, 131.
Hughes, Edward, 258, 263, 340.
Hughes, Elizabeth (Betsy), 167, **242.**
Hughes, Euphemia (Uphemia), 96, **217,** 369, 389, 431, 496, 497, 577, **581.**
Hughes, Even, 28.
Hughes, Francis, 269.
Hughes (Hughs, Huse), **James, 59, 61,** 70, 96, 98, 100, 102, 132, 361, 365, **369,** 389, 390, 392, 397, 398, 410, 413, **415,** 431, 439, 476, 496, 497, 504, 536, **540,** 548, 562, 577, 582.
Hughes, Jenny, 577.
Hughes, John, 63, 70, 73, 315, **356, 478,** 553.
Hughes, **Margaret, 96.**
Hughes, Mary, 577.
Hughes, Moses, 242.
Hughes, Samuel, 102, 282.
Hughes, Sarah, 478.
Hughes, Thomas, 134, 573.
Hughes, Timothy, 543.
Hughes, William, 150, 529.
Hughson, John, 167.
Hugler, Boston, 405.
Hulet, James, 593.
Huling(s), Andrew, 113, **472.**
Hull, Barbara, 224.
Hull, Daniel, 224, 232.
Hull, Francis, 232, 554, 555.
Hull, Frederick, 232.
Hull, George, 195.
Hull, John, 232.
Hull, Peter, 195, 305, 351, 412, 480, **570.**
Hull, Samuel, 7, 15, 51, 113, **114.**
Hull, Susanna, 232, 351, 412.
Hulse, James P., 584.
Humbert, Jacob, 251.
Humble, Charity, 498.
Humble, Conrad, 115, 135, 148, **150, 152,** 408, 433, 498, 551, 552.
Humble, Martin, 135, 148, 152, **408, 441.**
Humble, Michael, 133.
Humble, Uriah, 22, 36, 40, 43, 77, **123,** 345, 346, 406, 498.
Hume, G., 307.
Hume, John, 394.
Hume, Peter, 573.
Humphrey, David, 160, 525.
Humphry (Humphries), Uriah, **120, 490.**
Humphreys, Alexander, 181, 184, **197, 200,** 201, 202, 209, 589.
Humphreys, Bishop, 213.
Humphreys, James, 9, 404, 409, **487, 555,** 576, 578.
Humphreys, Joshua, 525, 545, 553.

Humphreys, Mary, 200.
Humphreys, Wiliam, 9, 451.
Humphries, John, 81.
Hungate, Ann, 12, 18.
Hungate, Charles, 12, 15.
Hunt, Charles, 178, 551, 556, 566.
Hunter, Alexander, 594.
Hunter, Andrew, 183, 205, 226, 237, 240.
Hunter, Ann, 212.
Hunter, Charles B., 564.
Hunter, Elizabeth, 256.
Hunter, Francis, 135, 226, 499, 504.
Hunter, Henry, 135, 226, 240.
Hunter, Hugh, 135.
Hunter, Isabella, 553.
Hunter, James, 52, 57, 360, 553.
Hunter, John, 43, 44, 71, 135, 226, 240, 361, 362, 377, 402, 403, 416, 432, 448, 474, 499, 504, 537, 556.
Hunter, Margaret, 180.
Hunter, Martha, 226.
Hunter, Mathew, 226, 240.
Hunter, Miles, 556.
Hunter, Nat, 212.
Hunter, Robert, 135, 226, 237, 361, 362, 416, 499.
Hunter, Samuel, 86, 87, 135, 144, 146, 162, 183, 184, 188, 208, 226, 240, 350, 361, 403, 499, 521.
Hunter, Susannah, 240.
Hunter, William, 30, 52, 220, 240.
Huntman, John, 146.
Hunton, Frances, 555.
Hunton, John, 548, 551, 555.
Huntsman, Lawrence, 59, 80, 81, 84.
Hupp, Philip, 53.
Hurst, Judith, 274.
Hurst, William, 291, 294.
Huse, Aaron, 383.
Huston, Agness, 365, 421.
Huston, Ann, 62.
Huston, Archibald, 52, 59, 63, 64, 66, 67, 68, 70, 79, 80, 85, 87, 88, 103, 113, 114, 118, 123, 124, 125, 129, 130, 132, 136, 137, 161, 166, 282, 313, 397, 413, 455, 509, 523, 531.
Huston, Benjamin, 236.
Huston, David, 413.
Huston, Elizabeth, 62.
Huston, Esther, 62.
Huston, George, 136, 151, 156, 192, 510, 531, 551.
Huston, Hugh, 413.
Huston, James, 54, 62, 93, 136, 264, 315, 365, 415, 421, 431, 443, 447, 448, 454, 499, 504, 531, 536, 562.
Huston, John, 14, 30, 34, 35, 45, 62, 132, 136, 142, 263, 265, 267, 287, 304, 315, 340, 361, 422, 464, 481, 520, 531, 546, 551, 570.
Huston, Joseph, 236.

Huston, Margaret, 34, 62.
Huston, Martha, 570.
Huston, Mary, 23, 62, 136, 455.
Huston, Mathew, 34, 78, 88, 148, 152, 352, 368, 402, 428, 464, 465, 570.
Huston, Nathan, 136, 151.
Huston, Rebeka, 137.
Huston, Robert, 24, 50, 62, 66, 266, 271, 287, 296, 304, 324, 350, 358, 359.
Huston (Houston), Samuel, 34, 50, 51, 62, 76, 79, 143, 148, 152, 273, 287, 304, 305, 313, 322, 333, 340, 341, 352, 388, 402, 415, 515.
Huston, Sarah (Sally), 236, 304.
Huston, Stephen, 136, 166, 341.
Houston, William, 578.
Hutchenson, Jane, 577, 578.
Hutcheson, Betsy, 233.
Hutcheson (Hutchison, Hutchinson), George, 8, 167, 233, 254, 278, 282, 297, 316, 327, 334, 340, 348, 360, 391, 402, 432, 453, 458, 459, 552, 592.
Hutcheson, John, 43, 49, 57, 208, 271, 282, 290, 296, 316, 322, 334, 340, 346, 343, 360, 401, 425, 432, 439, 458, 459, 546, 548.
Hutcheson, Margaret (Peggy), 231, 247, 322, 546, 548.
Hutcheson, Martha, 246.
Hutcheson, Mary, 334.
Hutcheson, Sarah, 123, 142, 172, 178, 205, 448, 539, 577, 578.
Hutcheson, Thomas, 123, 125, 142, 178, 448, 539, 577, 581.
Hutcheson, William, 5, 37, 119, 120, 127, 161, 162, 167, 290, 306, 340, 346, 354, 401, 436, 458, 459, 472, 492, 521, 534, 546, 552, 589.
Hutchinson, Eleanor, 254, 316.
Hutchinson, Frances, 8.
Hutchinson, Isabell, 94, 432, 459.
Hutchinson, James, 354, 467, 596.
Hutchinson, Jannet, 8.
Hutchison, Ann, 290, 340, 401.
Hutchison, Agnes, 123, 340, 346, 577, 578.
Hutchison, Ro, 246.
Hutson, Isbela, 135.
Hutson, Margaret, 135.
Hutson, Robert, 375.
Hutson, Thomas, 109, 135.
Hutton, Ally, 435.
Hutton, Andrew, 553.
Hutton, James, 110, 117, 379, 435.
Hyde, William, 100, 387, 397, 402, 417, 493.
Hyer, Ridle, 28.
Hyleton, Charles, 315.
Hynds, Anne, 152.
Hynds, Edward, 152, 156.
Hynds, Elizabeth, 152.
Hynds, Jenny, 152.

Inglebird, George, 491.
Ingleman, Peter, 216.
Ingleman (Engleman), Philip, 166, 217.
Ingles, Alexander, 417.
Ingles, John, 65.
Ingles (Inglish), Patrick, 67, **72.**
Ingles (Ingless, English), Thomas, 17, 18, 24, 26, 74, 85.
Inglish, Elizabeth, 491.
Ingleton, Anthony, 200, 589.
Ingram (Ingraham), Abraham, **586, 587.**
Ingram, Alexander, 25, 50, 301, **308, 309,** 340, 429.
Ingram, John, 308.
Ingram, William, 308.
Inman, Ezekiah, 36, 47.
Inman, Lazarus, 117, **157, 360.**
Inzer, Elizabeth, 475.
Ipsher, Ludwick, 401.
Ipsher (Ipher), Peter, **117, 401.**
Irwin, Margret, 244.
Irwin, Martha, 244.
Irvin, Nickle, **244.**
Irvin, Rebecca, 244.
Isaac, David, 211.
Isaac, Elisha, 74, 309, 310, 331, **423, 437.**
Isbell, Zachary, 338.
Isrel, Solomon, 187.

Jack, Catherine, 136.
Jack, John, 188.
Jack, Patrick, 351.
Jackson, Aaron, 5.
Jackson, Christopher, 5.
Jackson, David, 224.
Jackson, Elizabeth, 492.
Jackson, Francis, 87, 99, 119, **427, 463, 492.**
Jackson, James, 24, 104, 349.
Jackson, Jane, 21, 26.
Jackson, Jesse, 453.
Jackson, John, 24, 103, 144, 224, **238, 474,** 537, 543, 566, 590.
Jackson, Margaret (Peggy), **224, 245.**
Jackson, Martha, 537.
Jackson, Mary, 66, 127, 349.
Jackson, Robert, 41.
Jackson, Samuel, 74, 224, **238, 245.**
Jackson, Thomas, 129, 132, 224, 240, **493.**
Jackson, William, 21, 28, 37, 326, **427,** 492, 527, 528, 566, 567, 584.
Jaeger (Taeger, Teager), Andrew, **563.**
Jaffrey, George, 144.
James (Jemes, Jeames), Daniel, 272, **274,** 383, 441, 455, 456, 478, 487, **515, 549.**
James, David, 144.
James, James, 162.
James, Jane, 313.
James, Joseph, 13.
James, Joshua, 13.
James, Sarah, 13.
James, Thomas, 13, 83.

James (Jeames, Jemes), William, **5, 6, 8,** 9, 11, 13, 14, 15, 17, 158.
Jameson, George, 27, 80, 115, 117, **135,** 145, 148, 411.
Jameson, Jane (Jean), 71, 242.
Jameson, Margaret, 241, 493.
Jameson, William, 27, 91, 99, 105, **189,** 247, 268, 273, 280, 306, 418, 420, **453,** 473, 493.
Jamison, Andrew, 27, 202.
Jamison, James, 247.
Jamison, John, 27, 62, 68, 72, 73, 91, **139,** 142, 247, 278, 281, 302, 360, **422, 429,** 434, 489, 493, 565.
Jamison, Mary, 434.
Jamison, Mathew, 247.
Jamison, Robert, 167, 189, 500, **511, 522,** 535.
Jamison, Samuel, 247.
Jamison, Sarah (Sally), 27, **247, 511.**
Jankins, John, 102.
Jannet (Jennet), John, 6, 9.
Jarid, William, 579.
Jarvin (Garvin), David, **145.**
Jarvis, Elizabeth, 586.
Jarvis, John J., 406.
Jarvis, Thomas, 586.
Jasper, John, 167, 171.
Jeehon, Nicholas, 397.
Jefferson, Peter, 6.
Jefferson, Thomas, 462.
Jenkin, Abraham, 132.
Jenkins, Andrew, 167.
Jenkins, Joseph, 68.
Jennings, Gibbons, 259, 262, 290, **345, 403.**
Jennings, William, 53.
Jeremiah, John, 79, 100, 421.
Jervis, James, 121.
Jewell, Joseph, 199, 584.
Job (Jobe), Abraham, **6, 15, 17, 21.**
Job, Barbara, 14, 17.
Job, Caleb, 17.
Job, David, 17, 18.
Job, Elisha, 17.
Job, Elizabeth, 17, 18.
Job, Hannah, 17.
Job, Isaac, 17, 18, 106.
Job (Jobe), Jacob, 17, **65.**
Job, Joshua, 25.
Job, Margaret, 25.
Job (Jobb), Martin, 53, 121.
Job, Nathan, 17.
Job, Phoeby, 17.
Job, Rebecca, 17.
Job, Samuel, 17.
Johns, Isaac, 571, 583.
Johns, Joshua, 103.
Johns, William, 571.
Johnson (Johnston), **Andrew, 54, 98, 107,** 118, 274, 277, 287, 297, 363, 374, **400,**

405, 431, 454, 459, 476, 487, 504, 508, 545.
Johnson (Johnston), Anthony, 156, 505, 553, 559, 561, 565.
Johnson (Johnston), Arthur, 15, 48, 50, 54, 56, 65, 71, 72, 78, 282, 504.
Johnson, Chapman, 226.
Johnson (Johnston), Daniel, 383, 479, 512, 552.
Johnson (Johnston), David, 276, 294, 340.
Johnson (Johnston), Eleanor, 174, 193, 198.
Johnson (Johnston), Esther, 224, 234.
Johnson, Gennet, 71.
Johnson (Johnston), Isaac, 11, 39, 47, 92.
Johnson (Johnston), James, 39, 41, 61, 88, 89, 106, 115, 205, 209, 356, 383, 390, 479, 512.
Johnson (Jonson, Johnston), Jane (Jean), 54, 174, 224, 232, 248.
Johnson (Jonson, Johnston), John, 11, 13, 42, 54, 78, 118, 119, 174, 206, 215, 238, 248, 277, 325, 335, 351, 366, 368, 378, 406, 442, 445, 504, 541, 542, 555, 573, 584, 585.
Johnson, Joseph, 174.
Johnson (Jonson, Johnston), Margaret, 54, 65, 72, 174, 198.
Johnson (Johnston), Mary, 42, 54, 68, 119, 159, 199, 235, 335, 383, 389, 504.
Johnson (Johnston), Michael, 119, 291.
Johnson, Rebeckah, 174, 294.
Johnson, Rose, 389.
Johnson (Jonson), Sarah, 54, 174.
Johnson, Susanna, 479.
Johnson (Johnston), William, 22, 42, 43, 48, 51, 57, 59, 68, 94, 119, 123, 158, 171, 174, 189, 198, 202, 226, 227, 232, 254, 278, 279, 281, 282, 284, 286, 289, 295, 317, 330, 354, 357, 371, 378, 381, 289, 406, 423, 442, 467, 482, 495, 520, 550.
Johnston, Ann, 61, 179, 330, 482, 550, 577, 594.
Johnston, Arwaker, 359, 366.
Johnston, Barnabas, 550.
Johnston, Benjamin, 7, 256, 263, 264, 266.
Johnston, Hannah, 11.
Johnston (Johnson), Hugh, 105, 116, 406, 416, 439, 447, 448, 454, 514, 519, 557.
Johnston, Richard, 235.
Johnston, Rosannah, 121.
Johnston, Samuel, 544.
Johnston, Stephen, 45.
Johnston, Thomas, 8, 180, 594.
Johnston, Zachariah, 61, 123, 179, 185, 196, 279, 383, 459, 482, 529, 550, 571, 577, 585, 594.
Jones, Ann, 208.
Jones, Benjamin, 544.
Jones, Catherine, 228.
Jones, David, 95.

Jones, Eleanor, 251.
Jones, Elizabeth, 416.
Jones, Enos (Eness), 194, 229, 554, 565.
Jones, Evan, 206.
Jones, Gabriel, 6, 25, 34, 37, 39, 77, 85, 89, 94, 129, 140, 206, 255, 256, 257, 259, 260, 261, 264, 266, 290, 295, 300, 312, 318, 357, 383, 394, 395, 398, 406, 436, 444, 448, 459, 461, 466, 477, 480, 482, 485, 489, 504, 521, 529.
Jones, Hannah, 188.
Jones, Howel, 40.
Jones, Isaac, 21, 23, 243.
Jones, Isaiah, 229.
Jones, James, 33.
Jones, Jane, 530.
Jones, Jemima, 229.
Jones (Joans), John, 29, 49, 51, 79, 145, 294, 312, 336, 370, 416, 486, 507, 543.
Jones, John G., 485, 497, 503.
Jones, Jones, 165, 355.
Jones, Joshua, 251.
Jones, Lydia, 229.
Jones, Margaret, 208, 395, 444.
Jones, Peter, 229.
Jones, Robert, 229, 583, 585.
Jones, Sarah, 229, 231.
Jones (Joans), Thomas, 81, 90, 95, 102, 137, 167, 371, 538, 539, 543.
Jones, Valentine, 149.
Jones, William, 221.
Jordan, Andrew, 214, 580.
Jordan, Ann, 580.
Jordan, John, 81, 137, 150, 157, 553, 565, 580, 590.
Jordan, Mary, 560.
Jordan, William, 53, 128, 150, 167, 194, 505, 550, 553, 560, 561, 565, 580.
Jordone, Francis, 493.
Joseph, Daniel, 171, 216, 567, 569, 573, 592.
Joseph, Eve, 216, 569, 573, 592.
Joseph, Zephli, 40.
Jouett, John, 167.
Jsaton (Isaton), William, 159.
Judd, William, 404.
Judy, Henry, 141, 156, 495, 517.
Judy (Juddy, Juda, Juty), Martin, 141, 156, 405, 495, 517.
Judy, Nicholas, 141, 495.
Judy, Rosanna, 495.
Julias (Julius), Henry, 531.
Julius, Jacob, 531.
Justice, John, 302, 326, 360.

Kailor, James, 553.
Kairn (Karin), Nicholas, 522, 537.
Karsnar, Caspar, 543.
Kaufman, Barbara, 11.
Kaufman, David, 11.
Kaufman, Martin, 11, 14.
Kaufman, Michael, 11.

Kavanaugh, William, **438.**
Kaylor, Frederick, 530.
Kayser, James D., **236.**
Kayser, Martin, 449.
Keachy, James, 64.
Keal, David, 167.
Kear, Alexander, 238.
Kear, James, 238.
Kear, Jean, 238.
Kear, John, 238.
Kearr, Henry, 26.
Keasy, Archibald, 180.
Keely, Anthony, 435.
Keenan, Nelly, 167.
Keenan (Kenan), Patrick, **41, 210.**
Keening, Rose, 131.
Keenon, Hugh, **582.**
Keenon (Keening), John, **543, 582.**
Keer, Samuel, 23.
Keesle (Keesil, Keezell), George, **161,** 493, 536.
Keester (Kiester), Frederick, **127, 408.**
Keester (Kaster), Paul, **135.**
Keglan, John, 587.
Keith, Isaac S., 239.
Keith, John, 233.
Kella, Barbara, 250.
Kellar, George, 216, 553.
Kelley, Anna, 46.
Kelley, Margaret, 103, 435.
Kelly, Alexander, 60, 121, **468, 515.**
Kelly, Anthony, 103, 159, **406.**
Kelly, Cathereen, 139.
Kelly, Christopher, 26.
Kelly, Elizabeth M. Elwrath, 103.
Kelly, Henry, 219.
Kelly, James, 167.
Kelly, John, 103, 433, 457, **495, 529, 561.**
Kelly, Nathaniel, 539.
Kelly, Rebecca, 103, 159.
Kelly, Samuel, 103, 121, **495, 529.**
Kelly, Terence, 511.
Kelly, William, 103, 104, 120, **391, 435.**
Keloffer, Christopher, 190.
Kelso, Charles, 231, 379.
Kelso (Kelsey), Hugh, 102, 121, **135, 249,** 406, **495, 508, 521.**
Kelso, James, 591.
Kelso, Polly, 231.
Kennedy, Andrew, 86, 181, **380, 393,** 411, 524, 564, 579.
Kennedy, Arthur, 327, 335, **398.**
Kennedy, Elizabeth, 327, 333.
Kennedy, James, 69, 360, 380, **396, 407,** 426, 442, 565.
Kennedy, Jane (Jeane), 335, **336.**
Kennedy, John, 18, 393.
Kennedy (Canady), Joseph, 10, **14, 20,** 28, 31, 34, 48, 256, 273, 290, **299, 301,** 302, 303, 304, 306, 311, 327, **332, 333,** 335, 340, 349, 361, 363, 377, **380, 398,** 411, 436, 439, 442, 478, **511, 516.**

Kennedy, Margaret, 96.
Kennedy, Martha, 146, 171, **368.**
Kennedy, Mathew, 170.
Kennedy, William, 83, 90, 111, 146, **210,** 246, 327, 333, 352, 363, 368, 380, **396,** 410, 411, 439, 450, 565, 569, 586.
Kenner, James, 589.
Kennerley, Benjamin, 212, 221, 250.
Kennerley, Catren (Kitty), 238, **564.**
Kennerley, James, 122, 204, 236, **250, 275,** 481, 495, 501, 509, 545, 564.
Kennerley, John, 446, 545.
Kennerley, John J., 507.
Kennerley, Joseph, 27, 315.
Kennerley, Mary, 545.
Kennerley, Mary M., 275.
Kennerley, Philip, 223.
Kennerley, Reuben, 221, 250, 575.
Kennerly, Samuel, 250.
Kennerley, Thomas, 250, 275, 298, 561, **564,**
Kennerley, William, 206, 250, 545, **561,** 564, 582, 586.
Kennin, Charles, 159.
Kenny, Bryan, 131, 567.
Kear, Thomas, 135.
Keplinger, Johannis, 356, 366.
Kerkendall (Kuykendale), Benjamin, **19,** 406.
Kerler, Sarah, 246.
Kern, Michael, 531, 548.
Kern (Keern), Nicholas, 132, **135.**
Kerns, Alexander, 232.
Kerns, Katherine, 232.
Kerr, Andrew, 306, 319, 371, 380, **385.**
Kerr, Ann, 315.
Kerr, Catherine (Katherine), 311, **327,** 479.
Kerr, David, 311, 315, 327, 335, **479, 556,** 558, 563.
Kerr (Karr, Carr), Gilbert, 576.
Kerr, James, 75, 110, 113, 123, **127, 142,** 154, 165, 187, 188, 198, 202, 204, **286,** 302, 306, 357, 366, 377, 386, 412, **510,** 525, 568.
Kerr, Jes, 369.
Kerr (Keer), John, 113, 223, 254, **277, 286,** 297, 303, 306, 311, 315, 328, 357, **369,** 371, 407, 412, 418, 567, 476, 479, **494,** 497, 501, 517, 525, 583.
Kerr, Joseph, 153.
Kerr, Lucy, 277, 369, 371, 467.
Kerr, Margaret, 328, 558.
Kerr, Martha, 467.
Kerr, Mary, 153, 174.
Kerr, Rachel, 380, 385.
Kerr, Richard, 28, 74, 388.
Kerr, William, 47, 60, 82, 101, 120, **149,** 154, 174, 268, 298, 313, 319, 369, **371,** 385, 412, 467, 558, 573, 579, 583.
Kersh, Mathias, 103, 110, 122, 493.
Kersner, George, 533, 552, 547.
Kess, John, 361.

Kessenger, Mathias, 464.
Kester, Arnold, 53.
Kester, Richard, 135.
Kestor, Fardrick, 62.
Kether, Rose, 207.
Key, Henry, 458.
Keys, Agness, 528.
Keyes, Hamp, 215.
Keyl, Peter, 531.
Keyla, Alexander, 393.
Keyls, Jacob, 120.
Keys, Anne, 35.
Keys, Benjamin, 81, 463.
Keys, John, 31, 81, 313, 368, 528.
Keys, Margaret, 81, 82.
Keys, Nicholas, 76.
Keys, Roger, 31, 33, 35, 78, 81, 83, 271, 276, 313, 326, 336, 403.
Keys, Samuel, 39, 81.
Keys, Sarah, 35, 81, 82.
Keyster, Frederick, 55.
Kiblinger, Jacob, 472.
Kice (Rice), Betsy, 233.
Kice, George, 233.
Kice (Rice), Polly, 233.
Kidd, Anne, 402.
Kidd, Daniel, 84, 133, 134, 135, 137, 138, 140, 142, 149, 154, 163, 174, 178, 195, 297, 391, 402, 408, 409, 410, 415, 453, 459, 471, 484, 492, 496, 516, 530, 540, 550, 587, 589.
Kidd, Frances, 108, 111.
Kidd, William, 476.
Kidney (Cidney), Daniel, 29, 278, 297.
Kiff, Barberry, 503.
Kiff, George M., 503.
Kighter, John, 74.
Kilburn, James, 299.
Kile (Kyle), Alexander, 94, 352, 379.
Kile, David, 144.
Kile, Peter, 144.
Kilkeney, John, 231.
Kilkeney, Sarah, 231.
Kilkny, Peggy, 221.
Killpatrick, Jenet, 593.
Killpatrick, William, 593.
Kilpatrick, Alexander, 177, 463, 513, 548.
Kilpatrick, Charles, 84, 99, 339.
Kilpatrick, James, 189.
Kilpatrick, John, 189.
Kilpatrick, Mary, 548.
Kilpatrick, Robert, 136, 159, 287, 492.
Kilpatrick, Roger, 99, 115, 447, 463.
Kilpatrick, Thomas, 189, 433.
Kimberland, Jacob, 91.
Kimberland, Mary M., 91.
Kimmins, Joseph, 50.
Kimsey, Benjamin, 100.
Kimsey, Elizabeth, 52.
Kimsey, William, 492.
Kimsley, Conrad, 69.

Kinder, Conrad, 73, 321.
Kinder, Gasper, 67.
Kinder, George, 349, 390.
Kinder, Jacob, 15.
Kinder, Mary, 9.
Kinder, Michael, 73, 321, 390.
Kinder, Peter, 9, 12, 16, 50, 133, 330, 412, 478, 503.
King, Adam, 240.
King, Catherine, 14, 23, 30, 270, 508, 524.
King, Charity, 225.
King, Elizabeth, 14, 23, 507, 524.
King, Fany, 244.
King, George, 165, 565, 581.
King, Henry (Harry), 118, 168, 173, 186, 204, 244, 248, 369, 389, 589.
King, Isaac, 244.
King, Isabella, 225.
King, James, 139, 208, 586.
King, John, 14, 23, 70, 83, 92, 96, 108, 109, 174, 208, 211, 225, 261, 280, 310, 353, 368, 404, 407, 410, 413, 414, 438, 440, 441, 453, 458, 464, 465, 498, 500, 503, 507, 508, 509, 511, 543, 580, 585, 586, 588.
King, Joseph, 108, 110.
King, Margaret, 208, 225, 230.
King, Mary, 240, 248, 353, 407, 441, 458, 507, 509.
King, Mary A., 299.
King, Nelly, 108, 210, 589.
King, Nicholas, 108.
King, Robert, 14, 23, 30, 165, 208, 240, 257, 264, 270, 280, 337, 391, 394, 398, 507, 524, 561.
King, Samuel, 148, 208, 585.
King, Sarah, 14, 240, 524.
King, Susannah, 248.
King, Thomas, 240.
King, William, 14, 207, 225, 240, 277, 278, 292, 299, 302, 313, 345, 373, 414, 587, 588, 590.
Kingin, John, 156, 561.
Kinkade, George, 43, 55.
Kinkade, Leona (Lena), 457.
Kinkead, Andrew, 25, 38, 134, 141, 233, 500, 505, 513, 518, 530, 546, 555, 574, 590, 595.
Kinkead, Ann, 80, 202.
Kinkead, Anna H., 443, 500.
Kinkead, Archibald, 587.
Kinkead, Burrows, 80, 83.
Kinkead, David, 22, 75, 110, 145, 417, 499, 513, 570.
Kinkead, Elizabeth, 145, 370, 499, 503, 504, 513, 518, 546, 582.
Kinkead, Hannah, 546.
Kinkead, James, 513, 518.
Kinkead, Jean, 503.
Kinkead, John, 40, 107, 120, 122, 145, 182, 316, 330, 344, 379, 392, 413, 417, 443,

492, 499, 503, 504, 513, 518, **546, 570,** 574, 575.
Kinkead, Joseph, 53, 80, 126, 167, 385, **396,** 500, 505, 555.
Kinkead, Margaret, 344, **575.**
Kinkead, Mary, 555.
Kinkead, Mary A., 145.
Kinkead, Mathew, 143, 145, **148, 443, 457,** 504, 513, 518, 570.
Kinkead, Rebecca, 555.
Kinkead, Robert, 73, 77, 152, 397, **443, 457**, 482, 500.
Kinkead, Samuel, 68, 326, 341, 418, **485,** 575, 582.
Kinkead, Sarah, 145, 574.
Kinkead, Thomas, 30, 121, 330, **443, 499,** 503, 505, 523, 546, 584, 587.
Kinkead, William, 30, 108, 139, 141, **145,** 150, 344, 385, 413, 439, 436, 489, **492,** 499, 523, 530, 587.
Kinkead, Winifred, 499.
Kinley, Benjamin, 42, 147, 282, **292, 295,** 390, 408, 494, 506, 509, 552.
Kinnear, Agness, 144.
Kinnear (Krimer), Andrew, 144, 145, **148,** 528, 547.
Kinney, Agnes, 227.
Kinney, Chesley, 212.
Kinney, Elizabeth, 227.
Kinney, Jacob, 198, 200, 201, **202, 209, 210,** 215, 217, 230, 231, 234, 477.
Kinney (Kenny), James, 161, 164, **227,** 235.
Kinney, John, 227.
Kinney (Kenny), Mathew, 154, **155, 193,** 201, 202, 411, 513, 536, 559.
Kinney, Patrick, 94.
Kinney, Patience, 227.
Kinney, Phebe, 202, 227.
Kinney, Rebecca, 227.
Kinney (Kenny), Robert, 142, 154, **168,** 174, 176, 179, 184, 187, 188, 193, 194, 198, 200, 201, 202, 206, 211, 227, **283,** 411, 445, 513, 532, 548, 568, 571, **594.**
Kinode, John, 207.
Kinseys, Abigail, 19.
Kintner, George, 115, 541.
Kintner, Michael, 115, 541.
Kipp, George, 530.
Kipp, John G., 501.
Kirk, Agnes, 465.
Kirk, Alexander, 141, 142, 165, 465, **509,** 510, 562.
Kirk, George, 193.
Kirk, James, 25, 112, 145, 165, 192, **193,** 220, 232, 273, 353, 465, 509, 510, 562.
Kirk, Jane (Jean), 145, 165, 193, 208, **220,** 232, 510.
Kirk, John, 142, 165, 193, 206, 208, **220,** 233, 393, 403, 435, 443, 453, 465, 500, 509, 562, 591.
Kirk, Margaret, 164, 509.
Kirk, Martha, 165, 237.
Kirk, Mary, 208.
Kirk, Mary Ann, 220, **232.**
Kirk, Mathew, 208.
Kirk, Patrick, 523.
Kirk, Rachel, 220.
Kirk, Rachel Bell, 241.
Kirk, Robert, 165, 237.
Kirk, William, 220, 233.
Kirk, William B., 241.
Kirkham, Elizabeth, 12, **90, 350.**
Kirkham (Kircum), Hannah, 36, 350, **409,**
Kirkam, Henry, 5, 12, 32, 47, 48, 90, 91, 92, 109, 275, 288, 302, 407.
Kerkham, Henry H., 356.
Kirkham, Jane (Jean), 90, **350.**
Kirkham, John, 90, 91.
Kirkham, Joseph, 90.
Kirkham, Margaret, 12, **90,** 288.
Kirkham, Mary, 90, 109.
Kirkham (Kirkum), Michael, **5, 90.**
Kirkham, Nancy, 12.
Kirkham, Robert, 5, 12, **14, 36, 38, 74,** 90, 104, 309, 350.
Kirkham, Samuel, 90, 469.
Kirkham, Sarah, 12.
Kirkland, John, 431.
Kirkland, Rachel, 233.
Kirkpatrick, Agness, 563.
Kirkpatrick, Alexander, **404, 447.**
Kirkpatrick, Anny, 240, 245.
Kirkpatrick, Charles, 404, 475.
Kirkpatrick, George, 245.
Kirkpatrick, James, 240, 245, **521, 563.**
Kirkpatrick, John, 30, 68, 86, 164, 240, **337,** 360, 441, 475, 528, 539.
Kirkpatrick, Margret, 159, 227.
Kirkpatrick, Martha, 240, **245, 539.**
Kirkpatrick, Nancy, 240.
Kirkpatrick, Polly, 240.
Kirkpatrick, Robert, 287, **290, 304, 469.**
Kirkpatrick, Samuel, 520.
Kirkpatrick, Thomas, 26, 68, 81, 240, **245,** 279, 281, 290, 332, 337, 342, 441.
Kirtley, Elizabeth, 137, 409, **494, 496.**
Kirtley (Kirkley), Francis, **44, 67, 69, 113,** 137, 140, 142, 267, 287, 327, 328, 337, 384, 391, 408, 409, **447, 457, 460, 494,** 496, 505, 540, 559, **579.**
Kirtley, Honorius P., 137.
Kirtley, James, 384, 394, **447.**
Kirtley, John, 136, 137, **540, 579.**
Kirtley, Sinkle, 137.
Kirtley, Thomas, 327, 337, **394.**
Kirtley, William, 137, 337, **540, 579.**
Kiser, Henry, 145.
Kislin, Catherine, 133.
Kislin, Christiana, 133.
Kislin, Elizabeth, 133.
Kislin, Henry, 133.

Kislin, John, 133.
Kislin, Mathew, 133.
Kislin, Teterick, 133.
Kisling (Kislin), Christopher, 133, 151.
Kisling, John, 151, 547, 589.
Kislinger (Kishlinger), Christopher, 57, 134.
Kislinger, John, 522.
Kiss, John, 517.
Kissel, George, 535.
Kister, Frederick, 414.
Kister, Hannah, 414.
Kitchey, John, 124.
Kite, William, 510.
Kittrick, Adam, 47.
Kizer, Lettis, 197.
Kizer, Joseph D., 238.
Knapp, Moses, 176.
Knave, Dochther, 131.
Knave, Leonard, 53, 121.
Knight, Charles, 94, 99, 335.
Knoling, Andrew, 13.
Knowles, Archibald, 238.
Knowles, Catherine, 238.
Knowles, Daniel, 238.
Knowles, John, 30, 196, 238.
Knowles, Mary (Polly), 238.
Knowles, Sarah, 238.
Knowles, Susan, 238.
Knowles, William, 238.
Knox, Abigail, 123.
Knox, Elisha, 149.
Knox, Elizabeth, 123.
Knox, James, 5, 84, 86, 123, 380, 427, 441, 489.
Knox, Jane (Jean), 123, 427, 489.
Knox, John, 123.
Knox, Mary, 123.
Knox, Robert, 123, 413, 427, 441.
Koogler, George, 148.
Kook, Paul, 579.
Koontz, Elizabeth, 229.
Koontz, Michael, 229.
Koontz, William, 246.
Korp, Christian, 147.
Kountz, John, 246.
Kountz, Paul, 246.
Kountz, Peter, 246.
Kowan, James, 357.
Kring, John, 533, 553.
Krouse, Daniel, 192.
Kuhn, Peter, 583, 589, 591.
Kulpatrick, Michael, 247.
Kulpatrick, Samuel, 247.
Kurter, Arnold, 43.
Kurtz, John, 364.
Kuykendall, Ab, 152.
Kuykendall, James, 13.
Kuykendall, John, 13.
Kyle, Jane E., 169.
Kyle, Robert, 364.

Kyles, Joseph, 55.
Kyne, Michael, 392.

Labourn, Edward, 36.
Lackey, Dorcus, 153.
Lackey, Elizabeth, 507.
Lackey (Lakey, Leckey), James, 155, 461, 507, 513.
Lackie, Margaret, 248.
Lacky, Thomas, 521.
Lade, Edward, 171.
Lafone, Randall, 93.
Laghlin, Archibald, 162.
Lair, Andrew, 553.
Lair, Barbara, 129.
Lair, Catherine, 104, 128.
Lair, Ferdinando, 104, 129.
Lair, George, 104.
Lair, Joseph, 478, 553.
Lair, Margaret, 104.
Lair (Lear), Mathias, 88, 104, 128, 129, 478.
Laird, Ann, 249.
Laird (Lard, Leard), David, 94, 126, 131, 132, 136, 143, 249, 250, 355, 362, 497, 503, 529, 584.
Laird (Leard, Lard), James, 56, 57, 86, 162, 166, 208, 249, 362, 412, 467, 494, 564.
Laird, Samuel, 249.
Lamb, Abraham, 230, 235.
Lamb, Arbibald, 106.
Lamb, Catherine, 459.
Lamb, Conord (Conrod), 349, 459.
Lamb, Elin, 235.
Lamb (Lamme), Elizabeth, 187, 230.
Lamb (Lam), John, 193, 230.
Lamb, Michael, 115.
Lamb (Lamme), William, 11, 17, 60, 96, 131, 272, 274, 280, 348, 350, 367, 369, 382, 391, 411, 477, 495, 503, 535, 537, 539.
Lanier, Mary, 200.
Lamir (Lamor, Lanier), Jacob, 200.
Lamm, Nathan, 144.
Lamma, Anna, 411.
Lammar, William, 144.
Lamme, James, 218, 220, 411.
Lamme, Robert, 249.
Lancaster, John, 94.
Lance, Amy, 175.
Lance (Lince), Barnard, 100, 158, 175.
Lance, Barnet, 195, 581.
Lance, Chreestiania, 175.
Lance, Elizabeth, 175.
Lance, George, 175, 581.
Lance, Joseph, 158, 175, 581.
Lance, Margaret, 175.
Lance, Mary, 175.
Lancisco, Henry, 28, 30, 292, 340, 517.
Landon, Charlson, 462.

Landrum, John, 253.
Lane, Aaron (Aron), 521, 523.
Lane, Joseph, 312, 317, 330, 524.
Lane, Margaret, 312.
Lane, Thomas, 342.
Lane, William, 567.
Langdon, Ann, 118.
Langdon, Jonathan, 83, 101.
Langdon, Joseph, 16, 92, 101.
Langdon, Thomas, 516.
Lange, Charles, 518.
Lange, Arsilla, 518.
Lanlap, Samuel, 36.
Lansley, James, 157.
Lao, John W., 159.
Laporte, Peter, 246.
Lapsley, John, 33, 50, 342, 344.
Lapsley (Lapley), Joseph, 38, 41, 47, 48, 64, 81, 82, 87, 263, 265, 268, 288, 292, 304, 314, 329, 342, 349, 407, 443.
Lapsley, Mary, 144.
Lapsley, Samuel, 378, 555.
Lapslie, William, 344.
Larderson, George, 421.
Larew, Abraham, 207, 220, 237, 558.
Larew, Anny (Anna), 220, 237.
Larew (Larue), Benjamin, 228, 237.
Larew, Elizabeth, 207, 245.
Larew, Jacob, 220, 228, 237, 558.
Larew, John, 237.
Larew, Joseph, 228, 237.
Larew, Mary (Polly), 220, 237.
Larew, Peter, 207, 220, 237.
Larew, Reuben, 220, 237.
Larken, Henry, 421, 471.
Laslea (Leslea), Jacob, 572.
Lasnet, Sally, 251.
Lasnett, Joseph, 251.
Lasnett, Mary, 251.
Lasnett, Rebecca, 251.
Lasnett, Richard, 251.
Lastly, James, 8.
Laur, John, 201.
Laverty, Jane (Jean), 121, 127, 498, 500, 541.
Laverty, Rebekah, 578.
Laverty (Lafferty), Ralph, 6, 23, 28, 35, 45, 48, 50, 52, 58, 61, 80, 84, 124, 132, 167, 471, 489, 498, 500, 560, 578, 581.
Laverty, Robert, 541.
Laverty, William, 500, 541.
Law, John, 73, 403.
Law, Michael, 520.
Law, Robert, 122, 403, 404.
Lawderdale, James, 361.
Lawler, John, 18.
Lawler, Mary, 275, 298.
Lawler, Michael, 275, 298.
Lawless, Henry, 45, 48.
Lawrence, Frances, 135.
Lawrence, Henry, 47, 51, 56, 65.

Lawrence, James, 66, 98.
Lawrence, John, 18, 20, 394, 419.
Lawrence, Samuel, 142, 394, 395, 480.
Lawrentz, Hans, 18.
Laws, Robert, 515.
Lawson, James, 73.
Layburn, Henry, 87.
Layton, Jacob, 384.
Layton, Thomas, 210, 214.
Leaburn, Henry, 441.
Leakey, William, 516.
Leamer (Lemon), Jacob, 193.
Leane, William, 13.
Leard, Jane, 238.
Leary (Lary), Derby (Dorbe), 131.
Leas, Jacob, 215, 245.
Lease (Leese), Michael, 166, 541.
Leath, George, 10.
Leathers, George, 573.
Leburn, George, 196.
Leckey, Thomas, 148.
Lecky, Andrew, 159, 581.
Lecock, James, 370.
Ledderdale (Litherdale, Latherdale), James, 55, 60, 64, 97, 103, 274, 288, 375, 470.
Ledford, Henry, 74, 322.
Ledford, John, 110, 300, 397.
Ledford, William, 74, 110, 322.
Ledgerwood, Agnes, 468.
Ledgerwood, Rebecca, 394.
Ledgerwood, William, 11, 49, 54, 58, 63, 64, 84, 122, 281, 282, 298, 302, 303, 394, 468, 509, 520, 566.
Lee, Benjamin, 288.
Lee, Bridget, 157.
Lee, James, 46, 52, 57.
Lee, John, 22.
Lee (Lees), William, 74, 100.
Leech, James, 250.
Leedekey, George, 573.
Leedekey, Mary, 181.
Leeper, Andrew, 47, 56, 93, 96, 307, 312, 333, 353, 367, 432, 453.
Leeper, Elizabeth, 71, 89.
Leeper, Gawin, 333, 353, 355, 432, 548, 551, 556.
Leeper, George, 93.
Leeper, Hugh, 71, 89.
Leeper, James, 47, 71, 79, 83, 89, 93, 98, 267, 278, 285, 298, 307, 333, 355, 386, 430, 432, 505, 511, 524, 526, 554, 556, 559.
Leeper, Jean, 71, 333, 453.
Leeper, John, 93, 116, 430, 432, 505, 554.
Leeper, Margaret, 79, 93, 98, 307, 432.
Leeper, Nicholas, 93, 267, 298, 307, 331, 353, 361, 430, 432, 524, 526, 556, 559.
Leeper, Susanna, 554.
Lees, Henry, 149.
Leeven, Samuel, 170.

Leget, Alexander, 161.
Leister, James, 67, 70, 93, 107, **540**.
Leister, Robert, 569, 570.
Leister, Sarah, 570.
Leith, Ephraim, 17.
Lemon, George, 579.
Lemon, Joseph, 533, 552.
Lene. Abraham, 557.
Lenox, Hugh, 389.
Lentz, Bernhard, 143.
Leo, John, 438.
Leo, John W., 143, 542, 543, **544**.
Leo, Martha, 544.
Leonard, David, 240.
Lepham (Lipham), Frederick, 574, **575**.
Lepham (Lipham), Frederick J., 312, 575.
Leppard (Lippard), William, 73, 76, 110, 320.
Lessley, Agness, 142, 158, 199.
Lessley, Dolly, 158.
Lessley, Elizabeth (Betsy), 158, 198, **199**.
Laslea (Leslea), Jacob, 572.
Lessley, James, 116, 142, 155, 157, 158, 193, 198, 199, 259, 421, 422, 424, 522, 559.
Lessley, John, 120, 157, 193, 199.
Lessley, Mary, 142, 231, 559.
Lessley, Robert, 157, 193, 199.
Lessley, Samuel, 142, 158, 193, 199, 216.
Lessley, Sarah, 157, 158, 193, 199, 200, 216.
Lesslie, Joseph, 193.
Lester, Mary, 220.
Letcher, John, 537.
Lettimore, Mathew, 168.
Levier, Catherine, 236.
Levingston, Conrod, 480.
Leviston, William, 534.
Leviston, John, 7.
Levistone, Robert, 7.
Levistone, Thomas, 7.
Lewell, Abraham, 153.
Lewell, Andrew, 153, 154, **194**.
Lewell, Hanah, 153.
Lewell, Peter, 153.
Lewell, Rebecca, 153.
Lewell, Simon, 153.
Lewis, Aaron, 569.
Lewis, Andrew, 20, 22, **26**, 30, 31, 32, 58, 76, 89, 91, 95, 96, 98, 99, 102, 109, 112, 138, 248, 255, 267, 282, 291, 303, 304, 306, 312, 317, 342, 363, 364, 370, 373, 392, 413, 424, 430, 436, 441, 445, 448, 455, 458, 465, 466, 483, 485, 490, 502, 505, 507, 521, 549.
Lewis, Ann, 482, 511, **562**.
Lewis, Archibald, 241.
Lewis, Benjamin, 136, 339, 517.
Lewis, Charles, 50, 58, 67, 73, 76, 91, 107, 116, 121, 138, 139, 142, 338, 362, 373, 390, 421, 443, 482, 488, 495, 500, 520, 546.
Lewis (Luce), Elizabeth, 138, 210, 549.

Lewis, Fielding, 334, 365.
Lewis, Francis, 87.
Lewis, George, 35, 37, 87, 88, 138, **210**, 211, 339, 427, 459, 496, 512, 529.
Lewis (Lues), James, 210.
Lewis, Jean (Jane, Jenny), 167, 363, **549**.
Lewis, John, 5, 15, 17, 24, 40, 76, **80**, **88**, 89, 109, 124, 138, 140, 189, 191, 193, **249**, 253, 254, 255, 257, 262, 264, **267**, **268**, 270, 273, 280, 289, 291, 292, 293, **296**, 307, 316, 317, 330, 334, 339, **381**, **413**, 425, 437, 443, 457, 458, 468, 501, **517**, 521, 529, 550, 566, 567, 568, 579, **585**.
Lewis, Lawrence, 241.
Lewis, Margaret, 76, 138, 189, 193, **254**.
Lewis, Mary (Polly), 210, 235, 529.
Lewis, Rachel, 249.
Lewis, Rebecka, 210.
Lewis, Samuel, 171, 372, **447**, **466**.
Lewis, Sarah, 138, **482**.
Lewis, Susanna, 517.
Lewis, Thomas, 22, 27, 31, 32, **58**, 76, 89, 91, 116, 129, 137, 138, 167, 189, **252**, 253, 254, 258, 259, 261, 264, 268, 270, 273, 277, 288, 292, 299, 312, 316, **317**, 334, 339, 353, 363, 370, 377, 392, **424**, 425, 434, 437, 448, 457, 458, 460, **464**, 465, 521, 546, 549, 560.
Lewis, William, 26, 58, 76, 79, 81, 98, **100**, 134, 138, 139, 284, 292, 306, 317, **356**, 424, 482, 511, 526, 534, 546, 560, **561**, 562. 565, 580, 582.
Lewis, Zachariah (Zachary), 41, 117, **379**, 436.
Lewnis (Lewis?), Adam, 318.
Leybown, Jane, 227.
Liber, Francis, 375.
Life, Martin (Martian), 175, **195**.
Ligget, James, 233.
Ligget, Jane, 233.
Lightfooder, Christopher, 126.
Lightner, John, 298.
Likens, Dorraty, 124.
Likens, John, 527.
Lilly, John, 527.
Linch, Barnet, 535.
Linch, Neil, 92.
Lincoln, Abraham, 113, 115, **524**, **533**.
Lincoln, Isaac, 533.
Lincoln, Jacob, 533.
Lincoln, John, 147, 474, 533.
Lincoln, Rebecca, 533.
Lincoln, Sarah, 558.
Lindel, Joseph, 139.
Lindsey, Flow, 196.
Lindsey (Linsey), John, 102, 566.
Lindsey (Linsey), Margaret, 117, **391**.
Lindsey (Linsey), Samuel, 46, 362, **391**, 470, 480.
Lindsey, Walter, 470.
Lindwad. George, 92.
Lingal, Paul, 110.

Lingle, Ann, 488.
Lingle, Barbara, 148, 149.
Lingle, Elizabeth, 547.
Lingle (Lingell), Jacob, 75, 148, 321, 393, 488, 547.
Lingle, John, 133, 148, 547.
Lingle, Philip, 133, 148, 149, 172.
Link, Adam, 234, 243.
Link, Christian, 243.
Link, Daniel, 510.
Link, David, 243.
Link, John, 242, 243.
Link, Mary, 242.
Link, Mathias, 242, 243.
Link, Peter, 243.
Link, Sarah, 243.
Linsey, Mathew, 298.
Linwell, Eleanor, 256, 257.
Linwell, Hannah, 257.
Linwell (Linvell), Thomas, 257, 258, 339.
Linwell (Linvell), William, 255, 256, 257, 339, 371, 449, 473, 477, 513, 548.
Lionberger, John, 5.
Lister, Jean, 107.
Lister, John, 107.
Lister, Martha, 107.
Litching, Anthony, 563.
Litching, Susanna, 563.
Litster, James, 70.
Little (Lyttle), David, 457, 475.
Little, William, 80.
Livers, Francis, 59, 96.
Livingston, William, 516, 517, 556.
Lloyd, Thomas, 50, 55, 97, 99, 331, 335, 358, 451, 465.
Loagan, Ezekiel, 478.
Lock (Loch, Loff, Lough, Look), Adam, 127, 134, 144, 146, 150, 156, 494.
Lock, James, 128.
Lockhart, Catherine, 313, 337, 338.
Lockhart, Charles, 93, 99.
Lockhart, Elce, 164.
Lockhart, Francis, 312.
Lockhart, Hanna, 595.
Lockhart, Isabella, 547, 567.
Lockhart, Jacob, 99, 114, 164, 281, 283, 312, 336, 522, 528, 529, 595.
Lockhart, Jane, 164.
Lockhart, James, 11, 13, 24, 26, 27, 29, 35, 36, 40, 43, 44, 47, 48, 49, 54, 57, 68, 69, 72, 75, 76, 82, 90, 270, 280, 283, 284, 288, 304, 310, 312, 317, 328, 331, 334, 338, 339, 343, 355, 368, 369, 500, 510, 523, 529, 542, 554, 557.
Lockhart, John, 26, 262, 270, 273, 297, 357.
Lockhart, Levi, 164, 595.
Lockhart, Mary, 250, 312, 523, 529.
Lockhart, Patrick, 368, 369, 390, 399, 401, 426, 443, 457, 460, 462, 480, 485, 486, 490, 492, 493, 497, 506, 507, 523, 542, 549, 557.
Lockhart, Randal (Randolph, Ronald), 96,
353, 355, 363, 369, 389, 437, 439, 440, 464, 487, 488, 493, 496, 500.
Lockhart, Rebecca, 297.
Lockhart, Samuel, 14, 313, 336, 337, 338, 378, 441, 497, 529.
Lockhart, Sarah (Sally), 163, 547.
Lockhart, William, 355, 368, 369, 507, 523, 542, 545.
Lockmer, Christian, 103.
Lockridge, Agness, 207, 393, 440.
Lockridge, Andrew, 56, 67, 127, 134, 141, 156, 194, 215, 216, 219, 305, 414, 442, 457, 482, 489, 530, 547, 548, 550, 578, 583, 587.
Lockridge, Ann, 194, 215.
Lockridge (Louchridge), Elizabeth (Betsy), 194, 215.
Lockridge, Isabella, 344, 398.
Lockridge, James, 28, 37, 39, 194, 215, 253, 270, 306, 344, 361, 393, 398, 414, 453, 499, 587.
Lockridge, Jane (Jean), 120, 134, 194, 587.
Lockridge, John, 194, 207, 215, 587.
Lockridge, Lauty, 194.
Lockridge, Rebecca, 194, 417.
Lockridge, Robert, 55, 67, 194, 344, 395, 417, 442.
Lockridge, Samuel, 145, 189, 207, 213, 214.
Lockridge, Sarah, 194, 215.
Lockridge, William, 30, 34, 67, 88, 135, 156, 189, 194, 207, 215, 295, 325, 335, 341, 349, 393, 440, 488.
Lofland, Charles, 428.
Lofland, Smith, 518.
Lofftis, Sarah, 187, 554.
Lofftus, Ralph, 459, 478, 521, 549, 554, 561, 576.
Lofftus, Ralph A., 238, 239.
Logan (Loggan), Alexander, 152, 332, 333, 396.
Logan, Benjamin, 55, 101, 106, 109, 193, 249, 399, 432, 416, 449, 475, 482, 508, 518, 529, 530.
Logan, David, 9, 45, 53, 65, 70, 272, 274, 282, 377, 421.
Logan, Elizabeth, 276, 489, 511.
Logan, Hugh, 469, 486, 487.
Logan, Isabella, 495.
Logan, James (Jame), 76, 83, 93, 152, 362, 520.
Logan, Jean (Jane), 55, 109, 272, 596.
Logan, John, 36, 41, 71, 81, 83, 90, 152, 161, 231, 311, 327, 332, 396, 407, 475, 489, 503, 526, 536, 596.
Logan, Rachel, 231, 396.
Logan, Samuel, 152, 286, 383, 393, 448.
Logan, Thomas, 285, 396.
Logan, William, 48, 51, 57, 94, 97, 109, 152, 163, 276, 285, 286, 295, 348, 379, 431, 469, 475, 489, 495, 511, 551, 596.
Loge, Samuel, 402.
Loggan, Joseph, 152.

Loggan, Mary, 152, 448.
Loggan, Robert, 152.
Loggan, Sarah, 152.
Lohr, Peter, 591.
Lojo, David, 324.
Lonetally, Thomas, 315.
Long, Alexander, 117, 145, 153, 160, 181, 201, 205, 207, 235, 241, 586.
Long, Anna (Ann, Anne), 46, 109.
Long (Lung), Barbara, 514, 515, 531, 538.
Long (Lung), Catherine, 424, 429, 479.
Long, Charles, 479, 480, 490, 512, 513.
Long, David, 50, 153, 160, 199, 200, 235, 241.
Long, Dorcas, 235.
Long, Edward, 70, 100, 189, 369, 431, 500, 504, 518, 536, 588.
Long, Elizabeth, 46, 235, 241, 242, 583, 584, 586.
Long, Francis, 160, 211, 235, 241, 364.
Long, Gabriel, 540, 579.
Long, Gennet, 46.
Long (Lung), Henry, 23, 46, 69, 85, 97, 101, 132, 383, 415, 424, 429, 475, 479, 482, 514, 515, 531, 538.
Long, James, 160, 167, 199, 241, 586.
Long, Jane, 235.
Long, John, 46, 160, 189, 364, 415, 446, 577, 589.
Long, Joseph, 16, 32, 35, 46, 48, 160, 189, 232, 241, 299, 301, 338, 340, 415, 454.
Long, **Margaret, 58.**
Long (Lung), Paul, 5, 17, 28, 29, 259, 293, 406, 413, 429, 528.
Long (Lung), Philip, 293, 406, 413, 429, 449, 480, 482, 515.
Long, Rebecca, 235.
Long, Ruth, 46.
Long, Samuel, 46, 153, 160, 188, 199, 212, 215, 219, 221, 232, 235, 241, 415, 414, 446, 555, 582, 586.
Long, Ursilla, 512.
Long (Lang), William, 5, 10, 18, 29, 41, 44, 46, 58, 60, 116, 131, 132, 153, 160, 167, 180, 189, 235, 241, 274, 277, 273, 279, 280, 304, 324, 341, 358, 362, 364, 368, 379, 446, 508, 524, 578, 583, 584, 586, 588.
Longsdale, William, 140.
Look, Nicholas, 190.
Looker, James, 478.
Looker, Momas, 25.
Looker (Loker), Thomas, 9, 25, 455, 478.
Lookey, James, 455.
Lookey, Thomas, 42, 513.
Looney, Abraham, 102, 330, 331.
Looney, Adam, 37, 74, 308, 430, 446, 471, 474.
Looney (Luney), Daniel, 60, 64, 93, 330, 431, 438.
Looney (Luney), David, 60, 64, 67, 83, 93, 98, 102, 361, 369, 375, 401, 430, 431, 450, 451, 466.
Looney, Hanna 446.
Looney (Luney), John, 41, 67, 369, 446, 471.
Looney (Luney), Joseph, 103, 105, 417, 465.
Looney (Luney), Margaret, 41, 60, 93, 103, 382, 401, 430, 438.
Looney, Mary, 401, 451.
Looney, Peter, 58, 60, 62, 64, 74, 102, 103, 321, 430, 431.
Looney (Luney), Robert, 9, 11, 16, 42, 49, 102, 331, 358, 390, 395, 417, 430, 431, 438, 451, 466.
Lorrimer, John, 92.
Lorrimer, Thomas, 92, 105, 127, 356, 365, 400.
Lorton, Israel, 25, 26
Lorton, Jacob, 25, 73, 106, 110, 321, 451, 452, 465, 470, 487.
Lorton, Lydia, 465.
Lots, George, 592.
Lowderback, David, 502.
Louderdale, James, 362.
Loueraine, John, 76.
Loumer, John, 85.
Louts, Barnit, 126.
Love, Alexander, 363, 365, 368, 387, 392, 397, 407, 425.
Love, Daniel, 17, 36, 37, 39, 40, 45, 50, 54, 55, 62, 66, 68, 70, 82, 84, 113, 114, 376, 407, 413, 475, 512.
Love, Dorcas, 424.
Love, Elizabeth, 487.
Love, Ephraim, 15, 18, 20, 37, 40, 45, 47, 50, 51, 52, 55, 62, 63, 65, 71, 78, 141, 270, 315, 335, 336, 338, 349, 353, 360, 376, 402, 418, 475, 487, 534.
Love, James, 535.
Love, Jane (Jean), 113, 114, 407.
Love, Jennet, 18.
Love, Johanna, 333.
Love, John, 53, 69, 94, 130, 313, 333.
Love, Joseph, 9, 19, 36, 47, 49, 126, 167, 272, 277, 297, 307, 313, 385, 410, 423, 424, 434, 439, 543, 551, 556.
Love, Margaret, 297, 317.
Love, Mary, 410, 439, 551, 556.
Love, Phil, 98.
Love, Rachel, 543.
Love, Robert, 150, 159, 187, 199.
Love, Samuel, 19, 95, 111, 187, 357, 385, 396, 407, 410, 423, 424, 536, 543.
Love, Thomas, 232, 561.
Loveley, William, 167.
Lovingood, Ann, 588.
Lovingood (Levingood), Harman, 140, 177, 179, 185, 186, 539, 588.
Lovingood, John, 588.
Lovingood, Philip, 588.
Low, John, 80, 141, 315, 319, 340, 356.
Lower (Sower), Christian, 65, 141.

Lowman, Barnard, 240.
Lowman, Barnet, 234.
Lowman, Jacob, 234.
Lowney, John, 71.
Lowney, Patrick, 76.
Lowraine, David, 76.
Lowrey, Alexander, 147.
Lowrey, Benjamin, 557.
Lowrey, Isabel, 515.
Lowrey, Sarah, 557.
Lowry, David, 69.
Lowry, Elizabeth, 69.
Lowry, James, 69.
Lowry, Jean (Jane), 114, 499.
Lowry, Jennet, 69.
Lowry (Lowrie), John, 12, 25, 62, 69, 82, 99, 114, 161, 204, 267, 268, 284, 289, 294, 295, 302, 322, 330, 335, 341, 346, 347, 349, 403, 429, 443, 460, 478, 487, 499, 502, 515, 537, 549, 561, 591, 595.
Lowry, Jonathan, 487.
Lowry, Joseph, 204, 243, 591, 595.
Lowry, Mary, 204.
Lowry, Melvin (Malvin), 114, 204.
Lowry, Patrick, 114, 302.
Lowry, Rebeckah, 69.
Lowry, Robert, 69, 310, 311, 346, 349, 356, 478, 484, 515.
Lowry, William, 69, 515.
Loy, Catharine, 497.
Loy, Martin, 73, 321, 436.
Loy, Mary, 464, 503.
Loy, Stephen, 417, 436, 456, 464, 497, 503, 506, 550.
Lucas, Elizabeth, 16.
Lucas (Lucases), John, 70, 102.
Lucas, Richard, 16.
Ludspicke, William, 149.
Louisey, Samuel, 376.
Luke, Richard, 27.
Lukeback, Ann Elizabeth, 228.
Lumenberger, Catrine, 124.
Lunday, Thomas, 114.
Luney, Absolum, 430.
Luney, Elizabeth, 390.
Luney, Moses, 446.
Luney, Thomas, 60.
Lung, Emmaniel H., 538.
Luok, Hugh, 72.
Luse, Henry, 565.
Lusk, Agness, 10, 330, 504.
Lusk, Daniel, 510.
Lusk, Eleanor, 320.
Lusk, Elizabeth, 10, 119, 122, 351, 393.
Lusk, Hugh, 35, 304, 367.
Lusk (Loosk), James, 10, 135, 274, 284, 307, 319, 320, 346, 532.
Lusk, John, 10, 23, 89, 119, 275, 279, 337, 344, 351, 379, 393, 450, 464, 478, 505.
Lusk, Joseph, 119.
101, 102, 108, 209, 232, 248, 258, 268,
Lusk, Margaret, 119.
Lusk, Mary 119.
Lusk, Nathan, 10, 12, 257, 284.
Lusk, Robert, 19, 23, 49, 50, 80, 135, 275, 368, 464, 465, 481, 507, 555.
Lusk (Losk, Lisk), Samuel, 95, 255, 271, 272, 292, 313, 330, 463, 504, 523, 543.
Lusk, Sarah, 119.
Lusk, William, 49, 54, 61, 102, 104, 119, 122, 135, 263, 267, 282, 285, 296, 299, 304, 310, 311, 312, 315, 317, 324, 328, 334, 346, 352, 355, 358, 367, 379, 381, 384, 418, 433, 435, 472, 518.
Luttenton (Lutterington), Thomas, 74, 322.
Lyday, Andrew, 113.
Lyle, Daniel, 23, 24, 26, 33, 49, 60, 62, 66, 69, 80, 102, 119, 122, 129, 135, 175, 265, 284, 322, 355, 384, 435, 461, 511.
Lyle, Elizabeth, 49, 134.
Lyle, Esther, 49, 396.
Lyle, James, 102, 103, 119, 134, 135, 145, 175, 190, 200, 425, 477, 530, 551, 589, 596.
Lyle, Jean, 49.
Lyle, John, 20, 23, 31, 45, 49, 50, 103, 126, 134, 135, 137, 189, 258, 264, 266, 270, 276, 295, 299, 336, 347, 350, 358, 396, 443, 450, 477, 519, 531, 538, 555.
Lyle, Julia (Juliet), 200.
Lyle, Martha, 49, 134.
Lyle, Mathew, 13, 23, 26, 34, 44, 47, 49, 55, 72, 134, 258, 259, 267, 270, 276, 311, 318, 336, 350, 358, 396, 477.
Lyle, Robert, 467.
Lyle, Samuel, 34, 49, 60, 70, 80, 82, 101, 102, 114, 119, 124, 129, 135, 140, 143, 154, 266, 295, 387, 408, 414, 418, 461, 507, 518, 530, 537.
Lyle, Sarah, 49.
Lyle, William, 49, 200, 205, 229, 414.
Lynch, Charles, 83, 107, 121, 159.
Lynch, James, 230.
Lynch, Patrick, 30, 38.
Lynn (Linn), Andrew, 280, 286, 298, 303, 557.
Lynn, Jacob, 221.
Lynn, James, 26, 261, 265, 269, 273, 280, 286, 298, 303, 359, 468.
Lynn, Jean, 301.
Lynn (Linn), John, 19, 261, 262, 274, 278, 280, 281, 282, 283, 288, 296, 297, 298, 299, 301, 304, 395, 477, 485.
Lynn, Joseph, 8.
Lynn (Linn), Josiah, 264, 271.
Lynn, Margaret, 107, 304.
Lynn, Naomie, 297.
Lynn, Sarah, 26, 298.
Lynor (Liner), Henry, 94, 164, 498.
Lyon, Henry, 584.
Lyon, Humberston, 6, 102, 258, 341, 357.
Lyon, John, 386.

Lyon, Margaret, 417.
Lyon, Nathaniel, 62, 381, 417, 500.
Lyons, William, 225.

McAdan, Samuel, 215.
McAdow, William, 464.
McAfee, George, 394, 444, 507.
McAfee, James, 37, 50, 91, 117, 272, 299, 394, 436, 444, 450.
McAfee, Robert, 444.
McAffee, Jannet, 450.
McAghan, William, 38.
McAkee, John, 33.
McAleary (McAllery), Hugh, 174, 221.
McAllister (MacCalister), James, 414, 445.
McAllister, John, 594.
McAllister, Mary, 445.
McAlly, William, 158.
McAlvery, Samuel, 37.
McAnally (McNally), Charles, 19, 333.
McAnaire (McAnore, McNare, McNair), Daniel, 25, 26, 33, 73, 97, 112, 150, 169, 184, 195, 196, 252, 277, 297, 308, 319, 344, 358, 411, 438, 439, 544, 546, 562, 590.
McAnare (McAnore, McNare), Hannah, 252, 308, 344, 438.
McAxwell, John, 39.
McBride, Benjamin, 15.
McBride, Daniel, 334.
McBride, Francis, 15, 28, 33, 53, 66, 76, 306, 307, 322, 342, 371, 383, 449, 473, 513, 524, 533, 552.
McBride, James, 359.
McBride, Joseph, 95, 376, 386, 476.
McBride, Margaret, 33.
McBride, Martha, 488.
McBride, Mary, 33, 87, 322, 449, 513, 552.
McBride, Sarah, 33.
McBride, Thomas, 87, 95.
McBride, William, 33, 50, 95, 97, 113, 453, 476, 478, 488.
McCafferty, Cormick, 131, 182.
McCafferty, Hugh, 182, 216.
McCafferty, Jane (Jinny), 182, 216.
McCain, James, 102.
McCain, Margaret, 102.
McCall, James, 131.
McCallam, John, 361.
McCallam, Patrick, 388.
McCallim, Mary, 236.
McCallister, James, 83, 456, 530.
McCamas, Elizabeth, 149.
McCamey, James, 175.
McCampbell, Andrew, 62, 81, 119, 159, 173, 432, 433, 451, 508, 519.
McCampbell, James, 62, 71, 80, 93, 116, 120, 399, 471, 491, 520, 548, 596.
McCampbell, John, 104, 355, 426, 528.
McCampbell, Patrick, 97.
McCampbell, Samuel, 595.

McCampbell, William, 432, 433, 451, 498.
McCan, Daniel, 154.
McCan (McCann), James, 165, 572, 592.
McCan, Neil, 135, 178.
McCandles, Alexander, 533.
McCandless (McCanless, McCandls), William, 35, 36, 59, 71, 78, 82, 89, 93, 152, 181, 295, 305, 310, 346, 347, 402, 429, 439, 443, 468, 469, 498, 499, 504, 544.
McCarroll (McCarral, McCarrell), James, 305, 324, 364, 370, 377, 540.
McCarty, James, 476.
McCarty, John, 212, 213.
McCaslin (McCasling), Andrew, 173, 188.
McCaslin (McCaselon, McCastling), John, 85, 87, 119, 151, 482, 560.
McCaslin, William, 590.
McCaul, Alexander, 466.
McCaul, James, 73.
McCausland, James, 233, 240.
McCausland, John, 215, 233.
McCausland, Mary, 233.
McCaw, James, 587.
McCawley, Hugh, 563.
McCay (McCoy), Robert, 18, 255, 256, 259, 260, 579.
McCay, William, 577, 578.
McCherry, Luke, 73.
McChesney, Adam, 239.
McChesney, George, 178, 179.
McChesney, James, 156, 239, 529, 573.
McChesney, Jan, 195.
McChesney, Jane E., 239.
McChesney, John, 239, 242, 247.
McChesney, Rebecca, 239.
McChesney, Robert, 195, 239, 247, 529, 561, 587.
McChesney, Sally, 239.
McChesney, Samuel, 219, 524, 529, 543.
McChesney, Walter, 529, 543.
McChesney, William, 247.
McCinney, Alexander, 70.
McCinney, Ann, 70.
McCinney, John, 70, 71, 72.
McCinney, Margaret, 70.
McCinney, Mary, 70, 71.
McCinney, Sarah, 70.
McCintage, William, 476.
McCleary (McCleery), Alexander, 24, 26, 257, 266, 311.
McCleary (McCleery), James, 32, 54, 73, 85, 89, 99, 101, 105, 132, 145, 148, 150, 160, 334, 412, 531.
McCleary (McCleery), Margaret, 24, 145.
McCleary, Rachel, 24.
McCleery, John, 101, 145, 148, 150, 383.
McCleery, Samuel, 145.
McClehenny, Robert, 46.
McClelhill, Joseph, 53.
McClelland, Jean, 472.
McClellon (McClelan), Abraham, 450.

467.
McClellon (McClalon, McClellan, McCleland), John, 248, 369, 376, 436.
McClenachan, Alexander, 90, 91, 112, 113, 116, 138, 139, 140, 160, 162, 163, 171, 190, 197, 249, 250, 395, 464, 503, 534, 539, 555, 582, 583, 594.
McClenachan, Elijah, 45, 63, 123, 129, 144, 166, 167, 174, 175, 186, 187, 198, 209, 210, 271, 286, 303, 310, 394, 452, 495, 498, 511, 560, 561.
McClenachan, Elisha, 504.
McClenachan, Elizabeth, 191, 209.
McClenachan, Esther, 227.
McClenachan, Jane (Jenny), 89, 395.
McClenachan, John, 28, 90, 98, 116, 119, 138, 139, 160, 164, 197, 217, 286, 395, 472, 529, 534, 566, 563.
McClenachan, Lettice, 395.
McClenachan, Letucann, 209.
McClenachan, Lewis, 316.
McClenachan, Margaret, 138, 191, 209, 529, 568.
McClenachan, Nancy, 227.
McClenachan, Robert, 7, 8, 15, 23, 24, 30, 31, 32, 35, 38, 39, 47, 50, 51, 79, 86, 87, 98, 112, 113, 116, 126, 133, 137, 138, 139, 163, 197, 258, 259, 264, 270, 271, 277, 278, 286, 289, 291, 293, 295, 296, 297, 302, 303, 304, 310, 317, 323, 331, 357, 361, 377, 395, 402, 430, 436, 444, 456, 476, 479, 497, 504, 506, 519, 540, 549, 553.
McClenachan, Sarah, 197, 258, 286, 361, 377, 395, 444, 519, 534.
McClenachan, Thomas, 138, 160.
McClenachan, William, 107, 111, 112, 137, 144, 189, 227, 371, 414, 450, 453, 467, 475, 482, 488, 491, 534, 589.
McClinken, Robert, 131.
McClintock, Elizabeth, 173.
McClintock, John, 157, 173.
McClintock, Martha, 136, 173.
McClintock, Preepare, 136, 173.
McClintock, Samuel, 173.
McClintock (McClintick), William, 35, 136, 173, 177, 280, 281, 283, 294, 331, 332, 361, 390, 422, 473, 490, 493, 516, 558, 571, 586.
McClister, Neaiell, 60.
McClolon, Joseph, 72.
McCluer, Michael, 162.
McClug, Samuel, 584.
McClung, Elizabeth, 248.
McClung, Francis, 119.
McClung, Henry, 104, 122, 133, 408, 435.
McClung, James, 23, 172, 189, 235, 295, 296, 304, 324, 328, 355, 388, 435.
McClung, John, 40, 81, 97, 116, 119, 125, 145, 189, 353, 358, 388, 484, 537.
McClung, Joseph, 395, 489.

McClung, Margaret, 489.
McClung, Mary (Polly), 233, 435.
McClung, Samuel, 130, 435.
McClung, Thomas, 40, 484, 489.
McClung, William, 29, 44, 45, 137, 259, 284, 295, 238, 353, 407, 435.
McClure, Agnes, 34, 64.
McClure, Alexander, 34, 64, 101, 103, 109, 133, 154, 258, 292, 296, 299, 313, 342, 344, 375, 409, 516, 542.
McClure, Andrew, 64, 66, 94, 123, 125, 160, 185, 279, 281, 282, 283, 284, 294, 327, 348, 354, 364, 383, 426, 446, 448, 468, 473, 511, 514, 527, 529, 539, 564.
McClure, Arthur, 102, 109, 271, 274, 283, 296, 399, 428, 485.
McClure, Catherine, 296.
McClure, David, 185, 206, 209, 231, 248, 251.
McClure, Dorothy, 62.
McClure, Eleanor, 64, 185, 294.
McClure, Elizabeth (Betty), 185, 229, 475.
McClure, Esther, 64.
McClure, Finley (Finla, Phinley), 68, 343, 468.
McClure, Frances, 296.
McClure, Halbert, 34, 35, 62, 100, 101, 103, 106, 122, 125, 209, 232, 258, 260, 367, 433, 499, 516, 542, 551.
McClure, Hanah, 62.
McClure, Hugh, 60, 64, 126, 150, 248, 251, 306, 324, 354, 383, 511, 514, 548.
McClure, Isaac, 231, 248, 251.
McClure, Isabella, 8, 122, 313.
McClure, James, 62, 64, 67, 100, 101, 129, 189, 218, 272, 284, 384, 395, 441, 446.
McClure, Jean (Jane), 64, 248.
McClure, John, 22, 33, 34, 41, 45, 64, 67, 75, 79, 101, 109, 110, 115, 185, 192, 221, 249, 275, 281, 283, 284, 296, 299, 328, 342, 343, 373, 409, 413, 421, 446, 454, 475, 476, 481, 491, 503, 556, 564.
McClure, Josiah, 185.
McClure, Margaret, 62, 100, 101, 102, 103, 299.
McClure, Mary (Polly), 62, 100, 101, 103, 122, 229, 299, 308, 365, 409, 441, 446, 454, 475, 481, 485, 591.
McClure, Mathew, 66.
McClure, Moses, 9, 41, 62, 100, 101, 102, 103, 208, 209, 260, 268, 275, 299, 313, 329, 339, 344, 405, 409, 455.
McClure, Nathan, 62, 296, 342, 406.
McClure, Nathaniel, 20, 34, 62, 65, 100, 101, 102, 103, 209, 260, 268, 429, 441, 474.
McClure, Phebe, 122.
McClure, Patrick, 25.
McClure, Rebecca, 196.
McClure, Robert, 149.
McClure, Samuel, 12, 33, 34, 62, 64, 72,

273, 302, 308, 325, 329, 342, 365, 384, 385, 399, 408, 442, 460, 482, 485, 491, 527, 529, 539, 564.
McClure, Susanna, 344.
McClure, Thomas, 62, 100, 101, 229.
McClure, William, 64, 233, 445, 473, 485.
McCluskey, Patrick, 297, 338.
McCluster, Neal, 64.
McColgan, Edward, 49, 327, 432.
McColgan, Marion, 432.
McCollister, Elijah, 530.
McCollock (McClulock), Thomas, 126, 174, 497.
McCollom, Patrick, 60, 85, 86, 87, 102, 110, 289, 296, 387, 395, 413, 418, 450.
McCollum, John, 86, 87, 98, 148, 407, 450, 484.
McComb, Rebecca, 165.
McCombe, Andrew, 83, 136, 165, 179, 181, 183, 203, 527, 562.
McCombe, Barbara, 136.
McCombe, Jane (Jean), 179, 203.
McCombe, William, 179, 180, 562.
McCommus, Catherine, 34.
McCommus (McComas, McCaumus), David, 34, 317, 457.
McConkey, Samuel, 445, 538, 573, 574.
McConnel, Francis, 139.
McConnel, Patrick, 446.
McConnell, Alexander, 198, 209.
McConnell, Andrew, 287, 288, 354, 510.
McConnell, James, 337, 349, 355, 494.
McConnell, William, 570.
McConnigle, James, 595.
McConnolly (McConnolay), John, 303, 423, 428.
McConwell, Hugh, 346.
McCord, Adam, 29, 80.
McCord, Andrew, 279.
McCord, Benjamin, 80.
McCord, James, 17, 18, 80, 233, 303.
McCord, John, 76, 80, 83.
McCord, Joseph, 76, 80, 83.
McCord, Martha, 15.
McCord, Mary, 29, 76.
McCord, Sarah, 29.
McCord, William, 17, 18, 80.
McCorkle, Alexander, 17, 46, 325, 367, 399, 446.
McCorkle, Elizabeth, 182.
McCorkle (McCorkall), James, 16, 19, 24, 261, 262, 269, 275, 276, 290, 293, 301, 302, 306, 310, 394, 402, 452, 490, 491, 509.
McCorkle, Jane, 310.
McCorkle, John, 182.
McCorkle (McKorkle), Mary, 182, 446.
McCorkle, Patrick, 358, 387, 446, 507.
McCorkle, Robert, 182, 275, 302, 303.
McCorkle, Samuel, 182, 183, 246, 278, 279, 399.

McCorkle, Sarah, 182.
McCorkle, William, 182.
McCorley, John, 583.
McCormack, Polly, 242.
McCormick, Anne, 466.
McCormick, Daniel, 82, 96, 117, 397, 419, 428, 437, 466.
McCormick, Henry, 247.
McCormick, John, 247.
McCormick, Joshua, 73, 314, 397, 431, 456, 458, 466, 467.
McCormick, Martha, 96.
McCormick, Maxwell, 342.
McCormick, Robert, 150, 163, 212, 217.
McCormick, William, 226, 247.
McCoskery (McCoskry), James, 50, 51, 305, 311, 468.
McCoskry, Agness, 181.
McCoskry, Ann, 181.
McCoskry, David, 51, 181, 310, 322, 399, 499, 520.
McCoskry (McCroskry), Elizabeth, 50, 181, 579.
McCoskry, Esther (Esher), 181.
McCoskry, Grisel, 181, 520.
McCoskry, Jean, 181.
McCoskry, Martha, 181.
McCoven, John, 65.
McCown, Francis, 6, 7, 12, 13, 14, 17, 18, 35, 44, 60, 66, 67, 75, 97, 129, 255, 259, 275, 291, 295, 303, 308, 315, 319, 327, 346, 348, 349, 367, 422.
McCown, Francis F., 27.
McCown, Frank, 189.
McCown, George, 66.
McCown, Isbell, 66.
McCown, James, 39, 47, 48, 54, 55, 66, 88, 118, 189, 273, 275, 285, 286, 303, 312, 332, 349, 354, 394, 398, 406, 444.
McCown, Jane, 92.
McCown, John, 44, 60, 66, 85, 107, 285, 291, 295, 325, 329, 391.
McCown, Katrine, 66.
McCown, Malcom, 66, 85, 489.
McCown, Margaret, 66, 93, 255, 346, 349, 354, 398, 406.
McCown, Mary, 93.
McCown, Moses, 85, 92, 93, 291.
McCown, Nancy, 66.
McCown, Samuel, 84.
McCoy (McCay), James, 21, 48, 62, 84, 85, 87, 103, 186, 434, 442, 456, 461, 466, 525, 571, 584.
McCoy, Jane, 571.
McCoy (McCay), John, 52, 63, 65, 121, 125, 137, 139, 157, 163, 176, 179, 191, 344, 411, 434, 442, 456, 461, 525, 530, 535, 584.
McCoy, Mary, 18.
McCoy, Moses, 25.
McCoy, Oliver, 535, 587.
McCoy, Sarah, 442, 525, 530.

McCoy, Zacharay, 25.
McCrab, William, 316.
McCrary, James, 131.
McCray (McCrea), Alexander, 17, 246.
McCray, Archibald A., 219.
McCray, Jean, 219.
McCray, Margaret, 219.
McCrea, David, 159.
McCrea, Mary, 246.
McCreary (McCray), Jean, 194.
McCredie (McCready), Thomas, 388, 510.
McCredie, William, 510.
McCreery, Agness, 107, 302, 363, 403.
McCreery (McCreary), John, 26, 48, 88, 98, 107, 122, 139, 164, 302, 306, 339, 363, 386, 403, 427, 443, 517, 534, 565, 579, 590, 593.
McCreery, Martha, 579.
McCreery, Robert, 107, 139, 164.
McCreerey, William, 12.
McCroscery, James, 189.
McCroskry, Alexander, 50, 51, 268, 290, 322, 344, 491, 520.
McCroskry, John, 30, 50, 52, 71, 181, 263, 267, 284, 287, 322, 443, 579.
McCroskry (McCoskey, McCoskery), Samuel, 50, 51, 62, 322, 329, 349, 367.
McCroskry, William, 50, 51, 284, 311.
McCrosky, Mary, 167.
McCrown, Samuel, 8.
McCue, Allen, 235.
McCue, James A., 237.
McCue (McKeu), John, 292, 594.
McCue, Patrick, 26.
McCullagh, Isaac, 271.
McCullagh, Margaret, 271.
McCulley, John, 74.
McCulloch, Isabell, 66.
McCulloch, John, 66, 548.
McCulloch, Rachel, 66.
McCullock (McCollough), Robert, 215, 216, 573, 578, 583, 589.
McCullough, Mathew, 104, 447.
McCullough, Nancy, 243.
McCullough, Thomas Turk, 234.
McCune, Allen, 238.
McCune, Anne, 206, 222, 230.
McCune, Archibald, 206, 222, 230.
McCune, Elizabeth, 222.
McCune, Francis, 253, 256, 290, 293, 299.
McCune, James, 206, 238, 277.
McCune, James A., 206.
McCune, John, 206, 222, 230, 238, 568.
McCune, Margaret (Peggy), 222, 238, 252.
McCune, Mary, 222.
McCune, Samuel, 22, 51, 67, 166, 206, 222, 230, 238, 278, 279, 316, 324, 344, 432, 511, 522.
McCune, William, 206, 222, 231.
McCurey, Archibald, 484.

McCurry, William, 74, 118, 280, 458.
McCurtle, James, 278.
McCutchan, Jones, 219.
McCutchan, Mary, 219.
McCutchan, Robert, 219, 337, 351, 368, 373, 445, 451, 456, 569, 573.
McCutchen, Elizabeth, 52, 139, 535.
McCutchen, Francis, 257, 468, 469.
McCutchen, Grisal, 52.
McCutchen, Hannah, 206.
McCutchen, Isabella, 234.
McCutchen, James, 50, 52, 54, 219, 240, 277, 282, 334, 467, 500, 531, 535, 555, 582.
McCutchen, Jennate, 186, 188.
McCutchen, John, 52, 171, 172, 196, 206, 210, 219, 277, 282, 283, 284, 312, 383, 432, 467, 468, 469, 500, 511, 535, 569, 582, 596.
McCutchen, John Patrick, 234.
McCutchen, Margaret, 229, 246, 569, 573, 582.
McCutchen, Patrick, 52, 535.
McCutchen, Samuel, 12, 26, 50, 52, 90, 95, 104, 117, 132, 135, 150, 158, 159, 161, 162, 171, 190, 196, 201, 257, 274, 307, 312, 319, 320, 334, 346, 358, 427, 438, 467, 468, 469, 500, 501, 531, 564, 577, 582.
McCutchen, Sarah, 52.
McCutchen, Thomas, 240.
McCutchen, William, 11, 17, 52, 87, 90, 93, 95, 186, 196, 211, 225, 271, 277, 281, 312, 324, 325, 333, 337, 351, 358, 360, 368, 383, 396, 411, 416, 429, 432, 467, 500, 501, 569, 582.
McDade, John, 23.
McDanaght, John, 591.
McDaniel, John, 360, 384, 521.
McDavid, Martha, 562, 583.
McDavid, Patrick, 562, 563, 583.
McDavitt, William, 201, 202.
McDole, James, 62.
McDonal, Sarah, 139.
McDonald (McDonall, McDonnall), Alexander, 42, 53, 94, 101, 352, 390, 412, 472.
McDonald (McDanniel), Bryan, 45, 48, 55, 63, 73, 75, 82, 103, 110, 111, 113, 397, 423, 491.
McDonald, Catherine, 45, 55.
McDonald, Charles, 577.
McDonald, David, 521.
McDonald, Edmund, 33.
McDonald, Edward, 25, 39, 45, 49, 55, 59, 63, 74, 314, 318, 320, 371, 397, 451.
McDonald (McDonell), Elisabeth, 85, 397.
McDonald (McDonall), Francis (Fras), 57, 69, 85, 139, 359, 468, 561.
McDonald, Grany, 109.

McDonald (McDonnal), Henry, 121, 139, 561, 592.
McDonald (McDonell), Hugh, 74, 85.
McDonald, Isaac, 521.
McDonald, James, 45, 561.
McDonald (McDonnald), Jannet, 46, 55.
McDonald (McDonnel), John, 21, 22, 37, 53, 85, 101, 357, 365, 561.
McDonald, Joseph, 45, 50, 63, 73, 117, 318, 331, 334, 397, 465.
McDonald, Margaret, 472, 561.
McDonald, Martha, 561.
McDonald (McDonell), Mary, 59, 85, 331, 422.
McDonald, Patrick, 378.
McDonald, Prisla, 45.
McDonald (McDonall, McDonell), Randall (Randolph), 42, 46, 48, 89, 280, 541.
McDonald, Richard, 45.
McDonald (McDannal, McDonell), Samuel, 85, 121, 127, 566.
McDonell, Rebecca, 85.
McDonell, William, 85.
McDonough, Dianah, 166.
McDonough, Edward H., 166.
McDonough, John, 166, 169, 176, 179, 193.
McDougall, John, 525, 534, 554, 556, 576, 577.
McDowell, Alexander, 298, 308, 368, 393, 528, 541.
McDowell, Alice, 227.
McDowell, Elizabeth, 121, 227, 390, 456.
McDowell, Ephraim, 263, 336, 396.
McDowell, Francis, 415, 478, 479.
McDowell, Hugh, 181, 186, 202, 562, 580, 581, 589.
McDowell, James, 31, 39, 41, 68, 78, 79, 81, 82, 91, 93, 101, 105, 106, 109, 121, 126, 134, 258, 263, 276, 304, 335, 336, 346, 347, 358, 360, 368, 390, 394, 395, 399, 403, 414, 415, 417, 422, 429, 433, 435, 437, 439, 453, 456, 464, 469, 471, 478, 479, 483, 489, 491, 496, 521, 530, 564.
McDowell, John, 7, 35, 41, 201, 202, 215, 227, 228, 258, 259, 263, 270, 276, 325, 326, 336, 368, 385, 433, 437, 528, 530.
McDowell, Margaret, 227.
McDowell, Mary, 202, 346, 384, 385, 390, 414, 433, 437, 439, 475, 530.
McDowell, Mathew, 113, 414, 418.
McDowell, Robert, 200, 202, 215, 216, 589.
McDowell, Samuel, 31, 35, 47, 68, 77, 78, 81, 82, 91, 101, 103, 106, 107, 114, 121, 123, 129, 133, 134, 148, 336, 343, 346, 358, 368, 378, 384, 385, 387, 390, 394, 399, 403, 414, 429, 432, 433, 435, 437, 439, 447, 463, 464, 475, 484, 491, 528, 530, 537, 539, 549, 564.
McDowell, Sarah, 31, 202.
McDowell, William, 111, 126, 191, 227, 490, 493, 499, 549, 564, 575, 583, 589.
McDoyle, John, 28.
McElheney (McAlhany, McIlhenney, McElhenony), William, 46, 380, 381, 435, 484.
McElhenny, Francis, 422.
McElhenny (McIlhany), John, 474, 493, 575.
McElhenny, Robert, 48, 73, 286, 342, 348, 423, 469, 471, 498.
McElhenny (McIlhany), Thomas, 465, 491.
McElheny (McIlhenny), Mary, 418, 484.
McElheney, James, 484.
McElroy (McEleroi), Agness, 386, 559.
McElroy (McAlroy), Alexander, 37, 52, 385, 386, 559.
McElvain, Andrew, 194.
McElvain, Margaret, 139, 499.
McElvain, Moses, 398, 449, 499, 502.
McElwrath, Robert, 463.
McEntosh, Michael, 167.
McFadden, Elisabeth, 498.
McFadden, Hugh, 432, 464, 498, 525.
McFadden, John, 217, 235, 236.
McFall, Cornelius, 159.
McFall, John, 9, 64, 375.
McFarland, Alexander, 207.
McFarland, Duncan, 332, 450, 498.
McFarland, Elenor, 207.
McFarland, Francis, 577.
McFarland, Isabella, 207.
McFarland, James, 207.
McFarland (McFarling), John, 28, 205, 207, 401, 461, 577, 578.
McFarland, Mary, 207, 401, 461.
McFarland, Robert, 75, 330.
McFarlane, Margaret, 189.
McFarlin (Farling(land)), Daniel, 205, 207.
McFarling, Ann, 206, 207.
McFarling, William, 459.
McFaul, Neal, 187.
McFaul, Olive, 238.
McFeeters, Margaret, 556.
McFerran (McFerrin), Martin, 434, 485.
McFerran, Samuel, 485, 486.
McFerran (McFerrin), Thomas, 65, 80, 314, 485, 486.
McFerrin, Agnes, 62.
McFerrin, James, 62, 65, 78.
McFerrin (McFarron, McFerring), John, 65, 67, 78, 80, 277, 286, 290, 295, 376, 485.
McFerson, John, 442.
McFerson (McFarson), Robert, 11, 53.
McGarry (McGary, McGeery), Edward, 51, 54, 62, 71, 84, 92, 372, 406.
McGarry, John, 372, 401.
McGarry, Robert, 68, 70, 372.

McGarry, Sarah, 401.
McGary, Hugh, 71, 98.
McGaughey, William, 119.
McGavock, James, 68, 77, 81, 87, 89, 346, 447, 469, 480, 484.
McGee, Charles, 111, 113, 121.
McGee, Hugh, 159.
McGee, James, 55.
McGee, Jane (Jean), 57, 490.
McGee, Richard, 93.
McGee, Robert, 397.
McGee, William, 22, 43, 291, 346, 490, 499.
McGill, James, 51, 62, 503, 522.
McGill, John, 24, 51.
McGill, Margaret, 51.
McGill, Martha, 236.
McGill, Mary, 230.
McGill, Robert, 230.
McGill, Samuel, 149.
Magill, William, 9, 47, 490.
McGinney, Alexander, 557.
McGinnis, Edward, 15.
McGitre, Robert, 96.
McGlamery, John, 170.
McGlamry, Martha, 115.
McGlaughlan, Margaret, 68.
McGlaughlin, James, 149.
McGonagal, Margaret, 178.
McGonagle, Patrick, 566.
McGonegal, James, 201, 215, 583.
McGonegal, Newman, 331.
McGooney, James, 190.
McGouneig, Newman, 334.
McGowin, John, 37.
McGraw, Agnes, 144.
McGraw, Sally, 167.
McGriffin, Robert, 199.
McGuffey, James, 399, 467.
McGuiness, John, 287.
McGuire, Jack, 126.
McGuire, James, 161.
McGwillan, Robert, 570.
McHan, Robert, 45.
McHenry, Barnard (Bernard), 269, 440, 543.
McIlroy, Alexander, 159.
McIlvain, John, 587.
McIntire, John, 67.
McIntosh, George G., 215, 224, 236.
McKain (McKair), James, 103, 465, 470.
McKain, Margaret, 470.
McKane, William, 210.
McKanear, Hanah, 128.
McKarter, Thankful, 195.
McKay, Elizabeth, 25.
McKay, Hannah, 25.
McKay, Isaac, 18.
McKay, James, 25, 289, 294, 383, 474, 533.
McKay, John, 260.
McKay, Leah, 25.

McKay, Lydia, 474.
McKay, Margaret, 25.
McKay, Mary, 25, 383, 474.
McKay, Moses, 17, 25, 474, 533.
McKay (McCay), Robert, 13, 25, 274, 302, 308, 383, 474, 533.
McKay, Zackary (Zachoriah), 25, 474, 533.
McKeachvy, Cormick, 459.
McKeachy (McKachey, McKatchey), James, 19, 64, 70, 295.
McKearney, John, 289.
McKee, David, 573.
McKee, James, 62, 291, 341, 350, 433, 443, 537.
McKee, John, 76, 82, 90, 96, 99, 112, 246, 288, 306, 328, 349, 410, 422, 428, 437, 469, 471, 495, 511, 537.
McKee, Lydia, 433.
McKee, Rosanna, 537.
McKee, Samuel, 118, 180, 211, 450, 508, 510, 567, 573, 591.
McKee, William, 83, 92, 99, 112, 205, 220, 350, 367, 407, 428, 429, 435, 464, 473, 474, 476, 484, 495.
McKemey, Agness, 186, 247, 513.
McKemey, Elizabeth, 186, 209.
McKemey, Ellenor, 209.
McKemey, Isabella, 209.
McKemey (McKemy), James, 136, 171, 175, 186, 209, 218, 222, 247, 511, 534, 576, 581.
McKemey, Jean (Jane), 186, 247.
McKemey (McKemy, McKeemey), John, 152, 172, 175, 176, 181, 186, 201, 209, 215, 247, 271, 352, 513, 534, 549, 570, 577, 579.
McKemey, Margaret (Peggy), 186, 209.
McKemey, Nancy, 209.
McKemey, Polly, 209.
McKemey (McKemy), Robert, 186, 426.
McKemey (McKemy), William 66, 115, 157, 161, 186, 209, 212, 352, 451, 511, 513, 528, 582.
McKemy, Jo, 135.
McKendrick, Patrick, 287.
McKeney, Robert, 60, 97.
McKennan, William, 210.
McKenney, James, 571.
McKenny, Bernard, 426.
McKenny (McKenney), John, 99, 569, 571.
McKenny (McKemy), William, 99, 136, 571.
McKeters, William, 406.
McKibben (McKibbin), James, 580, 583.
McKibben, John, 583.
McKim, John, 218.
McKim, Robert, 105.
McKinney, Alexander, 596.
McKinney (McKiney), Jane, 196.

McKinney, John, 71, 196, 545, **596.**
McKinney, Robert, 596.
McKinsey, Alexander, 107.
McKirgan, Thomas, 236.
MacKitrick, Jame, 145.
McKitrick, Jane, 143, 420.
McKitrick, John, 170, 208.
McKitrick (McCittrick), Robert, 141, **143,** 171, 208, 324, 420, 500, 519, 562, **587.**
McKittrick, Isbell, 208.
McKittrick, James, 208.
McKittrick, Margaret, 208.
McKittrick, Sarah, 208.
McKittrick, William, 208.
McKnight, Daniel, 61.
McKnight (McNight), Elizabeth, **456,** 461.
McKnight, James, 239.
McKnight (McNutt), John, 573.
McKnight, Mary, 55, 215.
McKnight, Timothy, 192.
McKnob, William, 232.
McKown, French, 60.
McLain, Archibald, 493.
McLary, Hugh, 182.
McLaughlan (McLoughlin), **James, 201,** 589.
McLaughland, Archibald, 166.
McLean, Daniel, 140.
McLean, James, 567.
McLeary (McLeery), James, 332.
McLeary (McLeery), John, 271, 332, **573,** 574.
McLeery, Elizabeth, 574.
McLehenny, Robert, 117.
McLong, James, 41.
McMachan, John, 318, 382.
McMachan, William, 263, 312.
McMachen, Isabella, 382.
McMachen, Richard, 152.
McMahan, Isabella, 432.
McMahon, Deborah, 170, 560.
McMahon, Elizabeth, 170.
McMahon, John, 109, 116, 126, 134, **152,** 170, 171, 372, 403, 432, 485, **503, 560.**
McMahon, Margaret, 440.
McMahon, Mary, 170.
McMahon, Nancy, 170.
McMahon, Robert, 34, 35, 39, 170, **305,** 318, 369, 372, 527, 440, 463, 481, **485,** **503, 560.**
McMahon, Samuel, 35, 39, 318, 390.
McMahon, William, 170.
McManis, James, 167.
McManners, James, 187.
McMaster, John, 144, 252, 531.
McMath, James, 484.
McMath, Susanna, 484.
McMechan, Benjamin, 521.
McMillin, James, 100.
McMolan, Alexander, 81.

McMolan, Easter, 82.
McMolan, William, 81.
McMortry (McMurtery), Joseph, **64, 452.**
McMory (McMurry), William, 53.
McMullen (McMillin), Alexander, 19, **22,** 35, 294, 295, 311.
McMullen, Esther, 35.
McMullen, Sarah, 144, 146.
McMullen (McMillin), William, 92, **93,** 98, 355, 365, 400, 424, 467.
McMullin, Edward, 354.
McMullin, Mary, 400.
McMullin, Michael, 455.
McMurphey, Mary, 154.
McMurray, Barney, 166.
McMurray, Thomas, 293, 335.
McMurtrey, John, 358, 484.
McMurtry (McMurty), Samuel, 55, **62,** 73, 358, 367, 386, 446, 464, 484.
McMurtry, Sarah, **340.**
McMurty, Alexander, 55.
McNabb, Andrew, 271, 291.
McNabb, Baptist, 34, 62, 70, 100, 260, **283,** 297, 299, 366, 378, 388, 451, 519.
McNabb, Catherine (Kathren), 378, 519.
McNabb, Isabell, 473.
McNabb, James, 93, 349, 387, 437, **480,** 499, 500.
McNabb, John, 66, 97, 271, 288, 295, **296,** 480.
McNabb, Martha, 499, 500.
McNabb, Mary, 271.
McNabb (McKnab), Samuel, 397, **401,** 429, 434, 466, 473, 487, 500.
McNabb, Sarah, 142.
McNabb (McKnab), William, 167, **281,** 293, 284, 318, 323, 326, 477, 499, **500,** 567.
McNair, Elizabeth, 196.
McNare, Andrew, 581.
McNare (McNair), David, 168, 186, **196,** 197, 203, 208, 214, 223, 250, 591, **594.**
McNeal (McNeill), James, 14, 106.
McNeal (McNeil), Neal, 25, 38, 44, **45,** 67, 70, 75, 79, 87, 110, 319.
McNeal, Thomas, 453.
McNeall, George, 537.
McNeeley, David, 84, 164, 507, 542.
McNeeley, George, 177.
McNeeley, Sarah, 177.
McNeeley, William, 542.
McNeelly, Rebecca, 161.
McNees (McNiece), Jane, 524, 554.
McNees, John, 544.
McNees (McNiece), William, 524, 554.
McNeil (McNeal), Daniel, 121, 423, **458,** 461, 465, 470, 491.
McNeill, Annabella, 89.
McNeill, Hector, 88, 100, 102.
McNeill, Henrietta, 89.
McNeill, John, 88, 90, 100, **350.**

McNeill, William, 414.
McNeilly, Andrew, 375.
McNelie, Eleanor, 66.
McNelle, Hugh, 450.
McNulty, John, 102, 362.
McNutt, Alexander, 30, 115, 238, 311, 316, 333, 398, 407, 426, 517, 574, 575.
McNutt, Catren, 387.
McNutt, Daniel, 474.
McNutt (McKnut), James, 14, 15, 29, 30. 47, 115, 238, 286, 311, 398, 407, 517.
McNutt, Jane, 238.
McNutt, John, 69, 108, 326, 387, 454, 575.
McNutt, Margaret, 238.
McNutt, Samuel, 238.
McNutt, Robert, 30, 152, 238, 426, 432, 517.
McNutt, Samuel H., 246.
McNutt, Sarah, 517.
McPheeters (McFeeters), Alexander, 59, 63, 64, 66, 70, 134, 135, 214, 215, 262, 269, 281, 323, 334, 500, 531.
McPheeters (McFeeters), Ann, 63, 214.
McPheeters, James, 214, 231.
McPheeters, James A., 231.
McPheeters, Jean, 214.
McPheeters (McFeeters), Jannet, 63, 127.
McPheeters (McFeeters), John, 48, 49, 66, 86, 101, 121, 127, 157, 214, 289, 296, 297, 320, 323, 332, 346, 363, 379, 422, 485, 505, 553, 591.
McPheeters (McFeeters), Martha, 63, 127, 214.
McPheeters (McFeeters), Mary, 127, 129, 429.
McPheeters, Philander, 231.
McPheeters, Rachel, 231.
McPheeters (McFeeters), Rebecca, 63. 214, 553.
McPheeters, Robert, 214.
McPheeters (McFeeters), Samuel, 86, 99, 101, 128, 130, 415, 451, 456, 556, 590.
McPheeters, Sophronia, 231.
McPheeters, Theophilus, 231.
McPheeters (McFeeters), William, 5, 11, 21, 22, 25, 48, 58, 63, 66, 96, 105, 107, 115, 127, 128, 130, 132, 179, 183, 191, 207, 210, 231, 251, 267, 283, 289, 292, 295, 297, 302, 320, 331, 332, 351, 389, 415, 422, 429, 470, 503, 565, 576, 577, 593.
McPherson, Charles, 425.
McQuillen, Robert, 590.
McRandolph, Robert, 54.
McReeters, William, 349.
McRoberts, John, 121, 151, 164, 589.
McRoberts, Samuel, 48, 63, 67, 72, 75, 98, 101, 111, 121, 275, 401, 450, 473, 474, 486.
McRory, Margaret, 308.

McRory, William, 298, 307.
McRoy, James, 406.
McShery, Thomas, 491.
McSpadden, Moses, 475.
McSpaden (McSpedon), Thomas, 16, 24, 257, 259, 266, 353, 396, 399.
McSpeden, Archibald, 535.
McSwine, George, 32, 35, 314.
McTeer, Eliza, 239.
McTeer, Isabella, 240.
McTeer, Jane, 239.
McTeer, Mitchel, 239.
McTeer, William, 145, 239, 240.
McVey, George, 399.
McVey, James, 157, 179, 554, 556.
McVey, John, 157.
McVey, Margaret, 157.
Macwill, William, 124.

Maag, Rudolph, 5.
Maagill, Matha E., 208.
Macan, John, 37.
Mace (Maese), Ann, 390, 541.
Mace (Maese), Henry, 131, 362, 366, 390, 401, 496.
Mace (Maese, Mase), Nicholas, 40, 362, 366, 378, 390, 401, 496, 526, 541.
Machir, James, 293.
Mack, Felty, 63.
Macky, Betsy, 133.
Macky, Esther, 133.
Macky, Henry, 133.
Macky, Jane, 133.
Macky (Makev), John, 13, 23, 66, 133, 137, 328, 341, 388.
Macky, Mary, 133.
Macky, Robert, 523.
Macky, William, 133.
Macuell, John, 340.
Madey, James, 149.
Madison, Agatha, 296, 367, 372, 380, 502, 538.
Madison, Catherine, 114.
Madison, Gabriel, 479, 572, 574.
Madison, George, 63.
Madison, Humphrey, 44, 52, 114, 271, 277, 279, 314, 337.
Madison, James, 456.
Madison, John, 22, 34, 35, 43, 63, 76, 77, 78, 84, 89, 91, 92, 102, 104, 114, 115, 116, 121, 124, 126, 137, 138, 251, 253, 255, 257, 263, 265, 267, 270, 277, 280, 285, 288, 292, 293, 296, 297, 303, 312, 317, 329, 330, 331, 334, 337, 350, 353, 361, 367, 372, 375, 380, 395, 403, 422, 445, 457, 458, 476, 479, 483, 502, 503, 508, 516, 523, 525, 537, 538.
Madison, Lewis, 293, 310.
Madison, Mary, 52.
Madison, Priscilla, 172.

Madison, Richard, 151, 166, 172, 523, 534, 537.
Madison, Thomas, 107, 114, 116, 121, 124, 362, 381, 394, 409, 419, 429, 434, 448, 467, 470, 486, 487, 490, 491, 516.
Madison, William, 504.
Madison, William S., 509.
Mafet, James, 263.
Magart (Magot, Mageth, Magert), David, 21, 140, 142, 291, 494, 506, 507.
Magavock, James, 406.
Magee, Robert, 423.
Magee, William, 13, 57, 347, 450.
Magert, Catharine, 140.
Maggart (Magert), John, 70, 304.
Maggot, Samuel, 110.
Magill, Elizabeth, 14.
Magill (Megill), James, 14, 92, 140, 274, 296, 373, 478, 508.
Magill, Jean, 208, 481.
Magill (Megill), John, 14, 72, 140, 373, 492, 493, 503, 516, 522, 526, 534, 536.
Magill, Margaret, 14, 15.
Magill, Mary, 246, 373.
Magill, William, 14, 15, 34, 51, 72, 92, 359, 360, 393, 481, 546, 559.
Maglaken, Hugh, 92.
Magonel, James, 184.
Magot, Hance, 42, 44, 95.
Magret, Christian, 29.
Magruder, Nath D., 167.
Mahafey, Charles, 404.
Mahan, Martha, 25.
Maharfey, John, 498.
Mahey, John, 8, 50.
Maighan, John T., 45.
Maighan, Theobald, 58.
Mair, Charles, 148.
Mair (Mares), Hugh, 110, 363, 428.
Mair, James, 587.
Maitland, Robert, 542.
Make, Henry, 108.
Malarie, Mary, 192.
Malchier, Valentine, 377.
Malcom, Alexander, 434.
Malcom, Dorothy, 530.
Malcom (Malckom, Malkem), John, 45, 55, 61, 66, 84, 101, 121, 125, 339, 343, 404, 429, 434, 442, 511, 520, 521, 522, 534.
Malcom, Joseph, 139, 191, 434, 456, 461, 525, 530, 534, 576, 579.
Malcon, Alexander, 246.
Malden (Maulding), Richard, 259, 406, 429, 482, 531, 537.
Maley, James, 238.
Mallow, Adam, 127, 156.
Mallow (Mallo, Malloa), George, 110, 124, 419, 420, 432, 469, 549.
Mallow (Mallo), Michael, 49, 51, 56, 58, 62, 63, 84, 86, 89, 90, 99, 115, 119, 127, 130, 156, 471, 494, 523.
Malkem, George, 66.
Malkem, Margaret, 66.
Man, Ann M., 469.
Man, Barnet, 439, 469, 480, 533.
Man, Bernard, 53, 69, 94.
Man, Charles, 57, 69, 400.
Man (Mann), George, 85, 108, 394, 439, 469, 533.
Man, Jacob, 57, 383, 439, 469.
Man, Margaret, 439.
Manahon, Daniel, 493.
Mann, Damis, 416.
Mann, George B., 18.
Mann (Man), John, 25, 42, 59, 100, 102, 104, 388, 416, 422, 439, 469.
Mann (Man), Moses, 42, 271, 416.
Mann, Samuel, 109.
Mann, Thomas, 25, 119.
Mann (Man), William, 77, 102, 381, 416, 422, 453.
Mannin, Michael, 141, 158.
Mans, Peter, 596.
Mans, Rosannah, 404, 596.
Mara (Mora, Marra), Francis, 158, 164, 169, 203, 563.
March, Boston, 513.
March, Sebastian, 549.
March, William, 9.
Marchle, Charles, 581.
Mark, David, 148.
Mark (Marks), Jacob, 148, 552.
Mark, Mary, 148.
Mark (Marks), William, 92, 370.
Markle, Tobias, 200.
Markley, William, 517.
Marks (Marcs), John, 169, 306.
Marks (Mark), Margaret, 148, 552.
Marrett, Susanna, 509.
Marshal, Catherine, 23.
Marshall, Benjamin, 507, 516.
Marshall, George, 79, 197, 488, 522, 560.
Marshall, Gilbert, 111.
Marshall, Henry, 195.
Marshall (Marsall), James, 123, 133, 420, 433.
Marshall, Jane, 106.
Marshall John, 117, 288, 294, 356, 400, 547, 560.
Marshall, Lindsay, 214, 220, 223.
Marshall, Thomas, 210, 228.
Marshall, William, 106, 302, 326, 343, 387, 504.
Marten, Janet, 363.
Martin, Agness, 139, 420.
Martin, Andrew, 15, 16, 114.
Martin, Ann, 286.
Martin, David, 398, 478, 575.
Martin, Edward, 580.

Martin, George, 66, 94, 104, 114, 115, 396, 496.
Martin (Mardin), Hanah, 577.
Martin, Henry, 276.
Martin, Hugh, 12, 14, 15, 53, 64, 94, 128, 253, 259, 272, 284, 291, 293, 308, 316, 348, 360, 389, 392, 393, 411, 414, 418, 420, 442, 561.
Martin, Jacob, 49, 60, 79, 90, 278.
Martin, James, 114, 145.
Martin, Jane, 114, 409, 485.
Martin, Jesse, 577.
Martin, John, 81, 151.
Martin, Joseph, 5, 114.
Martin, Martha, 10.
Martin, Mary, 496, 561, 586.
Martin, Morris, 151.
Martin, Patrick, 7, 10, 11, 15, 25, 39, 48, 51, 90, 98, 105, 114, 117, 189, 272, 281, 283, 289, 295, 302, 331, 359, 360, 409, 412, 431, 445, 470, 485.
Martin, Richard, 287.
Martin, Robert, 286, 337, 339, 418, 448.
Martin, Salathiel, 575.
Martin, Thomas, 220.
Martin, William, 20, 90, 94, 290, 293, 307, 311, 316, 323, 338, 363, 366, 389, 411, 418, 420, 470, 493.
Mason, Alexander, 201.
Mason, James, 64.
Mason, Jannet, 64.
Mason (Meason), John, 12, 15, 17, 19, 42, 53, 64, 70, 79, 421.
Mason, Joseph, 64.
Mason, Leah, 64.
Mason, Margaret, 64.
Mason, Mary, 64.
Mason, Philip, 47.
Mason, Robert, 569.
Mason, William, 64.
Massie, Nathaniel, 230.
Massive, Thomas, 182.
Matchier, Valentine, 420, 481, 482.
Mathes, Alexander, 6.
Mathes, George, 169.
Mathes, Robert, 115.
Matheson, Alexander, 36, 43, 45.
Matheson, Gilbert, 44.
Matheson, John, 44.
Mathew, David, 151, 190, 192, 213, 546.
Mathews, Alexander, 10.
Mathews, Anne, 46, 84, 287, 315, 343, 443, 550, 560, 575.
Mathews, Archer, 46, 138, 241, 418, 425, 448, 459, 476, 478, 479, 496, 497, 506.
Mathews, Archibald, 443.
Mathews, Catherine, 230, 238, 589.
Mathews, Charles L., 241.
Mathews, Edward, 84.
Mathews, Elizabeth, 46, 100.
Mathews, Francis Meriwether, 241.
Mathews, George, 46, 82, 84, 86, 93, **96,** 98, 111, 112, 115, 116, 121, 124, **125,** 127, 134, 138, 141, 241, 343, 351, 377, 389, 425, 437, 439, 443, 448, 453, 454, 459, 460, 485, 488, 492, 497, 506, **512,** 518, 537, 550, 560, 568, 574, **575.**
Mathews, James, 201, 238.
Mathews, Jane, 46, 84.
Mathews, John, 22, 33, 36, 46, 48, 49, 54, 57, 63, 84, 93, 230, 238, 241, 259, **265,** 268, 280, 287, 292, 301, 306, 315, **317,** 318, 330, 331, 332, 341, 342, 343, **349,** 351, 371, 395, 396, 443, 453, 478, **496,** 543.
Mathews, Joseph, 208, 222, 238.
Mathews, Joshua, 36, 39, 46, 82, 93, **100,** 125, 287, 315, 318, 342, 351.
Mathews, Lettice (Lettis), 84, **506.**
Mathews, Margaret, 238.
Mathews, Martha, 125.
Mathews, Mary (Molly), 79, 167, 241, 395, 550, 560.
Mathews, Rachel, 46
Mathews, Richard, 46, 105, 153, 197, **204,** 238, 287, 318, 332, 343, 443, 476, **478,** 516, 580, 581, 590.
Mathews, Robert, 562.
Mathews, Sally, 576.
Mathews, Sampson, 32, 46, 70, 79, 84, **90,** 92, 93, 96, 98, 111, 115, 116, 121, **122,** 124, 125, 126, 127, 145, 176, 199, **202,** 204, 209, 230, 325, 331, 351, 359, 377, 382, 389, 395, 397, 425, 439, 444, **445,** 448, 453, 454, 459, 460, 476, 479, **485,** 488, 492, 496, 497, 506, 507, 523, **529,** 543, 547, 549, 550, 560, 568, 581, **582,** 585, 589.
Mathews, Samuel, 377.
Mathews, Samuel B., 241.
Mathews, William, 46, 63, 95, 105, **109,** 111, 133, 153, 232, 238, 241, 276, **351,** 365, 369, 442, 467, 478, 492, 528, **562,** 593.
Mathinearly, James, 565.
Matteson, John, 34.
Matthewson (Matheson), **Mathew, 44,** 120, 178, 529.
Mauk, Cathrine, 440.
Mauk (Mauck, Maught, Mack), **Rudolph** (Rude, Rudy), 17, 21, 108, 440, **448,** 479, 490, 512, 522, 531, 537.
Maupin, Cornelius, 187, 564.
Maupin, Jesse, 125.
Maurice, Hance (Haunce), 74, **75, 323.**
Maurray, Henry, 67.
Maurray, John, 111.
Maurry (Maury), James, 104, 542.
Mauzie, Peter, 28.
Maxwell, Adley, 283.
Maxwell, Alexander, 152.
Maxwell, Jacob, 177.

Maxwell, John, 25, 28, 33, 36, 43, 48, 64, 75, 78, 84, 261, 263, 271, 273, 277, 284, 287, 289, 292, 297, 317, 318, 343, 346, 350, 363, 434, 443, 447, 469, 488.
Maxwell, Mary, 317, 434.
May, Caleb, 102, 443.
May (Mays, Maise), Richard, 241, 550.
May, Rulen, 433.
May, Stephen, 176, 452, 549.
Mayberry, George, 575.
Mayer, Christenah, 510.
Mayer, Jacob, 132, 135, 137, 382, 510.
Mayes, Robert, 226.
Mays, Archibald, 241.
Mays, Ester, 241.
Mays, George, 198.
Mays (Maze), Isaac, 241.
Mays (Maze), James, 10, 43, 45, 50, 241.
Mays (Mayze, Mais), Joseph, 35, 37, 80, 164, 241, 334, 346, 442, 458, 500, 520, 587.
Mays, Margaret, 209.
Mays, Nancy, 241.
Mays (Maze), Rebekah, 241, 346, 500.
Mays, Sarah, 241.
Mays, William, 43, 50, 80.
Mead, John, 243.
Mealray, Elicksander, 20.
Means, Hugh, 23, 339.
Means, James, 80, 337, 397.
Means, Robert, 40.
Means, William, 408.
Mease, James, 26, 389.
Measl, James, 6.
Meckghew, Jacob, 167.
Medley, John, 74, 110.
Meek, Agnes, 179, 206, 216.
Meek, Daniel, 118, 167, 179, 216.
Meek, Elizabeth, 192.
Meek, Jane, 115.
Meek (Meaks), John, 61, 63, 77, 115, 153, 179, 416.
Meek, Samuel, 179.
Meek, Thomas, 49, 64, 77, 179, 180, 337, 351, 360, 416, 445.
Meek, William, 77.
Megarry (Megerry), John, 389, 402.
Megarry, Sarah, 402.
Megary, Edward, 40.
Meglamery, John, 561.
Megongal, James, 192, 195, 589.
Megongal, Margaret, 195.
Mehafey, Charles, 84.
Mehoney, Dennis, 201.
Melcomb, John, 303.
Melligan, Charles, 309.
Melser, Palser, 74.
Melvin, James, 100.
Menerley, David, 94.
Menken, Thomas, 174.
Mentire, John, 54.

Meredith, J., 492.
Meriwether, David, 48.
Meriwether, Rebecca, 241.
Meriwether, Thomas, 6, 574.
Merrila, Samuel, 201.
Merritt, Catherine, 221.
Merritt, Samuel, 171, 221, 578, 580, 588, 589.
Mertin, Lewis, 176, 181.
Messexs, Elihu, 157.
Meteer (Mateer), Elizabeth (Betsy), 201, 225, 313.
Meteer (Mateer), James, 124, 201, 222, 225, 239, 313, 520.
Meteer, Jenny, 229.
Meteer, Sally, 225.
Meteer, Samuel, 201, 222, 225.
Meteer, William, 150, 156, 201, 208, 225, 495, 499, 500.
Metsker, Henry, 144.
Miars, Henry, 53.
Michael, Christian, 214.
Michael, Elizabeth, 214.
Michael, Frederick, 214, 217, 395, 451, 587.
Michael, George, 214.
Michael, Jacob, 214.
Michael, John, 168, 214, 240.
Michael, William, 214.
Michelsneler, John, 289.
Michker, Paulser, 141.
Mickamy, James, 245.
Mickamy, Jane, 245.
Mickken, Gasper, 147.
Migrons, Christopher, 189.
Mildebarger, Nicholas, 412
Miles, James, 260, 313, 329, 351, 361, 471, 495.
Miles, John, 24.
Miliken, Arthur, 15.
Milikin, Joseph, 18.
Miliron, Christian, 93.
Miliron, Christian G., 406, 408, 452, 475.
Miliron, Mary, 452, 475.
Mill, Joseph, 379.
Mill, William, 467.
Millar, George, 538.
Millar, Hannah, 249, 269, 382, 394, 399, 449, 451.
Millbery, Barbara, 494.
Millbery, Nicholas, 32, 57, 94, 480, 494.
Miller, Abraham, 148, 350, 463, 477, 513, 553.
Miller, Adam, 40, 102, 269, 420.
Miller, Agnes, 191, 226.
Miller, Alexander, 44, 51, 62, 70, 71, 75, 97, 273, 310, 318, 327, 345, 348, 353, 361, 364, 382, 399, 415, 457, 458, 496.
Miller, Andrew, 95, 99, 437, 470, 474.
Miller, Ann, 84, 352, 452, 503.
Miller, Barbara, 259, 506.

Miller, Caspar, 569.
Miller, Catherine, 54, 104, 195, 324, 328, 555.
Miller, Christian, 15, 16, 311, 488, 537.
Miller, Daniel, 167, 195, 517, 586.
Miller, David, 34, 35, 61, 65, 74, 104, 108, 299, 323, 366, 375, 394, 406, 437, 438, 451.
Miller, Elenor, 432.
Miller, Elizabeth, 234, 546, 547, 553.
Miller, Francis, 144.
Miller, Henry, 40, 54, 56, 142, 174, 218, 231, 239, 249, 269, 385, 420, 432, 488, 517, 539, 552, 554, 555, 558, 572, 575, 576.
Miller, Jacob, 15, 20, 23, 26, 44, 54, 56, 87, 104, 105, 106, 115, 117, 121, 134, 142, 195, 220, 269, 285, 292, 303, 375, 420, 452, 473, 498, 537, 546.
Miller, James, 26, 27, 28, 73, 195, 217, 245, 249, 262, 270, 271, 278, 293, 294, 296, 324, 328, 331, 342, 372, 404, 415, 434.
Miller, James E., 105.
Miller, John, 6, 13, 14, 17, 21, 24, 28, 33, 40, 43, 54, 60, 64, 65, 72, 73, 78, 86, 95, 98, 99, 103, 125, 182, 198, 262, 264, 268, 269, 295, 307, 311, 314, 321, 322, 342, 352, 362, 366, 371, 375, 376, 377, 379, 380, 382, 389, 392, 394, 395, 413, 423, 425, 448, 449, 452, 457, 464, 469, 474, 480, 488, 490, 503, 506, 516, 526, 537, 554, 571, 583, 585.
Miller, Leonard, 545, 551, 555.
Miller, Magdalen, 517.
Miller, Margaret, 195, 449, 583, 585.
Miller, Mark (Marks), 44, 45, 47, 65.
Miller, Martha, 249, 571.
Miller, Martin, 231.
Miller, Mary, 65, 195, 480, 517.
Miller, Michael, 195, 517.
Miller, Morthew, 379.
Miller, Nancy, 230, 243.
Miller, Patrick, 164, 379, 380, 489.
Miller, Peter, 65, 69, 85, 94, 97, 106, 108, 116, 139, 144, 377, 383, 419, 421, 424, 480, 482, 519.
Miller, Robert, 21, 80, 449.
Miller, Samuel, 184, 195, 230, 248, 249, 517, 576, 586, 587, 592.
Miller, Sibil, 212.
Miller, Thomas, 83, 449, 452, 495, 503.
Miller, Valentine, 212.
Miller, West, 243.
Miller, William, 17, 19, 34, 35, 39, 53, 195, 230, 249, 306, 311, 322, 323, 427, 517.
Miller, Windle, 53.
Miller, Wit, 191.
Millican (Milligan, Milliken), Charles, 74, 263, 369, 376, 436.
Millican, James, 100.
Millican (Millikin), John, 446, 474, 495.

Mills, Agnes, 46.
Mills, Alexander, 46, 173
Mills, Ann, 314, 319, 320.
Mills, Charles, 82.
Mills, Elizabeth, 218.
Mills, George, 545.
Mills, Gilbert, 46, 47.
Mills, Hugh, 39, 74, 110, 308.
Mills, James, 268, 288.
Mills, Jane, 372.
Mills, Jenett, 19.
Mills, John, 12, 19, 61, 74, 75, 109, 110, 173, 190, 204, 207, 218, 268, 295, 301, 308, 309, 314, 319, 320, 336, 349, 350, 372, 376, 377, 388, 397, 401, 403, 417, 419, 428, 430, 447, 458, 462, 465, 474, 482, 491, 584.
Mills, Joseph, 280, 307, 410, 435, 595.
Mills, Mary, 372, 428, 430, 447, 474, 491.
Mill(s), Robert, 173, 218.
Mills, Samuel B., 207.
Mills, Susannah, 173.
Mills, William, 9, 46, 173, 301, 309, 313, 319, 364, 371, 377, 417, 482.
Millsap, Joseph, 57.
Millsap, Mary, 57.
Millsap, William, 57, 499.
Milsap, Anne, 499.
Milsap, Eleanor, 57, 78.
Milsap, Robert, 14, 57, 315.
Milsap, Thomas, 9, 57, 60, 78, 260, 269, 291, 313, 490, 499.
Milterbarger, Michael, 135.
Mines, Robert, 63.
Minger, Henry, 185.
Minnis, Robert, 65, 68, 71, 137, 139, 151, 494.
Minter (Mynter), William, 65, 81, 92, 382, 391, 398, 409, 460, 558.
Minzees, Ninian, 479.
Misker, Mich, 141.
Misscampbell, Andrew, 407.
Misscampbell (Maskamell), John, 51, 429, 433.
Misscampble, James, 429.
Mitchell, Alexander, 144.
Mitchell, Andrew, 8, 270, 328.
Mitchell, Ann, 221.
Mitchell, David, 53, 89, 259, 264, 314, 371, 434, 437.
Mitchell, Elenor (Helenor), 120, 357.
Mitchel, Elizabeth, 11, 120, 229, 383.
Mitchell, George, 215.
Mitchell, Helen, 262, 269.
Mitchell, Henry, 511.
Mitchell, Ibby, 229.
Mitchell, James, 53, 58, 84, 111, 112, 120, 123, 124, 162, 181, 188, 201, 218, 219, 226, 228, 229, 234, 272, 294, 313, 317, 334, 354, 383, 442, 468, 488, 498, 500, 531, 550, 568.
Mitchell, John, 8, 18, 26, 36, 42, 54, 120,

123, 129, 164, 189, 218, 229, 254, **261**,
262, 268, **269**, 290, 299, 302, 303, **306**,
313, 329, 407, 426, 428, 466, 467, **484**.
Mitchell, Margaret, 272, 306, 484.
Mitchell, Martha, 53, 54, 111, 157.
Mitchell, Mary, 120, 234, 254, 270, 328.
Mitchell, Rebecca, 536.
Mitchell, Robert, 106, 120, 189, 357, **499**.
Mitchell, Sarah, 466, 467.
Mitchell, Thomas, 111, 120, 147, 157, **184**,
185, 188, 221, 222, 225, 229, 240, 316,
368.
Mitchell, William, 164, 203, 210, 229, 254,
272, 273, 306, 497, 536.
Mitcher, Valentine, 110.
Mitsker, Valentine, 58.
Mitts, Charles, 75.
Moffett, Ann, 236, 241.
Moffett, Catherine, 27.
Moffett, Clarissa, 237.
Moffett, Eleanor, 227.
Moffett, Elizabeth, 84, 229, 236, 237, 566.
Moffett, George, 27, 48, 66, 77, 86, 96, 103,
134, 138, 142, 154, 156, 157, 158, **163**,
173, 174, 180, 237, 337, 441, 438, 463,
469, 472, 527, 542, 544, 546, 548, **578**,
590.
Moffett, Hannah, 27, 48, 237.
Moffett, James, 27, 84, 85, 174, 201, 210,
219, 227, 236, 237, 241, 246, 282, **294**,
302, 303, 468, 503, 558, 566, 588.
Moffett, Jane (Jean), 62, 84, 227, **447, 566**.
Moffett, John, 8, 12, 15, 27, 48, 77, 84, 105,
117, 128, 132, 140, 156, 162, 164, **191**,
227, 231, 237, 257, 286, 351, 389, **412**,
414, 445, 447, 480, 508, 511, 595.
Moffett, Joseph, 237.
Moffett, Magdalene, 237.
Moffett, Margaret, 237.
Moffett, Martha, 84, 237.
Moffett, Mary (Maria), 12, 27, 84, **229**,
237, 257, 546.
Moffett, Rachel, 246.
Moffett, Robert, 27, 165, 303, 304, 324, **361**,
414, 447.
Moffett, Sarah (Sally), 237, **239**.
Moffett, Thomas, 237.
Moffett, Waller, 150.
Moffett, William, 27, 77, 156, 193, 194, **208**,
214, 227, 237, 470, 544, 546, 559.
Moiren, Lawrence, 81.
Molar, Mathew, 76.
Mold, Edward, 145.
Moldrow, Andrew, 57.
Moll (Null), Nicholas, **285**.
Monahan, Daniel, 9.
Monation, Daniel, 308.
Money, Samuel, 333.
Monroe, John, 224.
Monrow, James, 587.
Monsey, Samuel, 15, 68, 97, **423**.

Montague, John, 111.
Monteer, William, 178.
Montgomery, Agnes, 236.
Montgomery, Alexander, 115, 189, **517**,
554.
Mountgomery, Ann, 44.
Montgomery, Easter (Esther), 235, **559**,
561.
Montgomery, Hugh, 401, 460.
Montgomery, Hughart, 235.
Mountgomery, James, 16, 38, 44, 113, **121**,
135, 152, 164, 256, 260, 273, 281, **294**,
368, 559, 561.
Montgomery, Jean, 490.
Montgomery (Mountgomerie), John, **12**,
27, 28, 54, 67, 68, 78, 88, 101, 111, 112, **113**,
130, 143, 157, 164, 186, 189, 194, **207**,
208, 210, 213, 235, 236, 239, 244, **263**,
313, 325, 330, 341, 344, 352, 368, **408**,
427, 429, 443, 464, 465, 559, 561.
Montgomery, Joseph, 113, 121.
Montgomery, Math, 169.
Montgomery, Robert, 49, 64, 67, 72, **113**,
121, 260, 294, 346, 401, 402, 403.
Montgomery, Samuel, 28, 98, 113, 475.
Montgomery, Sarah, 554.
Montgomery, Thomas, 235.
Mountgomery, William, 22, 28, 235, **471**,
490, 574.
Mooberry, John, 71.
Moody, Andrew, 474, 514, 564, 581, 585.
Moody, James, 41, 46, 67, 262, 267, **278**,
298, 361, 432, 507.
Moody, Rebecca, 267.
Moody, Robert, 41, 46, 51, 67, 177, **279**,
296, 324, 383.
Mook, Henry, 53.
Moon, Abraham, 106.
Mooney, Peggy, 231.
Moore, Alexander, 10, 13, 86, 131, **189**,
259, 273, 293, 325, 407, 452, 498.
Moore, Andrew, 13, 14, 120, 129, 146, **148**,
195, 325, 468, 499, 568.
Moore, Ann, 458.
Moore, Conrad, 53, 121.
Moore, David, 10, 12, 13, 17, 20, 27, 29,
30, 40, 61, 96, 147, 262, 269, 295, **297**,
308, 310, 316, 323, 325, 335, 381, **393**,
439, 488, 518, 521, 587.
Moore, Edward, 74.
Moore, Elizabeth, 27.
Moore, George, 584, 586.
Moore, James, 13, 19, 21, 37, 43, 46, 51, **75**,
83, 92, 110, 176, 189, 212, 249, 285, **292**,
296, 299, 301, 310, 333, 344, 345, **362**,
382, 391, 435, 443, 456, 495.
Moore, Jane (Jean), 224, 249, 292, **296**,
382.
Moore, Jinet, 249.
Moore, John, 10, 12, 13, 20, 23, 27, **30**,
31, 34, 35, 43, 45, 48, 64, 69, 71, 74, **78**,

86, 95, 103, 104, 124, 189, 200, 212, 215, 217, 249, 263, 265, 268, 272, 287, 290, 304, 310, 340, 359, 380, 382, 395, 422, 435, 443, 446, 454, 455, 489, 537, 563, 589.
Moore, Joseph, 132, 135, 249, 371, 381, 505, 508, 520.
Moore, Margaret, 219, 272.
Moore, Martha, 135.
Moore, Mary, 131, 249, 315, 382, 518.
Moore, Mary A., 212, 422.
Moore, Michael, 121.
Moore, Moses, 49, 118, 184, 429, 457, 573.
Moore, Phebe, 82, 118.
Moore, Philip, 47, 53.
Moore, Quanten, 13.
Moore, Rachel, 249.
Moore, Reuben, 458, 549.
Moore, Robert, 12, 48, 60, 72, 212, 217, 272, 485.
Moore, Samuel, 10, 13, 27, 36, 50, 67, 70, 72, 77, 105, 147, 273, 308, 325, 370, 381, 386, 402, 403, 408, 431, 436, 439, 448, 518, 526.
Moore, Thomas, 6, 11, 13, 22, 27, 28, 77, 269, 293, 294, 314, 315, 339, 382, 456, 465, 467, 492, 497, 509, 513, 530.
Moore, William, 13, 17, 29, 61, 71, 113, 129, 131, 148, 157, 189, 212, 273, 325, 359, 401, 440, 452, 468, 498, 518, 537, 538, 563.
Moore, William S., 218.
Moorehead, Mathew, 104, 120, 411, 445, 509, 515, 518.
Moorman, Zachariah, 107.
Moran (Morin, Morren), Dominick, 148, 399, 435.
Morgan, Benjamin, 274, 508.
Morgan, Lewis, 81.
Morice, Henry, 153.
Morisey, Francis, 366.
Morley, Daniel, 15, 77.
Morly, Catherine, 77.
Morra, Samuel, 380.
Morrall (Morrel), Samuel, 156, 399, 408.
Morrice, William, 476.
Morrin, Laurance, 414.
Morris, Elizabeth, 241.
Morris, Ezel, 85.
Morris, George, 241.
Morris, Isaac, 486.
Morris, Morris (Maurice), 520, 591.
Morris, Richard, 435.
Morris, Robert, 408.
Morris, William, 228.
Morrise, Daniel, 480.
Morrise, Ezekiel, 480.
Morison, Hugh, 214.
Morrison (Morson), James, 37.
Morrison, Nurnie, 147.
Morrison, Richard, 81.
Morrow, Adam, 121.

Morrow, James, 153, 553.
Morrows, William, 181, 313, 556, **570**.
Morten, John, **345**.
Mose, Nicholas, 433.
Moser, Cathrine (Cathron), 62, 63, **156**.
Moser, Eliza, 90.
Moser, Elizabeth, 91.
Moser, Eve, 156.
Moser, George, 49, 65, 91.
Moser, Peter, 23, 49, 50, 62, 63.
Moses, John B., 230.
Moses, Samuel, 145, 178.
Moss, Joseph, 175.
Moulding (Mouldin), Richard, 293, **531**.
Mountfield, Margaret, 167.
Mountony, Samuel, 50.
Moura, Lodwick, 565.
Mourie, Hance, 486.
Mourie, John, 486.
Mouse, Catherine, 77.
Mouse, Daniel, 23, 77, **531**, 538, **545**.
Mouse, Elizabeth, 89.
Mouse, Eve, 538.
Mouse, Frederick, 59, 86.
Mouse, George, 49, 50, 59, 63, 65, 86, 89.
Mowrey, Henry, 206, 212, 213, 250.
Mowrey, Mary, 206, 250.
Mowry, Ludwig, 211.
Mowyer, Henry, 555.
Moyer, Jacob, 97, 128.
Moyle, Jacob, 520.
Mucklewains, Elizabeth, 213.
Muldrough, Andrew, 7, 12, 43, 51, 53, **54**.
Muldrough, Hugh, 53.
Muldrough, Jane (Jean), 53, 93.
Muldrough, John, 53.
Mulphallan, William, 174.
Mull, William, 391.
Mullan, Michael, 535, 537.
Mullenax, Thomas, 195.
Mullinax, John, 195.
Mullene, Samuel 23.
Müller, Adam, 259.
Mullin, Edward, 40, 49.
Mummer, Betsy, 225.
Mummer, Christian, 589.
Muncy, Joseph, 69.
Muncy (Monsey), Obediah, 449, **533**.
Muncy, Samuel, 69, 70, 113, 467, 468.
Muncy (Monsey, Munsey, **Monsly**), Skidmore, 76, 99, 389, 533.
Munger, Henry, 535.
Munger (Monger), William, 113, **397**, 502, 514.
Munroe (Monrow), Daniel, 587.
Munroe, Elizabeth, 587.
Munsey (Monsie), Mary, 467, 533.
Munsey, William, 106.
Murley, Austas, 280, 305.
Murley, Cornelius, 280, 305, 312, **531**.
Murley, Daniel, 22, **280**, **312**, **449**.
Murley, Judith, 312.

Murphy, Daniel, 27.
Murphy, John, 81, 84, 214, 311.
Murphy, Lazarus, 160.
Murphy, Nancy, 214.
Murphy, Patrick, 144.
Murphy, William, 214, 490.
Murra, Ludwick, 543.
Murray, Adam, 174, 328, 421.
Murray, Barney, 481.
Murray, Henry, 72, 78, 143, 296, 312, 339, 587.
Murray, John, 100, 392, 445, 458, 460, 462, 472, 478.
Murray, Rosanna, 143, 587.
Murray, Thomas, 575.
Murray, William, 317, 327.
Mustoe, Anthony, 178, 181, 185, 186, 191, 573, 574, 575, 578, 583, 584, 585, 588.
Mustoe, Dorothy, 583.
Myer, Jacob, 523.
Myers, Elizabeth, 592.
Myers, Frederick, 592.
Myers, Lewis, 577.
Mynes, Elizabeth, 240.
Mynes, Martha, 586.
Mynes (Mines), Thomas, 558, 559, 586, 593.
Myrtian, Henry, 258.
Nahale, Jacob, 265.
Nall (Nalle), Martin, 140, 146, 538.
Nall, Robert, M. D., 172.
Nall (Nalle), William, 140, 538, 549.
Napier (Naper, Napper), William, 93, 97, 105, 189.
Nare, Peter, 84.
Nare, Sarah, 84.
Narle, Christian, 135.
Nation, Christopher, 527.
Nare, Christly, 204.
Neal, Ann, 254, 255.
Neal, James, 45, 515.
Neal (Neill), John, 34, 62, 195, 254, 275, 360, 362, 365, 373, 389, 402, 477, 480, 481, 484, 528.
Neal (Neil), Lewis, 34, 254, 312, 477, 480, 484, 528.
Neal, Lydia, 254.
Neal (Neil), Thomas, 127, 195, 389, 579.
Nealands, John, 266.
Nealls (Nicalls), Leavin, 188.
Neave, Leonard, 53.
Neavill, Joseph, 532.
Nedonstoone, John, 101.
Needham, Ann, 147.
Needham, Catherian, 147.
Needham, Eliner, 147.
Needham, John, 101, 147, 148.
Needham, Sniah (Siner), 147.
Neel, George, 14.
Neelley, Anna, 452.
Neeley (Nealy, Neilley), James, 6, 18, 19, 30, 38, 40, 74, 87, 99, 103, 109, 110, 111, 282, 298, 299, 308, 329, 339, 376, 452, 478, 488, 491.
Neeley (Neally, Neilly), John, 80, 82, 91, 98, 107, 111, 299, 314, 328, 378, 385, 438, 444, 452, 456, 491.
Neelley, Robert, 376, 401, 452.
Neelly, Jane, 491.
Neff, Hans Heinrich, 16, 18.
Neff, John Henry, 9, 20.
Neghly, Paulus (Negter, Pollis), 134.
Neglee, Jacob, 287.
Neglee, (Nägle), John, 287.
Neice (Nease), Margaret, 457.
Neice (Niece, Nease, Nees), Michael, 457, 487, 493, 509, 520, 523, 530.
Neidner, Elizabeth, 250.
Neif, Leonard, 141.
Neigley, Sebastian, 125.
Neil, Samuel, 207.
Neizbitt, Mary, 159.
Neizbitt (Nuzbet), Samuel, 159, 498, 499.
Nelley (Nilly), James, 14, 40, 102.
Nelly, John, 111, 115.
Nelson, Alexander, 198, 199, 201, 205, 580, 581, 589.
Nelson, Ann, 230.
Nelson, David, 53, 55, 65, 68, 69, 71, 91, 92, 288, 518.
Nelson, Henry, 289.
Nelson, Hugh, 230, 578.
Nelson, John, 91, 92, 240, 245.
Nelson, Joseph, 555, 557.
Nelson, Mary (Scott), 230.
Nelson, Sarah Carpenter, 241.
Nelson, Thomas, 159, 169, 240, 245, 251, 555.
Nerrity, Daniel, 88.
Nesbit, John, 118.
Nesbitt, William, 575.
Netherton, Henry, 18, 21, 289.
Newberry, Rosanna, 90.
Newberry, Samuel, 87, 90.
Newman, Jonathan, 9, 15, 20.
Newman, Leroy, 214.
Newman, Martha, 294, 398.
Newman, Samuel, 9, 14, 19, 20, 25, 26, 28, 41, 265, 269, 272, 291, 294, 296, 304, 311, 312, 314, 315, 398, 527.
Newman, William, 302.
Newport, John, 253, 255, 259.
Newton, Joseph, 153, 157, 190.
Nichol (Nichols), Jacob, 287, 297.
Nicholas, Barbara, 90.
Nicholas, Jacob, 18, 20, 42, 44, 47, 52, 56, 57, 65, 66, 69, 85, 97, 103, 115, 117, 120, 125, 129, 134, 141, 152, 292, 298, 383, 394, 397, 416, 419, 483, 488, 505, 519, 526, 528, 540, 549, 551.
Nicholas, James, 69.
Nicholas, Jean, 441, 526.
Nicholas, James, 69.
Nicholas, Jean, 441, 526.

Nicholas (Nicolas), John, 125, 147, 252, 373.
Nicholas, Nathan, 74.
Nicholas (Nicolas), Samuel, 115, 125, 142, 413, 543, 551.
Nicholas (Nickle), Thomas, 441.
Nichols, James, 579.
Nickel (Nickoll), Margaret, 226, 563.
Nickle (Nickoll), Andrew, 136, 204, 563.
Nickle (Nickall), Barbara, 136, 563.
Nickle (Nichol, Nickel, Nickoll), Elizabeth, 136, 196, 229, 563.
Nickle (Nickoll), Isaac, 136, 563.
Nickle (Nickoll, Nickel, Nicoll, Nichole), John, 22, 80, 133, 136, 161, 170, 212, 251, 277, 299, 347, 373, 563, 568, 593.
Nickle (Nickoll), Joseph, 136, 563.
Nickle, Nancy, 251.
Nickle, Sarah, 251.
Nickle, Thomas, 136.
Nickls, George, 126.
Nicolas, Elizabeth, 125.
Nicolas, Margaret, 125.
Nicolas, Mary, 125.
Nicolas (Nickolas), Peter, 145, 238, 592.
Nicolas (Nicholas), Phillip, 125, 543.
Noble, Alexander, 27, 330, 338.
Noble, Ezekiel, 27.
Noble, James, 27.
Noble, Jean, 27.
Noble, John, 16, 21, 26, 27, 28.
Noble, Mary, 26, 27.
Noble, Patrick, 27.
Noll, Elizabeth, 234.
Nomel, Jacob, 85.
Norris, Robert, 26, 28.
North, Catherine, 167.
North, John, 180.
North, Philip, 167, 176, 228, 583.
North, Roger, 167, 176, 547, 565, 575.
Northon, Thomas, 141.
Norton, Benjamin, 198.
Norton, John H., 593.
Norwood, Elizabeth, 422, 423.
Norwood, Samuel, 66, 82, 93, 253, 259, 287, 295, 328, 339, 350, 361, 367, 422, 423, 433.
Nuckens (Pickens), John, 254.
Null, Barbara, 480, 483, 531.
Null, George, 101, 113, 480, 483, 501, 531.
Null, Henry, 108, 113, 328, 503.
Null, Margaret, 101, 324, 357, 480.
Null, Michael, 341.
Null, Nicholas, 34, 46, 57, 67, 94, 97, 101, 103, 113, 275, 287, 291, 303, 307, 324, 357, 375, 394, 480, 483, 501, 531.
Null, William, 18, 568.
Nulls, Blaney, 482.
Nutt, Andrew, 276, 286.
Nutt, Eleanor, 269, 290.
Nutt, Nicholas, 43, 49, 50, 305.

Nutt, William, 30, 261, 262, 269, 276, 278, 280, 286, 290, 302, 310, 395, 402.
Nutts, Charles, 323.
O'Bryan, Ann, 387, 533.
O'Bryan, Benjamin, 21.
O'Bryan, Cornelius, 21, 23, 24, 387, 533.
O'Bryan, Elizabeth, 387.
O'Bryan, James, 73.
O'Bryan, John, 21, 23, 387, 533.
O'Bryan, Mary, 387.
O'Bryan, Rebecca, 21.
O'Bryan, Thomas, 21, 387, 533.
O'Dair, John, 131, 176.
O'Dear, Neal, 594.
O'Dear, Robert, 176.
O'Donald, Charles, 125.
O'Donnell, Margaret, 130.
O'Donnell, Mary, 101, 130, 131.
O'Donnel (O'Donald, O'Donnal, O'Donley), Michael, 68, 101, 115, 121, 125, 130, 131, 307.
Offreel (Offiriel, Ofrel), Moses, 26, 292, 313.
O'Friel, Catherine, 150.
O'Friel, Daniel, 142, 150, 559.
O'Friel, Eleanor, 151.
O'Friel, Jeremiah, 150, 559.
O'Friel, John, 151.
O'Friel, Joseph, 151.
O'Friel, Mary, 150.
O'Friel, Maurice (Morris), 16, 60, 92, 93, 105, 139, 150, 277, 302, 317, 345, 360, 420, 475, 481.
O'Harra, Elizabeth, 457.
O'Hara, Robert, 170.
O'Hara (O'Harra), Daniel, 43, 56, 457, 583.
O'Neal, Edmond, 104, 106.
O'Neal, James, 150.
O'Neal, John, 40, 43, 44, 45, 46, 317, 348, 506, 528, 534.
O'Neal, Joseph, 194.
O'Neal, Thomas, 44, 70, 418, 534, 551.
Oaler, William, 96, 514.
Ocheltree, Alexander, 160.
Ochelthe, Mary E., 243.
Ocheltree, Michael, 243.
Odell, Benjamin, 555.
Odell, Samuel, 14, 15.
Offill, John, 168.
Ogle, Benjamin, 26, 74, 309, 437.
Ogle, Thomas, 490.
Öhler (Ahlar), Anthony, 221.
Öhler, Barbara, 221.
Öhler, Catherine, 221.
Öhler, Elizabeth, 221.
Öhler (Ahler), George, 221.
Öhler, John, 221.
Öhler, Madelena, 221.
Öhler, Margaret, 221.
Öhler, Mary, 221.
Öhler, Susannah, 221.

Ohlpman, Felix, 92.
Older, Bartholomew, 553.
Oldham, William, 512, 534, 538, 558.
Olinger, Barbara, 177.
Olinger, Christopher, 577.
Olinger, Eve M., 186.
Olinger, Jacob, 177, 545.
Olinger, Juliana, 177.
Olinger, Katherine, 177.
Olinger, Philip, 177, 542, 545.
Olinger, Stophel, 175, 177.
Oliver, Aaron (Aron), 15, 132, 134, 358, 386.
Oliver, Elizabeth, 358.
Oliver, James, 73, 185, 227, 572, 587.
Oliver, Jean, 227.
Oliver, Jemina, 132.
Oliver, John, 197, 199, 556, 559, 572, 593.
Oliver, Mary, 227, 587.
Oliver, Sarah, 572.
Oliver, Thomas, 202.
Ollar, Adam, 45.
Oller, William, 40.
Olley, William, 60.
Olphid, Hansel, 169.
Onesney, A. M., 176.
Ong, Isaac, 589.
Ooley, William, 93.
Opp, Frederick, 63, 83.
Orban, Adam, 128.
Orr, Robert, 401.
Orr, William, 591.
Orrey, James, 109.
Orson, Stephen, 73.
Osborn, Ann, 106.
Osborn, Thomas, 106.
Osburn, Jeremiah, 76, 143, 374, 375.
Osburn, John, 171.
Ose, Thomas, 73.
Osinger, Philip, 210.
Osran, Prudence, 19.
Ostler (Osler), Bosten, 496.
Ostler, Paushton, 113.
Oswedy, Nicholas, 127.
Ott, David, 233.
Ott, Hannah, 240.
Ott, John, 233.
Ott, Mary, 233.
Ott, Michael, 208.
Ott, Sally, 233.
Our, John, 121.
Ove, Christopher, 141.
Owens, Jane (Jenny), 577, 581.
Owens, Margaret, 224.
Owens, Mary, 217.
Owens, Owen, 169, 413, 553, 581.
Owler, Mary, 94.
Owler, William, 94, 439, 502.
Oxer, Michael, 53.
Page, Allen, 235.
Page, Elizabeth, 328.

Page, Mary, 157.
Paget, Elizabeth, 294.
Paget, Reuben, 294.
Painter, Adam, 132, 201, 457, 509, 523.
Painter, Alexander, 24, 85, 347, 373, 509, 523, 530.
Painter, Catherine, 85, 86, 132, 248.
Painter, Christian, 132.
Painter, Christly, 509.
Painter, Elias, 158.
Painter, Elizabeth, 132, 523.
Painter, Henry, 248.
Painter, John, 131, 509.
Painter, Margaret, 509, 530.
Pal, John, 29.
Pall, Mary, 98.
Palmer, Ann, 212.
Palmer, Barbara, 242.
Palmer, George, 242.
Palmer, Jean, 228, 493.
Palmer, John, 177, 221.
Palmer, Martha, 212.
Palmer, Mary, 161, 212.
Palmer, Robert, 212.
Palmer, Stophel, 221.
Palmer, William, 57, 60, 123, 212, **282**, 283, 289, 296, 303, 348, 352, 360, **361**, 367, 388, 389, 420, 493.
Palsley, Elizabeth, 212.
Pancake, Joseph, 155.
Panniger, Peter, 490.
Pap, John Chrisman, 552.
Parent, Josiah, 14.
Paretree, Rebecca, 131.
Paris, Robert, 375.
Paris, Sarah, 347.
Park, Catherine, 167.
Park, Rebecka, 410.
Parker, Hugh, 17.
Parker, William, 151.
Parks, David, 236.
Parks, Elizabeth, 227, 250.
Parks (Park), James, 81, 236.
Parks (Park), John, 236, 393, 410, **439**, 510.
Parks, Joseph, 236.
Parks, Thomas, 236.
Parks, William, 41, 236.
Parris, Alexander, 242.
Parris (Parrus), Elizabeth, 192, 242.
Parris (Paris), George, 69, 242, 309, **366**, 375.
Parris, Hannah, 242.
Parris (Paris, Parrus), John, 144, 167, 180, 192, 242.
Parris, Thomas, 242.
Parris (Parrus), William, 54, 69, 192.
Parrus, Andrew, 192.
Parrus, Janet, 192.
Parry, David, 215, 248.
Parry (Perry), John, 337.

Parry, Joshua, 208, 589.
Parsinger, Barbara, 108.
Parsinger (Persinger, Passinger), Catherine (Catrina), 416, 419, 480, 523.
Parsinger, Christian, 108.
Parsinger (Persinger), Phillip, 59, 61.
Parsons, Esther, 436.
Parsons, Huldah, 409.
Parsons (Parson), James, 53, 158, 409, 436, 532, 539.
Parsons, Mary, 436.
Parsons (Persons), Thomas, 30, 53, 58, 87, 121, 158, 363, 436, 532, 580.
Patrick, Charles, 66, 75, 234, 237, 239, 243, 392, 456.
Patrick, George, 237.
Patrick, Jane, 234.
Patrick, John, 66, 107, 165, 174, 234, 237, 392, 418, 456, 481, 493, 509, 527, 578.
Patrick, Martha, 66.
Patrick, Mary, 174, 380, 381, 456.
Patrick, Rachel, 66.
Patrick, Rebeccah, 174.
Patrick, Robert, 66, 67, 258, 265, 276, 285, 302, 304, 330, 333, 345, 348, 392, 403, 456.
Patrick, William, 174, 229, 234, 235, 239, 380.
Patteet (Peteet), John, 252, 309.
Patten, Thomas, 228.
Patterson, Agness, 12, 13, 30, 114, 375.
Patterson, Ann, 455.
Patterson, Deborah, 243.
Patterson, Eleanor, 71, 159, 376.
Patterson, Elizabeth, 114, 123, 229, 286, 398, 524.
Patterson, Erwin (Ewin), 6, 17, 19, 22, 42, 50, 55, 74, 280, 289, 293, 294, 301, 306, 309, 315, 317, 320, 372, 376, 396, 460.
Patterson, George, 13, 60, 366, 397, 432, 434, 436.
Patterson, Isabell, 24, 159.
Patterson, Israel, 230, 241.
Patterson, James, 16, 24, 114, 123, 159, 175, 193, 204, 231, 233, 243, 272, 349, 388, 424, 439, 446, 520, 530, 536, 547.
Patterson, Jane, 114, 123, 129, 243.
Patterson, Janet (Jannet), 123, 131.
Patterson, Jean, 50, 123.
Patterson (Pattison), John, 5, 12, 14, 23, 24, 25, 30, 31, 114, 117, 123, 131, 137, 153, 154, 156, 158, 174, 177, 183, 243, 260, 272, 274, 286, 288, 290, 343, 356, 370, 385, 391, 434, 436, 447, 448, 458, 500, 514, 542, 578, 584.
Patterson, Joseph, 159, 218, 231, 233, 530, 558.
Patterson, Ledia, 229.
Patterson, Margaret, 366, 367.
Patterson, Martha, 24, 99, 101, 446, 566, 595.
Patterson, Mary, 113, 114, 123, 131, **172**, 204, 541.
Patterson (Pattison), Mathew, 24, **145**, 231, 233, 563.
Patterson (Pattison), Nathan, 24, 26, 37, 280, 563.
Patterson, Nathaniel, 18, 595.
Patterson, Rachel, 230, 241.
Patterson, Rebecca, 114.
Patterson (Pattison), Robert, 19, 23, 24, 35, 37, 38, 51, 99, 113, 114, 137, 138, 145, 148, 160, 167, 189, 261, 270, **280**, 283, 370, 398, 455, 468, 476, 500, **508**, 524, 532, 563, 578, 595.
Patterson, Robina, 16.
Patterson, Samuel, 24, 92, 243, **412**, **442**, 446, 455, 503, 520, 547.
Patterson, Sarah, 24, 536.
Patterson, Susanna, 248.
Patterson, Thomas, 58, 70, 114, 131, 137, 138, 139, 155, 201, 202, 206, 370, 391, 432, 458, 537, 546.
Patterson, Walter, 316, 318.
Patterson, William, 75, 95, 110, 114, **123**, 204, 243, 281, 297, 375, **410**, **411**, **541**, 576.
Patterson, William King, 248.
Pattison, Jane, 563.
Patton, Agness, 44, 49, 54.
Patton, Alexander, 333.
Patton (Patten), Elizabeth, 106, 228.
Patton, Francis, 514, 524, 529.
Patton, Hance, 558, 577.
Patton, Henry, 40.
Patton, Hester, 53.
Patton, Isabell, 44.
Patton, Jacob, 18, 33, 37, 38, 49, 61, 74, 75, 163, 185, 215, 323, 528, 558, 564, 577.
Patton, James, 6, 27, 33, 34, 40, 44, 73, 100, 110, 117, 118, 253, 257, 264, 265, 266, 267, 268, 270, 273, 274, 276, 279, 280, 284, 285, 288, 289, 294, 298, **299**, 300, 304, 306, 307, 308, 309, 314, **315**, 317, 318, 319, 320, 322, 324, 329, **330**, 335, 339, 350, 352, 362, 369, 370, **376**, 379, 381, 386, 388, 393, 412, 413, **417**, 423, 428, 430, 436, 437, 438, 442, 452, 455, 456, 457, 458, 462, 464, 465, 467, 468, 471, 479, 486, 488, 550, 551, **568**.
Patton, John, 22, 27, 30, 36, 44, 45, 49, 106, 145, 249, 264, 265, 292, 293, **306**, 335, 336, 337, 347, 384, 487, 494, **544**, 550.
Patton, Margaret, 40, 44.
Patton, Mary, 40, 185, 249, 253.
Patton, Mathew, 36, 39, 49, 50, 52, 54, **56**, 73, 75, 78, 92, 108, 125, 127, 128, **142**, 150, 151, 159, 249, 264, 292, 306, **323**, 336, 347, 373, 374, 392, 405, 408, **421**, 455, 458, 494, 520, 527, 543, 566.
Patton, Phebe, 577.

Patton, Roger, 158.
Patton, Samuel, 316.
Patton, Sarah, 323.
Patton, Susannah (Susan), 33, 49.
Patton, William, 44, 84, 145, 249, 432, 496, 520, 550, 557.
Paul, Audley, 93, 297, 340, 351, 434, 488.
Paul, Hugh, 586.
Paul, James, 46, 60, 231, 234, 284.
Paul, John, 7, 46, 82, 287, 325, 326, 336, 443, 444.
Paul, Margaret, 46.
Paul, Mary, 297, 444.
Paul, Peter, 207, 211.
Paul, William, 46, 48.
Paullen (Paulin), Henry, 99, 473, 486.
Paunton, John, 333.
Paxton, Elizabeth, 183, 229, 478.
Paxton, James, 475.
Paxton, John, 33, 35, 38, 39, 40, 43, 64, 65, 86, 90, 102, 107, 288, 308, 325, 329, 360, 364, 365, 378, 390, 407, 442, 450, 475, 478.
Paxton, Joseph, 39, 40, 41, 271.
Paxton, Martha, 218.
Paxton, Mary, 43, 399, 540.
Paxton, Rebeka, 405, 406, 491.
Paxton, Samuel, 39, 43, 45, 55, 72, 77, 102, 313, 399, 406.
Paxton, Sarah, 72.
Paxton, Stuart, 183, 229.
Paxton (Paxtun), Thomas, 8, 12, 25, 31, 39, 40, 43, 69, 72, 77, 102, 218, 267, 268, 275, 284, 293, 294, 304, 308, 313, 317, 323, 326, 339, 341, 350, 382, 398, 405, 406, 410, 413, 415, 429, 432, 468, 478, 489, 491, 499, 520, 540.
Paxton, William, 39, 144, 229, 478, 540.
Paxtun, Eloner, 144.
Payne, Ailer (Ailie), 556.
Payne, Richard, 551, 555, 556.
Peace, Joseph W., 90.
Peace, Joseph, 109.
Pearis, George, 309, 310, 331, 385.
Pearis, Margaret, 347.
Pearis, Rhoda, 392.
Pearis, Richard, 347, 389, 392.
Peartree, John, 541.
Peck, Andrew, 188.
Peck, Daniel, 224.
Peck, Elizabeth, 224.
Peck, Jacob, 149, 559, 570, 572.
Peck, John, 188.
Peck, Joseph, 204, 211.
Peck, Mary (Polly), 559.
Peden (Pedan, Peder), John, 166, 542.
Peebles, James, 152, 578.
Peebles, John, 142, 152, 156, 216, 593.
Peerie, Agness, 76.
Peerie, Elizabeth, 76.
Peerie (Peery, Peary), George, 76, 224, 498, 536, 580.
Peerie, Katherine, 477.
Peerie, Margaret, 76.
Peerie, Robert, 128.
Peerie (Peary, Perey), Thomas, 76, 91, 174, 281, 429, 446, 473, 477.
Peery, Ann, 220.
Peery (Peary, Perey, Pearey, Peerie, Peare), James, 68, 76, 177, 185, 198, 203, 206, 209, 215, 219, 220, 224, 281, 446, 473, 477, 490, 495, 561, 565.
Peery, Janet, 174, 220.
Peery (Peerie, Peary, Perey), John, 68, 73, 76, 91, 118, 224, 236, 429, 446, 473, 539, 578.
Peery, Martha, 224, 578.
Peery (Peerie, Perey), Mary, 68, 76, 429.
Peery (Peerie, Pearey), Sarah, 224, 446, 539.
Peery (Peerie), William, 76, 217, 224.
Peevie, James, 281.
Peevie, Thomas, 281, 283.
Peilentine, Elizabeth, 157.
Peir, Jersmons, 66.
Peirce, William, 305.
Pellum, William, 321.
Penaner, Henry, 126.
Pence, Adam, 65, 97, 387, 419, 479 547.
Pence, Barbara, 65, 144.
Pence, Catherine, 65, 69, 135, 338.
Pence, Felty, 298.
Pence, George, 106, 108, 482, 483.
Pence, Henry, 65, 144, 483.
Pence, Jacob, 18, 20, 22, 53, 65, 69, 70, 97, 106, 108, 285, 387, 416, 419, 424, 479, 482, 483, 519, 547.
Pence, John, 65, 106, 144, 480.
Pence, Katherine, 547.
Pence, Mary, 65, 144.
Pence, Sarah, 65, 144.
Pence, Valentine, 20, 31, 50, 52, 57, 62, 65, 66, 69, 94, 97, 106, 108, 144, 285, 292, 305, 324, 338, 377, 416, 419, 481, 482, 483, 519.
Pence, William, 106, 108.
Pendle (Pendleton), Gabriel, 196, 198.
Pendle, Margaret, 196.
Pendleton, Edmond, 92.
Pendleton, James, 298.
Penigar (Penninger, Penegor), Henry, 65, 71, 103, 158, 374, 581.
Penigar, Magdalene, 512.
Penigar (Pannenger), Peter, 512.
Penn, Catherine, 571.
Penn (Pen), Mathew, 156, 176, 571, 573, 583.
Penner, Margaret, 116.
Pennywait (Pennywite), John, 56, 314.
Penticost, William, 205.
Peoples, John, 133, 429, 540.
Peoples, Nathan (Nathaniel), 80, 112, 318, 377, 480, 495.
Peoples, William, 377, 480.

Pepper, Robert, 87.
Pepper, Samuel, 97, 104, 106, 118, 178, 451.
Pepper, William, 74, 309.
Percy, Christian, 576.
Percy, John, 214, 576.
Perey, Christian, 245.
Perey, Christopher, 209.
Perey, Hannah, 236.
Perey, Joseph, 236.
Perey, Rebecca, 236.
Perkey, Ann, 67, 531.
Perkey, Elizabeth, 67,
Perkey (Purkey), Henry, 46, 57, 67, 68, 70, 298, 307, 328, 345, 351.
Perkey (Pirkey), Jacob, 67, 364.
Perkey, Margaret, 67, 81, 107, 460.
Perkey, Mary, 67.
Perkins, Amos, 167.
Perkins, Isaac, 275.
Perrigin, William, 157.
Perrins, William, 157.
Perry, George, 283, 354.
Perry, John, 142, 304.
Perry, Joshua, 575.
Persey, Sarah, 171.
Persinger, Christopher, 419.
Persinger (Parsinger, Passenger), Jacob, 48, 51, 57, 59, 61, 63, 65, 70, 85, 87, 88, 351, 355, 387, 397, 412, 416, 419, 424, 439, 480, 519, 523.
Perthulls, James, 177.
Peskels, Henry, 99.
Peterfish, Conrad, 97, 110, 136, 477.
Peters (Peter), Jacob, 65, 101, 103, 110, 140, 409, 416.
Peters (Petter), John, 106, 149.
Peterson, Jacob, 51, 114.
Peterson, John, 20.
Peterson, Michael, 156.
Peterson, Thomas, 63.
Petterson, Jane, 130.
Pettyjohn, William, 157.
Pettrson, John, 114.
Petty, Ebenezer, 159.
Peyton, Francis, 581.
Peyton, Robert, 373.
Pfifer, Henry, 9.
Phears, John, 92.
Pheemster, Thomas, 169.
Phegan, Philip, 50.
Phelan (Pheland), Gerald, 156, 164, 168.
Pheus, John, 98.
Phifer, George, 206, 211.
Philip, Patsy, 230.
Philips, Evans, 131.
Philips, William, 291.
Phillips, Charles, 71, 102, 167, 475, 481, 544, 559.
Phillips, James, 10, 49, 59, 70, 71, 359, 447, 517, 545.

Phillips, Jane, 224, 585.
Phillips, John, 57, 71, 113, 274, 291, 320, 373, 397, 447, 472, 481, 545, 559, 584, 585.
Phillips, Joseph, 413, 585.
Phillips, Mary, 119, 345, 447, 517.
Phillips, Robert, 101, 116, 313, 345, 360.
Phillips, Stephen, 14.
Phillips, Thomas, 214, 235.
Philson, Martha, 173.
Philson, Mary, 191.
Phinney, Christopher, 289.
Phypher, George, 588.
Pickens, Abram, 132.
Pickens, Andrew, 5, 16, 251, 255, 283, 289, 297, 379.
Pickens (Pickings), Anne, 132, 289, 530.
Pickens, Eleanor, 259, 312, 334.
Pickens, Gabriel, 16, 37, 58, 65, 79, 274, 339, 384, 478.
Pickens, Israel, 274.
Pickens, John, 8, 16, 23, 258, 259, 267, 277, 282, 284, 312, 313, 319, 328, 334, 346, 363, 389, 422.
Pickens, Thomas, 115, 473.
Picket, Augustine, 132.
Picket, Henry, 427, 485, 508.
Picket, Jean, 485.
Pickins, William, 40, 78, 346, 368, 530.
Pickle (Pikle), Christian, 110, 141, 549.
Pickle (Pickles, Pickel), Henry, 83, 128, 405, 540.
Pierce (Pierie), Daniel, 95, 108.
Pierce, William, 324.
Piercey, John L., 515.
Pierson, George, 200, 209.
Piery (Peery), John, 286.
Pilson, Dorcas, 234.
Pilson, George, 234, 238, 554.
Pilson (Pillson), Richard, 39, 281, 282, 312, 407, 446.
Pilson, Samuel, 209, 360, 459, 514, 554.
Piper, Samuel, 117.
Pircy, Henry, 65.
Pirgy, Henry, 364.
Pirie, George, 282, 283.
Pirkey, Jacob, 449, 551.
Pirkey, John, 592.
Place, Thomas, 545.
Pleasant, John, 89.
Plesent, Robert, 26.
Plummer, Daniel, 40.
Plummer, Robert, 40.
Plummer, William, 38, 49, 74, 75, 100, 323.
Plunkett, John, 141, 192.
Poack, George, 134.
Poack, John, 22, 134, 299.
Poack, Robert, 134.
Poack, Thomas, 134.
Poack, William, 134.

Poag, Seth, 255.
Poage (Pong), Agnes, 184, 198, 217, 223, 225, 447.
Poage, Ann, 81, 184, 223, 391, 404, 467.
Poage, Easter McM., 82.
Poage (Pong), Elijah, 198, 223, 225, 561.
Poage, Elizabeth, 15, 184, 217, 223, 225, 254, 268, 272, 312, 313, 328, 330, 332, 334.
Poage, George, 104, 173, 184, 416, 431, 450, 488, 590.
Poage, Isabel, 217.
Poage, James, 124, 184, 217, 235, 280, 435, 551.
Poage, Jean, 202, 391.
Poage, John, 33, 36, 46, 53, 54, 60, 61, 72, 75, 81, 82, 83, 96, 113, 114, 115, 117, 122, 127, 131, 134, 136, 140, 150, 151, 152, 153, 154, 158, 159, 165, 168, 172, 173, 179, 184, 185, 197, 202, 211, 213, 217, 222, 223, 225, 226, 236, 242, 244, 245, 274, 280, 287, 288, 299, 306, 308, 312, 328, 330, 332, 340, 343, 346, 349, 350, 352, 356, 363, 371, 376, 381, 391, 398, 403, 404, 406, 408, 410, 417, 423, 424, 428, 432, 438, 441, 443, 446, 447, 453, 459, 472, 474, 485, 494, 496, 498, 507, 508, 513, 520, 521, 523, 526, 527, 548, 555, 560, 561, 564, 572, 578, 581, 593.
Poage, Jonathan, 181.
Poage, Margaret, 381.
Poage, Mary (Polly), 184, 202, 223, 308, 391, 423, 513.
Poage, Nancy, 583.
Poage, Rachel, 203, 431.
Poage, Rebecca, 226.
Poage, Robert, 14, 15, 20, 21, 24, 152, 184, 217, 223, 225, 254, 268, 270, 272, 274, 280, 294, 309, 312, 313, 323, 328, 330, 332, 334, 356, 362, 365, 371, 375, 381, 390, 391, 398, 399, 404, 406, 423, 428, 430, 444, 459, 462, 527, 545, 549, 552, 557.
Poage, Sarah, 217.
Poage, Thomas, 98, 116, 153, 174, 184, 188, 197, 202, 205, 223, 225, 335, 356, 391, 406, 425, 438, 454, 459, 539, 583, 593.
Poage, William, 70, 77, 87, 184, 189, 217, 223, 226, 236, 350, 356, 391, 467, 469, 473, 519, 572.
Poff, George, 213.
Poindexter, Elizabeth, 250, 495, 552, 567.
Poindexter, Joseph, 495, 552, 567, 578.
Poindexter, Richard, 509.
Pointer, Thomas, 51.
Points, Joseph, 215.
Poland, Loftus, 28.
Polis, Jacob, 206.
Polk, Ezekiel, 114, 524.

Pollock, James, 52, 76, 411, 429, 430.
Pollock, William, 429.
Polock, John, 124.
Pond, Mary, 67.
Ponder, Daniel, 66, 98, 101, 364, 391, 403, 409.
Ponder, Jemiah, 403.
Porter, David, 164.
Porter, Fanny, 246, 251.
Porter, Jane, 259.
Porter, John, 133, 229, 426.
Porter, Patrick, 133.
Porter, Samuel, 22, 428.
Porter, Thomas, 149.
Porter, William, 117, 133, 165, 259, 290, 325, 329, 480, 549.
Porterfield, James, 134.
Porterfield, John, 239.
Porterfield, Robert, 192, 194, 204, 206, 212, 217, 234, 235, 524, 578.
Porteus, James, 9, 19, 22, 255, 256, 259, 263, 264, 266, 275, 285, 287, 289, 293, 298.
Porteus, Samuel, 7.
Posey, Major, 203.
Posey, Thomas, 524.
Poss, Catherine, 585.
Poss, Henry, 585.
Post, Valentine, 141.
Potter, Gordon, 465.
Potter, James, 562.
Potter, John, 141, 142.
Potts, Amos, 401.
Potts, Jesse, 558.
Potts, John, 49, 58, 117, 319, 401.
Potts, Joseph, 75.
Potts, Joshua, 20.
Pound (Poutz), Maurice (Morris), 298, 305, 364, 434.
Pour, Adam, 126.
Pousel, Barbara, 314.
Pousel, Jacob, 314.
Powel, Gabriel, 509.
Powell, Ambrose, 168.
Powell, Caleb, 42.
Powell, Honorius, 384, 391, 408.
Powell, Jannet, 384, 408.
Powell (Powel), Joseph, 307, 518.
Powell, Simon, 69.
Power, Valentine, 340, 517.
Power, Walter, 518.
Powers, Charles, 103, 148, 544, 549.
Powers, Hannah, 544.
Powers, Susanna, 59, 112.
Poynter, Thomas, 58.
Poythress, Joseph, 573.
Prentice, Daniel, 101.
Preston, Elizabeth, 8, 68.
Preston, John, 8, 41, 254, 258, 264, 270, 423, 586.
Preston, Margret, 315.

Preston, Mary 41, 330, 380, 395, 398.
Preston, Susannah, 380, 408, 416, 428, 466, 525, 549, 561.
Preston, William, 23, 27, 34, 35, 37, 41, 50, 55, 56, 58, 59, 60, 61, 65, 67, 73, 80, 82, 91, 93, 95, 100, 109, 110, 111, 117, 118, 248, 268, 273, 274, 284, 292, 296, 298, 300, 307, 308, 309, 312, 314, 320, 323, 330, 331, 334, 350, 351, 354, 356, 357, 359, 361, 362, 366, 368, 370, 372, 380, 392, 394, 395, 397, 401, 408, 416, 423, 425, 428, 431, 437, 442, 444, 451, 458, 465, 466, 467, 470, 471, 477, 490, 492, 504, 525, 549, 561, 574.
Preush, Henry, 147.
Price, Aaron, 13.
Price, Adam, 364, 382.
Price (Preis), Augustine, 47, 56, 57, 58, 75, 85, 110, 113, 122, 123, 124, 130, 146, 148, 149, 321, 382, 397, 419, 420, 471, 528, 544.
Price, Calem, 94, 531.
Price, Daniel, 50, 57, 75, 117, 123, 127, 136, 321, 382, 400, 481.
Price, Elizabeth, 56, 131, 544.
Price, Evan, 131.
Price, Gill, 113.
Price, Hauverstine, 113.
Price, Henry, 60, 123, 321, 364, 382.
Price, James, 9, 75, 82, 254, 324.
Price, John, 89, 107, 200, 201, 212, 213, 215, 589, 595.
Price, Judith, 212, 215.
Price, Madlina, 85.
Price, Margaret, 222, 242.
Price, Michael, 75, 110, 147, 486, 487.
Price, Peter, 85.
Price, Richard, 253.
Price, Samuel, 222, 516.
Price, William, 85.
Prinder, Michael, 419.
Pringle, Richard, 287.
Pritchard, Abigail, 384.
Pritchard, James, 384.
Probeck, Joseph, 245.
Probeck, Rebecca, 245.
Probo, George, 144.
Probst, Daniel, 141.
Proops, Catharine, 502.
Props, Frederick, 128.
Props (Proopst, Probst), Leonard, 83, 141, 502.
Props (Proops), Michael, 63, 84, 373, 374, 502.
Props, Philip, 103.
Puckett, Drury, 117.
Puckett, Henry, 65.
Puffenberry, George, 158.
Pugh, Nathan, 242.
Puicer (Puiser), Francis, 318.
Puicer, Sarah, 318.

Pullen, Gidian, 157.
Pullen (Pulland), Loftus, 58, 75, 124, 142, 297, 362, 384, 468, 505.
Pullian, Borvell, 203.
Pullock, William, 538.
Puran, Prudence, 22.
Purdice, Alexander, 157.
Purkey, Jacob, 101.
Purkey, Margaret, 307.
Purkey, Margaret M., 328.
Purris, Andrew, 217.
Purris, John, 201, 203, 219.
Purris, William, 193, 310, 318, 341, 382, 388.
Purveance (Peerviance), William, 147, 358.
Pyper (Fyper), Augustine, 544.
Quin, David, 97, 464.
Quin (Guin), John, 512.
Quin (Queen), Patrick, 53, 147, 274, 378, 401, 496, 541.
Rab(b), John, 214, 586.
Rabuck, Jacob, 121.
Rackham, Mary, 167.
Rader (Raider, Reader, Reeder, Reder, Reider, Rider), Adam, 11, 13, 24, 27, 86, 108, 115, 128, 130, 131, 132, 298, 345, 346, 347, 372, 373, 451, 473, 509, 530, 552.
Rader (Reader), Anthony, 115, 128, 132, 552.
Rader (Reder), Barbara, 347, 373.
Rader (Reader, Rider), George, 128, 298, 373, 472.
Rader (Raider, Reader, Reeder, Reder), Mathias, 11, 115, 128, 347, 372, 373, 509.
Rady, Michael, 29.
Rafferty, Esther (Easter), 514.
Rafferty (Raferty), Thomas, 76, 411, 514.
Ragen, Jacob, 142.
Ragen, Jeremiah, 92.
Raiff, Abraham, 553.
Raiff, Tom, 553.
Raigh, Archibald, 492.
Railey, Francis, 436.
Railey, Michael, 28.
Rainey, Michael, 362.
Rains, Robert, 480.
Ralland, Ester, 232.
Ralstone, Andrew, 136, 440, 515.
Ralston, Ann, 37, 51, 406.
Ralston, Betsey, 237.
Ralstone, David, 37, 51, 99, 115, 132, 237, 338, 349, 366, 392, 406, 422, 434, 456, 557.
Ralston, Eleanor, 99, 237.
Ralston, George, 237.
Ralston, Henry, 587.
Ralston, James, 92, 168, 237, 502.
Ralston, John, 92, 299, 414, 587.
Ralstone, Martha, 294, 338, 349, 353.

Ralston, Mathew, 237, 467.
Ralston (Rallstone), Robert, 36, 68, 99.
  277, 292, 294, 315, 337, 338, 349, 353,
  392, 398, 450, 557, 593.
Ralston, Sally, 237.
Ralston, Samuel, 99, 237, 406.
Ralston, Thomas, 245.
Ralston, William, 61, 75, 99, 101, 110, 117,
  237, 299, 556, 578, 579, 587.
Rambo, Barbara, 9, 14.
Rambo, Jacob, 113, 293, 320, 373, 472.
Rambo, Jane, 291, 293.
Rambo, Swain (Swan), 9, 291, 293, 472.
Rambo, William, 272.
Ramsey, Agness, 461.
Ramsey, Alexander, 165, 170, 176, 594.
Ramsey, Andrew, 165, 170, 176, 185, 187,
  194, 221, 222, 229, 231, 234, 235, 247,
  565, 591, 594.
Ramsey, Daniel, 165, 170, 591.
Ramsey, George, 165, 170, 176, 594.
Ramsey, James, 60, 61, 80, 170, 176, 178,
  209, 231, 344, 358, 461, 591.
Ramsey, Jane, 457.
Ramsey, John, 34, 38, 39, 40, 42, 43, 44,
  48, 53, 73, 76, 85, 96, 97, 104, 112, 127,
  165, 169, 170, 176, 185, 194, 221, 236,
  253, 271, 277, 286, 296, 301, 304, 330,
  345, 352, 362, 384, 395, 399, 403, 412,
  420, 446, 453, 459, 468, 469, 472, 511,
  516, 525, 542, 548, 565, 567, 591, 592,
  594.
Ramsey, Josiah, 75, 106, 121.
Ramsey, Margaret, 60, 238, 388, 461.
Ramsey, Mary, 165, 176, 453, 469.
Ramsey, Robert, 8, 10, 29, 55, 56, 59, 111,
  157, 261, 264, 269, 279, 281, 297, 304,
  311, 313, 315, 388.
Ramsey, Samuel, 147, 548.
Ramsey, Sarah, 315.
Ramsey, Thomas, 58, 64, 72, 75, 113, 300,
  428, 432.
Ramsey, William, 103, 122, 133, 165, 170,
  176, 223, 236, 301, 313, 325, 384, 411,
  446, 452, 457, 461, 472, 496, 511, 516,
  594.
Randall, Elizabeth, 548.
Randall (Randalls, Randles), Francis, 60,
  97, 417.
Randall, James, 20, 38.
Randall, John, 548.
Randall, Thomas, 143.
Randall, Winnifor, 548.
Randels (Randall), Richard, 548.
Randerbush, Emanuel, 247.
Randolph, James, 273.
Randolph, Peyton, 571.
Randolph, William, 571.
Randolson, Francis, 432.
Rankin, Ann, 198.
Rankin, Armstrong, 198, 199.

Rankin, George, 58, 60, 198, 199.
Rankin, Isaac, 198, 199.
Rankin (Renkin), James, 58, 179, 182, 187,
  190, 194, 195, 198, 199, 200, 214, 219,
  228, 230, 232, 590.
Rankin, Jean, 58.
Rankin, John, 58, 165, 173, 187, 199.
Rankin, Joseph, 198, 199.
Rankin, Lettice, 239.
Rankin, Margaret, 235.
Rankin, Martha, 58.
Rankin, Mary, 58, 124, 157, 194, 197, 238.
Rankin, Richard, 199, 248.
Rankin, Robert, 58, 187, 190, 232.
Rankin, Samuel, 198, 199.
Rankin, Samuel S., 209.
Rankin, Thomas, 58, 170, 184, 187, 197,
  235, 515, 519, 526.
Rankin, William, 58, 187, 239.
Rapp, Job, 221.
Ratcliff, Daniel, 321.
Ratcliff, Reuben, 322.
Ratlif, Thomas, 452, 454.
Ratliff, Richard, 11.
Ratlive, Samuel, 490.
Ray (Reay), Bety, 180.
Ray, Daniel, 553, 565.
Ray (Rhea, Rhey), David, 38, 39, 188.
Ray (Reah, Reagh, Rhea), James, 173,
  437, 504, 510, 542, 557.
Ray (Reagh, Rhea, Reaugh), John, 82,
  118, 164, 211, 542.
Ray, Joseph, 98, 135, 174, 197, 246, 445,
  493, 566.
Ray, Thomas, 197, 217.
Raynolds, Elizabeth, 452.
Raynolds (Randels, Randals), Richard,
  452.
Rea, Daniel, 183, 205.
Reaburn, Adam, 94, 102, 562.
Reach (Reah), Archibald, 133, 135.
Reach, Margaret, 133.
Reach, William, 55, 132.
Reachey, Alexander, 498.
Reader, Elizabeth, 128.
Reader, Margaret, 472.
Readpath (Redpath, Ridpath), John, 454,
  457, 459, 496, 518, 523, 526, 587.
Ready, Patrick, 201.
Reager (Reeger, Regar), Anthony, 47, 53,
  150.
Reager, Barbara, 527.
Reager, Dorothy, 527.
Reager, Hance, 52.
Reager (Reagor), John, 38, 49, 92, 527.
Reagh (Rhea), Robert, 325, 327, 351, 433,
  436.
Reagh, Sara, 351.
Reagland, John, 151, 172.
Reagland (Regland), Nathan, 151, 172.
Reagland, Rachel, 172.

Reagland, Rebecca, 151.
Reagland, Sackey, 151.
Reagland, Susania, 172.
Reah (Reagh, Reaugh, Rhea), Archibald, 83, 90, 107, 174, 194, 211, 311, 333, 351, 407, 422, 433, 482, 516.
Reah (Ray, Rea Regh, Reagh, Reaugh, Rhea), Elizabeth, 150, 179, 443, 471, 487, 510, 515, 542, 557.
Reah, Martha, 179.
Reah (Ray, Regh, Reagh, Raigh, Rhea, Reaoh), William, 57, 63, 133, 150, 160, 211, 239, 286, 311, 312, 333, 351, 411, 437, 442, 454, 487, 492, 510, 515, 542, 557.
Realy (Railey), Michael, 30, 294.
Reamy, Michael, 12.
Reese, Mary, 26.
Reburn, Agness, 179.
Reburn (Reyburn), Edward, 34, 80.
Reburn, Elizabeth, 365.
Reburn (Rayburn, Reaburn), Henry, 34, 45, 80, 318, 364, 372, 520, 537, 538.
Reburn, Isabella, 213.
Reburn (Reaburn, Reyburn), James, 80, 84, 95, 102, 133, 136, 310, 365, 407, 555.
Reburn (Reaburn), Jean, 381, 441.
Reburn (Reaburn, Reybourn), John, 39, 213, 369, 410, 440, 441, 454, 491, 515, 546, 554.
Reburn (Reaburn), Joseph, 95, 111, 124, 126, 136, 340, 365, 441, 502, 508, 510, 528, 554, 564.
Reburn (Reaburn), Margaret, 34, 213, 510, 537, 538.
Reburn (Reaburn, Reyburn), Robert, 94, 134, 217, 372, 381.
Reburn, Sarah, 213.
Redburn, Joseph, 419.
Redenhouse, Elizabeth, 239.
Redford, Thomas, 114.
Rediford (Redeford, Rutherford), Joseph, 471, 472.
Redman (Redmont), Samuel, 176, 214, 561.
Redmon, John, 561.
Redmond, Joseph, 560.
Reece, James, 214.
Reed (Reid), Adam, 308, 393, 528.
Reed, Agness, 173.
Reed (Reid), Alexander, 167, 173, 182, 188, 202, 210, 355, 386, 412, 512, 542, 561, 562, 594.
Reed, Ann, 406.
Reed, Barbara, 393, 472, 519, 542.
Reed, Cathern, 310.
Reed, Deborah, 173.
Reed, Elizabeth, 202, 270.
Reed, Gaisper, 53.
Reed (Reid), George, 74, 110, 219.
Reed, Isabel, 173.
Reed, Jacob, 340, 387, 406.
Reed, James, 400, 564, 596.
Reed (Reid), John, 202, 210, 386, 412, 528, 529.
Reed (Read), Joseph, 100, 102, 125, 133, 262, 263, 270, 272, 297, 311, 326, 381, 414, 423, 480.
Reed, Leonard, 58.
Reed, Margaret, 540, 589.
Reed (Read, Reid), Mathew, 70, 104, 136, 387, 439, 454, 459, 485, 529, 538.
Reed, Owen, 69.
Reed, Peter, 58, 310.
Reede, Pally, 244.
Reed, Richard, 39.
Reed (Ried, Read), Robert, 59, 61, 67, 70, 72, 80, 98, 104, 173, 179, 180, 182, 183, 200, 202, 203, 214, 216, 338, 392, 402, 406, 416, 440, 454, 457, 472, 486, 496, 506, 512, 519, 534, 540, 542, 574, 575, 586, 594.
Reed (Reid), Thomas, 202, 223, 386, 412, 461, 520, 568, 584.
Reed (Read, Reid), William, 58, 189, 344, 345, 406, 524.
Reedy, Thomas, 31.
Reelson, Benjamin, 397.
Rees (Ree), David, 98, 476.
Rees, Persilla, 35.
Rees, Thomas, 25, 26, 28, 35.
Reese, Joseph, 26.
Reese, Priscilla, 37.
Reeves, Brewer, 497.
Reeves, John, 171.
Reeves, Thomas, 496.
Regan, Barney, 14.
Regan, Richard, 424.
Reid, Daddy, 223.
Reid, Hannah, 150.
Reider, Anna, 530.
Reiger, Jacob, 121.
Reiley, Francis, 293, 295, 473.
Reiley, John, 287.
Reiley, Michael, 47.
Reily, James, 387.
Reiney, Michael, 496.
Reisling, Christopher, 97.
Remy, Daniel, 34.
Renick, Ann, 169.
Renick (Rennack, Rennick), Elizabeth, 260, 271, 299.
Renick (Rennick, Rennix), Thomas, 86, 459, 462.
Rennald (Renalds, Reynolds), James, 19, 20, 99.
Rennick, George, 271.
Rennick (Renick, Rennock, Rennix), Robert, 21, 25, 32, 34, 37, 39, 46, 74, 75, 81, 86, 151, 199, 209, 254, 260, 268, 271, 276, 294, 299, 306, 308, 313, 318, 320, 346, 353, 381, 437, 573.

Rennock (Renick, Renocks), **William**, 189, 492, 567.
Rennolds, Job, 179.
Rentfro, Esther, 260.
Rentfro, Joseph, 372.
Rentfro (Rentfroe), Stephen, 9, **35**, **67**, **74**, **271**, **297**, **354**, **378**, **401**, **405**.
Rentfroe, James, 260.
Rentfroe, Margaret, 405.
Rentfrow, Joseph, 362.
Reoack, Archibald, 310.
Reoarch, William, 310.
Resburg (Risburg), Augustavus (**Gustavus**), 583, 589, 591.
Retsworth (Retsroth), Zachary, **156**.
Rew, Ab, 149.
Rexrode, Zeacriah (Zachariah), 110, **128**, 141.
Reynolds, Francis, 367.
Reynolds, John, 279, 528, 581.
Reynolds, Mary, 99.
Rhea, Hugh, 211, 492, 516.
Rhea (Reah), Thomas **Turk**, **234**.
Rhine, Elizabeth, 83.
Rhine (Ryan), Michael, 83, **84**.
Rhoads, Thomas, 123, **145**, **547**.
Rhodes, Robert, 184.
Rhuble, John, 533.
Rice, Benijah, 541.
Rice, Benjamin, 470.
Rice (Brice), George, 180.
Rice, John, 156, 535, 538.
Rice, Thomas, 205.
Rice, William, 759, 187, **536**.
Rich, Francis, 295.
Richard, Aron, 158.
Richards, Benjamin, 570.
Richards, Jacob, 40.
Richards, Phillemon, 197.
Richards, Samuel, 493.
Richards, William, 557, 558.
Richardson, Elizabeth, 30.
Richardson, Jane, 185.
Richardson, Robert, 131.
Richardson, William, 199.
Richason (Richardson), **Aaron (Aron)**, 152, 153, 154, 155.
Richason, Abraham, 153.
Richason (Richardson, Richeson), Daniel, 13, 26, 28, 30, 36, 38, 58, 141, 153, 312.
Richason (Richardson), **Ephraim**, **153**, 155, 159, 409, 416, 436.
Richason (Richardson), Rachel, 153, **155**.
Richeson, Jonathan, 431.
Richey (Ritchie), Alexander, 24, **38**, **46**, **268**, **293**, **294**, **308**, **318**, **326**, **353**, **361**, **395**.
Richey (Richie), Hugh, 564, 566.
Richey (Ritchey), James, 161, **427**, **462**, **475**, 518.

Richey (Ritchie), Mary, 146, 318, 442.
Richey, Patience (Peations), 204, 207.
Richey (Ritchie), William, 64, **74**, **75**, 149, 295, 319, 442, 485.
Richison, Joseph, 99.
Richman, John, 31.
Ricket, Thomas, 214.
Rickey, Martha, 251.
Riddle, James, 570.
Riddle, Lewis, 570.
Riddle (Ruddle), Stephen, 13, **139**, **293**, 315.
Riddle, William, 570.
Riddle, William P., 570.
Rider, Borket, 65.
Rieley, John, 22.
Rieley, William, 22.
Riely (Rieley, Riley), Francis, 117, **426**, 490.
Riggs, Margaret, 517.
Riggs, Mark, 455, 517, 544.
Rinehart, Lewis, 547.
Rinhart, Michael, 21.
Rinerd, Ludwick, 146.
Riney, Michael, 131.
Rinken, William, 543.
Rippy, Samuel, 96.
Risk (Rusk), David, 147, 176, 587.
Risk (Rusk), Elizabeth, 147, 175, **176**.
Risk (Rusk), Hannah, 147, 176.
Risk (Rusk), James, 77, 81, 82, 112, **118**, 135, 147, 175, 176, 360, 396, 429, 573.
Risk, Jane, 135, 233.
Risk (Rusk, Rush), John, 5, 11, 49, 60, **81**, 82, 140, 145, 147, 152, 167, 175, **176**, 220, 226, 254, 280, 281, 313, 316, **419**, 429, 516, 542, 564, 565, 587.
Risk (Rusk), Margaret, 82, 147, 176, **429**, 564.
Risk, Mary, 147.
Risk, Mathew, 147.
Risk (Rusk), Robert, 82, 118, 147, 175, 176, 443, 564.
Risk (Rusk), Samuel, 147, 176.
Risk (Rusk), William, 147, 167.
Ritchey (Richey), John, 147, 158, 178, **308**, 318, 326, 347, 352, 359, 369, 375, **400**, 440, 441, 561, 567.
Ritchey (Richey), Margaret, 352, **441**.
Ritchey, Mary M., 361.
Ritchey, Robert, 172.
Ritchie, Nancy, 247.
Rivellner, Jacob, 516.
Rivers, Martha, 250.
Rives, James, 227.
Rives, Martha, 227.
Roach, Ruben, 137.
Roads, Isaac, 8.
Roap, Nicholas, 144.
Roberts, Benjamin, 246, 575.
Roberts, George, 100.

Roberts, Isaiah, 217.
Roberts, James, 95.
Roberts, John, 235, 246, 275, 380, 530.
Roberts, Joseph, 70.
Roberts, Margaret, 250, 380.
Roberts, Nicholas, 28.
Roberts, Patsey, 246.
Roberts, Rebecca, 245.
Robertson, Alexander, 36, 116, 120, 165, 168, 174, 176, 179, 185, 187, 201, 202, 207, 213, 218, 220, 233, 238, 239, 244, 379, 519, 550, 557, 559, 594.
Robertson, Ann, 220, 238, 239.
Robertson, David, 189.
Robertson, Elijah, 238.
Robertson, Elizabeth, 36, 54, 56, 199, 455.
Robertson, George, 36, 220, 550.
Robertson, Isabella, 92, 199.
Robertson, James, 34, 36, 38, 43, 44, 84, 91, 165, 168, 176, 202, 220, 224, 238, 239, 253, 254, 286, 370, 428, 508, 550.
Robertson, Jane, 216, 220, 550.
Robertson, John, 42, 43, 92, 120, 121, 189, 199, 379, 406, 421, 440, 487.
Robertson, Lettice (Letis), 220, 239, 508.
Robertson, Margaret, 134, 199.
Robertson, Martha, 176, 286.
Robertson, Mary, 120, 158, 199, 202, 216, 238, 421.
Robertson, Mathew, 36, 43, 44, 120, 170, 177, 220, 237, 238, 245, 257, 283, 286, 405, 406, 445, 455, 508, 526.
Robertson, Ruth, 245.
Robertson, Simon, 70.
Robertson, William, 36, 42, 43, 92, 93, 103, 104, 112, 113, 120, 123, 127, 154, 155, 168, 176, 193, 211, 213, 220, 237, 239, 244, 286, 411, 426, 468, 471, 497, 508, 510, 519, 526, 547, 549, 556, 568, 579.
Robinson, Alexander, 61.
Robinson, Ann, 61.
Robinson, Annable (Annabale), 415, 428, 467.
Robinson, Catherine, 80, 139.
Robinson, Charles, 304, 346.
Robinson, Cornelius, 346, 347.
Robinson, David, 21, 33, 50, 95, 97, 105, 108, 110, 146, 275, 319, 339, 350, 366, 369, 378, 397, 403, 408, 415, 418, 428, 430, 467, 470, 544.
Robinson, Elinner, 139.
Robinson, Elizabeth, 162, 316.
Robinson, Esther, 30, 314, 316.
Robinson, Gartry, 169.
Robinson, George, 6, 7, 25, 38, 45, 55, 59, 64, 73, 80, 82, 96, 145, 146, 254, 266, 271, 273, 275, 284, 289, 297, 301, 305, 314, 315, 334, 339, 352, 354, 378, 384, 389, 397, 401, 420, 444, 451, 467, 493.
Robinson, Hannah, 105, 139, 426, 495.
Robinson, Henry, 585.

Robinson, Isaac, 21, 102, 103, 112, 139, 150, 462, 503, 544.
Robinson, Isabella, 105, 216, 319, 320, 346, 476.
Robinson, James, 10, 11, 12, 21, 22, 27, 29, 30, 61, 70, 80, 96, 105, 108, 139, 143, 146, 260, 270, 272, 297, 311, 312, 313, 316, 333, 354, 364, 365, 378, 408, 415, 426, 444, 460, 474, 476, 491, 495, 535, 544.
Robinson, Jane (Jean), 61, 105, 144, 146, 298.
Robinson (Robson), Joel, 101, 535, 552.
Robinson (Robeson, Robison), John, 10, 12, 34, 43, 45, 72, 74, 75, 80, 105, 108, 110, 144, 146, 276, 288, 294, 298, 309, 312, 313, 316, 317, 341, 396, 408, 413, 428, 430, 476, 479, 585.
Robinson (Robison, Robertson), Jonathan, 21, 378, 382, 398, 413, 533, 544.
Robinson, Joseph, 14, 17, 24, 33, 80, 87, 91, 120, 146, 316, 371, 416, 419, 428, 451, 456.
Robinson, Luke, 139.
Robinson, McKenny, 162, 163.
Robinson (Robison), Margaret (Margrey), 91, 105, 341, 535.
Robinson, Martha, 80, 96, 254, 304, 397, 401, 469.
Robinson, Mary, 21, 25, 43, 193, 316.
Robinson, Mathew, 19, 72, 312, 313, 396, 413, 461.
Robinson, Peter, 589.
Robinson, Priscilla, 80.
Robinson, Rachel, 105.
Robinson (Robison), Robert, 12, 184, 307, 315, 319, 320, 346.
Robinson, Samuel, 80, 96, 105, 401, 431.
Robinson, Sarah, 80, 413, 444.
Robinson, Simon, 467.
Robinson, Thomas, 316.
Robinson (Robison, Roberson), William, 29, 30, 54, 80, 83, 91, 108, 109, 146, 181, 264, 265, 268, 273, 276, 278, 279, 280, 298, 304, 310, 313, 314, 316, 361, 365, 379, 399, 408, 411, 420, 430, 433, 435, 469, 487.
Robson, James, 92.
Roche, Richard, 186.
Rockey, Henry, 592.
Rodeback, Adam, 116.
Rodes, Barbara, 135.
Rodes, David, 488.
Rodes (Roads), John 364, 382.
Rodes, Mathias, 129, 135.
Rodgers, Anthony, 440.
Rodgers, Elizabeth (Betty), 162, 391, 509, 572.
Rodgers (Rogers), George, 104, 105, 116, 282, 284, 323, 326, 334, 354, 366, 381, 391, 402, 406, 417, 422, 432, 453, 572.
Rodgers, Jacob, 440.

Rodgers, John, 495, 496, 518.
Rodgers (Roger), Margaret (Peggy), 199, 226.
Rodgers (Rogers), Robert, 142, 391, 406, 417, 446, 447, 453, 514, 559, 572.
Rodgers, Sarah, 162.
Rodgers (Rogers), Seth (Sith), 117, 447, 453.
Rodgers, Thomas, 495, 501, 509, 563.
Roe, George Hook, 171.
Roebuck, William, 497.
Roerty, John, 110.
Rogal, Philip, 572.
Roger, Mary, 158.
Rogers, Ann, 59.
Rogers (Rodgers), James, 59, 61, 496.
Rogers (Rodgers), William, 167, 226, 290, 403, 440, 454, 560, 565.
Roleman (Rollman, Rolsman), Christian, 103, 126, 356, 399, 411, 502.
Roleman (Rolman, Rollman), Jacob, 63, 83, 126, 128, 356, 399, 405, 411.
Roling, Peter, 65.
Roller, Paul, 244.
Rollman, Margaret, 399, 411.
Root, Hans, 11.
Root (Roote), Jacob, 159, 541.
Root, John, 11.
Rorebough (Roreback), John, 121.
Roreck (Rork), Michael, 111, 502.
Rorty, John, 75.
Rose, Alexander, 280.
Rose, Daniel, 473.
Rose, Robert, 22.
Roseborough (Roseboro), James, 280, 302, 327.
Roseborough, Margaret, 327.
Roseby, William, 82.
Roseman (Rosamon, Rosemand), John, 15, 26, 30, 54, 306, 311, 335, 344, 359, 383, 433.
Roseman, Sarah, 436.
Ross, Adam, 240.
Ross, David, 425.
Ross, Hugh, 15, 252, 386, 412, 472.
Ross, James, 198, 216.
Ross, Jane, 240.
Ross, John, 81, 240.
Ross, Letty, 240.
Ross, Margaret, 240.
Ross, Mary, 158.
Ross, Robert, 145, 158.
Ross, Samuel, 240, 321.
Ross, Sarah, 412.
Ross, William, 240.
Rothgab, Anna, 28, 29.
Rothgab, Barbery, 28.
Rothgab, Catherine, 28.
Rothgab, Elizabeth, 28.
Rothgab, John George, 28.
Rothgab (Rodgab), John Jacob, 28, 29.
Rothgab, Peter, 28.
Rouback, John, 375.
Roudenboush, Adam, 84.
Roundtree, Noah, 115, 119.
Rowan, James, 163, 193, 570.
Rowland, Bridgett, 547.
Rowland, George, 399.
Rowland, James, 98, 364, 397, 416, 582.
Rowland, Martha, 399.
Rowland, Richard, 547.
Rowland, Robert, 9, 41, 42, 64, 399, 480.
Rowland, Thomas, 480.
Rowland, William, 100, 107, 399, 458.
Rubble, George, 588.
Rucker, James, 573.
Rucker, Leonard, 573.
Rucker, Mary, 573.
Ruckman, John, 32, 110, 300, 386.
Ruckman, Thomas, 386.
Ruddle, Archibald, 13, 293, 315, 373.
Ruddle, Cornelius, 21, 106, 139, 166, 205, 315, 324, 370, 449, 543, 553, 556, 562.
Ruddle, George, 543.
Ruddle, Ingabo, 324, 562.
Ruddle, Isaac, 315.
Ruddle (Rudle, Ruddell, Ridle), John, 8, 13, 14, 15, 16, 17 18, 20, 22, 23, 25, 28, 32, 35, 95, 261, 498, 551.
Ruddle, Mary, 13, 315.
Rude, Jacob, 141.
Rufenough (Ruffnaugh, Rafner), Peter, 5, 10, 29, 253.
Ruh, Jacob, 113.
Rule, David, 65, 450.
Rule, Henry, 156, 405.
Ruleman, Christian, 128, 157.
Ruleman, Jacob, 157.
Rund, Ralph, 26.
Runkel, Samuel, 171.
Runkle, Anna Marie, 530.
Runkle (Runcle), Jacob, 481, 496, 514, 522, 530, 537, 547.
Runkle, Lewis, 504.
Runkle (Rankle), Peter, 146, 530, 547.
Runyan (Runnion), Henry, 133, 152, 533.
Rush (Rusk), Charles, 51, 113, 116, 120, 123, 124, 127, 129, 135, 136, 140, 152, 351, 412, 420, 450, 480, 531.
Rush, Jacob, 238.
Rush (Rusk), Jean, 167, 176.
Rush, John, 238, 551.
Rush, Marchius, 531.
Rush, Peter, 223, 480, 551.
Rusk, James, 85.
Rusk, Rachel, 176.
Rusmessel, Anny, 241.
Rusmessel, Christian, 241.
Russell, Adam, 231.
Russell, Alexander, 224.
Russell, Andrew, 43, 69, 70, 72, 99, 102, 117, 162, 164, 220, 224, 242, 290, 354, 371, 377, 384, 412, 472, 526, 551, 564.
Russell, Ann, 164, 224, 245.

Russell, Bryan, 84, 347.
Russell, Bryce, 57, 68, 71, 79, 157, 342, 382, 400, 485, 526.
Russell (Rusel), David, 152, 569, 596.
Russell, Elizabeth (Betty, Betsey), 164, 220, 224, 245.
Russell, Florence, 384.
Russell, George, 71, 89.
Russell, Hanna, 245.
Russell, Henry, 245.
Russell, Hugh, 71, 89.
Russell, Isabella, 89.
Russell, Isabella H., 71.
Russell, James, 164, 224, 245.
Russell, Jammiane, 245.
Russell, Jane (Jean), 164, 224, 240.
Russell, John, 224, 245, 558.
Russell, Joseph, 70, 245.
Russell, Joshua, 124, 355, 384, 413, 526, 564.
Russell, Margaret, 569.
Russell, Mary, 164, 240.
Russell, Mathew, 164, 224.
Russell, Moses, 240.
Russell, Nancy, 245.
Russell, Rachel, 71, 89, 526.
Russell, Robert, 137, 198, 245, 415, 526, 564.
Russell, Ruth, 245.
Russell, Samuel, 245.
Russell, Sarah (Sally), 245, 557.
Russell, William (W.), 37, 164, 167, 224, 255, 259, 260, 261, 264, 270, 273, 275, 277, 282, 284, 288, 289, 292, 300, 316, 318, 329, 340, 341, 348, 351, 352, 360, 374, 377, 405, 411, 420, 460, 493, 512, 545, 557.
Rutherback, Adam, 53, 375.
Rutherford, Arthur (Archer), 538.
Rutherford, Benjamin, 113.
Rutherford, Eliner, 539.
Rutherford, Elizabeth, 113.
Rutherford, Elliott, 118.
Rutherford, James, 104, 109, 333, 471.
Rutherford, John, 113, 226.
Rutherford, Joseph, 118, 318, 370, 403, 412, 413, 438, 538, 539.
Rutherford, Margaret, 104, 109, 135, 159.
Rutherford, Mary, 118, 534.
Rutherford, Reuben, 118, 131, 349, 370, 403, 471, 472, 491, 539.
Rutherford, Robert, 111, 118, 492, 511, 534, 538.
Rutherford, Samuel, 104, 135.
Rutherford, Thomas, 113, 118, 131, 269, 370, 383, 471, 472.
Rutledge (Ritledge), Edward, 23, 80, 94, 143, 149, 177, 178, 188, 195, 319, 371, 467, 570, 575, 579.
Rutledge, Elizabeth, 79.
Rutledge, George, 23, 27, 79, 177, 188, 195, 217, 221, 261, 284, 287, 326, 354, 371,, 387, 407, 411, 488, 503, 528, 542, 579.

Rutledge, James, 17, 27, 177, 188, 195, 266, 570.
Rutledge, Jean (Jane), 23, 29, 143, 195, 343.
Rutledge, John, 23, 195, 259, 269, 287, 288, 290, 295, 343, 355.
Rutledge, Katarine, 195.
Rutledge, Mary, 221.
Rutledge, Rebecka, 177, 188.
Rutledge, Rosanna, 177, 188, 217.
Rutledge, Sarah, 143, 177, 188, 217, 570, 579.
Rutledge (Ruttledge), Sarah, 143, 177, 188, 217, 570, 579.
Rutledge (Ruttchledge), Thomas, 23, 29, 68, 79, 100, 117, 166, 195, 197, 259, 260, 281, 343, 353, 354, 359, 371, 376, 392, 411, 473, 566.
Rutledge, William, 23, 315, 324, 343, 354, 370, 413, 543.
Rutlishberger (Rutleshber), Christian, 466.
Ryan, Edward, 13.
Ryan (Ryon), John, 13, 38.
Ryan, Joseph, 332.
Ryan, Michael, 67.
Ryan, Sarah C., 332.
Ryan, Timothy, 117.
Rydebogh, Adam, 121.
Ryley, Aaron, 87.
Ryley, Francis, 404.
Ryley, Pharaoh, 61, 73.
Rynard, Michael, 20
Ryndle (Reynolds), Patrick, 194.
Ryne, James, 22.

Sadowski, Andrew, 53.
Sagnarisera, 551.
Sale, John, 59.
Sallas, Jacob, 530.
Salles, Nicholas, 61, 124, 525.
Salling (Sally), Ann, 298, 317, 318, 325.
Salling, George, 87, 390.
Salling, George A., 38, 39, 364, 390, 410, 475.
Salling, John, 38, 364.
Salling (Sally), John Peter, 38, 39, 40, 298, 300, 325, 331, 332, 364.
Salling, Peter, 390.
Sallix, William, 115, 118, 479.
Sallord, John, 409.
Salmons, Jacob, 120.
Salsberry, John, 55.
Sample, Ann, 143.
Sample (Semples), Moses, 66, 94, 143, 406, 556, 557.
Sample (Samples, Sanpils), Robert, 143, 145, 383, 553.
Sample (Samples, Semple), Samuel, 49, 51, 72, 94, 130, 142, 143, 145, 157, 366, 367, 422, 445, 532.

Sample (Samples, Semples), William, 55, 69, 143, 498, 522, 533.
Samples, Hannah, 532.
Samples, Sarah, 498, 533.
Sampson, Edward, 432, 472, 478, 490, 504.
Sampson, William, 94, 501.
Sanderson, Francis, 504.
Sanger, Jacob, 199.
Sansabough, John, 543.
Sasinger, Elizabeth, 467.
Saunders, Mary, 251.
Saunders, William, 251.
Savage, Abraham, 167.
Sawin, Henry, 544.
Sawin, Jennet, 544.
Sawin (Sawings), Joseph, 543.
Sawin, Katherine, 543.
Sawyers, Ann, 169, 186.
Sawyers, David, 169, 186, 223, 230, 452.
Sawyers, Ester, 117.
Sawyers, George, 186.
Sawyers, George W., 169.
Sayers, Ann, 5.
Sayers, Cathren, 5.
Sayers, David, 43, 44, 69, 78, 272, 287, 297, 311, 326.
Sayers, Elizabeth (Elibeth), 5, 211.
Sayers (Sayer), Hannah, 44, 326.
Sayers, Margaret, 5.
Sayers, Rachel, 438.
Sayers (Sawyers), Robert, 5, 43, 44, 48, 97, 311, 323, 326, 417, 567.
Sayers, William, 5, 6, 21, 258, 272, 286, 299, 338, 341, 438.
Saylor, Christian, 563.
Saylor, Philip, 557, 560, 563.
Scaggs (Skeggs), Henry, 106, 490.
Sawyers, Hannah, 144, 169, 186, 199, 220, 590.
Sawyers (Sayers), James, 26, 48, 68, 72, 89, 92, 93, 109, 116, 144, 169, 170, 186, 188, 194, 220, 252, 260, 276, 318, 344, 437, 438, 452, 474, 564.
Sawyers, John, 93, 169, 188, 207.
Sawyers, Martha, 169, 186.
Sawyers, Nancy, 223.
Sawyers, Rachel, 169, 186, 437.
Sawyers, Rebecca, 169, 186, 188, 199, 230, 590.
Sawyers, Sampson, 160, 169, 188, 437.
Sawyers, Thomas, 169, 186, 188.
Sawyers, William, 110, 113, 542.
Saxton, William, 93.
Sayers (Sawyers), Alexander, 5, 6, 73, 97, 341, 351, 389, 397.
Scaggs (Skeggs, Skggs), James, 18, 73, 321, 490.
Scaggs, Rachel, 490.
Scarbrough, John, 147.
Sceleher, Mathew, 544.
Scheyder, Casper, 149.

Scholl (Sholl), Peter, 6, 14, 15, 17, 24, 25, 26, 45, 88, 260, 268, 269, 273, 291, 293, 302, 304, 311, 312, 314, 317, 530.
Scholl, William, 265.
Scholley (Scooly), Isaac, 16, 33.
Schom, Nicholas, 144.
Schoolar, William, 208.
Schoolcraft, James, 140, 154.
Schoon, John, 536.
Scilar (Siller), Plackard, 74, 75, 117, 323, 428, 465, 596.
Sciler, Peter, 562.
Sconce, Robert, 595.
Scoolcraft, Austin, 58.
Scoot, Anderson, 136.
Scot, Adonijah, 28, 31.
Scot, Judith, 24.
Scot, Phebe, 28.
Scot, Rachel, 28.
Scothorn, Joseph, 149.
Scott, Agness, 576.
Scott, Alexander, 22, 31, 224, 230.
Scott, Andrew, 45, 66, 92, 108, 140, 204, 230, 239, 250, 308, 312, 318, 560, 572, 576.
Scott, Ann, 11, 53, 58, 245, 272, 354, 404, 463.
Scott, Archibald, 173, 190, 229, 231, 239, 567.
Scott (Scot), Benjamin, 24, 28, 30, 31, 53, 58, 78, 84, 495.
Scott, Catherine, 230, 432, 524.
Scott, Charles, 569.
Scott (Scot), David, 28, 31, 64, 78, 103, 406, 415, 426, 428, 524.
Scott, Easter, 464.
Scott, Elizabeth, 230.
Scott, Fany, 205.
Scott, Frances, 245.
Scott, George, 11, 53, 69, 84, 92, 271, 272, 274, 290, 312, 318.
Scott, Gibly (Ibley), 225.
Scott, Jacob, 28, 83, 87, 471.
Scott, James, 20, 24, 28, 30, 54, 57, 78, 87, 168, 205, 224, 239, 302, 464, 465, 483, 571.
Scott, James S., 6.
Scott, Jean (Jane), 11, 56, 77, 93, 190, 225, 239.
Scott, Jennette, 245.
Scott (Scoot), John, 11, 22, 23, 24, 28, 36, 38, 56, 77, 80, 83, 87, 190, 192, 205, 224, 225, 230, 250, 287, 346, 353, 354, 367, 382, 401, 403, 404, 417, 418, 432, 463, 553, 558.
Scott, Rebecca, 224, 225, 230, 245.
Scott, Robert, 7, 11, 33, 53, 57, 58, 69, 72, 126, 136, 140, 178, 203, 205, 245, 258, 272, 274, 276, 295, 296, 297, 299, 421, 422, 464, 465, 471, 476, 504, 510, 511, 531, 541, 551.

Scott, Matilda, 239.
Scott, Peter, 335.
Scott, Joseph, 28, 78, 87, 406.
Scott, Julianna, 225.
Scott, Major, 167, 308.
Scott, Martha, 245.
Scott, Mary (Polly), 11, 71, 89, 245, 495.
Scott, Samuel, 10, 11, 17, 38, 53, 56, 58, 77, 78, 99, 106, 404, 418.
Scott, Sarah (Sally, Saley), 28, 205, 245, 250.
Scott, Thomas, 26, 66, 108, 117, 138, 141, 163, 176, 190, 204, 224, 230, 250, 290, 477, 563, 577.
Scott, William, 36, 44, 68, 74, 88, 90, 123, 130, 154, 167, 178, 205, 210, 224, 230, 239, 309, 325, 335, 370, 389, 450, 520, 540, 571, 575, 576, 579.
Scott, William H., 563.
Scott, William Joseph, 245.
Scraggs, James, 110.
Scull (Schall), John, 30, 465.
Sea (See), Frederick, 13, 22, 23, 42, 83, 107.
Sea, George, 13, 22.
Sea, Matain, 503.
Seamans, Nicholas, 150.
Seamen, Levers, 103.
Seamon (Seeman), Leonard, 84, 125, 436.
Seamon, Hans M., 84.
Searight, Anne, 251.
Searight, Margaret, 251.
Sears, James, 121.
Seaton, George, 81.
Seawright (Seeright), Alexander, 163, 584.
Seawright (Searight), George, 171, 172, 173, 174, 556, 559.
Seawright (Searight), James, 128, 174, 186, 191, 505, 512, 559, 594.
Seawright (Seeright), Jane (Jean), 584. 590.
Seawright (Searight), John, 15, 79, 93, 251, 261, 282, 322, 349, 484, 505, 529, 569, 577.
Seawright (Searight, Seeright), Sarah (Sharah), 251, 484, 584, 590.
Seawright (Seeright), William, 584, 590.
Seccafoose (Segenfoos), Jacob, 158, 169.
Seduskay (Sedusky), Andrew, 40, 66.
See, John, 42, 543.
Seehorn (Seehaven), Nicholas, 16, 21, 22.
Seeley, Jeremiah, 42, 100, 109.
Segerfoot (Segerfeet), Peter, 156, 158.
Seig, David, 247.
Seig, Jacob, 246.
Seig, John, 246.
Seig, Paul, 206, 246, 247.
Seig (Sieg), Susannah, 206, 247.
Selham, John, 200.
Sell, William, 220.

Seller (Sellers), Adam, 480, 506, 528.
Seller, Ellis, 15.
Seller (Sellar, Sellers), Henry 42, 364, 373, 449, 480, 528, 535.
Seller (Siller, Sellers), John, 110, 133, 134, 136, 140, 146, 373, 480, 481, 501, 517, 528.
Seller (Selers, Sellars), Peter, 50, 364, 373, 480.
Selone, John, 93.
Selzer, Henry, 132, 398.
Selzer (Celses, Celzar, Seltzer), Mathias, 5, 20, 21, 29, 265, 291, 302, 314, 328, 391, 398.
Semon, Nicholas, 405.
Semple, John, 39, 47, 337, 350.
Sennghors, 551.
Separs, John, 552.
Server, John, 156.
Sevenson, Mary, 150.
Sevents, Catron, 144.
Severt, Charles F., 472.
Sevier (Sevior), Joanna, 315, 441, 450, 534.
Sevier, John, 111, 504.
Sevier (Sevire, Severe, Sevear, Sevior, Seviear), Valentine, 11, 26, 257, 264, 272, 275, 276, 315, 347, 397, 441, 450, 456, 487, 490, 493, 496, 501, 534, 535, 538, 549.
Sewell, Thomas, 42.
Seybert, Nicholas, 155, 554, 558, 572.
Seyler, Anna C., 186.
Seyler, Anna M., 186.
Seyler, Dority, 186.
Seyler, Eve M., 186.
Seyler, Elizabeth, 186.
Seyler (Siler), Jacob, 186.
Seyler, Magdalene, 186.
Seyler, Mary C., 186.
Seyler, Philip, 186.
Seymore, Felix, 406.
Shackelford, Reuben, 198.
Shad (Shields?), Nancy, 241.
Shaddon, Mathias, 91, 95, 110.
Shaddon (Shadon), Susanna, 91, 127.
Shaddon, Lodwick, 133, 136.
Shafner, Ludwick, 146.
Shally, Michael, 124.
Shalkman, John, 75.
Shank, John, 548.
Shank, Michael, 548.
Shanklin, Andrew, 178, 192, 523.
Shanklin, Ann, 107.
Shanklin, Edward, 57, 68, 76, 107, 109, 140, 276, 301, 307, 511.
Shankland (Shaakland), Eleanor, 138, 368.
Shanklin, Elizabeth, 178.
Shanklin, Evan, 107.
Shanklin (Shankland), John, 55, 107, 109,

138, 178, 179, 182, 356, 368, **402**.
Shanklin, Jonathan, 107.
Shanklin, Joseph, 107.
Shanklin, Margaret, 107.
Shanklin, Molly, 192.
Shanklin, Rebecca, 549, 553.
Shanklin (Shankling), Richard, 71, **107**, 358, 397, 398, 511.
Shanklin (Shankland, Shankling), Robert. 29, 107, 109, 138, 178, 247, 276, 297, 299, 301, 315, 358, 368, 372, 385, **394**, 402, 483, 503, 511, 549, 553.
Shanklin (Shankland), Thomas, 138, **141**, 178, 179, 288, 299, 318, 336, 356, **358**, 368, 402.
Shannon, Ann, 223.
Shannon, James, 526.
Shannon, Jean (Jane), 421, 451, 487.
Shannon, John, 192.
Shannon, Martha, 526.
Shannon (Shannan), Robert, 98, 109, 454.
Shannon (Shinan), Samuel, 145, 174, 241, 447.
Shannon, Susan, 37.
Shannon (Shannin), William, 57, 359, 360, 392, 409, 421, 438, 451, 456, 476, 487, 526.
Shanour, Powel, 103.
Sharkey (Shockley, Shoukey), Patrick, 75, 110, 166, 306, 314, 394, 458, 473.
Sharp, Adam, 419, 523.
Sharp, Alexander, 251.
Sharp, Ann, 419.
Sharp, Edward, 93, 436, 462, 467.
Sharp, Ernest, 73.
Sharp, George, 320, 321.
Sharp, Harness, 320.
Sharp (Sharpe), John, 14, 73, 226, 246, 251, 419, 521, 523, 563, 574.
Sharp, Joseph, 246, 251.
Sharp, Lettis, 251.
Sharp, Mary, 251.
Sharp, Samuel, 109.
Sharp, Thomas, 226, 246, 251, 569.
Sharp, William, 115, 404, 407, 508, **550**, 564, 565.
Sharpe, James, 246.
Sharpe, Margery, 14.
Sharpe, Mathew, 97, 419, 523.
Sharpe, Robert, 246, 251.
Sharpley, John, 139.
Sharril, Rebecca, 182.
Sharyer, William, 589.
Shaup, Adam, 18, 355.
Shaup, John, 18, 355.
Shaup, Mathew (Mathias), 18, 20, **115**, 355.
Shaver (Shevar), Elizabeth, 124, 523.
Shaver, George, 155, 494, 500, 523.
Shaver, John, 580.
Shaver (Shever, Shevers), Paul (Powl), 50, 62, 65, 113, 124, 128, 501, 523.

Shaw, Andrew, 106.
Shaw, Grace, 560.
Shaw, James, 59, 102, 144, 357, 362, **430**, 436, 443, 448, 468, 523, 526, 590.
Shaw John, 31, 32, 37, **51**.
Shaw, Mary, 106.
Shaw, Mathias, 69.
Shaw, Robert, 162, 197, 214, 250, 350, **475**, 551, 560.
Shawdon, Mathew, 127.
Shawk, Catrine, 69.
Shawp, Margaret, 69.
Shay, Darby, 93.
Sheabler, Henry, 20.
Shearman, Martin, 551, 555, 556, **558**.
Shearman, Mary, 558.
Sheets (Shets), George, 179, 191.
Sheetz, Andrew, 234, 236.
Sheetz, Daniel, 234, 236.
Sheetz, Elizabeth, 234.
Sheetz, Henry, 234, 236.
Sheetz (Sheets), Jacob, 186, 197, **234**, 236.
Sheetz, John, 186, 234, 236.
Sheets, John A., 237.
Sheetz, Peter, 234, 236.
Sheetz, Philip, 234, 236.
Sheldon, John, 80, 86.
Shell, Jacob, 110, 451, 452, 481.
Shell, John S., 134.
Shellman, Felix, 403.
Shelly, Betsy, 241.
Shelly, Christian, 241.
Shelly, Daniel, 241.
Shelly, Fany, 241.
Shelly, Jacob, 241.
Shelly, John, 241.
Shelly, Mary, 241.
Sheltman, Ann, 147.
Sheltman, Cecily, 541.
Sheltman, Felix, 118, 157, 412, **424**.
Sheltman, John, 424, 541.
Sheltman, John I., 542.
Sheltman, Sarbrough, 147.
Shelton, John, 462, 478, 520, **544**.
Shelton, William, 520, 544.
Shelton, William P., 478.
Shepherd, James, 212.
Sheplar (Shipler), Henry, 13, **23**, **53**, **84**.
Shepter, Henry, 108.
Sherley, Jacob, 238.
Sherley, Jonathan, 248.
Sherman, John, 591.
Shields, Adam, 244.
Shields, Agnes, 196.
Shields, Alice (Ally), 222, **377**.
Shields, Eleanor, 232.
Shields, Jane (Jean, Gean), 15, 181, **201**, 205, 215, 232.
Shields, James, 12, 15, 17, 186, 208, **222**, 257, 306, 319, 346, 427, 531, 532.
Shields, John, 12, 15, 41, 93, 132, **133**,

189, 207, 221, 230, 240, 275, 284, 306, 317, 319, 320, 343, 354, 416, 430, 484, 511, 531, 532, 537, 566, 570, 576.
Shields, Margaret, 132, 195, 222, 531.
Shields, Mary, 132, 343.
Shields, Patrick, 232.
Shields, Rachel, 222.
Shields, Robert, 132, 232, 383, 565, 566.
Shields (Sheals, Shiels), Thomas, 41, 47, 132, 133, 150, 161, 232, 263, 271, 273, 275, 276, 292, 298, 313, 330, 354, 360, 362, 377, 416, 499, 537, 576.
Shields, William, 132, 168, 184, 188, 215, 217, 222, 558, 560, 566.
Shipley, Robert, 127.
Shipman, Elizabeth, 386, 414.
Shipman, Ezrah, 84.
Shipman, Isaiah, 18, 20, 134, 336, 386, 414, 516, 524.
Shipman, Jonathan, 176, 560.
Shippley, Henry, 58.
Shirer, Daniel, 211.
Shirer, Martin, 211.
Shires (Shire), William, 577, 581, 584.
Shirey, Michael, 211.
Shirkey, George, 104.
Shirkey, Patrick, 9, 260.
Shirley, Adam, 238.
Shirley, Anna, 238.
Shirley, Betsey, 238.
Shirley, Catherine, 238.
Shirley, Charles, 238.
Shirley, Henry, 238.
Shirley, Michael, 83, 110.
Shirley, Nicholas, 113.
Shirley, Valentine, 204, 238, 534, 580.
Shiry, Michael, 241.
Shiver (Shirey), John, 211.
Shives, William, 580.
Shlander, Conrad, 146.
Shoemaker, James, 105.
Shoemaker, John B., 159.
Shoemaker, Martin, 290.
Shoemaker, Peter, 537.
Shole, Martin, 150.
Sholl, Philip, 202.
Shoob (Shob), Martin, 65, 103.
Shoemaker, Elizabeth, 501.
Shoomaker (Shoemaker), George, 440, 441, 501, 543.
Shook, Peter, 121.
Shoultz, Catharine, 225.
Shoultz (Shultz), David, 219, 231, 236.
Shound (Shown), Andrew, 166, 580.
Shound, Catherine, 166.
Shound, Henry, 166.
Shound, Isaac, 166.
Shound, John, 166.
Shound (Shown), Leonard, 166, 580.
Shound, Mary, 166.
Shout, Herman, 54.
Shover, Paul, 112.
Shover, Peter, 321.
Shrewsberry, Samuel, 241.
Shriver, Lewis, 121.
Shroffe, Andrew, 592.
Shuey (Sliney), Caty, 240.
Shull, Jacob, 96, 110.
Shull, John, 125.
Shull, William, 76.
Shuls, Charles, 145.
Shultz, Adam, 236.
Shultz, Christiana, 236.
Shultz, George, 236, 246.
Shultz, Henry, 236.
Shultz, Jacob, 571.
Shultz (Shoultz), John, 217.
Shumate, Peyton, 237.
Shumate, Polly, 237.
Shuneman, George, 14, 21.
Shuye, John, 592.
Shyrigh, Jacob, 217.
Sibert, Andrew, 483.
Sibert (Siber), John, 483.
Sifort, Michael, 589.
Sights, Mary, 225.
Siler, Jacob, 130.
Siller (Silling), Casper, 545.
Silling, Ann, 229.
Silling, Pruhella, 229.
Sillings, William, 243.
Simman, Henry, 214.
Simmerman, David, 245.
Simmerman, Esther, 248.
Simmerman, May, 245.
Simmons, George, 544.
Simmons, Jacob, 544.
Simmons, Leonard, 83, 144, 476, 580.
Simmons, Mark, 580.
Simmons, Nicholas, 544.
Simmons, Peter, 580.
Simms, Charles, 542, 547.
Simon, Leonard, 143, 150.
Simond, Jacob, 142.
Simpson, Alexander, 559.
Simpson, Edward, 119, 166.
Simpson, Elizabeth, 106.
Simpson (Simson), James, 8, 13, 15, 24, 28, 38, 44, 48, 52, 53, 54, 57, 69, 70, 72, 80, 87, 341, 351, 352, 391, 447.
Simpson, Jane, 391.
Simpson, William, 99, 103, 106, 417, 452, 474, 483.
Sims, John, 331.
Sinck, Christiana, 229.
Sinckler, Charles, 252.
Sinder, Henry, 229.
Singleton, Richard, 172.
Singleton, Thomas, 53, 84, 306.
Sink (Sinks), Daniel, 45, 116, 127, 364, 514.
Sink, Jacob, 71, 94.
Sink, Philip, 229.
Sinters, John, 189.

Sircle, Catharine, 552.
Sircle, Eve, 373, 552.
Sircle, Michael, 552.
Sires, Hannah, 167.
Sisson, George, 214.
Sitlington (Sutlington), Andrew, 59, 61, 71, 126, 164, 167, 175, 475, 571.
Sitlington, Elizabeth, 591.
Sitlington (Sutlington), John, 140, 541, 591.
Sitlington (Sutlington), William, 126, 132, 170.
Siver (Sivers, Sivart, Sivert), Jacob, 43, 47, 49, 50, 65, 490.
Siver, John M., 116.
Siver, Windle, 65, 113.
Skags, John, 490.
Skaine, Jane, 9.
Skeegs, James, 293.
Skeen (Skean), John, 78, 320.
Skeen (Skaine), Mathew, 9, 14, 269.
Skellishner, Michael, 314.
Skidmore, Agness, 522.
Skidmore, Andrew, 151, 153, 159.
Skidmore, James, 113, 143, 486.
Skidmore, John, 65, 113, 126, 127, 129, 141, 143, 376, 522, 544, 570.
Skidmore, Joseph, 58, 90, 94, 103, 141, 151, 153, 155, 373, 376, 405, 455, 489, 522, 528.
Skidmore, Mary, 570.
Skidmore, Samuel, 119, 522.
Skidmore, Thomas, 146, 151, 522.
Skihawk, Aron, 150.
Skillern (Skilleron), Elizabeth, 6, 114, 379, 412, 452, 516, 525.
Skillern (Skileron, Skiliron)), George, 50, 61, 89, 92, 104, 108, 110, 347, 362, 366, 368, 372, 376, 379, 381, 396, 400, 412, 413, 415, 437, 439, 449, 452, 458, 470, 475, 482, 489, 516, 525.
Skillern (Skillem, Skillings), Mary, 203, 400, 495, 516.
Skillern (Skillem, Skillings), William, 6, 203, 268, 295, 377, 379, 381, 400, 415, 495, 508, 510, 516.
Skilson, Thomas, 6.
Skilton, John, 81.
Skyhaw, Aron, 141.
Slack, Sarah, 155.
Slack, Randell, 155.
Slagle, Cathrine, 212.
Slaton, Rachel, 251.
Slaughter, Ann, 510.
Slaughter, Francis, 256, 384.
Slaughter, Robert, 256, 510, 528.
Slaughter, Thomas, 256, 510.
Slaven, Elizabeth, 587.
Slaven, John, 553, 587.
Slemmon, John, 521.
Slemmons, Sarah, 521.
Sleven, Robert, 440, 441.

Sloan (Slown), John, 449, 518, 524.
Sloan, Robert, 361, 470.
Sloan, Margaret, 524.
Sloane, James, 285, 566, 388.
Slusher, Conrad, 171.
Slusher, Henry, 175.
Smalzer (Smelzer), Palzer, 321, 452.
Smelser, Poulson, 465.
Smiley, Alexander, 10, 12, 72.
Smiley, Andrew, 72.
Smiley, Archibald, 249.
Smiley (Smyley), John, 41, 75, 87, 100, 367, 399.
Smiley, Mary, 10.
Smiley (Smelly), Walter, 59, 75, 85, 383, 384, 385, 427, 444, 480, 518, 528, 534.
Smith, Abner, 414.
Smith, Abraham (Abram), 15, 32, 42, 47, 49, 51, 52, 54, 56, 60, 63, 66, 79, 89, 94, 96, 99, 113, 115, 126, 127, 140, 141, 320, 343, 355, 360, 384, 386, 388, 391, 395, 400, 417, 430, 449, 456, 458, 462, 477, 478, 487, 498, 500, 501, 519, 521, 528,, 539, 540, 541, 544, 552, 560, 570, 592.
Smith, Adam, 167.
Smith, Amelia, 420.
Smith, Amie, 343.
Smith, Andrew, 63, 71, 90, 103, 374.
Smith, Anne (Agness), 401, 444, 466, 492.
Smith, Anthony, 155.
Smith, Ballard, 236.
Smith, Barbara, 116, 117, 194, 513, 548, 554, 564, 592.
Smith, Benjamin, 214, 592.
Smith, Burton, 408.
Smith, Cemey, 409.
Smith, Charles, 98, 121, 147, 316, 390, 470.
Smith, Christiina, 214.
Smith, Daniel, 42, 44, 46, 49, 51, 54, 56, 58, 63, 64, 65, 66, 73, 76, 77, 78, 83, 90, 92, 96, 101, 104, 109, 113, 115, 118, 126, 127, 129, 130, 132, 133, 135, 137, 139, 140, 142, 167, 214, 276, 318, 339, 343, 344, 350, 366, 390, 391, 398, 403, 412, 417, 430, 437, 438, 442, 445, 461, 470, 477, 483, 490, 494, 501, 505, 513, 518, 521, 523, 524, 526, 532, 534, 538, 539, 540, 542, 544, 545, 547, 551, 553, 557.
Smith, David, 75, 102, 486, 487.
Smith, Edmond, 9.
Smith, Edward B., 224.
Smith, Elizabeth, 214, 547, 567, 576, 584.
Smith, Ericus (Eracker), 116, 529.
Smith, Francis, 95, 104, 108, 109, 369, 376, 385, 388, 394, 401, 403, 416, 418, 423, 424, 426, 434, 444, 451, 465, 466, 467, 470, 481, 490, 492.
Smith, Frederick, 306, 466.
Smith, Granville, 470.

Smith, Henry (Henery), 42, 52, 65, 73, 96, 343, 356, 384, 404, 409, 420, 451, 478, 487, 521, 558, 578.
Smith, Henry M., 236.
Smith, Isaac, 259, 275, 345.
Smith, Jane, 273.
Smith, Jacob, 116, 117, 214, 238.
Smith, James, 224, 276.
Smith, Jean (Jane), 297, 344, 438, 461, 524, 532.
Smith, Jeremiah, 143, 408.
Smith, John, 13, 14, 16, 25, 30, 32, 33, 36, 41, 42, 45, 47, 52, 54, 56, 58, 61 62, 63, 73, 75, 76, 83, 89, 96, 105, 110, 116, 130, 141, 167, 244, 248, 252, 255, 256, 265, 270, 273, 274, 276, 280, 294, 296, 300, 308, 314, 318, 336, 337, 342, 343, 358, 359, 369, 370, 373, 385, 386, 389, 392, 394, 395, 408, 416, 431, 437, 458, 462, 465, 466, 479, 482, 501, 503, 521, 539, 540, 542, 554, 587.
Smith, Jonathan, 62, 103, 107, 465, 470, 480.
Smith, Joseph, 137, 234, 521, 532, 553.
Smith, Lawens, 521.
Smith, Levy, 106.
Smith, Margaret, 62, 240, 274, 342, 470, 501, 554.
Smith, Mary (Polly), 45, 53, 71, 108, 228, 246, 406, 433, 482, 587.
Smith, Mathew, 179, 209.
Smith, Nicholas, 53, 55, 466.
Smith, Peter, 83, 84, 110, 150, 158, 581.
Smith, Rebecca, 244, 336.
Smith, Robert, 64, 372, 553.
Smith, Samuel, 569.
Smith, Sarah (Serah, Sarrah), 179, 417, 462, 478, 560, 570.
Smith, Stephen, 580, 581.
Smith, Thomas, 34, 45, 116, 134, 137, 144, 154, 160, 166, 324, 431, 457, 459, 463, 466, 476, 507, 530, 534, 537, 543, 546, 547, 548, 560, 562, 565, 573, 575, 576, 584, 595.
Smith, Tobias, 24, 280, 285, 306, 334, 362.
Smith, Valentine, 344.
Smith, William, 6, 27, 32, 33, 41, 42, 126, 152, 157, 182, 261, 272, 273, 281, 294, 297, 302, 311, 333, 351, 406, 408, 412, 433, 447, 482, 523, 535, 547, 570, 587.
Smith, Zechoriah (Zackariah, Zachary), 57, 84, 179, 180, 330, 383, 529.
Smither, Conrat, 509.
Smithers, Andrew, 87, 98.
Smithers, Archibald, 119, 127, 482, 555.
Smithers, Archibald A., 126.
Smithers, Cecilia, 555.
Smithers, Gabriel, 449, 450.
Smyth, Ad, 549, 566.
Snap, James, 217.
Snapp, Joseph, 237.
Snedecore, Christian, 158.

Snelson, John, 385.
Snider, Casper (Gasper), 154, 232, 562, 583.
Snider, Henry, 232.
Snider, Margaret, 583.
Snider, Martin, 245.
Snider, Nicholas, 15.
Snider, Philip, 28.
Snodgrass, James, 91, 127, 135.
Snodgrass, John, 49, 54.
Snodgrass, Joseph, 127, 540.
Snodgrass, Robert, 147.
Snodgrass, William, 48, 75, 117.
Snodon, Darkis, 107.
Snodon, Robert, 319.
Snodon (Snaden, Snodden), William, 53, 65, 107, 294, 324, 395.
Snyder, Catherine, 245.
Sollers, John, 294.
Solovane, Catherine, 496.
Solovane, Margaret, 496.
Solovane, Timothy, 496.
Somers, John, 83.
Somervil, Samuel, 202.
Sommers, Elizabeth, 12.
Somvalt, John, 580.
Sorals, Walter, 42.
Sorel, John, 68.
Sorn, Jacob, 40.
Sorn, Mary, 40.
Sowell, Edward, 245.
Sowell, Sally, 245.
Sowers (Sours), John C., 228, 245.
Spear, Hugh, 59.
Spear, Jean (Jane), 59.
Spear (Speer), John, 10, 59, 61, 315, 320, 558, 572.
Spears, Peter, 141.
Speece, Christena, 366.
Speece (Speice), George, 341, 366, 382, 423, 462, 537.
Speer (Spear, Speers), George, 99, 149, 398, 413, 463, 468, 502, 533.
Speers, Elizabeth, 63.
Spelman, John, 121.
Spence, Catherine (Kety), 214.
Spence, James, 161, 212.
Spence, William, 212, 216, 228.
Spencer, Thomas, 87, 119.
Spering, Henry, 184 589.
Spiller, John, 28.
Spindle, Ardolph (Adulf), 178, 588.
Spinler, Richard, 145.
Spouel, Margaret, 161.
Spring, Catherine, 170.
Spring, Nicholas, 170, 224, 572, 577.
Springer, Charles, 73.
Springer, Edward, 103, 451.
Springer, George, 248.
Springstone, Jacob, 156, 157.
Sproul, Andrew, 88, 89.
Sproul, Charles, 229, 246.
Sproul, James, 229, 246, 531.

Sproul, Jane (Jean), 366, 378, 385.
Sproul (Sprowl), John, 59, 229, 246, 313, 314, 318, 341, 461, 478, 484.
Sproul, Joseph, 229, 246.
Sproul (Sprowl), Margaret, 484, 536.
Sproul, Mary, 229, 246.
Sproul, Sarah, 93.
Sproul (Sprowl), William, 229, 242, 246, 356, 366, 378, 385, 386, 427, 468, 469, 489, 511, 532, 559.
Sproull, Alexander, 229, 246.
Sproull, Fanny, 229.
Sproull, Martha, 229.
Sproull, Nemsey, 229.
Sproull (Sprowl), Samuel, 229, 312, 337, 536.
Sproull, Susanna, 229.
Sproull, Oliver, 229, 246.
Sprout, Jace, 37.
Sprout, Jane, 37.
Sprout (Sprott), John, 37, 39, 75, 110, 300, 318, 331.
Sprout, Martha, 37.
Sprout, Mary, 37.
Sprout, Sarah, 37.
St. Clair (Sinclair), Alexander, 127, 138, 139, 142, 160, 164, 171, 181, 191, 197, 202, 208, 211, 215, 221, 395, 472, 491, 519, 520, 527, 534, 539, 445, 553, 563, 578, 581, 584, 588, 589, 591, 593.
St. Clair, James, 197, 586.
St. Clair (Sinclair), Jane (Jene), 197, 545, 584, 595.
St. Clair, Ro. B., 215.
Stafford, Henry, 486.
Stalp, Catherine, 128.
Stalp, Elizabeth, 128.
Stalp, Henry (Hennery), 128, 129.
Stalp, John, 128.
Stalp, Margaret, 128.
Stalp, Mary, 128.
Stalp (Stolp), William, 128, 129, 132, 516.
Stalnaher, Samuel, 30, 39, 40.
Stalsnaker, Elizabeth, 127.
Stalsnaker, Henry, 127, 135.
Stanley (Standley, Stanleys), David, 37, 299, 317, 453, 461.
Stanley (Standley, Standlee), John, 220, 299, 317, 461.
Stanton, Charity, 470.
Stanton, Richard, 394, 470.
Stapleton, Catherine, 320.
Stapleton, Charles, 302, 320.
Stapleton, Robert, 302, 320.
Starling, John, 189.
Starrat, Benjamin, 338.
States (Steats), John, 7, 10, 17, 22, 39, 269.
Staunton Fire Company, 588.
Staunton, Beverley, 244.
Staunton, Sayee (Gayee), 244.

Staunton (Stanton), Thomas, 327, 337, 394, 470, 473.
Steaton, Thomas, 518, 524.
Stedham, John, 74, 75, 323.
Steel, Elizabeth (Betsey), 86, 240.
Steel, Isabel, 512.
Steel, Margaret, 187, 208, 209.
Steel, Martha, 187.
Steel, Mary, 187, 208, 217, 218, 221, 427, 516, 537.
Steel, Moses, 8.
Steel, Nathaniel, 8, 85, 123, 187, 209, 211, 232, 270, 281, 341, 342, 440, 464, 465, 514.
Steel, Sarah (Sally), 86, 187, 217, 221, 222, 224, 225, 234, 358.
Steel, Thomas, 8, 41, 77, 224, 449, 464, 509, 512, 520, 535, 537, 542, 559.
Steel, Walter, 303.
Steel, William, 4, 8, 163, 179, 209, 218, 224, 225, 226, 236, 240, 251.
Steele, Andrew, 26, 41, 48, 52, 54, 71, 86, 87, 165, 170, 176, 187, 221, 222, 225, 275, 290, 335, 349, 360, 363, 382, 393, 478, 484, 491, 591, 594.
Steel, Catherine, 217, 224.
Steele, David, 8, 77, 146, 167, 171, 189, 201, 217, 218, 264, 265, 270, 359, 393, 464, 465, 502, 516, 522, 537.
Steele, James, 34, 81, 126, 151, 162, 170, 183, 186, 187, 190, 192, 195, 203, 204, 208, 217, 221, 222, 249, 540, 592.
Steele, Jane (Jean, Jenny), 208, 217, 221, 224.
Steele, Jannet, 8, 17, 41.
Steele, John, 133, 165, 209, 217, 218, 221, 222, 225, 249, 251, 344, 348, 512.
Steele, Kitty, 208.
Steele, Nancy, 208.
Steele, Polly Tate, 222.
Steele, Rebecca, 8.
Steele, Robert, 8, 41, 86, 107, 146, 148, 189, 217, 218, 224, 226, 240, 251, 281, 342, 353, 358, 393, 427, 434, 440, 537.
Steele, Rosannah, 209, 224, 232, 465.
Steele, Samuel, 29, 34, 41, 42, 47, 56, 59, 77, 79, 83, 85, 86, 87, 90, 93, 130, 132, 171, 177, 187, 189, 208, 209, 211, 217, 222, 225, 251, 264, 265, 269, 281, 283, 342, 344, 349, 358, 393, 411, 426, 427, 499, 503, 529, 542, 590.
Steenberger, Peter, 92.
Stephen, Adam, 409, 420, 539, 558.
Stephen, Agnes, 204.
Stephen, Isabella, 204.
Stephen, James, 204.
Stephen (Stevens), John, 117, 204.
Stephen, Lawrence, 42.
Stephen, Mary, 204.
Stephen, Nancy, 204.

Stephen (Stevens), Robert, 94, **164, 204,**
410, 420.
Stephen, Stephen, 204.
Stephen, William, 204.
Stephens, Lewis, 59.
Stephens, Thomas, 136.
Stephenson (Stevenson), Adam, 52, 58,
66, 72, 101, 121, 195, 247, 360, **442,**
455, 477, 554.
Stephenson (Stevenson), Andrew, 29,
284, 304, 313, 328, 443, 444.
Stephenson (Stevenson), David (D.), 39,
52, 177, 187, 188, 192, 200, 211, 213,
215, 217, 224, 244, 247, 381, 392, 414,
525, 539, 575, 579, 594.
Stephenson (Stevenson), Elizabeth, 52,
536, 546.
Stephenson (Stevenson), James, 39, 52,
58, 61, 83, 108, 148, 184, 196, 247, 279,
381, 390, 393, 461, 489.
Stephenson, Jane, 276, 410.
Stephenson (Stevenson, Stinson), John, 7,
10, 17, 20, 44, 45, 52, 56, 58, 63,
68, 69, 110, 112, 114, 116, **119, 124,**
126, 136, 217, 259, 261, 275, 282, 284,
288, 290, 293, 296, 299, 305, 307, 313,
339, 364, 382, 388, 397, 410, 442, 456,
460, 470, 477, 520, 531, 534, 541, 554,
551, 571.
Stephenson (Stevenson), Martha, **58, 124.**
Stephenson (Stevenson), Mary, **114, 244,**
247, 381.
Stephenson, Mathew, 52, 534.
Stephenson (Stevenson), Rebecca, **195,**
196, 335, 381, 442, **455.**
Stephenson (Stevenson), Robert, **116, 124,**
136, 170, 405, 450, 536, 549, 554, **562.**
Stephenson (Stevenson), Sarah, 52, **68,**
118, 313, 347, 443, 531.
Stephenson (Stevenson), Thomas, 10, 39,
53, 80, 92, 124, 169, 173, 191, **255, 276,**
289, 381, 398, 404, 414, 448, **455, 459,**
486, 536, 545, 546, 549, 554, 574.
Stephenson (Stevenson), William, 52, 55,
247, 264, 265, 337, 347, 381, 450, 534.
Steps, Joseph, 430.
Sterips, Robert, 182.
Sterling, John, 186, 558, 593.
Stern (Starn), Frederick, 21, 73, **104, 106,**
117, 474.
Stern, Sarah, 45.
Sterrett, David, 247, 248.
Sterrett, Henry, 247.
Sterrett, Isabella, 247.
Sterrett (Staret), James, 46, 248.
Sterrett, John, 247, 248.
Sterrett, Joseph, 247.
Sterrett, Samuel, 247, 248.
Sterritt (Starit), William, 160, **170, 188,**
194, 206, 208, 214, 216, 247, 582.
Stevens, Jacob, 364.
Stevens, John, 117.

Stevenson, Amoos, 414.
Stevenson (Stinson), George, **29, 73, 74,**
284, 293, 309, 335, 381, **393.**
Stevenson, Jean, 398.
Stevenson, **Margret, 456.**
Stewart, Ann, 47, 106.
Stewart, Iseble, 124.
Stewart, Janet, 66.
Stewart, Ralph, 78, 140, 154.
Stewart, Sebing, 98.
Stewart, Walter, 113, 117, 248, **463, 486.**
Stickleman, Elizabeth, 596.
Stickleman, John, 596.
Stiegel, Jacob, 206.
Stiffey, John, 165.
Stockdale, Mary, 210.
Stockton, Jesse, 584.
Stocton, Thomas, 169, 584.
Stone, Bastian, 561.
Stone, Godlieb, 224, 231.
Stone, Henry, 83, 84, 94, 100, **108, 126, 127,**
129, 148, 157, 405, 502, 527.
Stone, Sebastian, 175.
Stone (Staen), William, **541.**
Stoner, Jacob, 328.
Stookie, Jacob, 156.
Stophelmire, Michael, 110.
Storkley, Jacob, 588.
Story, Ann, 583.
Story, Elinor, 149.
Story, Elizabeth, 149.
Story, James, 149, 152, 190, **586.**
Story, John, 149, 152, **583, 585.**
Story, Martha, 149.
Story, Mary, 149, 392.
Story, Rebecca, 149.
Story, Sarah, 149, 586.
Story, Thomas, 23, 35, 149, 152, 168, **270,**
277, 288, 371, 392, 583, 585, **586.**
Stount, George, 581.
Stount, Mary, 581.
Stout, Ezekiah, 163.
Stover, Daniel, 10, 14, 21, 241, 243, **253,**
287, 532.
Stover, Isaac, 86.
Stover, Jacob, 275, 291, 293, **298, 300, 304,**
305, 329, 412, 420, 434, 460, 488, **494.**
Stover, Joseph, 505.
Stram, John, 515.
Stratton, Scriah, 160, 545.
Stribling, Erasmus, 243.
Strickler, Abraham, 5, 10.
Strickler, Isaac, 253.
Strickler, Jacob, 287.
Stricklar, James, 171.
Stringer, Daniel, 113, 322.
Stringer, Elizabeth (Eliza), **322.**
Strofer, Daniel, 6.
Strother, Anthony, 14, 27, 312, **363, 389.**
Strother, John, 545.
Strother, Joseph, 545.

Strother, Mary, 363.
Stroud, Adam, 83, 391, 392, 421, 482.
Stroud, Mary, 482.
Stroup, William, 321.
Stuart, Agatha, 189.
Stuart (Stewart), Alexander, 66, 126, 137, 179, 209, 210, 244, 419, 421, 423, 431, 442, 455, 465, 474, 484, 530, 557, 576, 595, 596.
Stuart (Stewart), Archibald, 34, 60, 66, 79, 182, 200, 210, 222, 223, 227, 231, 235, 244, 281, 297, 299, 375, 576, 584, 589, 595.
Stuart (Stewart), Benjamin, 34, 60, 66, 111, 112, 151, 159, 166, 183, 204, 210, 213, 222, 223, 233, 249, 591, 592.
Stuart (S. M.), Burnside, 203, 204.
Stuart (Stewart), Charles, 189, 352, 402, 567.
Stuart, Charles A., 247, 248.
Stuart (Stewart), David, 14, 24, 26, 27, 31, 33, 35, 38, 41, 43, 54, 60, 61, 67, 77, 81, 93, 98, 99, 112, 258, 262, 265, 267, 269, 270, 271, 277, 290, 291, 297, 302, 328, 331, 342, 362, 373, 377, 395, 425, 437, 440, 441, 445, 457, 473, 474, 479, 485, 496, 504, 539, 576, 577.
Stuart (Steward), Edward, 176, 181.
Stuart (Stewart), Eleanor, 66, 210, 235, 249, 595.
Stuart (Stewart), Elizabeth (Betsy), 98, 106, 120, 158, 183, 210, 229, 235, 418.
Stuart, Frances, 187, 200, 204, 207, 575.
Stuart (Stewart), Francis, 106, 426, 437.
Stuart, Grizel, 402.
Stuart (Stewart), James, 47, 48, 78, 84, 120, 124, 140, 154, 183, 189, 229, 244, 460, 465, 499.
Stuart (Stewart), Jane (Jean, Jenny), 120, 183, 200, 219, 221, 225, 229, 557.
Stuart, Julia, 183.
Stuart (Stewart), John, 49, 70, 75, 78, 79, 81, 82, 91, 92, 98, 106, 113, 119, 120, 123, 130, 149, 152, 158, 178, 187, 189, 190, 200, 210, 233, 286, 302, 346, 368, 377, 381, 389, 390, 392, 398, 406, 409, 410, 413, 421, 422, 427, 431, 434, 437, 445, 458, 469, 473, 475, 476, 487, 491, 504, 506, 508, 539, 549, 575, 577.
Stuart, Lydia, 444.
Stuart (Stewart, Steuert, Stewart), Margaret (Peggy), 70, 98, 187, 200, 207, 271, 377, 395, 463, 473, 474.
Stuart, Margaret S., 203, 204.
Stuart (Stewart), Mary (Polly), 106, 119, 120, 138, 183, 187, 200, 203, 204, 210, 229, 233, 427, 437, 576.
Stuart, Nancy, 233.
Stuart (Stewart), Robert, 30, 78, 138, 156, 183, 189, 205, 225, 229, 233, 237, 292, 311, 427, 521, 529, 541, 555, 560, 564, 576, 577, 584, 589, 595, 596.
Stuart (Stewart), Samuel, 15, 187, 200, 366, 367, 444.
Stuart (Stewart), Sarah (Sally), 170, 233, 381, 389, 392, 409.
Stuart (Stewart), Thomas, 19, 24, 29, 34, 41, 46, 59, 60, 66, 73, 84, 101, 106, 125, 131, 165, 183, 188, 189, 229, 279, 280, 283, 284, 297, 310, 328, 340, 357, 359, 365, 368, 371, 418, 448, 454, 508, 518, 524, 529.
Stuart (Stewart), William, 58, 106, 107, 112, 120, 121, 152, 158, 189, 355, 360, 361, 366, 378, 384, 420, 463, 533, 537, 575.
Stull, Frederick, 201, 382, 565.
Stulznaker, Henry, 129.
Stump, Cathrine, 121.
Stump, Michael, 8, 9, 15, 53, 121.
Stuneard, John, 554.
Stunkard, John, 576, 592.
Sturman, John, 292.
Sturtsnocker, Henry, 519.
Sudeth, William, 595.
Suesanger, Niclas, 196.
Sullivan, Dennis, 58.
Sullivan, Owen, 116.
Sullivan, Timothy, 62, 87, 119.
Summerfield, Joseph, 159.
Summerfield (Sumfield), Thomas, 156, 159.
Summers, Andrew, 229.
Summers, Catherine, 224.
Summers, David, 224.
Summers, Elizabeth, 224.
Summers, Eve, 224.
Summers, George, 229.
Summers, Henry, 224.
Summers, Isabel, 93, 484.
Summers, Jacob, 224.
Summers, John, 67, 78, 90, 109, 224, 229, 358, 359, 463, 484, 529, 593.
Summers, Margaret, 224.
Summers, Martha, 593.
Summers, Nicholas, 83.
Summers, Paul, 158, 563.
Summers, Philip, 229.
Summers, Samuel, 229.
Summers, Sarah, 229.
Summons, Leonard, 158.
Summy, Michael, 110.
Sumpster, Elizabeth, 73.
Sumter, Thomas, 112.
Sumwalt, Christopher, 559.
Sumwalt, Marilus, 559.
Supplee, Jonas, 139.
Surface, Jacob, 250.
Surface (Surfas), John, 164, 250.
Surface, Mary, 250.
Surface, Mortin (Martin?), 250.
Sutherland, George, 159, 187.
Sutton, Jeremiah, 5.
Swadley, Henry, 567.

Swadley (Swatley, Swedley), Mark, 43, 83, 100, 103, 110, 125, 128, 150, 374, 375, 411, 502, 567.
Swallow, Jacob, 218, 225, 246, 574.
Swallow, Mary, 246.
Swarm, Thomas, 581.
Swartsley, John, 594.
Swatzer, Henry, 144.
Swearingen, Van, 164, 587.
Stweet (Stuert), Elizabeth, 145.
Swelser, Paulser, 147.
Swink, Hannah, 229.
Swink, Henry, 183, 220, 221.
Swinks, Lawrence, 220, 244.
Swink, Margaret, 220.
Swink, Mathias, 220, 244.
Swink, Sarah, 182.
Swisher, Daniel, 237.
Switsard (Switchard), Henry, 75, 100.
Swoope, Jacob, 215, 221, 223, 228, 234, 240, 247.
Swoope, John, 591.
Swoope, G. Washington, 240.
Swoope, Mary 227.
Swoope, William, 227.
Sworback, John, 144.
Sword, Jacob, 40, 520.
Sybert, Jacob, 44, 336, 471, 494.
Sybert (Seybert), Nicholas, 494, 579.
Syer, David, 426.
Syer, Robert, 381.
Syers (Sayers), William, 268, 317, 319, 366.
Syford, Michael, 200, 201.
Syler, Jacob, 190.
Symes (Syms), Charles, 160, 167.
Symes, Christopher, 160.
Syms, John, 175.
Syver, Jacob, 40.

Tack, Henry, 357, 450.
Tacton, Richard, 19.
Tacton, Rosamond, 19.
Taff, James, 53.
Tafney, Hugh, 200.
Tagaaia, 551.
Tagart, Samuel, 215.
Talbert, Hugh, 191.
Talford, Robert, 60 470.
Taliaferro, Zachariah (Z.), 200, 584, 586.
Tallard, Mark, 59, 60.
Tallford, Alexander, 361.
Tallford, David, 60.
Talmann (Tolman), Benjamin, 165, 203, 562, 567, 568.
Talor, James, 102.
Talor, Jemmina, 102.
Talor, Martha, 102.
Tamewood, Henry, 110, 505, 538.
Tamson, William 355.
Tandy, Smith, 160.
Tankers (Tankersey), Elizabeth, 214.
Tankersly, Obadiah, 214.

Tanner, James (Indian), 163.
Tanner, John, 592.
Tap, Roger, 106.
Tapp, Vincent, 213, 215, 217, 234, 242.
Taplett, Francis, 125.
Tar, George, 49.
Tarbet, Hugh, 561.
Tarr, Edmond, 54.
Tarr, Edward, 49, 324, 435.
Tarr, George Peter, 74, 75.
Tarr, Joseph, 81.
Tarr, Peter, 74.
Tarr, Robert, 81.
Tarry, Jasper, 111.
Tasher, Christale, 121.
Tasher, Elizabeth, 121.
Tate, Agness, 592.
Tate (Teat), Ann, 453, 562.
Tate, David, 450, 471.
Tate, Elizabeth, 209.
Tate, Isaac, 213, 223, 249, 531.
Tate, James, 156, 159, 160, 168, 213, 249, 453, 505, 516, 531.
Tate, Jane (Jenny), 159, 220, 223.
Tate (Tat, Taite, Teat), John, 26, 106, 120, 123, 159, 168, 178, 187, 189, 191, 196, 202, 205, 208, 209, 210, 213, 218, 219, 220, 223, 249, 250, 262, 265, 270, 273, 286, 338, 349, 357, 359, 440, 465, 468, 479, 501, 505, 516, 558, 574.
Tate, Joseph, 9.
Tate, Mary (Polly), 213, 516, 558.
Tate, Patsey, 213.
Tate, Robert, 223, 249, 250, 289, 558.
Tate, Sarah (Sally), 159, 168, 213.
Tate (Teat), Thomas, 26, 42, 66, 69, 129, 144, 148, 159, 162, 249, 338, 353, 359, 414, 440, 453, 468, 474, 516, 562.
Tate, William, 123, 159, 168, 558, 592.
Tatham, John, 492.
Tavlor, Rev. Mr., 18.
Taylor, Andrew, 102, 418.
Taylor, David, 150, 548.
Taylor, Edward, 233.
Taylor, Eleanor, 7, 20.
Taylor, Elizabeth (Betty), 12, 76, 102.
Taylor, Esther, 124, 347.
Taylor, Gasper (Casper), 485, 545.
Taylor, George, 114, 189, 289, 387, 418.
Taylor, George, 465.
Taylor, Isaac, 8, 25, 75, 102, 110, 258, 259, 295, 300, 355, 384, 387, 388, 397, 418, 435, 454.
Taylor, Isabel (Isbell, Esabella), 102, 387, 388, 418.
Taylor, John, 6, 7, 9, 28, 29, 73, 106, 110, 117, 124, 126, 312, 347, 406, 408, 413, 414, 426, 438, 442, 447, 449, 454, 475.
Taylor, Leah, 25.
Taylor, Mary 438.
Taylor, Mathew, 192.
Taylor, Thomas, 12, 13, 81, 253, 309, 391.
Taylor (Talor), William, 15, 25, 97, 102,

104, 310, 384, 418, 461.
Tays, Joseph, 42.
Teaford, Catherniah, 228.
Teaford, Christenah, 228.
Teaford, Elizabeth (Betty), 228, 236.
Teaford, George, 228, 236.
Teaford, Henry, 228.
Teaford, Jacob, 181, 228.
Teaford, John, 228, 236.
Teaford, Polly, 228.
Tear, Eleanor, 46.
Teas (Tees), Charles, 41, 126, 410, 418, 434, 480, 481, 491.
Teas (Tees), Jane (Jean, Jeen). 42, 116, 150, 187, 385.
Teas, John, 8.
Teas (Tees), Joseph, 41, 276, 281, 297. 304, 307, 375, 385, 410, 439, 575.
Teas, Martha, 8.
Teas (Tees), Mary, 42, 150, 157, 187, 439.
Teas (Tees), William, 41, 93, 126, 150, 151, 157, 159, 187, 410, 418, 420, 424, 439, 444, 462, 491, 500, 524.
Teck, Margaret, 554.
Teck (Tick), Ronimous, 554.
Teder, Christian, 149.
Tedford, John, 135, 528, 548.
Tedford, William, 548.
Teebo, Abraham, 215.
Teenan, Anne, 151.
Teenan, Robert, 151.
Tees, Eleanor, 42.
Teford, Jeremiah, 189.
Telfair, Jane. 241.
Telford (Tedford), Alexander, 51, 70, 83, 117, 135, 347, 399, 489, 491, 499, 548, 595, 596.
Telford (Tedford), David, 62, 70, 83, 135, 347, 528.
Telford (Tedford), James, 97, 181, 329, 403, 421, 499.
Telford (Tedford), Robert, 51, 81, 117, 135, 347, 353, 382, 434, 463, 470, 478, 484, 519, 528.
Temple, Anne, 345.
Temple (Sample), Samuel, 345.
Templeton, James, 457, 481.
Templeton, Polly, 247.
Templeton, Samuel, 281, 283, 294, 296, 361.
Tenant, Catherine, 596.
Tenant (Tennant), John. 589, 596.
Terrel, Edward G., 212.
Terrol, Robert, 524.
Terry, Jasper, 9.
Terry, William, 9, 17.
Teter, Christian, 97.
Teter (Teetar), George, 94, 99, 474, 475.
Teter, Mathias, 48.
Teter, Paul, 94.
Tetrach, Christian, 57.
Teverbaugh, Paulser, 572.

Thackum, Thomas, 578.
Therspy, Thomas, 198.
Thomas, Catherine, 245.
Thomas, Conrad, 245.
Thomas, Eleanor, 251.
Thomas, Elizabeth, 26, 29, 245, 375.
Thomas, Evan, 52, 66, 433, 473, 501.
Thomas, Griffith, 314.
Thomas, Jacob. 13, 23, 26, 245, 272, 285, 375.
Thomas, James, 33, 50, 52, 71, 94, 370, 433, 464, 501, 543, 547, 551, 552 557.
Thomas, Jean, 52.
Thomas, John, 9, 40, 42, 43, 52, 53, 93, 106, 108, 125, 130, 140, 195, 197, 245, 311, 315, 373, 433, 459, 498, 503, 512, 513, 524, 533, 539, 541, 543, 544 547, 551, 552, 553, 568.
Thomas, Morgan, 29.
Thomas, Peter, 245.
Thomas, Rebekah, 501.
Thomas, Rees (Reece), 52, 54, 66, 115, 315, 408, 433, 494, 501, 524, 552.
Thomas, Richard, 549.
Thomas, Sarah, 433, 551.
Thomas (Thompson), Smith, 145.
Thomas, Thomas (Toms), 92, 245.
Thommer, Elizabeth, 25.
Thommer, Jacob, 25.
Thompson, Adam, 48, 108, 113, 124, 253, 255, 278, 281, 283, 284, 294, 296, 306, 318, 326, 341, 354, 361, 395, 485, 499.
Thompson, Agness, 161, 175, 203, 225, 529, 554.
Thompson, Alexander, 30, 83, 119, 123, 125, 161, 166, 175, 225, 252, 258, 261, 289, 296, 315, 330, 337, 344, 352, 353, 381, 388, 389, 420, 425, 493, 510, 511, 521, 536, 546, 575.
Thompson, Andrew, 208, 473, 485, 522.
Thompson, Annie, 485.
Thompson, Cathrine (Catrin), 129, 151, 569.
Thompson, Christopher, 143, 341, 413, 416.
Thompson, Cornelius, 523.
Thompson (Thomson), Edward, 40. 48, 49, 75, 82, 119, 130, 380, 393, 484.
Thompson, Eleanor (Eliner), 71, 89.
Thompson (Thomson), Elizabeth, 151, 255, 318, 341.
Thompson, Henry, 172.
Thompson, Hugh, 5, 22, 36, 53, 71, 79, 89, 253, 290, 312, 342, 382, 453, 485, 509.
Thompson (Thomson), James, 19, 20, 36, 40. 41, 71, 89, 94, 103, 125, 129, 133, 163, 189, 260, 268, 271, 273, 292, 296, 299, 313, 342, 344, 382, 392, 413, 444, 489, 529, 534, 557, 568, 569, 571.
Thompson, Jane (Jean), 85, 253, 265, 296, 382, 392, 458.

Thompson (Thomson), John, 22, 29, 67,
74, 94, 97, 103, 108, 110, 119, 124, 125,
129, 145, 154, 161, 172, 189, 215, 218,
222, 234, 244, 274, 279, 282, 289, 295,
296, 344, 352, 364, 375, 388, 389, 394,
401, 410, 417, 420, 425, 440, 443, 459,
482, 484, 489, 491, 496, 499, 511, 529,
532, 543, 571.
Thompson. John B., 296.
Thompson, Joseph, 129, 199, 535.
Thompson, Lindsay, 591.
Thompson (Thomson), Margaret, 29, 51.
67, 108, 161, 172, 225, 244, 529, 577.
Thompson, Martha, 29, 203, 225, 536.
Thompson. Mary, 29, 40, 57, 71, 129, 154,
182, 307, 317, 352, 413, 416, 486, 566,
568, 588.
Thompson (Thomson), Mathew, 11, 17,
29, 68, 70, 79, 131, 132, 133, 147, 154,
161, 168, 217, 220, 239, 272, 330, 339,
354, 377, 381, 430, 440, 465, 482, 510,
532, 535, 539, 540, 541, 542.
Thompson (Thomson), Moses, 48, 151,
153, 159, 253, 254, 262, 289, 296, 312,
347, 355, 392, 400.
Thompson, Nancy, 569.
Thompson, Naomie, 108.
Thompson, Patterson, 203, 225.
Thompson, Patterson W., 225.
Thompson, Polly, 225.
Thompson, Rachel, 196, 541.
Thompson, Rebecca, 108, 172, 174, 529.
Thompson, Robert, 42, 105, 119, 125, 130,
161, 165, 203, 225, 352, 389, 420, 425,
439, 453, 510, 528, 529, 546, 554, 569.
571, 591.
Thompson, Sarah, 119, 161, 225, 251, 425.
Thompson, Shem, 566.
Thompson, Smith, 192, 200, 201, 215, 589.
Thompson, Susanna, 394, 491.
Thompson (Thomson), Thomas, 28, 40,
45, 48, 57, 59, 61, 67, 72, 80, 85, 92.
94, 96, 106, 130, 246, 324, 352, 395,
529, 566, 571, 577, 588.
Thompson (Thomson), William, 6, 9, 23.
29, 30, 40, 41, 42, 55, 58, 71, 83, 87,
104, 110, 124, 129, 148, 150, 161, 183,
222, 225, 226, 239, 244, 248, 251, 253,
261, 265, 272, 273, 274, 279, 280, 283,
288, 290, 296, 297, 302, 307, 311, 312, 315,
317, 318, 326, 334, 344, 352, 360, 367,
368, 370, 376, 379, 380, 381, 382, 407,
417, 453, 455, 458, 482, 486, 499, 521,
531, 548, 557, 565, 566, 567, 568.
Thomson, Fanny, 246.
Thorn, Anthony, 71.
Thorn, Henry, 20, 52.
Thorn, Lazarus, 53.
Thorn, Michael, 47, 108, 121.
Thorn, Peter, 8, 20, 21, 23, 28, 30, 53, 310.
Thorn, Sarah, 20.

Thorn, Tobias, 53.
Thorn, Valentine, 190.
Thornhill, Samuel, 45, 494.
Thornton, Abraham, 70.
Thornton, Coats, 582.
Thornton, Francis, 92, 253.
Thornton, Henry, 248.
Thornton, Joseph, 248.
Thornton, Mary, 248.
Thornton, Nancy, 248.
Thornton, Susanna, 248.
Thornton, William, 103.
Thorp, Edward, 408.
Thorp, James, 119.
Thorp (Throp), Sarah, 193, 221, 232.
Throckmorton, Robert, 118.
Tice, George, 100.
Ticktom, Frederick, 17.
Ticktom, Joseph, 17.
Ticktom, Mary, 17.
Ticktom, Nanny, 17.
Ticktom (Tictom), Richard, 17, 19, 22, 40,
426.
Ticktom, Rose, 17.
Tilman, Rice, 248.
Tincher, Francis, 417.
Tincher, Margaret, 505.
Tincher, Mary, 474.
Tencher (Tincher). Samuel, 32, 40, 55,
292, 344, 505.
Tincher, William, 408, 474, 503.
Tindall, Dr., 176.
Tinsley, Peter, 588.
Tirkell, Peater, 129.
Tise, Mathias, 347.
Tiswaters (Fiswaters), Judy, 135.
Todd, George, 220.
Todd, James, 73, 220, 342, 376, 446, 476,
488.
Todd, Jane, 428.
Todd (Tode), John, 167, 370, 542, 543.
Todd, Low, 285, 286, 292, 348, 361, 385,
484, 489.
Todd, Nathen, 220.
Todd (Tod), Samuel, 99, 109, 114, 379,
386, 403, 428.
Todd, Susanna, 376.
Todd, William, 285, 286, 350, 379, 385,
435, 484.
Tolman, Nancy, 199, 230.
Tolman, Rebecca Ann., 230.
Tomison, Simon, 394.
Torbet, Hugh, 537, 571.
Torbet, Martha, 244.
Torbit, Samuel, 222.
Tosh, Agnes, 70.
Tosh, Mary, 441.
Tosh, Tasker, 15, 16, 22, 45, 70, 96, 295.
Tosh, Thomas, 16, 19, 44, 45, 55, 70, 79,
100, 295, 421, 441, 465, 467.
Tosher, Christian, 47, 108, 373.
Tosher, Mary, 121.

Tours, Charles, 172.
Tousand, John, 574.
Townsend, Ezekiel, 181.
Townsend, James, 588.
Townsend, Jesse, 102, 119.
Townsend, John, 181.
Townsend, Keziah, 181.
Townsend, Mary, 181, 293.
Townsend, Repentance, 37, 70, 256, **293**, 308.
Townsend, Zekail, 588.
Trace (Drais), Jacob, 545, 560, 580.
Tracey, John, 54.
Trader, Arthur, 52, 66, 92, 338.
Trader, **Peter,** 51.
Treper, Andrew, 397.
Tresler, Henry, 494.
Tresler, John P., 494.
Tresler, Peter, 494.
Trigg, Daniel, 553.
Trigg, Stephen, 94, 99, 451, 452, 461, 553.
Trimble, Allen, 255.
Trimble, Ann, 191, 313, 360.
Trimble, David, 10, 86, 91, 94, 97, **179,** 252, 272, 308, 310.
Trimble, Grace, 327.
Trimble, Hannah, 447.
Trimble, Isaac, 555.
Trimble, James, 12, 15, 17, 19, 22, 33, 35, 43, 46, 72, 78, 83, 86, 90, 93, 97, 102, 103, 105, 107, 108, 127, 143, 160, 161, 191, 208, 231, 251, 252, 254, 255, 257, 260, 267, 269, 273, 291, 300, 304, 307, 305, 312, 327, 332, 333, 347, 350, 352, 356, 363, 366, 376, 378, 379, 387, 395, 398, 399, 410, 411, 418, 436, 442, 446, 450, 454, 457, 470, 475, 482, 485, **517,** 525, 546, 547, 549, 555, 558.
Trimble, Jean, 195, 223, 454, 558.
Trimble, John, 5, 11, 24, 26, 44, 48, 51, 60, 71, 78, 86, 89, 93, 103, 107, 123, **124,** 131, 142, 185, 191, 195, 206, 216, 254, 263, 278, 283, 292, 295, 301, 302, 303, 308, 312, 313, 317, 320, 328, 331, 332, 345, 351, 358, 360, 385, 389, 421, **423,** 427, 450, 452, 454, 470, 485, **555,** 556.
Trimble, Joseph, 191.
Trimble, Mary (Polly), 86, 216, 385.
Trimble, Moses, 62, 114, 265, 268, **284,** 322, 328, 423, 433, 452, 464, 499.
Trimble, Peggy, 238.
Trimble, Robert, 191, 231, 438, 447, 571.
Trimble, Rosa, 272.
Trimble, Rosanna, 438.
Trimble, Sarah, 291, 347, 350, 356, 363, 376, 378, 379, 398, 399, 418, 436, **442,** 470.
Trimble Walter, 151, 191, 216, 272, 345, 421, 438, **447, 571, 579.**
Trobuch, Frederick, 589.
Tropough, **Nicholas, 579.**
Trother (Strother), Richard, **202.**

Trotter, David, 161, **162, 556.**
Trotter, James, 275, 320, 332, **345, 366,** 384, 386, 427, 445, 494, 507, **510, 526,** 528, 556, 561, 563, 564, 582, **589.**
Trotter, John, 238, 410, 539.
Trotter, Joseph, **425,** 577, 580.
Trotter, Mary, 332, 427, 494, 526, **556.**
Trotter, Richard, 211.
Trotter, Sally, 224, 238.
Trotter, Samuel, 494, 507, 510, **561.**
Trotter, William, 176, 185, **526, 573.**
Trout, Barbara, 494, 500.
Trout, Catharine, 164.
Trout (Trust), David, 164, 201, **586.**
Trout, George, 31, 60, 64, 94, 164, **343,** 396, 426, 439.
Trout, Jacob, 494, 500.
Trout, Mary, 426, 439.
Trout, Nicholas, 31, 32, 70, 94, 305, **307,** 387, 416, 494, 519.
Trout, Valentine, 494.
Trover, Hanirey, 287.
Trowerbough, Nicholas, 587.
Troxal, Peter, 225.
Trumbo (Trumboer), Andrew, 373, **440,** 512.
Trumbo, George, 115.
Trumbo (Trombar), Jacob, 105, **128, 305,** 311, 433, 530.
Trumbo, John, 152.
Trumbo, Mary, 530.
Trusler, Henry, 149.
Tudon, Benjamin, 379.
Tumelson, Thomas, 206.
Tunstall, Joseph, 594.
Tunstall, Richard, 288.
Turk, Esther, 164.
Turk, James, 89, 126, 234, 352, 386, **481.**
Turk, John, 262.
Turk, Margaret, 258, 265, 276, 352, **369,** 382, 426.
Turk, Mary, 164, 234, 386, 481.
Turk, Robert, 126, 127, 252, 258, **259, 265,** 266, 276, 282, 297, 304, 352, 369, **418,** 426, 481, 573, 594.
Turk, Samuel, 567.
Turk, Thomas, 89, 126, 164, 169, 221, **234,** 235, 352, 369, 382, 386, 426, **495, 501,** 509, 525 556, 561.
Turpin, Solomon, 15, 75, 92, 98, **120.**
Tustee, Peter, 13.
Tutt, William, 466.
Tuttle, Abner, 217.
Ty, Charles, 57.
Tybout, Andrew, 116.
Tyler, Eleanor, 296.
Tyler, Francis, 37, 60, 337, 390.
Tyler, John, 511.
Tyler, Leah, 13.
Tyler, Lewis, **476.**
Tyler, William, 13.

Uall, Andrew, 340.
Ufner, Peter, 10.
Underwood, James, 53, 81, 84, 85.
Underwood, Nathan, 252.
Underwood, Thomas, 37.
Unroo, John, 200.
Upp, Pet., 170.
Usher, Ann Jenny, 5.
Upshur, Jacob, 583.
Upshur, James, 583.
Upsher, Peter, 74, 75.
Upshur, Robert, 583.
Usher, Lewis, 568.
Usher, Lois, 553.
Usher, Mary, 568.
Usher, Robert, 232, 577.
Usher, William, 553, 568.
Utt, Casper, 41, 43.

Vachob (Vachub), Christopher, 120.
Vachob, Robert, 119.
Vachub, John, 99, 153, 179, 180, 206.
Vachub (Vachob), Joseph, 39, 77, 99, 324, 360, 548, 559.
Vachub, Mary, 179.
Vance, Benjamin, 162.
Vance, David, 25.
Vance, George, 29, 283, 306.
Vance (Vence), Handel, 546.
Vance, James, 162, 278.
Vance, Jennet (Jenat), 465, 484.
Vance, John, 62, 102, 127, 163, 335, 361, 430, 446, 476.
Vance, John P., 162.
Vance, Margaret, 162.
Vance, Mathew, 37, 162.
Vance, Mathias, 117.
Vance, Patrick, 50.
Vance, Samuel, 86, 108, 119, 133, 162, 191, 194, 436, 447, 552, 573, 585, 589, 590.
Vance, Thomas, 80, 102, 103, 119, 122, 426, 465, 484.
Vance, William, 162, 332, 546.
Vanderpoole, Abraham, 7, 13, 21, 23, 293.
Vanderpool, Rebecca, 293.
Vaneman (Venimon), Elizabeth, 65, 559.
Vaneman (Venimon, Finiman), Peter, 44, 65, 91, 114, 124, 129, 134, 474, 559.
Van Fossen, Jacob, 211, 581.
Vangemunday, Charles M., 88.
Vangemunday, George F., 88.
Vangemunday, Henry, 88.
Van Gemunday, Mary P. C., 88.
Vangemunday, Philip C., 88.
Van Hook, Laurence, 543.
Van Lear, Jacob, 165, 166, 169, 184, 205, 237, 324, 525, 588.
Van Lear, John, 169.
Van Lear, John H., 222.
Van Lear, Margaret, 169.
Van Lear, Nancy, 222.
Van Pelt, Margaret, 76.

Vansant, Isaiah, 571.
Vansant, Margaret, 571.
Vanscoy (Vanskoy, Vansye, Van Sky), Aaron (Aron), 141, 147, 156, 159.
Vansill, Edmund, 470.
Vanskiver, John, 183.
Vanvill, John, 58.
Vare, Ann, 338, 397.
Vare, Richard, 338, 397.
Varnum, Hannah, 201.
Varnum, John, 201.
Varnum, Julian, 201.
Varnum, Rebecca, 201.
Varrill, John, 53.
Vasteen, William, 208.
Vato, Paul I., 403.
Vaughan, James, 492.
Vanpeet, Tunis, 474.
Vauferson (Jefferson), Joaken, 540.
Vause (Voss, Vorse), Ephraim, 6, 12, 14, 20, 34, 50, 74, 277, 280, 282, 314, 322, 339, 361, 381, 389.
Vause, Theodosia, 322.
Velton, Jobb, 141.
Venus, Henry, 181, 579.
Verner, John, 102, 496.
Vernon, Henry, 555.
Vernon, Richard, 110.
Vernum, William, 202.
Via (Viers), David, 94, 96.
Vicker, Christopher, 398.
Vickers, Rebecca, 253.
Vickrey, Christopher, 527.
Vickrey, Hannah, 527.
Viers (Via), Francis, 94.
Viers (Vicers), Rebecca, 41.
Vigors, John, 240.
Villortin, Peter, 116.
Vinyard, Christopher, 70, 390, 433, 435.
Vinzent, Isaiah, 577.
Vinzent, Margaret, 577.
Virden, Egeniah (Egniar), 73, 421.
Voice, John, 590.
Volt, Sun, 126.
Votaw, John, 167.
Vought, Casper, 275.
Vought, John, 53.

Waady, James, 102.
Waaz (Haaz), Hannah, 568.
Waaz (Haaz), Peters, 568.
Waddell, Alexander, 519.
Waddell (Waddle), James, 171, 207, 550, 554, 557, 568, 569, 571, 594.
Waddell (Waddle), Joseph, 171, 179, 207, 209, 550, 554, 571.
Waddell (Wadle, Waddle, Woddall), Thomas, 19, 171, 186, 303, 340, 357, 513, 549, 550, 554, 589.
Waddle, Alese (Elise), 550.
Waddle, Dolly, 193.

Waddle, Elizabeth, 171.
Waddle, John, 171, 236, 565, 569.
Waddle, Martha, 171.
Waddle (Waddel), Mary, 565, 569, 594.
Wade, Alexander, 552.
Wade, Dawson, 94, 533.
Wade (Wades), John, 163, 228, 552.
Wade, Rachel, 533.
Wade, Thomas, 552.
Wagener, Henry, 84.
Wagener, Ludwig A., 502.
Waggoner, Christopher, 524, 533.
Waggoner (Waggner, Wagoner, Wagener), Ludwick, 50, 65, 103, 156, 337, 383, 384, 502.
Waggoner, Peter, 236.
Wahub, John, 90.
Wahob (Wachob, Wacob), Joseph, 43, 60 61, 80.
Wahub, Margaret, 147.
Waiett, William, 103.
Waildon, George, 173.
Waite (Waide), James, 67, 69, 70, 94, 124, 166, 201, 307.
Waldon, Edward, 111.
Wales, Margaret, 352.
Wales, Thomas, 101.
Walker, Alexander, 8, 21, 45, 48, 57, 75, 92, 95, 103, 104, 109, 114, 118, 120, 131, 135, 139, 172, 176, 188, 189, 300, 302, 304, 307, 309, 311, 312, 313, 318, 333, 345, 352, 362, 391, 406, 435, 440, 442, 445, 447, 463, 467, 476, 481, 494, 495, 508, 520, 527, 532, 546.
Walker, Andrew, 139, 149, 151, 154, 176.
Walker, Ann, 345.
Walker, Barbara, 139.
Walker, Charles, 140.
Walker, Edward, 145.
Walker, Elizabeth, 139, 176, 440, 532.
Walker, George, 156.
Walker, Hugh, 462.
Walker, Isabella, 139, 176.
Walker, James, 12, 16, 20, 45, 95, 104, 118, 120, 189, 192, 304, 306, 327, 406, 508.
Walker, Jane, 139.
Walker, John, 49, 104, 118, 119, 135, 139, 189, 202, 300, 307, 308, 309, 310, 316, 329, 332, 333, 345, 385, 426, 432, 433, 457, 503, 508, 546.
Walker, Joseph, 35, 37, 62, 73, 83, 90, 101, 109, 117, 231, 315, 330, 334, 340, 426, 455, 457, 475, 482, 485, 489, 508.
Walker, Margaret (Peggy), 130, 139, 149, 249.
Walker, Martha, 114, 131, 139, 176.
Walker, Mary, 139, 176, 406, 508.
Walker, Patsey, 231.
Walker, Robert, 139, 176.
Walker, Samuel, 25, 32, 36, 37, 188, 280.

301, 306, 317, 318, 328, 365, 447, 484.
Walker, Thomas, 117, 351, 362, 372, 376, 381, 412, 430, 455, 456.
Walker, William, 110, 248, 319, 428, 430, 496, 515, 522, 548, 568.
Wall, Adam, 74, 85, 87, 110.
Wall, Andrew, 85.
Wall, Apell, 85.
Wall, Conrad, 117, 129.
Wall, John, 61, 66, 85, 92.
Wall, Moses, 122.
Wallace, Agness, 561.
Wallace, Andrew, 221.
Wallace, David, 349, 435, 437.
Wallace, Elizabeth, 86, 92, 101, 240, 422, 423.
Wallace, Esther, 240.
Wallace, Frances, 158.
Walace, Frederick, 228.
Wallace (Wallis), James, 107, 135, 159, 228, 240, 249, 270, 353, 365, 495, 503.
Wallace, Jane (Jean), 135, 158.
Wallace, Jennet (Jannet), 92, 423, 572.
Wallace (Walles), John, 48, 53, 57, 62, 88, 90, 94, 104, 109, 135, 153, 182, 183, 187, 228, 333, 354, 370, 563.
Wallace, Joseph, 92.
Wallace, Margaret, 221, 348.
Wallace, Mary, 158, 453.
Wallace, Mathew, 569.
Wallace, Moses, 240.
Wallace, Peter, 7, 48, 87, 90, 92, 93, 292, 313, 346, 348, 349, 369, 378, 385, 484.
Wallace, Petty, 308.
Wallace, Rachel, 423, 572.
Wallace, Robert, 92, 102, 135, 142, 151, 153, 207, 214, 240, 391, 422, 453, 475.
Wallace, Robert P., 240.
Walace, Samuel, 22, 26, 86, 90, 92, 93, 101, 158, 249, 278, 299, 301, 302, 310, 360, 421, 422, 423.
Wallace, Thomas, 228.
Wallace, William, 67, 98, 158, 185, 270, 347, 353, 432, 458, 561, 569.
Waller, Benjamin, 379.
Waller, John, 595, 596.
Waller, William, 41, 379.
Walling, Mary C., 269.
Walling, William, 8, 10, 269.
Walls, Alexander, 93.
Walls, Arthur, 75.
Walsh, Agnes, 422.
Walsh, Edward, 220.
Walsh, John, 497, 506.
Walter, Henry, 596.
Walter, John, 308.
Walter, Rosanna, 596.
Walters, William, 369.
Walton, Edward, 189.
Walton, Wilton, 386.
Wamsley, David, 162, 163.
Wamsley, Dorcas, 162, 163.

Wamsley, James, 162, 163.
Wamsley (Warmsley, Wormsley), John, 158, 162, 163, 471, 559.
Wamsley, Joseph, 162.
Wamsley, Mary, 162, 163.
Wamsley, Mathew, 162.
Wamsley, Samuel, 162, 163.
Wamsley, Thomas, 162.
Wamsley, William, 162.
Wandless, Stephen, 587.
Wanless, Ralph, 182.
Wappaler, William, 18.
Warburton, John, 476.
Ward, Elizabeth, 129.
Ward, Isaac, 99, 451, 475.
Ward, Israel, 28.
Ward, James, 55, 70, 95, 99, 129, 361, 386, 389, 390, 439.
Ward, Janet, 443.
Ward, John, 28, 41, 49, 50, 124, 286, 302, 317, 325, 368, 434.
Ward, Joseph 379, 393, 443, 444.
Ward, William, 354, 384, 484, 567.
Warden, William, 33.
Wardlaw, Agness, 442.
Wardlaw, Andrew, 380.
Wardlaw, Hugh, 68, 69, 80, 86, 368, 380, 383, 396, 439.
Wardaw, James, 68, 69, 81, 86, 95, 196, 340, 380, 383, 411, 439, 442, 499, 520.
Wardlaw, Jeannet 68.
Wardlaw, John, 44, 49, 54, 68, 69, 88, 317, 327, 347, 433, 442, 443.
Wardlaw, Joseph, 68, 86, 442.
Wardlaw, Margaret, 68, 443.
Wardlaw, Martha, 520.
Wardlaw, Robert, 68, 484, 547.
Wardlaw, William, 68, 71, 86, 304, 344, 383, 442, 539.
Ware, James, 585.
Ware, Pleasant, 232.
War, Hatchet, 132.
Warhop, Joseph, 107.
Waring, Francis, 269.
Warner, Alexander, 585.
Warner, Edward, 71, 94, 151, 152, 159, 536.
Warner, Marthew, 151.
Warner, Mary, 182, 183.
Warnock, John, 14.
Warren, Anne, 113, 115, 483.
Warren (Weron), Caterian (Catherine), 147, 474.
Warren, Edmond, 113, 115, 149.
Warren, Elizabeth, 113.
Warren, Hannah, 113.
Warren (Waring), Jacob, 113, 115, 483.
Warren (Werren), John, 113, 115, 130, 532.
Warren, Mary, 115.
Warren (Waren, Waring, Wearon), Michael, 22, 23, 24, 27, 41, 60, 65, 72, 73, 78, 83, 113, 115, 121, 142, 148, 294, 346, 440, 474, 486, 506, 513, 523, 533.
Warren, Michael, 32.
Warren (Waring), Thomas, 113, 269.
Warren (Waren), Timothy, 115, 147.
Warren, William, 52.
Warrick (Warick, Warwick), Jacob, 138, 162, 191, 585, 587.
Warrick, Jenot, 40.
Warwell, John, 13.
Warwick (Warrick, Worrack, Worick), John, 37, 72, 140, 141, 152, 155, 353, 429, 586.
Warwick (Worwick), William, 31, 267.
Wason, Alexander, 208.
Wason, Robert 498
Wast, Thomas, 40.
Water, John, 84.
Waters, Mathew, 40.
Waterman, Asher (A.), 196, 584, 589.
Waterson, Ann, 554.
Waterson, Henry, 554.
Watkins, Doctor, 112, 167.
Watkins, Jane, 202.
Watkins (Wattkins), John, 116, 149, 463, 497, 506.
Watkins, John S., 464, 549.
Watkins, Louis Christiana, 549.
Watkins, Peter, 75, 92, 98.
Watkins, Philip, 49, 434, 485.
Watkins, Reece, 49, 75.
Watsai, Widdow, 199.
Watson, Benjamin, 12, 74, 75, 93, 322.
Watson, Elizabeth, 6.
Watson, John, 6, 141, 143, 144.
Watson, Joseph, 7, 488.
Watson, Mary, 141.
Watterson (Waterson), Mary, 149, 316, 337, 342, 349, 449.
Watterson (Waterson), Thomas, 149, 316, 337, 342, 349, 406, 449, 458, 494, 547, 548, 587, 592.
Watterson, William, 109, 149, 438, 459, 462, 470, 476.
Watts (Wats), Arther, 82, 268.
Watts, Edward, 304.
Watts, Elizabeth, 304.
Watts, William, 425.
Waugh, Isaac, 184, 199.
Waugh, Jean, 184.
Waugh, John, 184.
Waugh, Samuel, 184.
Waughub, Joseph, 368.
Wayland, Elizabeth, 243.
Wayland, Joseph, 251.
Wayland, Lewis, 248, 251.
Wayt, John, 215.
Wead, Elizabeth, 217.
Wead, John, 217.
Wead, Martha, 217.
Wealdon, Edward, 179.
Wear, George, 154.

Wear, Joseph, 148, 568.
Wear, Robert, 148.
Wear, Samuel, 581.
Wearly, Mary, 235.
Weavell, Conrad, 501.
Weaver, Adam, 242.
Weaver, Andrew, 185, 217.
Weaver, Ann M., 185.
Weaver, Christena, 185.
Weaver, Christian, 204.
Weaver, Elizabeth, 185, 596.
Weaver, George, 70, 185, 434, 549.
Weaver, John, 185, 204, 596.
Weaver, John G., 185, 188, 204, 596.
Weaver, Mary, 185.
Weaver, Michael, 81, 464 467.
Weaver Peter, 185, 539, 555, 596.
Weaver, Philip, 287.
Weaver, Samuel, 217.
Weaver, Windle, 113.
Webb, Adin, 216.
Webb, Mary, 216.
Weeble, Conrad, 129.
Weedon, George, 89, 100.
Weelson, David, 341.
Weems, Eleanor, 79, 398.
Weems, Thomas, 54, 58, 268, 330, 398.
Weifford (Wieford, Wiford), George, 186, 200, 582, 589.
Weir, George, 135, 152, 520, 531.
Weir (Wier), Hugh, 112, 189, 251 402, 468, 495, 497.
Weir, James, 189, 568.
Weir, Jane (Jean), 229, 246.
Weir (Wier, Wire), John, 155, 189, 428, 429, 440, 468, 515.
Weir, Joseph, 429.
Weir, Rebecca, 563.
Weir (Weer, Wier, Wire), Robert, 68, 189, 305, 316, 329, 335, 402, 563.
Weise, Lewis, 139.
Weitreith, Daniel, 291, 506, 553.
Weitreith, David, 553.
Weitreith, Margaret, 553.
Weitzel, Magdalena, 206.
Welch, William, 190.
Wellson, John, 210.
Wellton, Job, 121.
Welppert (Wilpper), John D., 296.
Welsh, Agatha, 542.
Welsh (Welch), Agnes, 34, 298, 427, 543.
Welsh, George, 533.
Welsh (Welch), James, 34, 105, 298, 320, 353, 385, 413, 427.
Welsh, John, 74, 127, 167.
Welsh (Welch), Nicholas, 117, 428, 473.
Welsh, Walter (Wat.), 74, 110.
Welshar, Nathaniel, 28.
Welson, Thomas, 189.
Welton, John, 30, 53.
West, Adam, 58.
West, Alexander, 115, 430.

West, Catens (Cathorine, Caian), 135.
West, Christiana, 298, 365.
West, Ebenezer, 322.
West, Elizabeth, 135.
West, James, 182, 527.
West, Thomas, 7, 17, 77, 135, 148, 263, 298, 329, 365, 513, 533, 539, 551.
West, William, 131, 539.
Westcoat (Wastcoat), Ebenezer, 11, 18, 321, 451, 452, 465, 481.
Western, Cyrus, 251.
Western, James, 251.
Western, Rachel, 251.
Western, Richard, 251.
Westfall, Abel (Able), 6, 7, 21, 23.
Westfall, Blandena, 30.
Westfall, Daniel, 155, 157, 159.
Westfall, Euric, 28.
Westfall, George, 140, 159.
Westfall, Jacob, 7, 24, 158.
Westfall, Joel, 154, 158.
Westfall, John, 7, 121, 156.
Westfall, Laya, 7.
Westfall, William, 158, 159.
Weton, George, 166.
Wever, Caspar, 106.
Whaling, Jared, 174.
Wharey, James, 66.
Whitacre, Charles, 28.
White, Alexander, 487, 492, 493, 507, 516, 523, 526.
White, Catharine, 152.
White, Christopher, 44.
White, Daniel, 169.
White, David, 139, 141, 152, 162, 239, 592.
White, Elizabeth, 33, 492, 493, 523, 526.
White, George, 44.
White, Gordon, 162, 592.
White, Isaac, 34, 46, 79, 162, 495, 508, 510, 546, 556, 592.
White, Isabella, 162.
White, James, 162, 546, 592.
White, Jane (Jean), 162, 592.
White, John, 16, 32, 191, 201, 318, 336, 341, 377, 469.
White, Katherine, 377.
White, Margret, 162.
White, Rebecca, 239.
White, Robert, 243.
White, Stophel, 60, 62, 70.
White, Valentine, 160, 549, 556, 573, 585.
White, William, 6, 8, 11, 13, 17, 22, 23, 25, 29, 32, 35, 152, 155, 243, 270, 293, 312.
Whitely (Whitly, Whitlow), Robert, 462, 467.
Whiteside, Moses, 24, 286, 294, 327, 329, 336, 339, 341, 367, 383, 468, 499, 535, 555.
Whitesides, Margaret, 383.
Whitesides, William, 287.

Whitley, Jonathan, 62, 287, 350, 454.
Whitley (Whitey), Paul, 87, 109, 287.
Whitley, Sarah, 287.
Whitley, Solomon, 416, 454.
Whitman, John, 176.
Whitt, Richard, 490.
Whitton, David, 150.
Whitzel, Elizabeth, 533.
Whitzel (Witzel, Witsell), Martin, 249, 365, 533.
Wice, Jacob, 532.
Wier, Margrate (Peggy), 246, 251, 497.
Wier, Samuel, 440, 497, 548.
Wigel, George, 588.
Wilcher (Wilshire), Nathaniel, 75, 330.
Wildings, William, 170.
Wildridge, William, 145.
Wiley, Alexander, 425, 575.
Wiley (Willey, Willy), James, 73, 110, 121, 329, 338.
Wiley (Willey Weiley), John, 10, 14, 18, 60, 65, 90, 92, 98, 109, 110, 114, 286, 342, 350, 386, 404, 425, 426, 431, 433, 442, 498, 536, 575.
Wiley, Peter, 92, 425.
Wiley, Robert, 122, 555.
Wilfong, Elizabeth, 84.
Wilfong, Michael, 156.
Wilhelm, Michael, 200.
Wilkey, Samuel, 15.
Wilkins, John, 20, 53, 282, 287, 289, 292, 324, 447.
Wilkins, Samuel, 9, 10, 53, 256, 282, 287, 289, 292, 301, 302, 395, 447.
Wilkins, Sarah, 256, 282.
Wilkins, Thomas, 20.
Willey, George, 10.
Willey, Jean, 10.
Willey, Margaret, 10.
Willey, Martha, 338.
Willey, Robert, 403.
William, George, 130.
Williams, Alexander, 196, 569.
Williams, Ann, 196.
Williams, Betsey, 237.
Williams, David, 72, 73, 95, 148, 196, 209, 237, 388, 395.
Williams, Edward, 21.
Williams, James, 21, 81.
Williams, Jane, 306.
Williams, Jo., 243.
Williams, John, 41, 81, 91, 123, 138, 196, 348, 407, 444, 497, 539, 593.
Williams, Margaret, 530, 553.
Williams, Mary, 494.
Williams, Moses, 76, 187, 196, 394, 395.
Williams, Phillip, 107, 113.
Williams, Richard, 593.
Williams. Robert, 17, 40, 49, 66, 74, 76, 323, 373, 380, 424, 430, 459, 530, 553.
Williams Sabina, 577.
Williams, Samuel, 577.

Williams, Sarah, 296, 298.
Williams, Thomas, 306, 318, 351, 396, 460.
Williams, William, 14, 20, 22, 69, 287, 296, 298, 334, 348, 354, 510, 566.
Williamson, Abby, 500.
Williamson, Arthur, 227.
Williamson, David, 146, 162.
Williamson, James, 146, 190.
Williamson, Jennet, 146.
Williamson, John, 37, 146.
Williamson, Jonathan, 146.
Williamson, Lurini, 146.
Williamson, Lyddy, 146.
Williamson, Pennellipy, 146.
Williamson, Richard, 386, 500.
Williamson, Smith, 131.
Willis, Stephen, 385.
Willkie (Wilke), James, 121, 150.
Willpink, Michael, 157.
Wills, William, 415, 420.
Willson, Barbara, 450.
Willson, Heloner, 226.
Willson, Jane, 5.
Wilmot (Wilmouth, Wilmuth), Thomas. 65, 141, 156, 555.
Wilmouth, Margaret, 57.
Wilmuth, Ann, 555.
Wilper, Anna C., 391.
Wilper (Wilpert), John D. (J. D.), 47, 48, 342, 371, 384, 391.
Wilson, Ab, 528.
Wilson, Agness, 35, 47, 230, 388, 395.
Wilson, Alexander, 190, 484, 512, 547.
Wilson, Andrew, 104, 111, 167, 443, 569, 588.
Wilson, Anne, 35, 49, 57, 105, 236.
Wilson (Willson), Benjamin, 152, 155, 157.
Wilson (Willson), Charles, 53, 84, 252, 303, 374.
Wilson, Christian, 92.
Wilson (Willson), David, 105, 160, 407, 582.
Wilson, Deborah, 243.
Wilson (Willson), Elenor, 120, 226, 370.
Wilson (Willson), Elibable (Eli Bab), 137, 156.
Wilson (Willson), Elizabeth, 5, 59, 116, 129, 183, 197, 216, 225, 226, 244, 352, 355, 357, 380, 466, 488, 532, 540, 582, 594.
Wilson, Ephraim, 67, 425, 439.
Wilson (Willson), Francis, 5, 461.
Wilson (Willson), George, 21, 26, 28, 31, 32, 33, 40, 41, 47, 53, 54, 56, 67, 69, 70, 76, 77, 217, 238, 248, 299, 300, 309, 312, 322, 335, 347, 348, 350, 351, 352, 355, 357, 380, 384, 431, 434, 442, 443, 444, 454, 466, 467, 519, 532, 560, 562, 582, 583, 593, 596.
Wilson, Harklas, 31, 32.
Wilson (Willson), Henry, 356, 393, 408.

Wilson, Isabella, 439.
Wilson (Willson), James, 35, 47, 51, 105, 106, 129, 182, 189, 197, 212, 217, 230, 238, 267, 301, 360, 361, 415, 443, 486, 511, 524, 585.
Wilson, Jean, 216.
Wilson, Ruth, 137, 169.
Wilson (Willson), Sampson, 137, 164.
Wilson (Willson), Samuel, 30, 50, 56, 58, 59, 61, 77, 78, 94, 106, 116, 129, 132, 137, 139, 183, 189, 230, 252, 265, 286, 301, 306, 338, 348, 352, 358, 359, 393, 464, 468, 484, 489, 535, 540, 541, 545, 563, 564, 583, 585.
Wilson (Willson), Sarah, 47, 226, 574.
Wilson, Stephen, 37.
Wilson, Steth, 57.
Wilson (Willson), Thomas, 56, 57, 59, 74, 106, 112, 116, 118, 120, 129, 131, 146, 148, 157, 173, 189, 216, 220, 306, 384, 415, 431, 442, 468, 484, 488, 499, 518.
Wilson (Willson), William (W.), 32, 35, 47, 54, 56, 57, 60, 61, 72, 73, 78, 81, 105, 107, 170, 174, 182, 183, 184, 196, 203, 204, 210, 211, 214, 216, 217, 219, 220, 221, 222, 224, 225, 226, 227, 229, 230, 233, 238, 239, 243, 245, 246, 247, 304, 306, 360, 369, 370, 388, 390, 395, 431, 450, 464, 498, 504, 518, 542, 564, 571, 586, 587, 591, 594.
Wilson (Willson), John, 5, 6, 17, 24, 30, 35, 36, 38, 42, 47, 49, 56, 59, 67, 73, 78, 121, 127, 138, 146, 152, 157, 176, 178, 182, 189, 195, 197, 210, 216, 226, 229, 230, 247, 255, 263, 268, 271, 272, 273, 274, 276, 279, 283, 286, 296, 298, 301, 307, 314, 317, 334, 340, 342, 345, 351, 360, 410, 439, 443, 454, 455, 476, 482, 502, 512, 516, 574, 577, 585, 592, 593, 595, 596.
Wilson (Willson), Joseph, 121, 199, 224, 238.
Wilson, Josiah, 51.
Wilson, Lettice, 105.
Wilson (Willson), Margaret, 197, 216, 566.
Wilson (Willson), Martha, 59, 116, 129, 182, 197, 226, 540, 563.
Wilson (Willson), Mary (Polly), 35, 105, 106, 108, 137, 225, 226, 244, 345, 351, 393, 408, 431, 464, 504, 518, 535.
Wilson (Willson), Mathew, 24, 73, 85, 124, 127, 129, 146, 148, 158, 210, 226, 272, 280, 370, 460, 540.
Wilson, Nancy, 81, 182, 225.
Wilson, Nathaniel, 129, 488.
Wilson (Willson), Patrick, 67, 69, 94, 113, 297, 305, 412, 434, 450, 480, 488.
Wilson (Willson), Rachel, 182, 216.
Wilson (Willson), Ralph, 137, 566.
Wilson, Rebekah, 129, 309.
Wilson, Richard, 84.

Wilson, Rhoda, 129.
Wilson (Willson), Robert, 5, 10, 12, 42, 47, 57, 59, 83, 105, 108, 129, 131, 134, 148, 150, 161, 182, 183, 189, 197, 216, 217, 219, 263, 267, 268, 272, 273, 283, 289, 311, 315, 316, 320, 323, 326, 334, 338, 357, 361, 362, 368, 381, 412, 415, 416, 440, 500, 521, 531, 571, 595.
Windlecoit (Windlekite), George, 470.
Windlecoit (Windlekite), John, 23, 26, 470, 471.
Windlecoit, Mary, 470.
Windlecoit, Philip, 471.
Windlecoit, William, 470.
Windlekite, Eve Elizabeth, 26.
Windon, James, 172.
Windon, John, 172.
Windor, John, 121.
Wine, Jacob, 238.
Wineman (Vineman), Peter, 156.
Wingord, Barbara, 51.
Wingord, Christopher, 57, 59.
Wingord, John, 51, 52, 57.
Winslow, Benjamin, 269.
Winslow, Richard, 259.
Winston, John, 311.
Winston, Richard, 41, 345, 403.
Wintermaker (Winters), Catharine, 225.
Wire, Benjamin, 155.
Wire, Daniel, 155.
Wire, (McGuire), Francis, 128, 155, 158.
Wire, Hannah, 155.
Wire, Solomon, 155.
Wise, Abraham, 53.
Wise (Wiss), John, 156, 215, 544.
Wiseman, Anna M., 214.
Wiseman, Catherena, 214, 232.
Wiseman, Christena, 214.
Wiseman, Elizabeth M., 214.
Wiseman, John G., 214.
Wiseman, Lodwick, 214, 215.
Wiseman, Magdalena, 215.
Wiseman, Margaret, 215.
Wiseman, Mary E., 215.
Wiseman, Peter, 214, 215.
Wiseman, Susanna, 214.
Wister, Henry, 539.
Witman, Charles, 40.
Woland, George, 179.
Woldridge (Woolridge), George, 84, 94, 375, 384, 400.
Wolfaart, Frederick, 512.
Wolfort, Sol, 589.
Wolson, Charles, 43, 76.
Wolson, William, 81.
Wolsy, W., 83.
Womer, Edward, 463.
Woneck, John, 570.
Wood, Abner, 157.
Wood, Alexander, 163.
Wood, Ann, 163, 225.
Wood, Benjamin, 102.

Wood, Ephriam, 266.
Wood, Erwin, 372.
Wood (Woods), James, 72, 193, 266, 270, 274, 275, 276, 288, 292, 301, 307, 316, 318, 322, 332, 338, 340, 342, 358, 370, 374, 383, 402, 405, 406, 411, 424, 444, 450, 465, 471, 487, 492, 493, 501, 512, 517, 521, 526, 527, 539, 585.
Wood (Woods), John, 81, 82, 167, 243, 244, 372, 475, 532, 560, 579.
Wood (Woods), Mary, 80, 243, 338, 370, 373, 374, 375, 391, 405, 471, 475, 487, 492, 493, 507, 511, 512, 521, 523, 526, 539, 579.
Wood, Med, 574.
Wood (Woods), Richard, 5, 7, 34, 35, 41, 46, 47, 55, 65, 77, 87, 90, 93, 97, 101, 255, 268, 288, 292, 294, 295, 299, 308, 313, 336, 346, 348, 350, 369, 378, 410, 473, 484, 485.
Wood, Robert, 487, 492, 493.
Wood, Searight, 163.
Wood, Thomas, 257, 270, 276, 284, 288, 292.
Wood, Tunis, 15.
Wood (Woods), William, 36, 49, 63, 94, 163, 169, 170, 243, 275, 292, 313, 328, 423.
Woodell, John, 212.
Woodlaw, William, 519.
Woodley, Grace, 456.
Woodley (Woodle), Jacob, 9, 16, 21, 41, 113, 272, 311, 441, 456, 497, 536.
Woodley (Woodle), John, 16, 18, 186, 539.
Woodrow, Thomas, 422.
Woods, Agnes, 239.
Woods, Andrew, 299, 438, 450, 461, 470, 480, 548.
Woods, Archibald, 275.
Woods, Arthur, 77, 414.
Woods, Charles, 77.
Woods, Dolly, 193.
Woods (Wood), Elizabeth, 19, 77, 83, 93, 346, 350, 523.
Woods, Esther, 77, 227.
Woods, Hannah, 157.
Woods, Jacob, 219, 243.
Woods, Jemima, 243.
Woods, Joseph, 243, 495.
Woods, Margaret, 362, 417.
Woods, Martha, 134.
Woods, Michael, 227, 480.
Woods, Patrick, 495.
Woods, Samuel, 77, 287, 292, 313, 466, 495, 554, 566.
Woods, Stephen, 557.
Woods, Susanna, 275.
Woody, James, 278.
Wooley, William, 97.
Woolf, John, 15.
Woolf, Sebastian, 588.

Woolffallier, John, 8.
Woolfort, Frederick, 522, 537.
Woolman, Easther, 234.
Woolvine, Elizabeth, 178.
Woolwine, Philip, 178.
Woolwine, William, 177.
Worden, Ezeriah, 92.
Workman, Daniel, 124.
Workman, John, 194.
Workman, Sina, 194.
Worley, Caleb, 397, 424.
Worthclaw, William, 12.
Worthington, Abigail, 384.
Wright, Abraham (Abram), 73, 113, 366, 518.
Wright, Alexander, 15, 34, 37, 39, 50, 70, 146, 274, 277, 279, 280, 285, 296, 301, 314, 315, 330, 331, 334, 338, 362, 363, 365, 400, 401, 415, 417, 422, 459, 464, 492, 576, 595.
Wright, Anne, 24, 26.
Wright, Charity, 546.
Wright, Deborah, 40.
Wright, Easter, 73.
Wright, Elizabeth, 73, 208, 313, 595.
Wright, James, 40, 73, 146, 148, 449, 547, 595.
Wright, Jane, 590.
Wright, Janet, 73.
Wright, John, 46, 62, 65, 66, 68, 70, 73, 75, 92, 146, 148, 208, 272, 291, 307, 345, 364, 366, 392, 403, 434, 445, 518, 546, 547, 562, 576.
Wright (Write, Right), Joseph, 37, 153, 163, 167, 208, 230, 243, 303, 340.
Wright, Joshua, 73, 148, 546.
Wright, Lydia (Lidy), 73, 291, 364, 445.
Wright, Margaret, 66, 286, 295, 576, 595.
Wright (Right), Mary, 73, 120.
Wright, Peter, 40, 41, 42, 48, 59, 84, 465.
Wright, Reatchel, 40.
Wright, Samuel, 146, 495.
Wright, Sarah, 73.
Wright, Susannah, 518.
Wright (Right), Thomas, 24, 33, 40, 155, 561, 590.
Wright, William, 39, 66, 101, 143, 146, 259, 265, 268, 279, 281, 282, 286, 295, 298, 304, 313, 352, 439, 461, 495, 595.
Wyley, John, 486.
Wylie, Alexander, 486.
Wylie, Mary, 486.
Wylie, Peter, 416, 486.
Wyms (Wynn), Jane, 243.
Wynes, Deborah, 243.
Wynes (Wymes), James, 243.
Wyse, John, 405.

Yager, John, 160.
Yancey, John, 154, 548.
Yancey, Susanna, 548.

Yardly (Yearly), Benjamin, 113, 187, 481, 508, 510, 511.
Yarhoss (Yarhass, Yarrass), Charles. 153, 550, 562.
Yates, Thomas, 488.
Yayers (Yayer), Adam, 294, 380.
Yeacon, Valentine, 107.
Yeager, Adam, 530.
Yeager, Andrew, 179, 191.
Yeakham, Philpole, 53.
Yeakly, Martin, 186.
Yeakly, Mary C., 186.
Yearout, Charles, 568.
Yeasill, Christopher, 121.
Yeates, George, 102.
Yegart, Andrew, 580.
Yeoman, Mathias, 58.
Yeorons (Yorehons), Charles, 194, 211.
Yoackum (Yoakham, Yoakam), Mathias, 340, 368, 425.
Yoacum, Valentine, 83.
Yocome, John, 153.
Youckam (Yoccum, Yeokim), George, 38, 121, 293.
Youell (Youel, Youl, Yoall), William, 207, 213, 561, 576, 584.
Young, Agnes, 10, 292, 493, 548.
Young, Alexander, 78.
Young, Allas, 62.
Young, Andrew, 165, 200, 226, 227, 244.
Young, Conrod, 531.
Young, Daniel, 75, 416, 421.
Young, Elizabeth, 99, 237, 355, 397.
Young, Esibala (Isabella), 62, 73, 165, 342.
Young, Hugh, 10, 33, 35, 40, 49, 52, 54, 57, 86, 122, 167, 240, 277, 278, 281, 283, 292, 302, 331, 332, 351, 360, 361, 366, 389, 470, 548.
Young, Isabel, 72.
Young, James, 7, 57, 60, 62, 76, 78, 86, 99, 111, 149, 156, 164, 165, 166, 170, 191, 196, 200, 201, 203, 211, 213, 216, 222, 226, 227, 231, 237, 267, 283, 285, 286, 290, 292, 315, 319, 323, 331, 332, 336, 338, 340, 342, 351, 353, 355 358, 363, 373, 379, 389, 390, 415, 416, 470, 493, 494, 498, 505, 516, 519, 553, 562, 572, 594.
Young, James C., 33.
Young, Jane (Jean), 83, 200, 235, 432, 541, 543.
Young, Jannet, 62, 78, 99, 390.
Young, John, 7, 8, 14, 33, 48, 59, 61, 86, 92, 111, 122, 126, 132, 136, 142, 154, 157, 159, 161, 162, 165, 167, 173, 174, 176, 177, 190, 191, 207, 209, 214, 216, 224, 227, 231, 232, 254, 272, 283, 331, 332, 351, 355, 390, 402, 403, 409, 432, 439, 450, 469, 472, 481, 484, 485, 494, 514, 545, 548, 568, 572.
Young, Joseph, 86, 332.
Young, Lydia, 200.
Young, Margaret, 165, 200, 226, 244, 494, 545.
Young, Mary, 162, 179, 187, 195, 231, 439, 450, 505, 572.
Young, Mary Eliot, 243.
Young, Mathew, 10, 19, 66, 285, 286, 292, 361.
Young, Patrick, 62, 65, 73, 78, 99, 315, 319, 340, 342, 353, 475.
Young, Peggy, 226.
Young, Rachel, 233.
Young, Rebeccah, 165.
Young, Robert, 7, 10, 20, 46, 78, 86, 90, 92, 96, 99, 103, 129, 165, 191, 195, 200, 226, 227, 231, 233, 243, 244, 263, 271, 281, 283, 284, 286, 331, 332, 355, 373, 385, 390, 398, 416, 432, 450, 484, 493, 494, 500, 508, 516, 541, 543, 545.
Young, Samuel, 51, 52, 67, 72, 78, 83, 233, 331, 332, 373, 390, 441, 445, 476, 493, 516, 587.
Young, Sarah, 62, 78, 99, 165, 191, 243, 315, 319, 342.
Young, Thomas, 226, 227, 233, 235.
Young, William, 35, 86, 103, 120, 127, 144, 159, 160, 161, 162, 164, 165, 168, 169, 173, 177, 178, 180, 181, 183, 191, 193, 194, 197, 200, 213, 219, 226, 227, 237, 243, 295, 332, 348, 349, 403, 404, 493, 494, 505, 512, 514, 519, 521, 541, 559, 572, 594.
Yourd, Robert, 99.
Youste, Hilnkele, 99.

Zane, Isaac, 526.
Zeburn (Zeborn), Nicholas, 441.
Zee, George, 26.
Zimmerman, Christian, 228.
Zimmerman, Christinia, 250.
Zimmerman, Christopher, 53.
Zimmerman, George, 142, 291, 307.
Zimmerman, Henry, 228.
Zimmerman, Jacob, 228.
Zimmerman, John, 142, 228.
Zimmerman, Lawrence, 228.
Zimmerman, Leonard, 142.
Zimmerman, Stophel, 228.
Zink, Daniel, 504.
Zinn, Garrett, 322, 389, 464.
Zinn, Henry, 74.
Zircle, Frederick, 472.
Zircle, Ludwick, 373, 472.
Zöller, John, 146.
Zorn, Catherine, 405, 411.
Zorn, Jacob, 43, 84.
Zrepbli, Joseph, 40.
Zumbro, George, 237.

Lightning Source UK Ltd.
Milton Keynes UK
UKHW021911050619
343950UK00006B/92/P